Birnbaum's
France

A BIRNBAUM TRAVEL GUIDE

Alexandra Mayes Birnbaum
EDITORIAL CONSULTANT

Lois Spritzer
Editorial Director

Laura L. Brengelman
Managing Editor

Mary Callahan
Senior Editor

David Appell
Patricia Canole
Gene Gold
Jill Kadetsky
Susan McClung
Associate Editors

HarperPerennial
A Division of HarperCollinsPublishers

To Stephen, who merely made all this possible.

BIRNBAUM'S FRANCE 95. Copyright © 1995 by HarperCollins Publishers.
All rights reserved. Printed in the United States of America. No part of this
book may be used or reproduced in any manner whatsoever without written
permission except in the case of brief quotations embodied in critical articles
and reviews. For information address HarperCollins*Publishers*, 10 East 53rd
Street, New York, NY 10022.

FIRST EDITION

ISSN 0749-2561 (Birnbaum Travel Guides)
ISSN 0749-2553 (France)
ISBN 0-06-278190-1 (pbk.)

95 96 97 98 ❖/CW 5 4 3 2 1

Cover design © Drenttel Doyle Partners
Cover photograph © Rex Ziak/AllStock
Saumur, France; Loire River Valley

BIRNBAUM TRAVEL GUIDES

Bahamas, and Turks & Caicos
Berlin
Bermuda
Boston
Canada
Cancun, Cozumel & Isla Mujeres
Caribbean
Chicago
Country Inns and Back Roads
Disneyland
Eastern Europe
Europe
Europe for Business Travelers
France
Germany
Great Britain
Hawaii
Ireland
Italy

London
Los Angeles
Mexico
Miami & Ft. Lauderdale
Montreal & Quebec City
New Orleans
New York
Paris
Portugal
Rome
San Francisco
Santa Fe & Taos
South America
Spain
United States
USA for Business Travelers
Walt Disney World
Walt Disney World for Kids, By Kids
Washington, DC

Contributing Editors

Colette Boulard
Frederick H. Brengelman
Rebecca Brite
David Burke
Bernard Cartier
Roger Collis
Charles Cupic
Karen Cure
Stephanie Curtis
Emily Emerson-Le Moing
Caro Frankel
Carolyn Friday
Alice Garrard
Edward Guiliano
Mireille Guiliano
Kathy Gunst
Jeffrey C. Haight
Ben Harte

Jill Herbers
Douglas Hill
David Howley
Susan Kelly
Harriet Leins
Marc-Alexandre Lile
Maguy Macario
Anne Manderson
Elise Nakhnikian
Nancy Nisselbaum
Anita Peltonen
Everett Potter
H. W. Rochefort
Margery Safir
Susan Shipman
Peter Simon
Phoebe Tait
David Wickers

Maps

B. Andrew Mudryk

Contents

Getting Ready to Go

Practical information for planning your trip.

The Cities

Thorough, qualitative guides to each of the 16 cities most often visited by vacationers and businesspeople. Each section offers a comprehensive report on the city's most compelling attractions and amenities— highlighting our top choices in every category.

Diversions

A selective guide to active and/or cerebral vacation themes, pinpointing the best places to pursue them.

Unexpected Pleasures and Treasures

For the Experience

For the Mind

For the Body

Directions

The most spectacular routes and roads; most arresting natural wonders; and most magnificent châteaux, manor houses, and gardens—all organized into 18 specific driving tours.

Glossary

Foreword

It sometimes seems easier to deal with France as just a chapter in a guide-book that deals with all of Europe than to try to treat this extraordinary country adequately all by itself. In a more general guidebook, it's possible to maintain the fiction that France is a truly homogeneous nation, with a single face and similar sensitivities in every corner of the country. But the diversity that flourishes across the Gallic landscape is extraordinarily broad, and in trying to lead readers to each separate region it sometimes feels as if there are at least a dozen different countries demanding attention, rather than several areas of a single sovereign nation. Trying somehow to connect the dour visages found along the Brittany coast with the exuberant Mediterranean mentality of Marseilles is quite a task; no less irreconcil-able is the Teutonic temperament of Alsatians when compared to the gentle demeanor of the denizens of the Dordogne.

That's why we've tried to create a guide to France that's specifically organized, written, and edited for today's demanding traveler, one for whom qualitative information is infinitely more desirable than mere quantities of unappraised data. We realize that it's impossible for any single travel writer to visit thousands of restaurants (and nearly as many hotels) in any given year and provide accurate appraisals of each. And even if it were physically possible for one human being to survive such an itinerary, it would of necessity have to be done at a dead sprint, and the perceptions derived there-from would probably be less valid than those of any other intelligent individual visiting the same establishments. It is, therefore, both impractical and undesirable (especially in a large, annually revised and updated guide-book *series* such as we offer) to have only one person provide all the data on the entire world. Instead, we have chosen what we like to describe as the "thee and me" approach to restaurant and hotel evaluation and, to a somewhat more limited degree, to the sites and sights we have included in the other sections of our text. What this really reflects is a personal sam-pling tempered by intelligent counsel from informed local sources.

This guidebook is directed to the "visitor," and such elements as restau-rants have been specifically picked to provide the visitor with a represen-tative, enlightening, and, above all, pleasant experience. Since so many extraneous considerations can affect the reception and service accorded a regular restaurant patron, our choices can in no way be construed as an exhaustive guide to resident dining. We think we've listed all the best places, in various price ranges, but they were chosen with a visitor's enjoyment in mind.

Other evidence of how we've tried to tailor our text to reflect modern travel habits is apparent in the section we call DIVERSIONS. Where once it was common for travelers to spend a foreign visit seeing only obvious sights, today's traveler is more likely to want to pursue a special interest or to venture off the beaten path. In response to this trend, we have collected a series of special experiences so that it is no longer necessary to wade through a pound or two of superfluous prose just to find exceptional pleasures and treasures.

Finally, I also should point out that every good travel guide is a living enterprise; that is, no part of this text is carved in stone. In our annual revisions, we refine, expand, and further hone all our material to serve your travel needs better. To this end, no contribution is of greater value to us than your personal reaction to what we have written, as well as information reflecting your own experiences while using the book. Please write to us at 10 E. 53rd St., New York, NY 10022.

We sincerely hope to hear from you.

Alexandra Mayes Birnbaum

ALEXANDRA MAYES BIRNBAUM, editorial consultant to the *Birnbaum Travel Guides,* worked with her late husband, Stephen Birnbaum, as co-editor of the series. She has been a world traveler since childhood and is known for her travel reports on radio on what's hot and what's not.

France

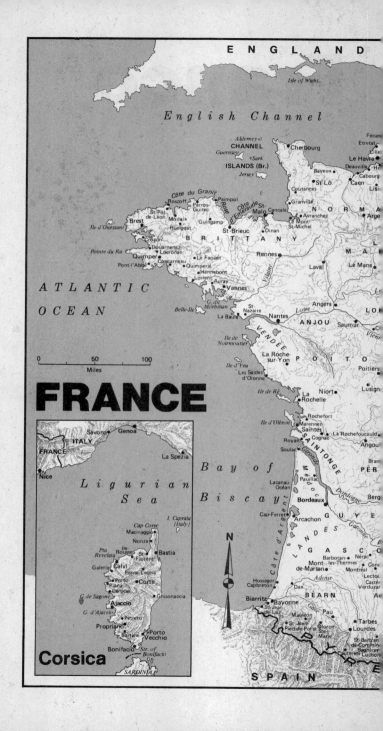

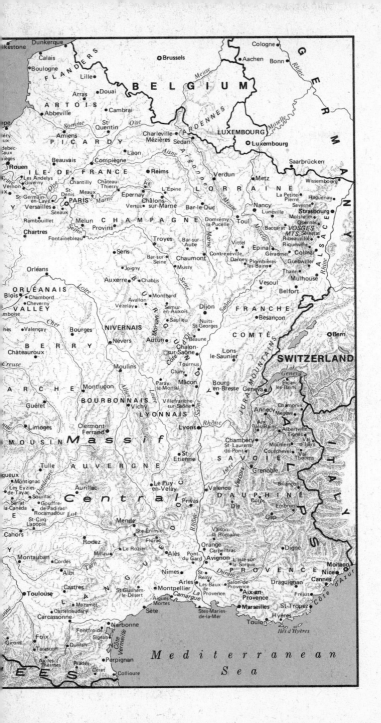

How to Use This Guide

A great deal of care has gone into the organization of this guidebook, and we believe it represents a real breakthrough in the presentation of travel material. Our goal is to create a more modern generation of travel books, and to make this guide the most useful and practical travel tool available today.

Our text is divided into five basic sections in order to present information in the best way on every possible aspect of a vacation to France. Our aim is to highlight what's where and to provide basic information—how, when, where, how much, and what's best—to assist you in making the most intelligent choices possible.

Here is a brief summary of what you can expect to find in each section. We believe that you will find both your travel planning and en-route enjoyment enhanced by having this book at your side.

GETTING READY TO GO

A mini-encyclopedia of practical travel facts with all the precise data necessary to create a successful trip to France. Here you will find how to get where you're going, currency information and exchange rates, plus selected resources—including pertinent publications, and companies and organizations specializing in discount and special-interest travel—providing a wealth of information and assistance useful both before and during your trip.

THE CITIES

Individual reports on the 16 cities in France most visited by travelers and businesspeople offer a short-stay guide, including an essay introducing the city as a historic entity and a contemporary place to visit; *At-a-Glance* contains a site-by-site survey of the most important, interesting, and unique sights to see and things to do; *Sources and Resources* is a concise listing of pertinent tourist information such as the address of the local tourism office, which sightseeing tours to take, where to find the best nightspot, play golf, or get a taxi. *Best in Town* lists our cost-and-quality choices of the best places to eat and sleep on a variety of budgets.

DIVERSIONS

This section is designed to help travelers find the best places in which to engage in a variety of exceptional experiences for the mind and body without having to wade through endless pages of unrelated text. In every case, our particular suggestions are intended to guide you to that special place where the quality of experience is likely to be the highest.

DIRECTIONS

Here are 18 itineraries that range all across the country, along the most beautiful routes and roads, past the most spectacular natural wonders, and through the most historic cities and countryside. DIRECTIONS is the only section of this book that is organized geographically, and its itineraries cover the touring highlights of France in short, independent journeys of five to seven days' duration. Itineraries can be "connected" for longer sojourns or used individually for short, intensive explorations.

GLOSSARY

This compendium of helpful travel information includes a climate chart, a weights and measures table, and *Useful Words and Phrases,* a brief introduction to the French language that will help you to make a hotel or dinner reservation, order a meal, mail a letter, and even buy toothpaste in France. Though most large hotels, restaurants, and attractions in major French cities have English-speaking staff, at smaller establishments and in rural, out-of-the-way towns and villages, a little knowledge of French will go a long way.

To use this book to full advantage, take a few minutes to read the table of contents and random entries in each section to get a firsthand feel for how it all fits together. You will find that the sections of this book are building blocks designed to help you put together the best possible trip. Use them selectively as a tool, a source of ideas, a reference work for accurate facts, and a guidebook to the best buys, the most exciting sights, the most pleasant accommodations, the tastiest foods—*the best travel experience* that you can possibly have.

Getting
Ready to Go

Getting Ready to Go

When to Go

France has a temperate climate, although there is considerable variation between regions. Towards the west, the Atlantic Ocean moderates extremes of temperatures, but also contributes to increased precipitation. Moving east, the climate becomes more typically continental, with colder winters and hotter summers. The south of France generally has milder winters and hotter—though less humid—summers, and less rain. In the Pyrénées and the Alps, the peaks are snow-covered all year long.

Mid-may to mid-September generally is the peak travel period. Travel during the off-season (roughly November to *Easter*) and shoulder seasons (the months immediately before and after the peak months) also offers relatively fair weather and smaller crowds. During these periods, travel can be less expensive.

If you have a touch-tone phone, you can call *The Weather Channel Connection* (phone: 900-WEATHER) for current worldwide weather forecasts. This service, available from *The Weather Channel* (2600 Cumberland Pkwy., Atlanta, GA 30339; phone: 404-434-6800), costs 95¢ per minute; the charge will appear on your phone bill.

Traveling by Plane

SCHEDULED FLIGHTS

Leading airlines offering flights between the US and France include *Aer Lingus, Air France, American, British Airways, Continental, Delta, IcelandAir, Northwest, Sabena, TAP Air Portugal, Tower Air, TWA, United,* and *USAir.*

FARES The great variety of airfares can be reduced to the following basic categories: first class, business class, coach (also called economy or tourist class), excursion or discount, and standby, as well as various promotional fares. For information on applicable fares and restrictions, contact the airlines listed above or ask your travel agent. Most airfares are offered for a limited time. Once you've found the lowest fare for which you can qualify, purchase your ticket as soon as possible.

RESERVATIONS Reconfirmation is strongly recommended for all international flights. It is essential that you confirm your round-trip reservations—*especially the return leg*—as well as any flights within Europe.

SEATING Airline seats usually are assigned on a first-come, first-served basis at check-in, although you may be able to reserve a seat when purchasing your ticket. Seating charts sometimes are available from airlines and also are included in the *Airline Seating Guide* (Carlson Publishing Co., 11132 Los Alamitos Blvd., Los Alamitos, CA 90720; phone: 310-493-4877).

SMOKING US law prohibits smoking on flights scheduled for six hours or less within the US and its territories on both domestic and international carriers. These restrictions do not apply to nonstop flights between the US and international destinations, and at press time, major carriers permitted smoking on flights to France. If the flight includes European connections, however, smoking may not be permitted on the intra-European leg of the trip. A free wallet-size guide that describes the rights of nonsmokers under current regulations is available from *ASH* (*Action on Smoking and Health;* DOT Card, 2013 H St. NW, Washington, DC 20006; phone: 202-659-4310).

SPECIAL MEALS When making your reservation, you can request one of the airline's alternate menu choices for no additional charge. Though not always required, it's a good idea to reconfirm your request the day before departure.

BAGGAGE On major international airlines, passengers usually are allowed to carry on board one bag that will fit under a seat or in an overhead bin and to check two bags in the cargo hold. Specific regulations regarding dimensions and weight restrictions vary among airlines, but a checked bag usually cannot exceed 62 inches in combined dimensions (length, width, and depth), or weigh more than 70 pounds. There may be charges for additional, oversize, or overweight luggage, and for special equipment or sporting gear. Note that baggage allowances may be more limited on intra-European flights. Check that the tags the airline attaches are correctly coded for your destination.

CHARTER FLIGHTS

By booking a block of seats on a specially arranged flight, charter operators frequently can offer travelers bargain airfares. If you do fly on a charter, however, read the contract's fine print carefully. Federal regulations permit charter operators to cancel a flight or assess surcharges of as much as 10% of the airfare up to 10 days before departure. You usually must book in advance, and once booked, no changes are permitted, so buy trip cancellation insurance. Also, make your check out to the company's escrow account, which provides some protection for your investment in the event that the charter operator fails. For further information, consult the publication *Jax Fax* (397 Post Rd., Darien, CT 06820; phone: 203-655-8746; fax: 203-655-6257).

DISCOUNTS ON SCHEDULED FLIGHTS

COURIER TRAVEL In return for arranging to accompany some kind of freight, a traveler pays only a portion of the total airfare (and sometimes a small registration fee). One agency that matches up would-be couriers with courier companies is *Now Voyager* (74 Varick St., Suite 307, New York, NY 10013; phone: 212-431-1616; fax: 212-334-5243).

Courier Companies

Discount Travel International (169 W. 81st St., New York, NY 10024; phone: 212-362-3636; fax: 212-362-3236; and 801 Alton Rd., Suite 1, Miami Beach, FL 33139; phone: 305-538-1616; fax: 305-673-9376).

F.B. On Board Courier Club (10225 Ryan Ave., Suite 103, Dorval, Quebec H9P 1A2, Canada; phone: 514-633-0740; fax: 514-633-0735).

Halbart Express (147-05 176th St., Jamaica, NY 11434; phone: 718-656-8279; fax: 718-244-0559).

Midnite Express (925 W. Hyde Park Blvd., Inglewood, CA 90302; phone: 310-672-1100; fax: 310-671-0107).

Way to Go Travel (6679 Sunset Blvd., Hollywood, CA 90028; phone: 213-466-1126; fax: 213-466-8994).

Publications

Insiders Guide to Air Courier Bargains, by Kelly Monaghan (The Intrepid Traveler, PO Box 438, New York, NY 10034; phone: 212-569-1081 for information; 800-356-9315 for orders; fax: 212-942-6687).

Travel Unlimited (PO Box 1058, Allston, MA 02134-1058; no phone).

CONSOLIDATORS AND BUCKET SHOPS These companies buy blocks of tickets from airlines and sell them at a discount to travel agents or directly to consumers. Since many bucket shops operate on a thin margin, be sure to check a company's record with the *Better Business Bureau*—before parting with any money.

Council Charter (205 E. 42nd St., New York, NY 10017; phone: 800-800-8222 or 212-661-0311; fax: 212-972-0194).

International Adventures (60 E. 42nd St., Room 763, New York, NY 10165; phone: 212-599-0577; fax: 212-599-3288).

Travac Tours and Charters (989 Ave. of the Americas, New York, NY 10018; phone: 800-872-8800 or 212-563-3303; fax: 212-563-3631).

Unitravel (1177 N. Warson Rd., St. Louis, MO 63132; phone: 800-325-2222 or 314-569-0900; fax: 314-569-2503).

LAST-MINUTE TRAVEL CLUBS Members of such clubs receive information on imminent trips and other bargain travel opportunities. There usually is an annual fee, although a few clubs offer free membership. Despite the names of some of the clubs listed below, you don't have to wait until literally the last minute to make travel plans.

Discount Travel International (114 Forrest Ave., Suite 203, Narberth, PA 19072; phone: 215-668-7184; fax: 215-668-9182).

FLY ASAP (PO Box 9808, Scottsdale, AZ 85252-3808; phone: 800-FLY-ASAP or 602-956-1987; fax: 602-956-6414).

Last Minute Travel (1249 Boylston St., Boston, MA 02215; phone: 800-LAST-MIN or 617-267-9800; fax: 617-424-1943).

Moment's Notice (425 Madison Ave., New York, NY 10017; phone: 212-486-0500/1/2/3; fax: 212-486-0783).

Spur of the Moment Cruises (411 N. Harbor Blvd., Suite 302, San Pedro, CA 90731; phone: 800-4-CRUISES or 310-521-1070 in California; 800-343-1991 elsewhere in the US; 24-hour hotline: 310-521-1060; fax: 310-521-1061).

Traveler's Advantage (3033 S. Parker Rd., Suite 900, Aurora, CO 80014; phone: 800-548-1116 or 800-835-8747; fax: 303-368-3985).

Vacations to Go (1502 Augusta Dr., Suite 415, Houston, TX 77057; phone: 713-974-2121 in Texas; 800-338-4962 elsewhere in the US; fax: 713-974-0445).

Worldwide Discount Travel Club (1674 Meridian Ave., Miami Beach, FL 33139; phone: 305-534-2082; fax: 305-534-2070).

GENERIC AIR TRAVEL These organizations operate much like an ordinary airline standby service, except that they offer seats on not one but several scheduled and charter airlines. One pioneer of generic flights is *Airhitch* (2790 Broadway, Suite 100, New York, NY 10025; phone: 212-864-2000).

BARTERED TRAVEL SOURCES Barter—the exchange of commodities or services in lieu of cash payment—is a common practice among travel suppliers. Companies that have obtained travel services through barter may sell these services at substantial discounts to travel clubs, who pass along the savings to members. One organization offering bartered travel opportunities is *Travel World Leisure Club* (225 W. 34th St., Suite 909, New York, NY 10122; phone: 800-444-TWLC or 212-239-4855; fax: 212-564-5158).

CONSUMER PROTECTION

Passengers whose complaints have not been satisfactorily addressed by the airline can contact the *US Department of Transportation* (*DOT;* Consumer Affairs Division, 400 Seventh St. SW, Room 10405, Washington, DC 20590; phone: 202-366-2220). Also see *Fly Rights* (Publication #050-000-00513-5; *US Government Printing Office,* PO Box 371954, Pittsburgh, PA 15250-7954; phone: 202-783-3238; fax: 202-512-2250). If you have safety-related questions or concerns, write to the *Federal Aviation Administration* (*FAA;* 800 Independence Ave. SW, Washington, DC 20591) or call the *FAA Consumer Hotline* (phone: 800-322-7873). If you have a complaint against a local travel service in France, contact the French tourist authorities or *La Partie Administrative du Tourisme* (2 Rue Linois, Paris 75015, France; phone: 33-1-44-37-36-00).

Traveling by Ship

Your cruise fare usually includes all meals, recreational activities, and entertainment. Shore excursions are available at extra cost, and can be booked in advance or once you're on board. An important factor in the price of a cruise is the location (and sometimes the size) of your cabin. Charts issued by the *Cruise Lines International Association* (*CLIA;* 500 Fifth Ave., Suite 1407, New York, NY 10110; phone: 212-921-0066; fax: 212-921-0549) provide information on ship layouts and facilities and are available at some *CLIA*-affiliated travel agencies.

The *US Public Health Service (PHS)* inspects all passenger vessels calling at US ports; for the most recent summary or a particular inspection report, write to Chief, Vessel Sanitation Program, *National Center for Environmental Health* (1015 N. America Way, Room 107, Miami, FL 33132; phone: 305-536-4307). Most cruise ships have a doctor on board, plus medical facilities.

For further information on cruises and cruise lines, consult *Ocean and Cruise News* (PO Box 92, Stamford, CT 06904; phone/fax: 203-329-2787). And for a free list of travel agencies specializing in cruises, contact the *National Association of Cruise Only Agencies* (*NACOA;* 3191 Coral Way, Suite 630, Miami, FL 33145; phone: 305-446-7732; fax: 305-446-9732).

A potentially less expensive alternative to cruise ships is travel by freighter—cargo ships that also transport a limited number of passengers. For information, consult the *Freighter Travel Club of America* (3524 Harts Lake Rd., Roy, WA 98580; no phone), *Freighter World Cruises* (180 S. Lake Ave., Suite 335, Pasadena, CA 91101; phone: 818-449-3106; fax: 818-449-9573), *Pearl's Travel Tips* (9903 Oaks La., Seminole, FL 34642; phone: 813-393-2919; fax: 813-392-2580), and *TravLtips Cruise and Freighter Travel Association* (PO Box 188, 163-07 Depot Rd., Flushing, NY 11358; phone: 800-872-8584 or 718-939-2400; fax: 718-939-2047).

A number of companies, both in the US and in Europe, offer cruises on the continent's inland waterways. For those interested in riverboat rentals, the *Syndicat National des Loueurs de Bateaux de Plaisance* (Port de Bourdonnais, Paris 75007, France; phone: 33-1-45-55-10-49; fax: 33-1-47-53-94-75) provides information and referrals for companies that offer rentals.

Ferries provide transportation between mainland France and its islands, and also link France with Great Britain, Ireland, Italy, and other countries. Nearly all of them carry both passengers and cars and most routes are in service year-round.

International Cruise Lines

Classical Cruises (132 E. 70th St., New York, NY 10021; phone: 800-252-7745 or 212-794-3200; fax: 212-517-4735).

Club Med (3 E. 54th St., New York, NY 10022; phone: 800-CLUB-MED or 212-750-1687; fax: 212-750-1697).

Crystal Cruises (2121 Ave. of the Stars, Los Angeles, CA 90067; phone: 800-446-6620 or 310-785-9300; fax: 310-785-0011).

Cunard (555 Fifth Ave., New York, NY 10017; phone: 800-5-CUNARD or 800-221-4770; fax: 718-786-0038).

Epirotiki Lines (901 South America Way, Miami, FL 33132; phone: 800-221-2470 or 305-358-1910; fax: 305-358-4807).

EuroCruises (303 W. 13th St., New York, NY 10014; phone: 800-688-3876 or 212-691-2099; fax: 212-366-4747).

Holland America Line (300 Elliot Ave. W., Seattle, WA 98119; phone: 800-426-0327; fax: 800-628-4855).

Marquest (101 Columbia, Suite 165, Aliso Viejo, CA 92656; phone: 800-510-7110 or 714-362-2080; fax: 714-362-2081).

P&O Cruises (c/o *Golden Bear Travel,* 16 Digital Dr., Suite 100, Novato, CA 94948; phone: 800-551-1000 or 415-382-8900; fax: 415-382-9086).

Pacquet Cruises (6301 NW Fifth Way, Suite 4000, Ft. Lauderdale, FL 33309; phone: 800-556-8850 or 305-772-8600; fax: 305-491-5099).

Princess Cruises (10100 Santa Monica Blvd., Los Angeles, CA 90067; phone: 800-421-0522; fax: 310-284-2844).

Raymond & Whitcomb (400 Madison Ave., New York, NY 10017; phone: 212-759-3960 in New York State; 800-245-9005 elsewhere in the US; fax: 212-935-1644).

Regency Cruises (260 Madison Ave., New York, NY 10016; phone: 212-972-4774 in New York State; 800-388-5500 elsewhere in the US; fax: 800-388-8833).

Renaissance Cruises (1800 Eller Dr., Suite 300, Ft. Lauderdale, FL 33316; phone: 800-525-2450; fax: 800-243-2987 or 305-463-8125).

Royal Caribbean Cruise Lines (1050 Caribbean Way, Miami, FL 33132; phone: 800-432-6559 in Florida; 800-327-6700 elsewhere in the US; fax: 800-722-5329).

Royal Cruise Line (1 Maritime Plaza, Suite 1400, San Francisco, CA 94111; phone: 800-792-2992 in California; 800-227-4534 elsewhere in the US; fax: 415-956-1656).

Royal Viking Line (95 Merrick Way, Coral Gables, FL 33134; phone: 800-422-8000; fax: 305-448-1398).

Seabourn Cruise Line (55 Francisco St., Suite 710, San Francisco, CA 94133; phone: 800-929-9595 or 415-391-7444; fax: 415-391-8518).

SSC Radisson Diamond Cruise (11340 Blondo St., Omaha, NE 68164; phone: 800-333-3333; fax: 402-498-5055).

Sun Line (1 Rockefeller Plaza, Suite 315, New York, NY 10020; phone: 800-872-6400 or 212-397-6400; fax: 212-765-9685).

Swan Hellenic Cruises (c/o *Esplanade Tours,* 581 Boylston St., Boston, MA 02116; phone: 800-426-5492 or 617-266-7465; fax: 617-262-9829).

Windstar Cruises (300 Elliott Ave. W., Seattle, WA 98119; phone: 800-258-7245; fax: 206-281-0627).

Freighter Companies

Bank Line Freighters of Britain (c/o *Freighter World Cruises,* 180 S. Lake Ave., Suite 335, Pasadena, CA 91101; phone: 818-449-3106; fax: 818-449-9573).

Egon-Oldendorff (c/o *Freighter World Cruises;* address above).

Grimaldi (c/o *Freighter World Cruises;* address above).

Mediterranean Great Lakes Line (c/o *Freighter World Cruises;* address above).

Mediterranean Shipping (c/o *Sea the Difference,* 420 Fifth Ave., Suite 804, New York, NY 10018; phone: 800-666-9333 or 212-354-4409; fax: 212-764-8592).

Inland Waterway Cruise Companies

Abercrombie & Kent (1520 Kensington Rd., Suite 212, Oak Brook, IL 60521; phone: 800-323-7308 or 708-954-2944; fax: 708-954-3324).

AHI International (701 Lee St., Des Plaines, IL 60016; phone: 800-323-7373 or 312-694-9330; fax: 708-699-7108).

Aqua Viva (Port de Grenelle, Paris 75015; phone: 33-1-45-75-52-60; fax: 33-1-45-75-52-31).

Bargain Boating, Morgantown Travel Service (PO Box 757, Morgantown, WV 26507-0757; phone: 800-637-0782 or 304-292-8471; fax: 304-292-0819).

The Barge Lady (225 N. Michigan Ave., Suite 324, Chicago, IL 60601; phone: 800-880-0071 or 312-540-5500; fax: 312-540-5503).

Blakes Vacations (1076 Ash St., Winnetka, IL 60093; phone: 800-628-8118 or 708-446-4771; fax: 708-446-4772).

Blue Lines (Le Grand Bassin, Boîte Postal 21, Castelnaudary 11400, France; phone: 33-68-23-17-51; fax: 33-68-23-33-92).

Le Boat (215 Union St., Hackensack, NJ 07601; phone: 800-922-0291 or 201-342-1838; 800-992-0291 in Canada; fax 201-342-7498).

Carlisle Cruises (9110 NE 73rd St., Vancouver, WA 98662; phone: 800-426-9297 or 206-253-5414; fax: 206-253-5411).

Cruise Company of Greenwich (31 Brookside Dr., Greenwich, CT 06830; phone: 800-825-0826 or 203-622-0203; fax: 203-622-4036).

Cunard EuropAmerica River Cruises (555 Fifth Ave., New York, NY 10017; phone: 800-221-4770; fax: 718-786-2350).

Elegant Cruises and Tours (31 Central Dr., Port Washington, NY 11050; phone: 800-683-6767 or 516-767-9302; fax: 516-767-9303).

Esplanade Tours (581 Boylston St., Boston, MA 02116; phone: 617-266-7465 in Boston; 800-426-5492 elsewhere in the US; fax: 617-262-9829).

Etoile de Champagne (89 Broad St., Boston, MA 02110; phone: 800-280-1492 or 617-426-1776; fax: 617-426-4689).

Europ' Yachting (11 Bd. de la Bastille, Paris 75012, France; phone: 33-1-43-44-00-65; fax: 33-1-43-07-66-37).

Europe Cruise Line (225 N. Michigan Ave., Suite 224, Chicago, IL 60601; phone: 800-880-0071 or 312-540-5500; fax: 312-540-5503).

European Waterways (represented in the US by *B & V Associates,* 140 E. 56th St., Suite 4C, New York, NY 10022; phone: 800-546-4777 or 212-688-9538; fax: 212-688-9467).

French Country Waterways (PO Box 2195, Duxbury, MA 02331; phone: 800-222-1236 or 617-934-2454; fax: 617-934-9048).

French Cruise Lines (*FCL;* 2500 Westchester Ave., Purchase, NY 10577; phone: 800-346-6525 or 914-696-3600; fax: 914-696-0833; and 323 Geary St., San Francisco, CA 94102; phone: 800-858-8587 or 415-392-8817; fax: 415-392-8868).

The French Experience (370 Lexington Ave., Suite 812, New York, NY 10017; phone: 212-986-1115; fax: 212-986-3808).

Frontiers International (100 Logan Rd., Wexford, PA 15090; 800-245-1950 or 412-935-1577; fax: 412-935-5388).

Hideaways International (PO Box 4433, Portsmouth, NH 03802-4433; phone: 800-843-4433 or 603-430-4433; fax: 603-430-4444).

Hoseasons Holidays Ltd. (Sunway House, Lowestoft, Suffolk NR32 2LW, England; phone: 44-1502-500555; fax: 44-1502-500535).

INTRAV (7711 Bonhomme Ave., St. Louis, MO 63105-1961; phone: 800-456-8100; fax: 314-727-0908).

KD River Cruises of Europe (2500 Westchester Ave., Purchase, NY 10577; phone: 800-346-6525 or 914-696-3600; fax: 914-696-3808; and 323 Geary St., San Francisco, CA 94102; phone: 800-858-8587 or 415-392-8817; fax: 415-392-8868).

Kemwel's Premier Selections (106 Calvert St., Harrison, NY 10528-3199; phone: 800-234-4000 or 914-835-5555; fax: 914-835-5449).

Maine Anjou Rivières (Chenillé Changé, Le Moulin 49220, France; phone: 33-41-95-10-83; fax: 33-41-95-10-52).

Rive de France (172 Bd. Berthier, Paris 75017, France; phone: 33-1-46-22-10-86; fax: 33-1-43-80-65-75).

Skipper Travel Services (1500 41st Ave., Suite 8B, Capitola, CA 95010; phone: 408-462-5333; fax: 408-462-5178).

Ferry Companies

Hoverspeed Ltd. (International Hoverport, Marine Parade, Dover, Kent CT17 9TG, England; phone: 44-1304-240241; fax: 44-1304-240088).

P&O European Ferries (Channel House, Channel View Rd., Dover, Kent CT17 9TJ, England; phone: 44-1304-203388; fax: 44-1304-223464).

Société Nationale Maritime Corse Méditerranée (*SNCM;* main office: Division Passages, 61 Bd. des Dames, Marseilles 13002, France; phone: 33-91-56-32-00; fax: 33-91-56-36-66).

Spena Sealink (Charter House, PO Box 121, Park St., Ashford, Kent TN24 8EX, England; phone: 44-1233-647047; fax: 44-1233-623294).

Traveling by Train

The government-owned and -operated French railway system—*Société Nationale des Chemins de Fer (SNCF)*, also known as *French National Railways*—is one of the world's most modern and extensive networks. *SNCF* trains include the high-speed *Train à Grande Vitesse (TGV)*, as well as *EuroCity (EC)* and *InterCity (IC)* trains, *rapides,* and expresses. The car-carrying *Train Auto-Couchette (TAC),* or *Motorail* train, is another convenience. In addition, *SNCF*'s *"Le Shuttle"* trains carry vehicles and passengers through the new Channel Tunnel (often called the "Chunnel") between France and Great Britain. *Eurostar TGV* trains, a joint venture of British, French, and Belgian railways, also link France and Great Britain via the Chunnel. A few minor railways—such as the *Chemins de Fer de Provence* (or *Provence Railways*), which operates between Nice and Digne—are not part of the *SNCF* system.

Most trains have both first and second class cars. Food service aboard French trains ranges from traditional dining cars—although these are being phased out—to vendors dispensing sandwiches, snacks, and beverages from carts. Overnight accommodations include *couchettes* (coach seats of a compartment converted to sleeping berths) and *wagons-lit,* or sleepers (bedroom compartments providing one to three beds). Luggage often can be placed just inside the doors; otherwise, you can use the overhead racks. For a set fee per item, you also can send up to three pieces of luggage, each weighing up to 30 kilos (about 66 pounds), as registered baggage. Note that your baggage may be transported on a different train—and could potentially arrive later than you do. In many stations, you'll find self-service luggage carts at your disposal, as well as baggage checkrooms and lockers.

Reservations are required for some trains (such as the *TGV*) and advisable on all trains during the summer months and holidays, as well as on popular routes. Various discount excursion tickets and rail passes also are available, including the Eurailpass (which covers train travel throughout much of Europe), the Europass (a more limited version of the Eurailpass), and the France Railpass (for travel only within France). Note that most rail passes must be purchased before you leave the US.

You can reserve and purchase tickets or passes in the US from travel agents or from *SNCF*'s North American representative, *Rail Europe* (phone: 800-4-EURAIL; fax: 800-432-1329); for *Eurostar* reservations, call 800-94-CHUNNEL. In France, tickets can be purchased at train stations, *SNCF* offices, travel agencies displaying the *SNCF* sign, and—usually for a surcharge—aboard trains. Packaged rail tours in France are offered by companies such as *Accent on Travel* (112 N. Fifth St., Klamath Falls, OR 97601; phone: 503-885-7330), which also sells French rail passes and individual tickets.

FURTHER INFORMATION

Useful information about European rail travel, including rail passes, is provided in *Europe on Track* and other publications available from *Rail Europe* (phone above). The *Thomas Cook European Timetable,* a compendium of European rail services, is available in bookstores and from the *Forsyth Travel Library* (9154 W. 57th St., PO Box 2975, Shawnee Mission, KS 66201-1375; phone: 800-367-7984 or 913-384-3440; fax: 913-384-3553). Other useful resources include the *Eurail Guide,* by Kathryn Turpin and Marvin Saltzman (Eurail Guide Annual, 27540 Pacific Coast Hwy., Malibu, CA 90265; no phone) and *Europe by Eurail,* by George and LaVerne Ferguson (Globe Pequot Press, 6 Business Park Rd., PO Box 833, Old Saybrook, CT 06475; phone: 203-395-0440; fax: 203-395-0312).

In France, there are information desks in the main train stations, and in most stations, racks display city-to-city timetables *(fiches horaire).* The *Guide Pratique du Voyageur* (available only in French) provides information on train travel throughout France; its companion *Guide du Voyageur TGV* focuses on France's high-speed trains.

Traveling by Car

Driving is the most flexible way to explore France. To drive in France, a US citizen needs a US driver's license. In addition, an International Driver's Permit (IDP) is recommended (although it is not required). The IDP—essentially a translation of your license into nine languages—can be obtained from US branches or the main office of the *American Automobile Association* (*AAA;* for locations, check the yellow pages or contact the main office: 1000 AAA Dr., Heathrow, FL 32746-5080; phone: 407-444-7000; fax: 407-444-7380).

Proof of liability insurance also is necessary and is a standard part of any car rental contract. To be sure of having the appropriate coverage, let the rental staff know in advance about the national borders you plan to cross. If buying a car and using it abroad, you must carry an International Insurance Certificate, known as a Green Card (*Carte Verte* in France), which can be obtained from your insurance agent or through the *AAA.*

Driving in France is on the right side of the road. The basic rule of the road is *priorité à droite* (priority to the right), which means that unless there is some indication to the contrary, the car coming from the right has the right of way—even if coming from a minor side street or entering a traffic circle from an approach road. Pictorial direction signs are standardized under the International Roadsign System, and their meanings are indicated by their shapes: Triangular signs indicate danger; circular signs give instructions; and rectangular signs provide information.

Except for stretches of free autoroutes in the vicinity of cities, most major highways (designated by A on pan-European maps) are *autoroutes à péage,* or toll roads. Free roads include *routes nationales* (designated by N) and secondary, or regional, *routes départementales* (designated by D).

Distances are measured in kilometers (km) rather than miles (1 mile equals approximately 1.6 kilometers; 1 kilometer equals approximately .62 mile) and speeds in kilometers per hour (kmh). French speed limits usually are 130 kmh (81 mph) on toll *autoroutes* (superhighways), 100 kmh (68 mph) on free *autoroutes* and dual carriageways (four-lane highways), and 80 kmh (56 mph) on other roads outside built-up areas. In towns, unless otherwise indicated, the speed limit usually is 60 kmh (37 mph); on the *boulevards périphériques* around Paris the speed limit is 80 kmh (50 mph).

Seat belts are compulsory for both front- and back-seat passengers; children under 10 must travel in the back seat. In Paris and some other cities, honking is discouraged during the day and forbidden at night; flash your headlights instead. If you park in a restricted zone, you may return to find a wheel "clamped," which renders the car inoperable and involves a tedious—and costly—process to get it freed. For more information, consult *Euroad: The Complete Guide to Motoring in Europe* (VLE Ltd., PO Box 444, Ft. Lee, NJ 07024; phone: 201-585-5080; fax: 201-585-5110).

MAPS

Road maps are sold at gas stations throughout France. Some free maps can be obtained from branches of the *French Government Tourist Office* in the US. Among the most comprehensive and up-to-date road maps of France are those available from Michelin Travel Publications (PO Box 19008, Greenville, SC 29602-9008; phone: 803-458-5000 in South Carolina; 800-423-0485 elsewhere in the US; fax: 803-458-5665). *The Hallwag Road Map of France* (Rand McNally, 8255 N. Central Park, Skokie, IL 60076; phone: 800-627-2897; fax: 800-673-0280) is another good resource. *Freytag & Berndt* maps cover most destinations in Europe (including France) and can be ordered—along with the maps of many other publishers—from *Map Link* (25 E. Mason St., Suite 201, Santa Barbara, CA 93101; phone: 805-965-4402; fax: 800-MAP-SPOT or 805-962-0884). The *American Automobile Association* (*AAA;* address above) also provides some useful reference sources, including a regional map of France and an overall planning map of Europe, as well as the *Travel Guide to Europe* and *Motoring in Europe.*

AUTOMOBILE CLUBS AND BREAKDOWNS

To protect yourself in case of breakdowns while driving to and through France, and for travel information and other benefits, consider joining a reputable automobile club. The largest of these is the *American Automobile Association* (*AAA;* address above). Before joining this or any other automobile club, check whether it has reciprocity with French clubs such as the *Automobile Club National* (5 Rue Auber, Paris 75009; phone: 33-1-44-51-53-99; fax: 33-1-49-24-93-99).

GASOLINE

Gasoline is sold in liters (about 3.8 liters = 1 gallon). Leaded, unleaded, and diesel fuel are available.

RENTING A CAR

You can rent a car through a travel agent or international rental firm before leaving home, or from a regional or local company once in France. Reserve in advance.

Most car rental companies require a credit card, although some will accept a substantial cash deposit. The minimum age to rent a car is set by the company; some also may impose special conditions on drivers above a certain age. Electing to pay for collision damage waiver (CDW) protection will add to the cost of renting a car, but releases you from financial liability for the vehicle. Additional costs include drop-off charges or one-way service fees. In conjunction with *Avis, French National Railways (SNCF)* also offers a car rental service at rail stations throughout France.

Car Rental Companies

Auto Europe (phone: 800-223-5555).
Avis (phone: 800-331-1084).
Budget (phone: 800-472-3325).
Dergi Location (phone: 33-1-45-87-27-04).
Dollar Rent A Car (known in Europe as *EuroDollar Rent A Car;* phone: 800-800-6000).
Europe by Car (phone: 212-581-3040 in New York State; 800-223-1516 elsewhere in the US).
European Car Reservations (phone: 800-535-3303).
Foremost Euro-Car (phone: 800-272-3299).
Hertz (phone: 800-654-3001).
Kemwel Group (phone: 800-678-0678).
Meier's International (phone: 800-937-0700).
National (known in Europe as *Europcar;* phone: 800-CAR-EUROPE).
Town and Country/ITS (phone: 800-248-4350 in Florida; 800-521-0643 elsewhere in the US).
Thrifty (phone: 800-367-2277).

Package Tours

A package is a collection of travel services that can be purchased in a single transaction. Its principal advantages are convenience and economy—the cost usually is lower than that of the same services purchased separately. Tour programs generally can be divided into two categories: escorted or locally hosted (with a set itinerary) and independent (usually more flexible).

When considering a package tour, read the brochure *carefully* to determine exactly what is included and any conditions that may apply, and check the company's record with the *Better Business Bureau.* The *United States Tour Operators Association* (*USTOA;* 211 E. 51st St., Suite 12B, New York, NY 10022; phone: 212-750-7371; fax: 212-421-1285) also can be helpful in determining a package tour operator's reliability. As with charter flights, to safeguard your funds, always make your check out to the company's escrow account.

Many tour operators offer packages focused on special interests such as the arts, nature study, sports, and other recreations. *All Adventure Travel* (5589 Arapahoe St., Suite 208, Boulder, CO 80303; phone: 800-537-4025 or 303-440-7924; fax: 303-440-4160) represents such specialized packagers. Many also are listed in the *Specialty Travel Index* (305 San Anselmo Ave., Suite 313, San Anselmo, CA 94960; phone: 415-459-4900 in California; 800-442-4922 elsewhere in the US; fax: 415-459-4974).

Package Tour Operators

Abercrombie & Kent (1520 Kensington Rd., Oak Brook, IL 60521; phone: 800-323-7308 or 708-954-2944; fax: 708-954-3324).

Above the Clouds Trekking (PO Box 398, Worcester, MA 01602; phone: 800-233-4499 or 508-799-4499; fax: 508-797-4779).

Adventure Center (1311 63rd St., Suite 200, Emeryville, CA 94608; phone: 510-654-1879 in northern California; 800-227-8747 elsewhere in the US; fax: 510-654-4200).

Adventure Golf Holidays (815 North Rd., Westfield, MA 01085; phone: 800-628-9655 or 413-568-2855).

Adventure Tours (10612 Beaver Dam Rd., Hunt Valley, MD 21030-2205; phone: 410-785-3500 in the Baltimore area; 800-638-9040 elsewhere in the US; fax: 410-584-2771).

Adventures in Golf (29 Valencia Dr., Nashua, NH 03062; phone: 603-882-8367; fax: 603-595-6514).

Adventures on Skis (815 North Rd., Westfield, MA 01085; phone: 800-628-9655 or 413-568-2855; fax: 413-562-3621).

AESU (2 Hamill Rd., Suite 248, Baltimore, MD 21210; phone: 800-638-7640 or 410-323-4416; fax: 410-323-4498).

AHI International (701 Lee St., Des Plaines, IL 60016; phone: 800-323-7373 or 312-694-9330; fax: 708-699-7108).

Alternative Travel Groups (69-71 Banbury Rd., Oxford 0X2 6PE, England; phone: 800-527-5997 in the US; 44-1865-310255 in Great Britain; fax: 44-1865-310299).

American Airlines FlyAAway Vacations (offices throughout the US; phone: 800-321-2121).

American Express Vacations (offices throughout the US; phone: 800-YES-AMEX).

American Museum of Natural History Discovery Tours (Central Park W. at 79th St., New York, NY 10024; phone: 212-769-5700).

Archaeological Tours (271 Madison Ave., Suite 904, New York, NY 10016; phone: 212-986-3054; fax: 212-370-1561).

Art and Anthropological Tours (322 Oakland St., Oakland, CA 94607; phone: 510-465-5528; fax: 510-763-4431).

AutoVenture (425 Pike St., Suite 502, Seattle, WA 98101; phone: 800-426-7502 or 206-624-6033; fax: 206-340-8891).

Bacchants' Pilgrimages (475 Sansome St., Suite 840, San Francisco, CA 94111; phone: 800-952-0226 or 415-981-8518; fax: 415-291-9419).

Backroads (1516 Fifth St., Berkeley, CA 94710-1740; phone: 800-462-2848 or 510-527-1555; fax: 510-527-1444).

Bike Tour France (5523 Wedgewood Dr., Charlotte, NC 28210; phone: 704-527-0955).

Bike Tours/Bike Events (PO Box 75, Bath, Avon BA1 1BX, England; phone: 44-1225-310859 or 44-1225-480130; fax: 44-1225-480132).

Blue Marble Travel (2 Rue Dussoubs, Paris 75002, France; phone: 33-1-42-36-02-34; fax: 33-1-42-21-14-77; in the US, contact *Odyssey Adventures,* 305 Commercial St., Suite 505, Portland, ME 04101; phone: 800-544-3216 or 207-773-0905; fax: 207-773-0943).

Brendan Tours (15137 Califa St., Van Nuys, CA 91411; phone: 800-421-8446 or 818-785-9696; fax: 818-902-9876).

British Airways Holidays (75-20 Astoria Blvd., Jackson Heights, NY 11370; phone: 800-AIRWAYS).

British Coastal Trails (California Plaza, 1001 B Ave., Suite 302, Coronado, CA 92118; phone: 800-473-1210 or 619-437-1211; fax: 619-437-8394).

Butterfield & Robinson (70 Bond St., Suite 300, Toronto, Ontario M5B 1X3, Canada; phone: 800-387-1147 or 416-864-1354; fax: 416-864-0541).

Caravan Tours (401 N. Michigan Ave., Chicago, IL 60611; phone: 800-CARAVAN or 312-321-9800; fax: 312-321-9810).

Catholic Travel (10018 Cedar Lane, Kensington, MD 20895; phone: 301-530-8963 or 301-530-7682; fax: 301-530-6614).

Catholic Travel Centre (7301 Sepulveda Blvd., Van Nuys, CA 91405; phone: 800-553-5233 or 818-909-9910; fax: 818-997-8981).

Central Holiday Tours (206 Central Ave., Jersey City, NJ 07307; phone: 800-935-5000 or 201-798-5777; fax: 201-963-0966).

Certified Vacations (110 E. Broward Blvd., Ft. Lauderdale, FL 33302; phone: 800-233-7260 or 305-522-1440; fax: 305-468-4781).

Classic Adventures (PO Box 153, Hamlin, NY 14464-0153; phone: 800-777-8090 or 716-964-8488; fax: 716-964-7297).

Collette Tours (162 Middle St., Pawtucket, RI 02860; phone: 800-752-2655 in New England; 800-832-4656 elsewhere in the US; fax: 401-727-4745).

Contiki Holidays (300 Plaza Alicante, Suite 900, Garden Grove, CA 92640; phone: 800-266-8454 or 714-740-0808; fax: 714-740-0818).

Continental Grand Destinations (offices throughout the US; phone: 800-634-5555).

Coopersmith's England (6441 Valley View Rd., Oakland, CA 94611; phone: 510-339-3977; fax: 510-339-7135).

Dailey-Thorp (330 W. 58th St., New York, NY 10019-1817; phone: 212-307-1555; fax: 212-974-1420).

Delta's Dream Vacations (PO Box 1525, Ft. Lauderdale, FL 33302; phone: 800-872-7786).

DER Tours (11933 Wilshire Blvd., Los Angeles, CA 90025; phone: 800-782-2424 or 310-479-4411; fax: 310-479-2239; and 9501 W. Devon Ave., Rosemont, IL 60018; phone: 800-782-2424 or 708-692-6300; fax: 708-692-4506).

DMI Tours (11757 Katy Fwy., Suite 250, Houston, TX 77079; phone: 800-553-5090 or 713-497-5666; fax: 713-497-8694).

Educational Adventures (815 North Rd., Westfield, MA 01085; phone: 800-628-9655 or 413-568-2855; fax: 413-562-3621).

Edwards & Edwards (1 Times Square Plaza, 12th Floor, New York, NY 10036-6585; phone: 212-944-0290 in New York State; 800-223-6108 elsewhere in the US; fax: 212-944-7497).

Equitour (PO Box 807, Dubois, WY 82513; phone: 307-455-3363 in Wyoming; 800-545-0019 elsewhere in the US; fax: 307-455-2354).

Escapade Tours (9 West Office Center, 2200 Fletcher Ave., Ft. Lee, NJ 07024; phone: 800-356-2405 or 201-346-9061; fax: 201-346-0511).

EuroConnection (2004 196th St. SW, Suite 4, Lynnwood, WA 98036; phone: 800-645-3876 or 206-670-1140; fax: 206-775-7561).

Europe Through the Back Door (PO Box 2009, Edmonds, WA 98020; phone: 206-771-8303; fax: 206-771-0833).

European Tours Limited (5725 77th St., Lubbock, TX 79424; phone: 800-722-3679 or 806-794-4991; fax: 806-794-8550).

Exodus (9 Weir Rd., London SW12 OLT, England; phone: 44-181-675-5550; fax: 44-181-673-0779; represented in the US by *Safaricenter,* 3201 N. Sepulveda Blvd., Manhattan Beach, CA 90266; phone: 800-223-6046 or 310-546-4411; fax: 310-546-3188).

Extra Value Travel (683 S. Collier Blvd., Marco Island, FL 33937; phone: 813-394-3384; fax: 813-394-4848).

FITS Equestrian (685 Lateen Rd., Solvang, CA 93463; phone: 800-666-3487 or 805-688-9494; fax: 805-688-2493).

Five Star Touring (60 E. 42nd St., Suite 612, New York, NY 10165; phone: 212-818-9140 in New York City; 800-792-7827 elsewhere in the US; fax: 212-818-9142).

Forum Travel International (91 Gregory La., Suite 21, Pleasant Hill, CA 94523; phone: 510-671-2900; fax: 510-671-2993 or 510-946-1500).

4th Dimension Tours (1150 NW 72nd Ave., Suite 333, Miami, FL 33126; phone: 800-343-0020 or 305-477-1525; fax: 305-477-0731).

Gadabout Tours (700 E. Tahquitz Canyon Way, Palm Springs, CA 92262-6767; phone: 800-952-5068 or 619-325-5556; fax: 619-325-5127).

Globus/Cosmos (5301 S. Federal Circle, Littleton, CO 80123; phone: 800-221-0090, 800-556-5454, or 303-797-2800; fax: 303-347-2080).

GOGO Tours (69 Spring St., Ramsey, NJ 07446-0507; phone: 201-934-3759).

Golf International (275 Madison Ave., New York, NY 10016; phone: 800-833-1389 or 212-986-9176; fax: 212-986-3720).

Golfing Holidays (231 E. Millbrae Ave., Millbrae, CA 94030; phone: 800-652-7847 or 415-697-0230; fax: 415-697-8687).

HF Holidays, Ltd. (Imperial House, Edgware Rd., London NW9 5AL, England; phone: 44-181-905-9558; fax: 44-181-905-9558).

Hiking Holidays (PO Box 750, Bristol, VT 05443-0750; phone: 802-453-4816; fax: 802-453-4806).

Himalayan Travel (112 Prospect St., Stamford, CT 06901; phone: 800-225-2380 or 203-359-3711; fax: 203-359-3669).

HSA Voyages (160 E. 26th St., Suite 5H, New York, NY 10010; phone: 800-927-4765 or 212-689-5400; fax: 212-689-5435).

In Quest of the Classics (PO Box 890745, Temecula, CA 92589-0745; phone: 800-227-1393 or 909-694-5866 in California; 800-221-5246 elsewhere in the US; fax: 909-694-5873).

Insight International Tours (745 Atlantic Ave., Suite 720, Boston, MA 02111; phone: 800-582-8380 or 617-482-2000; fax: 617-482-2425).

InterGolf (PO Box 500608, Atlanta, GA 31150; phone: 800-468-0051 or 404-518-1250; fax: 404-518-1272).

International Bicycle Tours (PO Box 754, Essex, CT 06426; phone: 203-767-7005; fax: 203-767-3090).

International Golf Vacations (PO Box 1129, Maplewood, NJ 07040; phone: 201-378-9170; fax: 201-378-9193).

INTRAV (7711 Bonhomme Ave., St. Louis, MO 63105-1961; phone: 800-456-8100; fax: 314-727-6198).

ITC Golf Tours (4134 Atlantic Ave., Suite 205, Long Beach, CA 90807; phone: 800-257-4981 or 310-595-6905; fax: 310-424-6683).

Jet Vacations (1775 Broadway, New York, NY 10019; phone: 800-JET-0999 or 212-247-0999; fax: 212-586-2069).

KLM/Northwest Vacations Europe (c/o *MLT,* 5130 Hwy. 101, Minnetonka, MN 55345; phone: 800-727-1111; fax: 800-655-7890).

Liberty Travel (for the nearest location, contact the central office: 69 Spring St., Ramsey, NJ 07446; phone: 201-934-3500; fax: 201-934-3888).

Marathon Tours (108 Main St., Charlestown, MA 02129; phone: 800-444-4097 or 617-242-7845; fax: 617-242-7686).

Marsans International (19 W. 34th St., Suite 302, New York, NY 10001; phone: 800-777-9110 or 212-239-3880; fax: 212-239-4129).

Matterhorn Travel Service (2450 Riva Rd., Annapolis, MD 21401; phone: 410-224-2230 in Maryland; 800-638-9150 elsewhere in the US; fax: 410-266-3868).

Maupintour (PO Box 807, Lawrence, KS 66044; phone: 800-255-4266 or 913-843-1211; fax: 913-843-8351).

Mercator Travel (122 E. 42nd St., New York, NY 10168; phone: 800-514-9880 or 212-682-6979; fax: 212-682-7379).

MLT Vacations (c/o *MLT,* address above; phone: 800-328-0025 or 612-989-5000; fax: 612-474-0725).

Mountain Travel-Sobek (6420 Fairmount Ave., El Cerrito, CA 94530; phone: 510-527-8100 in California; 800-227-2384 elsewhere in the US; fax: 510-525-7710).

Nantahala Outdoor Center Adventure Travel (13077 Hwy. 19 W., Bryson City, NC 28713-9114; phone: 800-232-7238 for reservations; 704-488-2175 for information; fax: 704-488-2498).

New England Vacation Tours (PO Box 560, West Dover, VT 05356; phone: 800-742-7669 or 802-464-2076; fax: 802-464-2629).

Odyssey Adventures (305 Commercial St., Suite 505, Portland, ME 04101; phone: 800-544-3216 or 207-773-1156; fax: 207-773-0943).

Olson Travelworld (970 W. 190th St., Suite 425, Torrance, CA 90502; phone: 800-421-2255 or 310-354-2600; fax: 310-768-0050).

Past Times Tours (800 Larch La., Sacramento, CA 95864-5042; phone: 916-485-8140; fax: 916-488-4804).

Petrabax Tours (97-45 Queens Blvd., Suite 600, Rego Park, NY 11374; phone: 800-367-6611 or 718-897-7272; fax: 718-275-3943).

Pleasure Break (3701 Algonquin Rd., Suite 900, Rolling Meadows, IL 60008; phone: 708-670-6300 in Illinois; 800-777-1885 elsewhere in the US; fax: 708-670-7689).

Progressive Travels (224 W. Galer Ave., Suite C, Seattle, WA 98119; phone: 800-245-2229 or 206-285-1987; fax: 206-285-1988).

Prospect Music and Art Tours (454-458 Chiswick High Rd., London W45TT, England; phone: 44-181-995-2151 or 44-181-995-2163; fax: 44-181-742-1969).

Regina Tours (401 South St., Room 4B, Chardon, OH 44024; phone: 800-228-4654 or 216-286-9166; fax: 216-286-4231).

Saga International Holidays (222 Berkeley St., Boston, MA 02116; phone: 800-343-0273 or 617-262-2262).

Select Travel Service (main office: Bridgefoot House, 159 High St., Huntington, Cambridgeshire PE18 7TF, England; phone: 44-181-480-433783; fax: 44-181-480-433514; US office: 795 Franklin Ave., Franklin Lakes, NJ 07417; phone: 800-752-6787 or 201-891-4143; fax: 201-847-0053).

Sierra Club Outings (730 Polk St., San Francisco, CA 94109; phone: 415-923-5630).

Smithsonian Study Tours and Seminars (1100 Jefferson Dr. SW, Room 3045, Washington, DC 20560; phone: 202-357-4700; fax: 202-786-2315).

Steve Lohr's Holidays (206 Central Ave., Jersey City, NJ, 07307; phone: 201-798-3900 in New Jersey; 800-929-5647 elsewhere in the US; fax: 201-693-0966).

Take-A-Guide (main office: 11 Uxbridge St., London W8 7TQ, England; phone: 44-181-960-0459; fax: 44-181-964-0990; US office: 954 Lexington Ave., New York, NY 10021; phone: 800-825-4946; fax: 800-635-7177).

Tauck Tours (PO Box 5027, Westport, CT 06881; phone: 800-468-2825 or 203-226-6911; fax: 203-221-6828).

Thomas Cook (headquarters: 45 Berkeley St., Piccadilly, London W1A 1EB, England; phone: 44-171-499-4000; fax: 44-171-408-4299; main US office: 100 Cambridge Park Dr., Cambridge, MA 02140; phone: 800-846-6272; fax: 617-349-1094).

Trafalgar Tours (11 E. 26th St., Suite 1300, New York, NY 10010-1402; phone: 800-854-0103 or 212-689-8977; fax: 212-725-7776).

TRAVCOA (PO Box 2630, Newport Beach, CA 92658; phone: 800-992-2004 or 714-476-2800 in California; 800-992-2003 elsewhere in the US; fax: 714-476-2538).

Travel Bound (599 Broadway, Penthouse, New York, NY 10012; phone: 212-334-1350 in New York State; 800-456-8656 elsewhere in the US; fax: 800-208-7080).

Travel Concepts (62 Commonwealth Ave., Suite 3, Boston, MA 02116; phone: 617-266-8450; fax: 617-267-2477).

Travent International (PO Box 800, Bristol, VT 05443-0800; phone: 800-325-3009 or 802-453-5710; fax: 802-453-4806).

TWA Getaway Vacations (Getaway Vacation Center, 10 E. Stow Rd., Marlton, NJ 08053; phone: 800-GETAWAY; fax: 609-985-4125).

United Airlines Vacations (PO Box 24580, Milwaukee, WI 53224-0580; phone: 800-328-6877).

Unitours (8 S. Michigan Ave., Chicago, IL 60603; phone: 312-782-1590 or 800-621-0557; fax: 312-726-0339).

Value Holidays (10224 N. Port Washington Rd., Mequon, WI 53092; phone: 800-558-6850 or 414-241-6373; fax: 414-241-6379).

Vermont Bicycle Touring (PO Box 711, Bristol, VT 05443-0711; phone: 802-453-4811; fax: 802-453-4806).

The Wayfarers (172 Bellevue Ave., Newport, RI 02840; phone: 800-249-4620 or 401-849-5087; fax: 410-849-5878).

Wide World of Golf (PO Box 5217, Carmel, CA 93921; phone: 800-214-4653 or 408-624-6667; fax: 408-625-9671).

Wilderness Travel (801 Allston Way, Berkeley, CA 94710; phone: 800-368-2794 or 510-548-0420; fax: 510-548-0347).

Worldwide Rocky Mountain Cycle Tours (PO Box 1978, Canmore, Alberta T0L 0M0, Canada; phone: 800-661-2453 or 403-678-6770; fax: 403-678-4451).

X.O. Travel Consultants (38 W. 32nd St., Suite 1009, New York, NY 10001; phone: 212-947-5530 in New York State; 800-262-9682 elsewhere in the US; fax: 212-971-0924).

Yamnuska (PO Box 1920, 1316 Railway Ave., Canmore, Alberta T0L 0M0, Canada; phone: 403-678-4164; fax: 403-678-4450).

Insurance

The first person with whom you should discuss travel insurance is your own insurance broker. You may discover that the insurance you already carry protects you adequately while traveling and that you need little additional coverage. If you charge travel services, the credit card company also may provide some insurance coverage (and other safeguards).

Types of Travel Insurance

Automobile insurance: Provides collision, theft, property damage, and personal liability protection while driving.

Baggage and personal effects insurance: Protects your bags and their contents in case of damage or theft at any point during your travels.

Default and/or bankruptcy insurance: Provides coverage in the event of default and/or bankruptcy on the part of the tour operator, airline, or other travel supplier.

Flight insurance: Covers accidental injury or death while flying.

Personal accident and sickness insurance: Covers cases of illness, injury, or death in an accident while traveling.

Trip cancellation and interruption insurance: Guarantees a refund if you must cancel a trip; may reimburse you for additional travel costs incurred in catching up with a tour or traveling home early.

Combination policies: Include any or all of the above.

Disabled Travelers

Make travel arrangements well in advance. Specify to all services involved the nature of your disability to determine if there are accommodations and facilities that meet your needs. Information about accessibility and transportation for the disabled in France is provided by the *Comité National Français de Liaison pour la Réadaptation des Handicapés* (38 Bd. Raspail, Paris 75007, France; phone: 33-1-45-48-90-13; fax: 33-1-45-48-99-21). For information on the accessibility of French airports, contact the US representative of the *Paris Airport Authority, Marketing Challenges International* (10 E. 21st St., Suite 600, New York, NY 10010; phone: 212-529-8484; fax: 212-460-8287).

The *French Government Tourist Office* in the US distributes the *Paris Hotel Guide* and *Paris Guide to Monuments and Museums,* both of which list wheelchair accessibility. Hotel and restaurant guides, such as the *Michelin*

Red Guide to France (Michelin Travel Publications, PO Box 19008, Greenville, SC 29602-9008; phone: 803-458-5000 in South Carolina; 800-423-0485 elsewhere in the US; fax: 803-458-5665), use a standard symbol of access (person in a wheelchair) to point out accommodations suitable for wheelchair-bound guests.

Organizations

ACCENT on Living (PO Box 700, Bloomington, IL 61702; phone: 800-787-8444 or 309-378-2961; fax: 309-378-4420).

Access: The Foundation for Accessibility by the Disabled (PO Box 356, Malverne, NY 11565; phone/fax: 516-887-5798).

American Foundation for the Blind (15 W. 16th St., New York, NY 10011; phone: 800-232-5463 or 212-620-2147; fax: 212-727-7418).

Holiday Care Service (2 Old Bank Chambers, Station Rd., Horley, Surrey RH6 9HW, England; phone: 44-1293-774535; fax: 44-1293-784647).

I.CARE (69-73 Av. du Général Leclerc, Boîte Postal 113, Boulogne 92106, France; phone: 33-1-46-09-91-96; fax: 33-1-46-21-50-80).

Information Center for Individuals with Disabilities (Ft. Point Pl., 27-43 Wormwood St., Boston, MA 02210; phone: 800-462-5015 in Massachusetts; 617-727-5540 elsewhere in the US; TDD: 617-345-9743; fax: 617-345-5318).

International Help for the Disabled (*IHD;* Boîte Postale 62, Puget-sur-Argens 83480, France; phone: 33-94-81-61-51; fax: 33-94-81-61-43).

Mobility International (main office: 228 Borough High St., London SE1 1JX, England; phone: 44-171-403-5688; fax: 44-171-378-1292; US office: *MIUSA,* PO Box 10767, Eugene, OR 97440; phone/TDD: 503-343-1284; fax: 503-343-6812).

Moss Rehabilitation Hospital Travel Information Service (telephone referrals only; phone: 215-456-9600; TDD: 215-456-9602).

National Rehabilitation Information Center (8455 Colesville Rd., Suite 935, Silver Spring, MD 20910; phone: 301-588-9284; fax: 301-587-1967).

Paralyzed Veterans of America (*PVA;* PVA/ATTS Program, 801 18th St. NW, Washington, DC 20006; phone: 202-872-1300 in Washington, DC; 800-424-8200 elsewhere in the US; fax: 202-785-4452).

Royal Association for Disability and Rehabilitation (*RADAR;* 12 City Forum, 250 City Rd., London EC1V 8AF, England; phone: 44-171-250-3222; fax: 44-171-250-0212).

Society for the Advancement of Travel for the Handicapped (*SATH;* 347 Fifth Ave., Suite 610, New York, NY 10016; phone: 212-447-7284; fax: 212-725-8253).

Travel Industry and Disabled Exchange (*TIDE;* 5435 Donna Ave., Tarzana, CA 91356; phone: 818-368-5648).

Tripscope (The Courtyard, Evelyn Rd., London W4 5JL, England; phone: 44-181-994-9294; fax: 44-181-994-3618).

Publications

Access Travel: A Guide to the Accessibility of Airport Terminals (Consumer Information Center, Dept. 578Z, Pueblo, CO 81009; phone: 719-948-3334).

Air Transportation of Handicapped Persons (Publication #AC-120-32; *US Department of Transportation,* Distribution Unit, Publications Section, M-443-2, 400 Seventh St. SW, Washington, DC 20590; phone: 202-366-0039).

The Diabetic Traveler (PO Box 8223 RW, Stamford, CT 06905; phone: 203-327-5832; fax: 203-975-1748).

Directory of Travel Agencies for the Disabled and Travel for the Disabled, both by Helen Hecker (Twin Peaks Press, PO Box 129, Vancouver, WA 98666; phone: 800-637-CALM or 206-694-2462; fax: 206-696-3210).

Guide to Traveling with Arthritis (Upjohn Company, PO Box 989, Dearborn, MI 48121; phone: 800-253-9860).

The Handicapped Driver's Mobility Guide (*American Automobile Association,* 1000 AAA Dr., Heathrow, FL 32746-5080; phone: 407-444-7000; fax: 407-444-7380).

Handicapped Travel Newsletter (PO Box 269, Athens, TX 75751; phone/fax: 903-677-1260).

Handi-Travel: A Resource Book for Disabled and Elderly Travellers, by Cinnie Noble (*Canadian Rehabilitation Council for the Disabled,* 45 Sheppard Ave. E., Suite 801, Toronto, Ontario M2N 5W9, Canada; phone/TDD: 416-250-7490; fax: 416-229-1371).

Holidays and Travel Abroad, edited by John Stanford (*Royal Association for Disability and Rehabilitation,* address above).

Incapacitated Passengers Air Travel Guide (*International Air Transport Association,* Publications Sales Department, 2000 Peel St., Montreal, Quebec H3A 2R4, Canada; phone: 514-844-6311; fax: 514-844-5286).

Ticket to Safe Travel (*American Diabetes Association,* 1660 Duke St., Alexandria, VA 22314; phone: 800-232-3472 or 703-549-1500; fax: 703-836-7439).

Travel for the Patient with Chronic Obstructive Pulmonary Disease (Dr. Harold Silver, 1601 18th St. NW, Washington, DC 20009; phone: 202-667-0134; fax: 202-667-0148).

Travel Tips for Hearing-Impaired People (*American Academy of Otolaryngology,* 1 Prince St., Alexandria, VA 22314; phone: 703-836-4444; fax: 703-683-5100).

Travel Tips for People with Arthritis (*Arthritis Foundation,* 1314 Spring St. NW, Atlanta, GA 30309; phone: 800-283-7800 or 404-872-7100; fax: 404-872-0457).

Traveling Like Everybody Else: A Practical Guide for Disabled Travelers, by Jacqueline Freedman and Susan Gersten (Modan Publishing, PO Box 1202, Bellmore, NY 11710; phone: 516-679-1380; fax: 516-679-1448).

Package Tour Operators

Accessible Journeys (35 W. Sellers Ave., Ridley Park, PA 19078; phone: 800-846-4537 or 215-521-0339; fax: 215-521-6959).

Accessible Tours/Directions Unlimited (Attn.: Lois Bonnani, 720 N. Bedford Rd., Bedford Hills, NY 10507; phone: 800-533-5343 or 914-241-1700; fax: 914-241-0243).

Beehive Business and Leisure Travel (1130 W. Center St., N. Salt Lake, UT 84054; phone: 800-777-5727 or 801-292-4445; fax: 801-298-9460).

Classic Travel Service (8 W. 40th St., New York, NY 10018; phone: 212-869-2560 in New York State; 800-247-0909 elsewhere in the US; fax: 212-944-4493).

Croisières Handy (Port Minervois, Homps 11200, France; phone: 33-68-91-16-48; fax: 33-94-81-61-43).

Dialysis at Sea Cruises (611 Barry Pl., Indian Rocks Beach, FL 34635; phone: 800-775-1333 or 813-596-4614; fax: 813-596-0203).

Evergreen Travel Service (4114 198th St. SW, Suite 13, Lynnwood, WA 98036-6742; phone: 800-435-2288 or 206-776-1184; fax: 206-775-0728).

Flying Wheels Travel (143 W. Bridge St., PO Box 382, Owatonna, MN 55060; phone: 800-535-6790 or 507-451-5005; fax: 507-451-1685).

Good Neighbor Travel Service (124 S. Main St., Viroqua, WI 54665; phone: 800-338-3245 or 608-637-2128; fax: 608-637-3030).

The Guided Tour (7900 Old York Rd., Suite 114B, Elkins Park, PA 19117-2339; phone: 800-783-5841 or 215-782-1370; fax: 215-635-2637).

Hinsdale Travel (201 E. Ogden Ave., Hinsdale, IL 60521; phone: 708-325-1335 or 708-469-7349; fax: 708-325-1342).

MedEscort International (*ABE International Airport,* PO Box 8766, Allentown, PA 18105-8766; phone: 800-255-7182 or 215-791-3111; fax: 215-791-9189).

Prestige World Travel (5710-X High Point Rd., Greensboro, NC 27407; phone: 800-476-7737 or 910-292-6690; fax: 910-632-9404).

Sprout (893 Amsterdam Ave., New York, NY 10025; phone: 212-222-9575; fax: 212-222-9768).

Weston Travel Agency (134 N. Cass Ave., Westmont, IL 60559; phone: 708-968-2513 in Illinois; 800-633-3725 elsewhere in the US; fax: 708-968-2539).

Single Travelers

The travel industry is not very fair to people who vacation by themselves—they often end up paying more than those traveling in pairs. There are services catering to single travelers, however, that match travel companions, offer travel arrangements with shared accommodations, and provide information and discounts. Useful publications include *Going Solo* (Doerfer Communications, PO Box 123, Apalachicola, FL 32329; phone/fax: 904-

653-8848) and *Traveling on Your Own,* by Eleanor Berman (Random House, Order Dept., 400 Hahn Rd., Westminster, MD 21157; phone: 800-733-3000; fax: 800-659-2436).

Organizations and Companies

Club Europa (802 W. Oregon St., Urbana, IL 61801; phone: 800-331-1882 or 217-344-5863; fax: 217-344-4072).

Contiki Holidays (300 Plaza Alicante, Suite 900, Garden Grove, CA 92640; phone: 800-466-0610 or 714-740-0808; fax: 714-740-0818).

Gallivanting (515 E. 79th St., Suite 20F, New York, NY 10021; phone: 800-933-9699 or 212-988-0617; fax: 212-988-0144).

Globus/Cosmos (5301 S. Federal Circle, Littleton, CO 80123; phone: 800-221-0090, 800-556-5454, or 303-797-2800; fax: 303-347-2080).

Insight International Tours (745 Atlantic Ave., Boston, MA 02111; phone: 800-582-8380 or 617-482-2000; fax: 617-482-2425).

Jane's International and Sophisticated Women Travelers (2603 Bath Ave., Brooklyn, NY 11214; phone: 718-266-2045; fax: 718-266-4062).

Marion Smith Singles (611 Prescott Pl., N. Woodmere, NY 11581; phone: 516-791-4852, 516-791-4865, or 212-944-2112; fax: 516-791-4879).

Partners-in-Travel (11660 Chenault St., Suite 119, Los Angeles, CA 90049; phone: 310-476-4869).

Singles in Motion (545 W. 236th St., Riverdale, NY 10463; phone/fax: 718-884-4464).

Singleworld (401 Theodore Fremd Ave., Rye, NY 10580; phone: 800-223-6490 or 914-967-3334; fax: 914-967-7395).

Solo Flights (63 High Noon Rd., Weston, CT 06883; phone: 800-266-1566 or 203-226-9993).

Suddenly Singles Tours (161 Dreiser Loop, Bronx, NY 10475; phone: 718-379-8800 in New York City; 800-859-8396 elsewhere in the US; fax: 718-379-8858).

Travel Companion Exchange (PO Box 833, Amityville, NY 11701; phone: 516-454-0880; fax: 516-454-0170).

Travel Companions (Atrium Financial Center, 1515 N. Federal Hwy., Suite 300, Boca Raton, FL 33432; phone: 800-383-7211 or 407-393-6448; fax: 407-451-8560).

Travel in Two's (239 N. Broadway, Suite 3, N. Tarrytown, NY 10591; phone: 914-631-8301 in New York State; 800-692-5252 elsewhere in the US).

Umbrella Singles (PO Box 157, Woodbourne, NY 12788; phone: 800-537-2797 or 914-434-6871; fax: 914-434-3532).

Older Travelers

Special discounts and more free time are just two factors that have given older travelers a chance to see the world at affordable prices. Many travel suppliers offer senior discounts—sometimes only to members of certain senior citizens organizations (which provide benefits of their own). When considering a particular package, make sure the facilities—and the pace of the tour—match your needs and physical condition.

Publications

Going Abroad: 101 Tips for Mature Travelers (*Grand Circle Travel,* 347 Congress St., Boston, MA 02210; phone: 800-221-2610 or 617-350-7500; fax: 617-423-0445).

The Mature Traveler (PO Box 50820, Reno, NV 89513-0820; phone: 702-786-7419).

Take a Camel to Lunch and Other Adventures for Mature Travelers, by Nancy O'Connell (Bristol Publishing Enterprises, PO Box 1737, San Leandro, CA 94577; phone: 510-895-4461 in California; 800-346-4889 elsewhere in the US; fax: 510-895-4459).

Unbelievably Good Deals & Great Adventures That You Absolutely Can't Get Unless You're Over 50, by Joan Rattner Heilman (Contemporary Books, 1200 Stetson Ave., Chicago, IL 60601; phone: 312-782-9181; fax: 312-540-4687).

Organizations

American Association of Retired Persons (*AARP;* 601 E St. NW, Washington, DC 20049; phone: 202-434-2277).

Golden Companions (PO Box 754, Pullman, WA 99163-0754; phone: 208-858-2183).

Mature Outlook (Customer Service Center, 6001 N. Clark St., Chicago, IL 60660; phone: 800-336-6330).

National Council of Senior Citizens (1331 F St. NW, Washington, DC 20004; phone: 202-347-8800; fax: 202-624-9595).

Package Tour Operators

Elderhostel (75 Federal St., Boston, MA 02110-1941; phone: 617-426-7788; fax: 617-426-8351).

Evergreen Travel Service (4114 198th St. SW, Suite 13, Lynnwood, WA 98036-6742; phone: 800-435-2288 or 206-776-1184; fax: 206-775-0728).

Gadabout Tours (700 E. Tahquitz Canyon Way, Palm Springs, CA 92262; phone: 800-952-5068 or 619-325-5556; fax: 619-325-5127).

Grand Circle Travel (347 Congress St., Boston, MA 02210; phone: 800-221-2610 or 617-350-7500; fax: 617-423-0445).

Grandtravel (6900 Wisconsin Ave., Suite 706, Chevy Chase, MD 20815; phone: 800-247-7651 or 301-986-0790; fax: 301-913-0166).

Insight International Tours (745 Atlantic Ave., Suite 720, Boston, MA 02111; phone: 800-582-8380 or 617-482-2000; fax: 617-482-2425).

Interhostel (*University of New Hampshire,* Division of Continuing Education, 6 Garrison Ave., Durham, NH 03824; phone: 800-733-9753 or 603-862-1147; fax: 603-862-1113).

Mature Tours (c/o *Solo Flights,* 63 High Noon Rd., Weston, CT 06883; phone: 800-266-1566 or 203-226-9993).

OmniTours (104 Wilmot Rd., Deerfield, IL 60015; phone: 800-962-0060 or 708-374-0088; fax: 708-374-9515).

Saga International Holidays (222 Berkeley St., Boston, MA 02116; phone: 800-343-0273 or 617-262-2262; fax: 617-375-5950).

Money Matters

The basic unit of currency in France is the French **franc** (abbreviated "F") which is divided into 100 **centimes**. The franc is distributed in coin denominations of 20F, 10F, 5F, 2F, 1F, and .50F, and 20 centimes, 10 centimes, and 5 centimes, and in bills of 500F, 200F, 100F, 50F, and 20F. Although the French use a comma in expressing numerical values where Americans use a decimal point (and vice versa), throughout this book we use the American style of notation. At the time of this writing, the exchange rate for French currency was 5.8 francs to $1 US.

Exchange rates are listed in international newspapers such as the *International Herald Tribune.* Foreign currency information and related services are provided by banks and companies such as *Thomas Cook Foreign Exchange* (for the nearest location, call 800-621-0666 or 312-236-0042; fax: 312-807-4895); *Harold Reuter and Company* (200 Park Ave., Suite 332E, New York, NY 10166; phone: 800-258-0456 or 212-661-0826; fax: 212-557-6622); and *Ruesch International* (for the nearest location, call 800-424-2923 or 202-408-1200; fax: 202-408-1211). In France, you will find the official rate of exchange posted in banks, airports, money exchange houses, hotels, and some shops. Since you will get more francs for your US dollar at banks and money exchanges, don't change more than $10 for foreign currency at other commercial establishments. Ask how much commission you're being charged and the exchange rate, and don't buy money on the black market (it may be counterfeit). Estimate your needs carefully; if you overbuy, you lose twice—buying and selling back.

CREDIT CARDS AND TRAVELER'S CHECKS

Most major credit cards enjoy wide domestic and international acceptance; however, not every hotel, restaurant, or shop in France accepts all (or in some cases any) credit cards. (Some cards may be issued under different names in Europe; for example, *MasterCard* may go under the name *Eurocard,* and *Visa* sometimes is called *Carte Bleue.*) When making purchases with a credit card, note that the rate of exchange depends on when the charge is processed; most credit card companies charge a 1% fee for converting foreign currency charges.

It's also wise to carry traveler's checks while on the road, since they are widely accepted and replaceable if stolen or lost. You can buy traveler's checks at banks and some are available by mail or phone. Keep a separate list of all traveler's checks (noting those that you have cashed) and the names and numbers of your credit cards. Both traveler's check and credit card companies have international numbers to call for information or in the event of loss or theft.

CASH MACHINES

Automated teller machines (ATMs—called "minibanques" in France) are increasingly common worldwide, and most banks participate in international ATM networks such as *CIRRUS* (phone: 800-4-CIRRUS) and *PLUS* (phone: 800-THE-PLUS). Cardholders can withdraw cash from any machine in the same network using either a "bank" card or, in some cases, a credit card. For instance, in France, ATMs that accept *MasterCard* or *Visa* are quite common. Additional information on ATMs and networks can be obtained from your bank or credit card company.

SENDING MONEY ABROAD

Should the need arise, you can have money sent to you throughout France via the services provided by *American Express MoneyGram* (phone: 800-926-9400 for information; 800-866-8800 for money transfers) or *Western Union Financial Services* (phone: 800-325-6000 or 800-325-4176). If you are down to your last cent and have no other way to obtain cash, the nearest *US Consulate* will let you call home to set these matters in motion.

Accommodations

For specific information on hotels, resorts, and other selected accommodations see *Checking In* in THE CITIES, *Best en Route* in DIRECTIONS, and sections throughout DIVERSIONS. The *French Government Tourist Office* issues regional guides listing tourist hotels officially graded by the government, as well as lists of selected, rated Paris hotels and US representatives of French hotels. Information on hotels in the Principality of Monaco is available from *SBM* (509 Madison Ave., New York, NY 10022; phone: 212-688-9890; fax: 212-935-2947) or the *Monaco Government Tourist and Convention Bureau* (845 Third Ave., New York, NY 10022; phone: 800-753-9696 or 212-759-5227; fax: 212-754-9320).

Tourist offices in over 50 French cities (and several larger airports and railway stations) provide a service called *Accueil de France*. For those touring France, this service can book a room at the next stop en route where there is another *Accueil* office.

RELAIS & CHÂTEAUX AND OTHER ASSOCIATIONS

Founded in France, the *Relais & Châteaux* association has grown to include hotels (and restaurants) in numerous countries. At press time, there were 154 members in France. All maintain very high standards in order to retain their memberships, as they are reviewed annually. An illustrated catalogue of properties is available from *Relais & Châteaux*

(11 E. 44th St., Suite 707, New York, NY 10017; phone: 212-856-0115; fax: 212-856-0193).

The smaller *Relais du Silence* (2 Passage du Guesden, Paris 75015, France; phone: 33-1-45-66-53-53 for reservations; 33-1-45-66-77-77 for information; fax: 1-40-65-90-09) is composed of former manor houses, rustic wayside inns, châteaux, and other properties, mostly in country settings—all with a focus on providing peace and quiet. Another group is the *Fédération Nationale des Logis de France* (43 Av. d'Italie, Paris 75013, France; phone: 33-1-45-84-70-00; fax: 33-1-45-83-59-66) with approximately 4,500 members in France. Member *logis* (literally lodging, dwelling, or home) are small family-run hotels in towns and villages throughout the countryside. Publications on both of these organizations are available free from branches of the *French Government Tourist Office* in the US.

A smaller French group offers overnight accommodations under the heading *Gîte de France–Chambre d'Hôte* (La Maison de Gîte de France, 35 Rue Godot de Nauroy, Paris 75439, France; phone: 33-1-49-70-75-75; fax: 33-1-49-70-75-76). The *gîte chambre d'hôte,* offering a room in a private house or on a farm, is the French version of a bed and breakfast establishment. At press time, there were about 6,000 *gîtes* in France, many in the countryside. Travelers interested in B&B stays also should contact the bed and breakfast association, *International Café Couette* (8 Rue de l'Isly, Paris 75008, France; phone: 33-1-42-94-92-00; fax: 33-1-42-94-93-12), and *Bed & Breakfast Reservations Services World-Wide* (PO Box 14841, Baton Rouge, LA 70898-4841; phone: 800-364-7242 or 504-336-4035; fax: 504-343-0672), an international association of B&B reservations services.

RENTAL OPTIONS

An attractive accommodations alternative for the visitor content to stay in one spot is a vacation rental. For a family or group, the per-person cost can be reasonable. To have your pick of the properties available throughout France, make inquiries at least six months in advance. The *Worldwide Home Rental Guide* (3501 Indian School Rd. NE, Albuquerque, NM 87106; phone/fax: 505-255-4271) lists rental properties and managing agencies.

Rental Property Agents

At Home Abroad (405 E. 56th St., Suite 6H, New York, NY 10022-2466; phone: 212-421-9165; fax: 212-752-1591).

B & V Associates (140 E. 56th St., Suite 4C, New York, NY 10022; phone: 800-546-4777 or 212-688-9538; fax: 212-688-9467).

Blakes Vacations (1076 Ash St., Winnetka, IL 60093; phone: 800-628-8118 or 708-446-4771; fax: 708-446-4772).

British Travel International (PO Box 299, Elkton, VA 22827; phone: 800-327-6097 or 703-298-2232; fax: 703-298-2347).

Castles, Cottages and Flats (7 Faneuil Hall Marketplace, Boston, MA 02109; phone: 800-742-6030 or 617-742-6030; fax: 617-367-4521).

Chez Vous (220 Redwood Hwy., Suite 129, Mill Valley, CA 94941; phone: 415-331-2535; fax: 415-331-5296).

Europa-Let (92 N. Main St., Ashland, OR 97520; phone: 800-462-4486 or 503-482-5806; fax: 503-482-0660).

The French Experience (370 Lexington Ave., New York, NY 10017; phone: 212-986-1115; fax: 212-986-3808).

Hideaways International (767 Islington St., Portsmouth, NH 03801; phone: 800-843-4433 or 603-430-4433; fax: 603-430-4444).

Hometours International (PO Box 11503, Knoxville, TN 37939; phone: 800-367-4668).

Interhome (124 Little Falls Rd., Fairfield, NJ 07004; phone: 201-882-6864; fax: 201-808-1742).

Keith Prowse & Co. (USA) Ltd. (234 W. 44th St., Suite 1000, New York, NY 10036; phone: 800-669-8687 or 212-398-1430; fax: 212-302-4251).

London Lodgings and Travel (3483 Golden Gate Way, Suite 211, Lafayette, CA 94549; phone: 800-366-8748 or 510-283-1142; fax: 510-283-1154).

Orion (c/o *B & V Associates,* address above).

Property Rentals International (1 Park W. Circle, Suite 108, Midlothian, VA 23113; phone: 800-220-3332 or 804-378-6054; fax: 804-379-2073).

Rent a Home International (7200 34th Ave. NW, Seattle, WA 98117; phone: 206-789-9377; fax: 206-789-9379).

Rent a Vacation Everywhere (*RAVE;* 383 Park Ave., Rochester, NY 14607; phone: 716-256-0760; fax: 716-256-2676).

Riviera Retreats (11 Rue des Petits Ponts, Mougins-le-Haut, Mougins, France 06250; phone: 33-93-64-86-40; fax: 33-93-64-00-80; in the US, contact *Suzanne Pidduck Rentals in Italy,* 1742 Calle Corva, Camarillo, CA 93010; phone 800-726-6702 or 805-987-5278; fax: 805-482-7976).

Sterling Tours (2707 Congress St., Suite 2G, San Diego, CA 92110; phone: 800-727-4359 or 619-299-3010; fax: 619-299-5728).

Vacances en Campagne (c/o *Heritage of England,* 22 Railroad St., Great Barrington, MA 01230; phone: 800-533-5405 or 413-528-6610; fax: 413-528-6222).

VHR Worldwide (235 Kensington Ave., Norwood, NJ 07648; phone: 201-767-9393 in New Jersey; 800-633-3284 elsewhere in the US; fax: 201-767-5510).

La Vie de Châteaux (c/o *B & V Associates,* address above).

Villa Leisure (PO Box 30188, Palm Beach, FL 33420; phone: 800-526-4244 or 407-624-9000; fax: 407-622-9097).

Villas and Apartments Abroad (420 Madison Ave., Suite 1105, New York, NY 10017; phone: 212-759-1025 in New York State; 800-433-3020 elsewhere in the US; fax: 212-755-8316).

Villas International (605 Market St., Suite 510, San Francisco, CA 94105; phone: 800-221-2260 or 415-281-0910; fax: 415-281-0919).

HOME EXCHANGES

For comfortable, reasonable living quarters with amenities that no hotel could possibly offer, consider trading homes with someone abroad. The following companies provide information on exchanges:

Home Base Holidays (7 Park Ave., London N13 5PG, England; phone/fax: 44-181-886-8752).

Intervac US/International Home Exchange (PO Box 590504, San Francisco, CA 94159; phone: 800-756-HOME or 415-435-3497; fax: 415-386-6853).

Loan-A-Home (2 Park La., Apt. 6E, Mt. Vernon, NY 10552-3443; phone: 914-664-7640).

Vacation Exchange Club (PO Box 650, Key West, FL 33041; phone: 800-638-3841 or 305-294-3720; fax: 305-294-1448).

Worldwide Home Exchange Club (main office: 50 Hans Crescent, London SW1X 0NA, England; phone: 44-171-589-6055; US office: 806 Brantford Ave., Silver Spring, MD 20904; phone: 301-680-8950).

HOME STAYS

United States Servas (11 John St., Room 407, New York, NY 10038; phone: 212-267-0252; fax: 212-267-0292) maintains a list of hosts worldwide willing to accommodate visitors free of charge (there is a membership fee). The aim of this nonprofit cultural program is to promote international understanding and peace, and *Servas* emphasizes that member travelers should be interested mainly in their hosts, not in sightseeing, during their stays. Another organization offering home stays with French families is *Friends in France* (40 E. 19th St., Eighth Floor, New York, NY 10003; phone: 212-260-9820; fax: 212-228-0576).

Time Zones

France and Monaco are both in the Greenwich Plus 1 time zone—which means that the time in these countries is six hours later than it is in East Coast US cities. France moves its clocks ahead an hour in the spring and back an hour in the fall, corresponding to daylight saving time, although the exact dates of the changes are different from those observed in the US. French timetables use a 24-hour clock to denote arrival and departure times, which means that hours are expressed sequentially from 1 AM—for example, 1:30 PM would be written as "13:30" or "13 h 30" ("13:30 heures" in French, "13:30 hours" in English).

Business and Shopping Hours

Most businesses and shops in France are open from 9 AM to 6 or 7 PM, with a one-hour lunch break starting at 12:30 or 1 PM. (Towards the south of

France, a more Mediterranean schedule is observed, with longer midday breaks.) Smaller retail establishments usually are open Tuesdays through Saturdays from 10 AM to noon, and from 2 to between 6 and 7 PM, and also may be open for a full or half-day on Mondays. Some shops in Paris and other major cities are open on Sundays from 9 AM to 5 PM. Department stores and other large emporia are open from about 9:30 AM to 6:30 or 7 PM (usually with no midday break), Mondays through Saturdays, and may stay open as late as 9 or 10 PM one or more days of the week; they also may offer additional hours during busy holiday seasons.

In Paris and other major cities, banks usually are open weekdays from 9 AM to 4:30 PM, with some staying open until 6 PM; some banks also may offer Saturday hours (usually from 9 AM to 3 PM). In the provinces, some banks are closed on Mondays, most close for an hour or two at midday, and few are open late. Saturday hours, where offered, usually are from 9 AM to noon. Money exchange houses—particularly at major airports—may stay open as late as 11 PM, seven days a week.

Holidays

France shuts down thoroughly on public holidays. Banks, offices, stores, museums, and public monuments—even most gas stations—are closed tight. Banks and some offices may close as early as *noon* the day before a holiday. Below is a list of the French national holidays and the dates they will be observed this year. (Note that the dates of some holidays vary from year to year; others occur on the same day every year.)

New Year's Day (January 1)
Easter Sunday (April 16)
Easter Monday (April 17)
Labor Day (May 1)
V-E Day (May 8)
Ascension Thursday (May 25)
Whitmonday (June 5)
Bastille Day (July 14)
Feast of the Assumption (August 15)
All Saints' Day (November 1)
Armistice Day (November 11)
Christmas Day (December 25)

Monaco celebrates many of the same holidays as France, as well as the following:

Feast Day of St-Dévoté (January 27)
Corpus Christi (June 2)
National Day (November 19)
Feast of the Immaculate Conception (December 8)

Mail

Post offices in France are indicated by signs reading *La Poste* and display-ing a picture of a blue bird against a yellow background. Most post offices are open weekdays from 8 AM to 7 PM and Saturdays from 8 AM to noon. Stamps also are sold at hotels, *tabacs* (tobacco shops), and some news-stands, as well as from public vending machines. Mail boxes (and stamp vending machines) are painted yellow.

Although letters to and from France have been known to arrive in as little as five days, allow at least 10 days for delivery in either direction. Note that the inclusion of postal codes in French addresses is essential; delivery of your letter or parcel may depend on it. If your correspondence is espe-cially important, you may want to send it via an international courier ser-vice, such as *Federal Express* (phone: 800-238-5355 in the US; 05-33-33-55, toll-free, in France) or *DHL Worldwide Express* (phone: 800-225-5345 in the US; 05-20-25-25, toll-free, in France).

You can have mail sent to you care of your hotel (marked "Guest Mail, Hold for Arrival") or to a post office (the address should include *Poste Restante*—the French equivalent of "General Delivery"). *American Express* offices also will hold mail for customers ("c/o Client Letter Service"); infor-mation is provided in their pamphlet *Travelers' Companion.* Note that *US Embassies* and *Consulates* abroad will hold mail for US citizens *only* in emer-gency situations.

Telephone

Direct dialing and other familiar services are available in France. In addi-tion, an increasing number of French homes are equipped with a phone computer called a *minitel,* which offers a wide range of information and services—from standard telephone listings to brief descriptions of films currently playing in Paris.

France is divided into two zones: Paris/Ile-de-France and the rest of the country (the provinces). All French telephone numbers have eight digits. For most destinations in France, these digits include the city code; how-ever, for Paris/Ile-de-France, it is necessary to dial an additional city code of "1" before the eight-digit number. The procedures for making calls to, from, or within France are as follows:

> *To call a number in the Paris/Ile-de-France area from the US:* Dial 011 (the international access code) + 33 (the country code for France) + 1 + the local eight-digit number.
>
> *To call a number in the provinces (outside the Paris/Ile-de-France area) from the US:* Dial 011 (the international access code) + 33 (the coun-try code for France) + the eight-digit number.

To call the US from anywhere in France: Dial 19 (wait for a dial tone) + 1 (the US country code) + the area code + the local number.

To call the provinces from the Paris/Ile-de-France area: Dial 16 (wait for a dial tone) + the eight-digit number.

To call the Paris/Ile-de-France area from the provinces: Dial 16 (wait for a dial tone) + 1 + the eight-digit number.

To call within the Paris/Ile-de-France area: Dial the eight-digit number (beginning with 4, 3, or 6—no extra "1"required).

To call between provinces or within a given province: Dial the eight-digit number.

Public telephones are found in post offices, cafés, and in booths on the street. Although some public telephones in France still take coins (inserted before dialing), in Paris and other major cities most accept only plastic phone cards called *télécartes*. These cards can be purchased in the US from *Marketing Challenges International* (10 E. 21st St., Suite 600, New York, NY 10010; phone: 212-529-9069; fax: 212-529-4838), or at post offices, transportation centers, tobacco shops, and newsstands in France.

Although you can use a telephone company calling card number on any phone, pay phones that take major credit cards (*American Express, MasterCard, Visa,* and so on) are increasingly common. Also available are combined telephone calling/bank credit cards, such as the *AT&T Universal Card* (PO Box 44167, Jacksonville, FL 32231-4167; phone: 800-423-4343). Similarly, *Sprint* (8140 Ward Pkwy., Kansas City, MO 64114; phone: 800-THE-MOST or 800-800-USAA) offers the *VisaPhone* program, through which you can add phone card privileges to your existing *Visa* card. Companies offering long-distance phone cards without additional credit card privileges include *Executive Telecard International* (4260 E. Evans Ave., Suite 6, Denver, CO 80222; phone: 800-950-3800), *MCI* (323 Third St. SE, Cedar Rapids, IA 52401; phone: 800-444-4444; and 12790 Merit Dr., Dallas, TX 75251; phone: 800-444-3333), *Metromedia Communications* (1 International Center, 100 NE Loop 410, San Antonio, TX 78216; phone: 800-275-0200), and *Sprint* (address above).

Hotels routinely add surcharges to the cost of phone calls made from their rooms. Long-distance telephone services that may help you avoid this added expense are provided by a number of companies, including *AT&T* (International Information Service, 635 Grant St., Pittsburgh, PA 15219; phone: 800-874-4000), *MCI* (address above), *Metromedia Communications* (address above), and *Sprint* (address above). Note that even when you use such long-distance services, some hotels still may charge a fee for line usage.

AT&T's Language Line Service (phone: 800-752-6096) provides interpretive services for telephone communications in French. Additional resources for travelers include the *AT&T 800 Travel Directory* (phone: 800-426-8686 for orders), the *Toll-Free Travel & Vacation Information Directory* (Pilot Books, 103 Cooper St., Babylon, NY 11702; phone: 516-422-2225; fax: 516-422-2227), and *The Phone Booklet* (Scott American Corporation, PO Box 88, W. Redding, CT 06896; no phone).

Important Phone Numbers
Emergency assistance:
15 for an ambulance.
17 for the police.
18 for the fire department.

Local information and operator: 12.
International operator: 19, wait for dial tone, then 3311.

Electricity

France uses 220-volt, 50-cycle alternating current. Travelers from the US will need electrical converters to operate the appliances they use at home, or dual-voltage appliances, which can be switched from one voltage standard to another. (Some large tourist hotels may offer 110-volt current or may have converters available.) You also will need a plug adapter set to deal with the different plug configurations found in France.

Staying Healthy

For up-to-date information on current health conditions, call the Centers for Disease Control's *International Travelers' Hotline*: 404-332-4559.

Travelers to France face few serious health risks. Tap water generally is clean and potable—if the water isn't meant for drinking, it should be marked *eau non potable*. Bottled water also is readily available in stores. Milk is pasteurized throughout France, and dairy products are safe to eat, as are fruit, vegetables, meat, poultry, and fish. Because of Mediterranean pollution, however, all seafood should be eaten cooked, and make sure it is *fresh*, particularly in the heat of the summer, when inadequate refrigeration is an additional concern.

When swimming in the ocean, be careful of the undertow (the water running back down the beach after a wave has washed ashore), which can knock you off your feet, and riptides (currents running against the tide), which can pull you out to sea. Sharks are found in coastal waters, but rarely come close to shore. Some small jellyfish, as well as eels and sea urchins, also may be present. Coral reefs (found off Corsica) can be razor sharp.

France has socialized medicine, and all hospitals are public facilities *(hôpitaux publiques)*. Low-cost medical care is available to French citizens;

however, visitors from the US and other countries that are not members of the European Economic Community (which provides reciprocal health coverage) will have to pay for most services.

French hospitals fall into three categories. At the top of the list is the *CHRU* (*Centre Hôpital Régional et Universitaire,* or Central Regional University Hospital), a large, full-service hospital associated with a major medical university. Others are the *CHR,* which designates a full-service regional hospital, and the *CH,* which means that the hospital is the central one in its town or city (and probably has 24-hour emergency service). There also are some private clinics (*cliniques privées*), which are like small hospitals and can provide medical aid for less serious conditions.

French drugstores, called *pharmacies,* are identified by a green cross out front. There should be no problem finding a drugstore in most major French cities. Night duty may rotate among local pharmacies—those that are closed provide the addresses of the nearest all-night drugstores in the window. Telephone operators and local hospitals also may have this information.

Should you need non-emergency medical attention, ask at your hotel for the house physician or for help in reaching a doctor. Referrals also are available from the *US Embassy* or a *US Consulate.* **In an emergency: Go to the emergency room of the nearest hospital, dial the nationwide emergency assistance number provided in** *Telephone,* **above, or call an operator for assistance. If possible, someone who can translate into French should make the call.**

Additional Resources

InterContinental Medical (2720 Enterprise Pkwy., Suite 106, Richmond, VA 23294; phone: 804-527-1094; fax: 804-527-1941).

International Association for Medical Assistance to Travelers (*IAMAT;* 417 Center St., Lewiston, NY 14092; phone: 716-754-4883; and 40 Regal Rd., Guelph, Ontario N1K 1B5, Canada; phone: 519-836-0102; fax: 519-836-3412).

International Health Care Service (440 E. 69th St., New York, NY 10021; phone: 212-746-1601).

International SOS Assistance (PO Box 11568, Philadelphia, PA 19116; phone: 800-523-8930 or 215-244-1500; fax: 215-244-2227).

Medic Alert Foundation (2323 Colorado Ave., Turlock, CA 95382; phone: 800-ID-ALERT or 209-668-3333; fax: 209-669-2495).

Travel Care International (*Eagle River Airport,* PO Box 846, Eagle River, WI 54521; phone: 800-5-AIR-MED or 715-479-8881; fax: 715-479-8178).

TravMed (PO Box 10623, Baltimore, MD 21285-0623; phone: 800-732-5309 or 410-296-5225; fax: 410-825-7523).

Consular Services

The American Services section of the *US Consulate* is a vital source of assistance and advice for US citizens abroad. If you are injured or become seriously ill, the consulate can direct you to sources of medical attention and notify your relatives. If you become involved in a dispute that could lead to legal action, the consulate can provide a list of English-speaking attorneys. In cases of natural disasters or civil unrest, consulates handle the evacuation of US citizens if necessary.

The *US State Department* operates an automated 24-hour *Citizens' Emergency Center* travel advisory hotline (phone: 202-647-5225). You also can reach a duty officer at this number from 8:15 AM to 10 PM, eastern standard time on weekdays, and from 9 AM to 3 PM on Saturdays. At all other times, call 202-647-4000. For faxed travel warnings and other consular information, call 202-647-3000 using the handset on your fax machine; instructions will be provided. With a PC and a modem, you can access the consular affairs electronic bulletin board (phone: 202-647-9225).

The US Embassy and Consulates in France

Embassy

Paris: 2 Av. Gabriel, Paris 75008, France (phone: 33-1-42-96-12-02 or 33-1-42-61-80-75; fax: 33-1-42-66-97-83); *Consular section,* 2 Rue St. Florentin, Paris 75001, France (same phone and fax numbers as the *Embassy*).

Consulates

Bordeaux: *Consulate,* 22 Cours du Maréchal-Foch, Bordeaux 33080, France (phone: 33-56-52-65-95; fax: 33-56-51-60-42).

Marseilles: *Consulate,* 12 Bd. Paul-Peytral, Marseilles 13286, France (phone: 33-91-54-92-00; fax: 33-91-55-09-47).

Nice: *Consular Agent,* 31 Rue du Maréchal-Joffre, Nice 06000, France (phone: 33-93-88-89-55; fax: 33-93-87-07-38).

Strasbourg: *Consulate,* 15 Av. d'Alsace, Strasbourg 67082, France (phone: 33-88-35-31-04; fax: 33-88-24-06-95).

Entry Requirements and Customs Regulations

ENTERING FRANCE

A valid US passport generally is the only document a US citizen needs to enter France, although immigration officers in French airports *may* ask for proof that you have sufficient funds for your trip, or to see a return or ongoing ticket. As a general rule, a US passport entitles the bearer to remain in France for up to 90 days as a tourist. (Resident aliens of the US may need different documents.) A visa is required for study, residency, work, or stays of more than 3 months. Proof of means of independent financial support is pertinent to the acceptance of any long-term–stay application. US citizens should contact the *French Embassy* or a *French Consulate* well in advance of their trip. Note that all individuals for whom a visa is necessary also must obtain a *Carte de Séjour* (residency permit) at the local police prefecture upon arrival in France.

You are allowed to enter France with the following items duty-free: 200 cigarettes or 250 grams of tobacco; 50 cigars; up to two liters of wine and either one liter of liquor over 38.8 proof or two liters of liquor under 38.8 proof; 50 grams of perfume; a quarter of a liter of cologne; 500 grams of coffee; 40 grams of tea. Note that only those over 18 (the legal drinking age in France) are permitted to bring alcohol into the country. Items designated as gifts and valued at less than 300F (about $52) per item also can be brought into France duty-free (children under 15 can bring in gift items valued at less than 150F (about $26).

DUTY-FREE SHOPS

Located in international airports, duty-free shops provide bargains on the purchase of goods imported to France from other countries. But beware: Not all foreign goods are automatically less expensive. You *can* get a good deal on some items, but know what they cost elsewhere. Also note that although these goods are free of the duty that *French Customs* normally would assess, they will be subject to US import duty upon your return to the US (see below).

VALUE ADDED TAX (VAT)

Called *taxe à la valeur ajoutée (TVA)* in France, this sales tax (typically 18.6%) is applicable to most goods and services. Although everyone must pay the tax, foreigners often can obtain a partial refund if their purchases in a single store total at least 2,000F (about $345 at press time). Note that a refund is *not* applicable to purchases of certain goods, such as food, wine, medicine, tobacco, and antiques and works of art worth over 30,000F—although the rules regarding artwork vary, depending on the age of the item.

Many stores participate in the *Europe Tax-Free Shopping (ETFS)* program, which enables visitors to obtain cash refunds at the airport upon departure. The procedure is as follows: Request a tax-free shopping voucher at the store when you make your purchase. At the airport, have this voucher stamped by *French Customs* officials, and then take it to the cash refund desk or agent (customs officials can direct you) for your refund.

If you purchase goods at a store that does not participate in the *ETFS* program, you still may be able to obtain a refund, although the procedure is somewhat more complicated and, unfortunately, subject to long delays.

Request special refund forms for this purpose when making your purchase. These must be stamped by *French Customs* officials at the airport upon departure, and then mailed back to the *store*, which processes the refund. The refund will arrive—eventually—in the form of a check (usually in francs) mailed to your home or, if the purchase was made with a credit card, as a credit to your account.

Note that stores are under no obligation to participate in either of the VAT refund programs, so ask if you will be able to get a refund *before* making any purchases. For additional information, contact the French office of *Europe Tax-Free Shopping* (90 Rue Anatole France, Levallois 92300, France; phone: 33-1-47-48-03-22; fax: 33-1-47-48-04-96) or the French tourist authorities.

RETURNING TO THE US

You must declare to the *US Customs* official at the point of entry everything you have acquired in France. The standard duty-free allowance for US citizens is $400. If your trip is shorter than 48 continuous hours, or if you have been outside the US within 30 days of your current trip, the duty-free allowance is reduced to $25. Families traveling together may make a joint customs declaration. To avoid paying duty unnecessarily on expensive items (such as computer equipment) that you plan to take with you on your trip, register these items with *US Customs* before you depart.

A flat 10% duty is assessed on the next $1,000 worth of merchandise; additional items are taxed at a variety of rates (see *Tariff Schedules of the United States* in a library or any *US Customs Service* office). Some articles are duty-free only up to certain limits. The $400 allowance includes one carton of (200) cigarettes, 100 cigars (not Cuban), and one liter of liquor or wine (for those over 21); the $25 allowance includes 10 cigars, 50 cigarettes, and four ounces of perfume. With the exception of gifts valued at $50 or less sent directly to the recipient, *all* items shipped home are dutiable.

Antiques (at least 100 years old) and paintings or drawings done entirely by hand are duty-free. However, to take archaeological finds or other artifacts worth more than 998,100 francs (over $170,000) out of France, you must obtain a certificate from the *Musée de France* (60 Rue des Francs-Bourgeois, Paris 75003, France; phone: 33-1-40-27-60-96; fax: 33-1-40-27-66-45), and bring this certificate to the *Service des Titres du Commerce Extérieur* (*SETICE;* 8 Rue de la Tour des Dames, Paris 75436, France; phone: 33-1-44-63-25-25; fax: 33-1-44-63-26-59), which will issue you an "authorization of exportation" permit.

FORBIDDEN IMPORTS

Note that US regulations prohibit the import of some goods sold abroad, such as fresh fruits and vegetables, most meat products (except certain canned goods), and dairy products (except for fully cured cheeses). Also prohibited are articles made from plants or animals on the endangered species list.

FOR ADDITIONAL INFORMATION Consult one of the following publications, available from the *US Customs Service* (PO Box 7407, Washington, DC 20044): *Currency Reporting; Importing a Car; International Mail Imports; Know Before You Go; Pets and Wildlife;* and *Pocket Hints. Travelers' Tips on Bringing Food, Plant, and Animal Products into the United States* is available from the *United States Department of Agriculture, Animal and Plant Health Inspection Service* (*USDA-APHIS;* 6505 Belcrest Rd., Room 613-FB, Hyattsville, MD 20782; phone: 301-436-7799; fax: 301-436-5221). For tape-recorded information on customs-related topics, call 202-927-2095 from any touch-tone phone.

For Further Information

Branches of the *French Government Tourist Office* in the US are the best sources of travel information. Offices generally are open on weekdays, during normal business hours. Note, however, that these offices do not accept telephone inquiries. For information by phone, call the *French Government Tourist Office*'s telephone information line, *France on Call* (phone: 900-990-0040); the cost is 50¢ per minute. (There is no charge for information requested in person or by mail from tourist office branches.) A number of free publications also are available from the *French Government Tourist Office,* including the 1995 *France Discovery Guide* and the *American Express Welcome Center Directory.*

Once you have arrived in France, you can take advantage of a computerized information system called *minitel.* Computer terminals are available in the lobbies of most French hotels rated two stars or above, as well as in many post offices. In addition, *American Express* provides an English-language, travel information hotline (phone: 05-20-12-02, toll-free, throughout France).

For information on entry requirements and customs regulations, contact the *French Embassy* or a *French Consulate* in the US.

French Government Tourist Offices

California: 9454 Wilshire Blvd., Suite 715, Beverly Hills, CA 90212 (phone: 310-271-6665; fax: 310-276-2835).

Illinois: 676 N. Michigan Ave., Suite 3360, Chicago, IL 60611 (phone: 312-751-7800; fax: 312-337-6339).

New York: walk-in office: 628 Fifth Ave., Suite 222, New York, NY (phone: 212-757-1125; fax: 212-247-6468); mailing address: 610 Fifth Ave., New York, NY 10020.

The French Embassy and Consulates in the US

Embassy

Washington, DC: 4101 Reservoir Rd. NW, Washington, DC 20007 (phone: 202-944-6000; fax: 202-944-6212).

Consulates

California: *Consulate General,* 10990 Wilshire Blvd., Suite 300, Los Angeles, CA 90024 (phone: 310-479-4426; fax: 310-312-0704); *Consulate General,* 540 Bush St., San Francisco, CA 94108 (phone: 415-397-4330; fax: 415-433-8357).

Florida: *Consulate General,* 1 Biscayne Tower, 2 S. Biscayne Blvd., Suite 1710, Miami, FL 33131 (phone: 305-372-9798; fax: 305-372-9549).

Georgia: *Consulate General,* Marquis Tower II, 285 Peachtree Center Ave., Suite 2800, Atlanta, GA 30303 (phone: 404-522-4226; fax: 404-880-9408).

Illinois: *Consulate General,* 737 N. Michigan Ave., Suite 2020, Chicago, IL 60611 (phone: 312-787-5359, 312-787-5360, or 312-787-5361; recorded visa information: 312-787-7889; fax: 312-664-4196).

Louisiana: *Consulate General,* 300 Poydras St., Suite 2105, New Orleans, LA 70130 (phone: 504-523-5772; fax: 504-523-5725).

Massachusetts: *Consulate General,* visa applications: 20 Park Plaza, Suite 1123, Boston, MA 02116 (phone: 617-482-2864; fax: 617-426-9236); all other business: 3 Commonwealth Ave., Boston, MA 02116 (phone: 617-266-1680; fax: 617-437-1090).

New York: *Consulate General,* 934 Fifth Ave., New York, NY 10021 (phone: 212-606-3688; recorded visa information: 212-606-3644, 212-606-3652, or 212-606-3653; fax: 212-606-3670).

Texas: *Consulate General,* 2777 Allen Pkwy., Suite 650, Houston, TX 77019 (phone: 713-528-2181; fax: 713-528-1933).

The Cities

Aix-en-Provence

According to polls, Aix is the provincial city that the French most admire, and the reasons are entirely understandable. There's the matter of size, for one thing. With 130,000 residents and a significant university population, the city is large and sophisticated enough to have its share of good restaurants, smart shops, art galleries, serious libraries and bookstores, cafés and nightclubs, theater and music, and other urban amenities. Yet almost everything is within easy walking distance, little of interest is ever more than 20 minutes away, and—miraculous in this age of urban sprawl—the countryside starts at the end of the bus lines (except if you're headed toward Marseilles).

Aix often *feels* small, too. Perhaps because of its Mediterranean character, daily life still proceeds at a comparatively slow pace, although this is changing. Despite the construction accompanying its recent rapid growth, most of its buildings still have comfortable proportions that are easily dwarfed by the limestone massif—the Montagne Ste-Victoire—that the talent of native son Paul Cézanne transformed into the most famous monument of the nearby landscape. Ste-Victoire was named for a battle fought at the bottom of the mountain by Marius, the popular Roman general who defeated the invading Teutonic tribes, killing more than 100,000 Teutons and taking as many prisoners in the process. To this day, many sons of the region still are named Marius.

Even the city's location strikes the perfect balance. It's close to the Mediterranean beaches, but aloof from the noise and the crowds; it's near the hills and valleys of rustic Provence, but far enough away to escape the torpor of the backcountry. And Aix is only three and a half hours from Paris via the *TGV* (*Train à Grande Vitesse,* or "fast train").

Even before Roman times, people came here for Aix's warm thermal springs. The area was occupied for centuries by a Celto-Ligurian tribe whose capital, Entremont, was on a plateau north of the present Aix and whose faith in the local water extended to a belief that it assured fertility. The Roman consul Caius Sextius destroyed Entremont in 123 BC; the following year, he established a fortified camp near the springs, calling it Waters of Sextius, or Aquae Sextius (its modern name is a contraction of the Latin words). The boulevards circling Aix today follow the line of the old ramparts, and a huge 18th-century spa stands on the Cours Sextius, near the site of the original Roman baths.

In the 12th century, the Counts of Provence made the town their capital, and their court soon became known for its love of music and poetry. This was the age of the troubadours, the poet-musicians who traveled from court to court singing their ballads in the Provençal tongue and spreading ideals of chivalry and romantic love throughout Europe. Perhaps the town's most civilized era, however, was the 15th century. In 1409, both the Université d'Aix and "Good King René" (1409–80) were born. Called "the last of the troubadours," René held the title of Count of Provence, among others (he was also Duke of Anjou and titular King of Naples), and he proved to be a remarkable exemplar of the culture of his time. He was not only a patron of the arts but also a poet, musician, painter, and student of classical languages, mathematics, and law. An unaffected man of the people, he organized popular festivals, tilled the soil, and introduced the muscatel grape to the region. The people were not happy, however, when he levied heavy taxes and printed worthless money to finance his cultural projects.

Provence became a part of the kingdom of France a few years after René's death, though Aix remained important as the seat of the provincial *parlement* (court of justice) from 1501 to 1790. It flourished during the 17th and 18th centuries, when wealthy magistrates, church officials, and merchants built many of the elegant *hôtels* (townhouses) that give the city its look today. The period also is remembered in Aix's main thoroughfare, the Cours Mirabeau, named for Count Mirabeau, a prominent Aix resident during the late 18th century. Before achieving the eminence that brought him immortality in the Cours Mirabeau, the count had achieved some notoriety by tricking a rich heiress of Aix into marriage and then running up debts large enough to bring about his imprisonment. The count's philanderings made him popular with the masses (if not with his fellow nobles), and in 1789, when Louis XVI summoned the Estates-General—a meeting that proved to be the first step toward ending the monarchy—Mirabeau was easily elected to represent the third estate of Aix-en-Provence. He went on to become the leading statesman of the first years of the French Revolution.

As Marseilles grew during the 19th century, Aix went into a period of decline, but it re-emerged in the mid-20th century with a vengeance. Since 1950, the population of Aix has more than doubled. Much of the growth is attributable to its successful light industry. Clothing is one of the town's better-known products; another is candy. Remarkably sweet Provençal almonds go into *calissons d'Aix,* oval-shaped candies that are protected and controlled, like fine wines, as an *appellation d'origine* item. In the 17th century, *calissons* were blessed by the bishop and distributed to the faithful in an annual ceremony commemorating the end of the plague of 1630. Now the rich candies are exported worldwide.

Meanwhile, Aix's thermal springs draw visitors from across Europe. The spa district has been completely renovated, and new shops and restaurants are continually opening here. Others come to Aix for the *Festival International d'Art Lyrique et de Musique* (International Festival of Lyric Art and Music), one of Europe's better-known music festivals (see *Special Events*). Before the festival begins, the tempo of the Provençal lifestyle accelerates, and for the three weeks of the festival itself, the city is filled with action.

Outside of those three weeks, Aix is a sleepy university town, where travelers gather to enjoy quiet pleasures—lingering at a café on the Cours Mirabeau, gazing at the lovely fountains, or strolling over to one of the nearby outdoor markets to savor the visual barrage of pulpy red tomatoes, dark green *courgettes* (zucchini), luscious melons, and other produce. Some people lament that such pleasures are becoming increasingly rare as the city grows and fast-food establishments mar the landscape along the Cours Mirabeau. Even so, when one needs a refuge from modern madness, there's always the silence of the *Cathédrale St-Sauveur,* and after a stroll through the inviting maze of Vieil (Old) Aix's pedestrian zones, benches seem to beckon everywhere. And you still can turn down almost any street and walk to one of the city's ever-present fountains, whose sounds soothe jangled nerves. Along with Aix's art and music festival, its thermal cure, and its diet-disrupting *calissons,* these endearing fountains make clear what matters most to this delightful city: Despite staggering growth, Aix rarely puts progress ahead of *douceur de vivre* (the sweetness of life).

Aix At-a-Glance

SEEING THE CITY

Outside the city, the best vista is from the excavations of the pre-Roman settlement, the *Oppidum d'Entremont,* on the Plateau d'Entremont, 2 miles (3 km) north of Aix via the road to Puyricard. It offers a striking view of the Montagne Ste-Victoire, too, which dominates Aix to the east. City bus No. 20 departs for the site at approximately half-hour intervals Mondays through Saturdays from in front of the *Banque National de Paris* on the Cours Sextius. Closed Tuesdays.

SPECIAL PLACES

Most of the sights in Aix are within the circle of boulevards that follow the outline of the city's ancient walls. North of the Cours Mirabeau is Vieil Aix (Old Aix), a zone of old squares and narrow streets, many of them pedestrian islands. South of the Cours is the Quartier Mazarin, a neighborhood of 17th- and 18th-century *hôtels* (townhouses). The entire area north and south of the Cours can be walked easily. Note that museums and other sites often close for lunch, usually between the hours of noon and 2 PM.

COURS MIRABEAU Four rows of shady plane trees distinguish this lovely wide east-west avenue, which has been the focal point of Aix since the 17th century. Evoking the old grandeur of the Champs-Elysées, a bit of the chic of the Boulevard St-Germain in the late 1940s, and a touch of the boisterousness of the Boulevard St-Michel in the 1960s, the Cours is so short that it can be walked in less than 10 minutes. The stately 17th- and 18th-century *hôtels* that line it have become, on one side, mostly banks. Note the giant caryatids holding up a wrought-iron balcony at No. 38, now a university building. On the other side are mostly bookshops, restaurants, and lively cafés. At each end is a 19th-century fountain. In the center of the circular Place de la Libération (popularly called La Rotonde), where the Cours begins, is a large fountain topped by three female figures; at the end, where the Cours runs into the Hôtel de Poët, is a smaller fountain with a statue of Good King René holding a bunch of grapes. But the main attractions of the Cours are its cafés. Stake out a sidewalk table at aperitif time and, especially when the university is in session and the weather is warm, you'll see more people than Aix seemingly could hold.

VIEIL AIX

CATHÉDRALE ST-SAUVEUR (HOLY SAVIOR CATHEDRAL) A curious blend of architectural styles, spanning 15 centuries, makes this massive cathedral an unusual sight. The baptistery, off to the far right (south) as you enter, is the oldest part, dating from the 4th and 5th centuries; its eight Roman columns are a stark contrast to the gilt 16th-century Renaissance cupola they support. From right to left, the church grows progressively younger. The southernmost, Romanesque aisle was the nave of a 12th-century church; to its left is a Gothic nave from the 13th to the 15th century, and to the left of that, a newer, Baroque aisle from the 17th century. One of the treasures of the church, the 15th-century *Triptyque du Buisson Ardent* (Triptych of the Burning Bush), is on the wall of the Gothic nave. It's usually closed, revealing only two panels in grisaille depicting the Annunciation, but if you ask the caretaker to open it, you'll see the brilliance of its colors (predominantly red) fairly gleaming in the interior dimness. Done by Nicolas Froment, court painter to King René, it shows the Virgin and Child in the center (along with the eponymous burning bush), with the king and his wife, Queen Jeanne, kneeling in the side panels. Upon request, the caretaker also will uncover another of the church's prized possessions, the 16th-century sculpted wooden doors on the exterior of the Gothic nave. Pl. de l'Université (phone: 42-23-45-65).

CLOÎTRE ST-SAUVEUR (HOLY SAVIOR CLOISTER) This delightful, small, Romanesque (12th-century) cloister is reached through a doorway on the right aisle of the cathedral or from the street. It's a favorite spot of Aix residents, who come to sit and chat or read a newspaper under its arches. These rest on pairs of delicate columns, some plain and some carved, with carved capitals. Pl. des Martyrs-de-la-Résistance.

MUSÉE DES TAPISSERIES (MUSEUM OF TAPESTRIES) Adjoining the cloister and cathedral, this small museum contains some rare Beauvais tapestries, including a series on the life of Don Quixote dating from the 17th and 18th centuries. A few pieces of furniture from the same period also are on display. The interior courtyard is the focal point of Aix's music festival in July and August (see *Special Events*), when it turns into an elaborate outdoor opera house. Closed Tuesdays. Admission charge. *Palais de l'Ancien Archevêché* (stairway on the left), 28 Pl. des Martyrs-de-la-Résistance (phone: 42-23-09-91).

MUSÉE D'HISTOIRE NATURELLE (MUSEUM OF NATURAL HISTORY) This museum displays archaelogical finds and prehistoric remains from around Aix. Don't miss the dinosaur egg exhibit; also pay particular attention to the painted wood panels from the 17th century. Closed Sunday mornings. Admission charge. *Hôtel Boyer d'Equilles,* 6 Rue Espariat (phone: 42-26-23-67).

PLACE DE L'HÔTEL DE VILLE (TOWN HALL SQUARE) The 16th-century clock tower at one corner of this square catches the eye first. On high, it has ornate wrought-iron trim, including an ironwork Provençal bell cage at the very top. Farther down and less prominent is a mechanical statue representing the season, one of four that rotate and make their appearance during the course of the year. The 17th-century building with the Italianate façade next to the clock tower is the *Hôtel de Ville* (Town Hall). Built by Parisian architect Pierre Pavillon, it is notable for its sculpted wooden doors as well as the beautiful wrought-iron balcony and archway in the interior courtyard. The building once contained an outstanding 300,000-volume library, the *Bibliothèque Méjanes,* named for the Marquis de Méjanes, who founded it in the 18th century. The library has since been moved to a former match factory near the *Gare Routière* on Espace Méjanes (closed Sundays and Mondays; admission charge; phone: 42-25-98-88). On the south side of the square is the old grain market, an 18th-century building decorated with carvings by Chastel, an Aix sculptor of the period, which now houses a branch of the post office. The square itself, surrounded by plane trees with a fountain at its center, is the site of a colorful flower market. When the vendors leave, the cafés put out their tables.

EGLISE STE-MARIE-MADELEINE (CHURCH OF ST. MARY MAGDALENE) Its west front was redone in the mid-19th century, though the church dates from the 17th century. Inside are some interesting works, including a large painting (in the aisle left of the altar) that has alternately been attributed to Rubens and to Rembrandt, and the center panel of a highly original 15th-century triptych of the Annunciation, with inexplicable diabolical figures. There is an 18th-century marble Virgin by Chastel, who is also credited with the *Fontaine des Prêcheurs* (Preachers' Fountain) out front. Place des Prêcheurs (phone: 42-38-02-81).

CHAPELLE DU SACRÉ-COEUR (CHAPEL OF THE SACRED HEART) A replica of the one in the palace at Versailles, this beautiful 17th-century Jesuit chapel was known to the public for 300 years by its ornate façade alone. In the last decade, however, it was reopened at the initiative of two art lovers, and its striking cream-colored architecture—with vaulted ceilings and stone columns—has since been an inviting setting for art exhibits. Its ongoing restoration is being financed by proceeds from such events as concerts (held in June and July). It's also a pleasant, refreshingly cool place in which to stroll. Open during exhibitions only; schedules are posted on the door and listed in a brochure available at the tourist office. 20 Rue Lacépède (phone: 42-38-03-74).

QUARTIER MAZARIN

MUSÉE GRANET Aix's museum of fine arts and archaeology took its name from the early 19th-century Aixois painter François-Marius Granet, a major donor (many of his own works are displayed, and there is a portrait of him by Ingres). Today, the museum is considered among the finest in Provence. In a 17th-century building, the former priory of the Knights of Malta, the museum contains three watercolors, two drawings, and eight oil paintings by Cézanne—all that there is in Aix of its native son's work—and a good collection of Provençal, Flemish, and Italian paintings from the 16th to the 19th century. There also are pieces from 20th-century masters such as Martung, Léger, and Matisse, and in summer temporary exhibitions of contemporary art are often held here. Also exhibited are archaeological finds such as death masks, warriors' torsos, and other examples of Celto-Ligurian statuary from the pre-Roman settlement at Entremont, as well as articles of Egyptian, Greek, and Roman origin. Closed Tuesdays and some winter holidays. Admission charge. Pl. St-Jean-de-Malte (phone: 42-38-14-70).

EGLISE ST-JEAN-DE-MALTE (CHURCH OF ST. JOHN OF MALTA) Once the chapel of the Knights of Malta priory, this 13th-century church is next door to the *Musée Granet*. It was the first Gothic building in Provence, and its interior is worth a visit for the lovely stained glass windows to the front and back and for the motif of the Maltese cross, which is repeated on pillars and windows throughout. Pl. St-Jean-de-Malte (phone: 42-38-25-70).

ELSEWHERE

PAVILLON DE VENDÔME (VENDÔME PAVILION) This elegant 17th-century mansion, just beyond Vieil Aix, was built as the provincial residence of the Cardinal de Vendôme. Its attraction lies primarily in its architecture and lovely grounds, which include a rose garden, a playground, and various semiprivate nooks, in addition to the main velvety green lawn dotted with boxwood carved into swirling shapes, like the tops of mad ice cream cones. All of this is hidden from the bustle of the town by a high wall. The Aixois who retreat here to push prams, read, or knit on park benches seem oblivious to the suffering of the two striking male figures that hold up the balcony of the building, visibly straining under its weight. Closed Tuesdays and some holidays. Admission charge. 32 Rue Celony (phone: 42-21-05-78).

ATELIER DE CÉZANNE (CÉZANNE'S STUDIO) The brown-shuttered house that the artist built in 1897 (and used until his death in 1906) affords visitors an intimate glimpse of his working conditions. Only the actual studio—one high-ceilinged room with a huge northern window and other windows overlooking the treetops to the south—can be visited. The studio has been preserved just as Cézanne left it, with his cap and cape on a wall hook, a coal stove, a few pieces of furniture, some sketches, letters, and books, and a profusion of vases, bottles, pitchers, dried flowers, and dried and fresh fruit (the latter are changed from time to time)—the subjects of numerous still lifes. The garden surrounding the house is quietly pleasant. Closed Tuesdays and some holidays. Admission charge. A bit of a walk uphill at the edge of the city, at 9 Av. Paul-Cézanne (phone: 42-21-06-53).

FONDATION VASARELY (VASARELY FOUNDATION) This huge building decorated with alternating black and white circles is hard to miss in the hilly suburb west of town. Devoted to the oeuvre of the Hungarian geometric artist Victor Vasarely, the largely glass structure consists of eight hexagonal main rooms. The giant floor-to-ceiling works include the artist's vibrantly colored wall murals, Aubusson tapestries, and multidimensional works, including a revolving sculpture. In an upstairs gallery, you can learn all about Vasarely and get a glimpse from overhead at some of his massive creations. Occasionally, there are shows of works by other artists. Closed Tuesdays. Admission charge. Take bus No. 12 from La Rotonde. 1 Av. Marcel-Pagnol, Jas-de-Bouffan (phone: 42-20-01-09).

EXTRA SPECIAL

The landscape surrounding Aix, with the stark white Montagne Ste-Victoire jutting dramatically above it, is much as it appears in so many Cézanne canvases. Route D17 leading east toward the village of Le Tholonet was enough of a favorite of the painter that it's now called the Route de Cézanne; to follow in his footsteps, whether by car, bicycle, or on foot, is a memorable part of a stay in Aix. From the top of the Cours Mirabeau, follow Rue Maréchal-Joffre, which eventually becomes Boulevard des Poilus, then Avenue des Ecoles-Militaires-St-Cyr-et-St-Maixent, and eventually D17. It's 3½ miles (6 km) to Le Tholonet, where you can sit down before turning back or proceeding to the mountain, which has paths for hikers. The paths are not as simple as they look, so be careful if you are not fit. Alternatively, you can join a guided tour to Cézanne-related sites organized by the Aix Tourist Office from July through mid-November for a modest fee (some include an English-speaking guide).

A footpath called "Sur les Pas de Cézanne" ("In the Footsteps of Cézanne") goes through Aix and into the suburbs; brass plates along the pavement guide visitors to 12 sites connected with the artist's life and work. An English-language brochure and map are available from the tourist office (see *Tourist Information*).

Sources and Resources

TOURIST INFORMATION

The *Office du Tourisme* (just off La Rotonde, at 2 Pl. du Général-de-Gaulle; phone: 42-16-11-70; fax: 42-16-11-62) has an English-speaking staff. Open daily (hours are shorter on Sundays and holidays), it stocks brochures listing hotels, restaurants, sights, sports facilities, villas and flats for rent, and other pertinent information. It also publishes an inexpensive monthly brochure, *Le Mois à Aix,* listing events in and around Aix; distributes free, large maps; and organizes guided tours of the city and surrounding area (some in English during summer months).

LOCAL COVERAGE *Le Provençal* and *Le Méridional* are two regional dailies with Aix editions. *La Semaine d'Aix* is a free weekly that can be picked up in a number of places; it gives mostly movie schedules and reviews. They all are in French. *Paradox* (2 Rue Reine-Jeanne; phone: 42-26-47-99) is a good English-language bookstore with material on the region.

TELEPHONE The city code for Aix-en-Provence is 42, which is incorporated into all local eight-digit numbers. When calling a number in Aix from the Paris region (including the Ile-de-France), dial 16, wait for a dial tone, then dial the eight-digit number. When calling a number from outside Paris, dial only the eight-digit number.

GETTING AROUND

The best way to see Aix is on foot; the streets are narrow and there are few parking spots. Illegally parked cars are swiftly towed away, especially if they have out-of-region plates.

BUS About a dozen main lines serve the city, most of them departing from La Rotonde or the *Gare Routière,* and there's also a limited minibus system. Tickets are sold individually on the bus for 6.50F (about $1.10 at press time) or in economical *carnets* (packets) of ten for 37F (about $6.30 at press time). Most lines stop running before 8 PM, and weekend service is infrequent. The tourist office and *Autobus Aixois* (phone: 42-26-37-28) have schedules.

The *Gare Routière* (on Rue Lapierre; phone: 42-27-17-91) is the depot for intercity bus service. There are regular buses to Arles, Avignon, Marseilles, and other points in Provence and along the coast as far as Nice. *Le Comette* buses (phone: 91-61-83-27) run frequently between *Gare Routière* and *Marignane Airport.*

CAR RENTAL *Hertz* (43 Av. Victor-Hugo; phone: 42-27-91-32) and *Avis* (11 Bd. Gambetta; phone: 42-21-64-16) are represented, as are other major international and European firms.

TAXI There are stands at the train and bus stations and around the city; cabs also can be hailed on the street. To phone for one, call *Taxi Mirabeau* (phone:

42-21-61-61) or *Les Artisans* (phone: 42-26-29-30); also reliable are the cab service at the train station (phone: 42-27-62-12) and the one at *Gare Routière* (phone: 42-27-20-92).

TRAIN The train station *(Gare SNCF)* is at the end of Avenue Victor-Hugo (phone: 42-27-51-63, 91-08-50-50, or 91-08-84-12), but Aix is not very well connected to its close neighbors by rail.

SPECIAL EVENTS
One of the country's most highly acclaimed music festivals dominates the special events calendar here.

FAVORITE FÊTE

Festival International d'Art Lyrique et de Musique Of France's 250-odd music festivals, this one ranks among the best, since it combines a high musical standard with meticulous organization and a delightful setting. From mid-July through early August, the festival offers works of all vintages, from early Rameau to late Berio, and on all instruments, with a special emphasis on vocal works. Three operas are traditionally staged each year (one of them almost always a work by Mozart), but budgetary constraints caused a last-minute reduction to one opera in 1994; confirm this year's schedule in advance. The operas are usually performed in any one of three theaters; concerts make lyrical use of the beautiful *Cathédrale St-Sauveur* and its cloister. A recent festival featured performing groups from the English *Baroque Soloists* to the *Ensemble Intercontemporain,* with Pierre Boulez wielding the baton. Bookings by mail should be made at least three months in advance, as the tickets sell out fast. Programs are available at French tourist offices abroad and throughout France; write for information and reservations directly to the festival office at the Palais de l'Ancien Archevêché, Aix-en-Provence 13100 (phone: 42-17-34-00).

A *Mardi Gras Carnival* is celebrated in February, and musical and theatrical events also take place during the spring. *Aix en Musique,* two weeks of primarily classical—but also jazz and ethnic—music (most of it presented free to the public), comes in late June or early July; the *Festival International de Danse* (phone: 42-63-06-75), with performances of modern dance and ballet, takes place in early July. A jazz festival (phone: 42-21-05-57) is held in August; music and theater festivals take place throughout the fall; a *Salon des Antiquaires* (antiques show) is held in November; and the wonderful *Foire aux Santons*, celebrating carved Provençal figures displayed at *Christmas,* takes place in December. For additional details on any special events, see *Le Mois à Aix* or consult the tourist office.

MUSEUMS

In addition to those mentioned in *Special Places,* Aix's museums of interest include the following:

MUSÉE PAUL-ARBAUD (PAUL ARBAUD MUSEUM) A large collection of old Provençal ceramics, paintings, and books on Provence. Open afternoons; closed Sundays and holidays. Admission charge. 2 Rue du Quatre-Septembre (phone: 42-38-38-95).

MUSÉE DU VIEIL AIX (MUSEUM OF OLD AIX) Recalls Aix's glorious past with old *Carnival* puppets and *santons* (wooden figures). Closed Mondays and the month of October. Admission charge. 17 Rue Gaston-de-Saporta (phone: 42-21-43-55).

SHOPPING

Some of the best-known souvenirs of Aix are ultra-rich sweets (surely not part of the thermal cure): The traditional almond-paste candies called *calissons d'Aix,* hazelnut-flavored nougat *victorines,* and unforgettable fresh chocolates from the nearby Puyricard chocolatiers are among France's best confections. Less caloric treats are the fragrant herbs of Provence and the Côtes de Provence and Côteaux d'Aix wines. For information about the Côteaux d'Aix wines and local producers who welcome visitors, as well as maps of the wine region, contact the *Syndicat des Côteaux d'Aix* (*Maison des Agriculteurs,* 22 Av. Henri-Pontier; phone: 42-23-57-14) or the tourist office.

Colorful and distinctive Provençal cotton fabrics, antiques, and designer clothes are among other treasures to be found in the lovely shops on such pedestrian streets as the Rue Fabrot, Rue Marius-Reinaud, and Rue des Cordeliers. The crafts and flea market held on the Place du Palais de Justice (also known as the Place de Verdun) on Tuesday, Thursday, and Saturday mornings is a good place to browse for interesting old postcards, maps, jewelry, and furniture. The *Village des Antiquaires,* 5 miles (8 km) from Aix on N7 toward Avignon, is a good bet for antiques.

A Provençal market is a market par excellence, and the produce market that takes place on Place de la Madeleine and Place des Prêcheurs on Tuesday, Thursday, and Saturday mornings is the crème de la crème. (There's also a daily market held mornings on the Place Richelme.) There's everything here to stock a larder or supply a memorable picnic: ripe fruit, vegetables, cheese, ham, sausage, pâté, herbs and spices, dozens of varieties of olives, and huge crusty country bread. The crowded, sprawling marketplace, alas, is a favorite with pickpockets.

The lovely, typically Provençal *Christmas santons* (wooden figures representing the holy family, the three wise men, and typical villagers) are still hand-carved by a number of local artisans. Inquire at the tourist office for a list of *santonniers* who welcome visitors. For standard shopping hours, see GETTING READY TO GO.

Bacchus A great wine cellar in which to find out about any kind of alcoholic beverage or bottled water. The proprietors speak little English. Closed one week in February. 27 Rue d'Italie (phone: 42-38-07-41).

Béchard The best pastry shop in Aix. 12 Cours Mirabeau (phone: 42-26-06-78).

La Boutique du Pays d'Aix Regional gift items, from Côteaux d'Aix wines and *calissons* to T-shirts and carved wooden *santons,* are for sale at this shop within the main tourist office. 2 Pl. du Général-de-Gaulle (phone: 42-16-11-61).

Chocolaterie de Puyricard An outlet of the nearby factory. 7 Rue Rifle-Rafle (phone: 42-21-13-26).

Galerie Manuel An art gallery featuring Aixois painters, with four exhibits each year. 4 Rue Manuel (phone: 42-27-59-40).

Hermès The famous Parisian source for fine clothing, scarves, and leather goods has a branch in Aix. 23 *bis* Rue Thiers (phone: 42-38-20-11).

Leonard Parli Established in 1874, it's among the oldest makers of *calissons d'Aix.* 35 Av. Victor-Hugo (phone: 42-26-05-71).

Les Olivades Provençal print fabrics by the yard and made into bags, eyeglass cases, bedspreads, and other articles. 5 Rue des Chaudronniers (phone: 42-23-57-47).

Santons Fouque For three generations the Fouque family has been creating *santons* right in the heart of Aix. Here you can see all the stages in the process of making these charming traditional figures. 65 Cours Gambetta (phone: 42-26-33-38).

Souleiado Beautiful Provençal prints—yard goods, ready-to-wear, and gift items. Pl. des Chapeliers (phone: 42-26-23-08).

SPORTS AND FITNESS

BICYCLING Bikes can be rented at *Cycles Naddeo* (Av. de Lattre-de-Tassigny; phone: 42-21-06-93) and at *Trocvélo* (62 Rue Bourlegon; phone: 42-21-37-40).

GOLF There is an 18-hole course at *Golf Club Aix-Marseille* (Domaine de Riquetti, Les Milles; phone: 42-24-20-41), and the *Golf International Pont Royal Country Club* (on N7 in Mallemort; phone: 90-59-44-80) boasts an 18-hole Ballestero-designed course.

HORSEBACK RIDING The tourist office has a list of riding clubs, some of which offer daily rates. Nearest to Aix is the *Club Hippique Aix-Marseille*, Av. au Club Hippique, Chemin des Cavaliers (phone: 42-20-18-26).

JOGGING A good course stretches along the Arc River at Pont de l'Arc under the trees.

SWIMMING The *Piscine Municipale* (Municipal Swimming Pool; not too far from the center of town, on Rte. du Tholonet; phone: 42-21-44-37) is covered in winter, uncovered in summer, and open daily year-round. Another pool, the *Piscine Municipale Plein Ciel* (Open-air Municipal Swimming Pool) is in suburban Jas-de-Bouffan (Av. Marcel-Pagnol; phone: 42-20-00-78).

TENNIS The Aix area boasts one of France's better tennis facilities.

CHOICE COURT

Country Club Aixois Offers five-day *stages* (instruction sessions) during school holidays and summer, with instruction from two and a half to five hours a day. Chemin de Cruyès, in Celony, 2 miles (3 km) north of Aix (phone: 42-92-10-41).

There are public courts at the municipal stadium (Rte. du Tholonet; phone: 42-26-64-58) and at the *Complex Sportif du Val de l'Arc* (Chemin des Infirmeries; phone: 42-61-02-50).

THEATER AND FILM

The *Théâtre Municipal* (Rue de l'Opéra; phone: 42-38-07-39) stages French classics and foreign plays in translation, plus other *spectacles,* including dance events. For listings of other theater performances (in French), see *Le Mois à Aix* or contact the tourist office. *Ciné Mazarin* (6 Rue Laroque; phone: 42-26-99-85) comprises three theaters that feature films in their original languages—which often is English—with French subtitles, as well as debates and appearances by guest stars. *Le Studio Keaton* (45 Rue Manuel; phone: 42-26-86-11) also shows films in English.

MUSIC

Not completely silent after the summer festival season is over, Aix's churches and cloisters continue to be the austere settings for concerts of classical music. Several operas and operettas—plus *chansons,* jazz, and rock—can be heard throughout the year, mostly at the *Théâtre Municipal* (see *Theater,* above). Consult *Le Mois à Aix, Le Provençal,* or the tourist office, or check posters for last-minute events.

NIGHTCLUBS AND NIGHTLIFE

The young, fashionable, disco-oriented crowd heads to the *Rétro 25* (N8, Pont de Luynes; phone: 42-24-01-00), an "in" club with videos and fashion shows. Popular discos include *Le Richelme* (Rue de la Verrerie; phone: 42-23-49-29) and *Oxydium* (outside town on the Route des Milles; phone: 42-27-92-16). Most clubs open at 10 PM and are closed Mondays. The older crowd goes dancing and sometimes can hear excellent live jazz at *Le Hot Brass* (Chemin de la Plaine-des-Verguetiers; phone: 42-21-05-57). *London Taverne* is a popular spot for beers, drinks and live jazz or rock on weekend nights (9 Rue des Bretons; phone: 42-38-59-58). *Le Blue Note* (10 Rue de la Fonderie; phone: 42-38-06-23) offers American food, along with live jazz and salsa on Tuesday and Friday evenings.

Café-theaters, which offer a combination of a meal and music and/or a theater performance, are popular in Aix. Among the possibilities are *Les Deux Garçons* (53 Cours Mirabeau; phone: 42-26-00-51); *La Petite Fonderie*, a cabaret (14 Cours St-Louis; phone: 42-63-12-11); *La Cour de Rohan* (Pl. de l'Hôtel de Ville; phone: 42-96-18-15), which offers a classical concert to accompany a special pastry every Thursday evening; and *Château de la Pioline* (see below).

Best in Town

CHECKING IN

Hotel rooms seem to vanish during Aix's summer festival. For a double room, expect to pay more than $175 at a very expensive hotel; from $125 to $175 at an expensive place; from $90 to $125 at a moderate one; and from $50 to $90 at an inexpensive place. Most rates do not include breakfast. Unless otherwise noted, all hotels listed below feature air conditioning, telephones, TV sets, and private baths in the rooms. Some inexpensive hotels have private baths in only some of their rooms; it's a good idea to confirm whether your room has a private bath when making a reservation. All hotels listed below are open year-round and accept major credit cards unless otherwise noted; some with restaurants require *demi-pension* (where the rate includes breakfast and either lunch or dinner) in summer.

VERY EXPENSIVE

Hôtel des Augustins Converted from a 15th-century convent, this beautiful place has 30 rooms with vaulted ceilings. Reserve in advance; ask for one of the two rooms (each has a terrace) overlooking the *Campanile des Augustins*. No restaurant, but breakfast is served in the garden. Just off the Cours Mirabeau, at 3 Rue de la Masse (phone: 42-27-28-59; fax: 42-26-74-87).

Château de la Pioline The 18 sumptuous rooms and three suites here overlook a fountain in the French-style, formal garden. The restaurant is one of the city's better, with elaborate dishes with a country-Provençal air, like grilled lamb with tiny stuffed vegetables. There is a pool. In Les Milles, about a mile (1.6 km) south of Aix by D9 (phone: 42-20-07-81; fax: 42-59-96-12).

Pullman Roi-René This luxurious property, with 131 rooms and three suites, is built in the Provençal style (creamy pink stucco and a few wrought-iron balconies). Amenities include a pool, a garden, and a full complement of business services. The restaurant, *La Table du Roi* (see *Eating Out*), is superb. 24 Bd. Roi-René (phone: 42-37-61-00; 800-221-4542; fax: 42-37-61-11).

Villa Gallici This hotel in a converted 18th-century *mas* (a large Provençal farmhouse) appears right at home in the lovely park it occupies. Each of the 17 luxurious rooms is unique, though all are spacious and beautifully decorated with Provençal furniture and fabrics. There's a lovely pool; *Le Clos de la Violette,* Aix's only one-Michelin-star restaurant (see *Eating Out*), is nearby. 18 *bis* Av. de la Violette (phone: 42-23-29-23; fax: 42-96-30-45).

EXPENSIVE

Le Domaine de Tournon The lovely surrounding countryside makes a detour to this luxury hotel an enjoyable trip. There are 59 comfortable rooms (none air conditioned), plus a pool, three tennis courts, and a restaurant that serves traditional fare. About 2 miles (3 km) out of town; take the Périphérique to Place Bellegarde, turn right on the Ancienne Route des Alpes, and follow D63C toward Les Pinchinats (phone: 42-21-22-05; fax: 42-21-38-61).

Les Infirmeries du Roi-René This former 16th-century *infirmerie* (nursing center) is now a luxurious hotel whose 66 units, decorated in a modern style, have kitchen facilities, but no air conditioning. Some of the rooms have mezzanines and terraces overlooking ancient plane trees. There is a sports center with two tennis courts, and a pool next door. With all its conveniences, this place is ideal for families. Chemin des Infirmeries (phone: 42-37-83-00; fax: 42-27-54-40).

Mas des Ecureuils A peaceful *mas* (farmhouse) with 19 rooms (none air conditioned) set in its own pine grove on the edge of Aix, this hotel's features include a pool, business facilities, and a good restaurant, *La Carraire,* that serves Provençal specialties. The hotel and restaurant are closed the last two weeks in December; the restaurant is also closed for Sunday lunch and on Mondays. A minibus shuttles guests to the center of town. Chemin de Castel Blanc (phone: 42-24-40-48; fax: 42-39-24-57).

Mercure Paul-Cézanne A member of the prestigious Mercure chain, this hotel is situated near the center of town and has antique furnishings and minibars in its 54 rooms, along with excellent service. 40 Av. Victor-Hugo (phone: 42-26-34-73; fax: 42-27-20-95).

Le Nègre-Coste In the oldest 18th-century *hôtel* on the Cours, this is a favorite among traveling thespians and journalists. Its 36 renovated rooms retain their period character and furnishings. There's no restaurant, but there is a garage. 33 Cours Mirabeau (phone: 42-27-74-22; fax: 42-26-80-93).

Le Pigonnet Tucked amid shady chestnut trees (which Cézanne is said to have painted) and lovely flowered grounds is this typical Provençal mansion, whose 50 carefully decorated rooms (some air conditioned) and two suites fulfill the promise of their bucolic setting. There's a fine restaurant that offers Provençal specialties. The restaurant is closed during school vacations in February and November, and for lunch on weekends except in July.

Near the outskirts of the city, at 5 Av. du Pigonnet (phone: 42-59-02-90; fax: 42-59-47-77).

Relais Ste-Victoire Outside town in beautiful Cézanne country, this small, 10-unit stopover for travelers has a pool and a tennis court. The one-Michelin-star restaurant (see *Eating Out*) is worth the drive, even if you don't plan to stay overnight. Closed the first week in January, and during school vacations in February and November. In Beaurecueil (phone: 42-66-94-98).

MODERATE

Hôtel des Quatre Dauphins A cheerfully decorated hotel with 12 rooms (none air conditioned) in a renovated mansion. Closed mid-February through early March. Centrally located at 54 Rue Roux-Alphéran (phone: 42-38-16-39; phone: 42-38-60-19).

Le Manoir A converted 14th-century cloister with 43 rooms (no air conditioning) and period furnishings. The public rooms have exposed beams and French Provincial furniture, and there's a pretty, shaded terrace on a gravel courtyard off the very quiet street. No restaurant. Closed mid-January through mid-February. Centrally located, at 8 Rue d'Entrecasteaux (phone: 42-26-27-20; fax: 42-27-17-97).

INEXPENSIVE

Cardinal Extremely pleasant, this is perhaps the best buy for the money in Aix. Its 31 simple rooms are comfortable and thoughtfully decorated; nearly all of them have private baths. The two small but cozy top-floor rooms have a lovely rooftop view. Most of the staff members speak English. Near the *Musée Granet,* at 24 Rue Cardinale (phone: 42-38-32-30; fax: 42-26-39-05).

EATING OUT

Provençal cooking draws inspiration from the celebrated local aromatic herbs and also makes good use of olive oil, garlic, tomatoes, and onions. The accent tends to be on light dishes, and seafood is common. Be aware that service often is unbearably slow, and most restaurants take their last orders before 9:30 or 10 PM. For a three-course dinner à la carte for two, including wine, tax, and service (usually added to the bill automatically), expect to pay more than $100 in expensive restaurants, $50 to $100 in moderate ones, and less than $50 in inexpensive ones. Unless otherwise noted, all restaurants listed below are open for lunch and dinner.

EXPENSIVE

Le Clos de la Violette By far the best dining room in Aix, and the only one with a Michelin star. Cooking is Provençal, with most of the herbs and some of the vegetables coming from the owner's garden. Closed Monday lunch, Sundays, and late March through mid-April. Reserve well in advance. Major credit cards accepted. 10 Av. de la Violette (phone: 42-23-30-71; fax: 42-21-93-03).

Les Frères Lani Inventive dishes like sweetbreads with wine vinegar and all kinds of chocolate desserts are served in an elegant setting. Closed Monday lunch, Sundays, two weeks in February, and August 1 through 15. Reservations advised. Major credit cards accepted. 22 Rue Victor-Leydet (phone: 42-27-76-16; fax: 42-22-68-67).

Puyfond In this elegant eatery, surrounded by a pine grove, authentic Provençal home cooking prevails. Closed Sunday dinner, Mondays, one week in January, mid-February through mid-March, and mid-August through early September. Reservations necessary. MasterCard and Visa accepted. In Rigoulon, about 3½ miles (6 km) north of town on routes N96 and D13 (phone: 42-92-13-77). ·

Relais Ste-Victoire A changing, seasonal menu of delightful Provençal specialties, plus views of dramatic Montagne Ste-Victoire from the restaurant's terrace, make the drive to this small inn outside town well worth it. Typical choices from the one-Michelin-star menu include *terrine de lapereau* (terrine of young rabbit), *agneau confit* (slow-cooked lamb), and pasta with fresh truffles. Closed Sunday dinner, Mondays, the first week in January, and during school vacations in February and November. In Beaurecueil (phone: 42-66-94-98).

La Table du Roi The chef has brought imaginative cuisine to this restaurant; the *langoustines à l'huile d'olive au thym* (Dublin Bay prawns with thyme-infused olive oil) are superlative. Open daily. Reservations advised. Major credit cards accepted. In the *Pullman Roi-René* hotel, 24 Bd. Roi-René (phone: 42-37-61-00; fax: 42-37-61-11).

MODERATE

Auberge Provençal This pleasant restaurant outside town has authentic regional specialties and local wines. Closed Tuesday dinner, Wednesdays (except in summer, when the restaurant is open daily), and two weeks in February. Reservations advised. MasterCard and Visa accepted. On N7, in Canet, 5 miles (8 km) southeast of Aix (phone: 42-58-68-54; fax: 42-58-68-05).

Les Bacchanales This new addition to Aix's restaurant scene has excellent regional dishes such as rabbit with wild thyme. Closed Sunday dinner and Mondays. Reservations advised. Major credit cards accepted. 10 Rue Couronne (phone: 42-27-21-06).

Le Bistrot Latin This friendly place offers excellent simple Provençal fare (avoid the more complicated dishes) and an extensive selection of local wines. Closed Sunday dinner and Monday lunch. Reservations advised. Major credit cards accepted. 18 Rue Couronne (phone: 42-38-22-88).

La Brocherie Attractively rustic with a pleasant courtyard, it specializes in meat grilled over a wood fire. With good service, this is an excellent buy. Closed Monday dinner, Sundays, and August 10 through September 10. Reservations essential for the courtyard. Major credit cards accepted. 5 Rue Fernand-Dol (phone: 42-38-33-21).

Côté Cour This dining room in an 18th-century house has good brasserie and bistro cooking, complemented by excellent service and a good selection of wines by the *pichet* (carafe). Closed Sunday dinner, Mondays, a week in January, and the first week of June. Reservations advised. Major credit cards accepted. 19 Cours Mirabeau (phone: 42-26-32-39).

INEXPENSIVE

Al Dente Only pasta is served here, but it's fresh, light, and well prepared. Open daily; closed Sunday lunch. No reservations. No credit cards accepted. 14 Rue Constantin (phone: 42-96-41-03).

Le Dernier Bistrot The name is derived from Truffaut, the decor from Fellini, but the food is definitely Provençal, and the service is friendly. Closed Sunday dinner and Mondays. Reservations advised. MasterCard and Visa accepted. 19 Rue Constantin (phone: 42-41-13-02).

BARS AND CAFÉS

Aix's premier sidewalk café is *Les Deux Garçons* (see *Nightclubs and Nightlife,* above). Outside, in the shade of the plane trees, or inside, soaking in its lovely rococo decor, it has been *the* place for people watching for more than 200 years. Open till 2 AM daily, it's one of the few places where you can order only coffee or tea any time of the day or night. Café-concerts take place here as well. *Le Petit Verdot* (7 Rue Entrecasteaux; phone: 42-27-30-12) is a wine bar that serves food; it's closed Monday lunch and Sundays. The "in" place in Aix for the young university crowd is *Bistro Aixois* (37 Cours Sextius; phone: 42-26-00-33). Live rock music is one of its draws. Cocktail bars include *Le Jungle Bar* (4 Bd. Carnot; phone: 42-21-47-44) and *Key Largo* (34 Rue de la Verrerie; phone: 42-38-47-10).

Avignon

On the traditional route from Paris to the Mediterranean, Avignon always has had the vibrant style of a crossroads town. But the city is a monument to one special period of glory, and to appreciate Avignon fully, one must consider its role as seat of the papacy in the 14th-century.

Early in that century, Pope Clement V refused—largely because of internecine violence in Italy—to take up residence in Rome. His decision to live in a relatively unknown town in Provence was not exactly a quirk of fate: The pope, a Frenchman by birth, was somewhat beholden to Philippe-le-Bel (Philip the Fair), then King of France, for his election; and, though Avignon was not a part of the French kingdom (it belonged to the Counts of Provence), it was close enough to be within the king's sphere of influence. It also had a strategic riverside location (just north of the intersection of the Rhône and Durance) and was situated within a papal territory, the Comtat Venaissin. Clement V arrived in Avignon in 1309, and while he lived for the most part in the peaceful countryside of the surrounding papal lands, his official presence transformed this obscure town into a capital of the Christian world.

For the next 70 years or so, seven popes, all French, reigned from Avignon. Clement V's successor, John XXII, was the first to establish his permanent residence in Avignon proper, moving into the episcopal palace. Pope Benedict XII, who succeeded John XXII in 1334, built his own palace, a structure that left no doubt of his intention to remain in Avignon. Nor was there any doubt in the mind of his successor, Clement VI, pope from 1342 to 1352, who bought the city from the Countess of Provence and spent the duration of his papacy adding to Benedict XII's palace, in effect creating an entirely new palace attached to the older one.

By 1352, when Innocent VI succeeded Clement VI, Avignon's main tourist attraction—the massive and staunch *Palais des Papes* (Palace of the Popes)—was essentially the same size and shape it is today. Innocent VI added reinforcements to the structure, including two towers; Urban V, his successor in 1362, added a gallery. Urban V tried to restore the papacy to Rome, leaving Avignon in 1367, only to return a few months before his death, in 1370, after finding the Eternal City too violent and another French king vehemently opposed to the move. The next pope, Gregory XI, succeeded in returning to Rome in 1377.

The city's papal period has been called the "Avignon Captivity," and even the "second Babylonian Captivity" because of charges that Avignon was another Babylon, a place of excessive worldliness, of which the flagrantly luxurious palace was a telling symbol. Across the river in Villeneuve-lès-Avignon, the sumptuous homes of the cardinals almost rivaled that of the popes. Throughout this period, the city also was the banking and commercial center of southern Europe.

With so much money flowing from the church's coffers, the arts flourished here. The Sienese painter Simone Martini worked in Avignon from 1339 to 1344, painting frescoes on the porch of the cathedral; he was followed by other Italian artists, who worked in the palace. The great Italian poet Petrarch spent many years in the city, and it was here that he met Laura, who inspired his famous love lyrics. Petrarch was a regular at the court of Clement VI (and in his later years an active champion of the return of the papacy to Rome). Troubadours, mountebanks, processions of penitents, religious minorities seeking the pope's protection, and miscreants of all stripes seeking refuge within the boundaries of the papal enclave all descended upon Avignon. A spirit of tolerance prevailed, and crime and prostitution prospered.

When Gregory XI moved the papacy back to Rome in the late 14th century, the city did not fade into obscurity: No sooner had a new pope, Urban VI, replaced Gregory XI than his attempt to introduce reforms caused the College of Cardinals to annul his election and choose a second pope, Clement VII, who returned to Avignon to occupy the palace from 1378 to 1394. During the resulting Great Schism, the Christian world had two popes reigning simultaneously, one in Rome and one in Avignon—each excommunicated by the other (with even a third pope during the later years). Meanwhile, Clement VII's successor, Benedict XIII, who held the Avignon papacy from 1394 to 1409, managed to prolong the city's period of glory past the turn of the century. By this time in Avignon's career as an ecclesiastical city, there were 35 monasteries and 60 churches here, whose bells rang so often that the French writer François Rabelais named it "La Ville Sonnante," the "ringing city."

The schism ended in 1415, when all popes but those of the Roman line were declared antipopes by the Council of Constance. Afterward, Avignon became merely an important provincial city, with merchants manufacturing silk and smuggling salt and tobacco. The palace now housed papal legates, who fought with the French kings until 1791, when Avignon became French territory.

As important as its 14th-century heyday is Avignon's entire long history, signs of which are still evident. Retreat north from the barren stone of the palace to the calm greenery of the *Rocher des Doms* (Doms' Rock) park, bearing in mind that ducks swim, pigeons roost, and children play on the very spot that was the cradle of Avignon, inhabited some 4,000 years before Christ. Across the Rhône is the square fortress built by Philip the Fair in the last decade of the 13th century. During the neighborhood's renewal in the 1960s, first-century pottery and other Gallo-Roman relics were unearthed in the upper class Balance quarter west of the palace, with its beautiful, restored, 17th-century townhouses. This was the site of Roman arcades, or "fusteries," as is evident from street names in the vicinity. Some relics are on display in the neighborhood. Nearby, the central Place de l'Horloge was the site of the Roman forum.

All told, today's town of nearly 90,000 people (fewer than 20% of whom live within the familiar ramparts) contains nearly 100 national historic monuments. Most of them—like the walls that are lined with open-air vegetable markets or parked cars and encircled by busy, six-lane streets, or the *Palais des Papes,* with its modern convention center—are now part of a living, thriving present.

In recent decades, Avignon has become a cultural center of sorts. A number of artists live on and enliven the beautiful Rue des Teinturiers, and art cinemas, galleries, and experimental theaters populate the inner city. Most important of all is the annual international *Festival d'Avignon,* one of France's liveliest arts events and its most important theater festival.

Five centuries after the departure of the popes, Avignon—the capital of Vaucluse, a charming province of southern France—still stands out as one of the remarkable cities of Provence.

Avignon At-a-Glance

SEEING THE CITY

On the far bank of the Rhône, directly opposite "Le Pont d'Avignon" at the entrance to the medieval town of Villeneuve-lès-Avignon, is the late-13th-century *Tour Philippe-le-Bel* (Philip the Fair Tower; phone: 90-27-49-49). From the top of this edifice there is a striking 180° view of Avignon, with the vast *Palais des Papes* in the foreground, the city's densely packed rooftops beyond, and Mont Ventoux in the distance. The tower is closed Tuesdays and the month of February. Admission charge.

SPECIAL PLACES

Enter the historic center at *Porte de la République;* then head straight along tree-lined Cours Jean-Jaurès and Rue de la République to Place de l'Horloge, Avignon's main square. At nearby Place du Palais are the immense *Palais des Papes,* the city's cathedral, the main museum, and a lovely public park. Across from the palace, signs point down a side street and steps to the famous bridge. Place de l'Horloge also gives access to a pedestrian shopping zone around Rue de la Bonneterie, which eventually leads to Rue des Teinturiers. All sights below are within walking distance of each other except Villeneuve-lès-Avignon, which is 2 miles (3 km) across the Rhône. Museums and churches generally close between noon and 2 PM.

CITY CENTER

PALAIS DES PAPES (PALACE OF THE POPES) This imposing fortress residence was the home of five of the seven popes of the Avignon Captivity and of two of the antipopes of the Great Schism. It's actually two palaces, with a total area of more than 150,000 square feet, whose differing styles reflect the differing personalities of the popes who commissioned them.

The austere Romanesque palace on the left was built from 1335 to 1342 under the ascetic Benedict XII, while the palace on the right, in the more ornate Flamboyant Gothic style, was built from 1342 to 1352 under the more worldly Clement VI. Unfortunately, both parts of the palace now are mostly bare: A fire in 1413 devastated paintings and ceilings in the two huge halls, the *Consistoire* (Consistory) and the *Grand Tinel* (Banquet Hall); looting and vandalism during the French Revolution destroyed furniture and statuary; and when the palace later served as a barracks and prison, frescoes were literally cut up and removed.

In recent years, centuries-old tapestries have been added throughout, and wooden ceilings have replaced lost ones in a few rooms (including the *Consistoire* and the *Grand Tinel*), but the palace's highlights are the rooms where the original decoration remains. Among these are the *Chapelle St-Jean,* with frescoes attributed to Matteo Giovanetti, and the *Chapelle St-Martial,* with frescoes by Giovanetti which are remarkable for the predominant, vivid lapis lazuli blue. (The quaint graffiti here date from the 15th century.) The walls of the *Chambre du Pape* (Pope's Bedchamber), covered with a pattern of foliage on a dark blue ground, may reflect the taste of either Benedict XII or Clement VI, who both used the room. The *Chambre du Cerf* (Deer Room), Clement VI's study, reveals an intact painted wooden ceiling that was protected by a false one in the 18th century; the walls are full of surprisingly secular hunting, fishing, and bird trapping frescoes.

The palace's imposing courtyard—the *Cour d'Honneur*—is closed to the public in late spring and early summer, when it becomes a setting for the *Festival d'Avignon* (see *Special Events*). The palace is open daily (except *Christmas* and *New Year's Day*), with regularly scheduled guided tours. From April through September, there are two hour-long tours daily (except May 1) in English, one in the morning, and one in the afternoon. The rest of the year, regularly scheduled guided tours are available in French only, but special tours are available year-round by reservation (and for a considerable fee) in several languages. Tours are often modified because of continuous restoration work. Admission charge. Pl. du Palais (phone: 90-27-50-74 for information; 90-27-50-73 to reserve a special tour; fax: 90-86-61-21).

CATHÉDRALE DE NOTRE-DAME DES DOMS (CATHEDRAL OF OUR LADY OF THE DOMS)

Up the hill from the palace is Avignon's cathedral. Dating from the 12th century, it was partly rebuilt from the 14th to the 17th century, and topped by a tall gilded statue of the Virgin in the 19th century. Inside are the tombs of Popes John XXII and Benedict XII; outside on the porch are sketches of two frescoes by Simone Martini (the upper layers have been removed and are on display in the palace). Pl. du Palais (phone: 90-86-81-01).

ROCHER DES DOMS (ROCK OF THE DOMS) This rocky promontory overlooking the Rhône is the highest point in the city. Inhabited in prehistoric times, it is now a delightful public park with sloping lawns, lovely trees and flowerbeds, a duck pond and a grotto for swans, a shaded playground, and a shaded café. The immense esplanade affords a broad view across the river to the vast green fields of Villeneuve-lès-Avignon (a viewing table at one corner identifies all the visible sights) or, looking back, over the red roofs of the city. Follow the esplanade around to the left to gaze down upon the Pont St-Bénézet. The park is a short climb north of the cathedral; a toy-like mini-train leaves regularly in season from Place du Palais.

MUSÉE DU PETIT PALAIS (MUSEUM OF THE LITTLE PALACE) Built in the 14th century after the arrival of the papacy in Avignon, this "little palace" became the official archbishop's residence when the "big palace" was constructed across the square for the popes. Remodeling in the 15th century gave the medieval building a Renaissance finish; today, the graceful structure houses a museum. On display are paintings and sculpture of the Avignon School from the 12th to the 16th century and Italian paintings from the 13th to the 16th century. Totaling about 300, these works represent but a minuscule selection of an enormous hoard accumulated by a rich 19th-century Roman count and amateur archaeologist, Gian Pietro Campana, whose passion for art depleted the coffers of the bank of which he was director, ending with his imprisonment for misappropriation of funds. His collection comprised approximately 15,000 objets d'art, including 1,100 paintings—so many that he ran his own restoration workshops, with not always felicitous results. The collection was eventually divided among the *Louvre* and 100 or so provincial museums; only recently have some of the paintings been reassembled here. Among the gems of the collection are a Virgin and Child by the Sienese Taddeo di Bartolo, a Holy Conversation by the Venetian Carpaccio, and an early Botticelli Madonna. Closed Tuesdays and holidays. Admission charge. Pl. du Palais (phone: 90-86-44-58).

PONT ST-BÉNÉZET According to legend, France's most famous bridge, "Le Pont d'Avignon," was built as a result of the divine vision of a young shepherd named Bénézet. Considered an engineering miracle upon its completion in 1185, it was 1,000 yards long and had 22 arches spanning the Rhône. Only four of the arches remain now, the rest destroyed in the middle of the 18th century by the Rhône's high waters, and the bridge stops tantalizingly short of the Ile de la Barthelasse, which divides the river into two branches. It was actually on the island and *under,* rather than *on,* the bridge—*sous le pont* rather than *sur le pont*—that everyone took part in the area's traditional circle dances. Still standing on the narrow cobblestone span is the two-story, 13th-century *Chapelle St-Nicolas,* which is bare but for modern graffiti, and in which Saint Bénézet is said to be buried. The entrance to the bridge is somewhat obscure: If you're coming from the *Porte du Rhône,* turn right, pass under the bridge, and go into the postcard shop just beyond

it. The new *Espace St-Bénézet* next to the entrance to the bridge has a multilingual audiovisual display on Avignon's history. Both the bridge and the
Espace St-Bénézet are open daily April through September; closed Mondays
the rest of the year, *Christmas* through January 2, and the last two weeks
of January, February, and March. Admission charge for the bridge (none
for the *Espace*). Rue Ferruce (phone: 90-85-60-16).

PLACE DE L'HORLOGE (CLOCK TOWER SQUARE) At the heart of Avignon is this
large bustling 15th-century square, teeming with sidewalk café patrons and
street performers until the wee hours of the morning in the summer. On
the left (if you're coming from the train station) is the stately *Hôtel de Ville*
(Town Hall), built in the mid-19th century around the old Gothic belfry
that gives the square its name. Enter to see its massive columns. Next door
is the elegant *Opéra d'Avignon* (see *Theater and Film*), from the same decade.
The square is on the site of a Roman forum, many of whose 1st-century
vestiges have been removed to the nearby corner of Rues St-Etienne and
Racine.

RUE DES TEINTURIERS This charming cobblestone street is lined on one side by a
narrow canal—part of the Sorgue River—whose brush-like waterwheels
rise above a stone wall. The waters once served the cloth dyers for whom
the street is named. On the other side of the street are old-fashioned uphol-
stery, photography, and antiques shops, restaurants, and café-theaters.

CITY WALLS The 3 miles of stone ramparts, complete with turrets and battlements,
that encircle Avignon's historic center were built in the 14th century as the
popes' first line of defense against marauders and foreign armies. If today
they don't seem high enough for defensive purposes, it's partly because the
surrounding moat—through which the Sorgue used to flow—has not been
excavated. Originally, also, there were only seven *portes* (gates) leading into
the city; the other openings were added in the 19th century, when the walls
were restored by the architect Viollet-le-Duc.

ENVIRONS

VILLENEUVE-LÈS-AVIGNON This area first was occupied by Gallo-Romans. After
Saint Caesaria's death in the 6th century, it became a site of devotion, where
Benedictine monks later built a small monastery and started a settlement.
Philippe-le-Bel founded the town as a stronghold in the late 13th century,
when Avignon belonged to the Counts of Provence and the territory on
this side of the river belonged to France. He began in 1293 by constructing the square keep of the *Tour Philippe-le-Bel,* to which an upper story and
watchtower were added in the 14th century (see *Seeing the City*). Later 14th-
century kings built the *Fort St-André* (Rue Montée de la Tour; phone: 90-
25-45-35), whose crenelated walls completely enclose the top of a nearby
hill and end in twin round towers defending a massive gateway. (Open daily;
closed holidays and during lunch hours September through June. Admission

charge.) But the development of the town really accelerated with the arrival of the papacy, when it was named Villeneuve-lès-Avignon (New City by Avignon). The cardinals built their grand residences here, turning Villeneuve into a wealthy residential suburb that witnessed a brilliant ecclesiastical life until the French Revolution.

There are several other sites of interest in this small and quiet medieval town. The ruined 14th-century *Chartreuse du Val-de-Bénédiction* (Valley of Benediction Charterhouse; Rue de la République; phone: 90-25-05-46) was once the largest and most important Carthusian monastery in France. It was founded in 1356 by Pope Innocent VI, whose white marble tomb is in a chapel of the church. It's open daily (except holidays); admission charge. The *Musée Municipal* (Rue de l'Hôpital; phone: 90-27-49-66), in a 17th-century building, contains many items from the charterhouse and a notable 15th-century painting, Enguerrand Charonton's *Coronation of the Virgin,* considered a masterpiece of the Avignon School. The parish *Eglise de Notre-Dame* (Pl. J.-Meissonier), founded as the collegiate church in the 14th century, holds another of Villeneuve's treasures: a small ivory Virgin and Child that follows the curve of the elephant's tusk from which it was carved. The festival of music and dance held here every summer is a perfect complement to the *Festival d'Avignon* (see *Special Events*). Two miles (3 km) northwest of Avignon, Villeneuve can be reached by bus No. 20 from the Avignon train station. (The bus takes you to, but not *into,* Villeneuve; ask where to get off.) There is a local tourist office (1 Pl. Charles-David; phone: 90-25-61-33); it's closed Sundays and during lunch hours.

ROQUEMAURE Ten miles (16 km) north on D980 is this town, whose 14th-century church, the *Eglise St-Jean-Baptiste,* on Place Clément-V, houses the remains of Saint Valentine, brought here in 1868 from Italy. Every February 14, lovers come from all over to receive the saint's blessings. For more information, contact the local tourist office at 66-90-54-34.

Sources and Resources

TOURIST INFORMATION

Avignon's *Office du Tourisme* (41 Cours Jean-Jaurès; phone: 90-82-15-98; fax: 90-82-95-03) is open daily from mid-June through mid-August; closed Sundays the rest of the year. It handles information and currency exchange and organizes guided tours (including in English) of Avignon and its environs. Just outside the train station, the hotel-run *Vaucluse Tourisme Hébergement (VTH)* reservation center (phone: 90-82-05-81) will change money on weekends.

LOCAL COVERAGE The regional dailies *Le Provençal, Vaucluse Matin, Gazette Provençale,* and *Le Méridional* all have Avignon editions (in French, naturally). The tourist office distributes *Avignon Pratique,* a free brochure that provides useful data on hotels, restaurants, and sights, along with a map. A free brochure on cultural events, *Rendez-Vous,* is published monthly except in July and August, when the *Festival d'Avignon* is held (see *Special Events*). The *maison de la presse* (newsstand and stationery store) opposite the tourist office carries English-language books, newspapers, and maps on Avignon and the surrounding region.

TELEPHONE The city code for Avignon is 90, which is incorporated into all local eight-digit numbers. When calling a number in Avignon from the Paris region (including the Ile-de-France), dial 16, wait for a dial tone, then dial the eight-digit number. When calling a number from outside Paris, dial only the eight-digit number.

GETTING AROUND

The ramparts and one-way streets make driving here difficult and slow. Almost everything within Avignon's walls can be seen best on foot; for the rest of the city or across the Rhône, alternatives are available.

BOAT *Grands Bateaux de Provence* (Allées de l'Oulle; phone: 90-85-62-25) offers day and evening cruises, which include lunch or dinner, to various vineyards and villages in the region.

BUS Tickets, which cost about 6F each (around $1 at press time), can be bought individually on the bus or in economical packets of ten, for about 40F (around $6.90 at press time) from booths in Place Pie and at *Porte de la République,* as well as at bakeries and *tabacs* (tobacco shops). Schedules, available at the same locations, also can be obtained from the tourist office (see *Tourist Information*). There's no evening service, and weekend service is spotty.

CAR RENTAL All the major firms, including *Avis* (at the train station; phone: 90-82-26-33) and *Hertz* (6 Rte. de Lyon; phone: 90-86-61-69), are represented.

TAXI There are stands at the train station and scattered around Avignon, or call *Radio Taxis* (phone: 90-82-20-20).

TRAIN The train station, *Gare SNCF,* is just outside *Porte de la République* at the foot of Cours Jean-Jaurès. Avignon is well served by trains en route between Paris and Nice. The high-speed *TGV* (*Train à Grande Vitesse,* or "fast train") brings you from Paris to Avignon in a mere four hours (phone: 90-82-50-50).

SPECIAL EVENTS

During the summer, modest, provincial Avignon is transformed into a polyglot United Nations of theater.

A FAVORITE FÊTE

Festival d'Avignon Begun in 1947, this is France's foremost theater festival—though to call it that alone is to fail to communicate its scope, because it's also an international festival of dance, film, music, and every other possible manifestation of the performing arts. Groups from all over the world—from Stuttgart's *Staatstheater* and England's *Footsbarn Travelling Theatre* to Milan's *La Scala* and a Japanese ritual dance troupe—converge on the city. Still, the festival's core is theater, and from early July through early August any French troupe of note will make an appearance here. The audience is full of Parisian playgoers trying to discern which way the French theater is heading, since a good number of the French productions are premieres of works by living playwrights of international reputation. These are interspersed with performances of Racine and other French classics and with productions by foreign companies of their ancients and moderns, occasionally including productions in English. The main stage is the courtyard of the *Palais des Papes,* but the list of parallel "Off Avignon" activities is by now so long that the entire city becomes a stage at this time, with concerts, debates, café-theater, and street theater going on in theaters, churches, cloisters, and squares. For details, contact the tourist office or the *Festival d'Avignon* at 8 *bis* Rue de Mons, Avignon 84000 (phone: 90-82-67-08) or *Avignon Public Off,* BP 5-75521 Paris 75001 (phone: 48-05-20-97), where you can receive an advance program of "Off Avignon" offerings (include a stamped, self-addressed envelope). Reservations are taken beginning in June.

In addition, the *Cheval Passion*, a festival honoring equestrian arts, takes place in January, and a month-long dance festival is held in January or February. Two secondhand dealers' fairs take place yearly by the river on Les Allées des Oulles, one in spring during *Pentecost* weekend and the other in early September. At the end of April or beginning of May, Villeneuve-lès-Avignon (see *Special Places,* above) celebrates the *Fête de St-Marc* with a *Foire aux Vins et Produits Régionaux* (Wine and Regional Products Fair). In Avignon proper, May brings the *Foire d'Avignon,* celebrating the best of Provençal food and arts, and in June a music festival is held. Villeneuve-lès-Avignon is also the site of a music and dance festival in the summer, and during the first week of July, the town hosts the highly regarded *Festival du Film Américain* (Festival of American Film); contact the *French-American Center* (10 Montée de la Tour, Villeneuve-lès-Avignon 30400; phone: 90-25-93-23). July also brings an annual artisans' fair to the area by the river. *Bastille Day* (July 14) is celebrated with extraordinary fireworks off the Pont St-Bénézet, with dancing on the bridge into the night. And the third Thursday in November, young Côtes du Rhône wine is celebrated during the *Baptêmes des Côtes du Rhône Primeur.*

MUSEUMS

In addition to those mentioned in *Special Places,* the following museums are of interest:

MAISON JEAN VILAR (JEAN VILAR HOUSE) A cultural center housed in the lovely 14th-century *Hôtel de Crochans* honors Jean Vilar (1912–71), the popular actor and theater director who founded the *Festival d'Avignon*. Conferences, exhibitions, and cultural events take place here, and there's a free library and media center on the premises. Closed Sundays; media center open afternoons only, or by appointment. Admission charge to some events. 8 Rue de Mons (phone: 90-86-59-64).

MUSÉE CALVET (CALVET MUSEUM) A diverse art collection (including works by David, Daumier, Delacroix, Soutine, Vlaminck, Dufy, and the 18th-century Avignon painter Joseph Vernet), archaeological artifacts, and a collection of wrought-iron hardware dating from the 15th to the 19th century are housed in a classic 18th-century mansion with exceptional grounds. Long closed for restoration, the museum partially reopened last year; the refurbishing will continue throughout most of this year. 65 Rue Joseph-Vernet (phone: 90-86-33-84).

MUSÉE LAPIDAIRE (LAPIDARY MUSEUM) Gallo-Roman objects are displayed in this former Jesuit chapel. Closed Tuesdays. No admission charge. 27 Rue de la République (phone: 90-85-75-38).

MUSÉE VOULAND Housed in the original collector's mansion, this small museum diplays a fine collection of 17th- and 18th-century decorative objects. Closed Sundays, Mondays, and holidays. Admission charge. 17 Rue Victor-Hugo (phone: 90-86-03-79).

SHOPPING

The side streets off Rue de la République—notably the pedestrian zone dominated by Rue de la Bonneterie—are filled with quality clothing and antiques shops. The parallel Rue Joseph-Vernet is another elegant shopping street, featuring well-known Parisian establishments. Local specialties include excellent *eaux-de-vie* and liqueurs made by the Manguin family on the Ile de la Barthelasse and tasty, liquor-filled chocolate candies called *papalines*. Also good buys are such regional items as colorful Provençal cottons and aromatic *herbes de Provence*–scented products. A flea market is held Saturday mornings on Place Crillon and Sundays at Place des Carmes. There are regularly scheduled auctions at the *Hôtel des Ventes* (2 Rue Rempart St-Lazare; phone: 90-86-35-35). For standard shopping hours, see GETTING READY TO GO. Among the other Avignon shops worth exploring are the following:

Antiquités Bourret The owners of this lovely shop focus on Provençal antiques, from pottery to gilded mirrors and handsome quilts. 5 Rue Linas (phone: 90-86-65-02).

Cristallerie des Papes Unique hand-crafted and hand-blown glass. Fontaine-de-Vaucluse, 15 miles (25 km) south of Avignon (phone: 90-20-32-52; fax: 90-20-20-16).

Hervé Baume This antiques shop, which focuses on locally produced objects, also carries decorative wrought-iron items. 17-19 Rue Petite Fusterie (phone: 90-86-37-66; fax: 90-27-05-97).

Librairie Roumanille A publishing house and bookstore selling rare books and manuscripts about Provence, as well as old prints. 19 Rue St-Agricol (phone: 90-86-12-40).

Salle d'Exposition, Espace St-Bénézet A group of artisans sell items ranging from almond cookies to herbal products to hand-painted scarves. Closed October through mid-March. Entrance on Rue Ferruce or on Quai de la Ligne, next to the bridge (phone: 90-85-60-16).

Souleiado Marvelous Provençal fabric, fashions, and gift items. 5 Rue Joseph-Vernet (phone: 90-86-47-67).

SPORTS AND FITNESS

BICYCLING Rental bikes are available at *Dopieralski* (80 Rue Guillaume-Puy; phone: 90-86-32-49) and *Masson* (19 Rue Florence; phone: 90-82-32-19). All-terrain bikes are available at *Transhumance* (34 Bd. St-Roch; phone: 90-95-57-81). Bikes also can be rented at the *SNCF* office at the train station (phone: 90-82-50-50). Call ahead to reserve a bike in the summer.

HORSEBACK RIDING The *Centre Equestre et Poney Club d'Avignon* on the Ile de la Barthelasse (phone: 90-85-83-48) offers guided rides, instruction, and pony rides for children.

MOUNTAIN CLIMBING Scale the slopes at Les Dentelles de Montmirail and around Fontaine-de-Vaucluse. For information, contact the *Club Alpin Français* (7 Rue St-Michel, Avignon 84000; phone: 90-38-14-77). The club is open only on Thursday afternoons for visits and Tuesday afternoons for phone information.

SWIMMING There is an Olympic-size pool on the Ile de la Barthelasse (phone: 90-82-54-25), open daily mid-May through early September. The municipal pool, the *Piscine du Stade Nautique* (phone: 90-87-00-90), is on Av. Pierre-de-Coubertin, part of the Route de Marseille. It's open daily from July through mid-September.

TENNIS Reserve in advance for the municipal courts at the *Tennis Club d'Avignon* (Av. Pierre-de-Coubertin; phone: 90-87-45-51), next to the municipal pool.

THEATER AND FILM

Drama is alive and well year-round here, but—except when it's really kicking during the *Festival d'Avignon* (see *Special Events*)—it is rarely in English. The *Opéra d'Avignon* (Pl. de l'Horloge; phone: 90-82-23-44) stages a wide range of established theatrical works and ballet. Important new works often originate at the *Théâtre du Chêne Noir* (8 *bis* Rue Ste-Catherine; phone: 90-86-58-11; fax: 90-85-82-05). The *Théâtre des Halles* (4 Rue Noël-Biret;

phone: 90-85-52-57) stages the works of contemporary playwrights. There's amateur theater at *La Tarasque* (14 Pl. d'Etudes; phone: 90-85-43-91). There's also much exciting café-theater, notably at the *Théâtre du Chien Qui Fume* (75 Rue des Teinturiers; phone: 90-85-25-87), with various performances from morning till night (closed Mondays), and at *La Tache d'Encre* (22 Rue des Teinturiers; phone: 90-85-46-03), a pleasant café-theater with weekend performances in its tiny back room.

The *Utopia* cinema complex, which has recently moved to a new location (La Manutention, Rue des Escaliers Ste-Anne; no phone at press time) features films in original languages, with many in English.

MUSIC

For classical or contemporary music, opera, or jazz, the eclectic *Opéra d'Avignon* (see *Theater,* above) is the place, as is the *Chapelle des Pénitents Blancs* (Pl. Principale; phone: 90-86-49-27). There's frequently jazz, folk, or rock at *La Tache d'Encre* (see *Theater*). Major rock acts perform at the *Parc des Expositions* in the *Avignon Parc Expo Loisirs* (Rte. de Marseilles, Montfavet; phone: 90-84-18-21), 4 miles (6 km) east of town on N7. For information on jazz concerts, contact the *A.J.M.I. Jazz Club*—part of the *Théâtre du Chêne Noir* (see *Theater*).

NIGHTCLUBS AND NIGHTLIFE

Sholmes (7 miles/11 km out of town, at Rochefort-du-Gard; phone: 90-31-73-73) is a splashy, upper class nightclub with a pool, a Moroccan restaurant, and a dance floor (no jeans or sneakers). Other spots include the *Ambassy Club* (27 Rue Bancasse; phone: 90-86-31-55) and *Club 5.5* (Porte St-Roch; phone: 90-82-61-32).

Best in Town

CHECKING IN

If you plan to be in Avignon during the peak festival period, make sure to reserve a room *well* in advance. If you're driving, consider the numerous two-star (*Ibis* and *Climat*) and three-star (*Mercure* and *Novotel*) chain hotels on the roads leading into town, none more than a 10-minute ride away. There also are many country hotels in villages on both sides of the Rhône, all the way to Arles. The tourist office's *Accueil de France* service will book you a room for a fee; the hotel-run *VTH* reservation center also books rooms in the area (see *Tourist Information* for both). Expect to pay $175 or more for a double room at very expensive hotels, $125 to $175 at expensive places, $90 to $125 at moderate ones, and less than $90 at inexpensive places. Most rates don't include breakfast. *Demi-pension* (a higher rate that includes breakfast and one other meal) is often required in July and August in hotels with restaurants. Unless otherwise noted, all hotels listed below feature air conditioning, telephones, TV sets, and private baths in the rooms.

Some less expensive hotels may have private baths in only some of their rooms; it's a good idea to confirm whether your room has a private bath when making a reservation. Hotels accept major credit cards and are open year-round unless otherwise noted.

For an unforgettable experience, we begin with our favorite Avignon hostelry, followed by our cost and quality choices of hotels, listed by price category.

A SPECIAL HAVEN

Le Prieuré Built in the 14th century as a residence for a cardinal and later used as a priory, this renovated *hostellerie,* a Relais & Châteaux member, is reason enough to cross the Rhône. It's removed from the sounds of the city, yet has a fine view, and it's set in shady grounds that include a large pool and two tennis courts. The modern annex, by the pool, has larger rooms (with better views) than those in the original building, but both sections are equally refined, and all 36 units are exquisitely furnished. Another plus is the friendly, one-Michelin-star restaurant, where diners may eat on the delightful outdoor terrace amidst lavender and roses. The *gigot* (leg of lamb) in aromatic herbs, the betruffled tournedos, and the lobster lasagna are delectable; the homemade *tapenade* (a spread of garlic, olives, and anchovies) is so popular that the kitchen packs it in jars to sell to departing guests. Closed from early November through mid-March. 7 Pl. du Chapitre, Villeneuve-lès-Avignon (phone: 90-25-18-20; fax: 90-25-45-39).

VERY EXPENSIVE

Cloître St-Louis This luxurious, quiet property ensconced in a 16th-century cloister has 77 rooms and three suites (none with air conditioning), an outdoor pool, and a restaurant. 20 Rue Portail Boquier (phone: 90-27-55-55; fax: 90-82-24-01).

Europe This former 16th-century palace, one of the best hotels in the city, has a graceful elegance. Aubusson tapestries decorate the high walls in the antiques-furnished public rooms, and the 50 bedrooms, with beamed dark wood ceilings, are richly appointed. Its restaurant, the one-Michelin-star *La Vieille Fontaine* (see *Eating Out*), has a setting as picturesque as its food is well prepared. 12 Pl. Crillon (phone: 90-82-66-92; fax: 90-85-43-66).

Les Frênes A member of the prestigious Relais & Châteaux group, this 19th-century house has an imposing garden with roses and century-old trees, 20 antiques-filled guestrooms, a free-standing villa which accommodates up to 10 people, and a pool. Its restaurant boasts a Michelin star. Closed mid-November through mid-March (restaurant opens April 1). Three miles (5 km) from Avignon via D53, on Av. Vertes Rives, in Montfavet (phone: 90-31-17-93; fax: 90-23-95-03).

La Mirande This pretty hotel is housed in a former 18th-century home with a garden. Its extremely formal—verging on the stuffy—restaurant, which has been awarded one Michelin star, features Provençal dishes. Most of the 20 rooms, furnished in the 18th-century manner with sumptuous white marble bathrooms, look out onto the *Palais des Papes*. 4 Pl. Amirande (phone: 90-85-93-93; fax: 90-86-26-85).

EXPENSIVE

Auberge de Cassagne All 21 guestrooms and three suites in this tranquil inn are simply yet tastefully furnished *à la Provençal,* and many overlook a beautiful garden. The one-Michelin-star dining room (see *Eating Out*) is a must. Closed early November through early December. 450 Allée de Cassagne, Rte. de Vedène (phone: 90-31-04-18; fax: 90-32-25-09).

La Magnaneraie A 15th-century residence with 19th-century furniture and 20th-century comforts in its 27 rooms, this place, now a link in the international Best Western chain, offers peace and quiet in a pine forest setting. The excellent restaurant, which serves traditional French and Provençal fare, boasts a good wine selection. Closed the month of February. 37 Rue Camp de Bataille, Villeneuve-lès-Avignon (phone: 90-25-11-11; 800-528-1234; fax: 90-25-46-37).

Mercure Palais des Papes Despite its location in the heart of the city, this is a remarkably quiet enclave, designed around a courtyard. The building is tastefully modern, its sandstone color blending harmoniously with the restored townhouses in the neighborhood. The 87 rooms have all the amenities of a classic luxury hotel. There's no restaurant, but there's a breakfast buffet (better than the breakfast served in the rooms). Midway between the Pont St-Bénézet and the *Palais des Papes,* on Rue Ferruce (phone: 90-85-91-23; fax: 90-85-32-40).

MODERATE

Angleterre Though modest, this place is very clean and pleasant. Some of the 40 rooms look out onto a large terrace; none are air conditioned, but most have private bathrooms. There's no restaurant. Closed from mid-December through late January. A short walk from the train station in a quiet neighborhood, at 29 Bd. Raspail (phone: 90-86-34-31; fax: 90-86-86-74).

Danieli This centrally located 19th-century hostelry is not as luxurious as its Venice namesake (it once was a brothel), but it is nevertheless a pleasant and comfortable place to stay. None of its 29 rooms is air conditioned, and it has no dining room. 17 Rue de la République (phone: 90-86-46-82; fax: 90-27-09-24).

La Ferme This old farmhouse in a tranquil setting is now a 20-room hotel. Its restaurant serves traditional dishes, and there's a pool on the premises. Closed January through early February. About 3 miles (5 km) from Avignon on Chemin des Bois, Ile de la Barthelasse (phone: 90-82-57-53; fax: 90-27-15-47).

La Ferme Jamet A true 16th-century Provençal farm, it has four guestrooms, three one-room bungalows with kitchenettes, and four apartments with kitchenettes and living rooms. None of the accommodations is air conditioned. There's also a private garden, a tennis court, and a pool, but no restaurant. Honey, jams, and wine are for sale. Closed November through February. Chemin de Rhodes, Ile de la Barthelasse (phone: 90-86-16-74; fax: 90-86-17-72).

Mignon Translated, it means cute, and it really is just that. It has 16 small but tastefully decorated rooms (none with air conditioning). Thirteen have private baths (the other three have private showers, but shared toilet facilities). There's no restaurant. Set 200 yards from the *Palais des Papes,* at 12 Rue Joseph-Vernet (phone: 90-82-17-30; fax: 90-85-78-46).

Le Rocher Pointu This bed and breakfast establishment, set in a farmhouse on seven isolated acres, has four guestrooms (each with either bath or shower). There are also a studio and a one-bedroom apartment, both with kitchenettes. None of the accommodations is air conditioned. A pool, a kitchen, a barbecue, and a lounge are at the disposal of the guests. Closed from early November through mid-March. In the hamlet of Aramon, 7½ miles (12 km) outside Avignon, at Plan-de-Dève (phone: 66-57-41-87; fax: 90-14-02-18).

INEXPENSIVE

Garlande This small hotel in the city center has been tastefully redecorated, and the management is friendly. There are 12 rooms (none air conditioned) but no restaurant. 20 Rue Galante (phone: 90-85-08-85; fax: 90-27-16-58).

Régina A conveniently situated budget hotel; ask for a quieter room in the back during the festival. Nothing fancy (only the lobby is air conditioned), but it's clean and comfortable. There's no restaurant. Closed November and December. No credit cards accepted. Off Place de l'Horloge, at 6 Rue de la République (phone: 90-86-49-45).

EATING OUT

Ever since the arrival of the popes, Avignon has been recognized as a culinary as well as an ecclesiastical center. But in addition to more formal dining places, pizzerias are plentiful and frequently quite good. Note that many restaurants take their last orders as early as 9 PM. Expect to pay $125 or more for a meal for two in an expensive restaurant, from $90 to $125 in a moderate one, and from $75 to $90 in an inexpensive one. Prices include service (usually included in the bill automatically) but not wine. Unless otherwise noted, all restaurants listed below are open for lunch and dinner.

EXPENSIVE

Aubertin This restaurant beneath the arcades of a lovely square is decorated in Art Deco style, but the cuisine is up to date, with a focus on local ingredients. Try the *rognons de veau au raifort* (veal kidneys with horseradish) served with a potato-mushroom cake. Closed Mondays. Reservations necessary. MasterCard and Visa accepted. 1 Rue de l'Hôpital, Villeneuve-lès-Avignon (phone: 90-25-94-84; fax: 90-26-30-71).

Brunel Inventive cooking and perfectly fresh products reign here, where specialties include hot oysters with curry, salmon with a sauce made from roast guinea hen, and a luscious chocolate *mille-feuille*. The prix fixe menu, available at lunch only, is an excellent bargain. Closed Sundays, Mondays, and mid-July through mid-August. Reservations necessary. Major credit cards accepted. 46 Rue de la Balance (phone: 90-85-24-83; fax: 90-86-26-67).

Christian Etienne The chef who presides over this one-Michelin-star eatery specializes in unusual flavor combinations, as evidenced in his grilled fish with black olive purée, *bourride* (a garlicky stew) with chicken instead of fish, and fennel sherbet. The restaurant is in one of Avignon's oldest (13th–14th century) residences, which housed the popes while the *Palais des Papes* was under construction. Closed the last two weeks in February, the last two weeks in August, Sundays (except in July), and Saturday lunch. Reservations necessary. Major credit cards accepted. 10 Rue de Mons (phone: 90-86-16-50; fax: 90-86-67-09).

Hiély-Lucullus The simple façade and unprepossessing location upstairs on a commercial street belie the exquisite dining experience offered here, at one of Avignon's best restaurants (one Michelin star). There is only a prix fixe menu, but the choice for each course is wide, cheese and dessert are included, and the value is extraordinary. The emphasis is regional, with such dishes as *pieds et paquets provençale* (mutton, tripe, and pigs' feet in a stew) and grilled Alpilles lamb. There are fine local Côtes du Rhône wines, and the service is gracious and professional. Closed Mondays, Sunday dinner, Tuesday lunch (except in July and August), and two weeks each in January and June. Reservations necessary. MasterCard and Visa accepted. 5 Rue de la République (phone: 90-86-17-07; fax: 90-86-32-38).

MODERATE

Auberge de Bonpas This local favorite has a loyal following for its strictly traditional Provençal cuisine, such as *gâteau d'aubergine* (eggplant terrine) and chopped beef with green beans. There are also 11 simple guestrooms. Open daily except for annual closings in winter (usually two weeks each in November and February, but call ahead). Reservations advised. Major credit cards accepted. Three miles (5 km) east of Avignon by D53, on Rte. de Cavaillon in Montfavet (phone: 90-23-07-64; fax: 90-23-07-00).

Auberge de Cassagne Philippe Boucher pays homage to the teachings of epicurean eminences Georges Blanc and Paul Bocuse in this cheerful dining room. Among his more tempting dishes are *terrine provençale* accompanied by foie gras, *filets de rouget poêlés au citron vert* (fried mullet filets in lime juice), and *émincé d'agneau et côtelettes de lapereau panées* (thinly sliced lamb and rabbit coated with breadcrumbs). Boucher's efforts have won the restaurant one Michelin star. Open daily. Reservations necessary. Major credit cards accepted. In the *Auberge de Cassagne,* 450 Allée de Cassagne, Rte. de Vedène (phone: 90-31-04-18).

Le Cintra This brasserie offers traditional French fare. The service is friendly, particularly in the early morning hours. Open daily from 7 AM until midnight (1 AM in July and August). No reservations. Visa and MasterCard accepted. 44 Cours Jean-Jaurès (phone: 90-82-29-80).

La Fourchette Long a popular favorite for good food and pleasant decor, this eatery offers delicious terrines, grilled sea bass with ratatouille, and homemade sherbets. Closed weekends and the last two weeks in June. Reservations necessary. MasterCard and Visa accepted. 17 Rue Racine (phone: 90-85-20-93).

Le Grangousier Hidden in a medieval courtyard, this restaurant has won a Michelin star for its inventive variations on Provençal recipes, such as *feuilleté d'asperges à la tapenade* (asparagus in puff pastry with olive pâté). Closed Sundays and the last two weeks of August. Reservations necessary. MasterCard and Visa accepted. 17 Rue Galante (phone: 90-82-96-60; fax: 90-85-31-23).

L'Isle Sonnante In this small, cozy restaurant, traditional French fare and Provençal dishes are served, accompanied by wines from nearby vineyards. Closed Sundays, Mondays, August 7 through 30, and *Christmas* week. Reservations necessary. MasterCard and Visa accepted. 7 Rue Racine (phone: 90-82-56-01).

Les Trois Clefs The menu at this small, pretty place reflects the personal style of the ambitious chef, whose specialties include delicious veal kidneys with a honey sauce, and eggs poached *à la cantadine.* The service is friendly, and the warm decor is highlighted by mounted photos of fin de siècle Avignon. Closed Sundays and one week each in February and November for school vacations. Reservations necessary. MasterCard and Visa accepted. 26 Rue des Trois Faucons (phone: 90-86-51-53).

La Vieille Fontaine In summer this pleasant one-Michelin-star restaurant serves meals in a lovely courtyard amid lush greenery, with a stone sundial over the doorway, and, naturally, an old fountain. The menu specializes in regional cuisine (emphasizing ingredients such as tomatoes, olives, goat cheese, and herbs like rosemary and thyme), with a wine list to match. Closed Saturday lunch and Sundays. In the *Europe* hotel, 12 Pl. Crillon (phone: 90-82-66-92).

INEXPENSIVE

Entrée des Artistes This friendly bistro has simple *plats du jour* and a boisterous atmosphere. Closed Saturday lunch and Sundays. Reservations advised. MasterCard and Visa accepted. 1 Pl. des Carmes (phone: 90-82-46-90).

BARS AND CAFÉS

For a late drink, the lively Place de l'Horloge is always a good bet, though prices are relatively high. One of the picks here is *Bar la Civette* (phone: 90-86-55-84), seedy and cool, where artists congregate. On the Cours Jean-Jaurès is *Le Pezet* (phone: 90-82-65-24), a comfortable bar.

Biarritz

The premier resort city on France's Atlantic coast is in the southwest corner of the country on the Bay of Biscay, at the edge of Basque country, about 20 miles (32 km) from the Spanish border. Biarritz was little more than a fishing village until the middle of the 19th century, when it became "the Beach of Kings and the Queen of Beaches," one of the most fashionable seaside watering spots in the world. Today, it remains a very popular and busy summer place, though its glory days are long gone.

Biarritz experienced a similar reversal of fortune once before in its history. Around the 12th century, it grew prosperous as a fishing village and whaling port, thanks in large part to nearby Bayonne, the major market for its catch and by-products. When the whales left the Bay of Biscay, the port saw a decline in fortunes. The *Eglise St-Martin* (see *Special Places*, below) is one of the few vestiges of Biarritz's early boom.

Over the centuries, Bayonne's inhabitants came here to enjoy the beauty of the coast and to bathe in the sea, a new activity that caught on quickly. They were followed by the Spanish nobility, especially exiles from the Carlist wars who were unable to set foot in nearby San Sebastián, in their native country. Most propitious for Biarritz was the arrival of the Countess de Montijo, who came here regularly with her two daughters, one of whom, Eugénie, married Napoleon III in 1853. Recalling her summers in Biarritz, Eugénie persuaded Napoleon to accompany her here in 1854, and he was charmed enough by the sight to set about building the extravagant *Villa Eugénie* (today's *Hôtel du Palais;* see *Special Places*), in which the couple spent their summers until 1868. Forthwith, Biarritz became the summer capital of France.

By the fall of the empire, the cachet of the city was well established. Avenues Reine-Victoria, Edouard-VII, and Alphonse-XIII are named after only a few of the European kings and queens who vacationed here. So many Russian princes and grand dukes regularly came that they even built their own church. Through the Belle Epoque and up to the Great Depression, Spanish and French aristocracy, English gentry, and American millionaires mixed at the gaming tables and at the balls, played golf, tennis, and water polo, strolled the promenades, and tooled about town in their Bugattis, Hispano-Suizas, and Rolls-Royces.

The city's star faded a bit during the 1950s, when the spotlight turned to the Mediterranean's Côte d'Azur and such chic spots as St-Tropez. As the Côte d'Azur becomes increasingly crowded and expensive and less friendly, however, a gradual shift back to the Atlantic coast seems to have begun. Visitors who've sampled life on both coasts find the residents of Biarritz approachable and sincere, even humble, in comparison to their compatriots to the east.

In recent decades, Biarritz has gained a reputation among the international surfing set as the scene of some of the world's best waves. In fact, nearly every imaginable sport can be pursued here, from golf to horseback riding to people watching. The grand promenade takes place nightly on Place Clemenceau, Place Ste-Eugénie, and the pathways that wind above the shore from one end of town to the other, laid out to take advantage of the city's splendid natural beauty. Otherwise, Biarritz, with a population of approximately 30,000 people, is refreshingly free of obligatory tourist sights. The main ones still are the wide sandy beaches, framed by rocky cliffs and green hills blooming with blue and pink hydrangeas. In this setting, the pale Victorian buildings—turn-of-the-century marvels that look like giant candy confections—add a touch of fantasy that gives the city a special appeal.

Biarritz At-a-Glance

SEEING THE CITY

The most outstanding of a number of panoramic vistas of Biarritz is from Pointe St-Martin, a high plateau at the northern tip of the city. It can be reached via the narrow paths that twist precariously through the Pointe St-Martin gardens along the tops of precipitous cliffs. From the point, one can take in most of the Biarritz waterfront. The St-Martin headland marks the dividing line between the Landes region north of Biarritz, characterized by sand dunes and forests, and the wild, rugged terrain of the Côte Basque to the south. The 240-foot-high lighthouse, dating from 1834, can be climbed daily; it is closed during lunch hours, the first two weeks of June, and October through April (except holidays). Admission charge by donation (phone: 59-24-01-29).

It also is possible to climb a few steps below the lighthouse to *La Grotte de la Chambre d'Amour.* According to legend, this cave was the secret meeting place of the son of a wealthy landowner and the daughter of a poor peasant family, forbidden by their parents to marry. One night the couple met in the cave as the tide was rising, and a sudden swell swept them to their deaths.

SPECIAL PLACES

Biarritz's seafront and the *promenade du bord de mer* that lines much of it are the resort's primary attractions. The promenade's sinuous paths, carved along plateaus and into cliffsides, transform the fern- and flower-carpeted rocks into a magnificent public park. From the Pointe St-Martin gardens, go down the staircase marked "Descente de l'Océan," which takes you to Allée Winston-Churchill, a paved walkway running along the Plage Miramar. After passing the stately *Hôtel du Palais* (see below), the path widens into the Quai de la Grande Plage. This is the main promenade, which continues to the opposite end of the city, where there is a final viewpoint overlooking the southernmost stretch of beach. At a leisurely pace, the walk requires about three hours; it takes you past most of the points of interest listed below and several magnificent seascapes. Note that some attractions such as museums are closed during lunch hours (usually from noon to 2 PM), especially in the off-season.

SEAFRONT

HÔTEL DU PALAIS (PALACE HOTEL) Biarritz's most arresting manmade sight is this large, red brick building with white trim and a gray roof, fronted by ample green lawn and set in a commanding spot on the Grande Plage. Originally Napoleon III's *Villa Eugénie* (dubbed by some "Eugénie's Basque folly"), it saw its share of eminent personages when Eugénie was in residence. Today, as a luxury hotel, it maintains its regal bearing. Even if you're not a guest, you can glimpse some of the palatial trappings in the public rooms or dine in style in one of its restaurants (also see *Checking In*). 1 Av. de l'Impératrice (phone: 59-41-64-00).

EGLISE ORTHODOXE RUSSE (RUSSIAN ORTHODOX CHURCH) This Byzantine Russian church, across from the *Hôtel du Palais,* was built in 1892 by the colony of Russian notables who wintered here. It has a striking, sky-blue dome. 8 Av. de l'Impératrice (phone: 59-24-16-74).

GRANDE PLAGE (GREAT BEACH) In the city's heyday around the turn of the century, this beach was the site of leisurely promenades by ladies with long, billowing skirts, wide-brimmed hats, and lacy parasols. Today, the scene is a lot less *habillé*—few of the female bathers bother to wear bathing-suit tops—and the beach is popular with surfers. Sprawled along the Grande Plage like an albino whale is the former *Casino Municipal,* now completely renovated and reopened last year as the *Casino de Biarritz* (phone: 59-22-77-77). (For additional details, see *Casinos Royale* in DIVERSIONS.) The giant blue and white wedding cake on the hill above the southern end of the beach was the *Casino Bellevue,* now the *Centre Bellevue* (Pl. Bellevue; phone: 59-24-11-22), the city's convention center. From the Grande Plage, the Plage Miramar extends north to Pointe St-Martin.

PLACE STE-EUGÉNIE From the southern edge of the Grande Plage, steps and a path lead past the Rocher du Basta to this gracious open plaza lined with hotels and terraced restaurants, one of the prime gathering places of the resort. From the newly renovated Place Ste-Eugénie, Rue Mazagran—full of pedestrians browsing through charming shops—climbs gradually to the Place Clemenceau, the city's main shopping area.

PORT DES PÊCHEURS (FISHERMEN'S PORT) This small fishing port below Place Ste-Eugénie is one of Biarritz's most picturesque places, crowded with boats, slight wooden houses and shacks backed up against a small cliff, and huge piles of lobster traps, driftwood, rope, and other fishing paraphernalia. There's also a collection of small harborside restaurants and cafés. The little harbor is protected from the surf by a system of manmade breakwaters and concrete walls; to reach open water, boats pass through several canals and compartments and then navigate between dangerous-looking rocks that jut out beyond the walls.

ROCHER DE LA VIERGE (VIRGIN'S ROCK) The rocky Plateau de l'Atalaye forms one side of the Port des Pêcheurs. The tunnel through the plateau, which was carved at the orders of Napoleon III, leads to an esplanade from which a metal footbridge stretches several hundred feet out into the sea to a magnificent rock islet, named for the statue of the Virgin crowning it, whose duty since 1865 has been to protect the sailors and fishermen of the Bay of Biscay. The metal footbridge, built during the 1880s under the direction of Alexandre-Gustave Eiffel (of tower fame), allows visitors to walk all the way out to the terraced edge of the rock, a dramatic spot high above the crashing surf, for unforgettable views of the sea and the coastline. Open daily. No admission charge. Esplanade du Rocher de la Vierge.

MUSÉE DE LA MER (MUSEUM OF THE SEA) The esplanade that gives access to the Rocher de la Vierge holds this museum, dedicated to the sea and its inhabitants. Founded in 1933, it has three floors of marine exhibits, maps of the ocean floor, and remnants of Biarritz's past whaling culture, including the impressive skull of a colossal blue whale. The museum's glass-walled aquariums currently shelter more than 150 species of marine life; the shark grotto is particularly dramatic. If you can, watch the three species of seals in the roof tank at feeding time—10:30 AM and 5 PM daily. Also on the esplanade is a simple but touching monument to the city's casualties during the two World Wars. Museum open daily year-round (until midnight from July 14 through August 15). Admission charge. Esplanade du Rocher de la Vierge, 14 Plateau de l'Atalaye (phone: 59-24-02-59).

LA PERSPECTIVE From Port Vieux, on the other side of the Plateau de l'Atalaye, a path leads up to yet another plateau, where the flower-lined promenade offers sensational views north, over the distance you have already covered, and south, over the vast, rocky Plage de la Côte des Basques as far as the mountains of Spain. Paved switchback paths lined with benches and stone balustrades crisscross the steep incline that drops from La Perspective to the beach, which is the wildest and most exposed in Biarritz and the one most highly regarded by surfers. At high tide, however, the entire stretch of the Plage de la Côte des Basques is forbidding, with breakers crashing at the base of the cliffs and splashing onto Boulevard du Prince-de-Galles only feet away from the seawall. In the cliff face over the boulevard are the remains of bunkers from World War II.

MUSÉE DE L'AUTOMOBILE MINIATURE (MINIATURE AUTOMOBILE MUSEUM) A collection of over 7,000 miniature cars, fire trucks, and other vehicles, plus an audiovisual presentation of the history of the automobile. Open daily. Admission charge. 13 Plateau de l'Atalaye (phone: 59-24-56-88).

EGLISE ST-MARTIN (CHURCH OF ST. MARTIN) Biarritz's only old religious monument is up the hill, away from the beaches and the town center. Probably begun in the 12th century, it was restored in 1541 and has a Flamboyant Gothic chancel. Rue St-Martin (phone: 59-23-05-19).

MUSÉE DU VIEUX BIARRITZ (MUSEUM OF OLD BIARRITZ) Housed in a former Anglican church, this museum displays paintings, costumes, objets d'art, and documents that illustrate Biarritz's two primary historical roles—as a port and, more recently, as a watering place for Europe's ruling classes. Several exhibits depict life during Biarritz's golden era, during and after the reign of Napoleon III. Closed mornings, Thursdays, and Sundays. Admission charge. Salle Saint Andrew's, Rue Broquedis (phone: 59-24-86-28).

ENVIRONS

MUSÉE BONNAT (BONNAT MUSEUM) This stately museum in nearby Bayonne was built at the end of the 19th century to house the artwork bequeathed to the city by a native son, the painter and collector Léon Bonnat. One of the country's outstanding art galleries, it features works from the 13th century to the Impressionists, among them Bonnat's own works, some lovely Aragonese primitives, paintings by such masters as Rubens, Rembrandt, Goya, Ingres, Delacroix, and Degas, and an archaeological collection. A formidable lode of drawings by Flemish, Dutch, Italian, French, and German artists from the Renaissance through the 19th century is displayed in changing exhibitions. Closed Tuesdays and holidays. Admission charge. 5 Rue Jacques-Laffitte, Bayonne (phone: 59-59-08-52).

Note that at press time the *Musée Basque* (phone: 59-59-08-98), a popular tourist attraction in Bayonne, was scheduled to be closed at least through next year for renovations.

EXTRA SPECIAL

One of the main reasons to make a day trip south along the Côte Basque is to visit St-Jean-de-Luz, 9 miles (14 km) away. If Biarritz is "the Queen of Beaches," then this delightful resort, about half its size but with a broad scallop of safe and sandy beach on a well-protected bay, is at least a crown prince or princess. After a stop in St-Jean-de-Luz, you can continue along the Corniche Basque (the coastal road) to Hendaye, another popular resort, about 9 miles (14 km) away at the Spanish border. The views are magnificent en route, and some people consider the beaches of Hendaye the best on the coast. For additional details on this part of the Côte Basque, see *The Pyrénées* in DIRECTIONS.

Sources and Resources

TOURIST INFORMATION

Biarritz's *Office de Tourisme* (Sq. d'Ixelles, near the corner of Av. Joseph-Petit and Rue Louis-Barthou phone; phone: 59-24-20-24) is ensconced in a suitably grand edifice: the *Palais Javalquinto,* former residence of the Spanish Dukes of Osuna. Next door is the public information office; both are closed *Christmas.* The tourist office's friendly, efficient staff, most of whom speak fluent English, will provide maps, hotel and restaurant listings, and any other information you might need, and will assist visitors in choosing a hotel or making reservations. A small pamphlet listing pertinent information about the city's amenities and essential services is available. The tourist office also furnishes guides for larger groups and supplies information about a number of local companies operating guided bus tours of the Pays Basque and other neighboring regions. There's also a tourist information booth open daily during the summer (mid-June through mid-September) at the train station, the *Gare de Biarritz–La Négresse.*

LOCAL COVERAGE The local daily newspaper is *Sud-Ouest. La Semaine du Pays Basque* is a widely distributed, French-language weekly guide to the entertainment, arts, and sports events in the area. Many bookstores and other shops in the heart of town carry English-language newspapers and magazines.

TELEPHONE The city code for the Biarritz area (including Anglet, Bayonne, and St-Jean-de-Luz) is 59, which is incorporated into all local eight-digit numbers. When calling a number in the Biarritz area from the Paris region (including the Ile-de-France), dial 16, wait for a dial tone, then dial the eight-digit number. When calling a number from outside Paris, dial only the eight-digit number.

GETTING AROUND

The most practical way to get around the center of town is to walk.

AIRPORT Biarritz's airport, the *Aéroport de Biarritz-Bayonne-Anglet* is located only a mile (1.6 km) from town, easily accessible by taxi or by the municipal bus company, *STAB* (phone: 59-52-59-52) bus No. 6. In addition to several other domestic routes, the airport schedules six flights a day from Paris's *Orly Ouest* airport on *Air Inter;* and from the last week of June through August, there's service from London two or three times a week on *Air Littoral.*

BUS Public buses operate within Biarritz and between Biarritz and neighboring communities. The standard fare is about 7F (around $1.20 at press time), and economical *carnets* (booklets) of 10 tickets are available for about 58F (around $10 at press time). Call the municipal bus company *STAB* (see above) for information on local buses and buses to Anglet and Bayonne;

ATCRB (phone: 59-26-06-99) for information on buses to St-Jean-de-Luz; and *TPR* (phone: 59-27-45-98) for information on buses to Pau. (Employees at all three usually speak some English.) The main *STAB* stop is located in front of the tourist office (see *Tourist Information*); there's also an information booth here, where a map of local bus routes may be obtained.

CAR RENTAL *Eurodollar* (63 Av. du Maréchal-Juin; phone: 59-43-98-43) currently has the best rates in town. Also represented are *Avis* (25 Av. Edouard-VII; phone: 59-24-33-44), *Budget* (32 Av. de Bayonne; phone: 59-63-11-77), *Europcar* (Rte. de Cazalis, near the airport; phone: 59-23-82-82), and *Hertz* (at the airport; phone: 59-43-92-92).

TAXI Though taxis don't generally cruise the winding streets in the heart of town, there's a station on Avenue de Verdun (phone: 59-24-16-13). You also can call *BAB Radio Taxi* (phone: 59-63-17-17). Most of the taxi dispatchers at both numbers speak some English.

TRAIN The *Gare de Biarritz–La Négresse* is about 2 miles (3 km) southeast of the center of town, about 10 minutes by bus. Biarritz is a regular stop for trains en route from Paris and Bordeaux to points in Spain. The *TGV* (*Train à Grande Vitesse,* or "fast train"; phone: 59-55-50-50) has cut the rail time from Paris to just under five hours. The trip from Biarritz to Bayonne takes approximately 10 minutes; to St-Jean-de-Luz, about 15 minutes. For train information, call 59-55-50-50. Many of the officials at both numbers speak some English; also, from mid-June through August, there's a helpful tourist office booth at the train station that's open daily.

SPECIAL EVENTS

Biarritz is the venue for a full calendar of activities. An annual *Salon des Antiquaires* (Antiques Show) comes to the *Centre Bellevue* (Pl. Bellevue; phone: 59-24-11-22) for the last week of March through the first week of April, and again for the third week of August. May brings the *Fêtes Musicales,* during which concerts take place at various locations, including the *Hôtel du Palais* (see *Special Places*), the *Eglise Ste-Eugénie* (Pl. Ste-Eugénie; phone: 59-24-07-43), and the sparkling *Palais des Festivals* (23 Av. du Maréchal-Foch; phone: 59-22-19-19). The *Festival International de Bridge* occurs in June. The city's *Bastille Day* fireworks (July 14) are stunning, and on August 15, *Nuit Féerique* (roughly translated as "Fairy Night"), a grand fireworks display lights up the Grande Plage and the cliffs along the seafront. The following Sunday, for the traditional *Fête de la Mer* (Sea Festival), a helicopter drops flowers on the Rocher de la Vierge in memory of Biarritz's sailors. There is a naval parade in late August.

The *Concours Hippique International,* a horse-jumping championship in which equestrians from about a dozen nations compete, is held in September at the *Stade Aguiléra* (see *Sports and Fitness*). Also in September are the *Quicksilver Biarritz Surf Masters,* the world championship of professional surfing, held off the Grande Plage; the *Festival International de Biarritz des*

Cinémas et Culture de l'Amérique Latine at the *Palais Bellevue,* devoted to Latin American films and culture; and the *Temps d'Aimer,* a month-long international festival featuring dance performances and art exhibits. An important golf tournament, the *Pro-Am de Bulles Laurent Perrier,* which draws as many as 800 participants annually, takes place the last week of September or the first week of October at the *Golf Municipal Biarritz–Le Phare* (see *Golf* in *Sports and Fitness*).

SHOPPING

The best shopping streets are Avenue Victor-Hugo, Rue Gambetta, Rue Mazagran, Avenue Edouard-VII, Avenue de Verdun, and Avenue du Maréchal-Foch, all of which converge on Place Clemenceau, the heart of town. Such well-known names as *Cartier, Hermès, Cacharel,* and *Kenzo* are represented here by boutiques. Particularly noteworthy are a handful of shops specializing in household linens and other articles made of the colorful cotton and wool of the nearby Pays Basque. You probably will pay more for them here than in the small towns in the Pyrénées, but the Biarritz shops offer a wider selection, and many accept credit cards. Biarritz's fine tradition of chocolate-making began in the 17th century, not long after Anne of Austria (who, despite her name, was a Spanish princess) married France's Louis XIII and brought the delectable substance from Spain. When chocolate then became *à la mode,* Spanish Jews fleeing persecution in their native country took up chocolate-making in Biarritz. Today four shops in particular—*Daranatz, Dodin, Henriet,* and *Pariès* (see below for all four)— carry on the tradition, though there are several other excellent chocolatiers. There also are several shops selling the gastronomic delicacies of the neighboring Landes and Gers regions—*confit d'oie* and *confit de canard* (respectively, flavorful preserved goose and duck), foie gras, and armagnac, to name just a few.

Shops in Biarritz, unlike in many other French cities, are generally closed Sundays, but open on Mondays. For standard shopping hours, see GETTING READY TO GO. Among the shops to explore are the following:

Arostéguy Maison An *épicerie* carrying everything from Petrossian caviar to canned cassoulet. 5 Av. Victor-Hugo (phone: 59-24-00-52).

Bakara Interesting antiques, old dolls, and curiosities. 23 Rue Mazagran (phone: 59-22-08-95).

Boutique Fancy A small specialty shop with a lovely, expensive selection of women's casual wear. 20 Pl. Clemenceau. A second shop, specializing in shoes, is next door, at 2 Av. du Maréchal-Foch (phone for both: 59-24-22-75).

Cannelle Another women's boutique, with *prêt-à-porter* for summer and winter. 12 Rue Mazagran (phone: 59-24-51-47).

Daranatz One of the best chocolate shops in Biarritz. 12 Av. du Maréchal-Foch (phone: 59-24-21-91).

Dodin The chocolate here is devastatingly tempting. Two locations: 9 Pl. Clemenceau (phone: 59-24-16-37) and 7 Rue Gambetta (phone: 59-24-16-37).

Galerie des Arceaux One of several local antiques shops, this one specializes in 19th-century furniture and porcelain. 14 Av. Edouard-VII (phone: 59-22-08-00).

Henriet Chocolates made with oranges, pistachios, and almonds. The *"rocher de Biarritz"* (orange peel and toasted almonds covered in chocolate) is a specialty. Pl. Clemenceau (phone: 59-24-24-15).

Maud Frizon A tiny boutique displaying the best of this designer's fancy (and sporty) footwear. 5 Av. Edouard-VII (phone: 59-24-04-03).

Mille et Un Fromages Cheese, wine, and other fixings for a picnic or a snack. 8 Av. Victor-Hugo (phone: 59-24-67-88).

Natacha Three boutiques next door to each other (same address) that stock merchandise from such famous names as Stéphane Kélian and Sonia Rykiel. 3 Av. Edouard-VII (phone: 59-24-55-44).

Parfumerie Royale The best names in perfume, including Yves Saint Laurent and Guerlain. 1 Rue Mazagran (phone: 59-24-00-17).

Pariès Another of Biarritz's great *chocolatiers,* in business since 1914. 27 Pl. Clemenceau (phone: 59-22-07-52).

St-Léon An extensive collection of Basque linen. 18 Av. Victor-Hugo (phone: 59-24-19-81).

SPORTS AND FITNESS

One of the city's strongest points is the wide range of sporting activities available—on the water, on land, and at the well-equipped *Parc des Sports d'Aguiléra* complex (east of town, on Rue Henri-Haget; phone: 59-23-93-42).

BICYCLING *Capdeboscq* (16 Av. Jaulerry; phone: 59-24-13-64) and *Sobilo* (24 Rue Peyreloubith; phone: 59-24-94-47) rent bikes.

BULLFIGHTS There are Spanish-style bullfights on July 14, August 13-15, and September 3-4 at the *Arènes Bayonne/Biarritz;* for additional details, consult the tourist office in Biarritz or in Bayonne (phone: 59-46-01-46).

FISHING Surf casting and fishing from the rocks are popular; contact the tourist office for information.

GOLF Wonderful weather year-round (similar to that of northern California) makes this region perfect for tee-time anytime. The oldest golf area in the country is the site of Europe's most extensive golf training center, the *Centre International d'Entrainement au Golf (Golf d'Ilbarritz,* Av. Reine-Nathalie, Bidart; phone: 59-23-74-65), in a valley right outside town. The *Stratton American School* at the *Comfort Inn* (19 Av. Reine-Victoria; phone: 59-22-

04-80; fax: 59-24-91-19) and the *Ecole de Golf Sabine Fourment* (*Golf Municipal de Biarritz–Le Phare,* Av. Edith-Cavell; phone: 59-41-27-26) offer training programs at the *Golf d'Ilbarritz,* using the facilities of the *Centre International d'Entrainement au Golf.* The *Ecole de Golf Sabine Fourment* also offers instruction at *Golf Municipal de Biarritz–Le Phare.* Greens fees at 18-hole courses in the Biarritz area vary depending on the day of the week and the time of year.

TOP TEE-OFF SPOTS

Chiberta Created in 1927, it is one of the most famous layouts in France. The course (18 holes, 6,400 yards, par 72) varies widely, from seven holes in a pine forest to wonderful holes at water's edge. 104 Bd. des Plages, Anglet (phone: 59-63-83-20).

Golf d'Arcangues In the rolling, oak-forested countryside is Ronald Fream's 6,700-yard, 18-hole, par 72 course. Duffers beware: The killer bunkers and tricky dips in the fairways make this a very demanding course. Route d'Arcangues, 3 miles (5 km) east of Biarritz in Arcangues (phone: 58-43-10-56).

Golf Club d'Hossegor This course (18 holes, 6,400 yards, par 72) is set in a pine forest typical of the Basque region. It is challenging, but high scorers will be mollified somewhat by the excellent lunch at the clubhouse. Av. du Golf, 15 miles (24 km) north of Biarritz in Hossegor (phone: 58-43-56-99).

Golf Municipal de Biarritz–Le Phare In its more than 100-year history, this lovely, short (5,900 yards) course right near the *Hôtel du Palais* and the Pointe St-Martin lighthouse has attracted some of the world's best players. Le Phare, Av. Edith-Cavell, Biarritz (phone: 59-03-71-80).

Golf de Seignosse Designed by Robert Von Hagge, this 18-hole course (6,800 yards, par 72) is considered one of the most spectacular in France. Beautifully situated in the midst of the Landes forest, it is demanding and hilly (luckily, carts are available). 23 miles (37 km) north of town via A63, in Seignosse (phone: 58-43-17-32).

HORSEBACK RIDING Horses may be rented on a daily or hourly basis from the *Centre Equestre* (Allée Gabrielle-Dorziat; phone: 59-41-27-32), which also offers instruction and organizes group rides along the beach.

PELOTE Biarritz's mind-bogglingly fast version of jai alai is called *cesta punta.* Frequent games of this popular spectator sport are played at the *Euskal-Jaï* fronton (phone: 59-23-91-09) in the *Aguiléra* sports complex. Other forms of *pelote* are played at the open-air fronton at *Parc Mazon* (Av. Maréchal-Joffre), at the fronton at *Plaza-Berri* (Av. du Maréchal-Foch; phone: 59-22-15-72), and at the *Trinquet St-Martin* (Av. Pasteur; phone: 59-23-11-23).

SAILING *Monsieur Hontebeyrie*, at Port des Pêcheurs, rents Hobie Cats. The *International Sailing School* (phone: 59-47-06-32 from mid-June through mid-September or 59-02-38-06 the rest of the year) in nearby Socoa, next to St-Jean-de-Luz, offers courses for all age groups at reasonable prices from mid-June through mid-September. *Haizean* (phone: 59-23-34-07) organizes day or weekend cruises.

SCUBA DIVING The ocean floor, at depths of 15 feet and more, can be very beautiful when the weather is good. For information about equipment and lessons, contact the tourist office or the *Union Sportive de Biarritz* (*U.S.B.;* Allée des Passereaux; phone: 59-03-29-29), which offers a full range of instruction and dives.

SPAS Biarritz is a saltwater spa town: The *Centre de Thalassothérapie Louison Bobet* in the *Miramar* hotel (see *Checking In*) and *Thermes Marins* (80 Rue de Madrid; phone: 59-23-01-22) both offer a variety of spa therapies. The latter occupies sun-flooded quarters overlooking the sea, with state-of-the-art equipment and facilities.

SQUASH *Milady Squash* (phone: 59-23-27-29), with two courts, is at 86 Rue de Simonnet.

SURFING Introduced in 1958, it is now one of Biarritz's big draws. The most intrepid surfers head for the Plage de la Côte des Basques; the Grande Plage is somewhat less exposed. *Ecole de Surf Plums* (5 Pl. Clemenceau; phone: 59-24-08-04) offers group and individual lessons. *Moraiz Surf Shop* (25 Rue Mazagran; phone: 59-24-22-09) offers classes, and sells and rents boards, as does the *Freedom Surf Shop* (2 Av. Reine-Victoria; phone: 59-24-38-40). *Biarritz Surf Training* (also at 2 Av. Reine-Victoria; phone: 59-23-15-31) offers lessons, too.

SWIMMING The safest beach is the Plage du Port-Vieux, the small horseshoe beach along the pathway from the Plateau de l'Atalaye. It's well protected by rocks, and the shallow, calm waters are favored by families with children. Besides that and all the other beaches, there is the *Piscine Municipale* (closed November; phone: 59-24-05-83), an indoor, heated, seawater pool on the Grande Plage; an indoor pool of heated sea water at the *Casino de Biarritz* (see *Special Places*); the heated outdoor seawater pools at the *Hôtel du Palais;* the outdoor pool at the *Miramar* hotel; and the outdoor freshwater pool at the *Régina et Golf* hotel (see *Checking In* for the last three); all can be used for a fee (there's no charge for registered guests to use the hotel pools).

TENNIS Biarritz boasts an outstanding tennis facility.

CHOICE COURT

Biarritz Olympique Tennis This tennis club has 14 courts: 12 clay, three lighted, and four covered. Professionals are available for lessons by the day or week. Open year-round. In the *Parc des Sports d'Aguiléra* complex, east of town on Rue Henri-Haget (phone: 59-41-20-80).

In addition, you can reserve one of the 17 courts at the *Côte Basque Country Club* (phone: 59-52-22-55; fax: 59-73-99-02), just outside Biarritz along N10.

WINDSURFING Lessons and boards are available at *Point Glisse Océan* (phone: 59-54-70-38; open July and August only) on the dock in Guéthary, about 4 miles (7 km) south of town via N10, or, a little farther south, at *Yacht Club Basque* (phone: 59-47-18-31; fax: 59-47-60-14) in Ciboure, near St-Jean-de-Luz, around 10 miles (16 km) from town.

THEATER AND MUSIC

Performances of Basque music and dancing take place frequently during the summer season. Two or three times a week, at either *Parc Mazon* or *Plaza Berri,* you'll be able to see a *pelote* match, perhaps accompanied by a folk-dancing exhibition at *Parc Mazon.* Much less often, the highly respected *Groupe Oldarra* presents its own Basque song and dance spectacle, also usually at *Parc Mazon.*

Concerts of classical, and occasionally modern, music by visiting and local artists and ensembles take place year-round in such venues as the *Eglise Ste-Eugénie* (Pl. Ste-Eugénie; phone: 59-24-07-43), the *Hôtel du Palais* (see *Special Places*), and the *Palais des Festivals* (23 Av. Foch; phone: 59-22-19-19). The tourist office can provide more information on all of the above.

NIGHTCLUBS AND NIGHTLIFE

Among the more popular of Biarritz's dozen or so nightclubs are the chic *Copacabana* (with its sister club, *Brasilia*), which specializes in Brazilian cocktails and salsa music (both at 24 Av. Edouard-VII; phone: 59-24-65-39); the *Play Boy* (15 Pl. Clemenceau; phone: 59-24-38-46), a disco that's an old favorite (though its popularity seems to be fading); *Le Caveau* (4 Av. Gambetta; phone: 59-24-16-17), where a chic crowd (both gay and straight) gathers; and *La Plantation,* the nightclub at the *Casino de Biarritz,* where there's also high-style and high-stakes gambling (see *Special Places*). *Magi's* (1 Bd. du Général-de-Gaulle; phone: 59-24-77-90) is a popular disco. For piano music, try *Le Piano Bar* at the *Hôtel du Palais* (see *Checking In*) and *Carlos* (7 Bd. du Prince-de-Galles; phone: 59-24-95-51), with a terrace overlooking the sea. The *Blue Note* (*Résidence Victoria Surf,* 21 *ter* Av. Edouard-VII; phone: 59-24-78-10) features jazz nightly. A rock band plays on weekends at *Le Green* (10 Pl. Clemenceau; phone: 59-24-22-68), a lively, sleek, but not overbearing café that's perfect for people watching. Dress is casual at all of the above.

Best in Town

CHECKING IN

At last count, Biarritz boasted nearly 1,700 guestrooms, spanning the entire gamut of comforts. Many rooms in all categories have ocean views, and there are a number of hotels in the neighboring beach communities of Bidart and Anglet. By all means reserve in advance for rooms during July or August. For a double room (meals not included), expect to pay $100 or more per night in an expensive hotel; from $60 to $100 in a moderate one; and under $60 in an inexpensive place. All prices are for the high season; rates drop by as much as 50% in the off-season. Unless otherwise noted, all hotels listed below feature air conditioning, telephones, TV sets, and private baths in the rooms; but note that even the highest-rated hotels in Biarritz frequently do not have air conditioned rooms, since the climate— not too hot in summer, not too cold in winter—is generally delightful year-round. Some less expensive hotels may have private baths in only some of their rooms; it's a good idea to confirm whether your room has a private bath when making a reservation. All hotels accept major credit cards and are open year-round unless otherwise noted.

For an unforgettable experience, we begin with our favorite Biarritz haven, followed by our cost and quality choices of hotels, listed by price category.

ROOM AT THE TOP

Hôtel du Palais This most patrician of lodging places dominating the Grande Plage looks much as it did when Eugénie and Napoleon III spent their summers here. Now a part of the Concorde group of hotels, it offers a renovated version of the Old World grandeur to which its original owners were accustomed: public rooms rife with marble floors, columns, chandeliers, and draperies; 140 rooms and 20 suites appointed with period furnishings (with fans, not air conditioning); and attentive service. There are stunning views of the sweeping coastline, an elegantly groomed private beach, and a gently warmed seawater pool on a terrace by the beach, with cabañas and a poolside restaurant perfect for casual lunches. There also are two more formal restaurants, *La Rotonde* and the one-Michelin-star *Grand Siècle* (see *Eating Out*). None of this comes cheap, of course; the empress herself probably couldn't afford to stay here today. Closed February. 1

Av. de l'Impératrice (phone: 59-41-64-00; 800-888-4747; fax: 59-41-67-99).

EXPENSIVE

Château de Brindos A charming Italianate villa hidden in a thick grove of trees at the edge of a lake filled with water lilies and some swans. The lovely surroundings, grand interiors, highly rated restaurant (see *Eating Out*), and availability of only 12 rooms (none air conditioned) make it a perfect choice for those who prefer tranquillity to proximity to the beach (though the hotel does have a heated pool and a tennis court). About 3 miles (5 km) southeast of Biarritz off N10, on Lac de Brindos, Anglet (phone: 59-23-17-68; fax: 59-23-48-47).

Miramar Although the building itself looks like a nuclear-age command center, the 126 rooms and suites within are undeniably comfortable, the service is excellent, and the restaurant, *Relais Miramar,* has earned a Michelin star (see *Eating Out*). Other draws include a lobby bar, boutiques, a gym, a sauna, a heated seawater pool (outdoor), and the *Centre de Thalassothérapie Louison Bobet* (a saltwater spa). 11 Av. de l'Impératrice (phone: 59-41-30-00; fax: 59-24-77-20).

Plaza Fairly modern and unpretentious, this place has a gracious air and a prime location overlooking the beaches and the center of Biarritz. The 60 rooms are spacious and well furnished, and most have balconies commanding an ocean view. There's a restaurant, and the bar is a rich, elegant room. Also, the staff speaks some English, and there are parking facilities. It's a good value. Av. Edouard-VII (phone: 59-24-74-00; fax: 59-22-22-01).

Président This typical "French modern" property might seem more at home in a business center than a resort. Nonetheless, its 64 rooms are comfortable (though not air conditioned), and it's handy for the beach, restaurants, and shopping. There's no dining room. Pl. Clemenceau (phone: 59-24-66-40).

Régina et Golf A luxury hostelry that offers old-fashioned grandeur on a small scale, it's set majestically above the city on a plateau near the lighthouse, public gardens, and municipal golf course. Many of its 71 rooms have breathtaking views (none is air conditioned). There's an outdoor pool, and a restaurant specializing in seafood. Closed mid-November through December 22. 52 Av. de l'Impératrice (phone: 59-41-33-00; fax: 59-41-33-99).

MODERATE

Le Château du Clair de Lune An exquisite miniature château, it is set back from the road and surrounded by gardens and woods. There are 17 individually decorated rooms (none air conditioned), but no restaurant; the ambience is that of a private home. Ten minutes from Biarritz, on 48 Av. Alan-Seeger, Rte. d'Arbonne (phone: 59-23-45-96; fax: 59-23-39-13).

Palacito Though the welcome here can be curt, this hotel is conveniently located and clean. There are 30 rooms (none air conditioned), but no restaurant. Closed January. 1 Rue Gambetta (phone: 59-24-04-89; fax: 59-24-33-43).

Le Petit Hôtel One of the best bargains in town, this place on a tiny street in the heart of Biarritz has a fresh, pretty lobby and 12 cheerful rooms (none air conditioned), though there's no restaurant. The owners are charming. 11 Rue Gardères (phone: 59-24-87-00; fax: 59-24-32-34).

Windsor The oceanside door of this hostelry is just a frog's leap from the Grande Plage. The welcome is friendly, and the 49 rooms, many with views, are decorated in a comfortable, modern style; the bathrooms have either a bath or shower. There is a restaurant, but no air conditioning. Closed January through mid-February. 11 Av. Edouard-VII, Grande Plage (phone: 59-24-08-52; fax: 59-24-98-90).

INEXPENSIVE

Edouard-VII Simple, with 16 clean, no-frills rooms (there's one TV set on the premises and no air conditioning) and a jovial proprietor. Closed October through February. No credit cards accepted. Up the hill from the beaches and town center, at 21 Av. Carnot (phone: 59-24-07-20).

EATING OUT

From a gastronomic point of view, Biarritz is ideally situated. A rich fishing center with all manner of fresh seafood, it also benefits from its proximity to the Landes and Gers regions, rich in foie gras, and to the Basque country, famous for air-cured ham, fish soups (such as the peppery *ttoro*), and cakes. The resort's restaurants are impressive in their number and variety, and the quality is, for the most part, high, while the prices remain reasonable. A boon for the traveler is the relatively recent proliferation of ample, inexpensive fixed-price meals at places that would otherwise be considered very pricey. Dinner for two, with service (usually included in the bill) but not wine, in an expensive restaurant will cost $85 or more; in a moderate place, between $60 and $85; and in an inexpensive place, less than $60. Try the regional Madiran and Jurançon wines with your meal. Unless otherwise noted, all restaurants listed below are open for lunch and dinner.

EXPENSIVE

Café de Paris Though it lost its Michelin star a few years back and even closed briefly last year, this airy, garden-like spot, once considered by some to be the best restaurant on France's Atlantic coast, seems primed for a triumphal comeback. Didier Oudill, the chef who earned high accolades (including two Michelin stars) for the remote Landais restaurant *Pain Adour et Fantaisie*, recently brought his talents here, where he delights diners with such specialties as giant fresh *crevettes* (shrimp) grilled and served with a spicy fresh fennel sauce, plus other dishes highlighting regional ingredients such as *chiperons* (tiny cuttlefish), sheep's milk cheese, fava beans, and seafood. For dessert try the apricot pastry topped with lavender ice cream. There also are 19 bright, modern guestrooms, some with terraces and all with ocean views. Closed Sunday dinner and Mondays off-season. Reservations advised. Major credit cards accepted. 5 Pl. Bellevue (phone: 59-24-19-53; fax: 59-24-18-20).

Château de Brindos The beautifully appointed dining room of this tranquil villa-hotel offers views overlooking the lake. The food won't let you down: Basque specialties and dishes include a *mousseline* of turbot encased in puff pastry. Open daily. Reservations advised. Major credit cards accepted. About 3 miles (5 km) southeast of Biarritz off N10 in the *Château de Brindos,* Lac de Brindos, Anglet (phone: 59-23-17-68; fax: 59-23-48-47).

Galion Ocean views, a marine motif, and nouvelle cuisine featuring fresh seafood are the attractions at this local favorite. Closed Sunday dinner, Mondays (except during July and August), and February. Reservations advised. MasterCard and Visa accepted. 17 Bd. du Général-de-Gaulle (phone: 59-24-20-32).

La Gascogne A staid, conservative, yet comfortable sort of place, where people talk in hushed tones above the tinkle of fine china. The fixed-price menus are a comparative bargain. For lunch, dishes such as *salade basquaise* (a salad with peppers and Bayonne ham) and *poulet basquaise* (chicken cooked with peppers, tomatoes, and onions) are featured; at dinner, try the fresh, giant oysters, followed by a three-layered fish pâté and a chicken dish served with a delicious tarragon and cream sauce. Open daily; closed Sunday lunch and Monday dinner. Reservations advised. Major credit cards accepted. 11 Av. du Maréchal-Foch (phone: 59-24-20-12).

Grand Siècle This restaurant brims with Belle Epoque charm and pomp. Its kitchen has won accolades (including a Michelin star) for dishes such as langoustines on a bed of *pipérade* (a Basque mixture of green and red sweet peppers, onions, and tomatoes), and veal wrapped in celery root. Open daily. Reservations necessary. Major credit cards accepted. *Hôtel du Palais,* 1 Av. de l'Impératrice (phone: 59-41-64-00).

Les Platanes This inviting Basque-style house is home to a one-Michelin-star restaurant. Nothing here is a cliché; everything reflects imagination and flair, from the Plexiglass-encased menu that changes every few days to the Gascony-inspired food to the decor (there's a huge tableau of nudes behind the bar). Closed Mondays and Tuesday lunch. Reservations advised. MasterCard and Visa accepted. Not far from the town center, at 32 Av. Beausoleil (phone: 59-23-13-68).

Relais Miramar Chef André Gauzère's inventive dishes—light yet luscious, with an emphasis, naturally, on seafood—have earned this hotel restaurant a

Michelin star. Specialties include *ravioli de homard aux cèpes* (lobster ravioli with wild mushrooms) and a fricassee of sole and crayfish with fresh pasta. Open daily. Reservations advised. Major credit cards accepted. In the *Miramar* hotel, 11 Av. de l'Impératrice (phone: 59-41-30-00).

La Table des Frères Ibarboure The Ibarboure family's large, pink house in the country is not easy to find. But once settled at a table on their lovely, flower-bedecked terrace sampling their dazzlingly inventive Basque cuisine, you'll be happy you made the effort. Specialties include *ravioles de morue à la biscayenne* (Basque-style codfish ravioli) and *foie chaud de canard aux agrumes confits* (warm duck liver with citrus preserves). Save room for dessert; the pastry chef is one of France's best. The restaurant has earned consistently high ratings, including a Michelin star. Open daily; closed mid-November through the first week of December, and Wednesdays from October through May. Four miles (6.5 km) south of Biarritz by N10 on Chemin de Ttalienia, Bidart (phone: 59-54-81-64; fax: 59-54-75-65).

MODERATE

Auberge de la Négresse Bright, active, and bustling is this dining spot whose simple, traditional specialties include foie gras, grilled *louvine* (*loup*, in local parlance, or sea bass), and roast milk-fed lamb. The head cook, a butcher, does wonders with meat dishes. Closed Mondays and the month of October. Reservations unnecessary. Major credit cards accepted. A bit tricky to find, but worth the search, it's near the train station, under the viaduct, at 10 Av. de l'Aérodrome (phone: 59-23-15-83).

La Belle Epoque The entrance to this genteel dining room is through a boutique selling crystal and silver. The decor is true to the name, with handsome wood and a central dining court with palm trees. The food, however, is modern and creative. The *ragoût du pêcheur* (fish stew) is particularly inspiring. Open daily; closed Mondays off-season and the last two weeks of January. Reservations advised. Major credit cards accepted. 10 Av. Victor-Hugo (phone: 59-24-66-06).

Chez Albert This is the largest and best known of a handful of delightful, casual seafood eateries tucked away in the Port des Pêcheurs. Dinner comes with informal entertainment, in the person of the flamboyant host. There's also a professional performer who sings Spanish songs. Closed Wednesdays and from December through March. Reservations advised. Major credit cards accepted. Port des Pêcheurs (phone: 59-24-43-84).

Les Flots Bleus Far from the commotion of the town center is this wonderful family place, where you can order anything from Italian fare to Moroccan couscous to *crêpes à la provençale,* though the specialties are seafood dishes of the region, including a fresh fish soup that could feed a boatload of people. Open daily. Reservations unnecessary. Major credit cards accepted.

Perched on the cliffs overlooking Plage de la Côte des Basques, at 41 Perspective Côte des Basques (phone: 59-24-10-03).

Tantina de Bourgos This place stands out among Biarritz's Spanish restaurants and *tapas* bars for its grilled fresh fish and meat. Open daily; closed Sunday dinner. Reservations advised. MasterCard and Visa accepted. 2 Pl. Beau Rivage (phone: 59-23-24-47).

Le Vaudeville A trendy spot, where residents and well-informed visitors enjoy fine food at reasonable prices. Closed Monday lunch and Tuesdays. Reservations advised. Major credit cards accepted. 5 Rue du Centre (phone: 59-24-34-66).

BARS AND CAFÉS

A popular spot with locals and visitors alike is *Les Colonnes* (4 Av. Edouard-VII; phone: 59-24-17-97), which has a wood, leather, brass, and bamboo interior, a terrace in front with tables and chairs under a portico, and a view of the ocean. On Place Clemenceau, there's the café/bar *Le Royalty* (phone: 59-24-01-34), where recorded pop/rock plays continually, and *La Coupole* (phone: 59-24-09-96), a café. *Le Corsaire,* on the tiny waterfront of Port des Pêcheurs, is a small and cozy bar, with stucco walls, brass lamps, and pop/disco issuing softly from the speakers. Other alternatives are tea at the *Miremont* (1 Pl. Clemenceau; phone: 59-24-01-38), where there's a spectacular view of the sea, or *tapas* at *El Callejón* (15 Pl. Clemenceau; phone: 59-24-99-15), a popular spot on a tiny street in the center of town.

Bordeaux

The 600,000 people of Bordeaux pronounce the name of their city slowly, rolling the syllables on their tongues and savoring each vowel as they do the fine wine that bears the city's name. In fact, there is much to be savored about Bordeaux, from its famous wine to its well-preserved 18th-century architecture to the beauty of the surrounding countryside.

Bordeaux was founded near the southwestern coast of France on the bank of the Garonne River, where the river deviates from its meandering path to take the shape of a gigantic crescent moon. The city also has assumed this shape, as have the two major roads that loop around it; it's only fitting, then, that Bordeaux's symbol is a crescent moon.

Originally a village of Gallic tribes, Bordeaux prospered as a military headquarters for the colonizing Romans, who called the town *Burdigala* and introduced grape growing to the region. After withstanding assaults by waves of Visigoths, Arabs, and Normans, Bordeaux achieved mercantile fame as an English city. It was part of the dowry of the colorful Eleanor (Alienor), daughter of the ruling Duke of Aquitaine and Count of Poitiers, to her husband, the future Louis VII of France. In 1152, after 15 years and two daughters, Louis sued for annulment and, in his eagerness to be rid of his high-spirited wife, tossed back the riches she had brought to the ill-fated union. Then 30 years old, Eleanor packed up and left, marrying the teenage Henry Plantagenet, Duke of Normandy and Count of Anjou, only two months later. The couple's combined territories in France equaled those of the French sovereign, and Henry's accession to the crown of England in 1154 set off a long struggle between the English and French for the possession of the Aquitaine region.

Throughout the Anglo-French wars of the next three centuries, the Bordelais were content to remain under the rule of England. The laissez-faire policies of the English crown granted a privileged independence to the city's shippers and traders, and the English taste for the red wines of Bordeaux allowed the wine growers to increase their production many times over. By the middle of the 14th century, the equivalent of a million modern cases of wine was leaving the port of Bordeaux yearly, much of it destined for the thirsty market across the English Channel.

Bordeaux, along with the rest of the province of Aquitaine, reverted to France in 1453, at the conclusion of the Hundred Years War. The English influence eventually waned, but the Parisian government did not really fill the power vacuum until the 18th century, when Louis XV ascended the throne. At the time, an economic boom was well under way in Bordeaux: The city was shipping wine, foodstuffs, and textiles as far away as the expanding colonial markets in America and the West Indies, and wine, armaments, hardware, and manufactured goods to Africa. Foreign ships brought fine wood, tobacco, rum, sugar, coffee, and raw materials into its port.

All this commerce provided a steady flow of cash for the vast program of public works that transformed Bordeaux into one of France's most handsome provincial cities. Louis XV, who was aware of Bordeaux's growing importance, appointed *intendants* (governors) to oversee the city, and it is to them that it owes its modern face. Each *intendant* tried to outdo his predecessor in clearing away slums, crowded alleyways, and swampy marshland to create broad quays, public parks, and splendid boulevards lined with mansions. Many of the mansions still stand today, now townhouses occupied by the wealthiest shippers and wine growers. The 18th-century complex of the Place de la Bourse—comprising the *Hôtel des Douanes* (Customs House), the *Hôtel de la Bourse* (Stock Exchange), the *Hôtel de Ville* (the Town Hall, originally the *Palais Rohan*), and the *Grand Théâtre*—dates from this era.

During the late 19th century, an invasion by an American vine louse decimated the Bordeaux region's vineyards, at an enormous cost to France. Eventually, however, the roots of native American species, which were immune to the parasite, were grafted onto French vine stocks, business resumed, and Bordeaux recovered its economic balance. Today, Bordeaux wines continue to play a significant role in the French economy.

Besides wine, Bordeaux is well known for its interest in architectural revival, particularly of 18th-century buildings. Restoration is in progress all over the city, and nowhere is this resurgence more evident than in Vieux Bordeaux, the old part of town by the river, and in the adjacent St-Michel quarter. Along the cobbled streets of these old neighborhoods, workers are busily scraping away dingy façades and exposing amber stone, drawing deserved attention to ancient doorways, window trims, gracefully curving stairways, ornamental ironwork, and lacy balcony railings.

Bordeaux is also a cultural and trade center and a popular vacation spot: In every direction, no more than an hour away, lie places offering relaxation, exercise, or cultural diversion. Due east is the picturesque medieval village and wine producing area of St-Emilion; due south, the serene forests of Landes, with tiny villages and bicycle and horse trails; southwest, the Arcachon Basin and the old resort town from which it takes its name; west and northwest, miles of forest-backed beaches and two large lakes perfect for swimming, fishing, and boating; and almost due north lies the Médoc, where the most noble vineyards in France are found. Bordeaux beckons travelers not only to a vital urban center with plenty to look at, stroll through, buy, and admire, but also to an entire region of abiding richness and beauty.

Bordeaux At-a-Glance

SEEING THE CITY

For a view of the Pont de Pierre and the river, go to Bordeaux's answer to the *Arc de Triomphe,* the *Porte Cailhau,* built in 1496 (see *Special Places*). For a view of the city and the cathedral, climb the *Tour Pey-Berland* (Pl. Pey-Berland; phone: 56-81-26-25). It's open daily; no admission charge. In the evening, cross the Pont de Pierre to the east bank of the Garonne, then head north until you are opposite the Place de la Bourse and *Porte Cailhau.* From here, you can see the impressive buildings along the quays and the entry to Vieux Bordeaux.

SPECIAL PLACES

Bordeaux's monuments are best seen on foot. Note that many sites close during lunch hours, usually between noon and 2 PM. Downtown, start at the centrally located Place de la Comédie, and wander up Cours de l'Intendance as far as Place Gambetta, stopping at *Eglise Notre-Dame* on Place du Chapelet (Rue Martignac leads there). At Place Gambetta, you can sip coffee at the outdoor café, *Le Dijeaux,* study a map, and people watch. From *Porte Dijeaux*—an early corruption of "Porte des Juifs" ("Jews' Gate")—follow Rue Bouffard to its end, where you will find *Cathédrale St-André* on your left and the *Hôtel de Ville* (Town Hall), backed by the *Musée des Beaux-Arts* on your right. Then follow the pedestrian Rue des Trois Conils along the modern St-Christoly commercial center toward the river as far as Place St-Projet, the city's oldest town square. Turn left onto Rue Ste-Catherine, which will take you back to the Place de la Comédie. If you have a little energy left, stroll along Allées de Tourny, surely one of the loveliest thoroughfares in Bordeaux, named after the *intendant* who perhaps did the most to beautify the city.

The most exciting area these days is Vieux Bordeaux (Old Bordeaux), which is undergoing continuing restoration. Twisting and turning from the river at *Porte Cailhau,* it's the kind of place that encourages you to get happily lost. Do be sure to find Rue des Argentiers and Rue des Bahutiers—silversmiths' and chestmakers' streets—named for the merchants who used to work along them.

DOWNTOWN

GRAND THÉÂTRE Designed by Victor Louis (the architect of the famous arcades of Paris's Palais-Royal) and completed in 1780, this theater, with its 12 Corinthian pillars, has served as a model for theaters around the world, including the *Opéra/Palais Garnier* in Paris. The 12 statues of muses and goddess-patrons of the arts, posed regally on the front balcony, extend an open invitation to enjoy a theatrical, operatic, or philharmonic event. The interior is richly decorated; the acoustics are nearly perfect. Except for scheduled performances, the theater is open only for a one-hour guided tour, by arrangement with the tourist office. Admission charge. Pl. de la Comédie (phone: 56-44-70-71 or 57-81-90-81; 56-48-58-54 for reservations).

MAISON DU VIN (HOUSE OF WINE) This striking, flatiron-shape building is a fascinating source of information about wine and the châteaux in the region that are open for tours and tastings. Changing exhibits as well as tastings in the handsome ground-floor center make it all the more interesting. Closed weekends, except Saturdays in summer. No admission charge. 1 Cours du 30-Juillet (phone: 56-00-22-88 or 56-00-22-66; fax: 56-00-22-77).

EGLISE NOTRE-DAME (CHURCH OF OUR LADY) An Italian Revival church of the late 17th and early 18th century, completely restored inside and out. Tucked away on Place du Chapelet at the end of Rue Martignac, just off Cours de l'Intendance (phone: 56-81-01-37).

MUSÉE DES BEAUX-ARTS (FINE ARTS MUSEUM) This small museum was created in the early 19th century at the behest of Napoleon Bonaparte, then the *premier consul* of France. It houses an important collection of paintings and sculpture, with an emphasis on French works (Delacroix, Redon, Corot, Matisse, Seurat, Renoir, and Rodin). Closed Tuesdays. No admission charge on Wednesdays. Guided tours by appointment. Entrance in the garden of the *Hôtel de Ville,* 20 Cours d'Albret (phone: 56-10-16-93).

The *Galerie des Beaux-Arts,* catercorner to the museum and accessible from Place du Colonel-Raynal, is open only for special exhibitions. Admission charge (phone: 56-96-51-60).

MUSÉE D'AQUITAINE (MUSEUM OF AQUITAINE) Bordeaux's oldest museum, dating from 1781, and now ensconced in a restored 1885 building, it houses permanent collections and temporary exhibitions covering the history, agriculture, aquaculture, viticulture, commerce, art, and daily life of the province from prehistoric times to the present. In the rooms, which occupy nearly an acre, are artworks, tools, and documents, plus books from the private library of the late Nobel Prize winner François Mauriac, one of France's most famous 20th-century writers. A Bordeaux native, Mauriac drew much inspiration for his work from the area. Closed Tuesdays. No admission charge on Wednesdays. 20 Cours Pasteur, at the corner of Cours Victor-Hugo (phone: 56-10-17-58).

HÔTEL DE VILLE (TOWN HALL) Housed in the *Palais Rohan,* this 18th-century mansion was originally built for the Prince-Archbishop, later Cardinal, de Rohan. Features of the lavish decoration include finely carved wainscoting, a grand staircase, and grisailles (monotone mural paintings) by the Bordelais painter Lacour in the grand dining room. The interior houses mainly offices and staterooms, but the exterior is worth a look for its simple, striking lines. Closed Sundays; guided tours on Wednesdays. The garden, flanked on one side by the *Musée des Beaux-Arts,* is open daily. No admission charge. Pl. Pey-Berland (phone: 56-90-91-60).

CATHÉDRALE ST-ANDRÉ (ST. ANDREW'S CATHEDRAL) The original structure was built during the 11th and 12th centuries, and parts were added during the boom period of British rule; when the funds ran out, the building-in-progress stopped. But to an amateur's eye, the existing hodgepodge, complete with flying buttresses, appears harmonious in its gracefully landscaped setting. Inside, the cathedral is surprisingly light and airy, and a magnificent organ occupies the rear. Viollet-le-Duc used moldings of some of the statues of the cathedral's impressive *Porte Royale* for his restoration of *Notre-Dame* in Paris: The representations of the Apostles, the Last Judgment, the Resurrection, and the Divine Court are particularly beautiful. Pl. Pey-Berland (phone: 56-52-68-10).

CENTRE NATIONAL JEAN MOULIN (JEAN MOULIN NATIONAL CENTER) The center is named for the writer, artist, and Resistance hero who was murdered by Klaus Barbie's Gestapo, headquartered at Lyons. It houses an extensive collection related to World War II, including documents and photographs detailing the history and achievements of the Resistance. Don't overlook the powerful paintings by Jean-Jacques Morvan on the second floor and the re-creation of Moulin's clandestine office on the third floor. Closed weekday mornings, weekends, and holidays. Admission charge. Pl. Jean-Moulin (phone: 56-10-15-80).

VIEUX BORDEAUX (OLD BORDEAUX)

PORTE CAILHAU (CAILHAU GATE) This gate, built from 1493 to 1496, is one of the entries to Vieux Bordeaux. Although it now stands alone, it's possible to see where the ramparts once were attached. It can be entered daily on afternoons from mid-June to mid-September, and on Saturday afternoons the rest of the year. There are guided tours every 45 minutes. Admission charge. North of Pont de Pierre at Quai de la Douane.

PONT DE PIERRE (STONE BRIDGE) It's impossible not to notice this graceful, low-slung bridge with its 17 arches looping the Garonne. It was Bordeaux's only bridge from 1822 until 1965, when Pont St-Jean was completed. It's most beautiful at dusk. Opposite Pl. de Bir-Hakeim.

PLACE DU PARLEMENT (PARLIAMENT SQUARE) Constructed mostly around 1760, this is one of the quietest and sunniest of Bordeaux's lovely *places*. Any one of the small streets branching from it inevitably leads to a restaurant or a tiny, treasure-filled shop.

PLACE DE LA BOURSE (STOCK EXCHANGE SQUARE) Completed in 1755, this beautiful grouping of warm, gold-tinged stone buildings laced with elegant wrought iron is a fitting symbol of the wealth and taste of the age. Quai de la Douane, west of the Pl. du Parlement.

LES QUAIS Walk along the quays from the Place de la Bourse to the *Eglise St-Michel*—braving the noise and car fumes—to appreciate the backdrop of

18th-century buildings. Most notable are the *mascarons* (carved faces) over doorways and in walls; they represent the people of Bordeaux at that time, as well as mythological and fantastical figures. Supposedly there are a couple of hundred *mascarons,* no two of them alike. Quais des Salinières, Quai Richelieu, and Quai de la Douane.

EGLISE ST-MICHEL (ST. MICHAEL'S CHURCH) The basilica of this church was badly damaged during World War II, but the restored, modern stained glass windows over the high altar work well in their 15th-century setting. Two windows from the 16th century remain in the transept. The 375-foot bell tower, built separately, is the tallest in the south of France. Pl. St-Michel at Rue des Faures (no phone).

GROSSE CLOCHE (GREAT BELL) This 13th- to 16th-century clock tower looks oddly out of place along busy Cours Victor-Hugo, which is lined with 18th- and 19th-century buildings. The bell used to signal the beginning of the grape harvest; now it chimes only on days of national rejoicing. Beside the tower is the tiny *Eglise St-Eloi,* which was built into the wall of Vieux Bordeaux. A movement is afoot to restore this church, named after the patron saint of ironworkers; it may be open to visitors by late this year. Rue St-James, just off Cours Victor-Hugo (no phone).

CITÉ MONDIALE DU VIN ET DES SPIRITUEUX (INTERNATIONAL CENTER FOR WINE AND SPIRITS) This ambitious new development is a five-acre trade and cultural center dedicated to the international, rather than merely regional, wine and spirits industry. It is in the Chartrons district, for centuries the center of the region's wine industry. The complex includes restored *chais* (wine storehouses), an international *maison des vins* (house of wines) and market, a wine museum, a research center (open to wine professionals only), shops, pedestrian walks, hotels, conference facilities, and restaurants. The museum is open daily; the shops are generally closed Sundays. No admission charge. Bordered by Cours Xavier-Arnozan, Cours de Verdun, and Quai des Chartrons, at 20 Quai des Chartrons (phone: 56-01-20-20; fax: 56-01-71-00).

CASA DE GOYA AND ESPACE GOYA (GOYA HOUSE AND GOYA SPACE) These two institutions in the house where the painter lived and died in exile include a permanent exhibition on Goya's life in Bordeaux, replicas of his rooms, and a Spanish cultural center. Guided tours of Goya's living quarters are offered on Monday, Tuesday, Wednesday, and Friday afternoons for a small fee. *Casa de Goya* is closed weekday mornings and weekends; *Espace Goya* is closed mornings and on Sundays. Admission charge to both. 57 Cours de l'Intendance (phone: 56-52-79-37 or 56-51-66-15).

ELSEWHERE

CENTRE D'ART PLASTIQUE CONTEMPORAIN/MUSÉE D'ART CONTEMPORAIN (CENTER FOR CONTEMPORARY VISUAL ARTS/MUSEUM OF CONTEMPORARY ART) This building used to be the storehouse for the coffee, rum, wood, and spices shipped to Bordeaux from the colonies; today, it serves as a storehouse for talent. The structure was remodeled to accommodate art exhibits and to house the *Musée d'Art Contemporain,* incorporating the *Centre d'Art Plastique Contemporain (CAPC).* Since then, the *CAPC* has blossomed into an increasingly important museum, considered southwest France's preeminent modern arts center. The museum café is pleasant and inexpensive. Closed Mondays. Admission charge. Near Quai des Chartrons and the Esplanade des Quinconces, on 7 Rue Ferrère at Rue Foy (phone: 56-44-16-35).

JARDIN PUBLIC (PUBLIC GARDEN) A 5-minute walk from the Place Tourny or Esplanade des Quinconces, this idyllic spot, surrounded by 19th-century townhouses, is the place to see the Bordelais—young and old—at rest and at play. The tiny pond is put to good use by swans, ducks, and children taking joy rides in small boats. There's also a charming old botanical garden. Open daily. Cours de Verdun.

PALAIS GALLIEN (ROMAN PALACE) A relic of Bordeaux's past, this 3rd-century Roman amphitheater could accommodate 15,000 spectators. The ruins are blocked from public access, but it is possible to get a couple of worthwhile views of them by following Rue du Palais Gallien to its end, in the direction of the traffic.

SITE PALÉO-CHRÉTIEN DE ST-SEURIN (ST. SEURIN PALEO-CHRISTIAN SITE) In the middle of a busy commercial and residential neighborhood, this is Bordeaux's oldest historical site. Evidence of early Christian worship—tombs, frescoes, and amphorae from the fourth through the eighth centuries—have been discovered in the grounds behind this church. An audiovisual display on the archaeological findings at the site is presented at the adjoining museum. Painters congregate in the garden here the first Saturday afternoon of each month. Open Tuesday and Saturday afternoons from April through August, or for private tours by arrangement with the tourist office. Admission charge. Pl. des Martyrs-de-la-Résistance (phone: 56-79-05-39).

QUARTIER MÉRIADECK (MÉRIADECK QUARTER) It's easy to miss this modern complex of chrome, concrete, and steel buildings if you don't know where to look: right across the street from the *Musée des Beaux-Arts.* Not only interesting as a contemporary center for living, working, and shopping in what is essentially an 18th-century city, it also deserves a look for its plaza and the varied styles of its buildings. Between Rues Jean-Fleuret and Claude-Bonnier, opposite the garden of the *Hôtel de Ville.*

CIMETIÈRE DE LA CHARTREUSE (CHARTERHOUSE CEMETERY) Graveyard lovers should wend their way a few blocks west of Mériadeck to the cemetery at the *Eglise St-Bruno.* The 18th-century church has a painting by Philippe de Champaigne and a statue by Bernini; the cemetery, also dating from the 18th century, has interesting tombs and a monument marking the spot where Goya was temporarily buried (he was later moved to his family's tomb in Spain). Open daily. No admission charge. Corner of Rue François-de-Sourdis and Rue Georges-Bonnac (phone: 56-93-17-20).

ENVIRONS

BLAYE Of the several boat excursions possible from Bordeaux, we highly recommend a trip to this small, late 17th-century walled city 30 miles (48 km) north of Bordeaux. Excursion days are posted in the tourist office, where tickets can be purchased. Pack a picnic or eat at *La Citadelle,* in the citadel in Blaye. The restaurant is good, if expensive; there are also 21 moderately priced rooms for rent. It's closed Mondays from October through March (phone: 57-42-17-10; fax: 57-42-10-34). To reach Blaye by land, either drive to Lamarque and take the ferry across the Gironde or follow the scenic route toward St-André-de-Cubzac, stopping to admire the view from the terrace of the *Château de Bourg.*

CHÂTEAU DE LA BRÈDE (LA BRÈDE CASTLE) The birthplace and home of Montesquieu from 1689 to 1775, this impressive dwelling, surrounded by a large moat, was built from the 13th to the 15th century. Closed mornings, Tuesdays, and November through February; open weekend afternoons only in March. Admission charge. About 12 miles (19 km) south of Bordeaux via N113 and D108 (phone: 56-20-20-49).

CHÂTEAU HAUT-BRION (HAUT-BRION CASTLE) This is the perfect place for travelers who want to visit a vineyard but haven't the time or transportation to go to the Médoc. In 1855, the wines of 60 or so of the 100 châteaux in the Médoc were classified according to excellence. The famous red wine produced at this château, only a few miles southwest of the center of Bordeaux, was the only one outside the Médoc to be included in the classification. Reservations are necessary for tours. Closed weekends and in August. No admission charge. In Pessac, via N650, or take a bus from Quai Richelieu in Bordeaux (phone: 56-00-29-30).

ST-EMILION This minuscule town, with its steep hills, winding cobblestone streets, small ocher stone houses with red tile roofs, and bustling square, is one of the most picturesque wine villages of France. It's just a 45-minute drive east of Bordeaux. At the top of the hill (and the town) is the *Eglise Collégiale.* This is the site of two major events: the June 20 celebration of the new *vin nouveau* and the famous celebration of the beginning of the grape harvest, held on the Sunday closest to September 20.

Walk to the Place du Clocher for a sweeping view of the Dordogne Valley and the town. The tourist office (15 Rue Clocher; phone: 57-24-72-03) has maps of St-Emilion (sometimes) and a list of the châteaux and vineyards open to the public. The tourist office is closed Sundays October through April, and Sunday afternoons May through September.

English is spoken at *Châteaux Ausone, Figeac, Cheval-Blanc, Beauséjour,* and *Haut-Sarpe,* where there also is a village; an English-speaking staff member is usually available at all châteaux in the summer. The *Maison du Vin de St-Emilion,* at Place Pierre-Meyrat (phone: 57-74-42-42), is a must not only for its exhibits on local viticulture but also for its bargains on local wines, including many from the *grand cru* vineyards. The staff speaks English and is very knowledgeable about the selection of vintages. It's open daily except *Christmas* and *New Year's Day.*

There also are exhibitions, lectures, and very good concerts in St-Emilion, especially in July, during the *Grandes Heures de St-Emilion,* when music is performed in ancient churches and private châteaux. And be sure to visit the *Cloître des Cordeliers* (Cordelier Cloisters), on Rue des Cordeliers, a 14th-to-15th-century convent and cloister that is now an arresting, overgrown shell of stone walls, stairways, and columns.

The most luxurious lodgings in town are in the recently opened *Château Grand Barrail* (phone: 57-55-37-00; fax: 57-55-37-49), an 18th-century château just west of St-Emilion on the tiny Route de Libourne. The *Hostellerie de Plaisance* (Pl. du Clocher; phone: 57-24-72-32; fax: 57-74-41-11) offers comfortable rooms and a moderately priced, one-Michelin-star restaurant. *Francis Goullée* (27 Rue Guadet, phone: 57-24-70-49) features regional cuisine and wines. And don't leave town without sampling the *truffes au vin* (chocolate truffles filled with St-Emilion wine) sold at the town's pâtisseries. Follow N89 and signs from Bordeaux to Libourne/Périgueux, and from Libourne those toward La Réole and Bergerac on D17E.

ENTRE-DEUX-MERS Just south of St-Emilion lies this charming region, a patchwork of green hills, windmills, water mills, small vineyards, abbeys, châteaux, and villages nestled between the Garonne and the Dordogne rivers. Visit the picturesque village of La Réole, the medieval towns of St-Macaire and Castelmoron-d'Albret, the *bastides* (medieval fortified cities) of Créon and Sauveterre-de-Guyenne, and the nearby Labarthe mill on the Gamage River. St-Ferme, the beautiful ruins of Blasimon, and La Sauve-Majeure are ancient abbeys. Among the châteaux to be explored are La Benauge, Cadillac, Duras, and Rauzan.

Sources and Resources

TOURIST INFORMATION

The *Office du Tourisme de Bordeaux* (12 Cours du 30-Juillet; phone: 56-44-28-41) can provide maps and information, arrange tours in and around the city, including tours to famed wine châteaux, and sell tickets permitting entry to 10 Bordeaux museums. There are branch tourist offices at the *Gare Saint-Jean* (phone: 56-91-64-70) and at the airport (phone: 56-34-39-39). All three offices are open daily. There's also an English-language telephone message (phone: 56-48-04-61) listing current events in town. Also useful, especially for sports and cultural activities, is the *Centre d'Information*

Jeunesse Aquitaine, a block south of *Cathédrale St-André* (5 Rue Duffour-Dubergier; phone: 56-48-55-50). The center, which has a bright red exterior, has a helpful staff that offers maps and information. Check the bulletin boards for announcements of concerts, movies, and lectures. The center is closed Sundays.

LOCAL COVERAGE In French, there are the daily *Sud-Ouest,* published in Bordeaux, and the *Bordeaux Journal Municipal d'Information,* published monthly by the mayor's office. The latter is packed with news about sports, expositions, and cultural events and is available free at the office of *L'Entrepôt Lainé* (3 Rue Ferrère; phone: 56-90-91-60) and at the *Hôtel de Ville* (see *Special Places*). The tourist office publishes a free quarterly newsletter, *Euro-Tourist,* that lists upcoming performances, cultural and sports events, expositions, and so on, in both French and English. The annual, student-produced, French-language *Le Bordeluche* is a guide to restaurants, entertainment, sports facilities, city services, and baby-sitters. English newspapers and other international publications are sold at the newsstand in front of the *Grand Théâtre* and at most large *maisons de la presse* (newsstands), including the one at 68 Rue St-Rémi, just below Rue Ste-Catherine. Tourist information also is available through *minitel,* France's computerized information system, with terminals available at some hotels and at most branches of the *PTT* (postal service and telephone). To gain access to the system, dial 3615-BORDEAUX on a phone hooked up to one of the special terminals. Some of the information is available in English. For maps, guidebooks, and phrase books, try *Bradley's Bookshop* (see *Shopping*).

TELEPHONE The main city codes for Bordeaux are 56 or 57, which are incorporated into all local eight-digit numbers. When calling a number in Bordeaux from the Paris region (including the Ile-de-France), dial 16, wait for a dial tone, then dial the eight-digit number. When calling a number from outside Paris, dial only the eight-digit number.

GETTING AROUND

AIRPORT The *Aéroport International de Bordeaux-Mérignac* (phone: 56-34-50-50) handles over two million passengers a year. To reach the center of town from the airport, take bus No. 73 (about a 30-minute ride), the *CCI* shuttle or *navette* (a shuttle bus that runs regularly from the airport to town), or a taxi.

BOAT TOURS Guided boat excursions of the Bordeaux harbor are offered; information and tickets are available on Wharf des Quinconces (or Wharf des Queyries on the other side of the river) and at the tourist office (see *Tourist Information*). To get a feel for Bordeaux as a major port, take a cruise down the Garonne, Dordogne, or Gironde rivers; contact the tourist office for information.

BUS The city bus system, *CGTFE* (phone: 57-57-88-88), serves Bordeaux and some of its suburbs. A single ticket, which must be stamped when you enter the bus, costs around 5F (about 85¢ at press time) and is good for only one ride. Buy a *carnet* (packet) of 10 tickets for around 40F (about $6.85 at press time); not only are they less expensive, but each can be used for four rides within an hour. Free maps and schedules are available at the major terminals at *Gare St-Jean* and Place Gambetta, near Place Tourny; at 10 Cours de Verdun; and at Place Jean-Jaurès, near the quays. Tickets may be purchased on the buses or at the terminals. Long-distance buses to the coast, the Arcachon Basin, and other points outside Bordeaux are provided by *CITRAM* (8 Rue Corneille; phone: 56-43-04-04).

CAR RENTAL Major companies, including *Avis* (phone: 56-92-69-38); *Budget* (phone: 56-91-41-70); *Europcar* (phone: 56-31-20-30); and *Hertz* (phone: 56-91-01-71) all have offices within a block or two of the train station *(Gare St-Jean)* and are easy to spot.

TAXI Distinguished by a small sign on top of the vehicle, cabs come in all shapes, sizes, and colors. Taxi stands are designated by a triangular sign with a "T." There's one at the Place Gambetta end of Cours Clemenceau and another at the corner of Rue Esprit-des-Lois by the *Grand Théâtre;* there's also one at the train station, *Gare St-Jean.* To call a cab day or night, dial 56-97-11-27 (at the airport) or 56-91-48-11 (near the train station); the dispatchers usually speak some English.

TRAIN *Gare St-Jean,* Bordeaux's main train station, is south of the center, just inland from the river and Pont St-Jean. For schedule and fare information (usually in French only, though sometimes someone will speak English), call 56-92-50-50.

SPECIAL EVENTS
Bordeaux is charged with creative energy, and calendars fill up more quickly than usual in May and November.

FAVORITE FÊTE

Festival International de Bordeaux Quite apart from its great artistic value, this festival—which takes over the city for the entire month of May—provides a lovely opportunity to get to know Aquitaine in the spring. Concerts featuring solo pianists, massed choirs, and jazz groups alternate between town and country; venues include the *Grand Théâtre,* the *Cathédrale St-André,* the *Château de la Brède,* a cruise boat on the Garonne, and castles and churches in the wine-rich villages of the surrounding countryside. For additional details, contact the tourist office.

A *Semaine Mondiale des Vins et Spiritueux* or *VINEXPO,* a week-long fair and conference on wines and spirits, takes place at the *Cité Mondiale du Vin et des Spiritueux* (see *Special Places*) every two years in June; the next session is planned for this year. The spotlight shifts to dance and contemporary arts for two weeks in November, when the annual *SIGMA* festival lures well-known international soloists and groups to Bordeaux. In the summer (sometimes September), the *Nuit du Vieux Bordeaux* (Night of Old Bordeaux) fills the streets of the St-Pierre quarter with music, crowds, and a holiday atmosphere. Additional information on all these events is available from the tourist office.

MUSEUMS

Noteworthy museums not mentioned in *Special Places* include the following:

MAISON DES MÉTIERS DE L'IMPRIMERIE (HOUSE OF THE PRINTING TRADES) Dedicated to the art of printing, this small museum's exhibits include a dozen or so old presses. Open Monday and Wednesday afternoons and Saturday mornings; closed in July. Admission charge. 10 Rue du Fort Louis (phone: 56-92-61-17).

MUSÉE DES ARTS DÉCORATIFS (MUSEUM OF DECORATIVE ARTS) One of the city's loveliest, this museum displays ceramics, glassware, ironwork, furniture, and other *objets,* many of them from 18th-century Bordeaux. There also are changing exhibitions. Closed mornings and on Tuesdays. No admission charge Wednesdays. 39 Rue Bouffard (phone: 56-10-15-62).

MUSÉE DES CHARTRONS (CHARTRONS MUSEUM) Devoted to wine making, this museum exhibits collections of old bottles, labels, and tools. Closed weekends and Mondays. Admission charge. 41 Rue Borie (phone: 56-44-27-77).

MUSÉE DES DOUANES (CUSTOMS MUSEUM) A well-restored floor of one of the 18th-century Place de la Bourse buildings is dedicated to customs history. Closed Mondays. Admission charge. 1 Pl. de la Bourse (phone: 56-52-45-47).

MUSÉE D'HISTOIRE NATURELLE (MUSEUM OF NATURAL HISTORY) Tucked away in the back of the *Jardin Public,* this small, well-maintained museum has simple but well-executed exhibitions. Be sure to see the butterflies on the third floor and the photographs that show how the museum's stuffed elephant was mounted and carried through the streets of Bordeaux to its present home in the lobby. Closed mornings and on Tuesdays. Admission charge. 5 Pl. Bardineau; enter through the gate of the garden or Rue Emile-Zola (phone: 56-48-29-86).

SHOPPING

If it's clothing you're after, traverse the "golden triangle," whose angles are Place Gambetta, Place Tourny, and Place de la Comédie and whose sides are Cours de l'Intendance, Cours Clemenceau, and Allées de Tourny. The *Galeries des Grands Hommes,* in the center of the triangle at the Place des

Grands Hommes, houses chic boutiques, including *Pierre Cardin, Charles Jourdan,* and *Laure Japy.* Place du Parlement is popular with a younger clientele for clothing, shoes, and accessories. If you prefer riding escalators to walking, head to the shopping center at Quartier Mériadeck (see *Special Places*) with its 100 boutiques.

If it's antiques you seek, the best bets are Rue Bouffard, Rue des Remparts, and Rue Notre-Dame; also try the small streets around the *Eglise St-Michel.* Don't overlook *Village Notre-Dame,* an old covered market filled with antiques shops, near *Eglise Notre-Dame* on the outskirts of the Chartrons district. Occasionally, an object of real value turns up among the run-of-the-mill wares at the Sunday-morning flea market in front of the church. The city also holds a flea market in May and November at Place des Quinconces. Antiques fairs are held annually in January at Le Lac exposition center, around 3 miles (5 km) north of the city center by the Allée de Boutant, and in February at *Hangar Cinq* (on the river).

For cheese, try *Jean d'Alos* (4 Rue Montesquieu; phone: 56-44-29-66). *La Comtesse du Barry* (2 Pl. Tourny; phone: 56-44-81-15) offers regional and national food specialties, some made from the recipes of well-known French chefs. *Cerruti* (21 Rue Voltaire; phone: 56-44-24-51) is a deluxe grocery with fresh, homemade products and a certain snob appeal. By contrast, the Thursday-morning market in front of the *Eglise St-Pierre,* on Place St-Pierre, looks like an encampment of Gypsies, bright tents and all. In fact, they are farmers and vendors of organically grown produce, homemade baked goods, and wines made from organically grown grapes. An equally colorful food market can be found on Saturday mornings near the *Eglise St-Michel.* If you find yourself reconnoitering Rue Ste-Catherine at lunchtime, pick up a sandwich of *jambon de Bayonne,* a ham similar to the famous Parma ham, from the stand called *Laurent Petricorena* (14 Pl. Gambetta).

The best wine stores in Bordeaux include *Badie* (62 Allées de Tourny; phone: 56-52-23-72); *La Vinothèque* (near the tourist office, on Cours du 30-Juillet; phone: 56-52-32-05); *Bordeaux Magnum* (3 Rue Gobineau; phone: 56-48-00-06); and *L'Intendant* (2 Allées de Tourny; phone: 56-48-01-29). For a more intimate experience, visit a *cave,* a dark, usually old shop where Bordelais buy simple wines. You also can make purchases from a local wine maker, such as Pierre Roubin, who sells on Thursdays at the organic market near the *Eglise St-Pierre* and on the weekends from his home in Bellefond, near Rauzan (phone: 56-23-93-71).

For standard shopping hours, see GETTING READY TO GO. Other Bordeaux shops to explore:

Atelier Basset-Nayad Decorative handmade enameled tiles are produced and sold in this old-fashioned shop. 230 Rue Camille-Godard (phone: 57-87-25-10).

Bradley's Bookshop Bordeaux's oldest English-language bookstore, it stocks phrase books, maps, guidebooks, dictionaries, best sellers, and classics. 32 Pl. Gambetta (phone: 56-52-10-57).

Cadiot Badie Excellent bonbons in pretty tin boxes. 26 Allées de Tourny (phone: 56-44-24-22).

Galerie Condillac Changing exhibits of up-and-coming painters, plus art supplies for sale. 24 Rue Condillac (phone: 56-79-04-31).

Galerie Plexus New, younger international artists are featured in revolving exhibitions. 10 Rue des Argentiers (phone: 56-81-89-90).

Interchasse Men's and women's clothing, hats, jewelry, and gift items in a quaint store filled with decorative objects and paintings with a hunting theme. 19 Rue des Remparts (phone: 56-44-56-83).

Jacqueline Dourthe Original dresses by the well-known Bordeaux designer. 18 Rue Lafaurie de Monbadon (phone: 56-52-35-78).

M. Mazuque A small gift shop that specializes in engraved glass and crystal. Items can be shipped home. In Vieux Bordeaux, at 6 Rue du Parlement Ste-Catherine (phone: 56-52-94-14).

Mollat Even if you don't read French, drop by this lovely bookstore, which is housed in an early 19th-century building on the spot where Montesquieu's last home once stood. The selection of books on Bordeaux is outstanding. It's closed Monday mornings. 9-15 Rue Vital-Carles (phone: 56-44-84-87).

La Soierie Silk and leather clothing and accessories for *les dames.* 27 Rue du Parlement St-Pierre (phone: 56-51-23-75).

Xavier Pariente A fine antiques shop purveying 17th- and 18th-century furniture, paintings, and other items. 60 Rue Bouffard (phone: 56-81-22-37).

SPORTS AND FITNESS

Bordeaux is less than an hour away from the Arcachon Basin and the Côte d'Argent, where golf, tennis, swimming, biking, and horseback riding can be enjoyed.

GOLF Visitors to Bordeaux have a unique opportunity to complement fairway action with fine wines.

GOLF AND GOBLETS

Le Golf du Médoc This set-up vies for honors as France's most deluxe golfing facility. Each of its 18 holes is sponsored by a different wine château—the 18th, for example, is Mouton Rothschild. If you make a hole-in-one at the par 3, 155-yard Pontet Canet (the fifth), you get a magnum of the wine. Regional wines also are served at the clubhouse's restaurant, with a minimal markup. Twenty miles (32 km) northwest of the city on D211, Chemin de Courmateau, Louens, Blanquefort (phone: 56-70-21-10).

·Just north of Le Lac are two 18-hole municipal courses (Av. de Pernon; phone: 56-50-92-42) where clubs can be rented; they're closed Tuesdays. There also is an 18-hole course at *Golf Bordelais* (Av. d'Eysines; phone: 56-28-56-04), which is closed Mondays.

HORSE RACING Every Sunday in spring and summer, races are run at two local *hippodromes* (racetracks): *La Teste Arcachon* (Route d'Oléron; phone: 56-54-74-26) and *Le Bouscat* (Av. d'Eysines; phone: 56-28-06-74).

ICE SKATING The large *patinoire* (rink) at the Mériadeck sports complex (Terrace Général-Koenig, Rue Corps Franc de Pommiers; phone: 56-93-05-85) is closed in summer; diehards who like to ice skate in the warm-weather months can use the rink in nearby Arcachon (Allée de Mimosa; phone: 56-83-24-56).

RUGBY Amateur clubs and university teams often play at the *Stade Municipal* (Pl. Johnston; phone: 56-93-25-83). For information about upcoming matches, call 56-85-94-01 or check the newspapers.

SOCCER The popular local team, *Les Girondins de Bordeaux,* plays at the *Stade Municipal* (see *Rugby,* above). Check newspapers for current schedules.

SQUASH Stop by *Jeu de Paume* (369 Av. de Verdun, Mérignac; phone: 56-97-51-12), where exercise can be rewarded with a drink at the bar or lunch or dinner at the pleasant restaurant. Bring your own athletic shoes and clothes; racquets are provided. There are three courts plus saunas. The center is sometimes closed in August.

SWIMMING A covered municipal pool is in the *Grand Parc* (6 Av. Généraux-Duché; phone: 56-50-31-97); it is accessible to disabled swimmers.

TENNIS Several clubs in the area open their courts to visitors. For information, contact the *Ligue de Guyenne* (53 Rue de Colonel-Moll, Talence 33400; phone: 56-37-02-90). The indoor courts at the Mériadeck sports complex (see *Ice Skating,* above) are open daily and can be rented by the hour.

THEATER

The *Grand Théâtre* (see *Special Places*) is the venue for ballets and plays. A few blocks away, at the *Théâtre Fémina* (Rue de Grassi; phone: 56-52-58-84)—not a feminist theater, as its name might imply—classical and contemporary plays are performed regularly. The *Théâtre du Port de la Lune* (Pl. Renaudel; phone: 56-91-99-44) also presents both classic and modern plays.

MUSIC

The Bordelais love music and have numerous opportunities to listen to it. The *Orchestre National Bordeaux-Aquitaine,* the *Orchestre de la Musique Municipale,* the *Jeunesses Musicales de France,* operatic ensembles, and chamber music groups perform most often at the *Grand Théâtre* and the *Théâtre*

Fémina (see *Theater,* above, for details on both). There are also occasional concerts at the modern *Centre André-Malraux–Conservatoire National de la Région* (22 Quai St-Croix; phone: 56-94-13-17); the *Palais des Sports* (Rue Ravez, off Cours d'Alsace et Lorraine; phone: 56-52-23-40), in the skating rink at Mériadeck (the acoustics are bad at the highest, least expensive tier); and in the cathedral and various other churches in the city.

NIGHTCLUBS AND NIGHTLIFE

A big night out for the Bordelais appears to be dinner and a movie. If you decide to follow suit, consult *Eating Out* (below) and then take in a classic or second-run avant-garde film at *Cinéma Trianon–Jean Vigo* (6 Rue Franklin; phone: 56-52-32-89). First-run films, primarily French and American, are shown at the *Gaumont, Marivaux, Ariel,* and *Français* cinemas, all near Place Gambetta.

The chic *Studio 21* (21 Rue Mably; phone: 56-44-35-22); *Sénéchal* (57 *bis* Quai de Paludate; phone: 56-85-54-80); and *Macumba* (Rte. du Cap-Ferret, Mérignac; phone: 56-34-05-48) are all popular discos, though most are off the beaten track. For cocktails, go to *L'Orchidée Noire* (2 Pl. Pey-Berland; phone: 56-44-40-04); for jazz, drop in at the *Black Jack* piano bar (35 Pl. Gambetta; phone: 56-81-71-38). Café-theaters include *L'Onyx* (11 Rue Fernand-Philippart; phone: 56-44-26-12); *Théâtre Boîte Jouer* (50 Rue des Lombards; phone: 56-50-08-24); and the *Théâtre l'Oeil–La Lucarne* (48 Rue Carpenteyre; phone: 56-92-25-06). For rock and jazz, go to *Le Café Carabosse* (Rue de Bègles between the railway station and the *Marché des Capucins,* or Capuchins Market; phone: 56-91-43-27) or the *White Spirit* (15 Rue Notre-Dame; phone 56-52-37-82). Clubs generally stay open until the wee hours, but whenever possible, call ahead to verify the days and times they are open, since these vary widely.

Best in Town

CHECKING IN

Bordeaux has many hotels within walking distance of almost anything a visitor might want to do or see. Expect to pay more than $150 per night for a double room at a very expensive hotel; $90 to $150 at an expensive one; between $70 and $90 at a moderate place; and less than $70 at an inexpensive hotel. Unless otherwise noted, all hotels listed below have telephones, TV sets, and private baths in the rooms. Some inexpensive hotels have private baths in only some of their rooms; it's a good idea to confirm whether your room has a private bath when making a reservation. In general, only expensive to very expensive hotels in Bordeaux have air conditioning, unless otherwise noted, and summers can be very hot. All hotels listed are open year-round and accept major credit cards unless otherwise indicated.

Burdigala This classic old building has been transformed into an elegant establishment with 70 rooms and 13 duplex suites, all offering modern comforts, plus a restaurant. In the Mériadeck section, at 115 Rue Georges-Bonnac (phone: 56-90-16-16; fax: 56-93-15-06).

Château Chartrons This deluxe property near *La Cité Mondiale du Vin et des Spiritueux* (see *Special Places*) was built by a major Bordeaux wine company, and the decoration of its 143 rooms and seven suites was inspired by the area's wine trade. There are two restaurants, a wine bar, and private parking. In the heart of Bordeaux's historic Chartrons quarter, at 81 Cours St-Louis (phone: 56-43-15-00; fax: 56-69-15-21).

EXPENSIVE

Grand Hôtel Français Since its renovation, this old standby has risen to new heights of comfort and elegance in its public areas and in the decoration of its 35 rooms. A grand stairway and gracious sitting rooms recall Vieux Bordeaux. There's no restaurant, but excellent room service fare is provided by a well-respected local caterer. 12 Rue du Temple (phone: 56-48-10-35; fax: 56-81-76-18).

Pullman-Mériadeck Modern and bustling, this hotel has 196 rooms (all with mini-bars), the elegant *Le Mériadeck* restaurant, and a bar. In the Mériadeck area, at 5 Rue Robert-Lateulade (phone: 56-56-43-43; 800-221-4542; fax: 56-96-50-59).

Sainte-Catherine Warm golden stones and wrought iron give this deluxe, recently refurbished hostelry a special charm. The 82 rooms and one sumptuous suite are large and comfortable. There's a restaurant and piano bar. In the heart of Vieux Bordeaux, at 27 Rue du Parlement-Ste-Catherine (phone: 56-81-95-12; fax: 56-44-50-51).

Sofitel Bordeaux–Le Lac If you plan to spend a lot of time in Le Lac (for, perhaps, a conference or an exposition), this is a comfortable, modern place to return to at the end of the day. It has 202 rooms, eight suites, a pool, and a restaurant. 4 Bd. Domergue (phone: 56-50-83-80; 800-763-4835; fax: 56-39-73-75).

MODERATE

Bayonne Quiet, comfortable, and modern, this 36-room hostelry decorated in Art Deco style is conveniently located near the *Grand Théâtre*. There's no restaurant. Closed the first week in January. 4 Rue Martignac (phone: 56-48-00-88; fax: 56-52-03-79).

Gambetta This old hotel that has been renovated inside, though not out. There are 31 comfortable, if small, rooms with mini-bars. There's also a lounge, and the management is friendly. Breakfast is available, but there's no restaurant. 66 Rue Porte-Dijeaux (phone: 56-51-21-83; fax: 56-81-00-40).

Hôtel des Quatre Soeurs Richard Wagner once slept in this pleasant 35-room hostelry. There's a perfectly preserved mid–19th-century bar and a meeting room; no restaurant, though. Near the *Grand Théâtre,* at 6 Cours 30-Juillet (phone: 57-81-19-20; fax: 56-01-04-28).

Hôtel de Sèze A comfortable 24-room hotel in a converted 18th-century home, with fin de siècle furnishings. There's no restaurant. 23 Allées de Tourny (phone: 56-52-65-54; fax: 56-44-31-83).

Hôtel du Théâtre The welcome is warm and the 23 rooms are pleasant at this hotel in an 18th-century townhouse in the heart of Bordeaux. There's a bar, a small meeting room, a sauna, and a solarium, but no restaurant. 10 Rue Maison-Daurade (phone: 56-79-05-26; fax: 56-81-15-64).

Normandie A classic hotel with a refurbished stone façade, it has 100 rooms (some with terraces) and a bar, but no dining room. In front of the tourist office, at 7 Cours du 30-Juillet (phone: 56-52-16-80; fax: 56-51-68-91).

Royal Médoc This charming place offers 45 modern, tastefully decorated rooms and a bar. There's no dining room, but room service is available from nearby restaurants. A few blocks from the Pl. de la Comédie, at 3-5 Rue de Sèze (phone: 56-81-72-42; fax: 56-51-74-98).

INEXPENSIVE

Vieux Bordeaux Guests are accorded a warm welcome at this neat 18th-century house. There are 11 simple, clean rooms (six with private baths); ask for one on the street side. There's no restaurant. Quartier St-Pierre, a couple of blocks from Pl. du Parlement and Pl. St-Pierre. 22 Rue du Cancéra (phone: 56-48-07-27; fax: 56-51-93-13).

EATING OUT

Bordeaux's vast array of restaurants offers ample opportunities to sample such regional delights as foie gras, *confit* (preserved fattened goose or duck), *cèpes* (wild boletus mushrooms), *entrecôte* (steak grilled over the coals of dried grapevine prunings and garnished with shallots), and seafood such as *lamproie* (eel, usually prepared *à la bordelaise,* in red wine sauce), *huîtres* (oysters, served with whole wheat or rye bread in these parts), and *alose* (a fish that usually is grilled and then presented in elegant and exciting ways). A few restaurants offer regional wines by the glass. Although it's easy to concentrate on only red Bordeaux wines, don't overlook the whites of Graves and Sauternes (a classic with foie gras). Many restaurants are housed in beautifully restored buildings. Expect to pay $130 or more for a meal for two at a very expensive restaurant; between $90 and $130 at an expensive one; between $75 and $90 at a moderate place; and less than $75 at an inexpensive one. Prices include service (which is usually added automatically to the bill) but not wine. Unless otherwise noted, all restaurants listed below are open for lunch and dinner.

VERY EXPENSIVE

Amat Despite its regal interpretations of local delicacies and an exhaustive wine list, this controversial establishment (formerly the *St-James*) lost one of its two Michelin stars in 1993. The addition of a new wing with 18 starkly modern (and expensive) guestrooms caused a stir, too. The restaurant seems to be back on track now (though the star has yet to be regained); try the *civet de canard aux cèpes* (braised duck with wild boletus mushrooms) or the *lamproie à la bordelaise.* The setting, high on a ridge with a commanding view of vineyards and the Garonne River, is, as always, sublime. The house's adjoining second restaurant, *Le Bistroy,* is highly recommended for its casual atmosphere and reasonably priced bistro fare. A member of the Relais & Châteaux group. Open daily. Reservations necessary. Major credit cards accepted. Across the Garonne and well away from the city center, in suburban Bouliac at 3 Pl. Camille-Hosteins (phone: 57-97-06-00; fax: 56-20-92-58).

EXPENSIVE

L'Alhambra The up-and-coming chef here favors traditional cuisine, such as beef filet with mustard cream sauce and poached eggs with sorrel. The wine list is excellent. No lunch on Saturdays; closed Sundays. Reservations advised. Major credit cards accepted. 111 *bis* Rue Judaïque (phone: 56-96-06-91)

Chapon Fin In this lovely landmark, whose turn-of-the-century decoration has been perfectly preserved, diners can feast on such one-Michelin-star delicacies as lobster with morel mushrooms and salmon filet with a crust of preserved garlic. The reasonably priced wine list is among the city's most extensive. Closed Sundays and Mondays. Reservations necessary. Major credit cards accepted. 5 Rue Montesquieu (phone: 56-79-10-10; fax: 56-79-09-10).

Le Clavel Saint-Jean Tasty variations on regional specialties, such as *lapereau à la royale* (rabbit stuffed with foie gras) and *lamproie à la bordelaise,* are served in a historic 19th-century structure with stonework decorations. There also is a 5,000-bottle wine cellar. Closed Saturday lunch and Sundays. Reservations advised. Major credit cards accepted. 44 Rue Charles-Domercq (phone: 56-92-63-07).

Jean Ramet This simple, well-loved place has friendly service, an intimate atmosphere, and well-prepared food that has earned a star from Michelin. Popular entrées include *salade tiède de homard* (warm lobster salad) and turbot braised with Médoc wine. Try the *délice glacé praliné* (frozen praline delight) for dessert. Lunch prices are agreeably low. Closed Saturday lunch, Sundays, and two weeks in August. Reservations advised. Major credit cards accepted.

Near Pl. de la Bourse, at 7 Pl. Jean-Jaurès (phone: 56-44-12-51; fax: 56-52-19-80).

Pavillon des Boulevards Another fine, one-Michelin-star restaurant, this one is notable for its various lobster dishes, rabbit with carrot and rosemary sauce, and chocolate puff pastries. The extensive wine list concentrates on red and white Bordeaux. Closed Saturday lunch, Sundays, and the last two weeks in August. Reservations advised. Major credit cards accepted. 120 Rue Croix de Seguey (phone: 56-81-51-02; fax: 56-51-14-58).

Les Plaisirs d'Ausone This lovely restaurant is becoming a local favorite for such specialties as scampi with baby cabbage and pear-honey gratin. There's also an excellent wine list. Closed Saturday lunch, Sundays, Mondays, and two weeks in both February and August. Reservations advised. Major credit cards accepted. 10 Rue Ausone (phone: 56-79-30-30; fax: 56-51-38-16).

Le Rouzic A one-Michelin-star restaurant with a family feel; the fare and extensive wine list, however, put this place in a luxury class. Specialties include a foie gras terrine with morel mushrooms, and puff pastry stuffed with rabbit and rosemary. Closed Saturday lunch and Sundays. Reservations necessary. Major credit cards accepted. 34 Cours Chapeau Rouge (phone: 56-44-39-11; fax: 56-40-55-10).

Le Vieux Bordeaux You'll appreciate the refined cooking—it has been awarded one Michelin star—and the elegant surroundings here. The menu's highlights include truffle omelettes, duck with peaches, and creative desserts, such as *nougat glacé au coulis de framboises* (iced nougat with raspberry sauce). Closed Saturday lunch, Sundays, and three weeks in August. Reservations necessary for dinner. MasterCard and Visa accepted. 27 Rue Buhan (phone: 56-52-94-36; fax: 56-44-25-11).

MODERATE

Le Bistrot du Sommelier The wine list here is outstanding and reasonably priced, as one would expect in a restaurant run by a former sommelier, and the bistro cooking is hearty and excellent; if you're feeling adventurous, the *pied de porc* (pig's foot) really is delicious. Closed Saturday lunch and Sundays. Reservations advised. MasterCard and Visa accepted. 167 Rue G. Bonnac (phone: 56-96-71-78).

Chez Philippe This friendly seafood restaurant on one of Bordeaux's loveliest squares is a great spot for a romantic tête-à-tête, especially at one of the tables outside in warm weather. Try the mussels with fresh herbs or various fish served with aioli (garlic mayonnaise). Closed Sundays, the first week of January, and the month of August. Reservations advised. Major credit cards accepted. 1 Pl. du Parlement (phone: 56-81-83-15; fax: 56-79-19-36).

Didier Gélineau The young chef at this welcoming restaurant is attracting a loyal following for dishes like sea scallops in their own roe and orange-flavored *crème brûlée*. Closed Saturday lunch in summer; Sundays, except for lunch in winter; and Mondays. Reservations advised. Major credit cards accepted. 26 Rue Pas-St-Georges (phone: 56-52-84-25; fax: 56-51-93-25).

Gravelier Recently opened in the Chartrons district, this restaurant features light, inventive dishes, such as couscous with tuna and *tarte tatin* (caramelized upside-down tart) with mangos. Closed Saturday lunch, Sundays, and two weeks in both January and August. Reservations necessary. MasterCard and Visa accepted. 114 Cours Verdun (phone: 56-48-17-15; fax: 56-51-96-07).

Le Mably This bustling brasserie's decor is so classic (moleskin benches and big mirrors) that at first it looks like a movie set, but it's for real. It has a huge local following, especially at lunch, when almost everyone seems to order the steak *tartare*. Closed Thursday, Friday, and Saturday dinner; Sundays; and two weeks in August. Reservations advised. Major credit cards accepted. 12 Rue Mably (phone: 56-44-30-10).

La Tupina The classic cooking of southwest France is the strength of this friendly restaurant. The *frites à l'ancienne* (potatoes sautéed in duck fat) and the *terrine de foie gras de canard aux truffes* (duck foie gras with truffles) are irresistible. Closed Sundays and holidays. Reservations advised. Major credit cards accepted. 6 Rue Porte-de-la-Monnaie (phone: 56-91-56-37; fax: 56-31-92-11).

INEXPENSIVE

Darricau This is the crème de la crème of pâtisseries/*salons de thé* (teashops). Sit in the upstairs salon if it's open (its windows look out onto the pleasant little square) and take a minute to admire the mirrored Art Deco doors (leading to *les toilettes*) on the landing. Open daily. Reservations unnecessary. Major credit cards accepted. 7 Pl. Gambetta (phone: 56-44-21-49).

Jegher Dating from 1856, it offers out-of-this-world pastries, chocolates, and ice cream in an Old World setting. Closed Sundays in summer. Reservations unnecessary. No credit cards accepted. Across from the *Jardin Public,* at 36 Cours de Verdun (phone: 56-52-15-28).

Le Port de la Lune This classic bistro is a favorite among Bordeaux's young and trendy night owls (it's open until 2 AM). Classic dishes include green salad with chicken livers, steak with french fries, and excellent raw oyster platters. The prix fixe menu, with wine included, is a real bargain. Open daily. Reservations advised. MasterCard and Visa accepted. 59 Quai Paludate (phone: 56-49-15-55).

BARS AND CAFÉS

L'Ecluse (15 Allées de Tourny; phone: 56-81-49-94), a branch of the chic Paris wine bar, is devoted exclusively to wines from the Bordeaux region. Simple dishes can be ordered to accompany the excellent selection of wines, which come by the glass or bottle.

Step through the door at *Le Lug* (5 Rue des Faussets; phone: 56-81-04-87), and you suddenly go from Vieux Bordeaux to Greenwich Village. This little coffeehouse is filled with Parsons tables and benches, original works by local artists, and a sideboard laden with cheeses, breads, and desserts. Come here for lunch or an evening snack; it's open until 1 AM (closed Sundays). When the weather chills, you can sip your coffee on the couch in front of the fire. Another popular coffee bar is *Brûlerie Gama* (off Pl. Gambetta, at 111 Rue Porte-Dijeaux; phone: 56-48-15-17), where you can quaff a quick cup of coffee or cappuccino counterside. It's open weekdays, during business hours only.

Cannes

Some towns are important as centers of political power, commerce, or industry, others as the focus of artistic creativity or religious pilgrimage. Cannes is none of these: Its raison d'être is pleasure, and whatever business transactions take place are likely to be done over a shrimp salad at a beachside restaurant or an aperitif on the terrace of one of the great seafront hotels. The majority of the 70,000 people who live in Cannes work in the service industry, and even they manage to make their labors their pleasures.

It would be difficult to have it otherwise along La Croisette, the splendid promenade of palms and plane trees that curves gently around the bay. It's lined on one side with dazzling white hotels—"palaces," the French call them—and condominiums; on the other, with the tempting gravelly sands of the well-kept beaches. The whole is framed by the Esterel plateau, its deep red, even purple, rocky soil thickly overgrown with pines, cork oaks, and lavender. The air is sweet with the scent of the roses, mimosa, and begonias of the town's gardens. In the old port, only a few diligent fishing boats bob up and down among the hundreds of motor launches and yachts of the idle rich.

Yet the French didn't realize the pleasurable possibilities of this exquisite bay until relatively recently. In 1834, Lord Brougham of England was obliged to spend the night in Cannes; the bouillabaisse he dined on that evening and his walk along the seafront the next morning persuaded him that Cannes offered a delightful respite from the winter chills of the north. After a distinguished political career, Brougham built a home here. He was followed by the fashionable aristocracy of Europe, who constructed grandiose villas, a yacht club, and a casino. Gradually, the French realized that in Cannes they might have a gold mine.

The French contingent was led by the writer Prosper Mérimée. Best known for the story of *Carmen* that inspired Bizet's opera, Mérimée first came to Cannes on a business trip. He ended up staying to cure his asthma and eventually died here in 1870. Other notables followed, including Guy de Maupassant, who sailed in Cannes Bay for many years, and Frédéric Mistral, who wrote poems about the city.

During the Belle Epoque, Cannes was clearly established as a major magnet for a sparkling society of princes, archdukes, successful artists, and their retinue of mistresses. Before he became King Edward VII, the Prince of Wales liked to sail his royal yacht into the harbor and dally there with his mistress of the moment. In the 1920s, the city came to represent the hedonism characteristic of that decade, and no edifice better epitomized the spirit of the times than the *Carlton,* the preposterous, glorious wedding cake of a hotel. Chartres may have its cathedral, and Versailles its palace, but Cannes has its grand hotels. People will argue forever over the relative merits of the *Majestic,* the *Martinez,* the *Noga Hilton*—or the *Carlton*—and though their budgets may not be able to afford the price of a room, they'll at least check out the bar on the terrace and, for a half hour or so, join the Cannes "elite."

The glitterati keep coming, too, along with expense-accounted visitors on convention junkets. Their real moment in the sun, as it were, is the *International Film Festival,* which has placed Cannes second only to Hollywood as a focus for the world's movie industry.

The Cannois are a colorful mixture of retired Parisians, affluent former refugees from Eastern Europe and North Africa, and wealthy transplants from the oil kingdoms of the Persian Gulf and war-torn Lebanon (you'll notice that the signs in many banks and jewelry shops are posted in French, English, and Arabic). The domain of the true Cannes natives is north and west of the Vieux Port (Old Harbor), and there you'll see men lobbing *boules* in the sandy gravel under the plane trees that shade the Allées de la Liberté. In the Vieux Port itself, seamen putter about in their boats, painting and varnishing, as in any other Mediterranean port. It's just a few yards away from the gaudy glitter of La Croisette, but it's a whole different world.

Cannes At-a-Glance

SEEING THE CITY

Cannes boasts (literally) an area unashamedly called Super-Cannes, high on a hill about 2½ miles (4 km) from the center of town, where the panorama of Cannes, the Iles de Lérins, the Esterel range, and the Riviera coast merits the name. To get to Super-Cannes, drive north on Boulevard de la République and east on Avenue de Vallauris, then turn left onto Chemin des Collines. Also recommended is the romantic nighttime view of the city lights from the tower and ramparts up on Le Suquet, a hill at the western edge of town (see below).

SPECIAL PLACES

The Vieux Port divides the two sections of Cannes. To the west (and north) is the "old town," topped by Le Suquet. East of the port is the more modern resort, strung along the tree-lined promenade that traces the curve of the bay.

LA CROISETTE Rarely has a town been so dominated by one street as Cannes is by the Boulevard de la Croisette, a seafront promenade that provides an indispensable introduction to the town's glossy elegance. A walk of a mile and a half will take you from the Vieux Port at its western end past cafés, antiques shops, art galleries, boutiques, and the great hotels—beware of Rolls-Royces gliding silently from the driveways—to the quieter residential neighborhood. The best time for people watching is between 11 AM and noon, when the late risers are looking for a salad-brunch on the beach, and at the end of the afternoon, when the "beautiful people" are out admiring each other's suntans and clothes (nighttime brings out male and female prostitutes). In the gardens of the more sedate condominium stretch of La Croisette is a marvelous profusion (according to season) of primroses, cyclamens, snapdragons, begonias, pink and white blossoming tamarisks, and red and purple bougainvillea. The best public displays are the 14,000 roses of the *Parc de la Roseraie,* just north of the modern Port Canto yacht basin.

LA MALMAISON Housed in this charming, renovated Italianate building is Cannes's directorate of cultural affairs. Also here are temporary art exhibits, which change about every six weeks. Closed Tuesdays and holidays. Admission charge for exhibits. 47 La Croisette (phone: 93-99-04-04).

POINTE DE LA CROISETTE This promontory at the far eastern end of La Croisette closes the bay of Cannes and embraces the town's second harbor, Port Canto, which has become the favored mooring spot for some of the Mediterranean's most luxurious yachts. The nearby *Palm Beach Casino,* once a symbol of Cannes's perennial insouciance, is now closed, and its future is uncertain. The *Palm Beach*'s own little harbor is the home of the ultra-swank *Yacht Club.*

BEACHES These spotless golden strands are the town's pride and joy, swept and sifted daily and reinforced with new sand at the slightest hint of erosion. They are divided into three areas: two stretches of mainly public beach—the Plages du Midi beyond the Vieux Port on the west side of town and the Plage Gazagnaire around Pointe de la Croisette on the east side of town—plus the mainly private beaches along La Croisette, attached to the big hotels or beachfront restaurant concessions. You can picnic and bathe for free on the public beaches—Gazagnaire is good for morning sun, the Plages du Midi better for the afternoon. But the more chic Croisette beaches are open to anybody willing to rent a beach mattress and/or umbrella. Waiters will serve you drinks, snacks, and desserts right there by your mattress. Pedal boats may be rented on the beaches, too.

PALAIS DES FESTIVALS (PALACE OF FESTIVALS) At the western end of La Croisette, overlooking the Vieux Port, this sprawling, five-tiered beige and white convention hall is the home of the *International Film Festival* and other shows throughout the year. Many find its north front a little forbidding—the film crowd calls it the "bunker"—but the formal gardens at the rear with a small amphitheater, fountains, and reflecting pools offer a pleasant refuge from the madding crowd. Besides a formidable array of business facilities, the *Palais* houses the city's tourist office (see *Tourist Information*) and the *Casino Croisette,* which also includes a nightclub, *Le Jimmy'z de Régine,* and a room filled with slot machines (see *Nightclubs and Nightlife*). The walkway around the *Palais* and adjoining the Esplanade Georges-Pompidou is a "starwalk" of sorts, where film actors (mostly French) have imprinted their hands in wet cement.

VIEUX PORT (OLD PORT) A great place to browse in the early morning, when the few remaining "old salts" are fixing up their boats. On the Jetée Albert-Edouard, which forms the eastern arm of the port, is the *Gare Maritime*, from which bay cruises depart to the Iles de Lérins (see *Boat*, below).

RUE MEYNADIER Before Cannes became a resort town, this was its Main Street. Splendid carved doors are still visible on the 18th-century houses of the town's wealthier merchants from that era (a particularly fine specimen is No. 18). Today, it's a lively pedestrian shopping zone (see *Shopping*, below).

ALLÉES DE LA LIBERTÉ Running east of the *Mairie* (City Hall) in front of the harbor, these delightful avenues of plane trees shelter a flower market every morning except Mondays, *boules* players in the afternoon, and a flea market on Saturdays. Just north of the Allées, in the little Square Brougham, is a statue of the English lord who "created" modern Cannes.

LE SUQUET Also known as Mont-Chevalier or *La Castre* (The Fortress), this is the little fortified hill to which old Cannes clung in medieval days under the nominal protection of the abbots of the Iles de Lérins. Narrow streets, some of them just a series of spiraling steps, wind their way up around the hill. Rue Louis-Perrissol takes you to the ramparts and square tower, the *Tour de Mont-Chevalier*, erected at the top between 1070 and 1385 as a lookout against invading pirates. The late Gothic church nearby, *Notre-Dame-d'Espérance* (phone: 93-39-17-49) was completed in the 17th century and has a madonna to which miraculous powers were attributed.

Just south of the church is the 12th-century Romanesque *Chapelle Ste-Anne* with its 15th-century woodcarvings, which is part of the *Musée de la Castre*. The museum draws on the wide-ranging archaeological collections donated to the town in the 19th century by the Dutch Baron Lycklama. Pride of place is given to sculpture, ceramics, and artifacts of the Mediterranean (Egyptian, Greek, Roman, Etruscan, and North African) and the Middle East (Babylonian and Persian). There also are fine pre-Columbian sculptures and weavings from Mexico; exhibits of Chinese porcelain and sculpture, Japanese military uniforms, and sculptures from Thailand and Laos; plus a fine collection of regional paintings. Closed Tuesdays and holidays. Admission charge (phone: 93-38-55-26).

EXTRA SPECIAL

The terrace of the *Carlton* hotel bar is perhaps the best-known spot in Cannes, yet many people—either motivated by reverse snobbery or intimidated by the price of a drink—steer clear of it. They are really missing out, for the terrace epitomizes the quintessence of Cannes's mystique, a stage for whatever is magical or merely gloriously vulgar about the town.

Think of the exorbitantly priced cocktail as your ticket to one of the great shows of European razzmatazz. Curtain time is around 9 PM nightly, and the show goes on, on balmy nights, into the wee hours of the morning (see *Checking In*).

Sources and Resources

TOURIST INFORMATION

The Cannes *Office du Tourisme* (*Palais des Festivals*; phone: 93-39-24-53 or 92-99-84-22) is open daily in July, August, and during the *Film Festival* in May; closed Sundays September through June. It provides brochures and maps and arranges guided tours of the surrounding countryside. There's a branch of the tourist office at the train station (Pl. Semard; phone: 93-99-19-77); it's closed weekends.

LOCAL COVERAGE The principal daily newspaper of the Côte d'Azur, *Nice-Matin*, has a regional edition for Cannes and Grasse worth consulting for information about movies, concerts, and other events. *Paris–Côte d'Azur* is a bimonthly magazine covering cultural and social events in Cannes; the monthly *Gault Millau* magazine publishes a detailed Cannes restaurant guide in its May issue to coincide with the film festival. Bookstores often stock back issues if you're here later in the summer. Newspapers and magazines can be found on newsstands along La Croisette. At the tourist office pick up the indispensable, free booklet *Le Mois à Cannes,* packed with useful addresses and information on what's happening, and *7 Jours et 7 Nuits,* a free weekly guide to the Côte d'Azur. Another weekly guide, the excellent *Semaine des Spectacles de la Côte d'Azur,* is on sale at bookstores. All of the above are in French.

TELEPHONE The city codes for Cannes are 92 and 93, which are incorporated into all local eight-digit numbers. When calling a number in Cannes from the Paris region (including the Ile-de-France), dial 16, wait for a dial tone, then dial the eight-digit number. When calling a number from outside Paris, dial only the eight-digit number.

GETTING AROUND

AIRPORT The nearest airport for domestic and international flights is the *Aéroport Nice–Côte d'Azur* (phone: 93-21-30-30 or 93-21-30-12), about 15 miles (25 km) east of Cannes. A taxi from the airport to Cannes costs about 350F (around $60 at press time). For about the same price, if you're traveling alone, you can take a 10-minute helicopter shuttle through *Héli-Air Monaco* (phone: 93-21-34-95, in Nice). A much cheaper alternative is the bus service which operates daily between the airport and the *Hôtel de Ville* terminus in Cannes; for more information, call *Rapides Côte d'Azur* (14 Rue François-Guisol; phone: 93-55-24-00 in Nice; 93-39-11-39 in Cannes) or

Autocars Nesa-Tavanti (*Gare Routière;* phone: 93-88-18-48), both in Nice, or the tourist office in Cannes. There's also hourly train service from the airport to Cannes (see *Train,* below, or call 93-87-50-50 or 93-25-54-54 for train information in Nice); the trip takes 20 minutes and costs around 29F (about $5 at press time).

BOAT Boats leave daily from the Jetée Albert-Edouard (phone: 93-39-11-82) for day trips to the Iles de Lérins. The excursion takes in Ile Ste-Marguerite, fragrant with eucalyptus and pine forests, and Ile St-Honorat, the site of an ancient fortified monastery. The legendary "man in the iron mask," immortalized by Alexandre Dumas *père,* was imprisoned on Ste-Marguerite in the *Fort Royal.*

BUS The terminus of the *Société des Transports Urbains de Cannes* (*STUC*; phone: 93-39-18-71) is at the Place de l'Hôtel-de-Ville. Seven main routes operate in town, and minibus No. 8 runs along La Croisette to Palm Beach, on the Pointe de la Croisette. The standard bus fare is about 7F (around $1.20 at press time), and economical *carnets* (booklets) of 10 tickets are available for about 48F (around $8.25 at press time). Buses also leave approximately every hour daily from the *Hôtel de Ville* terminus for the Nice airport (see *Airport,* above).

CAR RENTAL *Avis* (69 La Croisette; phone: 93-94-15-86); *Budget* (160 Rue d'Antibes; phone: 93-99-44-04); *Europcar* (3 Rue du Commandant-Vidal; phone: 93-39-75-20); and *Hertz* (147 Rue d'Antibes; phone: 93-99-04-20) are represented.

TAXI Meter rates operate inside town; set rates are used for excursions beyond the city limits. There are stands at the Place de l'Hôtel-de-Ville (phone: 93-39-60-80), at the train station (Pl. Pierre-Semard; phone: 93-38-30-79), and outside the main hotels, most conveniently at the *Majestic* (phone: 93-99-52-10) and the *Carlton* (phone: 93-38-09-76).

TRAIN Most trains running along the coast between Marseilles and Nice stop in Cannes. *Gare SNCF* (phone: 93-99-50-50 or 93-99-19-77) is at Place Pierre-Semard, a few blocks inland from La Croisette.

SPECIAL EVENTS

There are a number of citywide celebrations throughout the year, but the *Film Festival* gets top billing.

FAVORITE FÊTE

Festival International du Film For two weeks every May, the suntanned starlets, stogie-smoking producers, and phalanxes of tuxedoed moguls always portrayed in the tabloids are indeed part of the *Cannes Festival*—but that's only the glamorous tip of the moviedom iceberg. The festival also is a 24-hour-a-day bazaar where executives hailing from as far away as Hong Kong, Ankara, and New Delhi peddle and purchase hundreds of surefire hits along the lines of *Terminator XII* or *Die Hard X.* Some 40,000 cinema pros throng the *Palais du Festival* and the dozens of theaters and screening rooms between Rue d'Antibes and the sea. Some 400 pictures are shown that are not even competing for the coveted prize, the Palme d'Or. For just plain film fans, the mid-May fantasia is a chance to see everything that is old, new, borrowed, and especially blue in an atmosphere that blends Hollywood, the Riviera, and the suqs (open-air markets) of Damascus. If you're not accredited as a professional, you probably won't get tickets for the main festival screenings, but you can catch screenings of films that are not part of the competition. *Palais des Festivals* (phone: 93-39-01-01).

In January, the *Marché International du Disque et de l'Edition Musicale (MIDEM)* draws professionals of the classical and popular music recording and publishing industries. *Carnaval de Cannes* takes place on the last Sunday of March. In May, there's an international horse show, *Concours Hippique,* at the *Stade des Hespérides.* On *Bastille Day* (July 14), on *Ste-Marie,* or *Assumption, Day* (August 15), and on the anniversary of the 1944 liberation of Cannes (August 24), fireworks light up the bay. July also brings a music festival at Le Suquet, along with jazz and theater festivals. The *Yacht Club* stages a *Regatta* in September, and in October, *Vidcom* brings the video industry to town (the tourist office can tell you how to get into the convention to see the latest gadgetry).

SHOPPING

La Croisette is the location of most of the town's elegant shops, but many also are found inside the great hotels. For instance, the shopping center near the *Gray d'Albion* hotel, in the luxury complex of the same name, is perhaps the most opulent on the Côte d'Azur. The second main shopping street, running parallel to the seafront, is the Rue d'Antibes, with a slightly more democratic mix of prices, from the expensive to the downright moderate.

Cannes is *not* a good town for buying art and antiques, though there are plenty of both. There seems to be nothing really inexpensive here, but the best bet for a bargain is at the *Marché aux Puces* (Flea Market), held on the Allées de la Liberté on Saturdays. In addition, there are many shops under the medieval arches of Le Suquet (see *Special Places*), where a market is held every morning except Sundays.

The Rue Meynadier pedestrian zone is devoted mainly to high class food shops, many of which package wines and food delicacies for shipment abroad. This area is also popular among the attractive young Cannois for the bargains to be had in the trendy, open-air boutiques that overflow into the street. If you're buying food for immediate consumption, don't forget the *Marché Forville* (closed Mondays), the covered food market in Le Suquet near the Vieux Port.

For standard shopping hours, see GETTING READY TO GO. Here are some other noteworthy emporia:

Alexandra High class women's wear: Chloé, Jean-Louis Scherrer, Giorgio Armani, and Christian Lacroix. Rond-Point Duboys-d'Angers (phone: 93-38-41-29).

Cannes English Bookshop As advertised, this place stocks English-language books. 11 Rue Bivouac Napoléon (phone: 93-99-40-08).

Cannolive Over 100 years old, this shop features olive oil, Provençal liqueurs, and orange wine (a local aperitif). 16 Rue Vénizelos (phone: 93-39-08-19).

Cartier Home of the ultimate in jewelry and leather goods. 57 La Croisette (phone: 93-99-58-73).

Ernest A first class charcuterie specializing in exquisite pâtés. Its pastry shop is across the street. 52 Rue Meynadier (phone: 93-39-25-96; pastry shop, 93-39-19-07).

La Ferme Savoyarde Great for cheese. 22 Rue Meynadier (phone: 93-39-63-68).

Gérard Jewelry designs with a touch of fantasy. In the *Majestic,* 14 La Croisette (phone: 92-98-77-00).

Hermès Quite apart from the classic leathers and silks, they make the world's greatest beach towels. *Gray d'Albion Shopping Center,* 17 La Croisette (phone: 93-39-08-90).

Maiffret The venerable manufacturer of sinfully good chocolates and candy, particularly the local specialty, candied fruits. Watch them being made in the mezzanine "lab." 31 Rue d'Antibes (phone: 93-39-08-29).

Benito et Fils Classic and modern chinaware and silver. 109 Rue d'Antibes (phone: 93-38-54-06).

SPORTS AND FITNESS

For more information about sports, call the *Office Municipal de la Jeunesse,* 2 Quai St-Pierre (phone: 93-38-21-16 or 93-99-20-96).

BICYCLING Great for exploring the surrounding countryside, bicycles and motorcycles can be rented at *Fam Corot* (54 Rue Georges-Clemenceau; phone: 93-39-22-82); *Cannes Location Rent* (5 Rue Allieis; phone: 93-39-46-15); or the *Gare SNCF* (Pl. Pierre-Semard; phone: 93-47-01-01).

BOATING The *Centre Nautique Municipal* (Base du Mouré Rouge; 9 Rue Esprit-Violet; phone: 93-43-83-48) rents sailboats and offers instruction. Sailboats and motorboats are also for rent at *New Boat* (Port de la Napoule; phone: 93-93-12-34).

BOULES This is the most relaxing spectator sport in town, and it's free. Go to the *Boulodrome de la Pantiero* on Allées de la Liberté.

GOLF Two top-flight layouts are a short distance from Cannes.

TOP TEE-OFF SPOTS

Cannes Mandelieu This 6,300-yard, par 71 course, set among beautiful pine trees, is one of France's oldest clubs. It's also a popular one, hosting 60,000 players each year. The *Majestic* hotel offers golf packages here, and electric carts are available. Closed Tuesdays. In Mandelieu, 4 miles (6 km) west of town on N7 (phone: 93-49-5539).

Country-Club de Cannes-Mougins Home to 500 members from 28 countries, this club hosts the annual *Cannes-Mougins Open,* a stop on the PGA European Tour. The 18-hole course is 6,700 yards, par 72; the clubhouse is in a restored olive mill. Closed Mondays. Four miles (6 km) north of Cannes at 175 Rte. d'Antibes, Mougins (phone: 93-75-79-13; fax: 93-75-27-60).

SCUBA DIVING Contact the *Centre Nautique Municipal* (see *Boating,* above).

SWIMMING Pool fanciers who aren't lodging at one of the pricier hotels can try the *Piscine Municipale* (Av. Pierre-de-Coubertin; phone: 93-47-12-94). It's closed weekends.

SPORT FISHING Deep-sea fishing is organized by the *Club de Pêche Sportive de Cannes* (phone: 93-63-78-30). Fishing equipment is available at *La Cible 06* (13 Bd. Carnot; phone: 93-99-24-02) and at *Rizzi Serge* (5 Rue Félix-Faure; phone: 93-39-10-41).

TENNIS Your hotel can help you get one of 10 courts at the *Complexe Sportif Montfleury* (23 Av. Beauséjour; phone: 93-38-75-78); five clay courts at the *Gallia Tennis Club* (30 Bd. Montfleury; phone: 93-99-23-20); five clay courts at *Tennis de l'Aérodrome* (220 Av. Francis-Tonner; phone: 93-47-05-82); or 18 hard courts at *Tennis Municipal de la Bastide* (230 Av. Francis-Tonner; phone: 93-47-68-21). Lessons are available at the *Martinez* hotel's *Cannes Tennis Martinez* (11 Rue Lacour; phone: 93-43-58-85), which has seven outdoor courts.

WINDSURFING The *Centre Nautique Municipal* (see *Boating*) rents equipment and offers instruction.

MUSIC

The *Orchestre Cannes–Provence–Côte d'Azur* gives classical music concerts in the *Salle Claude-Debussy* of the *Palais des Festivals* (see *Special Places*). Chamber music recitals can be heard at *Notre-Dame-d'Espérance* on Le

Suquet; call the church at 93-39-17-49 for more information. The tourist office also can provide concert information.

NIGHTCLUBS AND NIGHTLIFE

The smartest discos—don't go before midnight—are *Jane's* in the *Gray d'Albion* (see *Checking In*) and *Le Jimmy'z de Regine* in the *Casino Croisette* (*Palais des Festivals;* phone: 93-68-00-07). Gays and celebrities—and gay celebrities—dance under laser beams at the *Whiskey-à-Go-Go* (115 Av. de Lérins; phone: 93-43-20-63). *La Chunga* (72 La Croisette; phone: 93-94-11-29) is another current hot spot. *L'Amiral,* the piano bar at the *Martinez* (see *Checking In*) showcases the considerable talent of American expatriate Jimmy McKissic, whose expansive personality is an attraction in itself.

The other action in town is gambling, and there are three places in Cannes where you can get in on it: the *Casino Croisette* at the *Palais des Festivals* (phone: 93-38-12-11), open from 5 PM to 4 AM; the *Carlton Casino Club* at the *Carlton* hotel (phone: 93-68-00-33), open from 4 PM to 4 AM weekdays, and to 5 AM Fridays and Saturdays; and the *Casino Riviera* at the *Noga Hilton* (phone: 93-68-43-43), open from 7 PM to 4 AM. The games available include French and English roulette, baccarat, punto banco, trente-et-quarante, chemin de fer, and craps. There's an admission charge at all three casinos, and you'll need your passport. Gentlemen must wear a jacket and tie.

The *Casino Croisette* also has a huge array of *machines à sous*—slot machines—which have made it the most heavily played casino on the Côte d'Azur. You can play them from 11 AM to 4 the next morning. No jackets and ties are required to play the slot machines. The *boule* room here also offers a more proletarian form of low-stakes roulette, in which a golf-size ball teeters around a tableful of numbers. For additional details on casinos, see *Casinos Royale* in DIVERSIONS.

Best in Town

CHECKING IN

It's neither possible nor desirable to do Cannes on the cheap. This is an expensive resort town where the Mediterranean is the whole story, and it's just no fun being in a third-rate hotel far from the sea. Double occupancy for less than $100 is hard to come by, unless you book several months in advance. During the film festival, in May, prices rise dramatically, and hotels always are booked; be prepared to reserve *very* early—possibly years in advance. In season, expect to pay $350 to $400 and way up per night for a double room with continental breakfast in very expensive hotels (the so-called palaces); $200 to $350 in expensive hotels; $100 to $200 in moderate places; and less than $100 in inexpensive ones. Unless otherwise noted, all hotels listed below feature air conditioning, telephones, TV sets, and private baths in the rooms. All are open year-round and accept major credit cards, unless otherwise indicated.

For an unforgettable experience, we begin with our favorite Cannes hostelries, all in the very expensive category, followed by our cost and quality choices of hotels, listed by price category.

ROOMS AT THE TOP

Carlton Inter-Continental This great white-turreted doyenne presides over La Croisette like some permanent sand castle for seaside royalty, complete with swaying green palm trees and blue and white umbrellas to shade some of the most beautiful bodies in Europe. The decor is decidedly Belle Epoque; the 325 rooms and 30 suites have modern comforts (including stereos, mini-bars, and in-room movies). The bathrooms alone are monumental enough to justify a good part of the price, and the view is magnificent. The 13-room penthouse Imperial Suite offers every imaginable comfort at $6,000 a day. Service is efficient without being obsequious—except during film festival time, when all bets are off. In addition to the famous main bar and terrace, there's a delightful, intimate, smaller bar off the lobby. The *Carlton Casino Club* (see *Nightclubs and Nightlife*) is one of Cannes's premier gaming rooms. There is also a fitness center where you can work off the to-die-for food you sampled at *La Belle Otéro* and *La Côte* restaurants (see *Eating Out* for both). There's a private beach, but no pool. Count on reserving *well* in advance. 58 La Croisette (phone: 93-68-91-68; 800-327-0200 in the US; fax: 93-38-20-90).

Majestic Many connoisseurs insist this is the best of the "palaces," more sophisticated than its more celebrated rival, the *Carlton*. Certainly the 248 rooms and 13 suites and their amenities are impeccable, and the service is very good. Its great asset is the lovely seawater pool in tree-shaded grounds that set the hotel quietly back from the bustling Croisette. Its restaurant, *Le Sunset,* is quite good, and the bar and terrace are a joy. 6 La Croisette (phone: 92-98-77-00; fax: 93-38-97-90).

Martinez The largest hotel in town, now part of the Concorde group, this luxurious establishment offers elegance and pluperfect service. All 418 rooms and 12 suites are tastefully appointed with Art Deco furnishings; no less magnificent are the restaurants, *La Palme d'Or* (see *Eating Out*), which has won two coveted Michelin stars for its fare, and *L'Orangerie,* a delightful bistro. Other amenities include a pool, a private beach, a tennis club with seven courts, and *L'Amiral,* a piano bar. Closed mid-November through mid-

January. On Cannes Bay, at 73 La Croisette (phone: 92-98-73-00; 800-888-4747; fax: 93-39-67-82).

Noga Hilton This 180-room, 45-suite, ultramodern hotel—the latest pretender to "palais" status—opened its doors in 1992. It was built, at a cost of more than $100 million, in the center of La Croisette on the site of Cannes's old *Palais des Festivals*. Everything about it shows a grandeur of design and a faultless attention to detail, from its cathedral-like white marble lobby to the bright, spacious rooms to the rooftop pool and terrace with spectacular views in all directions. All rooms are equipped with satellite TV, VCRs, fax lines, mini-bars, safes, and huge marble bathrooms. The hotel has a fine restaurant, *La Scala,* with a terrace overlooking La Croisette; a brasserie, *Le Grand Bleu;* a private beach with a restaurant open for lunch in season; and a piano bar in the lobby. It's all part of the *Palais Croisette* complex, which includes a luxury shopping mall, an 850-seat auditorium and conference center, and the *Casino Riviera.* 50 La Croisette (phone: 92-99-70-00; 800-221-2424; fax: 92-99-70-11).

EXPENSIVE

Grand The most discreet of the "palaces," set back at the end of an avenue of palms, this is the place to get away from the mob in perfect modern comfort. Service and amenities in the 76 rooms and two apartments have an appropriate refinement, though swingers may find the bar a little *too* quiet. There's a restaurant. 45 La Croisette (phone: 93-38-15-45; fax: 93-68-97-45).

Gray d'Albion One of the most modern of Cannes's properties is part of a huge luxury shopping and apartment complex. The 186 rooms and 14 suites boast all the most up-to-date comforts, including phones in the bathrooms and VCRs in the suites. Although it's set away from the sea, the eighth and ninth floors have a Mediterranean view. The hotel has its own discotheque, *Jane's,* a piano bar, a private beach, and a great restaurant, *Royal Gray* (see *Eating Out*). 38 Rue des Serbes (phone: 92-99-79-79; fax: 93-99-26-10).

Sofitel-Méditerranée This lovely hostelry has 150 rooms, five suites, and perhaps the best view on the entire Côte d'Azur. Amenities include a good restaurant, tennis courts, and a pool. Closed mid-November through mid-December. At the western end of the Vieux Port, at 2 Bd. Jean-Hibert (phone: 92-99-73-00; 800-763-4835 in the US; fax: 92-99-73-29).

MODERATE

Beau Séjour Well equipped, with 46 rooms, it has its own pool and garden. The service is efficient, and the restaurant, less pretentious than those of the "palaces," is a pleasant surprise. Closed from mid-October through mid-December. About 300 yards from the beach, at 5 Rue des Fauvettes (phone: 93-39-63-00; fax: 92-98-64-66).

Primotel-Canberra Here are 42 simple but nicely done rooms, a small bar, and a quiet little garden, but no restaurant. In the shopping district, and just a few steps away from the beach, at 120 Rue d'Antibes (phone: 93-38-20-70; fax: 92-98-03-47).

Novotel-Montfleury In the middle of a park looking down a hill to the sea, this is the luxury spot for the sporting crowd. Guests can avail themselves of the heated pool, tennis courts, volleyball court, and skating rink (winter only) of the *Complexe Sportif Montfleury*. It's perhaps the one place in Cannes where you won't mind not being near La Croisette. The 180 rooms, many with spacious balconies, and the Presidential Suite are ultramodern and superbly furnished. Ask for a room above the fourth floor for a good view of the sea. 25 Av. Beauséjour (phone: 93-68-91-50; 800-221-4542 in the US; fax: 93-38-37-08).

Splendid This marvelous, white, 1870 wedding-cake hotel between La Croisette and Le Suquet hit the jackpot in 1982 when the *Palais des Festivals* was built right across the street. Combined with a ringside view of the *boules* games on the Allées de la Liberté as well as a panoramic view of the Vieux Port, it has one of the best locations in town. The 64 rooms are neat, pleasant, and comfortable with modern amenities, and 40 come with kitchenettes for those who want to take advantage of the nearby food market. There is no restaurant, but the breakfast service is fine, and the friendly and efficient staff makes you feel right at home. Allées de la Liberté, entrance at 4-6 Rue Félix-Faure (phone: 93-99-53-11; fax: 93-99-55-02).

INEXPENSIVE

Corona Here are 20 modest, clean rooms, but no restaurant. What you save on the hotel bill you can spend at the *Gray d'Albion Shopping Center* across the street. Closed mid-January through mid-February. A short walk from La Croisette and the railroad station, at 55 Rue d'Antibes (phone: 93-39-69-85; fax: 93-99-09-69).

EATING OUT

The local cooking is not especially Provençal—no more so than the resident population. But the fruit and vegetable season is longer than in other parts of France, and fresh fish is in abundance, so you can be assured of eating light and quickly prepared dishes. For ice cream lovers, Cannes is a paradise: Besides the traditional flavors, there are cream cheese sherbets and licorice, ginger, and honey ices. As with hotel prices, restaurant prices must be seen in a specifically Cannois context. Expect to pay $150 to $200 for a meal for two at an expensive restaurant; $70 to $150 at a moderate one; and less than $70 (indeed, sometimes as little as $25) at an inexpensive place. Prices include service (usually included in the bill automatically), but not drinks or wine. Unless otherwise noted, all restaurants listed below are open for lunch and dinner.

For an unforgettable culinary experience, we begin with our Cannes favorite, followed by our cost and quality choices of restaurants, listed by price category.

HAUTE GASTRONOMIE

Le Moulin de Mougins Fifteen minutes from town in the hills above Cannes, this 16th-century olive oil mill houses one of the Riviera's most glamorous restaurants, with a clientele to match. Dark wood beams stand out against rustic white walls, and the exotic garden is the "beaker full of the warm south" for which an old French poet once pined. Chef Roger Vergé's braised slivers of Provençal duck in honey and lemon sauce stand out as one of the plainer selections on an entrancing two-Michelin-star menu. Hoard your francs and don't miss the *salade mikado* (mushrooms, avocado, tomato, and truffles); violet asparagus with truffles; artichokes, scallops, and smoked salmon in lime sauce; and, for dessert, *soufflé glacé aux fraises des bois* (cold wild strawberry soufflé). Some reports have it that Vergé's gastronomic magic isn't what it used to be, and prices have been lowered in an effort to boost its sagging reputation. There are also five guestrooms, and organic products are sold in the adjacent boutique. Closed Mondays off-season, Thursday lunch, and late January through *Easter*. Reservations are essential, as are a jacket and tie for men. Major credit cards accepted. On D3 at Notre-Dame-de-Vie, 4 miles (6 km) north of Cannes (phone: 93-75-78-24; fax: 93-90-18-55).

EXPENSIVE

La Belle Otéro *Minestrone de homard en bouillon de crustacés* (lobster in a crustacean broth) and *filet mignon de veau en jus de osso-buco* (filet mignon of veal stewed with veal shin bones) are just two of the delectable specialties at this two-Michelin-star temple of gastronomy. Order a Côtes de Provence wine from the excellent list. Closed most of February, the first two weeks of November, and Sundays and Mondays off-season. Reservations necessary. Major credit cards accepted. In the *Carlton-Intercontinental* hotel, 58 La Croisette (phone: 93-39-69-69).

La Côte One of the most beautiful dining rooms in the south of France, it offers fine, light food that more than deserves its Michelin star. Try the fresh pasta with seafood or any fish dish. Closed Tuesdays, Wednesdays, and mid-

February through March. Reservations necessary. Major credit cards accepted. In the *Carlton-Intercontinental* hotel, 58 La Croisette (phone: 93-68-91-68).

La Palme d'Or Served in an Art Deco room hung with photos of Hollywood stars, this establishment's delectable and delicate Provençal fare has garnered two Michelin stars. A meal here should end with the beautiful cheese selection, a superb dessert—or both. Closed Mondays, Tuesday lunch, and mid-November through mid-January. Reservations necessary. Major credit cards accepted. In the *Martinez,* 73 La Croisette (phone: 92-98-74-14).

Royal Gray Until recently, this restaurant overlooking a garden held two Michelin stars, thanks to chef Jacques Chibois, who has moved on to open his own restaurant in Grasse. It's too soon to tell whether his successor, Michel Bigot, will recapture Chibois's glory (though Chibois's current role as a consultant should help). Still, this is one of Cannes's finest, offering inventive interpretations of classic fare. The prix fixe menu is an excellent value. The service is courteous, efficient, and not pompous, and the terrace is famous in its own right. Closed Mondays, Sundays in the off-season, and the month of February. Reservations necessary. Major credit cards accepted. In the *Gray d'Albion,* 38 Rue des Serbes (phone: 93-99-79-60).

MODERATE

Gaston et Gastounette This comfortable place facing the Vieux Port offers a variety of fish and Provençal dishes. Closed two weeks in mid-January. Reservations advised in summer. Major credit cards accepted. 7 Quai St-Pierre (phone: 93-39-47-92).

Au Mal Assis The fish here is first class, the service amiable. Closed November through mid-December. Reservations advised in season. MasterCard and Visa accepted. Nicely situated on the Vieux Port, at 15 Quai St-Pierre (phone: 93-39-13-38).

Le Maschou This place stands out for its good charcoal-grilled steaks and its candlelit setting, where the plain look pretty and the pretty stunning. It's a favorite with the *jeunesse dorée* (the "beautiful people"). Open daily for dinner only; closed November through mid-December. Reservations necessary. MasterCard and Visa accepted. 17 Rue St-Antoine (phone: 93-39-62-21).

La Mère Besson A rarity in Cannes: an authentic Provençal restaurant. It's very fashionable, always crowded, and everybody table-hops. Try the fragrant *daube provençale* (beef stew). Closed Sundays and Monday lunch in the off-season, and one week in February. Reservations necessary. Major credit cards accepted. 13 Rue des Frères-Pradignac (phone: 93-39-59-24).

Au Bec Fin Fine, straightforward cooking prevails here. The excellent steaks are served thick, the plain grilled fish—local *daurade* (sea bream), *rascasse* (hogfish), or sea bass—is graced with perhaps a touch of fennel, and the salads are among the best in town. Closed Saturday dinner, Sundays, and mid-December through mid-January. Reservations necessary. No credit cards accepted. Near the railroad station, at 12 Rue du 24-Août (phone: 93-38-35-86).

Chez Astoux Great platters of oysters, clams, mussels, sea urchins, winkles, crabs, and shrimp—not to mention scrumptious chocolate profiteroles—attract diners to this seafood bistro, where the atmosphere is noisy, lively, and friendly. Open daily. Reservations advised. MasterCard and Visa accepted. Close to the Vieux Port, at 43 Rue Félix-Faure (phone: 93-39-06-22).

BEACH RESTAURANTS

Strung along La Croisette, some of these establishments are connected to the big hotels. All are relatively expensive, but they're still a delightful way to enjoy the beach at lunchtime. Your best bet is to have the prix fixe menu of the day or a salad—*niçoise,* shrimp, or crabmeat—plus a small carafe of wine or mineral water, and maybe some strawberries. Service is slow, but nobody's in a hurry on the beach. The best people watching locations are the *Maschou Beach,* also known as *Plage du Festival* (phone: 93-39-37-37); *Hawaii Beach* (phone: 93-38-17-47); *Lido Plage* (phone: 93-38-25-44); *Plage Club des Sports* (phone: 93-38-59-72), where volleyball players go; and the *Plage des Sports* (phone: 93-47-49-62). Reservations are essential for all. Also excellent are *L'Ondine* (phone: 93-94-23-15), with some of the best cooking on the beach at the best prices, and *Le Goéland* (phone: 93-38-22-05), where lots of fresh vegetables garnish the fish dishes. For good salads, try *Volier* (phone: 93-94-25-46).

BARS AND CAFÉS

The *Petit Carlton* (93 Rue d'Antibes; phone: 93-39-27-25) is a friendly, somewhat scruffy tavern. Staked out at festival time by movie buffs who can't or don't want to afford the "other" *Carlton,* to which this one bears no relation (or resemblance), it serves edible meals and retains its counterculture ambience the rest of the year. For an English pub atmosphere, complete with dart games and *Rolling Stones* music, join the young clientele at *The Swan* (4 Rue Clemenceau; phone: 93-39-05-57). At the risk of tiresome repetition, the best hotel bars remain the *Carlton* terrace and the *Majestic* (which features superior potato chips).

Chartres

There still are places in the world where the center seems to hold, to paraphrase Yeats, and Chartres is one of them. Not far to the southwest of Paris, the medieval town wraps itself around its treasures—an incomparable cathedral and an unrivaled collection of stained glass and sculpture. For anyone scaling the steep, winding streets or wandering along the banks of the Eure River, with its reedy waters and stone bridges, there are no jarring notes.

Though Chartres no longer is the bustling crossroads that supported the extravagant building projects of the 13th century, it is still a prosperous market town, sitting at the center of some of France's richest arable land. On Saturdays, when the region's gardeners come out in force for the *Marché des Fleurs* (Flower Market) and farmers stack their produce under the arches of the covered market, crowds of shoppers mill around well-kept stores in the pedestrian zones. In the back streets, matronly neighbors gossip from their windows, and inviting courtyards offer glimpses of ancient iron pumps and greenery within. On the feast days that draw backpack-laden pilgrims to special services at the cathedral, there may be a tousle-headed ascetic pacing the cobbles and wrangling with himself, a reminder of the many pilgrims who have passed this way.

Ongoing excavations have revealed that a settlement flourished here under the Romans, who called it "the town of the Carnutes"—after the Gallic tribe of the area—and built a forum, an amphitheater, and a temple on the banks of the Eure. Before Roman culture and, later, Christianity took hold, Chartres was an important druidic religious center; in fact, the Roman temple and the town's first Christian church, built in the 4th century on the temple site, appear to have been erected on a spot hallowed by the druids. After 876, when Charles the Bald, the French king, gave the city the *Sancta Camisia* (the robe Mary is said to have worn when she gave birth to Christ), Chartres became an important center of the cult of the Virgin Mary.

By the end of the 10th century, under the leadership of counts such as Thibaut the Cheat, Chartres had become one of Europe's most exciting cities. It was a center of learning, the home of Bishop Fulbert, who built a predecessor of Chartres's cathedral; of Bernard of Chartres, a theologian who lived here in the 12th century; of Saint Bernard, who came here to preach about the crusades; and of John of Salisbury, the secretary of Thomas à Becket. All the while, pilgrims flocked in with offerings to Mary's shrine.

In 1194, a fire razed the flourishing town, leaving only the early cathedral's crypt, parts of its façade, and its steeple. But the *Sancta Camisia* miraculously escaped damage, fueling enthusiasm for the construction of a new building on the old foundations. The main body of the cathedral that stands today was completed between 1194 and 1225, financed by gifts from the crowned heads of Europe and the well-heeled merchants of the city. Chartres's status as a spiritual center persisted into the 14th century, when the county became a dependency of the Kings of France, many of whom became its benefactors. In 1594 Henri IV of Navarre had himself crowned here, one of the few exceptions to the rule that French kings be crowned in Reims Cathedral.

By the 19th century, Chartres had lost its political importance, but its beauty attracted writers and artists (the musical tradition surrounding the cathedral had always been strong). The writer Théophile Gautier frequently stayed in the area, as did Anatole France and Alfred de Musset, who wrote a novella here. Corot painted a fine canvas of the cathedral, now in the *Louvre;* much later, the Lithuanian Jewish painter Chaim Soutine translated the landscapes of the Eure Valley into swirling canvases during the Nazi occupation, which he spent in hiding nearby. The town's World War II hero and one of the architects of the French Resistance was Jean Moulin, who was prefect of the Eure-et-Loir *département* at the beginning of the war.

Chartres's town leaders are working to ensure the city's continued evolution. Ambitious developments such as the multipurpose *Chartrexpo* exhibition hall and the *Centre International du Vitrail* (International Stained Glass Center; see *Special Places*) will usher this medieval city into the 21st century. Yet, despite all the evidence of its continuing vitality through the centuries, Chartres *is* its cathedral. It is in the clear gaze of its statues and the intense colors of its stained glass, undimmed by time, that Chartres lives most intensely.

Chartres At-a-Glance

SEEING THE CITY

Nobody forgets seeing the *Cathédrale de Notre-Dame de Chartres* for the first time, its two spires like the masts of a sailing ship afloat on a sea of grain. Because it sits on a spur of elevated ground, it looms on the horizon whether you arrive by road or by rail. As you approach, the layers of the city peel off: first the sprawling 20th century, then the sturdy bourgeois 19th century receding to expose the well-preserved medieval core. It all can be seen from the highly decorated turrets of the cathedral's *Tour du Nord* (North Tower), a winding walk up 350 narrow stairs (entrance inside the *Porte du Nord,* or North Door). Closed daily from 11:30 AM to 2 PM, Sunday mornings, and January. Admission charge.

The stone bridges on the Eure River along the Rue de la Foulerie-Frou and the Rue de la Tannerie in the Basse Ville (Lower Town) also afford an unforgettable view of the city. Flanked by sober medieval buildings, the narrow stream flows past tree-lined banks, carrying the eye up to the cathedral, and the low walls on either side provide a comfortable resting place for contemplation. A profile of the town's major churches can be glimpsed from the Pont de la Courtille at the extreme southeast of the Vieille Ville (Old Town), and a panorama of the rich countryside is available from the well-mown terraced lawns of the *Jardin de l'Evêque* (Bishop's Garden), immediately behind the cathedral.

Another lovely view of the city can be enjoyed from the 14th-century stone steps that descend precipitously from the *Musée des Beaux-Arts* (see *Special Places*) to Place St-André and the river.

SPECIAL PLACES

All the sights below except the *Eglise St-Martin-au-Val* are in the Vieille Ville, whose hub is the cathedral. The Haute Ville (Upper Town) takes in the cathedral and its southern and western environs, including the commercial center around Place des Epars. The Basse Ville (Lower Town) is east of the cathedral, running along the river. All of this is easily covered on foot; even St-Martin-au-Val is no more than a 15-minute walk from Notre-Dame. On your way back, be sure to wander along Rue aux Herbes, Rue de là Petite Cordonnerie, and the Place de la Poissonnerie, where curious old houses give one a sense of the medieval city come alive. The tourist office in front of the cathedral rents portable cassette players with tapes in English describing the monuments and other landmarks in the old parts of the city (see *Tourist Information*). Note that many sites of interest close at lunchtime, generally between noon and 2 PM.

CATHÉDRALE DE NOTRE-DAME DE CHARTRES (CATHEDRAL OF OUR LADY OF CHARTRES)

If the Parthenon sums up Greek civilization and St. Peter's in Rome epitomizes the Renaissance, the cathedral of Notre-Dame de Chartres is the last word in Gothic architecture. Today's cathedral is probably the fifth church to be built on the spot; fire and sword destroyed its previous incarnations. Because most of it was constructed within a period of about 30 years (1194–1225), it has an unusual architectural homogeneity. However, its two spires, which do not match and give it a lopsided look, are from completely different eras. The *Clocher Vieux* (Old Tower), on the right, is in the Romanesque style, elegantly sober and unadorned to the tip of its steeple. Completed in about 1160, it survived the fire of 1194. The base of the *Clocher Neuf* (New Tower), on the left, also survived that fire, and is even older than the *Clocher Vieux,* but its steeple was built by Jean Texier, or Jehan de Beauce, in the convoluted Flamboyant style of the early 16th century.

The 12th- and 13th-century statuary surrounding the cathedral's three main doorways—the *Portail Royal* (Royal Portal) in the western façade and the porches of the northern and southern transepts—is a gold mine of information on the people of the Middle Ages, and the cathedral's stained glass windows are considered the most beautiful in France. Archaeologists recently uncovered traces of the *maisons canoniales,* where priests lived during the

13th century, in front of the cathedral; remains of an important, Roman-era building also have been discovered here.

Note: The cathedral is open daily except Sunday mornings or during masses held at other times, when visitors not attending mass are prohibited from entering the nave (phone: 37-21-56-33).

NAVE The size of the nave, which is the broadest in France, staggers even the most blasé of modern observers; there can be few man-made structures, one feels, that enclose this much space. The ogival arches rise to 122 feet; the intricate webbing of flying buttresses so lightens the stone colossus that it seems almost poised for flight.

The walls are studded with 27,000 square feet of mostly medieval stained glass, the most complete collection anywhere in the world. Brilliant reds, yellows, and greens puncture the deep aquamarine background that has come to be known as Chartres blue, telling the familiar Bible stories over and over again. It's best to come armed with binoculars (available at the *Optique des Changes,* 9 Rue des Changes; phone: 37-21-51-39; and at *La Crypt,* 18 Cloître Notre-Dame; phone: 37-21-56-33) to appreciate, frame by frame, the detail of these luminous texts. Most prized are the three 12th-century lancet windows under the spire of the west front. These were retrieved, like the famous *Notre-Dame de la Belle Verrière* window (the Blue Virgin window) next to the choir, from the earlier Romanesque cathedral. They show the Tree of Jesse (on the right), scenes from the life of Christ (middle), and the Passion (left). Detailed English-language brochures are available here. Try to hear one of the frequent recitals on the restored 14th-century organ, among the finest in Europe.

CHOIR Like the massive Baroque altarpiece, which is a little out of place here but striking in its sweep and movement, the ornate stone tableaux of the choir screen were an afterthought, embellishments on the Gothic. Begun by Jehan de Beauce in 1516 and finally completed in 1716, they illustrate stories about the courtiers and seamstresses of the Renaissance, plus scenes from the lives of Christ and the Virgin.

CHAPELLE DE ST-PIAT Behind the choir, the cathedral's 14th-century treasure house displays the famous relic of the Virgin's robe, as well as embroidered vestments and other precious objects given to the church. Closed during lunch, Sunday mornings, Mondays, and the month of January.

CRYPT The third-largest in the world (after those at Canterbury Cathedral in England and St. Peter's in Rome), the U-shaped crypt houses some interesting 12th-century murals, statues rescued from the *Portail Royal,* and a carved Madonna that is a replica of one burned during the French Revolution. The crypt is the oldest part of the cathedral, most of it dating back to the 11th century; it contains an even earlier crypt (from a 9th-century church) and elements of Gallo-Roman origin. Guided tours (the only way the crypt can be visited) leave several times daily, except on religious holidays, from *La Crypte* (18 Cloître Notre-Dame; phone: 37-21-56-33), a souvenir shop just across from the cathedral. There is a small charge for tours, which are not given Sunday mornings.

PORTAIL ROYAL (ROYAL PORTAL) The sculpted columns and arches above the main entrance in the western façade survive from an earlier cathedral. Considered among the finest examples of French Romanesque art, they present the stern and ethereal mid–12th-century vision of Christ in majesty, the figures elongated, the lines pure.

PORCHE NORD (NORTH PORCH) The three 13th-century arches here concentrate on the Old Testament and the prophecies of Christ's coming—with, in parentheses, the story of the Creation and a fascinating series showing the months, the arts, and the virtues as seen through medieval eyes.

PORCHE SUD (SOUTH PORCH) Also carved in the 13th century, the sculpture above the *Portail Sud* (South Door) focuses on Christ, who is seen presiding at a vividly depicted Last Judgment, complete with sinners, demons, and phalanxes of martyrs and confessors of the church. The grisly end awaiting sinners makes for compulsive viewing, and there are some exquisite visions of the ideal courtly knight (look for Saint George and Saint Maurice, the outermost figures flanking the entrance).

ELSEWHERE IN TOWN

MUSÉE DES BEAUX-ARTS (MUSEUM OF FINE ARTS) Behind the cathedral is the *Jardin de l'Evêque* (Bishop's Garden), which falls in terraces toward the river, and the *Palais Episcopal* (Bishop's Palace), built during the 17th and 18th centuries. The palace now houses the *Musée des Beaux-Arts,* which contains tapestries, furniture, enamels, medieval wood carvings, an exceptional collection of 10 paintings by the Fauvist Maurice Vlaminck, and part of Vlaminck's collection of African sculpture. Closed Tuesdays and some holidays. Admission charge. 29 Cloître Notre-Dame (phone: 37-36-41-39).

CENTRE INTERNATIONAL DU VITRAIL (INTERNATIONAL STAINED GLASS CENTER) The fine ogival arches of the *Enclos de Loëns,* the 13th-century cellar of this structure, were built for a secular purpose: The priests stored wine here. The building's spacious beamed attic now houses displays of ancient and contemporary stained glass, and permanent exhibitions detail the history and techniques of stained glass making, an art that continues to flourish in workshops around town. There also are frequent temporary exhibitions. Open daily. Admission charge. Down a small side street north of the cathedral, at 5 Rue du Cardinal-Pie (phone: 37-21-65-72).

EGLISE ST-ANDRÉ (CHURCH OF ST. ANDREW) This 12th-century Romanesque church, deconsecrated since the Revolution, gave its name to Chartres's *Foire de la St-André* (see *Special Events*), which takes place at the church. The back wall of the churchyard carries the stump of a bridge, now covered with greenery, that used to reach over the river Eure. Rue de la Brèche, just beyond Place St-André (no phone).

EGLISE ST-PIERRE If Chartres ever lost its cathedral, it would still be remembered for this late-13th-century house of worship, once the church of a Benedictine abbey. The graceful ribs of its flying buttresses, each finished with a fearsome gargoyle, leave room inside for wall-to-wall stained glass (13th to 16th century) and a unique impression of light and air. Pl. St-Pierre (no phone).

EGLISE ST-AIGNAN Less elegant than the *Eglise St-Pierre* and balanced on a single flying buttress, this 16th-century structure has an interesting sculpted doorway and exquisite Renaissance stained glass windows, including one that shows the life of the Virgin (the fourth along from the entry). The highly decorative polychrome interior provides a colorful respite from Gothic sobriety. Pl. St-Aignan, off Rue des Grenets (no phone):

ESCALIER DE LA REINE BERTHE (QUEEN BERTHA'S STAIRCASE) This unusual, 16th-century, timbered spiral staircase is decorated with weatherbeaten wooden sculptures. The name recalls the wife of a 10th-century Count of Chartres who went on to marry a King of France. The interior of the house is closed to the public. 35 Rue des Ecuyers at Rue du Bourg (no phone).

EGLISE ST-MARTIN-AU-VAL (CHURCH OF ST. MARTIN-IN-THE-VALLEY) A fine crypt—some of whose pillars date from just before Charlemagne—and the tombs of 6th-century bishops are the prime attractions of this church. Pl. St-Martin-au-Val, off Rue St-Brice.

EXTRA SPECIAL

Malcolm Miller, the well-tailored Briton who conducts tours of the cathedral, has become something of an institution among English-speaking visitors here. He has made the cathedral his life's work, and his descriptions of the stained glass and sculpture have set audiences alight from Chartres to Kalamazoo. If he's not off lecturing somewhere else (which he often does in February and March), try to catch him holding court during his noon and 2:45 PM tours, held daily except Sundays from January through *Easter*. Private tours can be arranged in advance by contacting Miller in his superb medieval home at 26 Rue des Ecuyers (phone: 37-28-15-58; fax: 37-28-33-03).

Sources and Resources

TOURIST INFORMATION

Chartres's *Office du Tourisme* (left of the Pl. de la Cathédrale; phone: 37-21-50-00) dispenses maps, pamphlets, and information daily May through September; it's closed Sundays and holidays October through April. From

May through September, there is a currency exchange booth (open daily) on the square in front of the cathedral.

LOCAL COVERAGE There are two local dailies, *L'Echo Républicain* and *La République du Centre*. Books about Chartres and its cathedral can be purchased in the cathedral shop and at local bookstores. Malcolm Miller's books, in English, are excellent (see *Extra Special,* above). *Le Guide de Chartres* by Jean Villette (Flammarion; 30F) is good for those who read French. An English-language pamphlet on Chartres and its main attractions is available for a small charge at the tourist office.

TELEPHONE The city code for Chartres is 37, which is incorporated into all local eight-digit numbers. When calling a number in Chartres from the Paris region (including the Ile-de-France), dial 16, wait for a dial tone, then dial the eight-digit number. When calling a number from outside Paris, dial only the eight-digit number.

GETTING AROUND

A good pair of legs is the best vehicle for negotiating the steep and winding streets of the Vieille Ville, and pedestrian zones have been created in the commercial center.

AIRPORT The nearest airport is Orly in Paris, about 50 miles (80 km) away.

BUS A good network of local buses serves the immediate neighborhood; information can be obtained from the *Gare Routière,* adjacent to the train station on Place Pierre-Sémard (phone: 37-21-30-35). The standard bus fare is currently 5F (about 85¢ at press time).

CAR RENTAL *Avis* (36 Av. du Maréchal-Leclerc, in Lucé; phone: 37-28-37-37), *Hertz* (31 Rue de la Paix, phone: 37-36-77-81; and 30 Rue Georges-Fessard, phone: 37-36-77-81), and *Europcar* (16 Av. Jehan-de-Beauce; phone: 37-21-49-39) are represented.

TAXI Cabs congregate outside the train station at Place Pierre-Sémard, or call 37-36-00-00 (if you don't speak French, be ready with your phrasebook—the dispatchers don't always speak English). For a lightning visit of a few hours, if you split the fare with a couple of other people, it would be feasible to rent a cab for the 55-mile (88-km) ride from Paris.

TOURS For easy sightseeing of the charming old quarters along the banks of the Eure, take a ride on *Le Petit Train de Chartres,* which departs from the Place de la Cathédrale. This open-air trolley travels a 35-minute route, with commentary in English; for additional details, consult the tourist office. For tours of the cathedral in English, see *Extra Special,* above.

TRAIN The train station (Pl. Pierre-Sémard; phone: 37-28-50-50 or 37-18-60-60) is within walking distance of the cathedral. The trip between Chartres and Paris's *Gare Montparnasse* takes about an hour, and service is frequent.

SPECIAL EVENTS

Chartres's cathedral is, as one would expect, the focal point of the city's most important events.

FAVORITE FÊTES

Festival de l'Orgue and Concours International d'Orgue (Chartres Organ Festival and International Organ Competition) A massive restoration of the cathedral's 14th-century organ in 1971 once again placed it among Europe's noblest instruments. The organ festival, attracting performers from all over the world, takes place in July and August in the cathedral. The *Concours International d'Orgue,* one of the world's most important organ competitions, takes place in Chartres in mid-September of even-numbered years. Both events give visitors plenty of opportunity to hear the instrument's rich and majestic tones swelling and rising into the cathedral's celestial heights.

On Sundays in late April and May, student pilgrims crowd into Chartres after their 25-mile hike through the forest of Rambouillet. The pilgrimages are a tradition started early in this century by the Catholic poet Charles Péguy, who originally made the trip on foot from Paris when his son fell dangerously ill (the child survived). An antiques fair takes place every October at the *Eglise St-André.* The Sunday closest to *La Journée du St-André* (St. Andrew's Day; November 30) brings the *Foire de la St-André,* a riot of bumper cars and candy apples, held all over town, that has little to do with its historic origins.

MUSEUMS

Besides the one listed in *Special Places,* the following museums may be of interest:

COMPA (CONSERVATOIRE DU MACHINISME ET DES PRATIQUES AGRICOLES; CONSERVATORY OF AGRICULTURAL MECHANIZATION AND PRACTICES) This museum is devoted to the history and future of agrarian societies. This year, it features an exhibition during the spring on the ways diet has changed over the centuries; an exhibit on the art of the table, with displays of silverware and porcelain, will be held in fall and winter. Closed Saturdays. Admission charge. Near the train station, at 1 Rue de la République (phone: 37-36-11-30).

MAISON PICASSIETTE (PICASSIETTE HOUSE) This house's former owner decorated it with brightly colored murals made from pieces of broken plates—delightful and touching examples of *art naïf.* Closed Tuesdays and from November through *Easter.* Admission charge. East of town, at 22 Rue du Repos (phone: 37-34-10-78).

MUSÉE DE L'ECOLE (SCHOOL MUSEUM) Features a classroom dating from the end of the 19th century and a remarkable collection of authentic furniture and equipment, including microscopes and film projectors. Open Wednesdays during the school year and by appointment. Admission charge. 1 Rue du 14-Juillet (phone: 37-34-46-97 or 37-35-46-85).

MUSÉE DES SCIENCES NATURELLES (MUSEUM OF NATURAL SCIENCES) Displays prehistoric remains found in the region. Open Wednesday and Sunday afternoons. No admission charge. Sq. Noël Ballay, off Bd. de la Courtille (phone: 37-28-36-09).

SHOPPING

For a town of its size, Chartres boasts impressive shopping facilities. There is a branch of the *Au Printemps* department store (Rue Marceau), together with a healthy overspill of Paris fashions. *Galerie de France* is a mini-mall in the main shopping area just off Place des Epars on Rue Noël-Ballay. Its dozen or so shops include *Rodier* and a *maison de la presse* (newsstand).

In the newly expanded pedestrian zone near the cathedral, a flower market is held on Tuesdays, Thursdays, and Saturdays at Place du Cygne. There's also a vegetable and poultry market on Saturdays on the Place Billard at Rue des Changes, and a flea market on the fourth Sunday of each month at the Place St-Pierre.

The town's good burghers evidently are fond of food, judging by the appetizing terrines (Chartres's pâtés are a specialty) sold at local charcuteries. Local specialties also include the praline-filled chocolates called *mentchikoffs*, created in 1893 in honor of the Franco-Russian alliance. Attractive, glazed pottery, yet another local specialty, can be purchased at *Déco Faïence* (15 Pl. du Cygne; phone: 37-36-05-53).

For standard shopping hours, see GETTING READY TO GO. Chartres's shops of note include the following:

Ariane Original hand-knit sweaters, antique lace, linen, and children's wear. 39 Rue des Changes (phone: 37-21-20-68).

Darreau Charcuterie des Epars A variety of sausages, salamis, and pâtés. 6 Rue Delacroix (phone: 37-21-03-05).

Ferme Sainte-Suzanne More than 150 farm-fresh cheeses. 7 Rue de la Pie (phone: 37-21-88-24).

La Galerie du Cloître Featured in a beamed, stone loft are a wide variety of artworks—painting, sculpture, glasswork, tapestry—made mainly by local artists. 8 Cloître Notre-Dame (phone: 37-36-30-37).

La Galerie du Vitrail Old and new stained glass pieces are for sale; there also are audiovisual presentations on the subject. 17 Cloître Notre-Dame (near the cathedral; phone: 37-36-10-03).

Lassaussois Antiquités A variety of antique art and decorative objects and furniture. 17 Rue des Changes (phone: 37-21-37-74).

Tartine & Trottinette A charmingly cluttered toy and crafts shop with some unusual items. 38 Rue des Changes (phone: 37-36-03-38).

SPORTS AND FITNESS

BICYCLING Bicycles are available by the half day, the day, or longer at the train station (Pl. Pierre-Sémard; phone: 37-36-18-56).

BOATING In the leafy setting of the Eure at the Pont de la Courtille, the friendly man at *La Petite Venise* rents flat blue rowboats that seat four or five, from *Easter* through October (no phone).

HORSEBACK RIDING Among the riding schools in the area is the *Poney Club du Pays Chartrain* (Route du Nogent-le-Phaye; phone: 37-30-10-10).

HORSE RACING There are frequent horse races at the *Hippodrome* (Av. Jean-Mermoz; phone: 37-34-93-73).

SWIMMING The public swimming pools most convenient to the city center are the *Piscine Municipal* (Bd. Courtille; phone: 37-28-05-87) and the *Piscine Beaulieu* (Rue de Sours; phone: 37-28-66-68), both outdoor pools closed October through April.

TENNIS AND SQUASH The *Comité d'Eure-et-Loir de Tennis* (Av. Jean-Perrin; phone: 37-28-66-68) has five indoor hard courts and five outdoor clay courts for public use. Squash courts are available at *Horizon de Beaulieu* (8 Rue des Petits Clos; phone: 37-35-90-25).

THEATER

Artists occasionally give pre-premiere performances here before opening in Paris. The *Forum de la Madeleine* (1 Mail Jean-de-Dunois; phone: 37-35-08-83) stages frequent performances, predominantly *chanson française* and comedies; the *Théâtre Municipal* (1 Pl. Ravenne; phone: 37-21-57-29), with its Italianate interior, presents plays and modern dance from September through May.

MUSIC

In addition to the *Festival de l'Orgue* (see *Special Events*) are the chamber and choral concerts of the *Samedis Musicaux* (Musical Saturdays) series, which take place periodically in a variety of historic buildings. Programs of jazz and rock are part of the fare at the *Théâtre Municipal* (see above).

NIGHTCLUBS AND NIGHTLIFE

Hardly a specialty here, but there are a few popular nightspots, including two piano bars, *Saxophone* (20 Pl. des Halles; phone: 37-36-05-05) and *L'Escalier* (1 Rue du Bourg; phone: 37-28-11-25). Both are open late and feature live music. Oddly enough, Chartres boasts a roller disco, *Roller Star System* (off N10 at Bois-Paris; phone: 37-31-62-54).

Best in Town

CHECKING IN

Chartres is a cosmopolitan rendezvous from mid-April through mid-November; make sure to book ahead for this period. The tourist office can supply names of a few friendly families in the Vieille Ville who offer bed and breakfast in their homes. A double room will cost upward of $110 per night in a very expensive hotel; $75 to $110 in an expensive one; $40 to $75 in a moderate one; and less than $40 in an inexpensive one. Unless otherwise noted, all hotels listed below feature telephones, TV sets, and private baths in the rooms; hotels in Chartres generally do not have air conditioning, unless otherwise noted, and summers can get hot. Some inexpensive hotels have private baths in only some of their rooms; it's a good idea to confirm whether your room has a private bath when making a reservation. All hotels accept major credit cards and are open year-round unless otherwise noted.

VERY EXPENSIVE

Château d'Esclimont One of France's most elegant château hostelries, this 50-room Renaissance palace is surrounded by a tranquil park. A member of the Relais & Châteaux group, it offers a driving and putting range, a pool, two tennis courts, and a restaurant. Eleven miles (18 km) northeast of Chartres in St-Symphorien-le-Château (phone: 37-31-15-15; fax: 37-31-57-91).

Grand Monarque The town's most imposing establishment has a good (some would say overpriced) restaurant offering a mix of classic and nouvelle cuisine, and a popular bar with its own attempt at stained glass. Renovations have spiffed up the lobby and restaurant of the 19th-century structure and added a conference room, a winter garden, and 15 rooms with wood-beamed ceilings and modern marble baths. Most of the 37 older rooms, individually decorated, look onto the courtyard where horses once were stabled. Centrally located, at 22 Pl. des Epars (phone: 37-21-00-72; fax: 37-36-34-18).

EXPENSIVE

Le Manoir du Palomino In this elegant hostelry are 20 rooms, some more deluxe (and more expensive) than others; ask for the best, and book well in advance. Closed January through mid-February. The creditable restaurant is closed Mondays. Four miles (6 km) from Chartres, in St-Prest (phone: 37-22-27-27; fax: 37-22-24-92).

Mercure Chartres-Châtelet Part of a nationwide chain, this hotel has a mock medieval lobby and a modern wing that's cleverly angled toward the cathedral. Several of the 48 well-equipped rooms overlook the great landmark (others have views of an interior garden), making up for the lack of inspiration within. On the leafy avenue leading down to the train station, at 6-8 Av. Jehan-de-Beauce (phone: 37-21-78-00; fax: 37-36-23-01).

MODERATE

Boeuf Couronné Half of the 27 spotless rooms here have views of the cathedral; 17 have private baths. There are a bar, outside terraces, and a reasonably priced restaurant serving local specialties. Restaurant closed Mondays in off-season. At the top of the avenue leading to the train station, at 15 Pl. du Châtelet (phone: 37-21-11-26).

Ibis A member of a nationwide chain, this motel lacks Old World charm but compensates by offering such practicalities as meeting rooms, easy parking, and an inexpensive restaurant with fast service. About 15 of the 79 rooms overlook the cathedral. Beside the river, on Pl. de la Porte-Drouaise (phone: 37-36-06-36; fax: 37-36-17-20).

De la Poste Few of the 59 rooms have views of the cathedral, but most overlook a courtyard. All but 10 of the rooms have private baths. A relatively peaceful night is guaranteed. The restaurant has three copious menus. 3 Rue du Général-Koenig (phone: 37-21-04-27; fax: 37-36-42-17).

INEXPENSIVE

Saint-Jean A 19th-century bourgeois house with 16 simple, clean rooms; twelve have private, renovated baths (though five of these share toilet facilities), and 10 rooms have TV sets. There's no restaurant. Near the train station, at 6 Rue du Faubourg Saint-Jean (phone: 37-21-35-69).

EATING OUT

While Chartres's restaurants don't live up to the promise of the shopfronts of its butchers and bakers, one or two illustrious names have come to nest here. Don't miss the local specialty, *marsauceux,* a soft-crusted cheese wrapped in chestnut leaves. A meal for two costs $75 to $100 (and more) at an expensive restaurant; $50 to $75 at a moderate place; and $25 to $50 at an inexpensive one. Prices include service (usually part of the bill) but not wine. Unless otherwise noted, all restaurants listed below are open for lunch and dinner.

EXPENSIVE

Le Moulin de Ponceau With the Eure flowing slowly by, this is an idyllic spot to enjoy a leisurely cocktail. The drinks (including an exotic punch) do not come cheap, but the setting is impeccable. In winter, you may dine by a log fire; in summer, on a wooden patio over the water. The menu features very good nouvelle-inspired dishes. Closed Sunday dinner, Mondays, two weeks in

February, and the last two weeks in August. Reservations advised. MasterCard and Visa accepted. 21 Rue de la Tannerie (phone: 37-35-87-87).

Le Relais d'Authon A former coaching inn, this restaurant is worth the drive into the countryside for its friendly welcome and classic cuisine. Closed Sunday dinner and Mondays. Reservations advised. MasterCard and Visa accepted. About 8 miles (13 km) east of Chartres at 1 Rue des Rochers, St-Denis-d'Authon (phone: 37-49-40-32).

La Truie Qui File In an ancient house in the center of town, this restaurant serves such inventive dishes as whole roast salmon and, for dessert, warm pears with chocolate and caramel sauce. Closed Sunday dinner and Mondays. Reservations necessary. Major credit cards accepted. Pl. Poissonnerie (phone: 37-21-53-90).

La Vieille Maison Elegant dining in an old house. The chef uses the freshest produce to create a varied menu, which includes duck pâté and, for dessert, apple and nut cake. Though some say the prices are too high, there's no denying the quality of the cuisine. Closed Sunday dinner and Mondays. Reservations advised. Major credit cards accepted. Near the cathedral, at 5 Rue au Lait (phone: 37-34-10-67).

MODERATE

Le Buisson Ardent Just steps from the cathedral, this place is not the tourist trap one might expect. Simple bistro dishes with the freshest ingredients are featured. Open daily; closed Sunday dinner. Reservations advised. Major credit cards accepted. 10 Rue au Lait (phone: 37-34-04-66).

Café Serpente Ideally situated in the former post office building, which is classified as a monument and faces the cathedral, this place is done up as a turn-of-the-century bistro and features traditional cuisine. It also caters to the in-a-hurry tourist, with a selection of fast, but high quality, food. Open daily; closed the first two weeks of January. Reservations unnecessary. Major credit cards accepted. 2 Cloître Notre-Dame (phone: 37-21-68-81).

Le Pichet Moderately priced wines served in *pichets* (pitchers) and classic bistro cuisine draw crowds here. Closed Sunday dinner and Mondays. Reservations advised. MasterCard and Visa accepted. 19 Rue du Cheval-Blanc (phone: 37-21-08-35).

INEXPENSIVE

Les Epars A family feel prevails in this simple restaurant featuring bistro classics. Closed Sunday dinner and Mondays. Reservations advised. MasterCard and Visa accepted. 11 Pl. Epars (phone: 37-21-23-72).

Le Minou This is a place with low-key, traditional decor—copper cooking utensils on the wall, fresh flowers, simple wooden furniture—and a relaxed, convivial atmosphere. And yet the food is classic French cuisine, albeit with a home-cooked feel. Closed Saturday lunch, Sunday dinner, and Mondays. Reservations advised. MasterCard and Visa accepted. 4 Rue Lattre-de-Tassigny (phone: 37-21-10-68).

Les Trois Lys The short walk down to the river and the Basse Ville, where this *crêperie* sits nestled cozily in a crooked, old half-timbered house by the river, is rewarded with a pleasant atmosphere, affordable prices, and scenic surroundings. Closed Sundays year-round, and Monday dinner in the off-season. Reservations unnecessary. Major credit cards accepted. In one of the oldest parts of Chartres, at 3 Rue Porte-Guillaume (phone: 37-28-42-02).

Dijon

Arriving at the Dijon train station, a traveler has little sense of the enchanting medieval city just a few blocks away. The streets on the outskirts of town are very much a part of the 20th century, but a walk into the center of town reveals a place where the routines of modern life are woven unobtrusively into the ancient fabric of the city. Here is Dijon's most dazzling architectural sight, the *Palais des Ducs de Bourgogne* (Palace of the Dukes of Burgundy), and around it are narrow cobblestone streets lined with old houses, mansions, and churches.

Established by Roman times, Dijon was relatively unknown until 1015, when Robert I, the first Duke of Burgundy of the Capetian line, chose it as the capital of his duchy. But it was the four Valois dukes—beginning in 1364 with Philip the Bold, who was succeeded by John the Fearless, Philip the Good, and Charles the Bold—who transformed Dijon into a setting fit for their increasingly princely reign. The duchy's borders expanded to include other parts of France as well as sections of today's Belgium, Netherlands, and Luxembourg, and the power of the dukes came to equal that of the French king.

As patrons of the arts, the dukes attracted the greatest masters of the time to Dijon, leaving the city with an outstanding architectural and artistic heritage. Philip the Bold, who ruled for 40 years, embarked on the construction of the *Palais des Ducs;* Philip the Good, who ruled for 48 years, greatly enlarged the palace in the 15th century.

The Valois dukes were a powerful force in European politics. John the Fearless and Philip the Good allied themselves with the English against the French during the Hundred Years War; it was Philip the Good who delivered Joan of Arc to her English enemies after her string of victories for Charles VII, the French king. But Charles the Bold's conniving with the English against Louis XI led to the demise of the duchy of Burgundy. In 1477, after a reign of only 10 years, Charles was defeated and killed in battle, and Louis XI seized the duchy for the French crown. Dijon's most glorious age was over, though the city remained the capital of Burgundy and an important provincial town to the southeast of Paris.

The 18th century brought Dijon the *Université de Dijon* and the Canal de Bourgogne, a romantic body of water that weaves its way through the city, eventually flowing into the Saône (pronounced *Sown*) River. The 19th century was marked by the coming of the all-important railroad. Its arrival transformed Dijon into one of France's major transportation crossroads, increasing its population from 20,000 in 1850 to approximately 150,000 today (250,000 including the surrounding areas). Dijon also developed as an important industrial and commercial center, known especially for its gastronomic specialties—above all, of course, mustard.

Although mustard seeds date back to prehistoric times, local legend has it that it was the great Dukes of Burgundy who first gave mustard its name during their lengthy and elaborate banquets. At the time, it was difficult to preserve meat, so the dukes had their chefs create a sauce that would disguise the meat's often rancid smell and taste. *Moult me tarde,* meaning "a long time I delay my meal," was the term given to this condiment; later, the phrase was shortened to *moutarde* ("mustard").

Dijon has made many gastronomic contributions, and classic Burgundian dishes are featured in the city's numerous dining establishments. Many of these restaurants are housed in historic buildings, and among the best are the old family-run places—some of them run by third- and fourth-generation descendants.

Visitors often use Dijon as a starting point for a tour of the vineyards of Burgundy, traveling by waterway or taking the famed Route des Grands Crus (the highway linking the major wine producing communes of the nearby Côte d'Or, or "gold coast"). While the landscape around Dijon is certainly lovely, don't make the common mistake of heading directly out of town. Dijon is a beautiful city that deserves attention. Many of the old streets and buildings have been restored with loving care, and a walking tour through the center of the city takes you past some of the most impressive medieval mansions and Gothic churches in France.

Dijon At-a-Glance

SEEING THE CITY

Toward the middle of the 15th century, Philip the Good, the Duke of Burgundy, added a tall tower to his palace so that he would always be able to keep watch against invaders. Today that tower, *Tour Philippe-le-Bon,* offers the city's most spectacular views. There are 316 steps to the top; spread out below is the beauty of Dijon's colorful rooftops, dramatic church steeples, and tranquil surrounding valleys. Closed Tuesdays and some holidays year-round; open only Wednesday afternoons, Sundays, and holidays from mid-November through *Easter.* Admission charge. Pl. de la Libération (phone: 80-74-52-70).

SPECIAL PLACES

Note that some sites of interest, especially museums, may close during lunch hours, usually between noon and 2 PM.

IN THE CITY

PALAIS DES DUCS ET DES ETATS DE BOURGOGNE (PALACE OF THE DUKES AND OF THE ESTATES-GENERAL OF BURGUNDY) This huge, ornate set of buildings testifies to the power of the Dukes of Burgundy and to the importance of the city even after the duchy had been annexed by the French. Begun by

Philip the Bold in the 14th century, the palace grew substantially in the 15th century under Philip the Good. A great transformation came during the 17th and 18th centuries, when additions were created for the *Etats de Bourgogne,* a regional assembly, and the medieval ducal quarters acquired a classic veneer designed by Jules Hardouin-Mansart, the architect of Versailles. The palace was finally completed in the 19th century.

Today, part of the palace is Dijon's *Hôtel de Ville* (Town Hall) and as such is open to the public (you may have to ask to see specific rooms). Another section houses the *Musée des Beaux-Arts* (see below). Impressive architectural details—grand marble staircases and giant banquet halls—abound; ask to see the extravagantly decorated fireplace in the *Salon de la Renommée* in the *Hôtel de Ville* section. The kitchen built by Philip the Good—once the finest in all of Burgundy—is bare today, but its six fireplaces, each with its own chimney, are enormous. The huge glass window, made from the bottoms of wine bottles, is noteworthy, too. The most famous room in the palace, also dating back to Philip the Good, is the *Salle des Gardes* (Guard Room), entered through the museum. It contains the marble and alabaster tombs of Philip the Bold and John the Fearless. Philip's tomb, built between 1385 and 1410, is one of the masterpieces of the Flemish sculptor Claus Sluter. *Hôtel de Ville* closed Sundays and holidays; no admission charge. Pl. de la Libération (phone: 80-74-52-70).

Musée des Beaux-Arts (Museum of Fine Arts) This museum's eclectic collection is considered among the best in France. Installed largely in one of the newer sections of the *Palais des Ducs,* it includes paintings and sculptures ranging from early French and Flemish masters to such modern artists as Picasso, Matisse, and Rodin. Also displayed are Byzantine enamelwork; Renaissance furniture, including some of the palace's original furnishings, dating back to the 1500s; and masks and sculptures from Africa. Closed Tuesdays. Admission charge. Pl. de la Ste-Chapelle (phone: 80-74-52-70).

PLACE DE LA LIBÉRATION (LIBERATION SQUARE) Another legacy of Hardouin-Mansart is this late 17th-century square (actually a semicircle), which, taken together with the Louis XIV houses that line it and the palace façade, create a harmonious classical ensemble. Across the street from the *Palais des Ducs.*

EGLISE NOTRE-DAME (CHURCH OF OUR LADY) Built in the 13th century, this church is considered the finest surviving example of Gothic architecture in Burgundy. For the most dramatic view of its unusual exterior, walk around the corner from the Rue de la Chouette (Owl Street) and look directly up at the gargoyles sitting in three rows on the upper half of the façade. One of the church towers houses *Jacquemart,* the famous Flemish mechanical clock that Philip the Bold brought back from Courtrai as a war trophy in 1383. At that time, the clock featured a lonely little iron blacksmith, who hit the bell every hour on the hour. At the beginning of the 17th century, the people of Dijon "procured" for the blacksmith a wife, Jacqueline; about 100 years later, they had a son, Jacquelinet; a daughter, Jacquelinette, followed in 1881. Along the Rue de la Chouette, note the small stone owl set into the church's exterior: It is said that if you place your left hand on the owl, it will bring good luck. In a chapel to the right of the church's choir is the 11th-century *Vierge Noire* (Black Virgin), one of the oldest wooden statues in France and an object of veneration. Pl. Notre-Dame.

CATHÉDRALE ST-BÉNIGNE (ST. BÉNIGNE'S CATHEDRAL) The most interesting part of this primarily Gothic structure, built between 1280 and 1314, is what remains of the Romanesque basilica that formerly occupied the site: a 10th-century crypt containing the tomb of Saint Bénigne. The cathedral's 18th-century organ is outstanding. Pl. St-Bénigne.

MUSÉE ARCHÉOLOGIQUE (ARCHAEOLOGICAL MUSEUM) An impressive collection of Gallo-Roman and medieval artifacts is complemented by a famous bust of Christ by Claus Sluter. Closed Tuesdays. Admission charge. Next to the *Cathédrale St-Bénigne,* at 5 Rue Dr-Maret (phone: 80-30-88-54).

HISTORIC HOMES Dijon has a wealth of beautifully preserved townhouses and other buildings dating back to the 15th century. Many of them are now designated historic landmarks, identified with a plaque giving the date, original use, and outstanding architectural feature(s). Be sure to see the buildings along Rue de la Chouette, Rue des Forges, and Rue Berbisey. At 34 Rue des Forges is the 15th-century *Hôtel Chambellan,* which, with its beautifully carved staircase and balcony in the courtyard, is considered a fine example of Flamboyant Gothic architecture. The *Hôtel de Vogüé* (8 Rue de la Chouette), built in the early 17th century, sports an eye-catching, patterned-tile roof typical of Burgundian architecture. None of the above are open to the public.

LES HALLES CENTRALES (CENTRAL MARKET) Every Tuesday, Friday, and Saturday, the streets surrounding *Les Halles* fill with vendors and merchants selling everything from fresh braids of garlic from the south of France to antique kitchenware and books. The market itself—a huge, open building—is a wonderful place to gather picnic makings or simply to gaze at the glories of French food. There also are little coffee counters where you can grab an espresso and a croissant. Rue Quentin.

JARDIN DE L'ARQUEBUSE ET JARDIN BOTANIQUE (HARQUEBUS GARDEN AND BOTANICAL GARDEN) There are acres of these idyllic gardens to explore, scattered with elaborate flower beds and herb gardens. The name comes from the *Compagnie de l'Arquebuse,* which used the area in the 16th century for archery and harquebus (a gun of the times) practice. The *arquebusiers'* barracks now house a large flower, herb, and botany library, plus the *Musée de l'Histoire Naturelle* (see *Museums*). Open daily. No admission charge. Rue de l'Arquebuse (no phone).

CHARTREUSE DE CHAMPMOL (CHAMPMOL CHARTERHOUSE) In 1383, Philip the Bold founded a Carthusian monastery and set about establishing a necropolis for the dukes within its confines. Though the monastery was destroyed in 1793 and the site is now occupied by a psychiatric hospital, two important works of sculpture by Claus Sluter can still be seen: a chapel doorway and the *Puits de Moïse* (Well of Moses), actually the hexagonal pedestal of a former calvary group. Sluter was the greatest of the artists in service to Philip the Bold, and the six powerful figures of prophets on the well are notable as milestones in the development of realism in medieval sculpture. They rank as one of the Flemish artist's two masterpieces, along with the tomb of Philip now in the *Palais des Ducs.* Closed weekends. Admission charge. A 30-minute walk west of the center of town; entrance from Bd. Chanoine-Kir (phone: 80-42-48-48).

EXTRA SPECIAL

A good mustard should be hot enough to "tweak" your nose, but not so hot that it's unenjoyable. One of the best places in which to get a taste of the pungent spread is the *Grey Poupon* shop (32 Rue de la Liberté; phone: 80-30-41-02), whose product American visitors know from stateside supermarket shelves. It has been selling mustard since 1777, and residents still bring in empty crocks and jars to be filled with the golden paste. Be sure to see the collection of antique mustard jars belonging to the Grey and Poupon families; they are unusually beautiful. Assorted mustards, vinegars, and other condiments produced by Maille, one of the better Dijon brands, are also on sale, as are replicas of the old china crocks; they'll fill them with mustard and pack them for traveling.

Sources and Resources

TOURIST INFORMATION

The Dijon *Office du Tourisme* is in the center of town (Pl. Darcy; phone: 80-44-11-44); it provides maps, brochures, information about touring the surrounding wine country, guidebooks on all aspects of the city, and lists of hotels and restaurants in the city and its environs. Much of the information is in English. The office's bulletin board announces concerts, university events, sporting events, and festivals. Open daily.

LOCAL COVERAGE Consult the local French-language daily *Le Bien Public/Les Dépêches.* The tourist office also distributes the bilingual *Dijon Culture,* a pamphlet that lists theater, music, and dance events. The *maison de la presse* (newsstand) at 26 Rue de la Liberté (phone: 80-30-45-62) carries English and American newspapers.

TELEPHONE The city code for Dijon is 80, which is incorporated into all local eight-digit numbers. When calling a number in Dijon from the Paris region (including the Ile-de-France), dial 16, wait for a dial tone, then dial the eight-digit number. When calling a number from outside Paris, dial only the eight-digit number.

GETTING AROUND

The easiest and most pleasant way to see Dijon is on foot.

AIRPORT The nearest airport is in Lyons, 93 miles (150 km) away.

BUS City bus service is provided by the *Société des Transports Routiers Dijonnais (STRD),* which operates a user-friendly network through Dijon and its environs. Bus maps are available from the tourist office or from the central bus station (Pl. Grangier; phone: 80-30-60-90). In addition to individual tickets, which cost about 5F (around 85¢ at press time), you may purchase unlimited-travel tickets, good for one week, for about 100F (around $17 at press time). Buses stop running at 8:30 PM, and there is no bus service on Sunday mornings.

CAR RENTAL Near the train station are *Avis* (5 Av. Maréchal-Foch; phone: 80-43-60-76) and *Hertz* (18 *bis* Av. Maréchal-Foch; phone: 80-43-55-22). *Europcar* also has a local office (47 Rue Guillaume-Tell; phone: 80-43-28-44). There are underground parking facilities at several locations, including Rue du Bourg, Place Grangier, and in a garage under Place Darcy.

TAXI Taxis are available 24 hours a day at the train station (at the opposite end of Av. Maréchal-Foch from Pl. Darcy) and at the post office on Place Grangier. You also can call *Taxi Radio* (phone: 80-41-41-12); the dispatchers sometimes speak English, but be prepared to use your French phrasebook. Prices are reasonable, but fares double after 8 PM.

TOURS Guided walking tours of the city (in French) leave the tourist office at 3 PM daily during the summer (there is a small charge); ask at the tourist office for information about English-language tours. Taxi tours of the city—and various excursions out of town—are offered by *Taxi Radio* (see above), with English-language narration on cassette.

If you only have a day to explore Dijon and Burgundy's great vineyards, a guided bus tour (in English and French) of Dijon, Beaune, and the celebrated Clos de Vougeot is a practical solution. Tours are offered every Thursday and Saturday from late April through late October; they depart from Dijon in the morning and return at 6:30 PM. For information and reservations, call *Bourgogne Tour Incoming* (11 Rue de la Liberté; phone: 80-30-49-49).

Finally, a trip over Burgundian vineyards in a hot-air balloon can be thrilling on a clear day. You'll be picked up at a major Dijon hotel; all flights end with a bottle of burgundy wine. Contact *Air Escargot* (Remigny, Chagny;

phone: 85-87-12-30; fax: 85-87-08-84) or *Bourgogne Tour Incoming* for details.

TRAIN The renovated *Gare de Dijon-Ville* is at the opposite end of Avenue Maréchal-Foch from Place Darcy (phone: 80-41-50-50, information; 80-43-52-56, reservations). The station has a sleek *Salon d'Affaires,* a business lounge equipped with a fax machine, telephones, small conference rooms, video equipment, and other amenities for the business visitor to Dijon. For information and membership details, call 80-40-12-40; they'll have English-speaking employees on hand. Dijon is only an hour and a half from Paris by the *TGV* (*Train à Grande Vitesse,* or "fast train").

SPECIAL EVENTS
Naturally, Dijon's most important annual event is inextricably linked to the wines of Burgundy.

FAVORITE FÊTE

Fêtes de la Vigne et Folkloriade International (Wine and International Folk Dance and Song Festivals) This bacchanal combining folklore with wine lore takes place from late August through early September. Some 20 traditional singing and dancing groups from countries such as Israel, Japan, Romania, Sri Lanka, Turkey, and Russia join their French counterparts to make merry through all the vineyard villages of the Côte de Nuits and the Côte de Beaune. The concurrent wine celebrations allow for endless *dégustations* (tastings), both in Dijon and in all the nearby châteaux and villages. For additional details, contact the tourist office (see *Tourist Information*).

The huge *Salon des Antiquaires et de la Brocante* (Antiques Fair) takes place in mid-May in the *Parc des Expositions et des Congrès* just outside the center of town (3 Bd. de la Champagne; phone: 80-77-39-00). The *Eté Musical,* when local artists present classical and jazz concerts at many of Dijon's most beautiful monuments, occurs in June. *L'Estivade,* a festival of theater and music, runs from June through mid-August. The *Puces Dijonnaises* (Dijon Flea Market) comes to the *Parc des Expositions et des Congrès* (see above) in September. For true lovers of food and wine, and for those whose business they are, Dijon's most important event is the *Foire Internationale et Gastronomique* (International Food and Wines Fair), held the first two weeks of November at the *Parc des Expositions et des Congrès* (see above). One of the country's major trade fairs, it showcases the finest edibles and potables from all over France and the world, providing a perfect opportunity for some magnificent tasting. A *Salon de l'Artisanat d'Art et du Cadeau* (Crafts and Gifts Fair) usually takes place in December. Contact the tourist office (see *Tourist Information*) for more details on all events.

MUSEUMS

Dijon offers a special card that permits admission to all of its museums (except the *Espace Grévin*) for one reasonable fee. It's available at the tourist office (see *Tourist Information*) or at any of the participating museums. In addition to those mentioned in *Special Places,* the following museums may be of interest (all are closed Tuesdays unless otherwise noted, and many are closed during lunch hours, from noon to 2 PM):

ESPACE GRÉVIN (GRÉVIN SPACE) A franchise of Paris's well-known wax museum, it houses an exhibit of the history of the Burgundy region through Grévin's famous wax figures (M. Grévin was considered the Mme. Tussaud of Paris). There's a wine tasting facility next door (see *Wine Bars*). Open daily. Admission charge. 13 *bis* Av. Albert-I (phone: 80-42-03-03).

MUSÉE D'ART SACRÉ (MUSEUM OF SACRED ART) Ever-changing exhibits of religious art from the region's churches. Some works currently are being housed here while the churches they belong to undergo restoration. Admission charge. 15 Rue Ste-Anne (phone: 80-30-06-44).

MUSÉE DE L'HISTOIRE NATURELLE (MUSEUM OF NATURAL HISTORY) Geological and zoological specimens of the Dijon region. Closed mornings. Admission charge. In the old barracks of the *arquebusiers,* in the *Jardin de l'Arquebuse* (see *Special Places*), at 1 Av. Albert-I (phone: 80-41-61-08).

MUSÉE MAGNIN Housed in the *Hôtel Lantin,* a gorgeous renovated 17th-century mansion bequeathed to the city by Maurice Magnin, this collection documents elegant 17th-century life with period furniture and paintings. Closed Mondays. Admission charge. 4 Rue des Bons-Enfants, off Pl. de la Libération (phone: 80-67-11-10).

MUSÉE RUDE A local favorite dedicated to the works of the 19th-century sculptor François Rude, set up in the transept of a deconsecrated church. No admission charge. 8 Rue Vaillant (phone: 80-66-87-95).

MUSÉE DE LA VIE BOURGUIGNONNE (MUSEUM OF BURGUNDIAN LIFE) This museum occupies a 15th-century building. One room is filled with heraldry and authentically costumed models of medieval Burgundian knights; the other room, devoted to wine, features antique wine presses, corkscrews, bottles, labels, tools, and other equipment. Closed Tuesdays and some holidays. No admission charge. 17 Rue Ste-Anne (phone: 80-30-65-91).

SHOPPING

The city's best shopping is along the Rue de la Liberté; food and wine are among the best buys. Look for such regional specialties as mustard, *cassis* (black currant liqueur), *pain d'épice* (gingerbread), and burgundy wines. Not to be missed is *Les Halles Centrales* (Central Market; see *Special Places*), a glorious conglomeration of fresh foods, antique cookware, and other finds.

On the last Sunday of every month, there is a flea market at the *Forum* (Rue Général-Delaborde). Dijon is also a good place to hunt for antiques, especially 18th- and 19th-century Burgundian furniture. Several stores are on or near the Rue Verrerie near the *Eglise Notre-Dame,* including *Michel Guillemard* (22 Rue Verrerie; phone: 80-31-89-11); *Au Vieux Dijon* (8 Rue Verrerie; phone: 80-31-89-08); *Atelier de la Tour St-Nicolas* (61 Rue J.J.-Rousseau; phone: 80-73-41-69); *Monique Buisson* (21 Rue Verrerie; phone: 80-30-31-19), a specialist in 18th-century Burgundian furniture; and *Dubard* (25 *bis* Rue Verrerie; phone: 80-30-50-81), which also offers decorating advice.

For standard shopping hours, see GETTING READY TO GO. Other noteworthy shops:

La Boucherie Nouvelle This butcher shop/charcuterie is a good place to sample *jambon persillé* (ham in parsley-flavored aspic), a Burgundian specialty, perfect for a picnic lunch. 27 Rue Pasteur (phone: 80-66-37-10).

Escargots de Bourgogne Whether fresh, canned, or in sealed glass jars, only escargots are sold in this crowded little shop. 14 Rue Bannelier (phone: 80-30-22-15).

Galerie 6 Fine 17th- to 19th-century paintings are restored and sold here; there also are occasional art exhibitions. 6 Rue Auguste-Comte (phone: 80-71-68-46).

Mulot et Petitjean This is a good place for regional wines and foods, including *pain d'épice* (gingerbread) in a variety of shapes and tastes, some filled with *cassis* cream. Three locations: 1 Pl. Notre-Dame, 16 Rue de la Liberté, and 13 Pl. Bossuet (phone for all three: 80-30-07-10).

Occasions French, English, and Chinese furniture, as well as antique carpets. 29 Rue Auguste-Comte (phone: 80-73-55-13).

Oudebert Dijon's most established women's specialty shop, it carries everything from accessories to undergarments. 62-68 Rue de la Liberté (phone: 80-30-44-56).

Au Pain d'Autrefois Behind a fancified façade hides the heart and soul of this bakery—an old bread oven. Pick up some interesting breads to accompany your wine and cheese purchases. 47 Rue du Bourg (phone: 80-37-47-92).

Crèmerie Porcheret A dream of a cheese shop with some of the most wonderful aged cheeses likely to be found anywhere. Ask for *citeaux* made by local monks. 18 Rue Bannelier (phone: 80-30-21-05).

SPORTS AND FITNESS

BOATING Various companies offer week-long cruises on luxury hotel barges departing from Dijon; well-equipped self-piloted boats also may be rented for cruises of a day, a weekend, a week, or more. Contact the tourist office for information. Sailboats are available for rent at Lac Kir, the manmade lake west of downtown on N5 toward Paris (also accessible by Bus No. 18).

GOLF One of the closest courses to the city is the 18-hole *Golf de Quetigny* (phone: 80-46-69-00), 4 miles (6 km) away, in Quetigny. The 18-hole course at *Golf de Bourgogne* (Norges-la-Ville; phone: 80-35-71-10) is 6 miles (10 km) from Dijon. *Golf de Beaune à Levernois* (phone: 80-24-10-29), a public course in Levernois, is another option. To get there, drive 16 miles (26 km) south via A31, then at the Beaune exit, around 2 miles (3 km) southeast toward Verdun-sur-le-Doubs on D970.

JOGGING A number of parks throughout town are ideal for jogging. The most accessible is probably Place Darcy, the small park in the center. South of the city center, the Louis XIV–era *Parc de la Colombière* has 80 acres to roam. There's also Lac Kir (see *Boating,* above) and the beautiful *Parc de la Combe à la Serpent,* also west of town.

SWIMMING Indoor pools open to the public include *Piscine du Carrousel* (Cours du Parc; phone: 80-67-20-12), *Piscine de la Fontaine d'Ouche* (Fontaine d'Ouche, Av. du Lac; phone: 80-43-38-19), and *Piscine des Grésilles* (Bd. Champollion; phone: 80-71-37-35). Pools are also available at *Tennis La Fleuriée* (3 Rue En Paillery; phone: 80-73-31-81) and *Duck de Bourgogne,* around 4 miles (7 km) away in Gevrey-Chambertin (Chemin du Champ Franc; phone: 80-34-34-22).

TENNIS AND SQUASH The *Parc des Sports* (Pl. Gaston-Gérard; phone: 80-71-29-43) has 15 outdoor courts open to the public. *Duck de Bourgogne* (see *Swimming*) has four outdoor and three indoor tennis courts and six squash courts, as well as a gym and a bar/restaurant. *Tennis La Fleuriée* (see *Swimming*) has 11 tennis courts and five squash courts.

WINDSURFING Equipment can be rented at Lac Kir (see *Boating,* above).

THEATER AND MUSIC

The elegant *Théâtre Municipal* (Pl. du Théâtre; phone: 80-67-23-23), on one side of the *Palais des Ducs,* is Dijon's oldest theater and its main site for a full range of plays, operettas, operas, ballets, and classical concerts. The city's avant-garde theater, *Théâtre du Parvis St-Jean* (14 *bis* Rue du Chapeau Rouge; phone: 80-30-63-58 for information; 80-30-12-12 for reservations), stages a wide variety of experimental productions, as well as music and dance performances. The *Théâtre Espoir* (26 Rue Bannelier; phone: 80-30-08-92) also features experimental theater. *Université de Dijon* (phone: 80-66-64-13) holds a number of noteworthy theater, dance, and musical events. Various churches—especially *St-Bénigne* (see *Special Places*) and *St-Michel*—are used for organ recitals and choral and orchestral concerts. The *Eldorado* (21 Rue Alfred-de-Musset; phone: 80-66-12-34 or 80-66-51-89) is an old movie house specializing in "art films," frequently in English. The *Bistrot de la Scène* (203 Rue d'Auxonne; phone: 80-67-87-39), a café-theater, presents plays, jazz, and concerts. The *Théâtre des Feuillants* (9 Rue Condorcet; phone: 80-43-25-85) has theater and dance performances. Occasional concerts are given in the *Palais des Sports* (17 Rue Léon-Mauris; phone: 80-73-05-40). For more information or tickets to major cultural events in and around Dijon, contact the *Association Bourguignonne Culturelle* (Passage Darcy; phone: 80-30-59-78).

NIGHTCLUBS AND NIGHTLIFE

What most people do in Dijon for an evening's entertainment is eat and drink, often stretching dinner out to 10 or 11 PM and then lingering at the bar with a snifter of cognac or Burgundian *marc* (grape brandy). But because this is a university town, there are nightclubs and discos, such as *La Jamaïque* (14 Pl. de la République; phone: 80-73-52-19), a popular meeting spot with exotic cocktails and a West Indian beat, and *Rio* (in the *Hôtel de Paris*, at 9 Av. Maréchal-Foch; phone: 80-43-50-23). For a more tranquil setting, go to *Le Cygne* (Plombières-lès-Dijon; phone: 80-41-02-40), a terraced restaurant beside Lac Kir that offers a variety of dinner shows, ranging from contemporary theatrical comedies to evenings of jazz and French song. Clubs often stay open until well after midnight, but opening days and hours vary; it's a good idea to call ahead.

Best in Town

CHECKING IN

Compared with those in Paris, prices in Dijon are extremely reasonable. The tourist office can help you book rooms locally; for those without accommodations, a bulletin board outside the main tourist office lists available rooms. A double room in a very expensive hotel will cost from $100 to $200; in an expensive place, $70 to $100; in a moderate one, $50 to $70; and, in an inexpensive one, less than $50—but you may end up sharing a bathroom down the hall. Unless otherwise noted, all hotels listed below have TV sets, telephones, and private baths in the rooms. None has air conditioning, unless otherwise noted, and it can get very hot in the summer. Some less expensive hotels have private baths in only some of their rooms; it's a good idea to confirm whether your room has a private bath when making a reservation. Also, unless otherwise noted, hotels are open year-round, major credit cards are accepted, and breakfast is not included.

VERY EXPENSIVE

Le Chapeau Rouge This small, well-respected place next to the *St-Bénigne* cathedral is part of the Best Western group. A few of the 29 rooms and two suites have beautiful 18th-century furniture; the rest are tastefully decorated with a nice balance of old and new. Several side rooms have dramatic views of the cathedral. Ten rooms are air conditioned, and over half have been renovated; some include saltwater Jacuzzis. There is a highly rated restaurant (see *Eating Out*) and a bar. 5 Rue Michelet (phone: 80-30-28-10; 800-528-1234; fax: 80-30-33-89; 602-957-5895 in the US).

Sofitel La Cloche All that remains of the original structure—dating from 1424—are the exterior walls, including the façade. This elegant hostelry, formerly a link in the Pullman chain, has 80 attractively furnished, air conditioned rooms and suites enhanced by wonderful views of the Place Darcy and the hotel's own peaceful little garden. Though this is one of the grandes dames of Dijon hotels, recent visits have been disappointing, with lackluster service, mediocre breakfast, and some rooms looking a bit run down. The rooms *en duplex* (with mezzanines) are still charming, however, and there's an excellent restaurant, *Jean-Pierre Billoux* (see *Eating Out*), a bar, and a boutique. One hopes that the new management will straighten out the kinks. 14 Pl. Darcy (phone: 80-30-12-32; 800-221-4542; 914-472-0370 in New York; fax: 80-30-04-15; 914-472-0451 in the US).

EXPENSIVE

Holiday Inn Garden Court This new, 100-room member of the chain has all the familiar, modern conveniences (including air conditioning in the rooms). The hotel has a restaurant and a good location: in the *Toison d'Or* complex, with shops and a theme park. 1 Pl. Marie-Bourgogne (phone: 80-72-20-72; fax: 80-72-32-72).

Mercure-Altéa Château Bourgogne Convenient to the *Parc des Expositions et des Congrès,* this sleek, modern hotel is part of the national chain. The 114 rooms and seven suites are very comfortable, with air conditioning and extremely large bathrooms. Rear rooms all have views of the convention center. There's a restaurant, *Le Château Bourgogne* (see *Eating Out*), plus conference rooms, a bar, and a pool. About a 15-minute walk from the center of town in a new district, at 22 Bd. de la Marne (phone: 80-72-31-13; fax: 80-73-61-45).

MODERATE

La Flambée This comfortable hotel is in a completely renovated, thatch-roofed farmhouse in the quiet countryside. The 22 rooms and one suite have modern decor and are air conditioned. There is a restaurant. Rte. de Genève, Sennecy-lès-Dijon, 4 1/2 miles (7 km) southeast of Dijon by N5 and D905 (phone: 80-47-35-35; fax: 80-47-07-08).

Jacquemart The choice of visiting actors, artists, and antiques dealers, this 30-room, two-suite hotel in the city's prime antiques-shopping district is beautifully furnished. There's no restaurant. 32 Rue Verrerie (phone: 80-73-39-74; fax: 80-73-20-99).

Hôtel du Jura A friendly place with a lovely private garden on the main thoroughfare between Place Darcy and the railroad station. The 79 rooms are comfortable, with modern decor, and there's a bar, but no restaurant. Closed mid-December through mid-January. 14 Av. Maréchal-Foch (phone: 80-41-61-12; 800-927-4765; 212-689-5400 in New York City; fax: 80-41-51-13; 212-689-5435 in the US).

Hôtel du Nord Run by the same family for four generations, this charmer feels more like a country inn than a city hotel. The 29 rooms are clean and quiet, with fluffy down comforters on every bed, and large baths. The cellar wine bar is a convenient spot in which to try out the tastes of Burgundy. There is a restaurant, *La Porte Guillaume.* Closed *Christmas* through early January. 2 Rue de la Liberté (phone: 80-30-58-58; fax: 80-30-61-26).

Hôtel du Palais Visiting lawyers tend to stay in this fine old building, which offers friendly service and great value just down the street from the *Palais de Justice.* Many of the 16 renovated rooms have antique furnishings. No restaurant. In the historic quarter, at 23 Rue du Palais (phone: 80-67-16-26).

Philippe le Bon A simple, recently opened hotel, with 27 rooms equipped with mini-bars and all the modern comforts, plus a superb restaurant, *La Toison d'Or* (see *Eating Out*), decorated in 16th-century style. 18 Rue Ste-Anne (phone: 80-30-73-52; fax: 80-30-95-51).

Relais de la Sans Fond Formerly a private house, this 17-room lodging set in a large park is cozy and peaceful. There's a restaurant. The inn is closed Sundays. Five miles (8 km) outside of town, in Chevigny-Fenay, Rte. de Seurre (phone: 80-36-61-35; fax: 80-36-94-89).

Wilson This recently renovated 27-room hotel was once a 17th-century coaching inn. Its ceiling beams, warm stone hearths, and central courtyard, all relics of its past life, make this perhaps the most charming of the city's hotels. The *Thibert* restaurant (see *Eating Out*) has won considerable praise for its innovative menu. 10 Pl. Président-Wilson (phone: 80-66-82-50; fax: 80-36-41-54).

INEXPENSIVE

Terminus et Grande Taverne Small and family-run, it has been in business for more than a century. The 30 rooms are quiet, with simple, old-fashioned decor. There's a bar and a brasserie. Convenient to the train station, at 24 Av. Maréchal-Foch (phone: 80-43-53-78; fax: 80-42-84-17).

EATING OUT

Considered a capital of French cooking, Dijon is a wonderful place to sample such Burgundian classics as *escargots à la bourguignonne* (snails in garlic butter), *jambon persillé* (ham in parsley-flavored aspic), *oeufs pochés en meurette* (eggs poached in red wine with mushrooms and ham), *rognon de veau à la dijonnaise* (veal kidney in a Dijon mustard sauce), *coq au vin* (chicken in wine), *boeuf bourguignon* (beef stewed in wine), and *kir* and *kir royal* (aperitifs made of *cassis*—black currant liqueur—mixed with *aligoté*—a dry white wine or champagne). Burgundian food tends to be hearty and satisfying, though a number of chefs in town are producing lighter food, in the nouvelle style, with good results. Burgundy's vineyards yield some of the best wines of France, if not the world—pouilly-fuissé and romanée-conti come to mind—and Dijon's restaurants and bistros offer these, too, at extremely reasonable prices. Beaujolais nouveau often goes for as little as $10 a bottle.

Expect to pay $100 or more for dinner for two at expensive restaurants; between $50 and $90 at moderate ones; and less than $50 at inexpensive ones. Prices include service (usually added to the bill automatically), but not wine. Unless otherwise noted, all restaurants listed below are open for lunch and dinner.

EXPENSIVE

Le Chapeau Rouge The recipient of one Michelin star, this candlelit dining room serves excellent regional and nouvelle cuisine, presented with the lightest of sauces. Try the roast squab with celery root purée. Open daily. Reservations necessary. Major credit cards accepted. In *Le Chapeau Rouge* hotel, 5 Rue Michelet (phone: 80-30-28-10; fax: 80-30-33-89).

Le Château Bourgogne Housed not in the old-fashioned setting its name suggests, but in a spare, contemporary dining room, it offers up classic dishes, such as fresh duck foie gras and *ris et rognons de veau à la moutarde* (veal sweetbreads and kidneys in mustard sauce), with a light touch. The wine list is quite good. Open daily. Reservations necessary. Major credit cards accepted. In the *Mercure-Altéa Château Bourgogne* hotel, 22 Bd. de la Marne (phone: 80-72-31-13; fax: 80-73-61-45).

Breuil/La Chouette This small, medieval dining room in a lovely area of the city serves some of the best traditional cuisine in town. Try the delicate *lotte aux raisins* (monkfish with raisins in a Mercurey wine sauce), the *petits escargots à la crème aux herbes et champignons* (snails in cream sauce with herbs and mushrooms), the *rognons de veau à la moutarde*, and any of the first-rate desserts. Closed Monday dinner, Tuesdays, and the first two weeks in July. Reservations necessary. Major credit cards accepted. Down the street from the *Eglise Notre-Dame*, at 1 Rue de la Chouette (phone: 80-30-18-10; fax: 80-30-59-93).

Les Gourmets Overlooking a garden, this dining room has been awarded a Michelin star for its renditions of such dishes as lamb with eggplant and roast veal with orange sauce. Closed Sunday dinner, Mondays, and two weeks in February. Reservations advised. Major credit cards accepted. In Marsannay-la-Côte, south by the D122, on Rue Puits-de-Tête (phone: 80-52-16-32; fax: 80-52-03-01).

Jean-Pierre Billoux Considered by many to be Dijon's best chef, Billoux concocts refined, original fare—*pintade farcie d'échalote et de persil* (guinea hen stuffed with shallots and parsley) and *ris de veau aux poireaux frits* (veal sweetbreads with fried leeks), for example—that has been awarded one Michelin star. The elegant room is in the old *caves* (wine cellars) of the renovated, 15th-century *Hôtel de la Cloche,* but under different management than the hotel. Closed Sunday dinner, Mondays, and two weeks each in February and in August. Reservations necessary. Major credit cards accepted. 14 Pl. Darcy (phone: 80-30-11-00; fax: 80-49-94-89).

Thibert Locals come here for savory, refined dishes like *coquilles St-Jacques avec une cuvée de navet avec des truffes grises de Bourgogne* (sea scallops with turnip purée and truffles). Add to this sophisticated decor, recorded chamber music playing softly in the background, and an ideal location—on one of Dijon's most beautiful squares—and you'll understand why Michelin has granted the place a star. Closed Monday lunch, Sundays, and two weeks in August. Reservations necessary. Major credit cards accepted. In the *Wilson* hotel, 10 Pl. Président-Wilson (phone: 80-67-74-64 or 80-66-82-50; fax: 80-63-87-72).

La Toison d'Or (Restaurant de la Compagnie Bourguignonne des Oenophiles) Don't miss the experience of dining in this 17th-century mansion, whose original beams, huge stone fireplaces, tapestries, period furniture, and view onto a small garden give it the feel of an elegant country inn. The food is a mixture of hearty Burgundian specialties—*lapin en gelée* and *coq au vin*—and lighter, nouvelle dishes such as salmon, turbot, spinach terrine, and thinly sliced breast of duck with grapes. The wine list is especially strong in younger (and less expensive) choices; the *compagnie* also stocks its own wine for sale direct from growers. Before dinner, be sure to visit the adjoining 15th-century courtyard and *Musée de la Vie Bourgignonne* (see *Museums*). Closed Sunday dinner and two weeks in August. Reservations necessary. Major credit cards accepted. In the *Philippe le Bon* hotel, 18 Rue Ste-Anne (phone: 80-30-73-52; fax: 80-30-95-51).

MODERATE

Bistrot des Halles In this friendly establishment, which is the more casual, bistro restaurant of master chef Jean-Pierre Billoux (see above), Burgundian cuisine predominates. Closed Sundays. Reservations advised. Major credit cards accepted. 8 Rue Bannelier (phone: 80-30-11-00).

Le Chabrot The jovial, mustachioed owner offers a warm welcome, and the talented young chef is particularly versatile with *poisson:* The salmon menu has 15 versions of that fish alone. Besides the recently enlarged main dining room, there's a wine bar and a 12th-century *cave.* Closed Monday lunch and Sundays. Reservations advised. MasterCard and Visa accepted. 36 Rue Monge (phone: 80-30-69-61).

Le Chandelier This family-run restaurant features good, traditional Burgundian cuisine and local wines. Open late, it's a popular after-theater dining spot.

Closed Sunday dinner, Mondays, and two weeks in August. Reservations advised. MasterCard and Visa accepted. 65 Rue Jeannin (phone: 80-66-15-82).

Hostellerie de l'Etoile An ancient façade and a warm, wood-paneled dining room on one side contrast with the modern exterior and eating area on the other side of this restaurant, which occupies an entire block (there's an entrance on each side). Try the *oeufs pochés en meurette,* a Dijon specialty prepared perfectly here. Open daily. Closed Sunday dinner and Monday lunch. Reservations advised. Major credit cards accepted. 1 Rue Marceau (phone: 80-73-20-72; fax: 80-71-24-76).

Le Petit Vatel A long-standing favorite, featuring solid traditional French cuisine served in an old-fashioned setting. Try the *pâté d'escargots à la bourguignonne.* Closed Saturday lunch, Sundays, and mid-July through late August. Reservations advised. Major credit cards accepted. 73 Rue d'Auxonne (phone: 80-65-80-64).

INEXPENSIVE

Le Bouchon du Palais A small, friendly eating spot that features traditional dishes, with customers seated *coude à coude* (elbow to elbow). Regulars often lunch on big platters of charcuterie and a glass of wine at the bar. Closed Sundays. Reservations advised. Major credit cards accepted. 4 Rue Bouhier (phone: 80-30-19-98).

Le Dôme A favorite gathering spot after the Saturday market at *Les Halles.* Good home cooking, with an accent on classic recipes from southwest France, such as foie gras and *confit de canard* (salted duck cooked in its own fat). Closed Saturday dinner, Sundays, and Mondays. Reservations unnecessary. Major credit cards accepted. 16 *bis* Rue Quentin (phone: 80-30-58-92).

BARS AND CAFÉS

The *Concorde* (2 Pl. Darcy; phone: 80-30-69-43) is a turn-of-the-century brasserie and a favorite local hangout, where people congregate for a carafe of wine, a cold mug of beer, or a demitasse of coffee. Another place to people watch on Place Darcy is *Le Glacier* (phone: 80-30-05-17), a popular brasserie and café with a nice selection of wine and beer and a limited menu; sit by the window and you'll be mesmerized for hours. The *Brighton* (33 Rue Auguste-Comte; phone: 80-73-59-32) is an agreeable, English-style pub, and *Messire* (3 Rue Jules-Mercier; phone: 80-30-16-40) is another popular bar with a good selection of wine and beer. *Aux Délices d'Italie* (26 Rue Odebert; phone: 80-30-20-67) is a café serving pastries and espresso coffee.

WINE BARS

Dijon has a growing number of serious wine bars and tasting rooms, where visitors may sample some of Burgundy's fine wines by the glass. You can choose from among some 20 wines—the cost of sampling is about $10—at *Le Caveau de la Porte Guillaume* (Pl. Darcy; phone: 80-30-59-59), which offers tastings daily; no appointment necessary. *La Cave du Clos* (3 Rue Jeannin; phone: 80-67-64-62) has a renovated wine bar/tasting boutique, where a glass of Santenay Premier Cru, for example, can be tasted for about $10. A cold menu is offered as well. Appointments are recommended; closed Sundays and Mondays. *Les Caves de l'Espace Grévin* (13 Av. Albert-I; phone: 80-42-03-03), next to the *Espace Grévin,* has three vaulted-ceiling *caves* where tasters can choose from about 200 burgundy wines. Tastings are given for groups only, and only by appointment; organized tastings conducted in English are available.

Lyons

Lyons is a city of contradictions, which may have something to do with its geography. For one thing, it's essentially a northern city that faces south, so a whiff of the Mediterranean from Marseilles here is often mixed with a chilly blast from the Alps. For another, it's set halfway between the northern border of France and the southern Mediterranean coast at the junction of two great rivers, the Rhône and the Saône, making Lyons a crossroads where foreign traffic and trade have been heavy for centuries. At various times in its history, it has been the Roman headquarters of Gaul and part of the Holy Roman Empire; for a long time, it was only tenuously ruled by the French crown. During the German occupation of France in World War II, Lyons was a capital of the French Resistance, and daring patriots traversed its *traboules,* secret passages in the old sections that connect street to street.

Lyons's history begins on October 10, 43 BC, the day a former lieutenant of Julius Caesar founded a colony named Lugdunum on Fourvière, one of Lyons's hills. Lugdunum became the capital from which the Romans administered the three provinces of Gaul, and their emperors made it into a substantial city. Between 16 and 14 BC, Augustus built a 4,500-seat theater on Fourvière, which was enlarged in Hadrian's time to hold 10,000 people. The town also had a circus for chariot races (now gone) and the *Amphithéâtre des Trois-Gaules* (across the Saône on the slope of another hill, the Croix-Rousse). The amphitheater is believed to have been a gathering place for delegates of Gallic tribes and, in the 2nd century, the site of the martyrdom of early Christians. Another area, on the *presqu'île* (peninsula) that holds the heart of the city, was a commercial zone of warehouses and workshops and a wealthy residential district.

As the Roman Empire declined, so, too, did the influence of Lyons. It remained a city of religious consequence, however, ruled by archbishops, until it became a part of the French kingdom in the 14th century. Then, with the Renaissance, came its second great period. Already a crossroads of trade and commerce, Lyons became France's banking, printing, and silk manufacturing center. Charles VI helped secure the city's economic future in 1420 by authorizing its first trade fairs, events that continue today. Merchants flocked to the Lyons fairs from all over Europe, followed by bankers from Italy in the late 15th century.

In the first part of the 16th century, when François I granted the Lyonnais the privilege of manufacturing silk free of taxes (just as they had earlier been granted a monopoly in the sale of silk), silk weavers began to arrive from Genoa. Lyons soon was Europe's foremost silk producer, richer and more populous even than Paris. Merchants and bankers built impressive *hôtels* (townhouses) in the area between Fourvière and the Saône, now known as Vieux (Old) Lyon. But the city also was a renowned intellectual center. Printing shops flourished, attracting scholars and writers. Among them was Rabelais, who practiced medicine and published two volumes of his *Gargantua and Pantagruel,* in 1532 and 1534, while living here.

Lyons was then—and still is—a working city. Strikes by journeyman printers around 1540 were among the first real labor disputes in world history. The silk industry was subject to repeated boom-and-bust cycles, and the brutally repressed uprisings of the *canuts* (silkworkers) of the Croix-Rousse in the 1830s are landmarks in the history of the labor movement. Eventually, the introduction of the power loom during the 1870s put an end to the clacking of tens of thousands of hand looms in the ateliers of Lyonnais *canuts.* Today, the city is the center of a vast industrial agglomeration in which the manufacture of textiles is still important, along with the metallurgical and petrochemical industries. Lyons is France's third-largest city, with a population of more than 400,000 in the city proper and over a million in the greater urban area.

Lyons is also, more or less by common consensus, the gastronomic capital of France. Indeed, for many a traveler, food is just about the *only* reason to stop here. The institution of the two-hour high-speed *TGV* (*Train à Grande Vitesse,* or "fast train") between Paris and Lyons made it possible—and by no means unheard of—for a Parisian to visit Lyons for lunch and be back home in time for dinner. The Lyonnais are connoisseurs of the art of *bien manger,* and their patronage of this art supports a reported 700 to 800 restaurants. One reason for the city's high culinary standards is its location in the midst of a region of agricultural abundance; another may be some *je ne sais quoi* in the Lyonnais's genes that has produced the finest of cooks. Eminent chefs from the Lyons region have included Alain Chapel, Paul Bocuse, Georges Blanc, and Pierre Troisgros. But behind the "old boys" club of chefs is a tradition of female restaurateurs, the great *mères* or *cuisinières lyonnaises,* whose interpretations of home cooking gave rise to some of the classic specialties of Lyons. That tradition goes back at least to the 18th century, when Mère Guy de la Mulatière opened a restaurant that still exists in Lyons (under the name *Roger Roucou;* see *Eating Out*).

Among culinary cognoscenti circulates a fable that pretty much sums up the importance of food to the Lyonnais: It's said that in 1847, Mme. Célestine Blanchard opened a restaurant. One day her chef, Jacques Rousselot, concocted a chicken recipe for her that he dubbed *poulet Célestine.* The dish was so marvelous that Célestine fell in love with Jacques—and the two were married. Whether the story is true or not is beside the point: In Lyons it's easy to believe that cuisine could be the catalyst for *amour.*

Lyons At-a-Glance

SEEING THE CITY

There are two natural vantage points for a panoramic view of Lyons. One is from the *observatoire* of the *Basilique Notre-Dame* atop Fourvière, on the right bank of the Saône (see *Special Places*), where payment of the admission charge and a climb up the 300 or so steps (or a ride on the funicular) earns you a splendid view of the city and the surrounding countryside. The other vista is from the height of Croix-Rousse, between the two rivers north of the center. From here, you can descend toward the flat ground of the *presqu'île* by several routes that offer excellent, sometimes unexpected views. Head down via Rue des Pierres-Plantées and the Montée de la Grande-Côte, for instance, or via Place Bellevue and Rue des Fantasques; on the west, Place Rouville has a view of Fourvière and the bend in the Saône.

In addition, the *Panache Bar,* ensconced in the *Pullman Part-Dieu* hotel (see *Checking In*) in the cylindrical Crédit Lyonnais tower on the flat left bank of the Rhône, offers views toward the city or the Alps, depending on which side of the building you find yourself.

SPECIAL PLACES

Lyons can be broken down into distinct, compact areas, defined by the two rivers that meet here. The Saône flows into the city from the north, curving first around Croix-Rousse and then Fourvière; the Rhône flows in from the Jura Mountains to the northeast. The two run nearly parallel for a short distance before they converge, creating between them a narrow *presqu'île*, which is the city's center. To the west, on the right bank of the Saône at the foot of Fourvière, is Vieux Lyon, the old quarter. To the east is the left bank of the Rhône, where the main attractions are a park and La Part-Dieu, a modern urban complex with offices, shops, and cultural centers, whose construction began in the early 1970s. Note that many attractions, particularly museums, close for lunch, generally between the hours of noon and 2 PM.

FOURVIÈRE AND VIEUX LYON

VIEUX LYON Squeezed between the slope of Fourvière and the Saône River, this is the most extensive and authentic Renaissance city center surviving in France. Its three *quartiers* of St-Paul, St-Jean, and St-Georges include some 350 buildings dating from the end of the Gothic period through the 17th century, when this was the center of town. The area, which was in poor condition at the end of World War II, was extensively renovated and is now animated day and night. To explore it, walk along Rue St-Jean (the main street), Rue Lainerie, Rue Juiverie, and Rue du Boeuf, poking into courtyards and cutting through the *traboules* (see *Extra Special*).

CATHÉDRALE ST-JEAN (ST. JOHN'S CATHEDRAL) One of the prime reference points of Vieux Lyon, the historically important cathedral was the site of two church councils in the 13th century, the consecration of Pope John XXII in the 14th century, the marriage of Henri IV and Marie de Médicis in 1600, and the investiture of Richelieu as a cardinal in 1622. Begun in the 12th century with an apse in the Romanesque style, it was completed in 1420 in Flamboyant Gothic. Despite the mixture of styles, it forms a harmonious mass whose four relatively short towers give it a powerful, low-slung look. It is richly decorated, with interesting stained glass windows, some from the 13th century. A curiosity is the astronomical clock in the transept, which strikes on the hour from noon to 3 PM, accompanied by the crowing of a mechanical rooster and a procession of figures representing the Annunciation. Pl. St-Jean (phone: 78-42-11-04).

PLACE DU CHANGE (EXCHANGE PLAZA) On the uphill side of this square is the *Loge du Change,* a former commercial exchange building that now serves as a church. Though it does incorporate parts of the former structure, it owes its present aspect to the 18th-century architect Jacques Soufflot, the designer of Paris's *Panthéon.* Opposite, at No. 2, is the *Maison Thomassin,* which dates from the 14th and 15th centuries. Its Gothic façade and courtyard make it probably the finest pre-Renaissance house in Vieux Lyon.

TOUR ROSE (ROSE TOWER) With a splendid Florentine façade, this structure takes its name from the circular stair tower in the courtyard. Like many other Vieux Lyon buildings, it was built on a hill so steep that every floor was in effect a ground floor, with terraces and a hanging garden. It used to be said of such houses that the people lived downstairs and stabled their horses on the fourth floor. 16 Rue du Boeuf.

THÉÂTRES ROMAINS DE FOURVIÈRE (ROMAN THEATERS) Uncovered in the 1930s in archaeological digs, these two theaters, halfway up Fourvière from Vieux Lyon, are the most important visible remnants of Gallo-Roman Lugdunum. The larger theater, dating from around 43 BC, when Lugdunum was founded, is the oldest in France. It once held as many as 10,000 spectators. A smaller theater, or *odéon,* seating only 3,000, is nearby. Open daily. No admission charge. You can reach the site from Vieux Lyon by walking up the Montée de Gourguillon or by taking the funicular. 6 Rue de l'Antiquaille (phone: 78-25-94-68).

MUSÉE GALLO-ROMAIN (GALLO-ROMAN MUSEUM) Adjacent to the *Théâtres Romains de Fourvière,* this splendid museum, laid out as an assembly of spiral ramps, gives a comprehensive presentation of the history of the area from prehistoric through Roman times. Two inscriptions on bronze—the Gallic calendar from Coligny and the Claudian table—are among the most interesting exhibits. The former is the longest extant inscription in the Gallic language; the latter is the text of a speech delivered before the Roman Senate by the Emperor Claudius in AD 48. Also interesting are several mosaic floors, including the beautiful depiction of *Cupid and Pan Fighting*. Models of the *Théâtres Romains de Fourvière* as they were in ancient times are set up near floor-to-ceiling windows looking out onto the present-day ruins. Closed Mondays and Tuesdays. Admission charge. 17 Rue Cléberg (phone: 78-25-94-68).

BASILIQUE NOTRE-DAME DE FOURVIÈRE (BASILICA OF OUR LADY OF FOURVIÈRE) The top of Fourvière had already been a place of pilgrimage for centuries when, in 1870, the Archbishop of Lyons invoked the aid of the Virgin in keeping Prussian troops out of Lyons during the Franco-Prussian War. In return, he vowed to build a church worthy of the miracle. When the city was spared, he kept his promise. The resulting edifice, built during the last three decades of the 19th century and visible from almost everywhere in Lyons, is a curious mixture of every imaginable style; with its four ungainly towers (one of which can be climbed), it has been likened to an elephant on its back. Inside are mosaic murals and stained glass windows; the rest of the church, inside and out, is elaborately carved stone. The 12th-to-18th-century chapel to the right of the church (the original place of pilgrimage) contains the miracle-working statue of the Virgin. The esplanade to the left affords a view of the city stretching to and beyond the Rhône. The basilica and the tower are closed throughout this year for renovations. Pl. de Fourvière (phone: 78-25-51-82).

PRESQU'ÎLE (PENINSULA)

BASILIQUE ST-MARTIN-D'AINAY The basilica is all that remains of an important ensemble of buildings belonging to a Benedictine abbey on what used to be an island in the Rhône. Consecrated by Pope Pascal II in 1107, it is, despite later additions, considered a fine illustration of the Carolingian style. 5 Rue de l'Abbaye-d'Ainay.

PLACE BELLECOUR This square was laid out between 1710 and 1714, in the last years of the reign of Louis XIV, on what was then open land belonging to the Ainay abbey. The buildings that originally surrounded it were demolished during the Revolution; the present-day ones, in Louis XVI style, were put up when Napoleon came to power. The rectangular open space, which measures more than 200 by 300 yards, includes an equestrian statue of the Sun King, a replacement of one torn down during the Revolution, and the pavilion of the tourist office.

MUSÉE HISTORIQUE DES TISSUS (MUSEUM OF TEXTILE HISTORY) In the 18th-century *Hôtel de Villeroy,* this is perhaps the finest fabric museum anywhere and a reminder of Lyons's past importance as a silk center. Its 28 rooms house a collection of European, Near Eastern, and Far Eastern textiles ranging from cloth predating the time of Christ to modern fabrics designed by Raoul Dufy and Sonia Delaunay. The French collection is dominated by the work of Philippe de Lasalle, the 18th-century designer who created

Lyonnais silks for such personages as Marie-Antoinette and Catherine the Great of Russia. Closed Mondays and holidays; guided tours are offered. Admission charge includes entrance to the *Musée des Arts Décoratifs* (see below). 34 Rue de la Charité (phone: 78-37-15-05).

MUSÉE DES ARTS DÉCORATIFS (MUSEUM OF DECORATIVE ARTS) Next door to, and a logical extension of, the *Musée Historique des Tissus* (see above), this collection of furniture, woodwork, tapestries, silver, porcelain, and clocks is installed in an 18th-century *hôtel* (townhouse). Closed Mondays. Admission charge includes entrance to the *Musée Historique des Tissus*. 30 Rue de la Charité (phone: 78-37-15-05).

RUE MERCIÈRE AND QUAI ST-ANTOINE (MERCHANT STREET AND ST. ANTHONY'S QUAY) Over the centuries, the Via Mercatoria (Merchants' Street) of Roman times degenerated into an outright slum. Then, about a decade ago—along with the parallel Quai St-Antoine—it underwent a dramatic revival. It's now a center of Lyonnais nightlife and boasts several small restaurants and boutiques. In the mornings (except Mondays), the Quai St-Antoine is the scene of one of France's most colorful street markets for food and flowers. It's worth a visit even if you're not buying.

PLACE DES TERREAUX Roughly speaking, this is the spot where, in the city's early history, the Rhône and Saône converged (*terreaux* refers to the alluvial soil carried by the Rhône that made this area into terra firma). It lies at the foot of Croix-Rousse, bordered on the south by the *Palais St-Pierre* and on the east by the *Hôtel de Ville* (Town Hall). At the western end is a monumental fountain by Bartholdi (of Statue of Liberty fame), depicting a team of galloping horses that represents the rivers flowing to the sea. The city of Bordeaux, for which it was made, refused the structure, and the city fathers of Lyons apparently decided it could just as well represent Lyons's Rhône and Saône as Bordeaux's Garonne and Dordogne.

Hôtel de Ville (Town Hall) This town hall, one of the handsomest in France, was built in the mid-17th century by the Lyonnais architect Simon Maupin. Partly destroyed by fire in 1674, it was restored by the noted architects Jules Hardouin-Mansart and Robert de Cotte. It consists of an imposing rectangle of two-storied buildings which are separated by a colonnade and surround a central courtyard; the buildings contain several magnificently decorated ceremonial rooms. Closed Sundays. No admission charge. Pl. des Terreaux (phone: 78-27-71-31).

Musée des Beaux-Arts (Museum of Fine Arts) The *Palais St-Pierre,* built in the 17th century as an abbey for the Benedictine Dames de St-Pierre, now serves as a museum, and one of the principal pleasures of a visit is entering the arcaded cloister with its statues, among them works by Rodin and Bourdelle. The comprehensive collection includes both modern and ancient sculpture, as well as paintings by Veronese, Tintoretto, Rubens, El Greco,

Cranach, Impressionists and other 19th-century artists, and by Lyonnais artists of various periods. Closed Mondays, Tuesdays, and holidays. Admission charge. Pl. des Terreaux (phone: 78-28-07-66).

AMPHITHÉÂTRE DES TROIS-GAULES (AMPHITHEATER OF THE THREE GAULS) The ruins of this amphitheater on the slope of the Croix-Rousse came to light in 1958. It is believed to have been the site of combat between animals and gladiators, public executions, the martyrdom of early Christians, and annual meetings of delegates from the 60 Gallic nations which the Romans had divided into the three provinces of Gaul. Open daily. No admission charge. Entrance from 1 Rue Lucien-Sportisse (no phone).

THE LEFT BANK OF THE RHÔNE

PARC DE LA TÊTE D'OR (GOLDEN HEAD PARK) Created in 1856, this park covers more than 250 acres. It comprises a large lake, a zoo, botanical gardens, and a Guignol (puppet) theater. The 70,000-plant rose garden is heaven in June. Open daily. No admission charge. The main entrance is at Place du Général-Leclerc (phone: 78-89-01-39).

EXTRA SPECIAL

Unique to Lyons are its *traboules,* corridors that link one street to another by passing through two or more buildings. The word comes from the Latin *trans ambulare,* "to walk through," which also produced the French verb, *trabouler.* The *traboules* are found in the Vieux Lyon and Croix-Rousse quarters, both former centers of the silk industry. In Vieux Lyon they are of architectural interest, with vaulted Gothic ceilings; in Croix-Rousse, where they were the scene of the silkworkers' bloody uprisings in 1831 and 1834, they are part of a partly abandoned working class area, filthy but evocative.

The *traboules* probably were created originally to conserve land in cramped areas, and they provided a practical way to move bolts of silk from place to place in the rain without getting them wet. But the passages also lend themselves easily to the Lyonnais penchant for secrecy. In Croix-Rousse, a businessman could always appear to be going to or coming from some business appointment while in fact ducking through to an adjacent street of ill repute. It is possible to go from the top of Croix-Rousse to Place des Terreaux at the bottom by using *traboules* and their interior staircases for the descent, emerging into each street only long enough to cross it. A map such as those in the Michelin *Vallée du Rhône* guide or the *Miniguide du Vieux-Lyon* is an indispensable companion to an exploration of the *traboules;* just go into any substantial-looking bookstore and make your desire to *trabouler* known.

Sources and Resources

TOURIST INFORMATION

The city and regional tourist office has two locations. The centrally located *Pavillon du Tourisme* (Pl. Bellecour, by the florists' kiosks; phone: 78-42-25-75) is open daily in the summer. The *Centre d'Echanges de Perrache* (at the *Gare Perrache;* phone: 78-42-22-07) is closed Sundays. Both dispense general information, maps, and brochures. During the summer, there is an information center on the Esplanade de Fourvière. The tourist office organizes walking tours of various parts of the city and a general city tour by bus, available in English daily from June through August; during the rest of the year, check with the tourist office for schedules.

LOCAL COVERAGE In Lyons, English-language tourist guides are hard to come by. In French, there's the principal daily newspaper, *Le Progrès,* which carries information on entertainment and other events. Also available are *Lyon Matin* and the Lyons editions of two Paris dailies, *Libération* and *Le Figaro.* The most useful guide to theater, music, and the like is the weekly *Lyon Poche,* available at all newsstands. A virtually indispensable guide to restaurants in Lyons and environs is *Lyon Gourmand,* published annually; though its commentary is in French, a system of symbols makes it fairly easy to follow. If you are visiting Vieux Lyon and read a minimum of French, pick up the *Miniguide du Vieux-Lyon.* Both *Lyon Gourmand* and the *Miniguide du Vieux-Lyon* are part of a series of miniguides focusing on different aspects of Lyons and its environs that readers of French will find helpful; they're available at most bookstores and some newsstands, and each costs less than $5. The map and street guide of the *Plan Guide Blay* series is useful for finding out-of-the-way *rues;* it also contains a map of the métro (subway) system. Lyons is prolific in books about itself, from coffee table picture volumes to obscure histories and multi-volume works on the Lyonnais dialect and slang. Some large bookstores, such as *Flammarion* (across from the tourist pavilion at 19 Pl. Bellecour), group them all in one section for easy perusal.

TELEPHONE The city codes for Lyons are 72 and 78, which are incorporated into all local eight-digit numbers. When calling a number in Lyons from the Paris region (including the Ile-de-France), dial 16, wait for a dial tone, then dial the eight-digit number. When calling a number from outside Paris, dial only the eight-digit number.

GETTING AROUND

Vieux Lyon and the center of the city are best negotiated on foot and by public transportation.

AIRPORT Lyons's *Satolas International Airport* is served by direct *Air France* flights twice a week from New York's *JFK Airport,* as well as by daily flights from

Paris and other European cities. A major expansion has increased the facility's annual passenger capacity to eight million people.

BOAT For information on sightseeing boat rides on Lyons's two rivers, contact *Navig'Inter* (13 *bis* Quai Rambaud; phone: 78-42-96-81), whose boats leave every afternoon from April through October from the Quai des Célestins, on the left bank of the *presqu'île*. The company also runs lunch and dinner cruises aboard *L'Hermès,* departing from Quai Claude-Bernard, and a cruise down the Rhône on the *Elle.*

BUS Lyons's public transport system, *TCL (Transports en Common Lyonnais),* operates nearly 100 bus lines in the city and suburbs, four métro (subway) lines, and two funiculars. The same tickets are good for all three modes of transport (and combinations thereof). They can be used for one hour after validation, but not for return trips. Tickets may be purchased singly for around 5F (about 85¢ US at press time) or in books of six (for a 20% discount) from bus drivers and at *TCL* kiosks around the city, but the simplest method is to use the automatic coin machines in métro stations. The tickets must be validated in the ticket-stamping machines on buses or at the gates to métro trains and funiculars before boarding. Of particular interest to the short-term visitor is the *ticket liberté,* a reasonably priced one-day unlimited-travel ticket. The ticket can be purchased at the *Gare Perrache,* at the *TCL* office (43 Rue de la République; phone; 78-71-70-00), and at *TCL* kiosks. Maps of the system are available in the same places. Most bus lines run from 5 AM to midnight.

CAR RENTAL All the major firms are represented at the airport (a total of seven firms have offices here) and in the city, and the "Train + Auto" plan offered by *SNCF (Société Nationale des Chemins de Fer)* is available at Lyons's railroad stations.

FUNICULAR Known locally as the *ficelle,* two funiculars leave from *Gare St-Jean,* at the end of Avenue Adolphe-Max near the *Cathédrale St-Jean.* One goes to the top of Fourvière, depositing passengers in front of *Notre-Dame de Fourvière;* the other climbs the St-Just hill, making an intermediate stop at the Minimes station, near the *Théâtres Romains de Fourvière.* Bus-métro tickets are valid for the *ficelle,* but you also can buy a discounted round-trip ticket valid for a day. Service on the St-Just line stops at 9 PM; on the Fourvière line, at 9:30 PM.

MÉTRO The still-growing four-line subway system is easy to use, provided you have a map showing where to transfer from one line to another. Line A, the backbone of the system, runs north from the *Gare Perrache* to, among other destinations, Place Bellecour and the *Hôtel de Ville* (switch here to Line C for Place de la Croix-Rousse), then goes to the left bank of the Rhône and runs to the eastern fringes of the city. Switch to Line B at Charpennes for *Gare des Brotteaux* and La Part-Dieu. Line D goes from

Gorge de Loup to *Parc de Parilly.* The métro runs from 5 AM to midnight. (Also see *Bus,* above.)

TAXI Lyons is amply served by taxis. You can flag one on any of the principal thoroughfares, pick one up at cabstands at main squares and intersections, or call 78-28-23-23.

TRAIN Lyons has two train stations: the *Gare Perrache,* on the *presqu'île* at Cours de Verdun and Place Carnot, and the newer *Gare de la Part-Dieu,* in La Part-Dieu. Trains to and through Lyons, including the *TGV,* usually stop at both stations; trains originating in Lyons leave from *Gare Perrache.* For train information, call 78-92-50-50; to reserve a seat on the *TGV,* call 78-92-50-70.

SPECIAL EVENTS

A wine expo, *VINORAMA,* held at the *Eurexpo* complex, brings wine professionals to the city in January of this year. The *Foire Internationale de Lyon,* which traces its origins back to 1420, is now held at the *Heure d'Expo* in Chassieu, about 7 miles (11 km) east of Lyons. On sale here are a range of reasonably priced goods, from food and clothing to antiques; it will be held this year from April 1 through 10. The *Brocante du Vieux Lyon,* a flea market, is held annually in June, usually on the third weekend of the month. For 10 days in mid-September in even-numbered years, the *Festival International Biennal de la Danse Française* welcomes classical and contemporary artists and dance groups from around the world. Lyons's marathon, the *Marathon International de Lyon,* is run in September or October. The *Grand Prix de Tennis de Lyon* (phone: 78-23-45-45) takes place in October, along with another dance festival (for information, contact the *Maison des Festivals;* phone: 72-40-26-26) and an antiques show, the *Salon des Antiquaires.* During November and December, the *Festival de Musique Sacrée du Vieux Lyon* hosts concerts of sacred music whose venues include the city's churches.

Two dates on the church calendar celebrated in a decidedly lay fashion are the long weekend of *Pentecost* (the seventh Sunday after *Easter*), when a national *boules* tournament is held in the *Stade Municipal de Gerland* (see *Sports and Fitness*), and the *Feast of the Immaculate Conception* (December 8), when candles are lighted in windows throughout the city, the streets are illuminated, and the *Christmas* season is semi-officially ushered in to general merriment, Lyonnais style.

MUSEUMS

Besides those described in *Special Places,* the following museums may be of interest:

CENTRE D'HISTOIRE DE LA RÉSISTANCE ET DE LA DÉPORTATION (CENTER FOR THE HISTORY OF THE RESISTANCE AND THE DEPORTATION) Symbolically housed in the former Gestapo headquarters, this museum has a library, an audiovisual center, a study center designed for young people, an auditorium for conferences, and permanent and temporary exhibition space, all related to the Resistance movement and the persecution of Jews in Lyons during World War II. Closed Mondays and Tuesdays. Admission charge. 14 Av. Berthelot (phone: 78-72-23-11).

ESPACE LYONNAIS D'ART CONTEMPORAIN (ELAC; LYONS SPACE FOR CONTEMPORARY ART) This exhibition space hosts shows of contemporary art from all over the world. Open daily. No admission charge. On the top floor of the *Centre des Echanges* (Exchange Center) in the *Gare Perrache* (phone: 78-42-27-39).

MAISON DES CANUTS (HOUSE OF SILKWORKERS) A museum of silk weaving, featuring looms set up with work in progress, and a shop with a limited selection of merchandise, mostly silk ties. Closed Sundays and holidays. Admission charge for a guided visit; free otherwise. 10-12 Rue d'Ivry (phone: 78-28-62-04).

MUSÉE DE L'AUTOMOBILE HENRI MALARTRE (HENRI MALARTRE AUTOMOBILE MUSEUM) One hundred and fifty vehicles, including Hitler's Mercedes, are housed in an imposing château high on the left bank of the Saône. Open daily. Admission charge. Seven miles (11 km) north of Lyons on Vallée de la Saône, Rochetaillée-sur-Saône (phone: 78-22-18-80).

MUSÉE GUIMET D'HISTOIRE NATURELLE (GUIMET MUSEUM OF NATURAL HISTORY) Exhibits on Egyptology and natural history and collections of Far Eastern art. Closed Mondays and Tuesdays. No admission charge. 28 Bd. des Belges (phone: 78-93-22-44).

MUSÉE HISTORIQUE DE LYON (LYONS HISTORICAL MUSEUM) A survey of the city's history, beginning in Roman times. Closed Tuesdays. Admission charge. In the Renaissance *Hôtel de Gadagne,* on Pl. du Petit-Collège (phone: 78-42-03-61).

MUSÉE DE L'IMPRIMERIE ET DE LA BANQUE (MUSEUM OF PRINTING AND BANKING) It commemorates the city's importance as the birthplace of French printing and banking. Closed Mondays and Tuesdays. Admission charge. In the 15th-century *Hôtel de la Couronne,* at 13 Rue de la Poulaillerie (phone: 78-37-65-98).

MUSÉE INTERNATIONAL DE LA MARIONNETTE (INTERNATIONAL PUPPET MUSEUM) The heart of this museum is a history of Lyons's own puppet, Guignol (the original is here). There's also a collection ranging from European puppets to Indochinese shadow theater stage sets. Closed Tuesdays and holidays. Admission charge. In the *Hôtel de Gadagne,* along with the *Musée Historique de Lyon* (see above), at Pl. du Petit-Collège (phone: 78-42-03-61).

MUSÉE ST-PIERRE D'ART CONTEMPORAIN (ST. PETER MUSEUM OF CONTEMPORARY ART) In the same former monastery that houses the *Musée des Beaux-Arts* (see *Special Places*), but with a separate entrance, this annex displays a permanent collection of works dating from 1960, as well as temporary exhibitions of the works of contemporary artists. Closed mornings, Tuesdays, and holidays. Admission charge. 16 Rue Edouard-Herriot (phone: 78-30-50-66).

MUSÉE DE TRAIN MINIATURE DES BROTTEAUX (BROTTEAUX MINIATURE TRAIN MUSEUM) One of Lyons's newer museums, this houses a collection of miniature trains. Closed Sundays. Admission charge. 4 Pl. Jules-Ferry (phone: 78-34-31-17).

SHOPPING

Two pedestrian streets on the *presqu'île* form the main shopping axis: Rue Victor-Hugo, which runs from the *Gare Perrache* to Place Bellecour, and Rue de la République, which continues from Place Bellecour to the *Hôtel de Ville*. These streets, and the nearby parallel and cross streets (including the chic Rue Emile-Zola), include most of Lyons's fashionable shops, many of them outposts of famous Paris or London emporiums. The leading department store on the *presqu'île* is *Au Printemps* (42 Pl. de la République). In the ultramodern Part-Dieu section is the *Centre Commercial,* with several department stores (including *Galeries Lafayette* and *Jelmoli,* a Swiss store) and some 200 boutiques, and *Les Halles* (102 Cours Lafayette), the central food market.

The restoration of Vieux Lyon and the ongoing urban renewal centered on Rue Mercière and Quai St-Antoine have attracted a wide variety of specialty boutiques and crafts to these quarters. An ambitious development on the southern edge of the city, the *Cité Internationale de Lyon* (Quai Achille-Lignon; phone: 78-93-14-14; fax: 78-89-01-71) contains a conference center and the world headquarters of *Interpol* (the international anticrime force known to all fans of spy novels), and will eventually include luxury hotels, restaurants, and shops.

It's no surprise that Lyons is rich in fine charcuteries, pastry shops, and other specialty food stores. The city's outdoor food market, which stretches along the Saône River, is where great chefs like Paul Bocuse do their shopping. Silk is another matter: The old silkworkers' quarter on the slope of Croix-Rousse, while evocative of the past, no longer is a place to find small silk ateliers, although there are still some elsewhere in the city (see below). For antiques, browse along the Rue Auguste-Comte, just south of the Place Bellecour, or take a short taxi ride to the *Cité des Antiquaires* (Antiques Dealers' District), behind the *Parc de la Tête d'Or* at 117 Boulevard Stalingrad in the Villeurbanne district, where you'll find an antiques complex containing nearly 100 stores. It's open Thursdays, Saturdays, and Sunday mornings; closed October through March. A used-book market is held daily on the Quai de la Pêcherie. For standard shopping hours, see GETTING READY TO GO.

Some of our favorite Lyons shops are below:

Atelier de Guignol Hand-crafted puppets, Guignol and others, with heads made to order. 4 Pl. du Change (phone: 78-29-33-37).

Bernachon Some people take the *TGV* all the way from Paris to indulge in the bonbons sold in this justly celebrated *chocolatier*. All the chocolates are made on the premises and sold here only. 42 Cours Franklin-Roosevelt (phone: 78-24-37-98).

Caves de Lyon A fine wine shop. 6 Rue de la Charité (phone: 78-42-86-87).

Chorliet Perhaps the most Lyonnais of charcuteries, as well as a leading caterer. 12 Rue du Plat (phone: 78-37-31-95).

Hermès For elegant scarves from the Paris purveyors of things silk and leather. 95 Rue du Président-Herriot (phone: 78-42-25-14).

Maréchal Cheeses of enormous variety and superb quality. In *Les Halles* (phone: 78-62-36-77).

Au Petit Paris Silk and other textiles by the meter. 9 Pl. des Jacobins (phone: 78-37-08-21).

Le Petit Train Bleu Toy soldiers, model trains, and chess sets. 7 Rue de la Charité (phone: 78-37-61-81).

Sibilia Among the best—and most famous—*charcuteries* in town for sausages and other meat. In *Les Halles* (phone: 78-62-36-28).

Tourtiller Less renowned than *Bernachon* (see above), this is still an excellent place for exquisite chocolates. 4 Cours F.-Roosevelt (phone: 78-52-20-69).

SPORTS AND FITNESS

Lyons has a wide range of facilities for spectator sports, including the *Stade Municipal de Gerland* (Allée de Coubertin; phone: 78-72-66-06), home field of the city's *Olympique* soccer team, and the *Palais des Sports* (350 Av. Jean-Jaurès; phone: 78-72-62-02), where basketball games and boxing matches take place.

BICYCLING Rent bikes at *Loca Sport* (62 Rue Colombier; phone: 78-61-11-01).

BOULES Lyons claims to be the birthplace of this quintessentially French sport, and impromptu games take place almost anywhere there is flat dirt ground. A national annual tournament is held in the *Stade Municipal de Gerland* (see above) during the four days of *Pentecost* weekend.

GOLF The 18-hole, par 72 *Golf Club du Beaujolais* welcomes visitors. It's located in Lucenay-Anse, around 12 1/2 miles (20 km) north of Lyons off N6 (phone: 74-67-04-44; fax: 74-67-09-60).

ICE SKATING There are two municipal skating rinks (100 Cours Charlemagne, phone: 78-42-64-56; and 52 Rue Baraban, phone: 78-54-20-33). Both are closed Sundays and from May through August.

SWIMMING The centrally located *Centre Nautique* (Quai Claude-Bernard; phone: 78-72-04-50), which has two outdoor pools on the Rhône, is open daily June through August. The indoor *Piscine Garibaldi* (221 Rue Garibaldi; phone: 78-60-89-66) is closed Tuesdays and May through August.

TENNIS There are seven public courts at the *Stade Municipal de Gerland* (see above).

THEATER

The theater scene in Lyons is dominated by two institutions that couldn't be more different from each other.

CENTER STAGE

Théâtre de Guignol de Lyon At the end of the 18th century, an unemployed silkworker, Laurent Mourguet, invented a puppet named Guignol, who became the principal character—along with his wife, Madelon, and his friend, Gnafron—in countless comedies. Today, Guignol theaters are scattered all over France. Lyons's is in the basement of the *Palais du Conservatoire.* Here, performances of the classic Guignol repertory, mainly for children, are staged during the day; performances of new pieces intended for adults (because of their political, not sexual, content) take place evenings. The characters are spiritual ancestors of every Lyonnais, and their language is full of the almost forgotten local argot. Even Guignol's costume, with its pigtail and tight black hat, is that of a Lyons silkworker of the 18th century. Performance times vary, so check ahead. Rue Louis-Carrand (phone: 78-28-92-57).

Théâtre National Populaire (TNP) France's most successful experiment in bringing dynamic theater to a wider audience is this state-subsidized institution, located in the decidedly unglamorous suburb of Villeurbanne. Among the foremost theaters in France, it is run by the actor, author, and stage director Roger Planchon. At once "Establishment" and avant-garde, the theater started out leftist in its political orientation—which used to mean a lot of Brecht and daring productions of the classics—but the boundaries have blurred as of late. Supported by local management and labor organizations alike, it counts among its lengthy permanent roster of subscribers both patricians and proletarians. Planchon, one of French theater's *enfants terribles,* alternates easily between startling new visions of classics like Molière's *Tartuffe* and freshly minted works by young

unknowns. Whatever happens here is usually the talk of Paris. 8 Pl.
Dr.-Lazare-Goujon, Villeurbanne (phone: 78-03-30-50).

Lyons's other resident theaters range from the well established to flocks
of fly-by-nights. The city is also on the circuit for touring French and foreign productions. At the opposite pole from the *TNP* is the *Théâtre des
Célestins* (Pl. des Célestins; phone: 78-42-17-67), a handsome 19th-century
building where the repertory is eclectic (Molière, Wilde, Pinter, Feydeau,
Balzac, Shakespeare), but the style is traditional, appealing to a mainstream
audience—it's known familiarly as Lyons's *Comédie-Française*. The *Maison
de la Danse* (*Théâtre du 8e;* 8 Av. Jean-Mermoz; phone: 78-75-88-88) focuses
primarily on modern and contemporary dance. The *Théâtre de Lyon* (7 Rue
des Aqueducs; phone: 78-36-67-67) stages both traditional and contemporary works, from Maupassant to Mrozek. Ballet occasionally is presented
at the *Auditorium Maurice Ravel* (see below).

MUSIC

Ensconced in the modern Part-Dieu neighborhood is the *Auditorium Maurice
Ravel* (149 Rue Garibaldi; phone: 78-95-95-00), an enormous, ultramodern music palace where concertgoers might hear anything from a flute
sonata to Beethoven's "Ninth"—the spaces and the acoustics are equally
suited to small and large concerts. All the top names in French music appear
in the course of any year. The *Orchestre de Lyon,* under musical director
Emmanuel Krivine, makes its home here. The world-class *Opéra de Lyon*
has a striking new home (1 Pl. de la Comédie; phone: 78-28-09-50 or 78-
28-09-60); designed by the controversial architect Jean Nouvel, the completely new opera house is literally encased in the outer walls of the city's
old, 19th-century one. Visiting pop and rock groups that draw crowds usually perform at the *Palais des Sports* (see *Sports and Fitness*).

NIGHTCLUBS AND NIGHTLIFE

If you're in the mood for a pub crawl, head to the Rue Mercière–Quai St-
Antoine neighborhood (see *Special Places*), stopping in perhaps at the
Bouchon aux Vins, a wine bar (62 Rue Mercière; phone: 78-42-88-90); *Bar
du Bistrot* (64 Rue Mercière; phone: 78-37-18-44), an annex of the *Bistrot
de Lyon* restaurant (see *Eating Out*) and certainly one of the most popular
bars on this busy street; *Champagne 16,* a champagne bar (18 Rue Gasparin;
phone: 78-42-29-33); or the classy *Bar de la Tour Rose* (22 Rue du Boeuf),
part of *La Tour Rose* restaurant (see *Eating Out*), which features live jazz
and classical music. In Vieux Lyon, another popular late-night hangout is
the *Vieille Rhumerie* (12 Quai R.-Rolland; phone: 78-37-03-62), which is
also packed with video games. *Eddie et Domino* (6 Quai Gailleton; phone:
78-37-20-29) has a stunning collection of malt whiskies, and Eddie himself,
practically an honorary Scot, always is ready to discuss or instruct; closed
Sundays and holidays.

Among the more active jazz clubs is the *Hot Club* (26 Rue Lanterne; phone: 78-39-54-74); or there's the quiet and sophisticated *Fregoli* piano bar in the *Sofitel* hotel (see *Checking In*). For ballroom dancing, go to the *New Hollywood* (6 Rue Henri-Barbusse; phone: 78-69-42-77). Gamblers make their way to the sparkling *Casino le Lyon Vert,* a short drive west of Lyons in Charbonnières (200 Av. du Casino, La Tour de Salvagny; phone: 78-87-02-70); it's open daily from 3 PM to 2 AM (to 3 AM Fridays and Saturdays).

Best in Town

CHECKING IN

Most of Lyons's hotels are intended for the commercial traveler, and places fill up quickly during the week, even in the off-season. Most of those in the *presqu'île* are relatively modern, and there is a paucity of cozy, small, or quaint hostelries of the kind that one might find on the Left Bank in Paris. Expect to pay more than $200 per night for a double room at a very expensive hotel; between $100 and $200 at an expensive one; between $70 and $100 at a moderate place; and less than $70 at an inexpensive one. Unless otherwise noted, all hotels listed below feature telephones, TV sets, and private baths in the rooms. Some less expensive hotels may have private baths in only some of their rooms; it's a good idea to check whether your room has a private bath when making a reservation. Only expensive to very expensive hotels in Lyons have air conditioning, unless otherwise noted. Hotels accept major credit cards and are open year-round unless otherwise indicated.

VERY EXPENSIVE

Cour des Loges One of the city's most charming and unique hotels, this luxurious property combines the best of the old and the new. Creatively installed in four graceful, renovated Renaissance mansions, it features a spacious interior courtyard, 63 unusual rooms and suites (many of them duplexes), a restaurant, a piano bar, hanging gardens, an indoor pool, a sauna, meeting rooms, a garage, and superb service. On a winding street in Vieux Lyon, at 6 Rue du Boeuf (phone: 78-42-75-75; fax: 72-40-93-61).

Holiday Inn Crowne Plaza With 159 comfortable rooms, it offers all the comforts and services typically found in the top of the chain's line. There is a New Orleans–style restaurant. Near the Part-Dieu station, at 29 Rue de Bonnel (phone: 72-61-90-90; 800-HOLIDAY; fax: 72-61-17-54).

La Tour Rose When Philippe Chavent moved his highly rated restaurant *La Tour Rose* (see *Eating Out*) into new quarters in a 17th-century former convent, he decided to crown it with this deluxe 12-room hotel. The rooms have a warm, personal style, and are richly decorated with the textiles and silks for which Lyons is famous. In Vieux Lyon, at 22 Rue du Boeuf (phone: 78-37-25-90; fax: 78-42-26-02).

Villa Florentine One of the newest of the city's four-star establishments, this palatial hotel with 19 spacious rooms has been decorated in Florentine style, with ocher walls, a terrace with a pool, and a spectacular view of the city. Near La Fourvière at 25-27 Montée St-Barthélémy (phone: 72-56-56-56; fax: 72-40-90-56).

EXPENSIVE

Concorde While hardly deluxe, this quiet establishment counts in its favor 143 modern rooms and a central location. There is a restaurant, too. On the *presqu'île,* at 11 Rue Grolée (phone: 72-40-45-45; fax: 78-37-52-55).

Métropole The out-of-the-way location of this 122-room modern property is more than compensated for by a pool, three tennis and two squash courts, a restaurant, a grill, and a bar. On the left bank of the Saône, near La Croix-Rousse, at 85 Quai Joseph-Gillet (phone: 78-29-20-20; fax: 78-39-99-20).

Pullman Part-Dieu Its 245 rooms are stacked on the top 10 floors of the city's only real skyscraper, the 41-story, cylindrical Crédit Lyonnais tower. The view is unlimited; the style, functional luxury. There's also a creditable restaurant, *L'Arc en Ciel* (see *Eating Out*) and the *Panache Bar,* for the best view in town to accompany a leisurely cocktail. In La Part-Dieu, at 129 Rue Servient (phone: 78-62-94-12; 800-221-4542 in the US; fax: 78-60-41-77).

Pullman Perrache A renovated, turn-of-the-century grand railroad hotel with period charm. Its 124 rooms, many quite spacious, are only a few steps from the *Gare Perrache.* There's a restaurant. On the *presqu'île,* at 12 Cours de Verdun (phone: 78-37-58-11; 800-221-4542; fax: 78-37-06-56).

Royal Another traditional grande dame that has been modernized, and is now part of the Best Western chain. There are 80 rooms and a restaurant. Near the pedestrian shopping streets on the *presqu'île,* at 20 Pl. Bellecour (phone: 78-37-57-31; 800-528-1234; fax: 78-37-01-36).

Sofitel Modern and well equipped, with all the services one would find in an American urban hotel: shops, a hairdresser, a bank, a florist, a good restaurant, a snack bar that's open until 2 AM, and two bars, *Fregoli* and *Melhor.* There are 196 rooms and suites, some looking directly onto the Rhône. Not far from Pl. Bellecour, at 20 Quai Gailleton (phone: 72-41-20-20; 800-763-4835; fax: 72-40-05-50).

MODERATE

Altéa Park Completely renovated, this traditional place has 72 rooms, a garden, and a patio restaurant (open only in good weather). On the eastern side of the city, at 4 Rue du Professeur-Calmette (phone: 78-74-11-20; fax: 78-01-43-38).

Des Artistes Plain and quiet, with 46 modern, air conditioned rooms, this property is centrally situated on a peaceful square dominated by the *Théâtre des Célestins* (it's a favorite of the actors playing there). There's no restaurant. On the *presqu'île,* at 8 Rue Gaspard-André (phone: 78-42-04-88; fax: 78-42-93-76).

Berlioz Bright and cheerful, this remodeled hostelry has 40 small but functional rooms, but no restaurant. On the *presqu'île* behind the *Gare Perrache,* at 12 Cours Charlemagne (phone: 78-42-30-31; fax: 72-40-97-58).

Carlton In this turn-of-the-century hotel—a link in the Best Western chain—all 83 rooms are meticulously appointed with antique furnishings (60 are air conditioned). Traces of the old Belle Epoque decor linger, especially in the elegant, coffered lobby ceiling and the beautiful old elevator. There's no restaurant. On the *presqu'île* near the Pl. de la République, at 4 Rue Jussieu (phone: 78-42-56-51; 800-528-1234; fax: 78-42-10-71).

Charlemagne A good bet, this 116-room hotel is simple, clean, and comfortable. There's a restaurant on the premises. On the *presqu'île* near the *Gare Perrache,* at 23 Cours Charlemagne (phone: 78-92-81-61; fax: 78-42-94-84).

Créqui This is a small, modern spot with 28 rooms, some opening onto an interior garden. There's no restaurant. In La Part-Dieu, at 158 Rue de Créqui (phone: 78-60-20-47; fax: 78-62-21-12).

Grand Hôtel des Beaux-Arts Near the Places des Jacobins, this comfortable hotel, decorated in Art Deco style, has 79 air conditioned rooms. There's no restaurant. 73 Rue du Président Herriot (phone: 78-38-09-50; fax: 78-42-19-19).

Plaza République This 79-room hotel was recently totally refurbished. There's no restaurant, but a good buffet-style breakfast is included in the rate. Near the *presqu'île* at 5 Rue Stella (phone: 78-37-50-50; fax: 78-42-33-34).

INEXPENSIVE

Bayard Not only is this the best situated of the city's less pricey hotels, but charm lurks behind the modern entrance. The 15 rooms are quite nicely outfitted. There's no restaurant. On the *presqu'île,* at 23 Pl. Bellecour (phone: 78-37-39-64; fax: 72-40-95-51).

Bellecordière A small, 45-room hotel with brightly decorated, comfortable accommodations, but no restaurant. On the *presqu'île* near Pl. Bellecour, at 18 Rue Bellecordière (phone: 78-42-27-78; fax: 72-40-92-27).

Moderne A functional establishment in which about half of the 31 rooms have private baths, and a few have lovely old fireplaces. No restaurant. On the *presqu'île* between Pl. Bellecour and Pl. des Terreaux, at 15 Rue Dubois (phone: 78-42-21-83; fax: 72-41-04-40).

Morand Timeworn stone stairwells, Renaissance courtyards, and funky floral carpeting make this 24-room hotel a quaint mix of ancient and modern. During summer, guests can breakfast amid the flowers in the courtyard, but there's no restaurant. In La Part-Dieu, at 99 Rue de Créqui (phone: 78-52-29-96; fax: 78-24-87-88).

EATING OUT

Geography has played a major role in Lyons's gastronomic fortunes. Wine flows in from the Beaujolais and Burgundy regions just to the north, from the Côtes du Rhône to the south, and from the Jura to the northeast. The chicken of Bresse, the beef of Charolais, the fish of countless nearby rivers, and the robust cheeses of surrounding dairy regions all funnel into the city's markets and restaurants. The countryside surrounding Lyons is dotted with stellar restaurants headed by celebrated chefs, such as Pierre Gagnaire, Georges Blanc, and Pierre Troisgros (see *Haute Gastronomie* in DIVERSIONS for more on all three), who have flourished in Lyons's heady culinary environment.

The simplest kind of Lyonnais restaurant is a *bouchon,* often an unpretentious mom-and-pop enterprise, with marvelous regional wine served in a *pot lyonnais* (a heavy bottle containing about a pint) and simple cooking in which pork products weigh heavily. The word *mâchon* is used to describe the least expensive prix fixe menu, which might start with a *saladier lyonnais,* usually a rolling table loaded with a dozen or so cold dishes such as potato salad, lentils, herring and onion in oil, pig's (or sheep's) feet *rémoulade,* and the like. Lyonnais humor is reflected in the names of some dishes: *cervelle de canut* (literally, silkworker's brains) is a soft white cheese into which a variety of herbs has been mixed, and the *tablier de sapeur* (referring to the thick leather apron of a Napoleonic army engineer) is a slab of tripe breaded and grilled or sautéed. *Bouchons* usually also will have such familiar offerings as *boeuf bourguignon, coq au vin,* and quenelles, traditionally Lyonnais, mousse-like dumplings made of pike, veal, or poultry (although *brochet,* or pike, is by far the preferred ingredient), usually served with a rich sauce.

In Lyons and its immediate environs, a dinner for two with service (usually included in the bill) in a very expensive restaurant will run $200 or more; in an expensive one, $100 to $200; in a moderate place, $50 to $100; and in an inexpensive restaurant, less than $50. These prices do not include wine. Reservations are always a good idea; for the three-Michelin-star establishments, make them in advance *in writing.* If you're headed to a popular *bouchon* for lunch, don't arrive much later than midday, and don't be surprised to be turned away, for there may be only one sitting. In expensive places, you usually can limit the financial damage by ordering from the prix fixe menu; moderate restaurants can rapidly become expensive if the temptation to sample fine wine takes over. In the case of month-long summer closings, exact dates can vary, so call before visiting. Unless otherwise noted, all restaurants listed below are open for lunch and dinner.

For an unforgettable culinary experience, we begin with our Lyons (and environs) favorites, followed by our cost and quality choices of restaurants, listed by price category.

HAUTE GASTRONOMIE

Alain Chapel This lovely little inn with a whitewashed cloister and a manicured garden, part of the Relais & Châteaux group, was the base of operations of the late philosopher-chef Alain Chapel, a true star of French cuisine. Chapel's legacy remains; though the restaurant lost one of its three Michelin stars after his death, every morsel is still first class (with prices to match), whether a simple omelette, a complex lobster assemblage, or a *gâteau de foies blonds* (a pie of chicken livers and foie gras). A certain well-known pair of French food writers once admitted to having shed real tears over one of Chapel's creations. In warm weather, tables are placed outdoors on a lovely patio overlooking gorgeous gardens. Lodge in one of the 14 tasteful rooms (none with air conditioning) and you can start all over again the following day. Closed Mondays, Tuesday lunch, holidays, and most of January. Reservations necessary. Major credit cards accepted. Twelve miles (19 km) north of Lyons, on N83 in tiny Mionnay (phone: 78-91-82-02; fax: 78-91-82-37).

Paul Bocuse This three-Michelin-star culinary celebrity earned its reputation after generations in the Bocuse family. Regrettably, Bocuse is often away from his restaurant, tending to gastronomic affairs from Tokyo to *Walt Disney World;* still, there are those who'd cross continents to try the *soupe aux truffes noires* (truffle soup) and the *loup en croûte* (sea bass in a crust), two of the chef's most famous creations. Service can be indifferent—some would say downright rude—to first-timers, but for some the hauteur and astronomical prices are part of the appeal. Open daily; closed two weeks in August. Reservations necessary. Major credit cards accepted. Seven miles (11 km) north of Lyons on the right bank of the Saône, at 40 Rue de la Plage, Collonges-au-Mont-d'Or (phone: 72-27-85-85; fax: 72-27-85-87).

VERY EXPENSIVE

Léon de Lyon Jean-Paul Lacombe continues to serve the same traditional Lyonnais specialties his father did; his rendition of *gras double* (finely chopped tripe sautéed with onion, parsley, garlic, and white wine) is already legendary.

But Lacombe also has expanded his repertoire with nouvelle cuisine creations. The restaurant is a member of the Relais Gourmands, and in 1994 it was awarded a rare second Michelin star, a sign that Lacombe may even have improved on his father's legacy. Diners may choose to eat in a non-smoking dining room. The beaujolais selection is superlative. Closed Sundays, Monday lunch, and three weeks in August. Reservations necessary. Major credit cards accepted. 1 Rue Pléney (phone: 78-28-11-33; fax: 78-39-89-05).

Orsi Pierre Orsi is a well-established chef whose inspired and imaginative fare, served up in a renovated, *très-élégant* dining room, has won the place a Michelin star. Open daily; closed Sunday dinner and August weekends. Reservations necessary. Major credit cards accepted. 3 Pl. Kléber (phone: 78-89-57-68; fax: 72-44-93-34).

La Pyramide A French gastronomic shrine whose 60-seat dining room has a 1920s graciousness, it has been awarded two Michelin stars. There is a terrace and a garden, plus 21 guestrooms and four suites; the total effect is a fitting monument to the late Fernand Point, who some consider this century's greatest French chef. Closed Wednesdays, Thursday lunch, and February through March 7. Reservations necessary. Major credit cards accepted. Nineteen miles (30 km) from Lyons, at 14 Bd. Fernand-Point (recently renamed for the chef), Vienne (phone: 74-53-01-96; fax: 74-85-69-73).

La Tour Rose Philippe Chavent, one of Lyons's ambitious young chefs, has established himself grandly in Vieux Lyon, serving nouvelle cuisine in this one-Michelin-star dining room. Closed Sundays and the last two weeks of August. Reservations necessary. Major credit cards accepted. Chavent runs a shuttle between the restaurant and the parking lot on Quai Romain-Rolland. 22 Rue du Boeuf (phone: 78-37-25-90; fax: 78-42-26-02).

EXPENSIVE

L'Alexandrin This cozy, family-run restaurant with one Michelin star features generous portions of light dishes with a southern French accent, such as an omelette with red peppers, salmon, and leek purée. There's an excellent wine list. Closed Sundays, Mondays, most of August, and three weeks in December. Reservations advised. Mastercard and Visa accepted. Near the central market, at 83 Rue Moncey (phone: 72-61-15-69).

L'Arc en Ciel A fine hotel dining room, whose location—the 32nd floor of the Crédit Lyonnais tower—affords diners the best view in town, though it lost its Michelin star in 1994. Closed Sunday and Monday dinner and mid-July through mid-August. Reservations necessary. Major credit cards accepted. In the *Pullman Part-Dieu* hotel, 129 Rue Servient (phone: 78-62-94-12).

Bourillot Christian Bourillot is known for his classic cooking and for maintaining consistently high standards of excellence in this one-Michelin-star restaurant. The quenelles in lobster sauce are fabulous. Closed Sundays, Monday lunch, early July through early August, and holidays, including 10 days at *Christmas.* Reservations necessary. Major credit cards accepted. On an attractive square, at 8 Pl. des Célestins (phone: 78-37-38-64; fax: 78-38-20-35).

Le Fédora This lovely restaurant with a covered patio-garden offers perhaps the freshest seafood in town, with *homard en os à moelle* (lobster cooked with a marrow bone) as a gesture to meat-loving Lyons. Such inventiveness has earned one Michelin star. Closed Saturday lunch, Sundays, holidays, and December 23 through January 4. Reservations necessary. Major credit cards accepted. 249 Rue Marcel-Mérieux (phone: 78-69-46-26; fax: 72-73-38-80).

Le Gourmandin An old local favorite, it relocated several years ago to Lyons's long-abandoned Brotteaux train station. Superb traditional fare, such as *poulet aux morilles* (chicken with morel mushrooms), is served along with inventive new creations. Closed Saturday lunch and Sundays. Reservations advised. Major credit cards accepted. *Gare des Brotteaux,* 14 Pl. Jules-Ferry (phone: 78-52-02-52; fax: 78-52-33-05).

La Mère Brazier The *mère* has gone, but her one-Michelin-star place remains in family hands and adheres to the purest Lyonnais traditions. *Volaille demi-deuil* ("chicken in half-mourning"—the bird is poached with truffles, whose black color gives the dish its name) is sacrosanct here, as are the artichoke bottoms with foie gras, and quenelles with *béchamel* or lobster sauce. Closed Saturday lunch, Sundays, weekends in July, and the month of August. Reservations advised. Major credit cards accepted. 12 Rue Royale (phone: 78-28-15-49).

Nandron Gérard Nandron's one-Michelin-star restaurant is another place with a family tradition behind it; the menu falls midway between classic Lyonnais and innovative. Closed Saturdays and late July through late August. Reservations necessary. Major credit cards accepted. Overlooking the Rhône, at 26 Quai Jean-Moulin (phone: 78-42-10-26; fax: 78-37-69-88).

Le Passage Long a favorite with Lyonnais in the know, this lace-curtained Belle Epoque–style restaurant specializes in traditional fare. Chef Daniel Ancel is becoming well known for revolutionizing classic dishes with foreign seasonings. The more casual bistro annex next door, *Bar du Passage,* with red-plush seats amid walls covered with trompe l'oeil designs and velvet, has become the more popular of these two fine establishments; try the calf's liver with pan-fried potatoes. Closed Saturday lunch, Sundays, and holidays. Reservations advised. Major credit cards accepted. Hidden away in a passage near the Pl. des Terreaux, at 8 Rue Plâtre (phone: 78-28-11-16 for *Le Passage;* 78-28-12-61 for *Bar du Passage;* fax: 72-00-84-34 for *Le Passage;* 72-00-84-34 for *Bar du Passage*).

Les Quatre Saisons A traditional, bourgeois decor belies the nouvelle dishes produced here; everything from the duck with ratatouille and ginger to warm lobster with caper sauce is delicious. The simply grilled fish and the bouillabaisse are excellent, and the wine list offers more than its share of consistently good vintages. Closed Saturday lunch, Sundays, and two weeks in August. Reservations advised. Major credit cards accepted. 15 Rue Sully (phone: 78-93-76-07).

Roger Roucou (La Mère Guy) On the right bank of the Saône, this was a fishermen's eatery in the 18th century; today, it's one of the city's most elegant establishments, although relatively unknown to non-locals. Closed Sunday dinner, Mondays, and the month of August. Reservations necessary. Major credit cards accepted. South of the center, at 35 Quai Jean-Jacques-Rousseau, La Mulatière (phone: 78-51-65-37).

Le St-Alban Inventive interpretations of classic recipes, such as *pot-au-feu* made with duck instead of beef, and a rabbit terrine garnished with parsley, make this place a winner. Closed Saturday lunch, Sundays, one week in March, and three weeks in August. Reservations necessary. Major credit cards accepted. 2 Quai Jean-Moulin (phone: 78-30-14-89; fax: 72-00-88-82).

MODERATE

Les Adrets "Le Tire-Cul" Delightful atmosphere, good quality, and reasonable prices—especially for the lunch menu—make this place a local favorite. Closed weekends, a week in January, and three weeks in August. Reservations advised. No credit cards accepted. On a winding street in Vieux Lyon, at 38 Rue du Boeuf (phone: 78-38-24-30).

Bistrot de Lyon Jean-Paul Lacombe of *Léon de Lyon* (see above) is a partner in this booming enterprise. Open until 3 AM, it attracts all sorts of night people, including actors and their audiences after the theaters have rung down the curtain. The food is unpretentious, with a Lyonnais accent, and the wines and desserts are good. Open daily; closed 10 days at *Christmas*. Reservations advised. Major credit cards accepted. 64 Rue Mercière (phone: 78-37-00-62; fax: 78-38-32-51).

Le Bouchon aux Vins On the Champs-Elysées of Lyons *bouchons,* this pleasant place serves the usual fare as well as more refined dishes, such as duck breast with pears. About 30 wines are offered by the glass—from a rare white beaujolais to an old graves to the standard house red beaujolais. Closed Sundays. Reservations advised. Major credit cards accepted. 62 Rue Mercière (phone: 78-42-88-90; fax: 78-38-32-51).

Brasserie Georges Since 1836, this huge, bustling dining room has been serving wonderful classics like lentil salad with *chèvre* (goat cheese) and pears cooked in red wine. Open daily. Reservations advised for dinner. Major credit cards accepted. 30 Cours de Verdun (phone: 78-37-15-78; fax: 78-42-51-65).

Café-Comptoir Abel (Chez Abel) This lively, traditional *bouchon* is the place to go for *boudin noir* (black blood sausage) and huge *quenelles de brochet* (pike dumplings) that are light as a feather. Closed weekends (except for Saturday dinner in winter) and three weeks in August. No credit cards accepted. 25 Rue Guynemer (phone: 78-37-46-18; fax: 78-35-27-84).

Chez Hugon Another classic Lyonnais *bouchon,* complete with red-checkered tablecloths, tightly packed tables, rustic woods, and a motherly *cuisinière* at the stove serving up copious portions of simple, soul-satisfying local specialties. Open for lunch only; closed weekends. Reservations advised. Mastercard and Visa accepted. 12 Rue Pizay (phone: 78-28-10-94).

Le Comptoir du Boeuf Philippe Chavent offers a successful low-budget alternative to *La Tour Rose* (see above) with this colorful little café-restaurant, where you can snack on oysters or terrines or order a *plat du jour* until after midnight. Closed Sundays. Reservations advised. Mastercard and Visa accepted. In Vieux Lyon, at 3 Pl. Neuve-St-Jean (phone: 78-92-82-35; fax: 78-42-26-02).

Henry Among savvy Lyonnais, this is considered a sure bet for traditional food—particularly fish and game—prepared with finesse and served with style. Closed Mondays. Reservations advised. Major credit cards accepted. Off Pl. des Terreaux, at 27 Rue de la Martinière (phone: 78-28-26-08).

La Mère Vittet, Brasserie Lyonnaise The best reason for keeping this spot in mind is that it serves food all night—a rarity in France. It's a well-run establishment with decent fare and good wines. A lower-priced annex, *Le Bistrot de la Mère,* serves simpler dishes and good wines in carafes. Open daily; closed May 1. Reservations advised. Major credit cards accepted. Near the *Gare Perrache,* at 26 Cours de Verdun (phone: 78-37-20-17 for the brasserie; 78-42-16-91 for the bistro).

La Tassée A marvelously classic, appealing Lyonnais bistro decorated with amusing murals. The menu ranges from a *mâchon lyonnais* to solid bourgeois fare, and there is a wide range of excellent regional wines. A great spot for lunch. Closed Saturdays from July through August, Sundays, and 10 days at *Christmas.* Reservations advised. Major credit cards accepted. 20 Rue de la Charité (phone: 78-37-02-35; fax: 72-40-05-91).

Le Vivarais Robert Duffaud, a pupil of the late, great Alain Chapel, displays culinary panache in this upscale version of a classic *bouchon.* His artistic efforts give new meaning to the phrase "fashion plate," for each dish is imaginatively and exquisitely presented. Bresse chicken with a sauce that contains foie gras will produce a sigh of pleasure. Closed Sundays, mid-July through mid-August, and a week at *Christmas.* Reservations advised. Major credit cards accepted. 1 Pl. Dr.-Gailleton (phone: 78-37-85-15; fax: 78-37-59-49).

INEXPENSIVE

Bistrot de la Minaudière This simple place has a zinc bar and traditional bistro specialties like *boeuf bourguignon.* Open for lunch only; closed weekends.

Reservations advised. No credit cards accepted. 7 Rue Poullaillerie (phone: 78-37-32-96).

Bistrot d'En Face Another entry on the list of Lyons's chic bistros serving traditional cuisine, such as *coq au vin* and *escalopes de veau à la crème* (veal scallops in cream sauce) at moderate prices; the menu changes each week. Closed Sundays and the last three weeks of August. Reservations advised. Major credit cards accepted. Near the Part-Dieu train station at 220 Rue du Guesclin (phone: 72-61-96-16; fax: 78-60-59-97).

Le Bouchon de Fourvière In the Fourvière district overlooking the Saône, this friendly place has simple bistro dishes, such as grilled lamb chops and zucchini terrine, and a wonderful selection of Côtes du Rhône wines. Closed weekends and the month of August. Reservations advised. Major credit cards accepted. 9 Rue Quarantaine (phone: 72-41-85-02; fax: 78-37-46-28).

Café-Comptoir de Lyon (Chez Sylvain) Keep this traditional *bouchon* in mind when the weather is fine—it's one of the few in town with outdoor dining. The chef's classic offerings often include a touch of originality, such as *rillettes* (a spread made from goose fat and meat) with potatoes au gratin, and quenelles in a red-wine sauce. Closed weekends and mid-July through August 9. Reservations advised. No credit cards accepted. 4 Rue Tupin (phone: 78-42-11-98).

Café des Fédérations Highlights here include more typical Lyonnais *bouchon* fare, an excellent *pot de Morgon* (a variety of beaujolais), and a decor of sausages hanging from the ceiling and photos and old newspaper clippings on the walls. Closed weekends and August. Reservations unnecessary. Major credit cards accepted. 8 Rue du Major-Martin (phone: 78-28-26-00).

Le Garet At this long-established *bouchon,* the menu is classic Lyonnais, the service agreeable, and the beaujolais excellent. Closed weekends, holidays, August, and a week at *Christmas.* Reservations advised. Major credit cards accepted. 7 Rue du Garet (phone: 78-28-16-94).

La Meunière A 1930s *bouchon* with all the predictable trappings—worn tables and tiles, smoke-stained walls and ceiling—and some of the most generous and best offerings in town. If you haven't yet tried the local *poulet au vinaigre* (chicken in a tomato and vinegar sauce), do so here—it's exemplary. Closed Sundays, Mondays, and mid-July through mid-August. Reservations advised. Major credit cards accepted. 11 Rue Neuve (phone: 78-28-62-91).

Le Petit Léon This tiny, modest *bouchon* is the newest venture of superchef Jean-Paul Lacombe. Its menu, which changes daily, features dishes such as *boudin,* lentil salad, and *poulet au vinaigre.* Open for lunch only; closed Sundays. Reservations unnecessary. Major credit cards accepted. 3 Rue Pléney (phone: 72-00-08-10).

La Voûte (Chez Léa) In this down-to-earth *bouchon*, the prix fixe menu usually includes *tablier de sapeur* and the typically Lyonnais *salade de mesclun* (a mixture of wild greens). Closed Sundays and the month of July. Reservations advised. Major credit cards accepted. 11 Pl. Antoine-Gourju (phone: 78-42-01-33; fax: 78-37-36-41).

BARS AND CAFÉS

The best thing to do in Lyons at "happy hour" is to split a *pot* of beaujolais with a friend. Other possibilities include most of the bars listed under *Nightclubs and Nightlife* and two hotel bars with a view: *Le Melhor* in the *Sofitel* hotel and the *Panache Bar* in the *Pullman Part-Dieu* hotel (see *Checking In* for both). The *Grand Café des Négociants* (1 Pl. Francisque-Regaud) is a fine example of a fin de siècle grand café, while the *Cintra* (43 Rue de la Bourse) is a haven of Anglophilic understatement.

Marseilles

Modern Marseilles is above all else a port city, as it has been for 25 centuries. A natural port ideally situated for commerce in the western Mediterranean, it was founded in 600 BC by Phocaean Greeks from Asia Minor. Massilia, as it was first called, prospered at their hands. The city went into decline under Roman rule, but its fortunes picked up with the arrival of the Crusaders, whom the port provisioned with food and weapons; by that time, Marseilles was trading with Africa, the Near East, and the Far East.

The city was devastated in 1720 by the great plague, in which 50,000 of its citizens perished. Ever resilient, Marseilles rose to support the French Revolution: In 1792, 500 volunteers marched to Paris, exuberantly singing a war song composed at Strasbourg by a young officer named Claude-Joseph Rouget de Lisle. By the time the troops reached Paris, their expert chorus electrified all listeners. The song caught on and became France's stirring national anthem, "La Marseillaise," named not for the city but for those staunch choristers.

One hundred years after the Revolution, the opening of the Suez Canal assured the continued maritime success of Marseilles, and commercial traffic abandoned the small Vieux (Old) Port for a new one directly to the north. The new port—as well as much of the picturesque Old Quarter, known as Le Panier (French for "breadbasket")—was destroyed by the Germans during World War II. The new port was subsequently rebuilt and expanded, and nondescript, soulless buildings rose on the once vibrant site of Le Panier. But some reminders of Marseilles's tradition survive, and every ground breaking holds the possibility of unearthing still more traces of earlier civilizations. The most stunning discovery was made in 1967: As a new *Bourse* (Stock Market Building) was being constructed, vestiges of the ancient port of Massalia, previously thought to have been completely destroyed during various invasions, were unearthed. In 1974, a boat dating from the 3rd century was discovered in the same area. In recent years, an organization called the *Atelier du Patrimoine* has gained the right to refuse construction permits to buildings in the center of the city that threaten Marseilles's character and ancient landmarks.

Marseillais have as much in common with Italians and Greeks as they do with Parisians, and Marseilles's future in the new border-free Europe is expected to be linked more closely with its Mediterranean sunbelt neighbors—cities like Genoa, Nice, Montpellier, and Barcelona—than with far-away Paris. And with the opening last year of *L'Espace Mode Méditerranée* on the Canebière (see *Special Places*), Marseilles also is gearing up to become a Mediterranean fashion capital.

To the visitor, Marseilles offers palpable evidence of its link to the sensuous, boisterous world of the Mediterranean. Sailors from all over the world roam the Canebière, the famous street leading up from the Vieux Port, in search of women or excitement. The milieu of the French underworld endures, for Marseilles remains "the French Connection"; while many drug middlemen have moved on to Amsterdam or Berlin, Popeye Doyle would still recognize the place.

With almost 900,000 residents, Marseilles is France's second-largest city in terms of population, although not in terms of economics: The city is plagued by unemployment and burdened with debts to the French government. Numerous immigrants have settled in Marseilles, including a great number of industrial workers from the island of Corsica, Italians, and North Africans. Many impoverished Algerians, Tunisians, and Moroccans live in slums around the *Porte d'Aix* and the Rue Ste-Barbe, where shops sell inexpensive North African items. The area is perfectly safe in the daytime, and worth a visit for the colors and smells alone, but few people feel comfortable wandering here after dark.

Many visitors to Marseilles, en route to the Côte d'Azur, give short shrift to this bustling city. But there's sufficient reason to linger. Step into a café on the Vieux Port as the burning Mediterranean sun starts to sink in the sky and order a milky white *pastis,* an anise-flavored aperitif. Around you are spectacular white limestone hills; in front of you, a harbor filled with the accents of far-off lands. Who knows? You may, like the late American writer M.F.K. Fisher, fall in love with Marseilles and stay longer, soaking in its rich Mediterranean atmosphere and exploring its abundant historic remains.

Marseilles At-a-Glance

SEEING THE CITY

Take the No. 60 bus up to this hilly city's most imposing height, a 531-foot limestone bluff crowned by the half-Roman, half-Byzantine *Basilica of Notre-Dame-de-la-Garde* (Pl. du Colonel-Edon), known to the Provençal as *La Bonne Mère* (the good mother). The terrace affords an extraordinary view, particularly at sunset, of the boats on the Vieux Port, the white rocky islands, and the densely built city stretched out below. A sightseeing train called *Le Petit Train de la Bonne Mère* leaves daily afternoons from June through September from the Vieux Port to the basilica; consult the tourist office (see *Tourist Information*) for details and off-season schedules.

SPECIAL PLACES

Walk down the monumental staircase of the *Gare St-Charles* and continue on the Boulevard d'Athènes until you come to a busy central shopping street, the Canebière. The broad, plane-tree–lined concourse, which runs into the Vieux Port, is the city's main artery. This celebrated boulevard is Marseilles's answer to Paris's Champs-Elysées, but visitors are sometimes disappointed at its modern, occasionally tacky appearance. Note that some Marseilles sites of interest close for lunch, usually between noon and 2 PM.

IN THE CITY

VIEUX PORT (OLD PORT) Follow the Canebière down to the Quai des Belges and you'll arrive at the Vieux Port, the heart of Marseilles. A harbor for small fishing boats and yachts, it's far more picturesque than the burgeoning new port to the north. Its entrance is framed by the 17th-century forts of *St-Jean* and *St-Nicolas* (a Foreign Legion base). Terraced restaurants featuring bouillabaisse (at staggering prices) overlook the animated marina, and a fish market does a lively business every morning. One can ferry from one side of the Vieux Port to the other, an experience reminiscent of Marcel Pagnol's "Marseilles Trilogy" (the films *Marius, Fanny,* and *César*); ferries make the trip every 10 minutes daily.

MUSÉE DES BEAUX-ARTS (FINE ARTS MUSEUM) Housed in the 19th-century *Palais de Longchamp*—itself noteworthy for its impressive fountains and gardens—the museum offers a considerable display of art. Paintings from the Italian, Flemish, Dutch, and French (David, Courbet, Ingres) schools share the palace's left wing with works by Marseilles natives Honoré Daumier and Pierre Puget and other Provençal artists. The right wing of the palace contains a natural history museum, the *Musée de l'Histoire Naturelle*. Both museums are closed Mondays. Separate admission charge to each museum. Pl. Bernex (phone: 91-62-21-17, *Beaux-Arts*; 91-62-30-78, natural history museum).

ESPACE MODE MÉDITERRANÉE (MEDITERRANEAN FASHION SPACE) This complex contains a *Musée de la Mode* (fashion museum). Here, too, is the *Institut International de la Mode,* an organization presided over by top designer Azzedine Alaïa that has already helped launch the careers of many young designers from the Mediterranean region (Alaïa is a native of Tunisia). The museum holds special exhibits on fashion in general and on particular designers. Closed Mondays. Admission charge to the museum. 11 La Canebière (phone: 91-14-92-20).

MUSÉE GROBET-LABADIÉ Near the *Palais de Longchamp,* this showplace is furnished opulently with the furniture, art, and musical instruments that belonged to its former occupant, 19th-century musician Louis Grobet. Open daily. Admission charge. 140 Bd. Longchamp (phone: 91-62-21-82 or 91-08-96-04).

COURS JULIEN (JULIAN WAY) This unique public square has splashing fountains, interesting boutiques, bookstores, restaurants, and an innovative art gallery (see *Shopping*). It takes an hour to explore the whole plaza, but allow yourself the pleasure of real contact with the youth, vigor, and creativity of

Marseilles. To get here, walk north from the Vieux Port, up the Canebière, then east onto Bd. Garibaldi, which crosses Le Cours Julien.

MUSÉE DES DOCKS ROMAINS (MUSEUM OF THE ROMAN DOCKS) An unexpected benefit came from the Germans' 1943 bombing of this area, known as Le Panier: Fascinating remains of long-buried Roman docks and statuary were unearthed in the course of rebuilding the area. This museum incorporates the original area of the finds, plus objects retrieved offshore. Open daily. Admission charge. 28 Pl. Vivaux (phone: 91-91-24-62).

MUSÉE D'HISTOIRE DE MARSEILLE (MUSEUM OF MARSEILLES HISTORY) The excavations of the ancient Greek port and ramparts are now a museum. The open-air archaeological dig features the remains of a 3rd-century boat excavated on the site, and the adjacent *Jardin des Vestiges* contains the remains of Massilia. Closed mornings and Sundays. Admission charge. Pl. Belsunce (phone: 91-90-42-22).

LE PANIER (THE BREADBASKET) From the Quai du Port, the narrow streets climb toward what little remains of Marseilles's Old Quarter. Reminiscent of Paris's Montmartre (and beginning to suffer the same "renewal" fate), Le Panier is a maze of tiny streets reverberating with the exuberant sounds of daily life in a Provençal neighborhood. In the area are several worthwhile art galleries and interesting bistros. Behind the *Hôtel de Ville* (Town Hall), climb the steps to the left of *Notre-Dame-des-Accoules*'s bell tower, the remains of a 12th-century church.

LA VIEILLE CHARITÉ (OLD CHARITY) This Baroque, rose stone building sporting an egg-shaped cupola, built from 1640 to 1715, was designed as a prison hospital by Pierre Puget. Abandoned in the early part of this century, it was taken over by squatters until 1986, when a vast renovation restored the building to its original state. Currently home to several research institutes, it also houses temporary exhibitions of predominantly contemporary art and Egyptian and Greek artifacts, a *Musée d'Arts Africains, Amérindien, et Océanien* (a collection of African, Native American, and Oceanic arts), and a *Musée d'Archéologie Méditerranéenne* (Mediterranean Archaeology Museum). Closed weekends. Admission charge. In Le Panier, at 2 Rue de la Charité (phone: 91-56-28-38).

MUSÉE CANTINI (CANTINI MUSEUM) Ensconced in a former mansion, Marseilles's contemporary art museum is considered to be one of the best collections in France. Closed Mondays. Admission charge. 19 Rue Grignan (phone: 91-54-77-75).

CATHÉDRALES DE LA MAJOR (CATHEDRALS OF THE MAJOR) Reminiscent of Moslem mosques, the cathedrals' domes and cupolas dominate the Quai de la Tourette. The sadly battered *Ancienne* (Ancient) *Major* was built in the 12th century in pure Romanesque style on the ruins of the Roman Temple of Diana. The huge, ostentatious cathedral next to it was built in the 19th century in the Romanesque-Byzantine style. Pl. de la Major.

ABBAYE ST-VICTOR The present fortified Gothic church dates from the 11th to the 14th century, but the real interest lies below, in its crypt, which is actually an ancient basilica founded in the 5th century in honor of the 3rd-century martyr Saint Victor. This abbey contains a chapel and the tomb of two 3rd-century martyrs, in addition to pagan and early Christian catacombs. The crypt is closed Sundays. Admission charge. At the end of Rue Sainte (phone: 91-33-25-86).

CITÉ RADIEUSE (RADIANT CITY) The renowned architect Le Corbusier designed this *unité d'habitation* (housing development) from 1947 to 1952 to provide low-cost housing. Considered avant-garde for its time, it's still a landmark in modern functional architecture. 280 Bd. Michelet.

PARC BORÉLY (BORÉLY PARK) A lovely stretch of greenery where you can take some sun by the lake or rent a bicycle. There's also a quaint racetrack. Open daily. No admission charge. Promenade de la Plage and Av. Clot-Bey.

MUSÉE DES ARTS ET TRADITIONS POPULAIRES DU TERROIR MARSEILLAIS (MARSEILLES AREA MUSEUM OF POPULAR ARTS AND TRADITIONS) Among the exhibitions here are pottery, pewter, and glass displays. Closed mornings and Tuesdays. Admission charge. Just inside the city limits in the Château Gombert quarter; follow the autoroute north toward Lyons and exit at La Rose. 5 Pl. des Héros (phone: 91-68-14-38).

OUT OF TOWN

PROMENADE DE LA CORNICHE (BLUFF DRIVE) Also known as Corniche Président-J-F-Kennedy (President John F. Kennedy Bluff Drive), this scenic coast road winds for some 3 miles (5 km) south of the Vieux Port. It offers breathtaking views of the sea; Marseilles's most spectacular homes, including the *Château d'If;* and the Iles Frioul (see below). The road passes a picture-postcard fishing port, Vallon des Auffes, and lovely rocky coves before it becomes the Promenade de la Plage, in front of *Parc Borély.* The Promenade then continues to Cassis, 14 miles (22 km) from Marseilles, a beautiful fishing town and summer resort that has been celebrated by Derain, Vlaminck, Matisse, and Dufy. The lovely, sandy Prado Beach is also along the Corniche road; watch for signs. Pick up the Promenade in Marseilles at Rue des Catalans.

CHÂTEAU D'IF (YEW-TREE CASTLE) Set on a rocky island, this gorgeous castle was built in the 16th century for defense, and then turned into a state prison whose most famous inmate (though fictional) was Alexandre Dumas's Count of Monte Cristo. Inside some cells are carvings by Huguenot prisoners. The view of the port from the island is breathtaking. Open daily.

Admission charge. Boats to the château leave from the Quai des Belges (phone: 91-55-50-09) about every hour for the 20-minute ride.

ILES FRIOUL (FRIOUL ISLANDS) Southwest of Marseilles, these islands have sparkling creeks and simple restaurants that provide an idyllic retreat from the city's sometimes torrid atmosphere. Boats leave for the islands from the Quai des Belges (see above) daily every hour.

EXTRA SPECIAL

For unsurpassed and unspoiled natural beauty, don't leave the region without seeing the spectacular *calanques* along the coast between Marseilles and Cassis. The narrow, crystal-clear, fjord-like creeks, between stark white limestone cliffs that soar up to 650 feet, can be approached only by foot (about one-and-a-half hours each way) or by boat, thereby ensuring a minimum number of tourists. The closest *calanques*—Sormiou and Morgiou—lie at the terminus of bus No. 20. A free map of the *calanques* is available at the tourist office (see *Tourist Information*). For information on organized hiking ventures, visit *Les Excursionnistes Marseillais* (16 Rue de la Rotonde; phone: 91-84-75-52), open Tuesdays through Saturdays from 6 to 8 PM. Otherwise, boats leave from the Quai des Belges (see *Château d'If,* above) Wednesday and weekend afternoons from June 15 through September 15.

Sources and Resources

TOURIST INFORMATION

The English-speaking staff of the *Office du Tourisme* (4 La Canebière; phone: 91-54-91-11) provides hotel reservations, maps, guides, and advice; also ask for *La Charte de la Bouillabaisse,* which gives the real recipe for this often poorly imitated fish soup and provides a list of restaurants serving the authentic concoction. There is a second tourist office at *Gare St-Charles* (phone: 91-50-59-18). Both are open daily.

LOCAL COVERAGE The local newspapers, *Le Méridional* and *Le Provençal,* are available at any newsstand. *A Tout Marseille,* a quarterly magazine in French of what's happening, is distributed by the tourist office (see *Tourist Information*) free of charge. A good, street-indexed map is the *Carte et Plan Frézet,* available at major bookstores along the Canebière. They also carry English-language guidebooks. For a closer look at Marseilles, read *A Considerable Town,* by M.F.K. Fisher (Vintage; $14.95); it's a charming and personal account of a city she loved.

TELEPHONE The city code for Marseilles is 91 (the code for the airport is 42), which is incorporated into all local eight-digit numbers. When calling a number in Marseilles from the Paris region (including the Ile-de-France), dial 16, wait for the dial tone, then dial the eight-digit number. When calling a number from outside Paris, dial only the eight-digit number.

GETTING AROUND

AIRPORT The Modern *Aéroport Marseille-Marignane* (phone: 42-78-21-00) is 18 miles (29 km) northwest of the city. For a taxi into town, 24 hours a day, call 42-78-24-44; the ride should take about 30 minutes. Shuttle buses, a less expensive alternative, run every 20 minutes in both directions (to and from *Gare St-Charles,* the main train station; phone: 91-50-59-34).

BOAT Boats leave the Quai des Belges (phone: 91-55-50-09) approximately every hour daily for the Iles Frioul and the *Château d'If.* For information on trips to the *calanques,* see *Extra Special.*

BUS AND MÉTRO Marseilles's modern, attractive subway system is coordinated with the buses, allowing easy, free transfers between systems. The métro goes in only two directions, so it's difficult to get lost. Buy an economical *carnet* (packet) of six tickets instead of the single ticket, which costs around 5F (approximately 85¢ at press time). The métro shuts down each night at 9 PM, though many buses run later, some offering service through the night. For information, call 91-91-92-10.

CAR RENTAL *Avis* has offices at the airport (phone: 42-89-02-26); the *St-Charles* train station (phone: 91-64-71-00); 267 Boulevard National (phone: 91-50-70-11); and 92 Boulevard Rabatau (phone: 91-80-12-00). *Hertz* has locations at the airport (phone: 42-78-23-59); 16 Boulevard Charles-Nédelec (phone: 91-14-04-24); 40 Quai du Lazaret (phone: 91-90-52-10); 27 Boulevard Rabatau (phone: 91-79-22-06); and 59 Avenue de St-Just (phone: 91-66-00-82). *Budget* has offices at the airport (phone: 42-78-24-55) and at 40 Boulevard de Plombières (phone: 91-64-40-03). *Europcar* has three offices, including one at the airport (phone: 42-89-09-42).

FERRY For ferries to Corsica, inquire at *SNCM* (61 Bd. des Dames; phone: 91-56-62-05 or 91-56-32-00). The office is closed Sundays.

TAXI You can get a taxi at one of the cabstands around the city, or call *Taxi Tupp* (phone: 91-05-80-80); *Marseille Taxi* (phone: 91-02-20-20); *Maison du Taxi* (phone: 91-95-92-50); or *Taxi Radio France* (phone: 91-49-91-00).

TOURS From late May through September, three-hour guided bus tours of Marseilles are available in English upon advance request from *Protour* (4 Bd. Baille; phone: 91-94-00-44).

TRAIN The main station is the *Gare St-Charles* (Av. Général-Leclerc; phone: 91-08-50-50, information; 91-08-84-12, reservations). The extension of the Paris-Lyons high-speed *TGV* (*Train à Grande Vitesse,* or "very fast train") line to Valence, which continues to encounter resistance from locals who want to preserve the environment, will (if and when completed) cut travel time between Paris and Marseilles to just over three hours; in the meantime, it takes about four-and-a-half hours.

SPECIAL EVENTS

The annual *Fête de l'Ail* (Garlic Fair), when mounds of garlic cover the sidewalks of Cours Belsunce, is held June 15 through July 15. *L'Été Marseillais*, an extension of the traditional summer *Festival des Iles* (Islands Festival), runs from mid-June through mid-September and features a wide range of performances—from classical music and dance to jazz and theater—that take place in the city's parks, churches, and monuments, and on the islands off the port of Marseilles. Early July brings a *Festival International Folklorique* (International Folklore Festival) to the Château Gombert quarter. The colorful *Foire des Santons* (Santons Fair)—during which the traditional hand-painted clay statuettes, some as much as three feet tall, fill *Christmas* crèches all over the city—takes place from December 26 through January 2.

MUSEUMS

Besides those described in *Special Places,* the following museums may be of interest:

MUSÉE DE LA MOTO (MOTORCYCLE MUSEUM) The collection of motorcycles here includes a De Dion Bouton (1898), a Moto Guzzi (1947), a Motosacoche 215cc (1904), and many more. Closed Mondays. Admission charge. Traverse St-Paul, Quartier le Merlan (phone: 91-02-29-55).

MUSÉE DU VIEUX MARSEILLE (MUSEUM OF OLD MARSEILLES) A folklore museum set in the 16th-century *Maison Diamantée* (Diamond House), so called for the shape of its stone facing, it is best known for its *santon* collection (see *Shopping*). Open daily. Admission charge. Rue de la Prison (phone: 91-55-10-19).

SHOPPING

Major department stores, elegant couturier and gift shops, and enough shoe shops to satisfy a centipede are clustered in the frenetic area around the Canebière (Rue de Rome, Rue Paradis, and the pedestrian-only Rue St-Ferréol, where some of the *plus chic* shops are found). The flashy and trendy *Centre Bourse* is a shopping center north of the Canebière. Less expensive shops, usually selling North African items, are in the vicinity of the *Porte d'Aix* (the triumphal arch in Pl. Jules-Guesde at the end of Rue d'Aix).

The city's raucous market areas, on the Quai des Belges, where the fishermen and their wives sell their catch directly, are particularly alive in the mornings. Don't miss the food market on Rue Longue des Capucins (at Rue Vacon, near the Canebière), the flea markets near the industrial port, the daily book market on Le Cours Julien, and Rue St-Barbe in the Algerian quarter (but avoid this area after dark). Marseilles's suq (open-air market) is held every morning on the Rue d'Aubagne; the atmosphere is pure Istanbul. Other good outdoor markets are held on the Place Jean-Jaurès (Thursday and Saturday mornings) and the Place Castellane (every morning).

Typical Marseillais souvenirs include clay *santons,* which can be found during the *Christmas Foire des Santons* (see *Special Events*) at numerous booths set up on the Canebière, and year-round at the *Ateliers Marcel Carbonel* (47 Rue Neuve-Ste-Catherine; phone: 91-54-26-58), where they are made. These small, naively modeled and brightly colored figurines represent biblical figures and such traditional Provençal characters as the Gypsy, the shepherd, and the milkmaid. *Savon de Marseille,* another of the city's famous products, is a soap so pure it's used for babies' baths.

For standard shopping hours, see GETTING READY TO GO. The following are other browse-worthy shops:

Amandine This great *pâtisserie* has a small tearoom where you can indulge in an *assiette de gâteaux* (assortment of cakes). 69 Bd. Eugène-Pierre (phone: 91-47-00-83).

Les Arcenaulx A popular bookstore and publishing house, it sells both new and old editions; on the premises are a tearoom, a restaurant, and an antiques shop. 25 Cours Estienne d'Orves (phone: 91-54-77-06).

Benetto The city's best *charcuterie,* it's a great place for picnic provisions. 7 Pl. Notre-Dame-du-Mont (phone: 91-48-66-23).

Felio The most venerable hatmaker in Marseilles. Its *casquette Marseillaise* (a cap with a small brim) is a classic. 4 Pl. Gabriel-Péri (phone: 91-90-32-67).

Le Four des Navettes Try some *navettes* (flat biscuits flavored with orange-flower water) from this remarkable 200-year-old bakery. 136 Rue Sainte (phone: 91-33-32-12).

François Décamp This reliable antiques shop offers a wide variety of items, from 18th-century fans to furniture. 302 Rue Paradis (phone: 91-81-18-00).

Galerie Roger Pailhas An art gallery that promotes the work of international artists, including some of Marseilles's most original ones. 61 Cours Julien (phone: 91-42-18-01).

Galerie Wulfram-Puget An antiques shop specializing in Provençal antiques, including *boutis* (heavy quilted bedspreads). 39 Rue de Lodi (phone: 91-92-06-00).

Meffre This recently renovated shop is Marseilles's temple of classic men's and women's fashion. 14 Rue Paradis (phone: 91-33-01-40).

Puyricard The city's finest shop for chocolates. Try the ones stuffed with *pâte d'a-mande* (almond paste). Two locations: 155 Rue Jean-Mermoz (phone: 91-77-94-11) and 25 Rue Francis-Davso (phone: 91-54-26-25).

La Savonnerie du Sérail A soap factory specializing in *savon de Marseille,* with a boutique (closed weekends). 66 Rue Jules-Marlet (phone: 91-37-17-59).

Au Tastevin A slightly cluttered, old-fashioned shop where wines of the nearby Cassis and Bandol regions can be bought, as well as foie gras, truffles, and a limited selection of Fauchon fancy food products. 8 Rue Edmond-Rostand (phone: 91-37-10-62).

SPORTS AND FITNESS

FISHING Gilt-head and mackerel can be found off the Corniche, in the *calanques* and around the Iles Frioul (see *Special Places*), and in nearby fishing villages.

GOLF Tee off at *Golf de la Salette* (phone: 91-27-12-16), an 18-hole course less than 5 miles (8 km) from central Marseilles. To get there, take the autoroute east and exit at La Valentine.

HORSEBACK RIDING The *Centre Equestre de la Ville de Marseille* offers instruction. 33 Carthage (phone: 91-73-72-94).

JOGGING Take bus No. 21 to *Domaine de Luminy,* a park about 4 miles (6 km) from the city center. Or try *Parc Borély,* 3 miles (5 km) south of the city by the Promenade de la Corniche.

SAILING Contact *Centre Municipal de Voile* (Plage du Roucas-Blanc; phone: 91-76-31-60), which offers sailing classes on the Mediterranean.

SOCCER Marseilles's beloved soccer team, *L'Olympique de Marseille,* though highly ranked in Europe, has recently been embroiled in scandal. (There are allegations that their opponents have been paid to let them win!) For information and tickets, contact their office (441 Av. Prado; phone: 91-76-56-09).

SWIMMING Try the Olympic-size, public pool *Piscine Luminy* (Rte. Léon-Lachamp; phone: 91-41-26-59).

TENNIS AND SQUASH Try one of the 16 courts at *Tennis Municipaux* (Allée Ray-Grassi; phone: 91-77-83-89); or there's *Tennis St-Tronc* (81 *bis* Rue François-Mauriac; phone: 91-26-16-05), with five outdoor courts. For squash, there's *Set-Squash Marseille* (265 Av. de Mazargues; phone: 91-71-94-71), with nine courts, plus an indoor tennis court, pool, and fitness center, and *Prado Squash* (26 *bis* Bd. Michelet; phone: 91-22-83-90), with eight courts.

WATER SPORTS For information on what's available around Marseilles, call or drop in at the *Fédération des Sociétés Nautiques des Bouches du Rhône,* 10 Av. de la Corse (phone: 91-54-34-88).

THEATER AND DANCE

Despite the city's currently depressed economy, Marseilles offers a surprisingly good range of theater activity year-round.

TOP TROUPE

Ballet National de Marseille Roland Petit France's best-known dance company makes its home in Marseilles but travels nonstop both at home and abroad. Its dance pieces cross the austerity of the classical tradition with American musical comedy brashness to produce a personable style all their own that is never dark, stark, or aggressively experimental. The *compagnie* provides a fine introduction for the uninitiated who fear they may be bored by ballet. Don't miss the marvelously original *Coppélia,* in which the character that most companies portray as a lonely old man is a decadent roué in white tie and tails who attempts to bring to life the doll he has created—not to be the daughter he never had, but as a lover. If you're lucky enough to be in town when the company is here, you really should try to catch a performance. *Ballet National de Marseille Roland Petit,* 1 Pl. Auguste Carli (phone: 91-47-94-88 or 91-71-51-12).

Theatrical choices, featuring a wide variety of contemporary and classic theatrical and musical performances, include the *Espace Culturel Busserine* (6 Rue Busserine; phone: 91-58-09-27); the *Théâtre Toursky* (16 Impasse du Théâtre; phone: 91-02-58-35); the *Théâtre du Gymnase* (1 Rue du Théâtre Français; phone: 91-24-35-24); and the *Théâtre de l'Odéon* (162 La Canebière; phone: 91-42-90-90). There's also the more ambitious national theater, *La Criée* (30 Quai de Rive-Neuve; phone: 91-54-70-54).

For experimental theater and music, there's the *Théâtre de Lenche* (4 Pl. de Lenche; phone: 91-91-55-56; fax: 91-91-52-22); *Chocolat Théâtre* (59 Cours Julien; phone: 91-42-19-29); and *Espace Julien* (in the *Centre Culturel,* at 33 *bis*–39 Cours Julien; phone: 91-47-09-64). An exciting, original program of mostly contemporary drama is offered by the *Théâtre du Gyptis* (136 Rue Loubon; phone: 91-11-00-91). The *Théâtre des Bernardines* offers dance performances and concerts (17 Bd. Garibaldi; phone: 91-42-45-33). The *Théâtre Massalia* (41 Rue Jobin; phone: 91-62-39-51) features performances by marionette companies from all over Europe. The *Babadoum Théâtre* presents performances for children (16 Quai de la Rive Neuve; phone: 91-54-40-71). For more theater information and tickets, visit the office of the *FNAC* at *Centre Bourse,* north of the Canebière, or the tourist office (see *Tourist Information*).

MUSIC

The Marseillais know good opera as well as they know bouillabaisse. The *Opéra de Marseille* (Pl. de l'Opéra; phone: 91-55-00-70 or 91-55-14-99) offers major performances year-round (for reservations and information, go to the ticket office at 2 Pl. Ernest-Reyer). Unique *Espace Julien* (see above) offers occasional jazz and an open cabaret where anyone can perform, as well as lessons in everything from playing musical instruments to dance to gymnastics. The *Cité de la Musique* (4 Rue Bernard du Bois; phone: 91-39-28-28) offers musical instruction and performances of jazz and contemporary music. Chamber music and organ recitals take place often at major churches, such as the *Abbaye St-Victor,* and occasionally outdoors on the Vieux Port.

Popular music doesn't fare nearly as well, but concerts are occasionally held at the *Palais des Sports* (phone: 91-75-50-50).

NIGHTCLUBS AND NIGHTLIFE

Marseilles does not suffer from inactivity after dark, with action ranging from the sedate to the frenetic. In the former category, visitors will find soothing piano bars such as *Le Beauvau* in the *Pullman Beauvau* hotel (see *Checking In*), whose barman really knows his trade. *Le Pelle Mêle* (45 Cours d'Estienne-d'Orves; phone: 91-54-85-26) is a chic bar offering jazz and cocktails. The most "in" nightspots include *Bunny's Club* (2 Rue Corneille; phone: 91-33-29-15), with a packed dance floor and an excellent sound system, and *London Club* (73 Promenade de la Corniche; phone: 91-52-64-64), a friendly nightclub/disco. At the moment, the young set favors *Rock 'n' Roll* (5 Rue Molière; phone: 91-54-70-36). Other current popular spots include *L'Ascenseur* (118 Rue Dragon; phone: 91-33-15-37) and *Le Club 116* (116 Rue du Chantier; phone: 91-33-77-22).

Best in Town

CHECKING IN

Thanks to a fairly recent spurt of hotel construction, Marseilles now has an overabundance of higher priced, ultramodern rooms, but not much improvement in the lower price ranges. For a double room (not including breakfast), expect to pay $150 or more per night in a very expensive hotel; $100 to $150 in an expensive one; $70 to $100 in a moderate place; and less than $70 in an inexpensive hotel. Unless otherwise noted, hotels have air conditioning, telephones, TV sets, and private baths. Some less expensive hotels have private baths in only some of their rooms; it's a good idea to confirm whether your room has a private bath when making reservations. Hotels accept major credit cards and are open year-round unless otherwise indicated. Many require *demi-pension* (a higher rate that includes breakfast and either lunch or dinner) in July and August.

VERY EXPENSIVE

Concorde Palm Beach A supermodern 145-room hotel by the sea, it has an outdoor pool, two restaurants, and a private beach. 2 Promenade de la Plage (phone: 91-16-19-00; fax: 91-16-19-39).

Concorde Prado This palatial, 80-room modern hotel near the convention center offers guests access to the *Concorde Palm Beach* hotel's pool and beach.

There is a restaurant, where brunch is served on Sundays. 11 Av. de Mazargues (phone: 91-76-51-11; fax: 91-16-19-39).

Le Petit Nice Small (15 rooms and suites) and gracious, this member of the Relais & Châteaux group was built in the 19th century as a private villa. There's a shady garden, a seawater swimming pool, and the superb two-Michelin-star restaurant *Passédat* (see *Eating Out*), all overlooking the Mediterranean from a magnificent vantage on the Corniche. Hotel closed January and the first week in February. 160 Promenade de la Corniche (phone: 91-59-25-92; fax: 91-59-28-08).

EXPENSIVE

Holiday Inn Modern, with 120 rooms and six suites and all the comforts of the familiar chain, plus a terrace garden. In Marseilles's main business district near the *Palais des Congrès*, at 103 Av. du Prado (phone: 91-83-10-10; fax: 91-79-84-12).

Mercure This member of the luxury chain is distinguished by its taste, its pleasant piano bar, and its outstanding restaurant, *L'Oursinade* (see *Eating Out*). Its 200 rooms have all the expected luxury hotel amenities; nonsmoking rooms are available. Opt for a room on an upper floor for a spectacular view of the city and sea. A five-minute walk from the Vieux Port, on Rue Neuve-St-Martin (phone: 91-39-20-00; fax: 91-56-24-57).

Pullman Beauvau Most of the 71 rooms in this 19th-century property—one of Marseilles's best—face the Vieux Port. In a former incarnation the hotel housed George Sand, Chopin, and Lamartine; many of the rooms are furnished with antiques from that era. There is no restaurant. Next to the tourist office, at 4 Rue Beauvau (phone: 91-54-91-00; 800-221-4542; fax: 91-54-15-76).

Sofitel Vieux Port Magnificent and modern, with a splendid view from its perch above the entrance to the Vieux Port, it has 127 rooms, a heated outdoor pool, a cozy bar, and a fine restaurant. Nonsmoking rooms are available. 36 Bd. Charles-Livon (phone: 91-52-90-19; 800-763-4835; fax: 91-31-46-52).

MODERATE

Alizé Of the 35 rooms in this renovated portside hotel, ask for one with a view of the Vieux Port. There's no restaurant. 7 Quai des Belges (phone: 91-33-66-97; fax: 91-54-80-06).

Lutétia Although just off the Canebière, this modern, 29-room hotel offers quiet, light-filled rooms. Bathrooms have either a bath or a shower. Rooms are not air conditioned and there's no restaurant. 38 Allées L. Gambetta (phone: 91-50-81-78; fax: 91-50-23-52).

New Hôtel Bompard In a quiet park on a hill not far from the sea are 46 rooms—in a main building and surrounding bungalows—with kitchenettes, but no air conditioning. There's no restaurant. A five-minute drive on the Corniche from the bustle of the Vieux Port, at 2 Rue des Flots-Bleus (phone: 91-52-10-93; fax: 91-31-02-14).

St-Ferréol's This renovated, 19-room hotel is stylish and comfortable, with such extras as a Jacuzzi in some rooms, marble baths, elegant fabrics, and a cozy little bar for breakfast and drinks. There's no restaurant. Closed July 25 through August 23. Near the Canebière and the Vieux Port, at 19 Rue Pisançon (phone: 91-33-12-21; fax: 91-54-29-97).

INEXPENSIVE

Capitainerie des Galères In this modern hostelry are 141 smallish rooms, a restaurant, and a bar. Close to the Vieux Port, at 46 Rue Sainte (phone: 91-54-73-73; fax: 91-54-77-77).

Grand Hôtel de Genève Old, but modernized, this hotel has 43 rooms with minibars (20 are air conditioned), but no restaurant. In a quiet pedestrian precinct just behind the Vieux Port, at 3 *bis* Rue Reine-Elizabeth (phone: 91-90-51-42; fax: 91-90-76-24).

EATING OUT

Marseilles's restaurants are considered among France's finest for their renditions of both classic French cuisine and Provençal specialties. The city is best known for its bouillabaisse, a soup traditionally based on *rouget* (Mediterranean rockfish) but often containing other fish and shellfish, especially lobster and crab. Among the seasonings used, the standout is saffron, which gives the soup its golden color. Bouillabaisse often is served with rouille, a relish made of red pepper, garlic, and fish broth,while *bourride*, another Marseillaise fish stew, is often accompanied by aïoli, a delicious olive-oil–based garlic mayonnaise.

Other regional specialties include *anchoïade* (an anchovy-and-olive-oil paste that accompanies raw vegetables), *poutargue* (grated, pressed, and dried fish eggs), *navettes* (flat biscuits flavored with orange-flower water), and *fougasse* (flat, salty bread in leaf designs, flavored with walnuts, olives, bacon, or cheese). You also may wish to sample *pastis,* the anise-flavored aperitif, which is served diluted with ice water. Also try wines from Provence, particularly the dry, pleasant rosé.

For dinner for two (without wine), expect to pay $150 or more at an expensive hotel; $80 to $150 in a moderate one; and less than $80 in an inexpensive place. Prices include a service charge, which is usually added to the bill. Unless otherwise noted, all restaurants listed below are open for lunch and dinner.

For an unforgettable culinary experience, we begin with our Marseilles favorites, followed by our cost and quality choices of restaurants, listed by price category.

Patalain Marseilles's answer to the famous *mères* (female chefs) of Lyons is Suzanne Quanglia, a true Marseillaise whose cooking makes one feel like an honored guest in someone's home. From local specialties such as *langue d'agneau au vinaigre* (lamb's tongue in vinegar) and *morue fraîche* (fresh cod) to such inventive creations as crayfish with fresh ginger or sole filets with artichokes and fresh coriander, everything exudes the chef's lively Midi spirit. The atmosphere is friendly, and the prices are in the upper moderate range. Closed Saturday lunch, Sundays, holidays, and mid-July through early September. Reservations necessary. Major credit cards accepted. 49 Rue Sainte (phone: 91-55-02-78; fax: 91-54-15-29).

Passédat A two-star Michelin establishment that we feel deserves a third. The view alone is worth the very high price of admission, and the cuisine is even better than the view. The tomato tart appetizer is the most beautiful single menu item we've ever had on our *plats,* and the lobster ragout is equally impressive. Open daily; closed Saturday lunch and, from October through February, on Sundays except holidays. Reservations necessary. Major credit cards accepted. In the *Petit Nice* hotel, 160 Promenade de la Corniche (phone: 91-59-25-92; fax: 91-59-28-08).

EXPENSIVE

Chaudron Provençal Copper cauldrons hang from wide ceiling beams in this rustic little fish restaurant, where diners can choose from the day's fresh fish, displayed in baskets next to the tiny open kitchen and sold by weight. Closed Saturday lunch and Sundays. Reservations advised. Major credit cards accepted. In Le Panier, at 48 Rue Caisserie (phone: 91-91-02-37).

Les Echevins Don't miss the elaborate, beamed ceiling (built in 1637) of this elegant, antiques-filled restaurant. The cuisine includes local specialties as well as rich dishes; try the morel mushrooms cooked in sauterne, from the Périgord. Closed Saturday lunch, Sunday dinner, and August 1 through 16. Reservations advised. Major credit cards accepted. 44 Rue Sainte (phone: 91-33-08-08).

La Ferme In the opinion of many, this elegant restaurant featuring country cooking is one of the city's best. The terrine of *lapereau* (young rabbit), the fish dishes, and the casserole of veal kidneys are all excellent. Closed Sundays, holidays, and August. Reservations advised. Major credit cards accepted. 23 Rue Sainte (phone: 91-33-21-12).

Michel (Les Catalans) The menu is short and the seafood, succulent; this is a perfect place to sample bouillabaisse. Closed Tuesdays and Wednesdays. Reservations unnecessary. Major credit cards accepted. 6 Rue des Catalans (phone: 91-52-30-63).

Miramar Touted by locals as one of the best sources on the quay of the Vieux Port for authentic bouillabaisse, this modern, one-Michelin-star restaurant also serves a wide variety of other fish dishes and regional specialties. Closed Saturday lunch, Sundays, August 1 through 24, and *Christmas* through *New Year's*. Reservations advised. Major credit cards accepted. 12 Quai du Port (phone: 91-91-10-40; fax: 91-56-64-31).

L'Oursinade This place serves fine Provençal dishes in an atmosphere of understated elegance. Closed Sundays. Reservations advised. Major credit cards accepted. In the *Mercure Hotel,* Rue Neuve-St-Martin (phone: 91-39-20-00; fax: 91-56-24-57).

MODERATE

L'Ambassade des Vignobles This new restaurant features Provençal cuisine; the fish terrine with *aïoli* is a standout. The stunning wine list reflects the orientation of the owners, who are oenophiles; trust the sommelier's recommendations about what to drink with what. Closed Saturday lunch, Sundays, and August. Reservations necessary. Major credit cards accepted. 42 Pl. aux Huiles (phone: 91-33-00-25).

L'Assiette Marine A *nouvelle*-inspired eatery offering excellent and unusual seafood dishes like puff pastry with asparagus and crayfish, and a great orange mousse for dessert. Open daily; closed several weeks in summer—call ahead. Reservations advised. Major credit cards accepted. Near *Parc Borély,* at 148 Av. Mendès-France (phone: 91-71-04-04).

Les Arcenaulx This local favorite features regional cuisine; try the marinated fresh sardines or the rabbit with ratatouille. Closed Sundays. Reservations advised. Major credit cards accepted. 25 Cours d'Estienne d'Orves (phone: 91-54-77-06; fax: 91-54-76-33).

Chez Loury (Le Mistral) This dependable restaurant is favored for its bouillabaisse, puff pastry with seafood filling, and other fish dishes. Closed Sundays and the last two weeks in May. Reservations advised. MasterCard and Visa accepted. 3 Rue Fortia (phone: 91-33-09-73; fax: 91-33-73-21).

Au Jambon de Parme Italian food predominates here; you'll remember you're in Marseilles, though, when you try the excellent seafood. The authentic Roman-style *saltimbocca* (veal rolls) is hard to pass up. Closed Sunday dinner, Mondays, and July 11 through August 25. Reservations necessary. Major credit cards accepted. 67 Rue de la Palud (phone: 91-54-37-98).

Le Lunch In a splendid location overlooking the Calanque de Sormiou, this simple restaurant features super-fresh seafood (sold by weight) and home-style bouillabaisse. Open daily; closed mid-October through February. Reservations advised. MasterCard and Visa accepted. A 20-minute taxi ride from the Canebière, Calanque de Sormiou (phone: 91-25-05-37).

Les Petits Anges The bistro of chef Gérald Passédat, who masterminds *Passédat* (see above), serves strictly traditional regional dishes in a friendly atmosphere. Closed Sunday dinner and Mondays. Reservations advised. Major credit cards accepted. 44 Bd. E. Herriot (phone: 91-77-60-77).

René Alloin Alloin, an experienced chef who has served in many of France's finest restaurants, recently opened this one of his own. The focus is on seafood; try the *loup rôti au fenouil* (sea bass roasted with fennel) or the veal sweetbreads with morel mushrooms. No lunch on Saturdays; no dinner on Sundays. Closed Mondays. Reservations advised. Major credit cards accepted. 8 P. Amiral-Muselier (phone: 91-77-88-25; fax: 91-77-76-84).

INEXPENSIVE

Etienne Cassaro This Marseilles landmark and local legend offers wonderful pizzas, Sicilian-style pastas, and some seafood dishes, notably *supions* (cuttlefish). There's no menu, so listen carefully as the waiter recites the day's offerings. Closed Sunday dinner and Mondays. No reservations. No credit cards accepted. 43 Rue Lorette (no phone).

La Kahenas This Tunisian eatery offers daily specials, mint tea, and pastries. It gets very crowded at lunch. Closed Sundays. No reservations. No credit cards accepted. 2 Rue de la République (phone: 91-90-61-93).

BARS AND CAFÉS

Le Bistrot Thiars (38A Pl. Thiars; phone: 91-54-03-94) is an artists' haunt that becomes even more popular (and pricey) in the summer, when it attracts tourists and theater people for its alfresco dining. *Le Bar de la Marine* (15 Quai Rive-Neuve; phone: 91-54-95-42) is best known for its terrace, where scenes from some of Marcel Pagnol's films were shot. *La Samaritaine* (2 Quai du Port; phone: 91-90-44-95) is a local hangout where Midi-accented French (for franc, you'll hear "frang") prevails. One of the city's most *branché* (stylish) bars is the minuscule *L'X* (30 Rue St-Saëns; phone: 91-54-95-55); the terrace of *New York* (7 Quai des Belges; phone: 91-33-60-98) remains *the* place to see and be seen by *tout* Marseilles in summer.

Monaco
(and Monte Carlo)

One of the smallest states in Europe, the independent principality of Monaco is also one of its most renowned. It is a mixture of old and new, with sleek modern buildings juxtaposed with the pastel stucco and blue tile typical of French Mediterranean architecture and the extravagant silhouettes of the Belle Epoque. Everywhere, the emphasis is on sumptuous elegance: Yachts fill the port, and the shops display vintage wine, costly jewels, and *haute couture* clothes and furs.

Monaco's location, near the Italian border, between the Mediterranean and the foothills of the French Maritime Alps, gives it a climate much like that of Southern California. Winters are mild (in February, the average low temperature is 46F; the average high, 55F); summers are warm and pleasant (in August, temperatures hover in the 70s); and there is little rain. The vegetation, too, is like Southern California's, with orange and lemon trees, palms, and live oaks. The water temperature is ideal for swimming. In fact, the only shortfall in this natural endowment is an inadequate supply of beach. Monaco's most exclusive stretch of sand is actually just over the border, in France, and its own beach is all manmade.

What Monaco had from the very beginning was a harbor next to a high, rocky promontory jutting into the sea—a natural fortress. The rock itself first was colonized in the 6th century BC by the Monoikos Ligurian tribe (the probable origin of the name Monaco). Later, the Romans set up camp. By the late 12th century, this strategic configuration belonged to the Genoese, who in 1215 sent men and material to fortify Le Rocher (The Rock), as it is called. In the 13th century, the Republic of Genoa (along with the rest of Italy) was torn by strife between the Guelphs and the Ghibellines, opposing political parties favoring the pope and the emperor respectively. When the Ghibellines came to power in Genoa in 1295, they threw out the Guelphs, including the noble Ligurian Grimaldi family and one Francesco Grimaldi, known as Malizia (the Cunning One). Disguised as a monk and accompanied by a band of partisans, Malizia went to Le Rocher early in 1297 to ask for shelter. The guard agreed and opened the gates, and Malizia and his companions stormed the fortress and took it.

For more than 100 years, the Grimaldi family fought Genoa to maintain—or regain—control of its conquest, and in 1419, Jean Grimaldi officially founded the state, incorporating Menton and Roquebrune into Monaco. Afterwards, the tiny state still had to contend with other foreign influences. From 1524 to 1641, it was a protectorate of Spain; from 1641 to 1793, a protectorate of France. After the French Revolution, Monaco was annexed to France as part of the Alpes-Maritimes *département*. The 1814 Treaty of Paris restored it to sovereignty, but in 1815 it became a protectorate of the kingdom of Sardinia. By 1848, when Menton and Roquebrune declared themselves free cities, Monaco's identity had begun to dissolve.

The turning point came with Prince Charles III of Monaco. In 1861, Charles negotiated a treaty with France, again establishing Monaco as a sovereign nation, and underscoring the point by minting gold coins and issuing postage stamps. Because the loss of Menton and Roquebrune had reduced the revenues of the principality, Charles opened a gaming house to replenish the treasury, and the *Société des Bains de Mer (SBM;* Sea Bathing Society) was formed to run the enterprise and organize resort facilities. In 1864 the society debuted its first luxury hotel, the *Hôtel de Paris,* on the Spélugues plateau across the harbor from Le Rocher, and in 1865 the casino next door was opened. Four years later, the casino was so profitable that the prince was able to abolish direct taxes on his citizens. Monte Carlo (Mount Charles), as the development on the plateau was renamed in the prince's honor, had been born.

Charles's son, Prince Albert I (on the throne from 1889 to 1922), also took important steps to develop the principality. Passionately interested in oceanography, he undertook numerous scientific nautical expeditions and built the prestigious *Musée Océanographique* (Oceanographic Museum) to house the results and promote further research. (He also founded the *Institut Océanographique* in Paris in 1906.) Monaco is indebted to Albert I for the *Jardin Exotique* (Exotic Garden) and the *Musée d'Anthropologie Préhistorique* (Museum of Prehistoric Anthropology), for the construction of the port, for the establishment of numerous schools and a hospital, for its first constitution, and for its famous automobile race, the *Rallye Automobile Monte-Carlo* (see *Special Events*).

Prince Rainier III, the present ruler, who acceded to the throne in 1949, has changed the face of Monaco no less than his ancestors. His marriage to the late American actress Grace Kelly in 1956 turned the international spotlight on the principality as never before, making it a household word synonymous with fairy-tale romance. The great charm and beauty of Princess Grace (who died in an automobile accident in 1982), and the caliber of the international clientele she attracted to the social and cultural events of her new home, complemented the prince's efforts to overhaul the principality and its tourist industry. Modern high-rise apartment buildings, roads and tunnels, underground parking lots, public elevators, a port, hotels, parks, and beaches were constructed. Some of the development was on land that was reclaimed from the sea; the 77 new acres enlarged Monaco's area to a total of 482 acres. Because it has no taxes, Monaco also is something of a banking center; many an international deal has been closed at one of the city's after-work luxury spots.

The Monégasques (citizens of Monaco) enjoy a limited democracy. Since 1962, the principality has been administered by a national council, while the *Mairie de Monaco* (the Monte Carlo city hall) is ruled by a community council whose members are elected every four years. Although Monaco is a sovereign state, with its own postage stamps (favorites with collectors) and license plates, it enjoys a customs union with France, which means that there are no formalities crossing the border. The French franc is the medium of exchange, though Monégasque coins bearing Prince Rainier's likeness are circulated and are fully convertible in France. The principality's security is assured by French *gendarmes* and colorful local police. French is the primary language spoken, though Italian also is common; English is spoken in hotels, restaurants, and casinos. Less often will you hear the Monégasque dialect, a mixture of Italian and Niçois, though it is officially encouraged and is taught in the schools.

The majority of Monaco's population of 30,000 are foreigners, largely of French origin (14,000), but there also are Italian, Swiss, British, and American inhabitants. Only approximately 5,000 are Monégasques. Citizenship is difficult to come by, expensive, and not necessarily granted even to those born here. Those who possess it are excluded from the gaming tables, but in return do no military service and pay no income tax—privileges somehow fitting for the nationals of a country just the right size for the pages of a storybook.

Monaco At-a-Glance

SEEING THE CITY
Panoramic views are not in short supply in Monaco. The Place du Palais offers a breathtaking view of the harbor and Monte Carlo, a sight that should be seen at night, when the city lights glitter against their mountainous backdrop. From the *Jardin Exotique* (see *Special Places*), set even higher on a steep slope behind Le Rocher, the view takes in the whole of the principality and beyond to the Italian coast, including a grand expanse of blue Mediterranean. A sign directs you to the lookout point. Some of the most spectacular views of Monaco are found about 1 mile (1.6 km) from the city, on the Cannes-Nice highway (A8).

SPECIAL PLACES
Monaco is divided into four parts. Monaco-Ville, a traffic-free maze of narrow cobblestone streets and tile-roofed houses set atop Le Rocher, contains Monaco's Vieille Ville (Old City). Monte Carlo, the "new" city, is a seaside sprawl of modern luxury high-rises, broad avenues, and highways, with the respite of palm trees and gardens and several opulent examples of the architecture of the last century. Less interesting to tourists are La Condamine, the commercial harbor area between Monaco-Ville and Monte

Carlo (you'll often hear La Condamine referred to simply as Monaco), and Fontvieille, 20 acres of reclaimed land west of Le Rocher, now a commercial, residential, and industrial center. Note that many museums and other attractions close during lunch hours, especially in the off-season.

LE ROCHER (THE ROCK)

PALAIS PRINCIER (PRINCE'S PALACE) The first foundation stone of this manmade fortress was laid in 1215, and for a few hundred years thereafter the structure remained largely defensive. Its transformation into something fit for habitation by a prince was largely the work of two 17th-century Grimaldis, Prince Honoré II and Prince Louis I. During the French Revolution, the palace was looted, and it was used for a time as a military hospital; 19th-century restoration, continued modification, and the return of much lost furniture and artwork resulted in the palace of today. With its crenelated tower sporting an anachronistic clock and its cannon complete with neat piles of cannonballs, it looks like a castle from an operetta set, perfect for a miniature monarchy. The changing of the guard at the candy-striped sentry boxes takes place daily at 11:55 AM (go early for a good view). During the summer, you also can go inside the palace, where you'll see the *Cour d'Honneur* (central courtyard), surrounded by mainly 17th-century frescoes; the sumptuously decorated *Grands Appartements* (State Apartments); and the *Salle du Trône* (Throne Room). Guided tours last about 35 minutes. Open daily from June through October; admission charge. Atop Le Rocher, at Pl. du Palais (phone: 93-25-18-31).

Musée du Palais Princier (Prince's Palace Museum) Also known as the *Musée des Souvenirs Napoléoniens* (Napoleonic Museum), it houses Napoleonic memorabilia—such as his field glasses, watch, and decorations—gathered by Prince Louis II, Prince Rainier's grandfather. Documents relating to the history of the principality also are on display, along with a collection of rare 19th-century Monégasque postage stamps, a series of coins minted by the princes since 1640, and uniforms of the prince's guards. Open daily; closed Mondays, and from November through May. Admission charge. In the south wing of the *Palais Princier* (phone: 93-25-18-31).

JARDINS ST-MARTIN (ST. MARTIN'S GARDENS) The old fortifications surrounding Le Rocher have been turned into garden walks, a peaceful place to stroll amid Mediterranean flowers and shady trees. The gardens run roughly from the *Palais Princier* to the point of Le Rocher at *Fort Antoine*. Open daily; no admisssion charge (no phone).

CATHÉDRALE (CATHEDRAL) Near the *Jardins St-Martin* is this edifice, built in 1875 on the site of a 13th-century church. The white stone exterior is Romanesque in style; the interior, which contains two 16th-century altarpieces by Louis Bréa preserved from the original church, shows a Byzantine influence. The burial chapel is in the west part of the transept; the tombs of the Princes of Monaco—among whom Princess Grace was laid to rest—are in the crypt. Sunday mornings at 10 AM, mass is sung by the famous children's choir *Les Petits Chanteurs de Monaco.* 4 Rue Colonel-Bellando-de-Castro (phone: 93-30-88-13).

MUSÉE OCÉANOGRAPHIQUE ET AQUARIUM (OCEANOGRAPHIC MUSEUM AND AQUARIUM) Not only a museum but a working scientific research institute, this was the brainchild of Albert I. At the edge of a sheer drop on Le Rocher, the structure was considered bold for its day: Pillars had to be built from sea level to support it, and the rocks below had to be hollowed out to let in sea water for the aquarium. Work began in 1899, but the museum did not open until 1910.

Start your visit on the lowest level. Here is the aquarium, one of the finest in the world—not surprising when you learn that the director of the museum is Jacques-Yves Cousteau, whose films are shown in the conference hall. On the ground floor are zoological exhibits, skeletons of large marine mammals (including a 60-foot rorqual, or whale), and specimens that Prince Albert brought back from his expeditions. The top floor is perhaps the most interesting, with the prince's whaleboat and 19th-century navigational instruments and, in complete contrast, ultramodern diving equipment. Open daily. Admission charge. Av. St-Martin (phone: 93-15-36-00).

MONTE-CARLO STORY This 35-minute-long multivision slide presentation, given in five languages (including English), traces the history of the princes of Monaco. Open daily; closed December, and mornings from November through February. Admission charge. Near the *Musée Océanographique,* at the Terrasses du Parking des Pêcheurs (phone: 93-25-32-33).

MONTE CARLO

CASINO DE MONTE CARLO Even if you're not a gambler, this landmark is a must. Stop for a moment in front to appreciate the drama of the setting, the immaculate gardens adorned with sculptures, the comings and goings of glamorous patrons in elegant limousines and sports cars, and the building itself, designed by Charles Garnier, the architect of the Paris *Opéra.* Then enter the *Atrium,* a grand foyer paved with marble and lined with onyx columns supporting an elaborate second-story gallery and a stained glass ceiling.

To the left are the gaming rooms. The first is the *Salon Américain* (American Room), in all its rococo, gold splendor. It comes complete with American-rule gambling and some 140 incongruous slot machines, plus craps and blackjack tables, all staffed by Las Vegas–trained managers, as well as bartenders adept at making screwdrivers and Bloody Marys. The adjoining *Salon Rose* (Pink Salon), now a bar, used to be a smoking room (witness the cigar-puffing nudes painted overhead); the red-carpeted and -curtained *Salle Blanche* (White Salon) also has American games.

Dress is casual for gambling American style (women in pants and men without ties are welcome), but if you penetrate farther into the European gaming rooms, coats and ties are required for men (and you won't feel out of place in black tie or chiffon). Here are the *Salon Touzet* (Touzet Room), swathed in paintings; the large, regal *Salon Privé* (Private Room), reserved for high rollers; and, finally, a *Salon Super-Privé,* a cloistered sanctum catering to visiting royalty, celebrities, and the super-rich. Equipped with one table for *banque-à-tout-va,* the *Salon Super-Privé* is available by appointment only; the very knowledge that you have played there should forever banish the need to wear Gucci loafers or drive a Ferrari to establish your status.

To the right of the *Atrium,* past glass cases holding memorabilia and costumes from famous performances, is the unassuming entrance to the *Salle Garnier,* Monte Carlo's opera house. In six months, Garnier transformed a small concert room into a jewel of a theater, lavish with gold-leaf medallions, garlands, and scrolls; allegorical statues; a Romantic painted ceiling; and an 18-ton gilt bronze chandelier. Sarah Bernhardt starred on opening night in 1879, and the acts that followed were no less illustrious: Diaghilev created the *Ballets Russes de Monte Carlo* on this stage, Nijinsky danced here, and Caruso, Lily Pons, and other legends have sung here.

The casino is open daily; the *Salon Américain* and *Salon Touzet* open at noon, other rooms at 4 PM. There's no admission charge in the rooms before the European gaming rooms, though you must be over 21. A passport and an admission charge (waived for guests of one of the four *SBM* hotels— see *Checking In*) are required for the European gaming rooms. The *Salle Garnier* can be seen only by attending a performance. For additional details on the casino, see *Casinos Royale* in DIVERSIONS. Pl. du Casino (phone: 92-16-21-21, casino; 92-16-22-99, opera house).

MUSÉE NATIONAL (NATIONAL MUSEUM) One of the most complete collections of dolls and "automata" (mechanical dolls) in the world. The 2,000-plus objects here, mostly from the 18th and 19th centuries, include 400 exquisitely dressed dolls and the delicately crafted miniature furniture and accessories that surround them in their elegantly composed settings. The centerpiece is a remarkable 18th-century Neapolitan crèche. The museum is housed in another Garnier design, the beautiful *Villa Sauber,* whose grounds are rampant with roses and scattered with sculptures by Rodin, Maillol, and others. Open daily; closed holidays and during the *Grand Prix.* Try to come between 3:30 and 5:30 PM, when the automata come to life. Admission charge. 17 Av. Princesse-Grace (phone: 93-30-91-26).

ELSEWHERE

JARDIN EXOTIQUE (EXOTIC GARDEN) Another Albert I project, this is no ordinary cactus garden. It clings to the side of a rocky cliff at the western approach to Monaco, more than 300 feet above the sea. The inclination of the cliff provides protection from northern winds and maximum exposure to the winter sun, creating an environment in which 7,000 species of cacti and succulents, weird and wonderful specimens from semi-arid climes around the world (particularly from Africa and Latin America), thrive as well as they would in their native habitats. At the base of the cliff are the Grottes de l'Observatoire (Observatory Caves). Although today you're most likely to notice the stalagmites and stalactites, at one time the caves housed prehistoric man. You can take a guided tour of the caves, but note that the climb up and down totals 558 steps. Open daily; admission charge covers the garden, caves, and the *Musée d'Anthropologie Préhistorique* (see below). Bd. du Jardin-Exotique (phone: 93-30-33-65).

MUSÉE D'ANTHROPOLOGIE PRÉHISTORIQUE (MUSEUM OF PREHISTORIC ANTHROPOLOGY) The remains of Cro-Magnon man, primitive tools, and fossils and skeletons of fauna from 5000 to 500 BC, as well as some Roman jewelry and other relics discovered during excavations at the harbor in 1879, are on display. Open daily. Admission charge covers the *Jardin Exotique* and caves (see above). Bd. du Jardin-Exotique (phone: 93-15-80-06).

CENTRE D'ACCLIMATATION ZOOLOGIQUE (ZOOLOGICAL ACCLIMATIZATION CENTER) A tiny zoo at the foot of Le Rocher that is home to monkeys and apes, lions and other large cats, wild birds, an elephant, and many specimens of tropical (mainly African) fauna. Open daily. Admission charge. Pl. du Canton (phone: 93-25-18-31).

Sources and Resources

TOURIST INFORMATION

Monaco's tourist and convention bureau is above the gardens of the casino in Monte Carlo (2A Bd. des Moulins; phone: 92-16-61-66, 92-16-61-16, or 92-16-60-21/2; fax: 92-16-60-00). The English-speaking staff provides maps, detailed brochures on Monaco's sights, restaurants, and hotels, and, if necessary, assistance in making hotel reservations. Open daily; closed Sunday afternoons.

LOCAL COVERAGE The French daily *Nice Matin* covers the southeast of France, including Monaco. The free monthly brochure *Bienvenue à Monte Carlo,* published and distributed by the tourist office, lists events and other pertinent information in four languages, including English. *La Gazette,* an attractive bimonthly, bilingual newsmagazine that covers Monaco, the Riviera, and Europe in general, is more society-oriented, as is the slick *Riviera,* which is available in English. French and other international newspapers and magazines can be found at the *Café de Paris* (see *Eating Out*) or at the *Loews Monte Carlo* hotel (see *Checking In*). *Scruples* (9 Rue Princesse-Caroline; phone/fax: 93-50-43-52) is a bookstore that sells English-language books, maps, travel guides, and posters.

TELEPHONE The city codes for Monaco are 90, 92, and 93, which are incorporated into all local eight-digit numbers. When calling a number in Monaco from the Paris region (including the Ile-de-France), dial 16, wait for a dial tone, then dial the eight-digit number. When calling a number from outside Paris, dial only the eight-digit number.

GETTING AROUND

Monaco is one of the few countries visitors can see from one end to the other on foot. Transportation is simple and well organized, but driving is often tricky because the streets are narrow and steep.

AIRPORT The closest airport to Monaco for domestic and international flights is the *Aéroport de Nice–Côte d'Azur* (phone: 93-21-30-30 or 93-21-30-12), about 16 miles (26 km) west of the prinicipality. From the airport, taxis are available for the trip to Monaco (for a price—it will cost around 350F, or $60 at press time). Or take the 10-minute helicopter shuttle, about the same price as a taxi if you're traveling alone; contact *Héli-Air Monaco*. You can catch it at the heliport at Terre-Plein de Fontvieille in Monaco (phone: 92-05-00-50; fax: 92-05-76-17) or at either the baggage claim area at the national airport or the *Zone Affaire* at the international airport in Nice (phone: 93-21-34-95). There's frequent train service daily from Nice to Monaco (see *Train,* below); from the station nearest the airport (accessible by taxi), the fare is around 20F (about $3.50 at press time). A bus service also runs daily (approximately every hour) between Nice airport and Monaco, stopping at the Monaco train station (see *Train,* below) and at Place de la Crémaillère, near the casino in Beausoleil; the fare is around 75F (about $13 at press time). For more information on buses, call *Rapides Côte d'Azur* in Nice (14 Rue François-Guisol; phone: 93-55-24-00) or the tourist office (see *Tourist Information,* above).

BUS Of the four main bus lines, two (Routes 1 and 2) depart from Place de la Visitation in Monaco-Ville and go to the casino, and two (Routes 4 and 5) depart from the train station (see *Train,* below). Route 1 goes to the east border and St-Roman, taking in Monte Carlo, the *Musée National* (see *Special Places*), the beaches, and the *Monte Carlo Country Club* (see *Tennis and Squash* in *Sports and Fitness*); Route 2 goes to the west border and the *Jardin Exotique* (see *Special Places*); Route 4 goes east to the Larvotto beaches (see *Swimming* in *Sports and Fitness*); and Route 5 does a sort of figure eight, one loop encompassing Fontvieille, the other the *Centre Hospitalier Princesse Grace*. The local bus fare is about 5F (around 85¢ at press time), and discount cards good for four to eight trips, called *"cartes multivoyages,"* are also available. There are frequent stops; buses run about every 10 minutes during the week and on Saturdays and every 20 minutes on Sundays and holidays. Buses also depart from the train station and from Place de la Crémaillère in Beausoleil for Menton (where you can change to a bus for Italy) via Roquebrune-Cap-Martin and for the Nice airport (see *Airport,* above). For more fare and schedule information, contact the tourist office.

CAR RENTAL A car is hardly a necessity, but if you intend to roam the surrounding region, rentals are available, with or without chauffeur, from a number of agencies. *Avis* (9 Av. d'Ostende; phone: 93-30-17-53); *Europcar* (47 Av. de Grande-Bretagne; phone: 93-50-74-95); and *Hertz* (27 Bd. Albert-I; phone: 93-50-79-60) are represented, and the tourist office has a list of local firms. Note that Place de la Visitation, in Monaco-Ville, is closed to all traffic except local buses, taxis, and cars with Monégasque and French District of the Maritime Alps plates; other cars can park in the Chemin des Pêcheurs lot, linked with the Vieille Ville via public elevators.

ELEVATOR Six large public underground elevators facilitate pedestrian traffic between the various sections of the principality. They connect the *Jardin Exotique* to the port (near the Pl. Ste-Dévote end of Bd. Albert-I) and the center of Monte Carlo (Pl. des Moulins) to Avenue Princesse-Grace and the Larvotto beach area.

TAXI Taxis are expensive but worth it, since the fleets are composed mainly of comfortable Mercedes-Benzes, BMWs, and Peugeots. Call *Radio Taxi* (phone: 93-15-01-01), or walk to the nearest cabstand. The three major stands are at the train station (see below), at the casino end of Avenue des Beaux-Arts, and on Avenue Princesse-Grace.

TOURS The *Seabus* (phone: 92-16-18-20; fax: 92-16-18-21), a submarine, will take you down 100 feet for a one-hour exploration of marine flora and fauna, with shipwrecks and reefs providing added interest. The tour, offered daily except the second and fourth Mondays of every month, leaves from La Condamine, at the Quai des Etats-Unis. Daily during July and August, the *Azur Express* (phone: 92-05-64-38) operates two small trains that make guided tours of Monaco (available in English). One starts at the *Musée Océanographique* and goes around Le Rocher; the other, starting at the *Stade Nautique Rainier-III* on Quai Albert-I, links La Condamine with the Larvotto beaches during the day and makes a tour of Le Rocher in the evenings. Helicopter tours of the principality are also available through *Héli-Air Monaco* (see *Airport,* above).

TRAIN The *Gare de Monaco–Monte Carlo* (Av. Prince-Pierre, in the Condamine district; phone: 93-30-74-00) is a regular stop for French trains running along the Riviera; several international trains stop here as well. In summer, the *Métrazur,* a special *SNCF (Syndicat National de Chemins de Fer)* shuttle between Menton and Cannes, stops here every half hour. For train information, call 93-87-50-50 or 93-25-54-54; for reservations, 93-88-89-93. The station also offers currency exchange daily.

SPECIAL EVENTS

In January, specially souped-up cars are in abundance for the *Rallye Automobile Monte-Carlo,* a particularly prestigious motor rally that's been on the calendar since 1911, almost as long as cars have been in existence.

The *Fête de Ste-Dévote* (January 26 and 27) is a public holiday honoring the patron saint of the principality and its ruling family. In February, the Big Top is set up on the Fontvieille Esplanade for the *Festival International du Cirque,* five nights of competition to choose the best acts from the world's circuses. March brings the *Bal de la Rose* (Rose Ball), a gala charity event held at the *Monte-Carlo Sporting Club* (see *Nightclubs and Nightlife*) and sponsored by the royal family. High-caliber musical performances, some featuring the *Orchestre Philharmonique de Monte Carlo,* are held during the two or three weeks at *Easter* known as the *Printemps des Arts de Monte Carlo.* The *Championnats Internationaux de Tennis* (International Tennis Championships) at the *Monte Carlo Country Club* are the highlight of April, along with the *Exposition Canine Internationale de Monaco* (International Dog Show) at the *Espace Fontvieille* (phone: 93-25-18-68). May brings Monaco's *Grand Prix,* when the world's best drivers take state-of-the-art Formula One cars onto the Belle Epoque streets to compete on one of the most hazardous circuits in motor racing. In June there is the *Monte Carlo Open* golf tournament, held at the *Monte Carlo Golf Club* (see *Golf* in *Sports and Fitness*). In July and August, the *Festival International de Feux d'Artifice de Monte Carlo* (International Fireworks Festival) gives specialists of various nations a chance to fill the skies over the port with color and excitement. November 19 is the *Fête Nationale* (National Day), an excuse for a small parade in the Vieille Ville, fireworks, and other merriment.

MUSEUMS

Besides those described in *Special Places*, the following museums may be of interest:

MUSÉE DE CIRES (WAX MUSEUM) At this showcase, also called *L'Historial des Princes de Monaco,* 24 life-size scenes re-create the history of the principality and of the Grimaldi dynasty. Open daily. Admission charge. On one of Monaco's most picturesque streets, at 27 Rue Basse (phone: 93-30-39-05).

EXPOSITION DE LA COLLECTION DE VOITURES ANCIENNES DE S.A.S LE PRINCE DE MONACO (PRINCE RAINIER'S COLLECTION OF VINTAGE CARS) The prince recently opened his world-renowned antique automobile collection to the public. Closed Fridays and November. Admission charge. *Centre Commercial de Fontvieille* (phone: 92-05-28-56).

SHOPPING

Monte Carlo's Place du Casino and the Avenue des Beaux-Arts are lined with the fabulous boutiques of *Cartier, Bulgari, Van Cleef & Arpels, Christian Dior, Yves Saint Laurent,* and other purveyors of luxury goods. *Les Allées Lumières* (27 Av. de la Costa), the elegant shopping arcade of the *Park Palace Building,* at the top of the casino gardens, sells the wares of equally well known (and equally expensive) French designers. A shopping arcade called *Galerie du Sporting d'Hiver* is across the street from the *Hôtel de Paris.* In the *Métropole Palace* hotel are *Les Galeries du Métropole,* 130 elegant boutiques (see *Checking In* for both hotels). Shops offering moderately priced clothing, antiques, perfume, and gifts can be found among the more immoderate emporia on the Boulevard des Moulins, Boulevard Princesse-Charlotte, and Boulevard d'Italie, Monte Carlo's major shopping streets. In the Condamine district, the two main commercial streets are Rue Princesse-Caroline and Rue Grimaldi.

As befits its location in the south of France, Monaco is full of colorful food markets. To take the measure of one, and meet some real Monégasques, go to Place d'Armes, a small square at the base of Le Rocher in the Condamine district. The beautiful open-air market (held daily) is a riot of fruits, vegetables, flowers, pasta, bread, fresh fish, and more. There's another market at the renovated *Beausoleil* market building, just above Monte Carlo's *Eglise St-Charles,* on Rue du Marché; it's held daily, mornings only. The surrounding streets are full of indoor and outdoor markets and many specialty food shops. Finally, an antiques and flea market is held on the Fontvieille port every Saturday.

For standard shopping hours, see GETTING READY TO GO. The following are some of our favorite Monégasque shops.

Atmosphère Outstanding leatherwear. *Les Allées Lumières,* Monte Carlo (phone: 93-25-00-03).

Bijoux Cascio The best copies of designer jewels money can buy. 137 *Les Galeries du Métropole,* Monte Carlo (phone: 93-50-17-57).

Boutique du Rocher Created by Princess Grace to support local artisans, this place offers ceramics, embroidery, stuffed dolls, items made of Provençal fabrics, and other items suitable as souvenirs or gifts—all handmade. Two locations: 1 Av. de la Madone, Monte Carlo (phone: 93-30-91-17), and 11 Rue Emile-de-Loth, Le Rocher (phone: 93-30-33-99).

Christofle Pavillon A glistening array of crystal, silverware, and china. 42 Bd. des Moulins, Monte Carlo (phone: 93-25-20-20).

Jaguy A wide range of attractive men's suits, pants, and sweaters, at affordable prices. 17 Bd. Princesse-Charlotte, Monte Carlo (phone: 93-30-84-56).

Katy Christian Dior lingerie and an especially wide selection of women's bathing suits. 10 Bd. des Moulins, Monte Carlo (phone: 93-50-66-22).

Old River Exclusive men's fashions at competitive prices. Two locations: 17 Bd. des Moulins, Monte Carlo (phone: 93-50-33-85) and 17 Av. de Spélugues, Monte Carlo (phone: 93-50-06-01).

SPORTS AND FITNESS

BOATING The *Yacht Club de Monaco* (16 Quai Antoine-I; phone: 93-30-63-63) offers sailing lessons during July and August, weather permitting (it's best to call ahead); boat rentals are available too. You can charter craft (with or without a skipper) for day excursions at *Monte-Carlo Yachting* (40 Rue Grimaldi; phone: 93-25-36-33; fax: 93-50-67-02).

GOLF The local course is a real winner.

TOP TEE-OFF SPOT

Monte Carlo Golf Club On a clear day, this hilly 6,200-yard 18-holer has enchanting views of Monaco and the coast from St-Tropez to Italy. The course is actually in France, some 2,600 feet above sea level on top of Mont-Agel. Among the numerous tournaments that take place here throughout the year is the annual *Monte Carlo Open* (on the PGA European Tour) in June. It's a private club, so call in advance to make arrangements. There's a 50% discount on the greens fees for guests of any of the four *SBM* hotels (see *Checking In*). Closed Mondays October through May. About 20 minutes from the center of Monte Carlo by car via N7, in La Turbie (phone: 93-41-09-11).

SWIMMING This is a favorite year-round activity in Monaco. The *Plage du Larvotto* (phone: 93-15-28-76), the large, popular public beach off Avenue Princesse-Grace, is an artificial stretch of sand deposited along the shoreline between two strips of land that once upon a time did not exist. It's open from May through October (the rest of the year, it's barricaded to hold the sand in place), and there's no charge. Next door, the *Beach Plaza Sea Club* (22 Av. Princesse-Grace; phone: 93-30-98-80), a private bathing complex with two heated seawater pools, a heated freshwater pool, and a private beach, is for season members only, but it also is open (free of charge) to guests of the *Beach Plaza* hotel. The *Monte Carlo Beach Club* (Av. Princesse-Grace, St-Roman; phone: 93-28-66-66) is *the* place to be seen. It offers an Olympic-size, heated seawater pool, a snack bar, two restaurants, and a pebble beach lined with pretty striped cabañas, all on French territory, just beyond the eastern border of Monaco (perhaps the reason topless sunbathing is allowed here, unlike in Monaco proper). The club, which is open April through about mid-October, is free to guests of all *SBM* hotels (see *Checking In*); others pay a daily admission charge. The outdoor, Olympic-size, heated seawater pool at the *Stade Nautique Rainier-III* (Quai Albert-I; phone: 93-15-28-75) is open to the public from April through October for a small admission charge. The indoor heated freshwater pool at the *Stade Louis-II* (3-7 Av. Castelans; phone: 92-05-42-13) is closed in August. The luxurious *California Terrace* health spa (2 Av. de Monte Carlo; phone: 92-16-40-02) has, in addition to its spa facilities, an indoor heated seawater pool and a restaurant. It's open daily, and there's an admission charge (though use of the pool is free to guests of any of the four *SBM* hotels—see *Checking In*).

TENNIS AND SQUASH Monaco's best tennis spot is actually across the border in France, but don't let that stop you from experiencing one of the most sublime tennis layouts in either country.

CHOICE COURTS

Monte Carlo Country Club The 23 courts here, four of them lighted, are arranged on hillside terraces with spectacular Mediterranean views framed by column-like cypress trees. The clubhouse, with its sunny restaurant embellished with murals and its well-kept, old-fashioned locker rooms, is simply an extra delight. Prince Rainier III and his son, Crown Prince Albert, play doubles here. There also are two squash courts. Open daily. Guests of the four *SBM* hotels receive a 50% discount on court fees (see *Checking In*). Av. Princesse-Grace, Quartier St-Roman, Roquebrune-Cap-Martin (phone: 93-41-30-15).

The *Tennis Club de Monaco* (29 Bd. de Belgique; phone: 93-30-01-02) has 13 courts (five lighted), a sauna, and a clubhouse. The *Monte Carlo Squash Rackets Club* (*Stade Louis-II;* phone: 92-05-42-22) has four courts.

WINDSURFING Skim the water's surface at the *Monte Carlo Beach Club* (Av. Princesse-Grace, St-Roman; phone: 93-78-21-40) from April through October, or at the *Beach Plaza Sea Club* (see *Swimming,* above) from May through September.

THEATER AND MUSIC

The *Théâtre du Fort-Antoine* (Av. de la Quarantaine; phone: 93-15-83-03), an open-air theater in the old fortifications of Le Rocher, has a short season of plays, folkloric dance, and concerts from June through August. Tickets are sold at the theater 45 minutes before each performance. The lovely *Théâtre Princesse Grace* (12 Av. d'Ostende; phone: 93-25-32-27), designed by the late princess, presents a season of comedy and drama (anything from the French classics to the latest foreign plays in translation), variety acts, and concerts from October through May.

The *Orchestre Philharmonique de Monte Carlo,* with internationally known guest artists, can be heard from October through April in the 1,100-seat *Auditorium Rainier-III* at the *Centre de Congrès* (Bd. Louis-II; phone: 93-50-93-00), Monaco's largest theater. In July and August, the orchestra presents gala summer concerts in the *Cour d'Honneur* of the *Palais Princier.* Monte Carlo's opera company holds forth at the *Salle Garnier* in the *Casino de Monte Carlo* from December or January through March. The resident ballet company and visiting troupes also perform there during *Easter* and during the *Fête Nationale* (National Day; November 19), *Christmas,* and *New Year's* holidays. The box office for information and advance tickets for orchestra, opera, and ballet performances is in the atrium of the casino (phone: 92-16-22-99); closed Mondays.

NIGHTCLUBS AND NIGHTLIFE

Much after-dark excitement takes place in the *Casino de Monte Carlo* (see *Special Places*). There's also an all-American casino—the *Sun Casino*—in the *Loews Monte Carlo* hotel (12 Av. des Spélugues; phone: 92-16-21-23; fax: 93-30-36-93).

In summer, there's a casino in the *Monte Carlo Sporting Club* (Av. Princesse-Grace; main phone: 92-16-22-33; casino: 92-16-21-25). This lavish, modern pleasure complex, built on a spit of land reclaimed from the sea at the far end of Avenue Princesse-Grace, opens at 10 PM from July through mid-September. Its focal point is the large *Salle des Etoiles,* so called because of a roof that rolls back to reveal the stars. The room is the site of Monte Carlo's famous Friday night galas, grand dinner dances topped off with fireworks held to herald a new show or an international star's opening night—and to allow those in attendance to dress up *tenue de soirée.* On other nights, the dinner and show still take place, albeit *sans* fireworks and the formal dress requirement. Call 93-30-71-71 for information and reservations. Also at the sporting club is *Jimmy'z de la Mer* (phone: 93-25-14-14; 92-16-22-77 after 10 PM). Monte Carlo's most attractive (it overlooks a Japanese garden), chic, and expensive disco (you have to tip the bouncer to get in), it's open from 11 PM to dawn nightly in July and August. The sporting club also houses *Parady'z* (phone: 93-50-31-66), a second, less formidable disco (open in July and August only), and the *Maona* restaurant (phone: 92-16-36-36), a dinner-dance spot with tropical decor on one side and a Japanese theme on the other. From September through June, *Jimmy'z* moves to winter quarters (Pl. du Casino; phone: 93-50-80-80), where it's closed Mondays and Tuesdays from November through *Easter.*

There's also the *Living Room* (7 Av. des Spélugues; phone: 93-50-80-31), a popular piano bar and disco with a pleasantly old-fashioned atmosphere. *Flashman's* (in the *Résidence Sun Tower,* at 7 Av. Princesse-Alice; phone: 93-30-09-03), a fancy piano bar/restaurant, is good for late snacking on English food to easy-listening music until 4 AM. *Loews Monte Carlo* hotel has the *Folie Russe* supper club, where an elaborate Las Vegas–style show goes on every night but Mondays. A sophisticated evening in a more formal, old-fashioned setting is possible at the *Cabaret de Casino* (phone: 92-16-36-36), in what was formerly a concert room of the main casino, open from September through June; closed Tuesdays. An elevator in the *Salon Privé* takes you down, or you can enter from Place du Casino. *Le Bar Américain* in the *Hôtel de Paris* (Pl. du Casino; phone: 92-16-30-30) is a posh spot where the glitterati rendezvous. The experience is fun but expensive, and reservations are necessary for a good table, especially in summer.

Best in Town

CHECKING IN

The four *Société des Bains de Mer* (*SBM*) hotels—the *Hôtel de Paris, Hermitage, Mirabeau,* and *Monte Carlo Beach*—issue guests a Carte d'Or (Gold Card) at registration. This provides free entrance to the European gaming rooms at the casino, to the indoor pool at the *California Terrace,* and to the *Monte Carlo Beach Club* (see *Swimming* in *Sports and Fitness* for both); discounts of 50% on greens fees and court fees at the *Monte Carlo Golf Club* (see *Golf* in *Sports and Fitness*) and the *Monte Carlo Country Club* (see *Tennis* in *Sports and Fitness*); and the privilege of charging meals at any *SBM* establishment directly to your room.

For a double room in a very expensive hotel, expect to pay $300 and up (sometimes way up); in an expensive hotel, $200 to $300; in a moderate one, $100 to $200; and in an inexpensive place, less than $100. Unless otherwise noted, all hotels listed below feature air conditioning, telephones, TV sets, and private baths in the rooms. Some less expensive hotels may have private baths in only some of their rooms; it's a good idea to confirm whether your room has a private bath when making a reservation. Be aware that should you arrive in Monaco in the summer without a reservation, it will be practically impossible to find a room, though the tourist and convention bureau is ready to provide assistance. Unless otherwise indicated, hotels accept major credit cards and are open year-round.

For an unforgettable experience, we begin with our favorite Monaco hostelry, followed by our cost and quality choices of hotels, listed by price category.

ROOM AT THE TOP

Hôtel de Paris That this opulent (and opulently priced) Beaux Arts confection, which opened on New Year's Day in 1864, is the dowager queen of the Côte d'Azur is evident in its ample ornamentation—from the frescoes in the Empire dining room to the bare-breasted caryatids that line the facade and gaze across the rows of vintage Rolls-Royces parked at the casino across the square. The guestbook reads like a Who's Who of the century; Winston Churchill stayed here so often that the management named one of its palatial suites after him. The 129 spacious rooms and 69 suites have modern comforts and beautiful views, and guests have access to the indoor pool of the California Terrace spa (see *Swimming* in *Sports and Fitness*). The celebrated wine cellars, carved out of Le Rocher, are accessible to visitors, and it's possible to pick up a quick Dior in the lobby. The elegantly decorated

Louis XV restaurant, endowed with three Michelin stars, is one of the best on the Côte, while the one-Michelin-star Le Grill on the top floor offers the most incredible view in Monaco, plus dining under the stars (see Eating Out for both). There is also the sophisticated gathering spot Le Bar Américain. Pl. du Casino (phone: 92-16-30-00; fax: 93-25-59-17).

VERY EXPENSIVE

Hermitage Somewhat lower-key than its sister, the *Hôtel de Paris,* it's nonetheless splendorous in the best Belle Epoque tradition. The exquisite façade only hints at what's inside: a baroque dining room, where pink marble columns hold up an extravagant gilt and frescoed ceiling, and the Art Nouveau winter garden, a simpler, airier space encircled by a wrought-iron balcony and topped with a stained glass dome. The hotel is built on a rock that faces the harbor and Le Rocher, so many of its 240 luxurious rooms have enchanting views. All have period touches, such as brass beds, though the fixtures and fittings are mostly modern. There is also an indoor pool and a gym. Sq. Beaumarchais (phone: 92-16-40-00; fax: 93-50-47-12).

Loews Monte Carlo Huge and thoroughly modern, this American-managed hotel expresses a spirit entirely different from that of Monte Carlo's two landmark palaces. Set on pilings driven into the sea, it sprawls along the water at the foot of the casino. All 636 rooms and suites have terraces, many with sea views. The hotel has six restaurants, including the excellent *Le Pistou* (see *Eating Out*), its own casino, a nightclub, a lavish marble promenade level with attractive boutiques, an open-air heated pool on the roof garden, and a health and fitness club. 12 Av. des Spélugues (phone: 93-50-65-00; fax: 93-30-01-57).

EXPENSIVE

Beach Plaza Besides the *Monte Carlo Beach,* this is the only other hotel in Monaco with a beachfront location, and it's a great favorite with families. It has a heated freshwater pool and a private beach, in addition to the facilities (two more pools, more beach, and a mini-club for children) of the adjoining *Beach Plaza Sea Club.* The hotel is modern; its 313 rooms are nicely decorated, and many have sea views. In the summer, an open-air grill restaurant is set up by the pool. 22 Av. Princesse-Grace (phone: 93-30-98-80; fax: 93-50-23-14).

Métropole Palace A whopping $120 million was spent to restore this neoclassical-style establishment, one of Monte Carlo's Belle Epoque landmarks. It features 170 rooms and suites, plus an indoor-outdoor pool, three restaurants, and over 130 boutiques. A few blocks from the casino, at 4 Av. de la Madone (phone: 93-15-15-15; fax: 93-25-24-44).

Mirabeau Small and elegant, it occupies several floors of a modern high-rise. There are 103 comfortable rooms (all with terraces, some with sea views), a restaurant, *La Coupole* (see *Eating Out*), and its own heated seawater pool. Comfortable, if not particularly rich in character. Centrally located, at 1 Av. Princesse-Grace (phone: 92-16-65-65; fax: 93-50-84-85).

Monte Carlo Beach A compromise between the sumptuously baroque and the brashly modern look of the other deluxe properties, this terra cotta–roofed, crescent-shaped structure, built in 1928, sits at the edge of the sea. There are 46 small, elegant rooms, each with a balcony over the water; the ambience is quiet and private, less formal than the palaces, remote from Monte Carlo's nightlife, but full of charm. The hotel shares the beach, two pools, cabañas, and restaurants of the exclusive *Monte Carlo Beach Club* (also see *Swimming* in *Sports and Fitness*) literally at its front door. Hotel closed October through March; restaurant closed November through February. Beyond the eastern border of the principality, 1½ miles (2 km) from the casino, on Rte. du Beach, Monte Carlo, Roquebrune-Cap-Martin (phone: 93-28-66-66; fax: 93-78-14-18).

MODERATE

Abela Overlooking the sea, this property contains 192 rooms and suites with French windows and private terraces, plus a restaurant and a lobby bar. One floor is reserved for nonsmokers. Conveniently situated in Fontvieille, two minutes from the heliport and five minutes from the train station. 23 Av. des Papalins (phone: 92-05-90-00; fax: 92-05-91-67).

Alexandra A modest hostelry, it has 56 comfortable rooms (with either bath or shower), but no restaurant. At the intersection of two major shopping streets near the casino, at 35 Bd. Princesse-Charlotte (phone: 93-50-63-13; fax: 92-16-06-48).

Balmoral This traditional property has 77 rooms, some overlooking the harbor (with either bath or shower). A restaurant is on the premises (closed Sundays, Mondays, November, and *Christmas*). Conveniently located, at 12 Av. de la Costa (phone: 93-50-62-37; fax: 93-15-08-69).

Louvre A small hotel, it offers 33 cozy, comfortable rooms, some with sea views. There's no restaurant. On Monte Carlo's main shopping street, at 16 Bd. des Moulins (phone: 93-50-65-25; fax: 93-30-23-68).

INEXPENSIVE

Helvetia Another small, clean hotel, this one has 24 rooms (21 with private bathrooms and either bath or shower). None of the rooms is air conditioned. Its attractive restaurant, favored by locals, is a relative bargain. In the Condamine district, near the Place d'Armes market, at 1 *bis* Rue Grimaldi (phone: 93-30-21-71; fax: 92-16-70-51).

Terminus No view, but each of the 54 rooms is well equipped and comfortable (with either bath or shower). The restaurant is closed October and November. In the Condamine district, adjacent to the train station, at 9 Av. Prince-Pierre (phone: 92-05-63-00; fax: 92-05-20-10).

INEXPENSIVE OPTIONS

Beausoleil, the French community bordering Monaco several blocks north of the casino, has several hotels that are more down-to-earth and modestly priced than those in the principality, but just as conveniently located. Among them is the *Olympia* (17 *bis* Bd. Général-Leclerc, east of the *Crédit Lyonnais* bldg.; phone: 93-78-12-70; fax: 93-41-85-04). Only five minutes from the casino, its 32 rooms are affordable.

EATING OUT

Monaco's choice of restaurants ranges from haute cuisine to Italian restaurants and pizzerias serving very good, inexpensive food. Traditional Monégasque cooking—reminiscent of the cooking of Nice—can be sampled at bistros near the Place d'Armes marketplace or on Le Rocher. Among the traditional specialties are *barbagiuan* (a fried pocket of dough filled with zucchini, garlic, eggs, cheese, and rice), *pain bagnat* (a round bun "bathed" in olive oil, vinegar, garlic, and basil and stuffed with a *salade niçoise*), and stockfish (dried codfish stewed in a succulent wine and tomato sauce, with garlic, onions, and olive oil).

Dinner for two (excluding wine) will cost $120 to $220 in an expensive restaurant; $75 to $120 in a moderate one; and less than $75 in an inexpensive place. Service is usually included in the price of the meal, but it is customary to tip something extra if the service was good. Unless otherwise noted, all restaurants listed below are open for lunch and dinner.

For an unforgettable culinary experience, we begin with our Monaco favorite, followed by our cost and quality choices of restaurants, listed by price category.

HAUTE GASTRONOMIE

Le Louis XV When Prince Rainier decided to bring culinary greatness to his principality, he spared no expense in doing so. He hired Alain Ducasse, who trained at some of France's best restaurants, to be head chef, providing him with unlimited funds—which diners also may need to pay the tabs! The result is this wonderful restaurant, which earned three Michelin stars faster than any other dining spot in the history of that gastronomic bible. The Belle Epoque setting is perfect for such specialties as *homard thermidor* (lobster in a rich wine sauce), *pigeonneau cuit sur la braise* (braised squab), *légumes* *provençaux à la truffe noire* (Mediterranean vegetables with black truffles), and *fraises des bois et sorbet au mascarpone* (mascarpone sorbet with wild strawberries). In keeping with the pedigree of the place, women are provided with gilded brocade footstools for their handbags. The wines from one of Monaco's (and France's) best cellars help to make this an unforgettable dining experience. Open daily; closed Tuesday and Wednesday lunch off-season, the last two weeks of February, and December. Only 50 people can eat here at any one time, so be sure to reserve far ahead. Major credit cards accepted. *Hôtel de Paris,* Pl. du Casino (phone: 92-16-30-01; fax: 92-16-30-04).

EXPENSIVE

La Coupole The atmosphere in this one-Michelin star restaurant is contemporary, soft, and elegant; the food, refined nouvelle cuisine with an emphasis on seafood (try the flan of scallops and sea urchins). Don't forget the desserts—the chocolate ravioli with pistachio sauce is excellent. Open daily; closed for lunch July and August. Reservations necessary. Major credit cards accepted. *Mirabeau* hotel, 1 Av. Princesse-Grace (phone: 92-16-66-99; fax: 93-50-84-85).

Le Grill A swank rooftop restaurant (it's been awarded one Michelin star) with a delightfully romantic view of the casino's turrets on one side and the harbor and the Vieille Ville on the other. In summer, the ceiling opens up to the sky and stars. Among the *grillades* are succulent lamb noisettes, *côte de boeuf,* and veal paillard; there is a lobster tank; and, for dessert, there are delicate tangerine and raspberry soufflés. The wine cellar, carved out of Le Rocher about a decade after the hotel was built, holds some 200,000 bottles. Open daily; closed January. Reservations necessary. Major credit cards accepted. *Hôtel de Paris,* Pl. du Casino (phone: 92-16-30-02; fax: 92-16-30-04).

MODERATE

Café de Paris A true brasserie specializing in seafood, with two terraces for outdoor dining and people watching, it's in a shopping-and-casino complex restored to turn-of-the-century grandeur. Note the stained glass windows representing the four seasons and the zodiac signs, designed by Charles Garnier, the architect of Monte Carlo's casino. Open daily. Reservations unnecessary. Major credit cards accepted. Pl. du Casino (phone: 92-16-20-20; fax: 93-25-46-98).

Le Pinocchio Not one of the pasta dishes is likely to disappoint in this small, cozy spot with a vaulted ceiling. Closed mid-December through mid-January, and Wednesdays from September through March. Reservations advised.

MasterCard and Visa accepted. In the Vieille Ville, 30 Rue Comte-Félix-Gastaldi (phone: 93-30-96-20).

Le Pistou Good Monégasque and Provençal cooking is the draw of this rooftop restaurant. Try the *pissaladière* (Nice's version of onion pizza) or the *tian d'aubergines* (eggplant gratin). Closed from mid-September through mid-June. Reservations unnecessary. Major credit cards accepted. *Loews Monte Carlo,* 12 Av. des Spélugues (phone: 93-50-65-00; fax: 93-30-01-57).

Polpetta Delicious food and a warm Italian atmosphere make this lovely dining room popular. Closed Tuesdays off-season, Saturday lunch, three weeks in February, and two weeks in October. Reservations necessary. MasterCard and Visa accepted. 2 Rue Paradis (phone: 93-50-67-84).

Port In this charming place, which has outdoor tables in summer, the menu leans to local seafood, meat, and pasta. Closed Mondays and the month of November. Reservations unnecessary. MasterCard and Visa accepted. Near the port, on Quai Albert-I (phone: 93-50-77-21).

Santa Lucia This upstairs place is recommended for its pizza, risotto, and grilled meat. A pianist performing Italian songs and, on request, old American tunes animates the quaint Italian setting. Open daily for dinner only. Reservations unnecessary. MasterCard and Visa accepted. 11 Av. des Spélugues (phone: 93-50-96-77).

INEXPENSIVE

Castleroc The outside tables of this informal eatery command a view of the *Palais Princier* and the water. It's a fine place to try stockfish or other Monégasque specialties. Open for lunch only; closed Saturdays, December, and January. No reservations. Major credit cards accepted. Pl. du Palais (phone: 93-30-36-68).

BARS AND CAFÉS

The *Café de Paris* (see *Eating Out*), open daily until 4 AM, is the perfect place to sip a Campari while watching the comings and goings on Place du Casino. *Tip-Top* (11 Av. de Spélugues; phone: 93-50-69-13), a comparatively plain, small snack bar with sidewalk tables, is popular with Monaco's jet set after midnight in the summer (it stays open all night). Another unassuming place, the *Bar de la Crémaillère* (Pl. de la Crémaillère; phone: 93-50-66-24) is a bistro with small outside tables (closed Sundays and mid-December through mid-January). And don't forget *Harry's Bar* (19 Galerie Charles-III; phone: 93-30-41-06), Monaco's international rendezvous spot.

Nice

Those who remember the halcyon days of ornate villas, swaying palms, and languid luxury under an azure sky may shake their heads sadly at the Côte d'Azur of today, a real estate speculator's orgy of high-rise apartment blocks, pillbox hotels, honky-tonk pizza parlors, and shiny fast-food factories. Its once-quaint little marinas are linked by a permanent shoreline traffic jam, and the scene at some of its renowned beaches calls to mind a horde of people dangling their feet from the edge of a freeway.

Nice, long a gem of the Côte d'Azur nestled near Monaco and the border with Italy, has managed to keep its head above the concrete and retain its special flavor, but it is slowly becoming a place where tourism is more of a burden than a cultural exchange between visitors and natives. In the summer, the population of 340,000 swells with vacationers from Paris, Piccadilly, and Peoria, and an empty or moderately priced hotel room is harder to find than a winning lottery ticket. The streets become mobbed with traffic, and the deafening noise competes with the burning sun. But in mid-autumn, when the locals and a few visitors take advantage of the last hot days to dip into the still-warm sea, you can again begin to feel that Nice is nice.

The Greeks from nearby Massilia (today's Marseilles) founded the city in the 5th century BC as a little market town and auxiliary port, naming it Nikaia. Continuous lootings by pirates forced Nikaia's citizens to ask for help from the Romans, who built a military camp on the side of Cimiez Hill. The remains of their subsequent lavish colonization are evident today in the arena and the baths on the hill at Cimiez, now the city's elegant residential section. During the fall of the Roman Empire, barbarians from the north and pirates from North Africa invaded Nice and brought about its decline. The Counts of Provence brought the city back to its former glory in the 10th century, but in 1388 Nice was wrested from them by the House of Savoy, who would retain almost unbroken possession of the growing city for close to 500 years. In 1860, Victor Emmanuel II, the head of the House of Savoy and King of newly unified Italy, ceded the region to France in return for military support against an Austrian invasion.

Also in the 19th century, Nice became a haven for artists, including Rodin and Toulouse-Lautrec. Matisse spent the last years of his life close to Nice, and for many years Chagall lived nearby; their works can be seen in the city's new *Musée Matisse* and in the *Musée National Marc Chagall.*

Today, Nice's beauty and climate have made it the amusement park of the European aristocracy, an off-season refuge from harsh northern climes. The lapis lazuli of the Baie des Anges (Bay of Angels), the activity of the Vieux (Old) Port, and the timelessness of the city's towering Château—the name given to the hill that looms over the harbor—give Nice the look of a huge, gorgeous color postcard.

Nice At-a-Glance

SEEING THE CITY

Nice's beauty is best appreciated from a viewing platform at the summit of the 300-foot Château. It can be reached by an elevator (or a 300-step climb) at the end of the Quai des Etats-Unis, where the quay joins the Rue des Ponchettes. Open daily; admission charge. A train departs daily from the Esplanade Albert-I at the beginning of the Promenade des Anglais and goes through the Vieille Ville en route to the hills of the Château; from there, an exceptional panorama of Nice's port and the Baie des Anges unfolds before you. For information and reservations, call *Les Trains Touristiques* (phone: 93-18-81-58).

SPECIAL PLACES

Nice is a city to be ambled through casually, under a morning or late-afternoon sun.

IN THE CITY

PROMENADE DES ANGLAIS (PROMENADE OF THE ENGLISH) If you only have an hour in Nice, spend it strolling along this broad, fabled promenade, from the Place Masséna and the adjacent *Jardin Albert-I,* set against crimson buildings and cool graceful arcades, at one end, to the *Négresco* hotel, toward the other end. Ornate hotels grace one side, and a narrow, crowded strip of pebbled beach separates you from the brilliant blue of the bay. Lunch in your bathing suit on any of the several excellent private beaches along the promenade; prices are moderate, and the carafe wines are good.

VIEILLE VILLE (OLD CITY) This little, grand piano–shaped quarter huddled in the shadow of the Château is a tight labyrinth of winding streets and alleys, steep ascents between medieval buildings, and balconies festooned with rainbows of drying laundry—a pungently southern enclave that of late has shown indications of evolving into Nice's artists' quarter. Be sure to explore the Cours Saleya (the heart of the area), Rue Rossetti, the Rue de la Boucherie, or the Rue du Collet, crowding your way through teeming street markets. Stop in at the 17th-century *Cathédrale Ste-Réparate;* the *Eglise St-Martin-St-Augustin* (phone: 93-92-60-45); the 18th-century *St-François-de-Paule,* a good example of Niçois Baroque architecture; the 17th-century *Chapelle St-Giaume,* much of whose original interior is still intact; and the Vieille Ville cemetery.

MARCHÉ AUX FLEURS (FLOWER MARKET) On the edge of the Vieille Ville, just behind the Quai des Etats-Unis, Nice's wholesale flower market offers one of the city's most colorful spectacles. The variety of blossoms is dazzling, the aromas are heady, and there are a few well-placed cafés, where you can see, sniff, and sip, all at the same time. Closed Sunday afternoons and Mondays. Cours Saleya.

PALAIS LASCARIS (LASCARIS PALACE) A splendid 17th-century private palace in Genoese style, this is the former residence of the Count Lascaris-Ventimiglia. It is noted for its frescoed ceilings, its decorative woodwork, and its regal staircase. Closed Mondays, some public holidays, and November. Admission charge. 15 Rue Droite (phone: 93-62-05-54).

VIEUX PORT (OLD PORT) To the east of the Château, Nice's harbor is an artful array of multicolored boats, from small dinghies and kayaks to the white ferries that make the crossing to Corsica. To reach the port, go out around the base of the Château at the far end of Quai des Etats-Unis, or take Rue Cassini southeast from Place Garibaldi.

CATHÉDRALE ORTHODOXE RUSSE (RUSSIAN ORTHODOX CATHEDRAL) A reminder of the days when the royal Romanovs roamed the Riviera, this Belle Epoque cathedral was built from 1903 to 1912 under the auspices of Czar Nicholas II himself. Considered one of the most beautiful churches of its style outside of Russia, it supports a bouquet of ornate onion domes, and its exterior is a mixture of pink brick, grey marble, and colored ceramic tiles. Inside is a rich collection of icons and an impressive carved iconostasis (the screen that separates the altar from the nave in an Orthodox church). No visitors permitted during the Sunday morning service. Admission charge. Bd. du Tzaréwitch (phone: 93-96-88-02).

MUSÉE MATISSE (MATISSE MUSEUM) Henri Matisse had his studio here in the Cimiez section, and—after a five-year restoration project—this major repository of his work has been reopened to the public. The collection includes oils, drawings, engravings, sculpture, ceramic works, and some Oriental fabrics and clothing that Matisse used as props. In a completely renovated 17th-century Italianate villa surrounded by Roman ruins, the museum contains a multimedia research center and some of the artist's personal effects. Frequent temporary exhibits are held here, perhaps to compensate for the fact that the Matisse collection is often on the road. Matisse's tomb is in the nearby cemetery. Closed Tuesdays and holidays. Admission charge. 164 Av. des Arènes (phone: 93-81-08-08).

MUSÉE NATIONAL MESSAGE BIBLIQUE MARC CHAGALL (MARC CHAGALL BIBLICAL MESSAGE MUSEUM) Built on a wooded hill in Cimiez, this modern museum houses the 17 major canvases, executed over a 13-year-period, that make up Chagall's *Biblical Message*. Enhanced by a fine collection of preparatory sketches, as well as hundreds of gouaches, engravings, lithographs, sculptures, mosaics, and tapestries, the collection evokes the spirit of one of our century's most original artists. The unity of Chagall's poetic vision of man, nature, and the Bible is clear and present in every room. The lovely grounds and gardens, the reflecting pool, and the chapel glowing with stained glass all add to the experience. In summer, a tearoom is set up in the garden. Closed Tuesdays. Admission charge. Av. du Docteur-Ménard and Bd. de Cimiez (phone: 93-81-75-75).

MUSÉE D'ART MODERNE ET D'ART CONTEMPORAIN (MUSEUM OF MODERN AND CONTEMPORARY ART) The largest modern art complex in southern France displays works from such world-renowned artists as César, Klein, Christo, Warhol, Lichtenstein, Morris, and Louis. Its four towers afford great views of the city. Closed Tuesdays. No admission charge. Promenade des Arts (phone: 93-62-61-62).

EXTRA SPECIAL

The *Chapelle du Rosaire* (Rosary Chapel; Av. Henri-Matisse; phone: 93-58-03-26), designed and decorated by Matisse between 1947 and 1951, is the main reason so many people have rediscovered Vence, a picturesque old market town 13½ miles (22 km) northwest of Nice. Matisse considered the chapel his greatest masterpiece. He created the stunning stained glass windows to express his gratitude to the Dominican monks who protected him during World War II. The windows, the murals, and the church vestments created by Matisse may bring you here, but you'll also enjoy the setting—on a rock promontory, sheltered by the last foothills of the Alps—and the charm of the Old Town, enclosed in elliptical walls and entered through five arched gateways. The chapel is small, and public access is restricted, so it can get crowded, especially when a tour bus arrives. Open Tuesdays and Thursdays; other days by appointment made at least a day in advance. No admission charge. For additional details, see *The Côte d'Azur* in DIRECTIONS.

Perched on a rock spike 1,550 feet above the sea, the village of Eze—once a medieval fortress—offers a splendid panorama of the Riviera. Eze is less than 7 miles (11 km) from Nice, along the Moyenne (Middle) Corniche, on the way to Monte Carlo. For additional details, see *The Côte d'Azur* in DIRECTIONS.

Sources and Resources

TOURIST INFORMATION

The Nice *Office du Tourisme–Syndicat d'Initiative* has three branches: next to the train station on Avenue Thiers (phone: 93-87-07-07), at 5 Avenue Gustave-V (phone: 93-87-60-60), and near the airport (phone: 93-83-32-64).

LOCAL COVERAGE The daily newspaper of the area is *Nice-Matin*. *La Semaine des Spectacles,* a weekly, is also informative about current events. Both are in French, but they're easy to decipher. The brochure *Nice, Guide Pratique,* published by the tourist office and available in English, lists facilities for the handicapped in the city, as well as many other useful details. The *maison de la presse* (newsstand) at 1 Place Masséna carries English-language newspapers. The *Riviera Bookshop* and *The Cat's Whiskers* (see *Shopping* for both) carry English-language guidebooks. The *English-American Library* (12 Rue de France; phone: 93-97-23-54), with all English-language books, is a boon for those planning a longer stay, and visitors are welcome to peruse the library's periodicals (though only members may check out materials).

TELEPHONE The city code for Nice is 93, which is incorporated into all local eight-digit numbers. When calling a number in Nice from the Paris region (including the Ile-de-France), dial 16, wait for a dial tone, then dial the eight-digit number. When calling a number from outside Paris, dial only the eight-digit number.

GETTING AROUND

It's a good thing that central Nice is compact and easily accessible by foot, because traffic becomes ludicrous during the tourist seasons. Many areas— including Rue Masséna and some of its cross streets, and numerous streets in the Vieille Ville—are pedestrian zones.

AIRPORT *Aéroport de Nice–Côte d'Azur* (phone: 93-21-30-30 or 93-21-30-12), about 4 miles (6 km) west of the city, handles domestic and international traffic. An airport shuttle (part of the municipal bus network, *Transports Urbains de Nice;* 24 Rue Hôtel des Postes; phone: 93-62-08-08) leaves from Avenue Félix-Faure, next to the information office at the *Gare Routière,* about every 20 minutes, making runs to the airport from 6 AM to 8 PM and bringing passengers to Boulevard Jean-Jaurès, in town.

BOATS For ferries to Corsica and, in summer, day-trips along the coast, inquire at *SNCM* (Quai du Commerce; phone: 93-13-66-66). *Bateaux Gallus* (24 Quai Lunel; phone: 93-55-33-33) offers cruises along the coast and to outlying islands.

BUS You can hop on a bus for outlying districts, such as Cimiez, at the Place Masséna. The fare for a single ticket is around 5F (about 85¢ at press time), or you can purchase a discounted *carnet* (booklet) of six tickets. The central station for the municipal bus network, *Transports Urbains de Nice,* is at 10 Avenue Félix-Faure (phone: 93-62-08-08). Nearby, the main station for regional buses is the *Gare Routière* (Bd. Jean-Jaurès and Promenade Paillon; phone: 93-85-61-81). Companies offering service to various points along the Côte d'Azur include *Rapides Côte d'Azur* (14 Rue François-Guisol; phone: 93-55-24-00); *Autocars Broch* (phone: 93-31-10-52; fax: 93-

14-67-50); and *Autocars Nesa-Tavanti* (at the *Gare Routière;* phone: 93-88-18-48).

CAR RENTAL All the major firms are represented. *Avis* has two offices (Pl. Masséna, phone: 93-80-63-52; and at the airport, phone: 93-21-42-80). *Budget* has two offices (at the *Gare SNCF,* phone: 93-16-24-16; and at the airport, phone: 93-21-36-50). *Europcar* also has two locations (6 Av. Suède, phone: 93-88-64-04; and at the airport, phone: 93-21-36-44). *Hertz* has two offices (12 Av. Suède, phone: 93-87-11-87; and at the airport, phone: 93-21-36-72).

CYCLES If you want to move fast, rent a motorbike, moped, scooter, or bicycle from *Nicea Location Rent,* 9 Av. Thiers (phone: 93-82-42-71).

TAXI Cabs are expensive, so watch the meter, and remember streets often are clogged with traffic at certain hours. There usually are plenty of cabs at designated stands and at the airport, and they also can be hailed in the streets; or call 93-80-70-70.

TRAIN The *Gare SNCF* is on Avenue Thiers. For schedule and fare information, call 93-87-50-50 or 93-25-54-54. The *Gare de Provence* (33 Av. Malausséna; phone: 93-82-10-17) belongs to the *Chemins de Fer de Provence* (Provence Railways; 4 *bis* Rue Alfred Binet; phone: 93-88-28-56; fax: 93-16-28-71), a narrow-gauge railway that operates a scenic route daily between Nice and Digne, approximately 100 miles (160 km) to the northwest. The trip takes about three-and-a-half hours each way.

SPECIAL EVENTS

Nice celebrates two major annual events—*Carnaval* and Europe's biggest jazz festival.

FAVORITE FÊTES

Carnaval The history of Nice's *Carnaval* goes back to the 13th century, but it was the city's emergence as a fashionable winter resort during the last century that brought it to the full flower that visitors encounter today. The festivities begin with a Saturday night torchlight procession. The *Grand Corso Carnavalesque,* an afternoon parade held the next day, features fabulous floats and huge, leering dummies. Wednesday brings the famous *Batailles des Fleurs* (Battles of Flowers), when everyone throws mimosa branches. During the two-week period, there are four days and nights of parades (those during the day tend to be more restrained). The entire festival is crammed to the gills with all manner of regattas, masked balls, confetti and spray-can wars, and fireworks, culminating with the burning of King Carnival in effigy on the Sunday evening before *Mardi Gras* (the day preceding *Ash Wednesday,* which marks the start of *Lent*). With its throbbing music, steaming street food, prancing drum majorettes, and all those emphatically thronging throngs, Nice's *Carnival* is not a party for the faint of heart or, for that matter, for the faint of eardrum—and beware, it's a paradise for pickpockets.

Grande Parade du Jazz The brassiest jam in Europe, this event—held annually for 10 days in July—attracts just about every major jazz musician from the US and the Continent. Chick Corea, Fats Domino, Ella Fitzgerald, the late Dizzy Gillespie, Lionel Hampton, the late Woody Herman, Sonny Rollins, and a whole hall of fame's worth of others have performed here, in styles ranging from the best vintage New Orleans Dixieland to the last 12-tone word, from hot and bop to blue and cool. The music never stops: From late afternoon until midnight, music lovers can hear concerts in the gardens of the Roman amphitheater at Cimiez, and after that they can track down all-night jam sessions in the city's jazz joints. Food stalls dish out shrimp creole and *salade niçoise* in appropriately marathon fashion.

The *Fête des Mais* is a month of Sundays in May, with special merriment in the gardens of the Roman arena at Cimiez. In September, the *Triathlon de Nice* draws some of the world's best athletes, who swim across the Baie des Anges, run a marathon, and then compete in a long-distance bicycle race. To find out more about special events in Nice, contact the *Comité des Fêtes* (5 Promenade des Anglais; phone: 93-87-16-28).

MUSEUMS

In addition to those described in *Special Places* (see above), the following museums may be of interest. Note that some museums may close during lunch hours, generally from noon to 2 PM:

GALERIE-MUSÉE RAOUL DUFY (RAOUL DUFY GALLERY-MUSEUM) This small museum and gallery is devoted to Dufy and his contemporaries. Closed Sunday mornings and Mondays. No admission charge. 77 Quai des Etats-Unis (phone: 93-62-31-24).

MUSÉE ARCHÉOLOGIQUE DE CIMIEZ (CIMIEZ ARCHAEOLOGICAL MUSEUM) In the same complex as the *Musée Matisse* (see *Special Places*) is this collection of archaeological objects found at the Roman site of Cimiez, plus a fine array of Etruscan, Greek, and Roman ceramics. Closed Sunday mornings and Mondays. No admission charge. 160 Av. des Arènes (phone: 93-81-59-57).

MUSÉE DES BEAUX-ARTS JULES CHÉRET (JULES CHÉRET MUSEUM OF FINE ARTS) Nice's municipal art museum, with works by Fragonard, Renoir, Degas, and Picasso. Closed Mondays. No admission charge. 33 Av. des Baumettes (phone: 93-44-50-72).

MUSÉE D'HISTOIRE NATURELLE/MUSÉE BARLA (MUSEUM OF NATURAL HISTORY/ BARLA MUSEUM) Exhibitions on marine life, paleontology, and mineralogy.

Closed Tuesdays, some holidays, and from mid-August through mid-September. No admission charge. 60 *bis* Bd. Risso (phone: 93-55-15-24).

MUSÉE INTERNATIONAL D'ART NAÏF ANATOLE JAKOVSKY (ANATOLE JAKOVSKY INTERNATIONAL MUSEUM OF PRIMITIVE ART) Jakovsky's collection of almost 600 paintings documents primitive art from the 18th century to the present and represents nearly 30 countries. Closed Tuesdays and some holidays. No admission charge. *Château Ste-Hélène,* Av. Val-Marie (phone: 93-71-78-33).

MUSÉE NAVAL (NAVAL MUSEUM) From its perch atop the *Tour Bellanda* (a former residence of composer Hector Berlioz), this museum overlooks spectacular grounds. It houses ship replicas, arms, navigation instruments, and models of the port at various times in its history. Closed Mondays and Tuesdays, holidays, and mid-November through mid-December. No admission charge. *Parc du Château* (phone: 93-80-47-61).

MUSÉE DE PALÉONTOLOGIE HUMAINE DE TERRA AMATA (TERRA AMATA MUSEUM OF HUMAN PALEONTOLOGY) Artifacts from a 400,000-year-old prehistoric site. Closed Mondays and two weeks in September. No admission charge. 25 Bd. Carnot (phone: 93-55-59-93).

SHOPPING

Street market shopping in the Vieille Ville is relatively inexpensive and fun. Every Monday, the huge square where the *Marché aux Fleurs* is held (on Cours Saleya) becomes an antiques and bric-a-brac market of unusual allure. In the newer part of town, Rue Masséna, Place Magenta, and Rue Paradis are the best shopping areas; Rue Paradis especially is noted for its elegant stores. For standard shopping hours, see GETTING READY TO GO. Some to browse through:

Allées de la Côte d'Azur This shop has various unusual edibles; don't miss the dried figs wrapped in fig leaves. 1 Rue St-François-de-Paule (phone: 93-85-87-30).

Alziari Oils, spices, rustic wooden kitchenware, and olive oil soap. 14 Rue St-François-de-Paule (phone: 93-85-76-92).

Auer This beautiful 19th-century tearoom looks like a candy box and sells scrumptious handmade chocolates and every imaginable candied fruit, the latter made on the premises. 7 Rue St-François-de-Paule (phone: 93-85-77-98).

Casa Glacier Only natural flavors are used at this, the best ice cream shop in Nice. 8 Rue Lepante (phone: 93-85-17-00).

The Cat's Whiskers New and used books and magazines in English. 26 Rue Lamartine (phone: 93-80-02-66).

Cave Caprioglio This is where the locals come to fill up their wine bottles *au tonneau* (from the barrel). 16 Rue de la Préfecture (phone: 93-85-71-36).

Confiserie du Vieux Nice A candy factory with Provence specialties such as candied fruits and flowers. Watch the sweets being made downstairs, then make your selections upstairs. 14 Quai Papacino (phone: 93-55-43-50).

Louis Vuitton A branch of the famous Paris outfitter, selling handbags, luggage, and other items with the status initials. English is spoken, and prices are high. Check erratic seasonal opening hours. 2 Av. Suède (phone: 93-87-87-47).

Promenade des Antiquaires A complex of 22 antiques galleries. 7 Promenade des Anglais.

Riviera Bookshop A wide choice of new and secondhand books in English. 10 Rue Chauvain (phone: 93-85-84-61).

Victoria This pretty shop on one of Nice's most chic shopping streets has a wide range of stylish items for the home, including Provençal furniture, fabrics, and pottery. 12 Rue Alphonse-Karr (phone: 93-88-72-49).

SPORTS AND FITNESS

BOATING Small boats are available for hire in the Vieux Port. *Planches à voile* (windsurfers) can be rented at bathing establishments along the promenade.

FITNESS CENTER The *Centre Profil* at the *Méridien* hotel (phone: 93-87-73-57), with English-speaking instructors, is open to the public.

GOLF There are two good 18-hole courses near Nice—*Golf Bastide du Roi* (Av. Jules-Grec, Biot; phone: 93-65-08-48) and *Golf d'Opio Valbonne* (*Château de la Begude*, Rte. de Roquefort-les-Pins, Valbonne; phone: 93-12-00-45; fax: 93-12-26-00).

HORSE RACING Thoroughbred racing takes place at the *Hippodrome de la Côte d'Azur* in nearby Cagnes-sur-Mer (phone: 93-20-30-30). Call or check local newspapers or the national paper *L'Equipe* for schedules.

HORSEBACK RIDING Horses can be rented at the *Club Hippique de Nice* (368 Rte. de Grenoble; phone: 93-13-13-16).

JOGGING The wide sidewalk on the sea side of the Promenade des Anglais is good for an early-morning workout. The *Parc de Vaugrenier,* 5 miles (8 km) west of Nice on N7, has a jogging track equipped with exercise stations.

SCUBA DIVING The *Centre International de Plongée de Nice* (2 Ruelle des Moulins; phone: 93-55-59-50) offers a range of diving options.

SWIMMING The Ruhl Plage is the most central of Nice's bathing beaches. Castel Plage is set right into the rock of Pointe de Rauba Capeu below the *Château.* In winter, you can swim at the *Piscine Municipale J.-Médecin* (178 Rue de France; phone: 93-86-24-01) or the *Piscine Jean Bouin* (*Palais des Sports,* near the *Palais des Expositions;* phone: 93-13-13-13).

TENNIS AND SQUASH The *Nice Lawn Tennis Club* (*Parc Imperial,* 5 Av. Suzanne-Lenglen: phone: 93-96-17-70), delightfully away from the noisy beach and business districts in a residential section of the city, attracts a substantial number of better than average players. Suzanne Lenglen, who grew up across the street (now renamed to honor her), developed her distinctive balletic playing style on its courts. There are 19 in all, 13 of them clay. The *Tennis-Squash Club Vauban* (18 Rue Mar-Vauban; phone: 93-26-09-78) has seven tennis courts and four air conditioned squash courts.

THEATER AND FILM

In summer, alfresco performances take place in the Roman arena in Cimiez and in the Jardin Albert-I. *Théâtre Francis Gag* (4 Rue St-Joseph; phone: 93-62-00-03) features operettas and dance. For modern theater, try the *Théâtre de l'Alphabet* (10 Bd. Carabacel; phone: 93-13-08-88). The *Théâtre de Nice* (Promenade des Arts; phone: 93-80-52-60; fax: 93-62-19-46) presents a classical repertory and some dance. Check with the tourist office or the *FNAC* record store (30 Av. Jean-Médecin; phone: 93-92-09-09) for information on performance schedules at all of the above theaters. *Cinémathèque de Nice* (3 Esplanade Kennedy; phone: 92-04-06-66) shows classic films in the original language, including many in English.

MUSIC

The season at the *Théâtre de l'Opéra* (Quai des Etats-Unis) runs from November through April. The box office is at 4 Rue St-François-de-Paule (phone: 93-80-59-83, information; 93-85-67-31, reservations). The *Orchestre d'Harmonie de la Ville de Nice* (34 Bd. Jean-Jaurès; phone: 93-80-08-50) performs concerts throughout the year at various locales. Jazz can be heard from October through May at Cimiez's *Centre de Diffusion et d'Action Culturelle* (49 Av. de la Marne; phone: 93-81-09-09). There also are outdoor summer musical performances (see *Theater,* above).

NIGHTCLUBS AND NIGHTLIFE

Probably the best-known nightspot in Nice is the *Casino Ruhl,* on the ground floor of the *Méridien* hotel (1 Promenade des Anglais; phone: 93-87-95-87). Though their casino is smaller than its Monte Carlo counterparts, it does have slot machines, a Las Vegas–style cabaret, and a disco; there is also a chic piano bar, *Le Baccara,* in the hotel. *Le Relais* is a sophisticated piano bar in the *Négresco* hotel (see *Checking In*). *Blue Sea* (24 Quai Lunel; phone: 93-55-23-34) is a lively disco. *Chez Wayne* (15 Rue de la Préfecture; phone: 93-13-46-99), a British-owned bar, caters to a young crowd that likes beer and rock 'n' roll. There's also live music at *Le Pam-Pam Masséna* (1 Rue Desboutin; phone: 93-80-21-60).

Best in Town

CHECKING IN

Nice has a number of apartment hotels with furnished rooms for visitors who plan to stay a week or more; a brochure is available from the tourist office. *Résidence-Hôtel Ulys* (179 Promenade des Anglais; phone: 93-96-26-30; fax: 93-86-61-62) is among the finest of these.

Nice's hotels can be divided into those along the Promenade des Anglais, with a view of the bay (and the traffic), and those set back on quieter streets. For a double room, expect to pay $400 or more in a very expensive hotel (rates can be much higher for suites at palaces like the *Négresco*); $200 to $400 in an expensive hotel; $100 to $200 in a moderate one; and less than $100 in an inexpensive one. Unless otherwise noted, all hotels listed below feature air conditioning, telephones, TV sets, and private baths in the rooms. Some less expensive hotels have private baths in only some of their rooms; it's a good idea to confirm whether your room has a private bath when making a reservation. All hotels listed below are open year-round and accept major credit cards, unless otherwise noted. Some require *demi-pension* (a higher rate that includes breakfast and either lunch or dinner) in summer. Always be sure to make reservations in Nice.

For an unforgettable experience, we begin with our favorite haven in Nice, followed by our cost and quality choices of hotels, listed by price category.

ROOM AT THE TOP

Négresco Everyone should stay in this Côte d'Azur landmark at least once. It's a great wedding cake of a hotel with 131 rooms and 19 suites; Nice's only two-Michelin-star restaurant, *Chantecler* (see *Eating Out*); and staff attired in 18th-century livery. The elaborately and eclectically appointed rooms, some of which have canopied beds, overlook the promenade. In the central atrium, an enormous Baccarat crystal chandelier (a similar one is in the Kremlin) is suspended over what is allegedly the largest Aubusson carpet in the world. The 1913 building has been designated a national monument. 37 Promenade des Anglais (phone: 93-88-39-51; fax: 93-88-35-68).

VERY EXPENSIVE

Méridien With 314 rooms, this shiny, somewhat impersonal hotel is luxurious in a more streamlined way than the Victorian dowager hotels that gave the Riviera its reputation. There's a good restaurant, a piano bar, a roof terrace, a health club, a pool, and an underground parking lot offering access to the pedestrian zone. Above the *Casino Ruhl* near the *Jardin Albert-I,* at 1 Promenade des Anglais (phone: 93-82-25-25; fax: 93-16-08-90).

Palais Maeterlinck Every comfort imaginable—including lovely gardens, a pool, and exceptional views—is available in this quiet hotel, with eight rooms and 20 suites. The hotel's restaurant, *Le Mélisande,* is one of the city's best (see *Eating Out*). Closed early January through mid-February. Three miles (5 km) from the center of town, at 30 Bd. Maeterlinck (phone: 92-00-72-00; fax: 92-00-72-01).

EXPENSIVE

Abela A deluxe, modern, 332-room hotel boasting a very fine restaurant (closed July and August) and such lively activities as *thés dansants* (tea dances) and festive buffet lunches on Sundays. There's also a pool on the roof. Toward the airport, at 223 Promenade des Anglais (phone: 93-37-17-17; fax: 93-71-21-71).

Beau Rivage Near the opera house, this modern hotel with 106 rooms and 12 suites is a favorite among visiting divas. The rooms are quiet and comfortable, and the service is consistently good. There's a restaurant. 24 Rue St. François-de-Paule (phone: 93-80-80-70; fax: 93-80-55-77).

Elysée Palace This elegant 121-room, 22-suite hostelry boasts an excellent restaurant, a rooftop pool with a bar, a fitness room and sauna, and a garage. Set 100 feet from the sea, yet near the center of town, at 33 Rue François-I (phone: 93-86-06-06; fax: 93-44-50-40).

La Pérouse A charming, 65-room hostelry with a view of the entire bay, particularly spectacular at sunset. It offers gardens, a restaurant, a pool, and a sauna. One drawback is traffic noise on an uphill curve outside; since the rooms are now air conditioned, however, the summertime noise level has been considerably reduced. At the far end of the Quai des Etats-Unis, 11 Quai Rauba-Capeu (phone: 93-62-34-63; fax: 93-62-59-41).

Plaza Concorde A beautifully restored, palatial hotel with 183 rooms, it faces the *Jardin Albert-I* and the sea. The view from the rooftop terrace is magnificent. There's a restaurant. In the center of town, at 12 Av. de Verdun (phone: 93-87-80-41; fax: 93-82-50-70).

Sofitel-Splendid This dowager with 113 rooms and 16 suites has been run by the same family for three generations, though it's been updated with modern amenities. One floor is reserved for nonsmoking guests; there's a pool on the roof with a great view, a sauna, and a restaurant. 50 Bd. Victor-Hugo (phone: 93-16-41-00; 800-763-4835; fax: 93-87-02-46).

West End British-style elegance attracts a faithful clientele to this 130-room hotel. There's no restaurant. On the seafront, at 31 Promenade des Anglais (phone: 93-88-79-91; fax: 93-88-85-07).

Westminster Concorde This lovely 19th-century establishment—well located on the seafront—is in the grand tradition. There are 105 rooms (ask for one facing the bay) and a good restaurant, a bar, and a disco. 27 Promenade des Anglais (phone: 93-88-29-44; fax: 93-82-45-35).

Brice This old hotel with 66 rooms (none with air conditioning) is situated in a delightful flower garden with orange and palm trees. There is a dining room. Four blocks from the Promenade des Anglais, at 44 Rue Maréchal-Joffre (phone: 93-88-14-44; fax: 93-87-38-54).

Frantour-Napoléon This gracious, typically Niçois building has a warm and welcoming atmosphere. There are 83 rooms and a bar, but no restaurant. On a quiet corner near the pedestrian zone, at 6 Rue Grimaldi (phone: 93-87-70-07; fax: 93-16-17-80).

Grand Hôtel Aston Recommended for its central location and its creditable restaurant, this Art Deco–style establishment faces the fountains in the Place Masséna. There are 160 rooms, all with modern amenities such as minibars. 12 Av. Félix-Faure (phone: 93-80-62-52; fax: 93-80-40-02).

La Malmaison This inn has 50 large rooms with Louis XVI furniture; nonsmoking rooms are available. The restaurant features regional dishes. 48 Bd. Victor-Hugo (phone: 93-87-62-56; fax: 93-16-17-99).

L'Oasis This 38-room hotel really is an oasis, with its quiet garden right in the bustling center of town. The rooms are simply decorated but well equipped (though without air conditioning). There's no restaurant. 23 Rue Gounod (phone: 93-88-12-29; fax: 93-16-14-40).

Le Petit Palais It's worth the 10-minute drive from the city center to enjoy the views from this Belle Epoque mansion near the *Musée Matisse*. There are 25 rooms (none is air conditioned) but no restaurant. 10 Av. Emile-Bieckert (phone: 93-62-19-11; fax: 93-62-53-60).

Pullman Nice A five-minute walk from Place Masséna, this prime property has 200 rooms, but no restaurant. Among the hotel's attractions are a Polynesian bar, a pool and sauna, exotic interior gardens, and a great view from the rooftop terrace. In the center of town, at 28 Av. Notre-Dame (phone: 93-13-36-36; 800-221-4542; fax: 93-62-61-69).

Windsor Art dealers tend to congregate here, where frescoes of Nice decorate the walls. There are 60 rooms, and a light menu is served in a lovely garden. 11 Rue Dalpozzo (phone: 93-88-59-35; fax: 93-88-94-57).

INEXPENSIVE

Armenonville This quiet hideaway with 13 rooms (none air conditioned) is a good value, although it's about a 10-minute walk from the beach. There's no restaurant. No credit cards accepted. 20 Av. des Fleurs (phone: 93-96-86-00).

Le Floride Located on the most chic boulevard in the city, this simple 20-room hotel offers comfortable rooms (none air conditioned) and friendly service. There's no restaurant. 52 Bd. Cimiez (phone: 93-53-11-02).

Georges This family-run hotel near the beach has 18 rooms. Breakfast is served on a terrace overlooking the city's red-tiled roofs; there's no restaurant. 3 Rue Henri Cordier (phone: 93-86-23-41; fax: 93-44-02-30).

EATING OUT

Niçois cuisine is a curious mixture of Parisian, Provençal, and Italian. Among its culinary trademarks are *pissaladière* (pizza topped with black olives, onions, and anchovies), *stocaficada* (ragout of stockfish, with potatoes, tomatoes, peppers, and zucchini), *gnocchi à la niçoise* (potato dumplings), and *pain bagnat* (French bread soaked in olive oil and fillied with *salade niçoise*). *Soupe au pistou* is a vegetable bean soup containing a *pesto*-like paste. *Socca,* popular in the Vieille Ville and port, is an enormous pancake made from chick-pea flour and olive oil, baked like pizza or fried in oil. It is usually washed down with a solid red wine or a little glass of *pointu* (chilled rosé). Nice's best-known specialty is *salade niçoise,* which contains tuna, hard-boiled eggs, potatoes, string beans, tomatoes, and black olives. Also be sure to sample Nice's own Appellation Contrôlée wines—Bellet reds, whites, and rosés—during your stay here.

For a dinner for two, expect to pay over $160 at very expensive restaurants; $120 to $160 at expensive places; $70 to $120 at moderate restaurants; and less than $50 at inexpensive ones. These prices include service (usually added to the bill), but not drinks or wine. Unless otherwise noted, all restaurants listed below are open for lunch and dinner.

For an unforgettable culinary experience, we begin with our Nice favorite, which falls in the "very expensive" category, followed by our cost and quality choices of restaurants, listed by price category.

HAUTE GASTRONOMIE

Chantecler The setting is regal Regency at this elegant two-Michelin-star restaurant. Young wonder chef Dominique le Stanc concocts such specialties as *gourmandise de foie gras* (a luxurious pâté), a fish fantasy called *charlotte de St-Pierre,* and lobster ravioli. The *menu dégustation* features tiny, elegant portions of a dozen different dishes, and if *larme de chocolat* is proffered for dessert, be sure to taste this ambrosial "chocolate tear." Try one of the excellent Côtes de Provence wines. Open daily; closed mid-November through mid-December. Reservations necessary. Major credit cards accepted. In the *Négresco Hotel,* 37 Promenade des Anglais (phone: 93-88-39-51; fax: 93-88-35-68).

L'Ane Rouge *Moules farcies* (stuffed mussels), *oursins* (sea urchins), *loup de mer au fenouille* (sea bass grilled in fennel), *huîtres plates aux champagne* (oysters in champagne), *bourride* (fish stew), and just about anything else from the sea can be ordered either in the pretty, flowered dining room or outdoors on the terrace. Closed weekends, holidays, and mid-July through August. Reservations necessary. Major credit cards accepted. Vieux Port, at 7 Quai des Deux-Emmanuels (phone: 93-89-49-63).

Chez Don Camillo This tranquil, intimate place offers an appetizing taste of Italy with a Niçois accent. Closed Sundays, the last two weeks of August, and two weeks each in November and February. Reservations necessary. Major credit cards accepted. 5 Rue des Ponchettes (phone: 93-85-67-95).

Coco Beach A few yards from the sea, this large restaurant is popular with residents who appreciate good bouillabaisse, lobster, and grilled fish of all kinds. It gets *very* crowded during summer months. Closed Sunday dinner, Mondays, two weeks in March, and December. No reservations. MasterCard and Visa accepted. 2 Av. Jean-Lorrain (phone: 93-89-39-26).

Florian In this one-Michelin-star restaurant, savor such Niçois staples as fish with olives and garlic. The wine list, while extensive, is pricey. Closed Saturday lunch, Sundays, and late July through late August. Reservations advised. MasterCard and Visa accepted. 22 Rue A.-Karr (phone: 93-16-08-49; fax: 93-87-31-98).

Jean-François Issautier Although located in a less than scenic industrial zone, the two-Michelin-star food is worth the trip. Try the sea bass with tiny purple artichokes, accompanied by a Bellet wine. Closed Sunday dinner, Mondays, mid-February through mid-March, and a week in November. Reservations necessary. Major credit cards accepted. Fifteen miles (27 km) north of Nice, on N202 in St-Martin-du-Var (phone: 93-08-10-65; fax: 93-29-19-73).

Le Mélisande The magnificent view alone is worth the price of admission (ask for a table on the terrace in summer), but the food is also sublime; try the duck breast with avocado and warm goat cheese. The wine list is extensive—and the selections expensive. Closed Sunday dinner and Mondays. Reservations advised. Major credit cards accepted. In the *Palais Maeterlinck* hotel, 3 miles (5 km) from the center of town, at 30 Bd. Maeterlinck (phone: 92-00-72-00; fax: 92-00-72-01).

MODERATE

Auberge de Bellet Beautifully decorated, it is the ideal place to sample the range of local Bellet wines. Accompany them with braised chicken with mint or a fricassee of fish with herb butter. In summer, dine outdoors in the shaded garden. Closed Tuesdays and the first two weeks in February. Reservations unnecessary. Major credit cards accepted. A mile (1.6 km) west of St-

Pancrace (5 miles/8 km north of Nice), in St-Roman-de-Bellet (phone: 93-37-83-84).

Barale Here is a true Niçois restaurant, whose set menu includes such local specialties as *pissaladière* and ravioli. Closed Sundays, Mondays, and August. Reservations advised. MasterCard and Visa accepted. 39 Rue Beaumont (phone: 93-89-17-94).

La Belle Niçoise A popular, unpretentious seafood restaurant that displays its wares on the street and also prepares food to take out. Good for oysters. Closed Mondays and November. No reservations. Major credit cards accepted. 32 Cours Saleya (phone: 93-80-12-63).

Chez les Pêcheurs The specialties of this seafood spot include fish pâté and *loup de mer* (grilled sea bass). Closed Tuesday dinner in winter, Wednesdays, Thursday lunch in summer, and November through mid-December. Reservations unnecessary. Major credit cards accepted. In the Vieux Port, at 18 Quai Docks (phone: 93-89-59-61).

Dents de la Mer The fish swimming on view in a holding tank reflect the focus on freshness in this popular restaurant, decorated like a pirate ship that looks as if it came directly out of a Hollywood movie set. In summer ask for a table on the terrace. Open daily. Reservations advised. Major credit cards accepted. 2 Rue St-François-de-Paule (phone: 93-80-99-16).

Flo The place to see and be seen, this large, chic brasserie, which is open late, offers classics such as *choucroute garnie* and some regional dishes. Open daily. Reservations advised. Major credit cards accepted. 4 Rue Sacha-Guitry (phone: 93-16-08-49).

Grand Café de Turin By now a landmark, this restaurant has become the "in" place to enjoy simply cooked fresh seafood. There's a terrace under Italianate arcades. Closed Sunday dinner, Mondays, and part of February. Reservations advised. MasterCard and Visa accepted. 5 Pl. Garibaldi (phone: 93-62-29-52).

Le Grand Pavois (Chez Michel) This place has very good seafood dishes, especially fish soup, stuffed mussels, and sole *meunière*. Closed Mondays. Reservations advised. MasterCard and Visa accepted. 11 Rue Meyerbeer (phone: 93-88-77-42).

Mac-Mahon The specialty at this friendly brasserie (lots of bustle, beer on tap) is fresh seafood, but other dishes, such as rabbit with olives, also fare well. The wine list has bottles in all price ranges. Open daily. Reservations advised. Major credit cards accepted. 50 Bd. Jean-Jaurès (phone: 93-62-30-71; fax: 93-92-43-59).

La Mérenda A taste of pure Niçois tradition is offered in this family-run restaurant. Try the zucchini-blossom fritters or the mixed-greens salad with olive oil. The place is always packed. Closed weekends, Mondays, two weeks in February, and the month of August. No reservations. No credit cards accepted. Near the *Marché aux Fleurs,* at 4 Rue de la Terrasse (no phone).

Les Préjugés du Palais This excellent restaurant offers such nouvelle-inspired cuisine as *daurade rôti aux épices* (spicy roast sea bream). Closed Sundays and mid-October through mid-November. Reservations advised. Major credit cards accepted. 1 Pl. Palais (phone: 93-62-37-03).

Ruhl Plage The best of the beach restaurants along the Promenade des Anglais serves good grilled fish, salads, and carafe wines. A pool for children and all kinds of water sports facilities make it a popular summer lunch spot with the Niçois. Open from March through November, or as long as the weather stays warm. No reservations. Major credit cards accepted. Opposite the *Casino Ruhl,* on the Promenade des Anglais (phone: 93-87-09-70).

Le Safari Though this restaurant is currently a *très chic* hangout among artsy types, there's nothing bohemian about the cuisine, which includes elegant seafood dishes and some regional specialties. The bar is only for restaurant patrons. Open daily; closed Sunday and Monday dinner. Reservations advised. MasterCard and Visa accepted. 1 Cours Saleya (phone: 93-80-18-44).

La Toque Blanche This 10-table spot offers magnificent fish dishes; there's a prix fixe lunch weekdays. Closed Sunday dinner and Mondays. Reservations necessary. MasterCard and Visa accepted. 10 Rue de la Buffa (phone: 93-88-38-18).

L'Univers "César" A great place for pasta, served in all shapes and styles. *Loup de mer aux cèpes et artichaux* (sea bass with mushrooms and artichokes) is another specialty of the house. Open daily until 2 AM. Reservations necessary. Major credit cards accepted. 54 Bd. Jean-Jaurès (phone: 93-62-32-22).

INEXPENSIVE

Bièrerie Chez Nino You may find yourself the only out-of-towner in this small old bistro, whose clientele sports a democratic mix of business suits and leather jackets. The place features a hundred different beers (both bottled and draft) from 22 countries, and its friendly owner will help you choose the right one to accompany your meal. Try the grills or the stockfish. Closed Sundays and August. No reservations. MasterCard and Visa accepted. On a tiny street near the train station, at 50 Rue Trachel (phone: 93-88-07-71).

La Cambuse Niçois specialties are featured in this friendly local favorite. Closed Sundays. Reservations advised. MasterCard and Visa accepted. 5 Cours Saleya (phone: 93-80-12-31).

Chez Pipo Only the unadorned pancakes known as *socca* (see introduction to *Eating Out*) are served at this 65-year-old landmark. They are cooked on a wood-burning stove; order a glass of wine and enjoy a leisurely Niçois tradition. Open daily for dinner only. Reservations advised. MasterCard and Visa accepted. 13 Rue Bavastro (phone: 93-55-88-82).

La Nissarda The attractive decor provides a nice setting in which to sample a range of local specialties. Closed Sundays, holidays, and August. No reservations. MasterCard and Visa accepted. A 10-minute walk from Place Masséna, at 17 Rue Gubernatis (phone: 93-85-26-29).

La Pizza The best pizza this side of Ventimiglia, and good pasta, too. Young folks congregate here until 1 AM. Open daily. No reservations. MasterCard and Visa accepted. In the heart of the pedestrian zone, at 34 Rue Masséna (phone: 93-87-70-29).

Rive Gauche A small, friendly bistro with an Art Deco interior. Tasty dishes include calf's liver and duck. Closed Sundays. No reservations. MasterCard and Visa accepted. 27 *bis* Rue Ribotti (phone: 93-89-16-82).

BARS AND CAFÉS

The *Scotch Tea House* (4 Av. Suède; phone: 93-16-03-55) is very British and proper; *Auer* (see *Shopping*) is the most enchanting tearoom in town. *Café de France* (64 Rue de la France; phone: 93-88-50-81) is a landmark where old and young Niçois, as well as out-of-towners, drink coffee or beer or dine from a light menu. *Bar des Oiseaux* (5 Rue St-Vincent; phone: 93-80-27-33) is a colorful place where the owner carries a bird on her shoulder; ask for a *piconbière,* a beer with a sweetish syrup in it. For a late-night place, try *Bar-Tabac des Fleurs* (13 Cours Saleya), a bar near the *Marché aux Fleurs* that *opens* at 4 AM.

Paris

Paris—with its supreme joie de vivre and its passion for eating, drinking, and dressing well—always has attracted visitors and exiles from all corners of the earth. At the same time, it remains not so much a cosmopolitan city as a very French one, and a provincial one at that. Paris has its own argot, and each neighborhood retains its peculiar character, so that the great capital is still very much a city of 20 villages.

But parochialism aside—and forgetting about the consummate haughtiness of Parisians—the main attraction of the City of Light is its beauty. When you speak of the ultimate European city, it must be Paris, if only for the view from the Place de la Concorde or the *Tuileries* up the Champs-Elysées toward the *Arc de Triomphe,* or similarly striking sights beside the Seine. Here is the fashion capital of the world and the center of gastronomic invention and execution. Here the men all seem to swagger with the insouciance of privilege, and even the humblest shop girl dresses with the care of an haute couture model. Paris is the reason "foreign" means "French" to so many travelers.

Roughly elliptical in shape, Paris is in the north-central part of France, in the rich agricultural area of the Seine River valley. With a population of over two million people, it is France's largest city, an industrial and commercial hub, an important river port, and an undisputed center for arts and culture. The city has more than doubled in size in the last century; however, the population has decreased during the past decade as residential buildings have been converted to offices and the city has become too expensive for all but the very rich. The ring of mid-19th-century fortifications that once were well beyond its boundaries now serves as the city limits. At the western edge of Paris is the vast *Bois de Boulogne* and to the east is the enormous *Bois de Vincennes.* Curving through Paris, the Seine divides the city into the northern Rive Droite (Right Bank) and southern Rive Gauche (Left Bank). The Rive Droite extends from the *Bois de Boulogne* on the far west, through Place Charles-de-Gaulle (also known as Place de l'Etoile), which surrounds the *Arc de Triomphe,* farther east to the *Jardin des Tuileries* (Tuileries Gardens) and the fabulous *Louvre,* and on to the stately Marais district. North of the *Louvre* is the area of the Grands Boulevards, centers of business and fashion; farther north is the district of Montmartre, built on a hill and crowned by the domed *Basilique du Sacré-Coeur* (Basilica of the Sacred Heart), an area that has attracted artists since the days of Monet and Renoir.

The Rive Gauche sweeps from the *Tour Eiffel* (Eiffel Tower) in the west through the Quartier Latin (Latin Quarter), with its university and bohemian and intellectual community. Southwest of the Quartier Latin is Montparnasse, once inhabited by artists and intellectuals and laborers, now a large urban renewal project that includes a suburban-style shopping center around the *Tour Montparnasse* (Montparnasse Tower). To the south of Montparnasse are charming turn-of-the-century middle class residential districts.

In the middle of the Seine are two islands, the Ile de la Cité and the Ile St-Louis, the oldest parts of Paris. It was on the Ile de la Cité (in the 3rd century BC) that Celtic fishermen known as Parisii first built a settlement they named Lutetia, or "place surrounded by water." Caesar conquered the city for Rome in 52 BC, and in about AD 300, Paris was invaded by Germanic tribes, the strongest of which were the Franks. In 451, when Attila the Hun threatened to overrun Paris, a holy woman named Geneviève promised to defend the city by praying. She seems to have succeeded—the enemy decided to spare the capital—and Geneviève became the patron saint of Paris. Clovis I, the first Christian King of the Franks, made Paris his capital in the 6th century. As recently as last year, the city has yielded up evidence of this first ruling dynasty, the Merovingians; excavations in central Paris unearthed a spectacular burial site with nearly 60 tombs, including those of high-ranking Frankish dignitaries, dating from the 4th to the 7th centuries. The Merovingians gradually declined, and Paris's fortunes declined with them, until, in the mid-8th century, Pepin the Short took possession of the kingship. Pepin founded a new dynasty, the Carolingians, so named for his son, Charlemagne, who went on to rule not only France, but the entire Western world as head of the Holy Roman Empire. Still, after Charlemagne, relentless Norman sieges, famine, and plague curtailed the city's development, until at the end of the 10th century peace and prosperity were restored when the last of the now ineffectual Carolingian monarchs died, and Hugh Capet ascended the throne. The first of a long line of Capetian kings, Capet made Paris a great cultural center and seat of learning.

The Capetian monarchs contributed much to the growth of the city over the next few centuries. A defensive wall was begun in 1180 by Philip Augustus to protect the expanding Rive Droite business and trading center, as well as the intellectual quarter around the *Sorbonne,* the newly formed university on the Rive Gauche. He then built a new royal palace, the *Louvre,* just outside these ramparts, but never lived there. Medieval Paris was a splendid city, a leader in the arts and intellectual life of Europe. The *Sorbonne* attracted such outstanding scholars as Alexander of Hales, Giovanni di Fidanza (St. Bonaventure), Albertus Magnus, and Thomas Aquinas.

Work began on that splendid monument to medieval Paris, the *Cathédrale de Notre-Dame de Paris,* in 1163, under the direction of the energetic Bishop of Paris, Maurice de Sully. The rest of the Ile de la Cité remained a warren of narrow streets and wood and plaster houses, but the banks of the Seine continued to be built up in both directions. Renaissance kings, patrons of the arts, added their own architectural and aesthetic embellishments to the flourishing city. Major streets were laid out; some of Paris's most charming squares were constructed; the Pont-Neuf, the first stone bridge spanning the Seine, was completed; and Lenôtre, the royal gardener, introduced proportion, harmony, and beauty with his extraordinary *Tuileries.*

Louis XIV, who was responsible for many of the most notable Parisian landmarks, including *Les Invalides,* moved the court to Versailles in the late 17th century (for details on Versailles and the palace Louis XIV built there, see *Celebrated Cathedrals and Châteaux* in DIVERSIONS). Paris nevertheless continued to blossom, and it was under the Sun King's rule that France and Paris first won international prestige. Visitors were drawn to the city, luxury industries thrived, and the *Panthéon, Champ-de-Mars* parade ground, and *Ecole Militaire* were built.

French history reflects the conflict between the two extremes of the French character, both equally strong: a tradition of aristocracy and a penchant for revolution. The French aristocracy has erected some of the world's most magnificent palaces—the *Louvre,* the *Palais du Luxembourg,* and *Versailles.* But the French also have mounted their share of insurrections: from 1358, when the mob rebelled against the dauphin, to the Fronde in 1648–49, the 1830 and 1848 revolutions that reverberated throughout Europe, the Paris Commune of 1870–71, and the student rebellion of 1968, which nearly overthrew the Fifth Republic. The most profound uprising of all, of course, was the French Revolution of 1789. That historic rebellion was set off by the excesses of the French court and the consummate luxury of the *Versailles* of Louis XIV, which cost the French people dearly in taxes and oppression. The fiercely independent Parisians forced the French king to his knees with their dramatic storming of the Bastille in 1789. Inspired by the ideas of the French and English philosophers of the Enlightenment, just as the American founding fathers were in 1776, the French soon overthrew their monarchy.

During the Revolution, unruly mobs damaged many of the city's buildings, including *Sainte-Chapelle* and *Notre-Dame,* which were not restored until the mid-19th century. Napoleon, who came to power in 1799, was too busy being a conqueror to complete all he planned, though he did manage to restore the *Louvre,* construct the *Arc de Triomphe du Carrousel* (Carrousel Triumphal Arch) and the Place Vendôme victory column, and begin work on the *Arc de Triomphe* and the *Madeleine.* Napoleon's conquests spread the new ideas of the Revolution—including the Code Napoléon, a system of laws embodying the ideals of "Liberty, Equality, Fraternity"—to places as far away as Canada and Moscow.

Later in the 19th century, the great urban planner Baron Haussmann set about reorganizing and modernizing Paris. He instituted the brilliant system of squares as focal points for marvelous, wide boulevards and roads, and planned the Place de l'Opéra, the *Bois de Boulogne* and *Bois de Vincennes,* the railway stations, and the system of 20 *arrondissements* (districts) that make up Paris today. He also destroyed most of the center of the old Cité, displacing 25,000 people.

During the peaceful lull between the Franco-Prussian War and World War I, Paris thrived as never before. These were the days of the Belle Epoque, the heyday of *Maxim's,* the *Folies-Bergère,* and the cancan. Montmartre, immortalized by Toulouse-Lautrec, was so uninhibited that the foreign press dubbed Paris the "City of Sin." Later, in the two decades before World War II, this free-spirited city attracted artistic exiles by the dozens: Picasso, Hemingway, Fitzgerald, and Gertrude Stein were just a few. Only in Paris could such avant-garde writers as James Joyce, D. H. Lawrence, and, later, Henry Miller, find publishers. Paris witnessed the first Impressionist exhibition in 1874 and heard the first performance of Stravinsky's revolutionary *Sacre du Printemps* (Rite of Spring) in 1913.

However avant-garde in other areas, Parisians are a conservative lot when it comes to changes in the appearance of their city. When the *Eiffel Tower* was built in 1889, Guy de Maupassant commented, "I spend all my afternoons on the *Eiffel Tower;* it's the only place in Paris from which I can't see it." Not long ago, Parisians grumbled about the ultramodern *Centre Georges-Pompidou,* now a locus for every type of applied and performing art, and about *Le Forum des Halles,* an underground shopping complex in what was once *Les Halles,* the raucous, lively produce market. Today these are popular tourist attractions, symbols of the new, modern Paris. More recent issues that have sparked controversy include the I. M. Pei glass pyramids that now form the entrance to the *Louvre,* and the project to replace the *Bibliothèque Nationale* with a giant, glass library, due to be completed next year. However, other recent projects have been more popular among Parisians: the face-lift of the formerly rather tacky Champs-Elysées; the creation of a primarily pedestrians-only zone in the glorious Place Vendôme, once virtually clogged with cars; and the ongoing refurbishment of the *Louvre,* which already has resulted in the new *Richelieu Wing,* the elegant, underground *Carrousel du Louvre* shopping complex, and improvements in the surrounding *Jardin des Tuileries.*

Parisians accept innovations reluctantly because they want their city to remain as it has always been. They love their remarkable heritage inordinately, and perhaps it is this love, together with the irrepressible sense of good living, that has made Paris so eternally attractive to others.

Paris At-a-Glance

SEEING THE CITY

The most popular view of Paris is from the top of the *Eiffel Tower,* on the Rive Gauche; on a clear day, you can see for more than 50 miles. The terraces of the *Palais de Chaillot* afford excellent views across gardens and fountains to the *Eiffel Tower.* The tops of *Notre-Dame*'s towers offer close-ups of the cathedral's Gothic spires and flying buttresses, along with a magnificent view of the Ile de la Cité and the rest of Paris.

The most satisfying vantage point, if not the highest, is the top of the *Arc de Triomphe,* which commands a view of the majestic sweep of Baron Haussmann's 12 stately avenues radiating from the Place Charles-de-Gaulle, including the splendid vista down the Champs-Elysées to the Place de la Concorde, with the *Louvre* beyond. Visitors can take the elevator or climb the 284 steps up. The terrace of the *Basilique du Sacré-Coeur,* on the Butte Montmartre, provides an extraordinary view from its steps, especially at dawn or sunset. Other stunning vistas can be enjoyed from the landing at the top of the escalator of the *Centre Georges-Pompidou,* the top of the *Tour Montparnasse* complex, and the observation deck of *La Samaritaine,* the six-floor department store at the foot of the Pont-Neuf (see *Shopping*). For details on other sites described above, see *Special Places.*

Another spectacular cityscape can be seen from the *Grande Arche de la Défense,* to the west of the city (1 Cour de la Défense, Puteaux; phone: 49-07-27-57). The *Grande Arche* completes the axis that starts at the *Louvre* and runs through the Champs-Elysées and the *Arc de Triomphe.* It is open daily. There's an admission charge.

SPECIAL PLACES

Getting around this sprawling metropolis isn't difficult once you understand the layout of the 20 *arrondissements* (districts). Most bookshops and newsstands stock *Paris Indispensable* and *Plan de Paris par Arrondissement,* little lifesavers that list streets alphabetically and indicate the nearest *Métro* station on individual maps and an overall plan. Street addresses of the places mentioned throughout this chapter are followed by their *arrondissement* number.

JUST THE TICKET

The *Carte Musées et Monuments* (Museum and Monuments Pass) allows sightseers and art lovers to bypass ticket lines at 65 museums in and near Paris (though it's not valid for certain special exhibits). Available in one-, three-, or five-day passes, the *carte* is sold in *Métro* stations, museums, at the *Office du Tourisme de Paris,* and at tourist office branches in major train stations (see *Tourist Information* for more on tourist offices). It's also available in the US from *Marketing Challenges International* (10 E. 21st St., Suite 600, New York, NY 10010; phone: 212-529-9069; fax: 212-529-4838). The *Caisse Nationale des Monuments Historiques et des Sites* (see *Le Marais,* below) offers a card good for a year of free visits to monuments and sites both in Paris and throughout France.

LA RIVE DROITE (THE RIGHT BANK)

ARC DE TRIOMPHE AND PLACE CHARLES-DE-GAULLE This monumental arch (165 feet high, 148 feet wide) was built between 1806 and 1836 to commemorate Napoleon's victories (it was then the largest monument of its kind in the world). Note the frieze and its six-foot-high figures—the 10 impressive sculptures symbolizing triumph, peace, and resistance, and especially Rude's *La Marseillaise,* on the right as you face the Champs-Elysées. Also note the arches inscribed with the names of Bonaparte's victories, as well as those of Empire heroes. Beneath the arch is the *Sépulture du Soldat Inconnu* (Tomb of the Unknown Soldier) with its eternal flame, which is rekindled daily at 6:30 PM. A 284-step climb to the platform at the top is rewarded by a magnificent view of the city, including the Champs-Elysées and the *Bois de Boulogne.* (The platform also can be reached by elevator.) The arch is the center of Place Charles-de-Gaulle, once Place de l'Etoile (Square of the Star), so called because it is the center of a "star" whose radiating points are the 12 broad avenues, including the Champs-Elysées, planned and built by Baron Haussmann in the mid-19th century. The arch is open daily. Admission charge. Pl. Charles-de-Gaulle, 8e (phone: 43-80-31-31).

CHAMPS-ELYSÉES Paris's legendary promenade, the "Elysian Fields," was swampland until 1616. It once was synonymous with everything glamorous in the city, but the "Golden Arches" and schlocky shops have replaced much of the old *élégance.* Happily, the restoration and "greening" of what Parisians call the "Champs" have brought back some of the avenue's former cachet. The Champs-Elysées stretches for more than 2 miles between the Place de la Concorde and the Place Charles-de-Gaulle. Lined with rows of trees, shops, cafés, and cinemas, the broad avenue still is perfect for strolling, window shopping, and people watching. The area from the Place de la Concorde to the Rond-Point des Champs-Elysées is a charming park, where Parisians often bring their children. On the north side of the gardens is the *Palais de l'Elysée* (Elysée Palace), the official home of the President of the French Republic.

GRAND PALAIS (GREAT PALACE) Off the Champs-Elysées, on opposite sides of Avenue Winston-Churchill, are the elaborate turn-of-the-century *Grand Palais* and *Petit Palais* (see below), built of glass and stone for the *1900 World Exposition.* With its stone columns, mosaic frieze, and flat glass dome, the *Grand Palais* contains a large area devoted to temporary exhibits, the *Galeries Nationales,* as well as the *Palais de la Découverte,* a science museum and planetarium. Parts of the *Grand Palais* will be closed for structural repairs throughout this year. The *Galeries Nationales* are closed Tuesdays; the *Palais de la Découverte* is closed Mondays. Admission charge for both. Av. Winston-Churchill, 8e (phone: 44-13-17-17).

PETIT PALAIS (LITTLE PALACE) Built at the same time as the *Grand Palais,* it has exhibits on the city's history and a variety of fine and applied arts, plus special shows. Closed Mondays and holidays. Admission charge. Av. Winston-Churchill, 8e (phone: 42-65-12-73).

PLACE DE LA CONCORDE Surely one of the most magnificent in the world, this square is grandly situated in the midst of equally grand landmarks: the

Louvre and the *Tuileries* on one side, the Champs-Elysées and the *Arc de Triomphe* on another, the Seine and the Napoleonic *Palais Bourbon* on a third, and the pillared façade of the *Madeleine* on the fourth. Designed by Gabriel for Louis XV, the square was where his unfortunate successor, Louis XVI, lost his head to the guillotine, as did Marie-Antoinette, Danton, Robespierre, Charlotte Corday, and others. It was first named for Louis XV, then called Place de la Révolution by the triumphant revolutionaries. The square was given the name *"Concorde"* (peace) to erase the memory of the executions performed here during the Revolution. The 3,300-year-old, 220-ton, 75-foot-high *Obélisque de Louqsor* (Obelisk of Luxor) was a gift from Egypt in 1831.

JARDIN DES TUILERIES (TUILERIES GARDENS) Carefully laid out in patterned geometric shapes, with clipped shrubbery and formal flower beds, statues, and fountains, this is one of the finest examples of French garden design (in contrast to informal English gardens, exemplified by the *Bois de Boulogne*). It is currently undergoing extensive renovations, which will be completed in 1997. Along the Seine, between the Place de la Concorde and the *Louvre*.

ORANGERIE A museum on the southwestern edge of the *Jardin des Tuileries,* it displays Monet's celebrated paintings of water lilies, plus the art collection of Jean Walter and Paul Guillaume, with works by Cézanne, Renoir, Matisse, Picasso, and others. Closed Tuesdays. Admission charge. Pl. de la Concorde and Quai des Tuileries, 1er (phone: 42-97-48-16).

JEU DE PAUME (THE TENNIS COURT) This building was refurbished and reopened as a gallery for contemporary art in 1991 as part of the *Louvre* renovation project that began with the opening of the I. M. Pei pyramids. Facing the Place de la Concorde on the northeastern corner of the *Tuileries* opposite the *Orangerie*—and originally an indoor tennis court for France's royalty—the *Jeu de Paume* is the site where, in 1789, delegates met to declare their independence, marking the beginning of the French Revolution (a moment perhaps best commemorated in Jacques-Louis David's famous painting *The Tennis Court Oath,* which hangs in the *Louvre*). Previously home to the *Louvre*'s Impressionist collection (now in the *Musée d'Orsay;* see below), the extensively modernized museum houses exhibitions of contemporary works from 1960 on, including those of Takis, Broodthears, and Dubuffet. Closed Mondays and weekday mornings. Admission charge. Pl. de la Concorde, 1er (phone: 47-03-12-50).

RUE DE RIVOLI Running along the north side of the *Louvre* and the *Jardin des Tuileries,* this elegant but car-clogged old street has perfume shops, souvenir stores, boutiques, bookstores, cafés, and such hotels as the *Meurice* and the *Inter-Continental* under its 19th-century arcades.

LOUVRE This colossus on the Seine, born in 1200 as a fortress and transformed over the centuries from Gothic mass to Renaissance palace, served as the royal residence in the 16th and 17th centuries. It was then supplanted by suburban *Versailles*, becoming a museum in 1793 after the Revolution. Napoleon later turned it into a glittering warehouse of artistic booty from the nations he conquered. Today, its 200 galleries cover some 40 acres; to view all 297,000 items in the collections in no more than the most cursory fashion, it would be necessary to walk some 8 miles.

In addition to the *Mona Lisa, Venus de Milo,* and the *Winged Victory of Samothrace,* the *Louvre* has many delights that are easily overlooked— Vermeer's *Lace Maker* and Holbein's *Portrait of Erasmus,* for instance, not to mention van der Weyden's *Braque Triptych,* Ingres's *Turkish Bath,* Dürer's *Self-Portrait,* Cranach's naked and red-hatted *Venus,* and the exquisite 4,000-year-old Egyptian woodcarving known as the *Handmaiden of the Dead.* More of our favorites include Michelangelo's *The Dying Slave* and *The Bound Slave,* Goya's *Marquesa de la Solana,* Watteau's clown *Gilles* and his *Embarkation for Cythera,* Raphael's great portrait *Baldassare Castiglione,* Veronese's *Marriage at Cana,* Titian's masterpiece *Man with a Glove,* both *The Penitent Magdalen* and *The Card Sharps* by Georges de la Tour, Rembrandt's *Bathsheba,* and Frans Hals's *Bohemian Girl.* Also be sure to save time for any one of David's glories: *Madame Récamier, The Oath of the Horatii, The Lictors Bringing Back to Brutus the Body of His Son,* or *The Coronation of Napoleon and Josephine.* And don't miss *Liberty Leading the People* and *The Bark of Dante,* both by Delacroix, and Courbet's *The Artist's Studio, Burial at Ornans,* and *Stags Fighting.*

Nor is the outside of this huge edifice to be overlooked. Note especially the *Cour Carrée* (the courtyard of the old *Louvre*), the southwest corner of which is the oldest part of the palace (dating from the mid-1550s) and a beautiful example of the Renaissance style that François I introduced from Italy. Renovation of the *Cour Carrée* and other sections of the museum is in progress and will continue through 1997, but most of the external walls have already been cleaned. Note, too, the *Colonnade,* which forms the eastern front of the *Cour Carrée,* facing the Place du Louvre; classical in style, it dates from the late 1660s, not long before the Sun King left for *Versailles.* Newer wings of the *Louvre* embrace the palace gardens, in the midst of which stands the *Arc de Triomphe du Carrousel,* erected by Napoleon. From here, the vista across the *Tuileries* and the Place de la Concorde and on up the Champs-Elysées to the *Arc de Triomphe* is one of the most beautiful in Paris. I. M. Pei's glass pyramids, completed in 1989, sit center stage in the *Louvre's* grand interior courtyard, and the largest of the trio now is the museum's main entrance. The controversial structure houses the *Louvre's* underground shops and galleries connecting the north and south wings (the addition increased the museum's exhibition space by nearly 80%). Last year, the new *Richelieu Wing* opened, a stunning example of museum architecture just off the main *Louvre* entrance beneath the pyramid, as did the upscale *Carrousel du Louvre* shopping complex under the *Arc de Triomphe du Carrousel* (see *Shopping*).

Good guided tours in English, covering the highlights of the *Louvre,* are frequently available, but be sure to check in advance. Closed Tuesdays. Admission charge. Pl. du Louvre, 1er (phone: 40-20-51-51 for recorded information in French and English; 40-20-50-50 for more detailed information).

PLACE VENDÔME Just north of the *Tuileries* is one of the loveliest squares in Paris, the octagonal Place Vendôme, designed by Mansart in the 17th century. Now primarily a pedestrian zone, its arcades contain world-famous jewelers, perfumers, banks, the *Ritz* hotel, and the *Ministère de Justice* (Ministry of Justice). The 144-foot column in the center is covered with bronze from the 1,200 cannon that Napoleon captured at Austerlitz in 1805. Just off Place Vendôme is the famous Rue du Faubourg-St-Honoré, one of the oldest streets in Paris, which now holds elegant shops selling the world's most expensive made-to-order items. To the north is the Rue de la Paix, noted for its jewelers.

LA MADELEINE Starting in 1764, the *Eglise Ste-Marie-Madeleine* (Church of St. Mary Magdalene) was built and razed twice before the present structure was commissioned by Napoleon in 1806 to honor his armies. The design of the recently cleaned and restored church is based on that of a Greek temple, with 65-foot-high Corinthian columns supporting the sculptured frieze. The bronze doors are adorned with illustrations of the Ten Commandments, and inside there are many distinctive murals and sculptures. From its portals, the view extends down Rue Royale to Place de la Concorde and over to the dome of *Les Invalides.* Nearby are some of Paris's most tantalizing food shops. Open daily. Free concerts are held two Sundays per month at 4 PM. Pl. de la Madeleine, 8e (phone: 42-65-52-17).

OPÉRA/PALAIS GARNIER When it was completed in 1875, this imposing rococo edifice was touted as the largest theater in the world (though with a capacity of only 2,156, it holds fewer people than the *Vienna Opera House* or *La Scala* in Milan). Designed by Charles Garnier, it covers nearly three acres and took 13 years to complete. The façade is decorated with sculpture, including a copy of Carpeaux's *The Dance* (the original is now in the *Musée d'Orsay*). The ornate interior has an impressive grand staircase, a beautiful foyer, lavish marble from every quarry in France, and Marc Chagall's controversially decorated dome. At press time, the *Opéra* was closed for renovations through March 1996 at the earliest. Daytime visits may still be possible through the early part of this year. Call ahead for the current status of the renovations. Pl. de l'Opéra, 9e (phone: 40-01-24-93).

BASILIQUE DU SACRÉ-COEUR (BASILICA OF THE SACRED HEART) AND MONTMARTRE The white-domed *Basilique du Sacré-Coeur* is located on the Butte Montmartre, the highest of Paris's seven hills. The church's Byzantine interior is rich and ornate, yet at the same time light and well proportioned. Note the huge mosaics, one over the high altar depicting Christ; another, the Archangel Michael and Joan of Arc; and a third, of Louis XVI and his family. One of the largest and heaviest bells (19 tons) in Christendom is housed in the tall bell tower to the north. The church, including the cupola, is open daily. 35 Rue Chevalier-de-la-Barre (phone: 42-51-17-02).

The area around *Sacré-Coeur* was the artists' quarter of late 19th- and early 20th-century Paris, and the streets still look the same as they do in the paintings of Utrillo. The site of the last of Paris's vineyards, Montmartre contains old houses, narrow alleys, steep stairways, and carefree cafés enough to provide a full day's entertainment. And at night the district still comes alive as it did in the days of Toulouse-Lautrec, who immortalized Montmartre's notoriously frivolous Belle Epoque nightlife, particularly the dancers and personalities at the *Moulin Rouge*, in his paintings. The Place du Tertre, where Braque, Dufy, Modigliani, Picasso, Rousseau, and Utrillo lived, is still charming, but go early in the day; later, it's often filled with tourists and mostly under-talented artists. Spare yourself most of the climb to *Sacré-Coeur* by taking the modern, glass funicular, for which the fare is one *Métro* ticket, or the Montmartre bus (marked with an icon of *Sacré-Coeur* on the front instead of a number) from Place St-Pierre. Butte Montmartre, 18e.

LES HALLES The *Central Market* ("the Belly of Paris") that once stood on this 80-acre site northeast of the *Louvre* was razed in 1969. Gone are the picturesque early-morning fruit-and-vegetable vendors, butchers in blood-spattered aprons, and truckers bringing the freshest produce from all over France. In their places are the trendy shops and galleries of youthful entrepreneurs and artisans, small, charming restaurants, the world's largest subway station, acres of trellised gardens and playgrounds, and *Le Forum des Halles,* a vast, mainly underground complex of boutiques, as well as concert space and movie theaters. Touch-sensitive locator devices have been placed strategically throughout the complex. Rue Pierre-Lescot and Rue Rambuteau, 1er.

CENTRE NATIONAL D'ART ET DE CULTURE GEORGES-POMPIDOU (GEORGES-POMPIDOU NATIONAL ART AND CULTURAL CENTER) This stark creation of steel and glass, with its exterior escalators and blue, white, and red pipes, is better known as "Beaubourg," after the street it faces and the *quartier* it replaced. Outside, a computerized digital clock ticks off the seconds remaining until the 21st century. The wildly popular cultural center brings together art in all its contemporary forms—painting, sculpture, industrial design, music, literature, cinema, and theater—under one roof. In addition to housing the *Musée National d'Art Moderne* (National Museum of Modern Art) and the *Centre de Création Industrielle* (Industrial Design Center), it boasts a public information library and the *Institut de Recherches et de Coordination Acoustique/Musique* (*IRCAM;* Institute for Acoustic and Musical Research). The scene in the front courtyard, which serves as an impromptu stage for jugglers, mimes, acrobats, and magicians, often rivals the exhibits inside, which this year include special exhibitions of the work of Constantin Brancusi and Louise Bourgeois.

A massive renovation project, expected to cost more than $100 million, begins this year with work on the exterior of the center and on adjoining areas and buildings. Work on the interior is not slated to begin until 1997. The center as a whole will remain open throughout the project; sections under renovation will close in turn. Closed Tuesdays and weekday mornings. Admission charge for the *Musée National d'Art Moderne* and for special exhibitions only; no admission charge on Sundays. Entrances on Rue de Beaubourg and Rue St-Martin, 4e (phone: 44-78-12-33).

LE MARAIS A marshland until the 16th century, this district east of the *Louvre* in the 4th *arrondissement* became a fashionable neighborhood during the 17th century. As the aristocracy moved on it fell into disrepair, but over the last 30 years the Marais has been enjoying a complete face-lift, as preservationists have restored more than 100 of the magnificent old *hôtels* (in this sense the word means private mansions or townhouses) to their former grandeur. Among the *hôtels* to note are the *Hôtel Salé,* which now houses the *Musée Picasso* (see below); the *Hôtel de Soubise,* now the *Archives Nationales* (National Archives; 60 Rue des Francs-Bourgeois), with its 14th-century *Porte de Clisson* (58 Rue des Archives); and the *Hôtels d'Aumont* (7 Rue de Jouy); *Guénégaud,* designed by Mansart (60 Rue des Archives); *de Rohan* (87 Rue Vieille-du-Temple); *de Sens* (1 Rue du Figuier); and *de Sully* (62 Rue St-Antoine). The *Caisse Nationale des Monuments Historiques et des Sites* (National Commission for Historic Monuments and Sites), housed in the *Hôtel de Sully,* offers tours on weekends plus a pass good for a year of free visits to sites of interest in Paris and throughout France (phone: 44-61-21-50 for general information; 44-61-21-69/70, for information on tours).

PLACE DES VOSGES In the Marais district, the oldest square in Paris—and also one of the most beautiful—was completed in 1612 by order of Henri IV, with elegant, symmetrically arranged houses. Though many of the houses have been rebuilt inside, their original façades remain. Corneille and Racine lived here, and at No. 6 is the *Maison de Victor Hugo,* once the writer's home and now a museum. It's closed Mondays and holidays. Admission charge (phone: 42-72-10-16).

MUSÉE CARNAVALET Also in the Marais, this once was the home of Mme. de Sévigné, a noted 17th-century writer, and is now a museum with beautifully arranged exhibits covering the history of Paris from the days of Henri IV to the present. The museum's name is derived from that of an earlier owner of the building, the widow of François de Kernevenoy (corrupted to Carnavalet), tutor to Henri III, who bought the *hôtel* in 1572. It was built in 1550 by the architect Pierre Lescot, and over the years had many embellishments added by other architects. The museum's expansion through the *lycée* next door and into the neighboring *Hôtel Peletier de St-Fargeau* doubled the exhibition space, making it the largest museum in the world devoted to the history of a single capital city. The expansion created space for a major permanent exhibit on the French Revolution, and a new wing is set to open this year to house recent archaeological finds, including Neolithic canoes discovered during excavations at the Bercy development. Also watch for special exhibitions and occasional concerts. The gift shop offers a wealth of interesting items, from T-shirts to objets d'art; there's also an excellent bookstore. Closed Mondays. No admission charge on Sundays. 23 Rue de Sévigné, 3e (phone: 42-72-21-13).

MUSÉE PICASSO Housed in the beautiful, 17th-century *Hôtel Salé,* this museum displays a portion of the collection with which Picasso could never bring himself to part and provides a panoramic overview of the career of perhaps the century's greatest artist. More than 200 paintings, 3,000 drawings and engravings, and other objets d'art related to Picasso are arranged here in chronological order. Especially interesting is Picasso's own collection of works by other artists, including Cézanne, Braque, and Rousseau. There are also films on Picasso's life and work. Be sure to see the lovely fountain by Simounet in the formal garden. Closed Tuesdays. Admission charge. 5 Rue de Thorigny, 3e (phone: 42-71-25-21).

OPÉRA DE LA BASTILLE In sharp contrast to Garnier's *Opéra* (see above) is the curved glass façade of 20th-century architect Carlos Ott's Paris opera house. Set against the historic landscape of the Bastille quarter, this austere, futuristic structure houses over 30 acres of multipurpose theaters, shops, and urban promenades. In fact, it looks a lot like its namesake, the prison-fortress the storming of which ignited the French Revolution. Pl. de la Bastille, 11e (phone: 44-73-13-00).

AMERICAN CENTER AND BERCY A Parisian venue for performing artists from the US since 1931, the *American Center* reopened last year (after a seven-year hiatus) in a futuristic new building designed by Frank Gehry. The center (51 Rue de Bercy, 12e; phone: 44-73-77-77; fax: 44-73-77-55) comprises a theater, a cinema, a restaurant, a bookstore, classrooms, and performance and gallery spaces. Through an eclectic program of avant-garde dance, music, film, and art, it aims to encourage cross-cultural relations between the US and the rest of the world. It's closed Tuesdays. Admission charge for performances and special exhibits.

The *American Center* is located in eastern Paris's Bercy development, a former wine depot that's now also the site of France's *Ministère des Finances* and the *Palais Omnisports de Paris-Bercy,* a large sports complex. The much-talked-about new *Bibliothèque Nationale* (National Library) is slated to open here next year.

BOIS DE VINCENNES Designed as a counterpart to the *Bois de Boulogne* (see below), this park and zoological garden was laid out during Napoleon III's time on the former hunting grounds of the 14-century *Château de Vincennes,* which encompassed 2,300 acres on the city's east side. Visit the château and its lovely chapel, the large garden, and the zoo, with animals in their natural habitats. On the eastern edge of the *Bois de Vincennes* is the *Musée des Arts Africains et Océaniens* (Museum of African and Oceanian Art; see *Museums,* below).

CIMETIÈRE PÈRE-LACHAISE (PÈRE-LACHAISE CEMETERY) With over 100,000 tombs, sepulchers, and monuments, this is the most famous of France's cemeteries. The celebrated and the notorious alike are buried here, and it's a common weekend pastime of the French to visit its flowered walks and seek out the plots of famous writers, musicians, and politicians. Stop inside the entry and purchase a map before following the bizarre parade of adoring fans to the grave of rock star Jim Morrison of the *Doors* (Section 27). Other tombs of note include those of Edith Piaf, Proust, Chopin, Balzac, Modigliani, Sarah Bernhardt, and Oscar Wilde's morbid Sphinx statuary. It's hard to miss the legions of resident cats. Open daily. No admission charge. Bd. de Ménilmontant at Rue de la Roquette, 20e (phone: 43-70-70-33).

LA VILLETTE The *Cité des Sciences et de l'Industrie* (City of Sciences and Industry), a celebration of technology, stands in the *Parc de la Villette* on the northeastern edge of the capital. In it are a planetarium, the spherical *Géode* cinema (see *Film*), lots of hands-on displays, and a half-dozen exhibitions at any given time. The futuristic playground is a must for children. The *Cité de la Musique* (see *Museums*) and several restaurants and snack bars are also on the park grounds. Closed Mondays. Admission charge. 30 Av. Corentin-Cariou, 19e (phone: 40-05-70-00).

BOIS DE BOULOGNE Originally part of the Forest of Rouvre, on the western edge of Paris, this 2,140-acre park was planned along English lines by Napoleon. It's a great place to ride a horse or a bike, row a boat, trap shoot, go bowling, picnic on the grass, see horse races at *Auteuil* and *Longchamp,* visit a children's amusement park or a zoo, see a play, walk to a waterfall, or just smell the roses. A particularly lovely spot is the *Bagatelle* château and park; a former residence of Marie-Antoinette, it boasts a magnificent rose garden (on the Rte. de Sèvres in Neuilly, 16e; phone: 40-67-97-00). Avoid the *Bois* after dark, when it becomes a playground for prostitutes and transvestites who actively solicit passersby. Recent attempts by the French government to stop the nighttime activity by banning cars from the park have begun to alleviate the situation. The park is open daily; the château is closed November through mid-March. Admission charge to the château.

PALAIS DE CHAILLOT Built for the *Paris Exposition of 1937,* this structure houses a theater, a *Cinémathèque* (phone: 47-04-24-24), and four museums—the

Musée du Cinéma (Film Museum; phone: 45-53-74-39); the *Musée de l'Homme* (Museum of Man; phone: 44-05-72-72) with anthropological exhibits; the *Musée de la Marine* (Maritime Museum; phone: 45-53-31-70); and the *Musée des Monuments Français* (Museum of French Monuments; phone: 44-05-39-10), featuring reproductions of monuments. The terraces offer excellent views across gardens, fountains, and the Seine to the *Eiffel Tower* on the Rive Gauche. Closed Tuesdays and major holidays. Admission charge. Pl. du Trocadéro, 16e.

LA RIVE GAUCHE (THE LEFT BANK)

TOUR EIFFEL (EIFFEL TOWER) It is impossible to imagine the Paris skyline without this mighty symbol, yet what has been called Gustave Eiffel's folly was never meant to be permanent. Originally built for the *Universal Exposition of 1889,* it was due to be torn down in 1909, but was saved because of the development of the wireless—the first transatlantic wireless telephones were operated from the 984-foot tower in 1916 (the addition of television antennae in 1957 brought the tower's height up to 1,051 feet). It was the tallest structure in the world until New York's *Empire State Building* (1,284 feet) was completed in 1930. Extensive renovations (including the addition of modernized elevators) have taken place in more recent years, and a post office, three restaurants, and a few boutiques have opened up on the first-floor landing. We recommend the one-Michelin-star *Jules Verne* restaurant, though it is pricey and requires reservations a month or two in advance. It's open daily (phone: 45-55-61-44; fax: 47-05-29-41). The tower itself is also open daily. Admission charge. Champ-de-Mars, 7e (phone: 45-50-34-56).

LES INVALIDES Founded by Louis XIV in the 1670s as an asylum for wounded and aged soldiers, this vast structure was initially intended to house 4,000; it more often was a refuge for twice that number. The classically balanced buildings were designed by Libéral Bruant and have more than 10 miles of corridors. The royal *Eglise du Dôme* (Church of the Dome), part of the complex, was constructed from 1675 to 1706 and is topped by an elaborate golden dome designed by Mansart. Besides being a masterpiece of the 17th century, the church contains the impressive red-and-green granite *Tombeau de Napoléon Ier* (Tomb of Napoleon; admission charge). The monument is surrounded by 12 huge white marble statues, interspersed with 54 flags, each symbolizing one of Napoleon's victories. The church also has an impressive courtyard and noteworthy frescoes. In addition, at *Les Invalides* is the *Musée de l'Armée,* one of the world's richest museums, displaying arms and armor along with mementos of French military history. For yet another splendid Parisian view, approach the building from the Pont Alexandre III (Alexander III Bridge). Open daily. Admission charge. Av. de Tourville, Pl. Vauban, 7e (phone: 45-55-37-70).

MUSÉE RODIN This is one of France's most complete and satisfying museum experiences. By ambling through one of the great 18th-century Parisian aristocratic homes and its grounds, it's possible to follow the evolution of the career of Auguste Rodin, that genius of modern sculpture. Along the broad terraces and in the serene, elegant gardens are scattered fabled statues such as *The Thinker* and the *Bourgeois de Calais;* the superb statues of Honoré de Balzac and Victor Hugo; the stunning *Gate of Hell,* on which the master labored a lifetime; *Les Bavardes,* a sculpture by Rodin's mistress Camille Claudel; and more. Rodin's celebrated Ugolin group is placed dramatically in the middle of a pond. Closed Mondays. Admission charge. 77 Rue de Varenne, 7e (phone: 47-05-01-34).

MONTPARNASSE In the early 20th century, this neighborhood south of the *Jardin du Luxembourg* hosted a colony of avant-garde painters, writers, and Russian political exiles. Here Hemingway, Picasso, and Scott and Zelda Fitzgerald sipped and supped in such bars and cafés as *La Closerie des Lilas* (see *Nightclubs and Nightlife*); *Le Dôme* (108 Bd. du Montparnasse, 14e; phone: 43-35-25-81); *La Rotonde* (105 Bd. du Montparnasse, 14e; phone: 43-26-48-26 or 43-26-68-84); and *Le Select* and *La Coupole* (see *Eating Out* for both). The cafés, small restaurants, and winding streets still exist in the shadow of the *Tour Montparnasse* complex (see below).

TOUR MONTPARNASSE (MONTPARNASSE TOWER) Each day, the fastest elevator in Europe whisks Parisians and tourists up 59 stories (for a fee) to catch a view *down* at the *Eiffel Tower.* The shopping center here, *Maine Montparnasse,* boasts all the famous names, and the surrounding office buildings are the headquarters of some of France's largest companies. 33 Av. du Maine, 15e, and Bd. de Vaugirard, 14e (phone: 45-38-52-56).

MUSÉE D'ORSAY This imposing former railway station was transformed into one of the shining examples of modern museum design. Its eclectic collection includes the Impressionist paintings formerly displayed at the *Jeu de Paume* (see above), complemented by less sacred 19th-century achievements in sculpture, photography, and the applied arts, which together provide an excellent overview of the Victorian aesthetic. No detail of light, humidity, or acoustics has been left to chance, making this voyage around the art world a very comfortable one. Don't miss the museum's pièce de résistance—the van Goghs on the top floor, glowing under the skylight. There's also a restaurant. Closed Mondays. Admission charge is reduced on Sundays. 1 Rue de Bellechasse, 7e (phone: 40-49-48-14).

EGLISE ST-GERMAIN-DES-PRÉS (CHURCH OF ST.-GERMAIN-OF-THE-FIELDS) AND THE QUARTIER ST-GERMAIN-DES-PRÉS Probably the oldest church in Paris, it once belonged to an abbey of the same name. The original basilica, completed in AD 558, was destroyed and rebuilt many times, and the Romanesque steeple and its massive tower date from 1014. Inside, the choir and sanctuary are as they were in the 12th century, and the marble shafts used in the slender columns are 14 centuries old. Pl. St-Germain-des-Prés, 6e (phone: 43-25-41-71).

Surrounding the church is the Quartier St-Germain-des-Prés, long a center for Paris's fashionable intellectuals and artists, with art galleries, boutiques, and renowned cafés for people watching (though not necessarily for dining) such as the *Flore* (172 Bd. Saint-Germain, 6e; phone: 45-48-55-26), Sartre's favorite, and *Les Deux Magots* (6 Pl. Saint-Germain-des-Prés, 6e; phone: 45-48-55-25), once a Hemingway haunt.

QUARTIER LATIN (LATIN QUARTER) Extending from the *Jardin du Luxembourg* and the *Panthéon* to the Seine, this famous neighborhood still maintains its unique atmosphere. A focal point for *Sorbonne* students since the Middle Ages, it's a mad jumble of narrow streets, old churches, and academic buildings. Boulevard St-Michel and Boulevard St-Germain are its main arteries, both lined with cafés, bookstores, and boutiques of every imaginable kind. There are also some charming old side streets, such as the Rue de la Huchette, off Place St-Michel, and Rue St-André-des-Arts, which starts on the opposite side of Place St-Michel. And don't miss the famous *bouquinistes* (bookstalls) along the Seine, around Place St-Michel on the Quai des Grands-Augustins and the Quai St-Michel.

PALAIS ET JARDIN DU LUXEMBOURG Built for Marie de Médicis in 1615 in what once were the southern suburbs of Paris, this Renaissance palace became a prison during the Revolution and now houses the French *Sénat* (Senate). The palace is closed to the public except for a group tour organized by the *Caisse Nationale des Monuments Historiques et des Sites* (see *Le Marais,* above) on the first Sunday of each month. The classic, formal gardens, with lovely statues and the famous Médicis fountain, are popular with students and with neighborhood children. 15 Rue de Vaugirard, 6e (phone: 42-34-20-60).

PANTHÉON Originally built by Louis XV in 1764 as a church dedicated to Paris's patron saint, Geneviève, in 1791 it was declared a "nonreligious Temple of Fame dedicated to all the gods," where the *grands hommes* of French liberty (the first *grande femme* only arrived in 1885) would be interred. The tombs of Victor Hugo, the Resistance leader Jean Moulin, Rousseau, Voltaire, and Emile Zola are among those here. The impressive interior also features murals depicting the life of St. Geneviève. Closed some holidays. Admission charge. Pl. du Panthéon, 5e (phone: 43-54-34-51).

MUSÉE NATIONAL DU MOYEN AGE/THERMES DE CLUNY (CLUNY NATIONAL MUSEUM OF THE MIDDLE AGES/ROMAN BATHS OF CLUNY) One of the last remaining examples of medieval domestic architecture in Paris, the 15th-century residence of the abbots of Cluny, which was built on the site of 3rd-century Gallo-Roman baths and later became the home of Mary Tudor, is now a museum of medieval arts and crafts. The most famous work displayed here is the celebrated *Lady and the Unicorn* tapestry. Closed Tuesdays. Admission charge. 6 Pl. Paul-Painlevé, 5e (phone: 43-25-62-00).

MOSQUÉE DE PARIS (PARIS MOSQUE) Dominated by a 130-foot-high minaret in gleaming white marble, this is one of the most beautiful structures of its kind in the world. Take off your shoes before entering the pebble-lined gardens, full of flowers and dwarf trees. The *Salle de Prières* (Hall of Prayer), with its lush Oriental carpets, is closed to the public Fridays (the weekly prayer day for Muslims) and during lunch hours. Admission charge. Next door is a restaurant and a patio for sipping Turkish coffee and tasting Asian sweets. Pl. du Puits-de-l'Ermite, 5e (phone: 45-35-97-33).

EGLISE ST-SÉVERIN (CHURCH OF ST. SÉVERIN) This church still retains its beautiful Flamboyant Gothic ambulatory, considered a masterpiece of its kind, and lovely old stained glass windows dating from the 15th and 16th centuries. The small garden and the restored charnel house also are of interest. 3 Rue des Prêtres, 5e (phone: 43-25-96-63).

EGLISE ST-JULIEN-LE-PAUVRE (CHURCH OF ST. JULIAN THE POOR) One of the smallest and oldest churches (12th to 13th century) in Paris offers a superb view of *Notre-Dame* from the charming Place René-Viviani. 1 Rue St-Julien-le-Pauvre, 5e (no phone).

ILE DE LA CITÉ

The birthplace of Paris, settled by Gallic fishermen in about 250 BC, the Ile de la Cité is so rich in historical monuments that an entire day could be spent here and on the neighboring Ile St-Louis (see below). A walk all around the islands, along the lovely, tree-shaded quays on both banks of the Seine, opens up one breathtaking view (of the *Cathédrale de Notre-Dame*, the *Louvre*, the Pont Neuf) after another.

CATHÉDRALE DE NOTRE-DAME DE PARIS (CATHEDRAL OF OUR LADY OF PARIS) It is said that Druids once worshiped on this consecrated ground. Later, the Romans built their temple here, and many Christian churches followed. In 1163, the foundations were laid for the present cathedral, one of the world's finest examples of Gothic architecture. By 1270, when the funeral of Louis IX (St. Louis) was held here, the cathedral was essentially complete, but construction continued, working from the plans of a single anonymous architect, until 1345. Henri IV and Napoleon both were crowned here. At press time, a 10-year restoration project was beginning, the first major work on the cathedral since the mid-19th century. Unfortunately for visitors, scaffolding is expected to cover the exterior throughout this year, while the façade undergoes a high-tech cleaning process. Take a guided tour (offered in English at noon Tuesdays and Wednesdays and in French at noon other weekdays, 2:30 PM Saturdays, and 2 PM Sundays) or quietly explore on your own, but try to see the splendid 13th-century stained glass rose windows at sunset. Open daily. Pl. du Parvis de Notre-Dame, 4e (phone: 43-65-22-63).

PALAIS DE JUSTICE AND SAINTE-CHAPELLE (PALACE OF JUSTICE AND HOLY CHAPEL) This monumental complex was first the seat of the Roman military government, then the headquarters of the early kings of the Capetian dynasty, and finally the law courts. In the 13th century, Louis IX built a new palace, adding *Sainte-Chapelle* to house the Sacred Crown of Thorns and other holy relics. Its 15 soaring stained glass windows (plus a later rose window), with more than 1,100 brilliantly colored and exquisitely detailed miniature scenes of biblical life, are among the unquestioned masterpieces of medieval French art, and the graceful, gleaming 247-foot spire is one of the city's most beautiful and understated landmarks. Closed holidays. Admission charge. 4 Bd. du Palais, 1er (phone: 43-54-30-09).

CONCIERGERIE This remnant of the former royal palace sits like a fairy-tale castle on the Ile de la Cité. It served as a prison during the Revolution, and it was here that Marie-Antoinette, the Duke of Orléans, Mme. du Barry, and others of lesser fame awaited the guillotine. Documents and engravings dating from the time of Ravaillac, the 17th-century assassin of Henri IV, illustrate the past of this sinister palace. Don't miss Marie-Antoinette's cell, and the Girondins' chapel, where the moderate Girondin deputies shared their last meal. Closed holidays. Admission charge. 4 Bd. du Palais, 1er (phone: 43-54-30-06).

ILE ST-LOUIS

Walk across the footbridge behind *Notre-Dame* and you're in a charming, tranquil village. This "enchanted isle" has managed to keep its provincial charm despite its central location. Follow the main street, Rue St-Louis-en-l'Ile, down the middle of the island, past courtyards, balconies, old doors, curious stairways, the ornate *Eglise St-Louis* (St. Louis Church), built between 1664 and 1726, and discreet plaques bearing the names of illustrious former residents (including Mme. Curie, Voltaire, Baudelaire, Gautier, and Daumier). Pause along the way for some famous (and fabulous) *Berthillon* ice cream, either at their shop (see *Shopping*) or at one of the other small cafés that serve it. Then take the quay back along the banks of the Seine.

Sources and Resources

TOURIST INFORMATION

Paris's *Office de Tourisme* (127 Av. des Champs-Elysées, 8e; phone: 49-52-53-54 for general information, 49-52-53-56 for a recorded message in English on current events and exhibitions) is the place to go for information, brochures, maps, or hotel reservations. It's closed on *New Year's Day,* May 1, and *Christmas* only. If you call the office, be prepared for a four- to five-minute wait before someone answers. Other tourist offices, all closed Sundays, are found at the *Eiffel Tower* (phone: 45-51-22-15; closed October through April) and at train stations: *Gare du Nord* (15 Rue de Dunkerque, 10e; phone: 45-26-94-82); *Gare de Lyon* (Pl. Louis-Armand, 12e; phone: 43-43-33-24); *Gare de l'Est* (Pl. du 11-Novembre 1918, 10e; phone: 46-07-

17-73); *Gare Montparnasse* (17 Bd. de Vaugirard, 15e; phone: 43-22-19-19); and *Gare d'Austerlitz* (53 Quai d'Austerlitz, 13e; phone: 45-84-91-70).

LOCAL COVERAGE *Paris Selection,* in both French and English, is the official tourist office magazine. It lists events, sights, tours, some hotels, restaurants, shopping, nightclubs, and other information. Far more complete are the weekly guides *L'Officiel des Spectacles, 7 à Paris,* and *Pariscope.* All are in simple French (*Pariscope* even has a section in English) and are available at newsstands. English-language magazines are *Boulevard,* sold at newsstands; the monthly *WHERE,* distributed in hotels; and, available free at English-language bookstores and other locations, the monthly *Paris Free Voice,* and the biweeklies *Paris City* and *France-USA Contacts.* Among the city's English-language bookstores are *W. H. Smith and Sons, Brentano's,* and *Shakespeare and Company* (see *Shopping* for all three).

TELEPHONE All phone numbers in Paris begin with the prefix 4 (incorporated into the numbers given here); in the area surrounding Paris, they are preceded by either 3 or 6. When calling a number in the Paris region (including the Ile-de-France) from Paris, dial only the 8-digit number. When calling a number from outside the Paris region, dial 1, then the 8-digit number.

GETTING AROUND

AIRPORTS *Aéroport Charles-de-Gaulle* (Roissy, 14 miles/23 km northeast of Paris; phone: 48-62-12-12 or 48-62-22-80) has two terminals: *Aérogare 1,* for foreign airlines, and *Aérogare 2,* predominantly for *Air France* flights. The two terminals are connected by a free shuttle bus. *Air France* airport buses (phone: 42-99-20-18; 49-38-57-57 for a multilingual recorded message), open to passengers of all airlines, leave for the city, stopping at the *Palais des Congrès (Métro: Porte Maillot)* and the *Arc de Triomphe (Métro: Charles de Gaulle–Etoile),* every 12 minutes from 5:40 AM to 11 PM and take about 40 minutes; there's also an hourly bus that goes to the *Gare Montparnasse* on the Rive Gauche and takes about 45 minutes. The *RATP* (see *Bus,* below) operates the *Roissybus* (city bus No. 352), departing from the *Opéra/Palais Garnier* (Pl. de l'Opéra, 9e) for the airport every 15 minutes from 5:45 AM to 11:30 PM daily; the trip takes about 45 minutes, and the one-way fare is 30F (about $5.15 at press time). For more information, call 48-04-18-24 or the main *RATP* information number. *Roissy-Rail,* part of the *RER* B suburban train line, runs between the airport and the *Gare du Nord* every 15 minutes and takes about 35 minutes. (A shuttle bus connects the airport to Roissy station, and from there to the *Gare du Nord* is by train.) For more details, call the general *SNCF* information number (see *Train,* below).

    Aéroport d'Orly (9 miles/14 km south of Paris; phone: 49-75-52-52 or 49-75-15-15) has two terminals: *Orly Ouest,* mainly for domestic flights and flights to Geneva, and *Orly Sud,* for international flights. The two terminals are connected by a free shuttle bus. *Air France* buses (phone: 43-23-97-10; 49-38-57-57 for a multilingual recorded message) leave *Orly* for a terminus on the Esplanade des Invalides (*Métro* station: Invalides) every 12 minutes from 5:50 AM to 11 PM and take about 40 minutes. Another *RATP* service (see *Bus,* below) is *Orlybus* (city bus No. 215), which links the airport to Place Denfert-Rochereau in southern Paris, leaving every 13 minutes daily from 5:45 AM to 11:30 PM; the trip takes about 30 minutes, and the one-way fare is 27F (about $4.65 at press time). *Orlyval* is a service which connects by monorail the two Orly terminals with the Antony station on the *RER* C line, which links the suburbs with major stops in the city. The monorail shuttle departs every five to seven minutes from *Orly Sud* from 6:30 AM to 9:15 PM daily except Sunday, when hours are 7 AM to 10:55 PM. The trip takes 30 to 45 minutes, depending on the stop; the combined fare for the shuttle and the *RER* trip into Paris is 45F (about $7.80 at press time). A more direct service is *Orly-Rail,* part of the *RER* C suburban train line, which makes various stops in the city such as St-Michel and Invalides, with a shuttle bus from Orly station to the airport. The service runs every 15 or 30 minutes depending on the time of day and takes 35 to 50 minutes, according to the stop. For more details on *Orlyval* or *Orly-Rail,* call the general *SNCF* information number (see *Train,* below).

    Air France buses linking *Charles de Gaulle* and *Orly* airports run every 20 minutes and take from 50 to 75 minutes.

BOAT The *Batobus,* operated by *Bateaux Parisiens* (Pont d'Iéna, Port de la Bourdonnais, 7e, phone: 44-11-33-44; and Quai Montebello, 5e, phone: 43-26-92-55), carries passengers along the Seine daily from mid-April through September 26; stops (watch for the signs on the quays) are near the *Eiffel Tower,* the *Musée d'Orsay,* the *Louvre, Notre-Dame,* and the *Hôtel de Ville* (just east of the *Louvre*). The fare is 12F (about $2.10 at press time) for each leg of the trip, or 60F (about $10.35 at press time) for an all-day, unlimited travel pass; tickets may be purchased at the stops along the quays.

BUS They're slow, but good for sightseeing; a few do not run on Sundays and holidays. *Métro* tickets are valid on all city buses, but you will need a new ticket if you change buses. Unlike the *Métro,* buses charge by distance; two tickets are sometimes needed for a ride across town (into a different zone). The standard fare is 7F (around $1.20 at press time), but it's best to buy a *carnet* (booklet) of 10 tickets, only 41F (around $7.10 at press time); one of the special tourist passes for short stays in Paris; or a *carte orange,* a pass permitting either a week or a month of unlimited travel (see *Métro,* below, for more on tickets and passes). Bus lines are numbered, and both stops and buses have signs indicating routes. The Paris *Régional Autorité du Transit Provincial* (*RATP*; Regional Rapid Transit Authority; phone: 43-46-14-14 for general information), which operates the *métro* and bus system, has designated certain bus lines as being of particular interest to tourists; look for a panel on the front of the bus reading (in English), "This bus is good for sightseeing." On Sundays and holidays, a special *RATP* sightseeing bus, the *Balabus,* runs from the *Grande Arche de la Défense,* west of Paris, all the way east to the *Gare de Lyon.* The total trip time is 75 minutes; you can board the bus at any stop marked "Balabus Bb." The *RATP* has tourist offices at Place de la Madeleine, next to the flower market (8e; phone: 40-06-71-45) and on the Rive Gauche at 53 *bis* Quai des Grands-Augustins near Place St-Michel (6e; phone: 40-46-44-50 or 40-46-43-60) both organize bus tours in Paris and the surrounding region.

CAR RENTAL Book when making your plane reservation, or contact *Avis* (phone: 46-10-60-60, main reservations number in France; 5 Rue Bixio, 7e, phone: 44-18-10-50; *Charles de Gaulle* airport, phone: 48-62-34-34; and *Orly* airport, phone: 49-75-44-91); *Budget* (phone: 45-72-11-15); *Europcar* (phone: 46-51-44-03); or *Hertz* (phone: 47-88-51-51). Many car rental agencies also have offices in train stations.

MÉTRO Operating from 5:30 AM to about 1 AM, the *Métro* system is generally safe (although pickpockets abound in certain areas), clean, quiet, and easy to use, and since the *RATP* has been sponsoring cultural events and art exhibits in some 200 of Paris's 368 *Métro* stations, at times it is even entertaining. Different lines are identified by the names of their terminals at either end. Every station has clear directional maps, some with push-button devices that light up the proper route after a destination button is pushed. Handy streetside bus and *Métro* directions are now available in some *Métro* stations from *SITU* (*Système d'Information des Trajets Urbains*), a computer that prints out the fastest routing onto a wallet-size piece of paper, complete with the estimated length of the trip, free of charge. High-traffic spots such as the Châtelet *Métro* station, the *Gare Montparnasse,* and the Boulevard St-Germain now sport *SITU* machines.

Keep your ticket (you may be asked to show it to one of the controllers who regularly patrol the *Métro)* and don't cheat; there are spot checks. Tickets cost 7F (around $1.20 at press time); a *carnet* (10-ticket book) is available at a reduced rate, 41F (around $7.10 at press time). The same tickets can be used on buses, but on the *Métro* you will need only one ticket per ride. The *RATP* offers several economical tourist passes: The *Formule I* card is a one-day pass providing unlimited travel on the *Métro,* bus, and suburban trains; the *Paris-Visite* card entitles the bearer to three or five consecutive days of unlimited travel, plus discounts at several Paris attractions. A two-zone *Formule I* card (covering metropolitan Paris) costs 27F (about $4.70 at press time); three-day *Paris-Visite* cards cost 90F (about $15.50 at press time), and five-day cards cost 145F (about $25 at press time). The cards may be purchased upon presentation of your passport at 44 *Métro* stations, the four regional express stations, the six *SNCF* stations (see *Train,* below), or at the *RATP*'s tourist offices (see *Bus,* above); the cards also may be purchased in the U.S. from *Marketing Challenges International* (10 East 21st St., Suite 600, New York, NY 10010; phone: 212-529-9069; fax: 212-529-4838). The *carte orange,* a commuter pass, is available weekly (beginning on Mondays) or monthly (beginning the first of the month), and, like the tourist passes, provides unlimited travel. Though actually more economical than the tourist passes, the *carte orange* does require a small (passport-size) photo to attach to the card. For a two-zone pass (covering metropolitan Paris), the weekly *carte orange* costs 63F (about $10.90 at press time); the monthly pass sells for 219F (about $37.75 at press time). They are available at all *Métro* stations.

TAXI Taxis can be found at stands at main intersections, outside train stations and official buildings, and in the streets. A taxi is available if the entire "TAXI" sign is illuminated (with a white light); the small light *beside* the roof light signifies availability after dark; and no light means the driver is off duty. Be aware that Parisian cab drivers are notoriously selective about where they will go and how many passengers they will allow in their cabs. A four-some will inevitably have trouble since, by law, no one may ride in the front seat, but, also by law, a cab at a taxi stand must take you wherever you want to go. You also can call *Taxi Bleu* (phone: 49-36-10-10) or *Radio Taxi* (phone: 47-39-33-33); dispatchers usually speak at least some English. The meter starts running from the time the cab is dispatched, and a tip of about 15% is customary. Fares increase at night and on Sundays and holidays.

TOURS To orient yourself, we suggest taking one of the many excellent sightsee-ing tours offered by *Cityrama* (4 Pl. des Pyramides, 1er; phone: 42-60-30-14) or *Paris Vision* (214 Rue de Rivoli, 1er; phone: 42-60-31-25). Their bub-ble-top, double-decker buses are equipped with earphones for commentary in English. Reserve through any travel agent or your hotel's concierge. Both *Cityrama* and *Paris Vision,* among other operators, also offer organized "Paris by Night" group tours, which include at least one *"spectacle"*—a per-formance featuring women in minimal, yet elaborate, costumes, lavish sets and effects, and sophisticated striptease.

Another great way to see Paris is from the Seine, by boat. Prices are reasonable for a day or evening cruise on a modern, glass-enclosed river rambler, which provides a constantly changing picture of the city. Contact *Bateaux-Mouches* (Pont d'Alma, 7e; phone: 42-25-96-10); *Bateaux Parisiens* (see *Boat,* above); or *Vedettes Pont-Neuf* (Pl. Vert-Galant, 1er; phone: 46-33-98-38). *Paris Canal* (19-21 Quai de la Loire, Bassin de la Villette, 19e; phone: 42-40-96-97) and *Canauxrama* (13 Quai de la Loire, Bassin de la Villette, 19e; phone: 42-39-15-00) offer three-hour barge trips starting on the Seine and navigating through some of the city's old canals and locks (*Paris Canal* offers a subterranean route under the Bastille). An interesting commentary is given in both English and French, though *Canauxrama* only offers descriptive brochures in English when there aren't a minimum number of English-speaking passengers. *Paris Canal* offers two trips daily on weekdays, the first departing at 9:30 AM from the *Musée d'Orsay* (7e) and the second from the Bassin de la Villette at the *Parc de la Villette* at 2:30 PM; on weekends two additional trips are scheduled, departing from the Bassin de la Villette at 10 AM and the *Musée d'Orsay* at 2:25 PM. *Canauxrama* offers four trips daily (except *Christmas* and *New Year's*). They depart from the Bassin de la Villette at 9:30 AM and 2:45 PM, and from the Port de l'Arsenal at 9:45 AM and 2:30 PM; reservations are recommended. In addition to periodic theme cruises, *Paris Canal* also offers a full-day excursion on the Marne; boats leave from the *Musée d'Orsay* every Sunday in July and August at 9:30 AM and return at 5:30 PM; reservations are necessary. *Yachts de Paris* (Port de Javel-Hunt, 15e; phone: 44-37-10-20) offers dinner cruises, which, unlike other such operations, offer excellent food, with menus devised by a two-Michelin-star chef, Gérard Besson, in addition to romantic panoramas of Paris; there are two cruises nightly from May through September, one per night the rest of the year.

TRAIN Paris has six main *SNCF* (French national railroad) train stations, each one serving a different area of the country. Trains heading north depart from *Gare du Nord* (15 Rue de Dunkerque, 10e; phone: 49-95-10-00); east, *Gare de l'Est* (10 Pl. du 11-Novembre 1918, 10e; phone: 40-18-20-00); southeast, *Gare de Lyon* (Pl. Louis-Armand, 12e; phone: 40-19-60-00); southwest, *Gare d'Austerlitz* (53 Quai d'Austerlitz, 13e; phone: 45-84-14-18); west, *Gare Montparnasse* (17 Bd. de Vaugirard, 15e; phone: 40-48-10-00); west and northwest, *Gare St-Lazare* (20 Rue St-Lazare, 8e; phone: 42-85-88-00). For general information call 45-82-50-50; for reservations, 45-65-60-60 (there's usually someone who can speak English). For additional information in English, contact the tourist office within each station (see *Tourist Information*).

Most of the very fast *TGV*s *(Train à Grande Vitesse)*, leave from the *Gare de Lyon*, except for the Atlantic Coast run, which departs from the *Gare Montparnasse*, and the Lille-Calais run, which leaves from the *Gare du Nord* and connects at Calais to the "Chunnel," the trans-Channel tunnel connecting France and Great Britain. Reserved seats are necessary on all *TGV*s; tickets can be purchased from machines in all main train stations. A *TGV* station in Massy, 16 miles (25 km) south of Paris, is right near *Orly*; a 15-minute ride on the *RER*, the suburban *SNCF* service, it's ideal for those who are traveling to other parts of France and want to avoid going into Paris. *Orly-Rail* and *Roissy-Rail*, operated by the *RER*, link Paris with the two major airports, *Charles de Gaulle* and *Orly* (see *Airport*, above).

The *SNCF* has recently begun computerizing reservations, much in the same way airlines do. Known as *Socrate*, the new system's quirks have made many travelers wish they could give it hemlock. The bugs were still being worked out at press time, but what will not change is that the farther in advance (up to one month) tickets are purchased, the less expensive they are.

SPECIAL EVENTS

During summer and fall, the word "festival" here means something more akin to a musical orgy.

FAVORITE FÊTES

Festival Estival and Festival d'Automne The former, in July and August, brings a musical kaleidoscope of Gregorian chants, Bartók string quartets, Rameau opera, and more to the city's most picturesque and acoustically delightful churches. The *Festival d'Automne,* which takes up where the *Estival* leaves off, concentrates on the contemporary, generally focusing on one or two main themes or composers and including a certain number of new works. Its moving spirit is Pierre Boulez, France's top conductor. The *Festival d'Automne* also features theater and dance performances. For information, contact the *Festival Estival de Paris* (20 Rue Geoffroy-l'Asnier, Paris 75004; phone: 48-04-98-01) and the *Festival d'Automne* (156 Rue de Rivoli, Paris 75001; phone: 42-96-12-27).

Fashion shows come to Paris in January, when press and buyers pass judgment on the spring and summer haute couture collections; later, in February and March, more buyers arrive for the ready-to-wear shows (fall and winter clothes), which also are open to the trade only. Cat lovers will want to check out the *Exposition Internationale Féline* (International Cat Show) in early January. March brings the year's first *Foire Nationale à la Brocante et aux Jambons* (National Flea Market and Regional Food Products Fair), an event that is repeated in September; it's held on the Ile de Chatou, an island in the Seine west of Paris, accessible by the *RER* suburban train.

The running of the *Prix du Président de la République,* the year's first big horse race, takes place at *Auteuil,* in the *Bois de Boulogne,* in April. Late April through early May brings the *Foire de Paris,* a big international trade fair, to the *Parc des Expositions* (Porte de Versailles, 15e). In late April or May, the *Paris Marathon* is run; late May through early June is the time for the illustrious *Championnats Internationaux de France,* better known as the *French Open* tennis championship (in France it's informally called the *Roland Garros,* after the stadium in which it's held; 16e). Horse races crowd the calendar in June—there's the *Prix de Diane/Hermès* at *Chantilly,* the *Grand Prix de Paris* at *Longchamp,* the *Grande Steeplechase de Paris* at *Auteuil,* and the *Grand Prix de St-Cloud* (see *Horse Racing,* below, for details on all four). In the middle of June, the *Festival du Marais* begins a month's worth of music and dance performances in the courtyards of the Marais district's old townhouses. *Bastille Day* (July 14), which commemorates the fall of the *Bastille* and the beginning of the French Revolution in 1789, is celebrated with music, fireworks, parades (including one that goes down the Champs-Elysées), and dancing till dawn in many neighborhoods.

Cyclists arrive in Paris for the finish of the three-week *Tour de France* in late July. Also in July, press and buyers arrive to view the fall and winter haute couture collections, but the ready-to-wear shows (spring and summer clothes) wait until September and October, because August for Parisians is vacation time.

In even-numbered years, the *Biennale des Antiquaires,* a major antiques event, comes to the *Grand Palais* from late September through early October. With the finest pieces available in Europe and a range of exhibitors that includes all the top dealers from France and abroad, the *Biennale* may set the tone of the market for the following two years. Every year on the first Sunday of October, the last big horse race of the season, the *Prix de l'Arc de Triomphe,* is run at *Longchamp* (see *Horse Racing*). The first Saturday in October also brings the *Fête des Vendanges à Montmartre*, a celebration of the harvest of the city's last remaining vineyard, in Montmartre. The *Salon Mondial de l'Automobile* (World Motor Show) takes place at the *Parc des Expositions* in even-numbered years, usually in October. On November 11, ceremonies at the *Arc de Triomphe* and a parade mark *Armistice Day;* the *Open de Paris* tennis tournament is also played this month. The *Salon du Cheval et du Poney* (Horse and Pony Show) comes to the *Parc des Expositions* in early December; then comes *Noël* (Christmas), which is celebrated most movingly with *La Veille de Noël* (Christmas Eve) midnight mass at *Notre-Dame.* At midnight a week later, the *Nouvel An* (New Year) is ushered in with spontaneous street revelry in the Quartier Latin and along the Champs-Elysées.

MUSEUMS

Besides those described in *Special Places*, the following museums and sites may be of interest (unless otherwise indicated, an admission fee is charged).

BIBLIOTHÈQUE-MUSÉE DE L'OPÉRA (OPERA LIBRARY AND MUSEUM) These trace the history of opera in Paris from its 17th-century origins. Closed Sundays, holidays, and two weeks around *Easter. Opéra/Palais Garnier,* Pl. de l'Opéra, 9e (phone: 47-42-07-02).

CATACOMBES (CATACOMBS) Dating from the Gallo-Roman era, these ossuaries contain the remains of Danton, Robespierre, and many others. Bring a flashlight. Closed weekday mornings, during lunch hours on weekends, Mondays, and holidays. 1 Pl. Denfert-Rochereau, 14e (phone: 43-22-47-63).

CITÉ DE LA MUSIQUE Comprising concert halls, the *Conservatoire National Supérieur de la Musique,* and other music-related facilities, this complex also contains a music museum with a collection of 700 rare instruments. Closed Mondays. In the *Parc de la Villette,* 211 Av. Jean-Jaurès, 19e (phone: 40-05-80-00).

CRYPTE ARCHÉOLOGIQUE DE NOTRE-DAME (ARCHAEOLOGICAL CRYPT OF NOTRE-DAME) Exhibits in this ancient crypt on which the cathedral was built include floor plans that show the evolution of the cathedral and earlier religious structures built on this spot. Open daily. Under the square in front of *Notre-Dame,* at Parvis de Notre-Dame, 4e (phone: 43-29-83-51).

EGOUTS (SEWERS) This underground city of tunnels makes for a popular afternoon tour. Open daily. Pl. de la Résistance, in front of 93 Quai d'Orsay, 7e (phone: 47-05-10-29).

MANUFACTURE DES GOBELINS The famous tapestry factory has been in operation since the 15th century. Guided tours of the workshops take place Tuesdays, Wednesdays, and Thursdays (except holidays) from 2 to 3 PM. 42 Av. des Gobelins, 13e (phone: 43-37-12-60).

MÉMORIAL DE LA DÉPORTATION (DEPORTATION MEMORIAL) In a tranquil garden in the shadow of *Notre-Dame* at the tip of Ile de la Cité, this monument is dedicated to the 200,000 French citizens of all religions and races who died in Nazi concentration camps during World War II. Pl. de l'Ile-de-France, 4e.

MÉMORIAL DU MARTYR JUIF INCONNU (MEMORIAL TO THE UNKNOWN JEWISH MARTYR) A moving tribute to Jews killed during the Holocaust, this renovated memorial includes a museum displaying World War II documents and photographs. Closed Saturdays and Jewish holidays; the museum also is closed Sundays and other holidays. 17 Rue Geoffroy-l'Asnier, 4e (phone: 42-77-44-72).

MUSÉE DES ANTIQUITÉS NATIONALES (MUSEUM OF NATIONAL ANTIQUITIES) Archaeological specimens from prehistoric through Merovingian times, including an impressive Gallo-Roman collection, are exhibited. Closed during lunch hours and Tuesdays. Pl. du Château, St-Germain-en-Laye (phone: 34-51-53-65).

MUSÉE DES ARTS AFRICAINS ET OCÉANIENS (MUSEUM OF AFRICAN AND OCEANIAN ART) One of the world's finest collections of art from Africa and the Pacific Islands. Closed during lunch hours and Tuesdays. 293 Av. Daumesnil, 12e (phone: 43-43-14-54).

MUSÉE DES ARTS DE LA MODE ET DU TEXTILE (MUSEUM OF FASHION AND TEXTILE ARTS) Adjacent to the *Musée National des Arts Décoratifs* (see below), this museum chronicles the history of the fashion and textile industries with opulent exhibits. Closed Mondays and Tuesdays. 109 Rue de Rivoli, 1er (phone: 42-60-32-14).

MUSÉE DES ARTS ET TRADITIONS POPULAIRES (MUSEUM OF POPULAR ARTS AND TRADITIONS) Traditional arts and crafts from rural France are featured. Closed Tuesdays. 6 Av. du Mahatma-Gandhi, *Bois de Boulogne,* 16e (phone: 44-17-60-00).

MUSÉE BALZAC The house where the writer lived, with a garden leading to one of the prettiest little alleys in Paris. Closed Mondays and holidays. 47 Rue Raynouard, 16e (phone: 42-24-56-38).

MUSÉE CERNUSCHI A collection of Chinese art. Closed Mondays and holidays. 7 Av. Vélasquez, 8e (phone: 45-63-50-75).

MUSÉE DE LA CHASSE ET DE LA NATURE (MUSEUM OF HUNTING AND NATURE) Art, weapons, and tapestries relating to the hunt are displayed in the beautiful 17th-century *Hôtel Guénégaud*. Of particular interest is the courtyard, now decorated with sculpture, where horses once were kept. Closed during lunch hours, Tuesdays, and holidays. 60 Rue des Archives, 3e (phone: 42-72-86-43).

MUSÉE COGNACQ-JAY In a stunningly beautiful mansion in the Marais, this museum displays art, snuffboxes, and watches from the 17th and 18th centuries. Closed Mondays. 8 Rue Elzévir, 3e (phone: 40-27-07-21).

MUSÉE DES COLLECTIONS HISTORIQUES DE LA PRÉFECTURE DE POLICE (MUSEUM OF THE HISTORICAL COLLECTIONS OF THE POLICE PREFECTURE) On the second floor of this modern police station are historic arrest orders (for Charlotte Corday, among others), collections of contemporary engravings, and guillotine blades. Closed Sundays. 1 *bis* Rue des Carmes, 5e (phone: 43-29-21-57).

MUSÉE DAPPER This museum mounts splendid temporary exhibitions of African art in a charming former private house near the *Arc de Triomphe*. Open daily. 50 Av. Victor-Hugo, 16e (phone: 45-00-01-50).

MUSÉE EUGÈNE-DELACROIX A permanent collection of Delacroix's work as well as temporary exhibits of works by his contemporaries are displayed in the former studio and garden of the great painter. The museum was scheduled to reopen early this year after being closed for renovations. Closed Tuesdays. 6 Rue de Fürstemberg, 6e (phone: 43-54-04-87).

MUSÉE GRÉVIN Waxworks of French historical figures, from Charlemagne to present-day political leaders and celebrities. 10 Bd. Montmartre, 9e (phone: 47-70-85-05). A branch devoted to the Belle Epoque is in the *Forum des Halles* shopping complex. Pl. Carrée, 1er (phone: 40-26-28-50). Both branches are closed mornings.

MUSÉE GUIMET The *Louvre*'s Far Eastern collection. The museum's boutique, with reproductions inspired by the collection, is also well worth a visit. Closed Tuesdays. 6 Pl. d'Iéna, 16e (phone: 47-23-61-65).

MUSÉE GUSTAVE-MOREAU A collection of works by the early symbolist. Closed Tuesdays and during lunch hours Thursdays through Sundays. 14 Rue de la Rochefoucauld, 9e (phone: 48-74-38-50).

MUSÉE DE L'INSTITUT DU MONDE ARABE (MUSEUM OF THE INSTITUTE OF THE ARAB WORLD) Arab and Islamic arts from the 9th through the 19th century. Closed Mondays. 23 Quai St-Bernard, 5e (phone: 40-51-38-38).

MUSÉE JACQUEMART-ANDRÉ Eighteenth-century French decorative art and European Renaissance treasures, as well as frequent special exhibitions. Closed Mondays and Tuesdays. 158 Bd. Haussmann, 8e (phone: 42-89-04-91).

MUSÉE MARMOTTAN Superb Monets, including the nine masterpieces that were stolen in a daring 1985 robbery. All were recovered in a villa in Corsica and were cleaned, some for the first time, before being rehung. Closed Mondays. 2 Rue Louis-Boilly, 16e (phone: 42-24-07-02).

MUSÉE DE LA MODE ET DU COSTUME (MUSEUM OF FASHION AND COSTUME) A panorama of French contributions to fashion. Closed Mondays and Tuesday mornings. In the elegant *Palais Galliera,* 10 Av. Pierre-Ier-de-Serbie, 16e (phone: 47-20-85-23).

MUSÉE DE LA MONNAIE (MUSEUM OF COINS) More than 2,000 coins and 450 medallions, plus historic coinage machines. Closed mornings, Mondays, and holidays. 11 Quai de Conti, 6e (phone: 40-46-55-35).

MUSÉE DE MONTMARTRE Formerly artist Maurice Utrillo's house, it's now home to a rich collection of paintings, drawings, and documents depicting life in this quarter. Closed Mondays. 12 Rue Cortot, 18e (phone: 46-06-61-11).

MUSÉE NATIONAL DES ARTS DÉCORATIFS (NATIONAL MUSEUM OF DECORATIVE ARTS) Furniture and applied arts from the Middle Ages to the present, Oriental carpets, Dubuffet paintings and drawings, and three centuries of French posters. The *Galerie Art Nouveau–Art Deco* features the celebrated 1920s designer Jeanne Lanvin's bedroom and bath. Closed mornings, Mondays, and Tuesdays. 107 Rue de Rivoli, 1er (phone: 42-60-32-14).

MUSÉE NISSIM DE CAMONDO A former manor house filled with beautiful furnishings and art objects from the 18th century. Closed during lunch hours and Mondays, Tuesdays, and holidays. 63 Rue de Monceau, 8e (phone: 45-63-26-32).

MUSÉE DE SÈVRES Just outside Paris, next door to the Sèvres factory, it boasts one of the world's finest collections of porcelain. Closed Tuesdays. 4 Grand-Rue, Sèvres (phone: 45-34-99-05).

MUSÉE DU VIN (WINE MUSEUM) Housed in a 14th-century abbey whose interior was destroyed during the Revolution, the museum chronicles the history of wine and describes the wine-making process through displays, artifacts, and a series of wax figure tableaux. Closed mornings. Admission charge includes a glass of wine. 5-7 Pl. Charles-Dickens, 16e (phone: 45-25-63-26).

PAVILLON DES ARTS Located in the mushroom-shaped buildings overlooking the *Forum des Halles* complex, this space mounts a variety of art exhibits, from paintings to sculpture, ancient to modern. Closed mornings, Mondays, and holidays. 101 Rue Rambuteau, 1er (phone: 42-33-82-50).

VIDÉOTHÈQUE DE PARIS A treasure trove of information about the City of Light, this extensive computerized video archive contains thousands of films, documentaries, and videos dating from the turn of the century to the present. Closed mornings and Mondays. 2 Grand Galerie, 1er (phone: 44-76-62-00).

GALLERIES

Although fine galleries can be found all over the city, Paris's best are clustered on the Rive Droite around the *Centre Georges-Pompidou* and the Place de la Concorde, and on the Rive Gauche on or near the Rue de Seine. Here are some of our favorites:

ADRIEN MAEGHT Works by a prestigious list of artists that includes Miró, Matisse, Calder, and Chagall are displayed in this Rive Gauche gallery. 42 and 46 Rue du Bac, 7e (phone: 45-48-45-15).

AGATHE GAILLARD The best in photography, including works by Cartier-Bresson and the like. 3 Rue du Pont-Louis-Philippe, 4e (phone: 42-77-38-24).

ARTCURIAL Sculptures and prints by early moderns, such as Braque and Delaunay, are featured. The bookshop has an extensive, multilingual collection of art books. 9 Av. Matignon, 8e (phone: 42-99-16-16).

BEAUBOURG Well-known names in the Paris art scene, including Niki de Saint-Phalle, César, Tinguely, and Klossowski are found here. 23 Rue du Renard, 4e (phone: 42-71-20-50).

CAROLINE CORRE Exhibitions by contemporary artists, specializing in unique, handmade artists' books. 53 Rue Berthe, 18e (phone: 42-55-37-76).

CLAUDE BERNARD Francis Bacon, David Hockney, and Raymond Mason are among the artists exhibited here. 5 Rue des Beaux-Arts, 6e (phone: 43-26-97-07).

DANIEL MALINGUE Works by the Impressionists, as well as such notable Parisian artists from the 1930s to the 1950s as Foujita and Fautrier. 26 Av. Matignon, 8e (phone: 42-66-60-33).

DANIEL TEMPLON Major contemporary American and Italian artists. 30 Rue Beaubourg, 3e (phone: 42-72-14-10).

DARTHEA SPEYER Contemporary painting is featured in this gallery run by a former American embassy attaché. 6 Rue Jacques-Callot, 6e (phone: 43-54-78-41).

GALERIE DE FRANCE A prestigious gallery located in a majestic space features the works of historical avant-garde artists such as Brancusi and Gabo, as well as such contemporary artists as Matta, Aillaud, and Arroyo. 52 Rue de la Verrerie, 4e (phone: 42-74-38-00).

HERVÉ ODERMATT CAZEAU Early moderns—among them Picasso, Léger, and Pissarro—and antiques. 85 *bis* Rue du Faubourg-St-Honoré, 8e (phone: 42-66-92-58).

JEAN FOURNIER This dealer defended abstract expressionism in 1955 and remains faithful to the cause in his main gallery, where he also exhibits the works of promising young artists. 44 Rue Quincampoix, 4e (phone: 42-77-32-31).

LELONG The great moderns on view here include Tapiès, Bacon, Alechinsky, Donald Judd, and Voss. 13-14 Rue de Téhéran, 8e (phone: 45-63-13-19).

MARWAN HOSS In an elegant space near the *Tuileries* are displayed works by Hartung, Henri Hayden, Julio Gonzalez, and Zao Wou-Ki. 12 Rue d'Alger, 1er (phone: 42-96-37-96).

NIKKI DIANA MARQUARDT A spacious gallery of contemporary work opened by an enterprising dealer from the Bronx, New York. 9 Pl. des Vosges, 4e (phone: 42-78-21-00).

THORIGNY Marcel Duchamp, Man Ray, and other early avant-garde greats are exhibited here along with promising new artists. 13 Rue de Thorigny, 3e (phone: 48-87-60-65).

YVON LAMBERT A dealer with an eye for the avant-avant-garde, he also exhibits the works of major artists from the 1970s and 1980s, including Jammes, Lewitt, Serra, and Schnabel. 108 Rue Vieille-du-Temple, 3e (phone: 42-71-09-33).

ZABRISKIE Early and contemporary photography by Atget, Brassaï, Arbus, and others. 37 Rue Quincampoix, 4e (phone: 42-72-35-47).

SHOPPING

From street trends to classic haute couture, Paris sets the styles the world copies. Prices are generally high, but more than a few people are willing to pay for the quality of the merchandise, not to mention the cachet of a Paris label.

The big department stores are excellent places to get an idea of what's available. They include *Galeries Lafayette* (40 Bd. Haussmann, 9e; phone: 42-82-34-56; and other locations); *Printemps* (64 Bd. Haussmann, 9e; phone: 42-82-50-00); *La Samaritaine* (19 Rue de la Monnaie, 1er; phone: 40-41-20-20); *Le Bazar de l'Hôtel de Ville* (*BHV;* 52 Rue de Rivoli, 4e; phone: 42-74-90-00); and *Au Bon Marché,* located in two buildings on Rue de Sèvres (main store, 22 Rue de Sèvres, 7e, phone: 44-39-80-00; and the supermarket annex, *La Grande Epicerie,* 38 Rue de Sèvres, phone: 44-39-81-00). Three major shopping centers—*Porte Maillot* (Pl. de la Porte Maillot, 16e and 17e; phone: 45-74-29-09); *Maine Montparnasse* (at the intersection of Bd. du Montparnasse and Rue de Rennes, 6e); and the *Forum des Halles* (Rue Pierre-Lescot and Rue Rambuteau, 1er; phone: 44-76-96-56)—also are worth a visit, as is the lovely, glass-roofed *Galerie Vivienne* (main entrance at 4 Rue des Petits-Champs, 2e; phone: 42-60-08-23). Two new luxury shopping venues have opened recently: The *Carrousel du Louvre,* an underground complex beneath the museum, ranks among the world's most elegant shopping malls, with 50 fine stores and a central atrium containing an inverted version of the I. M. Pei pyramids (main entrance at 99 Rue de Rivoli, beneath the *Arc de Triomphe du Carrousel,* 1er; phone: 46-92-47-47); the complex is closed Tuesdays, when the museum is also closed. *Passy*

Plaza, located in the posh Passy district, is one of Paris's largest shopping centers (53 Rue de Passy, 16e; phone: 40-50-09-07).

Haute joaillerie—the jewelry with the most splendid designs and the highest prices—is sold on Place Vendôme. Haute couture can be found in the streets around the Champs-Elysées: Avenue George-V, Avenue Montaigne, Rue François-Ier, and Rue du Faubourg-St-Honoré. Boutiques are especially numerous on Avenue Victor-Hugo (16e), Rue de Passy (16e), Boulevard des Capucines (2e and 9e), in the St-Germain-des-Prés area (6e), in the neighborhood of the *Opéra* (9e), around the Place des Victoires (1er and 2e), on or near the Rue des Rosiers in the Marais district (4e), and in the shopping centers *Forum des Halles, Passy Plaza,* and *Carrousel du Louvre.* Rue de Rivoli is a souvenir shoppers' destination, the best place to find scarves decorated with Eiffel Towers and handkerchiefs imprinted with maps of the *Métro* system; it also abounds in shops selling perfume and other gifts. The Rue de Paradis (10e) is lined with crystal and china shops that offer amazing prices: Try *Boutique Paradis,* No. 1 *bis; L'Art et La Table,* No. 3; *Porcelain Savary,* No. 9; *Arts Céramiques,* No. 15; and *Cristallerie Paradis,* No. 17.

The best (and most expensive) antiques dealers are along the Rue du Faubourg-St-Honoré on the Rive Droite. On the Rive Gauche, there's *Le Carré Rive Gauche,* an association of more than 100 antiques shops in the area bordered by Quai Voltaire, Rue de l'Université, Rue des Sts-Pères, and Rue du Bac (all 7e). *Villages d'antiquaires,* which are something like shopping centers for antiques, have their prototype in the giant *Louvre des Antiquaires* (2 Pl. du Palais-Royal, 1er; phone: 42-97-27-00), 250 different shops housed in an old department store; it's closed Mondays and, in the summer, also on Sundays. Other *villages d'antiquaires* are *La Cour aux Antiquaires* (54 Rue du Faubourg-St-Honoré, 8e; phone: 42-66-38-60; closed Sundays and Monday mornings); *Village Suisse* (78 Av. Suffren, 15e; phone: 43-06-69-90; closed Tuesdays and Wednesdays); *Village St-Honoré* (91 Rue St-Honoré, 1er; phone: 42-36-57-45; closed Sundays); and *Village St-Paul* (entrance on Rue St-Paul just off the Quai des Célestins, 4e; phone: 48-87-91-02). For more on antiques, see *Antiques Hunting in France* in DIVERSIONS.

Antiques and curio collectors also should explore Paris's several flea markets, which include the *Puces de la Porte de Montreuil* (Av. de la Porte de Montreuil, 11e), which is held weekends and Mondays year-round and is especially good for secondhand clothing; the *Puces de la Porte de Vanves* (at Avenues Georges-Lafenestre and Marc-Sangnier, 14e, *Métro: Porte de Vanves*), held weekends year-round, for furniture and fine bric-a-brac (try to arrive early on Saturday morning); and the largest and best known, *Marché aux Puces de St-Ouen* (more commonly called the *Puces de Clignancourt;* between Porte de St-Ouen and Porte de Clignancourt, 18e), which is held weekends and Mondays year-round and offers an admirable array of antiques. The *Marché Biron* is one of the best of the smaller markets that make up the *Puces de Clignancourt;* it is especially good for fine bric-a-brac. Bargaining is a must at all the flea markets.

Paris boasts about 70 open-air and covered food markets, plus about 10 market streets and the central market—*Les Halles de Rungis,* 13e, successor to *Les Halles,* and now the world's largest wholesale market. Most numerous are the open-air roving markets that set up early in the morning two or three days a week on sidewalks or islands of major boulevards, only to tear down again at 1:30 PM. Most markets and market streets are closed Mondays. Among the best is the *Marché Batignolles* (17e, near Pl. Clichy), noteworthy for its reasonable prices and plethora of stands. More food shops line the streets surrounding the market. A typically tantalizing Rive Gauche market is the morning market that begins at the eastern end of Rue de Buci and winds around the corner onto Rue de Seine (6e). Paris's most popular market street is Rue Mouffetard (5e), which is criticized by locals for its high prices, dubious quality, and circus atmosphere. But the steep, winding street—about halfway between the *Jardin du Luxembourg* and the *Jardin des Plantes*—still has an old-fashioned flavor. The hustle and bustle of *Les Halles,* the vast central market that once occupied the same neighborhood, survives at the busy market on Rue Montorgueil (1er and 2e); some of Paris's chefs still do their marketing here. The open-air roving market under the elevated *Métro* in the center of Boulevard de Grenelle (15e), extending to the *La Motte–Picquet Métro* stop, though not necessarily the best for bargains, offers excellent high-quality items. Paris's most enjoyable market is probably the one set up on Wednesday and Saturday mornings on the Avenue du Président-Wilson (16e), between Place d'Iéna and Place de l'Alma, both of which have *Métro* stops. Other good roving markets appear in the Place Monge (5e) on Wednesdays, Fridays, and Sundays; on the Boulevard Raspail (6e) on Tuesdays, Fridays, and Sundays (when all goods are guaranteed to be organic); and on the Boulevard Edgar-Quinet (14e) on Wednesdays and Saturdays.

What follows is a sampling of the wealth of shops in Paris, many of which have more than one location in the city. Standard shopping hours are listed in GETTING READY TO GO.

TIPS FOR SAVVY SHOPPERS

In Paris, *soldes* (sales) take place during the first weeks in January and in late June and July. Any shop labeled *dégriffé* (the word means "without the label") offers year-round discounts on brand-name clothing, often last season's styles. For information on getting a refund of the Value Added Tax (VAT) on purchases, see *Shopping Spree* in DIVERSIONS.

Absinthe Chic is the word here—everything from one-of-a-kind silk hats to the latest clothes from up-and-coming designers. Near the Place des Victoires, at 74 Rue Jean-Jacques Rousseau, 1er (phone: 42-33-54-44).

Accessoire Very feminine footwear, often seen on the pages of *Elle* magazine. 6 Rue du Cherche-Midi, 6e (phone: 45-48-36-08) and other locations.

Agatha One of the best sources for chic costume jewelry. In the *Carrousel du Louvre* complex, entrance at 99 Rue de Rivoli, 1er (phone: 42-96-03-09) and other locations.

Agnès B Supremely wearable, trendy, casual clothes. Five stores on the block-long Rue du Jour, 1er: menswear at No. 3 (phone: 42-33-04-13); clothes for young children and infants at No. 4 (phone: 40-39-96-88); articles for the home at No. 5 (phone: 49-53-52-80); womenswear at No. 6 (phone: 45-08-56-56); and *Lolita,* for girls, at No. 10 (phone: 40-26-36-87). Also at 17 Av. Pierre-Ier-de-Serbie, 16e (phone: 47-20-22-44); 81 Rue d'Assas, 6e (phone: 46-33-70-20); and a new location with women's and children's clothing at 6 Rue Vieux-Colombier, 6e (phone: 44-39-02-60).

Après-Midi de Chien Women's and children's wear in what the French call "Anglo-Saxon"–style: tweedy jackets, jodhpurs, and print skirts. 10 Rue du Jour, 1er (phone: 40-26-92-78) and other locations.

Arnys Elegant, conservative men's clothing. 14 Rue de Sèvres, 6e (phone: 45-48-76-99).

Azzedine Alaïa Clothing by the Tunisian designer who redefined "body-conscious." 7 Rue de Moussy, 4e (phone: 42-72-19-19).

Baccarat High-quality porcelain and crystal. 30 *bis* Rue de Paradis, 10e (phone: 47-70-64-30), and 11 Pl. de la Madeleine, 8e (phone: 42-65-36-26).

La Bagagerie Perhaps the best bag and belt boutique in the world. 12 Rue Tronchet, 8e (phone: 42-65-03-40), and other locations.

Au Bain-Marie Beautiful kitchenware and table accessories, with an emphasis on Art Deco designs. 8 Rue Boissy-d'Anglas, 8e (phone: 42-66-59-74).

Balenciaga Ready-to-wear and haute couture from the classic design house. 10 Av. George-V, 8e (phone: 47-20-21-11).

Barthélémy In a city of great cheese stores, this is at the top of almost everyone's *fromagerie* list. 51 Rue de Grenelle, 7e (phone: 45-48-56-75).

Berthillon Heavenly ice cream—Parisians often line up outside. Flavors include wild strawberry, calvados crunch, and candied chestnut. Closed Mondays, Tuesdays, school holidays, and the month of August. 31 Rue St-Louis-en-l'Ile, 4e (phone: 43-54-31-61). Several cafés on the Ile St-Louis also serve scoops of Berthillon.

Biba Designer-label women's clothes, such as Gaultier and Junko Shimada. 18 Rue de Sèvres, 6e (phone: 45-48-89-18).

Boucheron One of several fine jewelers in the area. 26 Pl. Vendôme, 1er (phone: 42-61-58-16).

Boutique Le Flore You'll find silver-plated eggcups and other bistro accoutrements in this annex of the celebrated *Café de Flore*. 26 Rue St-Benoît, 6e (phone: 45-44-33-40).

Brentano's A variety of British and American fiction and nonficton, including travel, technical, and business books. 37 Av. de l'Opéra, 2e (phone: 42-61-52-50).

Cacharel Fashionable ready-to-wear in great prints, for children and adults. 34 Rue Tronchet, 8e (phone: 47-42-12-61); 5 Pl. des Victoires, 1er (phone: 42-33-29-88); and other locations.

Carel Beautiful shoes. 12 Rond-Point des Champs-Elysées, 8e (phone: 45-62-30-62), and other locations.

Carita Paris's most extensive—and friendliest—beauty/hair salon. 11 Rue du Faubourg-St-Honoré, 8e (phone: 42-68-13-40).

Cartier The legendary jeweler. 11-13 Rue de la Paix, 2e (phone: 42-61-58-56), and other locations.

Castelbajac Trendy designer clothes for men and women. 31 Pl. du Marché St-Honoré, 1er (phone: 42-60-78-40), and other locations.

Caves Taillevent One of Paris's best and most fairly priced wine shops, run by the owners of the three-star restaurant of the same name. 199 Rue du Faubourg-St-Honoré, 8e (phone: 45-61-14-09).

Céline A popular high-fashion women's boutique for clothing and accessories. 24 Rue François-Ier, 8e (phone: 47-20-22-83); 3 Av. Victor-Hugo, 16e (phone: 45-01-70-48); and other locations.

Cerruti For women's clothing, 15 Pl. de la Madeleine, 8e (phone: 47-42-10-78); for men's, 27 Rue Royale, 8e (phone: 42-65-68-72).

Chanel Classic women's fashions, inspired by the late, legendary Coco Chanel, now under the direction of Karl Lagerfeld. There are three individual buildings (one for shoes, another for clothing and cosmetics, and a third for watches) at 42 Av. Montaigne, 8e (phone: 47-23-74-12). Other locations include 29-31 Rue Cambon, 1er (phone: 42-86-28-00), headquarters for haute couture as well as ready-to-wear and accessories, and 5 Pl. Vendôme, 1er (phone: 42-86-28-00), which sells only Chanel watches.

Chantal Thomass Ultra-feminine fashions and sexy lingerie. Near the *Palais-Royal*, at 1 Rue Vivienne, 1er (phone: 40-15-02-36), and other locations.

Charles Jourdan Sleek, high-fashion footwear. 86 Av. des Champs-Elysées, 8e (phone: 45-62-29-28); 5 Pl. de la Madeleine, 1er (phone: 42-61-50-07); and other locations.

Charley Featuring an excellent selection of lingerie, plus personal attention and relatively low prices. 14 Rue du Faubourg-St-Honoré, 8e (phone: 47-42-17-70).

Charvet Paris's answer to Jermyn Street. An all-in-one men's shop, where shirts (they stock more than 4,000) and ties are the house specialties. 28 Pl. Vendôme, 1er (phone: 42-60-30-70).

La Châtelaine Where all of Paris shops for exquisite (and costly) toys and clothing for children. 170 Av. Victor-Hugo, 16e (phone: 47-27-44-07).

Chaumet Crownmakers for most of Europe's royalty. Expensive jewels, including antique watches covered with semiprecious stones. 12 Pl. Vendôme, 1er (phone: 42-60-32-82), and 46 Av. George-V, 8e (phone: 49-52-08-25).

Chloé Fashion for women. 54-56 Rue du Faubourg-St-Honoré, 8e (phone: 44-94-33-00).

Christian Dior One of the most famous couture houses in the world. Men's fashion, articles for the home, cosmetics, and *Baby Dior* (clothing for infants) are also here. 28-30 Av. Montaigne, 8e (phone: 40-73-54-44).

Christian Lacroix This designer offers the "hautest" of haute couture. 26 Av. Montaigne, 8e (phone: 47-23-44-40), and 73 Rue du Faubourg-St-Honoré, 8e (phone: 42-65-79-08).

Christofle The internationally famous silversmith. 9 Rue Royale, 8e (phone: 49-33-43-00).

Claude Montana Ready-to-wear and haute couture from this au courant designer. For both men's and women's clothes, 3 Rue des Petits-Champs, 1er (phone: 40-20-02-14); for women's clothes only, 31 Rue de Grenelle, 7e (phone: 42-22-69-56).

Coesnon Arguably one of Paris's finest charcuteries—in spite of its diminutive size—with the very best terrines, pâtés, *boudin blanc aux truffes,* and other temptations. 30 Rue Dauphine, 6e (phone: 43-54-35-80).

Commes des Garçons Asymmetrical-style clothing for both *des filles* and *des garçons.* 40-42 Rue Etienne-Marcel, 2e (phone: 42-33-05-21).

Comptoirs de la Tour d'Argent Glassware, napkins, silver items, and other objects bearing the celebrated restaurant's logo. 2 Rue de Cardinal-Lemoine, 5e (phone: 46-33-45-58).

Corinne Cobson The daughter of the founders of Dorothée Bis (below) is making a name for herself with her youthful, cheerfully sexy women's clothing. 43 Rue de Sèvres, 6e (phone: 40-49-02-04).

Courrèges Another bastion of haute couture. 40 Rue François-Ier, 8e (phone: 47-20-70-44), and 46 Rue du Faubourg-St-Honoré, 8e (phone: 42-65-37-75).

Cristalleries de Saint Louis Handmade lead crystal at good prices. They will pack and ship purchases. 13 Rue Royale, 8e (phone: 40-17-01-74).

Dalloyau Fine purveyor of pastries and inventor of the incredibly delicious *gâteau opéra*, a confection of coffee and chocolate cream frosted with the darkest of chocolate and topped with edible gold leaf. 99-101 Rue du Faubourg-St-Honoré, 8e (phone: 43-59-18-10); 2 Pl. Edmond-Rostand, 6e (phone: 43-29-31-10); and other locations.

Debauve et Gallais The decor of this shop, housed in a building dating from 1800, is as fine as the delicious chocolates sold here. 30 Rue des Sts-Pères, 7e (phone: 45-48-54-67).

Didier Lamarthe Elegant handbags and accessories. 219 Rue du Faubourg-St-Honoré, 1er (phone: 42-96-09-90).

Diners En Ville Irresistible antique glassware, dishes, and tablecloths. 27 Rue de Varenne, 7e (phone: 42-22-78-33).

Dominique Morlotti A current favorite of Paris's best-dressed men. 25 Rue St-Sulpice, 6e (phone: 43-54-89-89).

Dorothée Bis Colorful women's knit sportswear. 33 Rue de Sèvres, 6e (phone: 42-22-02-90), and other locations.

Les Drugstores Publicis A uniquely French version of the American drugstore, with an amazing variety of goods—perfume, books, records, foreign newspapers, magazines, film, cigarettes, food, and more, all wildly overpriced. 149 Bd. St-Germain, 6e (phone: 42-22-92-50); 133 Av. des Champs-Elysées, 8e (phone: 47-23-54-34); and 1 Av. Matignon, 8e (phone: 43-59-38-70).

E. Dehillerin An enormous selection of professional cookware. 18-20 Rue Coquillière, 1er (phone: 42-36-53-13).

Elle A clothes and home furnishings boutique run by the magazine that sums up Parisian feminine style. 30 Rue St-Sulpice, 6e (phone: 43-26-46-10).

Emmanuel Ungaro Haute couture for women. 2 Av. Montaigne, 8e (phone: 47-23-61-94).

Emmanuelle Khanh Feminine clothes in lovely fabrics, including embroidered linen. 2 Rue de Tournon, 6e (phone: 46-33-41-03).

Erès Avant-garde sportswear, including chic bathing suits, for men and women. 2 Rue Tronchet, 8e (phone: 47-42-24-55).

Fauchon No discussion of Parisian food is complete without a mention of this gastronomic institution, considered *the* place to buy fine food and wine of every variety, from *oeufs en gelée* to condiments and candy. At shops across from one another at 26 and 30 Pl. de la Madeleine, 8e (phone: 47-42-60-11 and 47-42-66-68 respectively). A pâtisserie/*boulangerie* is at 28 Pl. de la Madeleine, 8e (phone: 47-42-60-11).

Floriane Smart and well made clothes for children and infants. 45 Rue de Sèvres, 6e (phone: 45-49-97-61), and other locations.

Franck et Fils A department store for women's designer clothes, ranging from Yves Saint Laurent to Thierry Mugler. 80 Rue de Passy, 16e (phone: 46-47-86-00).

Fratelli Rossetti All kinds of shoes, made from buttery-soft leather, for men and women. 54 Rue du Faubourg-St-Honoré, 8e (phone: 42-65-26-60).

Galignani This shop, with books in English and French, has been run by the same family since the early 19th century. 224 Rue de Rivoli, 1er (phone: 42-60-76-07).

Georges Rech One of the most popular makers of classy, very Parisian styles, and at more affordable prices than other similar labels. 273 Rue du Faubourg-St-Honoré, 1er (phone: 42-61-41-14); 54 Rue Bonaparte, 6e (phone: 43-26-84-11); and other locations.

Gianni Versace This mega-store adorned with Empire antiques sells the designer's men's, women's, and children's lines. Across from the *Palais de l'Elysée* at 62 Rue du Faubourg-St-Honoré, 8e (phone: 47-42-88-02). A smaller Rive Gauche outlet featuring only women's clothing is located at 66 Rue des Sts-Pères, 6e (phone: 45-49-22-66).

Giorgio Armani The legendary Italian designer has two shops on the elegant Place Vendôme, 1er: No. 6 (phone: 42-61-55-09), for his top-of-the-line clothes, and *Emporio Armani,* No. 25 (phone: 42-61-02-34), for his less expensive line.

Givenchy Beautifully tailored clothing by the master couturier. 3 and 8 Av. George-V, 8e (phone: 47-20-81-31).

Guerlain For fine perfume and cosmetics. 2 Pl. Vendôme, 1er (phone: 42-60-68-61); 68 Champs-Elysées, 8e (phone: 45-62-52-57); 29 Rue de Sèvres, 6e (phone: 42-22-46-60); and 93 Rue de Passy, 16e (phone: 42-91-60-02).

Guy Laroche Classic, conservative couture. 30 Rue du Faubourg-St-Honoré, 8e (phone: 42-65-62-74), and 29 Av. Montaigne, 8e (phone: 40-69-69-50).

Hanae Mori The grande dame of Japanese designers in Paris. 9 Rue du Faubourg-St-Honoré, 8e (phone: 47-23-52-03), and 5 Pl. de l'Alma, 8e (phone: 40-70-05-73).

Hédiard A pricey but choice food shop, notable for its assortment of coffees and teas. There's a chic tearoom upstairs. 21 Pl. de la Madeleine, 8e (phone: 42-66-44-36).

Hermès For very high quality classic clothes, ties, scarves, handbags, shoes, saddles, and other accessories. 24 Rue du Faubourg-St-Honoré, 8e (phone: 40-17-47-17).

Hugo Boss Fine men's clothes and accessories at reasonable prices. 2 Pl. des Victoires, 1er (phone: 40-28-91-64).

IGN (French National Geographic Institute) All manner of maps are sold here. 136 *bis* Rue Grenelle, 7e, and 107 Rue La Boëtie, 8e (phone for both: 42-56-06-68).

Inès de la Fressange The former Chanel model has opened this chic shop, which sells everything from classic white silk shirts to furniture gilded with her signature oak leaf. 14 Av. de Montaigne, 8e (phone: 47-23-08-94).

Issey Miyake An "in" shop, selling women's clothing made by the Japanese artist-designer. Miyake's latest collections are at 3 Pl. des Vosges, 4e (phone: 48-87-01-86); a lower-priced line is featured at *Plantation,* 17 Bd. Raspail, 7e (phone: 45-48-12-32).

Jean-Paul Gaultier Designer clothes for men and women. 6 Rue Vivienne, 2e (phone: 42-86-05-05).

Jil Sander The first boutique in Paris for the leading German womenswear designer. 52 Av. Montaigne, 8e (phone: 44-95-06-70).

John Lobb What are said to be the finest men's shoes in the world (and probably the most expensive) are sold here. 51 Rue François-Ier, 8e (phone: 45-62-06-34).

Junko Shimada Formfitting clothes from the chic Japanese designer. 54 Rue Etienne-Marcel, 2e (phone: 42-36-36-97).

Karl Lagerfeld Women's clothing in a more adventurous spirit than those he designs for Chanel. 19 Rue du Faubourg-St-Honoré, 8e (phone: 42-66-64-64).

Kenzo Avant-garde fashions by the Japanese designer. A *Kenzo* children's shop is located in the passageway next to the store. 3 Pl. des Victoires, 1er (phone: 40-39-72-03). *Kenzo Studio,* with a lower-priced sportswear line, is at 60 Rue de Rennes, 6e (phone: 45-44-27-88).

Kitchen Bazaar Specializes in everything imaginable for the smart kitchen. 11 Av. du Maine, 15e (phone: 42-22-91-17). A second store, *Kitchen Bazaar Autrement,* features kitchen utensils from all over the world. 6 Av. du Maine, 15e (phone: 45-48-89-00).

Lalique The famous crystal. 11 Rue Royale, 8e (phone: 42-66-52-40), and in the *Carrousel du Louvre,* entrance at 99 Rue de Rivoli, 1er (phone: 42-86-01-51).

Lanvin Another fabulous designer, with several spacious, colorful boutiques under one roof. For women's and men's clothes, 15 and 22 Rue du Faubourg-St-Honoré, 8e (phone: 44-71-33-33); for men's clothes only, 2 Rue Cambon, 1er (phone: 42-60-38-83).

Legrand Fille et Fils Fine wines and spirits and articles for the *cave* and table, such as *rattes* (wrought-iron candle holders used in real wine cellars), plus excellent maps of French wine regions. 1 Rue Banque, 2e (phone: 42-60-07-12).

Lenôtre Specializes in pastries and other desserts—from exquisite éclairs and fruit mousses to charlottes and chocolates. 44 Rue d'Auteuil, 16e (phone: 45-24-52-52), and several other locations.

Lescêne-Dura Everything for the wine lover or maker, except the wine itself. 63 Rue de la Verrerie, 4e (phone: 42-72-08-74).

Limoges-Unic Two stores on Rue de Paradis (10e), the first selling more expensive items, the second offering many varieties of Limoges china as well as a good selection of typically French Porcelaine de Paris. No. 12 (phone: 47-70-54-49), and No. 58 (phone: 47-70-61-49).

Lolita Lempicka Iconoclastic, formfitting womenswear. 3 *bis* Rue de Rosiers, 4e (phone: 42-74-42-94), and other locations.

Louis Vuitton High-quality luggage and handbags. The agreeable, efficient, and well-mannered staff at the modern Avenue Montaigne branch are a pleasure after the chilly reception at the original Avenue Marceau shop. 54 Av. Montaigne, 8e (phone: 45-62-47-00), and 78 *bis* Av. Marceau, 8e (phone: 47-20-47-00).

Lumicrystal In the building where artist Jean-Baptiste-Camille Corot lived and died, this fine china and crystal store carries Baccarat, Daum, Limoges, and Puiforcat. 22 Rue de Paradis, 10e (phone: 47-70-27-97).

La Maison du Chocolat Robert Linxe, perhaps the most talented chocolate maker in Paris, produces delicate, meltingly delicious confections. 225 Rue du Faubourg-St-Honoré, 8e (phone: 42-27-39-44).

La Maison de l'Escargot This shop prepares (and sells) more than 10 tons of snails annually, following a well-guarded secret recipe. 68 Rue Fondary, 15e (phone: 45-77-93-82).

Maison de la Truffe The world's largest retailer of truffles. There are fresh black truffles from November through March, and the fresh white variety are offered from mid-October through December; the rest of the year they're preserved. 19 Pl. de la Madeleine, 8e (phone: 42-65-53-22).

Maria Luisa Haute couture and daring new looks from Paris's top designers. 2 Rue Cambon, 1er (phone: 47-03-96-15).

Marie Mercié Fashionable hats, including turbans and velvet berets. 56 Rue Tiquetonne, 2e (phone: 40-26-60-68), and 23 Rue St-Sulpice, 6e (phone: 43-26-45-83).

Marithée & François Girbaud Not just jeans at this shop for men and women. 38 Rue Etienne-Marcel, 2e (phone: 42-33-54-69).

Maud Frizon Sophisticated, imaginative shoes and handbags. 83 Rue des Sts-Pères, 6e (phone: 42-22-06-93).

Max Mara Carries six distinct collections of Italian ready-to-wear, from classic chic to trendy, at surprisingly affordable prices. 37 Rue du Four, 6e (phone: 43-29-91-10); 265 Rue du Faubourg-St-Honoré, 1er (phone: 40-20-04-58); and other locations.

Michel Swiss The best place to buy perfume in the city, offering a voluminous selection, cheerful service, and excellent discounts. American visitors who spend more than 2,700F (about $466 at press time) get a refund of 25%; the VAT refund brings the total discount to almost 44%. 16 Rue de la Paix, 2e (phone: 42-61-71-71).

Miss Maud High-style shoes for young folks' feet. 90 Rue du Faubourg-St-Honoré, 8e (phone: 42-65-27-96), and other locations.

Missoni Innovative Italian knitwear. 43 Rue du Bac, 7e (phone: 45-48-38-02).

Moholy-Nagy Superb shirts, most in cotton, for men and women. 2 *Galerie Vivienne,* 2e (phone: 40-15-05-33).

M.O.R.A. One of Paris's "professional" cookware shops, though it sells to amateurs as well. Just about any piece of equipment you can imagine, and an interesting selection of cookbooks in French. 13 Rue Montmartre, 1er (phone: 45-08-19-24).

Morabito Magnificent handbags and luggage at steep prices. 1 Pl. Vendôme, 1er (phone: 42-60-30-76).

Motsch et Fils Fine hatmaker for men and women since 1887—the film star Jean Gabin was a customer. 42 Av. George-V, 8e (phone: 47-23-79-22).

Muriel Grateau An eclectic shop, with silk blouses and fine table linen. *Jardin du Palais-Royal,* under the arcade, 1er (phone: 40-20-90-30).

Les Must de Cartier Actually two boutiques, on either side of the *Ritz* hotel, offering such Cartier items as lighters and watches at prices that, though not low, are almost bearable when you deduct the 25% VAT. 7-23 Pl. Vendôme, 1er (phone: 42-61-55-55).

Au Nain Bleu The city's greatest toy store. 408 Rue du Faubourg-St-Honoré, 8e (phone: 42-60-39-01).

Nina Ricci Women's fashions, as well as the famous perfume. 39 Av. Montaigne, 8e (phone: 49-52-56-00).

L'Olivier Olives and olive products, with a variety of olive oils, plus other fine cooking oils, from hazelnut to walnut. 23 Rue de Rivoli, 4e (phone: 48-04-56-59).

Paco Rabanne Men's and women's clothes by a French designer famous for dresses mixing fabric and metals. 7 Rue du Cherche-Midi, 6e (phone: 42-22-87-80).

Papier Plus One of Paris's finest *papeteries* (stationery stores). 9 Rue du Pont Louis-Philippe, 4e (phone: 42-77-70-49).

Per Spook One of the city's best younger designers. 40 Av. Montaigne, 8e (phone: 42-99-60-00), and other locations.

Au Petit Matelot Classic sportswear, outdoor togs, and nautical accessories for men, women, and children. Especially terrific are their Tyrolean-style olive or navy loden coats. 27 Av. de la Grande-Armée, 16e (phone: 45-00-15-51).

Pierre Balmain Women's fashions from the classic couturier. 44 Rue François-Ier, 8e (phone: 47-20-98-79), and other locations.

Pierre Cardin The famous designer's own boutique. 27 Av. de Marigny, 8e (phone: 42-66-92-25), and other locations.

Poilâne Considered by many French to sell the best bread in the country; the large and crusty, round country-style loaves dubbed *pain Poilâne* are delicious with soup, pâté, cheese, or cassoulet. 8 Rue du Cherche-Midi, 6e (phone: 45-48-42-59).

Popy Moreni Unusually designed unisex clothes inspired by commedia dell'arte costumes. On one of the loveliest squares in the city, at 13 Pl. des Vosges, 4e (phone: 42-77-09-96).

Porthault Expensive but exquisite bed and table linen. 18 Av. Montaigne, 8e (phone: 47-20-75-25).

Puiforcat Art Deco tableware in a beautiful setting. 22 Rue François-Ier, 8e (phone: 47-20-74-27).

Robert Clergerie Some of Paris's finest footwear, these slightly chunky, thick-soled shoes and boots will actually stand up to the perils of cobblestone streets. 5 Rue du Cherche-Midi, 6e (phone: 45-48-75-47), and other locations.

Romeo Gigli Men's and women's arty ready-to-wear and haute couture. 46 Rue de Sévigné, 3e (phone: 48-04-57-05).

Shakespeare and Company This legendary English-language bookstore, opposite *Notre-Dame,* is something of a tourist attraction in itself. 37 Rue de la Bûcherie, 5e (phone: 43-26-96-50).

Sidonie Larizzi Heavenly handmade women's shoes. 8 Rue Marignan, 8e (phone: 43-59-38-87).

Sonia Rykiel Stunning sportswear and knits. 175 Bd. St-Germain, 6e (phone: 43-54-60-60), and other locations.

Souleiado Vibrant, traditional Provençal fabrics made into scarves, shawls, totes, tableware, even bathing suits. 78 Rue de Seine, 6e (phone: 43-54-62-25), and 83 Av. Paul-Doumer, 16e (phone: 42-24-99-34).

Stéphane Kélian High-fashion, high-quality, and high-priced (but not completely unreasonable) men's and women's shoes. 66 Av. des Champs-Elysées, 8e (phone: 42-25-56-96), and other locations.

Tartine et Chocolat Clothing for children, from infancy to 12 years old, and dresses for moms-to-be. 90 Rue de Rennes, 6e (phone: 42-22-67-34).

Ted Lapidus A compromise between haute couture and fine ready-to-wear. 23 Rue du Faubourg-St-Honoré, 8e (phone: 44-60-89-91); 35 Rue François-Ier, 8e (phone: 47-20-56-14); and other locations.

Thierry Mugler Dramatic ready-to-wear for women. 10 Pl. des Victoires, 2e (phone: 42-60-06-37), and other locations.

Trussardi Italian ready-to-wear from a designer whose leather goods and canvas carryalls are much appreciated by the French and Japanese. 21 Rue du Faubourg-St-Honoré, 8e (phone: 42-65-11-40).

La Tuile à Loup Crafts from the provinces, including Burgundy pottery and Normandy lace. 35 Rue Daubenton, 5e (phone: 47-07-28-90).

Valentino Ready-to-wear and haute couture fashions for men and women from the Italian designer. 17-19 Av. Montaigne, 8e (phone: 47-23-64-61).

Van Cleef & Arpels One of the world's great jewelers. 22 Pl. Vendôme, 1er (phone: 42-61-58-58).

Vicky Tiel Strapless evening gowns decorated with beads and bows, as well as contemporary sweaters and baseball jackets. 21 Rue Bonaparte, 6e (phone: 44-07-15-99).

Victoire Ready-to-wear from up-and-coming designers such as André Walker, with attractive accessories and jewelry. 10 and 12 Pl. des Victoires, 2e (phone: 42-60-96-21 or 42-61-09-02), and other locations.

Virgin Megastore The British have taken over the Parisian market in CDs, audiocassettes, and videocassettes. Though the selection is staggering, the store is usually so crowded that browsing is impossible. 56-60 Champs-Elysées, 8e, and in the *Carrousel du Louvre,* entrance at 99 Rue de Rivoli, 1er (phone: 49-53-50-00 for both stores).

Walter Steiger Some of the capital's most expensive footwear for men and women. The flagship shop displays satin slippers like precious jewels—with prices to match. 83 Rue du Faubourg-St-Honoré, 8e (phone: 42-66-65-08).

W. H. Smith and Sons The largest English-language bookstore in Paris (with more space now that the upstairs tearoom has been converted into additional shelf space). It sells the Sunday *New York Times,* in addition to many British and American magazines. 248 Rue de Rivoli, 1er (phone: 42-60-37-97).

Yohji Yamamoto This Japanese designer offers highly unusual outerwear. For women, 25 Rue du Louvre, 1er (phone: 42-21-42-93); for men, 47 Rue Etienne-Marcel, 1er (phone: 45-08-82-45).

Yves Saint Laurent The world-renowned designer's flagship boutique is here, on the Rue du Faubourg-St-Honoré. 38 Rue du Faubourg-St-Honoré, 8e (phone: 42-65-74-59); 6 Pl. St-Sulpice, 6e (phone: 43-29-43-00); and other locations.

BEST DISCOUNT SHOPS

If you (like us) are among those shoppers who believe that the eighth deadly sin is buying retàil, you'll treasure the following inexpensive outlets, including some of Paris's best *dépôt-vente* shops, where merchandise is sold on consignment, at a discount. Several discount designer fashion outlets line the Rue d'Alésia (14e), from *Sonia Rykiel* at No. 64, to *Chevignon* at No. 122.

Anna Lowe Yves Saint Laurent, Valentino, and others, at a discount. 35 Av. Matignon, 8e (phone: 43-59-96-61).

Anne Parée Great buys on French perfume, Dior scarves, men's ties, Limoges china, and Vuarnet sunglasses. A 40% discount (including VAT) is given on purchases totaling 1,500F (about $260 at press time) or more. Mail order, too. 10 Rue Duphot, 1er (phone: 42-60-03-26).

Bab's High fashion at reasonable prices. 29 Av. Marceau, 16e (phone: 47-20-84-74), and 89 *bis* Av. des Ternes, 17e (phone: 45-74-02-74).

Bidermann Menswear from Saint Laurent, Kenzo, Courrèges, and more in a warehouse of a store in the Marais. 114 Rue de Turenne, 3e (phone: 44-61-17-00).

Boëtie 104 Good buys on men's and women's shoes. 104 Rue La Boëtie, 8e (phone: 43-59-72-38).

Cacharel Stock Surprisingly current Cacharel fashions at about a 40% discount. 114 Rue d'Alésia, 14e (phone: 45-42-53-04).

Catherine Baril Women's ready-to-wear by designers such as Chanel and Jean-Louis Scherrer. 14 Rue de la Tour, 16e (phone: 45-20-95-21). The men's store down the street carries labels such as Armani and Hermès. 25 Rue de la Tour, 16e (phone: 45-27-11-46).

Chercheminippes One of the best Parisian *dépôt-vente* shops for high-quality children's clothes. The women's *dépôt-vente* collections just down the street are also worth a visit. Children's clothes, 160 Rue du Cherche-Midi, 6e (phone: 42-22-33-89), plus two stores for women, at No. 109 (phone: 42-22-45-23) and No. 111 (phone: 42-22-53-76).

Dépôt des Grandes Marques A third-floor shop featuring up to 50% markdowns on Louis Féraud, Cerruti, Renoma, and similar labels. Near the stock market, at 15 Rue de la Banque, 2e (phone: 42-96-99-04).

Dorothée Bis Stock The well-known sportswear at about 40% off. 74 Rue d'Alésia, 14e (phone: 45-42-17-11).

Eiffel Shopping Another bastion of fine French perfumes at discounted prices, it also stocks Lalique crystal, watches, and upscale costume jewelry. 9 Av. de Suffren, 7e (phone: 45-66-55-30).

Eve Cazes Bijoux d'Occasion A *dépôt-vente* for pre-owned fine jewelry, operated by a gem expert. Prices are about 40% lower than new. 20 Rue de Miromesnil, 8e (phone: 42-65-95-44).

Jean-Louis Scherrer Haute couture labels by Scherrer and others at about half their original prices. 29 Av. Ledru-Rollin, 12e (phone: 46-28-39-27).

Kashiyama Check out the upper level of this store for designer clothes from the previous season at a discount. 80 Rue Jean-Jacques Rousseau, 1er (phone: 40-26-46-46).

Mendès Less-than-wholesale prices on haute couture, especially Yves Saint Laurent and Lanvin. 65 Rue Montmartre, 2e (phone: 42-36-83-32).

Miss Griff The very best of haute couture in small sizes (up to size 10) at small prices. Alterations, too. 19 Rue de Penthièvre, 8e (phone: 42-65-10-00).

Mouton à Cinq Pattes Ready-to-wear clothing for men, women, and children at 50% off original prices. 8 and 18 Rue St-Placide, 6e (phone: 45-48-86-26), and other locations.

Nina Ricci Stock Discounted fashions by this designer. 17-19 Rue François-Ier, 8e (phone: 47-23-78-88).

Réciproque Billed as the largest *dépôt-vente* in Paris, this outlet features names like Chanel, Alaïa, Lanvin, and Scherrer, as well as fine objets d'art. Several hundred square yards of display area are arranged by designer and by size. Five locations on the Rue de la Pompe, 16e: No. 89 for artwork; No. 93 for women's eveningwear; No. 95 for women's sportswear; No. 103 for men's clothing and accessories (phone: 47-04-30-28 for these four); and No. 123 for women's coats and accessories (phone: 47-27-30-28).

Soldes Trois Lanvin fashions at about half their normal retail cost. 3 Rue de Vienne, 8e (phone: 42-94-99-67).

If haute couture prices paralyze your pocketbook, several shops in the city offer pre-owned, high-style clothes with down-to-earth price tags. *L'Astucerie* (105 Rue de Javel, 15e; phone: 45-57-94-74) offers designerwear and accessories, from Hermès scarves to Vuitton luggage; *La Marette* (25 *Galerie Vivienne*, 2e; phone: 42-60-08-19) carries designer items including a selection of stylish children's outfits and accessories; *Didier Ludot*, under the arcades of the *Jardin du Palais-Royal* (19-24 Galerie Montpensier, 1er; phone: 42-96-06-56), offers an array of museum-quality designer fashions, most from the 1940s, '50s, and '60s; and *Troc'Eve* (25 Rue Violet, 15e; phone: 45-79-38-36) also has an impressive stock of pre-owned designer clothes in perfect condition.

SPORTS AND FITNESS

BICYCLING Rentals are available in the *Bois de Boulogne* and the *Bois de Vincennes*, or contact *Bicyclub* (8 Pl. de la Porte-de-Champeret, 17e; phone: 47-66-55-92) or *Paris-Vélo* (2 Rue du Fer-à-Moulin, 5e; phone: 47-07-67-45). For a membership fee, you can take advantage of group outings in Paris and the surrounding region, maps of cycling routes in the area, and other information especially for cyclists from the *Fédération Française de Cyclo-Tourisme* (*FFCT;* 8 Rue Jean-Marie-Jégo, 13e; phone: 44-16-88-88; fax: 44-16-88-99); contact them for a detailed brochure in English. In addition to renting bicycles, *Paris by Cycle* (78 Rue de l'Ouest, 14e; phone: 40-47-08-04 for rentals and for excursions outside Paris; 48-87-60-01 for Paris tours) arranges guided group tours of the city and of Versailles, as well as bike trips alternating with horseback rides. *Mountain Bike Trip* (6 Pl. Etienne-Pernet, 15e; phone: 48-42-57-87 or 49-29-93-91) also arranges group rides in and around Paris. The world-famous *Tour de France* bicycle race takes place in July, ending in Paris.

FITNESS CENTERS The *Gymnase Club* (208 Rue de Vaugirard, 15e; phone: 47-83-99-45; and many other locations); *Club Quartier Latin* (19 Rue de Pontoise, 5e; phone: 43-54-82-45); *Club Jean de Beauvais* (5 Rue de Jean-de-Beauvais, 5e; phone: 46-33-16-80); *Espace Beaujon* (208 Rue du Faubourg-St-Honoré, 8e; phone: 42-89-12-32); and *Espace Vit'Halles* (48 Rue Rambuteau; phone: 42-77-21-71) are open daily to non-members for a fee.

GOLF Although there are no 18-hole courses within the city, several major layouts are close by.

TOP TEE-OFF SPOTS

Euro Disneyland This 18-hole, competition-level course is part of Disney's "megaresort" project (which, when complete, will be nearly one-fifth the size of Paris). The Ron Fream design is laid out around a lush landscape including manmade lakes with stepped tees and characteristic mouse-ear–shaped sand bunkers. *Euro Disneyland,* Marne-la-Vallée, 20 miles (32 km) east of Paris (phone: 64-74-30-00).

Golf Club de Chantilly Known for its lace, Chantilly is also famous for the *Château de Chantilly,* one of France's royal palaces, and this elegant club, only five minutes from the historic castle. With Old World charm and aristocratic ambience, the two British-designed, 18-hole courses (each 6,820 yards) wind through an impressive forest. In July and August, non-members may play for a fee every day except Thursdays; the rest of the year non-members may play on weekdays except Thursdays. Twenty-five miles (41 km) north of Paris, in Chantilly (phone: 44-57-04-43).

Golf National Owned and operated by the *Fédération Française de Golf* (see below), this huge public golf complex comprises three courses. The first, the 18-hole, 7,400-yard stadium course *Albatros* (designed by Hubert Chesneau and Bob Von Hagge) is host to the *French Open.* Water hazards abound. 2 Av. du Golf, in St-Quentin-en-Yvelines, 19 miles (30 km) southwest of Paris (phone: 30-43-36-00).

Golf des Yvelines Set in a protected park, here are an 18-hole, par-72 forest course and a nine-hole course. Its clubhouse is in a château. Greens fees are higher on weekends. Twenty-eight miles (45 km) southwest of Paris, in La Queue-lès-Yvelines (phone: 34-86-48-89).

Urban Cély Golf Club This perfectly manicured and landscaped course (18 holes, 6,500 yards, par 72) has a beautiful clubhouse that resembles a medieval castle. Electric carts are available. Close to Fontainebleau, Barbizon, and Milly-la-Forêt. Le Château, Rte. de St-Germain, Cély-en-Bière (phone: 64-38-03-07; fax: 64-38-08-78).

The *Fédération Française de Golf* (69 Av. Victor-Hugo, 16e; phone: 45-02-13-55) and the *French Ministry of Tourism* have set up a system whereby travelers and others who are not members of a local golf club can play. Greens fees vary according to the day and season, but are usually higher on weekends. Call ahead to reserve. There is a nine-hole municipal course at the *St-Cloud* racecourse (1 Rue du Camp Canadien, St-Cloud; phone: 47-71-39-22), west of the city.

HORSE RACING If Paris has a sporting passion, it's horses. The French invented the pari-mutuel betting system (based on equally distributed winnings), and in and around the city there are eight tracks, a half-dozen racing sheets, and several hundred places to bet during a season that runs year-round. Here are our odds-on favorites for a great day at the races.

Auteuil Opened in 1870 for steeplechase only, *Auteuil* features over 40 permanent obstacles spread across 30 acres. More than 60,000 Parisians turn out for the fashionable *Grande Steeplechase de Paris* on the third Sunday in June (this is where Hemingway took Ezra Pound to the races). The best tip for this track is a reservation at the *Panoramique de l'Hippodrome* restaurant (phone: 45-24-00-38). Or take your winnings over to the neighboring *Pré Catelan* (see *Eating Out*). *Bois de Boulogne* (phone: 45-27-12-25).

Longchamp The temple of thoroughbred racing since 1855, *Longchamp* is Paris's most prestigious racetrack and the one for which hopeful entries train at nearby *Maisons-Laffitte, Enghien, Chantilly, Evry,* and *St-Cloud.* The track's two highlight events are the *Grand Prix de Paris* in late June, which carries a purse of one million francs, and the *Prix de l'Arc de Triomphe* in early October, which at five million francs is one of Europe's most lucrative races. *Bois de Boulogne* (phone: 44-30-75-00).

St-Cloud This course offers flat racing from spring to fall, with the prestigious *Grand Prix de St-Cloud* held the first Sunday in July. West of Paris, in the chic suburb of St-Cloud (phone: 46-02-62-29).

Vincennes A taxi ride into the woods, the *Champs de Courses de Vincennes* is the scene of night racing, particularly trotting. Popular with diehard bettors, the track has a rough reputation. The major highlight of the Vincennes season is the *Prix d'Amérique* for trotters, in the dead cold of January. Reservations are advised for the track restaurant, *Le Paddock* (phone: 43-68-64-94). *Bois de Vincennes* (phone: 49-77-17-17).

From late April through early September, a number of other historic tracks around Paris open for selected racing dates. In late spring, races are scheduled in Fontainebleau; and the French equivalent of *Ascot*, the *Prix de Diane/Hermès*, is held at *Chantilly* (phone: 44-62-91-00), about 25 miles (40 km) north of Paris, as part of the *Grande Semaine*. The best way to find out times, dates, and racing tips is by reading *Paris-Turf, Tiercé, France-Soir,* or *L'Equipe*, all available at newsstands.

OFF-TRACK BETTING

The words "win," "place," and "show" are as dear to a Frenchman's heart as liberty, fraternity, and equality. Identifiable by their bright green and red logos, there are over 7,000 *PMU (Pari-Mutuel Urbaine)* outlets in French cafés and tobacco shops for off-track betting. The overall system is the third-largest public service industry in France, and is easier to play than the lottery. The traditional system involves marking an entry card for the day's feature race. A minimum bet is 6F (about $1 at press time) for the *tiercé* (picking the first three horses to cross the finish line), or 10F (about $1.70 at press time) for a simple winner. More modern developments are course cafés. These neighborhood betting parlors, which charge an admission fee, offer satellite broadcasts of a full slate of day or night racing direct from trackside, and payouts are immediate. The food is often good, and the ambience convivial. There are presently about two dozen of these cafés in Paris, and their numbers are growing rapidly. Try the *Boul' Mich* (116 Bd. St-Germain at Carrefour de l'Odéon, 6e; phone: 46-33-76-66), where the barman usually has a winning tip.

JOGGING There are a number of places where you can jog happily; one of the most pleasant is the *Bois de Boulogne*. Five more centrally located parks are the *Jardin du Luxembourg* and the *Jardin des Tuileries* (see *Special Places* for both); the *Parc du Champ-de-Mars* (behind the *Eiffel Tower*, 7e); *Parc Monceau* (Bd. de Courcelles, 8e); and the *Jardin des Plantes* (Pl. Valhubert, 5e).

SOCCER There are matches from early August through mid-June at *Parc des Princes* (24 Rue du Commandant Guilbaud, 16e; phone: 42-88-02-76).

SQUASH *Stadium Squash Club* (44 Av. d'Ivry, 13e; phone: 45-85-39-06) has 14 air conditioned courts.

SWIMMING Among pools in Paris open to visitors (all of the following charge admission) are the indoor *Piscine des Halles* (10 Pl. de la Rotonde, 1er; phone: 42-36-98-44), open daily; the indoor *Piscine Pontoise* (19 Rue de Pontoise, 5e; phone: 43-54-82-45), open daily; the outdoor *Butte-aux-Cailles* (5 Pl. Paul-Verlaine, 13e; phone: 45-89-60-05), open daily; the outdoor *Stade Nautique Robert-Keller* (14 Rue de l'Ingénieur-Robert-Keller, 15e; phone: 45-77-12-12), closed Mondays; the indoor *Jean-Taris* (16 Rue Thouin, 5e; phone: 43-25-54-03), open daily; the indoor *Tour Montparnasse* (beneath the tower at 66 Bd. du Montparnasse, 15e; phone: 45-38-65-19), open daily; *Piscine Georges-Vallerey* (148 Av. Gambetta, 20e; phone: 40-31-15-20), which is covered, but can be converted to open-air in good weather, open daily; and *Aquaboulevard* (5 Rue Louis-Armand, 15e; phone: 40-60-10-00), a combination health club/water park, with facilities such as a wave pool, a manmade beach, and water slides, open daily.

TENNIS On the outskirts of Paris are several top-flight tennis clubs.

CHOICE COURTS

Tennis Club de Longchamp Weekly instruction sessions are available in English on this club's 20 courts. The club can also arrange a match with a player at the same competitive level. Call a day in advance to·reserve a court or arrange lessons. Down the road from *Stade Roland-Garros,* in the *Bois de Boulogne,* at 19 Bd. Anatole-France (phone: 46-03-84-49).

Tennis Forest Hill This club has eight indoor courts and offers instruction, in French only. Closed August. Six miles (9 km) from Paris, at 111 Av. Victor-Hugo, Aubervilliers, Seine-St-Denis (phone: 47-29-91-91).

Tennis de Villepinte Here are two outdoor and five indoor courts. Weekend and extended courses in English are available. Fourteen miles (22 km) from Paris, at Rue du Manège, Villepinte, Seine-St-Denis (phone: 43-83-23-31).

Tennis Club Vitis Lessons are available in English on this club's seven outdoor and four indoor courts. Call at least a day in advance to reserve a court or arrange lessons. 159 Rue de la République, La Défense-Puteaux (phone: 47-73-04-01).

UCPA With 14 outdoor courts (two covered), this club offers a seven-hour weekend instruction program (though it's not always available in English). Call a day in advance to reserve a court or arrange lessons. Rue de Tournezy, Bois-le-Roi, Seine-et-Marne (phone: 64-87-83-00).

In addition to those right outside the capital, six courts are available in the *Jardin du Luxembourg* for a nominal fee, but be certain to arrive early, as this is a popular spot. For general information on courts in Paris, call the *Ligue Régionale de Paris* (74 Rue de Rome, 17e; phone: 45-22-22-08), or the *Fédération Française de Tennis* (*Stade Roland-Garros,* 2 Av. Gordon-Bennett, 16e; phone: 47-43-48-00).

THEATER AND OPERA

The most complete listings of theaters, operas, concerts, and movies are found in *L'Officiel des Spectacles* and *Pariscope,* weekly publications that are available at newsstands. The season generally extends from September through May. Less expensive than in New York, tickets can be obtained at each box office; at any of the large *FNAC* stores (136 Rue de Rennes, 6e, phone: 49-54-30-00; in the *Forum des Halles,* 1er, phone: 40-41-40-00; also other locations); at the two *Virgin Megastores* (56-60 Champs-Elysées, 8e, and the *Carrousel du Louvre* shopping center, 99 Rue de Rivoli, 1er; phone: 49-53-50-00 for both); through brokers (*American Express* and *Thomas Cook* are good ones); or through your hotel's concierge. Tickets can also be purchased at high-tech *Billetel* machines at the *Galeries Lafayette* (see *Shopping*), near the *Centre Georges-Pompidou* (6 Bd. de Sébastopol; phone: 48-04-95-27), and other locations. Insert a credit card into a slot in the Billetel and choose from over 100 upcoming theater events and concerts.

The device will spew out a display of dates, seats, and prices, from which you can order your tickets, which then will be printed on the spot and charged to your account. Half-price, day-of-performance theater tickets are available at *Kiosque* (15 Place de la Madeleine, 8e); it's closed mornings and Mondays. The curtain usually goes up at 8:30 PM.

What follows is a selection of our favorite Parisian theaters and opera houses.

CENTER STAGE

Comédie-Française As much a national monument as the *Eiffel Tower,* the undisputed dowager queen of French theater presents lavish productions of great classics by Corneille, Racine, Molière, Rostand, and the happy few 20th-century playwrights like Anouilh, Giraudoux, and Sartre who have been received into the inner circle of French culture. The *CF* is polishing up its fin de siècle image (the theater itself was entirely renovated last year), but even at its stodgiest, it's well worth seeing. 2 Rue de Richelieu, 1er (phone: 40-15-00-15). The company also presents productions of contemporary plays in the renovated 350-seat *Théâtre du Vieux-Colombier* (21 Rue du Vieux-Colombier, 6e; phone: 42-22-77-48).

L'Odéon–Théâtre de L'Europe The chameleon-like *Odéon* has, for years, been the joker in the French theatrical pack. After the turbulent period when it hosted the fabled company under the direction of the late Jean-Louis Barrault and Madeleine Renaud and ranked among the most popular houses in the city, it became an annex of the *Comédie-Française.* Now it can be seen in yet another incarnation, as the *Théâtre de l'Europe.* Headed by one of Europe's foremost men of the theater, Giorgio Strehler of Milan's *Piccolo Teatro,* it has become a kind of theatrical Common Market, with original-language productions from all over Europe. Pl. de l'Odéon, 6e (phone: 44-41-36-36).

Opera in Paris In a futuristic opera house on the Place de la Bastille, the *Opéra de la Bastille* began regular performances in 1990 under the baton of Myung-Whun Chung (no longer with the company), while the *Opéra/Palais Garnier,* at the melodramatic end of Avenue de l'Opéra, now hosts the best in ballet (see *Special Places* for details on both opera houses). At press time, the *Opéra/Palais Garnier* was closed for renovations (until at least March 1996); all ballet performances are currently being held at the *Opéra de la Bastille.* The other mainstays of Paris opera are the *Théâtre National de l'Opéra Comique,* at the *Salle Favart* (Pl. Boïeldieu, 9e; phone: 42-96-12-20), and the *Théâtre du Châtelet/Théâtre Musicale de Paris* (1 Pl. du Châtelet, 1er; phone: 40-28-28-98). The latter, once the stronghold of the frothy operetta, now does everything from early Offenbach to late Verdi, importing productions from other European opera companies as well. The touch is light and stylish, the accent utterly French. The *Opéra-Comique* isn't especially comic. It's smaller and its performers are generally less well known than those at the *Opéra de la Bastille,* but it has a wider repertoire.

The city has numerous smaller theaters and companies as well. Known for its continually evolving and inventive style, the *Théâtre des Amandiers* (7 Av. Pablo-Picasso; phone: 46-14-70-00) is in Nanterre, a working-class suburb of Paris. Recent presentations have included such time-honored classics as the *Oedipus* trilogy by Sophocles, but a trip to the box office can turn up any number of theatrical surprises. The theater is about 20 minutes by the *RER* city-rail from downtown Paris. New formats, odd curtain times, and a constant redefining of theater and its audience are the trademarks of the *Théâtre National de Chaillot* (Pl. du Trocadéro et du 11-Novembre, 6e; phone: 47-27-81-15), whose repertory ranges from *Hamlet* to *Faust* for children— performed by marionettes—to new texts by Algerian workers, plus contemporary musical happenings. And *Théâtre du Soleil* (La Cartoucherie de Vincennes, Rte. du Champ de Manoeuvres, *Bois de Vincennes,* 12e; phone: 43-74-24-08 or 43-74-87-63), housed in an old cartridge factory, always has had a colorful, sweeping style with a popular mood and political overtones. That was true in the dazzling production *1789,* which made the troupe's international reputation during that other year of French upheaval, 1968, and in the more recent Shakespeare series as well. *Bouffes du Nord* (37 *bis* Bd. de la Chapelle, 10e; phone: 46-07-34-50) is a magical place, where the simple stagings and excellent acoustics lend power to the Peter Brook company's productions, from Shakespeare to the *Mahabharata. Théâtre Marie-Stuart* (4 Rue Marie-Stuart, 2e; phone: 45-08-17-80) produces contemporary drama, including some American works (though they're performed in French).

Paris's many café-theaters offer amusing songs, sketches, satires, and takeoffs on topical issues and events. Among them are *Café de la Gare* (41 Rue du Temple, 4e; phone: 42-78-52-51) and *Café d'Edgar* (58 Bd. Edgar-Quinet, 14e; phone: 42-79-97-97). In addition, several vessels moored along the quays offer theatrical performances, ranging from classical French plays to magic shows. The *Péniche Opéra* boat (200 Quai de Jemmapes, 10e; phone: 43-49-08-15) is berthed on the Canal St-Martin on the Rive Droite; it's closed during the summer. Nearby is the *Metamorphosis* (35 Quai de la Tournelle, 5e; phone: 42-61-33-70), which offers magic shows. At the Quai Malaquais, on the Rive Gauche, are *L'Ouragan* (phone: 40-46-01-24) and the *Mare au Diable* (phone: 40-46-90-67).

FILM

With about 200 movie houses, Paris is a real treat for film buffs. No other metropolis offers such a cinematographic feast—current French chic, recent imports from across the Atlantic, grainy 1930s classics, and the best of Third World and Eastern European offerings. The French often get their favorite American flicks up to six months late, but, then again, many of the front-runners at Cannes hit the screens here well before they wend their way stateside.

Pariscope and *L'Officiel des Spectacles,* which come out on Wednesday (the day the programs change), are available at newsstands and contain complete listings for each week. Films shown with their original-language soundtracks are called VO *(version originale),* worth noting if you want to avoid wincing at a French-dubbed version of an English-language film, called VF *(version française).* Broadly speaking, the undubbed variety of film flourishes on the Champs-Elysées and on the Rive Gauche, and it's a safe bet to avoid the mostly French-patronized houses of the Grands Boulevards north of the *Louvre.* There's more room in the big movie houses on the Champs-Elysées, but the cozier Quartier Latin establishments tend to specialize in the unusual and avant-garde.

At the *Cité des Sciences et de l'Industrie* complex (see La Villette in *Special Places*), the *Géode* (phone: 36-68-29-30 for a recorded message; 40-05-50-50 after 7 PM), the ultimate in high-tech, offers a B-Max hemispherical screen, cupped inside a reflecting geodesic dome. The program is limited, however, to a single scientifically oriented film at any given time. Located in La Défense, west of Paris, *Le Dome Imax* (Parvis de la Défense, La Défense; phone: 46-92-45-45) is billed as the largest of these hemispherical screens in the world.

The *Forum Horizon* (7 Pl. de la Rotonde, 1er; phone: 36-65-70-83), in the underground section of the *Forum des Halles* (see *Shopping*), offers a choice of six first-run movies and has one of the city's best sound systems, while the *Gaumont Kinopanorama* (60 Av. de la Motte-Picquet, 15e; phone: 43-06-50-50) boasts one of the widest screens in Paris. Other big screens are the *Grand Rex* (1 Bd. Poissonnière, 9e; phone: 42-36-83-93) and the *Gaumont Grand Ecran Italie* (30 Pl. d'Italie, 13e; phone: 45-80-77-00). The remodeled *Max Linder Panorama* (24 Bd. Poissonnière, 9e; phone: 48-24-00-47; 48-24-88-88 for a recording of screening times) has a spacious lobby in which you can wait in comfort. Some out-of-the-way venues such as the *Olympique Entrepôt* (7 Rue Francis de Pressence, 14e; phone: 45-43-41-63) and the *Lucernaire Forum* (53 Rue Notre-Dame-des-Champs, 6e; phone: 45-44-57-34) are social centers in themselves, incorporating restaurants and/or other theaters.

The *Cinémathèque* at the *Palais de Chaillot* (see *Special Places*) runs a packed schedule of revivals at rates lower than those of commercial cinemas. Daily programs from the museum's eclectic archive of over 20,000 films often include several running concurrently, so that a James Cagney gangster epic can share billing with a 1950s British comedy and a Brazilian thriller; come early, as seating is limited. The *Cinémathèque* also operates theaters in the *Centre Georges-Pompidou* (see *Special Places;* phone: 44-78-

12-33) and in the *Palais de Tokyo* (13 Av. President-Wilson, 16e; phone: 47-04-24-24). The *Vidéothèque de Paris* (see *Museums*), in the *Forum des Halles,* is an innovative public video library. Visitors can select individual showings or attend regularly scheduled screenings of films and television programs chronicling Paris's history.

There are two period movie houses almost worth a visit in themselves. *Le Ranelagh* (5 Rue des Vignes, 16e; phone: 42-88-64-44), where both film screenings and live theater performances are held, has an exquisite 19th-century interior. *La Pagode* (57 *bis* Rue de Babylone, 7e; phone: 47-05-12-15), decorated with flying cranes and cherry blossoms, and complete with a tearoom, is built around an authentic Japanese temple.

MUSIC

July and August bring the *Festival Estival,* which is followed by the *Festival d'Automne* (see *Special Events* for both). The *Orchestre de Paris* is based at the *Salle Pleyel,* Paris's *Carnegie Hall* (252 Rue du Faubourg-St-Honoré, 8e; phone: 45-63-07-96). The *Nouvelle Orchestre Philharmonic* performs at a variety of venues, including the *Grand Auditorium* at *Maison de Radio France* (116 Av. du Président-Kennedy, 16e; phone: 42-30-22-22). Classical concerts and recitals also take place at the *Salle Gaveau* (45 Rue La Boëtie, 8e; phone: 49-53-05-07); the *Théâtre des Champs-Elysées* (15 Av. Montaigne, 8e; phone: 49-52-50-50); and the *Palais des Congrès* (2 Pl. Porte Maillot, 17e; phone: 40-68-22-22). Special concerts frequently are held in Paris's many places of worship, with moving music at high mass on Sundays.

The *Palais des Congrès* and the *Olympia* (28 Bd. des Capucines, 9e; phone: 47-42-25-49) are the places to see well-known international pop and rock artists. Innovative contemporary music is the province of the *Institut de Recherche et de Coopération Acoustique/Musique (IRCAM;* 31 Rue du Cloître-St-Merri, 4e; phone: 44-78-48-43), whose musicians can be heard in various auditoriums of the *Centre Georges-Pompidou* (see *Special Places*). The *Musée Carnavalet* (see *Special Places*) rents out its concert hall to various music groups.

NIGHTCLUBS AND NIGHTLIFE

Typically lavish *Folies-Bergère*–style stage shows are a featured part of the "Paris by Night" group tours offered by a number of tour operators (see *Tours*). In addition, most music halls offer a package (usually far from discount) that includes dinner, dancing, and a half bottle of champagne. To save money, try going to one of these places on your own, skipping dinner and the champagne (both usually are below par), and sitting at the bar to see the show. The most famous extravaganzas occur nightly at *Crazy Horse* (12 Av. George-V, 8e; phone: 47-23-32-32); *Lido* (116 *bis* Champs-Elysées, 8e; phone: 40-76-56-10); *Moulin Rouge* (Pl. Blanche, 18e; phone: 46-06-00-19); and *Paradis Latin* (28 Rue du Cardinal-Lemoine, 5e; phone: 43-29-07-07). An amusing evening can also be spent at such smaller cabarets as *Au*

Lapin Agile (22 Rue des Saules, 18e; phone: 46-06-85-87) and *Michou* (80 Rue des Martyrs, 18e; phone: 46-06-16-04). Reserve a few days in advance for any of the above.

There's one big difference between discotheques and so-called "private" clubs. The latter, fashionable "in" spots such as *Le Palace* (8 Rue Faubourg-Montmartre, 9e; phone: 42-46-10-87); *Régine* (49 Rue de Ponthieu, 8e; phone: 43-59-21-13); *Chez Castel* (15 Rue Princesse, 6e; phone: 43-26-90-22); *Olivia Valère* (40 Rue de Colisée, 8e; phone: 42-25-11-68); *L'Arc* (12 Rue de Presbourg, 16e; 45-00-45-00); and *Les Bains* (7 Rue du Bourg-l'Abbé, 3e; phone: 48-87-01-80) superscreen potential guests. To gain entrance, go with a member or regular, dress to fit in with the crowd, and show up early and on a weeknight, when your chances of getting past the gatekeeper are at least 50-50. (One expensive way to get into *Régine, Chez Castel,* or *Les Bains* is to have your hotel make dinner reservations there for you.) Just as much fun and usually more hospitable are *Le Balajo* (9 Rue de Lappe, 11e; phone: 47-00-07-87), where the "in" crowd dances to music from rumba to rock; *Le Café Vogue* (50 Rue de la Chaussée-d'Antin, 9e; phone: 42-80-69-40), a restaurant and disco that is, as its name suggests, a favorite haunt of fashion models and other beautiful people; *Keur Samba* (73 Rue de la Boétie, 8e; phone: 43-59-03-10), for an African mood; *Chapelle des Lombards* (19 Rue de Lappe, 11e; phone: 43-57-24-24), for a Brazilian beat; *Le Cirque* (49 Rue de Ponthieu, 8e; phone: 42-25-12-13), a mainly gay nightclub; *Niel's* (27 Av. des Ternes, 17e; phone: 47-66-45-00), chic and popular with the film crowd; and *L'Ecume des Nuits,* in the *Méridien* hotel (see *Checking In*).

A natural choice for an American in Paris is the celebrated *Harry's New York Bar* (5 Rue Daunou, 2e; phone: 42-61-71-14), which has been serving classic cocktails to transatlantic transplants like Ernest Hemingway, Gertrude Stein, and George Gershwin since 1911; a *Harry's* tradition decrees that on the night of a US presidential election, only card-carrying Americans are allowed in the place, where they can watch election returns on the bar's TV set. Other pleasant, popular spots for a nightcap include *Bar de la Closerie des Lilas* (171 Bd. du Montparnasse, 6e; phone: 43-26-70-50); *Fouquet's* (99 Champs-Elysées, 8e; phone: 47-23-70-60); *Ascot Bar* (66 Rue Pierre-Charron, 8e; phone: 43-59-28-15); *Bar Anglais* in the *Plaza-Athénée* hotel (see *Checking In*); and *Pub Winston Churchill* (5 Rue de Presbourg, 16e; phone: 40-67-17-37).

Jazz buffs can choose from among the *Caveau de la Huchette* (5 Rue de la Huchette, 5e; phone: 43-26-65-05); *Le Bilboquet* (13 Rue St-Benoît, 6e; phone: 45-48-81-84); *New Morning* (7-9 Rue des Petites-Ecuries, 10e; phone: 45-23-51-41); *La Villa* (in *La Villa* hotel, 29 Rue Jacob, 6e; phone: 43-26-60-00); *Le Petit Journal* (71 Bd. St-Michel, 6e; phone: 43-26-28-59); *Arbuci* (25 Rue de Buci, 6e; phone: 45-23-51-41); *Le Petit Opportune* (15 Rue des Lavandières-Sainte-Opportune, 1er; phone: 42-36-01-36); *Le Baiser Salé* (58 Rue des Lombards, 1er; phone: 42-33-37-71); and *Au Duc des Lombards*

(42 Rue des Lombards, 1er; phone: 42-33-22-88). *Au Duc des Lombards* and *New Morning* are the best of the bunch.

Enghien-les-Bains, 8 miles (13 km) away in Enghien-les-Bains (3 Av. de Ceinture; phone: 34-12-90-00), is the only casino in the Paris vicinity. Open from 3 PM to about 4 AM, it's easily reached by train from the *Gare du Nord.*

Best in Town

CHECKING IN

Paris offers a broad choice of accommodations, from luxurious palaces with every service to more humble budget hotels. Below is our selection from all categories; for a double room, expect to spend $450 or more (sometimes much more) per night in the "palace" hotels, which we've listed as very expensive; from $250 to $450 in the expensive ones; $150 to $250 in the moderate places; and less than $150 in the inexpensive hotels.

Hotel rooms usually are at a premium in Paris. To reserve your first choice, we advise making reservations at least a month in advance, even farther ahead for the smaller, less expensive places listed. Watch for the dates of special events, when hotels are even more crowded than usual.

Street addresses of the hotels below are followed by the number of their *arrondissement.* Unless otherwise noted, all hotels listed feature air conditioning, TV sets, telephones, and private baths in the rooms. Some less expensive hotels may have private baths in only some of their rooms; it's a good idea to confirm whether your room has a private bath when making a reservation. Most of Paris's major hotels have complete facilities for the business traveler. Those hotels listed below as having "business services" usually offer such conveniences as an English-speaking concierge, meeting rooms, photocopiers, computers, translation services, and express checkout, among others. All hotels listed are open year-round and accept major credit cards, unless otherwise indicated.

For an unforgettable experience, we begin with our favorite Paris hostelries (all offer complete business services), followed by our cost and quality choices of hotels, listed by price category.

ROOMS AT THE TOP

Bristol Headquarters to dignitaries visiting the *Palais de l'Elysée* (Elysée Palace, the French *White House*), just a few steps down the street, this elegant establishment boasts 154 rooms and 41 suites, all beautifully decorated, and a one-Michelin-star restaurant with two dining rooms—one for summer and another for winter. The first is a light, airy glassed-in room overlooking the garden; the second is a wood-paneled room, a reassuring reminder of Old World craftsmanship. The open and exquisite elevator recalls an earlier age, the marvelously designed marble bathrooms are veritable oases of comfort, and the service is nothing short of superb. An elegant and comfortable lobby and bar add to the charm; there's also a new fitness center and business center, as well as a heated pool on the sixth-floor terrace, an amenity seldom found in Paris hotels. 112 Rue du Faubourg-St-Honoré, 8e (phone: 42-66-91-45; 800-223-6800; 212-838-3110 in New York City; fax: 42-66-68-68).

Crillon Today's heavy traffic gives the Place de la Concorde a frenetic atmosphere at odds with its 18th-century spirit. But here, within the Sienese marble foyers and the 163 elegant rooms and suites (plus three master suites) of this Relais & Châteaux member, guests are largely insulated from the world outside. Diplomats from nearby Embassy Row, observed by ever-present journalists, buy and sell countries in the bar (one of the city's most sophisticated meeting places) or dine in the two restaurants, *L'Obélisque* and the two-Michelin-star *Les Ambassadeurs* (see *Eating Out* for the latter). Rooms facing the street, though rather noisy, have a view *sans pareil;* those on the courtyards are just as nice and more tranquil. Business services are available. 10 Pl. de la Concorde, 8e (phone: 44-71-15-00; 800-888-4747; fax: 44-71-15-02).

George V The lobby is a League of Nations of private enterprise; it also seems to be where the *Cannes Film Festival* crowd spends the other 11 months of the year, so numerous are the movie folk who stay in the hotel's 298 rooms and 53 suites and dine in its two restaurants, including the one-Michelin-star *Les Princes*. The *Eiffel Tower* is just across the river, the Champs-Elysées down the block, and the *Arc de Triomphe* around the corner; most of the rest of Paris can be seen from the windows of rooms on the higher floors. Even those who can't afford one of them—or the tranquil chambers facing the gracious courtyard—should be sure to stop in for an utterly lyrical croissant at breakfast or a mean martini in the lively and chic bar. Business services are available. 31 Av. George-V, 8e (phone: 47-23-54-00; fax: 47-20-40-00).

Lancaster If location is everything, this charming 19th-century townhouse has it all: It's steps from the Champs-Elysées and two blocks from the Faubourg-St-Honoré. Admired by literati, dignitaries, socialites, Americans in the know, and even the haughtiest of Parisians, this Savoy Group establishment exudes an air of gentility, calm, and, above all, coziness. Aside from its handsome, 18th-century antiques and objets d'art, every one of its only 50 rooms and nine suites has individual charm. Try to book accommodations on the sixth (top) floor, where there's sure to be a view of the *Eiffel Tower, Sacré-Coeur,* or the hotel's delightful garden from a balcony or a terrace. There's an old-fashioned bar with garden murals, a delightful spot for taking mid-morning coffee, afternoon tea, or a post-prandial liqueur, and a relaxed and refined restaurant, with alfresco dining when the weather permits. If the pleasure of truly personal service and gracious surroundings with nary a glimmer of glitz are your preference, this is the place. Business services are available. 7 Rue de Berri, 8e (phone: 40-76-40-76; 800-223-6800; fax: 40-76-40-10).

Plaza-Athénée This European hotel is ever elegant and charming—from the 215 rooms and 41 suites done in Louis XV and XVI style to the *Relais Plaza* grill, where *tout Paris* seems to be eternally lunching, and the idyllic one-Michelin-star *Régence* restaurant, which is like a set for some Parisian *Mikado,* with its chirping birds, pools, and bridge. There's also the *Bar Anglais,* a classic Parisian spot for cocktails. A little more sedate and a little more French than the *George V* (above), this property is an haute bastion that takes its dignity very seriously (a discreet note in each bathroom offers an unobtrusive route in and out of the hotel for those in jogging togs). Business services are available. 25 Av. Montaigne, 8e (phone: 47-23-78-33; fax: 47-20-20-70).

Ritz The Rive Droite establishment that César Ritz made synonymous with all the finer things in life is such a Paris legend, that, seeing it for the first time, it's almost hard to believe it still exists, much less reigns as majestically as ever over the Place Vendôme. Marcel Proust wrote most of *Remembrance of Things Past* here, and Georges-Auguste Escoffier put France at the top of the culinary Olympus from its kitchen, still highly rated today as the two-Michelin-star *L'Espadon* restaurant. The *Ritz Club* is a nightclub and discotheque open to guests and club members only, and there's a deluxe spa. But even if you can't afford to stay in one of the 142 rooms or 45 suites, have a glass of champagne in the elegant bar. Business services are available. 15 Pl. Vendôme, 1er (phone: 42-60-38-30; fax: 42-60-23-71).

VERY EXPENSIVE

Grand Part of the Inter-Continental chain, this property has long been a favorite of Americans abroad, with its *Café de la Paix.* It has 545 rooms and luxurious suites, plus cheerful bars, two restaurants, and a prime location next to the *Opéra/Palais Garnier.* There is also a fitness center, and a wide range of business services is available. 2 Rue Scribe, 9e (phone: 40-07-32-32; 800-327-0200; fax: 42-66-12-51).

Inter-Continental The 452 rooms and suites have been meticulously restored to recreate turn-of-the-century elegance with modern conveniences. The cozy, top-floor Louis XVI "garret" rooms look out over the *Tuileries*. There's an American-style coffee shop, a grill, and a popular bar. Extensive business services are also offered. 3 Rue de Castiglione, 1er (phone: 44-77-11-11; fax: 44-77-14-60).

Lutétia With 286 rooms and 21 suites, this aristocrat of elegantly ornamented stone has reigned over the Rive Gauche since 1910. From gray-striped balloon awnings and bowers of sculpted stone flowers framing its arched windows to the regal red lobby appointed with crystal chandeliers, Art Deco skylights, and intricately carved wrought iron, this is a quintessentially Parisian place, with some of the most fantastic views in the city from its upper floors. The best perspective is from No. 71, whose balcony commands a view of nearly all of Paris's most famous monuments. There's also a restaurant, the one-Michelin-star *Le Paris,* and a brasserie. A range of business services is available. 45 Bd. Raspail, 6e (phone: 49-54-46-46; fax: 49-54-46-00).

Pont Royal Right in the midst of Paris's most exclusive antiques and shopping district, this former 18th-century *hôtel particulier* (private home) has been a well-kept secret. Each of the 73 spacious rooms and 10 suites is tastefully appointed with fine French antiques and sumptuous fabrics. The formal dining room, *Les Antiquaires,* serves first-rate fare, and business services are available. Closed for renovations at press time, the hotel was scheduled to reopen early this year. 7 Rue Montalembert, 7e (phone: 45-44-38-27; fax: 45-44-92-07).

Prince de Galles An excellent location (a next-door neighbor of the pricier *George V*) and impeccable style make this hostelry a good choice. All 169 rooms and suites are individually decorated and were renovated just last year. This Sheraton member has a restaurant and an oak-paneled bar, and parking and business services are available. 33 Av. George-V, 8e (phone: 47-23-55-11; 800-334-8484; fax: 47-20-96-92).

Raphaël Less well known among the top Paris hotels is this spacious, stately place, with a Turner in the lobby downstairs and paneling painted with sphinxes in the generous guestrooms. Its 87 rooms, including 38 suites, attract film folk and the like, and for those who savor strolling down the Champs-Elysées, it's only a short walk away. Most, but not all, of the rooms are air conditioned. There's a restaurant, and a wide range of business services is offered. 17 Av. Kléber, 16e (phone: 44-28-00-28; fax: 45-01-21-50).

Relais Carré d'Or For longer stays, this hostelry provides all the amenities of a luxury hotel, plus a variety of accommodations—from studios to multi-room apartments—all with modern kitchens, marble bathrooms, and lovely, understated furnishings. Most have balconies overlooking the hotel's garden or Avenue George-V. There's a restaurant, and extensive business services are available. 46 Av. George-V, 8e (phone: 40-70-05-05; fax: 47-23-30-90).

Royal Monceau This elegant, impeccably decorated 180-room, 39-suite hotel has three restaurants (one in an attractive garden setting), two bars, a fitness center, a pool, a Jacuzzi, and a beauty salon. The rooms are spacious, and the Sunday brunch is a delight. A range of business services also is offered. Not far from the *Arc de Triomphe,* at 37 Av. Hoche, 8e (phone: 45-61-98-00; fax: 45-63-28-93).

La Trémoille Built in 1886, this charming former *hôtel particulier* is a true gem. Each of the 110 spacious rooms is beautifully appointed. The atmosphere is one of understated elegance, and the location, just off Avenue Montaigne, a bonus. There's a restaurant, and business services are available. 14 Rue de la Trémoille, 8e (phone: 47-23-34-20; fax: 40-70-01-08).

EXPENSIVE

Abbaye St-Germain On a quiet street, this small, delightful place once was a convent. The lobby has exposed stone arches, and the 46 elegant rooms (we especially admire No. 4, whose doors open onto the charming courtyard) are furnished with antiques, tastefully selected fabrics, and marble baths; none is air conditioned. Unfortunately, there continue to be some complaints about the service. There's no restaurant. Some business services are available. 10 Rue Cassette, 6e (phone: 45-44-38-11; fax: 45-48-07-86).

Balzac Very private, this luxurious, charming hotel has 70 rooms and suites, plus the Paris branch of Milan's *Bice* restaurant. The nocturnally inclined can dance until dawn in the discotheque, and business services are available. Ideally located off the Champs-Elysées, at 6 Rue Balzac, 8e (phone: 45-61-97-22; fax: 45-25-24-82).

Colbert Each of the 34 rooms and two suites in this Rive Gauche hostelry has a balcony and a mini-bar, but no air conditioning. There's no restaurant, but breakfast is included. Limited business services are available. 7 Rue de l'Hôtel-Colbert, 5e (phone: 43-25-85-65; 800-755-9313; fax: 43-25-80-19).

Duc de St-Simon In two big townhouses in a beautiful, quiet backwater off the Boulevard St-Germain, this elegant 29-room, five-suite establishment veritably screams Proust. None of the rooms is air conditioned, and there's no restaurant. Some business services are available. No credit cards accepted. A five-minute walk from the *Musée d'Orsay,* at 14 Rue de St-Simon, 7e (phone: 45-48-35-66; fax: 45-48-68-25).

L'Hôtel Small but chic, this Rive Gauche hostelry is favored by experienced international travelers, and though it's growing a bit shabby around the edges, it still has great charm. It's also where Oscar Wilde died (room No. 16 is a re-creation of the room in which he lived briefly in 1900) and where the Argentinian writer Jorge Luis Borges lived. The 24 rooms and three suites are tiny, but beautifully appointed with antiques, fresh flowers, and marble baths; they also have mini-bars and safes. The attractive restaurant serves first-rate fare. Business services are available. 13 Rue des Beaux-Arts, 6e (phone: 43-25-27-22; fax: 43-25-64-81).

Jeu de Paume The architect-owner of this former tennis court has artfully married old and new in this addition to the Ile St-Louis's collection of exclusive hotels. High-tech lighting, modern artwork, and a sleek glass elevator are set against ancient ceiling beams and limestone brick hearths. Each of the comfortable 30 rooms and two suites overlooks the lovely garden; none is air conditioned. There is also a music salon, but no restaurant. Business services are available. 54 Rue St-Louis-en-l'Ile, 4e (phone: 43-26-14-18; fax: 40-46-02-76).

Méridien *Air France*'s modern, well-run hotel is American style, but with all the expected French flair. The 1,025 rooms are on the small side, but they're tastefully decorated, quiet, and boast good views. There are four attractive restaurants (one, *Le Clos Longchamp,* has a Michelin star, while another serves Japanese fare), a shopping arcade, three lively bars, and a chic nightclub, *L'Ecume des Nuits.* Business services are available. 81 Bd. Gouvion-St-Cyr, 17e (phone: 40-68-34-34; fax: 40-68-31-31).

Méridien Montparnasse With 952 rooms, this ultramodern giant has a futuristic lobby, efficient service, a coffee shop, two bars, the one-Michelin-star *Montparnasse 25* restaurant, and in summer, a garden restaurant. There is also an excellent, ample Sunday brunch. A full range of business services is available. In the heart of Montparnasse, at 19 Rue du Commandant-René-Mouchotte, 14e (phone: 44-36-44-36; fax: 44-36-49-00).

Meurice Refined Louis XV and XVI elegance and a wide range of services are offered for a franc or two less than at the other "palaces." The hotel, a member of the CIGA chain, has 179 rooms and 35 especially nice suites, a popular bar, the one-Michelin-star restaurant *Le Meurice* overlooking the Rue de Rivoli, and a chandeliered tearoom. Business services are available. Ideally located at 228 Rue de Rivoli, 1er (phone: 44-58-10-10; fax: 44-58-10-15).

Montaigne This unpretentious establishment is a true find. Each of its 29 rooms is comfortable, clean, and chicly decorated. There's a bar and a breakfast room, but no restaurant. 6 Av. Montaigne, 8e (phone: 47-20-30-50; fax: 47-20-94-12).

Montalembert Privacy is the hallmark of this exquisite little place, whose 56 rooms and suites are available in two styles—traditional, with restored period armoires and sleigh beds, or contemporary, with straight geometric lines and fireplaces. (If you're over six feet tall, ask for one of the modern rooms—the beds are longer.) Bathrooms are small, but high-tech. The hotel's *Le Montalembert* restaurant, which replaced *L'Arpège,* serves delicious fare;

there's also a cozy bar, and business services are available. On the Rive Gauche at 3 Rue Montalembert, 7e (phone: 45-48-68-11; 800-628-8929; fax: 42-22-58-19).

Le Parc Victor Hugo A sumptuous 122-room hotel, decorated in the style of an English country house, it features a large interior garden. Its excellent restaurant was set up by super-chef Joël Robuchon, whose own three-Michelin-star, self-named establishment (see *Eating Out*) is next door. Business services are available. 55 Av. Raymond-Poincaré, 16e (phone: 44-05-66-66; fax: 44-05-66-00).

Paris Hilton International Of the 455 modern rooms here, those facing the river have the best views. *Le Western* serves American staples like T-bone steaks, apple pie à la mode, and brownies (mostly to French diners), and the coffee shop is a magnet for homesick Americans. Complete business services are available. A few steps from the *Eiffel Tower,* at 18 Av. de Suffren, 15e (phone: 42-73-92-00; 800-932-3322; fax: 47-83-62-66).

Pavillon de la Reine Under the same ownership as the *Relais Christine* (see below), the Marais's only luxury hotel is similarly appointed. It's blessed with a supreme location on the elegant Place des Vosges, and the 55 rooms (most are on the small side) look out on a garden or courtyard. There's no restaurant. Some business services are available. 28 Pl. des Vosges, 3e (phone: 42-77-96-40; fax: 42-77-63-06).

Régina This hotel's 116 rooms and 14 suites are spacious and furnished with antiques. The restaurant has a lovely garden, and there's also a bar and a small fitness center. Business services are available. Centrally located, overlooking the *Louvre* and the *Tuileries,* at 2 Pl. des Pyramides, 1er (phone: 42-60-31-10; fax: 40-15-95-16).

Relais Christine Formerly a 16th-century cloister, this lovely place boasts 34 rooms and 17 suites with modern fixtures and lots of old-fashioned charm. Ask for a room with a courtyard or garden view; the suites and the ground-floor room with a private *terrasse* are particularly luxurious. There's no restaurant. Some business services are offered. 3 Rue Christine, 6e (phone: 43-26-71-80; fax: 43-26-89-38).

Relais Médicis With the same owners as the *Relais Saint-Germain* (see below), this elegant 16-room establishment in an 18th-century building boasts marble bathrooms and beamed ceilings. There's no restaurant. 23 Rue Racine, 6e (phone: 43-26-00-60; fax: 40-46-83-39).

Relais Saint-Germain In a 17th-century building, this hostelry with 19 guestrooms and one suite is ideally situated on the Rive Gauche, just steps from the Boulevard St-Germain and the area's best shops, eateries, and galleries. It is attractively decorated, and charming down to its massive ceiling beams and huge flower bouquets. A rare find. There's a breakfast parlor, but no restaurant. 9 Carrefour de l'Odéon, 6e (phone: 43-29-12-05; fax: 46-33-45-30).

Résidence Maxim's No expense has been spared to create sybaritic splendor in Pierre Cardin's luxurious venture, a distinguished favorite of the rich and famous. Its clever decor combines modern statuary with Belle Epoque appointments. There are 37 suites and four rooms, as well as a classic lobby, a secluded bar (*Le Maximin,* open late), and a world class restaurant. Complete business services are available. Near the Champs-Elysées and the *Palais de l'Elysée,* at 42 Av. Gabriel, 8e (phone: 45-61-96-33; fax: 42-89-06-07).

Résidence du Roy This establishment offers 36 self-contained studios, suites, and duplexes, complete with kitchen facilities. There's no restaurant, but business services are available. Within easy reach of the Champs-Elysées, at 8 Rue François-Ier, 8e (phone: 42-89-59-59; fax: 40-74-07-92).

St. James Paris Like something out of an Evelyn Waugh novel, this secluded 19th-century château—with 17 rooms and 31 suites, a walled courtyard and fountain, a library bar, a fitness center, an elegant restaurant overlooking a rose garden, and a more relaxed grill—gives one a sense of being a guest at an English country estate. Though the place is billed as a private club, hotel guests are welcome to stay after paying a temporary membership fee of about $10. (Non-members not staying at the hotel, however, may not dine or sip cocktails here.) Business services are available. A stroll from the *Bois de Boulogne,* at 5 Pl. Chancelier-Adenauer, 16e (phone: 47-04-29-29; 212-956-0200 in New York City; fax: 45-53-00-61; 212-956-2555 in the US).

San Régis Guests are made to feel at home at this elegant place with a comfortable ambience. There are 34 rooms and 10 suites, all beautifully appointed, as well as a restaurant and bar. Business services are available. 12 Rue Jean-Goujon, 8e (phone: 44-95-16-16; fax: 45-61-05-48).

Sofitel CNIT La Défense The city's sights and pleasures are easily reached from this modern luxury hotel in suburban La Défense. The 147 rooms and six suites are outfitted with mini-bars and other up-to-date amenities. There's also a shopping arcade, a bar, and the one-Michelin-star restaurant, *Les Communautés.* Business services are available. Steps away from the *Centre National des Industries et des Techniques* (*CNIT;* National Center for Industry and Technology) and the *Grande Arche,* at 2 Pl. de la Défense, La Défense (phone: 46-92-10-10; 800-763-4835; fax: 46-92-10-50).

Le Stendhal Named for the famous novelist who died here, this luxurious hostelry's 21 rooms feature antiques, Jacuzzis, and mini-bars. The suites are particularly charming—especially Nos. 52 and 53. There's a cozy bar, but no restaurant. Near the Place Vendôme, at 22 Rue Danielle-Casanova, 2e (phone: 44-58-52-52; fax: 44-58-52-00).

Tuileries With a good location in a "real" neighborhood in the heart of the city, this 26-room, four-suite hotel has a well-tended look and attractive, carved wood bedsteads. All the rooms have mini-bars and safes. There's no restaurant. This is also one of the few Parisian members of the Relais de Silence, an association of hotels that meet requirements for being especially quiet. 10 Rue St-Hyacinthe, 1er (phone: 42-61-04-17 or 42-61-06-94; fax: 49-27-91-56).

Le Vernet Guests staying in the 60 modern rooms and three suites here have complimentary access to the fitness center at the elegant *Royal Monceau* (see above), its sister establishment. There's an excellent restaurant, the one-Michelin-star *Les Elysées,* and business services are available. A few steps from the *Arc de Triomphe,* at 25 Rue Vernet, 8e (phone: 44-31-98-00; fax: 44-31-85-69).

De Vigny A small, elegant 25-room, 12-suite Relais & Châteaux member, it features lots of mahogany and chintz. Suite 504 has its own stairway leading to a glass-roofed *salon* with a spectacular view. There's a bar, but no restaurant; this is one of the few hotels in the neighborhood where nonsmoking rooms and parking are available. 9 Rue Balzac, 8e (phone: 40-75-04-39; fax: 40-75-05-81).

Westminster This establishment, which in recent years has regained some of its lost luster, has a traditional decor complete with wood paneling, marble fireplaces, and parquet floors. Some of the 101 rooms (including 16 suites) overlook the street; others look down into an inner courtyard. There's also a one-Michelin-star restaurant, *Le Céladon,* and a bar. Business services are available. Between the *Opéra/Palais Garnier* and the *Ritz,* at 13 Rue de la Paix, 2e (phone: 42-61-57-46; fax: 42-60-30-66).

MODERATE

Angleterre Its 29 classic, unpretentious rooms and one suite (none with air conditioning) are in what was the British Embassy in the 18th century; the building is now a national monument. There's no restaurant. Some business services are offered. 44 Rue Jacob, 6e (phone: 42-60-34-72; fax: 42-60-16-93).

Bretonnerie This restored, 17th-century townhouse with 28 rooms and one suite (none air conditioned) takes itself seriously, with dark wood furnishings and several beamed attic rooms that overlook the narrow streets of the fashionable Marais area. There's no restaurant. 22 Rue Ste-Croix-de-la-Bretonnerie, 4e (phone: 48-87-77-63; fax: 42-77-26-78).

Britannique A Quaker mission house during World War I, this friendly hotel now offers 40 rooms, all equipped with mini-bars, hair dryers, and satellite TV, but not air conditioning. There's no restaurant. Within minutes of the *Louvre* and *Notre-Dame,* at 20 Av. Victoria, 1er (phone: 42-33-74-59; 800-755-9313; fax: 42-33-82-65).

Danube St-Germain The 40 rooms and six elegant suites, all with four-poster bamboo beds, are comfortable, and some of them overlook an attractive courtyard typical of the Rive Gauche. None of the rooms is air conditioned, and 10 lower-priced rooms have baths, but shared toilets and no TV sets. There's no restaurant. Some business facilities are available. American Express only accepted. 58 Rue Jacob, 6e (phone: 42-60-34-70; fax: 42-60-81-18).

Deux Continents The cozy red sitting room of this quiet, 40-room establishment on the Rive Gauche looks invitingly onto the street. Eleven of the rooms are air conditioned. There's no restaurant. 25 Rue Jacob, 6e (phone: 43-26-72-46).

Deux Iles On the historic Ile St-Louis, this beautifully restored 17th-century house has a garden with a Portuguese fountain, but no restaurant. Though small, the 17 rooms are nicely decorated with French provincial fabrics and Louis XIV ceramic tiles in the bathrooms; none is air conditioned. Limited business services are available. No credit cards accepted. 59 Rue St-Louis-en-l'Ile, 4e (phone: 43-26-13-35; fax: 43-29-60-25).

Duminy-Vendôme This 19th-century building has been completely renovated and decorated in 1920s style. There's no restaurant, but the 79 rooms are comfortable, with such amenities as mini-bars and hairdryers, though no air conditioning. Business services are available. In a centrally located neighborhood, near the Place Vendôme, at 3 Rue du Mont Tabor, 1er (phone: 42-60-32-80; fax: 42-96-07-63).

Ferrandi This no-frills hostelry with a winding wood staircase and a quiet lounge is popular with international business travelers. The 41 rooms and one suite (none air conditioned) have antique furnishings. There's no restaurant. 92 Rue du Cherche-Midi, 6e (phone: 42-22-97-40; fax: 45-44-89-97).

Fleurie This lovely, family-run hotel in a former 18th-century townhouse has 29 well-equipped rooms with mini-bars and safes. The service is friendly, and there's a bar, but no restaurant. 32-24 Rue Grégoire-de-Tours, 6e (phone: 43-29-59-81; fax: 43-29-68-44).

Grand Hôtel de l'Univers Modern and tucked away on a quiet street, this hotel has 34 rooms, all with mini-bars and safes. There's no restaurant. Near St-Germain-des-Prés and the Quartier Latin, at 6 Rue Grégoire-de-Tours, 6e (phone: 43-29-37-00; fax: 40-51-06-45).

Grandes Ecoles This is the sort of place that people recommend only to the right friends (even the proprietress wants to keep it a secret). Insulated from the street by a delightful courtyard and garden, it is a simple 19th-century private house that's long on atmosphere even though the 48 rooms offer plain comforts (they lack air conditioning and TV sets, and some do not have private baths). There aren't many like it in Paris, but beware: Booking is difficult, and the owner has been known to give away reserved rooms.

There's no restaurant. 75 Rue Cardinal-Lemoine, 5e (phone: 43-26-79-23; fax: 43-25-28-15).

Le Jardin des Plantes In addition to a magnificent setting across from Paris's botanical gardens, this hotel offers 33 airy rooms with mini-bars and hair dryers, some with safes; some also have alcoves large enough for extra beds for children. None of the rooms is air conditioned. Art exhibits and classical music concerts are held on Sundays in the vaulted cellar. There's also a sauna in the basement, but no restaurant. 5 Rue Linné, 5e (phone: 47-07-06-20; fax: 47-07-62-74).

Lenox St-Germain Small and tastefully done, this hotel has 32 rooms (none air conditioned) and a cozy bar, but no restaurant. It's popular with the fashion crowd. Between the busy St-Germain area and the boutiques nearby, at 9 Rue de l'Université, 7e (phone: 42-96-10-95; fax: 42-61-52-83).

Lord Byron On a quiet street off the Champs-Elysées, it has a pleasant courtyard and 31 comfortable, homey rooms (none is air conditioned). The staff is friendly and speaks good English. There's no restaurant. 5 Rue de Chateaubriand, 8e (phone: 43-59-89-98; fax: 42-89-46-04).

Lutèce Here are 23 smallish, but luxurious rooms (one split-level; none air conditioned) on the charming Ile St-Louis. The decor is positively ravishing, with exquisite toile fabric and wallpaper and raw wood beams. There's no restaurant. No credit cards accepted. 65 Rue St-Louis-en-l'Ile, 4e (phone: 43-26-23-52; fax: 43-29-60-25).

Madison This place offers 55 large, bright rooms, with such amenities as mini-bars and safes; some have balconies. There's no restaurant. 143 Bd. St-Germain, 6e (phone: 40-51-60-00; fax: 40-51-60-01).

Des Marroniers An excellent location in the heart of the Rive Gauche makes this 37-room hotel a real bargain. The rooms are not air conditioned. There's a garden courtyard and pretty breakfast room, but no restaurant. No credit cards accepted. 21 Rue Jacob, 6e (phone: 43-25-30-60; fax: 40-46-83-56).

Novanox This 27-room hotel is ultramodern, with high-tech furniture, but it offers old-fashioned extras such as brioches for breakfast, served on an outdoor terrace. All the rooms have mini-bars and safes, but no air conditioning. There's a bar, but no restaurant. Service is exceptionally friendly. 155 Bd. du Montparnasse, 6e (phone: 46-33-63-60; fax: 43-26-61-72).

Odéon Small (29 rooms), modernized, and charming, it's in the heart of the St-Germain area on the Rive Gauche. There's no restaurant. 13 Rue de St-Sulpice, 6e (phone: 43-25-70-11; fax: 43-29-97-34).

Parc St-Séverin An interesting little hotel on the Rive Gauche, it has 27 rooms (none air conditioned), including a top-floor penthouse with a wraparound balcony. The decor is modern but understated, and the overall ambience is appealing, even though the neighborhood is not the quietest in Paris. There's no restaurant. 22 Rue de la Parcheminerie, 5e (phone: 43-54-32-17; fax: 43-54-70-71).

Pavillon Bastille There's a 17th-century fountain in the courtyard of this small, 19th-century *hôtel particulier.* The 24 smallish rooms and one suite are all cheerfully decorated in contemporary style and equipped with mini-bars. There's a bar and a breakfast room, but no restaurant. Conveniently located near the Place de la Bastille, at 65 Rue de Lyon, 12e (phone: 43-43-65-65; fax: 43-43-96-52).

Perreyve This quiet, 30-room hotel with understated, traditional decor is ideally located near the *Jardin du Luxembourg.* There's no restaurant. 63 Rue Madame, 6e (phone: 45-48-35-01; fax: 42-84-03-30).

Pierre et Vacances In a sleepy corner of Montmartre, this residential hotel charges nightly, weekly, and monthly rates. The apartments have kitchens, and some overlook a peaceful garden; none is air conditioned. There's no restaurant. Near the leafy square of the *Théâtre de l'Atelier,* at 10 Pl. Charles-Dullin, 18e (phone: 42-57-14-55; fax: 42-54-48-87).

Récamier An amazing bargain for those who manage to reserve a room, this is a simple, clean, and very peaceful 30-room hotel. The rooms are not air conditioned and have no TV sets; eight share baths (though all have private toilet facilities). There's no restaurant. 3 *bis* Pl. St-Sulpice, 6e (phone: 43-26-04-89).

Regent's Garden This small hotel has 39 spacious rooms, some with large marble fireplaces, and three suites; none of the accommodations is air conditioned, but all have amenities such as mini-bars and hair dryers. A country atmosphere pervades, and the young hoteliers who run the place make guests feel completely at home. There's also a garden and parking, but no restaurant. On a quiet street near the *Arc de Triomphe,* at 6 Rue Pierre-Demours, 17e (phone: 45-74-07-30; fax: 40-55-01-42).

Royal Saint-Honoré Newly renovated, the 68-room, seven-suite hotel is one of the city's best values for this prime location. Some rooms have terraces overlooking the *Jardin des Tuileries.* There's no restaurant, but business services are available. 221 Rue Saint-Honoré, 1er (phone: 42-60-32-79; fax: 42-60-47-44).

St-Germain-des-Prés In the heart of one of Paris's loveliest districts, this comfortable 30-room hotel is a good bargain. Request a room on the courtyard, as the street can be noisy. There's no restaurant. 36 Rue Bonaparte, 6e (phone: 43-26-00-19; fax: 40-46-83-63).

Le St-Grégoire A small 18th-century mansion on the Rive Gauche, this hostelry has an intimate, cozy atmosphere, a warm fire in the hearth, and 19 tastefully furnished rooms and one suite. Two of the rooms have terraces overlooking a garden, and only two of the rooms are air conditioned. There's no restaurant. 43 Rue de l'Abbé-Grégoire, 6e (phone: 45-48-23-23; fax: 45-48-33-95).

St-Louis Marais This tiny hotel is a short walk from the Place des Vosges, the quays along the Seine, and the Bastille-quarter nightclubs. Dating from the 18th century, when it was part of the Celestine Convent, it has 15 small rooms with safes and hair dryers (none has a TV set or air conditioning). There's no restaurant, and historical landmark status has barred the installation of an elevator. On a quiet residential street on the edge of the chic Marais district, at 1 Rue Charles-V, 4e (phone: 48-87-87-04; fax: 48-87-33-26).

Sofitel Porte de Sèvres Located in southwest Paris, this modern luxury hotel features 635 comfortably furnished rooms with all the conveniences (such as mini-bars). There's also a glass-enclosed fitness center and pool with marvelous views, the one-Michelin-star *Relais de Sèvres* restaurant, a brasserie, jazz bar, and even a movie theater. Business services are available. Right by the *Parc des Expositions,* at the Porte de Versailles, 8 Rue Louis-Armand, 15e (phone: 40-60-33-11; 800-763-4835; fax: 45-57-04-22).

Solférino A cozy place with Oriental rugs scattered about. The 34 tiny rooms have floral wallpaper; none has air conditioning or a TV set. There's a plant-filled breakfast and sitting room, but no restaurant. 91 Rue de Lille, 7e (phone: 47-05-85-54; fax: 45-55-51-16).

Suède A delightful hotel in a quiet area, just around the corner from the prime minister's residence. All 40 rooms and one suite are beautifully appointed (none has air conditioning or a TV set); those overlooking the garden are smaller but much prettier. There's no restaurant, but breakfast is served in a simple salon or, in good weather, in the beautiful courtyard. 31 Rue Vaneau, 7e (phone: 47-05-18-65; fax: 47-05-69-27).

Villa des Artistes Quiet luxury is the drawing card of this popular Quartier Latin hotel, with 59 rooms and its own patio-garden. There's no restaurant. 9 Rue de la Grande-Chaumière, 6e (phone: 43-26-60-86; fax: 43-54-73-70).

INEXPENSIVE

Caron de Beaumarchais Named after the 18th-century playwright who once lived on this street, this elegant, new hotel in the Marais has 19 rooms, all with fax lines, cable TV, safes, and mini-bars, and some with small balconies. There's a breakfast room that opens onto a small garden, but no restaurant. 12 Rue Vieille-du-Temple, 4e (phone: 42-72-34-12; fax: 42-72-34-63).

Delavigne With a good location (down the street from the *Odéon* theater) and an enlightened manager who says he isn't interested in simply handing out keys, but enjoys introducing foreigners to Paris, this 34-room hotel is a good value. None of the rooms is air conditioned. There's no restaurant. 1 Rue Casimir-Delavigne, 6e (phone: 43-29-31-50; fax: 43-29-78-56).

Deux Avenues A quiet, 32-room hotel offering friendly service, near a lively street market. None of the rooms is air conditioned; most don't have TV sets. Some rooms do not have private baths. There's no restaurant. 38 Rue Poncelet, 17e (phone: 42-27-44-35; fax: 47-63-95-48).

Esmeralda Some of this hotel's 19 rooms look directly at *Notre-Dame* over the gardens of *Eglise St-Julien-le-Pauvre,* one of Paris's oldest churches. The oak beams and furniture enhance the medieval atmosphere. Don't look for air conditioning or TV sets here, though the rooms do have safes and hair dryers, and all but three have private baths. Small and friendly, it's especially popular with the theatrical crowd. There's no restaurant. No credit cards accepted. 4 Rue St-Julien-le-Pauvre, 5e (phone: 43-54-19-20; fax: 40-51-00-68).

Jeanne d'Arc This little place doesn't get top marks for decor, and its facilities are simple, but somehow word of its appeal has spread from Minnesota to Melbourne. It's well placed, near the Place des Vosges, and the management is friendly. There's no restaurant. On a quiet street in the Marais, at 3 Rue de Jarente, 4e (phone: 48-87-62-11; fax: 48-87-37-31).

Marais Ideal for families traveling with children, this simple, 39-room hotel with friendly management has several connecting rooms available. None of the rooms is air conditioned. There's no restaurant. Near the Bastille, at 2 *bis* Rue Commines, 3e (phone: 48-87-78-27; fax: 48-87-09-01).

Oriental This simple but comfortable 32-room hotel is near *Notre-Dame.* There's no restaurant. 2 Rue d'Arras, 5e (phone: 43-54-38-12; fax: 40-51-86-78).

Prima-Lepic The cheerful young owners have decorated the 38 rooms in this Montmartre hotel with pretty floral wallpapers and one-of-a-kind furnishings—a wicker chair, a mirrored armoire, a 1930s lamp (no air conditioning, though). No. 56, on the top floor, looks out over Paris, and travelers with children should make special note of room No. 2, which connects to an adjoining room. The public spaces are charming, too. There's no restaurant. 29 Rue Lepic, 18e (phone: 46-06-44-64; fax: 46-06-66-11).

Le Vieux Marais This agreeable Marais hostelry has 30 pretty, if not very large, rooms; none is air conditioned. The breakfast room (there's no restaurant) has an impressive wall-size engraving of the Place des Vosges, which is not far away. Near the *Centre Georges-Pompidou,* at 8 Rue du Plâtre, 4e (phone: 42-78-47-22; fax: 42-78-34-32).

Welcome Overlooking the Boulevard St-Germain, it's simple but comfortable. There are 30 rooms; those on the street are relatively noisy, in spite of double windows, and none is air conditioned. The sixth floor garret rooms are very romantic, with great views. There's no restaurant. No credit cards accepted. 66 Rue de Seine, 6e (phone: 46-34-24-80; fax: 40-46-81-59).

EATING OUT

Paris considers itself the culinary capital of the world, and you will never forget food for long here. Whether you grab a fresh croissant and café au lait for breakfast or splurge on an epicurean fantasy for dinner, this is the city in which to indulge all your gastronomic dreams. Remember, too, that there is no such thing as "French" food; rather, Paris is a gastronomic mosaic, where one can try cuisines from Provence, Alsace, Normandy, Brittany, and other regions.

For a dinner for two, including service, but not wine, a very expensive restaurant will charge $250 or more; an expensive one, $150 to $250; a moderate place $100 to $150; an inexpensive restaurant, $50 to $100; and a very inexpensive one, $50 or less. A service charge of 15% usually is included in the bill, but it's customary to leave a small additional tip for good service. Street addresses of the restaurants below are followed by their *arrondissement* number. Unless otherwise noted, all restaurants listed below are open for lunch and dinner.

Although the city of Paris has passed a law requiring that all restaurants provide nonsmoking areas, nonsmokers can't claim victory yet. The general dearth of space in Paris restaurants, combined with the large numbers of French people who smoke (around 80% of the population, according to one recent survey), means that nonsmokers are still rarely seated very far from a smoker. And, what's more, compliance with the law is erratic: Ask restaurateurs in Paris about what is known there as the law *"à l'Américaine,"* and most will just laugh!

REMEMBER, CALL AHEAD

To save frustration and embarrassment, always *reconfirm* dinner reservations before noon on the appointed day. Also remember that some of the better restaurants do not accept credit cards, and many close over the weekend, as well as for part or all of July or August. It's best to check ahead on these matters to avoid disappointment at the restaurant of your choice. It's also worth remembering that many restaurants offer special lunch menus at considerably lower prices.

For an unforgettable culinary experience, we begin with our Paris favorites, followed by our cost and quality choices listed by price category.

HAUTE GASTRONOMIE

L'Ambroisie Promoted to three-star status by Michelin in 1988, this elegant establishment is the showcase for Bernard Pacaud's equally elegant cuisine. The menu is limited to only a few sublime entrées, such as a fresh truffle in puff pastry, rack of Pauillac lamb in a truffle crust, and *crème de homard aux Saint-Jacques* (lobster with sea scallops in a cream sauce). Closed Sundays, Mondays, two weeks in February, and the first three weeks in August. Reservations necessary. Major credit cards accepted. 9 Pl. des Vosges, 4e (phone: 42-78-51-45).

Amphyclès A former sous-chef of Joël Robuchon (see below), Philippe Groult prepares fine contemporary cuisine, which bears both bourgeois and southern French influences. There are splendid creamy soups, lamb stew with rosemary, lobster salad with sweet red peppers, and a rock lobster risotto. If the brightly lit modern decor of his small two-Michelin-star establishment is forgettably neutral, the food is unquestionably memorable. Closed Saturday lunch, Sundays, and most of July. Reservations necessary. Major credit cards accepted. Near the Place des Ternes, at 78 Av. des Ternes, 17e (phone: 40-68-01-01; fax: 40-68-91-88).

L'Arpège The minimalist decor of this two-Michelin-star establishment belies the succulent, generous cuisine prepared by Alain Passard. Peppery tuna filet, veal sweatbreads with rosemary, and lemon soufflé flavored with cloves are just a few of the possibilities. The prix fixe lunch menu is a relative bargain. Closed Saturdays and Sunday lunch. Reservations necessary. Major credit cards accepted. 84 Rue de Varenne, 7e (phone: 45-51-47-33; fax: 44-18-98-39).

Guy Savoy In spite of the fact that he now operates several bistros throughout Paris (see *La Butte Chaillot* and *Le Bistrot de l'Etoile-Lauriston,* below), Savoy, unlike many globe-trotting celebrity chefs, still mans the kitchen at his handsome, two-Michelin-star restaurant. The menu is small and constantly changing, with such recent successes as a peppery, jellied duck foie gras served with celery-root purée, and *volaille confite et laquée au vinaigre* (chicken stewed in and glazed with vinegar). Inventive desserts (which may be ordered in half portions) include a grapefruit terrine with tea-flavored sauce. There had been some complaints about the high prices, some disappointing dishes, and chilly service, but the restaurant seems to be back on track now. Closed weekends and most of August. Reservations necessary. Major credit cards accepted. 18 Rue Troyon, 17e (phone: 43-80-40-61; fax: 46-22-43-09).

Joël Robuchon A legend in his own time, Joël Robuchon is already ranked in France among the greatest chefs of any era, alongside Taillevent, Carême, and Escoffier. Robuchon's revolutionary cuisine, which he calls *moderne,* is neither traditional French nor nouvelle cuisine, but a happy medium. Like nouvelle cuisine, Robuchon's creations are lighter than traditional recipes, employing less butter and cream. They're based on intense reductions of vegetable, fish, and meat essences, as well as highly flavored, typically French ingredients such as truffles (a Robuchon favorite—the finest available pop up frequently in his signature dishes). But Robuchon also favors earthy, bistro-style ingredients that would never find their way onto the usual nouvelle cuisine menu. Mere words can't do justice to menu offerings such as *gratin de macaroni aux truffes et foie gras* (macaroni with truffles and foie gras), and *langouste rôtie au cumin et au romarin* (roast rock lobster with cumin and rosemary), served topped with aged Parmesan and chopped fresh truffles. Robuchon's three-Michelin-star restaurant now goes by his name (it was formerly *Jamin*) and has a new locale, in a turn-of-the-century townhouse with the warm feel of a Victorian British country estate. Robuchon has said he'll retire in 1996 (at the ripe old age of 50), depriving the world of his genius, so now is the time to experience it. Closed weekends and the month of July. Reservations necessary far in advance. Major credit cards accepted. 55 Av. Raymond-Poincaré, 16e (phone: 47-27-12-27).

Lasserre The waiters are in tails, the ceiling glides open to reveal the stars, the decanted burgundy is poured over the flame of a candle to detect sediment, and the impeccable service makes diners feel that somehow they deserve all this. The two-Michelin-star cuisine—heavy on foie gras, caviar, truffles, and rich sauces—is traditional French at its most heavenly, and the wine cellar is a virtual museum of French oenology. Not surprisingly, making dinner reservations here is akin to booking seats for a sold-out Broadway musical, so think way ahead. Closed Sundays, Monday lunch, and the month of August. Reservations necessary. Major credit cards accepted. 17 Av. Franklin-Roosevelt, 8e (phone: 43-59-53-43; fax: 45-63-72-23).

Lucas-Carton This lush, plush Belle Epoque dining room, under the watchful eye of chef/owner Alain Senderens, is the place to sample a few bites of truffle salad, lobster with vanilla, or anything else on the ever-changing menu. Diners also have the opportunity to order each course with a perfectly matched glass of wine. Senderens' quirky and innovative cooking combines many tenets of nouvelle cuisine with Asian influences, and Michelin lost no time in awarding it three stars. The utensils and serving pieces are almost as alluring as the food. The prix fixe lunch menu is a good value. Closed weekends, most of August, and December 24 through January 3. Reservations necessary. Major credit cards accepted. 9 Pl. de la Madeleine, 8e (phone: 42-65-22-90; fax: 42-65-06-23).

Michel Rostang Rostang seems to be at the top of his form these days, with an inventive repertoire that takes its inspiration mainly from the cuisine of Savoie, Lyons, and Provence. The restaurant has two dining rooms, one of which has a large glass wall overlooking the kitchen. Specialties include *oeufs de caille en coque d'oursin* (quail's eggs in a sea urchin shell), *feuilleté de canard et foie gras au chou rouge* (duck and foie gras in puff pastry with a red cabbage sauce), and Scottish salmon with sesame seeds and artichokes. Desserts include warm chocolate tart, and pears roasted in sauternes. Closed Saturday lunch, Sundays, and the first two weeks of August. Reservations necessary. Major credit cards accepted. 20 Rue Rennequin, 17e (phone: 47-63-40-77; fax: 47-63-82-75).

Taillevent Named after a famed medieval chef, this three-Michelin-star dining room occupies a distinguished 19th-century mansion complete with fine paintings, porcelain dinnerware, and aristocratic decor, making it look as if the French Revolution was really just a bad dream. Longtime chef Claude Deligne has retired, but the traditions he established and many of his recipes are being kept alive by Philippe Legendre, who also has added new items to the menu. The rabbit in pastry with spinach and *sarriette* (summer savory), the sea-urchin mousse, and the many stunning desserts are sure to please, while the wine list is one of the city's best and most reasonably priced. One of the hardest-to-get restaurant reservations in France—but do try. Closed weekends, part of February, and most of August. Reservations necessary. Major credit cards accepted. 15 Rue Lamennais, 8e (phone: 45-61-12-90; fax: 42-25-95-18).

La Tour d'Argent For many, this place is touristy, overrated, and overpriced, but Paris's senior three-Michelin-star restaurant continues to amaze and entertain with its cuisine and the most romantic view of any restaurant in the city. The gold-toned room brings to mind Cole Porter's "elegant, swellegant party"; in fact, Porter occasionally dined here, as have a host of other luminaries, from Franklin Roosevelt to Paul McCartney, Greta Garbo to the Aga Khan. The specialty is a Charente duck pressed at tableside just as it was a century ago; also not to be missed are the classic quenelles in mornay sauce with fresh black truffles. The spectacular wine list is one of France's best. Because it has a reservations book thicker than the Manhattan telephone directory, it's often impossible to get dinner reservations at certain times of the year. Best tip: Book a windowside table for lunch on a weekday, when there's a prix fixe menu; the view of *Notre-Dame* and the Seine is just as splendid by daylight. Closed Mondays. Reservations necessary. Major credit cards accepted. 15 Quai de la Tournelle, 5e (phone: 43-54-23-31; fax: 44-07-12-04).

Vivarois Claude Peyrot is unquestionably one of France's finest chefs. His small, elegant establishment features *la cuisine du marché,* meaning that offerings vary according to what is available at the market. A splendid grilled turbot with capers is usually on the menu. Michelin has awarded it two stars. Closed weekends and the month of August. Reservations necessary. Major credit cards accepted. 192 Av. Victor-Hugo, 16e (phone: 45-04-04-31; fax: 45-03-09-84).

VERY EXPENSIVE

Les Ambassadeurs A two-Michelin-star establishment that offers a soul-satisfying meal gracefully presented in an elegant dining room with 20-foot-high ceilings, massive crystal chandeliers, and stunning views of the Place de la Concorde. Delicious dishes such as *gratin dauphinois de homard avec crème au caviar* (potatoes au gratin with lobster in caviar sauce) and veal sweetbreads in a light wine sauce are perfectly complemented by one of the exceptional wines from the *cave.* The prix fixe lunch menu is a good value. Open daily. Reservations necessary. Major credit cards accepted. In the *Crillon Hotel,* 10 Pl. de la Concorde, 8e (phone: 44-71-16-16; fax: 44-71-15-02).

L'Ami Louis The archetypal Parisian bistro, small and charmingly unassuming, but with huge portions of generally marvelous, if extremely expensive food (though these days the place seems to be coasting on its reputation and its appealing ambience). Specialties include foie gras, roast chicken, spring lamb, ham, and burgundy wines. A favorite among Americans, this is the place to sample authentic French fries. Closed Mondays, Tuesdays, and most of July and August. Reservations necessary. Major credit cards accepted. 32 Rue de Vertbois, 3e (phone: 48-87-77-48).

Le Grand Véfour Established in 1760 in the stately courtyard of the *Palais-Royal,* this restaurant has rich carpets and mirrors framed by ornate frescoes, and the choice, two-Michelin-star dishes are named for dignitaries who have discussed affairs of state here since the time of Robespierre. These delectable dishes, such as crayfish with olive oil and spices, or potato-truffle terrine, are every bit as enthralling as the restaurant's rich history. In honor of both, men still are required to wear jacket and tie. The prix fixe lunch menu is a good value. Closed Saturday lunch, Sundays, and the month of August. Reservations necessary. Major credit cards accepted. 17 Rue de Beaujolais, 1er (phone: 42-96-56-27; fax: 42-86-80-71).

Laurent This *grand luxe* restaurant has regained its former glory under Philippe Braun, who trained with super-chef Joël Robuchon. The finest products are cooked to perfection—the freshest fish served with rare morel mushrooms, and game in season—and the wine list is one of Paris's best. Closed Saturday lunch, Sundays, and part of August. Reservations necessary. Major credit cards accepted. Near the Champs-Elysées, at 41 Av. Gabriel, 8e (phone: 42-25-00-39; fax: 45-62-45-21).

Maxim's Paris's most celebrated Belle Epoque restaurant was a century old in 1991; unfortunately, it has seen better days—it's now often half empty, with a façade that could use a face-lift. In fact, there are rumors that owner Pierre Cardin may be thinking of selling. But, with scenes like tableaux from Colette around its elegant salons, Maxim's will always be Maxim's, and with care could recapture its past glory. The service is impeccable, with excellent sommeliers to help with the extensive and intelligent wine list. The food is sometimes surprisingly good; try the *Challans canard aux cerises* (Challans duck with cherries). Fridays remain a strictly black-tie-only tradition, with an orchestra for dancing from 9:30 PM to 2 AM. Closed Sundays in July and August. Reservations necessary. Major credit cards accepted. 3 Rue Royale, 8e (phone: 42-65-27-94; fax: 40-17-02-91).

Pré Catelan This dreamy dinner palace is a wonderful special occasion spot—particularly in summer, when guests can dine on the flower-decked terrace. The food—which has earned two Michelin stars—lives up to the promise of the ambience. Offerings include pumpkin soup with crayfish, braised whole sole, and rack of lamb with coriander. Closed Sunday dinner, Mondays, and two weeks in February. Reservations necessary. Major credit cards accepted. Rte. de Suresnes, *Bois de Boulogne,* 16e (phone: 45-24-55-58; fax: 45-24-43-25).

EXPENSIVE

Apicius Jean-Pierre Vigato's highly original recipes have earned this restaurant two Michelin stars. Favorites include *tourte de canard* (duck in pastry), potato purée with truffles, and *crème brûlée* with cherries. Closed weekends and the month of August. Reservations necessary. Major credit cards accepted. 122 Av. de Villiers, 17e (phone: 43-80-19-66; fax: 44-40-09-57).

L'Assiette The chef, Lulu, is very much present in her slightly scruffy bistro, which attracts a fashionable clientele for delicious and generous servings of roast duck, potato salad with fresh truffles, and *coquilles St-Jacques* (sea scallops in cream sauce). The wine list is sublime. Closed Mondays, Tuesdays, and the month of August. Reservations necessary. Major credit cards accepted. 181 Rue du Château, 14e (phone: 43-22-64-86).

Auberge des Deux Signes This place was once the cellars of the priory of *St-Julien-le-Pauvre;* try to get an upstairs table overlooking the gardens. Auvergnat cooking (ham, charcuterie, cabbage, and potato dishes) is prepared with a light touch. Closed Saturday lunch, Sundays, and the month of August. Reservations necessary. Major credit cards accepted. 46 Rue Galande, 5e (phone: 43-25-46-56; fax: 46-33-20-49).

Beauvilliers With its intimate dining rooms and hydrangea-rimmed summer terraces, this one-Michelin-star restaurant is one of the most romantic spots in Paris. The rich, generous fare, prepared in the classic tradition of the restaurant's namesake, a famous 18th-century chef, complements the setting. Try the rabbit and parsley terrine, *turbot au jus de jarret* (turbot cooked in veal shank gravy), and the remarkable praline chocolate cake. Closed Sundays and Monday lunch. Reservations necessary. Major credit cards accepted. On the northern slope of the Butte Montmartre, at 52 Rue Lamarck, 18e (phone: 42-54-54-42; fax: 42-62-70-30).

Bistro 121 Hearty food and excellent wines are offered in a modern setting that's always chic and crowded. Try one of the many first-rate fish dishes or an original creation such as *canard au fruit de la passion* (duck with passion fruit). Open daily until midnight. Reservations advised. Major credit cards accepted. 121 Rue de la Convention, 15e (phone: 45-57-52-90).

Le Carré des Feuillants Alain Dutournier of *Au Trou Gascon* (see below) has set up shop in the heart of the city, offering such creations as *perdreau sauvage* (wild partridge) with cumin, apricots, and fresh coriander. Michelin has awarded the establishment two stars. The prix fixe lunch menu is a good value. Closed Saturday lunch, Sundays, and the month of August. Reservations necessary. Major credit cards accepted. 14 Rue de Castiglione, 1er (phone: 42-86-82-82; fax: 42-86-07-71).

Chez Benoît A pretty, unpretentious bistro with wonderful, old-fashioned Lyonnais cooking and exquisite wines. Just about at the top of the bistro list, it's rated one Michelin star. Closed weekends and the month of August. Reservations necessary. No credit cards accepted. 20 Rue St-Martin, 4e (phone: 42-72-25-76; fax: 42-72-45-68).

Chez Pauline In this quintessential bistro which has earned one Michelin star, ask to be seated in the tiny, wood-paneled downstairs room. Try the oysters in a watercress sauce or the assortment of seafood with a saffron sauce, and save room for dessert—the mille-feuille of orange with raspberry sauce is sublime. Closed Saturday dinner, Sundays, the month of July, two weeks in August, and December 24 through January 2. Reservations advised; make them well in advance. Major credit cards accepted. 5 Rue Villedo, 1er (phone: 42-96-20-70; fax: 49-27-99-99).

Chiberta Elegant and modern, this two-Michelin-star restaurant boasts the nouvelle cuisine of Philippe da Silva. Try the goat cheese ravioli, or the fish with ginger and mango in puff pastry. Closed weekends, the month of August, and December 24 through January 3. Reservations necessary. Major credit cards accepted. 3 Rue Arsène-Houssaye, 8e (phone: 45-63-77-90; fax: 45-62-85-08).

La Coquille This is a classic bistro, where the service is unpretentious and warm, and the food consistent, although the seafood (except the scallops) is usually overcooked. From October through mid-May, as its name suggests, the restaurant specializes in *coquilles St-Jacques,* a version that consists of scallops roasted with butter, shallots, and parsley. Closed Sundays, Mondays, late July through early August, and December 23 through January 3. Reservations advised. Major credit cards accepted. 6 Rue du Débarcadère, 17e (phone: 45-72-10-73).

Le Divellec This bright and airy, two-Michelin-star place serves exquisitely fresh seafood. Try the sea bass, the *rouget* (mullet), or the sautéed turbot. The latter is served with a thick pasta flavored with squid ink—an unusual and delicious concoction. Closed Sundays, Mondays, the month of August, and December 24 through January 3. Reservations necessary. Major credit cards accepted. 107 Rue de l'Université, 7e (phone: 45-51-91-96; fax: 45-51-31-75).

Drouant Founded in 1880, this perennial favorite has an ambitious chef who favors classic French recipes, particularly fish dishes and *agneau de Pauillac,* a lamb specialty from the Médoc region. Last year, Michelin awarded it a coveted second star. Open daily. Reservations necessary. Major credit cards accepted. 18 Rue Gaillon, 2e (phone: 42-65-15-16; fax: 49-24-02-15).

Duquesnoy Jean-Paul Duquesnoy, one of Paris's most promising young chefs, is in his element in this enchanting two-Michelin-star establishment. Warm, carved woods and tasteful decor set the stage for specialties that include squab with foie gras, and fresh sardines grilled with almond butter; for dessert, the *crème brûlée* with walnuts is a delight. Closed Saturday lunch, Sundays, and three weeks in August. Reservations necessary. Major credit cards accepted. 6 Av. Bosquet, 7e (phone: 47-05-96-78; fax: 44-18-90-57).

Elysée-Lenôtre Arguably one of Paris's most elegant dining rooms, this restaurant in a former private house on the Champs-Elysées serves fine traditional cuisine with a focus on seafood. Closed Saturday lunch and most of August. Reservations advised. Major credit cards accepted. 10 Av. des Champs-Elysées, 8e (phone: 42-65-85-10; fax: 42-65-76-23).

Faucher Chef/owner Gerard Faucher has drawn praise (and one Michelin star) for his light touch with fish dishes and desserts. Closed Saturday lunch, Sundays, and one week in August. Reservations necessary. Major credit cards accepted. 123 Av. Wagram, 17e (phone: 42-27-61-50; fax: 46-22-25-72).

Faugeron Awarded two stars by Michelin, this place combines a nouvelle cuisine approach with bistro influences and more generous portions. Specializing in such simple, but exquisitely prepared, dishes as soft-boiled eggs with truffle purée and slices of sea scallops with lentils, it offers excellent service, a first-rate wine list, and one of Paris's prettiest settings, in what was once a school. Closed weekends (except Saturday dinner October through April), and the month of August. Reservations necessary. Major credit cards accepted. 52 Rue de Longchamp, 16e (phone: 47-04-24-53; fax: 47-55-62-90).

La Ferme St-Simon Among our favorites for wholesome *cuisine d'autrefois* (old-fashioned cooking), this place offers nothing very chichi, just well-prepared, authentic dishes, which have earned the restaurant a star from Michelin. Leave room for dessert; the owner once was a top assistant to France's famed pastry chef Gaston Lenôtre. It's also a perfect place for lunch. Closed Saturday lunch, Sundays, and three weeks in August. Reservations advised. Major credit cards accepted. 6 Rue de St-Simon, 7e (phone: 45-48-35-74; fax: 40-49-07-31).

Gérard Besson Michelin has given this small, formal eatery two stars. The service is impeccable, and the classic menu includes specialties such as *ris de veau poêlé à la truffe* (veal sweetbreads sautéed with truffles). Closed Sundays, and from September through December for lunch. Reservations necessary. Major credit cards accepted. 5 Rue Coq-Héron, 1er (phone: 42-33-14-74; fax: 42-33-85-71).

Goumard-Prunier Chef Jean-Claude Goumard relies on a network of Breton and Mediterranean fishermen to provide the finest seafood obtainable; his inventive creations, such as scallop mille-feuilles, have earned him two Michelin stars. Closed Sundays and Mondays. Reservations necessary. Major credit cards accepted. 9 Rue Duphot, 1er (phone: 42-60-36-07; fax: 42-60-04-54).

Jacques Cagna This establishment has a quintessentially Rive Gauche look and a mix of nouvelle and classic dishes, which Michelin has awarded two stars. The talented eponymous chef always provides an interesting menu at this charming spot near the Seine. Closed weekends (except Saturday dinner twice a month), three weeks in August, and *Christmas* week. Reservations necessary. Major credit cards accepted. 14 Rue des Grands-Augustins, 6e (phone: 43-26-49-39; fax: 43-54-54-48).

Jean-Claude Ferrero This inventive chef prepares eclectic cuisine, from authentic bouillabaisse to chicken with asparagus. The restaurant is one of the city's prettiest. Closed weekends (except Saturday dinner October through March), two weeks in May, and most of August. Reservations advised. Major credit cards accepted. 38 Rue Vital, 16e (phone: 45-04-42-42).

Ledoyen This grand dowager of Paris restaurants has been given a breath of life by a new chef, Ghislaine Arabian, who favors hearty, classic dishes such as *coquilles St-Jacques* (sea scallops in cream sauce). Last year, her efforts were rewarded with a second Michelin star. There's also an excellent, more moderately-priced lunch menu. The view from the upstairs dining room—of the Champs-Elysées, but with trees blocking the traffic—is superb. Closed weekends and most of August. Reservations necessary. Major credit cards accepted. Carré des Champs-Elysées, 8e (phone: 47-42-23-23; fax: 47-42-55-01).

La Marée Its exterior is unobtrusive, but there is great comfort within—also the freshest of fish, the best wine values in Paris, and fabulous desserts. Michelin has awarded it one star. Closed weekends, holidays, and the month of August. Reservations advised. Major credit cards accepted. 1 Rue Daru, 8e (phone: 43-80-20-00; fax: 48-88-04-04).

Miravile Gilles Epié's one-Michelin-star cuisine features such memorable dishes as *lapin aux olives* (rabbit with olives) and other Provençal-inspired recipes. Closed Saturday lunch and Sundays. Reservations necessary. Major credit cards accepted. 72 Quai de l'Hôtel-de-Ville, 4e (phone: 42-74-72-22; fax: 42-74-67-55).

Morot-Gaudry This one-Michelin-star restaurant is perched on the top floor of a 1920s building with a great view of the *Eiffel Tower,* especially from the flowered terrace. Among the inventive dishes is *pigeon en papillote* (squab steamed in its own juices); many dishes have a Mediterranean accent. Closed weekends. Reservations necessary. Major credit cards accepted. 8 Rue de la Cavalerie, 15e (phone: 45-67-06-85; fax: 45-67-55-72).

Au Petit Marguery This true, family-run bistro on the Rive Gauche serves excellent, if rather pricey, old-fashioned cuisine and *petit crus* wines. Closed Sundays, Mondays, the month of August, and December 23 through *New Year's Day.* Reservations advised. Major credit cards accepted. Bd. du Port Royal, 13e (phone: 43-31-58-59).

Le Petit Montmorency In his location near the Champs-Elysées, chef Daniel Bouché presents one of the most consistent menus in Paris, offering such specialties as a fresh truffle roasted in pastry (in winter) and a *soufflé aux noisettes* (hazelnut soufflé). Closed weekends and the month of August. Reservations necessary. Major credit cards accepted. 26 Rue Jean-Mermoz, 8e (phone: 42-25-11-19).

Pile ou Face The name means "heads or tails," but you won't be taking any chances at this one-Michelin-star bistro; super-fresh ingredients come from the owners' own farm. Try the *lapin en marmelade de romarin* (rabbit in a rich, rosemary-flavored sauce). Closed weekends, the month of August, and *Christmas* through *New Year's Day.* Reservations advised. Major credit cards accepted. 52 *bis* Rue Notre-Dame-des-Victoires, 2e (phone: 42-33-64-33; fax: 42-36-61-09).

Le Port Alma This elegant establishment with a view of the *Eiffel Tower* offers some of the finest seafood in town, such as baby clams in a thyme-flavored cream sauce. Closed Sundays and the month of August. Reservations necessary. Major credit cards accepted. 10 Av. de New-York, 16e (phone: 47-23-75-11).

La Timonerie At this one-Michelin-star restaurant, specialties include *filet de maquereau* (mackerel filet) with an herb salad, and a superb chocolate tart. Especially recommended is the very affordable prix fixe lunch. Closed Sundays, Mondays, and one week in August. Reserve at least three days in advance. MasterCard and Visa accepted. 35 Quai de la Tournelle, 5e (phone: 43-25-44-42).

Le Toit de Passy Not only is the food here good (Michelin has awarded chef Yannick Jacquot one star), but the rooftop view in one of Paris's more exclusive districts is spectacular. Try specialties such as *pigeonneau en croûte de sel* (squab in a salt crust) while dining outdoors. Closed Saturday lunch, Sundays, and *Christmas* week. Reservations necessary. Major credit cards accepted. 94 Av. Paul-Doumer, 16e (phone: 45-24-55-37; fax: 45-20-94-57).

Le Train Bleu The pricey traditional cuisine is adequate, but it's really the setting that makes this place worthwhile—in a train station whose Baroque decor is so gorgeous that the spot has been declared a national monument. Open daily. Reservations advised. Major credit cards accepted. *Gare de Lyon,* 20 Bd. Diderot, 12e (phone: 43-43-38-39; fax: 43-43-97-96).

Au Trou Gascon Alain Dutournier created this restaurant's inspired and unusual cooking, featuring southwestern French specialties and augmented by a vast choice of regional wines and armagnacs. He now has set up operations in a more elegant neighborhood at *Le Carré des Feuillants* (see above), while his wife holds down the fort at this one-Michelin-star restaurant. Closed weekends, the month of August, and *Christmas* week. Reservations advised. Major credit cards accepted. 40 Rue Taine, 12e (phone: 43-44-34-26; fax: 43-07-80-55).

Vancouver One of Paris's newest seafood restaurants, this modern establishment has already won a Michelin star for dishes with a Pacific flair, such as sweet-and-sour shrimp with fresh seaweed, and crayfish wrapped in coriander leaves. Closed weekends and most of August. Reservations advised. Major credit cards accepted. 4 Rue Arsène-Houssaye, 8e (phone: 42-56-77-77; fax: 44-71-15-02).

MODERATE

Ambassade d'Auvergne The young chef here creates delicious, classic Auvergnat dishes with an innovative touch. Try the lentil salad and the sliced ham or the *aligot* (a purée of potatoes and young cantal cheese); for dessert opt for a slice of one of the wonderful cakes. Closed August 1 through 16. Reservations advised. Major credit cards accepted. 22 Rue du Grenier-St-Lazare, 3e (phone: 42-72-31-22; fax: 42-78-85-47).

Atelier Maître Albert Unlike most other eateries on the Rive Gauche, this one is pleasantly roomy, with a prix fixe menu of classic French cuisine and a cozy log fire in winter. The spectacle of *Notre-Dame* looming before you as you walk out the door and onto the quay adds the finishing stroke to a charming meal. Closed Sunday dinner. Reservations advised. Major credit cards accepted. 1 Rue Maître-Albert, 5e (phone: 46-33-13-78).

L'Auberge Nicolas Flanel Believed to be the oldest restaurant in Paris (an inn opened in the half-timbered building in 1407), its menu includes such good, simple fare as grilled tuna, and leg of lamb. Closed Saturday lunch, Sundays, and the first two weeks in August. Reservations advised. MasterCard and Visa accepted. 51 Rue de Montmorency, 3e (phone: 42-71-77-78).

L'Avenue This chic brasserie, as fashionable as the district, offers grilled meat, raw oysters, and old-fashioned desserts in a dining room with a view of the *Eiffel Tower*. Closed most of August. Reservations advised. Major credit cards accepted. 41 Av. Montaigne, 8e (phone: 40-70-14-91).

Balzar Perhaps because of its location next to the *Sorbonne,* this mirrored brasserie has always attracted well-heeled intellectuals. The steaks and *pommes frites* are definitely worth a visit. Open until midnight; closed the month of August, and *Christmas* through *New Year's Day*. Reservations necessary (and often difficult to get). Major credit cards accepted. 49 Rue des Ecoles, 5e (phone: 43-54-13-67).

Baracane This reasonably priced bistro has excellent cuisine from southwestern France. Try the *lentilles au magret d'oie séché* (lentils with dried goose breast) or the cassoulet. Closed Saturday lunch, Sundays, and most of August. Reservations necessary. MasterCard and Visa accepted. 38 Rue des Tournelles, 4e (phone: 42-71-43-44).

Bistro de la Grille The decor of this old-fashioned spot is right out of a Cartier-Bresson photo, and the excellent food, from the raw oysters to the *andouillette* (grilled tripe sausage), is as classic as the setting. The *première étage* (upstairs) is preferable to the noisy downstairs. Closed most of August. Reservations advised. MasterCard and Visa accepted. In the stylish St-Germain-des-Prés district, at 14 Rue Mabillon, 6e (phone: 43-54-16-87).

Le Bistrot d'à Côté Flaubert Michel Rostang, impresario of the topflight restaurant that bears his name (see above), here offers *cuisine de terroir* (back-to-basics regional fare) in a turn-of-the-century bistro. Closed Saturday lunch, Sundays, and the first two weeks of August. Reservations advised. Major credit cards accepted. 10 Rue Gustave-Flaubert, 17e (phone: 42-67-05-81; fax: 47-63-82-75).

Le Bistrot du Sommelier The wine list is sublime in this bistro operated by 1992's *Meilleur Sommelier du Monde* (World's Best Sommelier), and there's hearty bourgeois cuisine to match. The special wine-lover's menu at dinner features six dishes served with six different wines. Closed weekends, the month of August, and *Christmas* through *New Year's Day*. Reservations advised. Major credit cards accepted. 97 Bd. Haussmann, 8e (phone: 42-65-24-85; fax: 42-94-03-26).

Le Boeuf sur le Toit A haunt of Jean Cocteau, Antoine de St-Exupéry, and other Paris artists and writers in the 1940s, this eatery is managed by the Flo group, well known for good value in atmospheric surroundings, although here these far outrank the classic brasserie fare. The piano bar is open until 2 AM. Open daily. Reservations advised. Major credit cards accepted. Off the Champs-Elysées, at 34 Rue du Colisée, 8e (phone: 43-59-83-80; fax: 45-63-45-40).

Bofinger This magnificent Belle Epoque place is one of Paris's oldest brasseries, and its beauty makes up for the occasionally mediocre food. Ask to be seated on the ground floor, and order onion soup and *choucroute* (sauerkraut)—you won't be disappointed. Open daily. Reservations advised. Major credit cards accepted. 15 Rue de la Bastille, 4e (phone: 42-72-87-82; fax: 42-72-97-68).

Brasserie Lipp This famous brasserie (a beer hall distinguished by its brass dispensers), where the Paris intelligentsia have flocked for over a century, is fashionable for a late supper of *choucroute* and Alsatian beer and for people watching indoors and out, although guests not known to the staff sometimes receive less than welcoming treatment. Closed July and August. Reservations advised. Major credit cards accepted. 151 Bd. St-Germain, 6e (phone: 45-48-53-91).

Brissemoret Popular with Parisians, this pleasant eatery features basic, high-quality food: excellent foie gras, raw salmon marinated in fresh herbs, and great sauces—try the breast of duck in wine sauce. Closed weekends, and most of August. Reservations necessary. Major credit cards accepted. 5 Rue St-Marc, 2e (phone: 42-36-91-72).

La Butte Chaillot A starkly modern bistro operated by celebrated chef Guy Savoy (also see his self-named restaurant, above, and *Le Bistrot de l'Etoile-Lauriston,* below) features such old-fashioned dishes as roast chicken with mashed potatoes, and an unusual lentil soup with crayfish. Closed *Christmas* and *New Year's Day.* Reservations advised. Major credit cards accepted. 112 Av. Kléber, 16e (phone: 47-27-88-88; fax: 47-04-85-70).

La Cagouille This Rive Gauche bistro prepares fish to one-Michelin-star perfection; try the steamed clams or the *bar* (sea bass) with vegetables. Closed three weeks in August and *Christmas* through *New Year's Day.* Reservations advised. Major credit cards accepted. 12 Pl. Constantin-Brancusi, 14e (phone: 43-22-09-01; fax: 45-38-57-29).

Le Caméléon In a true bistro atmosphere—with marble tables, moleskin banquettes, and the spirit of 1920s Montparnasse—try the superb casserole-roasted veal and *morue provençale* (salt cod in tomato sauce with garlic mayonnaise). Closed Sundays, Mondays, and the month of August. Reservations advised. No credit cards accepted. 6 Rue de Chevreuse, 6e (phone: 43-20-63-43).

Campagne et Provence The bistro alternative to the fine *Miravile* (see above), this tiny Quartier Latin spot has a lovely *tapenade de lapin* (rabbit with olive purée) and a garlicky mixed green salad. Closed Saturday lunch, Sundays, Mondays, and most of August. Reservations necessary. MasterCard and Visa accepted. 25 Quai de la Tournelle, 5e (phone: 43-54-05-17; fax: 42-74-67-55).

Canard'avril This friendly place features such southwestern French specialties as roast duck, cassoulet, foie gras, and potatoes sautéed with garlic; there's also a good selection of fish dishes. Closed weekends. Reservations advised. MasterCard and Visa accepted. 5 Rue Paul-Lelong, 2e (phone: 42-36-26-08).

Le Caroubier A family-run couscous restaurant, it has some of the best hand-rolled couscous grains in town, accompanied by good vegetables, grilled meat, and a delicious *pastilla,* a flaky pastry with a spicy meat filling. Pour the vegetable broth on the delicate couscous, add a little hot pepper sauce, and you'll feel as if you've been transported to Morocco. Closed Sunday dinner, Mondays, and the month of August. Reservations advised. MasterCard and Visa accepted. 122 Av. du Maine, 14e (phone: 43-20-41-49).

Chez Marius A real find—the rotund chef really loves his work, and the three-dish prix fixe dinner is a great deal. Specialties are bouillabaisse and grilled fish. The atmosphere is Old World cozy, though there have been complaints of late about the service. Closed Saturday lunch, Sundays, most of August, and a week at *Christmas.* Reservations advised. Major credit cards accepted. 5 Rue Bourgogne, 7e (phone: 47-05-96-19).

La Coupole A big, brassy brasserie, once the haunt of Hemingway, Josephine Baker, and Picasso, it's now owned by the Flo group. The atmosphere is still great, and the food is improving. Open until 2 AM; closed the month of August and *Christmas Eve.* Reservations advised. Major credit cards accepted. 102 Bd. du Montparnasse, 14e (phone: 43-20-14-20; fax: 43-35-46-14).

Fontaine de Mars A simple, family-style restaurant with dishes from southwestern France, such as salad with *magret de canard* (slices of smoked duck breast) and chicken with morel mushrooms. In summer, there's outdoor dining on the patio. Closed Sundays and the month of August. Reservations advised. Major credit cards accepted. Near the *Eiffel Tower,* at 129 Rue St-Dominique, 7e (phone: 47-05-46-44; fax: 45-50-31-92).

Fouquet's Bastille Sister restaurant to the Champs-Elysées institution (see *Cafés,* below), this postmodern brasserie next to the *Opéra de la Bastille* serves traditional fare, such as shellfish platters and simple *plats du jour,* with a modern touch. Closed Saturday lunch, Sundays, and the month of August. Reservations advised. Major credit cards accepted. 130 Rue de Lyon, 12e (phone: 43-42-18-18).

Au Gamin de Paris Combining the coziness of a classic bistro with the chicness of a historic Marais building, it serves well-prepared, imaginative food. Specialties include grilled salmon and *magret de canard;* for dessert, try the *crème brûlée* or *tarte tatin* (caramelized apple tart). Open daily. Reservations unnecessary. Major credit cards accepted. 51 Rue Vieille-du-Temple, 4e (phone: 42-78-97-24).

Le Grizzli The wonderful food here is southwestern French in accent, featuring duck and plenty of garlic. Closed Sundays and Monday lunch. Reservations advised. Major credit cards accepted. 7 Rue St-Martin, 4e (phone: 48-87-77-56).

Jo Goldenberg The best-known eating house in the Marais's quaint Jewish quarter, with good, albeit overpriced, chopped liver and cheesecake and a range of Eastern European Jewish specialties. Try the mushroom and barley soup. It's also a fine place to sip mint tea at the counter in the middle of a busy day. Open daily. Reservations unnecessary. Major credit cards accepted. 7 Rue des Rosiers, 4e (phone: 48-87-20-16).

Le Maraîcher This tiny Marais eatery has excellent bourgeois cooking (try the cassoulet). Closed Sundays, Monday lunch, the month of August, and *Christmas* week. Reservations advised. Major credit cards accepted. 5 Rue Beautrellis, 4e (phone: 42-71-42-49).

Marie et Fils Marie and her son have found a successful formula: great bistro food, an authentic Rive Gauche atmosphere, and reasonable prices. Reservations advised. MasterCard and Visa accepted. Closed Sundays and Monday lunch. 34 Rue Mazarine, 6e (phone: 43-26-69-49).

Moissonnier Over the past 30 years little has changed (except the prices) on the menu of this Lyonnais restaurant, across the street from what was once Paris's wine depot. The seafood, tripe dishes, and beaujolais may not be anything new, but this is bourgeois cuisine par excellence. Closed Sunday dinner and Mondays. Reservations advised. MasterCard and Visa accepted. 28 Rue Fossés-St-Bernard, 5e (phone: 43-29-87-65).

Le Muniche St-Germain's best brasserie is a bustling place with a rather extensive menu. Open daily until 1:30 AM. Reservations advised. Major credit cards accepted. 22 Rue Guillaume-Apollinaire, 6e (phone: 47-34-01-06).

Ostréade Seafood is king at this bustling, loft-like Montparnasse brasserie. Try the salad of potatoes and baby clams or the whole roast fish, and don't miss the tiny Breton oysters known as *boudeuses.* Open daily. Reservations necessary. Major credit cards accepted. 11 Bd. de Vaugirard, 15e (phone: 43-21-87-41).

Le Poquelin The excellent bourgeois cooking includes splendid *magret de canard en croûte d'épices* (duck breast in a spicy crust). Closed Saturday lunch, Sundays, and three weeks in August. Reservations advised. Major credit cards accepted. 17 Rue Molière, 1er (phone: 42-96-22-19; fax: 42-96-05-72).

Robert et Louise With a warm, paneled decor and high standards in the kitchen, this family-run bistro is a great place to try *boeuf bourguignon* or open-fire–grilled *côte de boeuf*. Also good are the *fromage blanc* and the *vin en pichet*. Closed Sundays, holidays, and the month of August. Reservations advised for Friday and Saturday dinner. No credit cards accepted. 64 Rue Vieille-du-Temple, 3e (phone: 42-78-55-89).

La Rôtisserie du Beaujolais A de rigueur spot for Paris's "in" set is Claude Terrail's casual canteen on the quay in the shadow of his three-star gastronomic temple, *La Tour d'Argent*. Most of the restaurant's meat, produce, and cheese comes from Lyons; try the offerings with a superb Georges Duboeuf beaujolais. Closed Mondays. No reservations. Major credit cards accepted. 19 Quai de la Tournelle, 5e (phone: 43-54-17-47).

La Rôtisserie d'en Face Comfortably low-key decor, tiled floors, and an open, uncluttered atmosphere provide the backdrop for the bistro fare of noted chef Jacques Cagna (also see his self-named restaurant, above), such as grilled chicken, roast leg of lamb, and thick steaks. Closed Saturday lunch and Sundays. Reservations advised. MasterCard and Visa accepted. 2 Rue Christine, 6e (phone: 43-26-40-98; fax: 43-54-54-48).

La Tour de Montlhéry This bistro offers great bourgeois cooking. Closed weekends and the month of August. Reservations necessary. MasterCard and Visa accepted. In *Les Halles,* at 5 Rue des Prouvaires, 1er (phone: 42-36-21-82).

Le Valençay A small, popular bistro with classic bourgeois fare and wines by the glass or the bottle. Closed Sundays and the month of August. No reservations. Major credit cards accepted. 11 Bd. du Palais, 4e (phone: 43-54-64-67).

Yvan Creative bistro fare, such as squab with polenta, and sardines with tomatoes, along with a wonderful cheese selection, keeps this restaurant almost always full. The place also boasts a stylish atmosphere and very reasonable prices. Closed Saturday lunch and Sundays. Reservations necessary. Major credit cards accepted. 1 *bis* Rue Jean-Mermoz, 8e (phone: 43-59-18-40; fax: 45-63-78-69).

Les Zygomates This friendly bistro occupies a converted fin de siècle charcuterie with lots of mirrors and marble counters. The menu includes fish, as well as classic bistro meat dishes and gooey chocolate desserts. Closed Saturday lunch, Sundays, most of August, and December 26 through January 4. Reservations necessary. MasterCard and Visa accepted. In an out-of-the-way location, at 7 Rue Capri, 12e (phone: 40-19-93-04).

INEXPENSIVE

L'Ami Jean This place offers good Basque cooking. Closed Saturday dinner and Sundays. No reservations. No credit cards accepted. 27 Rue Malar, 7e (phone: 47-05-86-89).

Astier An honest-to-goodness neighborhood spot that always is packed, it offers the staples of lovingly prepared bourgeois cooking. Closed weekends, late April through mid-May, and late August through early September. Reservations advised. Major credit cards accepted. 44 Rue Jean-Pierre-Timbaud, 11e (phone: 43-57-16-35).

Auberge de Jarente This Basque restaurant is the place to sample classic *pipérade* (omelette with ham and tomato), and cassoulet. Closed Sundays, Mondays, and the month of August. Reservations advised. Major credit cards accepted. In the heart of the Marais, at 7 Rue de Jarente, 4e (phone: 42-77-49-35).

Bistrot de l'Etoile-Lauriston One of superchef Guy Savoy's bistros (also see his self-named restaurant and *La Butte Chaillot,* above) offers innovative variations on classic bistro themes, such as lamb with rosemary and *bisque d'étrilles,* a soup made from tiny crabs. Closed Saturday lunch and Sundays. Reservations advised. Major credit cards accepted. 19 Rue de Lauriston, 16e (phone: 40-67-11-16; fax: 45-00-99-87).

Brasserie Fernand A nondescript hole-in-the-wall place that produces surprisingly tasty dishes. The pot-au-feu, steaks with shallots, and fish pâté all are first-rate, but the real lure is the huge tub of chocolate mousse served for dessert—a chocoholic's fantasy come true. Open daily for dinner only. Reservations advised. MasterCard and Visa accepted. 13 Rue Guisarde, 6e (phone: 43-54-61-47).

Cartet This tiny, friendly place serves Lyonnais specialties with a focus on char-cuterie and meat, such as *côtes de veau aux morilles* (veal chops with morel mushrooms). Closed weekends and the month of August. Reservations advised. Major credit cards accepted. 62 Rue de Malte, 11e (phone: 48-05-17-65).

Casa Olympe Dominique Nahmias, the former doyenne of *Olympe,* has her own restaurant again, a chic and intimate place in a charming neighborhood. Her copious servings of fine bistro classics with a Mediterranean touch at reasonable prices (the menu is prix fixe only) have made reservations difficult to get, but keep trying. Closed weekends and most of August. Reservations necessary. Major credit cards accepted. 48 Rue Saint-Georges, 9e (phone: 42-85-26-01; fax: 45-26-49-33).

Le Grand Colbert This restaurant near the lovely *Galerie Vivienne* has authentic turn-of-the-century decor and good brasserie specialties like herring with potatoes in vinaigrette and duck *confit* with garlic-laden potatoes. Closed mid-July to mid-August. Reservations advised. Major credit cards accepted. 2 Rue Vivienne, 2e (phone: 42-86-87-88; fax: 42-86-82-65).

La Lozère Here you'll find authentic country cooking from the Lozère region in the south of France, with an emphasis on charcuterie and cassoulet. Closed

Sundays, Mondays, and the month of August. Reservations advised. No credit cards accepted. 4 Rue Hautefeuille, 6e (phone: 43-54-26-64).

Le Passage This bistro serves 70 excellent wines by the glass (try the chinon) and has a varied menu of bistro classics like *foie de veau sauté* (sautéed calf's liver) and friendly service. Closed Saturday lunch, Sundays, and most of August. Reservations advised. MasterCard and Visa accepted. 18 Passage de la Bonne-Graine, 11e (phone: 47-00-73-30).

Polidor Regulars here, who have included such starving artists as Paul Verlaine, James Joyce, Ernest Hemingway, and, more recently, Jean-Paul Belmondo, still keep their napkins in numbered pigeonholes. The *Collège de Pataphysique,* founded by Raymond Queneau and Eugène Ionesco, continues to meet here regularly for the good family-style food. But a drawback to this customer loyalty is that foreigners are often banished to the back room. Closed the month of August. Reservations unnecessary. No credit cards accepted. 41 Rue Monsieur-le-Prince, 6e (phone: 43-26-95-34).

La Route du Beaujolais This is a barn-like workers' bistro serving Lyonnais specialties and beaujolais wines. Don't miss the charcuterie and the fresh bread here, and try the *tarte tatin* for dessert. Closed Saturday lunch and Sundays. Reservations unnecessary. MasterCard and Visa accepted. On the Rive Gauche, at 17 Rue de Lourmel, 15e (phone: 45-79-31-63).

Thoumieux This family-run bistro has been reliable for decades. Come here for tripe, cassoulet, and *boudin aux châtaignes* (blood sausage with chestnuts). Open daily. Reservations advised. MasterCard and Visa accepted. 79 Rue St-Dominique, 7e (phone: 47-05-49-75; fax: 47-05-36-96).

Aux Tonneaux des Halles Wine by the glass, an old-fashioned setting, and typical bistro dishes like *navarin d'agneau* (lamb stew) make this a popular spot among Parisians. Closed Sundays and Mondays. Reservations advised. MasterCard and Visa accepted. 28 Rue Montorgueil, 1er (phone: 42-33-36-19).

Le Trumilou The formidable proprietress sets the tone of this robust establishment on the Seine, which serves huge, steaming portions of game in season, *truite aux amandes* (trout with almonds), and chicken, all beneath a frieze of some excruciatingly bad rustic oil paintings. Try the *charlotte aux marrons* (chestnut parfait) for dessert. Amazingly cheerful service. Closed Mondays. Reservations unnecessary. Major credit cards accepted. 84 Quai de l'Hôtel-de-Ville, 4e (phone: 42-77-63-98).

VERY INEXPENSIVE

Bistro de la Gare Michel Oliver offers a choice of three appetizers and three main courses with *pommes frites,* excellent for a quick lunch. Open daily. No reservations. Major credit cards accepted. Ten locations, including 1 Rue du Four, 6e (phone: 43-25-87-76); 59 Bd. du Montparnasse, 6e (phone: 45-48-38-01); and 30 Rue St-Denis, 1er (phone: 40-26-82-80).

Chartier This huge, turn-of-the-century place serves lots of down-to-earth food for the price. The famous pot-au-feu is still served on Mondays. Open daily. No reservations. No credit cards accepted. 7 Rue du Faubourg-Montmartre, 9e (phone: 47-70-86-29).

Drouot A favorite of locals, the younger member of the Chartier family (see above) proffers simple fare at bargain prices. To avoid a long wait for a table, arrive before 9 PM. Open daily. No reservations. No credit cards accepted. 103 Rue de Richelieu, 2e (phone: 42-96-68-23).

Le Petit Gavroche A hole-in-the-wall bistro-cum-restaurant with a lively clientele and a classic menu. Closed Sundays. Reservations unnecessary. No credit cards accepted. 15 Rue Ste-Croix-de-la-Bretonnerie, 4e (phone: 48-87-74-26).

Le Petit St-Benoît French cooking at its simplest, in a plain little place with tiled floors and curlicued hat stands. Closed weekends. Reservations unnecessary. No credit cards accepted. 4 Rue St-Benoît, 6e (phone: 42-60-27-92).

Au Pied de Fouet This former coach house has had its habitués, including celebrities as diverse as Graham Greene, Le Corbusier, and Georges Pompidou. Service is fast and friendly, and the daily specials are reliably good. Save room for the marvelous desserts, such as *charlotte au chocolat.* Arrive early; it closes at 9 PM. Closed Saturday dinner, Sundays, two weeks at both *Easter* and *Christmas,* and the month of August. No reservations. No credit cards accepted. 45 Rue de Babylone, 7e (phone: 47-05-12-27).

CAFÉS

Paris without cafés would be like Madrid without tapas bars, Dublin without pubs, or New York without delis. The corner café is the glue that holds the French neighborhood together; it's a place for coffee and gossip, or just a spot in which to sit and watch the world go by. Reservations are never needed; just a claim a table, and it's yours for as long as the spirit moves you. And, possibly best of all, it's almost always easy on the wallet. Of the more than 5,000 cafés in Paris, the following are our favorites:

Café Costes Philippe Starck's postmodern design, inspired by Fritz Lang's *Metropolis,* helped make this café the trendiest of trendsetters for *branché* ("with-it") Parisians; now its fame is such that it has rated a mention in *Time* magazine. Open daily. Major credit cards accepted. In the Beaubourg district, near the *Centre Georges-Pompidou,* at 4 Rue Berger, 1er (phone: 45-08-54-38/9).

Café de la Paix Designed by Charles Garnier to complement his baroque *Opéra,* this grande dame is best for afternoon tea; keep your eye out for the elusive pastry cart (the service in general can be elusive at times). Open daily until 1:30 AM. Major credit cards accepted. Two entrances, at 12 Bd. des Capucines and 2 Rue Scribe, 9e (phone: 40-07-32-32).

Fouquet's Arguably Paris's best-located café—it's part of the eponymous regal restaurant, now an official historic monument—this institution is far from perfect: The drinks are too expensive; the sidewalk is often too crowded; and the downstairs dining is forgettable one night and downright mediocre the next. But if there is still magic in the world, it can be found here at dusk, when the lights come up on the *Arc de Triomphe*. Open daily from 9 PM to midnight. Major credit cards accepted. 99 Av. des Champs-Elysées, 8e (phone: 47-23-70-60).

Ma Bourgogne Set beneath the vaulted arcades of the Place des Vosges, this is a great spot for an afternoon stop, not so much for the food as for the view of Paris's most beautiful square. Try their specialty of sausages from Auvergne with a glass of burgundy or bordeaux. Closed Mondays. MasterCard and Visa accepted. 19 Pl. des Vosges, 4e (phone: 42-78-44-64).

La Palette A Rive Gauche hangout on a tiny square, with outdoor tables during the summer, it stays lively with a young crowd until 2 AM. Closed Sundays, holidays, and the month of August. No credit cards accepted. 43 Rue de Seine, 6e (phone: 43-26-68-15).

Le Piano Zinc Tiny and authentic, this hole-in-the-wall place with a classic, zinc-topped, horseshoe-shaped bar has a regular and eclectic clientele of artists and workers. Closed the month of August. No credit cards accepted. Central to Marais shopping, museums, designer boutiques, and the *Hôtel de Ville*, at 49 Rue des Blancs-Manteaux, 3e (phone: 42-74-32-42).

La Rhumerie This longtime hangout of Rive Gauche literati has a pleasant, elevated terrace, salads and Caribbean-style cuisine for light lunches, and 15 varieties of mostly rum-based punch. Open daily until 2 AM. Mastercard and Visa accepted. 166 Bd. Saint-Germain, 6e (phone: 43-54-28-94).

Le Select Opened in 1925 at the height of Paris's Jazz Age, this was the first Montparnasse café to stay open all night. Edna St. Vincent Millay, Erik Satie, and Leonard Foujita adored the place; in 1927 Isadora Duncan got into a fistfight here with an American newspaperman. (History records that the dancer won by a decision.) The café hasn't changed much since, and it has some of the liveliest early-morning and late-night scenes imaginable. Open daily until 2 AM. MasterCard and Visa accepted. 99 Bd. du Montparnasse, 6e (phone: 42-22-65-27 or 45-48-38-24).

Le Voltaire An often-overlooked gem, this tiny café along the Seine was the place where Baudelaire wrote *Les Fleurs du Mal* (he lived at 19 Quai Voltaire), Wagner wrote the words for *Die Meistersinger* (his home was at No. 22), and the eponymous Voltaire died. Closed Sundays, Mondays, and the month of August. No credit cards accepted. Opposite the *Louvre* and near the *Musée d'Orsay,* at 27 Quai Voltaire, 7e (phone: 42-61-17-49).

WINE BARS

Though wine bars are now a Parisian institution, they actually originated among oenophilic Londoners. They vary widely in decor and the types of wines they purvey, but all offer wines by the glass only and a convivial atmosphere; if food is served, it's simple and specially chosen to accompany the wine. While some wine bars offer very expensive wines and edibles, all have some inexpensive wines on their lists. Unless otherwise noted, reservations are unnecessary; however, at lunch hour, if you don't have a reservation and want only a glass of wine, some very busy places may ask you to stand at the bar. The following are some of our favorites among Paris's true wine bars:

L'Ange-Vin This place boasts Paris's best collection of sweet white wines from the Loire Valley (try the Côteaux-du-Layon '89), good *plats du jour* and snacks, and a real nonsmoking section. Open 11AM to 8:30 PM (to 2AM Tuesdays and Thursdays); closed weekends. MasterCard and Visa accepted. 24 Rue Richard-Lenoir, 11e (phone: 43-48-20-20).

Bistrot des Augustins Just across the street from the booksellers on the quays, this old-fashioned café with an excellent *plat du jour* at lunch has fine beaujolais and other wines by the glass. Closed the month of August. No credit cards accepted. 39 Quai des Grands-Augustins, 6e (phone: 43-54-41-65).

Le Bouchon du Marais One of the capital's newer wine bars, it specializes in Loire Valley wines (the owner has a vineyard in Chinon) and simple light snacks. Closed Sundays, the month of August, and daily from 3 to 7 PM. No credit cards accepted. 15 Rue François-Miron, 4e (phone: 48-87-44-13).

Caves Saint-Gilles This Spanish wine bar serves generous tapas (try the *pipérade,* a Basque omelette), rioja and sangria by the glass, and an ample *plat du jour.* Closed the month of August. Reservations accepted for a full meal at lunch only. No credit cards accepted. Appropriately located near the *Musée Picasso,* at 4 Rue St-Gilles, 3e (phone: 48-87-22-62).

La Cloche des Halles The dim lighting and dark wood paneling at this cozy establishment add to the pleasure of sampling the wine here. Those with hunger pangs can order the generous cheese platter or try a plate of charcuterie. Closed Saturday evenings, Sundays, and the month of August. No credit cards accepted. 28 Rue Coquillière, 1er (phone: 42-36-93-89).

L'Ecluse This unassuming wine bar overlooking the Seine has fathered several other, more sophisticated places—on the Rue François-Ier, at the *Madeleine,* at the *Opéra* (both the *Palais Garnier* and the *Bastille*), in *Le Forum des*

Halles, and in Neuilly. Its red velvet benches and wooden tables—not to mention its bordeaux and the fresh, homemade foie gras and spectacular chocolate cake—remain unchanged. Open daily. Major credit cards accepted. 15 Quai des Grands-Augustins, 6e (phone: 46-33-58-74), and several other locations.

L'Enoteca This wine bar in the Marais features a vast assortment of Italian wines by the glass or bottle, along with Italian fare at lunch. Closed part of August. Major credit cards accepted. 25 Rue Charles-V, 4e (phone: 42-78-91-44).

Espace Hérault Attached to the Hérault *département*'s tourist office, it features wines and simple dishes from Languedoc. Closed Saturday mornings, Sundays, the month of August, and daily between 2 and 7:30 PM. Major credit cards accepted. 8 Rue de la Harpe, 5e (phone: 43-33-00-56).

Au Franc Pinot A restaurant has operated on this spot for 350 years, making this Paris's oldest wine bar. In a lovely setting on the Ile St-Louis, it offers regional wines, many from the Loire, and delicious snacks. Closed Sundays, Mondays, the month of August, and daily from 3 to 7 PM. Major credit cards accepted. 1 Quai Bourbon, 4e (phone: 43-29-46-98).

Jacques Melac An old-fashioned wine bar run by a young, extravagantly mustachioed man from the Auvergne, who bottles and sells his own rustic wines and even stages a harvest celebration in honor of the restaurant's vineyard. Closed weekends and the month of August. MasterCard and Visa accepted. 42 Rue Léon-Frot, 11e (phone: 43-70-59-27).

Juveniles This friendly spot has excellent wine and top-quality snacks, as well as several fine sherries. The British owners have a loyal British and American following. Closed Sundays. MasterCard and Visa accepted. 47 Rue de Richelieu, 1er (phone: 47-97-46-49).

Millésimes An ideal location next to the renovated St-Germain-des-Prés covered market, plus a wide choice of wines and good *tartines* (open-face sandwiches) and charcuterie platters make this one of the most popular wine bars on the Rive Gauche. Open 7 AM to 1 AM; closed Sundays. MasterCard and Visa accepted. 7 Rue Lobineau, 6e (phone: 46-34-21-15).

Le Pain et Le Vin Operated by four top Parisian chefs, including Alain Dutournier of *Le Carré des Feuillants* and *Au Trou Gascon* (see *Eating Out* for both), this place features 40 wines by the glass and daily hot lunch specials. Closed Sundays, the month of August, and daily between 3 and 7 PM. Major credit cards accepted. 1 Rue d'Armaillé, 17e (phone: 47-63-88-29).

Relais Chablisien As the name implies, this wine bar, with its wood-beamed ceilings and warm atmosphere, specializes in chablis. Sandwiches and excellent *plats du jour* also are available. Closed weekends and two weeks in August. Reservations advised for meals. Major credit cards accepted. 4 Rue Bertin-Poirée, 1er (phone: 45-08-53-73).

Le Repaire de Bacchus A tiny wine bar specializing in unusual regional wines, displayed in crowded rows. You can buy wine by the bottle to take home or on a picnic, or sip it at the counter with cheese and charcuterie. Closed Sundays and Mondays. MasterCard and Visa accepted. 13 Rue du Cherche-Midi, 6e (phone: 45-44-01-07).

Le Rouge-Gorge Near the antiques shops of the St-Paul *quartier,* this place has changing, thematic menus that feature the wines and foods of a particular region for two-week periods. Some patrons have complained of indifferent service, however. Closed Sundays and the month of August. No credit cards accepted. 8 Rue St-Paul, 4e (phone: 48-04-75-89).

Le Rubis A tiny corner bar, it has an old-fashioned atmosphere and a selection of about 30 wines. Try the pork *rillettes,* savory meat pies made on the premises. Closed Saturdays after 4 PM, Sundays, and two weeks in August. No credit cards accepted. 10 Rue du Marché-St-Honoré, 1er (phone: 42-61-03-34).

Le Sancerre A hospitable spot featuring nothing but Sancerre wines—red, white, and rosé. Simple lunches of omelettes, charcuterie, apple tarts, and *petits goûters* (snacks) such as goat cheese marinated in olive oil are the perfect accompaniment for the excellent wine. Open 7 AM to 8:30 PM; closed Saturday afternoons and evenings, Sundays, and the month of August. Major credit cards accepted. 22 Av. Rapp, 7e (phone: 45-51-75-91).

Au Sauvignon The couple who run this tiny corner bar seem to be in perpetual motion, pouring the sauvignon blanc (or the white Quincy and beaujolais nouveau in November and January) and carving up chunky *tartines* with bread from the famous *Poilâne* bakery not far away. Closed Sundays, two weeks in January, *Easter,* and the month of August. No credit cards accepted. 80 Rue des Sts-Pères, 7e (phone: 45-48-49-02).

La Tartine An old, authentic bistro where Trotsky was once known to sip a glass or two of wine. There's a colorful local clientele and a good selection of mostly inexpensive wines by the glass. Closed Tuesdays, Wednesday mornings, and most of August. No credit cards accepted. 24 Rue de Rivoli, 4e (phone: 42-72-76-85).

Taverne Henri IV A selection of nearly 20 wines is offered by the glass, along with generous servings of simple food such as open-face sandwiches of ham, cheese, sausage, or the more exotic terrine of wild boar. Closed Saturday evenings, Sundays, and most of August. No credit cards accepted. On the Pont Neuf, at 13 Pl. du Pont-Neuf, 1er (phone: 43-54-27-90).

Willi's An enterprising Englishman set up this smart little wine bar, a pleasant walk through the *Palais Royal* gardens from the *Louvre.* The wine selection—a list of 150—is one of the best in Paris, with an emphasis on Côtes du Rhône. The chef creates some appetizing salads as well as *plats du jour.*

Closed Sundays. Major credit cards accepted. 13 Rue des Petits-Champs, 1er (phone: 42-61-05-09).

TEAROOMS

In Paris, taking tea provides a revitalizing mid-afternoon break from frantic sightseeing and window shopping. The *salon de thé* originally was the refuge of patrician Parisian ladies, who lingered over ambrosial pastries and fragrant, steaming cups of *cerise* (cherry) tea between social calls. Today, tearooms still lure Parisians and visitors alike to partake of their caloric treats. *L'Arbre à Canelle* (57 Passage des Panoramas, 2e; phone: 45-08-55-87) offers scrumptious chocolate pear and apple tart in a stylish setting. Those with discriminating tea tastes frequent *A La Cour de Rohan* (59-61 Rue St-André-des-Arts, 6e; phone: 43-25-79-67), which offers over 20 varieties described in almost religious detail. You'll find a *plus raffiné* Belle Epoque atmosphere at *Ladurée* (16 Rue Royale, 8e; phone: 42-60-21-79), where it would be a shame to ignore the masterfully decorated petits fours, marrons glacés, and macaroons. Nowhere in Paris is tea taken more seriously than at *Mariage Frères* (30-32 Rue du Bourg-Tibourg, 4e, phone: 42-72-28-11; and 13 Rue des Grands-Augustins, 6e, phone: 40-51-82-50); with a supply of 450 different kinds of tea, it's perhaps wisest to close your eyes and choose a blend at whim. Neoclassical art and classical music contribute to the tranquil ambience at *A Priori Thé* (35-37 *Galerie Vivienne,* 2e; phone: 42-97-48-75), set in one of Paris's lovely *passages* (turn-of-the-century glass-roofed shopping arcades). In another *passage* is the new *Thé S. F.* (Passage du Grand Cerf, 2e; phone: 40-28-08-76), which features 45 teas, a scrumptious chocolate terrine, scones, and cheesecake; quiches and a cheese platter are also available. The *Tea Caddy* (14 Rue Julien-le-Pauvre, 5e; phone: 43-54-15-56), one of the oldest tea shops in Paris, is very British—from its name to its fine teas and scones. *Tea and Tattered Pages* (24 Rue Mayet, 6e; phone: 40-65-94-35), a combination tearoom and used-English-books store, is a great place to pick up some reading material for a rainy day. And the *Crillon* hotel (see *Checking In*) is one of the city's most elegant spots in which to take very expensive afternoon tea, complete with an assortment of sublime pastries.

AND FOR CHOCOHOLICS

The best hot chocolate in Paris, if not the universe, is served at *Angelina* (226 Rue de Rivoli, 1er, phone: 42-60-82-00; 86 Av. de Longchamp, 16e, phone: 47-04-89-42; 40 Bd. Haussmann, 9e, phone: 42-82-34-56; and in the *Palais des Congrès, Porte Maillot,* 17e; phone: 40-68-22-50). To accompany your cup of sweet ambrosia, order *chocolat l'Africain,* a dessert made with delicious dark chocolate.

Reims

Reims is in many ways more French than Paris, because it is more resistant to change. Just 141 kilometers (87 miles) east of Paris and surrounded by the gently rolling woodlands and cultivated hills of the Champagne region (also see the *Champagne* route in DIRECTIONS), it offers a little of everything that the mind's eye tends to include in a mental image of France: a glorious cathedral, impressive medieval churches, sidewalk cafés, eminent restaurants, elegant shops, river and canal barges, and, in the immediate vicinity, champagne cellars, famous vineyards, and elegant châteaux. Reims has also played a major role in French history. For nearly seven centuries, the kings of France were crowned here, and Reims has been at the crossroads of numerous historical conflicts, including World Wars I and II.

During Caesar's rule of Gaul from 58 to 51 BC, Reims, which had served for centuries as the capital of the Gallic tribe known as the Remi, was renamed Durocortorum. Under the Romans, this formerly unremarkable settlement on the Vesle River flourished, becoming one of Gaul's most beautiful and commercially important cities and outstripping the village of Paris in stature. Later the name became Rheims, reflecting its Gallic origins, and in the 18th century the "h" was dropped, leaving today's Reims (pronounced *Rance*—it rhymes with France).

The history of France may be said to have begun in Reims in 496, when Saint Remigius, the Bishop of Reims, baptized and crowned Clovis I King of all the Franks in a church that preceded the *Cathédrale Notre-Dame de Reims*. Though Clovis (a name that in time evolved into "Louis") chose Paris as his capital, it was in memory of this ceremony that Reims later became the city of coronations. From Louis VII, who ascended the throne in 1137, to Charles X, who was crowned in 1825, it was customary for the Kings of France to be crowned in the *Cathédrale Notre-Dame de Reims*.

The most famous of the coronations was that of Charles VII in 1429. In trying to end the Hundred Years War with England, Charles's father had agreed to a treaty appointing the King of England heir to France. Though the disinherited Charles repudiated the treaty and undertook to rule, his authority was limited to a small realm and contested by both the English and their French allies. It was at this point that Joan of Arc, driven by visions and voices, appeared in aid of her beleaguered king. After rallying his forces and leading them to an important victory at Orléans, she insisted that he go to Reims, where he was crowned Charles VII.

Geographically speaking, Reims stands in a fateful position. The region of Champagne is largely open, level land that has been a route of invasion throughout European history. As a consequence, between the 5th and 10th centuries, Reims was flattened to the ground seven times by war. But no recent conflict left its mark on the body and spirit of the city more than World War I. The Germans occupied the city of Reims for 10 days in 1914, but they also gained control of the surrounding heights, from which they bombarded the city for four horrifying years (from September 19, 1914 to November 11, 1918). About 80% of its homes were destroyed, and most public buildings were severely damaged, including the soaring Gothic *Cathédrale Notre-Dame de Reims,* commonly ranked with *Notre-Dame de Paris* and *Notre-Dame de Chartres* among the world's most magnificent cathedrals.

During World War II, the German occupation again lasted four years. After Allied soldiers liberated Reims in 1944, US General Dwight D. Eisenhower established his headquarters in a large high school here, and it was in one of its classrooms that the unconditional surrender of the Third Reich was signed on May 7, 1945.

Today, most visitors to Reims go to see the *Cathédrale* and to tour the cellars of the great champagne houses, stocked with millions of bottles of the only authentic versions of the golden, sparkling wine universally associated with joy and celebration.

Reims At-a-Glance

SEEING THE CITY
The vine- and tree-covered hills surrounding Reims offer a plethora of panoramic views. Be aware that the modern buildings on the outskirts of the city sometimes block out its most impressive structure, the *Cathédrale Notre-Dame de Reims,* and that the ancient church you see may be the *Basilique St-Remi* rather than the cathedral itself (see below for detailed descriptions of each). In the center of the city, you can survey the area from the cathedral's towers (entry permitted daily at 11 AM and 3, 4, and 5 PM).

SPECIAL PLACES
Long, wide Place Drouet-d'Erlon, lined with hotels, cafés, and arcaded houses, is a good place to begin a tour of the city. Near one end of it is the Rue de Vesle, from which you can easily walk to the cathedral and surrounding sights. At the other end, across from the railroad station and at the midpoint of a huge mall, it runs into Boulevard Foch–Boulevard Général-Leclerc. The Place de la République, with its grand arch known as *Porte Mars,* is at the northern extreme of the mall, and from here, the Rue de Mars will lead you toward the *Cathédrale,* while the Rue du Champ-de-Mars heads toward the *Chapelle Foujita* and the cellars of several of the major champagne firms. Note that many attractions, such as museums and churches, are closed during lunch hours (usually from noon to 2 PM), especially in the off-season.

CATHÉDRALE DE NOTRE-DAME DE REIMS This magnificent cathedral is one of the most historically important structures in France. The first church on the spot was the *Cathédrale de St-Nicaise,* in which Remi baptized Clovis I and, in 496, crowned him King of the Franks. That event set an early precedent for a later practice; from the early 12th through the 19th century, nearly all the kings of France were crowned here. This cathedral is also one of the most important monuments of French artistic heritage. The second church was destroyed by fire in 1210, and the edifice seen today was begun the next year; it was nearly complete a century later, although the towers were not added until the 15th century. Consequently, the style of the main cathedral structure, conceived by master builder Jean d'Orbais, is pure 13th century, representing the golden age of French Gothic architecture. The cathedral suffered heavy shelling during World War I, which burned the roof, damaged the apse, and caused a section of arches to fall down, requiring a long restoration of the original features. Also in this century, some of the original statuary was removed from the exterior for restoration or protection from the further ravages of war and the environment. (They are now on display at the museum at the *Palais du Tau;* see below.) Replicas take the place of the original statues.

The cathedral's western façade is one of the most splendid conceptions of the 13th century. Its three-deep doorways constitute a Bible in sculpted stone, with the central doorway dedicated to the Virgin, the left door to the saints and martyrs, and the right door to Christ and the prophets. Among the glorious statues, note the groups representing the Visitation and the Presentation to the Temple in the central door, and the two angels flanking the scalped Saint Nicaise in the left door. One of these, the *ange au sourire* (the smiling angel), is the most famous of the cathedral's many angels; it's also known as the *sourire de Reims* (the smile of Reims). The upper part of the façade is ornamented with a gallery of colossal statues of kings.

Inside, the tall windows, the clerestory, and the spectacular stained glass windows provide superb lighting for the nave. Much of the 13th-century glass, including the awe-inspiring rose window of the western façade and the rose window in the northern transept, was restored after World War I. Other windows are completely modern, including the six windows in the axial chapel, which were drawn by Marc Chagall and executed in 1974. Not to be overlooked is the interior sculpture, especially the remarkable ensemble of statues in niches surrounding the smaller rose window of the façade and the beautiful capitals of the columns. Seventeen handsome tapestries help dispel some of the somberness of the interior.

Be sure to see the façade and stained glass–lit nave in the early morning or at twilight, when they are at their most exquisite. For a lovely view of the spectacular flying buttresses, stand in the garden of the adjacent

Palais du Tau (see below). Son-et-lumière (sound-and-light) shows are presented at the cathedral after dark on Saturdays from late June to mid-August. Enter the cathedral from Pl. du Cardinal-Luçon. For additional information, call the *Office du Tourisme* (see *Tourist Information,* below).

PALAIS DU TAU This rebuilt archbishop's palace takes its name from the shape of the original plan of the building (the Greek letter "T," or "tau"). It was the residence of the king at the time of the coronations and the site of post-coronation banquets. Now a museum, it contains monumental sculptures from the exterior of the *Cathédrale;* magnificent 16th-century tapestries of the life of the Virgin; and the cathedral treasury, whose collection includes a 9th-century pendant said to have been the talisman of Charlemagne, a 12th-century chalice used in numerous coronations, and mementos of the coronation of Charles X. Open daily except major holidays. Admission charge. Pl. du Cardinal-Luçon (phone: 26-47-74-39).

BASILIQUE ST-REMI If it weren't overshadowed by the *Cathédrale Notre-Dame de Reims,* the glories of this ancient Benedictine abbey church would be far more celebrated. Dedicated in 1049, it is the oldest of Reims's churches, and was painstakingly restored after being damaged during World War I. Most impressive are its Romanesque nave and transept, which date from the middle of the 11th century, and its immense choir, an example of the primitive Gothic style of the 12th century. The Flamboyant (flame-patterned) Gothic façade of the southern transept dates from the 16th century. The church also contains a 19th-century reconstruction of Saint Remi's tomb. A son-et-lumière show is presented free of charge Saturdays after dark from late June through early October. Open daily. Rue Simon (phone: 26-85-35-22).

MUSÉE DES BEAUX-ARTS In this museum is a rich collection of tapestries and ceramics, 13 sketches of German princes by both the elder and younger Cranach, and French paintings from the 17th century to the present. Corot, with 27 canvases on display here, is the most heavily represented of the French painters, but there are also paintings by pre-Impressionists, Impressionists, and their successors, including Boudin, Pissarro, Monet, Sisley, Renoir, Dufy, Matisse, and Picasso. The gardens also may be visited. Closed Tuesdays and holidays. Admission charge. 8 Rue Chanzy (phone: 26-47-28-44).

PLACE ROYALE The main square of the city is a beautiful example of 18th-century architecture, a legacy of the reign of Louis XV, whose statue, by Pigalle, stands in the middle. It's between Place de la République and the *Cathédrale* at Rue Vesle.

PORTE MARS A remnant of Gallo-Roman times, this imposing 3rd-century triumphal arch is a memorial to Augustus Caesar. During the Middle Ages, it became a gate in the city's ramparts, and today, one can just make out some of the very worn out bas-reliefs that adorn it, such as Jupiter and Leda. Pl. de la République.

CHAPELLE FOUJITA (ALSO KNOWN AS NOTRE-DAME DE LA PAIX) This striking Romanesque-style chapel was designed by Léonard Foujita, the famous Japanese painter of the School of Paris, who converted to Catholicism late in his life. The color, freshness, and individuality of the stained glass windows and frescoes is stunning. A gift of Mumm Champagne to the city, the chapel was opened in 1966. Closed Wednesdays, holidays, and in very cold weather (there's no heat). Admission charge. 33 Rue du Champs-de-Mars (no phone).

SALLE DE REDDITION (HALL OF THE SURRENDER) On May 7, 1945—VE Day—the Germans signed an unconditional surrender in this simple schoolroom, which served as General Eisenhower's headquarters during the final days of World War II. The room has been preserved as it was that day, with operational maps on the wall. Closed Tuesdays and holidays. Admission charge. Behind the railroad station, at 12 Rue Franklin-Roosevelt (phone: 26-47-84-19).

CHAMPAGNE CELLARS

Some of Reims's champagne cellars date back to ancient times, when the Romans excavated huge *crayères* (chalk pits) in the limestone base of the city, creating inverted funnels that they probably used as cool pantries. These gigantic cones often were connected underground, and in recent centuries, it was discovered that conditions in this netherworld were perfect for the aging of champagne. (For an overview of the history of champagne and how it is made, see *Champagne* in DIRECTIONS.) Today, the underground tunnels have been expanded so that there are miles and miles of them, some with the bare chalk walls still exposed, some covered by brick, tile, and other materials.

Of the more than a dozen champagne houses in Reims that open their cellars to visitors, a number are beyond the Place de la République in the Champ-de-Mars section of the city; others are beyond the *Basilique St-Remi* around Place des Droits-de-l'Homme and nearby streets, including Avenue du Général-Giraud, Boulevard Henri-Vasnier, and Rue des Crayères.

If you plan to descend into a champagne *cave,* bring warm clothes; a constant temperature in the upper 40s F makes the cellars ideal for champagne making but cool for visitors. Also wear sturdy shoes, because in most cases you'll be doing a fair amount of walking on slightly damp, uneven surfaces in dimly lit passageways.

Some champagne houses court large tour groups, while others prefer small groups of visitors with a sincere interest in learning about champagne production. All champagne houses listed below offer some form of guided tour. Most require appointments, but those which do not are usually open weekdays (except holidays and during August) 9 AM to noon and 2 to 5 PM.

While most houses offer tours in English, travelers should verify that an English-speaking guide will be available.

With the exception of Taittinger and Piper-Heidsieck, which levy a nominal charge, the tours are free, and they usually end with a complimentary champagne tasting. Note: Due to recent recessionary pressures, frequency of tours may be further limited; call to verify.

CHARLES HEIDSIECK Fifty rooms of pure chalk linked by galleries. The Gallo-Roman *crayères* were rediscovered in the 18th century. Visits by appointment only. 4 Bd. Henry-Vasnier (phone: 26-84-43-50).

KRUG This serious champagne house still has the venerable oak barrels used for its first fermentation. Tours are given by appointment only, for groups of 10 or less, and you must write or call well in advance and indicate what aspect of the cellars you are interested in. Visits can be arranged year-round on weekdays. 5 Rue Coquebert, Reims 51100 (phone: 26-84-44-20; fax: 26-84-44-49).

LANSON Its beautiful wine presses make this a particularly interesting visit. Tours by appointment only. 12 Bd. Lundy (phone: 26-78-50-50).

LOUIS ROEDERER The enormous oak casks here are extraordinary. Make reservations well in advance. Closed Friday afternoons and during July. 21 Bd. Lundy (phone: 26-40-42-11; fax: 26-47-66-51).

MUMM No appointment is required to tour the 11 miles of gigantic cellars. The informative tour (available in English) is one of the best. Open daily from March through October; closed weekends and holidays in winter. 34 Rue du Champ-de-Mars (phone: 26-49-59-70; fax: 26-49-59-01).

PIPER-HEIDSIECK No appointment is required here, where part of the visit takes place aboard an electric train. Open daily March through November; closed Fridays and most weekends in December through February. English-speaking guides are available. 51 Bd. Henry-Vasnier (phone: 26-84-43-44; fax: 26-84-43-49).

POMMERY These are fascinating cellars: Down 116 steps are 11 miles of avenues with crossroads, statues (including a 14th-century Virgin), bas-reliefs, and extraordinary *crayères* that form pyramidal wells reaching through smooth white walls to daylight. Open daily from mid-March through October; closed weekends from mid-January through mid-March; to visit at other times, request an appointment. 5 Pl. Général-Gouraud (phone: 26-61-62-63; fax: 26-61-63-98).

RUINART PÈRE & FILS This dedicated champagne house, which bills itself as the oldest in Champagne, prefers to give tours to groups of ten or fewer. The pyramidal *crayères* date from the 2nd century BC and are the only ones in the region classified as a historic landmark. Tours are by appointment only. 4 Rue des Crayères (phone: 26-85-40-29).

TAITTINGER An interesting historical slide show precedes the tour of cellars set up in the crypt of the former abbey of Saint Nicaise, which is remarkable for its pointed arches. Other cellars are in beautiful triangular *crayères* of the 3rd and 4th centuries. Open daily March through November, and December through February by appointment only. 9 Pl. St-Nicaise (phone: 26-85-45-35; fax: 26-85-17-46).

VEUVE CLICQUOT PONSARDIN These extraordinary funnel-shaped *crayères*, which date from Gallo-Roman times, include 15 miles of underground galleries with splendid bas-reliefs carved into the walls. Closed Sundays from April through October. 1 Pl. des Droits-de-l'Homme (phone: 26-40-25-42; fax: 26-40-60-17).

ENVIRONS

FORT DE LA POMPELLE This 1880 fort, which defended Reims during World War I, contains a museum of war mementos—decorations, uniforms, arms, and an exceptional collection of German helmets—of interest to military history buffs. Open daily. Admission charge (no charge for World War I veterans). Three miles (5 km) east of Reims via N3 and N44 (phone: 26-49-11-85).

EXTRA SPECIAL

If you have a car, don't miss a drive through the undulating hills and valleys of the Montagne de Reims, the Valley of the Marne (of war and, more recently, *Euro Disney* fame), and the Côte des Blancs, where the grapes that become champagne are grown. You will see some of the finest vineyards in the world, travel through tiny villages with 12th and 13th century churches, and see acres of pastoral farmland, all elements of idyllic French provincial life. (In Reims proper, we recommend that you walk or use public or tour buses, since the largely one-way street system can get drivers in a tangle.) For a suggested itinerary, see *Champagne* in DIRECTIONS.

Sources and Resources

TOURIST INFORMATION

The Reims *Office de Tourisme* is on the Square du Trésor, left of the *Cathédrale* (2 Rue Guillaume-de-Machault; phone: 26-47-25-69; fax: 26-47-23-63); pick up some of their useful free brochures.

LOCAL COVERAGE Consult Reims's French-language daily, *L'Union*.

TELEPHONE The city code for Reims is 26, which is incorporated into all local eight-digit numbers. When calling a number from the Paris region (including the Ile-de-France), dial 16, wait for the dial tone, then dial the eight-digit number. When calling a number from outside Paris, dial only the eight-digit number.

GETTING AROUND

The best means of transportation in Reims is your own two feet. Many of most interesting shops, sites, and monuments are within walking distance of the *Cathédrale*. It is a hike, though, from there to the *Basilique St-Remi* and to many of the champagne cellars; see below for some of the alternatives.

AIRPORT *Aéroport Reims-Champagne* (Bétheny, 4 miles/7 km out of town; phone: 26-07-15-15) accommodates a limited number of regional flights and special charters. In addition, there are shuttle bus services from *Orly* and *Roissy* airports near Paris. For information, contact *Jet Home,* 204 Rue de Cernay (phone: 26-07-32-70) or *Ligne Directe,* 7 Rue des Poissonniers (phone: 26-88-32-43).

BUS For local buses, pick up maps and schedules from the *Office du Tourisme* or the *TUR* (*Transports Urbains Reims;* 6 Rue Chanzy; phone: 26-88-25-38). Tickets are sold on the bus; a *simple* (single, one-way ticket) costs 5F (about 85¢ at press time). Or else you can buy a *carnet,* a book of 10 tickets, for 30F (about $5.10 at press time) at the *TUR.* For long-distance buses, contact *Trans Champagne Evasion* (86 Rue Fajnières; phone: 26-65-17-07).

CAR RENTAL Among the major firms represented are *Avis* (Cour de la Gare; phone: 26-47-10-08); *Budget* (76 Rue Vesle; phone: 26-40-01-02); *Europcar* (76 Bd. Lundy; phone: 26-88-38-38); and *Hertz* (26 Bd. Joffre; phone: 26-47-98-78).

TAXI Other than a rented car, a taxi is probably the best way to get around this area on wheels. Find one at a designated stand—at the train station, for instance, and in plenty of other spots—or telephone for one (phone: 26-47-05-05, 26-02-15-02, or 26-04-03-02).

TOURS Perhaps the best way to experience Champagne's vineyards and villages is from aloft, on one of the long, breathtaking balloon flights (with licensed pilots) offered from April through October. Call either *Vols en Montgolfière* (15 *bis* Pl. St-Nicaise; phone: 26-82-59-60; fax: 26-82-48-62) or *Club Tonus* (36 Rue Léo-Lagrange; phone: 26-82-80-04; fax: 26-85-58-13) to verify flight times, which are determined by weather conditions. You also might want to tour the rivers and navigable canals around Reims by boat; although the views are not extraordinary compared to those from land, such tours might suit those who are in the mood to be on the water. Contact the *Halte Nautique* (Vieux Port; Bd. Paul-Doumer; phone: 26-40-52-60).

For leisurely viewing from terra firma, try a 45-minute jaunt on the sightseeing train called *Petit Train de Reims* (phone: 26-82-88-08). The trains operate weekends and holidays May through June, and daily July through August. Or you can take a horse-drawn carriage ride (*tour en calèche;* phone: 26-02-95-23), which are offered in July and August, except Tuesdays and rainy days. Both the carriages and the trains depart from the *Cathédrale,* where tickets are sold. For additional details on tours of Reims and its environs, consult the *Office du Tourisme* (see above).

TRAIN The Reims train station (*Gare SNCF;* phone: 26-88-50-50) is on Boulevard Joffre, across the mall from the north end of Place Drouet-d'Erlon. There are several trains daily to Paris (1½ hours) and to Epernay (25 minutes).

SPECIAL EVENTS

If you plan to be in Reims during January and February—especially if you have children with you—don't miss the annual performances given by France's national circus school, the *Centre des Formations des Arts du Cirque* (*Le Cirque,* 2 Bd. du Général-Leclerc; call the *Comité Central des Fêtes* number below for information). There's an antiques show in late January (contact the *Office du Tourisme* for details) and a vintage car show in mid-March (phone: 26-47-42-06). An international horse show takes place in May, as does an annual canoe-kayak regatta. The second weekend in June brings the historical parades and secular and religious plays and songs of the *Fêtes de Jeanne d'Arc,* celebrating Saint Joan's return to Reims with the *dauphin* for his coronation. Coinciding with these events is *Les Sacres du Folklore,* a weekend-long festival during which folkloric groups from around the world, dressed in native costume, parade through the streets, and a *Foire Médiévale,* featuring artisans selling crafts in the old streets in the center of the city. From late June through August, the city sponsors *Flâneries Musicales* (Musical Strolls), a series of public concerts (most of them free) featuring international artists such as Yehudi Menuhin. A *bal populaire* (dancing in the streets) takes place in the center of the city on July 13, the eve of *Bastille Day,* which is celebrated by a fireworks display in *Parc Léo-Lagrange* on July 14. In early fall (usually the third weekend in September), the city's *Journées de Patrimoine* (Heritage Festival) draws 100,000 visitors to the Place de la République for fairs and fireworks. The Reims *Marathon,* one of France's most important, takes place in late October or early November and attracts up to 8,000 runners. A large antiques show is regularly held in mid-November.

Contact the *Comité Central des Fêtes* (phone: 26-82-45-66) for information about all special events in and around Reims.

MUSEUMS

Besides those described in *Special Places,* the following museums may be of interest. Note that museums are among the attractions that tend to close during lunch hours, usually from noon to 2 PM.

MUSÉE DE L'AUTOMOBILE FRANÇAISE This is the private collection of engineer/inventor Philippe Charbonneaux, featuring 130 automobiles dating from 1897 to today. There also is a remarkable collection of toy and model cars and old posters. Open daily April through October; weekends only (or by appointment) November through March. Admission charge. 84 Av. Georges-Clemenceau (phone: 26-82-83-84).

MUSÉE-ABBAYE ST-REMI (ALSO KNOWN AS MUSÉE D'HISTOIRE ET D'ARCHÉOLOGIE)
This former abbey, constructed in the late 12th century, is now an archaeological museum. Its collection, dating from prehistoric times to the Middle
Ages, includes some interesting Gallo-Roman mosaics and tombs. There's
also an exhibit on regional military history. There are free son-et-lumière
shows Saturdays at 9:30 PM from July through September. Closed mornings and some holidays. There is an admission charge. It's adjacent to the
Basilique St-Remi, at 53 Rue Simon (phone: 26-85-23-36).

MUSÉE-HÔTEL LE VERGEUR/MUSÉE DU VIEUX REIMS (MUSEUM OF OLD REIMS)
Here are sculptures, paintings, drawings, and plans relating to the history
of Reims and to the splendors of the coronations. There are two rooms of
works by Flemish and Dutch artists, including a collection of Dürer engravings, and attractive suites with 19th-century furnishings. Closed mornings,
Mondays, and holidays. Admission charge. 36 Pl. du Forum (phone: 26-47-
20-75).

SHOPPING

Much of the best shopping in Reims can be found on the streets and malls
near the *Cathédrale.* Local specialties are champagne and biscuits, and if
you wish to stock up on the former, prices in the wine shops near the cathedral are slightly lower than those found in Paris. Better clothing shops for
men and women line the Cours Langlet and the Rue de Vesle. On the first
Sunday of every month except August, a flea market takes place at *Site
Henri Farman* at the *Parc des Expositions* (Rt. de Châlons-sur-Marne);
there's a smaller flea market Saturdays through Mondays at 6 Boulevard
Jamin.

For more on shopping hours and days in France, see GETTING READY
TO GO. Meanwhile, here are some shops to explore:

Fossier This is generally considered to be the best place to buy Reims's delicious
croquignolles (dry biscuits). 25 Cours Langlet (phone: 26-47-59-84).

La Garinie High-quality arts and crafts are sold here. 6 Rue de l'Université (phone:
26-88-43-91).

Maison Coeuriot/Au Cochon Sans Rancune The finest charcuterie (cold cuts) can
be bought here, for picnics or a snack. 47 Rue de Vesle (phone: 26-47-
33-35).

Le Marché aux Vins There's no better place to stock up on bottles of fine champagne and wine from all over France. Closed Monday mornings and Sundays.
3 Pl. Léon-Bourgeois (phone: 26-40-12-12).

Pâtisserie Durot Visit this elegant pastry shop and tearoom for a sweet pick-me-
up. 13 Rue du Cadran St-Pierre (phone: 26-47-51-49).

La Petite Friande Chocolate champagne corks are this confectioner's specialty. 15
Cours Langlet (phone: 26-47-50-44).

Aux Spécialités Remoises Savory *biscuits de Reims* (assorted, locally baked cookies) to accompany champagne and wonderful *pain d'épices* (gingerbread) are among the incredible edibles found here. Place du Cardinal-Luçon (phone: 26-40-43-85).

SPORTS AND FITNESS

Anyone interested in jogging or walking on the hilly country lanes of Champagne can find many places to do so just outside Reims. For other forms of exercise, see below.

GOLF The private 18-hole course at *Le Golf de Reims* in nearby Gueux (Château des Dames de France; phone: 26-03-60-14) often admits non-members for a fee. From Reims, take the Reims-Tinqueux road, turn onto N31 toward Soissons, and then quickly turn off it onto D27 toward Gueux. Farther away (31 miles/50 km south of Reims via D20) is *La Vitarderie* (Chemin de Bourdonnerie; phone: 26-58-25-09), a public 18-hole course. There is a driving range at the *Hippodrome de Reims* race course (3 Rue du Président-Kennedy; phone: 26-06-03-67); closed mornings March to November, and weekdays the rest of the year and in poor weather.

SWIMMING Among the public pools is the *Piscine Olympique* (41 Chaussée Bocquaine; phone: 26-82-60-00).

TENNIS AND SQUASH There are tennis courts at *Parc Pommery* (10 Av. du Général-Giraud; phone: 26-85-23-29), and squash courts at 10 Rue Gabriel-Voisin (phone: 26-85-40-80).

THEATER

La Comédie de Reims/Centre Dramatique National (3 Chaussée Bocquaine; phone: 26-48-49-10) has a varied repertory. The main venue for ballet is the *Grand Théâtre* (9 Rue Chanzy; phone: 26-47-43-41). A multipurpose cultural center, *Le Manège* (2 Bd. du Général-Leclerc; phone: 26-47-30-40), hosts a variety of live performances, including dance and theater.

MUSIC

The *Grand Théâtre* (see above) is the place for opera and concerts; *Le Manège* (see above) also features concerts. Popular music can be heard in some of the bars and cabarets listed below.

NIGHTCLUBS AND NIGHTLIFE

Though the people of Reims are reputed to be serious, family-oriented stay-at-homes who do their champagne drinking over dinner with friends and relatives, somebody is keeping the bars, cafés, and cabarets open at night. The champagne bar at *Boyer Les Crayères* (see *Checking In*) is open Tuesdays through Sundays from 11 AM to 1 AM. Other champagne and wine bars are *Le Petit Cellier* (5 Cours Anatole-France; phone: 26-47-16-31) and *Le Vintage* (1 Cours Anatole-France; phone: 26-40-40-82). *Le Club St-Pierre* (41 Bd. du Général-Leclerc; phone: 26-88-26-13) has dancing to disco and other kinds of music. Other bars and cafés with music are *La Boîte à Cocktails* (6 Pl. du Forum; phone: 26-47-56-58), with a pianist nightly except on Sundays and from mid-July to mid-August, when it's closed; *Bar de la Comédie,* a piano bar and artists' hangout (3 Chausée Bocquaine; phone: 26-48-49-20), closed Mondays and August; and *Les Ombrages,* in the *Altéa Champagne* hotel (see *Checking In*), an "American bar" where the live music includes some mild jazz, and where up to four dozen brands of champagne are in stock. *Le Croque-Notes* (24 Rue Ernest-Renan; phone: 26-88-41-28) is a lively jazz spot.

Best in Town

CHECKING IN

Although Reims has plenty of beds, visitors with cars might consider staying in one of the lovely country inns nearby, some of which are listed below (also see *Champagne* in DIRECTIONS). For a double room, expect to pay $150 or more in a hotel we list as very expensive; $100 to $150 in an expensive one; $60 to $100 in a moderate place; and less than $60 in an inexpensive hotel. Unless otherwise noted, all hotels listed below feature air conditioning, telephones, TV sets, and private baths in the rooms. Some less expensive hotels have private baths in only some of their rooms; it's a good idea to confirm whether your room has a private bath when making a reservation. All the properties listed below accept major credit cards and are open year-round unless otherwise noted.

For an unforgettable experience, we begin with our favorite Reims hostelry, followed by our cost and quality choices of hotels, listed by price category.

SPECIAL HAVEN

Boyer Les Crayères Ensconced in a stunning 19th-century château, this Relais & Châteaux member is set on nearly 20 beautifully landscaped acres, a stone's throw from the twin towers of the *Cathédrale.* If you want the best—and are willing to pay for it—this is the place to stay. Some of the 16 large, sumptuous rooms and three suites open onto terraces overlooking the gardens. All of them are decorated differently, mainly in the styles of the Louis Philippe era, with Provençal prints; each has an entry hall, a dressing room, and a sizable bathroom. The main attraction of the place, however, remains the glorious three-Michelin-star restaurant (see *Eating Out*). Closed December 23 through mid-January. 64 Bd. Henri-Vasnier (phone: 26-82-80-80; fax: 26-82-65-52).

Château de Barive This former hunting lodge in its own 1,000-acre park has been converted into a lovely 13-room, three-suite inn with a heated pool, a sauna, a tennis court, and a restaurant. Arriving along the long graveled driveway makes you feel like royalty. To get there, take the N44 or A26 to Laon, then the D977. About 20 miles (32 km) from Reims, at Liesse (phone: 23-22-15-15; fax: 23-22-08-39).

Château de Fère This Renaissance château set in a 14-acre park is worth the trip—29 miles (48 km) west of Reims—not only for its luxurious 19 rooms and six suites (all renovated last year), but also for the fish and other specialties served in its one-Michelin-star dining room. Between Château-Thierry and Fismes, in the village of Fère-en-Tardenois (phone: 23-82-21-13; fax: 23-82-37-81).

Grand Hôtel des Templiers In this lovely, renovated, 19th-century bourgeois mansion are 19 large, individually decorated rooms and suites with sleek marble baths. Guests also can enjoy a winter garden, an indoor pool, a sauna, a steambath, and a tanning room. There's no restaurant. It is on a quiet street removed from the city center, at 22 Rue des Templiers (phone: 26-88-55-08; fax: 26-47-80-60).

Altéa Champagne This is one of the largest hotels in the region. The 115 rooms and nine suites are ultramodern and comfortable (40 have color TV sets and air conditioning). A restaurant is on the premises, and by night, you might want to check out the live music at the hotel's "American bar," *Les Ombrages*. 31 Bd. Paul-Doumer (phone: 26-88-53-54; fax: 26-40-35-51).

L'Assiette Champenoise Set in its own large park, this inn has 62 spacious rooms, a covered pool, a sauna, and a fine restaurant. Just outside the city limits, at 40 Av. Paul-Vaillant-Couturier, Tinqueux (phone: 26-04-15-56; fax: 26-04-15-69).

Les Consuls This 28-room hotel in the center of town has smallish but cozy rooms, a bar, and room service. 7-9 Rue Général Sarrail (phone: 26-88-46-10; fax: 26-88-66-33).

Holiday Inn No surprises at this 84-room member of the worldwide chain, which opened in late 1993 in a renovated 1930s building. You will be able to relax in the unremarkable but sturdily furnished rooms, and the seventh-floor bar/restaurant offers a great view of the city. 46 Rue Buirette (phone: 26-47-56-00; fax: 26-47-45-75).

Liberty-Must The 80 comfortable rooms in this modern hostelry are soundproof, and most have a view of the canal. The restaurant, *Orphée* (see *Eating Out*), is one of the city's best. 55 Rue Boulard (phone: 26-40-52-61; fax: 26-47-27-38).

La Paix This is one of the best bets in the city—a friendly, efficiently run property with 105 well-equipped rooms. The pleasant bar opens onto a small garden. 9 Rue Buirette (phone: 26-40-04-08; fax: 26-47-75-04).

INEXPENSIVE

Du Nord An old-fashioned hostelry, it was renovated to include comforts and charm that come as a surprise after passing through its drab entryway. Located in the heart of Reims, it offers excellent value and 50 clean rooms. Closed December 24 to January 6. 75 Pl. Drouet d'Erlon (phone: 26-47-39-03; fax: 26-40-92-26).

EATING OUT

Regional cuisine includes anything cooked *au champagne* (with champagne), *potée champenoise* (a hearty meat stew), and *coq au vin*. Spectacular local cheeses include *brie de meaux* (named for a nearby city to the west, and considered the king of bries), *chaource* (a creamy, delicately flavored white cheese), and tangy, richly scented *maroilles* (whole milk cheese that is salted and washed in beer).

For a full lunch or dinner for two, excluding beverages but including service, expect to pay $150 or more at an expensive restaurant; $80 to $150 at a moderate place; and less than $80 at an inexpensive one. Service usually is included in the prices listed in the menu, although the French tip extra for good service.

For an unforgettable culinary experience, we begin with our Reims favorite, followed by our cost and quality choices of restaurants, listed by price category.

HAUTE GASTRONOMIE

Boyer Les Crayères Nary a pilgrim leaves this temple of haute cuisine (and haute prices) in less than a state of bliss. Gérard Boyer and his wife, Elayne, have earned three stars from Michelin for what is surely one of the finest restaurants in France. The warmth and glow here quickly translate into the comfort of its diners. The inspired seasonal menu leans toward foods that marry well with champagne. Try the *escalope de foie gras,* the delicate and elegant fish dishes, the sweetbreads with celery root purée and truffles, Boyer's famous *truffe en croûte* (truffle in puff pastry), or the local cheeses. Save room for the riches of the dessert cart, which might include *soupe au chocolat* (chocolate soup) served with a slice of *pain d'épices* (gingerbread), and a *glace au pain d'épices* (gingerbread topped with ice cream). The *cave,* a wine lover's dream, is stocked with rare champagnes. Closed Monday and Tuesday lunch, and when the hotel closes, from December 23 through mid-January. Reservations essential. Major credit cards accepted. 64 Bd. Henri-Vasnier (phone: 26-82-80-80; fax: 26-82-65-52).

EXPENSIVE

Le Florence This luxurious one-Michelin-star restaurant offers refined cooking characterized by delicate sauces; some locals feel it offers the best food for the money in town. It's especially strong on game and on fish dishes using crayfish, lobster, turbot, and oysters. Tantalizing desserts and a remarkable selection of champagne also are offered. In the summer, you may want to request a table on the terrace. Closed two weeks in August; closed Sundays except holiday Sundays. Reservations advised. Major credit cards accepted. 43 Bd. Foch (phone: 26-47-12-70; fax: 26-40-07-09).

La Garenne Specialties at this Michelin-star-holder include *ris de veau aux champignons des bois* (veal sweetbreads with wild mushrooms) and, for dessert, nougatine ice cream with mint sauce. Closed Sunday evenings, Mondays, and three weeks in August. Reservations necessary. Major credit cards accepted. Four miles (6 km) outside of Reims, on the N31 in Champigny (phone: 26-08-26-62; fax: 26-84-24-13).

Orphée Inventive nouvelle cuisine dishes—sea scallops with olive oil and fresh cilantro, for example—predominate at this eatery. The wine list abounds in champagnes. Closed Sundays. Reservations advised. Major credit cards accepted. In the *Liberty* hotel. 55 Rue Boulard (phone: 26-40-52-61).

MODERATE

Le Chardonnay This establishment unfailingly serves meals that many feel deserve a Michelin star or two. Try the quail stuffed with wild mushrooms or the frogs' legs in puff pastry. Prices were greatly reduced last year in a recession-fighting measure, so it's a real bargain. Closed Saturday lunch, Sunday dinner, most of August, and December 24 to mid-January. Reservations advised. Major credit cards accepted. 184 Av. d'Epernay (phone: 26-06-08-60).

La Côte 108 This restaurant has an elegant, recently remodeled dining room, and features such specialties as *feuilletés* with wild mushrooms, wild duck *magrets* (slices of boneless breast), and lamb medallions with garlic cloves. The balanced *menu dégustation* is a feast. Closed Sunday dinner, Mondays, two weeks in July, and from December 26 through mid-January. Reservations advised. Major credit cards accepted. In Berry-au-Bac, 7½ miles (12 km) from Reims via N44 (phone: 23-79-95-04; fax: 23-79-83-50).

Au Petit Comptoir The bistro trend continues, and like many of France's celebrity chefs, Gérard Boyer (see *Les Crayères,* above) has opened his own version.

A cozy, casual spot, it has all the requisite elements—a frosted glass façade, marble tables, a zinc bar, and well-prepared, refined French fare. Closed Saturday lunch, Sundays, two weeks in August, and two weeks in December. Reservations advised. Major credit cards accepted. In the heart of the old market area, at 17 Rue de Mars (phone: 26-40-58-58).

Vonelly Gambetta This modern restaurant has a following among local vintners. Some of the outstanding dishes are the warm lobster salad and a whole sole stuffed with crab. The prix fixe menus are a good bargain. Closed Sunday dinner, Mondays, one week in March, and late July to mid-August. Reservations advised. Major credit cards accepted. 9-13 Rue Gambetta (phone: 26-47-22-00; fax: 26-47-22-43).

INEXPENSIVE

Au Petit Bacchus Old and new mix harmoniously in this wine bar and lunch spot. Daily specials on blackboards announce light lunchtime platters, including cheese trays, smoked salmon, and caviar. As the name implies, wines take priority; the *cave* is excellent. Open daily. Reservations advised. Major credit cards accepted. On a small street behind the *Cathédrale,* at 11 Rue de l'Université (phone: 26-47-10-05).

Le Vigneron Local cuisine par excellence is the stock in trade of the two small dining rooms in this 17th-century house. The rooms are decorated with old posters and a collection of rare wine labels; the atmosphere is friendly and very French. Among the menu choices are Reims ham with grapes, pike in a champagne sauce, and *potée champenoise* (a stew of smoked ham, bacon, sausages, and cabbage). The reasonable wine list features an extensive selection of champagne and local still wines. Closed Saturday lunch, Sundays, two weeks in August, and from *Christmas* to early January. Reservations necessary. Mastercard and Visa accepted. Pl. Jamot (phone: 26-47-00-71).

Rouen

"Oh, Rouen, art thou then my final resting place . . . ?" With this plaintive cry, Joan of Arc was led off to her execution, an act that bound her to this city forever. Indeed, for the visitor this strong association tends to obscure other aspects of Rouen's history and current importance.

Roeun's location in Normandy, near the mouth of the Seine and the English Channel, has played a pivotal role in its history. The ever-efficient, occupying Romans established Rouen, choosing as its site the first point upstream from the English Channel where a bridge could be built. They settled on the right bank of the great loop in the river, in the natural amphitheater created by the steep surrounding hills that remains the heart of the city. Rouen is now Paris's main port, the fourth-largest in France (by road, Rouen is only 86 miles (139 km) from the French capital).

The fourth century saw the arrival of the first bishops, who came to Rouen to convert the locals to Christianity. Soon after, the Romans and their city disappeared into the shadows of the Dark Ages, when invading barbarians swept away nearly all of the physical and spiritual manifestations of the Pax Romana and plunged Europe into disorder. The city's recorded history resumed with the creation of the duchy of Normandy in 911, when the new duke—Rollo—chose Rouen as his capital.

Even after the Norman Conquest of 1066, Rouen was second only to London in importance among the possessions of the Norman-English kings, and it maintained that standing until 1204, when the luckless King John of England lost his Norman possessions to Philippe-Auguste of France, who annexed them to the French crown. Rouen soon became one of the most sought-after prizes in the on-again, off-again tug-of-war between France and England that reached its climax in the Hundred Years War (1337–1453). In 1418 and 1419, Rouen endured a six-month siege that ended with its capitulation to the English.

It was during Rouen's tenure under English control that Joan of Arc walked into the pages of history. Born in Domrémy (Lorraine) in about 1412, she heard voices and saw visions at an early age that urged her to go to the aid of the feeble heir to the French throne, the future King Charles VII. In an attempt to end the Hundred Years War, Charles's father had agreed in 1420 to a treaty naming Henry V, King of England, his successor as King of France. Though the young Charles repudiated the treaty when his father died in 1422, he ruled over only a small realm, confined to the area south of the Loire, while the English, with the help of the Dukes of Burgundy, extended their rule over an increasingly larger part of France north of the Loire. The important town of Orléans probably would have fallen to the English, too, had not the young peasant girl convinced the fainthearted Charles of her divine inspiration and led his troops to raise the months-long siege in 1429. She then led her king to be crowned in the cathedral of Reims, lending legitimacy to his royal title.

The next spring, the "Maid of Orléans," as Joan of Arc came to be known, was captured by the Burgundians during the defense of Compiègne. Her influence—more talismanic than tactical—was strong enough to make the English commanders anxious to have her destroyed. Richard de Beauchamp, Earl of Warwick, paid her Burgundian captors to release her to his custody, then handed her over to the ecclesiastical court of Rouen to be tried for heresy and witchcraft. Joan's prison was in a tower of the castle that Philippe-Auguste had built 200 years before, where she was shown some persuasive instruments of torture. The keep, now called *Tour Jeanne-d'Arc,* is all that remains of the castle. On May 24, 1431, she was taken to the cemetery of the *Abbey of St. Ouen* (now the garden of the *Hôtel de Ville*), where she publicly renounced the "voices" she had heard. In return for recanting, her inquisitors condemned her to life imprisonment rather than death, with the condition that she wear only women's clothes (she had worn male garb while fighting).

Not satisfied, the English pressed for more definitive measures until the Maid was tricked into donning men's clothing. She was duly accused of breaking her oath, and, on May 29, in a room of the *Archevêché* (Archbishop's Palace), she was condemned to death. The next day, on Place du Vieux-Marché, she was burned at the stake, and her remains were thrown into the Seine.

The English finally left Rouen in 1449, and during the next 100 years building flourished in the city on an unprecedented scale. The *Eglise St-Maclou,* one of the most perfect examples of the Flamboyant Gothic style in Europe, belongs to this period, as do the *Cathédrale de Notre-Dame's Tour de Beurre* (Butter Tower) and the superb Renaissance *Hôtel de Bourgtheroulde* and *Palais de Justice.* Along with the famous *Gros-Horloge* (Great Clock), these structures form a spectacular visual unity, especially when set against the simple *maisons de pans de bois*—homes with exposed beams, gables, *colombages* (half-timbered exteriors), and leaded windows— that survive in profusion in Rouen.

The city remained a prosperous trade center for the next 400 years. Today, the rich agricultural lands of surrounding Normandy, as well as the chemical, petroleum, paper, metallurgical, and textile industries operating in greater Rouen, all profit from the port's proximity to Paris, fueling an economy that supports more than half a million people. But the city suffered greatly during World War II.

A final stop en route to the capture of Paris, Rouen was taken by Rommel's Fifth Panzer Division on June 10, 1940, and was occupied for the next four years. Bombarded first by advancing German forces and then by Allied air attacks aimed at the invaders, Rouen experienced near-total destruction; the area between the cathedral and the river, for example, was obliterated. By August 30, 1944, when the city was liberated by Canadian forces, 1,600 people had been buried in the rubble; hundreds of acres of land had been destroyed; and 9,500 houses and 14 monuments had been razed. Luckily, many of the town's treasures—stained glass windows, paintings, ceramics, and book collections—had been stowed away for protection.

Rouen is a survivor. Except for the destroyed *Eglise de St-Vincent,* the major architectural wonders that were damaged were repaired, and those demolished were rebuilt. Despite the losses of war, Rouen has preserved the profound spirit of its past, incorporating it into the continuing rush of its present. The *Cathédrale de Notre-Dame,* whose architecture represents several centuries' worth of styles cobbled together in one enormous, bombastic structure, has been made famous in many renderings by the painter Monet. The ancient building at 31 Place du Vieux-Marché exists still as a restaurant, *La Couronne;* the school that Pierre Corneille attended and that is now named for him still drums Latin, Greek, and logic into the heads of tomorrow's leaders; scenes from *Madame Bovary* still draw fans of native son Gustave Flaubert; and the city's hundreds of bells still call the faithful to mass twice a day.

Rouen At-a-Glance

SEEING THE CITY

The best view of Rouen is from the viewing table on the Côte Ste-Catherine (St. Catherine's Hill), southeast of the center. Taking in the city's towers and belfries as well as the serpentine Seine, it is especially attractive in the glow of early evening. The summit of N182 in Canteleu, on the other side of town, commands a view eastward down the valley, over the docks to the city. Another fine view—across the roofs and gables of Le Vieux Rouen (the Old Town)—is from the *Beffroi* (Belfry) of the *Gros-Horloge* (see *Special Places*). Also worth seeing are the quays of the Seine, which hum with industrial activity, revealing an important facet of contemporary Rouen. Rue Grand Pont leads down to the Seine from in front of the cathedral; the best way to get there is by bicycle or on foot.

SPECIAL PLACES

All the sights below are within walking distance of each other in Le Vieux Rouen, on the right bank of the Seine. On the left bank is the modern St-Sever quarter. Note that a large number of attractions close at lunchtime, usually from 12 to 2 PM. Unless otherwise noted, churches and outdoor sites such as cemeteries and parks are open daily and charge no admission.

CATHÉDRALE DE NOTRE-DAME DE ROUEN The best way to approach this famous structure, whose architecture can best be described as *dentelle en pierre* (lacy stone), is from narrow Rue du Gros-Horloge. As you approach the Place de la Cathédrale, the extraordinary contours of the great west façade beloved of Monet gradually appear, a mesmerizing spectacle of statues, pinnacles, and mismatched towers that amounts to a lesson in 400 years of ecclesiastical architecture. To the left as you face the church is the Romanesque base of the *Tour St-Romain* (St. Romanus Tower), a vestige of the ancient Romanesque church that burned down in 1200. In addition, styles from four different Gothic periods are represented: primitive Gothic, in the middle tiers of the *Tour St-Romain;* pure Gothic, in the *Portails St-Jean-Baptiste* and *St-Etienne* flanking the main door; Rayonnant (a late 13th-century style employing great sheets of glass interrupted only by narrow fingers of masonry) in the windows above the *Portail St-Stephen* and the four major pinnacles of the façade; and Flamboyant (usually 15th or 16th century French, and characterized by wave-, fan-, or flame-like forms) in the famous *Tour de Beurre,* which was named for the local gourmands who paid for it by buying indulgences so they wouldn't have to give up butter during *Lent.* And rising from the central lantern tower is a 19th-century cast-iron spire that replaced the original wooden one. The detail of the west portals, as well as that of the north door (the *Portail des Libraires,* or Booksellers' Door) and the south door (the *Portail de la Calende*), is full of narrative, often of humor. In the *Cour des Libraires* (named for the booksellers that used to congregate here), leading to the door, is a workshop where sculptors chisel away at reproductions of the medieval saints that will replace those disfigured beyond repair.

The interior has more architectural unity, reflecting the pure Gothic style of the 13th century, when the nave—with its four great stories of arches, false tribunes, triforia, and high windows—was completed. The choir was lovingly restored after extensive damage in World War II; the carvings of the 15th-century misericords, which survived the bombing, provide a colorful illustration of the costumes, customs, and work implements of the period. Some 13th-century stained glass survives in the ambulatory, most notably in the windows of St-Julien l'Hospitalier; here, too, are several 13th-century tombs, including that of Richard Coeur de Lion, whose lion heart alone is buried below his effigy, his other earthly remains resting elsewhere. (The heart of Charles V is entombed in the nearby crypt, another of the few parts of the ancient Romanesque church still extant.)

In the north arm of the transept, the 15th-century *Escalier des Libraires* (Booksellers' Staircase) is famous for its lace-like banister. The *Chapelle de la Vierge* (Chapel of the Virgin) in the apse contains 14th-century stained glass windows depicting 24 of Rouen's bishops and archbishops. It is dominated by two 16th-century tombs: On the right facing the altar, the two cardinals d'Amboise, Georges I and his nephew Georges II, kneel in prayer above their sumptuously decorated burial place. Constructed between 1515 and 1525 in the overlush style of the early Renaissance, the tomb is a monument of arabesque and Italianate details at once gorgeous and grotesque. The tomb of Louis de Brézé (the husband of Diane de Poitiers, mistress of Henri II of France), on the left facing the altar, reflects a more sober

Renaissance style; its simple Corinthian columns and graceful caryatids provide a marked contrast to the tomb of the cardinals. A wonderful 17th-century Spanish-style reredos, painted in gold and crowned by a statue of the Virgin with Child, has a charming painting, *The Adoration of the Shepherds* by Philippe de Champaigne, at its center.

Guided tours of the cathedral (in French) take place several times daily during the summer (with a shortened schedule on Sundays and religious holidays), and on weekend afternoons the rest of the year; participants gather in the nave. The *Chapelle de la Vierge* is closed weekdays, except during guided tours (check with the office of the archbishop for tour times and information; phone: 36-71-20-52). The *Portail de la Calende,* on the Rue des Bonnetiers side of the cathedral, opens at 7 AM to admit worshipers. The cathedral takes on a magical quality at night, when the spire is illuminated; the entire exterior of the cathedral is lit on weekend nights and religious holidays. The cathedral is open daily except during Sunday mass and major Christian holidays. Pl. de la Cathédrale.

PLACE DE LA CATHÉDRALE The cobbled square where Monet painted is overwhelmed by the cathedral that inspired him. The former *Bureau des Finances,* a beautiful early-16th-century building that now houses the *Office du Tourisme* (see *Tourist Information,* below, for details), is also located here; make sure to look inside its marvelous courtyard. On the south side of the square are several brasseries—good places to drink beer and people watch.

GROS-HORLOGE (GREAT CLOCK) Rouen's best-known secular monument used to be in the *Beffroi* (Belfry) next door, but in 1527 the town's proud burghers decided to show it off to greater advantage, building the present gatehouse-like clock tower that spans the street. The extraordinary conglomeration is best seen from the west side of the gatehouse, where the eye can take in a collage of buildings whose styles span four centuries. The two lower stories of the Beffroi are 13th-century Rayonnant Gothic; the top story is Flamboyant; the clock tower is in the Renaissance style of the late 1520s and 1530s; the half-timbered houses nearby are in the simpler domestic style of the same epoch; the gatekeeper's house nestling against the clock tower and the Beffroi is 17th-century classical; and the vaguely Baroque fountain next to it dates from the reign of Louis XV, in the 18th century.

The gilded and painted clock face marks the hour with only one hand. The clock also tells the days of the week and the phases of the moon. The clockwork mechanism inside the cupola is among the oldest still functioning in Europe. One of the clock's two bells, named the Cache-Rimbaud, has been in service since 1260. Closed Tuesdays, some holidays, Wednesday mornings from *Easter* through September, and from October through *Easter Sunday.* Entrance to the *Musée des Beaux-Arts* and the *Musée Le-Secq-des-Tournelles* (see below) is included in the admission charge. Rue du Gros-Horloge.

RUE DU GROS-HORLOGE For close to two centuries, Rouen's most famous street has also been its main strip. Despite the boutiques, burger joints, and bars, several old houses give a faint hint of what this street was like before it became so highly concentrated with commercial establishments. The house at No. 161 dates from the early 1500s, No. 146 from a little later. The corner house next to the *Beffroi* on the Rue Thouret side was the city's original town hall, completed in 1608.

ARCHEVÊCHÉ (ARCHBISHOP'S PALACE) Behind the cathedral, this great Gothic mansion can be visited only by special arrangement (ask at the *Office de Tourisme;* see *Tourist Information,* below). Its most outstanding feature is the *Great Hall*, called the *Hall of the Estates of Normandy*, with four 18th-century pictures by Hubert Robert of Dieppe, Le Havre, Gaillon, and Rouen. Entrance on Rue des Bonnetiers.

RUE ST-ROMAIN This picturesque street is famous for its medieval and Renaissance half-timbered houses. Some of them (such as Nos. 11 and 13, which date from the early 1400s) have overhanging upper stories, constructed so that slops thrown from the top floors would not soil people leaning from windows below. Next to the *Cour des Libraires,* the wall of the *Archevêché* bears a plaque marking the spot below the room, no longer extant, where Joan of Arc was sentenced to death. Standing underneath the overhanging housefront opposite the plaque, you can peer through the moss-covered stonework of the walls of the archbishopric to view the massive central spire of the *Cathédrale*. The house at No. 56 almost certainly was standing in Joan's day.

EGLISE ST-MACLOU (CHURCH OF ST. MACLOU) Behind the cathedral, across Rue de la République, is this striking church, which was built in the 15th and 16th centuries and dedicated to St. Maclou, the Welsh saint who turns up in Brittany as St-Malo. Connoisseurs agree that the west façade, with its fan-shaped porch of five pinnacled arches, is one of the most perfect examples of Flamboyant Gothic in France. Inside, the visitor is struck by the soaring vertical lines of the nave, which give an impression of dynamic upward surge. The decorative carvings on the door panels are splendid examples of late 16th-century wooden sculpture. Twentieth-century technology was employed to scour centuries of grime from the church's exterior, returning it to a gleaming white. Pl. Barthélémy.

PLACE BARTHÉLÉMY In front of the *Eglise St-Maclou,* this square once consisted of several narrow streets and tiny blocks. Some years ago, the central buildings were torn down, revealing a view of the church's façade so stunning that no one dared replace the buildings. In addition, the half-timbered houses on either side also were seen from a new perspective that showed off their gables and fine exterior staircases to excellent advantage. The lower floors of these handsome houses, restored after massive damage during World War II bombardments, are almost all antiques shops.

RUE MARTAINVILLE Some of the 17th- to 18th-century houses on this street, once occupied by prosperous merchants and other professionals, are today bookshops and galleries.

AÎTRE ST-MACLOU (ST. MACLOU OSSUARY) Walk under the arch at 186 Rue Martainville, through an ancient courtyard, and under a gatehouse, and suddenly you are in a tree-lined quadrangle enclosed by a charming group of low, timbered buildings. This was once a burial ground for plague victims. The complex was founded in 1348, when 100,000 Rouennais succumbed to the "Black Death"; more victims were claimed during the plagues that raged from the 14th to the 17th centuries. The buildings, erected in 1526, 1533, and 1640, were once bone depositories, or ossuaries: Because the burial ground filled up so quickly, older corpses' bones were habitually dug up and stored in the ossuaries to make room in the cemetery. On the buildings' supporting timbers are macabre carving of skulls, crossbones, spades, hoes, and crosses.

There are no longer any bones in the ossuaries, and the cemetery has not been used for burial purposes since 1780. The buildings were restored in 1851, and the entire complex functioned as a girls' school for many decades. Since 1940, it has housed the *Ecole des Beaux-Arts*. In a corner by the entrance to the courtyard, a glass case embedded in the wall contains the mummified remains of a cat, supposedly a witch's familiar. This is the only grisly feature left in what is otherwise a serene retreat. Open daily. No admission charge. 186 Rue Martainville.

RUE DAMIETTE Along this street are more older residences, many of which now house antiques shops. Especially worth a glance is the 17th-century *Hôtel de Senneville* at the end of an alley at No. 30. Rue Damiette leads into the colorful Place Lieutenant-Aubert; there is an outstanding 15th-century house with a sculpted porch at No. 6. The view of the tower of *Eglise St-Ouen* (see below) from Rue Damiette is splendid.

RUE EAU-DE-ROBEC Now lined with antiques shops, this street was described by Gustave Flaubert in *Madame Bovary*. The houses at the western end have overhanging eaves built so that their medieval residents, mostly dyers, could hang wool out to dry.

EGLISE ST-OUEN (CHURCH OF ST. OUEN) This abbey church is long, high, and austere-looking. Although it took 300 years to build, beginning in 1318, the pure Gothic lines of the original plan were rigidly followed. Thus, the arches, triforium, and clerestory add up to a textbook example of how a Gothic church should look. Most of the glass in the windows, dating from the 14th to the 16th centuries, was removed to ensure safety (and preservation) at the beginning of World War II and has since been returned. Especially remarkable are the rose windows in the north and south transepts, the latter a treatment of the Tree of Jesse. Note, too, the organ, built in 1630 and famous enough for its tone to draw organists from all over Europe. Outside on the north flank of the church are the one remaining gallery of the old *St. Ouen* abbey cloister and 18th-century abbey buildings now serving as the *Hôtel de Ville* (Town Hall). The gardens behind the *Hôtel de Ville* and the church were once the abbey cemetery, where Joan of Arc was brought to renounce her voices. Pl. du Général-de-Gaulle.

MUSÉE DES BEAUX-ARTS One of France's greatest provincial collections is stored here. The exhibits emphasize European paintings, from the Flemish primitives (Gerard David's somber *Virgin and the Saints*) to the Impressionists and post-Impressionists (among them Dufy's *Beach at Ste-Adresse*). One room is devoted to Delacroix's *Justice of Trajan,* another to works by Rouen-born Géricault, including his *Slaves Stopping a Horse* and *Portrait of Delacroix.* There are views of Rouen by Van Ruisdael and Van Goyen in rooms devoted to Dutch and Flemish masters; among the Monets is one of his series of paintings of the cathedral. A first-floor room contains portraits by Jacques-Emile Blanche of his contemporaries (Claudel, Cocteau, Stravinsky, Montherlant, Giraudoux, and Maeterlinck) in the heady years before and after World War I. There also is a celebrated ceramics collection showing the development and decline of Rouen faïence from 1550 to 1800. Closed Tuesdays, Wednesday mornings, and holidays. Admission charge also covers entrance to the *Gros-Horloge.* Sq. Verdrel (phone: 35-71-28-40).

MUSÉE LE-SECQ-DES-TOURNELLES Here are thousands of pieces of ironwork, dating from the Dark Ages (the 5th to 8th centuries) to the 19th century. It is a feast of intricately wrought lamps, gates, balconies, grilles, keys, weapons, kitchen utensils, candelabra, and religious and secular ornaments, beautifully hung or mounted in what was formerly the *Eglise St-Laurent,* a Flamboyant Gothic edifice. Closed Tuesdays, Wednesday mornings, and holidays. Admission charge also covers entrance to the *Gros-Horloge* and the *Musée des Beaux-Arts.* Rue Jacques-Villon (phone: 35-71-28-40).

MUSÉE DE CÉRAMIQUE A visit here will demonstrate why Rouen ceramics have been prized for centuries, especially the faïence work created in the 16th through 19th centuries. The collection is housed in the historic *Hôtel d'Hocqueville,* formerly a private mansion. Closed Tuesdays, Wednesday mornings, and holidays. Admission charge. 1 Rue Faucon (phone: 35-07-31-74).

MUSÉE DES ANTIQUITÉS A Gallo-Roman mosaic from nearby Lillebonne is one of the outstanding sights at this museum, housed in the *Aître Ste-Marie,* a former 17th-century convent. The emphasis is on holdings with a Norman connection; a 13th-century *Virgin and Child* in ivory and a famous 15th-century tapestry, *Les Cerfs Ailés* (The Winged Stags), are especially appealing. Furniture, corbels, cornices, statues, ornaments, and household items from medieval Rouen throw a fascinating light on what some of the wonderful houses a few blocks from the museum once contained. Closed

Tuesdays and holidays. Admission charge. 198 Rue Beauvoisine (phone: 35-98-55-10).

TOUR JEANNE-D'ARC (JOAN OF ARC TOWER) A round keep is all that remains of the castle built by Philippe-Auguste in the early 13th century. The part of the castle in which the Maid of Orléans was imprisoned is no longer standing, but the starkly simple round room in which she was interrogated and threatened with torture is open to the public. Closed Tuesdays, holidays, and November. Admission charge. Rue du Donjon (no phone).

EGLISE ST-PATRICE (CHURCH OF ST. PATRICK) This was the parish church of a quarter that once was inhabited by Irish merchants and traders. Flamboyant Gothic in style, the church is famous chiefly for its 16th- and 17th-century stained glass windows. It also contains a collection of religious paintings. 22 Rue St-Patrice; entrance on Rue de l'Abbé-Cochet.

PALAIS DE JUSTICE (PALACE OF JUSTICE) Students of architecture consider this an exquisite example of the Flamboyant Gothic style. As you look at the famous façade, note that the decoration becomes increasingly richer the higher it goes, so that the pinnacles atop the buttresses on the roof resemble intricately carved icicles. The main part of the building was built from 1508 to 1509, and the left wing from 1493 to 1508; the right wing is a 19th-century reconstruction. Ironically, the newest part was spared the ravages of World War II, which particularly damaged older sections, including the *Salle des Procureurs* (Procurer's Room). It was in this room that Pierre Corneille appeared as king's counsel. The interior is not open to the public, but you are allowed into the *Cour d'Honneur* (Courtyard of Honor) to take in more of the fine architecture. Pl. Foch, Rue aux Juifs.

MONUMENT JUIF (JEWISH MONUMENT) Some 20 years ago, excavations in the courtyard of the *Palais de Justice* unearthed the remains of a 12th-century Romanesque building. Certain graffiti and Hebrew inscriptions indicated that it had been a center of some importance to the Jews of Rouen, who lived in the adjacent ghetto until they were expelled by Philip the Fair in the early 14th century. Since there already was one synagogue serving the community, it has been suggested that the building housed a *yeshiva* (school), making it one of the oldest universities in Europe. It can be visited on Sundays from May through August, and on Saturdays from September through April, but only with a guide; book your visit at least two days in advance at the *Office du Tourisme* (see below). Admission charge. Rue aux Juifs.

EGLISE STE-JEANNE-D'ARC One of France's most modern churches, it was built on the site where Joan of Arc was burned. It incorporates stained glass windows that date from the 16th and 17th centuries; they were originally in the chancel of the *Eglise St-Vincent,* which stood here until it was destroyed in World War II. The windows are devoted to traditional religious themes.

Many show figures in the garb of the various trades and guilds that paid for them. In the background (bottom right) of the window devoted to St. Peter are clear depictions of the churches of St. Maclou and St. Ouen. Pl. du Vieux-Marché.

EXTRA SPECIAL

Only 8 miles (13 km) south of Rouen (on the N138 and then the D64), at the first big curve the Seine makes on its way to the sea, is a remarkably well-preserved bit of medieval France: the village of La Bouille. Every street seems to have its own relics of medieval architecture, from half-timbered houses to tiny alleyways where one would not be surprised to meet a roving minstrel. That atmosphere is especially evident in summer, when the whole town seems to be decked out in flowers. Notice the house decorated with an archangel on Place St-Michel.

Sources and Resources

TOURIST INFORMATION

For brochures, maps, and listings of hotels and restaurants, go to the *Office de Tourisme* (25 Pl. de la Cathédrale; phone: 35-71-41-77), which is open daily; closed from 12:30 to 2:30 PM weekends and holidays.

LOCAL COVERAGE The regional newspaper *Paris-Normandie* is published daily in Rouen. Readily available in bookshops is the French-language *Le P'tit Normand,* a sort of yellow-pages-cum-encyclopedia of Rouen and the region. There are no monthly or weekly guides to Rouen in English, but *The City of Rouen,* published in English by *Editions Ouest France,* is a useful, illustrated guide to the city's most famous historical points. It is available for a few dollars in all bookshops and in most places where postcards are sold. For English-language books, try the *ABC Book Shop* (see *Shopping*).

TELEPHONE The city code for Rouen is 35, which is incorporated into all local eight-digit numbers. When calling a number in Rouen from the Paris region (including the Ile-de-France), dial 16, wait for a dial tone, then dial the eight-digit number. When calling a number from outside Paris, dial only the eight-digit number.

GETTING AROUND

BUS This is the best way to penetrate the suburbs and the hills above the Seine. The *Station du Théâtre des Arts,* at the foot of Rue Jeanne-d'Arc (phone: 35-52-52-52), is the main terminal for city and suburban buses, which are operated by two companies: *SATAR* (Rue des Charrettes; phone: 35-71-81-71) and *TCAR* (79 Rue Thiers; phone: 35-98-02-43). Monthly, weekly, and 20-trip tickets can be purchased at the main station at reduced rates;

one- to three-day *Sympabus Tourisme* passes, allowing unlimited rides on local buses, can be purchased at the *Office du Tourisme* (see above) or the station. The station also has timetables and maps of the 26 lines served. *Autocars* (long-distance buses) to Dieppe, Le Havre, and Fécamp operated by *CNA* (phone: 35-71-81-71) leave from the *Gare Routière* (Rue des Charrettes, close to the *Station du Théâtre des Arts*). Another line, *Bus Verts* (phone: 31-44-74-44), goes to Le Havre, Deauville, Honfleur, and Caen.

CAR RENTAL Among the firms represented are *Europcar* (17 Quai Pierre-Corneille; phone: 35-70-18-30); *Avis,* with two locations (8 Rue Verte, and at the *Gare SNCF,* at the top of Rue Jeanne-d'Arc; phone: 35-89-87-05); and *Hertz* (38 Quai Gaston-Boulet; phone: 35-98-16-57), which offers special rates for trips to *Orly* or *Charles de Gaulle Airports* in Paris.

TAXI Relatively inexpensive, cabs congregate outside the *Gare SNCF* (Rue Jeanne-d'Arc) and at Place Foch; they can be flagged down when passing. The best way to get one is to telephone *Radio Taxis* (67 Rue Thiers; phone: 35-88-50-50) or the group of independent drivers operating out of 18 Rue Wagner (phone: 35-61-20-50).

TOURS The *Office du Tourisme* (see above) provides guided walking tours of Rouen's historical neighborhoods daily from mid-June through September, and weekends and holidays from *Easter* to mid-June. Tours are conducted in French, but you can request an English-speaking guide. Visitors also can take a 40-minute guided tour of the city by miniature train, which goes along the city's principal streets and crosses the river to the left bank. The train leaves from the Place de la Cathédrale from April through November. For additional details, contact the *Office du Tourisme.* For a tour of the countryside from a different perspective, Paul Fleury (1453 Rue de l'Eglise, Bois-Guillaume; phone: 35-60-59-59) pilots balloon flights over the region for an hour or a day.

TRAIN Trains for Paris (about an hour-long trip) leave several times daily from the *Gare SNCF,* at the top of Rue Jeanne-d'Arc (phone: 35-98-50-50).

SPECIAL EVENTS

Rouen is a great market, exhibition, and festival town, and often these events attract throngs of people. Secondhand furniture is the order of the day at the *Puces Rouennaises,* a large flea market held at *Parc des Expositions* in mid-February. The *Salon des Antiquaires,* an annual antiques fair at the *Halle aux Toiles,* is held in April or early May. The *Fêtes Jeanne d'Arc* (Festival of Joan of Arc), on the weekend nearest May 30, the day of her death in 1431, brings pageants and plays about the saint to the Place du Vieux-Marché and the *Aître St-Maclou.* A *Salon des Artistes Indépendents Normands* (Normandy Independent Artists' Show) is held in the *Halles aux Toiles* in late June. The second half of October brings Rouen's major antiques event, the *Salon National des Antiquaires,* to the *Parc des Expositions* in Quevilly, about 4 miles (7 km) south of Rouen. From mid-October to mid-November is the *Tapis de Fleurs,* a beautiful display of chrysanthemums that carpet the square in front of the cathedral. From mid-October to mid-November, the *Foire St-Romain,* with a circus, food, crafts booths, and other activities, is held on the Quais Bas (South Bank) of the city. For additional details on any special events in Rouen, contact the *Office du Tourisme* (see above).

MUSEUMS

Besides those discussed in *Special Places,* the following museums may be of interest. Note that some are closed from 12 to 2 PM.

MANOIR PIERRE-CORNEILLE The former country place of Pierre Corneille is a delightfully timbered, many-gabled house containing books, manuscripts, prints, and pictures, all relating to the playwright. Closed Tuesdays and holidays. Admission charge. Rue Pierre-Corneille, in the suburb of Petit-Couronne, 5 miles (8 km) southwest of the city's center. For information, contact the *Office du Tourisme* (see above).

MUSÉE CORNEILLE Pierre Corneille's birthplace is a fine old Rouennais townhouse that gives a wonderful idea of how a well-to-do lawyer lived in the 17th century. The library is full of finely bound first editions and translations of the great dramatist's works and related tomes. Closed Tuesdays, Wednesday mornings, and holidays. Admission charge. 4 Rue de la Pie (phone: 35-71-63-92).

MUSÉE FLAUBERT ET D'HISTOIRE DE LA MÉDECINE The writer's birthplace is full of 17th- and 18th-century medical equipment and statues of saints famed for curing incurable ailments (his father and brother were surgeons). In another room are manuscripts, books, photographs, and other Flaubert memorabilia. Closed Sundays, Mondays, and holidays. Admission charge. 51 Rue de Lecat (phone: 35-08-81-81, ext. 52467).

MUSÉE D'HISTOIRE NATURELLE Dioramas of animals *chez eux* (in their natural habitats) are presented here. Local prehistoric finds and pre-Norman ethnography are well illustrated. Closed Sunday mornings, Mondays, Tuesdays, and holidays. Next to the *Musée des Antiquités* at 198 Rue Beauvoisine (phone: 35-71-41-50).

MUSÉE JEANNE-D'ARC A super-kitschy wax museum with life-size tableaux showing the saint's progress from her home in Domrémy to the spot in Rouen where she was burned. More interesting than the grisly dioramas are the few contemporary seals and charters struck in commemoration of this famous female martyr and patriot, as well as the intricately built cardboard models of the events in her life. Closed Mondays in winter. Admission charge. 33 Pl. du Vieux-Marché (phone: 35-88-02-70).

PAVILLON FLAUBERT In what remains of the riverside house where Flaubert wrote *Madame Bovary* are furniture, bibelots, and other mementos of the author not found in the *Musée Flaubert et d'Histoire de la Médecine* (see above). Closed Tuesdays, Wednesday mornings, and holidays. Three miles (5 km) west of Rouen via D51 in Croisset (phone: 35-36-43-91).

SHOPPING

Antiques are Rouen's shopping specialty, and the Rue Eau-de-Robec, Place Barthélémy, Rue Damiette, and Rue St-Romain, all in the heart of Le Vieux Rouen, are the best places to find them. Prices are significantly lower than they would be for comparable items in the United States. Ask at the *Office du Tourisme* (see above) for the leaflet *Rouen Ville d'Art*, which lists antiques shops, galleries, and artists' and artisans' studios.

Besides the shops, antiques auctions are scheduled year-round at the *Salles des Ventes* (25 Rue du Général-Giraud, phone: 35-71-13-50; and 20 Rue de la Croix-de-Fer, phone: 35-98-73-49). A flea market is held at Place St-Marc weekends and at Place des Emmurés on Thursdays (though both spots are heavier on blue jeans than antiques). On the first Saturday of each month, bric-a-brac and antiques are sold at the market set up along the stream on Rue Eau-de-Robec. Smaller *foires à la brocante* (antiques fairs) are organized throughout the year in various locations; check with the *Office du Tourisme* (see above) or watch for posters advertising the event. For a more colorful experience, head over to the covered marketplace at the Place du Vieux-Marché Tuesdays through Saturdays, where flowers, produce, and fish are sold.

Faïence de Rouen (ceramicware once made locally in traditional patterns) is everywhere. Beautifully bound books, some with delicate tooling, are abundant and comparatively inexpensive, as are old prints. *Coffrets de Rouen* (wooden chests with colorful hand-painted decorations, popular in the 18th and 19th centuries) make a wonderful souvenir of Normandy; copies abound, so to be sure you get the real thing, check with one of the city's reliable antiques dealers (see below).

For more on shopping hours and days in France, see GETTING READY TO GO. Meanwhile, here are some shops to explore:

ABC Book Shop A selection of English-language guidebooks as well as literature and cookbooks. 11 Rue des Faulx (phone: 35-71-08-67).

Antic St-Maclou Antique silver jewelry, ivory bibelots, and books with fine bindings are sold here. 178 Rue Martainville (phone: 35-89-52-61 or 35-98-36-31).

Atelier St-Romain Specialties include old French and English prints, plus a wide variety of antique objets d'art. 28 Rue St-Romain (phone: 35-88-76-17).

E. Bertran Carved wooden furniture from the 18th and 19th centuries, as well as rare books from the 15th century to modern times. 108 Rue Molière (phone: 35-70-79-96).

Herboristerie St-Romain The time-worn domain of a local herbalist; worth a visit if only to admire the half-timbered 15th-century structure. 74 Rue St-Romain (phone: 35-71-28-23).

M. Bertran Owned by the brother of E. Bertran (see above), this shop specializes in French paintings from every era. 100 Rue Molière (phone: 35-98-24-06).

Du Mesnil Gaillard The shop sells antique decorative items and 18th- and 19th-century furniture. 54 Rue des Bons Enfants (phone: 35-71-05-97).

Michel Carpentier Discriminatingly crowded with reproductions of engravings of Rouen's street scenes and churches, this outfit has the same owner as the faïence shop next door. 26 Rue St-Romain (phone: 35-88-77-47).

Michel Garnier Lamps of all ilk, including antiques in faïence, ceramics, glass, and brass; Tiffany lamps; and lamps from the Far East. 11 Rue Damiette (phone: 35-88-66-85).

Minitrain Model trains, reproductions, and miniatures in wood and metal. 28 Rue Jeanne-d'Arc (phone: 35-70-70-58).

Monique Women's hats that are soigné, outré, *raffiné,* and just plain passé, all at prices that Paris cannot cap. 58 Rue St-Romain (phone: 35-98-07-03).

M. et Mme. Ester A colorful variety of eggcups, decanters, fluted champagne glasses, and other bibelots jam this beautiful, attic-like antiques store. 190 Rue Eau-de-Robec (phone: 35-98-04-26).

P. Chasset Old glasses and bottles, fascinating antique playing cards, tarot cards, and children's games in beautifully decorated boxes. 12 Rue de la Croix-de-Fer (phone: 35-70-59-97).

Paillard Chocolates, nougats, pastries . . . ecstasy for all who enter here. 32 Rue du Gros-Horloge (phone: 35-71-10-15).

Poulingue Nineteenth-century Norman furniture prevails. 4 Pl. Barthélémy (phone: 35-98-09-56).

SPORTS AND FITNESS

BICYCLING For rentals try *Rouen Cycles et Motos*, at 45 Rue St-Eloi (phone: 35-71-34-30).

GOLF There are 18 holes overlooking the city at *Golf de Rouen,* on Rte. Maromme, in Mont-St-Aignan (phone: 35-74-10-91 or 35-75-38-65).

HIKING Contact the *Association Rouennaise de Randonnée Pédestre* (Walking Tour Association of Rouen; 58 Rue du Général-Giraud; phone: 35-62-02-49), for details on local trails.

HORSEBACK RIDING You can hire a steed at the *Centre Hippique des Cateliers* (Houppeville; phone: 35-59-14-06), for riding through the Forêt Verte, or at the *Centre Hippique de Génétey* (St-Martin-de-Boscherville; phone: 35-32-00-44), for riding through the Forêt de Roumare.

SQUASH Try *Rouen Squash,* 1 Quai Gaston-Boulet (phone: 35-89-47-80), but bring your own racket.

TENNIS There are three outdoor courts across the river at the *Centre St-Sever La Maison* (10 Rue St-Julien; phone: 35-72-10-32). For indoor courts, try the *Tennis Club de l'Ile Lacroix* (Rue Stendhal; phone: 35-88-85-36).

THEATER

The *Théâtre des Arts* (Rue du Docteur-Rambert; phone: 35-98-50-98) is the place to see touring hits from Paris, variety shows, plays staged by famous provincial troupes, and ballet. Experimental theater and dance companies use the *Théâtre Maxime-Gorki* (Rue Paul-Doumer, in nearby Petit-Quevilly; phone: 35-72-67-55). *L'Espace Duchamp-Villon* (Centre St-Sever; phone: 35-62-31-31) is a center for theater, dance, music, and film. The resident company at *Théâtre des Deux Rives* (48 Rue Louis-Ricard; phone: 35-70-22-82) mounts avant-garde productions and, occasionally, unconventional versions of French classics. The *Théâtre de L'Echarde* (16 Rue Flahaut; phone: 35-89-42-13) presents both classic and contemporary works.

MUSIC

Rouen is a regional opera center; a season of eight operas and six operettas is presented at the *Théâtre des Arts* (see *Theater,* above). *L'Espace Duchamp-Villon* (see *Theater,* above) has an annual program of concerts in which such international artists as Jean-Pierre Rampal perform with the *Orchestre de Chambre de Haute Normandie* and other local groups. A summer program of organ recitals and chamber music takes place at the *Eglise St-Maclou* each July and August (for information, call 35-70-84-90). The *Salle Ste-Croix des Pelletiers* (Rue Ste-Croix des Pelletiers; phone: 35-71-59-90 or 35-08-69-00) is the venue for classical concerts, including performances by young prize winners of international competitions appearing under the auspices of the *Rencontres Internationales de Musique en Normandie* (phone: 35-71-43-61). *Rouen Jazz Action* (phone: 35-98-15-91) arranges appearances in town by well-known artists.

NIGHTCLUBS AND NIGHTLIFE

Among Rouen's discos are *La Bohème* (12 Pl. St-Amand; phone: 35-71-53-99), which attracts an older crowd; *Sunset Boulevard* (66 Rte. de Bonsecours; phone: 35-71-12-18), which boasts distorted mirrors as part of its idiosyncratic decor, making one question the rather strict dress code; and *Boy Club Gay* (16 Av. de Bretagne; phone: 35-03-29-36), which is popular with gay men. As in most French cities, cafés abound and are open long hours; the lively *Green Onions Café* (29 Bd. des Belges; phone: 35-07-76-20), which has a restaurant, seems mainly to attract an over-30 crowd.

Best in Town

CHECKING IN

Because Rouen is only an hour from Paris and less than an hour from the scores of fine hostelries along the Normandy coast, it has become a city that people visit rather than stay in overnight. The result is a dearth of first-rate hotels, especially in the expensive and moderate categories. A double room with a private bath at a very expensive hotel will cost $125 or more; at an expensive place, $85 to $125; at a moderate one, $60 to $85; and at an inexpensive place, less than $60. Unless otherwise noted, all hotels listed below feature air conditioning, telephones, TV sets, and private baths in the rooms. Some less expensive hotels have private baths in only some of the rooms; it's a good idea to check when making a reservation. Hotels accept major credit cards and are open year-round unless otherwise indicated.

VERY EXPENSIVE

Royal Crosne With 45 modern rooms, this is ranked as one of Rouen's top luxury hotels. Amenities include a bar, a restaurant, and a parking garage. In the center of the city, at 26 Rue de Crosne (phone: 35-89-89-25; fax: 35-71-07-79).

EXPENSIVE

Colin's This is a very quiet, contemporary 48-room hostelry, tucked into a medieval courtyard, that offers the most modern, if not particularly charming, comforts in Le Vieux Rouen. There's a bar, a garden court, and a garage, but no dining room. Ask for a room with a view of the city's rooftops. 15 Rue de la Pie (phone: 35-71-00-88; fax: 35-70-75-94).

Dieppe This establishment's older wing has the atmosphere of a pre-war palace, while the newer wing is spare, clean-cut, and functional, with prints and the odd antique to alleviate an otherwise spartan atmosphere. There are 42 comfortable rooms, and the service is excellent. The hotel's *Le Quatre Saisons* restaurant (see *Eating Out*) is one of the city's better eating places. Close to the station and 10 minutes by foot from Le Vieux Rouen, on Pl. Bernard-Tissot (phone: 35-71-96-00; fax: 35-89-65-21).

Mercure Centre Although it's modern, this 129-unit hotel—formerly the *Pullman Albane*—blends surprisingly well into Le Vieux Rouen. Guests can avail themselves of the amenities expected of an up-to-the-minute hostelry—mini-bars and TV sets, for example—and, at the same time, look out into streets redolent of the Middle Ages. Service at the front desk is sometimes distracted, though most staff members speak English. There's no restaurant, but there is a bar. Rue de la Croix-de-Fer (phone: 35-52-69-52; fax: 35-89-41-46).

Carmes Here, you can enjoy the cozy, intimate feel of an old family hotel while staying in one of the comfortable 15 modern rooms. There is no restaurant. Centrally located, at 33 Pl. des Carmes (phone: 35-71-92-31).

Cathédrale The most famous and colorful hotel in Le Vieux Rouen. There's nothing uniform about any of the 24 rooms, which may be decorated in one of several styles, including Norman rustic, Mediterranean-influenced, or Directoire (between Louis XVI and Empire style). Request a room overlooking the flower-filled courtyard. Unfortunately, you cannot dine in this picturesque setting, as there is no restaurant. Near the cathedral, on a quiet, narrow street known for its old houses. 12 Rue St-Romain (phone: 35-71-57-95).

L'Europe In a remodeled 19th-century building, this old-fashioned hotel has 27 rooms (four without private baths), all decorated in rustic Norman style. Next to the Vieux Marché, at 87-89 Rue aux Ours (phone: 35-70-83-30).

Gros-Horloge The elegance of its Louis XVI furnishings has faded somewhat, and the hotel's entrance is cluttered with pinball machines, but its 62 rooms are comfortable and clean. Rooms on the Rue du Gros-Horloge offer a close-up of the famous clock. 91 Rue du Gros-Horloge (phone: 35-70-41-41; fax: 35-88-44-45).

Le Manoir de St-Adrien A turn-of-the-century manor house with 18 tastefully appointed rooms, in a wooded setting overlooking the Seine. Half-timbered and quaint outside, it has a cozy charm inside. The restaurant serves traditional regional dishes. Six miles (10 km) southeast (toward Vernon) of Rouen at 6 Chemin de la Source, St-Adrien (phone: 35-23-32-00).

Versan A modern hotel, with 34 comfortable rooms and friendly management, but no restaurant. Near the *Eglise St-Ouen,* at 3 Rue Thiers (phone: 35-71-00-88; fax: 35-70-75-94).

Lisieux Five minutes from the cathedral, in an ugly postwar complex close to the Seine, is this property, with little character but pleasant management. The 30 rooms are clean and comfortable. There's no restaurant. 4 Rue de la Savonnerie (phone: 35-71-87-73; fax: 35-89-31-52).

EATING OUT

Forget about dieting. True, apples are an integral part of Normandy cuisine—but so are cream and butter. Rich meats and cheeses are also common: Duck, ham, rabbit, or hare poached in cider precede desserts laced with calvados, and such Norman cheeses as camembert, livarot, and pont-l'evêque turn up in crêpes and sauces or are served with fresh apples and pears at the end of a meal. Be sure to try a traditional dish called *caneton à la rouennaise* (pressed duck with sauce made from the duck's blood).

On the other hand, some of the great fishing grounds of the English Channel are less than an hour away, so the city also is a great place for seafood. Turbot, sole, and brill, in cream sauces and occasionally in cider, are favorite dishes. Also order an *assiette de fruits de mer* (a platter of seafood that includes crayfish, crabs, oysters, clams, mussels, winkles, and shrimp). As a beverage, locally made hard cider often displaces the *grands crus* of Bordeaux and Burgundy. Real cider aficionados tolerate only cider served in *pichets* (stone jugs), which is slightly bubbly, very dry, and sometimes quite potent. If you prefer cider on the dry side, be sure to request *brut*.

Dinner for two (excluding wine and drinks) at an expensive restaurant will cost $90 or more; at a moderate place, $55 to $90; and at an inexpensive one, less than $55. Service usually is included in menu prices, but the French tip extra for good service. Unless otherwise noted, all restaurants listed below are open for lunch and dinner.

EXPENSIVE

Le Beffroy The recipient of one Michelin star, it's Norman in atmosphere, with superb fish dishes and a classic *caneton à la rouennaise*. Apple desserts predominate. Closed Sundays, Mondays, and August. Reservations necessary. Major credit cards accepted. 15 Rue Beffroy (phone: 35-71-55-27).

La Butte This enchanting family-run country inn of brick and beams, with traditional Norman furnishings, merits a Michelin star for specialties such as *salade tiède de homard frais* (warm, fresh lobster salad) and *andouillette de Vire aux chou rouge* (tripe sausage from Vire with red cabbage). Closed Sunday and Wednesday evenings, Thursdays, August, and during the *Christmas* period. Reservations necessary. Major credit cards accepted. In Bonsecours, 2 miles (3 km) outside of Rouen, on Rte. N14 in the direction of Pontoise/Paris (phone: 35-80-43-11).

Les Capucines In a modern building of little character, the dining room of this restaurant is decorated in typically Norman autumnal tones. However, it's the duck pâté, braised sweetbreads with celery, and apple sherbet, to name a few dishes, that make the short ride from Rouen worthwhile. Closed Sunday evenings. Reservations necessary. Major credit cards accepted. 16 Rue Jean-Macé, in Le Petit-Quevilly, 2 miles (3 km) southwest of Rouen (phone: 35-72-62-34; fax: 35-03-23-84).

La Couronne Rouen's most famous restaurant is also reputedly the oldest in France. The ancient interior is lovely, with exposed beams, carved woodwork, medieval porcelain in glass cases, and a fire when there's a cold snap in the air. *Caneton à la rouennaise* is the famous dish here; the *pieds de mouton* (sheep's feet) and *cassolette de homard* (lobster casserole with fresh vegetables) are equally good. Open daily. Reservations advised. Major credit cards accepted. 31 Pl. du Vieux-Marché (phone: 35-71-40-90; fax: 35-71-05-78).

Dufour A huge stone fireplace, exposed beams, antique statues of saints, and a vast display of fresh seafood in one corner make this the sort of place where you expect to see the Three Musketeers drop by any minute to sample a huge *assiette de fruits de mer,* oysters, *coquilles, paupiette de saumon fumé aux huîtres* (smoked salmon with oysters), duck pâté, or *caneton à la rouennaise.* Closed Sunday dinner, Mondays, and three weeks in August. Reservations advised. Major credit cards accepted. 67 *bis* Rue St-Nicolas (phone: 35-71-90-62).

L'Ecaille This one-Michelin-star restaurant is paradise for seafood lovers. Try truly Norman treats like *bouillabaisse de la Manche* (made with fish from the English Channel) and caramelized apples in puff pastry. Closed the first three weeks of August, Saturday lunch, Sunday dinner, and Mondays. Reservations necessary. MasterCard and Visa accepted. 26 Rampe Cauchoise (phone: 35-70-96-52).

L'Episode The surroundings may be cramped, but the portions are ample, and if delicacies such as asparagus with chives and the freshest of fish with sage sauce don't warm the cockles of your heart, then the engaging staff will. Closed Wednesday evenings and Sundays. Reservations essential. Major credit cards accepted. Conveniently located between the *Cathédrale* and the *Gros-Horloge,* at 37 Rue aux Ours (phone: 35-89-01-91).

Gill Gilles Tournadre, the young chef at this two-Michelin-star-establishment, has cultivated the culinary art of subtlety, making even simple dishes like a warm salad of asparagus and Brittany lobster, or duck liver with leeks, seem special. The *ragoût de homard* (lobster stew) and *panaché de poissons* (mixture of fish) both come highly praised. Closed Sundays, the first two weeks of January, and the last week of August to mid-September. Reservations necessary. Major credit cards accepted. 9 Quai de la Bourse (phone: 35-71-16-14; fax: 35-71-96-91).

Les Nymphéas This one-Michelin-star dining spot features seafood and duck dishes, such as *canard à la rouennaise.* Closed Sunday evenings. Reservations advised. Major credit cards accepted. 9 Rue de la Pie (phone: 35-89-26-69).

Pascal Saunier Housed in a remodeled 1930s building, this restaurant has what many consider the city's best view of the Seine and of Rouen. The food is as fine as the vista; try the salmon with rosemary or stuffed rabbit. Closed

Sunday evenings, Mondays, and late July to mid-August. Reservations necessary. MasterCard and Visa accepted. 12 Rue Belvédère (phone: 35-71-61-06; fax: 35-89-90-87).

Les P'tits Parapluies The Belle Epoque interior of this small, charming restaurant once housed an umbrella shop. Try the hot oysters with salmon roe and *pigeon rôti* (roast squab). Closed Sunday evenings, Mondays for lunch, two weeks in February, and the first three weeks of August. Reservations unnecessary. Major credit cards accepted. 46 Rue Bourg-l'Abbé (phone: 35-88-55-26).

Le Quatre Saisons This is a classic example of the truism that, in France, unprepossessing-looking buildings close to railways house exceptional restaurants. A favorite with discerning business types, its kitchen turns out a wonderful salad of smoked fish in sour cream, a splendid duck pâté, and a much-admired pressed duck. Open daily. Reservations advised. Major credit cards accepted. In the *Dieppe Hotel,* Pl. Bernard-Tissot (phone: 35-71-96-00).

La Toque d'Or A warren of rooms with whitewashed walls, beams going every which way, and flagstone corridors make this the most rustic restaurant in Le Vieux Rouen. It's possible to eat here for as little as $15 a head, but dining well on a brioche of salmon with herbs, sweetbreads in port, salad, cream cheese, and *crème caramel* costs more. Open daily. Reservations necessary. Major credit cards accepted. 11 Pl. du Vieux-Marché (phone: 35-71-46-29; fax: 35-71-79-82).

MODERATE

Le Boeuf Couronné A terrine of snails and salmon, or oysters cooked in cream, makes dining here an unusual pleasure. As befits the name, there are also better than average beef dishes. Closed Saturday dinner and Sundays. Reservations advised. Major credit cards accepted. 151 Rue Beauvoisine (phone: 35-88-68-28).

La Marmite Dining by candlelight at this small, comfortable spot is very relaxing. Specialties include duck in cider, lamb with white beans, and a casserole of sweetbreads with *cèpes,* a particularly tasty variety of mushroom. Open until 2 AM; closed Sundays. Reservations advised. Major credit cards accepted. 3 Rue Florence (phone: 35-71-75-55).

Pain, Amour et Fantaisie This funky little tea salon–cum–boutique offers a variety of English cakes, scones, tarts—savory and sweet—and salads. Shelves are cluttered with teas, jams, dried flowers, and other items for purchase. Open from 11 AM to 6:30 PM; closed Sundays and Mondays. Reservations unnecessary. No credit cards accepted. 25 Rue Cauchoise (phone: 35-07-52-74).

La Petite Auberge At this undiscovered spot, seafood is the specialty, and the fish soup and mussels in cream are recommended, though the chicken with lemon and curry also is excellent. The size of the portions is breathtaking. Closed Monday dinner. Reservations unnecessary. Major credit cards accepted. 164 Rue Martainville (phone: 35-70-80-18).

Grande Poste At this café-brasserie, a local institution, waiters *à l'ancienne* (with Old World style) cater to patrons of all ages, at nearly all hours, every day of the year. Reservations unnecessary. Major credit cards accepted. 43 Rue Jeanne-d'Arc (phone: 35-70-08-70).

La Tarte Tatin Though this is a *crêperie,* it's a rather smart one. Camembert, ham, creamed mushrooms, and crab are among the many fillings available in the beautifully prepared pancakes that are its trademark. It is also a *salon de thé* (tearoom). Closed Sundays. Reservations unnecessary. Major credit cards accepted. 99 Rue de la Vicomté (phone: 35-89-35-73).

BARS AND CAFÉS

Two favorites with young Rouennais and visitors are *Le Big Ben Pub,* in the shadow of the *Gros-Horloge* (30 Rue des Vergetiers; phone: 35-88-44-50), and *La Taverne* (11 Rue St-Amand; phone: 35-88-51-38), a Rouen landmark that counted Sartre among its patrons in the 1930s. Visiting singers and jazz groups occasionally come to *Le Bâteau Ivre* (17 Rue des Sapins; phone: 35-70-09-05); for softer music in a Louis XV atmosphere, try *Le Club XV* (81 Rue Ecuyère; phone: 35-98-60-41). For a nightcap in an intimate ambience, there is the *Bar Le Frégate,* the cocktail bar of the *Mercure Centre* hotel (see *Checking In*). The *Altéa Champs de Mars* hotel (Av. Aristide-Briand; phone: 35-08-09-08) has a pleasant piano bar. Many of Rouen's bars stay open until 2 AM most nights of the week; some close at least one day a week.

St-Tropez

St-Tropez first became a household word in the 1950s, when Roger Vadim filmed *And God Created Woman,* starring a shockingly nubile Brigitte Bardot, on the white sands of the Plage de Pampelonne. Soon, the erstwhile fishing port metamorphosed into the headquarters for a coterie of blond, pouty-lipped, long-legged Bardot look-alikes, trailed—with poodle-like devotion—by bronzed Nordic gods. Topless sunbathing, said to have originated in nearby La Ramatuelle, only enhanced the town's already considerable notoriety, and St-Tropez gained a reputation for sybaritic hedonism.

The miracle of St-Tropez is how well it has survived its success. Its incredible light and marvelous climate—give or take a mistral bluster or two around August 15—endures, and its mystique always triumphs over the formidable menace of the annual high summer invasion. In fact, in July and August, about 100,000 visitors crowd the town, and decent hotel rooms are impossible to get at the last minute. But those who do brave the traffic jam into town will find the multitudes at the portside cafés and boutiques magically radiating, if only for the short season of their stay, what could be termed the St-Tropez look, a certain aesthetic flair and delightfully meretricious chic that seduces even the most blasé visitors. For years, the town set trends in summer fashions, with no apparent end to their colorful craziness, and the clothes still manage to look their sexiest when worn in St-Tropez at six in the evening at *Sénéquier,* one of the "in" cafés on the waterfront.

Like many Mediterranean ports, St-Tropez has seen the destruction of pillage and war, but it has managed fairly well to resist the equally devastating assaults of modern real estate development. The city was almost completely destroyed during World War II, and its reconstruction was carried out with an eye toward preserving the enchanting allure of the old buildings, especially those with pink and ocher façades that used to line the main harbor—and, in facsimile, do so once again. Elsewhere, the narrow streets of cream stone houses and the broad, plane tree–shaded main square are unmistakably Provençal. Thankfully, the incursion of fast-food chains and faceless condominium blocks has been kept to an inconspicuous minimum here.

Isolated at the end of a rocky, hilly peninsula, St-Tropez has always been most easily approached by sea, a natural port of call for ships traveling from Italy to Spain. First a Greek settlement called Athenopolis, the town became Heraclea under the Romans. In AD 68, the current washed in a boat with an unlikely trio of passengers: a headless Roman centurion, a dog, and a cockerel. The Roman was Torpes, a converted Christian beheaded by the Emperor Nero; the dog and cockerel were sent along, as was the custom, to devour his body. But they left the martyr intact, prompting pious fishermen to erect a shrine to Saint Torpes (the name was eventually gallicized into St-Tropez). Torpes is still venerated in Pisa, Italy, which claims to have the martyr's head, and the anniversary of his arrival here is celebrated annually in St-Tropez with *Les Bravades* (May 16 through 18), during which a bust of the saint is paraded around town.

Ruled by Saracen pirates in the Middle Ages, St-Tropez underwent a continuous cycle of destruction and reconstruction until 1470, when the Genoese Raffaele Garezzio arrived with 60 families, authorized by the rulers of Provence to guarantee its defense in exchange for tax exemption. St-Tropez thus became an independent republic, governed by a council made up of the heads of all families and two elected consuls, until 1672, when Louis XIV incorporated it into France.

It remained a quiet little fishing village until the end of the 19th century, when Guy de Maupassant immortalized St-Tropez after visiting the "charming and simple daughter of the sea" during a Mediterranean cruise. His description attracted the attention of the painter Paul Signac, who was soon followed by Pierre Bonnard, Charles Camoin, Henri Matisse (for a short while), and, later, André Dunoyer de Segonzac, all drawn by the bewitching light of this isolated port. The painters in turn attracted the writer Colette, who, in summering here in the 1920s, scandalized the outside world by going around with bare legs. (The influx of celebrity-hungry tourists drove her away in 1938, prompting many to lament—as they still do today—that St-Tropez wasn't what it used to be).

In the years since, hordes of superbly narcissistic Scandinavians, Germans, Britons, Italians, Americans, and French have come here to dance and make love till dawn, sleep in the sun, and return to the quay the next evening to do it all over again. The 5,700 Tropezians, who've weathered other invasions, watch it all with a bemused eye, for they know the place is infuriatingly irresistible.

St-Tropez At-a-Glance

SEEING THE CITY

The best way to experience the beauty of St-Tropez is by sea, perhaps on one of the boats that depart from Port Grimaud, St-Raphaël, or Ste-Maxime. If you can't approach St-Tropez by sea, go directly to the Môle Jean-Réveille, the pier along the north side of the harbor, glancing back frequently at the unfolding panorama of portside houses embracing yachts and fishing boats. From the pier, you can take in the Vieille Ville (Old Town) at the foot of the *Citadelle* on the eastern heights and, to the west across the Golfe de St-Tropez, the castle ruins of Grimaud set against a mountain plateau, the Massif des Maures. The play of light at daybreak is dramatically different from that at sunset, so catch both. For a rear view of the town and gulf, walk up to the ramparts of the *Citadelle* above the pretty cemetery.

SPECIAL PLACES

Nearly everything here is within easy walking distance of everything else. Bear in mind that in St-Tropez, people are a very important part of the scenery—and that means that, wherever you go (the beach in particular), you're fair game for gawkers, too.

THE PORT St-Tropez's few remaining fisherfolk have to contend with falling prices and a diminished catch from the pollution-plagued Mediterranean, but the port is still the soul of the town. Most of the social and commercial life takes place along the quays, and the spectacle around the cafés, the boutiques, and the boats themselves is an essential sight of St-Tropez.

Smaller boats—fishing vessels and such—anchor around Quai Frédéric-Mistral, protected by the Môle Jean-Réveille. Luxury yachts are moored around the junction of Quai Jean-Jaurès and Quai Suffren. Farther along, a bronze statue pays tribute to Vice-Admiral Pierre André de Suffren, a St-Tropez resident who became one of the great sailors of 18th-century France. Artists display their works along the west side of the harbor, on the Quai de l'Epi.

MUSÉE DE L'ANNONCIADE (ANNONCIADE MUSEUM) One of France's most exquisite little museums of modern art is set back on the west side of the harbor in a deconsecrated 16th-century chapel. Beautifully converted to a bright museum, the former house of worship today houses the collection of Georges Grammont, including French painting and sculpture from 1890 to 1940. Around Maillol's sensual bronzes hang some fine canvases of Signac, Matisse, Bonnard, Seurat, Derain, Braque, Van Dongen, and Vlaminck; some of the best pieces are studies of St-Tropez. Closed Tuesdays; afternoon hours June through September; morning hours October through May; November; and some holidays. Admission charge. Pl. Georges-Grammont, Quai de l'Epi (phone: 94-97-04-01).

VIEILLE VILLE (OLD TOWN) Somehow spared the dynamite of the German army in 1944, La Glaye, the tiny bay in St-Tropez's Vieille Ville, offers a delightful alternative to the quayside bustle. Start at the *Tour du Portalet* (Portalet Tower), where old men sit on their *banc des mensonges* ("bench of lies") spinning yarns about fish and other wild creatures that got away. The tower is part of the old fortifications whose houses, built right out of the rock on the little bay of La Glaye, still present a formidable barrier on the seaward side.

A couple of blocks inland, the Place de la Mairie is graced by a remarkably unbombastic *Hôtel de Ville* (Town Hall) and, opposite, by a house with a huge, splendidly ornate carved wooden door brought back from Zanzibar by a local sailor. Stroll down the medieval Rue de la Miséricorde; note the blue, green, and gold tile roof of the *Chapelle de la Miséricorde* on the Rue

Gambetta; and visit the food market in the Place aux Herbes (mornings only). Among the tallest buildings are the 10th-century *Tour Souffren* and the *Tour du Portalet* and *Tour Vieille,* both from the 15th century.

EGLISE PAROISSIALE (PARISH CHURCH) This dignified, neoclassical 19th-century building, whose simple bell tower dates from 1634, is most notable for the contents of its chapel, which include a bizarre bust of the city's patron saint, Saint Torpes. The gaily colored wooden sculpture of the mustachioed saint wears a helmet and bejeweled crown, a bemedaled sash, and a slightly dazed look—perhaps because beneath this bust is a depiction of the circumstances of his arrival, featuring a headless version of Torpes, accompanied by dog and cockerel, in the boat that brought his body to town. He's also surrounded by ex-voto gifts, including some smashed blunderbusses and a bosun's whistle. At *Christmas,* a beautiful 19th-century nativity scene with Provençal wooden figures called *santons* is set up in the church. Rue du Clocher, in the Vieille Ville.

PLACE DES LICES The town's main square is the traditional gathering place of true Tropezians—year-round residents and seasonal regulars—who appreciate that moment at the end of the afternoon when the shade of the plane trees and the click of the *pétanques* (metal balls used in the popular eponymous game) provide the perfect setting for a cool *pastis.* On Tuesday and Saturday mornings, the square is the site of a food, flower, and used clothing and furniture market. Inland from Quai Suffren, the square is identified on some maps by its little-used newer name, Place Carnot.

CITADELLE The fortress that France's Henri IV ordered built at the end of the 16th century was an unpopular symbol of St-Tropez's transformation from an independent republic into just another French town, an assertion of the military authority over the region that was a constant bone of contention between Provençal nobles and the French monarchy. Its most recent military role was that of the Germans' last bastion of resistance to the American invasion of 1944; Tropezians participated in its recapture on August 15 of that year. The hexagonal 16th-century dungeon now houses the *Musée Naval,* full of the history of St-Tropez and of Mediterranean shipping. Among its exhibits are an attractive collection of maritime paraphernalia, ship models, engravings, paintings, and documents, including a graphic account of the Tropezians' heroic routing of a Spanish fleet in 1637. Closed Tuesdays and mid-November through mid-December. Admission charge. On the eastern edge of town (phone: 94-97-06-53).

BEACHES The dazzling stretches of white sand and umbrella pines, while just outside town, are inseparable from the entity that is St-Tropez. The elite arrive at the beach by boat; for those lesser mortals who must walk, the most accessible beach is La Bouillabaisse, popular with families and a quick 10 minutes southwest of the harbor. Almost as close, but to the east, is Les Graniers, favored by Tropezians during their lunch break. More fashionable are the

Tahiti, around the southern side of the peninsula in Ramatuelle, and its glorious extension, the 3-mile-long, less mobbed Pampelonne; both are a short car or taxi ride, or a more leisurely bike ride, 2½ miles (4 km) along the road toward Ramatuelle. Other St-Tropez beaches are Les Canoubiers and Les Salins.

EXTRA SPECIAL

In St-Tropez, vanity is most properly indulged at the *Sénéquier* café (at the hub of the port; phone: 94-97-00-90). If this town is the ultimate in street theater, the play must be seen from Act One: Between 8 and 9:30 in the morning, have breakfast in one of *Sénéquier's* scarlet canvas chairs. With a newspaper from the nearby *maison de la presse* (newsstand) and coffee and a fresh croissant or brioche from the café's own bakery, watch the performers, eccentric and otherwise, as this craziest of resorts comes to life (and a few of last night's owls head for bed). Act Two begins around 6 PM at the *Sénéquier,* when the same crowd, a little more tanned than at breakfast, returns for the ritual *café glacé* (iced coffee), parading their stuff and preparing for their evening's entertainment.

Sources and Resources

TOURIST INFORMATION

St-Tropez's *Office du Tourisme* (Quai Jean-Jaurès; phone: 94-97-45-21; fax: 94-97-82-66) is open daily. It provides the usual maps and brochures, information about accommodations, and schedules for local events, hotels, and museums.

LOCAL COVERAGE The French-language daily *Nice Matin* has special gossip-laden St-Tropez and Ste-Maxime editions.

TELEPHONE The city code for St-Tropez is 94, which is incorporated into all local eight-digit numbers. When calling a number in St-Tropez from the Paris region (including the Ile-de-France), dial 16, wait for a dial tone, then dial the eight-digit number. When calling a number from outside Paris, dial only the eight-digit number.

GETTING AROUND

AIRPORT The closest domestic airport is in Toulon, 44 miles (71 km) west of St-Tropez, with service from Paris. Nice has the closest international airport, the *Aéroport Nice–Côte d'Azur,* 63 miles (101 km) east of St-Tropez.

BOAT For excursions around the bay and along the coast, contact *Messageries Marines du Golfe* (*MMG*; Quai Jean-Jaurès, in St-Maxime; phone: 94-99-08-00) or *Taxi Bateau* (Chemin de Bemaignan, Cogolin; phone: 94-54-40-

61). For information on boat-taxis to St-Raphaël and St-Maxime, call the tourist office (see *Tourist Information*).

BUS Buses serve the surrounding villages of Grimaud, Gassin, Cogolin, Ramatuelle, La Garde–Freinet, and Croix-Valmer, as well as the railroad stations in St-Raphaël and Toulon. For information, contact the tourist office (see *Tourist Information,* above) or the local bus company, *Sodetrav* (phone: 94-54-62-36 in Cogolin; 94-65-21-00 in Hyères; 94-95-24-82 in St-Raphaël; 94-93-11-39 in Toulon).

CAR RENTAL In the summer it is imperative to make your reservation well ahead of arrival. Among the major firms represented are *Avis* (Av. du 8 Mai 1945; phone: 94-97-03-10); *Europcar* (Résidence du Port; phone: 94-97-15-41 or 94-97-21-59); and *Hertz* (Rue Nouvelle Poste; phone: 94-97-22-01).

TAXI Pick one up by the Quai de l'Epi in front of the *Musée de l'Annonciade* or call 94-97-05-27.

TRAIN There is no train service to St-Tropez; St-Raphaël (see *Bus,* above) is the closest station on the rail line. For information, call *SNCF* (Société Nationale des Chemins de Fer Français; phone: 94-95-13-89 in St-Raphaël).

SPECIAL EVENTS

The biggest of St-Tropez's celebrations is undeniably *Les Bravades.* The first and most important of these uniquely Tropezian commemorations, the *Grande Bravade,* begins on May 16, the eve of the legendary arrival of Saint Torpes. Following a tradition dating back to 1558, the bust of the martyr is paraded through the streets for 2½ days by gaily uniformed men firing off blunderbusses behind a band of fifes, bugles, and drums. Starting at the Place de la Mairie, it's a raucous celebration of civic pride punctuated by an occasional solemn blessing of the *bravadeurs'* antique arms and by the less solemn tippling of *pastis* or vermouth. A slightly less boisterous *Bravade des Espagnols,* on June 15, celebrates the Tropezians' victory over the hostile Spanish fleet in 1637.

Fishermen celebrate *St. Peter's Day* (June 29) at the old Port des Pêcheurs at the end of Rue de la Ponche. On August 14 and 15, Americans are particularly welcome for the anniversary of the 1944 landings and liberation, with fireworks and a midnight mass in the *Chapelle Ste-Anne* (2 miles/4 km south of the town center by Av. Paul-Roussel). There also are music-filled evenings scheduled throughout July, August, and September, as well as Provençal dancing, *pétanques* tournaments, and medieval jousting matches. The end of September and beginning of October bring *La Nioulargue,* a series of sailboat races.

SHOPPING

An amazing number of shops in St-Tropez change name, management, or location from season to season, a turnover that reflects more than anything else the ever-shifting whims of this most faddish of resorts. Many big Paris fashion names are taking over in town, and though St-Tropez is no longer regarded as *the* arbiter of resort *couture,* the St-Tropez flair remains, and the port provides the right ambience for the more outrageous clothes you might not risk back home.

Don't forget the Tuesday and Saturday morning markets at Place des Lices, good for clothing, antiques, food, and flowers. If you're around in late August or early September (it varies from year to year), don't miss the *Salon des Antiquaires* (Antiques Fair), also at Place des Lices. Paintings can be bought from artists along the harbor.

There are three main shopping areas: the port; the galleries, or *passages,* between Quai Suffren and Place des Lices; and the Vieille Ville (Old Town), around the *Hôtel de Ville.* For standard shopping hours, see GETTING READY TO GO. Below is a selective list of the more enduring shops that St-Tropez has to offer:

Carrelages Pierre Basset Hand-decorated glazed wall tiles. 30 Bd. Louis-Blanc (phone: 94-97-75-06).

Choses Trendy dresses, bathing suits, shirts, jeans, and T-shirts. Quai Jean-Jaurès (phone: 94-97-03-44).

Daniel Crémieux Great for men's shirts and classic casual wear. 101 Passage du Port (phone: 94-97-24-44).

Façonnable Beachwear and sandals. 6 Rue François-Sibilli (phone: 94-97-29-98).

Galeries Tropéziennes Provençal decorative items, both modern and antique, for the home. 56 Rue Gambetta (phone: 94-97-02-21).

Jacqueline Thienot A fine antiques shop, especially good for armoires, buffets, ceramics, and baskets. 12 Rue Georges-Clemenceau (phone: 94-97-05-70).

Josiane Abrial Specializes in silk—slinky clothes and grandly ornate bed linen. Quai Ste-Anne (phone: 94-97-31-08).

Les Petites Canailles For children who follow in their parents' fashion footsteps. 34 Rue Georges-Clemenceau (phone: 94-97-25-11).

SPORTS AND FITNESS

Other than people watching, the only serious spectator sport in town is *pétanques;* the courts are at the Place des Lices.

BICYCLING Rent a bicycle or a motorcycle from *Louis Mas* (Rue Josef-Quaranta; phone: 94-97-00-60) or *Easy Biker* (12 Av. du Général-Leclerc; phone: 94-97-73-79).

BOATING AND WINDSURFING *Get Offshore* (Corniche des Arbousiers, Le Canadel; phone: 94-05-50-85) rents boats with skippers year-round; you can also rent one with or without a captain from *Suncap Company* (15 Quai de Suffren; phone: 94-97-11-23). *Thyenis III* (phone: 45-06-30-04 or 01-99-57-22), a 15-meter ketch complete with crew, can be rented for a day or longer; it carries 20 people. For those who like living in style, *Sportmer* (8 Pl. Blanqui; phone: 94-97-32-33) rents houseboats.

The *Ecole de Voile* (Sailing School) is in session in the summer at the Baie des Canoubiers (phone: 94-97-12-58), and there is good windsurfing along Pampelonne and Tahiti beaches. You also can learn to sail or wind-surf at *La Moune* in Gassin (*Club Nautique de Gassin;* phone: 94-97-71-05). Rent windsurfers at *Windsports* (Rue Paul-Roussel; phone: 94-97-43-25) or *St-Tropez Surf* (Rte. des Plages; phone: 94-97-45-35). Make sure not to go out when the mistral is blowing; you might have trouble getting back.

HORSEBACK RIDING Consult the *Centre Hippique des Maures* (just outside town at Beauvallon; phone: 94-56-16-55).

SCUBA DIVING This is organized by *Les Plongeurs du Golfe,* whose boat is anchored off the Môle Jean-Réveille from June through September. Inquire at the Nouveau Port (phone: 94-97-08-39).

SPORT FISHING Deep-sea angling excursions are offered by *MMG* and *Taxi Bateau* (see "Boat" in *Getting Around,* above).

TENNIS Play at the *Tennis Club deï Marres* (Rte. des Plages; phone: 94-97-24-87), which has eight clay courts and a pool; the *Tennis-Club de St-Tropez* (Rte. des Plages, St-Claude; phone: 94-97-80-76); or *Les Tennis de St-Tropez* (Rte. des Salins; phone: 94-97-36-39), which has six clay courts.

MUSIC
Recitals and chamber music concerts are held at the *Château de la Moutte,* at the east end of the peninsula. Consult the *Office du Tourisme* for details.

NIGHTCLUBS AND NIGHTLIFE
Most of the super discos are distinguished from one another mainly by the people they let in or keep out. The two smartest, both in the *Byblos* hotel (see *Checking In*), are *Les Caves du Roy* (entrance off Pl. des Lices), which offers a good live band in season, and *Le Krak des Chevaliers,* a little more subdued. The *Papagayo* (Quai de l'Epi; phone: 94-97-07-56) has a pleas-ingly insane ambience, with Chinese exotica and local eccentrics. *Le Bal* at the *Résidence du Nouveau Port* restaurant (Nouveau Port; phone: 94-97-14-70) is fun for all. *L'Octave Café* (Rue Garonne; phone: 94-97-22-56) is a lively disco with a mixed-age crowd.

Best in Town

CHECKING IN
St-Tropez's hotels compare favorably in price with those found in other Côte d'Azur resorts. For a double room in a very expensive (read palatial) hotel, expect to pay more than $300; an expensive one will cost between $150 and $300; in a moderate place, expect to pay from $75 to $150; and

in an inexpensive hotel, less than $75. Prices given are for the high season. For anything less expensive, inquire well in advance through the *Office du Tourisme* about renting a furnished flat, available during the summer, or about camping and *villages de vacances* (holiday villages), which are available near Grimaud, Gassin, Ramatuelle, and La Garde-Freinet. From June through mid-September, it's absolutely necessary to book all accommodations as far ahead as possible. Unless otherwise noted, all hotels listed below feature air conditioning, telephones, TV sets, and private baths in the rooms. Some less expensive places may have private baths in only some of their rooms; it's a good idea to confirm whether your room has a private bath when making a reservation. Hotels accept major credit cards and are open year-round unless otherwise indicated.

For an unforgettable experience, we begin with our favorite St-Tropez getaway, followed by our recommendations of cost and quality choices of hotels listed by price category.

SPECIAL HAVEN

Villa de Belieu This villa-hotel is outstanding—and expensive—even by sybaritic Côte d'Azur standards. Vestiges of Roman construction have been found on the property, but the main building is typically Mediterranean, with pink walls, shutters, and rooms with beamed ceilings. The property is located just outside town on the *Domaine Bertaud,* a fine vineyard whose wines are available to hotel guests. Many of the furnishings are valuable Italian antiques, and each of the 18 rooms and suites has its own distinctive decor, from British to neo-Roman, with such amenities as mini-bars and Jacuzzis. There's more than a touch of the baroque here, but it is opulence with taste and good humor. Amenities include a restaurant, indoor and outdoor pools, tennis, and a health club. Gassin, 5 miles (8.5 km) outside St-Tropez (phone: 94-56-40-56; fax: 94-43-43-34).

VERY EXPENSIVE

La Bastide de St-Tropez A small, elegant hotel with 15 rooms and 11 suites. The lovely pool is surrounded by a garden; there's also an outdoor Jacuzzi, a cooking school for guests of the hotel, and a private boat (with a skipper) that may be rented for the day. The restaurant, *L'Olivier* (see *Eating Out*), earned a star from Michelin last year. Closed the month of January. Rte. des Carles, south of town by Av. Paul-Roussel (phone: 94-97-58-16; fax: 94-97-21-71).

Byblos Bearing little resemblance—physical or otherwise—to traditional Riviera "palaces," this place evokes the atmosphere of a self-contained Provençal village. The constantly expanding range of amenities includes Jacuzzis, a sauna, an excellent restaurant, *Les Arcades* (see *Eating Out*), and two top-notch nightclubs (see *Nightclubs and Nightlife*). The 58 rooms and 45 suites are beautifully and cheerfully furnished, and the service is personal and unpretentious. Lunch at the heated pool is *the* great midday rendezvous away from the beaches. Closed mid-October through mid-March. Av. Paul-Signac (phone: 94-97-00-04; fax: 94-97-40-52).

Château de la Messardière In this palatial turn-of-the-century mansion, part of the Sofitel chain, are 96 overwhelmingly luxurious rooms and 24 suites, all with private gardens or terraces. The restaurant is sumptuous (see *Eating Out*), and the entire place offers a stunning view of the bay and beaches. Conference facilities, a pool, and other sports facilities are available. Closed mid-October through March. In a large park high on a hill, at Rte. de la Belle Isnarde, a mile (1.6 km) southeast of town (phone: 94-56-76-00; 800-763-4835; fax: 94-56-76-01).

Domaine de l'Astragale This luxurious, 34-room hotel is surrounded by a large park and has a pool, a fitness center, tennis courts, a good restaurant, and its own private beach. Closed mid-October through mid-May. Chemin de la Gassine, a mile (1.5 km) outside town by N98 (phone: 94-97-48-98; fax: 94-97-16-01).

La Mandarine Designed like a small, pink-walled village, it has 38 brightly furnished rooms and four suites separated by hedges, vines, and graveled walks and arranged around a quiet courtyard. There is also an elegant restaurant with a terrace. In addition to its own pool, the hotel maintains a private beach at Pampelonne, about half a mile from town. Closed mid-October through March. Rte. de Tahiti (phone: 94-79-06-66; fax: 94-97-33-67).

Mas de Chastelas This lovely old farmhouse converted to a luxury hotel, with 21 rooms and 10 suites (none with air conditioning), is an oasis of calm in the countryside. A pool and tennis courts are on the property. Closed November through late April. Two miles (3 km) outside of town on Rte. de Gassin (phone: 94-56-09-11; fax: 94-56-11-56).

La Ponche One of the oldest and most charming of the in-town hotels, it has an exceptionally friendly staff. Several of the 20 small but nicely done units have private terraces that provide a splendid view of the Golfe de St-Tropez, a delight at breakfast time (although the street noise may bother some). The restaurant (see *Eating Out*) and the bar are very popular. Closed from late October through March. In the heart of the Vieille Ville (Old Town), by the Port des Pêcheurs, at 1 Pl. du Révelin (phone: 94-97-02-53; fax: 94-97-78-61).

Résidence de la Pinède This comfortable, recently renovated Relais & Châteaux member caters mainly to the sporting crowd. For those not content with the pool, saunas, or solarium, the private beach offers windsurfing and water skiing. The 36 rooms and five suites are spacious and prettily furnished in traditional Provençal style. The restaurant has earned a star from Michelin (see *Eating Out*). Closed from October through March. Plage de la Bouillabaisse (phone: 94-97-04-21; fax: 94-97-73-64).

Yaca It's quiet at this shady, 23-room hostelry—no mean claim in this noisy town— though the best rooms are still on the upper floors. The restaurant is open during the summer, and the cocktail bar features live jazz piano. There's also a pool. Closed from mid-October through early April; open two weeks at *Christmas* and *New Year's*. At the edge of the Vieille Ville (Old Town), at 1-3 Bd. d'Aumale (phone: 94-97-11-79; fax: 94-97-58-50).

EXPENSIVE

La Barlière This peaceful, modern hotel, built in the Provençal style in its own gardens, offers a respite from the resort scene; there are 14 rooms (none air conditioned). There's a pool, but no restaurant. Closed most of January. Only minutes from the beaches, on Av. Foch (phone: 94-97-41-24; fax: 94-97-47-85).

L'Ermitage One of the few hotels with a panoramic view of the town, this place offers 28 rooms and four suites, with ceiling fans but no air conditioning. The service is excellent and very friendly. There's no restaurant. On Av. Paul-Signac, the road leading past the *Citadelle* (phone: 94-97-52-33; fax: 94-97-10-43).

Le Levant On the road where Colette used to live, this property is tranquilly set in a lovely garden by the sea. It has a huge heated pool, beside which the restaurant serves a lunchtime barbecue, and there are 28 modern guestrooms housed in bungalows; none of the rooms is air conditioned. The hotel is closed from mid-October through mid-March; restaurant closed from mid-September through mid-June. Rte. des Salins, 1.5 miles (2.5 km) southeast of town (phone: 94-97-33-33; fax: 94-97-76-13).

Sube-Continental This place has 30 renovated rooms, with ringside views of the most amusing resort show on the Côte d'Azur, plus a popular restaurant. Make room reservations well in advance. On the harbor, behind the statue of Vice-Admiral Suffren, at 15 Quai Suffren (phone: 94-97-30-04; fax: 94-54-89-08).

MODERATE

Lou Troupelen There are a total of 44 rooms (none with TV sets or air conditioning) in these two pink-washed, Provençal-style houses. Set in a delightful garden surrounded by vineyards, the hostelry is only a short walk from the center of town and an easy ride to the beaches. There's no restaurant. Closed early November through March. Chemin des Vendanges (phone: 94-97-44-88; fax: 94-97-41-76).

La Tartane This establishment has 14 rooms in a cluster of bungalows (with two or more rooms in most of them), each with a terrace, surrounded by gardens, and just steps from the beach. There's a pool, but no restaurant. Closed November through March 15. Rte. des Salins, 2 miles (3 km) southeast of town (phone: 94-97-21-23; fax: 94-97-09-16).

Lou Cagnard A garden, friendly service, and a quiet atmosphere are the draws at this 19-room establishment. None of the rooms has air conditioning or a TV set, and there's no restaurant. No credit cards accepted. Not far from Place des Lices, on Av. Paul-Roussel (phone: 94-97-04-24; fax: 94-97-09-44).

EATING OUT

In St-Tropez's restaurants, ambience, table hopping, and people watching usually take precedence over sophisticated cuisine. You can eat well, though, especially if you stick to the excellent local fish, grilled or baked in Provençal herbs, accompanied by a local Côtes de Provence wine (try the rosé). While you're sampling, taste the local nougat and the *tarte tropézienne,* a pastry filled with cream and pineapple. A meal for two in an expensive restaurant will cost $150 or more; in a moderate one, $100 to $150; and in an inexpensive place, less than $100. Prices include service (usually included in the bill) but not wine. Closing periods vary from year to year, but most places are open from *Easter* on, through the winter. Unless otherwise noted, all restaurants listed below are open for lunch and dinner.

Les Arcades Fish and inventive dishes are the order of the day at this poolside restaurant. Open daily. Closed mid-October to March 1. Reservations unnecessary. Major credit cards accepted. In the *Byblos* hotel, Av. Paul-Signac (phone: 94-97-00-04; fax: 94-97-40-52).

Château de la Messardière Even if you don't stay in the palatial hotel, you can enjoy such inventive delights as steamed rock lobster, and roast duck with ginger. There's an excellent wine list; try the local wines or ask the knowledgeable young sommelier's advice. Closed October through February. Reservations advised. Major credit cards accepted. In the *Château de la Messardière* hotel, Rte. de la Belle Isnarde (phone: 94-56-76-00; fax: 94-56-76-01).

L'Olivier A charming place whose chef experiments with Mediterranean flavors in such classics as duck with honey and the *très* Provençal rack of lamb with basil. Last year, Michelin awarded it one star. Open daily; closed Mondays and Tuesday lunch in the off-season, and January. Reservations advised. Major credit cards accepted. In *La Bastide de St-Tropez,* Rte. des Carles (phone: 94-97-58-16; fax: 94-97-71-21).

Résidence de la Pinède In St-Tropez's senior one-Michelin-star restaurant, try the *St-Pierre au fenouil* (John Dory with fennel), smoked salmon ravioli, or young rabbit with garlic. The service is superb, as is the wine list. Closed October through February. Reservations necessary. Major credit cards accepted. In the *Résidence de la Pinède,* Plage de la Bouillabaisse (phone: 94-97-04-21; fax: 94-97-73-64).

MODERATE

Le Girelier A good place to enjoy very fresh fish, gaze out on the yachting harbor, and people watch. Closed January through mid-March. Reservations advised on Saturdays. Major credit cards accepted. Quai Jean-Jaurès (phone: 94-97-03-87 or 94-97-04-47; fax: 94-97-43-86).

Leï Mouscardins The new Italian owners have added pasta to the menu of old-fashioned Provençal cooking in this St-Tropez landmark in the Vieille Ville. Request one of the prized tables on the terrace, which commands a superb view of the gulf. Open daily; closed from mid-October through February. Reservations advised. Major credit cards accepted. Rue Portalet (phone: 94-97-01-53).

La Ponche This pleasantly calm terrace spot serves a marvelous saffron mussel soup and giant *gambas* (shrimp) in tarragon sauce; there's also a bargain lunch menu with such offerings as *soupe de poisson,* a fine *navarin* (lamb stew), and a definitive lemon pie. Closed Mondays and late October through March. Reservations unnecessary. Major credit cards accepted. In *La Ponche* hotel, Pl. du Révelin (phone: 94-97-02-53).

La Table du Marché The chef at this chic and popular establishment draws a devoted following with such dishes as rotisseried *poulet de Bresse* (the queen of French poultry), unusual risottos, and a fine *crème brûlée* for dessert. There's also an adjoining take-out shop (run by the chef) that's open until 1:30 AM. Restaurant open daily. Take-out shop open daily; closed Mondays in winter. Reservations necessary for the restaurant. Major credit cards accepted. 38 Rue Georges-Clemenceau (phone: 94-97-85-20; fax: 94-97-67-13).

La Table du Pêcheur No surprise that this restaurant near the port, "The Fisherman's Table," should specialize in the freshest possible seafood, served simply. Closed Wednesdays, and Monday lunch except in summer. Reservations advised. Major credit cards accepted. 3 Rue V.-Laugié (phone: 94-97-42-63).

INEXPENSIVE

Lou Revelen Try the *tapenade* (anchovy paste, minced olives, and garlic), great grilled sardines, and *bourride* (a cream-based, whitefish bouillabaisse). The restaurant has its own very honorable wines. Open daily *Easter* through December; weekends only the rest of the year. Reservations unnecessary. MasterCard and Visa accepted. 4 Rue des Remparts (phone: 94-97-06-34).

BARS AND CAFÉS

Tropezians and visitors in the know spend nights at the *Café des Arts* (Pl. des Lices; phone: 94-97-02-25), where they share elbow room at the great zinc bar with the *pétanques* players; the back room behind the bar and through the kitchen is a perennially fashionable hangout that serves standard bistro food. *Le Gorille* (Quai Suffren; phone: 94-97-03-93), the classic café-bar on the port, is full of sailors and those who went out for a pack of cigarettes and never came back; they serve a great *moules-frites* (mussels cooked in white wine with a side of French fries). No credit cards are accepted at *Le Gorille*. The most beautiful people on the port can be found at sundown in the bar at the back of *L'Escale* (9 Quai Jean-Jaurès; phone: 94-97-00-63). For quieter conviviality, try the bar of *La Ponche* (see *Eating Out*). The "in" place for young locals is the *Bar à Vins* (13 Rue des Féniers; phone: 94-97-46-10), where you can play billiards and get a quick bite to eat at the small bistro tables. And again, the scene at the *Sénéquier* (see *Extra Special*) can't be beat.

Strasbourg

As the headquarters of the Council of Europe since 1949 and the meeting place of the European Parliament since 1979, Strasbourg is truly a world class city. However, its residents seem not to notice their city's newfound international prominence, making this perhaps the most amiable of metropolises.

Strasbourg is a warm, cozy kind of city. Some sections date back to the 15th century, while others were built only after the considerable damage Strasbourg suffered during World War II. The overall effect is that of a live-in museum whose "hands-on exhibits" include high, narrow, half-timbered houses (that is, constructed of wood framing filled in with masonry); steep, massive tile roofs overhanging birdhouse-like dormer windows; and mazes of winding pedestrian streets.

The city is rich in art, music (including three weeks of first-rate classical concerts at the annual *Festival International de Musique*), and the intellectual ferment that comes from having a renowned four-century-old university (now with some 50,000 students) with major schools of medicine and Catholic and Protestant seminaries. Strasbourg is also France's main Rhine River port and a major commercial center, but despite the bustle and frequent congestion on Rue des Francs-Bourgeois, the Grand'Rue, the Rue des Grandes-Arcades, and along the quays that circle the central city, there is a pedestrians-only street, an escape for the wanderer, around nearly every corner.

The Germans have a word—*gemütlich,* meaning comfortable and pleasant—that perfectly describes this place, and as it happens, German is understood easily here. Strasbourg, the ancient capital of the province of Alsace, is at the very eastern edge of France. The city's port is on the Rhine, and its German neighbors just across the river have at times—during the Franco-Prussian War, and both world wars, for instance—considered it to be on the western edge of Germany. As a consequence, most Strasbourgeois speak both French and German and sometimes their own Alsatian dialect, a sort of smoothed-out German. Strongly regional, the Strasbourgeois have retained a certain isolation from the rest of France, especially from Paris. They have embraced elements of both French and German culture and traditions, while retaining their own Alsatian individuality. As a result, a visit to this part of France is akin to experiencing three countries at once.

Settled in 12 BC by Roman legions, who called it Argentoratum and later Strateburgum (City of the Roads), Strasbourg became in the 10th century a part of the Germanic kings' revival of the Holy Roman Empire. It achieved a measure of independence in the 13th century as a free imperial city. As such, it carried on a flourishing trade that would bring about, in the 14th century, the first of its annual fairs, the first bridge across the Rhine, and its first customs house, which still stands. Prosperity, in turn, attracted artisans, artists, and intellectuals, including a German from Mainz, Johannes Gutenberg, whose invention of printing from movable type may well have happened during the time he lived here in the mid-15th century.

In the 16th century, when the Reformation swept in from the east, Strasbourg became an important center of Protestantism. One result was the founding of the *Université de Strasbourg,* whose alumni would include Goethe and Metternich. In 1681, Louis XIV, taking advantage of the effective undoing of the Holy Roman Empire by the Thirty Years' War, surrounded the city with his army and annexed it to France. While assuming control of Strasbourg's defense and diplomacy, he allowed it the free exercise of the Protestant faith and a measure of autonomy in political, economic, and social institutions, which endured until the French Revolution.

By then, the Strasbourgeois felt French enough to defend the principles of "Liberty, Equality, Fraternity" from enemies within and without. In fact, in 1792, with invasion by Austrian and Prussian forces imminent, Claude-Joseph Rouget de Lisle, a poet, musician, and soldier, wrote a rousing marching song called the "Chant de Guerre pour l'Armée du Rhin" for a Strasbourg battalion. The song later was adopted by a volunteer battalion from Marseilles (hence its more familiar name, "La Marseillaise") and went on to become the French national anthem.

In 1870, during the Franco-Prussian War, the Germans captured Strasbourg; along with the rest of Alsace and part of Lorraine, it remained German for 44 years, returning to French rule only after Germany's defeat in World War I. From 1940 to 1944, it suffered two aerial bombardments and again was occupied by Germany, before French forces recaptured it as Allied armies moved east. Today, with about 250,000 inhabitants in the city proper and another 180,000 in the metropolitan area, it ranks as France's sixth largest city, although many of its older citizens were born German.

Perhaps because of its location, Strasbourg remains virtually undiscovered by Americans. Yet the city offers plenty to see, beginning with one of France's most important cathedrals. A few yards away is what might inelegantly be called Museum Row: An 18th-century palace houses three museums; three more museums are in neighboring, older buildings; and a seventh one lies over the bridge across the Ill. A 10-minute walk from the cathedral is La Petite France, once a tradesmen's quarter and now a tangle of shops and ateliers, restaurants, cafés, a tearoom or two, and even a few discos, tucked in amid crooked streets, tiny bridges, and picturesque corners. Nowhere in Strasbourg are you far from a café or pastry shop, so sit down between sights, order a cold Alsatian beer or some rich pâtisserie, and relax as you savor this unique face of France.

Strasbourg At-a-Glance

SEEING THE CITY

For a spectacular overview, climb the 330 steps up to the platform of the cathedral tower (also see *Special Places*); there's an admission charge. The restaurant and tearoom atop *Au Printemps* department store (see *Shopping*) and the 14th-floor *Valentin Sorg* restaurant (see *Eating Out*) are other spots from which to contemplate the rooftops of Strasbourg, while the *Barrage Vauban* (see *Special Places*) offers a reasonably close bird's-eye view of the Ponts Couverts (Covered Bridges) and La Petite France, with the cathedral in the background.

SPECIAL PLACES

Central Strasbourg is a flat little island bound on the south by the Ill River and on the north by the Fossé du Faux-Rempart, a narrow canal that once served as a moat. Most of Strasbourg's sightseeing attractions and main squares—Place Gutenberg, Place Kléber, Place Broglie, and Place de la Cathédrale—are found in this small area. To explore the island, start at the cathedral; from there, hardly anything else listed below is more than a 10-minute walk, except for the *Palais de l'Europe,* the park, and the *Brasserie Kronenbourg.* Note that many attractions, such as museums, close during lunch hours, usually from noon to 2 PM.

CATHÉDRALE DE NOTRE-DAME DE STRASBOURG (CATHEDRAL OF OUR LADY OF STRASBOURG) This is the physical and emotional heart of Strasbourg, and it can be glimpsed from virtually everywhere in the city. One of Europe's most striking examples of Gothic architecture, the rosy-hued cathedral was built of pink sandstone from the nearby Vosges mountains. Work began in 1015 in the Romanesque style. After the church burned several times in the 12th century, work began again, this time in pure Gothic. In 1439, when the cathedral was finally completed, its lacy openwork spire made it the tallest building in Christendom (466 feet), and so it remained for some 400 years. The building has witnessed much of the turbulent history of Alsace and even served the Protestant faith during the Reformation. Louis XIV and Louis XV both worshiped here, and in 1770, Marie-Antoinette was greeted formally by a member of the clergy here on the way to her wedding to Louis XVI. During the Revolution, many of the cathedral's statues were torn down (a good number of them have since been restored or replaced by copies, with the originals remaining in the *Musée de l'Oeuvre Notre-Dame*). The spire also was threatened (its height offended the principle of *égalité*), but was saved by being crowned with a huge red Phrygian cap, a symbolic part of the revolutionaries' uniform. The wars of the 19th and 20th centuries also damaged the structure.

Before going inside, note the rich sculptural decoration of the west façade, especially that of the middle of the three doorways, which almost in itself sums up medieval religious belief. Then go around to the double doorway of the south transept, known as the *Portail de l'Horloge* (Clock Portal). The two female figures to the right and left of the doors, allegories for the Synagogue (the blindfolded figure) and the Church (the one with the Cross), are counted among the masterpieces of the cathedral's sculpture, as is the moving *Death of the Virgin* in the left tympanum, a 13th-century original.

Stained glass is the marvel of the cathedral's interior. Particularly stunning are the large rose window (ca. 1316) in the west front, the windows of the *Chapelle Ste-Catherine* (ca. 1340), and the cathedral's oldest windows (late 12th and early 13th century) in the north transept. Also noteworthy are the exquisitely intricate late Gothic pulpit in the nave and the two attractions in the south transept: the *Pilier des Anges* (Angels' or Doomsday Pillar), a 13th-century masterpiece (if it's dark, put a franc in the box to illuminate it); and the hard-to-miss 16th-century astronomical clock, an ingenious device that displays the day of the week, sunrise and sunset, saints' days, eclipses of the sun and moon—and the time. Set according to the meridian of Strasbourg, it strikes noon at precisely 12:31 PM each day, and this is the time to see it in action. Toward noon, visitors are asked to leave the south transept and to reenter by the *Portail de l'Horloge* (after paying a small admission charge). A taped recitation in French, German, and English begins at 12:15. When the small cherub on the left (look carefully) strikes the time, the cherub on the right turns over an hourglass, an old man passes before Death, the Twelve Apostles parade before Christ, and the cock above flaps its wings, crowing three times. Guided tours of the cathedral in French or German are offered daily from July through mid-September; by reservation the rest of the year. Admission charge. There is a son-et-lumière show from April through October nightly at 8:15 PM (commentary in German) and at 9:15 PM (commentary in French). Pl. de la Cathédrale (phone: 88-32-75-78).

PLACE DE LA CATHÉDRALE The half-timbered house to one side of the square, wonderfully carved with signs of the zodiac, biblical figures, and ancient and medieval heroes, is the *Maison Kammerzell,* a 16th-century merchant's house that is now a restaurant (see *Eating Out*). The less ornate timbered building facing the cathedral at the corner of Rue Mercière is the *Pharmacie du Cerf,* the oldest pharmacy in France. It dates from 1268, though it has undergone various transformations since then.

CHÂTEAU DES ROHAN Off the south side of the cathedral, this Episcopal palace was commissioned by Cardinal Armand-Gaston de Rohan-Soubise, one of several members of the famous French family to be Archbishop of Strasbourg in the 18th century. It was built from 1730 to 1742 according to the plans of Robert de Cotte; during the course of its history, it welcomed such illustrious guests as Louis XV, Marie-Antoinette, and Napoleon, whose Imperial Quarters recently have been restored. Various rooms of the bishops' apartments can be seen—including a dazzling black and white marble salon with two giant faïence (ceramic) stoves, an inviting library, and a chapel—in addition to three museums. The *Musée des Arts Décoratifs* is notable for its collection of ceramics, especially those produced by the Hannong family of Strasbourg in the 18th century. The *Musée des Beaux-Arts* contains paintings by Italian (Botticelli, Tintoretto, Veronese, Tiepolo), Spanish (El Greco, Zurbarán, Murillo), Flemish and Dutch (Memling, Rubens, Van Dyck, De Hooch), and French (Lorrain, Watteau, Boucher, Fragonard) masters from the 14th to the 19th centuries. The renovated *Musée Archéologique,* in the basement of the château, traces Alsatian civilization from Paleolithic through Celtic, Gallo-Roman, and Merovingian times and is regarded as one of the most significant of its kind in France. All are closed Tuesdays and some holidays. Admission charge. 2 Pl. du Château (phone: 88-52-50-00).

MUSÉE DE L'OEUVRE NOTRE-DAME (MUSEUM OF THE WORKS OF THE CATHEDRAL OF OUR LADY) The *Maison de l'Oeuvre Notre-Dame* was built from the 14th through the 16th centuries to house the *Oeuvre Notre-Dame,* whose purpose it was to collect money for and oversee the construction and maintenance of the cathedral. Now the *maison* houses part of this museum, the rest of which rambles through the adjoining 14th-century *Hôtellerie du Cerf* and a 17th-century house that was reconstructed here. Only part of the museum is devoted to the *Cathédrale de Notre-Dame;* its broader scope is Alsatian art of the Middle Ages and the Renaissance. On display are drawings of the raising of the cathedral from the 13th to the 15th century and originals of many of the cathedral statues, plus paintings, sculpture, stained glass, furniture, and objets d'art. The courtyard is lined with magnificent, freshly restored 17th-century wood balconies. Closed some holidays. Admission charge. 3 Pl. du Château (phone: 88-32-88-17).

MUSÉE HISTORIQUE (HISTORICAL MUSEUM) This collection, which occupies a 16th-century slaughterhouse, includes arms, uniforms worn by the Strasbourgeois and Bas-Rhinois from the 18th through the 20th centuries, and regiment after regiment of antique *petits soldats de Strasbourg* (toy soldiers). A highlight is a 1:600 scale model of the city made in 1727 by the king's military engineers. Closed Tuesdays. Admission charge. 3 Pl. de la Grande Boucherie (phone: 88-52-50-00).

MUSÉE ALSACIEN (ALSATIAN MUSEUM) The charming exhibits here document the folk arts, traditions, and way of life of rural Alsace. There is a reconstructed early 19th-century *chambre paysanne* featuring a large iron stove, table and chairs, a rocking horse, a swinging cradle, and a plump alcove bed complete with bedside slippers and a chamberpot. The rest of the exhibitions—occupying three floors in a characteristic 17th-century house and spilling over into a courtyard and adjacent buildings—include other reconstructed rooms, furniture, ceramics, kitchenware, clothing, work tools and agricultural implements, and religious items from baptismal certificates to *Passover* plates. Closed Tuesdays and some holidays. Admission charge. 23-25 Quai St-Nicolas (phone: 88-35-55-36).

MUSÉE D'ART MODERNE (MUSEUM OF MODERN ART) The city's impressive permanent collection of modern paintings, sculpture, and stained glass is temporarily housed behind the post office at the Place de la Cathédrale until 1996, when a new, modern home for the collection is scheduled to open. In the meantime, only a small selection of the works is displayed here; it includes pieces by Monet, Degas, Gauguin, Braque, Chagall, Rodin, Renoir, Klee, and Strasbourg native Jean Arp. Open daily. Admission charge. 5 Pl. du Château (phone: 88-52-50-00).

EGLISE ST-THOMAS (CHURCH OF ST. THOMAS) Built in the 13th and 14th centuries, this has been an important Protestant church—called the cathedral of Lutheran Protestantism—since the 16th century. It is a hall church, a style common in Germany and the Netherlands but fairly rare in France. Inside, note the mausoleum of the Maréchal de Saxe by the 18th-century sculptor Jean-Baptiste Pigalle and the 18th-century Silbermann organ, on which Albert Schweitzer played concerts commemorating the death of Johann Sebastian Bach. Rue St-Thomas (phone: 88-22-32-08).

LA PETITE FRANCE (LITTLE FRANCE) This most picturesque quarter of Strasbourg, extending roughly from the *Eglise St-Thomas* to the Ponts Couverts (see below), used to be the home of the city's fishermen, millers, and tanners. It is full of 16th- and 17th-century houses mirrored in the waters of the small canals and the Ill River, with swans gliding and small boats and barges nudging through the locks. Walk along Rue de la Monnaie and Rue des Dentelles to Place Benjamin-Zix; at the edge of the water to the left is the huge, flower-bedecked *Maison des Tanneurs,* dating from 1572 and now a restaurant (see *Eating Out*). Other buildings that formerly housed tanners are beyond the *place* on Rue du Bain-aux-Plantes. Be sure also to walk along Rue des Moulins and Quai de la Petite France, which leads to the Ponts Couverts; lined on one side with old houses and a willow or two dipping into the water, the quay is especially appealing.

PONTS COUVERTS (COVERED BRIDGES) The three bridges and four towers at the dividing point of the Ill are vestiges of the city's 14th-century fortifications. Originally, the bridges were of wood and uncovered; from the 16th through the 18th century they had roofs; in the 19th century, they were rebuilt in stone. Today they provide a scenic promenade, and via the Quai de l'Ill, they give access to the *Barrage Vauban*.

BARRAGE VAUBAN (VAUBAN DAM) When Strasbourg was annexed to France in the late 17th century, its fortifications were modernized and extended by the French military engineer Sébastien Vauban, who built this dam across the Ill near the Ponts Couverts. You'll also find it identified on maps both as

L'Ecluse (The Floodgate), because it allowed the flooding of the southern part of the city if necessary, and as the *Terrasse Panoramique,* because that is its function today: The view from here is sensational. Open daily; admission charge from mid-October through mid-March only. Quai de l'Ill (phone: 88-36-16-98).

EGLISE ST-PIERRE-LE-VIEUX (CHURCH OF ST. PETER THE OLD) This unusual structure houses both Catholic and Protestant churches, each with a different architectural design. Among its treasures are its 16th-century carved wall panels. Pl. St-Pierre-le-Vieux (phone: 88-32-72-83).

PALAIS DE L'EUROPE (PALACE OF EUROPE) This 1977 building is noteworthy for its striking architecture—particularly its semicircular interior chamber (the hemicycle)—and for its symbolic purpose, representing the cornerstone of European cooperation. It is the seat of the 32-nation Council of Europe and the meeting place, for a week each month, of some 518 directly elected members of the 12-nation European Parliament. The building is open to the public; guided tours in English are offered, by reservation only, weekdays from April through September. Individuals may tour only when Parliament is not in session; groups may view Parliament in action. Call the Parliament (phone: 88-17-20-07) to arrange to attend a session. No admission charge. Av. de l'Europe.

PARC DE L'ORANGERIE (ORANGERIE PARK) Across the road from the *Palais,* this park was created by Le Nôtre (the landscape artist responsible for the gardens at *Versailles*) in 1692, although it was transformed in the 19th century. It contains a lake, a zoo, and a pavilion built for Empress Josephine in 1805, which is now used for exhibitions.

BRASSERIE KRONENBOURG This brewery in a northwestern suburb is the home of Strasbourg's most famous beer. Guided tours in English are offered; tours take place on weekdays (except holidays). No admission charge. 68 Rte. d'Oberhausbergen (phone: 88-27-41-59).

EXTRA SPECIAL

Wandering among the old streets and passages of this romantic city is an experience in itself. Just off Place du Corbeau is a large, pink-sandstone building with an old-fashioned roof that is otherwise nondescript. Walk inside the cobblestone courtyard, however, and you will see the kind of high, angled wooden balconies, weathered by age, that one can imagine the Three Musketeers leaping from. This is the *Hostellerie du Corbeau,* a coaching inn that dates back at least to 1538; among its guests was Frederick the Great, King of Prussia, who stayed here incognito in 1740. The Quai St-Nicolas's juxtaposition of buildings from the 15th through the 19th century constitutes a lesson in architecture; the entire picture is best seen from across the river. The Pont du Corbeau used to be the site of executions by drowning. Stroll up the narrow Rue de l'Ecurie, which begins at the *Ancienne Douane* (Old Customs House), becomes Rue de l'Epine, and crosses Rue des Serruriers and Rue Gutenberg. En route are 16th- to 18th-century homes and courtyards encrusted with sculptured lions and ugly faces to scare away the devil, pierced with oval *oeil-de-boeuf* (ox-eye) windows—also known as concierges' windows—and affixed with oriel windows, a form of bay window attached to the corners of the buildings. The steeply sloped tiled roofs are set with myriad dormer windows, which provided air circulation and a kind of refrigeration for the Strasbourgeois, who used their attics for food storage. Look, too, for the occasional stork's nest on the roofs. Now rare in Alsace, the stork has long been considered a lucky bird and a symbol of the region.

Sources and Resources

TOURIST INFORMATION

The *Office de Tourisme* of Strasbourg and its region has a central office (17 Pl. de la Cathédrale; phone: 88-52-28-28) that's open daily. There are two additional branches. One is across from the train station (Pl. de la Gare; phone: 88-32-51-49); it's open daily. The other is near the German border (Pont de l'Europe; phone: 88-61-39-23); it's open daily April through October; closed weekends November through March.

LOCAL COVERAGE The daily French-language *Les Dernières Nouvelles d'Alsace* keeps the Strasbourgeois up to date on local news, and for listings of current cultural and sports events, they refer to the monthly *Strasbourg Actualités,* available at all newsstands. A billboard in front of the *Marks & Spencer* department store (Pl. Kléber) posts movie and theater timetables, and kiosks along the city streets sport posters advertising the latest cultural happenings. The tourist offices (see above) offer free brochures on museums and other sights, plus an English-language booklet, *Strolling in Strasbourg* (about 20F, or $3.45 at press time), with five itineraries for exploring the architecture of the city from the Middle Ages to 1900. The *Librairie Kléber* (1 Rue des Francs-Bourgeois; phone: 88-32-03-88) is a good source of books in English on various local topics.

TELEPHONE The city code for the Strasbourg region is 88, which is incorporated into all local eight-digit numbers. When calling a number in Strasbourg from the Paris region (including the Ile-de-France), dial 16, wait for the dial tone, then dial the eight-digit number.

GETTING AROUND

Your feet are the best mode of transportation here, because the city is small and many streets in the vicinity of main points of interest are pedestrian zones.

AIRPORT The *Aéroport International de Strasbourg-Entzheim* is about a 20-minute taxi ride from the heart of town (phone: 88-64-67-67). Shuttle buses, which leave for the airport from Rue du Vieux Marché aux Vins and Place de la Gare about an hour before the departure of major flights, cost 37F (about $6 at press time).

BUS Service is good, although on Sundays it can be infrequent. Single tickets may be bought on the bus; the fare is about 5F (around 85¢ at press time). *Carnets* of five tickets, representing a discount of about 30% off the price of singles, can be bought at the tourist office or in *tabacs* near the bus stops (the nearest location is marked at the stop). Once punched, tickets are good for an hour.

CAR RENTAL Various firms at the airport and in town rent cars. Strasbourg's narrow streets and proliferation of pedestrian zones, however, make a car here more a burden than a convenience; if you do have one, leave it in an underground garage.

TAXI Given the city's size, cabs in Strasbourg are relatively inexpensive; they're also plentiful, except on weekends. Call *Taxi 13* (phone: 88-36-13-13) or *Novotaxi* (phone: 88-75-19-19), day or night.

TOURS Two-hour guided walking tours, in French and one other language (either English, German, or Italian), depart from the main tourist office (see *Tourist Information*) daily in July and August. The tourist office also offers a series of French-language theme tours for groups of 15 or more. Call or stop in to find out when English-language tours are offered. Mini-trains leave from the south side of the cathedral (Pl. du Château) from *Easter* through October; they roll along a 45-minute route that takes in the scenic sections of the Old City, or a longer route that includes the *Parc de l'Orangerie* and the *Palais de l'Europe*. For information and reservations, contact *CTS* (14 Rue Gare aux Marchandises; phone: 88-77-70-03). Boat tours of the Ill are offered through the *Port Autonome de Strasbourg* (15 Rue de Nantes; phone: 88-84-13-13) daily every half hour from late March through late October, and three times a day the rest of the year. Cruises on the Rhine are available from *Alsace Croisières* (12 Rue de la Division-Leclerc; phone: 88-76-44-44). *Nymphe de l'Ill* and *L'Alligator* are boat restaurants, offering *promenades gastronautiques* (cruises on the city's waterways that include meals); they are operated by the *Société Rhénane de Restauration* (15 *bis* Rue de Nantes; phone: 88-84-10-01; fax: 88-34-55-38).

TRAIN The *Gare Centrale SNCF* is west of the Old City, across Pont Kuss at the end of Rue du Maire-Kuss (phone: 88-22-50-50 for schedule and fare information; 88-32-07-51 for reservations). Strasbourg is a rail hub of northeastern France, with good connections to such European cities as Basel, Zurich, Stuttgart, Frankfurt, and Brussels. Paris is less than four hours away; when completed, the *TGV* line will cut travel time down to two hours (although at press time, work on it still had not started).

SPECIAL EVENTS

The *Foire de Printemps* (Spring Fair), a commercial fair, takes place in late April and early May, and the *Marathon de Strasbourg* is held in mid-May. June brings the world class *Festival International de Musique,* which features three weeks of classical concerts by first-rate guests and ensembles performing mainly in the *Palais de la Musique et des Congrès* (see *Music*) and also in the cathedral and various other churches. Information and reservations are available from the festival office (24 Rue de la Mésange, Strasbourg 67081; phone: 88-32-43-10); bookings by mail may be made about three months in advance. The *Strasbourg Jazz Festival,* which draws performers such as Herbie Hancock and B. B. King, takes place the first week of July. The commercial *Foire Européenne* (European Fair) is held for 12 days in early to mid-September. *Musica,* a festival of contemporary music, takes place here in late September and early October, often in such unlikely venues as the planetarium and the municipal pool. It draws more than 30,000 people each year (for information, phone: 88-21-02-21). From the last Saturday in November until December 24, a very festive *Christmas* market takes place. Most of the booths are set up at Place Broglie, but there are also many at Place de la Cathédrale and a few at Place Kléber.

MUSEUMS

Besides those discussed in *Special Places*, the following museums may be of interest:

MUSÉE ZOOLOGIQUE DE L'UNIVERSITÉ (UNIVERSITY ZOOLOGICAL MUSEUM) A small but interesting natural history museum, with a focus on endangered species and on Alsace's bird of good fortune, the stork. Closed during lunch (except on Sundays) and Tuesdays. No admission charge for those under 18 or over 65. 29 Bd. de la Victoire (phone: 88-35-85-35).

PLANETARIUM One of the best in France. There are astronomy shows four times daily Tuesdays through Fridays and twice daily on weekends. Guided tours of the dome are offered Tuesdays through Fridays. Reservations required. Admission charge. Rue de l'Observatoire (phone: 88-21-20-40).

SHOPPING

In terms of range and variety of goods, Strasbourg compares unfavorably with Paris and Lyons, although there's still an ample selection of the designer clothes, shoes, furniture, jewelry, tableware, and kitchen equipment for which France is well known. Most of the handicrafts and special products of the region are sold in the smaller towns where they originate, within 25 miles (40 km) of the city: pottery and ceramics in Soufflenheim and Betschdorf, embroidery and needlework in Eckbolsheim, and weaving and table linen at Muttersholtz. In Strasbourg itself, the best buys tend to be of the epicurean variety, including the Alsatian *eaux de vie*—"waters of life"—distilled from local fruits, and *kugelhopf,* sweet yeast cake baked in a fluted pan. The block-long Rue des Orfèvres has some excellent clothing and jewelry boutiques, including *Céline;* it is also the perfect place to shop for the ingredients of an Alsatian picnic. Among the street's tenants are *Au Vieux Gourmet* (No. 3), specializing in cheese; *Naegel* (No. 9), in pâtisserie; *Frick-Lutz* (No. 16), in charcuterie; *Nicolas* (No. 18), in wine; and *Bretzels Burgard* (No. 22), in pretzels. Dart through the small alley on Rue des Orfèvres to *Ziegler* for fresh fruits and vegetables on the quiet Place du Marché Neuf. Monday, Wednesday, and Friday mornings, there is a centrally located farmer's market at Place Broglie.

Strasbourg has a branch of *Au Printemps,* one of France's major department stores (on Pl. de l'Homme de Fer), and a *Marks & Spencer* (on Pl. Kléber), the British chain specializing in practical clothing at moderate prices. On Wednesday and Saturday mornings, a small flea market takes place in Place du Marché-aux-Cochons-de-Lait and Rue du Vieil-Hôpital; it's worth picking through for books, prints, glassware, and the odd piece collected and discarded more than a few times during the course of the century. For standard shopping hours, see GETTING READY TO GO. Other shops to explore:

Boulangerie au Vieux Strasbourg (Charles Woerlé) For cookies, sweets, bread in all shapes and sizes, a two-pound *kugelhopf* of pure butter, or a smaller one with almonds and walnuts. 10 Rue de la Division-Leclerc (phone: 88-32-00-88).

La Brocanterie An eclectic collection of dolls, old glassware, lamps, vases, and miniatures. 18 Rue du Vieil-Hôpital (phone: 88-32-52-79).

Faïencerie à la Petite France This quaint shop, in a half-timbered building in La Petite France, is chock-full of pottery and porcelain—new and old—from all over France. Prices are fair, and the gentleman who owns the shop is friendly and very informative. 33 Rue du Bain-aux-Plantes (phone: 88-32-33-69).

Fruhauf Original jewelry made by a passionate artist. Rue du Chaudron (phone: 88-32-52-27).

La Sommelière Local wines; Alsatian *eaux de vie* made from raspberries, plums, pears, and nearly every other available fruit of the region; and foie gras and caviar packed in handsome porcelain jars. 1 Rue du Fossé-des-Tailleurs (phone: 88-32-78-59).

SPORTS AND FITNESS

Consult the tourist office or the *Office Municipal des Sports* (2 Rue Baldung-Grien; phone: 88-36-61-29) for more information on sports facilities in the city.

BICYCLING Strasbourg is small and flat, ideal for cycling. Rentals are available at the train station, 3 Bd. du Président-Wilson (phone: 88-75-41-63).

FISHING Licenses can be obtained from the *Fédération de la Pêche,* 1 Rue de Nomeny (phone: 88-34-51-86).

GOLF Among the 18-hole courses in the area are the *Golf Club de Strasbourg* (just south of the city, on the Rte. du Rhin, Illkirch-Graffenstaden; phone: 88-66-17-22), *Le Kempferhof Golf-Club* (9 miles/15 km south of the city in Plobsheim; phone: 88-98-72-72), and *Le Golf de la Wantzenau* (6 miles/10 km northeast in La Wantzenau; phone: 88-96-37-73).

HORSE RACING From March through June and September through October, racing, with pari-mutuel betting, takes place 10 miles (16 km) north of Strasbourg in Hoerdt (phone: 88-51-32-44 for the track; 88-36-08-82 for the horse federation).

HORSEBACK RIDING Instruction is available at the *Centre Equestre de Strasbourg* (1 Rue des Cavaliers, Le Port du Rhin; phone: 88-61-67-35) and *Waldhof* (La Wantzenau; phone: 88-96-60-57).

ICE SKATING *Patinoire du Wacken* (Allée du Printemps; phone: 88-36-60-45) is open from mid-October through February and rents skates.

SWIMMING There is an indoor municipal pool at 10 Bd. de la Victoire (phone: 88-35-51-56) and an indoor, Olympic-size public pool on the Rue de Turenne in suburban Schiltigheim (phone: 88-33-24-20). Open-air pools are in the suburb of Wacken, not far from the exhibition ground on Rue Pierre-de-Coubertin (phone: 88-31-49-10), and at the *Parc du Rhin,* at the *Oceade* amusement park and club (phone: 88-61-9230).

TENNIS AND SQUASH Rent tennis and squash courts by the hour at *Tennis Loisirs* (31 Rte. du Rhin; phone: 88-34-58-79). You can also rent tennis courts at the *Ill Tennis Club* (15 Rue de la Fourmi; phone; 88-41-92-11) and the *Lawn Tennis Club* (Rue Wenger-Valentin; phone: 88-36-69-51).

THEATER

The *Théâtre National de Strasbourg* (Pl. de la République; phone: 88-35-63-60) and its highly respected drama school, *L'Ecole Supérieure d'Art Dramatique,* are an outgrowth of the post–World War II government effort to make Alsace completely French. Today, the repertory company performs the great classics and unjustly overlooked works of France's golden age of theater—the 17th century—along with plays by contemporary French and European dramatists. The *Théâtre Alsacien* performs in Alsatian at the *Théâtre Municipal* (19 Pl. Broglie; phone: 88-75-48-00). The *Maillon* (13 Pl. André-Maurois; phone: 88-27-61-81) presents contemporary theater and film. *D'Choucrouterie* (20 Rue St-Louis; phone: 88-36-07-28) is a lively, popular theater featuring comedies, satirical pieces, and song, mostly in Alsatian; its restaurant offers 13 different kinds of *choucroute* (sauerkraut).

General information on theater in Strasbourg is available from the tourist office.

MUSIC

The *Palais de la Musique et des Congrès* (Av. Schutzenberger; phone: 88-37-67-67) is Strasbourg's main classical music hall. It is home to the *Orchestre Philharmonique de Strasbourg* (phone: 88-52-14-00), a leading European orchestra, from October through June; the venue for most of the concerts of the *Festival International de Musique*; and the site of many concerts by visiting groups and soloists. From November through June, the *Opéra du Rhin* performs at the 19th-century opera house, *Théâtre Municipal* (19 Pl. Broglie; phone: 88-75-48-23). A certain number of seats are set aside for drop-ins and can be reserved up to six days before each performance; remaining tickets go on sale 30 minutes before curtain time. Another local group, the widely known *Percussions de Strasbourg*, featuring approximately 150 percussion instruments from around the world, plays at 15 Place André-Maurois (phone: 88-26-07-09). Check with the tourist office for information about Alsatian folk dances that are performed frequently during summer months in the courtyard of the *Château des Rohan*. Troupes from other nations also occasionally give international folk music and dance shows.

NIGHTCLUBS AND NIGHTLIFE

Although Strasbourg is a cosmopolitan city with plenty of international tourism, it is still in many ways a provincial town with provincial entertainment, and it becomes surprisingly quiet after dinner. Discos do come and go: *Apollo* (1 Rue du Miroir; phone: 88-32-63-94) and *Rock's* (56 Rue de Jeu-des-Enfants; phone: 88-32-31-22) are currently popular. The largest and most famous of Strasbourg's discos is *Le Chalet* (on the edge of town, at 376 Rte. de la Wantzenau; phone: 88-31-18-31). All are open until 4 AM; closed Sundays and Mondays.

Best in Town

CHECKING IN

While Strasbourg boasts a good number of hotels for a city of its size, there are relatively few in the top class. These are often snatched up by the European bureaucrats and business travelers who come here frequently, especially during sessions of the European Parliament (normally the second week of each month except August, and two weeks in the middle of October). So always be sure to make hotel reservations in advance. For a double room in an expensive hotel, expect to pay $120 or more; in a moderate place, about $70 to $120; and in an inexpensive one, $70 or less. Unless otherwise noted, all hotels listed below feature air conditioning, telephones, TV sets, and private baths in the rooms. Some less expensive hotels have private baths in only some of their rooms; it's a good idea to confirm whether your room has a private bath when making a reservation. All the properties listed below accept major credit cards and are open year-round unless otherwise noted.

Baumann Kammerzell The magnificent landmark building *Maison Kammerzell,* home of the restaurant of the same name (see *Eating Out*), has nine ultramodern guestrooms in a neighboring building, as well as conference and banquet rooms. 16 Pl. de la Cathédrale (phone: 88-32-42-14; fax: 88-23-03-92).

Beaucour A handsome, exceedingly comfortable new hotel in a lovingly converted 17th-century, half-timbered mansion with a quiet courtyard. Despite the modern amenities—whirlpool baths, built-in hair dryers, and computer and fax connections—in the 49 rooms, an Old World mood prevails. The rooms on the top floor have exposed wood beams; those in the front offer a view of the cathedral. There are two conference rooms, a bar, and a breakfast room, but no restaurant. The concierge is very knowledgeable. A few minutes' walk from *Baumann Kammerzell,* on 5 Rue des Bouchers (phone: 88-76-72-00; 800-332-5332; fax: 88-76-72-60).

Grand The best among the eight hotels facing the train station on a colorless square, this modern hostelry, a member of the Concorde chain, is frequented mainly by business and government travelers. It's convenient for tourists, too—only a 15-minute stroll from the cathedral and museums, and even less from La Petite France. There are 84 pleasant rooms and two suites (none air conditioned), a bar, two breakfast rooms, a drawing room, and several conference rooms, but no restaurant (there's one next door). 12 Pl. de la Gare (phone: 88-32-46-90; 800-888-4747; fax: 88-32-16-50).

Hilton International The chain's first French hotel outside Paris is large (246 rooms), comfortable, and equipped with such amenities as a health club with a sauna, a lounge and disco, and two restaurants, including the fine *La Maison du Boeuf* (as its name suggests, it specializes in steaks). The rooms are equally well equipped, with amenities such as mini-bars. In a quiet area across from the park surrounding the *Palais de la Musique et des Congrès* (see *Music*)—just a bus ride or a 10-minute walk from downtown, on Av. Herrenschmidt (phone: 88-37-10-10; 800-932-3322; fax: 88-36-83-27).

Holiday Inn This modern 170-room hotel offers familiar comforts, including a restaurant, tennis courts, a health club, and an indoor pool. Near the *Palais de la Musique et des Congrès* (see *Music*), at 20 Pl. Bordeaux (phone: 88-37-80-00; 800-HOLIDAY; fax: 88-37-07-04).

Le Régent Contades Here are 44 well-appointed rooms and suites, complemented by a fitness center and a bar. There's 24-hour room service, but no dining room. 8 Av. de la Liberté (phone: 88-36-26-26; 800-872-8372; fax: 88-37-13-70).

Régent Petite France On the banks of the Ill River is this 19th-century ice factory, transformed into a 21st-century luxury hotel, a member of the SRS chain. Its bright, aggressively modern lobby may be jarring to travelers in quest of old Alsace, but the 72 rooms are elegant and offer all the conveniences one would expect in a first class hotel. The large cocktail lounge and handsome restaurant overlook the river, and there are three modern conference rooms. The massive 19th-century ice-making machinery has been preserved as a museum, contrasting with the modern decor and contemporary artwork throughout the hotel. In La Petite France, at 5 Rue des Moulins (phone: 88-76-43-43; 800-223-5652; fax: 88-76-43-76).

Sofitel A modern member of the reliable chain, it boasts a quiet bar, a good dining room, boutiques, and a pleasant patio and garden. The 154 rooms have cable TV, 24-hour room service, laundry service, and a host of other comforts. In an excellent location, on a relatively quiet corner in the center of town, on Pl. St-Pierre-le-Jeune (phone: 88-32-99-30; 800-763-4835; fax: 88-32-60-67).

MODERATE

Cathédrale An old building houses this hostelry, with a crisply modern lobby and 32 tastefully decorated rooms, many with fantastic views of the cathedral and square. None of the rooms is air conditioned. Guests have access to a nearby health and fitness club. There's no restaurant. In front of the cathedral, at 12 Pl. de la Cathédrale (phone: 88-22-12-12; fax: 88-23-28-00).

Dragon Slightly off the beaten track is this appealing hostelry, whose 17th-century exterior belies an ultramodern Bauhaus interior. Its 32 rooms (none air conditioned) have reproduction Mallet Stevens chairs; some rooms have views of the cathedral. It's a favorite of members of the European Parliament. There's no restaurant. In a calm corner of town, at 2 Rue de l'Ecarlate (phone: 88-35-79-80; fax: 88-25-78-95).

L'Europe Old and slightly worn but entirely functional and clean, its 60 rooms (all with either bath or shower, none air conditioned) are furnished in heavy antiques and reproductions. There is no restaurant. Well located for touring La Petite France, at 38 Rue du Fossé-des-Tanneurs (phone: 88-32-17-88; 800-927-4765; fax: 88-75-65-45).

Maison Rouge With Art Deco reproductions, this hotel is more original than most—each of the 142 guestrooms (none air conditioned) has its own color scheme and furnishings. There are several conference rooms and an efficient, cooperative staff, but no restaurant. Centrally situated, at 4 Rue des Francs-Bourgeois (phone: 88-32-08-60; 800-332-5332; fax: 88-22-43-73).

Des Rohan Though it looks like a historic landmark, this small place has been completely modernized. The 36 rooms are all decorated differently in 17th- and 18th-century styles, each with either bath or shower. There's no restaurant.

On a pedestrian street near the cathedral, at 17-19 Rue du Maroquin (phone: 88-32-85-11; 800-223-1356; fax: 88-75-65-37).

Royal A pleasant little 52-room hotel, it offers modern amenities such as meeting rooms and a Jacuzzi, but is brimming with Alsatian touches—hand-painted furniture, prints by local artists, and hand-crafted door plates—that add warmth and charm. None of the rooms is air conditioned, and there's no restaurant. On the street leading from the train station to the business center, at 3 Rue du Maire-Kuss (phone: 88-32-28-71; 800-927-4765; fax: 88-23-05-39).

Terminus Plaza Next to the *Grand* hotel, this marble-and-crystal structure comprises a large country-inn kind of dining room, the *Cour de Rosemont,* with a fireplace and a cozy bar, and 78 rooms, some decorated in grand style (none with air conditioning). 10 Pl. de la Gare (phone: 88-32-87-00; 800-528-1234; fax: 88-32-16-46).

INEXPENSIVE

Gutenberg Housed in an 18th-century mansion, this small and simple hostelry is clean, if rather spare. Ten of the 50 rooms do not have private toilets; only 17 have a private bathtub or shower. Four rooms are air conditioned, and most have TV sets; many include an extra bed. There's no restaurant. A few steps off Place Gutenberg, at 31 Rue des Serruriers (phone: 88-32-17-15; fax: 88-75-76-67).

Ibis This modern, austere hotel has 97 functional rooms; none is air conditioned. Children under 12 stay in their parents' room for free. No restaurant. Atop the *Centre Halles* commercial complex, at 1 Rue Sébastopol and Quai Kléber (phone: 88-22-14-99; fax: 88-23-02-89).

Le Relais de Strasbourg An elegant façade and a high-ceilinged lobby hint at the former grandeur of this relic, where the 72 rooms have been renovated in a modern, minimalist style. There's no restaurant. Between the train station and the center of town, at 4 Rue du Vieux-Marché-aux-Vins (phone: 88-32-80-00; fax: 88-23-08-85).

EATING OUT

Alsatian cooking is fragrant, and the aromas travel through the streets beginning early in the morning. Everything is rich and can claim some relationship to pork, cabbage, or both. Although the city claims its fair share of restaurants specializing in fine French fare, other, more typically Alsatian dining spots are emphasized below.

Almost every Alsatian restaurant has *choucroute garnie,* a mound of warm sauerkraut, often flavored with juniper berries, heaped with boiled potatoes and varying combinations of ham, slab bacon, pork loin or shoulder, and at least three kinds of sausage. In Alsatian restaurants, portions are often huge and can easily be shared, which restaurant staffs seem willing to allow. *Baeckeoffe* ("baker's oven") is a stew of pork, beef, lamb (sometimes), potatoes, and onions served in an earthenware cooking pot; *jambon en croûte* is ham baked in a pastry crust; *tarte à l'oignon* is a light onion pie; and *tarte flambée* is the Alsatian rendition of pizza, a thin crust covered with onions, cheese, cream, bacon chunks, and nutmeg, baked crisp and served on a flat board. Desserts include *kugelhopf* (a yeast cake) and *tarte alsacienne* (a fruit tart with vanilla cream). The white Alsatian wines include Riesling (try *coq au Riesling,* the local version of coq au vin, served with tiny dumplings called *spaetzle*), Gewürztraminer, Sylvaner, and Tokay d'Alsace (Pinot Gris); among the beers are Kronenbourg 1664 and Meteor.

The Alsatians eat heartily and, as a rule, early. *Winstubs* are essentially wine bars that serve food; they are generally less formal than a standard restaurant, and many close at lunchtime. For a meal for two with service (usually included in the bill), but without wine in a very expensive restaurant, expect to pay $150 or more; in an expensive place, $100 to $150; in a moderate one, $50 to $100; and in an inexpensive place, less than $50. Unless otherwise noted, all restaurants listed below are open for lunch and dinner.

VERY EXPENSIVE

Buerehiesel A big, old half-timbered château houses this beautifully appointed dining room, where the ambience is softly personal. Last year it garnered a rare and coveted third Michelin star for chef Antoine Westermann's basically French menu, with excellent fish and, in season, game birds; there's also a large selection of fine wines. It's favored by many visiting European parliamentarians, but everyone is treated equally by the solicitous staff. Closed Tuesday dinner and Wednesdays, one week at the end of February, and two weeks in late August. Reservations necessary. Major credit cards accepted. In a lovely park, at 4 Parc de l'Orangerie (phone: 88-61-62-24; fax: 88-61-32-00).

Le Crocodile This elegant, three-Michelin-star establishment offers French cuisine with an Alsatian touch; the fish and game specialties, including eel and frogs, are outstanding. The wine list is one of the finest in the region. It's a wonderful choice for a special evening out. Closed Sundays, Mondays, from early July through early August, and for one week at *Christmas.* Reservations necessary. Major credit cards accepted. 10 Rue de l'Outre (phone: 88-32-13-02; fax: 88-75-72-01).

Julien This lively restaurant with a 1920s *années folles* decor has earned a Michelin star for its inventive fish and game dishes. The cuisine is strictly French. Closed Saturday lunch, Sundays, the first three weeks of August, and *Christmas* through *New Year's Day.* Reservations necessary. Major credit cards accepted. Across the river from the museums, at 22 Quai des Bateliers (phone: 88-36-01-54; fax: 88-35-40-14).

Maison Kammerzell A 16th-century architectural monument in its own right, it holds down the best corner in town. There is a comfortable dining room downstairs and a more formal room upstairs overlooking Place de la Cathédrale. The sale of this local institution to Guy Baumann, an Alsatian chef who made it big in Paris with a chain of quality *choucroute* restaurants, doesn't seem to have diminished its popularity or quality; some insist Baumann's classic *choucroute alsacienne* is the city's best. For a variation on this delicious theme, there's also *choucroute au poisson* (with fish). The menu offers some very reasonably priced offerings, and there are English-speaking waiters. Open daily. Reservations advised. Major credit cards accepted. 16 Pl. de la Cathédrale (phone: 88-32-42-14; fax: 88-32-03-92).

Maison des Tanneurs This beautiful half-timbered building, dating from 1572, today is a restaurant justly reputed to produce one of the best *choucroutes* in Strasbourg. It offers fine dining on other traditional dishes as well, all in lovely wood-paneled surroundings. Some of the staff speak English. Closed Sundays, Mondays, the second half of July, and late December through late January. Reservations advised. Major credit cards accepted. In the heart of La Petite France, at 42 Rue du Bain-aux-Plantes (phone: 88-32-79-70).

Valentin Sorg On the 14th floor of an undistinguished-looking office building, it offers fine French fare served in a pretty, surprisingly small dining room with a beautiful view of the quaint rooftops of Strasbourg and the towering cathedral above them. The overall tone may be slightly stiff, but this is still a good choice for a romantic and elegant dinner. Closed Saturday lunch, Sundays, two weeks in late February, and two weeks in late July and early August. Reservations necessary. Major credit cards accepted. In the middle of town, at 6 Pl. de l'Homme-de-Fer (phone: 88-32-12-16).

La Vieille Enseigne Once a mere *winstub,* this cozy restaurant has a club-like atmosphere that makes it popular with politicians. The food and service have improved over the years, and are now at a very high level. Don't miss the *crème brûlée.* Closed Saturday lunch and Sundays. Reservations necessary. Major credit cards accepted. 9 Rue des Tonneliers (phone: 88-32-58-50; fax: 88-75-63-80).

MODERATE

L'Ami Fritz This is a small, neat, friendly place for Alsatian food. It doesn't have the view enjoyed by some of its larger neighbors, but it's less pretentious. Closed Sunday dinner, Mondays, and the month of January. Reservations advised. Major credit cards accepted. In La Petite France, at 8 Rue des Dentelles (phone: 88-32-80-53).

Bierstub l'Ami Schutz A favorite of young businesspeople getting away from downtown, it has a terrace overlooking the water and La Petite France. It's a pretty place, albeit slightly stuffy, whose setting counts for more than the traditional-style cuisine. The hand-painted dishware is for sale. Open daily. Reservations unnecessary. Major credit cards accepted. Well situated, at 1 Ponts-Couverts (phone: 88-32-76-98; fax: 88-32-38-40).

S'Burjerstuewel (Chez Yvonne) A true *winstub,* featuring checkered tablecloths and a modish, noisy crowd. The specialties include *tarte à l'oignon* and baked ham that comes with *cornichons* (tiny sweet pickles) and horseradish. Or just perch at the small bar and drink the local wine. Open until 1 AM; closed Sundays, Monday lunch, mid-July through mid-August, and *Christmas* through *New Year's Day.* Reservations unnecessary. Major credit cards accepted. 10 Rue du Sanglier (phone: 88-32-84-15).

Le Clou One of the best *winstubs* in town for rubbing elbows with the outgoing Strasbourgeois. Businesspeople, plain folks, and students jam together at shared tables with a sense of jovial well-being. The service is gracious and bustling, with portions easily sufficing—and willingly divided—for two. This is a good spot to be introduced to *baeckeoffe.* Good local wines come by the pitcher. Open for dinner only; closed Sundays and holidays, the first week in January, and the last two weeks in August. Reservations accepted only for parties of four or more. Major credit cards accepted. 3 Rue du Chaudron (phone: 88-32-11-67).

Jean dit Carolis The air in the tiny rooms of this lively regional eatery is fragrant with such Alsatian specialties as *choucroute garnie* and *tarte à l'oignon.* Closed Saturday lunch and Sunday dinner. Reservations advised. Major credit cards accepted. 5 Rue de Zurich (phone: 88-37-04-44).

La Petite Alsace Rustic wood beams, white lace tablecloths, and a typical Alsatian menu characterize this pleasant spot. Closed Sunday dinner, Mondays, and the month of February. Reservations advised. Major credit cards accepted. In the heart of La Petite France, at 23 Rue du Bain-aux-Plantes (phone: 88-22-04-05).

Au Pont du Corbeau A modern little restaurant catering to businesspeople, it serves French rather than strictly Alsatian food, and you can top off your meal with a *tarte au fromage blanc,* a moist cheesecake that should not be missed. Open daily. Reservations unnecessary. Major credit cards accepted. A few steps from the *Musée Alsacien,* at 21 Quai St-Nicolas (phone: 88-35-60-68).

Au Pont St-Martin Located in a beautiful, large half-timbered building, this *winstub*-style restaurant has many tables overlooking the water and the locks. It stays open late at night, and when someone's playing the piano, anybody can sing. The mood is better than the food, but the view is fine. Open daily. Reservations advised. Major credit cards accepted. In La Petite France, at 13-15 Rue des Moulins (phone: 88-32-45-13; fax: 88-75-77-60).

St-Sépulcre (Hailich Graab) Small, noisy, crowded, and fun. Strangers share long tables, the menu is postcard-size, the food is good, and the service is fast. The management happily splits dishes. Closed Sundays, Mondays, and mid-July through early August. Reservations unnecessary; for lunch, it's best to arrive before 1 PM. Major credit cards accepted. 15 Rue des Orfèvres (phone: 88-32-39-97).

INEXPENSIVE

Aux Armes de Strasbourg This large, crowded room with a dark wooden ceiling and yellowed walls is the setting for good, solid food; the waitress will tot up the bill on the paper tablecloth. Closed Tuesdays and Wednesdays. Reservations unnecessary. Major credit cards accepted. 9 Pl. Gutenberg (phone: 88-32-85-62).

Chez Tante Liesel If Norman Rockwell had an Aunt Liesel, this would have been her kitchen. The cheerful tiny room has only nine wooden tables, which quickly become piled with traditional dishes from family recipes, plus such unexpected treats as a slab of muenster cheese with a little pot of caraway seeds to dip it in. Closed Tuesdays, Wednesday lunch, *Christmas,* and *New Year's Day.* Reservations advised. Major credit cards accepted. 4 Rue des Dentelles (phone: 88-23-02-16).

Au Gutenberg Small and friendly, with a stack of pretzels on each table and typical Alsatian fare. Open from 10 AM to 1 AM daily. Reservations unnecessary. Major credit cards accepted. 8 Pl. Gutenberg (phone: 88-32-82-48).

Au Petit Bois Vert A simple spot serving regional dishes, it has a pretty terrace under a giant plane tree beside the canal. Closed Wednesdays in winter. Reservations unnecessary. Major credit cards accepted. 3 Quai de la Bruche (phone: 88-32-66-32).

Pfifferbrieder In a little corner house that looks like something Disney would have drawn for Geppetto, this place serves Alsatian fare, without frills or fanfare. Closed Sundays and the month of August. Reservations unnecessary. Major credit cards accepted. 9 Pl. de la Grande Boucherie (phone: 88-32-15-43).

Zum Strissel Reliable Alsatian food, a good selection of Alsatian wines, traditional rustic decor, and a quintessential Alsatian atmosphere have made this one of the more popular places among Strasbourgeois. Closed Sundays, Mondays, the last week in February, and the last three weeks in July. Reservations advised. Major credit cards accepted. Between the museums and the cathedral, at 5 Pl. de la Grande Boucherie (phone: 88-32-14-73; fax: 88-32-70-24).

TAKING TEA (AND COFFEE, TOO)

Christian Meyer (10 Rue Mercière; phone: 88-22-12-70) has a chocolate and pastry shop downstairs and a tearoom serving coffee, tea, and fine, rich pastries upstairs. The *Salon de Thé Suzel* (corner of Rue du Bain-aux-Plantes and Rue des Moulins; phone: 88-23-10-46) is a tiny, welcoming place to drop in for tea and homemade pastries after trooping through La Petite France. It's closed mornings, Sundays, and Mondays. And if you're an early jogger looking for coffee and a croissant or a slice of *kugelhopf* after a sprint along the quays, try the *Expresso* (17 Rue du Maire-Kuss; phone: 88-32-02-19), between the canal and the train station. It opens at 5 AM every day except *Christmas* and the day after.

BARS AND CAFÉS

Local watering holes include the *Bugatti Bar* at the *Hilton International* and *Le Thomann* at the *Sofitel* (see *Checking In* for both). Two bars across the street from each other behind the cathedral are popular with the young crowd: *Les Aviateurs* (12 Rue des Soeurs; phone: 88-36-52-69) and *Le Nid d'Espions* (3 Rue des Soeurs; phone: 88-37-02-83). *La Rhumerie Waikiki* (6 Pl. de l'Homme-de-Fer; phone: 88-75-05-45) is favored by the professional thirtysomething crowd. A little off the beaten track is *L'Abreuvoir* (3 Pl. de l'Abreuvoir; phone: 88-36-09-36), a pleasant middle class bar.

Diversions
Unexpected Pleasures and Treasures

For the Experience

Quintessential France

Sprawling from the shores of the Rhine to the far-flung *départements* of Guadeloupe and Martinique in the Caribbean, France encompasses the Teutonic types of Alsace, the fractious faction of Basque separatists, the stoic Celts of Brittany, and the glitterati of Cannes. And France always is evolving, as the smoky bistros of Paris's Marais fill with North Africans and eastern European Jews, and the *Burger King* on the Champs-Elysées gradually becomes just as Parisian as the *Café de la Paix*. But France's unique flavor hasn't been boiled out of the French melting pot: Authentic bouillabaisse still requires *rouget* scooped fresh from the Mediterranean, *vin ordinaire* sipped in a crowded café always will be elevated far above pure plonk, and the stubborn Gauls still smooch by the Seine, argue using every available limb for emphasis, and happily dance in the streets on *Bastille Day*. Here are some quintessential French experiences to prove the point.

BOULEVARD ST-MICHEL, Paris In the gleam of street lamps and the evening glow from floodlit *Notre-Dame,* there is a simmering mix of arguing students, strumming guitars, roasting chestnuts, and sizzling street-corner crêpes—a feast that hasn't moved since Hemingway's day. Latin no longer is the lingua franca of this *quartier,* but you'll hear plenty of Greek, Arabic, Farsi, and Wolof, and sharing billboard space in front of the multilingual movie theaters are posters for the latest films from Hollywood to India. The bookstalls along the Seine hold anything from a first edition of Proust to a Simenon whodunit to a single, illuminated page from a medieval manuscript.

MEGALITHS OF BRITTANY, Pérros-Guirec and Carnac The Celts settled along the western rim of the liveable world, where the earth juts out into water and fog. And on this gray-green tongue of Europe they still speak a language closer to Gaelic than to French. On the northern coast of Brittany, between Pérros-Guirec and Ploumanac'h, the sea has chiseled and the wind has polished huge sculptures of rose-colored granite, challenging humans to match them. Across the Breton peninsula is the competition—the thousands of great stone *menhirs* of Carnac, aligned since prehistoric times like petrified cheerleaders in some cosmic half-time show. Long after the *Eiffel Tower* has collapsed into a twisted heap of scrap metal, this druidic trail marker for the gods will remain a symbol of France. Luckily, there is no quick way to cross Brittany from north to south. So after lying on the sun-warmed, smooth pink boulders perched delicately on a sheer cliff side, wander from

Carnac to St-Malo, with plenty of stops for fish soups, cider, and seafood crêpes.

BUBBLES, TRUFFLES, AND STAINED GLASS, Reims The 11 miles of catacombs under the Pommery vineyards hold that celebratory essence of France first brought to life by a 17th-century monk, Dom Pérignon. Since then conditions in Champagne have been honed to fastidious perfection, from the grapes grown close to the ground to absorb heat from the chalky soil, to the cellars' naturally constant temperature, to the patient *remueurs* who give each of millions of bottles the requisite fraction of a turn. At the restaurant *Boyer "Les Crayères"* (see *Reims* in THE CITIES), you will be treated as lovingly as a magnum of Roederer Cristal 1979. If famed chef Gérard Boyer comes to your table in the mansion's lavish dining room to ask if everything is to your liking, the *poulard demi-deuil* (young chicken with truffles) should give you reason enough to be sincerely ecstatic. The only possible disturbance to dessert on the terrace overlooking the bucolic estate might be the whirr of a helicopter as it deposits a guest from Paris on the restaurant's private landing pad. After dinner floodlights give a pale yellow tinge to the spikes, spires, and statues that adorn the façade of Reims's Gothic cathedral. But do try to get here during the day, when the principal ornament of the stark interior is the jeweled glimmer thrown by the stained glass windows on the gray stone floor.

ON HORSEBACK THROUGH CORSICA Take a deep breath when you get to Corsica—in the late spring the mingled scents from the undergrowth of honeysuckle, lavender, thyme, and mint mix with the salty froth of the Mediterranean and the last snow still clinging to the mountains. Avoid the resorts and the worn roads, and instead canter through the chestnut forests, the glacial streams, the olive groves, and terraced gardens carved out of steep granite and dense brush. Spend an evening listening to throaty *lamenti,* a kind of Corsican blues sung in the wine bars and cafés of minuscule port towns. This island was created with a postcard palette—the *maquis* flowering white in May, the electric-colored houses on Cap Corse, the red rock of the Calanques dropping into a sapphire sea at Piana. This banished bit of France, with its Genoese watchtowers and its dialect akin to Sardinian, is so close to Italy that Napoleon could almost see his native Corsica from the Tuscan island of Elba where he was exiled.

LOIRE VALLEY BY BOAT, BALLOON, OR BICYCLE Ever since the Middle Ages aristocrats, with a love of rural living but no taste for roughing it, have made the Loire Valley into the ultimate exurb. Go in the fall, when the traffic thins on the rivers, gravel paths, and marble stairways, and when, from the basket of a balloon, you can see the châteaux ensconced in the auburn parkland of their thousand-acre backyards. Don't visit too many, and concentrate on the outsides: It's better to remember the fairy-tale turrets of Chambord or the graceful arches of Chenonceaux spanning the Cher River than to have it all meld into a sumptuous haze of polished wood and tarnished mirrors and the very chair where Louis the Something sat. Whether you float, fly, or pedal from the catapult-proof towers of Loches to the flower beds of Villandry, the point is to take it slow. Stop during the hottest part of the day for some goat cheese and a glass of dry Vouvray, and bask for a while in the delightful silence.

D-DAY BEACHES, Normandy Save a gray day for this blowy, empty coast. Roll up your pant legs and wade along the silent, sandy flats, and listen in a seashell for the sputter of field radios, the crackle of machine guns, and the long-ago (a year over half a century, to be exact) crunch of boots on the beach. Or scan the coastline for the vast American cemetery, the German pill-boxes on the murderous cliff at Pointe du Hoc, and the landing craft and giant bulkheads sunk in the sand at Arromanches—the scars from one of the greatest operations in military history. You cannot help but be moved, whether you're 20 and read about Omaha Beach in a book, or 70 and have a buddy buried beneath one of the white marble crosses or Stars of David at St-Laurent-sur-Mer. June 6, 1944, the date of the Normandy landings, divides European history into before and after, much as 1066, the date the Normans landed in England, did centuries before.

TURQUOISE, EMERALD, AND GOLD—THE CÔTE D'AZUR Squeezed between mountains and the Mediterranean, the Côte d'Azur is a glittering strip of low-cut bathing suits and Alps-high prices, the meeting spot of Europe's wealthy worshipers of sun and self. With a croissant and *café crème* on the Promenade des Anglais in Nice comes a ringside seat for people watching—in July and August it's hard to see the beaches for the suntanned bodies. After a long day of windsurfing and body burnishing, take a sunset convertible ride on the Grande Corniche to the castle town of Roquebrune–Cap Martin, to look down on the feathery trails left by waterskiers eking out the last glow of twilight. Look west over the pines and the cactus-covered cliff side of the Riviera toward Monte Carlo, where most of what glistens really is gold, and where suitable attire should include an extra shirt, in case you lose the one you're wearing. From a table in *Le Grill* atop Monte Carlo's *Hôtel de Paris,* survey the yacht harbor, watering hole of the world's jet set. After dinner take a deep breath of flower-scented air and walk across the Place du Casino for an evening of serious play among the mirthful rococo motifs and poker-face croupiers in the casino's *Salon Privé.*

HARVEST TIME IN BURGUNDY, Beaune The well-being of Beaune is safeguarded by the phalanx of vines laid out in disciplined rows on the hills outside the city's high medieval walls. The town's veneration of *vin* is such that there is no marked separation between church and grape—the brothers of the *Ordre des Chevaliers du Tastevin* dress in priestly vestments for their tastings in the nearby *Château du Clos de Vougeot,* whose fabled vineyards were planted by Cistercian monks. A former mansion of the Dukes of

Burgundy now houses a wine museum, the *Musée du Vin de Bourgogne,* honoring Beaune's royal vintages. At harvest time the ripening grapes and turning leaves give the vineyard-patterned hills the same hues as the wine-colored tile designs that adorn Beaune's spectacular *Hôtel-Dieu,* a 15th-century hospital. Thousands of harvesters, armed with shears and giant baskets, fan out among the vines and round up the fruit to be pressed, stomped, aged, and bottled in a Nuits-St-Georges or a Pouilly-Fuissé. Visit the cellars for a tour and a taste, even if you decide not to bring home a case—you're sure to learn something, whether you've never touched the stuff or already know the difference between an impudent little rosé and a dignified, full-bodied red.

RUE DU FAUBOURG-ST-HONORÉ AND RUE ST-HONORÉ, Paris Like the *Grand Bazaar* of Istanbul, the souk of Marrakesh, and the agora of ancient Athens, the mile-long stretch of designer sidewalks between the *Palais de l'Elysée* and the *Palais-Royal* offers one of the world's all-time great shopping experiences. It has the finest names in everything and an unsurpassed array of retailers specializing in chocolate, leather, and lingerie. Try *Au Nain Bleu* for a miniature tea set in Limoges porcelain, *Hermès* for an equestrian-print umbrella, or *Raymond* for gold-plated faucets. Nearby, on the Place de la Madeleine, visit *Fauchon* for plum mustard or a salmon mousse sprinkled with caviar, and if you can't live without something nobody else can have, tour the galleries and antiques dealers, and stop in at that ultimate purveyor of the unique—the *Louvre des Antiquaires* on the Place du Palais-Royal.

THE BORDER BLEND, Alsace Often the rope in a Franco-German tug-of-war, Alsace now is the French capital of both foie gras and *choucroute.* Although the air is tinged with Riesling and the curvy Route des Vins defines the greatest distance between two nearby points, the people here do not live by wine alone—Alsace also produces France's best, most German beer. Alsace is the birthplace of the national anthem that got named for Marseilles and of the invention of movable type by a German. Over the years the same Strasbourg artery has been named for Napoleon, Kaiser Wilhelm II, the French Republic, Adolf Hitler, and Charles de Gaulle. The city even has a French quarter—La Petite France. The town of Riquewihr, with its gables, cobbles, old wells, storks' nests, and ancient walls, has the "Hansel and Gretel" look of 16th-century Germany. In the fairly large medieval city of Colmar, the *Musée d'Unterlinden* houses the glowing *Issenheim Altarpiece* by Matthias Grünewald. A bedraggled, tortured Christ, who hangs from twisted limbs covered in crimson rivulets of blood, is resurrected in a radiant aura, able-bodied and blond.

PAINTERS' PROVENCE, Arles and Aix-en-Provence A brooding Dutchman came to Arles and saw the light that soaks the earth here, and it gave him the luminous brushstroke that the world now immediately recognizes as Vincent van Gogh's. That same Provençal sun shines through the big picture windows of a studio in Aix, lighting up a canvas that still waits patiently on an easel for Cézanne to finish it. The revolutionary painter was born in this sleepy city cooled by fountains and shaded by the trees on the Cours Mirabeau. A walk out of town along the Route de Cézanne leads to the Montagne Ste-Victoire, still dressed in ocher and pine-tree green, still posing for a Postimpressionist landscape. Arles, too, looks like a canvas come to life, with its brightly painted shutters, its rich surrounding fields of sunflowers and wheat, its sunbaked Arlésiens tossing *boules* on a dusty pitch. Paul Gauguin lived here for awhile with van Gogh, and Picasso loved the town so much that he gave it 57 drawings—now housed in the *Musée Réattu.*

Romantic French Hostelries

In an increasingly homogeneous and anonymous world, the fine French hotel remains one of the last bastions of charm and luxury. From the first warm, flaky croissant to the last turned-down eiderdown, a stay in one of them is a study in pampering that makes for an inimitable experience.

France also boasts another unique species of hostelry, the wonderful establishment with a quality of romance that goes beyond mere luxury. Such a hotel may have a sleek, urbane lobby throbbing with the pulse of Paris, a languid arbor in a flower-filled garden overlooking the Mediterranean, or historic, antiques-filled salons and a dozen or so crackling fireplaces. These hostelries exist in harmony with their settings; they seem to be part of the local life rather than something apart from it. They have a special warmth, and their staffs make you feel that you count and they care. In many fine hotels with restaurants, *demi-pension* (breakfast and one other meal) is added to the room rate at a fixed price and required in July and August; be sure to verify whether rates are *demi-pension* when making reservations. In general, all the establishments described below feature telephones, TV sets, and private baths; are open all year; and accept major credit cards—unless otherwise noted. Some hotels in the cooler northern regions of France, such as Champagne and Brittany, are not air conditioned.

For information on special lodging places in or near major cities, see the *Checking In* sections of the individual chapters in THE CITIES. The list that follows is a selection of some of the best hostelries (listed alphabetically by town) in the smaller cities and towns, in the countryside, and along the French coasts.

HÔTEL DU CAP–EDEN ROC, Antibes, Alpes-Maritimes Believed to be the setting for F. Scott Fitzgerald's *Tender Is the Night,* this Riviera landmark, with 121 rooms, nine suites, and a 20-acre park crowded with pines, is perched on the tip of the rocky promontory at Cap d'Antibes, one of the most exclusive spots on the Côte d'Azur. It's *the* place to stay during the *Cannes Film*

Festival—if you can get a room. From the edge of the turquoise pool it's possible to dive right into the aquamarine sea; whole afternoons can be spent simply inhaling the fragrance of wisteria between serves on the five tennis courts. Sea-view dining on the patios of the *Pavillon Eden Roc,* one of the Riviera's most distinguished restaurants, is another paramount feature. And all for only pennies more than the price of a Renoir. Closed October through mid-April. Information: *Hôtel du Cap–Eden Roc,* Bd. Kennedy, Antibes 06602 (phone: 93-61-39-01; fax: 93-67-76-04).

CHÂTEAU D'AUDRIEU, Calvados This stately, historic monument has been lovingly preserved by the family that built it some two centuries ago. Now their castle is a member of the Relais & Châteaux group—complete with 30 luxurious rooms and suites, exquisite formal gardens, a heated pool, a full complement of antique furniture, two splendid dining rooms (see *Haute Gastronomie* in this chapter), more than 60 acres of verdant parkland, and a location just a few miles away from the beaches of Normandy—so close, in fact, that the castle narrowly escaped destruction during the *D-Day* invasion. Many of the ancient trees still bear shell scars. Closed December through February. Information: *Château d'Audrieu,* Audrieu 14250 (phone: 31-80-21-52; fax: 31-80-24-73).

OUSTAÙ DE BAUMANIÈRE, Les Baux-de-Provence, Bouches-du-Rhône Eleven miles (18 km) northeast of Arles is this gracious, verdant oasis in the dramatic, sun-drenched landscape of the Alpilles foothills. A member of the Relais & Châteaux group, its centerpiece is a venerable old manor house fitted out with accommodations that are nothing short of princely. Fireplaces crackle under vaulted ceilings, and four-poster beds in the hotel's 11 rooms and 13 suites cradle bodies wearied from swimming or horseback riding. Tapestries surround diners in the two-Michelin-star restaurant (see *Haute Gastronomie* in this chapter). Closed mid-January through early March. Information: *Oustaù de Baumanière,* Les Baux-de-Provence, Maussane 13520 (phone: 90-54-33-07; fax: 90-54-40-46).

NORMANDY, Deauville, Calvados At its most proud during the city's August racing season, when the casino is wall-to-wall tuxedos and all of Paris has come down for a stroll on the boardwalk, this imposing Norman mansion by the sea has a special, more solitary romance during the winter, when wind and rain froth the ocean and lash the Norman coast. Neither discourages the roulette players or the diners at *Le Ciro's,* Deauville's famous boardwalk restaurant (see *Haute Gastronomie* in this chapter). Inside, the hotel is as sumptuous as can be: Huge pillows and soft velvet spreads adorn the beds in the 260 rooms and 26 suites, most of them completely remodeled. The tables and easy chairs are elegant reproductions of the Louis XVI era, and the bathrooms are spacious. Although the place has a reputation for snobbery, the staff seems pleasant. Extensive sports facilities, a good restaurant—*La Potinière*—and a children's dining room complete the picture.

Information: *Hôtel Normandy,* 38 Rue Jean-Mermoz, Deauville 14800 (phone: 31-98-66-22; fax: 31-98-66-23).

CHÂTEAU DE DIVONNE, Divonne-les-Bains, Ain In a peaceful arboretum in the foothills of the Jura Mountains, golfers can test their skills on *Golf de Divonne* (phone: 50-40-34-11), one of France's finest courses; sailors can sample the winds on a sizeable artificial lake; hedonists can choose from 57 varieties of thermal baths; and gourmands can enjoy lavish predawn dining in the restaurant of France's liveliest casino. Geneva is only 15 minutes away, so at any given moment the demographics in this placid border village strike a pleasant balance between farmers' daughters and international businessmen. Of the many grand hotels in town, this Relais & Châteaux member is a standout, featuring 22 exceptionally large rooms (plus five suites), superb breakfasts, and a one-Michelin-star restaurant, all just steps from the golf course. Information: *Château de Divonne,* 115 Rue Bains, Divonne-les-Bains 01220 (phone: 50-20-00-32; fax: 50-20-03-73).

LE ROYAL, Evian-les-Bains, Haute-Savoie At this Edwardian-era palace hotel (it was built for England's King Edward VII himself in 1907) perched high above Lake Geneva, almost all of the 156 rooms and suites have a sunny balcony facing across the lake to Switzerland or south toward the Mont-Blanc range. Set in about 30 acres of woodland, this formerly staid center for sylvan pastimes now brims with athletic options, including a half-dozen Greenset tennis courts (three lighted) and a tennis academy; an archery range with daily instruction; saunas and hydrotherapy facilities with trained personnel; and fitness programs, including a jogging circuit with obstacles. The five restaurants, including *La Rotonde,* which specializes in spa cuisine, serves delightful repasts to anticipate while sweating. There is also shuttle service to the renowned casino and to the 18-hole *Royal Club Evian* golf course, to which guests staying a minimum of two days have free access. The property also offers complete business services. Closed December and January. Information: *Le Royal,* Rte. du Mateirons, Evian-les-Bains 74500 (phone: 50-26-85-00; fax: 50-75-61-00).

CHÂTEAU DE LA CHÈVRE D'OR, Eze-Village, Alpes-Maritimes This small hotel in a medieval village is perched so splendidly high (1,300 feet) above the Côte D'Azur that it's utterly peaceful compared to the resorts by the sea, even at the peak of summer. A member of the Relais & Châteaux group, it has 15 rooms and three suites with refreshingly rustic appeal, enhanced by stone walls and down comforters and all overlooking the sea. The one-Michelin-star restaurant offers hearty country cuisine with sophisticated touches; try the lobster mousse or the rack of lamb. Top off your meal with the wild strawberry soufflé, then work it off in one of the two pools. Monte Carlo and Nice are only a few miles away, but you just may decide to save them for another trip. Though the village's narrow streets tend to clog with day-trippers, and it's a bit of a climb from the parking lot *up* to the hotel's front door, it's worth every step. Information: *Château de la Chèvre d'Or,* Eze-Village 06360 (phone: 93-41-12-12; fax: 93-41-06-72).

CHÂTEAU DE LOCGUÉNOLÉ, Hennebont, Morbihan Visiting this stately château, a member of the Relais & Châteaux group that has been owned by the same family for more than 500 years, is like attending a courtly house party. A 250-acre woodland park surrounds the property, cushioning guests from the busy beaches of the Breton coast and any other brush with "real life." If your mood is regal, choose a large velvety room with French doors on the second floor; if your tastes run more to the rustic, the exposed beams and flowery prints of the attic floor will charm you. The rooms afford stupendous views over the well-tended grounds, which slope down to the edge of the Blavet River behind the château. Antiques, paintings, and tapestries collected over the centuries ornament the salons, which manage to be comfortable and welcoming despite their formality. The finely executed nouvelle cuisine specialties on the one-Michelin-star menu change according to the season; the fresh crab tart with cilantro and the young rabbit with truffles are noteworthy. Swimming, tennis, and fishing are possible without ever stepping off the grounds, and there is a fine 18-hole golf course nearby, the par-72 *Golf de Val Queven.* Information: *Château de Locguénolé,* Rte. de Port-Louis, Hennebont 56700 (phone: 97-76-29-04; fax: 97-76-39-47).

FERME SAINT-SIMÉON, Honfleur, Calvados Monet, Renoir, and Corot all painted at Honfleur. After a day outdoors the artists played dominoes and drank cider with the local farmers at this 17th-century inn, now a member of the Relais & Châteaux group. Today the modern 19-room annex is cozy and bright, but the original 19 rooms and four suites are more romantic. Ask for a room with a view of the Atlantic, and then watch the clouds move against a brilliant blue sky. Set the morning aside to explore the port of Honfleur; the evening, to savor the lobster stew at the one-Michelin-star restaurant, where—weather permitting—you can eat on the terrace amid flower boxes and under colorful umbrellas. If that's not enough activity for one day, you can always click chips at the Deauville casino. The hotel's fitness center includes a pool and sauna. Information: *Ferme Saint-Siméon,* Rue Adolphe-Marais, Honfleur 14600 (phone: 31-89-23-61; fax: 31-89-48-48).

MAS DU LANGOUSTIER, Ile de Porquerolles, Var On the Mediterranean near Toulon, this luxurious 57-room, four-suite inn was the hangout of many an artist and writer at the turn of the century. It has since become one of the most exclusive hotels on the Côte d'Azur, prized for its unspoiled setting, superb beach, and refreshing lack of TV sets and nightlife. People come here truly to get away from it all. The one-Michelin-star restaurant's specialties include a stunning aioli with fish and vegetables and made-to-order bouillabaisse. Closed November through April. Information: *Mas du Langoustier,* Ile de Porquerolles 83400 (phone: 94-58-30-09; fax: 94-58-36-02).

LA CÔTE ST-JACQUES, Joigny, Yonne Explore the true meaning of self-indulgence at this luxurious complex on the shore of the Yonne River, bordering Burgundy wine country. Many of the 25 rooms and four suites of this Relais & Châteaux member have been redecorated in Flamboyant style, some in an elegant annex separate from the hotel (many with soothing river views). On the premises are a pool, two tennis courts, and a superb restaurant (see *Haute Gastronomie* in this chapter), housed in a traditional 18th-century country home. You can stagger from repasts of foie gras and truffles to a flower-bedecked bed through the glamorously lit, vaulted tunnel that connects the two halves of the inn underground. Closed January through early February. Information: *La Côte St-Jacques,* 14 Faubourg de Paris, Joigny 89300 (phone: 86-62-09-70; fax: 86-91-49-70).

LE CHÂTEAU DE MARÇAY, Marçay-Chinon, Indre-et-Loire Housed in a 15th-century fortified château with 12th-century wine cellars, this luxury hotel, a member of the Relais & Châteaux group, has 34 rooms and six suites—some in the château itself and others, less expensive but still quite comfortable, in an adjoining building. The rooms in the château are spacious, with large windows, beamed ceilings, and huge bathrooms complete with granite double sinks. The large park surrounding the hotel contains a heated pool and a tennis court. The restaurant, which has garnered one Michelin star, focuses on local products, while the wine list is also exceptionally strong in Loire Valley varieties. The warm, gracious service adds the finishing touch to an already storybook stay. Closed mid-January through mid-March; restaurant also closed Sunday dinner and Mondays from November through April except on holidays. Information: *Château de Marçay,* Marçay-Chinon 37500 (phone: 47-93-03-47; fax: 47-93-45-33).

CHALET-DU-MONT-D'ARBOIS, Megève, Haute-Savoie In the French Alps certain establishments still represent the ultimate in jet-set cachet; they're places where the beautiful people brush the snow from their stretch pants and sip mulled wine by the fire. This 20-room member of the Relais & Châteaux group is one of those places. At 4,000 feet, it lies on a country road above the town, only 330 yards from the slopes. The chalet-style decor is woody and warm; there's a restaurant and tennis courts. Closed April through mid-June and November. Information: *Chalet-du-Mont-d'Arbois,* Rte. du Mont-d'Arbois, Megève 74120 (phone: 50-21-25-03; fax: 50-21-24-79).

CHÂTEAU D'ARTIGNY, Montbazon, Indre-et-Loire Many travelers who have spent the day visiting the châteaux of the Loire Valley experience an unquenchable desire to spend the night sleeping in one—and this Relais & Châteaux member is about as close as they can get. Built by François Coty (of perfume fame) on the site of an 18th-century château, this structure has a decorous mansarded exterior that cloaks an interior with 51 rooms and two suites as ornate and resplendent as any latter-day lord or lady could desire. A heated pool and two tennis courts are just a couple of the improvements that have been made since the establishment's construction; golf and horse-back riding are available nearby. In the excellent dining room try the duck with figs or the fish specialties. Classical music concerts enliven the fall and winter seasons. Closed late November through early January. Information: *Château d'Artigny,* Rte. de Monts, Veigné, Montbazon 37250 (phone: 47-26-24-24; fax: 47-65-92-79).

DOMAINE DES HAUTS-DE-LOIRE, Onzain, Loir-et-Cher Less awe inspiring perhaps than some of its fellow châteaux in the Loire Valley, this gracious Relais & Châteaux member was once the hunting lodge of the Count de Rostaing. A family-size château with rough oak beams and gleaming copper caul-drons, it has a pleasant, almost homey feel that's mirrored in the friendly, thoughtful service. Most of the 25 rooms—plus the nine suites in a newer but equally charming annex—are exquisitely decorated with antiques and have modern bathrooms. The elegant dining room has earned two well-deserved Michelin stars; fresh salmon, parsley mousse in hazelnut oil, and hot apple tart are among the house specialties. There also is a tennis court and a lake stocked with pike and carp. Spring, when flowers bloom in pro-fusion around the velvety lawns and swans glide on the placid pond, is a particularly entrancing time to visit. Closed December through February; restaurant also closed Mondays and Tuesday lunch, October through May. Information: *Domaine des Hauts-de-Loire,* Rte. de Herbault, Onzain 41150 (phone: 54-20-72-57; fax: 54-20-77-32).

MOULIN DE LA GORCE, La Roche-l'Abeille, Haute-Vienne A mill has existed at this spot in the countryside near Limoges from the time of the Valois, but the *moulin* here today serves not farmers, but seekers of tranquil enjoyment. Jean Bertranet, a former chef at the *Palais de l'Elysée* (the French *White House*), fell in love with the beauty of these Limousin surroundings and built a lovely establishment that recalls a more unhurried era. The nine rooms and one suite at this member of the Relais & Châteaux group are exceptionally comfortable and tastefully furnished, some located in a sep-arate building between a small pond and a rushing trout stream. Meals in the two-Michelin-star restaurant are served on the terrace overlooking a park and the pond or, in cooler weather, in the beautiful Louis XVI din-ing room with its massive brick fireplace. The rich, traditional specialties include *oeufs brouillés aux truffes* (scrambled eggs with truffles) and *mélange gourmand de homard et foie gras* (foie gras and lobster). Sumptuously endowed with wines of the Périgord and Bordeaux regions, the *cave* is noth-ing less than superlative. Closed January through early February; restau-rant also closed Sunday dinner and Mondays from mid-September through April. Information: *Moulin de la Gorce,* La Roche-l'Abeille 87800 (phone: 55-00-70-66; fax: 55-00-76-57).

GRAND HÔTEL LION D'OR, Romorantin-Lanthenay, Loir-et-Cher About 56 miles (91 km) southeast of Tours, in the game-rich Sologne region between the Loire

Valley's famous châteaux and the vineyards of Burgundy, this is one of France's most elegant hostelries. The old inn, now part of the Relais & Châteaux group, has a Renaissance fountain on its patio and one of the country's most admired chefs, Didier Clément, in its kitchen. The 13 luxurious rooms and three suites are each decorated in a unique style, some reflecting scenes from French novels. Clément's ever-changing two-Michelin-star menu features local products as well as Mediterranean fish and Atlantic oysters; specialties include game in season and unusual desserts such as pear flan with curry and caramel sauce. Closed January through mid-February. Information: *Grand Hôtel Lion d'Or,* 69 Rue Georges-Clemenceau, Romorantin-Lanthenay 41200 (phone: 54-76-00-28; fax: 54-88-24-87).

GRAND HÔTEL DU CAP-FERRAT, St-Jean-Cap-Ferrat, Alpes-Maritimes This jewel of a hotel on an isolated peninsula on the Côte d'Azur has been a winter haven for royalty since the beginning of the century. Open year-round, it abounds in summertime activities. The *Club Dauphin,* set by the sea, has a spectacular heated saltwater pool with an equally spectacular view, a sauna, sunbathing areas, cabañas, and an alfresco restaurant—perfect for lunch. A funicular takes guests back up to the hotel, where there is a piano bar designed to look like the bottom of the ocean and a one-Michelin-star restaurant (we think it deserves more). Renovated by its Japanese owners, the elegant yet light and airy, 50-room member of the Relais & Châteaux group is set in a 14-acre park filled with tropical flora. Information: *Grand Hôtel du Cap-Ferrat,* Bd. du Général-de-Gaulle, St-Jean-Cap-Ferrat 02690 (phone: 93-76-00-21; fax: 93-76-04-52).

MAS D'ARTIGNY, St-Paul-de-Vence, Alpes-Maritimes How can a hotel with 29 small pools be ignored? This ultramodern, ultra-luxurious bastion of the 20th century (and another member of the Relais & Châteaux group) is a complex of 53 guestrooms and 29 villas, each of the latter graced by its own private garden and pool. The units are arranged in a horseshoe around a main building, which itself boasts a more than adequate pool. The hotel's seafood restaurant, which has won a Michelin star, is the perfect place to sample *bourride de baudroie provençale* (anglerfish stew, Provence-style). Other pluses include tennis courts, parking, even a helicopter pad. Nice and the sea are only a short drive away. Information: *Mas d'Artigny,* Rte. des Hauts de St-Paul, St-Paul-de-Vence 06570 (phone: 93-32-84-54; fax: 93-32-95-36).

L'ESPÉRANCE, St-Père-sous-Vézelay, Yonne The finest of the 34 rooms and six suites in this serene, antiques-filled country manor house overlook the beautiful garden and the Cure River—be sure to request the very best; it's worth it. The principal indoor activity occurs in the glass-enclosed dining room, where three-Michelin-star food (such as potato *tourte* with caviar, and lobster with saffron sauce) is served with just the right degree of unfussy concern for your comfort. The restaurant's popularity sometimes seems to eclipse that of the glowing Romanesque *Basilique Ste-Madeleine,* in the village of Vézelay. A member of the Relais & Châteaux group. Closed January through early February; restaurant also closed Tuesdays and Wednesday lunch. Information: *L'Espérance,* St-Père-sous-Vézelay, Vézelay 89450 (phone: 86-33-20-45; fax: 86-33-26-15).

LE VIEUX LOGIS, Trémolat, Dordogne In one of the prettiest and least traveled regions of France, this enchanting member of the Relais & Châteaux group is one of the most picturesque yet least known of fine French hostelries. Installed in a typical old Périgord house with rustic furnishings, ivied walls, and flowered bowers, it offers 19 rooms and five suites, fine regional fare in its one-Michelin-star restaurant (with all the truffles the connoisseur could fancy), a lovely garden and pool, and good hunting and fishing grounds nearby. Closed January through early February; restaurant also closed Wednesday lunch and Tuesdays off-season. Information: *Le Vieux Logis,* Trémolat 24510 (phone: 53-22-80-06; fax: 53-22-84-89).

CHÂTEAU DU DOMAINE ST-MARTIN, Vence, Alpes-Maritimes Set 1,700 feet up in a park overlooking the blue waters of the Mediterranean, this 17-room, 10-villa country estate and castle has a magnificent view of the surrounding area, plenty of pure air, and a heart-shaped pool among the olive trees. Although the Relais & Châteaux member is incredibly tranquil, it is within easy striking distance of the bustling activity of Nice, Cannes, and Monte Carlo. Also on the property are tennis courts and a one-Michelin-star restaurant that serves Provençal food, much of it featuring the château's own products. Closed mid-November to mid-March; restaurant also closed Wednesdays (except for hotel guests). Information: *Château du Domaine St-Martin,* Rte. de Coursegoules, Vence 06140 (phone: 93-58-02-02; fax: 93-24-08-91).

TRIANON PALACE, Versailles, Yvelines Attached by private gardens to *Versailles,* this renovated palace is one of France's most historic hotels. Its vaulted-ceilinged, marble dining room, resembling a great mirrored ballroom, has played host to the likes of Marcel Proust, Colette, and Marlene Dietrich. Sarah Bernhardt used to arrive in a horse-drawn carriage, wrapped from head to wooden leg in tulle and feathers. When King Edward VIII abdicated the throne of England for the woman he loved, he and the former Wallis Simpson honeymooned here. The 157 rooms and 42 suites are furnished with antiques, and a covered pool and two terraces face the château's park, home to a flock of docile white sheep. Chef Gérard Vié presides over the kitchens of *Les Trois Marches,* which offers perfect service and highly original two-Michelin-star cooking; his foie gras is famous, as are his oysters and wild goose. The wine selection, with especially fine burgundies, is excellent, too. The beauty salon and spa, an exclusive Givenchy operation, are stocked with the designer's signature cosmetics and perfumes. There's also a conference center, shops, two tennis courts, and underground parking. Restaurant closed Sundays, Mondays, and August. Information: *Trianon Palace,* 1 Bd. de la Reine, Versailles 78000 (phone: 39-84-38-00, hotel; 39-50-13-21, restaurant; 800-772-3041; fax: 39-51-57-79).

Haute Gastronomie

Inspiring the same fierce passions and loyalties that soccer does in Brazil, eating is the French national sport. The French talk about food instead of the weather, reminisce about one meal while downing another, and select restaurants as if they were putting together an investment portfolio. The light, sauce-free fashion of nouvelle cuisine, which brought a few mouthfuls of moderation to the nationwide gourmandising, now is being supplanted by traditional *cuisine de bistrot,* and, happily, France is once again awash in béchamel and ablaze with cognac.

The best word of advice we can give to those planning a pilgrimage to a temple of gastronomy: Write for reservations months in advance of your anticipated arrival, since tables at the most favored restaurants are sometimes booked months ahead. And don't forget to *reconfirm* reservations once you arrive on French soil, even if no request for reconfirmation has been made formally. Reservations at the top restaurants are often automatically canceled without timely reconfirmation. When making your reservations, check to determine if credit cards are accepted and, if so, which ones; many restaurants accept MasterCard and Visa.

For information on our favorite restaurants in France's major cities, see the *Eating Out* sections of the individual chapters in THE CITIES. The following is our selection of culinary highlights (listed alphabetically by town) in the smaller cities and towns, in the countryside, and along the French coasts. Although we note the *fermetures annuelles* (yearly closings), bear in mind that last-minute changes frequently do occur. *Bon appétit!*

CHÂTEAU D'AUDRIEU, Audrieu, Calvados According to local legend, the first lord of the 60-acre park that surrounds this beautiful 18th-century castle was the personal chef to no less than William the Conqueror. Today the château's two tasteful and intimate dining rooms serve one-Michelin-star cuisine. The crown jewels are the *soupe de homard et d'escargots* (lobster and snail bisque) and the *aiguillettes de canard aux pêches* (duck in peach sauce). A very fine *menu dégustation* includes a sampling of the chef's finest creations. Closed Mondays, except at dinner for hotel guests, and December through February. Information: *Château d'Audrieu,* Audrieu 14250 (phone: 31-80-21-52; fax: 31-80-24-73).

OUSTAÙ DE BAUMANIÈRE and CABRO D'OR, Les Baux-de-Provence, Bouches-du-Rhône These two restaurants, a snail's throw from each other and under the same management, are in charming old Provençal manor houses in richly verdant settings. Seated under vaulted ceilings and wooden beams or on a terrace overlooking a fairy-tale duck pond, guests are graciously presented with some of France's most highly acclaimed cooking. At the former, a recipient of two Michelin stars, *filets de rougets au vinaigre* (mullet fillets with a vinegar sauce), *pigeon farci au foie gras* (squab stuffed with foie gras), and *gigot d'agneau en croûte* (leg of lamb in a pastry crust) are among the specialties. Wines are selected from the 35,000 bottles in the restaurant's famous cellars. The latter restaurant, which has one Michelin star, offers a fine *terrine de légumes au confit de tomates* (vegetable terrine with a tomato sauce). *Oustaù* is closed mid-January through early March, and Wednesdays and Thursday lunch from November through March; *Cabro* on Mondays, Tuesday lunch, and mid-November through mid-December. Information: *Oustaù de Baumanière*, Les Baux-de-Provence, Maussane-les-Alpilles 13520 (phone: 90-54-33-07; fax: 90-54-40-46); *Cabro d'Or*, same address (phone: 90-54-33-21; fax: 90-54-45-98).

AUBERGE DES TEMPLIERS, Les Bézards, Loiret Named for the austere order of Knights-Templars once headquartered here, this elegant eatery nestles languorously in a quiet oak grove. Guests can relax and enjoy a drink in front of the immense brick fireplace before moving on to one of the dining rooms, where 18th-century tapestries drape from the timbered ceilings to the Oriental-carpeted floor. In summer lunch is served under the rose-entwined trellises on the terrace. Michelin has awarded the place two stars for specialties such as those featuring fish fresh from the nearby Loire, and the extensive wine list boasts a 1947 Château Lafite-Rothschild. Closed February. Information: *Auberge des Templiers*, Les Bézards, Boismorand 45290 (phone: 38-31-80-01; fax: 38-31-84-51).

LA MAISON DE BRICOURT, Cancale, Ille-et-Vilaine Named France's Chef of the Year for 1994 by prestigious *Gault-Millau* magazine, Olivier Roellinger has a distinctive style that he traces to nearby St-Malo, once a center of the international spice trade. His specialties—such as a soup of Bélon oysters with local herbs—involve intensely flavored reductions of fish broths and unusual combinations of herbs and spices, recalling the traditional availability of an array of spices in the busy port. Roellinger relies on the freshest seafood (such as the giant Cancale oysters harvested in Mont St-Michel's bay) and the finest produce and meat provided by Breton farmers. Try such delights on the ever-changing menu as *Saint-Pierre retour des Indes* (John Dory with Indian spices) and crab with baby vegetables in a wild fennel sauce. The service is exceptional, and the wine list is an oenologist's dream. The restaurant, which has garnered two Michelin stars and is a member of the Relais & Châteaux group, is housed in an 18th-century townhouse with a rock garden and duck pond overlooking Cancale. The Roellingers also operate two luxury hotels, *Les Rimains* (adjoining the restaurant) and *Le Château Richeux*, and a seafood bistro, *Le Coquillage*. Closed Tuesdays and Wednesdays (except for dinner in July and August) and mid-December through mid-March. Information: *La Maison de Bricourt,* 1 Rue Duguesclin, Cancale 35260 (phone: 99-89-64-76; fax: 99-89-88-47).

LE CIRO'S, Deauville, Calvados Crowded but cozy, especially on summer Sundays when the Norman rains empty the beach, this bastion of the very rich on Deauville's celebrated boardwalk is owned by the *Casino de Deauville.* White napery and well-polished silver and glassware provide an appropriate setting for the classical seafood that is the specialty. The fine view of the ocean is a bonus. Information: *Le Ciro's,* Promenade des Planches, Deauville 14800 (phone: 31-88-18-10; fax: 31-98-66-71).

LES PRÉS D'EUGÉNIE, Eugénie-les-Bains, Landes Michel Guérard is to French gastronomy what Joe DiMaggio was to baseball, and this little spa resort in southwestern France is where he cooks his home runs. Guérard's three-Michelin-star *cuisine minceur* (slimming cuisine), the subject of his best-selling cookbook, is notable for allowing diners to make *cochons* (pigs) of themselves and stay slender at the same time. The more sybaritic will opt for his *cuisine gourmande,* creative, beautifully presented dishes that have earned Guérard the highest accolades from critics in France and abroad. The natural products of the region—the basis of these gustatory masterpieces—are selected by him and his staff with the meticulous care of an art dealer shopping for a Monet. The wine list represents a fine selection of the best the region has to offer, not to mention first-rate burgundies, bordeaux, and so on; the service is immaculate. Closed Wednesdays and Thursday lunch (except from mid-July through mid-September and holidays) and early December through mid-February. Information: *Les Prés d'Eugénie,* Eugénie-les-Bains 40320 (phone: 58-05-06-07; fax: 58-51-13-59).

AUBERGE DE L'ILL, Illhaeusern, Haut-Rhin Serene and exceptionally elegant, this three-Michelin-star establishment on the willow-shaded shores of the Ill River, surrounded by lovely gardens, serves Alsatian food at its pungent and aromatic best: a creative and elegant mix of the best of two cuisines, delicate French and vigorous German. The flower-filled dining room is the place to sample wild hare salad, frog soup, or pike mousse, or simply to dip into one of the almost innumerable pâtés. Venison in a light pepper sauce and salmon soufflé are among the other delights. Whatever the selection, let the fruity local riesling flow like the river outside. Closed Mondays (except for lunch from April through October), Tuesdays, and February. Information: *Auberge de l'Ill,* Rue de Collonges, Illhaeusern, Ribeauvillé 68150 (phone: 89-71-83-23; fax: 89-71-82-83).

LA CÔTE ST-JACQUES, Joigny, Yonne Housed in an 18th-century villa, this three-Michelin-star establishment is a Lorain family affair: Michel is chef; his son Jean-Michel, lieutenant in the kitchen; and his wife, Jacqueline, mistress of the wine cellar. Inside, fabric-covered walls, fresh flowers, and porcelain and silver tableware, all aglow in candlelight, set an elegant stage for the main event. The menu offers *cuisine traditionelle,* which includes three

courses of lobster, and *cuisine créative,* which features such novel preparations as a *galette de pommes de terre et de pigeon à la muscade* (a "pancake"
of potatoes and squab, seasoned with nutmeg). Must-try specialties include
sea bass in caviar cream sauce, an ethereal *poularde à la vapeur de champagne* (chicken with a delicate champagne sauce), and truffle ravioli.
Particularly strong in chablis, the wine list is sublime. Some Parisians make
the two-hour drive simply to dine here. Closed January through early
February. Information: *La Côte St-Jacques,* 14 Faubourg de Paris, Joigny
89300 (phone: 86-62-09-70; fax: 86-91-49-70).

LES FRÈRES TROISGROS, Roanne, Loire Brothers Pierre and Jean studied under
the late Fernand Point at Lyons's *La Pyramide* (see *Lyons* in THE CITIES),
then returned in the 1950s to take over their father's 20-room hostelry.
After the death of Jean, Pierre, along with his son Michel, continued the
tradition of concocting dishes in which natural flavors are delicately enhanced
and underscored. The haute-priced, three-Michelin-star menu changes with
the seasons to use the area's fresh vegetables, poultry, shrimp, and snails
to best advantage. From the vegetable terrines and sorrel-sauced salmon
(the restaurant's most celebrated dish, now a French standard) to the chicken
breasts served in vinegar-spiked and walnut oil–flavored bouillon, the menu
is a tribute to the kaleidoscopic richness of the French countryside. Recent
renovations have modernized the decor and include a dramatic glass and
brass façade. Closed Tuesday dinner, Wednesdays, the last two weeks in
February, and two weeks in August. Information: *Les Frères Troisgros,* Pl.
Jean-Troisgros, Roanne 42300 (phone: 77-71-66-97; fax: 77-70-39-77).

PIERRE GAGNAIRE, St-Etienne, Loire Housed in an opulent Art Deco building, this
restaurant—yet another to rate three Michelin stars and a member of the
Relais Gourmands—definitely is not the place to go for bourgeois cuisine
or prices. Gagnaire's iconoclastic menu, which changes often to suit market offerings and the seasons, features inventive dishes such as *laitue farcie de tourteau* (lettuce stuffed with crab). You're not likely to find cuisine
as delightfully surprising anywhere else in France. Closed Sunday dinner,
Wednesdays, a week in mid-August, and two weeks in November.
Information: *Pierre Gagnaire,* 7 Rue de la Richelandière, St-Etienne 42100
(phone: 77-42-30-90; fax: 77-42-30-95).

LA CÔTE D'OR, Saulieu, Côte d'Or With soberly decorated dining rooms overlooking
a garden, this splendid inn offers some of France's finest cuisine, evidenced
by its three Michelin stars. Chef Bernard Loiseau creates distinctive sauces
using almost no fats, but there is nothing austere about the taste of his *ris
de veau* (calf sweetbreads) and *foie aux champignons* (liver with mushrooms).
The menu, which titles every dish simply, offers no clue to the exciting, elusive flavors of the sauces. The wine list is outstanding, particularly in burgundies. Closed Mondays from November through March and Tuesday
lunch. Information: *La Côte d'Or,* 2 Rue d'Argentine, Saulieu 21210 (phone:

80-64-07-66; 800-FRANCOISE; 212-757-0874 in New York City; fax: 80-64-08-92; 212-757-1377 in New York City).

AUBERGE DU PÈRE BISE, Talloires, Haute-Savoie Lakes, a principal drawing card for European vacationers in prewar days, are, like spas, coming back into fashion, and Lac Annecy and its picturebook environs make a persuasive case for choosing a tranquil lake over a teeming seaside. The village of Talloires, elegant and serene, is the backdrop for this family-owned, two-Michelin-star restaurant and inn on the lakefront. With mountains to the left and serene water to the right, there's no choice but to give in to the temptation to lunch outdoors, perhaps on duck, lobster tails, and a wicked chestnut pastry. Outstanding hors d'oeuvres and specialties like fish terrine and filet of turbot in basil-tomato sauce add up to a meal you won't forget, but expect to pay for the pleasure. The excellent wine cellar includes outrageously priced *grand crus* and the more reasonable wines of the Savoie. Spend the night in one of this Relais & Châteaux group member's 27 deliciously plush rooms (with balconies). Closed mid-November through mid-February. Information: *Auberge du Père Bise,* Rte. du Port, Talloires 74290 (phone: 50-60-72-01; fax: 50-60-73-05).

L'ABBAYE ST-MICHEL, Tonnerre, Yonne In the middle of the idyllic Burgundy countryside, this 10th-century Benedictine abbey has a cool, stone-vaulted dining room, a gently blossoming garden, a selection of almost lyrical wines from the surrounding vineyards, and superbly refined two-Michelin-star cuisine that outshines even the celestial setting; *carré d'agneau aux petites fèves* (rack of lamb with baby fava beans) is only one example. Closed Tuesday lunch, Mondays from November through April, and January through early February. Information: *L'Abbaye St-Michel,* Rue St-Michel, Tonnerre 89700 (phone: 86-55-05-99; fax: 86-55-00-10).

GEORGES BLANC, Vonnas, Ain One of the stars in Lyons's culinary firmament, Blanc has created a menu combining traditional Burgundian and nouvelle cuisine that has won his restaurant three Michelin stars of its own. Items include braised sweetbreads in spinach and lamb tenderloin with fresh wild mushrooms; the dessert cart brims with nearly 20 pastry selections. Located in the picturesque Bresse region on the bank of the Veyle River, there are also 24 deluxe guestrooms. Closed Wednesdays, Thursdays (except for dinner in summer), and January through mid-February. Information: *Georges Blanc,* Vonnas 01540 (phone: 74-50-00-10; fax: 74-50-08-80)).

Shopping Spree

For centuries France has been producing the world's most fashionable clothing, its most delicious food and wine, and its most bewitching perfumes. All of these benefit from the same flair and good taste that characterize just about everything to which the French put their hearts and hands, so it's no wonder that shopping in this country is such a delight. In the provinces regional specialties are among the best buys—calvados in Normandy, sausage in Toulouse, perfume in Grasse, and wine almost everywhere, but especially in the Bordeaux, Burgundy, and Loire Valley growing areas.

All over France—particularly near the Côte d'Azur—are little ateliers whose potters, weavers, wood-carvers, and glassblowers sell their wares from tiny shops, in the sunny open-air markets of Nice and Cannes, or in the picturesque roving crafts fairs that periodically visit neighboring towns. Buy a local newspaper or an information booklet, which may advertise crafts exhibits. Gift-shop owners also may know how to contact artisans in their areas. In addition, the local tourist office almost always can answer specific questions. Shopping in the provinces offers its own pleasures, mostly related to the leisurely pace that affords time for personal contact between buyer and seller. There seldom is any savings, however, in buying a name-brand cast-iron skillet in the south of France and lugging it back to Paris. French storekeepers nationwide adhere more closely than their American counterparts to manufacturers' list prices, and if there is any price difference, it may well be that the skillet actually will cost *more* in that isolated shop than in a Paris department store. By the same token, the French capital also boasts the widest selection available of practically every type of merchandise.

Shoppers also should be aware that the values available on certain merchandise become even more compelling when the French government's refund to visitors of its Value-Added Tax (VAT)—usually 18.6%—is taken into account. At press time a visitor must spend a minimum of 2,000F (about $345) in a single shop to be eligible for a refund.

Following is an item-by-item guide to what to buy in France. For listings of recommended shops in France's major metropolises, see the *Shopping* sections of the individual chapters in THE CITIES.

ANTIQUES France is an excellent hunting ground for antiques, with a wide range of dealers, auction houses, and noncommercial institutions that offer many items at bargain prices. For additional details, see *Antiques Hunting in France* in this chapter.

CHILDREN'S CLOTHING Gorgeous hand-smocked and -decorated clothing for babies and older children still can be found in France—but at painfully high prices. For all but the most indulgent grandparents, the best idea is to head for department stores, which generally display a wide selection of charming clothing for youngsters, often embellished with very French motifs.

CRYSTAL AND CHINA France has crystal and china to make the humblest table gleam like a royal banquet hall, and there are two good ways to get an overview of the nation's best: a stroll the length of the Rue de Paradis in

Paris or a visit to a porcelain- producing center. The town of Limoges, in the Limousin region of southwestern France, is renowned the world over for its fine porcelain. (For a detailed description of shopping in Limoges, see *Périgord* in DIRECTIONS).

FABRIC The colorful and distinctive cotton fabrics of the south of France make delightful souvenirs.

FOOD AND WINE Almost anywhere in France it's possible to put together a sumptuous picnic by making four stops: at the charcuterie, a cross between a butcher shop and a deli; the *fromagerie,* or cheese store; the *marchand de vin,* or wine merchant; and the *boulangerie,* or bakery. Usually these shops will be within a block or two of one another, sometimes right next door, but plan ahead: Most are closed from 1 to 4 PM and on Sunday afternoons and Mondays.

A visit to a colorful open-air food market should head any travel itinerary to France. Wherever you are, find out (from the local tourist office) when the market is held and where, then plunge into the action with camera and shopping bag. Even if you buy no more than a bag of cherries— probably the sweetest you'll ever taste—you'll be glad you saw it all. In Normandy, at Dieppe's Saturday-morning market, which reaches inland behind the port, pots of jam made on nearby farms by the women who sell them are among the more alluring wares. Farm women, their bicycles laden with cartons of just-gathered eggs, freshly pulled carrots, and the like, pedal to the charming market held each Saturday morning in Mont-de-Marsan, in the Landes region of southwestern France. Children will love the live chickens, ducks, and rabbits; adults, the cooked ones. St-Pol-de-Léon, a small town on Brittany's north coast near Morlaix, has one of the liveliest wholesale produce markets in France. Every morning between January and September farmers gather in the Kérisnel *quartier* to sell their produce by public auction to wholesalers and dealers. In the small Dordogne town of Sarlat-la-Canéda a lively market takes place every Saturday and Wednesday morning in the Place des Oies (Place du Marché) and the Place de la Liberté. Another Dordogne town with a wonderful market, ancient Thiviers is now known for its Saturday morning *marché au gras* (literally, "fat market"), held in the Place Foch from November through February. It's famed for its foie gras, fattened ducks and geese, and truffles.

HOUSEWARES *Castorama,* with about a hundred branches throughout the country, carries 45,000 different European-designed basics for the home—from a simple flowerpot to a sophisticated security system. Although you may not want to cart home a bidet or a set of wrought-iron andirons (*Castorama* does *not* arrange shipping), you will find dozens of moderately priced and stylish smaller items—doorknobs, soap dishes, coat hooks, decorative door plaques—that travel well. Forget about electrical wall switches and anything else you have to connect to existing wiring; US and European systems are not compatible.

KITCHENWARE In a country that ranks cooking among the highest arts, it is not surprising to find an abundance of kitchen items at nearly every turn. The small, rural Norman town of Villedieu-les-Poêles (21 miles/34 km south of St-Lô) takes its name from the copper *poêles* (frying pans) that have been made there for 300 years. From one end of the main street to the other, copper gleams through the shop windows. Pots come in all different gauges and sizes, and prices vary accordingly. It is possible to save money over stateside prices for comparable merchandise, but the variety is such that it's necessary to come armed with exact specifications.

LEATHER GOODS It is a pleasure to shop for leather goods in France, especially in the best establishments, where every piece of merchandise from key cases to steamer trunks is impeccably designed and perfectly crafted. Bear in mind, however, that lower-quality leather goods are probably more expensive and not as well made as comparable items in the US. Americans also should be aware that some exotic skins sold legally in France—certain species of alligator, crocodile, ostrich, and lizard—are on the Endangered Species List in the United States and may be seized on arrival back home. For details on checking current US customs regulations, see GETTING READY TO GO.

LINGERIE The lacy, frilly, undergarments sold in France, often covered with polka dots or dripping with ribbons, are the stuff of which fantasies are made, and lingerie makes a delightful souvenir. Most department stores carry a wide selection of brands, styles, and sizes and display their wares clearly, making choices simpler than in small shops, where much of the stock may be tucked in boxes behind the counter.

MEN'S CLOTHING Men's clothing is not generally considered a good buy in France, and many a male has gone into shock after looking at a Parisian price tag. Yet for some the blend of classic styling and French flair is irresistible.

PERFUME For centuries the French have been making enticing scents which are synonymous with luxury and romance, so it's not surprising that perfume heads the shopping lists of many visitors to France. Department stores around the country, which generally carry the best selections of all the well-known brands (except Guerlain, which sells only from its own shops), do a booming business among tourists. By shopping in the right places and following the rules for getting VAT refunds, it's possible to purchase some of France's most expensive and sought-after perfumes at prices 30% lower than in the US. Even without the additional reduction afforded by the refund, the cost of French perfume in a department store is roughly 90% of what you would pay stateside.

Do not be taken in by the flashy "tax free" signs sported by perfume stores all over the country. Most shops, major department stores included, sell basically the same brands and sizes, at rates set by the manufacturers. Perfume becomes tax free only after you have purchased enough of it at a single store to qualify for the refund set up by the government. The exception is airport duty-free shops, which do not add tax, even on small bottles of inexpensive perfumes; the selection is more limited than in city stores, however.

Grasse, in the hills 10 miles (16 km) from Cannes, has been an international perfume-making center since the 17th century; for a detailed description of shopping there, see *The Côte d'Azur* in DIRECTIONS.

SHOES France is full of places to buy footwear that is not only stylish but also comfortable, probably because the French walk a good deal and seemingly refuse to wear ugly shoes. Look for the *André* and *Raoul* chains, which stock surprisingly inexpensive shoes in the latest styles and colors.

Antiques Hunting in France

The history of France may best be seen in cathedrals and châteaux, but it is best felt by holding a fragment of a sculpted choir stall or an Art Deco soup ladle, by touching the satiny surface of a marquetry wedding chest, or by slipping on the signet ring that once belonged to a scheming marquise. Such morsels of the nation's past can be savored at some 13,000 French antiques shops and auction houses or at a country-wide and year-round array of fairs and markets, from Abbeville to Zonza.

AUCTIONS

Once something of a professional club for dealers only, auctions—known in French as *ventes aux enchères*—have become the favorite indoor sport of the *haute bourgeoisie* in the last few years, so in the *salles des ventes* (salesrooms) of France there are fewer bargains around than there used to be. However, those who know their market may still save as much as a third of the retail price; even for those who don't, auctions are hard to beat for pure theater.

The auction situation in France is different than in the US, for all sales take place under the aegis of a government-authorized auctioneer known as the *commissaire-priseur*. The houses in the various cities are basically cooperatives managed by the local guild of *commissaires-priseurs;* reputations for probity and expertise are on the line, rather than those of specific salesrooms or companies. By law, French auctioneers are responsible for the authenticity of any item they sell for 30 years after the sale. Besides Paris, the most important *salles des ventes* are in Angers, Brest, Cannes, Chartres, Dijon, Enghien, Fontainebleau, L'Isle-Adam, Lille, Lyons, Morlaix, Toulouse, and Versailles. The weekly *Gazette de l'Hôtel Drouot* (10 Rue du Faubourg-Montmartre, Paris 75009; phone: 47-70-93-00), available at newsstands, prints a calendar of auction sales throughout France and a running tally of the results.

The true center of France's auction world is the *Hôtel des Ventes Drouot-Richelieu* (9 Rue Drouot, Paris 75009; phone: 48-00-20-20; fax: 48-00-20-33), on the Rive Droite. Some 600,000 lots go through its 16 salesrooms every year, and the activity is frantic. If you find yourself in a room full of plumbers' fittings or vintage cognacs when what you really wanted was antiques, just go up to the next floor. It's closed Sundays. Sales also are held at the *Drouot-Montaigne* (15 Av. Montaigne, Paris 75008; phone: 48-00-20-80).

A bidding-free variation on the auction theme is the *dépot-vente,* a salesroom where private sellers leave lots on consignment with a dealer who sets the price and takes a commission. These generally are well patronized by bargain-hunting professionals. The largest is the immense *Dépôt-Vente de Paris* (81 Rue de Lagny, Paris 75020; phone: 43-72-13-91).

ANTIQUES

No little village in France would be complete without its *Petite Galerie* (Little Gallery) or its *Au Bon Vieux Temps* (In the Good Old Days). Some are true *antiquaires,* antiques dealers who handle pieces of established value and pedigree; others are *brocanteurs,* secondhand dealers whose stock may run the gamut from Second Empire snuffboxes to broken 78-rpm Edith Piaf records. Many dealers belong to either the *Syndicat National des Antiquaires* (National Antiques Dealers' Association) or the *Syndicat National du Commerce de l'Antiquité* (National Association of Antiques Businesses), two reputable guilds whose members have pledged to be truthful about all items they sell. For an important purchase, the wise buyer will request a certificate of authenticity. With furniture, in particular, the dealer should be precise about just which parts have been restored and how; a number of "antiques" are really superbly carpentered composites of partly salvaged pieces, and there is a thriving industry in the recycling of genuinely ancient wood into pieces of "antique" furniture that actually were born yesterday.

A trend of the past decade has been the clustering of individual shops into *villages d'antiquaires,* something like shopping centers for antiques, with dozens of dealers housed under a single roof. Among the better ones are *La Treille des Antiquaires* (23-25 Rue des Chats-Bossus, Lille), the *Cour des Antiquaires* (7 Rue de l'Industrie, Nantes), and the *Marché des Antiquaires* (Vallauris, between Cannes and Antibes). Most are open on weekends and make a pleasant excursion.

ANTIQUES EXPOSITIONS, FAIRS, AND SALONS

These are three names for roughly the same ritual—an annual antiques fair that lasts a week, give or take a few days, and attracts dealers from all over the region, the nation, or Europe, depending on its importance in the trade. There are so many salons in France now that many dealers have no home base at all; they simply travel the circuit from one fair to the next, selling, buying, trading, and sizing up the competition. One of the biggest and best is the *Salon des Antiquaires Languedoc-Midi-Pyrénées,* in Toulouse. For 10 days, usually beginning the second week in November, more than 400 dealers spread their wares throughout the giant *Parc des Expositions.* The merchandise is some of Europe's finest, and the crowd includes all of the country's top professionals. It's a bit like ambling through the *Louvre,* but with everything for sale.

Besides those in Paris and Bordeaux (see the individual reports in THE CITIES), other top salons include the *Salon Européen des Antiquaires,* staged in late January or early February at *Alpexpo,* Grenoble; and the *Salon des Antiquaires et Brocanteurs,* which takes place in late April in Nancy.

FLEA MARKETS

The range of France's countless *marchés aux puces*—literally, "markets with fleas"—extends from the vast, sprawling bric-a-brac city that is Paris's *Marché aux Puces de St-Ouen* (better known as the *Puces de Clignancourt*) to two folding tables in the town square in Poubelle-les-Bains. The merchandise varies from lower-echelon antiques to very rare rubbish, and it may be necessary to comb your way through ten boxes of bent spoons and a decade of back copies of *Paris-Match* before finding the Picasso of your dreams. But dealers stock up in precisely this fashion, and flea markets are where everybody in Paris or Poubelle seems to be on nearly every sunny Saturday. The *Syndicat d'Initiative* in whatever town you may be visiting can tell you the time and place of the nearest *marché.* The flea markets in major cities are described in the individual shopping sections in THE CITIES. Among other delightfully dilapidated *marchés aux puces* are those held in Antibes (Thursdays and Saturdays on Pl. Aubertini), Lille (Sunday mornings at the *Marché Wazemmes*), Nantes (Saturday mornings on Pl. Viarme), Nîmes (Mondays on Rue Jean-Jaurès), Toulon (Sunday mornings in the Quartier Ste-Musse), and Toulouse (Saturdays, Sundays, and Mondays at the *Marché St-Germain*).

HOT SPOTS FOR ANTIQUES

Nearly all roads in France lead to antiques. For a list of the best antiques shops in the capital, consult the shopping section in *Paris,* THE CITIES. The regions described below are perhaps the richest in antiques, both historically and commercially. A word to the wily: The Riviera has the thinnest stylistic traditions and the thickest prices in the country; save your money for areas where the local antiques were once household objects rather than bathing-season baubles.

BURGUNDY Besides vintage wines, you'll find the flower of French furniture and sculpture in Burgundy. The town of Beaune is a good bet, especially for those in search of an antique mantelpiece; the villages of Mâcon and Nevers also can yield treasures.

LOIRE VALLEY The forest of princely châteaux here was synonymous with France itself in the 16th and 17th centuries, and many of its treasures have remained in the region. Drive from Blois to Orléans along one bank of the Loire and back along the other, and you'll find dozens of shops in all the villages en route.

Tours The most rewarding browsing is at the *Salle des Ventes* (20 Rue Michel-Colombe); at the *Salon des Antiquaires (Parc des Expositions),* held annually on the fourth weekend in March; and in the shops along Rue de la Scellerie. Wednesdays and Saturdays are flea market days at the Place des Victoires.

NORMANDY Wonderful Norman carvings in oak, particularly massive armoires, are among the more splendid finds in this corner of France.

Caen There's often a treasure or two at the *Marché aux Puces,* held the first Saturday of every month on Rue du Vaugueux, and in the shops on Rue Ecuyère. The *Salon des Antiquaires,* held in mid-June at the *Palais des Expositions,* brings new dealers and fresh wares.

Honfleur Antiques shops are a special attraction of this picturesque port town. The greatest concentration is around the Place Ste-Catherine and in the half-timbered houses along its side streets.

PROVENCE AND LANGUEDOC An antiques hunter will turn up all manner of oldies but goodies in the south of France at a handful of exceptional locations. The Sunday flea market at Isle-sur-la-Sorgue is the best of its kind in the region.

Montpellier On Saturday mornings the town's antiques lovers can be found prowling through the *Marché aux Puces* on the Place des Arceaux. Every year in late April or early May all eyes turn to the good-size *Salon des Antiquaires et de la Brocante* at the *Parc des Expositions.*

Nîmes On Mondays dealers congregate at the *Marché à la Brocante* in the Allée Jean-Jaurès. On Sundays there's the little flea market in the Place des Carmes. The year's activity climaxes in December with the *Salon des Antiquaires* at the *Parc des Expositions.*

RULES OF THE ROAD FOR AN ODYSSEY OF THE OLD

Buy for sheer pleasure and not for investment. Forget about the carrot of supposed resale value that dealers habitually dangle in front of amateur clients. If you love something, it probably will ornament your home until the next Revolution.

Don't be afraid to haggle. This is true even in the most awesomely elegant boutique on the Rue du Faubourg-St-Honoré. Everything is negotiable, and the higher the price, the harder (and farther) it falls.

Buy the finest example you can afford of any item, in as close to mint condition as possible. Chipped or broken "bargains" will haunt you later with their shabbiness.

Train your eye in museums. These probably are the best schools for the acquisitive senses, particularly as you begin to develop special passions. Collections like those of tapestries at Aubusson, of porcelain at Limoges, and of furniture in the *Louvre* will set the standards against which to measure purchases.

Peruse French art and antiques magazines. French newsstands abound in them. The best include *Connaissance des Arts, L'Estampille, Beaux-Arts,* and *L'Oeil. Trouvailles* deals with bric-a-brac and flea markets.

Get advice from a specialist when contemplating a major acquisition. Members of the various national guilds of antiques experts are well distributed throughout the country. For more information, contact the *Chambre Nationale des Experts Spécialistes en Antiquités* (4 Rue Longchamp, Nice 06000; phone: 93-82-21-40) or the *Syndicat Français des Experts Professionnels en Oeuvres d'Art* (81 Rue St-Dominique, Paris 75007; phone: 47-05-50-26).

Casinos Royale

To anyone brought up on the high-rolling, honky-tonk gambling supermarkets of Las Vegas and Atlantic City, the hushed elegance of France's many casinos, Europe's most elaborate gaming network, will require some adjustment—and perhaps some classier clothes. But even for those who only toss an occasional chip onto those lush meadows of felt, the spectacle at the great pleasure domes of Monte Carlo and Deauville is well worth the modest price of admission. Set in some of France's major resort towns (but forbidden within 60 miles/96 km of Paris by Napoleonic decree), they draw a heady mixture of Parisian chic and Arab sheik. Behind all the glitter is a system of tight surveillance by the *Brigade des Jeux,* France's gaming police, and a code that regulates everything from the odds on the slot machines to the dinner jacket on the croupier—which has, by law, no pockets. The result is an almost totally aboveboard industry, though players are nonetheless fairly certain to lose their money, according to the inexorable laws of mathematics.

Passports are required for admission to all casinos described below. Though marathon games of chemin de fer are allowed to continue until the players drop, most French casinos open daily in mid-afternoon and close at 3 or 4 AM. Dress has become far more casual in recent years, but there still are many casinos where jacket and tie are de rigueur for gentlemen; in any case, it's always better to err on the side of decorum. The staples of the French casino diet are roulette, baccarat, and *boule;* craps and blackjack increasingly are in evidence, the result of creeping Americanization. If you're not familiar with the rules or the vocabulary, many casinos will provide an explanatory booklet. Still others have roving *chefs de partie* (game chiefs), who will be more than happy to help the player who doesn't mind looking like a greenhorn in the midst of all that savoir faire.

AIX-LES-BAINS, Savoie At this ancient thermal resort where the Romans once frolicked, titled matrons fresh from the sulfurous mud baths hoard their chips in silver mesh purses. There is a vaguely fin de siècle feeling to it all, from the gaming tables of the *Casino Grand Cercle* in the *Palais de Savoie,* one of France's most distinguished and stately, to the more contemporary *Nouveau Casino* (where you will find slot machines and a movie theater), only a chip's throw away. The town nestles at the foot of the Alps on the east bank of lovely Lac du Bourget. When the chips are up, try the half-day boat tour of the lake, which includes a visit to the *Abbaye de Hautecombe.* Information: *Casino Grand Cercle,* Rue du Casino, Aix-les-Bains 73100 (phone: 79-35-16-16); *Nouveau Casino,* 36 Av. Victoria, Aix-les-Bains 73100 (phone: 79-35-10-00).

ANNECY, Haute-Savoie Annecy's *Casino Impérial* is part of the complex of the *Impérial Palace,* a sumptuous Belle Epoque hotel on a peninsula jutting out into Lac Annecy. Modern and traditional games are offered. The crowd here tends to become intensely involved in play; conversation practically ceases after the initial cry of *"Les jeux sont faits!"* If the appeal of the dice fades after a lost fistful of francs, take one of the hotel's shuttles to the picturesque historic quarter of Annecy, a taxi-boat to the town center, or drive to the magnificent shores of the lake. Information: *Casino Impérial,* 32 Av. d'Albigny, Annecy 74000 (phone: 50-09-30-00; fax: 50-09-33-33).

LA BAULE, Loire-Atlantique Gambling is so deeply ingrained in the spirit of this busy, pleasure-mad resort in southern Brittany that the main waterfront promenade, the Esplanade François-André, is reverently named after the founder of a great chain of French casinos. In a manicured park opposite the stately *Royal* hotel is the town's casino, whose original building was demolished and replaced several years ago. Its restaurant, *La Brasserie du Casino* (phone: 40-60-30-33), is open until 1 AM, and its nightclub, *Le Paradise* (phone: 40-60-80-23), has dining and dancing until dawn in season. Anyone who should happen to rise before the next evening's gaming can shine for a few hours on the resort's splendid 3-mile sweep of beach or on the several perfectly maintained clay tennis courts. The resort also boasts a state-of-the-art saltwater spa, *Thalgo* (phone: 40-24-44-88), next to the *Royal.* Yacht basins, equestrian centers, and all manner of other facilities effectively banish boredom at La Baule. Information: *Le Casino,* Esplanade François-André, La Baule 44500 (phone: 40-60-20-23).

BIARRITZ, Pyrénées-Atlantiques The two casinos in this most aristocratic resort attracted kings and princesses to the Atlantic coast long before the reign of the Riviera. Queen Victoria vacationed here, and it was here that King Farouk, a regular, once tossed his solid-gold lighter across the roulette table to a lady in need of a light—and then watched while she promptly handed it to the croupier as a tip. The refurbished *Casino Municipal,* now known as the *Casino de Biarritz,* on the sand of the Grande Plage, took over last year as the center of Biarritz's gaming activities. The *Casino Bellevue*, on the other hand, set on the cliffs and guarding the beach below like a sentry, now serves as the city's convention center. Just beyond the Grande Plage, great gilt-edged hotels like the *Hôtel du Palais, Miramar*, and *Régina et Golf*, which line the Avenue de l'Impératrice, gaze out to sea on a cluster of tiny islands. Information: *Office du Tourisme*, Pl. d'Ixelles, Biarritz 64200 (phone: 59-24-20-24).

CANNES, Alpes-Maritimes The classy *Palm Beach*, whose receipts were once among the highest in France, has closed its doors indefinitely, now supplanted by the *Casino Croisette*, opposite the old harbor. Thanks to its huge array of *machines à sous*—slot machines—the *Croisette* is now the most heavily played casino on the Riviera. It is housed in the modern *Palais des Festivals*, which, in addition to hosting the *International Film Festival* each year, is also home to the city's tourist office, an amphitheater, a nightclub, and lovely formal gardens. Other contenders on Cannes's casino scene are the *Carlton Casino Club* at the *Carlton* hotel and the spectacular *Casino Riviera* at the *Noga Hilton*. Traditional and newer games are offered at all three, and gentlemen will need to don a jacket and tie before hitting the tables. Information: *Casino Croisette, Palais des Festivals*, Jetée Albert-Edouard, Cannes 06406 (phone: 93-68-00-07); *Carlton Casino Club, Carlton Hotel*, 58 La Croisette, Cannes 06406 (phone: 93-68-00-33); *Casino Riviera, Noga Hilton*, 50 La Croisette, Cannes 06414 (phone: 93-68-43-43).

DEAUVILLE, Calvados A gleaming villa by the sea, the *Casino de Deauville* and its environs have often been called the "21st Arrondissement of Paris." A playground of the 19th-century version of the jet set, Deauville is in its patrician prime during the August horse-racing season, when formal dress still may be de rigueur in certain of the casino's sanctums. The Deauville casino also owns two of the town's other delights—the Norman, wooden-gabled *Hôtel Normandy* and a deluxe seafood restaurant named *Le Ciro's*, both on the eminently strollable boardwalk and both described at greater length in *Romantic French Hostelries* and *Haute Gastronomie* in this chapter. Trouville, Deauville's neighbor across the Touques River, offers comparable sport, not to mention horseback riding from one end of the beach to the other. Information: *Casino de Deauville*, 1 Rue Edmond-Blanc, Deauville 14800 (phone: 31-98-66-66).

DIVONNE-LES-BAINS, Ain Open year-round, Divonne is France's top money-making casino. In a sleepy border village at the foot of the Juras, it is only about 10 miles (16 km) from vice-free Switzerland and a quarter of an hour from the *Geneva Airport*. Consequently, among the varied clientele are many people visiting Geneva for reasons of foreign commerce or private finance. The local thermal baths are invigorating; the lush golf course is superb; and there is tranquil sailing on the artificial lake. The centerpiece of a luxurious park and hotel complex, the casino sponsors most of the town's cultural events—most notably the highly reputed summer chamber music festival. Everything from rustic Jura specialties to Iranian caviar is available in the casino's excellent restaurant, right on the gaming-room floor. Free champagne is offered with dinner on Mondays and Wednesdays. The dress code for men is strict—ties are required, and no jeans are allowed. Information: *Le Casino,* Av. de la Divonne, Divonne-les-Bains 01220 (phone: 50-40-34-34).

EVIAN-LES-BAINS, Haute-Savoie Divonne's competitor for the Swiss connection, Evian is 25 miles (40 km) by road from Geneva or 35 minutes by boat across Lake Geneva. Its casino—a late-19th-century gaming palace that complements another Evian pleasure dome, its thermal baths—is just a few yards from the boat dock. The oldest casino in France, it was immortalized by Ian Fleming in the James Bond novel *Casino Royale.* While men need jackets and ties to get into the first-floor salon, casual dress is permitted on the ground floor, where the slot machines are found. A large, strobe-lit disco adjoins the casino. The more nostalgic will enjoy strolling past the baths along the animated, flower-decked Quai de Blonay, where the highborn and high rollers alike contemplate the lake at cocktail hour. Take a room at *Le Royal,* the most sumptuous hotel in the region (for additional details on the hotel, see *Romantic French Hostelries* in this chapter). Information: *Casino Municipal,* Evian-les-Bains 74500 (phone: 50-75-03-78).

FORGES-LES-EAUX, Seine-Maritime Just outside the 60-mile (96-km) roulette-free zone that Napoleon decreed around Paris, Forges attracts all the capital's players who don't want to risk the wheels at the city's various *clandés,* as its clandestine gaming dives are called. Those who can't face the predawn drive back to Paris can stay at the *Continental* hotel, right in the casino complex—and those who lose enough in the course of the evening are guests of the management. Information: *Casino de Forges,* Av. des Sources, Forges-les-Eaux 76440 (phone: 35-09-80-12).

JUAN-LES-PINS, Alpes-Maritimes The *Eden Beach,* the casino in Juan-les-Pins, was founded in 1928 by a Riviera regular, the American railroad tycoon Frank Jay Gould. Nestled between emerald pines and the royal blue sea, it shortly thereafter became—and remains today—a principal center for all that is sleek on the Côte d'Azur nightlife scene. The restaurant is right on the beach, and those who go out for a breath of air between rounds of chemin de fer can hear the rhythmic throb of the all-night jazz clubs that animate the town. Nearby, in Antibes, is the huge *Siesta Casino* entertainment complex, which resembles nothing so much as a Mexican village for plutocrats, with three restaurants and five dance floors (three of them under the stars). Information: *Eden Beach Casino,* Bd. Edouard-Boudoin, Juan-les-Pins 06160 (phone: 92-93-71-71); *Siesta Casino,* Rte. du Bord de Mer, Antibes 06600 (phone: 93-95-00-99).

MONTE CARLO, Principauté de Monaco When the brash and brassy Las Vegas–style *Sun Casino* in the *Loews Monte Carlo* hotel began cutting into the receipts of the staid dowager, the *Casino de Monte Carlo,* this most legendary casino in Europe went slumming, turning the rococo *Salon de l'Europe* into the *Salon Américain.* Now this Monte Carlo landmark, designed by Charles Garnier, the architect of the *Opéra/Palais Garnier* in Paris, is aclatter with slot machines, fitted out with craps and blackjack tables, and staffed by Las Vegas–trained managers and bartenders adept at making screwdrivers and Bloody Marys. The *Salon Américain* is free of charge and has no dress code. Not to worry, though: The rest of the casino is still properly Belle Epoque, with paintings, murals full of nudes, and similar touches throughout. The old, elegant *Salon Privé* (Private Room) is as decorous as ever; a passport and admission fee must be presented at the door. The cloistered sanctum known as the *Salon Super-Privé,* with a table for *banque-à-tout-va,* is open by appointment only. Take time to get a glimpse of the casino's fabled theater, a lavish study in gold leaf, scrolls, and garlands. Information: *Société des Bains de Mer,* Pl. du Casino, Monte Carlo, Principauté de Monaco 98000 (phone: 92-16-21-21).

Most Visitable Vineyards

It's hard to know just what to expect at a vineyard or *cave* (cellar) in France. Arrive when the wine maker is in a chatty, outgoing mood, and you may end up staying for hours, sharing recent vintages and discussing French politics and the state of French wine. Another day you may find yourself in the hands of an ambitious young peasant farmer just getting started in the business, and the next you'll be visiting a château where a wealthy wine maker follows family rules and techniques that go back centuries. In almost every case a vineyard visit includes a wander through the château's tasting room, normally attached to the cellars, where guests settle down and the most recent vintages are uncorked. Usually these tastings are free; the wine also is available for purchase. Though almost every vineyard in France welcomes visitors, it always is a good idea to call ahead. Spring and summer visitors are more welcome than those who come in fall, when the harvest keeps the staff occupied nearly around the clock. Note that although many do not keep official hours—wine makers are farmers, after all—it's most polite to arrive between 10 AM and noon or between 2 and 5 PM.

Consider taking a summer course in wine wisdom with the *Centre d'Informations, de Documentations et de Dégustations,* which includes in its program visits to vineyards and cellars. The center has a wide range of activities in English, and occasionally holds an open house to introduce little-known wines to the public. Its Paris office is open weekday afternoons. Information: *CIDV,* 45 Rue Liancourt, Paris 75014 (phone: 43-27-67-21; fax: 43-20-84-00).

The following is a sampling of France's most visitor-friendly vineyards and *caves* (listed alphabetically by region and town).

ALSACE The wines of this area are fragrant, fruity, and white, ordinarily drunk while still young. They are named for the variety of grape from which they're made. Gewürztraminer is dry and spicy, with a certain zing. Pinot gris, also known as tokay d'Alsace, is broad and full-bodied. Riesling is at once dry and fruity, crisp and elegant. And sylvaner, the most plentiful of all, has a distinctive freshness that makes it a fine apéritif. For additional details on the region and its wines, see *Alsace* in DIRECTIONS.

Léon Beyer, Eguisheim, Haut-Rhin The Beyer family, tending its vineyards since 1850, makes one of the best and best-known wines in Alsace. Their riesling shows up on the wine lists of such famous three-Michelin-star restaurants as *Taillevent* in Paris and *L'Auberge de l'Ill* in Illhaeusern. The firm's tasting room is in Eguisheim, a historic and attractive town full of tidy stone and timber houses with geranium-filled window boxes. Centered around a main square with a handsome Renaissance fountain, the town is on the Route du Vin, which takes in several other wineries in the area. The tasting room is open weekdays by appointment only. Information: *Léon Beyer,* Eguisheim 68420 (phone: 89-41-41-05; fax: 89-23-93-63).

Hugel et Fils, Riquewihr, Haut-Rhin Visitors to these *caves*—in a pair of 16th-century houses that have been gutted to make room for the winery—can see what's believed to be the oldest cask in the world still in constant use. It was made in 1715 and holds more than 8,800 quarts. *Hugel* is respected for its elegant, supple, well-balanced wines, particularly the dry riesling, with its round bouquet, and the rich, spicy, full-bodied gewürztraminer. The entire town is a historical monument, and the main street, packed with remarkably well-preserved houses, warrants a visit in its own right. The *caves* are open weekdays by appointment only. Information: *Hugel et Fils,* Riquewihr 68340 (phone: 89-47-92-15; fax: 89-49-00-10).

BORDEAUX This flat terrain with its precise rows of vines punctuated by red roses near the roadsides and dotted with attractive villages is the home of some of the richest wine country in the world. The vines of the Médoc, the region that stretches along the left bank of the Gironde River between Bordeaux and the Bay of Biscay, set the standard. In Bordeaux's principal towns—Margaux, Pauillac, St-Estèphe, and St-Julien—as well as in small villages, the wine business occupies everyone, from the joiners who knock together the crates to the printers of the labels. The area has road signs for nearly every wine-producing château. The *Maison du Vin* in Bordeaux (1 Cours du 30-Juillet, Bordeaux 33075; phone: 56-00-22-66 or 56-00-22-88; fax: 56-00-22-77) can provide a list of those open to the public. The *Cité Mondiale du Vins et des Spiritueux* (20 Quai des Chartrons, Bordeaux 33080 CEDEX; phone: 56-01-20-20; fax: 56-01-71-00), an ultramodern commercial development designed as an international center for the wines and spirits indus-tries, has exhibits and conferences year-round. Also see *Bordeaux and the Médoc* in DIRECTIONS.

Château Palmer, Cantenac, Gironde Although the famous 19th-century turreted château that's pictured on the distinctive label of this vineyard's wine can be visited much of the year, it is most popular at harvest time, usually in October, since it is one of the few places where visitors can see the old-fashioned destalking of grapes by hand. The Dutch, French, and British flags fluttering outside honor its successful (if rather unusual) tri-national ownership. Visits are generally possible weekdays (except during lunch hours). Information: *Château Palmer,* Cantenac 33460 (phone: 57-88-72-72; fax: 57-88-37-16).

Château Prieuré-Lichine, Cantenac, Gironde The late Alexis Lichine, the most respected American wine producer in France and author of the *Guide to the Wines and Vineyards of France,* worked to make the wines of *Château Prieuré-Lichine*—a 16th-century Benedictine priory—among the finest and most fragrant from the more than 3,000 vineyard acres cultivated around Margaux. After parking on the side of the road opposite the gateway, walk through the courtyard; at the office at the end of the gravel walk you'll find an English-speaking guide who will escort you through the *chai.* The remains of the old cloister are decked out with fanciful antique cast-iron firebacks that Lichine collected from all over Europe. The craggy-beamed vat room was built by the monks who tended the vines, but the gleaming stainless-steel vats and wine- making equipment are among the most modern in the Médoc. Visits are possible daily; call for an appointment. Information: *Château Prieuré-Lichine,* Cantenac 33460 (phone: 57-88-36-28; fax: 57-88-78-93).

Château Beauséjour-Bécot, St-Emilion, Gironde A visitor who comes to this friendly wine maker's château with a few hours on his or her hands almost certainly will hear the story of how the small but now prosperous 16-acre property was rescued from decline some years ago. M. Bécot loves to quote Baudelaire, to sing the well-deserved praises of St-Emilion (both the wine and the charming hilltop village), and to receive visitors. When the spirit moves him, he sometimes passes out "before" and "after" samples to doc-ument the changes that have occurred since his arrival. Information: *Château Beauséjour-Bécot,* St-Emilion 33330 (phone: 57-74-46-87; fax: 57-74-48-40).

BURGUNDY Burgundian wines include the dry and flinty white made in Chablis; the aromatic, full-bodied reds and whites made south of Dijon in the Côte d'Or; and the light and fruity reds made in Beaujolais. The region's famous wine-producing villages include Chambertin, Chassagne-Montrachet, Gevrey-Chambertin, Meursault, Mâcon, Morey-St-Denis, Nuits-St-Georges, Pommard, Puligny-Montrachet, Pommard, and others. The *Musée du Vin de Bourgogne* in Beaune (Rue d'Enfer; phone: 80-22-08-19) documents the history of viticulture and wine making; there are tours in English daily on the hour. Also see *Burgundy* in DIRECTIONS.

Domaine Henri Gouges, Nuits-St-Georges, Côte d'Or The village of Nuits-St-Georges produces some admirable reds known for their characteristic earthy flavor; and some of the best known come from *Domaine Henri Gouges,* which supplies Paris's *Taillevent* with the remarkable and rare white wine of the region as well as full-bodied reds. The amiable M. Gouges receives visitors by appointment only. Information: *Domaine Henri Gouges,* 28 Rue du Moulin, Nuits-St-Georges 21700 (phone: 80-61-04-40).

Domaine de la Romanée-Conti, Vosne-Romanée, Côte d'Or The main gate of one of the world's most famous vineyards is hidden in the back streets of Vosne-Romanée, and visitors are received by appointment only. But then the wines of the Domaine—including the fabulously expensive Romanée-Conti (of which only 6,000 bottles are produced each year) and the equally well-known La Tâche—are among the most expensive and revered in the world. The likes of such notables as Nikita Khrushchev have signed their names in the crimson-and-gold guest book. Information: *Romanée-Conti* (phone: 80-61-04-57; fax: 80-61-05-72). Appointments may also be made through *Négociant Leroy,* Auxey-Duresses, Meursault 21120 (phone: 80-21-21-10; fax: 80-21-63-81).

CAHORS One of the principal gateways to the south of France, this tranquil village is most famous for the hearty red wine made from the grapes grown on the hills along the Lot River to the west of town. Also see *Périgord* in DIRECTIONS.

Clos de Gamot, Prayssac, Lot This establishment is a good place to sample some of the so-called "black" wine of Cahors. Jean Jouffreau, a gregarious grower, tends his vines without chemical sprays and ages his wine in oak casks. The result is a liquid that is dark and weighty—with overtones of cassis, some say; others love it for its vigor and ability to stand up to the robust food of the region—cassoulet, truffles, *confit,* and hearty breads. Information: *Clos de Gamot,* Prayssac 46220 (phone: 65-22-40-26).

CHAMPAGNE The Romans planted the first grapes in this region, the northernmost vine-growing area in the country. Despite a succession of wars, from the Hundred Years to World War II, the Champenois have been tending their vines, harvesting their grapes, and bottling their vintages nearly ever since. The sparkling beverage known as champagne, made according to a process developed at the end of the 17th century, is still the lifeblood of the region. Tourist information offices throughout the area publish standard itineraries and maintain signs along the routes. Also see *Champagne* in DIRECTIONS.

Ricciuti-Révolte, Avenay-Val-d'Or, Marne This bubbly is often described as the champagne with the Baltimore flavor, because the wine maker, Albert Ricciuti, is a Baltimore native who married a Frenchwoman from a champagne-producing family. It all started in 1944, when Ricciuti, then an American soldier, helped liberate the village of Avenay-Val-d'Or. He met a young Frenchwoman, corresponded with her for 18 years, then returned for a visit. Marriage followed, and since 1963 he's been part of the family business. Mr. Ricciuti is an outgoing, jovial man who loves showing visitors around his vineyards and cellars. Open year-round by appointment only. Information: *Ricciuti-Révolte,* 18 Rue Lieutenant de Vaisseau, Avenay-Val-d'Or, Ay 51160 (phone: 26-52-30-27).

Moët & Chandon, Epernay, Marne The best way to learn about champagne is to observe the painstaking care with which it is made. One of the best spots to do this is *Moët & Chandon,* whose impressive cellars, if not the most beautiful in the area, are certainly the largest, with 17 miles of galleries. Most impressive is the sight of the *rémueurs,* the men who carefully and rapidly turn each bottle precisely one quarter turn (a process called "riddling"). Afterward guides offer each visitor a drink of the famous nose-tickling wine. Entertaining tours are offered daily (except during lunch hours) from April through October; weekdays only the rest of the year. Information: *Moët & Chandon,* 20 Av. de Champagne, Epernay 51205 (phone: 26-54-71-11; fax: 26-54-84-23).

CÔTES DU RHÔNE The wines of this area usually are red and robust; Châteauneuf-du-Pape, the most famous from these southern vineyards, and the flavorful Gigondas, a close second, are just two examples. Those specifically labeled "Côtes du Rhône" and "Côtes du Rhône-Villages" are particularly soft and flavorful. Also see *Provence* in DIRECTIONS.

Caves des Vignerons, Beaumes-de-Venise, Vaucluse The sweet white wine from Beaumes-de-Venise and fresh melon from nearby Cavaillon make one of the finest food combinations in the world. The cooperative at Beaumes-de-Venise sells one of the better-known versions of the naturally sweet local dessert wines as well as a variety of other wines, including Côtes du Rhône-Villages and Côtes du Ventoux. Information: *Caves des Vignerons,* Beaumes-de-Venise 84190 (phone: 90-62-94-45).

Domaine de Mont-Redon, Châteauneuf-du-Pape, Vaucluse In the spotless tasting rooms at this largest, best-known, and most respected Châteauneuf-du-Pape estate, visitors may sample various recent vintages of red, a hearty blend of 13 different grape varieties, as well as a lesser-known white that rarely finds its way out of the region. The estate also is proud of its eau-de-vie, a clear liquor made from grape pressings; only about 2,000 bottles are produced each year, and most are sold at the château. Information: *Domaine de Mont-Redon,* Châteauneuf-du-Pape 84230 (phone: 90-83-72-75).

Gigondas, Vaucluse In the center of this sleepy little village, visitors will find a tasting room where more than 20 different varieties of Gigondas, a heady local red, may be sampled. One of the finest comes from Georges Faraud, whose farmhouse is at the edge of the village; visitors are given a most cordial welcome. Information: *Syndicat d'Initiative,* Gigondas 84190 (phone: 90-65-85-46).

Domaine de la Gautière, La-Penne-sur-Ouvèze, Drôme In the heart of French lavender country, the Tardieus run a small organic farm where they raise bees for honey, tend ancient olive trees that yield exquisite black fruit and golden oil, and produce a delicious red country wine that seems to taste best when sipped on the family patio. The honey, the olives, the oil, and the wine are all for sale here, and there's a campground attached to the property. Information: *Domaine de la Gautière,* La-Penne-sur-Ouvèze, Buis-les-Barronies 26170 (phone: 75-28-09-58).

Cooperative Vinicole Vinsobraise, Vinsobres, Drôme The French of this region usually buy their wine in bulk, and usually from a cooperative such as that at Vinsobraise, a large, active group just outside the village of Vinsobres, which makes a strong, substantial red that ages well and some lesser-known whites and rosés. All can be sampled at the *Cooperative*'s bar, where visitors also will see local makers bringing in their wines and buyers coming in with huge plastic containers for refilling. Information: *Cooperative Vinicole Vinsobraise,* Vinsobres 26110 (phone: 75-27-64-22; fax: 75-27-66-59).

Learning the Culinary Arts: Cooking Schools

France's cooking schools are as varied as its landscape and regional cuisine. Visitors can study with such famous chefs such as Gaston Lenôtre and Roger Vergé; they can gain hands-on experience at the most classic of all schools, *Le Cordon Bleu;* and they can take courses with farm wives in the rustic kitchens of the Quercy and the Dordogne in the southwest. Many schools will tailor special courses for groups of ten or more. Translators are usually available, and programs tend to be casual, geared to novices and experts alike. The point is to go with an open mind and a willing spirit, ready to acquire a few additional skills and authentic French experiences—and have a good time besides. Most schools operate year-round, and courses in Paris are good anytime; those offered in the southwest and in Provence are probably better in late spring and early fall, when the countryside is at its most beautiful and the pace is a bit less hectic. In any case, be sure to send away for brochures and read them carefully before booking so that you know exactly what to expect. The schools below are listed alphabetically by city or town.

PROVENÇAL COOKING SCHOOL, Gordes, Provence Sylvie Lallemand, an English-speaking culinary expert, learned to cook at her Provence-born mother's knee. She passes on the best of the region's recipes and the skills necessary to prepare them, as well as an appreciation of regional wines, to guests who stay in her pine-rimmed country house (with pool) in Gordes, 30 miles (48 km) east of Avignon. Mornings are dedicated to investigating the local food markets, afternoons are spent honing culinary skills, and evenings are given over to gastronomic indulgence and critique. Week-long courses begin on Saturday afternoons. Closed July and August. Information: *Provençal Cooking School*, Les Mégalithes, Gordes 84220 (phone: 90-72-23-41).

ECOLE DE CUISINE LA VARENNE, Joigny, Burgundy This well-known school, run by English cookbook author, journalist, and food historian Anne Willan (most recently in the spotlight for her PBS cooking series, "Look and Cook"), makes its home in a Burgundy château. With classes taught by a staff of French chefs, the school is particularly popular with Americans. Students may sign up in the summer or fall for week-long participation and demonstration courses in regional cooking, bistro cooking, pastry preparation, and contemporary and classic French cuisine. In addition, intensive five-week professional diploma courses are offered; to qualify for these, students must have previous training or experience in the field and an understanding of traditional French cooking. Classes are in French, but English translations are provided (though an understanding of French is most helpful). Students are housed within the château. Information: *Ecole de Cuisine La Varenne*, PO Box 25574, Washington, D.C. 20007 (phone: 800-537-6486).

FARM COOKING WEEKENDS, Ladornac, Dordogne Dany and Guy Dubois work a farm in the lush and hilly Dordogne in France's southwest. They also conduct informal weekend cooking classes that may include a visit to the town bakery or to an old but still working walnut-oil mill. Students may choose a weekend *du cochon*, which covers the preparation of such pork products as blood sausage and the curing of a ham, or a weekend devoted to foie gras, *confit*, and *rillettes*, all using the force-fed geese raised on the farm. Courses, which are taught in French, are limited to six students, and reservations must be made several months in advance. Meals and lodging are included, and the Dubois family will pick up students at the train station in nearby Brive. Open September through April. Information: *Dany and Guy Dubois*, Peyrenègre, Ladornac 24120 (phone: 53-51-04-24).

INITIATION A LA CUISINE PROVENÇALE, Marseilles, Bouches-du-Rhône A movable feast combining travel and kitchen wizardry has been cooked up by *La Couqueto*, a group dedicated to preserving Provençal culture. Classes (followed by a meal) are held at 2:30 and 7 PM on the first Thursday of every month; students are asked to reserve a place by calling between 6 and 7 PM on the previous Tuesday or by writing ahead. Classes are in French, and students are requested to contribute toward the cost of the meal prepared.

Information: *La Couqueto,* 12 Rue de la Bibliothèque, Marseilles 13001 (phone: 91-42-35-66).

ROGER VERGÉ'S ECOLE DU MOULIN, Mougins, Alpes-Maritimes Acclaimed chef Roger Vergé runs a school designed for home cooks. Touring American couples come by the dozen for the week-long course taught by various chefs from his celebrated restaurants, the two-star *Moulin de Mougins* (outside the charming village of Mougins) and *L'Amandier* (in Mougins). The participation-demonstration classes take place above the latter restaurant; each weekday students prepare two dishes derived from the varied cuisine of Provence. Students also can sign up for a single two-hour session. Classes are available in English. Information: *Ecole du Moulin, Restaurant L'Amandier,* Mougins, Alpes-Maritimes 06250 (phone: 93-75-35-70; fax: 93-90-18-55).

CFT FERRANDI, Paris This *Centre de Formation Technique (CFT)* is the only Paris cooking school to offer professionally motivated foreigners preparatory courses for a CAP, the French government's culinary certification. Though its basic course runs for nine months (five days a week) and is recommended only for the most serious students, shorter programs—including biannual week-long pastry and cuisine courses—also are offered. Owned by the *Paris Chamber of Commerce,* the *Ferrandi* school has been endorsed by such famous French chefs as Joël Robuchon and Pierre Troisgros. Information: *CFT Ferrandi,* 11 Rue Jean-Ferrandi, Paris 75006 (phone: 49-54-29-03).

LE CORDON BLEU, Paris This famous school has been instructing an international group of students in French cooking and pastry making since 1895. During the summer special four-week courses are offered in cooking and pastry, while 10-week sessions are available throughout the year. Intensive one-week "gourmet" sessions on such subjects as bistro cuisine, bread making, and *cuisine légère* also are conducted. All of these programs give credits toward certificates and diplomas. Visitors may reserve a few days ahead for one-day workshops or afternoon demonstrations, with menus available up to three months in advance. Most courses are translated into English. Students are responsible for their own lodging, but the school can help with referrals. Information: *Le Cordon Bleu,* 8 Rue Léon-Delhomme, Paris 75015 (phone: 48-56-06-06; 800-457-2433; 914-741-0606 in New York State; fax: 48-56-03-96).

LA CUISINE DE MARIE-BLANCHE, Paris The outgoing, enthusiastic Princess Marie-Blanche de Broglie teaches small groups of students in classes that last 1, 3, 5, 10, or 20 days. These include demonstration courses that deal with cooking professionally, the harmony of wines and foods, pastry, the art of entertaining, and French regional cooking. Courses may be arranged in English. Programs run year-round, except August; students are responsible for their own lodging. Reserve at least a month in advance. Information:

Marie-Blanche de Broglie, *La Cuisine de Marie-Blanche,* 18 Av. de la Motte-Picquet, Paris 75007 (phone: 45-51-36-34; fax: 45-51-90-19).

ECOLE DE GASTRONOMIE FRANÇAISE RITZ-ESCOFFIER, Paris The *Ritz* hotel, where the legendary chef Escoffier made his debut in the last century, houses the ultimate cooking school. Courses last one to six weeks and involve 25 hours of instruction weekly. There is also a course in making cakes, ice cream, chocolate, and candy, and there's a 12-week program for professionals. Instruction is in French and English. Information: *Ecole de Gastronomie Française Ritz-Escoffier,* 38 Rue Cambon, Paris 75001 (phone: 42-60-38-30; fax: 40-15-07-65).

ECOLE LENÔTRE, Paris Working in groups of up to a dozen under France's best-known and most respected pastry chef, Gaston Lenôtre, professionals and serious amateurs study French pastry, chocolate, bread, ice cream, charcuterie, and catering in the huge, modern, and spotless Lenôtre laboratory in the suburb of Plaisir, about 17 miles (27 km) outside Paris. Courses, which are conducted in French, generally last five days and include breakfast and lunch (students are responsible for their own lodging and transportation). Reserve at least a month in advance. Information: *Ecole Lenôtre,* 40 Rue Pierre-Curie, Plaisir 78370 (phone: 30-81-46-46; fax: 30-54-73-70).

For the Mind

Memorable Museums and Monuments

The stunning achievements of French art are an exhilarating hymn to human potential, from the spires of Mont-St-Michel to the treasures of the *Louvre,* from the prehistoric cave paintings of Les Eyzies to the science-fiction Tinkertoy that is Paris's *Centre Georges Pompidou.* There is a breathtaking elegance to French artistic endeavors, whatever the century. It can be seen in the intricate weave of an Aubusson tapestry, in the airy geometry of the *Eiffel Tower,* in the angular grace of a Toulouse-Lautrec chanteuse; everywhere the cool complexity of the Gallic mind is in evidence, together with that exquisite sense of taste.

Sip these pleasures—don't gulp them. Mix monuments with merriments. Try a few casual nibbles at a museum rather than a single marathon banquet. As soon as you feel a sense of duty creeping over you, it's time to look for the nearest glass of beaujolais. And always remember that a rainy Monday in February is far better for quiet contemplation than tourist-mad midsummer. If you must travel in August, at least present yourself at the gates for their early morning opening—or visit at lunch hour, when the hordes usually forsake Leonardo for pâté.

Memorable museums and monuments in the country's major cities are detailed in the individual reports in THE CITIES; what follow are the most compelling that France has to offer elsewhere (listed alphabetically by town).

MUSÉE FESCH, Ajaccio, Corsica This early 19th-century palace belonged to Cardinal Fesch, Napoleon's uncle, and is home to some 16,000 paintings assembled by this man of the cloth. Considered to be among France's best museums, it looks out onto the Bay of Ajaccio; its white, modern setting is perfect for some of the finest Italian primitive and Renaissance paintings found outside Florence, Italy, and the *Louvre.* Especially noteworthy are Botticelli's *Madonna and Child* and Tura's *Madonna and Child with St. Jerome.* There also is a collection of Napoleon memorabilia. Closed Sundays. Admission charge. Information: *Musée Fesch,* 50 Rue Fesch, Ajaccio, Corsica 20000 (phone: 95-21-48-17).

MUSÉE TOULOUSE-LAUTREC, Albi, Tarn Born of a noble family in this charming town on the banks of the Tarn, Henri de Toulouse-Lautrec, that crippled and tormented genius, became a creature of the Parisian night and immortalized its prostitutes, cabaret dancers, and café denizens. The museum, installed within the austere, brooding walls of the 13th-century *Palais de la Berbie,* bursts with the multicolored animation of his special world. This is the richest Toulouse-Lautrec collection anywhere, with more than 500 works, including the famous posters that marked the beginning of an entirely new art form. Closed Tuesdays off-season. Information: *Musée Toulouse-Lautrec, Palais de la Berbie,* Albi 81000 (phone: 63-54-14-09).

MUSÉE PICASSO, Antibes, Alpes-Maritimes Picasso lived and worked at the 16th-century *Château Grimaldi* in 1946—one of the most prolific years of his career—and later donated the entire production of that happy period to the town of Antibes, on the condition that the works remain forever at their birthplace. The 23 major paintings in the collection, displayed in a stunning site overlooking the sea, fairly sing with the Mediterranean's joys; there are also lithographs, drawings, etchings, and a fine assortment of ceramics. Wander out on the exotic, flower- and statue-filled terrace for the same gull's-eye view that inspired Picasso. Closed Tuesdays and November. No admission charge on Wednesdays. Information: *Musée Picasso, Château Grimaldi,* Pl. du Château, Antibes 06600 (phone: 93-34-91-91).

AUBUSSON TAPESTRIES, Aubusson, Creuse During the Renaissance, the tapestries of this ancient Limousin town, which had been an important weaving center as early as the 9th century, were world renowned; during the 20th century they have had their own renaissance at the hands of master weaver Jean Lurçat. On Avenue des Lissiers the *Centre Culturel et Artistique Jean Lurçat,* a tapestry museum, documents the art from ancient times to the present. On Rue Vieille it's possible to visit an old weaver's studio, the *Maison du Vieux Tapissier,* and a score of private galleries full of tapestries to buy—or just admire. Information: *Office de Tourisme,* Rue Vieille, Aubusson 23200 (phone: 55-66-32-12).

CITÉ DE CARCASSONNE, Carcassonne, Aude Perched on a hilltop above the Garonne Valley, this movie-set forest of turrets, battlements, and drawbridges is Europe's most perfect example of medieval military architecture. Romans, Gauls, Visigoths, Arabs, Franks, and later French royalty assembled it over a period of some 13 centuries, and the celebrated architect Eugène Viollet-le-Duc restored it lovingly in the 19th century. For the best views of its 52 towers, make the promenade around the Lices between the inner and outer ramparts, starting from the *Porte Narbonnaise.* Be sure to see the *Basilique St-Nazaire,* a wonderful marriage of Romanesque and Gothic styles with Renaissance stained glass. Whatever you do, stay until nightfall; the illumination of the Cité is high drama. Information: *Office de Tourisme,* 15 Bd. Camille-Pelletan, Carcassonne 11012 (phone: 68-25-07-04).

CAVES OF LES EYZIES, Les Eyzies-de-Tayac, Dordogne Ever since the caves at Lascaux were closed to the public, sleepy little Les Eyzies, at the confluence of the Vézère and Beune Rivers, has been France's center for the prehistoric. In 1868, when a path was being cut through the valley for the railroad, workers unearthed bones that proved to be the remains of Cro-Magnon man. Of the huge numbers of cave dwellings discovered during extensive excavations in the cliffs that rise above the town, the most fascinating (and one of the few to offer a daily tour in English) is the Grotte de Font-de-Gaume, a deep, narrow cave whose walls are decorated with more than 200 early Paleolithic wall paintings. These 15,000-year-old artworks present remarkably fluid depictions of bison, deer, mammoths, and horses colored with red and black oxides. The way these so-called "primitive" peoples used the contours of the cave walls to convey the shape and bulk of the animals is particularly fascinating. Many of the drawings were defaced by people who used the caves in the 18th and 19th centuries, unaware of their importance. In an effort to preserve them from deterioration, the number of visitors is limited to 100 a day, so arrive early; in season, tickets are sold only in the morning. Also compelling is the Grotte des Combarelles, which has 300 animal drawings, albeit very faint, dating from about the same period; again, entrance is limited. Also try to see the nearby Abri du Cap-Blanc, for its superb frieze of horses, and the Grotte du Grand Roc, which is rich in stalactite formations and offers, from its entrance, a panorama of the entire valley. Signs for all sites are clearly posted. In general, the caves are open daily, except the Grotte de Font-de-Gaume, which is closed Tuesdays. Information: *Syndicat d'Initiative des Eyzies,* Pl. Mairie, Les Eyzies-de-Tayac 24620 (phone: 53-06-97-05).

MUSÉE NATIONAL ADRIEN-DUBOUCHÉ, Limoges, Haute-Vienne For centuries this town has been Europe's most celebrated center of porcelain and enamel crafts, and its museums are consecrated to their glories. This particular one boasts the world's most extensive porcelain collection, more than 10,000 pieces in all. Delft, Wedgwood, and the work of China and France—ancient and modern alike—are all represented. Information: *Musée National Adrien-Dubouché,* Pl. Winston-Churchill, Limoges 87000 (phone: 55-77-45-58), and the *Office de Tourisme,* Bd. Fleurus, Limoges 87000 (phone: 55-34-46-87).

LOURDES, Hautes-Pyrénées Neither a museum nor a monument, this is a bona-fide shrine. Every year nearly five million people, both the faithful and the merely curious, flock to this mountain village where, in 1858, a 14-year-old farm girl named Bernadette Soubirous had her famed visions of the Virgin Mary. The official recognition of this miracle by the Catholic church has made Lourdes one of the world's major pilgrimage sites. Thousands of believers—particularly the ill and the handicapped—join in passionate group prayer here. Cast-off crutches dangle at the entrance to the Grotte Miraculeuse, the cave where Bernadette saw the apparitions. Although the town, with its religious supermarkets stocked with windup Virgins and holy water hip flasks, has a tawdry, commercial side, Lourdes is still unique and unsettling to the religious and nonreligious alike. Information: *Office Municipal de Tourisme,* Pl. du Champ-Commun, Lourdes 65100 (phone: 62-94-15-64).

MONT-ST-MICHEL, Manche This 11th-century Benedictine monastery carved out of natural granite is one of the world's most spectacular sights. Legend has it that Archangel Michael appeared in 708 to St. Aubert, Bishop of Avranches, and persuaded him (allegedly denting his skull in the process) to build a chapel or oratory on what was then Mont-Tombe, a rocky outcrop in the forest. (Geologists speculate that some natural phenomena, probably tidal waves, occurred in the region during the first part of the 8th century, which would explain the sinking of the forest around the mount.) Most of what remains of the Norman Romanesque parts of the abbey were completed during the 11th and 12th centuries, the period in which the monastery became a powerful force in Normandy. The abbot soon became the feudal lord over dozens of nearby villages and other fiefdoms, and a reputation for learning and miracles soon attached itself to the mount and its denizens. When Normandy passed into the hands of the Kings of France in 1204, Philippe Auguste undertook the construction of *La Merveille* (The Marvel), as the French call the Gothic abbey church and buildings on the mount's north side, which were completed by 1230. The abbey continued to gain in political power, becoming like a small city, with the community of brothers overseeing the administration of the vast tracts of forest in the abbatial domains. During the Hundred Years War the military role of Mont-St-Michel—which had been fortified in the 13th century—often superseded its spiritual one. Since 1879 a 2,000-yard causeway has connected the mainland and the island's single main street, thereby permitting visitors to flock to the island in droves. To appreciate the place fully, however, plan to stay overnight in one of the unpretentious small inns on the island, or at least remain for one of the scheduled nighttime openings when the Mont is spectacularly illuminated (from mid-June through September). Once the day tourists are gone, the place has a resonant silence that speaks more eloquently of its long history than all the tourist literature ever written. Information: *Office de Tourisme,* Bd. Avancée, Mont-St-Michel 50116 (phone: 33-60-14-30).

MUSÉE NATIONAL DE L'AUTOMOBILE, Mulhouse, Haut-Rhin The *National Automobile Museum* documents the vehicle's history with some 500 cars representing nearly 100 different makes, from an 1878 Jacquot to a freshly minted Formula I Ferrari. Two Swiss industrialists forfeited the collection in lieu of paying taxes owed to the French government. Arranged between mile-and-a-half-long rows of antique lanterns, the jam-packed exhibition contains Hispano-Suizas, vintage Rolls-Royces (including a 1910 Silver Ghost with silver-plated fittings), a Dion Bouton (gaily painted blue and red, with facing seats and no roof, it resembles an open stagecoach), and the Bugatti T16 Garros, which the French aviator had built with a transparent plastic body that reveals the motor. In addition, there are vehicles that once belonged to Charlie Chaplin, Juan Fangio, and Emperor Bao-Dai—all in perfect, gleaming condition. The museum is closed Tuesdays in winter.

Information: *Musée National de l'Automobile,* 192 Av. de Colmar, Mulhouse 68100 (phone: 89-42-29-17), and the *Office de Tourisme,* 9 Av. Maréchal-Foch, Mulhouse 68100 (phone: 89-45-68-31; fax: 89-45-66-16).

ROMAN AMPHITHEATER, Nîmes, Gard A virtual twin of the arena in nearby Arles, the Nîmes amphitheater, which dates from the 1st century, is one of the most stunningly preserved of the 70 known to have been built by the Romans. Used as a fortress by the Visigoths, it had long since degenerated into ghetto dwellings pieced together with chunks of Roman rubble when it was rehabilitated in the 19th century. Today's visitors can ramble at will through the galleries of the arena. Every spring and summer more than 20,000 spectators jam its elliptical grandstands for bullfights; sporting matches and various shows also take place here. Information: *Office de Tourisme,* 6 Rue Auguste, Nîmes 30000 (phone: 66-67-29-11; fax: 66-21-81-04), and the *Comité Départemental du Tourisme du Gard,* 3 Pl. des Arènes, Nîmes 30000 (phone: 66-21-02-51).

PONT DU GARD, Remoulins, Gard Another wondrous and perfectly preserved relic of ancient Rome's far-flung empire: a 180-foot-high, 2,000-year-old stretch of the aqueduct that once brought water to Nîmes from the mountain springs near Uzès. The pastoral setting in the middle of the Gardon Valley has a subtle way of putting you in closer contact with the grandeur that was Rome than the more obvious and far more frequented sites in Italian cities. Visitors can walk across all levels of the three-tiered, arched stone structure, though it's very dangerous (particularly the top tier) when there are strong winds. The bottom tier has six arches, the middle tier 11, and the top tier, which carried the water, 35. The aqueduct is about 14 miles (22 km) northeast of Nîmes on the way to Avignon. Information: *Comité Départemental du Tourisme du Gard,* 3 Pl. des Arènes, Nîmes 30000 (phone: 66-21-02-51).

ROCAMADOUR, Lot In 1166 the remains of a man believed to be St. Amadour were unearthed here, in the Périgord region in the south of France. Though the saint's identity has long been debated, legend has it that he was Zaccheus, a disciple of Christ and husband of St. Veronica. As the story goes, after Christ's death the couple were persecuted in Palestine and escaped to this part of France. When Veronica died, Zaccheus retreated to a rock on a high plateau and, when he died, was buried there. Shortly after the discovery of the remains, miracles began to occur, word spread, and the pious came in droves, among them the English King Henry Plantagenet. Until the 13th century Rocamadour—breathtakingly sited on the face of a sheer rock canyon wall some 500 feet above a gorge—ranked in religious importance with Rome, Santiago de Compostela, and Jerusalem. Although it is still the site of an annual pilgrimage, the floods of worshipers have been superseded by waves of tourists; unfortunately, the village (pop. 650) carries the scars and blemishes that accompany such renown. Nonetheless, if you make your way through it all and climb to the top of the 216 steps (called the *Escalier des Pèlerins,* or Pilgrim's Stairs, and climbed by pilgrims on their knees), your effort will be rewarded by the sight of a lovely little square surrounded by seven chapels. This is the Cité Religieuse, with several fine buildings: the fortified *Evêché* (Bishop's Palace); the 11th- to 13th-century *Basilique St-Sauveur;* the *Chapelle St-Michel,* known for its fresco of the Annunciation; St. Amadour's crypt; and most entrancing of all, the *Chapelle Miraculeuse.* This last was destroyed twice, then rebuilt during the 19th century; it houses the intriguing *Black Virgin and Child,* made of walnut covered with silver plate and believed to have been carved in about the 9th century. Here also, suspended from the roof, is the miraculous bell that is said to ring of its own accord to foretell miracles. On the wall outside the chapel are 13th- and 14th-century frescoes that depict St. Christopher and the Dance of Death. On the square near the *Chapelle Miraculeuse* is the *Musée Trésor,* in which valuable religious items are displayed. Farther up the hill via a crooked dirt path is a fortress built in the 14th century to protect pilgrims. The adjacent 19th-century château now is inhabited by the chaplains of Rocamadour; the only parts open to the public are the ramparts, which command a breathtaking view of the village and the surrounding countryside. Information: *Office de Tourisme, La Mairie,* Rocamadour 46350 (phone: 65-33-62-59).

The Liveliest Arts:
Theater, Opera, and Music

In the past, when a French citizen uttered the word *province,* usually with a certain wrinkling of the nose, he or she was referring to any part of the country that wasn't Paris. Nothing of any significant artistic interest was deemed to occur there, for the capital held an unquestioned monopoly on culture. But the byword of the past decade has been *décentralisation,* and the theatrical/musical map of France has undergone some startling changes. The provinces now fairly bristle with first-rate repertory companies and orchestras, financed by generous subsidies from the central and regional governments. Top French directors like Patrice Chéreau and Roger Planchon chose working class areas in Nanterre and Lyons, respectively, as their base of operations. The renowned *Centre de la Musique Electronique* (Center for Electronic Music) is situated in the otherwise quiet town of Bourges. The operas of Nancy, Toulouse, and Strasbourg have been outdoing their staid Parisian cousins in critical acclaim, and the spectacular new Lyons opera house symbolizes that city's enthusiasm for the arts.

Many of these companies spend a good part of their season on tour to smaller towns in their region and to other parts of the country. So keep an eye on kiosks and wall posters; if you miss the *Théâtre de la Salamandre* in Lille, you might still catch it in some Breton upland village. And don't bypass an evening in the theater just because your French is a high-school relic;

this is still a fine way to become a part of local life. In your favor is the current style for splashy, highly visual productions where spectacle trumps text. Where classics are concerned, French versions of English ones generally can be found in a city of any size—after all, France's most-performed playwright is the *formidable* Guillaume Shakespeare.

In addition to those found in the major cities (for details, consult the individual reports in THE CITIES), the following music or theater companies (listed alphabetically by town) are among France's best.

CENTRE DRAMATIQUE NATIONAL DES ALPES, Grenoble, Isère Grenoble was one of the first provincial cities to be allotted a *maison de la culture* (cultural center), during the reign of de Gaulle's renowned minister André Malraux. Like many of the more successful centers, this one eventually spawned a flourishing theater group. The original productions often dismantle and reassemble traditional works like *Lorenzaccio* and *King Lear* with flashy theatricality; the productions are always lively, often controversial, and never predictable. Information: *Centre Dramatique National des Alpes,* 4 Rue Paul-Claudel, Grenoble 38034 (phone: 76-25-54-14).

ORCHESTRE NATIONAL DE LILLE, Lille, Nord The thriving commercial-industrial complex of Lille-Roubaix-Tourcoing, at the Belgian border, enjoys one of the richest cultural lives outside Paris. This excellent young orchestra is under the direction of Jean-Claude Casadesus of the famous French musical dynasty, and he has stocked it with the finest new talent. If you have trouble hearing the orchestra on its home ground, you may just find it performing at major music festivals like the one at Aix-en-Provence. Information: *Orchestre National de Lille,* 3 Pl. Mendès-France, Lille 59000 (phone: 20-12-82-40).

THÉÂTRE DE LA SALAMANDRE, Lille, Nord One of the first-rate provincial theaters subsidized by the national government, this company of 15 performs under the direction of the exciting Gildas Bourdet. The repertoire may include anything from works by Racine and Corneille, the twin pillars of French classical theater, to Gorky's *Lower Depths* or stage versions of Jack London stories. An offer to perform with this troupe is prestigious enough to pull first class talent away from Paris. Information: *Théâtre de la Salamandre,* 9 Rue Crespel Tilloy, Lille 59200 (phone: 20-30-82-80).

ORCHESTRE PHILHARMONIE DE LORRAINE, Metz, Moselle The entire population of this stately town on the banks of the Moselle is music-mad and music-proud, and at any given performance at the 19th-century concert hall, *L'Arsenal,* those who manage to procure a ticket will find themselves surrounded by an audience of both long-haired, tight-jeaned high schoolers and elders of the Légion d'Honneur—and a great many others in between. The orchestra especially excels at works by the first rank of French composers: Berlioz, Bizet, Debussy, Fauré, Franck, Gounod, and Saint-Saëns.

Information: *Orchestre Philharmonie de Lorraine,* 25 Av. Robert-Schumann, Metz 57000 (phone: 87-55-12-02), and *L'Arsenal,* Av. Ney, Metz 57000 (phone: 87-39-92-00).

THÉÂTRE DU CAPITOLE, Toulouse, Haute-Garonne A longtime rival for national preeminence with the *Opéra/Palais Garnier* in Paris, it has often been a proving ground for the finest new singers in French opera. The orchestra, which usually plays for both opera and concert seasons in the stately 19th-century *Capitole,* even did a triumphal tour of the United States, and has brought both operas and a memorable Beethoven's *Ninth* to sellout audiences in the city's sprawling *Palais des Sports.* France is in the throes of a frantic opera renaissance, so to avoid rock concert–style lines of sleeping-bagged music lovers, it's wise to book seats well in advance. Information: *Théâtre du Capitole,* Pl. du Capitole, Toulouse 31000 (phone: 61-23-21-35).

Festivals à la Française

Direct descendants of the Greek drama marathons and the first *Olympic* games, festivals are celebrations of the pleasures of creating, competing, or just plain existing. They let a visitor cram the best and most of any given experience into the shortest possible time—whether it's auto racing or chamber music, wine tasting or bullfighting.

A word of sober caution to those planning to hurl themselves into the merriment at one of France's frothier celebrations: Crowds are very much a part of most festivals, so be prepared for crowded hotels, crowded restaurants, crowded auditoriums, and crowded bathrooms. Though advance planning will ward off much of the discomfort, it's still necessary to prepare yourself mentally for being jostled, for waiting in line, and for paying $5 for a can of warm cola. Keep in mind that festivals tend to offer some of France's most savory street eating, so avoid the meals offered in jammed, festival-priced restaurants in favor of crêpes stands, oyster bars, and wine booths. You'll be surprised how well Beethoven's *Ninth* goes with French fries.

In addition to those that take place in major cities (for details, consult the individual reports in THE CITIES), the following is a selective survey of the most festive fêtes (listed alphabetically by town) France has to offer.

LES TROIS GLORIEUSES, Beaune, Clos-de-Vougeot, and Meursault, Côte d'Or The event whose name translates as "The Three Glorious Days"—France's most important wine festival—takes place in three Burgundian towns on the third Saturday, Sunday, and Monday in November. The weekend begins with the great banquet of the oenophiles of the Chevaliers du Tastevin at Clos-de-Vougeot. It continues on Sunday with the famed *Les Hospices de Beaune* wine auction, which attracts merchants and bon vivants from all over the drinking world. The grand finale is *La Paulée,* a celebration in

Meursault, the village that produces some of the world's most exquisite white wines. Some of the activity is for professionals, and tickets for the banquets often disappear a year in advance, but there is plenty of wine tasting, folk dancing, and general merrymaking for casual visitors. Information: *Comité Départemental du Tourisme,* 14 Rue Préfecture, Dijon 21000 (phone: 80-63-66-00; fax: 80-49-90-97), and the *Office de Tourisme,* Rue de l'Hôtel-Dieu, Beaune 21200 (phone: 80-22-24-51; fax: 80-24-06-85).

FESTIVAL DE MUSIQUE DE BESANÇON ET DE FRANCHE-COMTÉ, Besançon, Doubs

Inaugurated after World War II in an ancient town tucked into a lyre-shaped bend of the Doubs River, this September festival has spread to a whole cluster of other towns in the region. Chamber music has a special preeminence. A number of the charming settings here are the perfect size for a string quartet. New York's distinguished *Beaux-Arts Trio* has been a highlight, along with pianist Claudio Arrau and mezzo-soprano Teresa Berganza. Followers of the festival's international competition for young conductors will be hooked on its drama. For an unforgettable philharmonic orgy, try the *abonnement complet,* a subscription ticket that grants admission to all of the festival's concerts. Information: *Festival de Musique de Besançon et de Franche-Comté,* 2D Rue Isenbart, Besançon 25000 (phone: 81-80-73-26).

LE QUATORZE JUILLET, Carcassonne, Aude

Bastille Day (July 14)—France's biggest and most colorful holiday—is celebrated in especially high style at the medieval citadel of Carcassonne. The nighttime fireworks spectacular known as *L'Embrasement de la Cité,* literally, "The Setting on Fire of the Old City," conjures up visions of boiling oil, flaming arrows, and besieging Crusaders as, like a stupendous blaze, it illuminates the city's 50 fantastic towers. The holiday also is the centerpiece of the *Festival de la Cité,* a two-week feast of ballet, music, and theater; Ray Charles, Yehudi Menuhin, Rudolf Nureyev, and France's major orchestras have all made appearances. Here, as in the rest of France, there really is dancing in the streets. Information: *Office de Tourisme,* 15 Bd. Camille-Pelletan, Carcassonne 11012 (phone: 68-25-07-04), and the *Festival de la Cité, Théâtre Municipal,* BP 236, Carcassonne 11000 (phone: 68-71-30-30).

LES 24 HEURES DU MANS, Le Mans, Sarthe

June's *24 Heures du Mans* (24 Hours of Le Mans), a grueling endurance contest at which speeds can reach 210 mph, has been one of European auto racing's premier events since 1923. The race is only the centerpiece of a week-long celebration of man and motor that begins with *le pesage* (the weighing in) and gathers steam with the trial heats. A ticket for the *Enceintes Générales* gets you inside the 7.8-mile circuit, where there is space for cars and camping; the classiest observation post is a loge seat in the *Tribune Citroën* beside the dignitaries of the Automobile Club de l'Ouest. During the festivities don't fail to visit the *Musée de l'Automobile,* inside the circuit, which has 150 stunning vintage vehicles, starting with an 1884 De Dion Bouton. Information: *Automobile Club de l'Ouest, Circuit des 24 Heures, Office de Tourisme, Hôtel des Ursulines,* Rue de l'Etoile, Le Mans 72040 (phone: 43-28-17-22).

SON-ET-LUMIÈRE, Loire Valley, Indre-et-Loire and Loir-et-Cher Invented in the Loire Valley in the early 1950s, these 30- to 90-minute sound-and-light pageants are offered today by virtually every major château. Admittedly corny yet undeniably gripping, they are an ingenious weave of mellifluous voices, music, and roving floodlights—part slick spectacle, part crash course in French history. Some start as early as *Easter* week, and most run until mid-September, with several châteaux offering performances in English on alternate nights. The best are held at the castles of Chambord and Chenonceaux, described at length in *Celebrated Cathedrals and Châteaux* in this section. Information: *Office de Tourisme,* 3 Av. Jean-Laigret, Blois 41000 (phone: 54-74-06-49; fax: 54-56-04-59), and the *Office de Tourisme,* 78 Rue Bernard-Palissy, Tours 37042 (phone: 47-70-37-37; fax: 47-61-14-22).

FESTIVAL INTERCELTIQUE, Lorient One of France's liveliest festivals is the celebration of Celtic culture held annually during the first two weeks of August in this town in western Brittany. The Celts of today are often Europe's outsiders, heirs to traditions and dialects that were gradually supplanted by the dominant ones in their countries, but which are still proudly kept alive. Participants from all over Europe—including Ireland, Scotland, Wales, Galicia and Asturias in Spain, as well as Brittany—gather at Lorient's Port de Pêche (Fishing Port) for theater and dance performances, sea chanteys, tales told by professional storytellers, and food and drink, all with a Celtic accent and flavor. Information: *Festival Interceltique de Lorient,* 2 Rue Paul-Bert, Lorient 56100 (phone: 97-21-24-29) or *Office de Tourisme, Maison de la Mer,* Quai de Rohan, Lorient 56100 (phone: 97-21-07-84).

FOLK-EPIC SPECTACLE, Puy du Fou, Vendée A remarkable marriage of oral tradition and high-tech computerized effects, this outdoor spectacular is a retelling of the history of France from the Middle Ages to the present through the eyes of a Vendean peasant family named Maupillier. A modern descendant of the son-et-lumière shows developed in the Loire, like them it is set against the stark background of a ruined château, but the hundreds of local actors and superb effects—as well as the renewal of area folk traditions—make this a unique experience. Performances take place Fridays and Saturdays from early June through July and from mid-August through early September. Thousands attend each show, and it is necessary to reserve ahead. There is also a replica of a medieval village, complete with musicians, jugglers, and artisans of the period and falconry and horsemanship exhibitions. It is open from early June through mid-September; closed Mondays. Information: *Secrétariat du Puy du Fou,* 30 Rue Georges-Clemenceau, Les Epesses 85590 (phone: 51-57-66-66, general information; 51-64-11-11, reservations; fax: 51-57-35-47).

GRAND PÈLERINAGE DE MAI, Stes-Maries-de-la-Mer, Bouches-du-Rhône Every May 23, 24, and 25, some 15,000 Gypsies from all over Europe flock to the Mediterranean village of Stes-Maries-de-la-Mer, in the Camargue, to honor their patron saint, Sarah of Egypt, who was the servant of two legendary followers of Jesus, Mary Salome and Mary Jacobe. According to the story, the two St. Marys, expelled from the old kingdom of Judea, were cast adrift with their servant girl, but they miraculously washed ashore at this town that now bears their name. In the 15th century a chapel was built, and the local Gypsies began to worship the two Marys and Sarah. The colorful ceremonies include a candlelight vigil in the church crypt and an exuberant procession to the sea with the sacred statues of the saints borne aloft in a sculpted boat. For three days the whole town—already richly atmospheric with its bullfights, flocks of flamingos, marshes, and legends of wild white horses—fairly vibrates with the gaudy rhythms and colors of Gypsy life. Information: *Office de Tourisme,* 5 Av. Van-Gogh, Stes-Maries-de-la-Mer 13460 (phone: 90-97-82-55).

Celebrated Cathedrals and Châteaux

For half a millennium the Gothic cathedral and the Renaissance château reigned as the most sublime reflections of the French spirit. These structures were the statements of the power, both religious and secular, that was France, and their massive stone shadows colored the life of the towns and surrounding countryside they inhabited.

The Gothic mode took shape in the northern part of the country during the middle of the 12th century and then spread throughout Western Europe. With its vaults and spires straining heavenward and its pointed arches, the cathedral was a celebration of both God and engineering. Searching for ever greater elevation and ever more light, its architects replaced the massive walls of earlier styles with airy windows and raised the vaults higher and higher. The result was a whole new system of stress and support, characterized most obviously by the famous flying buttress.

The onset of the Hundred Years War in 1338 put an end to the golden age of Gothic cathedral building. But the end of the conflict in the middle of the 15th century marked the beginning of the château-building years, when new generations of nobility subjected the placid Loire Valley to an orgy of regal real-estate development. As decoration replaced defense as a prime architectural motivation, the once stolid and brooding medieval fortress gave way to the fanciful wonder that is the Renaissance château.

Since cathedrals and châteaux share a number of stylistic features, there's a risk of aesthetic indigestion if you try to see too many of them on successive days. To get the most out of your visits, vary your sightseeing menu as much as possible. Take in an evening organ concert at one cathedral and attend early morning mass at another, for instance, or try bicycling between a pair of Loire castles and tour the interior of one and only the gardens of another.

For a description of the most important châteaux and cathedrals in France's major cities, see the individual reports in THE CITIES. The historic structures described below (listed alphabetically by town) are located in smaller towns or in the French countryside.

CATHÉDRALE STE-CÉCILE, Albi, Tarn This great crimson citadel stands like a fortress with high towers, sheer brick walls, and narrow windows; in fact, it was built to serve as a fortress as well as a place of worship. Its cornerstone was laid in 1282 by the Archbishop of Albi, during an era when the church was conducting holy wars against the heretical Catharis. Today the church is considered the country's finest example of the simple, austere Midi Gothic style of architecture. On the south side is the 15th-century main entrance, a wonderfully ornate and frilly contrast to the stark simplicity of the walls. The interior, characterized by a column-free nave whose 100 feet of elevation equals the span of its base, was richly decorated at the beginning of the 16th century by a team of sculptors from Burgundy and painters from Bologna, Italy. Superb intricate carvings of biblical characters and saints are arrayed around and inside the choir, and an almost surrealistic 15th-century fresco of the Last Judgment decorates the wall behind the altar; note the morbid imagination that went into the variety of punishments for the perpetrators of each of the Seven Deadly Sins. The breathtaking view from the tower over the town and the Tarn River is worth the heavenward trudge. Information: *Office de Tourisme,* 19 Pl. Ste-Cécile, Albi 81000 (phone: 63-54-22-30).

CATHÉDRALE NOTRE-DAME, Amiens, Somme While its 261,400 cubic yards make this cathedral the largest in France, its harmony of style and the airy grace of its immense spaces make it one of the most beautiful as well. The west portal, with its fine statuary, is one of the high points of Gothic art. Inside, don't miss the oak choir stalls, where some 3,600 carved figures depict scenes from the Old and New Testaments, and be sure to see the unique bronze reclining statues of the two bishops who spent their part of the 13th century supervising the construction of this grand monument to the age. Information: *Office de Tourisme,* 12 Rue du Chapeau de Violettes, Amiens 80000 (phone: 22-91-79-28).

AZAY-LE-RIDEAU, Azay-le-Rideau, Indre-et-Loire Often described as the most "feminine" of French châteaux, *Azay-le-Rideau* was built between 1518 and 1529 under the supervision of Philippa Lesbahy, the wife of the great financier Gilles Berthelot. A cheerful white manor, military in style but not in spirit, it stands gracefully astride a branch of the Indre River and is reflected in its waters. With its surrounding English gardens and beautiful avenue of trees, the château has a certain domesticity that seldom fails to inspire thoughts of how lovely it would be to live there. Evidently experiencing similar longings, François I confiscated it from its original owners. Those who tire of meandering about the luxuriant grounds should note the fine collection of Renaissance furniture and tapestries inside. The son-et-lumière performance here is especially striking, with woods and water dramatically illuminated and the château perfectly mirrored in its moat, as spectators follow elaborately costumed youths carrying tall torches on a one-hour stroll around the grounds. Information: *Office de Tourisme,* Pl. Europe, Azay-le-Rideau 37190 (phone: 47-45-44-40; fax: 47-45-31-46), and the *Office de Tourisme,* 78 Rue Bernard-Palissy, Tours 37042 (phone: 47-70-37-37; fax: 47-61-14-22).

CATHÉDRALE ST-PIERRE, Beauvais, Oise At Beauvais, an easy hour's journey from Paris, the Gothic architects' ceaseless quest for ever more height and light and the church's ongoing efforts to outdo itself in earthly tributes to heaven's glory ended in disaster: First, with too much space between the support piers and too little mass in the ribbing, the choir collapsed in 1284. Just as its reconstruction was completed, the Hundred Years War began, halting further work on the cathedral until the 16th century, when the transept was begun. After its completion, instead of starting work on the nave, the builders added an ambitious tower above the transept, which crashed to the ground in 1573. It was never restored, and the nave was never built. As a result, the 20th century's inheritance at Beauvais is an unfinished symphony of Gothic art with splendid stained glass windows and a priceless collection of Beauvais, Gobelin, and Flemish tapestries. Information: *Office de Tourisme,* Rue Beauregard, Beauvais 60000 (phone: 44-45-08-18; fax: 44-45-63-95).

PALAIS JACQUES COEUR, Bourges, Cher A banker to King Charles VII and one of the 15th century's most powerful merchants, Jacques Coeur built his palace at Bourges with profits, not an inheritance, and for many years the *palais* functioned as much as a warehouse as a sumptuous bourgeois dwelling. The practical burgher spirit is evident in everything from the efficient modern plumbing to ornamental details depicting cattle and turnips instead of the usual aristocratic unicorns and fleurs-de-lis. The ample courtyard is the site of the annual June *Festival International de Musique Electroacoustique* (International), a major international event on the busy French contemporary music calendar. Information: *Office de Tourisme,* 21 Rue Victor-Hugo, Bourges 18000 (phone: 48-24-75-33; fax: 48-65-11-87).

CHÂTEAU DE CHAMBORD, Chambord, Loir-et-Cher This quintessentially elegant, marvelously balanced, 440-room creation in the Italian Renaissance style was the brainchild of château-mad François I, who, at the outset of the 16th century, diverted a river to make way for it and emptied church coffers and melted down silverware to finance it. On the site of an old hunting lodge in the middle of the great forest domain of the Counts of Blois, it is the largest castle in the Loire Valley, and it is surrounded by the longest wall in France—20 miles around—as well as a 13,600-acre national game reserve. (Horses may be rented for rides through the park—a special delight in the golden light of late afternoon or on a misty morning.) A long alley carved through the park frames the central spire of the château, until the road at last opens onto the whole magnificent structure. The château is renowned for its roof terrace, crowded with black slate turrets, chimneys, dormers, and buttresses ornamented with an almost frenzied array of pediments, capitals, and statues, and for its ingenious double staircase soaring from ground floor to roof terrace in two spirals superimposed on one another, so that one person can ascend and another descend simultaneously without meeting. There are 84 additional staircases and 365 chimneys within its maze-like interiors. Molière stayed here as the guest of Louis XIV, and it was also here that *Le Bourgeois Gentilhomme* had its world premiere. The castle was sacked during the Revolution, and since many of the rooms have not yet been refurbished, much of it is empty. Be sure to stroll on the splendid roof terrace, from which the royal court stargazed, watched falcons, and applauded the jousting in the tournaments held below. The château also was the site of the world's first son-et-lumière performance, set to the music of Jean-Baptiste Lully, who composed and performed here in the 17th century. The château is open daily except holidays. Information: *Château de Chambord,* Chambord 41250 (phone: 54-20-31-32 or 54-20-34-86).

CHÂTEAU DE CHENONCEAUX, Chenonceaux, Indre-et-Loire The approach to this most graceful and majestic palace is down a long avenue shaded by plane trees, with ducks and swans swimming in canals alongside, then over a drawbridge onto a terrace surrounded by moats. To the left is the Italian garden of Diane de Poitiers, who was given the château in 1547 by her lover, King Henri II, 20 years her junior; to the right is the rival garden of Catherine de Médicis, the king's wife, who evicted Diane and took over Chenonceaux after Henri II was killed by a lance thrust in a tournament in 1559. Several other women played major roles in the history of the beautiful château, including Catherine Briçonnet, who supervised its building from 1513 to 1521, and Louise of Lorraine, daughter-in-law of Catherine de Médicis, who retired to Chenonceaux to mourn after the assassination of her husband, Henri III. The château's interior is largely intact, if somewhat worn, and there is a warm feeling about the place that makes it especially pleasant to visit. Make a special effort to see the tiny library, with windows overlooking the Cher, that was used by Catherine de Médicis; the downstairs kitchens, a labyrinth of rooms set into the château's piers almost at water level; and, above the kitchens, spanning the river, the beautiful gallery built by Catherine on top of a bridge previously constructed by Diane de Poitiers. In the bright, 65-yard-long gallery, where today taped Renaissance music plays softly, 2,254 wounded people were given medical care during World

War I, when the château was turned into a temporary hospital by its owners, members of the Menier chocolate-manufacturing family. Also noteworthy is the *Musée de Cires* (Waxworks Museum), where 15 scenes depict château life. One of the special pleasures of Chenonceaux is that there's no obligatory guided tour; visitors may stroll through at their own pace, reading full descriptions of each room from a free brochure. (An English version is available.) The château and museum are open daily. Admission charge. A haunting son-et-lumière spectacle is performed on the grounds on summer evenings from mid-June through mid-September at 10:15 PM. Information: *Office de Tourisme,* 13 Rue Château, Chenonceaux 37150 (phone: 47-23-94-45; closed October through May), or call the château directly (phone: 47-23-90-07).

CHÂTEAU DE FONTAINEBLEAU, Fontainebleau, Seine-et-Marne Set in a verdant forest 40 miles (64 km) south of Paris, Fontainebleau was built, expanded, redecorated, or otherwise touched by all the greats of French royalty. In the early 16th century François I transformed what had been a 12th-century hunting lodge into a palace. Henri IV created its lakes and carp-filled pond, Louis XIII was born here, Louis XIV signed the revocation of the Edict of Nantes here in 1685, and Louis XV was married here. Napoleon turned Louis XIV's bedroom into his own throne room, signed his abdication here, and bade farewell to his Old Guard from the great horseshoe staircase. The most beautiful sections of the interior are the *Galerie de François I* and the *Salle de Bal* (Ballroom), but Josephine's bedroom and Marie-Antoinette's boudoir are worth a look as well. Closed lunch hours and Tuesdays. Admission charge. Information: *Office de Tourisme,* 31 Pl. Napoléon-Bonaparte, Fontainebleau 77300 (phone: 64-22-25-68), or call the château directly (phone: 64-22-27-40).

DOMAINE DE VAUX-LE-VICOMTE, Melun, Seine-et-Marne On the evening of August 17, 1661, Louis XIV's superintendent of finance, Nicolas Fouquet, proudly welcomed his 23-year-old king to the new castle on whose construction he had just spent his entire personal fortune. To build *Vaux-le-Vicomte,* Fouquet had hired the greatest talents of the day: Le Vau as architect, Le Brun as decorator, and Le Nôtre as landscape architect. Serenades especially composed by the renowned Lully, a stage production by Molière, a fabulous five-course banquet, and a fireworks display all heralded the occasion. Three weeks later the jealous Louis XIV had Fouquet clapped into jail for life on trumped-up charges and hired his former superintendent's illustrious team to whip him up a pied-à-terre called *Versailles. Vaux-le-Vicomte,* Fouquet's castle, is today the largest private property in France; its magical, stylized gardens alone cover more than 125 acres. It is full of lovely fountains, placid pools, sculpted lawns, and fields of flowers that look like giant illuminated medieval manuscripts. The Vaux-aux-Chandelles (Vaux-by-Candlelight) tours show off all of the château's splendors at their most dramatic. The tours take place on the second and last Saturdays of each month. The château is open daily. Admission charge. Information: *Service Touristique,* Domaine de Vaux-le-Vicomte, Maincy 77950 (phone: 64-14-41-90).

CHÂTEAU DE VERSAILLES, Versailles, Yvelines Many consider Versailles the most magnificent of all the French châteaux, and it's just 13 miles (21 km) southwest of Paris. During the 1660s Louis XIV began enlarging a small hunting lodge used by Louis XIII; by 1682 he had really outdone himself, having created a palace whose splendor would help him earn the title of "Sun King." The vast, intricate formal gardens, designed by the great Le Nôtre, cover 1,800 acres and include 24 major fountains (with a total of 600 jets of water), for which a river had to be diverted. Besides a nucleus of 1,000 nobles, Louis XIV's retinue consisted of some 9,000 men-at-arms and an equal number of servants. At any given moment between 5,000 and 6,000 people were living here, which only begins to suggest the scale of this royal commune. Seeing it all in one visit is about as relaxing as running the *Boston Marathon,* but before you drop, be sure to squeeze in the cream-and-gold chapel where the kings said mass, the state apartments (many recently renovated), the fabled *Galerie des Glaces* (Hall of Mirrors), and the *Grands Appartements.* On the grand green grounds is the *Grand Trianon,* a smaller palace often visited by Louis XIV, and the *Petit Trianon,* a favorite of Marie-Antoinette, who also liked *Le Hameau* (The Hamlet), a model farm where she and her companions played at being peasants. More than 20 additional rooms—the apartments of the dauphin and the dauphine—are open to visitors Thursdays through Saturdays. Between May and September, on specified afternoons, the 50-odd fountains and pools in the gardens are all turned on; it's a spectacular sight. Versailles is accessible by public transportation from downtown Paris. Closed Mondays; guided tours in English are available from 10 AM to 3:30 PM. The *Grand Trianon* and the *Petit Trianon* are closed Mondays, and from October through April during lunch hours on weekdays. Admission charge for the palace and *Trianons* but not for the gardens. Information: *Office de Tourisme,* 7 Rue des Réservoirs, Versailles 78000 (phone: 39-50-36-22; fax: 39-50-68-07), or Av. Général-de-Gaulle, Versailles 78000 (phone: 39-53-32-11; fax: 39-53-31-63).

For the Body

Sensational French Skiing

Unsophisticated skiers may think of Switzerland when they daydream about the Alps, but savvy downhill devotees know that the Alps in France boast slopes equal to any in the world. French ski resorts, isolated centers of pleasure concentrated in the Haute-Savoie, are scenic and relaxing, and nightlife in the French mountains gave the world the term "après-ski," the all-inclusive phrase that describes all that's fun at the end of a hard day on the slopes.

Most major French ski resorts offer economical packages that include room, board, equipment, and lift passes—irresistible deals for those looking for the highest quality of European ski experience at the lowest possible cost. It is best to insist on half board—breakfast and one other meal—since returning to a lodging place for lunch almost always is inconvenient, although some hotels include lunch at a designated mountain restaurant for their full-board guests. Prices fluctuate according to the season: Late November and early December are considered low season, and *Christmastime* and February are high season. January, when conditions often are as good as they are a month later, usually falls somewhere in between. The *French Alps Tourism and Trade Commission* in New York City (610 Fifth Ave., New York, NY 10020; phone: 212-582-3439) can provide information about special package fares and bonuses for US skiers. The annually published *French Alps Guide* is available free of charge from the "France on Call" hotline (phone: 900-990-0040). All resorts offer special discounts based on length of stay, age group, and customer loyalty (so hold onto last year's lift ticket!) There are also group and family rates and inter-resort ski passes—for example, the *Forfait Mont-Blanc* (Mont Blanc Ski Pass), which permits access to no less than 12 resorts in the Chamonix area, and the *Forfait Olympique,* a similar pass good for resorts in the Tarentaise Valley. For those interested in exploring the French Alps on skis, *Skiez 12 Vallées* (phone: 79-00-00-95) offers week-long excursions through the Tarentaise Valley on both marked and unmarked trails. During the ski season there are two numbers you can call for snow conditions in the French Alps: 36-68-02-73 for the Savoie, and 36-68-02-74 for the Haute-Savoie.

Besides traditional downhill skiing, most resorts are equipped for the "new" snow sports—mono-skiing, snowboarding, free-style skiing, speed skiing, heli-skiing, and mogul-skiing. Because of several almost snowless seasons, resorts in the French Alps have developed equipment to attract enthusiasts: Snow guns have been installed, and new lifts have been built to bring skiers to higher elevations where year-round glacier skiing is available. Some resorts offer indoor fitness and sports centers and schools and nurseries.

All sites described below have a branch of the national ski school, the *Ecole du Ski Français* (most have English-speaking teachers), which provides instruction for skiers at every level—from beginners to those interested in the challenges of *off-piste* (off the marked trails) skiing, snow safaris, or heli-skiing. Ski accident insurance also is available at the *Ecole;* called *La Carte Neige,* it also entitles the purchaser to discounts in some shops and restaurants.

Each town, no matter how small, has a tourist office that can provide up-to-date information about hotel availability, unusual tours, ski schools, equipment rental, and so on. For each ski center, we have listed a few favorite hotels by price range: Very Expensive (VE), Expensive (E), Moderate (M), and Inexpensive (I). The tourist offices can provide more information on the hotels. To learn more about France's Alpine regions, see *The Alps* in DIRECTIONS. For a list of tour operators, including those that offer ski trips to France, see GETTING READY TO GO.

___

L'ALPE D'HUEZ, Isère Built after World War II, this is one of France's most up-to-date and well-cared-for ski resorts. With a dozen trails for experts (including the 10-mile Sarenne run), it has particular appeal for accomplished skiers. But among its 100 trails are options for everyone, and the network of lifts connecting the three main sections of the skiing terrain keeps waiting time down. Tennis, swimming, horseback riding, skating, and glacier skiing allow the resort to remain open year-round. Information: *Office de Tourisme,* L'Alpe d'Huez 38750 (phone: 76-80-35-41; fax: 76-80-69-54). Hotels: *Royal Ours Blanc* (E), *Petit Prince* (M), *L'Eclose* (I).

CHAMONIX, Haute-Savoie Ever since the first *Winter Olympics* were held here in 1924, this valley town (sandwiched between the Mont-Blanc range and the Aiguilles-Rouges) has had a reputation as an important center for mountain pursuits, and it unquestionably is one of the best ski resorts in the French Alps. The scenery is as good as the skiing—most of the more than 50 trails on the mountains above the busy, small town are within sight of Mont-Blanc, whose 15,771-foot summit makes it the highest peak in the Alps. Experts can join a guided tour down the challenging Vallée Blanche, a 14-mile-long glacier run. Information: *Office de Tourisme,* Pl. du Triangle de l'Amitié, Chamonix 74400 (phone: 50-53-00-24; fax: 50-53-58-90). Hotels: *Albert Ier* (E), *Alpina* (M), *Les Rhododendrons* (I).

COURCHEVEL, Savoie With 92 trails and some 380 miles of skiing, this resort offers some of the finest and certainly the most extensive skiing in France. The resort—actually a collection of skiing centers named according to their altitude in meters (1,850, 1,650, 1,550, and 1,300)—is part of Les Trois Vallées, Europe's largest ski area. A network of 200 lifts and 311 miles of marked trails links Courchevel with the resorts of Méribel, Les Menuires, and Val-Thorens. The brilliant sun here makes for pleasant skiing, though the slopes are not terribly challenging. At 1,850 meters (6,070 ft.), La Saulire peak commands a spectacular view of Mont-Blanc and other surrounding mountains. Just before arriving at 1850 you'll pass a 119-foot-high pinnacle of ice—used for climbing—that adds to the exotic appeal of the landscape. Courchevel is popular with celebrities and well-heeled skiers, and its prices reflect its clientele. Information: *Office de Tourisme,* La Croisette, Courchevel 73120 (phone: 79-08-00-29; fax: 79-08-33-54). Hotels: *Byblos des Neiges* (VE), *La Sivolière* (E), *Le Chamois* (E).

FLAINE, Haute-Savoie At an altitude of 5,250 feet at the base and 8,860 at the summit, this small but appealingly modern ski station is the highest resort in the Grand Massif of the Haute-Savoie. With more than 150 miles of slopes and trails served by 80 lifts, it offers skiing of a quality that vindicates the vision of its developers. The *Grandes Platières* cable lift whisks skiers up to a breathtaking view of Mont-Blanc. Information: *Office de Tourisme,* Flaine 74300 (phone: 50-90-80-01; fax: 50-90-86-26). Hotels: *Totem* (E), *Le Flaine* (M), *Aujon* (I).

MEGÈVE, Haute-Savoie Built around a lovely little 13th-century Savoyard village, with Mont-Blanc as its backdrop and a burbling little stream as its backbone, Megève is one of the country's most fashionable ski resorts. While the magnitude and quality of the slopes and trails do not measure up to those at Val-d'Isère or Chamonix, Megève does attract a contingent of *World Cup* racers each winter. Chair lifts and a gondola have brought the number of trails to over 120, and cross-country skiing is good. Since snow conditions are reliable only in January and February, the vacation season starts late and ends early here. Information: *Office de Tourisme de Megève,* Rue de la Poste, Megève 74120 (phone: 50-21-27-28; fax: 50-93-03-09). Hotels: *Parc des Loges* (VE), *Au Coin du Feu* (E), *Les Sapins* (I).

MORZINE-AVORIAZ, Haute-Savoie Only a chair lift away from Switzerland, this resort actually is two towns—traditional Morzine, a sunny, spread-out valley village at an altitude of only 3,000 feet, and modern Avoriaz, perched on a 5,400-foot plain. They are both part of the huge Franco-Swiss ski system called *Les Portes du Soleil.* Their trails interlock, and there's plenty to challenge an adventurous skier. Off-slope hours can be spent at Morzine's beautiful indoor skating rink; evenings, at one of its fine restaurants. Avoriaz is a friendly resort whose ambience attracts many families. It hosts a yearly *Festival du Film Fantastique* (Fantasy Film Festival) in early January. Information: *Office de Tourisme,* Morzine-Avoriaz 74110 (phone: 50-79-03-45; fax: 50-79-03-48). Hotels: *Le Dahu* (E), *Beau Regard* (M), *La Musardière* (I).

TIGNES, Savoie One of France's largest ski resorts, this town handles the spillover from neighboring Val d'Isère during busy seasons. Called "L'Espace Killy," since most of it was designed by 1968 *Olympic* star Jean-Claude Killy, Tignes has 61 trails, 90 miles of runs, and 2,100 acres of skiing off the main trails, but since it's so easy to travel to Val d'Isère on skis, there is even more skiing here than these statistics suggest. The entire ski area—including Val d'Isère—boasts 100 ski lifts and nearly 200 miles of slopes. The possibility of traveling between Tignes and La Plagne, another bustling ski center nearby, with a mountain guide or ski instructor increases the downhill possibilities still further. Tignes offers skiing year-round at the Grande Motte glacier, almost 12,000 feet high; a funicular carries passengers to the top in about five minutes. Information: *Office de Tourisme,* BP 51, Tignes 73320 (phone: 79-06-15-55; fax: 79-06-45-44). Hotels: *Ski d'Or* (E), *Curling* (M), *Campanules* (I).

VAL-D'ISÈRE, Savoie One of the highest resorts in the Savoie, Val-d'Isère is neither as impressive as Chamonix nor as attractive as Megève, but it has nonetheless attracted serious Alpine enthusiasts since the turn of the century. Val-d'Isère was the site of the men's downhill skiing events in the 1992 *Winter Olympics;* it has produced no less an international champion than Jean-Claude Killy; and its world-famous downhill course is a traditional stop on the *World Cup* racing tour. As a result, the resort draws big spenders who ensure an atmosphere of high fashion. There are innumerable slopes for every level of skier, and one can whoosh along at altitudes of well over 11,000 feet. Before or after skiing down the Tête de Solaise, stop at the cafeteria at the base of the slopes for something warm to eat or drink. Even in the coldest weather it's a good spot for relaxing on recliners and enjoying the strong sun. Summer skiing is possible on the 10,000-foot Grand Pissaillas glacier. Information: *Office de Tourisme, Maison de Val-d'Isère,* Val-d'Isère 73150 (phone: 79-06-06-60; fax: 79-06-04-56). Hotels: *Christiania* (VE), *Altitude* (M), *Kern* (I).

VAL-THORENS, Savoie The highest resort in Western Europe is the place for the true sports enthusiast. The altitude—7,545 feet at the base and 11,155 feet at its highest point—assures good conditions throughout the season. From here it's possible to ski virtually without interruption for half a day before arriving at Mottaret, the village at the bottom of the next valley. Val-Thorens is one of the resorts of Les Trois Vallées, which means that it's possible for an average skier to go from Val-Thorens to Les Menuires to Méribel to Courchevel and back (or vice versa) in the same day, using only 12 lifts. Nearly 90% of the skiing here is *off-piste,* allowing the adventurous to go off on their own to ski on the fantastic powder snow. Summer skiing on the glacier is also popular. Most hotels are located right on the runs, enabling serious skiers to roll out of bed onto the slopes. Information: *Office de Tourisme, Maison de Val-Thorens,* Val-Thorens 73440 (phone: 79-00-01-08; fax: 79-00-08-41). Hotels: *Fitz Roy* (E), *Trois Vallées* (M), *La Marmotte* (M).

Great French Golf

Food, wine, châteaux, and cathedrals are what first come to mind when thinking about France—not golf. But golf has been a tradition in Gaul since 1856, when the first course was laid out in Pau (in the Pyrénées). Since that time the game has grown enormously in popularity. By the end of 1993 there were 482 courses around the country, and 25 more are expected to be completed by the end of this year. In fact, except for England, France has more courses than any other country in Europe, including Scotland!

Leave it to the French to make golf even more attractive than it already is. With the beautiful courses found in Bordeaux, Burgundy, and the Loire Valley, it is possible to spend the mornings on the fairway and the afternoons at some of the world's finest vineyards. For a list of tour operators, including those that offer golf trips to France, see GETTING READY TO GO.

The *Fédération Française de Golf* (69 Av. Victor-Hugo, Paris 75116; phone: 44-17-63-00) and the *French Ministry of Tourism* have set up a system whereby those who are not members of a local golf club can play. Greens fees vary according to the day and season but are always highest on weekends. Call ahead to reserve.

Several major cities in France—Cannes, Biarritz, and Paris, among others—boast top-flight layouts; for information on those courses, consult the individual reports in THE CITIES. Below, we offer a survey of the courses somewhat off the beaten track that are considered among the best in the country. But be forewarned: Golf is considered more sport than leisure in France. Motorized carts are forbidden on most courses, but pull carts are available everywhere.

ATLANTIC COAST The mellow Charentais region attracts golfers with a yen for the area's famous oysters, not to mention cognac, the aristocratic elixir that takes its name from one of the region's towns.

Golf Club du Cognac The Martell cognac vineyards are the setting for this 6,950-yard, par 72 course. During harvest time players are treated to the aroma of fermenting grapes. It is an easy 18-holer, but well worth playing for the ambience. Wine tasting and golf packages are available. Information: *Golf Club du Cognac,* Rue St-Brice, Cognac 16100 (phone: 45-32-18-17).

BRITTANY This region, similar to parts of Ireland and northern California and home to small fishing villages and wild moors, has some interesting layouts.

Golf de Dinard One of the country's older courses, and also one of its shortest. But be forewarned: If the wind is blowing, the 5,700 yards will very quickly seem far longer. The views from the links are breathtaking. Information: *Golf de Dinard,* St-Briac-sur-Mer 35800 (phone: 99-88-32-07).

Golf des Ormes This inland course (18 holes, 6,750 yards, par 72) is part of the estate of the La Chesnais family. A few guestrooms are available in the

18th-century manor house set in the middle of the course. There are electric carts for rent. Information: *Golf des Ormes,* Dol-de-Bretagne 35120 (phone: 99-73-49-60).

Golf Public de Baden This public 18-hole, 6,700-yard forest layout is a stone's throw from St-Laurent. Information: *Golf Public de Baden,* Kernic, Baden 56870 (phone: 97-57-18-96).

Golf St-Laurent Ploërmel Set in a forest, this 27-hole, 6,800-yarder has often been chosen as the site of the *French PGA Championship.* Very popular during the summer, it is located near Carnac, known for its giant prehistoric stone formations. Information: *Golf de St-Laurent Ploërmel,* Auray 56400 (phone: 97-56-85-18).

CÔTE D'AZUR Famous for its beaches and casinos, the French Riviera is tops with tourists.

Barbaroux Long tees and a splendid setting against a backdrop of pine forests characterize this course, the first Pete Dye layout to be built in France. A private course (18 holes, 7,000 yards, par 72), it is cleverly designed to provide many challenges, and at times is quite difficult to read. Carts are available. Information: *Barbaroux,* Domaine de Barbaroux, Brignoles 83170 (phone: 94-59-07-43).

Golf de l'Estérel This pleasant course (18 holes, 6,500 yards, par 72) designed by Robert Trent Jones Sr. is on the grounds of the *Latitudes* hotel and resort (hotel guests may play for free). Its spectacular 15th hole (par 3) is set in water. There also is a 9-hole course. Information: *Golf de l'Estérel,* Av. Golf, St-Raphaël 83700 (phone: 94-82-47-88).

LANGUEDOC-ROUSSILLON Running along the Mediterranean Sea to the Spanish border, this part of southern France is one of the fastest growing golf areas in the country. Most of the courses here are new and in excellent condition, and the weather is ideal almost year-round.

Golf du Cap d'Agde Something of a French hot spot, this extremely difficult 18-holer is a full 7,000 yards long. It's better to play off-season than in the summer, when it is jammed toe to tee. Information: *Golf du Cap d'Agde,* Cap d'Agde 34300 (phone: 67-26-54-40).

Golf Club de Campagne These 6,800 yards are particularly challenging when the wind is blowing (which is quite often). In fact, the club suggests that only those with handicaps under 30 play at all. The 18th hole is next to a beautiful pond surrounded by weeping willows. The clubhouse is approached by a splendid alley of sycamore trees. Information: *Golf Club de Campagne,* Rte. de St-Gilles, Nîmes 30000 (phone: 66-23-33-33; fax: 66-70-33-14).

Golf Club de la Grande Motte Designed by Robert Trent Jones Sr., this resort has 9-hole and 18-hole courses. The warm climate, flat land, ponds, flamingos, and the Southern US–style architecture of the club will make folks from Florida feel right at home. As with the *Campagne* course (above), the wind can be a real challenge. This is the qualifying site of the *PGA* European tour. Information: *Golf Club de la Grande Motte,* La Grande Motte 34280 (phone: 67-56-05-00).

LOIRE VALLEY Set among the famous châteaux of this region are many golf courses, with several more under construction. The mildness of the area's climate (except in winter) makes it ideal for playing a few rounds after visiting the castles.

Golf d'Ardrée Laid out on a former private hunting preserve, the course features a small château on the property and a modern clubhouse. Electric carts are available to get around the 6,500 yards. Located eight miles (13 km) north of Tours. Information: *Golf d'Ardrée,* St-Antoine-du-Rocher 37360 (phone: 47-56-77-38; fax: 47-56-79-96).

Golf International Les Bordes Texas architect Robert Von Hagge designed this championship course with the goal of respecting the landscape, resulting in a beautiful 7,100-yard layout. There is water on 12 of its 18 holes, and the greens fees are among the highest in the country—two possible explanations for the fact that so few come here to tee off. Electric carts are available. Ten miles (16 km) southwest of Orléans. Information: *Golf International Les Bordes,* St-Laurent-Nouan 41220 (phone: 54-87-72-13; fax: 54-87-78-61).

NORMANDY Because of its relative proximity to the capital, Normandy has become a popular weekend haven for Parisians. There are nearly 40 golf clubs scattered throughout the region; the following is our favorite. For a complete list of Normandy's courses, contact the *Comité Régional de Tourisme de Normandie* (14 Rue Charles-Corbeau, Evreux 27000; phone: 32-33-79-00; fax: 32-31-19-04).

New Golf de Deauville Designed in 1920, it is one of the oldest golf clubs in France. Its 6,600 yard, 18-hole course (plus another 9-hole layout) make this a golfer's don't-miss. The views of the Norman houses and the surrounding coast are spectacular from the back 9 of the championship course. Information: *New Golf de Deauville,* St-Arnoult 14800 (phone: 31-88-20-53).

Game, Set, and Match: Tennis in France

The number of tennis courts and camps in France is on the increase, and there are hundreds of tennis clubs—both private and public. The surface of choice is red clay, though there are a fair number of all-weather and hard courts scattered around the countryside.

TENNIS CLUBS

France's many tennis clubs are organized by *département* or league. Most require annual membership, and virtually all are closed to outsiders who aren't personally acquainted with a member. However, some are less exclusive than others, and occasionally it's possible for business associates to provide an entrée. In resort areas the best clubs are open to any player willing to pay the sometimes substantial admission fee. Many offer *stages* (instruction sessions) to the general public on a weekend or weekly basis. Instruction usually is in French. A complete list of addresses for tennis clubs in France is available from the *Fédération Française de Tennis* (*FFT; Stade Roland-Garros,* 2 Av. Gordon-Bennett, BP 33316, Paris 75767; phone: 47-43-48-00).

In addition to those located in major cities (consult the individual reports in THE CITIES for details), the following clubs are the best France has to offer.

ARCACHON, Gironde This breezy beach town has just the right climate for summer tennis. There are 22 courts at the *Tennis-Club* (7 Av. du Parc) and five more at *Abatilles Tennis Courts* (165 Bd. de la Côte-d'Argent). Information: *Office de Tourisme,* Pl. Roosevelt, Arcachon 33120 (phone: 56-83-01-69; fax: 57-52-22-10).

LA BAULE, Loire-Atlantique The *Tennis Country Club* has the best opportunities in a town that boasts more than 80 courts. An establishment worth crossing the Atlantic to experience, it has a half-timbered clubhouse with squared hedges, an active tournament schedule, four all-weather courts, and 25 superbly tended red clay courts. Suzanne Lenglen reigned here for many years. Now owned by a hotel chain, it offers a wide variety of tennis packages that include lodging. Information: *Tennis Country Club,* 113 Av. du Maréchal-de-Lattre-de-Tassigny, La Baule 44500 (phone: 40-11-46-26; fax: 40-60-53-08).

DEAUVILLE, Calvados The town itself owns 23 courts by the sea and sponsors numerous tournaments, but should you strike it rich at the casino, consider one of the two classic Deauville hotels—the *Normandy* or the *Royal*—or the *Hôtel du Golf,* in nearby St-Arnoult. The *Normandy,* an oversize Norman cottage in the heart of town, faces its own 21 tennis courts as well as the Atlantic Ocean. Should the weather disappoint you, jog the underground passage to the casino or swim in the covered, heated *Olympic*-size saltwater pool. Down the street is the *Royal,* with 23 courts, and just outside town is the *Hôtel du Golf,* with additional racquet facilities. Information: *Hôtel Normandy,* 38 Rue Jean-Mermoz, Deauville 14800 (phone: 31-98-66-22; fax: 31-98-66-23); *Hôtel Royal,* Bd. Eugène-Cornuché, Deauville 14800 (phone: 31-98-66-33; fax: 31-98-66-34); *Hôtel du Golf,* St-Arnoult, Deauville 14800 (phone: 31-88-19-01; fax: 31-88-75-99).

EVIAN-LES-BAINS, Haute-Savoie World famous for its casino (see *Casinos Royale* in this section), Evian also boasts a tennis club with 13 courts. If money is no object, *Le Royal* hotel (see *Romantic French Hostelries* in this section) offers an intensive six-day tennis program combining exercise and two hours of daily play on its own six courts. Information: *Office de Tourisme,* Pl. d'Allinges, BP 988, Evian 74502 (phone: 50-75-04-26; fax: 50-75-61-08); *Le Royal,* Rte. du Mateirons, Evian 74502 (phone: 50-26-85-00; fax: 50-75-61-00).

HENDAYE, Pyrénées-Atlantiques The club in this beach town on the Spanish border has 13 clay courts, two of them indoors. It's most active in July and August. Information: *Tennis Club Parc des Sports,* Rue Elissacilio, Hendaye 64700 (phone: 59-20-02-73).

LA PLAGNE, Savoie *Stages* on the 16 hard courts at this popular ski and summer resort, which include full room and board, are available in July and August. Information: *Eric Loliée Résidence de Plagne Belle-Côte,* Aime 73210 (phone: 79-09-29-00); *Office du Tourisme,* BP 36, Plagne-Centre, Aime 73210 (phone: 79-09-79-79; fax: 79-09-70-10).

TIGNES, Savoie The instruction program at this ski and summer resort is intensive, with more than four hours of instruction a day for six days. But after a day of tennis on the 15 hard courts, it's possible to go sailing in the mountain lake, golf, or even ski. Information: *Stage Caujolle, Club Omni-Sports,* Tignes-le-Lac 73320 (phone: 79-06-30-28); *Club des Sports,* Tignes-le-Lac 73320 (phone: 79-06-53-87; fax: 79-06-46-56).

TROUVILLE-SUR-MER, Calvados The tennis club in this Atlantic-pounded Normandy resort town offers seven clay courts, two hard courts, and a single indoor court plus instruction on a weekly basis. Golf, horseback riding, swimming, and windsurfing are also possible. Open from April through September. Information: *Trouville Tennis Club,* Trouville-sur-Mer 14360 (phone: 31-88-91-62).

TENNIS CAMPS

French tennis camps, with highly qualified instructors, offer more intense tutoring than the clubs, usually by the week.

L'ALPE D'HUEZ, Isère A popular skiing center in the winter, this most up-to-date and well-cared-for of French resorts offers organized tennis instruction from mid-July through mid-August. Lessons are given on a weekly basis, with lodging in local hotels. Information: *Office de Tourisme,* L'Alpe d'Huez 38750 (phone: 76-80-35-41; fax: 76-80-69-54); *Club des Sports,* BP 40, L'Alpe d'Huez (phone: 76-80-34-42; fax: 76-80-49-38).

LES ARCS, Savoie *Arc 1600* and *Arc 1800,* a pair of ski resorts whose numbers refer to their altitude in meters, both offer six-day tennis camps in July and August, with three to four hours of instruction per day. There are 40 hard courts and, at Arc 1800, a pool and a golf course. Lodging is in local hotels. Information: *Maison des Arcs,* 94 Bd. du Montparnasse, Paris 75014 (phone: 43-22-43-32); *Office de Tourisme,* BP 45, Arc 1800, Bourg St-Maurice 73700 (phone: 79-07-12-57; fax: 79-07-45-96).

ARLES, Bouches-du-Rhône The camp at *Les Villages du Soleil* offers four-and-a-half-hour sessions for five days on either the seven indoor courts or the 23 outdoor hard courts, depending on the season. Lodging with half board is available at the camp, which also has a pool, a sauna, and squash and volleyball facilities. Information: *Les Villages du Soleil,* Mas de Véran, Arles 13200 (phone: 90-18-49-49).

CAP D'AGDE, Hérault Founded by former tennis star Pierre Barthès, this famous camp in the Languedoc consumes the life of the village. The instruction programs last for six days, with lessons four hours a day; most of the instructors speak English. There are 64 courts with about as many surfaces as a tennis player can name. Students can lodge at the camp hotel or at any of the numerous hotels and bungalows in the area. Information: *Club Pierre-Barthès,* Cap d'Agde 34305 (phone: 67-26-00-06).

FLAINE, Haute-Savoie The tennis camp in this modern mountain ski and summer resort may have as many as 10 students per instructor, but there is ample room for practice on the 26 hard courts. *Stages* are offered in July and August. Students lodge in ski chalets or hotels in the area. Information: *Stages Georges-Deniau, Sepad Loisirs,* 23 Rue Cambon, Paris 75001 (phone: 42-61-55-17); *Office de Tourisme,* Flaine 74300 (phone: 50-90-80-01; fax: 50-90-86-26); *Maison de Flaine,* 99 Bd. Haussmann, Paris 75008 (phone: 40-07-07-06; fax: 40-07-01-65).

LES HAUTS-DE-NÎMES, Gard Run by the same company that operates the camp at Flaine (above), this one, in the south of France, offers sessions of either two or four hours for each of six days on 33 courts (four indoors). Some instructors speak English. Lodging is available at the camp or in town. Information: *Le Tennis Club des Hauts-de-Nîmes,* Les Hauts-de-Nîmes, Rte. d'Anduze, Nîmes 30900 (phone: 66-23-14-67).

OPIO, Alpes-Maritimes Some of the best spots for playing tennis in Europe are at the "vacation villages" of *Club Mediterranée,* which consistently offer extensive facilities, first-rate instruction, and settings maintained with ecological fervor. The *Club Med* not far from the Côte d'Azur at Opio spreads out over 125 acres and has 15 tennis courts, seven of which are lighted. Information: *Club Med,* 40 W. 57th St., New York, NY 10019 (phone: 800-CLUB MED; 212-750-1670 in New York City).

TOURNAMENT TENNIS

There are two major international tournaments in France each year. The *French Open,* or *Championnats Internationaux de France,* known in France as the *Roland Garros,* takes place during the last week in May and the first week in June in Paris. The world's premier red clay–court tournament and one of the four *Grand Slam* events (the other three are *Wimbledon,* the *US Open,* and the *Australian Open*), it attracts most of the top international players. Tickets for early-round matches generally are easy to obtain as late as early May at the *Stade Roland-Garros* box office or by mail through the *Fédération Française de Tennis* (see *Tennis Clubs,* above); tickets for the semifinal and final matches, on the other hand, must be reserved well in advance. The *FFT* also can supply a roster of club tournaments open to visiting players and other competitive events of interest to spectators.

The Monte Carlo Open, France's other big clay-court event, also draws most of the world's best. The tournament takes place in April. For tickets and information, contact the *Monte Carlo Country Club* (Quartier St-Roman, Roquebrune-Cap-Martin 06190; phone: 93-41-30-15).

A handful of other tournaments on the intermediate circuit of the *Grand Prix* professional schedule—that is, the *Challenge Series* tournaments—attract competitors familiar to anyone who follows tennis regularly. The annual tournament in Nice is one of the most popular; there are others in Nancy (March), Aix-en-Provence (April), Bordeaux (September), Toulouse (October), and Paris (November). The *FFT* (see *Tennis Clubs,* above) can supply specifics.

Sun, Sea, and Sand: France's Best Beaches

The Riviera is almost everything it is touted to be. The water is clear and tame, the sun reliable, the celebrities abundant. It is a paradise of cool drinks by day and clubs and casinos by night. To those who are seeking a glitzy getaway, the Riviera will not disappoint. But most of the beaches are pebbled rather than sandy, and in August, when almost all of France shuts down so that workers can take the month of vacation that is guaranteed by law, it seldom is possible to find an open patch on which to spread a towel, and it's equally difficult to locate an empty hotel room.

France boasts some 1,200 miles of beachfront in all, and most of them have a lot more natural scenery to offer than the Côte d'Azur, however glamorous it may be. From the rugged cliffs of Normandy and Brittany down the expansive Atlantic coast to the Mediterranean hideaways of Languedoc, there are scores of places where a beach vacation can be mixed with the pleasure of exploring a country and its culture.

Note that some beaches are specially designated *naturiste,* connoting nude bathing. However, sunning and swimming in the buff are common enough in other places as well—usually on the fringes of the greatest concentration of swimmers—and topless bathing is the norm for women.

Below is a sampling of the most interesting seaside resorts, following the French coastline counterclockwise from Normandy.

NORMANDY Best known to the world today as the site of the Allied invasion in 1944, the Normandy coastline is a rugged stretch of sandy beaches and craggy cliffs. Omaha Beach, Utah Beach, and other spots are legendary (though they're not swimming beaches); others, among them the western side of the Cotentin Peninsula, are less well known and therefore more interesting to the visitor who wants to beat his or her own path. For information about any of the beaches below, contact the *Comité Régional du Tourisme de Normandie* (14 Rue Charles-Corbeau, Evreux 27000; phone: 32-33-79-00).

Deauville, Calvados This town and neighboring Trouville-sur-Mer, both affluent former fishing villages with sandy beaches and seaside restaurants, have drawn the rich and famous over the decades to their casinos, racetracks, chic hotels, and other attractions.

Plages du Débarquement, Calvados The landing beaches, as this stretch of coastline is known, bore the brunt of the Allied invasion. Luc-sur-Mer, with its museum of seashells, and Bernières-sur-Mer, whose 219-foot belfry is the highest on the Normandy coast, are especially pleasant.

Les Côtes des Grandes Marées, Manche Before reaching Mont-St-Michel, the motorist arrives at a stretch of magnificent beaches, including Granville, St-Pair-sur-Mer, Jullouville, and Carolles. The cliffs just beyond Carolles give a fine view of the northern Brittany coast, while Vauville, farther up the Cotentin Peninsula, is noted for its sand dunes.

BRITTANY The coastline of this especially scenic province, a picturesque mélange of rocky cliffs, small fishing ports, and sandy coves, has many faces. The northern area offers well-developed beach towns, some as glitteringly sophisticated as those on the Riviera and some low-key and family oriented. The south tends to be a little wilder, particularly around Quiberon.

St-Cast-le-Guildo, Côtes-du-Nord Many French families spend August in this area, known as the pride of the Côte d'Emeraude (Emerald Coast), one of Brittany's largest resorts. There are a dozen public tennis courts and a 9-hole golf course, among other diversions. Information: *Office de Tourisme,* Pl. Général-de-Gaulle, St-Cast-le-Guildo 22380 (phone: 96-41-81-52).

Bénodet, Finistère It is not always as warm on the pebbled beaches of Bénodet as it is on the sandy beaches farther south, and the water is often chilly. But this district at the mouth of the Odet River in folklore-rich Finistère is renowned for its beautiful camping areas and fine sailing school. A few miles down the coast is the beautiful, piney Beg Meil. The boat ride along the Odet to Quimper is a popular diversion. Information: *Syndicat d'Initiative,* 51 Av. de la Plage, Bénodet 29118 (phone: 98-57-00-14).

La Baule, Loire-Atlantique Many believe that the 3 miles of sandy beach at this busy and fashionable resort, farther east along the stretch of Brittany coastline known as the Côte d'Amour, are the loveliest in the country. The area—built up enough to be almost urban—draws a middle class clientele to its casino and discotheques, 70 tennis courts, two equestrian centers (with more than 200 horses), 18-hole golf course, and flying club. Information: *Office de Tourisme,* 8 Pl. de la Victoire, La Baule 44500 (phone: 40-24-34-44).

Baie de Quiberon, Morbihan The most favored beaches in the area around the Golfe du Morbihan, in the south of Brittany, are at Carnac—as famous for its prehistoric megaliths as for its resort facilities—at nearby La Trinité, and at Quiberon, at the end of a long, rocky peninsula. While the nights can be cool, the scenery is rugged—just what most visitors travel to Brittany to find. Quiberon is the departure point for trips to Belle-Ile, the largest island in the province and a beach lover's destination in its own right. The terrain rises sharply from the sands that border it, allowing for some spectacular coastal views. Information: *Office de Tourisme,* 74 Av. des Druides, Carnac 56340 (phone: 97-52-13-52).

UPPER ATLANTIC COAST This area is the site of several charming islands plus romantic La Rochelle.

Ile d'Oléron, Charente-Maritime The popularity of France's second-largest island, linked to the mainland by a bridge, has somewhat diminished its charm, but it does have an abundance of marvelous sandy beaches that draw youths by the thousands. At night the island bustles; by day you can visit oyster farms, take sailing lessons, and explore medieval ruins. Information: *Office de Tourisme, Le Château,* Pl. de la République, Le Château-d'Oléron 17480 (phone: 46-47-60-51; fax: 46-47-73-65).

Ile de Ré, Charente-Maritime Aptly named the "White Island" because of the plenitude of sunshine that graces it, this is an 18-mile-long treasure of tiny villages, whitewashed cottages, and undeveloped land. There's a bird sanctuary, a bicycle livery, a satisfying number of well-marked beaches, and a handful of comfortable hotels. Access is provided by the 2½-mile Pont l'Ile de Ré, the longest span in France. Information: *Syndicat d'Initiative,* Quai Sénac, La Flotte, Ile de Ré 17630 (phone: 46-09-60-38; fax: 46-09-64-88).

La Rochelle, Charente-Maritime A thriving port in medieval times, this city boasts Europe's largest pleasure boat basin and a charming fortified old city that was once English and remained something of an outsider even after it became French territory. With a population of 72,000, it is no quaint village: Night or day, the city dazzles. The city's antique carousel and the white sand beaches in its environs—including those on Ile de Ré (see above)—are lovely. The main harborside street, Quai Duperre, is closed to traffic on summer weekend evenings. Information: *Office de Tourisme,* Pl. de la Petite-Sirène, Le Gabut, La Rochelle 17025 (phone: 46-41-14-68; fax: 46-41-99-85).

Ile d'Yeu, Vendée About 75 minutes by ferry from Fromentine, this island is so notched by rocky promontories on the south side that the shore is known as the Côte Sauvage. But elsewhere there are lovely beaches and simple port towns. Marshal Pétain, head of the Vichy government during World War II, was imprisoned here from 1945 to 1951. It is possible to tour the island in a day on foot or by bicycle. Information: *Office de Tourisme,* 1 Pl. du Marché, Port-Joinville 85350 (phone: 51-58-32-58).

Les Sables-d'Olonne, Vendée The 7 miles of beach here make these strands among the most popular of all the Atlantic resorts. Many visitors go horseback riding through the dunes or visit the aquarium or zoo. La Tranche-sur-Mer, a few miles farther down the coast, is famous for its tulip fields in April and May and its vast sandy beaches all summer long. Information: *Office de Tourisme,* 8 Rue du Maréchal-Leclerc, Les Sables-d'Olonne 85100 (phone: 51-32-03-28; for hotel reservations only, 51-32-59-59; fax: 51-52-84-49).

St-Jean-de-Monts, Vendée The vast beach of St-Jean-de-Monts is perfect for families because of its exceptionally calm waters. The fact that there are only a few hotels suggests just how quiet the place can be. Information: *Office de Tourisme, Palais des Congrès,* St-Jean-de-Monts 85160 (phone: 51-58-00-48).

LOWER ATLANTIC COAST With almost 150 miles of sand, this stretch of beach backed by the Landes forest and running from the mouth of the Gironde River to the Basque country is one of the longest in the world. Environmental regulations have left some sections of the coast delightfully undeveloped; other sections have been allowed to grow so that there are comfortable hotels and restaurants aplenty. Note that the waters often are rough and dangerous, so it is advisable to swim only in designated areas and when there's a green flag flying—meaning that a lifeguard is on duty and swimming is safe.

Arcachon, Gironde Along the 40-mile perimeter of the Arcachon Basin, where Celts lived around 500 BC, there are about 30 beaches and oyster farms, pine trees by the thousands, and, near Pyla-sur-Mer, an immense sand dune (375 feet and still growing)—taller than any other in Europe. Thousands of sailboats moor here, and in the town of Arcachon proper, the old beachfront hotels, the handsome 19th-century villas, and the promenade edged with feathery tamarisk trees recall the town's Belle Epoque heyday, when English gentry visited to socialize and French artists like Manet and Toulouse-Lautrec came to paint. Nearby, at La Hume, a restored medieval village is full of craftspeople wearing period costumes. Information: *Office de Tourisme,* Pl. Roosevelt, Arcachon 33120 (phone: 56-83-01-69; fax: 57-52-22-10).

Lacanau-Océan, Gironde Visitors to this clean and modern resort can enjoy not only the sprawling beaches along the coast but also the forest immediately inland and two large freshwater lakes of almost 5,000 acres. There is an 18-hole golf course, more than 25 tennis courts, and a sailing school on nearby Lac Lacanau, as well as excellent cycling and windsurfing. Information: *Office de Tourisme,* 438 Pl. de l'Europe, Lacanau 33680 (phone: 56-03-21-01; fax: 56-03-11-89).

Soulac-sur-Mer, Gironde A thriving monastic community in the Middle Ages, Soulac was one of the stops along the pilgrimage route to Santiago de Compostela, Spain. Just south of the Pointe de Grave, this tidy little town full of color-fully trimmed brick houses welcomes about 100,000 vacationers each summer. Most prefer to spend at least some of their time away from the strand to explore the old town, with its 12th-century Romanesque church and other relics. There are also tennis courts, a gym, a cinema, a casino, and horses for rent. Information: *Office de Tourisme,* Rue de la Plage, Soulac-sur-Mer 33780 (phone: 56-09-86-61; fax: 56-73-63-76).

Hossegor and Capbreton, Landes Hossegor, a modern oyster center, and Capbreton, an old fishing village, combine to form one of the loveliest resorts on the south Atlantic coast. The beach is sandy, safe, and vast, and the lake between the two towns tends to be a few degrees warmer than the ocean. A little farther down the coast are other popular beaches, most notably Labenne-Océan and Ondres-Plage. Information: *Office de Tourisme,* Pl. Louis-Pasteur, Hossegor 40150 (phone: 58-41-79-00; fax: 58-41-70-15); *Office de Tourisme,* Av. Georges-Pompidou, Capbreton 40130 (phone: 58-72-12-11; fax: 58-41-00-29).

BASQUE COUNTRY At times more Spanish than French, this is one of France's most exciting areas.

St-Jean-de-Luz, Pyrénées-Atlantiques Louis XIV was married to Maria Theresa of Spain in 1660 in the *Eglise St-Jean-Baptiste,* and the old town has not changed much since. The harbor still bustles with fishermen bringing in their tuna and sardines. The vast and well-patrolled beach has a reputation for being one of the country's safest. Information: *Office de Tourisme,* Pl. du Maréchal-Foch, St-Jean-de-Luz 64500 (phone: 59-26-03-16; fax: 59-26-21-47).

LANGUEDOC-ROUSSILLON There are more than 100 miles of good sandy beaches backed by the Pyrénées along the Mediterranean coast north of the Spanish border, and resorts of all types: ancient fishing villages, modern pleasure grounds, and huge campsites. In this part of the country sunshine is practically guaranteed.

Cap d'Agde, Hérault More than 7 miles of white sand at the foot of an extinct volcano make this one of the Languedoc's best modern summer resorts. The handful of hotels are expensive; it's better to rent a studio apartment by the week. Information: *Office de Tourisme, Palais des Congrès,* Cap d'Agde 34305 (phone: 67-26-38-58).

Argèles-Plage, Pyrénées-Orientales The population of this massive modern seaside resort swells from its normal level of 5,000 to 300,000 in summer, and there are literally dozens of places to lodge or camp in the area, if you don't mind crowds. During the summer there's a casino open in Argèles-sur-Mer, a mile or so inland. Information: *Office de Tourisme,* Pl. de l'Europe, Argèles-sur-Mer 66700 (phone: 68-81-15-85).

Collioure, Pyrénées-Orientales This old port, a favorite of Matisse and Braque, boasts a 15th-century donjon that Philip II of Spain transformed into a citadel and a medieval château with a view of the surrounding beaches—the town's main drawing cards. Information: *Office de Tourisme,* Pl. 18-Juin, Collioure 66190 (phone: 68-82-15-47).

Leucate and Le Barcarès, Pyrénées-Orientales Between these two ports is a 6-mile stretch of beach that has developed rapidly in the course of the last decade or so, offering sailing, tennis, and water skiing. It is large enough not to seem overcrowded, even when it's teeming with tourists. Information: *Office de Tourisme,* Pl. du Village, Port-Barcarès 66420 (phone: 68-86-16-56).

St-Cyprien-Plage, Pyrénées-Orientales This futuristic resort is one of a handful in France designed to approximate a seaside paradise. There's a lake inhabited by flamingos and surrounded by sweet-smelling trees, a pair of golf courses, a thousand acres of lovely landscaping, and miles and miles of sandy beach. Information: *Office de Tourisme,* Quai Rimbaud, St-Cyprien-Plage 66750 (phone: 68-21-01-33).

CÔTE D'AZUR Many of the beaches are more stony than sandy, but the Côte d'Azur has a multitude of them, and they attract thousands of tourists. While hardly the place to get away from it all, the Côte offers spectacular scenery: gracefully curved bays and wildly beautiful coves, often backed by white cliffs, silvery olive and cypress trees, and dark green pines. The water is a dazzling shade of turquoise that almost matches the brilliant blue of the sky, and the light still possesses the exquisite brightness that lured many of the nation's most distinguished painters to work here at one time or another. There are hotels in all price ranges all along the coast. For people watching, the famous resorts such as Bandol, Cannes, Nice, and St-Tropez can't be beat; for peace and quiet, there are scores of smaller resorts.

Juan-les-Pins, Alpes-Maritimes About halfway between Cannes and Nice, Juan-les-Pins is as chic and as night-crazed as St-Tropez, with activity focused on the casino, which occupies a cool garden set just away from the sea. During the annual *World Jazz Festival,* things are even more active. The diving and sailing schools have a good reputation, and some three dozen hotels rise along the white sandy beach. Information: *Maison du Tourisme,* 51 Bd. Guillaumont, Juan-les-Pins 06160 (phone: 93-61-04-98).

Mandelieu and La Napoule, Alpes-Maritimes Just west of Cannes the old village of Mandelieu and nearby La Napoule, with its superb sandy beach, make up a spectacular resort with tennis courts, golf courses, and camping facilities. Anyone who scrambles down the stony cliffs from the Corniche de l'Esterel between Cannes and St-Raphaël might claim some picturesque little crescent of sand for the afternoon—to enjoy completely alone. Information: *Maison du Tourisme,* Av. de Cannes, Mandelieu–Là Napoule 06210 (phone: 93-49-14-39).

Ste-Maxime, Var While this resort lies just across the bay from St-Tropez, its lifestyle is light-years away. Some female sunbathers wear tops as well as bottoms, and disco takes second place to quiet dinners and daytime strolls through the many boutiques. Young families are the primary clientele. There also are more than a dozen tennis courts, a 9-hole golf course, a sailing school, a marina full of pleasure craft, and—most delightful of all—a sensational view of mountains and coast just a mile north at the Sémaphore. Information: *Office de Tourisme,* Promenade Simon-Lorière, Ste-Maxime 83120 (phone: 94-96-19-24).

Sanary-sur-Mer, Var Not far from the famous beaches at Bandol and La Ciotat, Sanary is a quiet place with a beach, an old town, and an open-air theater. Together with the islands of Bendor and Embiez, it is also a fabulous center for water sports. Hotel facilities are limited, so inquire well in advance. Information: *Maison du Tourisme,* Jardins de la Ville, Sanary-sur-Mer 83110 (phone: 94-74-01-04).

Horsing Around

Holidays on horseback in France unquestionably are among the country's best-kept secrets. Seeing the countryside astride a spirited steed can be pure delight: Whether the animal hauls your belongings while you walk alongside, pulls your wagon, or carries you from farm to village through deep woods, you will travel through stretches of France that few visitors ever see, where the rugged beauty is only enhanced by the creaking of saddle leather and the steady thud of hooves.

EQUESTRIAN REGIONS

Several areas of France lend themselves particularly well to holidays on horseback.

BRITTANY For those with the yen, Brittany's miles of mainly unspoiled, uncrowded beaches and numerous *centres équestres* (riding centers) offer an unusual holiday experience for beginners or experienced riders. One possibility is the *Centre Equestre du Trégor* (Kerianou 56193; phone: 96-95-67-41), on the outskirts of the north-coast town of Tréguier, which offers rides along the nearby Presq'île Sauvage (Wild Peninsula) or to the Point du Château at the tip of another peninsula, for splendid views of the Côte du Granit Rose (Coast of Pink Granite). Information: *Ligue du Tourisme*

Equestre de Bretagne, 8 Rue de la Carrière, Josselin 56120 (phone: 97-22-22-62).

CORSICA More than 500 miles of riding trails crisscross this mountainous Mediterranean island, and many of them still are used by shepherds and forest rangers. Picturesque villages along the way offer accommodations ranging from the primitive to the comfortable, and dozens of equestrian centers will organize expeditions that run from a few days to a couple of weeks. Information: *Comité Régional du Tourisme de Corse,* 17 Bd. Roi-Jérôme, Ajaccio, Corsica 20176 (phone: 95-21-56-56; fax: 95-51-14-40).

DORDOGNE For those who want to experience the luxuriant French countryside at a slow pace (around 4 miles per hour), the Dordogne tourist board offers *roulotte à cheval* (horse-drawn cart) rentals. The *roulottes,* which are wooden trailers, accommodate four people and are equipped with a portable stove, kitchen utensils, and bed linens (but no electricity). They can be rented by the weekend or week from April through September, and they depart from Bergerac along a *bastide* (fortified village) route or from Quinsac through the unspoiled, agricultural Périgord Vert (Green Périgord). Planned nightly stops are in areas where water and shelter for the horse and bathing facilities for the passengers are provided. A week's rental (which includes a training session in operating the *roulotte,* food for the horse, and insurance) costs as much as $1,000 during the high season, less at other times. Information: *Maison du Périgord,* 6 Rue Gomboust, Paris 75001 (phone: 42-60-38-77); *Office Départemental du Tourisme de la Dordogne,* 16 Rue Wilson, Périgueux 24009 (phone: 53-53-44-35; fax: 53-09-51-41).

NORMANDY A sunset gallop along the beach in Deauville, in the ancient province of Calvados, still ranks among France's prime existential delights. This is one of the equestrian capitals of Europe, with well-attended yearling sales from late August to early September, where each thoroughbred is sold for an astronomical price. Summer witnesses an orgy of polo and racing, but excellent riding programs and facilities are available year-round. The wonderful seafront mansion known as the *Hôtel Normandy,* for instance, offers vacation packages that include free access to the *Club Hippique d'Oxer* (Oxer Horse Club) and lessons in manège, dressage, and jumping. For additional details on the hotel, see *Romantic French Hostelries* in this section. Information: *Hôtel Normandy,* 38 Rue Jean-Mermoz, Deauville 14800 (phone: 31-98-66-22).

RIDING FACILITIES AND PROGRAMS

Equestrian holidays come in a variety of breeds. There are centers with riding instruction, multi-day horseback excursions, and week-long expeditions in horse-drawn carts. Highly organized centers provide expert instruction for every level of rider, including the beginner, while guest farms specialize in horseback *randonnées* (rambles) along their area's wooded paths and country roads, with accommodations that can vary from tent to straw-littered barn to cozy hotel. Pastoral-pure air, authentic country food, a relaxed pace, and an almost total absence of tourist hordes (and sometimes even motorized vehicles) are the chief allures. Each center can provide specific details on the *randonnées* it offers. Reserve well in advance, since horse farms and riding hotels always are small, family-run affairs with a loyal clientele. For more information about riding in France, contact the *Association Nationale pour le Tourisme Equestre et l'Equitation de Loisirs,* Ile Saint-Germain, 170 Quai de Stalingrad, Issy-les-Moulineaux 92130 (phone: 46-48-83-93).

Below, we offer a selective survey of the best equestrian programs France has to offer (listed alphabetically by city or town).

CENTRE EQUESTRE DE ZANIÈRES, Ardes-sur-Couze, Puy-de-Dôme A friendly atmosphere prevails at this family-oriented center specializing in week-long *randonnées* around the volcanoes, valleys, and lakes of this varied region. Accommodations are simple, both at the center and on trips into the surrounding area. The horses are well trained; the riders, who travel up to ten in a group, generally are highly accomplished. *Randonnées* are scheduled from May through September. It's also possible to leave a teenager behind in a specially designed riding program for young people. Information: *Centre Equestre de Zanières,* Ardes-sur-Couze 63420 (phone: 73-71-84-30).

LA CHEVAUCHÉE DES DEUX MERS, Aubiet, Gers Twice each summer, a dozen or so experienced riders cross southeastern France from the Atlantic to the Mediterranean, caravan-style. The 300-mile trip, which includes a stop in the enchanting fortress city of Carcassonne, is a wonderful fortnight's exploration of a seldom visited slice of the country. Information: *Le Cheval Vert,* Lussan, Aubiet 32270 (phone: 62-65-93-47).

CERCLE HIPPIQUE DU CHÂTEAU LA DOUVE, Le Bourge d'Ire, Maine-et-Loire This handsome hotel is a château that has been transformed with riders in mind. Facilities are located in the park that surrounds the hotel. Accommodations are more luxurious here than the often rustic lodgings found elsewhere. Information: *Cercle Hippique du Château La Douve,* Le Bourge d'Ire 49780 (phone: 41-61-54-54).

LES RANDONNÉES SAUVAGES DE L'HABITARELLE, Châteauneuf-de-Randon, Lozère For the hardy and adventurous, this place offers five- to eight-day riding odysseys in the Cévennes Mountains. Other routes go around the volcanoes of the Haut Vivarais area, through the Gorges du Tarn, or even across Corsica. The trips are for experienced riders only, in particular those unfazed by tentless, starlit nights in sleeping bags. Information: *Les Randonnées Sauvages de l'Habitarelle,* Châteauneuf-de-Randon, Lozère 48170 (phone: 66-47-90-10).

CLUB MÉDITERRANÉE, Pompadour, Limousin At this green paradise, riders wander around chestnut-shaded paths or take lessons in the covered riding school, while others can use the 22 tennis courts, the 9-hole pitch-and-putt golf course, and the heated pool. The regal facilities include a pony club for children. Information: *Club Med,* Domaine de Noailles, Arnac-Pompadour 19230 (phone: 55-73-39-00 or 55-97-30-00; 800-CLUB-MED).

FERME EQUESTRE DU VAL D'ADOUR, Rabastens de Bigorre, Hautes-Pyrénées In the high valley of the Adour River, this farm offers hour-long, weekend, and week-long riding programs in the lush farmland of a little-known corner of France not far from the *Haras de Tarbes,* the national stud farm, home of some magnificent examples of Anglo-Arabian stallions. Run by a family of horse breeders, this is a serious professional center which can guide a visitor from his or her first time in the saddle to the highest level of the sport. Mornings are usually spent on the trail; afternoons customarily are devoted to group instruction. Every sort of accommodation is available, from campsites on the farm to luxurious quarters at nearby hotels. The atmosphere is intimate, with no more than 10 riders accepted at any given time. Information: *Ferme Equestre du Val d'Adour,* Rabastens de Bigorre 65140 (phone: 62-96-59-44).

LES BEIGES, La Roche-l'Abeille, Haute-Vienne Set in a forest-bordered valley in a verdant and undisturbed region, this farm offers something for everyone—from three hours of daily instruction at the farm for the inexperienced to overnight excursions in the surrounding area with stops in neighboring farmhouses for more expert riders. Non-riders can join the latter group each evening, arriving in style in horse-drawn carriages. Teenagers who ride well can join week-long excursions especially designed for them or stay on their own at the farm for daily instruction. Information: *Les Beiges,* La Roche-l'Abeille 87800 (phone: 55-00-70-92).

CLUB EQUESTRE LOISIRS "LA GRANDE VIGNOBLE," St-Julien-de-Crempse, Dordogne Surrounded by acres of woods and meadows deep in the countryside, this converted manor house built in the days of Louis XIV offers luxurious accommodations, gleaming stirrups, and saddles that look as if they were crafted by Hermès. Aside from the outstanding riding facilities and instruction that completes the picture, there are tennis courts, a heated pool, programs for children, bikes to rent, and a sauna to soothe away sore muscles after an active day. Information: *Club Equestre Loisirs "La Grande Vignoble,"* St-Julien-de-Crempse 24140 (phone: 53-24-23-18; fax: 53-24-20-89).

L'ETRIER DU MONT-HEDIN, Tarzy, Signy-le-Petit, Ardennes The beautiful Champagne region is exceptionally well supplied with riding facilities. From *Easter* through August this one offers accommodations in rustic but comfortable quarters. Besides a complete program of riding instruction and excursions, there's glorious champagne to make every adventure just that much more effervescent. Information: *L'Etrier du Mont-Hedin,* Tarzy, Signy-le-Petit 08380 (phone: 24-54-32-52).

CARRIAGE TRADE

Lessons in the genteel art of carriage driving (*attelage* to the French) are offered in the exceedingly pleasant and refined surroundings of the Loire Valley and *Château Le Fresne,* home of the Marquis de Brantes, president of one of France's principal *Carriage Driving Association* chapters. A flexible schedule can be tailored to individual requests. Accommodations can be arranged at nearby country inns and bed and breakfast establishments. Information: Sue de Brantes, *Le Fresne,* Authon 41310 (phone: 54-80-33-04; fax: 54-80-34-41).

HORSE RACING

In France, horse racing is divided into three disciplines—*courses d'obstacles* (steeplechasing), *courses de plat* (flat racing), and *courses de trot* (trotting races, both mounted and with sulkies)—with a special racecourse (hippodrome) for each. Paris and its environs are the site of the country's more prestigious contests; for details on those, consult our *Paris* report in THE CITIES. The August racing season at Deauville, on the Normandy coast, is one of the country's major social and sporting highlights; the *Grand Prix de Deauville,* at the end of the month, is a highlight. From June to mid-September stately old Vichy offers the ultimate in stylish horse racing in an atmosphere of thermal baths, palm-lined promenades, and twirling white parasols; the *Grand Prix de Vichy* in late July is one of the high points. Chantilly, in the Ile-de-France, is the venue for the elegant *Prix du Jockey-Club,* which takes place in early June.

At most provincial courses racing is a casual affair, where it's possible to wander among the horse vans and watch trainers saddling up their charges. Some of the main provincial racing events are at Pau (Pyrénées-Atlantiques) throughout the winter; Craon (Mayenne) in August and September (especially the first weekend in September, the main meeting for the west of France); Corlay (at a particularly scenic location on a hill in central Brittany, southwest of St-Brieuc) in June and July; and at Saumur and Lion d'Angers (Maine-et-Loire) in spring and summer. Lion d'Angers also has a three-day-event course that attracts some of the top horse-trial riders worldwide. For additional information on France's horse-racing calendar, contact the *Fédération Nationale des Sociétés de Courses de France,* 22 Rue de Penthièvre, Paris 75008 (phone: 42-25-96-71), or check with local tourist offices.

Freewheeling by Two-Wheeler

To understand just how seriously the French have always taken the sport of bicycling, a visitor has only to consider the annual *Tour de France,* held in July. The world's premier bicycle competition, it has the French people cheering from the valleys of the Loire to the mountain passes of the Alps.

Though this competition is reserved for professional cyclists, the passion that spawned it is felt by many, and there are all kinds of other activities and competitions for the less serious at every level. Among them is a distance program, with merit certificates that recognize accomplishment in a variety of categories; those who cover a stipulated territory and pass through certain checkpoints in the various *départements,* complete certain short but difficult itineraries, or make certain long-distance trips may earn special certificates. For details, contact the *Fédération Française de Cyclotourisme* (*FFCT;* 8 Rue Jean-Marie-Jégo, Paris 75013; phone: 44-16-88-88; fax: 44-16-88-99).

Less ambitious visitors take advantage of the itineraries provided through the various regional societies of the *FFCT* (above). These *randonnées permanentes,* which can be followed by individuals or groups at any time of year and normally cover several hundred miles over country roads, are designed to be completed over a period of days or weeks, with stops specified at intervals of a dozen or so miles. While written in French, the place names, route numbers, and distances are comprehensible even to those who do not speak the language. The *FFCT* can supply specific information for all of the routes described below, as well as maps, information about where to rent multispeed bicycles, and a list of the train stations in France where simple one-speed bicycles may be rented and returned to another station. For information about organized biking tours all over France, contact *Bicyclub* (8 Pl. de la Porte-de-Champeret, Paris 75017; phone: 47-66-55-92). Some tour operators offering biking trips in France also are listed in GETTING READY TO GO.

BASQUE COUNTRY Using the seaside resort of Biarritz as the starting point, this excursion passes through the green hills of the French and Spanish Basque country to Bayonne, and to Bonloc, a popular rest stop along the pilgrimage route to Spain's Santiago de Compostela. After crossing into Spain at Arnéguy, it takes in Santesteben, known for its picturesque houses, and San Sebastián, which has a magnificent beach. In Fuenterrabía is a fine *parador,* once a medieval fortress and now an inn (phone: 943-642140 in Spain), which makes a pleasant overnight stop before the route returns once again to France and Ciboure, where the composer Maurice Ravel was born (and his house still stands). 337 miles (539 km).

BOURBONNAIS The ancient province of Bourbonnais, famous for its landscape, lies almost in the dead center of the country west of Burgundy. The area covered on this tour begins and ends in Vichy, famous for its mineral water and for having been the collaborationist government headquarters during World War II. Traveling west and then clockwise around the *département* of Allier, the route shows off soft mountains, an 11th-century church at Veauce, the Forêt Château-Charles, the Tartasse Valley near Ronnet, the ancient market town of Hérisson and its splendid ruined 14th-century château, the spa at Bourbon-l'Archambault that has been serving rheumatics since Roman times, the magnificent Romanesque church at Château-Montagne, and the museum of prehistory at Glozel. One of the most interesting areas is the Forêt-de-Tronçais, whose 26,000-acre oak grove is reputed to be the most beautiful in the country. 325 miles (520 km).

BRITTANY Beginning in cosmopolitan Nantes, this itinerary quickly leads into more rural scenery, taking in the fishermen's hamlet of Pont-St-Martin, the fortified city of Guérande, the eerie megaliths at Carnac, the rocky and surf-pounded coast at Quiberon, and Brittany's folkloric center, Quimper. Modern Brest and the islet of Mont-St-Michel—perhaps France's best-known monument after *Notre-Dame* and the *Eiffel Tower*—also are on the tour. 852 miles (1,363 km).

BURGUNDY Setting out from Dijon, the old capital of the Duchy of Burgundy, this trip meanders along winding country roads, through villages full of flower-bedecked stone buildings that date from the 16th century, and past immense cathedrals and imposing abbeys and châteaux. There is an undeniable tranquillity to it all. Going roughly counterclockwise around Burgundy, the route encompasses St-Germain-Source-Seine, where the famous river begins; the ruins of a 12th-century château at Maisey-le-Duc; and Ancy-le-Franc, where one of the most magnificent Renaissance châteaux in Burgundy is open to the public. Tonnerre, a comfortable small town on a hill full of vines and greenery, is another stop, as is Noyers, a handsome fortified city that has remained virtually unchanged since the Middle Ages, right down to the twisting outdoor stairways, the ancient stone walls, and the half-timbered architecture. Beaune, famous for its wine, is one of some three dozen other towns on the tour. 750 miles (1,200 km).

CALVADOS Best known for its eponymous apple brandy, this area of Normandy appeals to cyclists because of its diverse geography. The *FFCT* itinerary runs along the coast through the picturesque old port of Honfleur, takes in the splendid beaches of Deauville and Arromanches, visits the Louis XIII château in beautiful, peaceful Cérisy-la-Forêt (Cerisy Forest), and includes the Orne Valley and the caves and high rocky cliffs of "Swiss" Normandy, which center on Clécy. 287 miles (459 km).

CATHARIST SITES A large area of south-central France is known for its many fortresses and other remains from the 12th and 13th centuries, when it was inhabited by Cathari, members of a medieval Christian sect that believed that Christ was of angelic, rather than human, origin. The tour begins in Toulouse, known for its many churches and its famous *Hôtel de Ville* (Town Hall), and continues through Carcassonne, the 13th-century walled city that is Europe's largest fortress. Subsequent stops include the ancient blockhouse of Mirepoix, the ruins of the *Château de Puilaurens,* the fortified 14th-century village of Lagrasse, and the wine city of Béziers. 482 miles (771 km).

CHÂTEAUX OF THE LOIRE Probably no region of France is better suited to quiet pedaling than this area surrounding the quiet Loire River. The colorful villages, the spectacular valleys, and the beautiful châteaux combine to draw thousands of tourists each summer. The *FFCT* recommends four itineraries, all beginning in La Folie. The first takes in Balzac's birthplace at Tours and the châteaux near Vallière, Langeais, La Gaudinière, and Le Lude. The second, which travels southeast to Montbazon, famous for its ancient dungeon, includes the châteaux near Azay-sur-Indre, Montrésor, Valençay, Orbigny, and Montpoupon. The third heads west to the châteaux near Candé, Pont-de-Ruan, Chinon, Saumur, and Montsoreau. And the fourth follows an easterly route through Montrichard, Fougères-sur-Bièvre, Chambord, and St-Gervais-la-Forêt. 443 miles (709 km).

DORDOGNE That there are more than a thousand châteaux and country manors in this lush area of rolling hills, fern-carpeted forests, and cliff-edged rivers—more than in any other *département* in France—is just one of the charms of this tour. It begins in Périgueux, the capital of truffles and foie gras, and proceeds through one of the sections of the country that is richest in ruins and religious art. Splendid vistas are the norm, and there are innumerable small villages full of stone churches and old houses dating to the Middle Ages. Serene Brantôme is one of the highlights for its abbey founded by Charlemagne, its excellent restaurants, and the hyacinth-edged Dronne River that meanders through the village. 370 miles (592 km).

EDELWEISS ARIEGEOIS Ariège, in the vast, beautiful Pyrénées, is perfect for the conditioned cyclist. The tour begins in the heart of the Pyrénées in tiny Pamiers and includes prehistoric sites, pine forests, and a moving 12th-century monastery at Montjoie. 538 miles (861 km).

GIRONDE Anyone familiar with fine wine will recognize many of the stops on this tour of the green Bordeaux region, around the Dordogne: attractive little Pauillac, St-Emilion, Monségur, and the walled city of Blaye. Beginning in Bordeaux proper and moving through the Dordogne Valley before circling westward again, the tour spends a good deal of time southwest of the city in the quiet Landes forest, an amazing trail-crossed tract of regal conifers. Especially in the Médoc the terrain often is flat, and the parallel rows of vines, with every plant trimmed to the same height, are a study in elegant precision. 478 miles (765 km).

HAUTE-PROVENCE Covered with lavender fields and olive groves, this dry, mountainous region in southeast France offers exceptionally scenic terrain for the cyclist. The route begins at Dignes, the capital of the so-called "Lavender Alps," and extends spoke-like in four directions. The southern spoke travels through Moustier-Ste-Marie, an ancient village whose maze of alleys is set in the shadows of some fantastic boulders. East is picturesque Castellane, a village noted for Romanesque churches and magnificent views. To the north is Seyne-les-Alpes, where Louis XIV built an interesting citadel; the view from its ramparts is a favorite with visitors. The western route leads to the ancient fortress town of Sisteron, to Forcalquier, noted for its 16th-century Gothic fountain, and to the old market town of Manosque. 325 miles (520 km).

JOAN OF ARC ROUTE This pilgrimage, which runs from Lorraine through the Loire country to Normandy, begins in Domrémy-la-Pucelle, where the peasant girl was born in 1412, continues on a line through Tonnerre and Auxerre in Burgundy, passes through Chinon, and takes in Troyes, Reims, sections of Normandy, and Rouen, where Joan was executed in 1431. 934 miles (1,494 km).

MONT-BLANC TOUR A demanding route that circles Mont-Blanc, the highest peak in the Alps, this itinerary begins in Albertville at 1,132 feet, continues through the popular ski resorts of Megève and Chamonix, and penetrates into Switzerland, where, in the village of Col de la Forclaz, at 5,009 feet, it descends rapidly—with the Rhône Valley always in view—to the small Swiss town of Martigny, at 1,561 feet. This marks the beginning of a steep climb into Italy via an 8,100-foot mountain pass that has been well traveled since the Bronze Age. Aosta, in Italy, founded by Augustus in 25 BC, and Bourg-St-Maurice, back in France, are among the final stops. 200 miles (320 km).

Boating: France's Wonderful Waterways

Given France's vast coastline and 5,000 miles of inland rivers, canals, and lakes, it's little wonder that when the weekend rolls around, scores of pleasure seekers roll back the tarps of their boats and head out for some serious cruising. Avid sailors can challenge the waters of the Atlantic or Mediterranean and dock overnight in a charming old port town for a fine seafood meal in a waterside café. Or they may relax on the tame inland lakes. The canoe or kayak enthusiast can find adventure on the Loire, Rhône, and Vézère Rivers or in the white water of the Alps and Pyrénées. Also available are leisurely cruises on hired craft through the canals of Burgundy, Bordeaux, and the south of France. Boating novices can sign up for any number of sailing, cruising, or canoeing courses of varying duration.

Foreigners sailing their own boats in France must have a *permis de circulation,* a license available free of charge at French government tourist offices in foreign countries; depending on the size and type of vessel, other permits may be necessary as well, so check with the French tourist authorities before sailing to France.

What follows is a selective survey of France's best boating venues.

SAILING

The *Fédération Française de la Voile* (55 Av. Kléber, Paris 75016; phone: 44-05-81-00) has full details about sailing in France. Below, our favorite shores.

BRITTANY COAST Many sailors rave about the Raz de Sein, that stretch of rugged water off the westernmost point in France between the Pointe du Raz and the stony, isolated Ile de Sein. The rocky scenery is unequaled anywhere, but the wind can be fierce, and islanders call these waters the "Sailors' Graveyard," so be prepared. Farther down the coast in the Baie de la Forêt are the lovely fishing ports of Pont-Aven, a favorite retreat of the painter Gauguin, and Concarneau, where one- and two-week sailing courses are available throughout the year. The island-filled Golfe de Morbihan west of Vannes provides an opportunity to go for a sail in a *sinagot*, a traditional fisherman's boat. Many ports in Brittany offer sailing lessons. Information: *Fédération Française de la Voile* (see above) or the *Ecole de Voile les Glénans*, Quai Louis-Blériot, Paris 75016 (phone: 45-20-01-40).

CÔTE D'AZUR The Mediterranean teems with sailboats in summer, and it is easy to navigate the entire French section of the coastline—perhaps stopping in Monte Carlo for an evening at the casino and then setting out for a couple of days in Corsica. The loveliest section is the stretch between Cap Croisette and Cassis, where there are scores of secluded *calanques* (creeks with ports accessible only by water). The opportunity that these destinations offer to escape the madness of Marseilles and the other large Riviera harbors may well justify wrestling with a stiff eastern wind or even the mistral to reach them. Cassis is a charming port, with sand and pebble beaches; in July and August sailing courses lasting from one to three weeks are available. Information: *Maison de Cassis*, Pl. Pierre-Baragnon, Cassis 13260 (phone: 42-01-71-17).

EASTERN MEDITERRANEAN COAST West of Marseilles is the mouth of the Grand Rhône, and from Port St-Louis-du-Rhône it's possible to drive on up to Arles, Cézanne's favorite hideaway. En route, just shy of the fork of the Petit Rhône, is the exceptional bird sanctuary of the *Parc National de Camargue* (Camargue National Park). Near Sète at St-Gilles along the Petit Rhône is the fortification of Aigues-Mortes, whence St. Louis departed on an Egyptian crusade in 1248. Farther toward Sète and the Etang de Thau, a small bay, are the picturesque ports of Balaruc, Bouzigues, Marseillan, and Mèze, where there are sailing courses year-round. Information: *Comité Régional du Tourisme de PACA*, 2 Rue Henri-Barbusse, Marseilles 13006 (phone: 91-39-38-00).

NORTHERN COAST The small port of St-Valéry-en-Caux, about 20 miles (32 km) west of Dieppe and a bit removed from the heavy Channel traffic, makes a good starting point for northeasterly sails under the spectacular white cliffs that edge the English Channel. Before setting out, visit *Notre Dame* *du Port,* a 13th-century church, and the former residence of Henri IV next door. The Somme estuary, beyond Dieppe, is enlivened by the many varieties of birds that migrate there; on one side is beach-blessed Le Croitoy, on the other, St-Valéry-sur-Somme, a recommended port of call and one of the many points from which you can navigate by canal to Paris. Sailing lessons are available in July and August. For information about this and other sailing opportunities in Normandy, contact the *Comité Régional du Tourisme de Normandie,* 14 Rue Charles-Corbeau, Evreux 27000 (phone: 32-33-79-00; fax: 32-31-19-04).

SOUTHERN ATLANTIC COAST The hundred miles of coastline along the Landes Forest south of Bordeaux offer very few ports for yachts, and the Atlantic is generally rough and dangerous. However, there is nice, leisurely boating in the Bay of Arcachon and near St-Jean-de-Luz, not far from the Spanish border. The former is relatively calm, and the port itself has fine beaches and oyster beds. The rocky coastline outside the latter is more challenging, and the port at Ciboure is so small that it may be necessary to sail on into Spanish waters to find docking facilities. Information: *Comité Régional du Tourisme d'Aquitaine,* 2 Rue René-Cassin, Bordeaux 33000 (phone: 56-39-88-88; fax: 56-43-07-63).

CANOEING AND KAYAKING

As in North America, in France streams are graded in order of difficulty from categories I through VI, with VI being the most difficult and therefore suited to only the most accomplished sportspersons. Communities along the French rivers usually have canoe and kayak clubs to advise on conditions and arrange lessons and group outings. The *Fédération Française de Canoe/Kayak* (BP 58, Joinville-le-Pont 94340; phone: 45-11-08-50) can provide specifics on local clubs.

AVEYRON The Aveyron is only one of several fast-flowing rivers in the forested northwestern section of the *département* of Tarn; the Tarn and the Agoût Rivers also are recommended. Information: *Comité Régional du Tourisme,* 12 Rue Salambo, Toulouse 31200 (phone: 61-47-11-12).

DORDOGNE The trip on the Dordogne River toward the Garonne is magnificent, especially the 75 miles or so before the charming medieval village of Sarlat-le-Canéda, with its forested gorges and limestone rocks. From Argentat to Trémolat the water is category I and II. The only non-navigable point is at Beaulieu, about 15 miles downstream from Argentat, where it is necessary to portage past an obstruction. The tranquil Vézère, a tributary of the Dordogne, also is well suited to canoeing; the usual trip is from Montignac to Les Eyzies. Except just after a storm, when the waters swell and the current speeds up, the waters are swift but not dangerous. Points of interest en route include the unusual caves in the hills around Les Eyzies and Sarlat, farther downstream. For white-water trips, with or without instruction, the Gorges de Vézère has sections classed I and II for beginners and II, III, and IV for experienced kayakers. Information: *Office Départemental du Tourisme de la Dordogne,* 16 Rue Wilson, Périgueux 24009 (phone: 53-53-44-35; fax: 53-09-51-41), or the *Maison du Périgord,* 6 Rue Gomboust, Paris 75001 (phone: 42-60-38-77).

LOIRE France's longest river, which runs from its source high in the Massif Central to Nantes in Brittany and its mouth in the Atlantic, offers a wealth of possibilities. There are some lovely ruins of a château not far from the source, between Arlempdes and Goudet, and there are torrential waters farther downstream at the Gorges de Peyredeyre. The river, which is navigable all the way to the Atlantic, is rated category I from Roanne to Nantes. Information: *Comité Régional du Tourisme,* 2 Rue de la Loire, Nantes 44000 (phone: 40-48-24-20).

RHÔNE This is one of the most popular rivers among French canoeing and kayaking enthusiasts because it is navigable for almost 500 miles, from the Swiss city of Brig all the way to the Mediterranean. Anyone who manages to go the distance ends up on the Riviera—a suitable reward. The water is category II from Geneva to Lyons, category I the rest of the way.

RIVER AND CANAL CRUISING

There hardly exists a finer way to see the French countryside than to travel on a slow boat along some section of the nation's thousands of miles of river. Dozens of companies in France rent riverboats for leisurely cruises, with or without captains and accommodations. A handful of American firms also offer cruising through specified areas. For a list of organizations that organize cruises on French waterways and rent self-piloted boats in France, see GETTING READY TO GO.

ALSACE In the northeast corner of the country, the Grand Canal d'Alsace weaves in and out of the Rhine and runs along the Alsatian wine route south of Strasbourg. Adjoining canals—the Canal de la Marne au Rhin, which leads from Strasbourg into Lorraine, and the Canal du Rhône au Rhin, which crosses the region of Franche-Comté on its way to Burgundy—are also excellent for cruising. Information: *Association Départementale du Tourisme du Haut-Rhin, Hôtel du Département,* Colmar 68006 CEDEX (phone: 89-20-10-68; fax: 89-23-33-91).

BRITTANY The Nantes-Brest Canal, which ribbons through the heart of Brittany, provides access to many fine country hotels. But since the cruising speed on all canals in Brittany is limited to 3.5 mph (5.5 km), be prepared to take your time. The Vilaine River, which flows north to St-Malo, is another good destination. Information: *Syndicat d'Initiative/Office de Tourisme,* Pl. Parlement, Redon 35600 (phone: 99-71-06-04; fax: 99-71-01-59).

BURGUNDY The network of rivers and canals in this part of France happens to be especially dense. Here the rivers of the north and west of France—the Seine, the Loire, and the Marne—are connected to the rivers of the south and east—the Saône, the Rhône, and eventually the Rhine and even the Garonne—and cruising possibilities are limited only by time. The Canal de Briare, begun in the early 17th century and one of the oldest in France; the 19th-century Canal Latéral à la Loire, running along the middle section of the Loire; the Canal du Centre and the Canal de Bourgogne, in the heart of Burgundy; and the Canal de la Marne à la Saône and the Saône itself all provide wonderfully tranquil vantage points from which to view rural France. The Canal du Nivernais in particular provides a window on the beauties of Burgundy. Stopping every half hour or so to pass through the locks and exchange pleasantries with the keepers, tasting the marvelous wines and cheeses of the region, and docking in the afternoon to visit an interesting Romanesque church or a charming medieval town like Corbigny make for an unforgettable cruise. A good starting point is Auxerre, which has a splendid Gothic cathedral. Most boats have full accommodations. Information: *Office de Tourisme,* Pl. Darcy, Dijon 21022 (phone: 80-44-11-44), or the *Comité Régional du Tourisme de Bourgogne,* BP 1602, Dijon 21035 (phone: 80-50-10-20; fax: 80-30-59-45).

THE SOUTH The Canal du Midi runs southeast from the center of Toulouse through the corn and wheat fields of the Lauragais to Carcassonne, Béziers, and the Languedoc coast, in effect linking the Atlantic and the Mediterranean. Following its course gives you a real feeling for the south of France, with its red tile rooftops, its powder-blue sky, and its dark-green cypress trees at every turn. Adjacent canals include the Canal Latéral à la Garonne, running alongside the Garonne west of Toulouse and extending into the wine region of Bordeaux, and the Canal du Rhône à Sète, skirting the wild, marshy expanse of the Camargue from Sète to the Rhône River. Most boats in the area offer accommodations and meal facilities to allow for extensive cruises. Information: *Office de Tourisme, Donjon du Capitole,* Rue Lafayette, Toulouse 31000 (phone: 61-11-02-22).

Directions

Introduction

As the largest country in Western Europe, France lends itself to an infinite variety of driving tours. While visits to the major French cities reveal something of this diverse country and its people, there are aspects of Gallic life that can only be experienced outside city limits—in small fishing villages in Brittany or mountain campsites in the Pyrénées, on rocky beaches along the Côte d'Azur or on hairpin turns in the Alps, along the lush Loire Valley or the rugged terrain of Corsica, or through the wildlife preserve of the *Parc Régional de Camargue* (Camargue Regional Park).

France has captured the imagination of travelers for centuries. In this land that offers a range of climates, scenery, and cultures, there is much for visitors to absorb beyond its urban centers—museums, monuments, churches, and châteaux, to name the most obvious attractions. Outdoor activities—from swimming on the beaches of the northern, western, and southern coasts to skiing down the slopes of the Alps—also are part of the French experience.

What follows are 18 driving tours through France's very varied provinces. From Normandy to Provence, they traverse the country's most spectacular routes and roads, most arresting natural wonders, and most magnificent historical sites, offering unforgettable views of azure lakes, winding rivers, dramatic mountain peaks, and virgin forests. They travel through not only the most distinctively French regions of the country, but into areas where other heritages thrive. In Alsace and Lorraine, German dialects are spoken; in Brittany, Breton; in the Pyrénées, Euskara (the Basque language); and in Languedoc, an old Provençal tongue. There are journeys, too, into France's past; the routes enable travelers to follow in the footsteps of the early cavemen of Lascaux in the Dordogne or the Résistance fighters in the mountains of Corsica.

Each route begins with an introduction to the region, then describes suggested driving tours, each designed to take five to seven days. It is possible to string together several routes to form longer itineraries, but if you are pressed for time, you will find that by following any single itinerary you will see most of the sites and sights (and enjoy the best restaurants and accommodations) in the area. Each route offers suggestions for our favorite hotels and restaurants along the way, from simple pensions to deluxe châteaux, from cozy bistros to three-Michelin-star dining rooms.

These tours are not exhaustive—there is no effort to cover absolutely everything in each region. But the places recommended and activities described were chosen to make your drives memorable ones.

The Ile-de-France

The first thing to know about the Ile-de-France (Island of France) is that it is not an island at all. It is the region surrounding Paris to a radius of roughly 50 miles, and its name alludes to the fact that its boundaries are delineated by rivers and waterways. The Epte, the Aisne, the Eure, the Ourcq, the Autonne, the Essonne, and other rivers form an irregular circle around the area, while the mighty Marne and the regal, ubiquitous Seine coil through its heart. The rivers define the land here, and lend their names to the valleys that lie between them. The Ile-de-France can be divided into eight subregions: Paris and seven other *départements* (Seine et Marne, Yvelines, Essone, Hauts de Seine, Seine St-Denis, Val de Marne, and Val d'Oise) that wrap around the French capital, cradling it in a temperate basin.

Blessed with natural and manmade treasures, the Ile-de-France constitutes what art critic and author John Russell described as "one vast national park of fine living." This is the region of the French kings and their châteaux. The special quality of the light here has inspired numerous painters, while writers and poets have found their inspiration in the area's character.

No other part of France has a higher concentration of cathedrals and abbey churches, exquisite Gothic stone witnesses to a fervent religious past played out over centuries. The same locally quarried stone chiseled for these masterpieces was used in the châteaux and other countless small gems dotting the countryside.

The modern landscape of the Ile-de-France is full of contrasts: quaint market squares, medieval fortresses, deep woods, and serpentine rivers are juxtaposed against bleak industrial pockets and urban sprawl. Despite the encroachment of modern times and suburbanization, nature still firmly holds its own here, and there are places within minutes of the Paris periphery that are truly secret havens.

Besides the rivers and their soft green valleys, the most characteristic natural feature of the region is its majestic forests. Once princely hunting grounds, these tens of thousands of acres include Fontainebleau, Compiègne, Chantilly, and Rambouillet forests. Head out of Paris in almost any direction and you're likely to run into one of these woodlands, some tended and tamed, others wild and untouched by time. These forests, and the peaceful country-style inns that frequently can be found in their shadows, are rare pleasurable retreats for modern travelers.

We suggest that you make Paris your base for forays into the region, particularly if your time is limited. Sundays and Mondays, when many of Paris's shops and restaurants are closed, are ideal days to take advantage of the nearby countryside. For tourist information on sights of interest and accommodations in the Ile-de-France, write the *Comité Régional d'Ile-de-France* (73 Rue Cambronne, Paris 75015; phone: 45-67-89-41), or visit the Ile-de-France booth at the *Office du Tourisme de Paris* (127 Av. des Champs-Elysées; phone: 49-52-53-54). The latter is open daily (except *New Year's Day,* May 1, and *Christmas*).

The route suggested here begins at St-Denis in the north, then winds clockwise around the capital, occasionally spilling over into areas outside the official boundaries of the Ile-de-France. Every site on the route makes a comfortable day trip or can be combined with other stops to fill out a weekend jaunt.

Because of their proximity to Paris, country inns in the Ile-de-France tend to have city prices, and reservations almost always are required. For a double room for one night, expect to pay $200 or more in a very expensive hotel; $100 to $200 in an expensive one; $60 to $100 in a moderate place; and less than $60 in an inexpensive hotel. Most hotels listed below feature telephones, TV sets, and private baths in all of their rooms. However, some less expensive hotels may have private baths in only some of their rooms; it's a good idea to confirm whether your room has a private bath when making a reservation. Very few of the hotels in this temperate region, except a handful of deluxe establishments, have air conditioned rooms. Unless otherwise indicated, all hotels accept major credit cards and are open year-round.

For a dinner for two, with service (usually included in the bill), but not wine or drinks, expect to pay $150 or more at a very expensive restaurant; $105 to $150 at an expensive one; $60 to $105 at a moderate place; and less than $60 at an inexpensive restaurant. Unless otherwise noted, all restaurants are open for lunch and dinner. For each location, hotels and restaurants are listed alphabetically by price category.

ST-DENIS This otherwise dreary suburb is made visit-worthy by the *Basilique de St-Denis.* At the northern gate of Paris (off A1, about 2 miles/3 km north of the *Porte de la Chapelle*), it is perhaps one of the greatest, albeit one of the least visited, of the Ile-de-France's ecclesiastical monuments. Considered the cradle of French Gothic style, the church is noteworthy not only as an architectural milepost but also for its magnificent tombs of French kings and queens, which date back 12 centuries.

A church has stood on this holy ground since before the 5th century. Saint Denis, who is depicted throughout the church in stained glass and stone with his severed head in hand, was an evangelist. Along with two fellow missionaries named Rustique and Eleuthère, he brought Christianity to pagan Lutetia (later named Paris) in about AD 250. So successful were the trio at preaching that they were decapitated at Montmartre (whose name is said to derive from *mons martyrium,* or "Martyr's Mount") by leaders jealous of their influence. Legend has it that the decapitated Saint Denis picked up his head and walked north into the countryside until he collapsed. The spot where he fell and was buried became a pilgrimage site, and a modest abbey eventually was erected there.

At the behest of Saint Geneviève, work on a larger church began in the 5th century, and in 638, King Dagobert sponsored the construction of the abbey church. Nearly 600 years later, the Abbot Suger, Louis VII, and architect Pierre de Montreuil conspired to promote a new style that included the first rose windows, ogival arches, and buttresses (concealed at this early stage), marking the earliest manifestations of Gothic architecture. Much of what the visitor sees today is a result of excellent 19th-century restorations undertaken by Viollet-le-Duc.

Note the restored central portal representing the Last Judgment. The one on the right depicts the last communion of Saint Denis; that on the left, the torture of the saint and his fellow missionaries.

Equally impressive are the tombs grouped around the transept, a sketchbook in stone of France's monarchs and their loved ones. Among those buried here were Clovis, the first king of the Franks; Dagobert; Charles Martel; and Pepin the Short. Elaborate Renaissance structures, many of them created by the sculptor Germain Pilon, represent Catherine de Médicis and Henri II, Louis XII and Anne de Bretagne, and, most moving of all, Louis XVI and Marie-Antoinette. Most of the tombs now are empty—the royal remains were exhumed during the French Revolution and heaped into a nearby communal grave. There are other tombs in the crypt, as well as excavations of the churches that preceded the present one on this site. Regular guided tours of the transept are available for a fee. Visitors may also rent headphones with commentary in any of several languages. Open daily; closed Sunday mornings (phone: 48-09-83-54).

BEST EN ROUTE

Mets du Roy An inviting stone façade fronts this rather formal restaurant serving traditional fare. Closed Saturday lunch, Sundays, two weeks at *Easter,* and two weeks in July. Reservations advised. Major credit cards accepted. Across the square from the cathedral, at 4 Rue de la Boulangerie (phone: 48-20-89-74). Expensive.

Cour de l'Abbaye This casual restaurant leans heavily on the hearty fare of France's southwest; the service is friendly. Open daily for lunch, and for dinner Fridays only. Reservations unnecessary. Major credit cards accepted. Within walking distance of the cathedral, at 8 Rue de Boucherie (phone: 48-09-84-13). Inexpensive.

En Route from St-Denis Take N16 north for 12 miles (19 km) to Ecouen.

ECOUEN This drab town (pop. 5,000) is noteworthy for its superb *Château d'Ecouen,* and the *Musée National de la Renaissance* (National Museum of the

Renaissance) that it houses. Perched on a hill and surrounded by a park, *Château d'Ecouen* dates from the early 16th century and rivals *Chenonceaux* (see *The Loire Valley* in DIRECTIONS) in elegance, though far fewer travelers visit it. Its columned interior porticoes, delicately chiseled stone, and ribbed vaulting are Renaissance hallmarks. Anne de Montmorency, a powerful adviser to François I, commissioned two of the epoch's masters—Jean Goujon and Jean Bullant—to construct this palace for the king.

It would be hard to imagine a more appropriate home for a museum devoted to the Renaissance. In it is an outstanding assemblage of 16th- and early 17th-century pieces, particularly works from the decorative arts—furniture, carved wood panels, tapestries, ceramics, and enamels. Not to be missed is the 250-foot-long series of tapestries depicting the story of David and Bathsheba. Woven in silk, wool, and silver threads, it dominates the west wing of the museum's first floor and ranks among the most beautiful 16th-century tapestries in France. Note also the painted mantelpieces depicting biblical scenes in the style of the Fontainebleau School. The museum is closed during lunch hours, Tuesdays, and holidays. There's an admission charge (phone: 39-90-04-04).

Before leaving Ecouen, visit the *Eglise St-Acceul*, near the center of town. Its remarkable stained glass windows, attributed to Jean Cousin, date from 1545. Jean Bullant, who was responsible for much of the design of the *Château d'Ecouen*, is thought to be the architect of this church.

En Route from Ecouen Take N16 for 4 miles (6 km), and then turn west on to D922 and D909 to *Royaumont*.

ROYAUMONT This is one of the best preserved medieval abbeys in France. Founded in 1228 by Blanche of Castille, then Regent of France, and her 12-year-old son, the future Louis IX (Saint Louis), this immense Cistercian abbey has a regal character reflected in its name. The wealth and beauty still apparent here attest to the protection and interest lavished on Royaumont by kings after Louis IX. Visit the vaulted refectory with its five monolithic columns and the tomb of Henri of Lorraine sculpted by the artist Coysevox (phone: 30-35-40-18).

En Route from Royaumont Continue northeast on N16 for a few more miles to Chantilly.

CHANTILLY This town is famous for its château, its park, and its racetrack, on which horse races have taken place since 1836. The surrounding 5,187-acre Forêt de Chantilly (Chantilly Forest) is crisscrossed by roads and horse trails, many of them closed to automobiles. Over the last 2,000 years, five different châteaux have stood on this site. The Montmorency family owned Chantilly's château until 1632, when it passed into the possession of the Prince de Condé. The present château was built between 1875 and 1881 by Nicolas-François Mansart at the behest of the Duc d'Aumale, a son of King Louis-Philippe. Resembling an island rising out of the surrounding moat, the château is small but exceptionally elegant. It now houses the *Musée Condé,* an excellent museum with over 2,000 artworks, including more than 600 oils by French, Flemish, and Italian masters of the 16th through 18th centuries. The collection also features some superb manuscript illuminations from the 15th and 16th centuries, including *Les Très Riches Heures du Duc de Berry,* a 15th-century book of hours which is considered the finest extant example of its kind. You also can tour other parts of the château, including the library, with its prodigious collection of rare books. Closed during lunch hours November through February, and Tuesdays; admission charge (phone: 44-57-03-62 or 44-57-08-00).

The château's stables have been transformed into the *Musée Vivant du Cheval* (Living Museum of the Horse), which is open daily in May and June; closed Tuesday mornings July and August; Tuesdays in April, September, and October; mornings and Tuesdays November through March; and the first two weeks of December. There's an admission charge (phone: 44-57-13-13). Also visit the chapel, where the descendants of the last owner gather for Sunday services. Take time, as well, to wander through the 17th-century gardens and park, created by the renowned royal landscaper Le Nôtre. Among the other buildings of interest in the park are the *Maison de Sylvie,* named for the Duchesse de Montmorency, who hid Théophile de Viau here after he was condemned to death for his licentious poems. The house, rebuilt in 1684, later was the site of a mysterious romantic liaison that ended in the death in a "hunting accident" of the Duc de Joyeuse, Louis de Melun. It is closed year-round, but can be seen from the outside. Connected to the main château is the *Petit Château,* a lovely castle built in 1560 by Jean Bullant. It is closed Tuesdays.

BEST EN ROUTE

Hostellerie du Lys A modest 35-room hotel in a calm, beautiful park. There is a restaurant on the premises. 63 Av. Septième, Lys-Chantilly (phone: 44-21-26-19; fax: 44-21-28-19). Moderate.

Le Relais Condé Small and bright, with a beamed ceiling and huge stone fireplace, this restaurant serves classic fare, including sweetbreads and a good selection of fish. Closed Mondays. Reservations advised. Major credit cards accepted. 42 Av. du Maréchal-Joffre (phone: 44-57-05-75). Moderate.

En Route from Chantilly St-Leu-d'Esserent, 3 miles (5 km) northwest of Chantilly via N16 on D44, is the site of a mellow, beautiful 12th-century stone church. Renowned for its architectural excellence, it is in a prime location, with a wonderful view of the Oise River. From here, head east on N924 to the charming town of Senlis.

SENLIS Dominating this town is the *Ancienne Cathédrale de Notre-Dame* (Pl. Notre-Dame), which was begun in 1153. Of particular interest is the portico, dedicated to the Virgin and used as the prototype for the porticoes of the cathedrals of Chartres, Paris, and Reims. Also worth a visit are the old *Eglise St-Pierre* (Pl. St-Pierre; phone: 44-53-06-40); the *Château Royal* (Pl. du Parvis Notre-Dame); and, in front of the château, the *Musée de la Vénerie* (Hunting Museum). The museum is closed Mondays, Tuesdays, and Wednesday mornings; there's an admission charge (phone for both the château and the museum: 44-53-00-80, ext. 1315). The *Enceinte Gallo-Romaine,* a Gallo-Roman defense wall on the château's perimeter, provides a good vantage point from which to view all the principal monuments.

En Route from Senlis Take the D932 for 19 miles (30 km) to Compiègne.

COMPIÈGNE On the banks of the Oise, this village is famous for its palace (Pl. du Palais). While the exterior is somewhat austere, the rich and exquisite interior has been beautifully preserved. It's closed Tuesdays.

Compiègne has played a significant role in French history: Most of the kings of France visited it at one time or another, and Joan of Arc was taken prisoner here in 1430. More recently, the armistice of November 11, 1918, was signed here (the exact site—Clairière de l'Armistice—is marked in a clearing in the woods surrounding the palace). Tragically, from 1941 to 1944, Compiègne served as a deportation center for some French Jews en route to concentration camps.

The forest of Compiègne, with nearly 35,000 acres, has majestic avenues, ponds, and picturesque villages, such as Vieux-Moulin and St-Jean-aux-Bois. Just beyond the forest, via D85, is the splendid 12th century château-fortress of *Pierrefonds,* once the property of Napoleon. It's closed Tuesdays and during lunch hours; there's no admission charge.

BEST EN ROUTE

A la Bonne Idée Peaceful countryside surrounds this 24-room hostelry, which has a fine restaurant. St-Jean-aux-Bois, 7 miles (11 km) southeast of Compiègne via D332 and D85 (phone: 44-42-84-09). Moderate.

En Route from Compiègne Retrace the route back to Senlis and turn southeast onto N330 toward Meaux. Seven miles (11 km) south is the town of Chaâlis.

CHAÂLIS Here are the picturesque ruins of a 13th-century Cistercian abbey, with a lovely rose garden. It's closed Tuesdays; there's an admission charge. Also here is a château, a park north of the entrance to the château, and a museum containing the *Galerie du Souvenir de Jean-Jacques Rousseau,* three rooms devoted to memorabilia of Rousseau, who died in 1778 in Ermenonville, 2 miles (3 km) south. The museum is closed Tuesdays and from early November through early March; there's an admission charge (phone for information on all of the above Chaâlis sites: 44-54-00-01).

En Route from Chaâlis Continue on N330 for 15 miles (24 km) south to Meaux.

MEAUX A market town (pop. 50,000) in the center of the wheat fields of the Brie plain, Meaux (pronounced *Mow*) is renowned for its rich, creamy brie cheese and for a bishop named Jacques-Bénigne Bossuet, who was known for the perfection of his prose style.

Bossuet, one of the city's most illustrious citizens, served for 12 years as tutor to the young dauphin. In 1682 his grateful student, then Louis XIV, named Bossuet bishop of Meaux. Bossuet held the post for 22 years. His religious and moral convictions, as well as his literary gift, earned him a place in posterity under the title L'Aigle de Meaux (the Eagle of Meaux). In his vast library, Bossuet composed five famous eulogies—most notably the funeral oration for Marie-Thérèse, Louis XIV's wife.

Meaux's 14th-century *Cité Episcopale,* in the heart of the Old City, is one of the rare bishopric complexes in France that has remained almost entirely intact. The *Cathédrale St-Etienne,* constructed between the 12th and the 13th centuries, illustrates the evolution of the Gothic style: The elegant south façade is Rayonnant Gothic, while the main façade is later Flamboyant Gothic. Connected to the cathedral is the 13th-century chapter house, with a covered 16th-century staircase. Forming a rectangular courtyard with the chapter house and the cathedral is the *Ancien Evêché* (Old Episcopal Palace), built during the 12th century and modified in the 17th century. Today, it houses a museum that displays Bossuet's personal effects and writings.

In the chapel is a collection of sacred art, including medieval sculpture, fabrics, and religious relics. Part of the palace displays works of art by regional painters and other artists, including Millet, Courbet, and Van Loo. The palace complex is closed Tuesdays and holidays; there is an admission charge (phone: 64-34-84-45). From here, visit Le Nôtre's beautiful miter-shape garden and the old ramparts, parts of which date from the 4th century. The terrace atop the ramparts affords a beautiful view of the garden, the palace, and the cathedral.

Visit the nearby market area and the core of medieval streets that wrap around it. The first *halle* (market) was built here in 1722; the current structure is stocked with the best food products from the generous Brie plain. Be sure to pick up a wedge of the area's famous cheese.

A spectacular son-et-lumière show takes place in the summer on Friday and Saturday evenings in the courtyard of the chapter house; check with the tourist office (2 Rue Notre-Dame; phone: 64-33-02-26) for performance schedules. It's closed Sundays.

BEST EN ROUTE

Champs de Mars Locals recommend this traditional establishment for its consistent good quality regional fare and pleasant ambience. Closed Tuesday lunch, Friday dinner, and weekends. Reservations advised. Major credit cards accepted. 16 Av. Victoire (phone: 64-33-13-96). Expensive.

En Route from Meaux Take A4 approximately 15 miles (24 km) west to the Marne-la-Vallée/Val d'Europe exit and *Euro Disneyland.*

EURO DISNEYLAND The $4.5 billion European home-away-from-home of Mickey, Minnie, Donald, et al. opened in 1992. More than 11 million visitors passed through in its first year alone (though attendance figures still failed to live up to Disney's expectations). At press time the park was experiencing serious financial difficulties, and although it was recently saved from ruin by the sale of most of its shares to a single investor, its future remains uncertain. Familiar Disney attractions include Main Street USA, Frontierland, Adventureland, Fantasyland, and Discoveryland (known as Tomorrowland in the US parks), although there are some French additions, such as a fire-breathing dragon at Sleeping Beauty's castle and a theater that features videos and live entertainment (it turns into a disco at night). Disney-philes can enjoy a variety of shops, restaurants, an 18-hole golf course, and *Festival Disney,* an entertainment center and the site of the *Buffalo Bill Wild West Show.* The park is open daily. A special, reduced-price admission for "Star Nights" is offered for adults who enter the park after 5 PM. Note that this *Disney* park and its hotels are much pricier than their US counterparts (phone: 64-74-30-00).

BEST EN ROUTE

For *Euro Disneyland* hotel reservations, ask for an English-speaking operator if necessary (phone: 60-30-60-53; 407-W-DISNEY in the US; fax: 60-30-60-65.) All rooms accommodate up to four people, and cabins at *Camp Davy Crockett* accommodate six. For a double room at *Euro Disneyland,* expect to pay about $350 a night in a very expensive hotel; $250 in an expensive one; $150 in a moderate place; and $100 in an inexpensive hotel.

Disneyland This deluxe gingerbread-style hotel, with 500 rooms and 21 suites, is reminiscent of a turn-of-the-century Victorian hostelry. There are four restaurants, a bar, a lounge, a health club, an indoor heated pool, and shops (phone: 60-45-65-00; fax: 60-45-65-33). Very expensive.

New York Designed by Michael Graves to look like a cluster of Manhattan buildings, this 610-unit property's interiors are pure Art Deco. There are two restaurants, a health club, two tennis courts, a pool, and a skating rink designed to resemble the one in Rockefeller Center (phone: 60-45-73-00; fax: 60-45-73-33). Expensive.

Camp Davy Crockett Those longing for pine trees and squirrels can stay in one of the 181 campsites created to evoke the American "great outdoors." The re-created forest offers secluded wooded areas studded with log-cabin-style trailers; there are also many areas where you can simply pitch a tent. Each of the 414 log cabins accommodates up to six people, but none has a private bath; comfort stations with showers and restrooms are located nearby, as are an indoor pool and laundry facilities. The campsite is laced with winding nature trails and bicycle and jogging paths (phone: 60-45-69-01; fax: 60-45-69-37). *Moderate.*

Cheyenne More family-oriented than the other *Euro Disney* properties, it simulates a Wild West frontier town, complete with a log fort and observation tower, a corral, and a covered wagon. Each of the 1,000 rooms has bunk beds for children; two restaurants and a bar complete the picture (phone: 60-45-62-00; fax: 60-45-62-33). *Moderate.*

Newport Bay Club Dormer windows and awnings, an expansive front porch, and even a croquet lawn distinguish this property, which is intended to resemble a Rhode Island seaside resort. There are 1,098 rooms and 15 suites, an indoor and an outdoor pool, a health club, and three restaurants (phone: 60-45-55-00; fax: 60-45-55-33). *Moderate.*

Sequoia Lodge Here are 1,011 rooms and 14 suites, set in what looks like a US national park. On the premises are six lodges, three restaurants with garden views, a fireplace lounge, an indoor and an outdoor pool, and even two rivers. The rooms have patchwork quilts and checkered curtains, all designed to recall the atmosphere of a hunting lodge. Amenities include a health club, a bar, and shops (phone: 60-45-51-00; fax: 60-45-51-33). *Moderate.*

Santa Fe This adobe-style property has 1,000 smallish rooms. Four complexes are reached by trails landscaped with New Mexican flora, and the decor uses artifacts and desert tones that conjure up the southwest US. There's a Tex-Mex restaurant on the premises (phone: 60-45-78-00; fax: 60-45-78-33). *Inexpensive.*

En Route from *Euro Disneyland* Take D231, which intersects A4 just before the turnoff to *Disneyland,* southeast to Provins.

PROVINS Nowhere in the Ile-de-France are roses more prevalent than in Provins (pop. 12,000). According to legend, it was Thibaud IV, King of Navarre, Comte de Champagne, and religious crusader, who imported the first rose to France on his return to Provins from the Holy Land in the 13th century. He brought it as a gift to Blanche of Castille, his cousin and the mother of Saint Louis. Not long after, the red "rose Gallica," which came to be called *"La Rose de Provins,"* was incorporated into the coat of arms of Edmund of Lancaster when he married the widow of Henri le Gros, Comte de Champagne; here, as the emblem of the house of Lancaster, it gave its name to the 15th-century Wars of the Roses. Ever since it arrived, the rose has flourished in the fertile Brie plain, symbolizing the prosperity of this town, which remains one of France's most important and least discovered medieval relics.

During the Middle Ages, Provins was the third largest city in France after Paris and Rouen, boasting some 80,000 residents. Behind the city's wealth was the *Foire de Champagne,* a twice-yearly trade fair, sponsored by the powerful Counts of Champagne, that attracted merchants from all over Europe.

The Ville Haute (Upper Town), a fortification on a promontory jutting out over the valleys of the Voulzie and the Durteint rivers, already was a key post in 800, when Charlemagne sent his governors to oversee the settlement. The Ville Basse (Lower Town) was founded in 1049, when one of the Counts of Champagne built a chapel in the chestnut forest below. By the 10th century, powerful Provins was even minting its own currency.

Numerous vestiges of Provins's former prominence remain. The wide stone ramparts of the Ville Haute—which date from the 12th and 13th centuries—are reminiscent of the famous walled city of Carcassonne. Visit the *Porte St-Jean* and the *Porte de Jouy,* and walk along the ramparts or stroll down the quaint, interior cobbled streets. Near the edge of the Ville Haute is the pride of Provins, the *Tour de César,* a curious 150-foot-high stone tower built over the foundations of a 12th-century dungeon. The wall at its base, added by the British in 1432 when they occupied the tower during the Hundred Years' War, was dubbed "English Pie." When the French recaptured the tower, they hurled the executed English into the moat, which henceforth became known as the "English Pit." The tower is open daily; no admission charge.

Nearby is the *Eglise St-Quiriace* (phone: 64-00-05-31). Work on the present structure began in the 12th century, but its completion was plagued by lack of funds, and the façade wasn't added until nearly four centuries later. Shortly afterward, a fire destroyed many of *St-Quiriace*'s early treasures, though the 12th-century choir stalls and the north and south doorways (built during the 12th and 13th centuries) remain.

Provins has an exceptional number of underground passages. Dug over 1,000 years ago, these formed a bizarre labyrinth, winding from the Ville Basse to the Ville Haute. Whether they were used as simple refuges, places of worship, or for meetings of secret societies (whose symbols are carved in the earthen walls) is unknown. Guided tours in English of the only part of the passages open to tourists are available for a fee; they begin at the *Hôtel-Dieu* on Rue St-Thibault. This was the 12th-century palace of the Comtesses de Blois and Champagne, notable for its 13th-century portal and Renaissance stone altarpiece. Beneath the palace is the vast vaulted gallery from which tours depart. Consult the tourist office (Pl. Honoré-de-Balzac; phone: 64-60-26-26) for details on days and times; the office is closed Sundays.

Also worth visiting is the *Eglise St-Ayoul,* on the site of the first chapel built in the Ville Basse. Parts of it date from the 12th century, though much of it was rebuilt during the 16th century. If you visit in June, be sure to attend the colorful medieval festival that takes place every year in the Ville Haute (check with the tourist office for dates).

A worthwhile side trip is to the *Eglise St-Loup-de-Naud,* 4 miles (7 km) southwest on D403 and D49. A beautiful little building, it has a magnificent 12th-century main door and is surrounded by sculpture that rivals Chartres's cathedral portals. In 1432, the English destroyed the monastery that stood here.

BEST EN ROUTE

Croix d'Or Claiming to be the oldest inn in France, this 13th-century stone hostelry has five spacious rooms. Both of the dining rooms are warmed by great hearths. Restaurant closed Sunday dinner and Mondays. 1 Rue des Capucines (phone: 64-00-01-96). Moderate.

Aux Vieux Remparts In the newer part of this structure are a garden and 25 modern rooms. The older section houses a rustic, beamed restaurant, with a menu featuring refined interpretations of local specialties, most notably fish dishes. In the Ville Haute, at 3 Rue Couverte (phone: 64-08-94-00). Moderate.

En Route from Provins Take N19 west to the junction of N36 and follow it south to *Vaux-le-Vicomte,* a 17th-century château and park that ranks among the most beautiful in Europe. Many of the splendid rooms of *Vaux-le-Vicomte* are open to the public daily. Special candlelight visits are offered on the second and last Saturdays of each month. There's an admission charge (phone: 64-14-41-90). For a detailed description of the château, see *Celebrated Châteaux and Cathedrals* in DIVERSIONS.

Continue south on N36 past Melun to the forest and town of Fontainebleau, 39 miles (63 km) from Provins.

FONTAINEBLEAU Set in 50,000 acres of forest, this fabulous Renaissance palace was the old hunting preserve of the kings of France. Today the grounds are open to the public, and picnicking, hiking, or horseback riding among the trees, ravines, and ponds makes a perfect counterpoint to a day of city sightseeing. It's closed during lunch hours, Tuesdays, *New Year's Day,* May 1, and *Christmas.* There's an admission charge (phone: 64-22-27-40). For a detailed description of the palace, see *Celebrated Châteaux and Cathedrals* in DIVERSIONS.

BEST EN ROUTE

L'Aigle Noir At this elegant, family-run establishment facing the château gardens, the style is Napoleonic—fittingly grand lodgings for visitors to the château of which the emperor was so fond. The 57 units include five suites; there's also an elegant, one-Michelin-star restaurant, an indoor pool, a workout room, and a courtyard garden. Near the heart of the city, at 27 Pl. Napoléon-Bonaparte (phone: 64-22-32-65; fax: 64-22-17-33). Expensive.

En Route from Fontainebleau On the edge of the forest lies Barbizon, made famous as an artists' and writers' colony in the 19th century by the likes of Honoré Daumier, Alfred de Troyon, and George Sand. The Barbizon school of painters was founded by Théodore Rousseau; just behind the *Monument aux Morts,* a war memorial, is his house (55 Grande-Rue; phone: 60-66-22-38). It's closed Tuesdays; weekend lunch hours from April through September (except holidays); and mornings from October through March.

BEST EN ROUTE

Hôtellerie du Bas-Bréau In existence since 1867, it has housed such personages as Robert Louis Stevenson and Napoleon III. A Relais & Châteaux member, the hostelry boasts 12 rooms, seven suites, and a separate villa, all furnished with antiques and fine linen, with modern bathrooms. There's also an intimate bar and a one-Michelin-star restaurant, warmed by a flickering fire in fall and winter, though some have complained of the chilly service. An outdoor pool and clay tennis court round out the amenities. Hotel and restaurant closed January. Reservations necessary. Major credit cards accepted. 22 Rue Grande, Barbizon (phone: 60-66-40-05; fax: 60-69-22-89). Very expensive.

En Route from Barbizon Head toward Paris via A6 and turn west on N446 for a tour through what many French consider the prettiest countryside in the Ile-de-France—the Vallée de Chevreuse. Follow N446 to the intersection with N118, then go north until you reach Saclay, then southwest on N306. Picturesque villages abound: Châteaufort, named for a 12th-century fortress that once stood here; St-Rémy-lès-Chevreuse; St-Lambert; Dampierre; and Les Vaux de Cernay, one of the loveliest valleys in France. The 16th-century château in Dampierre, with its large park designed by Le Nôtre, is particularly noteworthy. Early morning tours are offered for a fee from April through September. It's open daily; there's an admission charge (phone: 30-52-53-24). Just south of Les Vaux de Cernay on N306 is *Rambouillet,* the château that served as a rural retreat for Louis XVI and Napoleon and is used today by the French President. Originally a medieval fortress, it retains its impressive 14th-century tower. The château is open to tourists when Mitterrand is not around; closed during lunch hours and Tuesdays. There's an admission charge (phone: 34-83-00-25).

From Rambouillet, take N10 for 19 miles (31 km) to Versailles.

VERSAILLES The construction of *Versailles* nearly bankrupted France. About 6,000 people once lived in this incredibly lavish palace, and its vast gardens, laid out by the royal landscape designer Le Nôtre in the formal French style, are spread over 1800 acres. A river was diverted to keep the 600 jets of its fountains flowing. A gleaming monument to the French monarchy at its most ostentatious, *Versailles* epitomizes the excesses that sparked the French Revolution, changing the course of history. The palace is under continuous restoration, so be prepared for temporary closings of certain rooms. To get the most from your visit, join an English-language tour or read up in advance. (For further details, see *Celebrated Châteaux and Cathedrals* in DIVERSIONS.) *Versailles* is closed Mondays; guided tours in English are available from 10 AM to 3:30 PM. There is an admission charge for the château, but not for the gardens. The *Grand Trianon* and the *Petit Trianon* are closed Mondays, and weekday lunch hours from October through April; there's an admission charge for each (phone: 30-84-74-00).

BEST EN ROUTE

Trianon Palace In operation since 1911, Versailles's most prestigious hotel has 157 rooms and 42 suites, plus a superb two-Michelin-star restaurant, *Les Trois Marches.* For additional details, see *Romantic French Hostelries* in DIVERSIONS. Restaurant closed Sundays, Mondays, and August. 1 Bd. de la Reine (phone: 30-84-38-00 for the hotel; 39-50-13-21 for the restaurant; 800-772-3041 for both; fax: 39-51-57-79). Very expensive.

En Route from Versailles Take A86 and D2 southeast to nearby Châtenay-Malabry, where you'll find the *Maison de Chateaubriand* (87 Rue de Chateaubriand, Vallée aux Loups; phone: 47-02-08-62), the former home of the writer and today a museum dedicated to him and his fellow Romantics. Closed mornings and Mondays; open for group visits only Tuesdays and Thursdays. There's an admission charge.

From the *Maison de Chateaubriand,* Sceaux is 2 miles (3 km) northeast.

SCEAUX Even in this region of lush woods and kings' gardens, *Sceaux* (pronounced *Sew*) stands out, with its cascading fountains, reflecting pools, grand canal, and precisely manicured, emerald lawns. In 1670, Colbert, the minister of buildings for Louis XIV, called on the greatest architectural and landscaping talents of the time to contribute to this grandiose project; the collaborators included Claude Perrault, Le Brun, Girardon, Coysevox, and Le Nôtre. The inauguration in 1677, with the Sun King as honored guest, was a spectacular affair, including the first performance of Racine's *Phèdre.* Transformed into a de rigueur stop for royalty and nobility, Sceaux entered its golden age.

About two decades after Louis XIV and his mistress (later wife) Mme. de Maintenon were received at Sceaux, their son, the Duc de Maine, bought the château and its gardens. His ambitious wife, the Duchesse de Maine, added to Sceaux's renown with her lively salons and spectacular festive evenings, called *nuits de Sceaux,* that drew *tout* Paris and Versailles. The duchess entertained her illustrious guests with productions of plays by Racine and Molière, which were performed in the *Orangerie* (northeast of the château), constructed by Jules Hardouin-Mansart in 1684. To the right of the *Orangerie* is the *Pavillon de l'Aurore,* built by Perrault, and behind it a series of neatly kept French gardens.

Colbert's sumptuous 17th-century château was replaced in the 19th century by the more modest one that stands today, nearly overwhelmed by the park's grandeur. Since 1937 the château has housed the *Musée de L'Ile-de-France* (Museum of the Ile-de-France), which documents the history and topography of the region. It's open daily; admission charge (phone: 46-61-06-71).

Take time to wander through the grounds to the west and south of the château. Laid out by Le Nôtre, this is one of the most beautiful public parks in the Paris region. Most spectacular is the *Allée de la Duchesse* leading to the *Grandes Cascades,* where tumbling water flows down 10 broad terraces into a sculpture-flanked, octagonal pool. To the west is the Grand Canal; beyond a putting-green-perfect lawn is the curious *Pavillon de Hanovre,* which was constructed in 1760 on Paris's Boulevard des Capucines, with funds extorted from Hanoverians during the Seven Years' War. The structure was moved to Sceaux in 1832. (It is not open to the public.)

Exit the park at the northwestern gate to visit the town. Visit the 16th-century *Eglise St-Jean-Baptiste,* which houses some mementos of the Duc and Duchesse du Maine, as well as a medallion of the Virgin, attributed to Coysevox. The French fabulist Florian is buried in the *Jardin des Félibres,* behind the church, where there are busts of Mistral and other provincial poets. Here also are the tombs of Pierre and Marie Curie. Nearby is yet another garden, the *Jardin de la Ménagerie.* Sceaux's little winding main street is a quaint pedestrian walkway lined with shops, many selling cheese, meat, and bread perfect for a picnic.

En Route from Sceaux Head north toward Paris on N20, then go west on the ring road until you reach N13. Take N13 west to the château of *Malmaison.*

MALMAISON This château was bought by Josephine Bonaparte in 1799, three years after her marriage to Napoleon. It became the empress's favorite residence; she settled here after her divorce in 1809 and stayed until her death in 1814. It now is a museum containing impressive artworks of the Napoleonic period, as well as some of the house's original furnishings and a survey of the era's history through documents and mementos. The château is closed during lunch hours and Tuesdays; there's an admission charge (phone: 47-49-20-07).

En Route from Malmaison Continue on N13 for 5 miles (8 km) to St-Germain-en-Laye.

ST-GERMAIN-EN-LAYE This former home of kings is today a favorite weekend retreat for Parisians. The gardens and terraces are splendid, and the extensive forest surrounding the town offers all manner of recreational activity. The château was begun during the 12th century but completely rebuilt in the 16th century to bring it up to Renaissance standards. Two floors now are occupied by the *Musée des Antiquités Nationales,* which houses prehistoric and Celtic artifacts, plus early Gallic tools, jewelry, ceramics, and other objects dating up to the time of Charlemagne. It is closed Tuesdays; there's an admission charge (phone: 34-51-53-65).

The town itself is one of the most chic in the Paris environs. The pedestrian shopping street that curves away from the château leads to boutiques-lined streets that are worth exploring. Also visit the *Musée du Prieuré* (Priory Museum; 2 *bis* Rue Maurice-Denis; phone: 39-73-77-87), a few minutes' walk southwest of the main shopping streets. Dedicated to the works of artists from the Symbolist and the Nabis schools and particularly to the museum's benefactor, artist Maurice Denis, the museum has a noteworthy collection of works from the mid-19th through the mid-20th century. Denis made this former hospital his home and studio from 1914 to 1943. Be sure to see *La Chapelle St-Louis,* the chapel of the old hospital, which Denis decorated in blue frescoes and stained glass. The museum is closed Mondays and Tuesdays; there's an admission charge.

BEST EN ROUTE

La Forestière A charming, traditional country inn with modern conveniences (recently renovated), set among beautiful gardens, this Relais & Châteaux member has 24 rooms and six suites. There's also a fine restaurant, *Cazaudehore,* that serves classic cuisine and Basque specialties such as *pipérade* (eggs with peppers, ham, and hot sausages). Restaurant closed Mondays. Reservations necessary. MasterCard and Visa accepted. 1 Av. Président-Kennedy (phone: 39-73-36-60, hotel; 34-51-93-80, restaurant; fax: 39-73-73-88). Expensive.

Pavillon Henri IV This old-fashioned hostelry has 42 plush rooms and apartments, and a delightful atmosphere. There's also a pleasant restaurant (where, incidentally, béarnaise sauce was first concocted) overlooking the Seine Valley. 21 Rue Thiers (phone: 39-10-15-15; fax: 39-73-93-73). Expensive.

Auberge Morainvilliers An attractive country inn and restaurant, it's set in private gardens with a pool. Morainvilliers-Orgeval, west of St-Germain-en-Laye via N13 and D198 (phone: 39-75-87-57). Moderate.

Brasserie du Théâtre The front room of this bustling, archetypally French eatery provides a great view of the château, just across the square. The decor is Art Deco; the service, friendly. The food is classic brasserie fare, including a fresh raw bar, grilled meat, steak tartare, and *choucroute* (Alsatian-style sauerkraut). Open daily until 1 AM; closed *Christmas.* Reservations unnecessary. MasterCard and Visa accepted. Pl. Charles-de-Gaulle (phone: 30-61-28-00). Moderate.

En Route from St-Germain-en-Laye About 12 miles (19 km) north of St-Germain-en-Laye via N184 and D927, outside Pontoise, is *Mirapolis* (phone: 30-75-14-91), France's first theme park. It's worth a visit if you have children along. The park is open daily; closed mid-October through mid-May. There's an admission charge.

From here, Beauvais is 31 miles (50 km) north.

BEAUVAIS Although the town is located in a less than attractive area, a visit to its imposing *Cathédrale St-Pierre* makes the trip worthwhile. The cathedral, whose Gothic style is in rather jarring contrast to that of the rest of the city, has had an erratic history, plagued by overambition and underfinancing. The architects were not equal to the challenge presented by the soaring choir section; begun in 1247, it collapsed 37 years later. In 1500, another generation of bishops decided to continue the work, undertaking its financing by the sale of indulgences. But again the architects literally let Beauvais down: The supporting pillars of the experimental cross tower gave way in 1573. Since then, the cathedral has remained a magnificent, if unfinished, monument.

The vaulted interior of the cathedral rises to startling, almost dizzying, heights. Light streams through the well-preserved stained glass windows, illuminating the church's magnificent tapestries, which attest to the city's renown as a weaving center.

Before leaving the city, also look at the *Eglise St-Etienne* (Rue de l'Etamine and Rue de l'Infanterie), whose choir section has some beautiful examples of Renaissance stained glass windows.

BEST EN ROUTE

Avenue Modern facilities, 60 rooms, and an outdoor pool—but no restaurant—are offered at this comfortable hotel. Av. Montaigne, Quartier St-Lazare (phone: 44-02-80-80; 800-221-4542; fax: 44-02-12-50). Moderate.

En Route from Beauvais N1 leads to Paris, 47 miles (76 km) away.

The Loire Valley

Beginning just one and a half hours southwest of Paris, this region bristles with the turrets of medieval châteaux soaring above the deep green branches of forests where the Kings of France once hunted wild boar. Many of the Loire's stately palaces, often set in the heart of centuries-old villages, function today as inns or museums of aristocratic life in France. This lush valley is fed by the gentle, reflective waters of several rivers (the principal being the Loire) which curve around wooded islands. On their shores neatly tended vineyards, orchards, and vegetable fields stretch under a wide, limpid blue sky.

The mild climate of this region is tempered by winds blowing inland from the Atlantic, into which the Loire River—at 635 miles, the longest river in France—flows 100 miles (160 km) west of the city of Angers. The Loire Valley includes two ancient provinces: Touraine (with Tours at its center), where the area's most famous châteaux are found, and equally beautiful but less visited Anjou, centered around Angers. Spring comes early here—Loire Valley gardeners send asparagus and strawberries to Paris markets before Parisians are out of their winter coats—and summer often lingers late.

Supremely tranquil today, the Loire Valley has seen considerable drama. Kings and counts fought over each piece of high ground here, gaining naturally well-defended positions (and, in the process, spectacular views). Among the dramatic, sometimes bloodthirsty characters who lived and died in the châteaux and abbeys of the Loire Valley were Eleanor of Aquitaine and her son, Richard the Lion-Hearted, François I, Marie de Médicis, François Rabelais, Honoré de Balzac, and Leonardo da Vinci. And it was here that Jeanne d'Arc (Joan of Arc) won the allegiance of the dauphin and rode into history and immortality under his banners.

Going back even farther, you also can visit remarkable prehistoric stone dolmens (slabs that often mark tombs) and menhirs (primitive monoliths), especially in the Saumur-Gens area. In the cliffs you will see troglodyte dwellings—cave homes—some large and comfortable, with surprisingly elegant stone façades. People still live in them or use them for garages or wine cellars.

Much of this area is flat, with well-surfaced country roads meandering past pretty fields and enchanting waterways. Hence bicycling is a popular pastime, and bicycles can be rented in several towns. You can canoe, kayak, and even windsurf on the Loire and its tributaries. Fishing is also popular, and places like Chinon and Langeais are full of shops selling tackle. With the French national riding school located near Saumur (see below), the area offers many opportunities for equestrians. And the truly adventurous can fly over Touraine in hot-air balloons; tours are organized by a number of companies, including *Bombard Balloon Adventures* (phone: 80-26-63-30 in Burgundy; fax: 80-26-69-20).

Mealtime is another pleasure in this region, whose rivers, forests, and fields produce an abundance of fine foods: Delicious fish, sausages, pâtés, and meats are usually exquisitely sauced, accompanied by excellent vegetables and the delightful fruits, cheeses, and wines of the Loire. Regional dishes include *andouillette* (sausage made from chitterlings), coq au vin (chicken in wine sauce), *matelote d'anguille* (stewed eel), *rillons* (spicy, cubed pork), and *rillettes de porc* (minced pork usually spread on crisp bread). One of the most savory sauces in traditional French cuisine, *beurre blanc,* originated in the western Loire Valley. It's made of wine, vinegar, shallots, and clarified white butter.

In 1882 Henry James said: "It is half the charm of the Loire that you can travel beside it. A wide river, as you follow a wide road, is excellent company." This driving route covers about 330 miles (528 km), beginning at Orléans, 81 miles (130 km) south of Paris. It progresses generally west past châteaux, through forests, and along rivers on the southern side of the Loire to Angers, then turns east, following the northern bank of the river back to Tours. It's also possible to zigzag back and forth across the river west of Tours and end the route at Angers (Michelin map No. 64 contains all but a short southern dip of the route).

A caveat: Attempts to cover all the stops mentioned in a single trip could lead to château burnout, so you might choose to concentrate on the sections of the route that most intrigue you and save the rest for return trips. However, distances between one point of interest and the next are relatively short—Blois and Angers are only 100 miles (160 km) apart, and the direct distance from Angers to Tours is a scant 66 miles (106 km)—making it possible to cover the entire route, with stops, in just a few days. Some châteaux and museums close one day a week, usually Monday or Tuesday, and many close daily from noon to 2 PM. Admission prices vary dramatically, but most are low.

For up-to-date information on all aspects of life in this area, consult regional and local *Syndicats d'Initiative* (tourist offices). The main tourist office in Tours (78 Rue Bernard-Palissy, Tours 37042; phone: 47-70-37-37; fax: 47-61-14-22), near the train station, annually publishes a detailed series of English-language brochures covering food and wine, hotels, monuments and museums, events, driving routes, and even unusual things to do and see in Touraine—the eastern Loire. The *Comité Départemental du Tourisme de l'Anjou* (Pl. Kennedy, Angers; phone: 41-23-51-51; fax: 41-88-36-77) is equally helpful with information about the Anjou area—the western Loire.

For a double room per night in a very expensive hotel, expect to pay $180 or more; in an expensive one, $120 to $180; in a moderate place, $75 to $120; and in an inexpensive one, less than $75. Unless otherwise indicated, all hotels accept major credit cards and are open year-round. Reserve as early as possible. This area is as popular with Parisians as it is with other tourists, and some towns have only one or two especially pleasant hotels. Almost all hotels with restaurants require *demi-pension* (a higher rate that includes breakfast and either lunch or dinner) in July and August; inquire when reserving. At other times of the year they usually charge extra for breakfast; check the card on the back of your hotel room door for both room and breakfast rates. Most hotels feature telephones, TV sets (less frequently), and private baths in all of their rooms. However, some less expensive places may have private baths in only some rooms; it's a good idea when making a reservation to confirm whether your room has a private bath. Very few hotels have air conditioning. A meal for two with service (usually included in the bill) and a bottle of regional wine will cost more than $150 in a very expensive restaurant; $100 to $150 in an expensive one; $50 to $100 in a moderate place; and under $50 in an inexpensive restaurant. The French customarily tip extra for good service. Unless otherwise noted, all restaurants listed below are open for lunch and dinner. For each location hotels and restaurants are listed alphabetically by price category.

ORLÉANS Now, as in centuries past, an industrial center, this city (pop. 135,000) is often chosen as the beginning of a tour of the Loire Valley. World War II was not kind to Orléans, yet a few treasures remain. And then there's its historic association with the legendary St. Joan of Arc, who was dubbed the "Maid of Orléans" after she liberated the city from the English in 1429.

A visit to Orléans should include the following three sights, all on or just off Rue Jeanne-d'Arc: The Gothic *Cathédrale Ste-Croix,* begun in the 13th century, was partially destroyed by the Huguenots (who made Orléans their headquarters briefly in 1568); it was not completed until the 19th century. Its chancel contains outstanding woodwork executed in the early 18th century by Jules Degoullons, who designed the stalls in *Notre-Dame de Paris* and contributed to the decoration of *Versailles.* The *Musée des Beaux-Arts* (1 Rue Fernand-Rabier; phone: 38-53-39-22), near the splendid 15th-century *Hôtel de Ville* (Town Hall), contains some outstanding works of primitive art from the 15th century, portraits from the 18th century, and 19th- and 20th-century art, including works by Gauguin and Max Jacob. It is closed Tuesdays; no admission charge. Finally there's the small, lovely *Musée Historique et Archéologique,* in the restored 16th-century *Hôtel Cabu* (Pl. de l'Abbé-Denoyers; phone: 38-53-39-22), which features local arts and crafts from the 17th through the 19th century. It is closed Tuesdays; there's an admission charge. A statue of Joan of Arc on horseback, erected in 1855, dominates Place du Martroi, into which Rue Royale dead-ends. Every May 7 and 8 the city celebrates its "maid" with great pageantry. For more information about sights and events in Orléans, contact the tourist office (Pl. Albert-I; phone: 38-53-05-95; fax: 38-54-49-84).

From Orléans excursions can be made easily into the *Forêt d'Orléans,* 124,000 acres of pine and oak, and beyond it to the *Basilique St-Benoît-sur-Loire,* in the village of St-Benoît-sur-Loire, 25 miles (40 km) upstream from Orléans via N60 and D60, on the north bank of the river. This exquisite Romanesque structure, perhaps the finest in France, is crowned with a beautifully carved belfry. A Roman mosaic brought from Italy in 1531 graces the floor, and the restored crypt looks the same as it did eight centuries ago.

About 13 miles (21 km) south of Orléans via N20 is the *Château La Ferté-St-Aubin,* a private castle open to the public. Though there has been a château on this site since the 11th century, most of this exceptional building was built in the 17th century by Henri de Saint-Nectaire. It's closed mornings from mid-November through mid-March; admission charge (phone: 38-76-52-72).

BEST EN ROUTE

Les Antiquaires The specialties in this elegant, one-Michelin-star restaurant, situated in a lovely old house, include game in season and *blini* with smoked salmon and leek purée. Closed Sundays, Mondays, two weeks in April, the first three weeks of August, and the week between *Christmas* and *New Year's Day.* Reservations necessary. Major credit cards accepted. 2-4 Rue au Lins (phone: 38-53-52-35; fax: 38-62-06-95). Expensive.

Mercure Here are 109 large rooms with all the comforts you might expect from this luxury hotel chain. The terrace around the heated pool overlooks the Loire. There's a restaurant. 44-46 Quai Barentin (phone: 38-62-17-39; 800-221-4542; fax: 38-53-95-34). Expensive.

La Poutrière In a remodeled *auberge* (inn), this one-Michelin-star restaurant serves contemporary renditions of traditional dishes, such as roast lamb with curry-flavored potato purée. Closed Sunday dinner, Mondays, two weeks in April, and December 24 through January 4. Reservations necessary. Major credit cards accepted. 8 Rue Brèche (phone: 38-66-02-30; fax: 38-51-19-38). Expensive.

En Route from Orléans Follow A10 west for 37 miles (59 km) to Blois.

BLOIS Rising above the right bank of the Loire River, its skyline dominated by the hulking, medieval *Château de Blois* (Pl. du Château), this pleasant city of 50,000 is mainly a business center for the surrounding farming region. The home of several French kings, Blois has a rich historical heritage, eloquently expressed in its architecture, especially the château. The multi-winged building reads like a summary of the evolution of French architecture: Separate sections date from the 13th-century feudal period, the 15th-century Gothic-Renaissance transition period, the 16th-century Renaissance, and the 17th-century classical period. Dastardly deeds and intrigues aplenty are evoked on a visit here. In 1588 the Duc de Guise was assassinated in King Henri III's second-floor bedroom; in 1619 Marie de Médicis, then a stout, middle-aged woman, escaped at night down a rope ladder into the moat after two years of banishment here ordered by her son, Louis XIII; and 237 carved wooden panels in Catherine de Médicis's study still conceal her secret cupboards. The château is closed major holidays; there's an admission charge.

Other places to visit in Blois include the fine *Eglise St-Nicolas,* the *Cathédrale St-Louis* and the picturesque streets stretching down from it toward the Loire, and the former *Bishop's Palace,* now the *Hôtel de Ville* (Town Hall), with a terrace overlooking the river and an 18th-century humpbacked bridge across it. The statue of Joan of Arc on the terrace is the work of an American sculptor, Anna Hyatt Huntington. There also is a statue of Denis Papin, Blois's most famous son, who discovered the principle of the steam engine in 1707 and also invented what he called a "digester," the forerunner of the pressure cooker.

On clear days in summer, helicopter flights lasting from 10 minutes to an hour can be arranged at the tourist office (3 Av. Jean-Laigret; phone: 54-74-06-49; fax: 54-56-04-59).

BEST EN ROUTE

Hostellerie la Malouinière Formerly the residence of Bernard Lorjou, a Loire Valley painter, this white stucco and red brick building is now an elegant country inn and restaurant. The 10 guestrooms are decorated with antique furniture, and the bathrooms are large and luxurious. A sunny terrace, garden, park, pool, and rose-filled, one-Michelin-star dining room add to the pleasure. Chef-owner Claude Berthon's specialties include *consommé aux truffes* (with truffles), grilled Brittany lobster, and *ris de veau aux morilles* (calf sweetbreads with morel mushrooms). Closed January through early March. MasterCard and Visa accepted. About 4 miles (6 km) east of Blois via N152, at 1 Rue Bernard-Lorjou, St-Denis-sur-Loire (phone: 54-74-76-81; fax: 54-74-85-96). Very expensive.

Au Rendez-Vous des Pêcheurs Despite the folksy name, "At the Fishermen's Meeting Place," this is an elegant, one-Michelin-star restaurant whose menu offers dishes for meat lovers, such as calf kidneys with chives, in addition to perfectly prepared fish, all drawing on regional ingredients. Closed Sundays, Monday lunch, one week in February, and most of August. Reservations advised. Major credit cards accepted. 27 Rue Foix (phone: 54-74-67-48; fax: 54-74-47-67). Expensive.

Le Médicis A homey atmosphere prevails in both the hotel and its restaurant. Some of the 12 individually decorated rooms have Jacuzzis; the large covered terrace is another plus. Just behind the train station, at 2 Allée François-I (phone: 54-43-94-04; fax: 54-42-04-05). Moderate.

En Route from Blois Cross Blois's main highway bridge over the Loire, with lovely views of sandbars and sometimes small boats, toward Chambord, 10 miles (16 km) away, turning right just at the south end of the bridge and then right again under it to follow D951 along the picturesque south bank of the river. Like many in the Loire region, the road has only two lanes but a good surface. It passes well-tended fields, pretty camping areas, and the remains of an old aqueduct on the right. On the left is an excellent view across the river of the *Château de Menars* and its terraces. Turn south on D84, which curves gently through cornfields and tiny villages, until you reach a sign warning you to reduce your speed; deer and wild boars roam freely through the forest of Chambord.

CHAMBORD The largest of the Loire Valley châteaux, *Château de Chambord* is also one of the most spectacular. For a detailed description, see *Celebrated Châteaux and Cathedrals* in DIVERSIONS. It's open daily except holidays (phone: 54-20-31-32 or 54-20-34-86).

BEST EN ROUTE

Grand St-Michel This would be a comfortable place to stay anywhere, but it happens to have an idyllic location directly across a narrow road from *Château de Chambord,* surrounded by Chambord's vast forest. Stay in one of the 38 rooms and, at dusk, after the busloads of tourists have gone, drive to an observation platform to spy on deer and boars. Return to the hotel's spacious dining room, which specializes in game in season and such Loire specialties as *rillons* and poached salmon and trout. Then (only in season) watch a son-et-lumière performance from your bedroom window, or simply gaze at the château as it glows silver by moonlight or rosy at dawn. Closed mid-November through mid-December (phone: 54-20-31-31). Moderate.

En Route from Chambord Take D112 south for 5 miles (8 km) through the cool forests of Chambord and Boulogne. At the pleasant little town of Bracieux take D102 west 6 more miles (10 km) to Cheverny.

CHEVERNY This lordly mansion, the *Château de Cheverny,* is unusual in the Loire for having been built all in one piece in 17th-century classical style. Many of its handsomely furnished rooms are open to the public. Even more memorable are its hunting museum, in an outbuilding with one room containing 2,000 sets of stag antlers, and kennel, where you can see a pack of 70 hounds that are a crossbreed between the English foxhound and the French *poitevin.* Your ears will guide you right to it. There are weekly stag hunts in the surrounding forests in season.

Château du Breuil In this elegant château in its own park are 16 spacious rooms and two suites. The one-Michelin-star restaurant features local dishes. Closed December through March; restaurant also closed Sunday dinner (except in summer) and Monday lunch (except holidays). MasterCard and Visa accepted. Two miles (3 km) west of Cheverny by D52, Rte. de Fougères-sur-Bièvre (phone: 54-44-20-20; fax: 54-44-30-40). Expensive.

Trois Marchands A former coaching inn, this pleasant dining place bustles, especially at noon, and the food, featuring lots of fish specialties, is fresh and delicious. There also are 38 guestrooms. Closed late January through mid-March and Mondays from October through mid-January. Cour-Cheverny (phone: 54-79-96-44; fax: 54-79-25-60). Moderate.

St-Hubert This quiet inn has 20 rooms; the restaurant specializes in game in season and regional dishes. Closed January; restaurant also closed Wednesdays. Close to the *Château de Cheverny,* Rue Nationale, Cour-Cheverny (phone: 54-79-96-60; fax: 54-79-21-17). Inexpensive.

En Route from Cheverny Head south on D102 for 6 miles (10 km), cutting across an edge of the Cheverny forest. At Contres pick up D956, which crosses the Cher River 12 miles (19 km) farther on at Selles-sur-Cher, whose château's towers are reflected in the water. Proceed to Valençay, 9 miles (14 km) away.

VALENÇAY Far enough off the main route of tour buses to preserve its tranquillity even at the peak of summer, Valençay is small and pleasant, with tree-shaded avenues that lead to a château whose builder, Jacques d'Estampes, was inspired by Chambord's château. Dating from 1540, the *Château de Valençay* was owned in the early 19th century by Talleyrand, the French statesman. King Ferdinand VII of Spain was comfortably confined here by Napoleon from 1808 to 1814. And you can see the table used for the Congress of Vienna in 1814–15, when a new map of Europe was drawn up in the wake of the Napoleonic Wars. The château's elegantly furnished 17th-century west wing is now the scene of musical and theatrical productions in the summer.

Probably the château's most unusual feature is its large park filled with deer, llamas, buffalos, peacocks, swans, and flamingos, a joy especially for youngsters. Included in the admission price to the castle is admission to the *Musée de l'Automobile* on the grounds and the *Musée de Talleyrand* within the château, filled with souvenirs of the statesman (phone: 54-00-10-66 for all three).

Espagne This beautiful old coaching inn's main connection with Spain seems to be that King Ferdinand VII's staff was housed here while he was confined to Valençay's château, a few steps away. Since 1875 four generations of the

Fourré family have welcomed guests to this elegant Relais & Châteaux member, with eight rooms and six suites built around a flower-filled courtyard; many have private balconies. The one-Michelin-star dining room serves *ris de veau aux morilles* (calf sweetbreads with morels), lamb filet with tarragon, *sandre* (pike perch), and flambéed peaches. Closed January through mid-February. 9 Rue du Château (phone: 54-00-00-02; fax: 54-00-12-63). Expensive.

En Route from Valençay Head west along pretty, sunflower-bordered D960 for 14 miles (22 km) to the tiny village of Nouans-les-Fontaines; watch for its strangely shaped church spire, which looks something like a rocket soaring over the fields, or you may drive through without realizing it. This unassuming village church, however, dates from the 13th century and contains one of the finest French works of art of the late 15th century, a moving *Descent from the Cross,* also called the *Nouans Pietà.* It was painted on wood in somber colors by artists from the school of Jean Fouquet. A five-franc piece placed in a slot illuminates the painting and sends a detailed commentary in French, English, or German echoing through the usually empty interior. Take D760, continuing west across rolling fields of sunflowers, 5 miles (8 km) to Montrésor.

MONTRÉSOR In this pretty Indrois River town, somebody has gone to the trouble of lining the main road with trees of alternating red and green foliage. The church here is known for its fine doorway and the 16th-century tomb of the Basternays, overlords of Montrésor. The *Château de Montrésor* is one of 20 in the Loire Valley built by Foulques Nerra (971–1040), a Count of Anjou and one of the most dramatic and violent personalities in the region's history. He spent his life battling the Counts of Blois and building fortresses to use in this fight; then, during periodic fits of repentance for his unscrupulous and sometimes criminal acts, he raised churches and went on pilgrimages to Jerusalem. Take a walk around the fortified promontory on which the château is perched, high above the river.

En Route from Montrésor Follow D760 5 miles (8 km) west to the long wall that indicates the *Chartreuse du Liget.*

CHARTREUSE DU LIGET These are the impressive ruins of a Carthusian monastery founded in the 12th century, supposedly by Henry II of England in expiation for the murder of St. Thomas à Becket, Archbishop of Canterbury. Park near the monumental 18th-century gateway, walk through it, and obtain permission from the caretakers to visit the vast cloisters near the brook called the Liget and the open, grass-floored ruin of the 12th-century chapel. Standing alone in a field west of the monastery, the *Chapelle St-Jean-de-Liget* contains interesting frescoes. An ideal place to stage a memorable picnic is just outside the walls of the monastery amid the tiny wildflowers.

En Route from the Chartreuse du Liget Continue west on D760 for 6 miles (10 km) to Loches.

LOCHES Off the standard tourist route yet one of the special treasures of the Loire Valley, this attractive little town on a hill above the Indre River has modern stores and friendly inhabitants. Loches has been fortified since its earliest history; captured in a three-hour surprise attack by Richard the Lion-Hearted in 1195, it was regained 10 years later for France by Philippe-Auguste after a year-long siege. Loches then became the state prison of the kings of France.

The town's large and fascinating medieval quarter, the Cité Médiévale, features a château full of history and dungeons with grim memories. The *Château de Loches* holds the lovely sculpted tomb of Agnès Sorel, mistress of Charles VII. The remains of *"la dame de beauté,"* as she was known, are no longer here; originally buried in the *Eglise St-Ours,* they were scattered to the winds during the French Revolution by soldiers who mistook Agnès for a saint. In the keep, a group of fortified towers at the southern end of the Cité Médiévale, are the dungeons, some of the more unsettling remnants of this age you are ever likely to see, complete with torture instruments and inscriptions carved or painted on the walls by the prisoners. (In more recent times a handful of Nazi collaborators was briefly jailed here.) Loches's château and dungeon are closed Wednesdays off-season and all of December and January. Also in the Cité Médiévale are the *Musée Lansyer* (1 Rue Lansyer; phone: 47-59-05-45) and, in the same building, the *Musée du Terroir* (Folklore Museum). The former is devoted to the works of a local landscape artist; the latter affords a lovely view of Loches. Both museums are closed Fridays from October through March, and both have an admission charge. The *Eglise St-Ours,* also in the Cité Médiévale, has two unusual pyramids rising between its towers.

En Route from Loches Start north on N143, picking up D764 east, then D31 north just outside town for 16 miles (26 km) through fields and vineyards to the busy little town of Bléré. Twist through town and turn east on N76 toward Chenonceaux, 4 miles (6 km) away.

CHENONCEAUX Leapfrogged splendidly across the Cher River like a fantasy bridge, with views of decorative gardens and water from almost all of its beautifully furnished rooms, the *Château de Chenonceaux* is perhaps the most photographed of all the region's châteaux. For a detailed description, see *Celebrated Châteaux and Cathedrals* in DIVERSIONS. The château and museum are open daily; admission charge (phone: 47-23-90-07).

BEST EN ROUTE

Château de Chissay This 12th-century château is now a luxury hotel complete with mosaic bathrooms in its 23 rooms and eight suites, a heated pool, and a restaurant; it's a member of the Relais & Châteaux group. Closed January through mid-March. Three miles (5 km) east of Chenonceaux on N76 (on the north bank of the Cher), in Chissay-en-Touraine (phone: 54-32-32-01; fax: 54-32-43-80). Expensive.

Château de Gué Péan Stop by just to visit or stay on awhile in this 23-room, 17th-century château, which is set in a private forest and furnished in 18th-century style. It has an elegant dining room. No credit cards accepted. About 12 miles (19 km) east of Chenonceaux, via N76 and tiny D21, in Monthou-sur-Cher (phone: 54-71-43-01). Expensive.

Bon Laboureur et Château *The* place to stay in the tiny village of Chenonceaux is a short walk from the château. Low and vine-covered, it has window boxes bright with flowers and a dining room that serves an abundance of well-prepared Loire Valley fish, other specialties, and good regional wines. A breakfast of fresh croissants and jam is served in the 36 rooms (some in an annex). There is also an outdoor pool with a bar and another grill-style restaurant. Closed mid-November through mid-March. 6 Rue Dr.-Bretonneau (phone: 47-23-90-02; fax: 47-23-82-01). Moderate.

Hostellerie de l'Isle Relax in the warm family atmosphere of this cozy 18th-century manor house with 10 rooms. The well-prepared meals are served by the fire on chilly days or under the trees in the surrounding garden-park, with pond, on warmer ones. Less than a mile (1.6 km) from the village of Chenonceaux via D40 west, in Civray-de-Touraine (phone: 47-23-80-09; fax: 47-23-82-91). Moderate.

En Route from Chenonceaux The most scenic route for the 7 miles (11 km) north to Amboise is D81; pick it up in Civray-de-Touraine, less than a mile (1.6 km) west of the village of Chenonceaux via D40. The road winds through vineyards under the overhanging greenery of the *Forêt d'Amboise.*

AMBOISE The village of Amboise offers the fine *Château d'Amboise* perched high on a promontory, with magnificent views over the Loire and surrounding countryside, and a lovely 15th-century clock tower. The château has a rich history, having played a part in the lives of 15th- and 16th-century kings (this was the birthplace of Charles VIII) and as the site of a massacre: Huguenots (French Protestants) were hanged from the castle walls or thrown from its battlements into the river in 1560. Its most illustrious resident was Leonardo da Vinci, who spent his last few years working here (his remains are entombed in the château's *Chapelle St-Hubert,* in the north transept). The château is open daily; there's an admission charge (phone: 47-57-00-98).

After touring the château, stroll about a third of a mile east along Rue Victor-Hugo to the *Clos Lucé,* the charming 15th-century manor house that François I, a patron of the arts, turned over to Leonardo after bringing him here from Italy in 1514. Pass through a gateway under a pretty little gallery with wooden arches, the oldest part of the red brick house, and past a lovely park with paths and benches to find this quotation from Leonardo just inside the front door: "A well-filled day gives a good sleep. A well-filled life gives a peaceful death." Over 60 years old when he arrived here with a paralyzed right hand, the artist nevertheless painted and sketched actively until his death on May 2, 1519. Some say François I was with him when he died. The lowest floor of the *Clos Lucé* holds a fascinating collection of 40 models of intricate machines constructed by *IBM* from plans by Leonardo, demonstrating his engineering genius in precursors of the first airplane, helicopter, military tank, and bridge designed to swing open. The house is open daily; there's an admission charge. For more information on sights in Amboise, contact the tourist office (phone: 47-57-09-28).

BEST EN ROUTE

Domaine des Hauts-de-Loire With 25 rooms and nine suites, this former hunting lodge is a real gem; the two-Michelin-star restaurant is reason enough to stop here. For additional details, see *Romantic French Hostelries* in DIVERSIONS. Hotel closed December through February; restaurant also closed Mondays and Tuesday lunch from October through May. Fourteen miles (22 km) northeast of Amboise, via N152 and D1, Rte. de Herbault, outside Onzain (phone: 54-20-72-57; fax: 54-20-77-32). Very expensive.

L'Aubinière This one-Michelin-star restaurant has a lovely view of the surrounding valley. Its specialties include fish cooked in Touraine wine and sautéed snails, and there is an excellent selection of Loire wines. Closed Tuesday dinner, Wednesdays, mid-February through early March, and the first two weeks of September. Major credit cards accepted. Rue J. Gauthier, Saint-Ouen-les-Vignes, 4 miles (6 km) northwest of Amboise via D431 (phone: 47-30-15-29; fax: 47-30-02-44). Expensive.

Château de Pray On a bluff overlooking the Loire, this picturesque old château with 17 rooms has a dining room with a fireplace and beamed ceiling and, for pleasant summer lunches, a terrace overlooking part of its own formal walled-in garden and the Loire. Adjoining the garden, with its graveled paths and geraniums, is a wild, woodsy park with trails. Closed January through mid-February. Two miles (3 km) northeast of Amboise via D751 (phone: 47-57-23-67; fax: 47-57-32-50). Expensive.

Le Choiseul This member of the Relais & Châteaux group offers 28 elegant rooms and four suites (ask for one overlooking the garden), a full complement of business services, and a swimming pool. The one-Michelin-star dining room boasts a superb view of the countryside; the chef excels in classic dishes with a light touch, such as pot-au-feu of lamb with garlic purée. Closed late November through mid-January. MasterCard and Visa accepted. 36 Quai Charles-Guinot (phone: 47-30-45-45; fax: 47-30-46-10). Expensive.

Le Manoir St-Thomas A Renaissance manor house–turned-restaurant whose excellent menu and fine selection of wines have earned it the best reputation in town. Closed Wednesday dinner except in summer, Mondays, and mid-January through mid-March. Reservations advised. Major credit cards accepted. Pl. Richelieu (phone: 47-57-22-52; fax: 47-30-44-71). Expensive.

Au Lion d'Or Choose one of the back rooms in this comfortable 22-room, one-suite dwelling, for a quiet spot with shuttered windows that face the château. The dining room exudes the atmosphere of a hunting lodge: A large fireplace fills one end, and game trophies line the walls. Try the *foie gras frais de canard* (fresh duck foie gras), *pain d'épinards à la crème* (spinach soufflé covered with a delicate cream sauce), or *navarin de cidre* (pork stew with potatoes, turnips, and a pungent cider sauce). Closed mid-January through mid-February; restaurant also closed Sunday dinner and Mondays in off-season. MasterCard and Visa accepted. 17 Quai Charles-Guinot (phone: 47-57-00-23). Moderate.

En Route from Amboise Good roads on both sides of the Loire lead to Tours, 15 miles (24 km) west; D751 on the south bank and N152 on the north provide good views of the river, its islands, and sandbars. One advantage of the northern route is that it allows a short detour on the marked Route du Vouvray past vineyards and through the hamlets of Noizay and Vernou to the little town of Vouvray, which produces the best-known white wine of Touraine. Watch for the signs of wine producers offering visits and tastings.

TOURS The major city of a region rich in magnificent châteaux, fine food and wine, and some of the most beautiful countryside in France, Tours is the home of 130,000 people (and another 120,000 in the outlying areas), and has been an important metropolis since Gallo-Roman times. It was bombed heavily in World War II, so it greets you with ugly 20th-century apartment towers instead of the elegant château turrets of its Loire neighbors. The city nevertheless is a good base for visitors who prefer to sleep in the same bed every night while exploring the Loire Valley, and it is easy to reach from Paris, three hours by autoroute or just 70 minutes by rail via the *TGV Atlantique.*

The charms of this city are hidden and must be sought out. Stop at the large, well-run tourist office in front of the train station (78 Rue Bernard-Palissy; phone: 47-70-37-37; fax: 47-61-14-22), then visit the *Cathédrale St-Gatien,* which could illustrate an art history text on the evolution of the Gothic style; it was begun in the early 13th century and not finished until the 16th. Be sure to see the fine stained glass windows dating from the 13th to the 15th centuries. The cathedral's cloister was the setting for native son Honoré de Balzac's novel *Le Curé de Tours* (The Vicar of Tours). In the nearby *Musée des Beaux-Arts* (18 Pl. François-Sicard; phone: 47-05-

68-73), formerly the archbishop's palace, hang paintings by Mantegna, Rubens, Rembrandt, Degas, and Delacroix. It's closed Tuesdays and major holidays; there's an admission charge. A few blocks to the west of the museum, on Rue Nationale, is the *Eglise St-Julien,* part of a former Benedictine abbey, whose cellars now house the *Musée du Compagnonnage* (Museum of the Craft Guilds; 8 Rue Nationale), where the works and tools of a variety of artisans are displayed, and the *Musée des Vins de Touraine–Celliers St-Julien* (16 Rue Nationale), which will delight devotees of the many local wines. Both museums are closed Tuesdays (except in summer), January, February, and major holidays; there's an admission charge to each (phone: 47-61-07-93).

Keep walking west to reach Vieux Tours (Old Tours), with half-timbered houses that lean into charming narrow streets. The *Musée du Gemmail* (Rue du Mûrier; phone: 47-61-01-19), which focuses on the *gemmail* artistic technique of superimposing pieces of glass to produce painting-like works, is in this area, as is a honeycomb of little streets known as Les Artisans du Petit St-Martin, whose shops feature painted jewelry, marionettes, made-to-measure lamp shades, and many items of silk, wood, and leather. The museum is closed Mondays and mid-October through February. The *Musée St-Martin* (3 Rue Rapin; phone: 47-64-48-87) is devoted to the life and works of the saint who was born in this city. It is closed Mondays and Tuesdays; there's an admission charge.

There are frequent concerts here, especially in the summer. A classical music festival, the annual *Fêtes Musicales en Touraine,* is held the last weekend in June at the *Manoir de Meslay,* a vast 13th-century barn that was part of a fortified farm; it is about 5 miles (8 km) north of Tours on N10, toward Château-Renault. Another festival, the *Semaines Musicales de Tours,* takes place in churches and halls in Tours itself, usually during July. The city also stages a folksy *Foire de l'Ail et du Basilic* (Garlic and Basil Fair) each summer on *St. Anne's Day,* July 26.

Bicycles are available for rental at the train station (Pl. de la Gare; phone: 47-20-50-50), *Au Col de Cygne* (46 *bis* Rue Docteur-Fournier; phone: 47-46-00-37), and at other small bicycle sales and repair shops.

BEST EN ROUTE

Charles Barrier This venerable restaurant, a member of the Relais & Châteaux group, has garnered top culinary ratings in Tours for decades and continues to merit two stars from Michelin for refined versions of regional specialties. A fixed-price menu puts the pleasures of the elegant dining room within reach of those of more moderate means. Closed Sunday dinner. Reservations necessary. Major credit cards accepted. 101 Av. de la Tranchée (phone: 47-54-20-39; fax: 47-41-80-95). Very expensive.

Château d'Artigny Built on the site of an 18th-century château, this world-famous hotel has 51 elegant rooms and two suites. It also features a heated pool, two tennis courts, a good restaurant, and classical music performances in the fall and winter. Closed late November through early January. For additional details, see *Romantic French Hostelries* in DIVERSIONS. Nine miles (14 km) south of Tours on N10 to Montbazon, then a mile (1.6 km) southwest on D17 (phone: 47-26-24-24; fax: 47-65-92-79). Very expensive.

Domaine de la Tortinière In this storybook château are 15 small, romantic rooms and six suites, surrounded by towers and turrets and overlooking grounds that slope gently toward the river. A garden-style restaurant adds to the pleasure, with fine fish and good sauces. The chef sometimes holds week-long cooking classes for groups of 10 or more at the hotel; English translation is provided by Americans living in the area. Closed December 20 through February. Eight miles (13 km) south of Tours on N10; then watch for signs on the right for D287 (phone: 47-26-00-19; fax: 47-65-95-70). Very expensive.

Jean Bardet Installed in a grand old mansion is Monsieur Bardet's sumptuous 16-room, five-suite hotel, a member of the Relais & Châteaux group. The restaurant has earned two Michelin stars, but though some find it outstanding, recent visitors have reported a less-than-warm welcome. Specialties include truffled guinea hen, farm rabbit with artichokes, and *brochet au vin de Loire* (pike in Loire Valley wine sauce). The wine list is superlative. Breakfast here is particularly good. Hotel closed mid-February through March; restaurant also closed Sunday dinner and Mondays in winter. In a park near the center of Tours, at 57 Rue Groison (phone: 47-41-41-11; fax: 47-51-68-72). Very expensive.

Château de la Bourdaisière Once the home of Gabrielle d'Estrées, a mistress of King Henri IV, this lovely Renaissance château was recently converted to a luxury hotel with 10 spacious rooms and two sumptuous suites. (A restaurant may open later this year, but no specific information was available at press time.) The hotel also offers a heated pool and tennis courts in its extensive private park. The rest of the château is open year-round for hotel guests, but visits by non-guests are permitted only from mid-March through mid-November. 25 Rue Bourdaisière, Montlouis-sur-Loire, 6 miles (10 km) east of Tours off D751 (phone: 47-45-16-31; fax: 47-45-09-11). Expensive.

Les Hautes Roches Here, in one of the country's most unusual hotels, are 11 luxurious rooms, eight of them cleverly carved into the soft limestone cliffs of the Loire riverbank. They are like caves, with cool, mellow stone walls, vaulted bathrooms, and striking views of the water. There is a riverside terrace and a one-Michelin-star restaurant featuring local fish, in the pretty 19th-century château perched on a natural stone cliff in front of the cave dwellings. Closed mid-January through mid-March; restaurant also closed Monday lunch. 86 Quai de la Loire, Rochecorbon (phone: 47-52-88-88; fax: 47-52-81-30). Expensive.

L'Hôtel de Groison In a quiet neighborhood across the Loire from the heart of Tours is this 18th-century townhouse transformed into a lovely hotel. Most of the 10 individually decorated rooms overlook a garden, and the restaurant, *Le Jardin du Castel,* has one of the city's prettiest dining rooms. The hotel is closed three weeks in January; the restaurant is closed Sundays, Mondays, Tuesday lunch, and mid-January through mid-February. 10 Rue Groison (phone: 47-41-94-40; fax: 47-51-50-28). Expensive.

La Roche Le Roy This local favorite housed in a Renaissance manor house has garnered one Michelin star for dishes like Breton lobster sautéed with vanilla, and farm-raised chicken stuffed with foie gras and truffles. Closed Saturday lunch, Sundays, two weeks in February, and late July through late August. Reservations advised. Major credit cards accepted. 55 Rte. St-Avertin (phone: 47-27-22-00; fax: 47-28-08-39). Expensive.

Rôtisserie Tourangelle A longtime local favorite, this brasserie's house specialties include homemade foie gras, snails in red wine, and local fish in a *beurre blanc* sauce. Closed Sunday dinner, Mondays, and February. Reservations advised. Major credit cards accepted. 23 Rue du Commerce (phone: 47-05-71-21). Moderate.

Les Tuffeaux This highly regarded restaurant boasts a scenic location near the cathedral. The Loire fish is especially good here, as are the puff pastry desserts. Closed Sundays and Monday lunch. Reservations advised. Major credit cards accepted. 19 Rue Lavoisier (phone: 47-47-19-89). Moderate.

Hôtel du Cygne Ensconced in a 17th-century building, this 19-room hostelry claims to be one of Tours's oldest. The balconies are filled with geraniums, and there's a cozy fireplace in the lounge. There's no restaurant. On a quiet street near the center of town, at 6 Rue du Cygne (phone: 47-66-66-41; fax: 47-20-18-76). Inexpensive.

Les Trois Rois This pleasant pub serves lunches of toasted sandwiches and salads, but no evening meals. The 15th-century house is a wonderful place to sip a cold drink on a hot summer afternoon. Open daily. No reservations or credit cards accepted. On the most charming square in Vieux Tours, Pl. Plumereau (phone: 47-20-61-20). Inexpensive.

En Route from Tours Follow D7 11 miles (18 km) west to Villandry. For those interested in such curiosities, the three-quarter-mile "petrifying" *grottes* (grottoes) are about 2 miles (3 km) before Villandry, at Savonnières. The caves, which are connected to the *Château de Villandry* (see below) by an underground passage, are the scene of continuous dripping that allegedly petrifies objects in a matter of months. Hour-long guided tours are given daily except mid-December through January and Wednesdays in February and March. Bring along a sweater to ward off the chill. For further information on the caves or castle, contact the tourist office in Tours (see above), or call the caves directly (phone: 47-50-00-09).

VILLANDRY The hamlet of Villandry faces the Cher River near the point at which it joins the Loire. Its château was the last great one of the Renaissance to be built in this area; Jean le Breton, a financier and minister to François I, finished it in 1536. Unlike many neighboring châteaux, the *Château de Villandry* always has been privately owned (but is now partially open to the public), and the interests of its owners have given it a special flavor. Le Breton, who served as the French ambassador to Italy, was knowledgeable in architecture and garden design. His attractive château, which includes a moat and elegant courtyard, is purely French in style, but the gardens, which manifest both French and Italian influences, are more renowned.

This is probably the only place in the Loire Valley where a château's splendor is eclipsed by its gardens. The three tiers of large, superimposed terraces include a lake, hedges, bushes trimmed into precise patterns representing, among other things, different kinds of love (tender, passionate, adulterous), an extensive garden of herbs and plants, and, most unusual, a large 16th-century kitchen garden whose colorful patterns are formed by carefully planted fruit trees and vegetables.

The 16th-century gardens were torn out in the 19th century, when the owners decided to plant an English-style garden. Happily, the original gardens were replanted according to old plans and drawings early in this century by Dr. Joachim Carvallo, whose grandson now owns and lives in the château with his family. The part of the château open to the public includes a fine collection of Spanish paintings and an intricate Moorish ceiling brought from Spain. Visitors should climb to a vantage point over the gardens and then wander through them at leisure. The château is open daily from mid-March through November 12; the gardens are open year-round (phone: 47-50-02-09).

BEST EN ROUTE

Cheval Rouge This pleasant 20-room hotel and restaurant is a short stroll from the château gardens. The menu offers homemade foie gras and smoked salmon; Loire fish, including *sandre* (pike perch); and good regional wines. Closed mid-January through mid-March; restaurant also closed Sunday dinner and Mondays in winter (phone: 47-50-02-07; fax: 47-50-08-77). Moderate.

En Route from Villandry Follow D7 west, then D39 south for 7 miles (11 km) to Azay-le-Rideau.

AZAY-LE-RIDEAU Pocket-sized and charming, Azay boasts a handful of picturesque old streets, some interesting shops, and in its heart, the Gothic *Château d'Azay-le-Rideau,* one of the jewels of the Loire Valley. For a detailed description, see *Celebrated Châteaux and Cathedrals* in DIVERSIONS. Because it stands where the road between Tours and Chinon crosses the Indre River, Azay was fortified early in its history. Originally named for one of its overlords, Ridel, or Rideau, of Azay, the village was known for centuries as Azay-le-Brulé (Azay-the-Burnt), because in 1418 Charles VII, then dauphin, avenged a verbal insult from a guard by executing 350 soldiers and torching the town. The nickname was dropped in the early 16th century, when the present château was built. Today the village has immense trees and expanses of greenery.

If you're interested in either Honoré de Balzac or wicker (or both), consider the following side trip. The site of the *Musée Balzac* is the *Château de Saché,* on the Indre River in the tiny town of Saché, 4 miles (6 km) from Azay via D84 east and D9 south. Among the rooms is Balzac's boudoir, which has been arranged to represent as closely as possible the way it appeared from 1829 to 1848, when he lived and wrote here. The museum is closed December through January; there's an admission charge (phone: 47-26-86-50). Just a block away, outside the *Hôtel de Ville* (Town Hall), a striking stabile with blue and red arms testifies to the former presence of Alexander Calder, whose home and workshop were near the village.

From Saché zigzag west and south (D17 to D217) for 3 miles (5 km) to Villaines-les-Rochers, an entire village of basket makers. Some 80 families, many working in troglodyte homes dug into walls of rock, belong to the village's wicker cooperative. Their big showroom (phone: 47-45-43-03) is an excellent place to buy baskets, wicker furniture, and such novelties as wicker babies' rattles with pebbles woven inside. In an adjoining workroom you can watch craftspeople at work. Some artisans invite visitors to their own workrooms; the shop of Joël Metezeau, sporting a big sign (visible on the right as you enter the village from Saché), is a pleasant place cluttered with picnic baskets, cradles, armchairs, and bracelets, all produced by amiable men weaving on the floor in the back room.

BEST EN ROUTE

Grand Monarque If a stay here doesn't relax you, probably nothing can. The hotel and its outbuildings ramble around a large graveled, tree-shaded courtyard, where tables are set up for lunch in the summer. The 25 rooms and one suite are old-fashioned, quiet, and comfortable. The pretty flower-filled dining room is the venue for such tasty offerings as *andouillette* and several good fish dishes. The château is a three-minute walk away; for a treat after its son-et-lumière show, return to the hotel lobby for a cognac or raspberry liqueur. Breakfast is included in the room rate. Hotel closed mid-December through mid-January; restaurant closed mid-November through mid-March. In the center of town, on Pl. de la République (phone: 47-45-40-08; fax: 47-45-46-25). Hotel, moderate; restaurant, expensive.

En Route from Azay-le-Rideau Head southwest on D751 for 13 miles (21 km) to Chinon. The road includes long, roller- coaster dips through the green *Forêt de Chinon* (Chinon Forest).

CHINON The mention of Chinon makes most people think first of the delightful red wine produced here and only later of this pleasant town astride the Vienne River. It was in the *Château de Chinon* that Joan of Arc recognized the dauphin, later Charles VII, in 1429, as he tried to hide himself in a crowd of followers, and it was also in Chinon that she won his trust. The English King Henry II died here in 1189, as did his son Richard the Lion-Hearted, ten years later. In 1321, a year before all Jews were expelled from France, the Jews of Chinon were massacred in a fire on the Ile de Tours, the island in the Vienne opposite the town, after a local uprising and accusations of well poisoning.

François Rabelais was born a little over 3 miles (5 km) outside of Chinon in La Devinière in 1494; he spent his early years in this area. His birthplace, the 15th-century *Maison de la Petite Devinière,* houses a literary museum containing editions of Rabelais's own writings as well as books he loved to read; it stages changing exhibitions related to the writer. From Chinon take D749 south to D751 east; turn left on D759, then right on D24, which becomes D117, where the museum is located. It's closed Wednesdays, mid-January through mid-March, and the last 10 days of April. There's an admission charge (phone: 47-95-91-18).

The *Château de Chinon* is mostly in ruins on a hilltop spur that dominates the town; you enter it through a clock tower containing a small Joan of Arc museum (entrance is included in the château admission charge). Peacocks stroll near the historic walls, and there is a deep moat and good views of the vineyard-covered countryside. Call 47-93-13-45 for seasonal changes in opening times.

From the château a short walk brings you to the wine-tasting shop of the *Couly-Dutheil* vintners; their Clos de l'Echo is among the best of the Chinons. A few dozen yards farther, down a road cryptically marked "A l'Echo" ("To the Echo"), you can experience one of the most amusing simple pleasures of the Loire Valley. A small sign adjacent to a vineyard denotes "l'Echo." Climb up on a concrete platform, face the walls of the castle (across the ravine), give a few shouts of different pitches, and enjoy the fun. When the weather is clear and there aren't too many people around to muddy the acoustics, the echo is amazingly clear and strong. If possible, try the queries that generations of residents have used to tease their wives and girlfriends:

"Les femmes de Chinon, sont-elles fidèles?"
("The women of Chinon, are they faithful?")
Echo: *"Elles?"* ("Them?")
"Oui, les femmes de Chinon." ("Yes, the women of Chinon.")
Echo: *"Non."* ("No.")

Below the castle experience medieval Chinon with a walk down Rue Voltaire, where red and yellow banners stretch between stone buildings and rosebushes bloom in lovely courtyards. Pedestrians, who have priority on the narrow street, can admire at leisure the pretty 17th-century *Hôtel du Gouvernement* (Hall of Government) and the *Maison des Etats-Généraux* (House of the Estates-General), in which, according to local legend, Richard the Lion-Hearted died of a wound he received at Châlus. The structure now houses an interesting museum, the *Musée du Vieux Chinon et de la Batellerie,* which focuses on the town of Chinon and on boats. The museum is closed Tuesdays and February; there's an admission charge (phone: 47-93-18-12). Chinon holds a medieval fair the first weekend in August, when residents dress in period costumes and everybody makes merry.

BEST EN ROUTE

Château de Marçay This 15th-century fortress has metamorphosed into a luxury hotel, a member of the prestigious Relais & Châteaux group, with 34 elegantly appointed rooms and six suites. (Some of the rooms, located in a modern annex, are both smaller and less expensive. In the one-Michelin-star dining room try the soft-boiled eggs with puréed morels or the snails in tiny crêpes; the wine list is a commendable tribute to the Loire. For additional details, see *Romantic French Hostelries* in DIVERSIONS. Closed mid-January through mid-March; restaurant also closed Sunday dinner and Mondays from November through April except on holidays. Reservations necessary. Four miles (6 km) south of Chinon via D749 and D116, in Marçay (phone: 47-93-03-47; fax: 47-93-45-33). Very expensive.

Château de Danzay Yet another captivating château conversion, this place has eight large rooms and one suite with exposed beams and stone walls. They are luxuriously decorated in traditional French style (elegant floral fabrics and antique furniture). There is a large private park with a heated pool, and a restaurant for guests only. Closed mid-November through mid-March. In Beaumont-en-Véron, 3 miles (5 km) northwest of Chinon via D749 (phone: 47-58-46-86; fax: 47-58-84-35). Expensive.

Château de la Poitevinière A touch of the US in the Loire Valley, this château was purchased and renovated by Francophile Americans. Stay in one of the five large rooms, or if you prefer, rent the entire château for about $6,000 a week. There's no restaurant. No credit cards accepted. Two miles (4 km) north of Chinon via D16 toward Huismes, followed by D118 east toward Avoine (phone: 47-95-58-40; 415-922-4795 in San Francisco; fax: 47-95-43-43; 415-928-2863). Expensive.

Hostellerie Gargantua A charming 15th-century building, its eight guestrooms and kitchen have been renovated. On Friday evenings guests are received by staff dressed in medieval costume. The house specialty is the *omelette Gargamelle,* with herbs and mushrooms. Closed mid-November through mid-March; restaurant also closed Wednesdays, and Thursday lunch in off-season. In the heart of Old Chinon, just beneath the château. 73 Rue Voltaire (phone: 47-93-04-71). Expensive.

Manoir de La Giraudière This picturesque 15th-century manor house in the beautiful countryside offers simple charm and the convenience of kitchenettes in some of its 25 rooms. There is also a restaurant. Swimming, tennis, and horseback riding are available nearby. Restaurant closed Tuesdays and Wednesdays off-season and all of January. Three miles (5 km) northwest of town, via D749 and the turnoff to Savigny (phone: 47-58-40-36; fax: 47-58-46-06). Expensive.

En Route from Chinon Take D751 west, turning south on D947, 12 miles (19 km) to Fontévraud-l'Abbaye. Shortly before the turnoff for the abbey, D751 becomes especially pretty; tree-shaded, it passes fields, small châteaux, and the scenic Vienne River close on the right. The stretch through La Chausée and St-Germain-sur-Vienne is most charming; you may want to pull off the road for a picnic. At the very least, slow down a bit to admire the flowers in the window boxes of the storybook houses, and be prepared for the occasional herd of cattle or flock of sheep crossing the road.

FONTÉVRAUD-L'ABBAYE Another relatively unknown treasure of the Loire Valley, the vast abbey here, *L'Abbaye de Fontévraud,* gives visitors a chance to explore one of the most intact monastic complexes still standing in France. Founded in 1099 by Robert d'Arbrissel, a Breton hermit, the Fontévraud order was remarkable for its aristocratic nature, for having been overseen by a succession of 36 abbesses—all from noble families—and for opening the doors of five separate monasteries to monks, nuns, lepers, the sick, and aristocratic women who wished to withdraw to a life of prayer and contemplation. The abbey church, consecrated in 1119 by Pope Calixtus II, is a huge Romanesque structure with a single nave. It contains the tombs of Henry II Plantagenet, Count of Anjou, who became King of England in 1154 and who asked on his deathbed to be buried at Fontévraud; Eleanor of Aquitaine, his widow, who withdrew to the abbey for the 15 years preceding her own death; Richard the Lion-Hearted, their son, who also requested that his remains be buried here; and Isabelle of Angoulême, the second wife of Richard's brother, King John Lackland. Their four beautiful, recumbent statues lie just to the right of the nave. There also are tranquil cloisters with noteworthy Renaissance and Gothic carvings, a medieval herb garden, and an unusual octagonal tower that served as the abbey kitchen, said to be the only one of its kind from the Romanesque period remaining in France. French revolutionaries destroyed some monastery buildings in 1793. In 1804 Napoleon converted most of the remaining buildings into a national prison, which operated until 1963. Today the French government and regional cultural agencies use *L'Abbaye de Fontévraud* for concerts, art exhibitions, and theatrical productions.

Also of note in the small town are the *Eglise St-Michel* (St. Michael's Church), across Place des Plantagenets and Rue du Logis Bourbon from the abbey, and the 13th-century *Chapelle St-Catherine,* off a pretty avenue of lime trees leading from the church.

BEST EN ROUTE

Hôtellerie du Prieuré Saint Lazare This elegant hotel in a restored priory has such amenities as mini-bars in all of its 53 rooms, although the place's greatest draw is the view of the abbey and its gardens. The hotel's restaurant is in a restored cloister. Closed for several weeks in winter; call ahead to check. Restaurant also closed Sunday dinner and Mondays (phone: 41-51-73-16; fax: 41-51-75-50). Expensive.

La Licorne Attractive and elegant, with a young and hospitable owner, this small one-Michelin-star restaurant adds extra sparkle to a visit to Fontévraud-l'Abbaye. If the weather is good, reserve one of the little tables on the patio adjacent to a walled flower garden. The inside is pleasant, too, with artwork focusing on *la licorne* (the unicorn). Loire fish with sorrel sauce, beef with tarragon sauce and homemade, carrot-tinted noodles, and the house's special chocolate cake all are excellent. The wine list is superb. Closed Sundays and Mondays in winter, two weeks in February, late August through early September, and *Christmas* through *New Year's.* Reservations advised. Major credit cards accepted. Allée Ste-Catherine (phone: 41-51-72-49; fax: 41-51-70-40). Expensive.

En Route from Fontévraud-l'Abbaye Route D947 follows the river west for 9 miles (14 km) to Saumur. Outside Fontévraud is Montsoreau, with a its pretty *Château de Montsoreau* and its *Musée des Goums* (French cavalry units recruited in Morocco). The museum contains souvenirs of the Moroccan conquest. There's an admission charge (no phone). Nearby are some picturesque troglodyte houses, an old windmill on a ridge, and wine cellars where you can taste Saumur wine.

SAUMUR With a many-arched old bridge over the Loire, attractive shops, and busy streets, Saumur is most famous for its national riding school, the *Ecole Nationale d'Equitation* (in Terrefort, southwest of town; phone: 41-50-21-35; fax: 41-67-63-08), home of the elite *Cadre Noir* (Black Squadron), which draws eager crowds to a military tattoo and riding spectacle every summer in late July. The school offers guided tours through the stables and areas where the *Cadre Noir* may be practicing. It's closed Sundays and Monday mornings from April through September.

Saumur is also renowned for its wines, the sparkling mousseux white and the light red Saumur-Champigny, served chilled. A *Maison du Vin*

(House of Wine; 25 Rue Beaurepaire; phone: 41-51-16-40) run by the wine producers' association is on Place de la Bilange, next door to the tourist office. The *Maison du Vin* is closed Sundays September through June, and Mondays from October through May.

The dramatic *Château de Saumur* soars high above the town on a sheer promontory. Several fortresses have stood here; the present one, dating from the late 14th century, contains a museum of decorative arts and another tracing the history of the horse. The château is closed Tuesdays and major holidays; the admission charge includes entrance to the museums.

En Route from Saumur Route D751 snakes northwest for 32 miles (51 km) to Angers. For an interesting detour, follow N147 through Saumur, over the Thouet River and into the southern suburb of Bagneux, which has one of the largest dolmens (prehistoric stone structures with side and roof slabs) in France. Standing in a yard by a café at the end of Rue du Dolmen, the monument, built some 5,000 years ago, is 70 feet long and divided into two chambers. The granite slabs that make up its sides and roof weigh as much as 35 tons.

Another Loire Valley curiosity, this one on D751 just west of St-Hilaire-St-Florent, is the *Musée du Champignon* (Mushroom Museum), where you can take a half-hour tour of a labyrinth of caves carved out of the porous limestone called tufa, during which you can see all the stages of growth of the white mushroom inaccurately called the *champignon de Paris*. Just inside the entrance to the caves is an exhibit of the various ways in which the famous tufa (*Westminster Abbey* in London is made from this stone) has been extracted over the years. As much as 40% of the world's canned mushrooms come from the Saumur region, where a full 500 miles of caves are used to grow them. One of the secrets of their successful cultivation is that much of the manure in which they thrive comes from the nearby riding school. You can buy mushrooms, fresh or canned, at the museum entrance. It's closed mid-November through mid-February; there's an admission charge (phone: 41-50-31-55).

A beautiful church dating from the 11th to the 13th century graces the pleasant village of Cunault, 3 miles (5 km) west of Chênehutte-les-Tuffeaux on D751. The belfry is Romanesque; the west front is fortified, with a fine 13th-century sculpture of the Adoration of the Virgin. Inside are traces of the painted decoration used to emphasize the main architectural lines of medieval churches, in addition to richly carved capitals and a rare 13th-century painted wooden shrine, riddled with wormholes but still lovely. The nave of this large church tapers slightly to make it appear even longer than it is. Just beyond Cunault four dolmens rise dramatically in the hills behind the village of Gennes; several menhirs (upright stones) stand in nearby fields.

The 21 miles (34 km) from Gennes to Angers along D751 are a pastoral jaunt through fields of corn and sunflowers, vineyards, old windmills, and sleepy villages where little seems to stir except the church bells that mark the hours.

Auberge Jeanne de Laval This quintessential family-run Loire Valley inn boasts a one-Michelin-star restaurant featuring such Anjou specialties as Loire fish with *beurre blanc* sauce and local wines and cheeses. Ten comfortable rooms open onto a tranquil, flower-filled garden. Closed January through early February; restaurant also closed Mondays. MasterCard and Visa accepted. 54 Rte. Nationale, in the tiny village of Les Rosiers-sur-Loire, just across the river from Gennes (phone: 41-51-80-17; fax: 41-38-04-18). Expensive.

Le Prieuré One of the most splendid hostelries of the Loire Valley, famous for its quiet, wooded setting with a sweeping view of the Loire, elegant quarters in a 12th- and 15th-century priory, and an excellent dining room, sits on a bluff above Chênehutte-les-Tuffeaux. A member of the Relais & Châteaux group, it offers a tennis court, a heated pool, and 35 rooms, 15 in the château and the rest in bungalows scattered over the grounds. The dining room features such items as *foie gras de canard* (duck foie gras), *veau à l'angevine* (veal with wine sauce), and a *menu dégustation* (tasting menu) with small portions of many specialties. The view from your table will be spectacular, especially at sunset. Closed January through early March. Make room reservations several months in advance for the summer and as early as possible the rest of the year. Chênehutte-les-Tuffeaux, 5 miles (8 km) west of Saumur via D751 (phone: 41-67-90-14; fax: 41-67-92-24). Expensive.

ANGERS Although the Loire River flows on for another 80 miles (128 km) before reaching Nantes and the Atlantic Ocean, the city of Angers (pop. 141,000) is generally considered the western end of the Loire Valley. Conquered by the Romans and later by the Normans, Angers lived through an especially brilliant period under the Counts of Anjou, from the 10th to the 12th century. Now a bustling regional center, it still boasts the imposing 13th-century *Château d'Angers,* built by Louis IX in a feudal style patterned on the crusaders' castles in Palestine; its 17 large towers are connected by a high curtain wall, and deer grazing in the dry moat add a whimsical note. Displayed within is the huge and splendid *Tapisserie de l'Apocalypse* (Apocalypse Tapestry), woven in Paris between 1373 and 1380 for Louis I of Anjou; its colors are still vivid.

The other sightseeing highlight in Angers, the *Cathédrale St-Maurice,* has a single nave with the first Gothic vaulting constructed in Anjou, an impressive late Romanesque façade with fine sculptures surmounted by three towers, and a good collection of stained glass windows. The oldest window, in the north aisle, dates from the 12th century.

The lovely *Musée Jean Lurçat* (4 Blvd. Arago; phone: 41-87-41-06) is devoted to contemporary tapestry, displayed in a stunning vaulted space. It's closed Mondays from October through May; the admission charge also includes entry to the nearby abbey. The *Musée des Beaux Arts* is in the *Logis Barrault* at 10 Rue du Musée (phone: 41-88-64-65; fax: 41-88-09-04). It's open daily; there's an admission charge. On the streets between the château and the cathedral are some interesting 16th- and 18th-century buildings.

The popular *Festival of Anjou,* held here in July, includes ballets, concerts, plays, and other cultural activities. The very efficient tourist office in front of the château on Place Kennedy (phone: 41-88-69-93; fax: 41-88-36-77) publishes a variety of helpful brochures (many in English). Bikes can be rented at the train station on Place de la Gare.

Also on Place Kennedy is the *Maison du Vin de l'Anjou* (No. 5; phone: 41-88-81-13), with samples of some of the region's contemporary treasures. Anjou wines such as the rare dry Savennières as well as wines from the Layon Valley and from around Saumur can be tasted and purchased in this shop just across from the château. It is closed Tuesdays from April through August, Mondays and Tuesdays from October through December, and January through February.

Off the usual tourist track, just northwest of Angers via N162, is the *Château de Plessis-Macé,* one of the Loire Valley's most impressive. Its fortress-like exterior is belied by a lovely interior courtyard; its most distinctive feature is a balcony carved of white stone, one of the few remaining in France from which medieval ladies watched jousting matches. There is also a 15th-century chapel with a carved wooden gallery in the Flamboyant style. The château is closed Tuesdays, mornings from March through May and October through December, January, and February. There's an admission charge (phone: 41-32-06-01).

BEST EN ROUTE

Pavillon Paul Le Quéré This fine hostelry in a converted late 19th-century home has four splendid suites and six elegant guestrooms, all decorated individually and all with luxurious bathrooms. The one-Michelin-star restaurant, in an elegant Victorian dining room, features "modern" cuisine (the chef studied with Joël Robuchon) such as tiny cabbages stuffed with crab, and lamb with basil. The wine list favors the Loire Valley. Restaurant closed Sunday dinner. In the center of town, at 3 Bd. Maréchal-Foch (phone: 41-20-00-20; fax: 41-20-06-20). Very expensive.

Château de Noirieux This handsome 19-room luxury hotel is housed in two historic buildings—a converted 17th-century château and a 15th-century manor house, both overlooking the Loire River and a large park. The restaurant's new chef excels in updated classics like Loire River fish stuffed with foie gras. There's also a 16th-century chapel on the premises. A pool, tennis court, and Jacuzzi complex round out the amenities. Closed mid-January through February; restaurant also closed Sunday dinner and Mondays from mid-October through mid-April. Near Briollay, 11 miles (18 km) north of Angers via D52 and east on D109, at 26 Rte. du Moulin (phone: 41-42-50-05; fax: 41-37-91-00). Expensive.

Hôtel d'Anjou An old-fashioned but refurbished hotel with 53 spacious rooms and three suites, fine service, and an excellent restaurant, *La Salamandre,* which features such local specialties as Loire fish in Anjou wine sauce. Restaurant closed Sundays. In the center of town, at 1 Bd. Maréchal-Foch (phone: 41-88-24-82, hotel; 41-89-99-55, restaurant). Expensive.

Le Toussaint This comfortable place features simple and creative cooking such as calf sweetbreads, *foie gras au vin de Layon,* and fresh fruit sherbets. Closed Sunday dinner, Mondays, and one week each in February and August. Reservations advised. Major credit cards accepted. 7 Pl. Kennedy (phone: 41-87-46-20). Expensive.

France This hostelry has 55 attractive rooms, one suite, and a restaurant, *Plantagenets,* that offers fine food and service. Closed December 22 through January 7; restaurant also closed Saturdays. Opposite the train station, at 8 Pl. de la Gare (phone: 41-88-49-42; fax: 41-86-76-70). Moderate.

En Route from Angers Backtrack east from Angers along the Loire's northern bank on D952 and N152. Route D952 provides enchanting views of the river and its tree-covered islands as well as glimpses of towns and villages with big stone quays that were once prosperous river ports. The highway hugs the edge of the river through Saumur, where it becomes N152 to continue its scenic route eastward. Follow it to Port-Boulet, across the Loire from the enormous stacks and globes of the Avoine nuclear power plant, begun in 1957 and one of the first in France. Then turn north for 3 miles (5 km) on D749 to Bourgueil, a total of 40 miles (64 km) from Angers.

BOURGUEIL A charming little town with the remains of a powerful 10th-century Benedictine abbey, Bourgueil produces one of the two acclaimed red wines of the Loire Valley (the other being that of Chinon, 11 miles/18 km south; see above). You can drive for miles past vine-covered slopes and find innumerable merchants happy to let you taste and buy their full-bodied, ruby red Bourgueil. It was in Bourgueil that the deaf French poet Pierre de Ronsard met the inspiration for his famous love poems.

BEST EN ROUTE

Château des Réaux This charming 15th-century château built by the Briçonnet family, who later constructed the *Châteaux of Chenonceaux* and *Azay-le-*

Rideau, is now a small hotel. All 12 guestrooms in the main château and five more in an annex are charmingly appointed with antiques. There is a small restaurant on the premises, and guests have access to nearby tennis courts. (phone: 47-95-14-40; fax: 47-95-18-34). Expensive.

Château des Briottières Seemingly lost in the countryside, this truly inviting 18th-century château has been in the same family for generations. Visitors who stay in one of the nine elegantly decorated guestrooms overlooking the château's park are treated like friends by the hosts, who speak English. There is a heated pool and a billiard room; an 18-hole golf course in nearby Champigné is available to guests. Children are welcome. Although there is no restaurant per se, the owners prepare a prix fixe dinner nightly for guests who request it, and join them for an aperitif. Closed *Christmas.* Near the village of Champigné (call ahead for directions), east of Angers on the way to Bourgueil (phone: 41-42-00-02; fax: 41-42-01-55). Moderate.

En Route from Bourgueil Route D35 east connects with N152, which leads to Langeais.

BEST EN ROUTE

Château de Rochecotte This converted château once owned by Talleyrand has 26 rooms, two suites, a formal French garden, and a chef of the first rank. Her nouvelle specialties include fish with coconut curry sauce; the decor of both the hotel and restaurant is contemporary, complementing the cuisine. Closed February. Four miles (6 km) east of Bourgueil on D35, in St-Patrice (phone: 47-96-91-28; fax: 47-96-90-62). Expensive.

LANGEAIS This crowded town 12 miles (19 km) east of Bourgueil boasts store windows filled with enough fishing gear to tempt any visitor into testing the waters of the Loire, a few steps away. In its center reposes another of the region's idiosyncratic and memorable castles. Although much smaller than those of Chambord and Blois, the 15th-century *Château de Langeais* is unusual in that it was built entirely within a five-year period by Louis XI and has remained unaltered ever since. The building, whose entrance is a drawbridge between two solid towers, looks like a powerful medieval fortress. It was intended to occupy a strong defensive position in case of an attack from Bretons heading from Nantes up the Loire Valley toward Touraine. Such worries were put to rest on December 16, 1491, when the son of Louis XI, Charles VIII, married Anne of Brittany in this castle, thereby uniting Brittany and France. Its apartments contain an excellent collection of 15th- and 16th-century antiques, among them Anne's marriage chest. The château is open daily; there is an admission charge (phone: 47-96-72-60).

BEST EN ROUTE

Hosten In this charming, comfortable inn are 11 rooms, most situated on winding corridors over an inner courtyard, well isolated from traffic noise. The rustic decor of chintz and country furniture is confined to the cozy bedrooms; the bathrooms are decidedly modern. The elegant, one-Michelin-star restaurant, *Le Langeais,* full of dark wood and fresh flowers, serves dishes like lobster salad with foie gras. Hotel closed mid-January through early February; restaurant also closed Monday dinner and Tuesdays from late June through early July. 2 Rue Gambetta (phone: 47-96-82-12; fax: 47-96-56-72). Hotel, moderate; restaurant, expensive.

En Route from Langeais Continue 3 miles (5 km) east on N152 to Cinq-Mars-la-Pile.

CINQ-MARS-LA-PILE This tiny village has two noteworthy monuments: its château and *La Pile,* a unique Gallo-Roman tower. The *Château de Luynes,* now only two overgrown 11th- and 12th-century towers, provides a fine cliff-top view over the Loire and its south bank. It was once the property of a favorite courtier of Louis XIII, Henri d'Effiat, the Marquis de Cinq-Mars, who was convicted of conspiracy against Richelieu and beheaded at the ripe old age of 22. *La Pile,* visible from the highway, is a square masonry structure 98 feet high surmounted by four small pyramids. A path leads up a ridge to its base, but its solid interior doesn't invite climbing. Its purpose remains a mystery, as does the name of the town, which in earlier times was called St-Mars.

En Route from Cinq-Mars-la-Pile To get to Luynes, the last stop on this route and 7 miles (11 km) west of Tours, turn off N152 onto D76, a little more than 2 miles (3 km) beyond Cinq-Mars.

LUYNES This town lies under the shadow of a 13th-century feudal château. Privately owned and occupied by the same family since 1619, the château can be viewed only from below. There are many troglodyte houses in this area, and signs lead through the pretty countryside behind and above the town to the ruins of a Roman aqueduct.

BEST EN ROUTE

Domaine de Beauvois Another luxurious Loire Valley château and a member of the Relais & Châteaux group, this one offers 32 rooms and four suites surrounded by woods. There are riding stables, a pool, a tennis court, and a restaurant. Culinary specialties (of inconsistent quality) include an eel terrine, bass cooked with truffles and leeks, and, for dessert, *feuilleté aux pruneaux* (puff pastry with prunes). Closed January through mid-March. Two miles (3 km) northwest of Luynes via D49 (phone: 47-55-50-11; fax: 47-55-59-62). Hotel, very expensive; restaurant, expensive.

Normandy

Normandy owes its name to the Northmen, or Norsemen, those Scandinavian invaders who swept down the Seine River valley in AD 820. This was neither the first, nor the last, time that an invasion would play a momentous part in the province's history. Whether the early Celts, whose descendants remain in neighboring Brittany, were settlers or conquerors when they arrived in the region in the 5th century BC is unclear. The Romans who sent many of them fleeing to the west were certainly conquerors, and their legions stayed long enough to build the towns where Evreux, Rouen, and Coutances now stand, leaving evidence of their presence in the ruins at Lillebonne. Saxon and German raiders disturbed the Roman peace, effecting the withdrawal of the legions toward the end of the 4th century and leaving Normandy a battleground between warring factions, a condition to be repeated on several occasions.

The area was under Frankish domination from 500 to the early 9th century, and that influence is reflected in the region's major religious houses from the period. Although the Norsemen plundered and sometimes destroyed many of those establishments, by the early 10th century the invaders had become settlers, and in 911 the Norman chieftain Rolf the Ranger became Rollo, Duke of Normandy. The most famous of Rollo's progeny was William the Bastard, who, thanks to his successful invasion of England in 1066, was accorded the sobriquet William the Conqueror.

Normandy's potential as a threat to the French throne dominated its history for the next 138 years, especially after the English King Henry II added to his empire the vast territories of Aquitaine by his marriage to the colorful Duchess Eleanor. Henry's son Richard, realizing that the duchy's position was vulnerable, built the formidable *Château Gaillard* on the Seine, close to the border of the French territories. Richard's foresight notwithstanding, his brother, the unloved and unwise John Lackland, lost Normandy in 1202, when Philippe Auguste invaded the duchy to avenge John's murder of his nephew Arthur of Brittany. From 1204 Normandy was united with the French crown, first as a duchy held by the sovereign and later as a province with its own governing body at Rouen. But it still served as a battleground during the dynastic quarrels of the French and English kings, especially during the Hundred Years' War, which ended in 1453 with the routing of the English.

For the next hundred years or so, Normandy enjoyed peace and prosperity, seeing the construction of such great castles as the *Châteaux d'O* and *Fontaine-Henry*. Rouen and Caen became free cities during this period, and the increasingly important merchant classes built the lovely half-timbered houses that still line the old streets of Rouen.

For the next several centuries, Normandy was relatively quiet—until 1944, when in the World War II battle to liberate France from the Nazis, more than 200,000 buildings and nearly 600 towns and villages—among them Le Havre, St-Lô, Caen, Lisieux, and Evreux—were almost completely destroyed. Of all the great ancient Norman cities, only Bayeux and its two great treasures, the cathedral and the *Tapisserie de la Reine Mathilde* (Queen Matilda's Tapestry), remains virtually intact. Still, while the war changed the urban face of Normandy radically, the more resilient rural landscape retains much of the lush green pasturage and forest that must have attracted the early Norsemen.

Normandy is bordered on the west by Brittany and the English Channel, on the north by the Channel as it narrows toward the Straits of Dover, on the northeast and east by Picardy and the Ile-de-France, and on the south by the Loire Valley. Although small by American standards, the province is divided by geography and tradition into distinct regions. The Cotentin Peninsula in the northwest, stretching to the Channel around Cherbourg, is famous for horse breeding and dairy farming. Dairy farming also is important in the Bessin, the area between Bayeux and the coast, a region also known for its handsome gray stone farmhouses. The *bocage* (a region of small fields divided by stone walls or hedgerows) south of the Bessin is most renowned for its dairy farming and the cider that comes from the apple and pear trees that blossom with astonishing beauty during April and May. On the prairie-type terrain around Caen cereals have become a major postwar crop. East of Caen, in the Pays d'Auge and Calvados (known for apple brandy), are more apple orchards, often surrounded by half-timbered farms and run-down barns that make this part of France especially picturesque. The dairy farms in the Pays d'Auge provide the milk that is used to produce three celebrated cheeses: camembert, livarot, and pont-l'évêque. South of the plains around Caen, near Flers, Clécy, and Falaise, are dramatic gorges. Across the Seine, in the triangle formed by Dieppe, Le Havre, and Rouen, are the rolling hills and valleys of the Pays de Caux, bordered on the Channel by great white chalk cliffs that drop precipitously into the sea.

Commercial fishing has remained an important activity for the people of Normandy, some of whom go as far as Newfoundland, where they harvest the cold North Atlantic for cod. The fruit of their labors graces the tables of most Norman restaurants and homes. The regional specialty, *assiette de fruits de mer* (a platter of fresh shellfish), might include crayfish, crabs, shrimp, oysters, clams, cockles, mussels, and periwinkles, often served on a bed of damp seaweed. Another favorite, *marmite dieppoise,* can consist of sole, turbot, brill, mackerel, whiting, shrimp, and crab, all simmered in their own juices to make a substantial stew/soup to which is added another Norman staple, fresh cream. What is not cooked in cream in Normandy is often cooked in hard cider. Normandy's other famous beverage is calvados, a classy applejack that takes up to 15 years to mature. Additional regional specialties include Caen tripe; oysters from St-Vaast-la-Hougue; *agneau pré-salé* (lamb fed on saltwater grasses near Mont-St-Michel); the omelette *à la Mère Poulard,* named for the famous restaurateuse on Mont-St-Michel who created the enormous, soufflé-like concoction; and sauces featuring thick *crème fraîche,* slightly sour cream.

This tour can be divided into three distinct sections. The first, which starts at Vernon, traverses the Pays de Caux from Rouen to Dieppe, travels down the coast to Le Havre, and crosses the Seine by the great Pont du Tancarville, heading for Honfleur, Trouville-sur-Mer, Deauville, and Cabourg, where it turns inland to Caen. The second leg of the route, a loop originating and ending in Caen, takes in the Normandy beaches immortalized on *D-Day.* The third section, starting again in Caen, leads northwest to Bayeux, then southwest to St-Lô, Coutances, and Granville, on the west coast of the Cotentin Peninsula, before climaxing at hauntingly brooding Mont-St-Michel. Throughout the region events are held to commemorate *D-Day;* for information, contact the very helpful *Comité Régional du Tourisme de Normandie* (14 Rue Charles-Corbeau, Evreux 27000; phone: 32-33-79-00; fax: 32-31-19-04) or any local tourist office. Also note that museums and other sites in the area may keep longer hours during these events to accommodate the extra tourists.

Expect to pay $190 or more per night for a double room in a very expensive hotel; between $150 and $190 in an expensive place; from $90 to $150 in a moderate hotel; and less than $90 in an inexpensive one. Hotels in Deauville and Cabourg are exceptionally expensive in July and August, often charging closer to $250 for a double room. In any season a sea view can add $30 to $40 to a room's price. Hotels with restaurants often require *demi-pension* (breakfast plus one other meal) in July and August; be sure to inquire in advance. Unless otherwise indicated, all hotels accept major credit cards and are open year-round. Most feature telephones, TV sets, and private baths in all of their rooms. However, some less expensive ones may have private baths in only some rooms; it's a good idea when making a reservation to inquire whether your room has a private bath. Most hotels in the region do not have air conditioning. Dinner for two in a very expensive restaurant will cost $160 or more; in an expensive one, $110 to $160; in a moderate place, $55 to $110; and in an inexpensive spot, less than $55. Prices include service but not wine or drinks. All restaurants listed below are open for lunch and dinner unless otherwise noted. For each location hotels and restaurants are listed alphabetically by price category.

VERNON TO CAEN

VERNON Although much of the town was destroyed in World War II, its site on the left bank of the Seine, backed by the Forest of Bizy and opposite the great Forest of Vernon, has attracted visitors ever since the 12th century, when Louis IX (St. Louis) came here to escape the heat of Paris. The collegiate *Eglise Notre-Dame,* which largely escaped damage in the war, was originally built in the 12th century and added to and modified in the 15th and 16th centuries. The splendid rose window on the west front is adorned on both sides by galleries with flying buttresses. The 15th-century nave, taller than the transept, is lofty and narrow, its cool lines enhanced by the grace of the triforium and the elegance of the high windows. In the precincts of *Notre-Dame* are a few 15th-century half-timbered houses that escaped the bombing, including one next door to the church and others on Rue Carnot. The *Musée Alphonse-Georges Poulain* (12 Rue du Pont; phone: 32-21-28-09) has a collection of animal paintings and Impressionist works in a half-timbered dwelling. Closed mornings and Mondays; admission charge. About a mile (1.6 km) outside of town, hidden behind stately trees, is the 18th-century *Château de Bizy,* the home of the Duke of Albuféra. The interior, handsomely decorated in the Empire style, contains some splendid tapestries and paneling and a collection of souvenirs of the Napoleonic era. The gardens are adorned with waterfalls and Baroque fountains that suggest Italy rather than northern France. The château is open from April through October; closed Fridays; admission charge (phone: 32-51-00-82).

From Vernon we highly recommend a short side trip to the town of Giverny. Cross the bridge to the suburb of Vernonnet, which affords a pleasant view of forested islands upstream and down. Also here are the remains of the original 12th-century bridge and the donjon of the small fortress that guarded it on the right bank. Turn right on D5, and about a mile (1.6 km) upstream from the bridge is Giverny.

GIVERNY Nestled against the hillside, this charming little village was home to Claude Monet from 1883 to 1926. His house, the *Musée Claude-Monet* (84 Rue Claude-Monet; phone: 32-51-28-21), owes its present condition—a somewhat idealized version of the way it was when he lived here—to an international group of sponsors who rescued it from dilapidation. The painter's love affair with color can be appreciated in the exterior's pink walls, white highlights, and green jalousies; the blue motif of the old-fashioned country kitchen; and the wonderful primrose-yellow dining room. The interior—with platters on the walls, dressers in the dining room, and pots on the yellow chimneypiece—was restored to look as it did when Renoir, Sisley, Cézanne, Manet, and Pissarro dropped by for a bite and a chat. Monet's much-loved Japanese prints largely have been returned to the places he allotted them. His bedroom is an unexpectedly elegant enclave, with none of the Bohemian ambience one associates with late 19th-century painters. Most appealing is his drawing room/studio, complete with couch, armchairs, and basketwork chairs, which evokes the atmosphere of the good talk, cigar smoke, and wine that must have prevailed here.

One of Monet's great passions was his garden, which has been meticulously re-created so that what one sees at any time of the year is, as far as possible, what he saw. Anyone who has seen pictures of the water-lily pool with its Japanese bridge will recognize the original immediately, now regrettably separated from the main gardens by a road. The irises, peonies, heliotropes, Judas trees, willows, and water lilies all appear here just as they do on canvas. In spring wisteria blooms over the bridge, and in the extensive gardens closer to the house, fruit trees burst into a blizzard of white and pink flowers not far from great masses of daffodils. In summer morning glories appear, along with snapdragons, nasturtiums, foxglove, sweet peas, columbine, phlox, gentian, and sage. In fall the garden is ablaze with the outrageous colors of dahlias and sunflowers, subtler asters, and lofty hollyhocks. Seen in any of the three flowering seasons, Giverny leaves an indelible impression. There is a small restaurant on the premises for simple meals. The museum is open from April through October; closed Mondays; admission charge.

The *Musée des Impressionistes Américains* (next to the Monet gardens, at 99 Rue Claude-Monet; phone: 32-51-94-65) showcases important American Impressionists influenced by Monet and other great French 19th- and 20th-century painters. Open April through October; closed Mondays; admission charge.

BEST EN ROUTE

Château de Brécourt This elegant Louis XIII château in a large park complete with indoor pool and tennis courts has 29 luxurious rooms and a restaurant serving traditional cuisine. There are no TV sets. In Pacy-sur-Eure, 9 miles (14 km) south of Vernon via D181 (phone: 32-52-40-50; fax: 32-52-69-65). Expensive.

Le Relais Normand/Hôtel d'Evreux This 18th-century townhouse is a typically French family-run hotel/restaurant with 18 rooms, homey touches, fine food, and friendly service. Restaurant closed Sundays. 11 Pl. d'Evreux, Vernon (phone: 32-21-16-12; fax: 32-21-32-73). Moderate.

En Route from Vernon Take D313 north to Les Andelys to see the remains of *Château Gaillard,* built by Richard the Lion-Hearted in the 12th century. The view over Les Andelys along the river, romantically dominated on the left bank by cliffs, is spectacular. From Les Andelys take D1 north to D2 and Ecouis, site of one of the most famous churches in the Vexin (as the surrounding territory is known); built in 1310, it contains a 14th-century wooden sculpture of St. Veronica and an unusual statue supposedly of St. Agnès, whose robe is formed from her flowing hair. About 3 miles (5 km) north on D2 turn right onto D12; the church at Lisors is worth a stop to see the beautiful 14th-century statue of Our Lady, Queen of Heaven. From there D715 north leads to the picturesque ruins of the 12th-century Cistercian *Abbaye de Mortemer,* surrounded by trees and lawns.

Continuing on D715 and turning left onto D6, you pass through Lyons-la-Forêt, the center of a beech forest, once the favorite hunting grounds of the Norman dukes and still the site of formal hunts, with much scarlet livery and black velour headgear in evidence between April and September. The town's 12th-century church, the *Eglise St-Denis,* contains several huge wooden statues, and there are many ancient half-timbered houses, one the former home of Maurice Ravel.

Turn left onto D321 and follow it for about 10 miles (16 km) to the *Abbaye de Fontaine-Guérard,* on the banks of the Andelle River. This Cistercian convent now is owned by the Salvation Army. The remains of the abbey church, chapter house, nuns' parlor, and study hall reveal interesting early-Gothic features. The abbey is open from April through October; closed Mondays; admission charge (phone: 32-49-03-82).

Backtrack on D321 to D1 and take that north about 6 miles (10 km) to the restored *Château de Vascoeuil,* where one finds—surprisingly—sculptures by Braque, Léger, and Calder, as well as works by David and Bernard Buffet. Open daily, April to November; admission charge (phone: 35-23-62-35). Just north of Vascoeuil off D1, N31 leads west to Martainville and its château, a small, sensible-looking red brick affair that now serves as a showplace of Norman arts, crafts, and traditions. The kitchen, with its huge brick fireplace and dozens of implements, is a joy. The château is closed Tuesdays, Wednesdays, and holidays, April through October, Mondays through Fridays in winter. There is an admission charge (phone: 35-23-40-13).

From Martainville continue west on N31 to Rouen, 8 miles (13 km) away.

ROUEN For a detailed report on the city, its sights, its hotels, and its restaurants, see *Rouen* in THE CITIES.

En Route from Rouen Take D982 west to Canteleu, which offers a good view along the Seine from the top of the hill. You can reach St-Martin-de-Boscherville by crossing the corniche on D982, but a more interesting—and circuitous—route is via the turnoff on D51 from Rouen, running along the cliff top above the river south to Sahurs, then turning right on D351 to drive north through the Roumare Forest. St-Martin boasts the Benedictine *Abbaye de St-George de Boscherville,* founded in 1114 by Guillaume de Tancarville on the site of a structure built in 1050 by his father, Raoul. One of the finest examples of Romanesque architecture in Normandy, the church is astonishingly pure in design, with a minimum of trappings to distract from the simple arches. Two jousting knights, typical of the era in which the church was constructed, adorn the capitals in the south transept. For more information, contact the *Association Touristique de l'Abbaye Romane* (Pl. Abbaye; phone: 35-32-10-82.)

From St-Martin take D982 to D65 and the Benedictine *Abbaye de Jumièges.* The ruins of the abbey are among the most romantic in France;

monks lived here from the 7th century until the Revolution, during which time *Jumièges* was one of the area's great ecclesiastical establishments. The remains include the nave and parts of the transept and chancel; in the center of the square cloister is a yew tree that romantics claim is almost as old as the abbey itself. Open daily; admission charge (phone: 35-37-24-02).

Return to D982 via D143 and continue west about 6 miles (10 km) to the *Abbaye de St-Wandrille* (phone: 35-96-23-11), whose Benedictine community still thrives; monks have lived here, with interruptions, since the 7th century. St. Wandrille, a count at Dagobert's court, became a monk, was ordained at *St-Ouen* in Rouen, and eventually founded the abbey named for him. The cloister, which can be viewed only on a guided tour (offered daily at 3 and 4 PM), has an interesting 16th-century lavabo (a ceremonial washbasin). Vespers (sung in Gregorian chant) and mass take place daily.

Continue west on D982 to Caudebec-en-Caux, 2 miles (3 km) from St-Wandrille and 22 miles (35 km) from Rouen.

BEST EN ROUTE

Auberge des Ruines This four-room hotel is wonderfully rustic, with a romantic arboreal bower and the exquisite abbey ruins nearby. The restaurant is decent, and no one minds if you linger by the fire. Closed late December through mid-January and for four weeks in the summer; restaurant also closed Monday dinner and Tuesdays. MasterCard and Visa accepted. 1 Pl. de la Mairie, Jumièges (phone: 35-37-24-05). Restaurant, moderate; hotel, inexpensive.

CAUDEBEC-EN-CAUX The extraordinary view over the Seine, especially from the steps of the *Hôtel de Ville* (Town Hall), makes Caudebec an attractive spot, even though most of the half-timbered houses that once lined its streets were burned down by the Germans in 1940.

The fine Flamboyant Gothic *Eglise Notre-Dame,* with its celebrated organ, dates from the 15th and 16th centuries. Sculpted on the balustrade surrounding the church are some of the words from the *Magnificat* and the *Salve Regina.* The 15th-century window over the north door is of English glass, rare in France. The *Musée Biochet-Bréchot* in the wonderful *Maison des Templiers* (Templars' House) has pictures and artifacts of local history from prehistoric times to the present. It is open daily from mid-June to mid-September; admission charge. For information in the off-season, contact the tourist office (Pl. Charles-de-Gaulle; phone: 35-96-20-65.) The Saturday morning food market on the Place du Marché has existed since 1390.

BEST EN ROUTE

Manoir de Rétival On a bluff overlooking the valley of the Seine, this restaurant in an elegantly restored manor house has earned a Michelin star. It is the place to sample *nouvelle normande* cooking, such as an almost fat-free meat terrine and a delicate apple tart with caramel sauce. There's a large selection of fine local ciders on the wine list. Closed Mondays, Tuesday lunch, and two weeks each in the summer and winter. Reservations advised. Major credit cards accepted. The two small but charming guestrooms must be reserved well in advance. 2 Rue St-Clair (phone: 35-96-11-22; fax: 35-96-29-22). Expensive.

En Route from Caudebec Take D81 out of Caudebec to Villequier, about 3 miles (5 km) west.

VILLEQUIER This charming riverside spot is sheltered by wooded hills. Victor Hugo stayed here often at his son-in-law's family home, which is now the *Musée Victor-Hugo* (Quai Victor-Hugo; phone: 35-56-78-31). It contains manuscripts, autographs, and letters by or concerning the author, as well as portraits and furniture. The museum is open daily; admission charge. Continue on D81 for 8 miles (13 km) to Lillebonne.

LILLEBONNE Back when the Romans controlled Gaul, this city, which was then called Juliobona, was a major metropolis. Today only the grass-covered remains of Lillebonne's Roman theater, which can be seen from the Place de l'Hôtel de Ville, recall its early importance. William the Conqueror found Lillebonne strategically useful, building a fortress whose keep's formidable walls and several towers still remain. It was here that William gathered his barons before crossing to Hastings in 1066. The *Musée Jardin Jean-Rostand* (Rue Victor-Hugo; phone: 35-38-53-73) exhibits various items, including tools and crafts important to the life of the area. It is open afternoons, May through August (closed Tuesdays); open afternoons on Sundays and holidays only, September through April; no admission charge.

En Route from Lillebonne Take D173 5 miles (8 km) to Bolbec, where there are four handsome 18th-century houses on Rue de la République; then follow meandering D149 toward Dieppe, 51 miles (82 km) away. The road passes through typical Pays de Caux countryside, characterized by large half-timbered farmhouses standing in orchards, with the whole farm sometimes ringed by windbreaking rows of oak and beech trees. Here and there barns have been remodeled with chic doors and window boxes, testifying to their new role as country retreats for city dwellers.

Longueville boasts a ruined castle that once belonged to Dunois, the Bastard of Orléans, who appears sympathetically in Shaw's *Saint Joan*. Turn left at the junction with D1 and continue to Arques-la-Bataille, 5 miles (8 km) southeast of Dieppe. Here, poised high on a rock, are the remains of a much larger castle, dating from the 12th century and surrounded by a moat. There are good views over the valley from the keep, the highest point of the castle, though the temptation to wander inside the walls should be avoided, since crumbling masonry can be a danger.

BEST EN ROUTE

Auberge du Clos Normand Regional specialties are served either in the wood-beamed and copper decor of the dining room or in the garden, which has a footbridge-laced stream running through it. Quiche lovers should request the *tarte aux moules* (with mussels). There are seven rooms and two suites available, all overlooking a garden and the river. Restaurant closed Monday dinner and Tuesdays off-season, one week in April, and from mid-November to mid-December. Reservations advised. Four miles (6 km) from Dieppe in Martin-Eglise, at 22 Rue Henri-IV (phone: 35-82-71-01). Moderate.

Restaurant St-Denis Excellent traditional cuisine with inventive touches (such as trout with watercress) reigns in this restaurant with a half-timbered façade. Closed Tuesday dinner and Wednesdays. Reservations advised. MasterCard and Visa accepted. Héricourt-en-Caux (phone: 35-96-55-23). Moderate.

DIEPPE The main attraction of this major Channel seaport is its beachfront, which stretches for nearly a mile between cliffs dominated at the west end by a castle and at the east by the port itself. The basins of the port, lined here and there with 18th-century houses, extend deep into the town along Quai de Quesle and Quai de Norvège. Dieppe became a fashionable seaside resort in the 19th century, when it was visited by the Duchess of Berry, Empress Eugénie, and her husband, Napoleon III.

The most interesting of the town's churches is the *Eglise St-Jacques,* dating from the 13th century but with later additions. In its Flamboyant Gothic *Sacred Heart Chapel,* a frieze shows Brazilian Indians, recalling the 16th century, when Dieppe was an important point of embarkation for Atlantic explorers. There still are some picturesque old houses in the neighborhood of *St-Jacques,* especially along Grande-Rue, which leads to another church, the part Gothic, part Renaissance *St-Rémy.* Beyond *St-Rémy* via Rue de Chastes is a much-restored but still imposing 15th-century castle that commands excellent views of the town and its surroundings from the terraces. The town's château-museum is notable for its extensive collection of ivory carvings. It's open daily June through September; closed Tuesdays the rest of the year; admission charge (phone: 35-84-19-76).

On August 19, 1942, Dieppe was the scene of Operation Jubilee, the first Allied landing after the retreat from Dunkirk. A force of 7,000, mostly Canadians, crossed the Channel, hoping to secure a foothold on the northern shore of the Continent. But the Allies did not know how strongly the port was defended, and the operation was a failure, costing the lives of 5,000 soldiers. The so-called Dieppe Raids did, however, teach the Allies two major lessons: first, that since the Germans expected major attacks to come via the ports, plans should be made to attack via the beaches and cliffs instead; second, that aerial and naval bombardment would be essential before land forces could gain a foothold. Almost two years later these lessons were put into effect successfully west of Dieppe, beyond the Orne River, on *D-Day.*

BEST EN ROUTE

Auberge de la Bucherie Small and flower-filled, this restaurant features traditional fare. Closed Sunday dinner, Mondays, late June through early July, and *Christmas* through January 2. Reservations advised. Major credit cards accepted. Rte. de Rouen, in Les Vertus, near Offranville (phone: 35-84-83-10; fax: 35-84-18-19). Moderate.

Marmite Dieppoise The obvious choice here is the *marmite dieppoise*, but there also are other delicious Norman classics. Closed Sunday dinner, Mondays, Thursday dinner (except in July and August), *Christmas* through mid-January, and two weeks in July. Reservations advised. MasterCard and Visa accepted. 8 Rue St-Jean (phone: 35-84-24-26; fax: 35-84-31-12). Moderate.

La Mélie At this one-Michelin-star restaurant, seafood is king. Sublimely fresh products are served in inventive ways, such as the *médaillon de lotte au vinaigre de cidre* (monkfish in cider vinegar). Closed Sunday dinner, Mondays, and mid-September through mid-October. Reservations advised. MasterCard and Visa accepted. Near the port, at 2 Grande Rue du Pollet (phone: 35-84-21-19). Moderate.

La Présidence An inviting place with 88 comfortable rooms, one suite, and a restaurant that offers good seafood dishes and wines plus a fine view of the water. 2 Bd. Verdun (phone: 35-84-31-31; fax: 35-84-86-70). Moderate.

Univers A small yet very popular hotel whose 30 rooms are decorated with beautiful antiques; a restaurant is on the premises (reservations necessary). Closed two weeks in February. 10 Bd. Verdun (phone: 35-84-12-55; fax: 35-40-20-40). Moderate.

En Route from Dieppe D75 climbs the cliff just beyond the castle and runs for a little over a mile along the coast before it turns inland to reach Varengeville-sur-Mer. There one can visit the *Manoir d'Ango* (call the *Hôtel de Ville* at 35-85-12-46), the country home of a famous Dieppe merchant-adventurer whose privateers broke the Portuguese trade monopoly on the west coast of Africa in the 16th century. The manor house, dating from 1530, is a wonderfully asymmetrical pile of brick and stone with sturdy Romanesque arches and a circular dovecote of ornate red and black brick. It is open Tuesdays, Thursdays, weekends, and holiday afternoons from *Easter* through October; admission charge. Varengeville's *Eglise St-Valéry* dates from the 12th century but has been much modified. The church stands in a lonely spot on the cliff's edge, bordered by a cemetery that holds the remains of the celebrated Cubist artist Georges Braque, who designed the *Tree of Jesse* window inside the church.

From the *Phare d'Ailly* (Ailly Lighthouse) in nearby Ste-Marguerite, is possible to see about 40 miles up and down the cliff-lined coast. The lighthouse is open from 8 AM until about an hour before dusk, and its keeper is not averse to accepting a small tip. Ste-Marguerite's 12th-century church, much altered in the 16th century, is notable for its high altar, dating from 1160.

At St-Aubin-sur-Mer turn left off D75 onto D237 to make a delightful 2-mile (3-km) detour along the Dun Valley to Bourg-Dun. The unusual spire on the town's church tower is shaped like the head of an ax.

Return on the same road and turn left onto D68, the coast road, toward Veules-les-Roses, picturesquely situated in a wooded valley through which runs what is supposed to be the shortest river in France. Continue to St-Valéry-en-Caux, 20 miles (32 km) from Dieppe.

BEST EN ROUTE

Les Galets Its seafood specialties, desserts, and superb selection of local cheeses have won this small, modern restaurant much praise. Closed Sunday dinner off-season, Tuesday dinner, Wednesdays, and January through early February. Reservations necessary. Major credit cards accepted. Near the beach, at 3 Rue Victor-Hugo, Veules-les-Roses (phone: 35-97-61-33; fax: 35-57-06-23). Expensive.

ST-VALÉRY-EN-CAUX Like many other coastal towns, the fishing port of St-Val, as it is locally known, is a breach in the great chalk cliffs. Most of its arterial streets run parallel to the colorful yacht and fishing basin that penetrates deep into town. St-Val was badly damaged in 1940, during the retreat of the British 10th Army, but was rebuilt and has become a popular seaside and sailing resort.

BEST EN ROUTE

Port Unusual combinations of fish and sauces can make dining in this restaurant overlooking the port an esoteric culinary experience. Closed Sunday dinner and Mondays. Reservations advised. Major credit cards accepted. 18 Quai d'Amont (phone: 35-97-08-93; fax: 35-97-28-32). Moderate.

En Route from St-Valéry-en-Caux Take the cliff-top road, D79, for 24 miles (38 km) to Fécamp.

FÉCAMP Set between great white cliffs, this is one of France's largest fishing ports. The colorful boats lying placidly at anchor along the quays may be waiting for a tide that will take them to the cold, rough fishing grounds off Newfoundland. Fécamp also is a resort, with a gambling casino and a shopping center that draw people from surrounding villages.

The most interesting sight here is *La Trinité,* an early-Gothic abbey church. The present structure, built between 1175 and 1225 and subsequently embellished, is impressive. Its massive, 210-foot lantern tower dominates the valley of Fécamp, and the interior is no less commanding: Its 416-foot length makes it one of the longest churches in France. The 10 awesome bays in the nave are marvelously free of ornament. When present, however, decoration is elaborate, especially in the sumptuous gilded baldachin, which hovers above the high altar, poised on marble pillars. In the *Lady Chapel* are four famous wooden medallions, including one with a veiled figure of Christ on the cross. Opposite the *Lady Chapel* at the back of the high altar is the *Tabernacle of the Precious Blood,* carved in white marble in 1505. In the south transept is a remarkable *Dormition of the Virgin* (1495) with nine saints and friends in attendance, all sculpted in wonderful detail. Following the humanist tradition of the early Renaissance, the figures are idiosyncratic personalities, suggesting that real models were used.

This abbey was the home of the Benedictine Brother Vincelli, who in 1510 experimented with the herbs he found on the nearby cliffs to produce a soothing liqueur. Closely guarded by the monks, his secret recipe was nonetheless lost during the Revolution; it was recovered in 1863, when a local businessman named Alexandre Le Grand happened upon an old manuscript that turned out to be the recipe. Le Grand called the resulting distillation Bénédictine. The factory where it is made, the *Musée de la Bénédictine* (110 Rue Alexandre-Le-Grand; phone: 35-10-26-00), is open daily from late March to mid-November; admission charge. It houses a sweet-smelling room piled with sacks of dried herbs and lined with bottles from all over the world. In the distillery are handsome old copper vats, and in the cellars, casks where the liqueur matures. And there is much more: Le Grand was a lover of paintings and objets d'art, and his collection, predominantly religious in theme, contains some extraordinary pieces. Just the ivory Spanish triptych of the life of Christ; the ivory, wood, and marble bas-relief *Presentation at the Temple;* and the 12th-century missal merit a visit to the museum. There are scores of other bas-reliefs, statues, and a variety of items rescued from the abbey during the Revolution as well as a fine ironwork collection and 600 oil lamps from the days of the Roman Empire.

BEST EN ROUTE

Auberge de la Rouge This half-timbered restaurant, with a tiny garden for summertime dining, offers fresh seafood and meat dishes. Closed Sunday dinner, Mondays, and two weeks in February. Reservations advised on weekends. MasterCard and Visa accepted. Upstairs are eight simple guestrooms. St-Léonard, about 1 mile (1.6 km) south of Fécamp on D940 (phone: 35-28-07-59; fax: 35-28-70-55). Moderate.

Le Viking The view of cliffs and sea from the dining room gets you in the mood for the well-prepared seafood specialties. Closed Sunday dinner from November through March and Mondays. Reservations advised. MasterCard and Visa accepted. 63 Bd. Albert-I (phone: 35-29-22-92; fax: 35-29-45-24). Moderate.

L'Univers A small, family-run hotel that offers a warm welcome. Some of the 16 rooms have TV sets. There's no restaurant. MasterCard and Visa accepted. In the center of town, at 5 Pl. St-Etienne (phone: 35-28-05-88). Inexpensive.

En Route from Fécamp Take D940, passing at the top of the hill on the right St-Léonard, which boasts some beautiful old half-timbered cottages and farms. Just past St-Léonard switch to the coast road, D211, and follow it down to Yport; from there to Etretat (7 miles/11 km), the road climbs over cliffs that look like moorland, covered with gorse, ferns, and brambles and often shrouded in mist. Along the way look for signs offering fresh fruit and *chèvre* (goat cheese) for sale.

ETRETAT A small, quiet resort, Etretat is little more than a cleft between the precipitous Falaise d'Aval (Aval Cliff), to the left as you face the ocean, and the Falaise d'Amont (Amont Cliff), to the right. The famous opening in the cliff to the left, which looks like a flying buttress, is known as the Porte d'Aval (the Aval Gate), and jutting from the sea close by is the needle rock. The scene will be startlingly familiar to any fan of Claude Monet's work.

The stairway and path from the Aval end of the beach lead to a vantage point offering a view of the cliffs from above, a thrilling perspective when the fog eddies below, around, and above you. The extremely steep path leads past grim World War II–era gun emplacements to the edge of the cliff, where a very narrow pathway, which falls away treacherously on either side, leads to what look like ramparts. A warning about the path: It is narrower on the inland side than on the ocean side; jumping from the narrow side to the cliff's edge, where it is broader, is not too difficult; jumping back, especially in a high wind, can be very dangerous. The flat, milky, blue-white of the ocean here explains why this is known as the Côte d'Albâtre (Alabaster Coast).

On the other side of Etretat the Falaise d'Amont is accessible by car. It is less dramatic than the Falaise d'Aval, although the nearby *Chapelle Notre-Dame-de-la-Garde* is worth seeing. On the beach at Etretat is a small open-air bar, where in the late morning, fishermen sometimes break into song, sea chantey–style.

BEST EN ROUTE

Dormy House Some of the 52 rooms in this tranquil inn offer an exceptional view of the Etretat cliffs. There is a restaurant. Closed mid-November through

March (except for weekends in January). On D940 (phone: 35-27-07-88; fax: 35-29-86-19). Moderate.

En Route from Etretat Take D940 to Le Havre, 17 miles (27 km) to the south.

LE HAVRE About 90% of this port, the second-largest in France, was destroyed in World War II. Its proximity to the English coast made it the target of RAF bombings intended to preclude a German invasion of Great Britain; by 1945 it was the most damaged port in Europe. One of the city's more compelling attractions is the *Musée des Beaux-Arts André-Malraux* (23 Bd. Clemenceau; phone: 35-42-33-97), which contains outstanding works by Eugène Boudin (296 pieces, 50 on permanent display) and Le Havre–born Raoul Dufy. There also are important paintings by Corot, Sisley, Monet, and Pissarro. The museum is closed Tuesdays and holidays; admission charge. Also interesting is the *Cathédrale Notre-Dame* (Rue de Paris), which, devastated in the war, has been almost completely restored, with the result that it has a pristine quality lacking in Normandy's more ornate churches.

Another ecclesiastical site worth visiting is the *Abbaye de Graville* (Vierge Noire; phone: 35-47-14-01), in what is now a suburb of Le Havre. The present edifice is a restoration of the one built in the 12th and 13th centuries. The buildings to the right, where Henry V stayed during the siege of Harfleur in 1415, are now a museum containing a collection of painted wooden houses representing different types of popular architecture found throughout France. The abbey and museum are closed Mondays and Tuesdays; admission charge to the museum.

Ste-Adresse, a suburb on the cliffs northeast of town, features Edwardian-era cliff-top villas and a tiny chapel, *Notre-Dame-des-Flots* (Our Lady of the Tides), lined with plaques thanking the Virgin for guiding a loved one to a safe harbor. Ste-Adresse was the provisional capital of Belgium during World War I, and the Belgian coat of arms has been incorporated into that of the village.

Harfleur, now another suburb of Le Havre, was a port of considerable importance until the 16th century. During the Hundred Years' War the English laid siege to the town no less than nine times, though they were successful in penetrating the walls only once, in 1415. At the time, Henry V was a guest at Graville, and the moment was immortalized in Shakespeare's *Henry V,* when the king says, "Once more unto the breach, dear friends, once more, or close the wall up with our English dead!" By the bard's time the Breach (La Brèque) had become the common name for the neighborhood of Harfleur where the wall had been breached. Parts of Harfleur's old wall are visible near the *Porte de Rouen* (Rouen Gate).

The striking 272-foot-high bell tower that dominates Harfleur belongs to the *Eglise St-Martin,* built in the 15th and 16th centuries. Inside, the decorative capitals on the pillars on the north side and the Renaissance organ are worth noting. Among the not always attractive 19th- and 20th-century buildings, you still can glimpse parts of the Old Town; Rue des 104, Rue de l'Eure, and Rue Thiers are the most rewarding.

BEST EN ROUTE

Foch This is a quiet 33-room hotel with no dining room. In the center of town near the port, at 4 Rue Caligny, Le Havre (phone: 35-42-50-69; fax: 35-43-40-17). Moderate.

Le Montagné Norman ingredients prepared with a modern touch are featured in this elegant restaurant near the port. Try the sea scallops sautéed with oysters and fresh herbs. Closed Saturday lunch, Wednesdays, and for some school vacations. Reservations advised. Major credit cards accepted. 50 Quai M. Féré, Le Havre (phone: 35-42-77-44). Moderate.

Nice-Havrais Seafood and other regional specialties abound here, among them turbot in raspberry vinegar, sweetbreads and lobster in tarragon sauce, shrimp and lobster crêpes, and steak with oysters cooked in champagne. Closed Sunday dinner, Mondays, and several weeks in summer. Reservations advised. MasterCard and Visa accepted. 6 Pl. F.-Sauvage, in the Le Havre suburb of Ste-Adresse (phone: 35-46-14-59). Moderate.

En Route from Le Havre Take N182 to the spectacular Pont de Tancarville, a suspension bridge completed in 1959 and nearly a mile long. After crossing the bridge, turn right onto N178. The south side of the Seine here is known as the Marais Vernier (Vernier Marsh), which was drained by Dutch engineers and laborers during the reign of Henri IV. The marshy plain is today a rich alluvial pastureland crisscrossed by canals and dotted with dairies and fruit farms. The plain and the surrounding hills can be seen to great advantage from the Pointe de la Roque, just off N178 between the Pont de Tancarville and Foulbec, whence a coast road leads to Honfleur, 34 miles (54 km) from Le Havre.

HONFLEUR Imagine a bright blue sky in the west, nervous gray clouds in the east, and, where they meet, luminous edges shedding a watery, silver light that illuminates an old port. Picturesque fishing boats lie at anchor, and tall narrow houses, their sides lined with gray slate, loom over the quays. This is Honfleur, a colorful antique but a working one. The picturesque boats are functional, and their casual comings and goings may be to and from places as remote as St-Pierre and Miquelon, off Newfoundland. Honfleur is quiet on Sundays, but on other days the fishermen, ships' engineers, and carpenters lend a sense of urgency to the place.

The Honfleur-born painter Eugène Boudin brought Monet, Renoir, Sisley, Pissarro, and others here, where their experiments with light eventually gave the world Impressionism. Honfleur also was the birthplace of Samuel de Champlain, who set off from here in 1608 on an expedition that resulted in the discovery of Quebec. The *Vieux Bassin* (Old Dock), from which he sailed, remains the town's most celebrated sight.

The *Musée du Vieux-Honfleur* (Quai St-Etienne; phone: 31-89-14-12), in a former church, contains antique arms, costumes, ceramics, and furniture illustrating the town's past, dating back to Gallo-Roman times. It is open daily from July to mid-September; weekends off-season; admission charge.

The most celebrated curiosity in Honfleur is the double-naved *Eglise Ste-Catherine,* shaped like an upturned keel, an ancient concept that has special meaning here because the ceilings of its two naves were built by shipwrights, not masons. Even though the naves are unequal in length and there is a makeshift quality to the church (though it has been here for 500 years), it is exceptionally appealing. Chief among the decorative items are a number of wooden statues, which harmonize beautifully with the church's rustic atmosphere. Seventeen carved panels on the 16th-century banister of the organ loft show mythological figures playing what amounts to an inventory of the musical instruments of the period. The church belfry, also of wood, was built across the road from the church and now seems to exist almost independently as a small museum, *La Tour Ste-Catherine* (St. Catherine's Tower; no phone), with liturgical objects and the records of the Confrérie de St-Léonard, a local guild. The church and tower frequently appear in paintings by Boudin, Monet, and others. They are open *Palm Sunday* through September; closed Tuesdays.

The modern *Musée Eugène-Boudin* (Pl. Erik-Satie; phone: 31-89-54-00, ext. 27) shares a courtyard with a typical 19th-century apartment house. Oblivious to the tourists below, residents put eiderdowns and colorful bedspreads out to air on their windowsills, just as they would have in Boudin's day. Besides the work of Boudin, Monet, and other Impressionists, the museum displays antique lace caps, children's bonnets, collars, and the instruments used in making them. The third-floor gallery affords a good view over the town, showing just how it is placed in relation to the Seine Estuary and the Channel. The museum is closed January, February, Tuesdays from mid-March through September, and weekday mornings in winter; admission charge.

There are some fine old houses within easy walking distance of one another; apart from those surrounding the *Vieux Bassin* and the church, Rue Haute and Rue du Puits are especially rewarding.

BEST EN ROUTE

La Chaumière The chef at *La Ferme St-Siméon* (see below) oversees the small dining room at this lovely Relais & Châteaux member, a nine-room inn housed in a half-timbered building overlooking an orchard and the Channel.

Restaurant closed Tuesday dinner. Two miles (3 km) west of Honfleur on D513, in Vasouy (phone: 31-81-63-20; fax: 31-89-59-23). Very expensive.

La Ferme St-Siméon Much frequented by the Impressionists, this half-timbered 17th-century inn now has a modern, 19-room annex, in addition to its original 19 rooms and four suites; all are sumptuously decorated. The kitchen has earned one Michelin star. For additional details, see *Romantic French Hostelries* in DIVERSIONS. Rue Adolphe-Marais (phone: 31-89-23-61; fax: 31-89-48-48). Very expensive.

L'Auberge du Vieux Puits The charming proprietors of this establishment in a rustic old Norman house will help you select a memorable meal (be sure to hint that a taste of the bewitching local trout would be most welcome). Closed Monday dinner, Tuesdays (except in summer), and mid-December to mid-January. Reservations advised. There are also 12 simple guestrooms that should be reserved well in advance. Sixteen miles (26 km) south of Honfleur on A13, at 6 Rue Notre-Dame-du-Pré, Pont-Audemer (phone: 32-41-01-48). Restaurant, expensive; hotel, inexpensive.

Le Cheval Blanc This half-timbered 15th-century inn offers 33 attractively refurbished rooms. Winter weekend packages include painting courses. The restaurant features seafood and excellent local dairy products. Closed January. Overlooking the port, at 2 Quai des Passagers (phone: 31-89-13-49). Expensive.

Le Butin de la Mer Following the trend of fine chefs opening lower-priced bistros as companions to their main restaurants, *La Ferme St.-Siméon*'s chef, Denis Le Cadre, has opened this seafood bistro in a converted manor house near the Butin lighthouse. Try the spectacular fresh oysters and St-Pierre (John Dory) roasted with fennel. Closed Mondays. Reservations advised. Major credit cards accepted. *Le Manoir, Phare de Butin,* Honfleur (phone: 31-89-06-06; fax: 31-89-54-54). Moderate.

L'Ecrin In the center of town, this quiet 22-room luxury hotel in a converted manor house is set in its own large park; the spacious rooms have canopy beds, and the opulent neo–turn-of-the-century decor includes fine rugs and tapestries. There are no in-room telephones and no restaurant. 19 Rue E. Boudin (phone: 31-89-32-39; fax: 31-89-24-41). Moderate.

En Route from Honfleur Take D513 for a scenic ride past old farms and views of the Channel through the apple orchards. The apple trees and flowers blooming on the cliffs that bracket the fine sandy beaches in this region, together with the sometimes exotic plantings by hillside villas and seaside homes, have given this corner of Calvados the name Côte Fleurie (Flowered Coast). At Cricqueboeuf, just before Villerville, look for a romantic, ivy-covered, 12th-century church next to a pond. Villerville itself, about 5 miles

(8 km) from Honfleur, is little more than a cleft in the cliffs, which shelter a small, attractive beach. Continue on D513 to Trouville and then Deauville.

TROUVILLE-SUR-MER In the heady days of Napoleon III, the affluent boulevardiers (men about town) of Paris brought their wives, children, and children's nannies to this fishing village-turned-resort for the season while they disported themselves with their mistresses a stone's throw away, across the Touques River at Deauville (see below). Boudin's masterly drawings and paintings of the beach at Trouville, showing women with bustles and parasols, illustrate what it must have been like when Empress Eugénie made it the most fashionable beach in France. The *Musée Montebello* (64 Rue Général-Leclerc; phone: 31-88-16-26) exhibits paintings by Boudin and others. It's open daily from 2:30 to 6 PM, April through September; no admission charge.

Today Trouville stays busy long after Deauville has put up its shutters for the winter. The fishing boats still go out in the morning; at day's end the nets still hang out to dry along the wall by the side of the river while the fishermen, in dungarees and navy sweaters, smoke their pipes and chat.

Bearing right at the Trouville seafront and walking toward the yacht club, you will find several blocks of villas, most of them still privately owned, which add up to an extravaganza of Gothic, Norman, and half-timbered follies that vie to outdo one another in turrets, towers, arches, and fantastic windows. Beyond the yacht club, at the end of Rue Lieutenant-R.-Morane under a low cliff, lies a golden sand beach that is much quieter here than at the Deauville end of it. The last week of July there is a sand castle contest at the Deauville end, in front of the casino, in which amateur architects attempt to reproduce some of the more dramatic buildings in the neighborhood. Also in July is Trouville's most important festival, the annual *Fête de la Mer,* and in May and November the city hosts antiques shows. Trouville is the site of an excellent complex of tennis facilities, the *Trouville Tennis Club* (for additional details, see *Game, Set, and Match: Tennis in France* in DIVERSIONS).

There is still gambling at the *Casino de Trouville* (Pl. Maréchal-Foch; phone: 31-87-75-00), whose atmosphere is decidedly less snooty than that in Deauville. Part of the building has been turned into a cinema and a concert hall, where entertainers from Paris sometimes perform in season. The lively fish market on the riverbank is open daily; try *Chez Saiter* (Quai Fernand-Moureaux; phone: 31-88-13-55) for take-out *soupe de poisson* (fish soup) and *bisque de homard* (lobster bisque).

BEST EN ROUTE

Le Moulin à Grains The dining room in this old Norman grain mill, with exposed beams and two fireplaces, is known for its generous portions of meat and seafood. The shrimp in calvados and meat grilled over the fireplace are popular dishes. A prix fixe dinner includes lobster, scallops, and shellfish pies; a seafood shish kebab; crab sausage; black pudding; tripe; and dessert crêpes with apple brandy. Closed Sunday dinner and Mondays. Reservations advised. Major credit cards accepted. Trouville-Alliquerville (phone: 35-38-04-46). Moderate.

Les Roches Noires For fine fare with a focus on simple seafood dishes, locals recommend this slightly out-of-the-way restaurant, perched above a sandy beach on the road to Honfleur near an old mansion of the same name. Arrive in time to watch the sun set over the Channel. Closed Mondays, Wednesdays, Tuesday dinner off-season, and two weeks in February. Reservations advised. Major credit cards accepted. 16 Bd. Louis-Bréguet (phone: 31-88-12-19). Moderate.

Les Vapeurs The name means "The Steamships," which are represented in red and white Art Deco tiles. This brasserie has a dedicated jet-set following for several reasons: The service is exceptionally friendly, the *moules marinières* (marinated mussels) and *soupe de poisson* (fish soup) are generous, and the sole is ultra-fresh. Closed Wednesdays off-season and January through early February. Reservations advised. Major credit cards accepted. 160 Quai Fernand-Moureaux (phone: 31-88-15-24; fax: 31-88-20-58). Moderate.

DEAUVILLE It was Napoleon III's half brother Charles, Duc de Morny, who established Deauville as the summer headquarters for the smart set, and its cachet lingers even today. This fashionable resort has a very short season—mid-July through September—during which visitors flock here to shop (in the town center are such designer boutiques as *Cartier, Chanel, Hermès,* and *Yves Saint Laurent*); sail in regattas; golf on two fine courses, including the *New Golf de Deauville* (for details, see *Great French Golf* in DIVERSIONS); gambol on the beaches; and gamble in Deauville's elegant casino (1 Rue Edmond-Blanc; phone: 31-14-31-14), which remains open year-round (for additional details, see *Casinos Royale* in DIVERSIONS).

The highlight of the season is the *Grand Prix de Deauville,* a horse race in late August that draws some of the most famous breeders and punters from around the world. Anyone interested in ogling celebrities will certainly find them here then; the Aga Khan and the Rothschilds are just a few of the fancy folk who may have reservations for lunch at *Le Ciro's* (see *Best En Route*). Besides the casino, the racetrack, and *Le Ciro's,* the place to be seen is on the *planches,* the wooden walkways along the beach, or on the beach itself, which is filled with innumerable brightly colored beach umbrellas. For a less rarefied experience, walk along the jetty in town on the west side of the Port-de-Deauville; it's especially nice at sunset, when pleasure craft make their way through the buoys into the harbor. Or sample some aged calvados at *La Cave de Deauville* (48 Rue Mirabeau; phone: 31-87-35-36), a wine and spirits shop. Also take a moment to gaze at the *Villa Strassburger,* the lavishly detailed Belle Epoque building that recalls an architectural era of turrets, spreading balconies, overhangs, and dormers.

BEST EN ROUTE

Hostellerie de Tourgéville A steeply pitched roof and half-timbered walls give this modern hotel in its own huge park a traditional Norman look. Inside, the six rooms and 19 suites, some with fireplaces, are comfortably furnished, with lovely picture windows and large baths. There are tennis facilities, a pool, and a sauna. Chemin de l'Orgueil, Tourgéville-Deauville (phone: 31-88-63-40; fax: 31-98-27-16). Very expensive.

Hôtel du Golf A palatial 169-room, 10-suite hotel facing the sea, recently renovated, next to the *New Golf de Deauville* layout and with many other sports facilities. Its restaurant, *La Pommeraie,* has a splendid view of the sea and fine seafood dishes. Closed November through February. On D278, 1½ miles (2 km) south of town, in St-Arnoult (phone: 31-88-19-01; fax: 31-88-75-99). Very expensive.

Normandy Its half-timbered gables and balconies make this property one of Deauville's focal points, with 260 rooms and 26 suites. For a detailed description, see *Romantic French Hostelries* in DIVERSIONS. 38 Rue Jean-Mermoz (phone: 31-98-66-22; fax: 31-98-66-23). Very expensive.

Le Royal A traditionally luxurious hotel whose 270 rooms and 17 suites are decorated comfortably, yet somewhat formally, in French Provincial style. The view of the sea from the upper-floor rooms is magnificent. (Be sure to specify a room facing the water.) The restaurant and lobby are dominated by floor-to-ceiling windows, crystal chandeliers, and ornamental plasterwork. A heated pool, a sauna, and parking all are available. This property, the *Hôtel du Golf*, and the *Normandy* (see above) are owned by the same group, and guests of any one of the hotels can use the facilities at the other two. Closed mid-November to mid-March. Bd. Eugène-Cornuché (phone: 31-98-66-33; fax: 31-98-66-34). Very expensive.

Le Ciro's Make no mistake about it: This is *the* place to eat during the high season, when the jet setters from Paris, London, and Hollywood are in town. For a detailed description, see *Haute Gastronomie* in DIVERSIONS. Open daily. Reservations necessary. Major credit cards accepted. Promenade des Planches (phone: 31-88-18-10; fax: 31-98-66-71). Expensive.

Le Spinnaker This increasingly popular spot near the main drag is a superior place to dine. The young chef shows considerable promise; his preparations, such as sole and rock lobster sautéed with fresh pasta, have earned the establishment a Michelin star. Closed Tuesdays off-season, Wednesdays except in August, and mid-January to mid-February. Reservations necessary. 52 Rue Mirabeau (phone: 31-88-24-40; fax: 31-88-43-58). Moderate.

Le Trophée It offers 22 modern rooms and two suites (some rooms have Jacuzzis), a rooftop sun deck, a pleasant restaurant, and a complete range of services. In the center of town, a short walk from the beach, at 81 Rue du Général-Leclerc (phone: 31-88-45-86; fax: 31-88-07-94). Moderate.

En Route from Deauville D513 passes through four popular Norman resort towns—Bénerville-sur-Mer, Blonville-sur-Mer, Villers-sur-Mer, and Houlgate—on the way to Cabourg, 11 miles (18 km) from Deauville. Bénerville and Blonville, nestled at the foot of pleasant, wooded hillsides studded with summer homes, are the quietest of this quartet of seaside spots. The beach at Villers is long but crowded in July and August, with a promenade along much of it. Houlgate, the brassiest of the bunch, is much favored by the residents of nearby Caen. Between Villers and Houlgate is one of the chief sights of the Côte Fleurie, the Falaise des Vaches Noires (Black Cow Cliffs), which, unlike the almost sheer chalk cliffs of the Pays de Caux, seem to tumble like a series of canyons down to the water. They are famous for yielding fossils. It is possible to walk at low tide underneath the cliffs from Villers to Houlgate or vice versa (remembering to start when the tide is going out) or to walk on top of them from Auberville, a tiny hamlet between the two resorts.

BEST EN ROUTE

L'Escale Rustic Norman furniture and walls lined with fishnets suggest the menu here: seafood Norman-style, abundant and good. Closed Monday dinner, Tuesdays, Wednesdays, January, and two weeks in December. Reservations advised. Major credit cards accepted. Pl. de l'Hôtel-de-Ville, Blonville (phone: 31-87-93-56). Moderate.

CABOURG A long stretch of beach and the most pleasant formal promenade of the Côte Fleurie are Cabourg's chief charms. The center of the promenade is dominated by the *Pullman Grand* hotel (see below) and the casino. Marcel Proust loved Cabourg and often stayed at the *Grand* as a child; he used Cabourg as one of the prototypes for Balbec in the "A l'Ombre des Jeunes Filles en Fleurs" section of *Remembrance of Things Past*. There is a pleasant walk at the east end of the beach along dunes above the estuary of the Dives River. The tourist office is in the *Jardins du Casino* (phone: 31-91-01-09).

BEST EN ROUTE

Pullman Grand Dripping with lavish turn-of-the-century details—marble columns, crystal chandeliers, elaborate plasterwork, and plush draperies—this hotel has 100 rooms and 10 suites, all recently remodeled. Its fine restaurant serves such well-prepared basics as lobster, tournedos, rack of lamb, shrimp and avocado salad, and lush desserts. Parking is available. Promenade Marcel-Proust (phone: 31-91-01-79; 800-221-4542 in the US; fax: 31-24-03-20). Very expensive.

L'Amiral The white tables and chairs with blue umbrellas outside this beachfront bar-restaurant look inviting, as does the interior—light, modern, and airy, with exposed beams and tiles of Norman and Breton women in traditional dress. *Fruits de mer,* tripe in cider, and shrimp in butter sauce are among the specialties. The food is well prepared; the service is good, except on crowded Sundays. Closed mid-November to *Easter.* Reservations advised. Visa accepted. Promenade Marcel-Proust (phone: 31-91-50-66). Moderate.

En Route from Cabourg Although this stretch of Normandy is usually associated with its lovely coastline and elegant resorts, you should make at least one excursion to the inland countryside here, known as the Auge, considered by many to be the most typical part of rural Normandy. Here you'll find placid herds of cattle, farms where magnificent thoroughbred racehorses are bred and trained, verdant rolling hills, and orchard after orchard of apples (used for making cider and calvados) and pears (used for making pear cider, called *poiré*). The traditional houses and barns are half-timbered, most of them carefully restored. One of the loveliest typically Norman villages is Beuvron-en-Auge, 8 miles (13 km) south of Cabourg on D49, which begins in Dives-sur-Mer just east of Cabourg (don't miss the splendid covered market, just off the main town square, in Dives-sur-Mer), or on quicker but less scenic D400, which picks up D49 south of A13. Take the time to stroll around Beuvron's village square, surrounded by magnificent half-timbered houses. Two local farmers' wives have opened farm-product operations here, just east of the main square, where they sell cider, calvados, fresh cream, *confiture de lait* (carmelized milk spread), and other locally produced goods.

From Beuvron take D146 north to Clermont-en-Auge, following the signs to "Chapelle de Clermont Panorama." The chapel, reached by a footpath, contains 16th-century statues, but its main attraction is the view of the green Vie and Dives Valleys below. Next follow tiny D85 south to the village of Cambremer, which, along with Beuvron-en-Auge, is on the "Route du Cidre," a route along farm roads with apple-shaped signs to tell you that you're in cider country. In Cambremer every year, local farmers compete for the chance to display the "Cru de Cambremer" sign designating fine, traditional cider; such farms, open to visitors, demonstrate cider making and offer tastings. For information about the 1995 route, contact the tourist office in Cabourg (see above) or Caen (see below).

From Cambremer you can either take D101 south to Crèvecoeur-en-Auge and then N13 to Caen, or wind your way to Caen along the "Route de Fromage," which links producers in and around some of France's most famous cheese towns, including the tiny and picturesque village of

Camembert, which has its own camembert cheese museum (no phone). For information and a map of the route, contact the tourist office in the lovely market town of Vimoutiers (10 Av. Général-de-Gaulle; phone: 33-39-30-29). To reach Vimoutiers from Cambremer, drive south on D101 to D16; follow D16 south to St-Pierre-sur-Dives (7 miles/11 km), then head east on D4 to Livarot, home of another great cheese (10 miles/16 km); from Livarot take D579 south to Vimoutiers (6 miles/10 km). Be on the lookout for farms with a "Calvados Fermier" sign; you can buy calvados directly from farmers who produce the popular applejack.

BEST EN ROUTE

Le Pavé d'Auge A lovely half-timbered, one-Michelin-star restaurant housed in what used to be a covered market. Its decor and cuisine sum up the glories of rural Normandy. Try the chicken *Vallée d'Auge* (with apples and cream). Closed Mondays (except for lunch from March to November), Tuesdays, January 6 to 28, and the first two weeks of December. Reservations advised. MasterCard and Visa accepted. Eight miles (13 km) south of Cabourg on D49, in Beuvron-en-Auge (phone: 31-79-26-71; fax: 31-39-04-45). Expensive.

CAEN Of all the French towns devastated by the bombs of World War II, none was as severely ravaged as Caen. Its old central quarter, which burned for 10 days, was completely destroyed, but some buildings have been nicely restored. Fortunately for Caen, its two great churches, the *Abbaye aux Hommes,* also known as the *Eglise St-Etienne,* and its sister institution, the *Abbaye aux Dames,* also known as the *Eglise de la Trinité,* survived. William the Conqueror and his wife, Matilda, built the abbeys as penance for their marriage, which took place even though they were cousins and had been denied papal dispensation.

The *Abbaye aux Hommes* is best viewed from Place Louis-Guillouard, across a broad vista of lawns and formal gardens, beyond which are the 18th-century residential quarters of the abbey, now the *Hôtel de Ville* (Town Hall). Crossing the *place* and turning into Rue Guillaume-le-Conquérant and then left again brings you around the church to a point right under the domineering west front, its simple Romanesque lines almost as massive and forbidding as the Etretat cliffs. The lovely 14th-century early-Gothic apse and choir blend subtly with the earlier parts of the church to form a monumental whole. In front of the pink marble high altar is the tombstone of William the Conqueror, who was buried in the abbey in 1087. His wife was buried in the *Abbaye aux Dames.*

The *Abbaye aux Dames* is smaller and appears more human in scale, despite the great arches over the nine lordly bays. The delightful 13th-century Gothic chapel, in the south transept, has delicately worked ribs and columns; female heads are carved on the supporting arches. The 16 pillars in the 11th-century crypt make it look like a stone copse. A slab marking the spot where Matilda was buried can be seen in the choir, although the tomb itself was desecrated during the Revolution.

Caen's castle, built by William in 1060 and now a truly magnificent ruin, encloses lawns and sylvan walkways where its great towers once stood. A platform provides a pleasant view over the city, but the chief attraction is the splendid *Musée des Beaux-Arts* (Esplanade du Château; phone: 31-85-28-63). The impressive collection includes many pieces accumulated by Napoleon in his forays across the Continent. Highlights are a magnificent *Marriage of the Virgin* by Perugino and Bordon's *Annunciation.* Veronese, Titian, Tintoretto, and Jacob van Ruisdael all are notably represented. The museum also houses more than 40,000 prints, including works by Rembrandt, Callot, Van Dyck, and Rubens. Few modern buildings sit so well in ancient surroundings; here the great gray stone slabs of the museum building merge handsomely with the medieval battlements. Closed Tuesdays and holidays; admission charge.

The *Caen Mémorial Musée pour la Paix* (Museum of Peace; Esplanade Général-Eisenhower; phone: 31-06-06-44; fax: 31-06-06-70), on the site of a German underground command post, features sobering exhibits that emphasize not military victories, but the suffering of people in wartime. A special gallery honors winners of the Nobel Peace Prize. The museum is closed *Christmas* and the first two weeks of January; admission charge. Caen's tourist office is at 12 Pl. St-Pierre (phone: 31-86-27-65).

BEST EN ROUTE

La Bourride In this 400-year-old dwelling-turned-restaurant, chef Michel Bruneau takes advantage of the best, freshest ingredients from Normandy's farms and fishing ports; his efforts have won the place two Michelin stars. Closed Sundays, Monday holidays, and two weeks each in January and August. Reservations necessary. Major credit cards accepted. 15 Rue Vaugueux (phone: 31-93-50-76; fax: 31-93-29-63). Expensive.

Daniel Tuboeuf This creative chef, who has returned to his native Normandy after a stint in Paris, attracts the locals to his one-Michelin-star restaurant with fine renditions of regional specialties plus a superb wine list. Closed Sundays, Mondays, and August. Reservations necessary. Major credit cards accepted. 8 Rue Buquet (phone: 31-43-64-48). Expensive.

Friendly Cozy British comfort is the theme here, from the pub-style bar to the 90 chintz-filled rooms; there's also a small heated pool. No restaurant. 2 Pl. Boston, Hérouville-St-Clair, a suburb of Caen (phone: 31-44-05-05; fax: 31-44-95-94). Moderate.

Relais des Gourmets There are 23 clean, comfortable rooms and five suites with baths in this pretty hotel near *Saint-Pierre* church. The restaurant serves traditional dishes. 15 Rue de Géôle (phone: 31-86-06-01; fax: 31-39-06-00). Moderate.

Hôtel St-Pierre A simple, traditional-style hostelry run by a
welcome sets it apart from others in its class. Ten o'
vate baths. There's no restaurant. In the heart o'
at 40 Bd. des Alliés (phone: 31-86-28-20). Iney

D-DAY INVASION BEACHES

From Caen we highly recommend a detour to Sword, June,
and Utah Beaches, the 50 miles of shore that played such a.
role in the events of *D-Day*, June 6, 1944. Virtually no one com.
from a visit to these famous beaches without at least a twinge of pat.
tism. Looking out over sweeping stretches of seascape, now so picturesque
and serene, it's difficult to imagine the devastation that took place on *D-
Day*, but the French have not forgotten; *The Longest Day*, an American
film depicting the event, is broadcast on French television (in French)
every year on June 6.

It had been agreed at meetings between Winston Churchill and Franklin
D. Roosevelt in 1942 and 1943 that an Allied invasion of Europe through
France would be launched somewhere in the north of the country at some
propitious time. After the abortive attempt to seize Dieppe in 1942, it
became clear that the beaches of Calvados were ideal. The Germans considered them a most unlikely landing spot for Allied troops, who would
have to overcome unreliable weather patterns, strong sea currents, and
steep cliffs in order to succeed. The umbrella name for the invasion was
Operation Overlord; General Dwight D. Eisenhower was appointed
Supreme Commander of the Allied Expeditionary Forces in charge of
strategic planning, and tactical coordination of all ground troops fell into
the hands of General Bernard Law Montgomery of Great Britain. The
unusual preparations for the invasion included training British Commando
and American Ranger units in cliff climbing; building vast floating docks
for an artificial port; and creating an elaborate intelligence plan to per-
suade the Germans that the action would take place at Calais. The invasion was projected for the early part of June, when the weather could be
expected to be good, the tides would be right, and the moon would be full
enough to provide light for the airborne troops scheduled to be dropped
behind the German coastal defenses (the "Atlantic Wall") a few hours
before the landings.

In the early hours of June 6 the US 101st and 82nd and the British 6th
Airborne Divisions dropped into France, the first two on the western flank
of the beaches just north of Carentan, the latter on the eastern flank around
Bénouville, on the Orne River. Their mission was to divert the enemy as
much as possible from the seaborne assault troops steaming across the
English Channel: General Omar Bradley's 1st American Army, headed for
Utah and Omaha Beaches, where they landed at 6:30 AM, and the British
2nd Army, under General Miles Dempsey (whose forces also included the

adian 3rd Infantry Division), headed for Gold, Juno, and Sword Beaches. about noon low-lying Utah Beach had been secured, and a unit of the 3rd Battalion of the 8th Infantry Regiment had forged inland about 8 miles to meet up with the 82nd Airborne. By the end of the day 23,250 men and 17,000 vehicles had come ashore there.

Of all the Normandy beaches, Omaha was the hardest to conquer. The cliffs along its shoreline proved a predictably tough barrier, especially with rough seas at their foot. These harsh conditions became even worse for the troops that followed the initial landing force, since by then the Germans had opened fire. Despite heavy losses, 225 US Rangers managed to scale and capture Pointe du Hoc, holding it against heavy counter-fire until they were relieved on June 8.

The near-legendary Northumberlands, the 50th British Infantry Division, were part of the British 2nd Army that landed at Gold Beach around 7:25 AM, and the Royal Marine Commandos pushed west to Port-en-Bessin, where they joined the American troops on June 8. The Canadian 3rd Infantry Division landed at Juno Beach around 7:10 AM, and by 5 PM the 7th Brigade had taken the beautiful hamlet of Creully, a few miles inland. The British 3rd Infantry Division, its objective Caen, came ashore on the part of Sword Beach between Lion-sur-Mer and Riva-Bella at about 7:30 AM. They captured a few small villages but met heavy resistance from the German 21st Panzer Division after 4 PM. A Franco-British Commando unit under Commander Philippe Kieffer took Riva-Bella and continued on to Bénouville, where they met up with the British 6th Airborne. The *Cimetière Militaire Américain* (American Military Cemetery; phone: 31-22-40-62) near Colleville is a poignant reminder of the day's losses. The Battle of Normandy lasted about 11 weeks more, finally ending shortly after the capitulation of the German 7th Army on August 19 at Chambois.

En Route from Caen Route D515 out of Caen leads north to Bénouville, where a sign with a blue flying horse marks Pegasus Bridge on the Orne. This important crossing was taken in the early hours of *D-Day* by members of the British 6th Airborne Division, and Bénouville's *Hôtel de Ville* (Town Hall) was the first in France to be liberated. A description of what happened can be found at the *Musée du Débarquement Pegasus Bridge/Musée des Troupes Aéroportées* (Pegasus Bridge Landings/Airborne Troops Museum; Pont de Bénouville; phone: 31-44-62-54), which is open daily from April through mid-October; admission charge. Bénouville also has an interesting 18th-century château, famous for its monumental staircase.

Here the road becomes D514 and continues to Ouistreham and its neighbor Riva-Bella, which formed the ancient port of Caen. Now this is a popular pleasure-boating center, and in summer the harbor is filled with the colorful sails of yachts from many northern European countries. British frogmen swam ashore here just before the invasion to clear the canals of obstacles. The *Musée du Débarquement No. 4 Commando* (Pl. Alfred-

Thomas, Ouistreham; phone: 31-96-63-10) concentrates on the French involvement in the invasion under Commander Kieffer, with displays of arms, equipment, documents, uniforms, and photographs. Open weekends from *Palm Sunday* through May; closed Wednesdays from June through September; admission charge.

Lion-sur-Mer, 4 miles (6 km) from Riva-Bella and halfway down Sword Beach, reveals little evidence of the chaos of *D-Day*. It is a typical resort town of the area, with a sandy beach, small hotels, tennis courts, and beach-front cafés. At Bernières-sur-Mer, 6 miles (10 km) farther on, two monuments commemorate the Canadian forces that created one of the essential bridgeheads in the operation. The 13th-century belfry of the church, with charming corner turrets over a small porch, is exceptionally fine, rising to a height of 220 feet. At Courseulles-sur-Mer, known for its oysters, ships were deliberately sunk during Operation Overlord to form a temporary harbor. Early in the operation Winston Churchill, George VI, and Charles de Gaulle landed here to visit the battlefields.

High on the cliff just before Arromanches (19 miles/30 km from Caen) is the point called St-Côme-de-Fresne, still surrounded by German gun emplacements. Take a look at the orientation table, at the top of a flight of steps, which offers a perfect perspective of the beaches from Sword to Utah. In front are the remains of the breakwaters of the great artificial port built at Arromanches.

ARROMANCHES Set between cliffs around a sandy beach, this town has the finest of all Normandy museums commemorating Operation Overlord: the *Exposition Permanente du Débarquement* (Permanent Exhibition of the Landings; Pl. du 6-Juin; phone: 31-22-34-31). The museum is famous for its vivid dioramas and models, chief among them one of Mulberry Harbor B, the great artificial port that was created to compensate for the coast's lack of natural protection. Eighteen old merchant ships were scuttled to form the first shelter behind which smaller units could unload their cargoes. The sunken ships were followed by more than 100 concrete pontoons—some weighing as many as 6,000 tons—forming a 7-mile-long breakwater. Forty of the pontoons can still be seen in a semicircle offshore. Floating steel platforms, created for unloading purposes, were linked to the shore by floating roadways made of small pontoons connected by "Bailey" bridges, each about 4,000 feet long and capable of withstanding the weight of jeeps and other heavy cargo. Just six days after the invasion began, 326,000 men and 54,000 jeeps had been put ashore. Also on view in the museum are parachutes of the 101st and 82nd Airborne Divisions, aerial bombs, high explosives, and uniforms of various regiments and squadrons. A Royal Navy film shot on June 6, 1944, shows what took place around Arromanches that day. The museum is closed *Christmas* and *New Year's Day*. The Arromanches tourist office (Rue Maréchal-Joffre; phone: 31-21-47-56) is open April through September.

En Route from Arromanches Seven miles (11 km) out of town, still on D514, a turnoff to the right leads down to the fishing harbor of Port-en-Bessin, a cleft in the cliffs at the mouth of the Drôme River, where American and British forces finally made contact on June 8. Even in summer Port-en-Bessin is relatively quiet, although the granite jetties occasionally are jammed with fishermen, and the action at the early morning fish auctions on Mondays, Wednesdays, and Thursdays can be colorful.

A road to the right off D514 between Colleville-sur-Mer and St-Laurent-sur-Mer leads to the *Normandy American Military Cemetery and Memorial,* on a cliff right above Omaha Beach and the Channel. An overlook with an orientation table details the landing beaches. The cemetery contains the graves of 9,386 military personnel, including 307 unknown, each marked by a plain white marble cross or Star of David. In one instance, simple headstones mark where a father and son lie side by side; in about 30 others, where brothers lie next to one another. The experience is, needless to say, a moving one.

There is another right turn off D514 at St-Laurent onto a small road that follows the beach at sea level as far as Vierville-sur-Mer for about 2 miles (3 km). At the east end, a post marks the spot where the first American casualties were buried. The western end of this pleasant seafront road is where the heaviest casualties on Omaha took place, with the majority of the 116th Regiment killed or injured. Vierville-sur-Mer's church is worth noting. Its current belfry replaces one that was an important German lookout and stronghold; it was destroyed on *D-Day* by offshore shelling.

Pointe du Hoc is reached by yet another short side road off D514 beyond Vierville. On *D-Day,* 225 American Rangers under Colonel James Earl Rudder scaled these cliffs, using grappling hooks and firemen's ladders (among other equipment) amid smoke from offshore barrages and relentless German fire from the cliff top. Today the cliff top is still shell-scarred. At the cliff's edge is a modest stone column dedicated to the Ranger Commandos of the 116th Infantry.

About a mile (1.6 km) south of the junction of D514 and N13 is Isigny-sur-Mer, which was liberated on June 9, 1944. Today the town is famous throughout France for its butter. The next stop on the route, 7 miles (11 km) west of Isigny, is Carentan, another prosperous dairy-farming market town, bordered by the marshes typical of the southeastern corner of the Cotentin Peninsula. There is a memorial to the 101st Airborne Division near the *Hôtel de Ville* (Town Hall).

Beyond Carentan turn off N13 onto D913; follow D913, passing Ste-Marie-du-Mont, to reach the monument at La Madeleine at the south end of Utah Beach on D421. The memorial consists of a former German blockhouse honoring the American 1st Engineer Special Brigade. Route D421 follows the coast, though the sea is often obscured by dunes. Utah Beach stretches for nearly 2 miles (about 3 km) as far as Les Dunes-de-Varreville. This is where the American 4th Division met formidable German resistance on *D-Day,* although before nightfall the men were able to meet up with the paratroopers who had been dropped inland around Ste-Mère-Eglise. Just off the road marked Route des Alliés at Les Dunes-de-Varreville, a pinkish granite marker is a reminder of French General Leclerc's arrival on August 1, 1944, with his 2nd Armored Division.

A little beyond Varreville turn left and pick up D15 to Ste-Mère-Eglise, 42 miles (67 km) from Arromanches.

STE-MÈRE-EGLISE This is where parachutists of the 82nd and 101st Airborne dropped just before dawn on *D-Day.* Unfortunately, the air drop wasn't the surprise it was meant to be, since a fire had awakened just about everyone in town, including the Germans. Many American soldiers were shot as they touched the ground. The best known of the soldiers who participated in the air drop was John Steele, who came down on top of the church spire and dangled there for hours, pretending to be dead; captured by the Germans, he escaped after two days. Outside the *Hôtel de Ville* (Town Hall) is the first milestone of Liberty Way, marked out by the American troops as they crossed France. The parachute-shaped *Musée des Troupes Aéroportées* (Airborne Troops Museum; Pl. du 6-Juin; phone: 33-41-41-35) contains documents, photographs, arms, uniforms, dog tags, and, outside, a Sherman tank—all part of the story of the early morning hours of the invasion. The museum is open daily, April through mid-November, and weekends only, mid-November to mid-December, February, and March; closed mid-December through January; admission charge.

The stained glass window over the main portal of Ste-Mère-Eglise's 13th-century church depicts the Virgin Mary and Child surrounded by American soldiers parachuting from the sky to liberate the town.

A new museum, the *Musée des Forces Aériennes Alliés* (Allied Air Forces Museum), in Ecausseville, 4 miles (6 km) north of Ste-Mère-Eglise, is set to open this year. It will trace the exploits of the American 9th Air Force, the RAF, and French forces.

En Route from Ste-Mère-Eglise Following N13, return to Caen, 55 miles (88 km) away.

BEST EN ROUTE

La Chenevière An inn with 11 rooms and four suites in its own park, and a fine restaurant with a cheese assortment that should not be missed. Closed Mondays and January. In Escures, 1½ miles (2 km) south of Port-en-Bessin (phone: 31-21-47-96; fax: 31-21-47-98). Expensive.

France et Fuchsias Located near the village fishing port, this friendly restaurant/hotel, with a flower-filled interior courtyard, specializes in the freshest possible seafood. The 32 rooms and one suite overlook a garden; the owners organize a chamber music festival every August. Closed January and February. Restaurant also closed Mondays in winter and Tuesdays. In

Saint-Vaast-la-Hougue, 12 miles (19 km) north of Utah Beach via D421 and D14 (phone: 33-54-42-26; fax: 33-43-46-79). Moderate.

CAEN TO MONT-ST-MICHEL

En Route from Caen Take N13 west 19 miles (30 km) to Bayeux.

BAYEUX Few towns in the world are famous for a piece of embroidery, but such a possession has indeed made this beautifully preserved town celebrated for centuries. With its fine cathedral and ancient streets, Bayeux was the only town close to the Norman coast that escaped the devastation of World War II.

Bayeux was an important center in Julius Caesar's day, and successive waves of Celts, Saxons, and Vikings later came to occupy the city. Around 1050 William the Conqueror gave the episcopal land here to his half brother Odo, who, as bishop, built the original cathedral. Over the years William's three sons engaged in power struggles for the English throne and the Duchy of Normandy. It was during one of these conflicts that Henry I came here and burned the cathedral (most of the present structure dates from the 13th century), along with the rest of the city. In the 19th century novelist Honoré de Balzac enjoyed well-earned respites here, and on June 7, 1944, Bayeux was the first town in France to be liberated by the Allies.

It is the tapestry, however, that draws most people here. Called *La Tapisserie de la Reine Mathilde* (Queen Matilda's Tapestry, or sometimes simply the *Bayeux Tapestry*), it is on display daily at the *Centre Guillaume-le-Conquérant* (13 *bis* Rue de Nesmond; phone: 31-92-05-48). Nineteen inches wide and 231 feet long, it tells the story of the events surrounding the Norman conquest of England, including the flight of the English after King Harold's death in the Battle of Hastings. Legend has it that the tapestry was commissioned by Bishop Odo and worked by William's wife, Matilda, and her ladies-in-waiting, although more prosaic minds have insisted that the stitching suggests it was sewn by Saxon women in England. Regardless, the tapestry is a remarkable and lively document comprising 58 distinct scenes, each with a Latin legend summarizing the picture. The costumes, uniforms, food, boats, furniture, and pets of the period are all vividly illustrated, and the borders are decorated with an awesome bestiary of real and imaginary monsters. The tapestry, which is laid out in a glass case, can be followed section by section with an excellent commentary in English on a listening device.

The two Romanesque towers with 13th-century Gothic spires dominating Bayeux and the surrounding countryside belong to the *Cathédrale Notre-Dame* (Rue du Bienvenu). Entering the cathedral from the west door, one is immediately struck by the formidable Romanesque arches of the nave. The walls of the nave are profusely decorated with saints, leaves, flowers, abstract designs, and various creatures. The nine chapels date from the first half of the 14th century. In the *Chapelle de Bonne Nouvelle* an extraordinary stone tableau shows the Virgin with all the sacred symbols connected with her. The *Chapelle de St-Michel* has a 15th-century fresco worked in a variety of blues and pinks showing Mary's Visitation to Elizabeth following the Annunciation.

Behind the cathedral is the *Musée Baron Gérard* (1 Rue de la Chaîne; phone: 31-92-14-21), which displays local porcelain and the lacework for which Bayeux is famous. The museum is open daily; no admission charge. Bayeux's few remaining lace makers can be seen at their craft at the *Atelier du Centre Norman de la Dentelle aux Fuseaux* (5 Pl. aux Pommes; no phone). The *Musée de la Bataille de Normandie* (Bd. Fabien-Ware; phone: 31-92-93-41) has a slide show and other exhibits commemorating the Normandy invasion.

On Saturdays the town's main shopping street, Rue St-Jean, is enlivened with brightly dressed shoppers, as is the Place St-Patrice, which becomes a bustling market with stalls selling clothes, bric-a-brac, finely bound old books, and food. From the beautiful, fortified farms of the surrounding Bessin countryside and from the nearby Channel ports come farmers and fishermen with refrigerated trailers laden with cheeses, seafood, charcuterie, vegetables, and fruit.

The countryside east of Bayeux, between N13 and the coast, is considered one of the most beautiful and serene parts of Normandy. Along N13 near Caen the landscape tends to be flat, with acres of grain fields; closer to the coast tiny roads undulate through gentle valleys and copses, twisting around modest hills. The farmhouses are not half-timbered as in the neighboring Pays d'Auge around Lisieux and in the Pays de Caux, but are built of stone. Take N13 southeast for a short distance; then pick up D35, following it to St-Gabriel-Brécy. Here is an 11th-century priory, a delightfully haphazard conglomeration of buildings with towers, turrets, arched windows, and stone entrances, staircases, and balconies. It is now a horticultural college for the region, but permission to look around can be obtained at the reception office. About a mile (1.6 km) farther is Creully, one of the most perfectly preserved feudal villages in Normandy. In the adjacent community of Creullet is a charming manor house in a pasture, where General Montgomery established his headquarters in a trailer just after *D-Day*. In Creully itself is a château (with parts dating from the 12th through the 16th centuries) that was the BBC's headquarters just after the invasion. Standing in lordly fashion on a hill above the Seulles River, the château now houses the *Hôtel de Ville* (Town Hall), which is open to the public daily.

From Creully continue south on D22 to pick up D141 to *Château Fontaine-Henry,* home of the family d'Harcourt for centuries and a triumph of Renaissance domestic architecture. The château is most notable for its steeply pitched roof. Inside is a fine Gothic staircase dating from the reign of François I; in the main room hangs a portrait by Mignard of the infant Louis XIV. There is a charming private chapel on the grounds. The château is open Wednesdays, weekends, and holidays from *Easter* through May and mid-September through October; closed Tuesdays and Fridays from June through mid-September; closed November through *Easter.* There is an admission charge (phone: 31-80-00-42). Return to Bayeux.

BEST EN ROUTE

Château d'Audrieu In its own park, this splendid 18th-century château has been converted to a luxury 21-room, nine-suite member of the Relais & Châteaux group. Its one-Michelin-star restaurant is truly aristocratic. For additional details on the hotel, see *Romantic French Hostelries* in DIVERSIONS; for additional details on the dining room, see *Haute Gastronomie,* also in DIVERSIONS. Closed December through February; restaurant also closed Mondays except for dinner in summer for hotel guests only. MasterCard and Visa accepted. In Audrieu, right outside Bayeux (phone: 31-80-21-52; fax: 31-80-24-73). Very expensive.

D'Argouges This 18th-century mansion is a very quiet, comfortable hotel that combines Old World charm with modern amenities. The 25 rooms and suites face either the inner courtyard or the back garden. Breakfast is served in the dining room, but there is no restaurant. TV sets are available on request. 21 Rue St-Patrice, Bayeux (phone: 31-92-88-86; fax: 31-92-69-16). Moderate.

Lion d'Or The best restaurant in Bayeux has been open since 1640 and operated by the same family since 1929. The one-Michelin-star menu of classic Norman cooking features brill, lobster, sole, salmon, and other favorites; service is friendly and unhurried. Reservations necessary. There are 25 clean, airy rooms and two suites upstairs. Closed late December to late January. Reservations necessary. Major credit cards accepted. 77 Av. St-Jean (phone: 31-92-06-90; fax: 31-22-15-64). Moderate.

En Route from Bayeux Take D572 south, turning almost immediately onto D67; go about 3 miles (5 km) to a sign on the left reading "Abbaye de Mondaye." Although this 18th-century abbey of the Premonstratensian order is open only for guided tours on Sunday afternoons (phone: 31-92-58-11), the classical church and conventual buildings can be seen at any time. They form a graceful unity, often offset by cows grazing almost up to the abbey walls.

Continue on D67 until it meets D13; then turn right and drive 6 miles (10 km) to the *Château de Balleroy,* built in the early 1600s by François Mansart, for whom the mansard roof is named. The symmetrical main buildings are of brick and stone, and gardens by Lenôtre add to the overall formality. The painted ceiling in one of the halls reveals classical allegories of the four seasons and portraits by Mignard of Louis XIII, Anne of Austria, Louis XIV, and Madame de Maintenon. The château also houses the *Musée des Ballons* (Museum of Balloon Flight), with old prints, blueprints, maps, documents, and instruments pertaining to lighter-than-air flight from the experiments of the Montgolfier brothers in the late 1700s to the present. Among the interesting dioramas is one showing the part dirigibles played in the *D-Day* invasions. The château and museum are open from mid-April through October; closed Wednesdays; admission charge (phone: 31-21-60-61).

Follow D13 5 miles (8 km) west of Balleroy to Cérisy-la-Forêt and the ruins of the 11th-century abbey, which has son-et-lumière shows on Saturday evenings from mid-July through August. It also is open Sundays and holidays from April through October (phone: 33-56-10-01). The church is imposing, especially when seen through the trees across the nearby meadows. Inside, the Romanesque choir with its simple oak stalls is considered by experts to be the finest in Normandy. The 13th-century convent buildings, the chapel, the porter's lodge, and the hall of justice have been converted into a museum containing 14th- and 15th-century religious manuscripts and books and 16th- and 17th-century furniture.

Retrace D13 from Cérisy toward Balleroy; turn right on D572 (which becomes D972) and follow it into St-Lô, which is about 22 miles (35 km) from Bayeux.

ST-LÔ So devastated was this ancient town in the 1944 Battle of Normandy that it was dubbed the "capital of the ruins." One of the few buildings to escape complete destruction was the *Eglise Notre-Dame,* which today has been almost completely rebuilt, although some parts were left damaged as a memorial to those terrible times. For centuries St-Lô was an important fortified city, and the ramparts—beautifully exposed by the bombardments—are a favorite promenade from which to view the rebuilt town. The *Musée des Beaux Arts* (Pl. du Champ-de-Mars; phone: 33-57-43-80) is worth a visit for its series of eight tapestries worked in Bruges in the 16th century. They provide a humorous, down-to-earth glimpse of peasant life, showing the flora, fauna, work implements, and musical instruments that were all accoutrements of Flemish life at that time. The museum also has a collection of portraits of the Matignon-Grimaldi family, ancestors in a circuitous line of the Prince of Monaco, and paintings by Corot, Rousseau, and Boudin. The museum is closed Tuesdays; admission charge.

The *Haras* (National Stud Farm; Rue du Maréchal-Juin; phone: 33-57-14-13) is open to visitors daily year-round; various French breeds of horses as well as a collection of carriages can be viewed.

BEST EN ROUTE

Château de la Salle A small château in a lovely private park, with 10 spacious, elegant rooms. The restaurant, with a huge fireplace and vaulted ceiling, prepares traditional cuisine in the grand manner—such as asparagus in puff pastry with shellfish cream sauce. Closed January through late March. In Montpinchon, 14 miles (22 km) southwest of St-Lô via D38 and D273 (phone: 33-46-95-19; fax: 33-46-44-25). Expensive.

En Route from St-Lô Continue east along D972 for 18 miles (29 km) to Coutances.

COUTANCES This city on a hill is dominated by its cathedral, a gray stone beacon that appears almost silver in sunlight. Go to the Place du Parvis for your first close look at the west façade, which has two towers with spires and pinnacles. The cathedral was begun in 1030 but ravaged by fire in 1218, soon after which a Gothic structure was superimposed on the original shell. The result is a fine, harmoniously proportioned example of Norman Gothic. Especially interesting is the large octagonal lantern tower, which crowns the transept and reaches a height of about 135 feet, and the chapels, separated from one another by delicately worked stone screens. The central chapel in the apse is much revered locally as the setting for the 14th-century statue of the Virgin known as *Our Lady of Coutances*. The *Chapelle St-François* has a 17th-century woodcarving showing Judas's betrayal of Christ with a kiss. The three 13th-century windows in the north transept depict St. George, St. Blaise, and St. Thomas à Becket.

The fine *Jardin Public* (Public Garden) features terraces, rose-filled flower beds, stone staircases leading down grassy slopes, and lots of trees. It is open daily; in summer there is a son-et-lumière show involving the gardens and the cathedral. The town's small museum (2 Rue Quesnel-Morinière; phone: 33-45-11-92) has an interesting bust of Emperor Hadrian; among what remains of its collection of paintings (much damaged in World War II) is a Rubens. The museum is usually closed Sunday mornings and Tuesdays; no admission charge.

En Route from Coutances Follow D971 south for about 19 miles (30 km) to Granville.

GRANVILLE On a promontory jutting out over the turquoise ocean, this resort city has been called the "Monaco of the North" for its flowers and sea views, though not for its cool and often blustery weather. The sea air is considered so healthful that a large, luxurious *Centre de Thalassothérapie* (Seawater Treatment Spa; 3 Rue Jules-Michelet, in the Haute Ville; phone: 33-90-31-12) has been established here; it is closed in January. The *Aquarium* (Pointe du Roc; phone: 33-50-19-10) is worth a visit, especially for its indoor garden filled with rare butterflies and its views of the bay of Mont-St-Michel. It is open daily from April to mid-March; admission charge. There are more spectacular views of the bay from a path around the ramparts (begin in front of the *Eglise Notre-Dame*, near the *Aquarium*).

A four-day *Mardi Gras* celebration features dancing in the streets, parades, and a flea market. One of western France's most famous *pardons* (religious parades and celebrations in honor of the local saint) is held here the last Sunday in July; if you're in the area, don't miss it. Ferries leave year-round from the city's lively port for the Channel Islands and the tiny nearby Iles de Chausey (about one hour each way), which are famous for the lobster fished off their rocky shores, and where much of the granite was quarried for use in building Mont-St-Michel abbey. Ferries operate several times daily in summer; schedules depend on the tides. For information, contact *Emeraude Lines* (1 Rue Lecampion; phone: 33-50-16-36); *Vedettes Jolie France* (in the yacht port; phone: 33-50-31-81); or the *Maison du Tourisme* (4 Cours Jonville; phone: 33-50-02-67).

BEST EN ROUTE

Bains Next door to the spa and overlooking the water (ask for a room with a view of the sea), this old-fashioned but regularly refurbished hotel offers 44 rooms and five suites. There is a restaurant featuring seafood dishes. 19 Rue G.-Clemenceau (phone: 33-50-17-31; fax: 33-50-89-22). Expensive.

La Citadelle Fine traditional cooking is the draw at this local favorite, which occupies a converted mansion. Try the lobster with foie gras or the duck with currants. Closed Mondays, except for dinner in summer; Tuesdays, except for dinner from March through October; and two weeks each in January and September. Reservations advised. MasterCharge and Visa accepted. 10 Rue Cambernon (phone: 33-50-34-10). Expensive.

Hérel This modern hotel offers 43 quiet rooms in a great setting: on a small peninsula overlooking the yacht port. There's a dining room (closed Sunday dinner and Monday lunch). Port de Plaisance (phone: 33-90-48-08; fax: 33-90-75-95). Moderate.

La Mougine des Moulins à Vent This seven-room hotel overlooking the sea has a lovely flower-filled garden but no restaurant. In Bréville-sur-Mer, 2 miles (3 km) northeast of Granville (phone: 33-50-21-41; fax: 33-50-63-11). Moderate.

En Route from Granville The most picturesque route to Avranches, 15 miles (24 km) away, is the turning and twisting coast road, D911, which occasionally has splendid views over the bay of Mont-St-Michel and distant prospects of the abbey itself, especially from Cabane Vauban, near the beach resort of Carolles. The route continues south to the village of Dragey, which has one of the largest concentrations of steeplechase horses and trainers in western France (there are more horses than people living here). The village beach (follow the sign to *"plage"* in the center of town) has trails through the dunes where the sleek steeplechasers are taken on their early-morning gallops. (Avoid standing in the trails, which are unmarked; the thoroughbred horse, not the tourist, is prized here!) The beach is unspoiled, largely because dramatic tides and undertows make it dangerous for swimming; development also has been restricted ever since this section of the bay was made a World Heritage Site by UNESCO.

Farther south along D911 is the village of Genêts, named for the yellow Scotch broom that blooms here all summer. The Bec d'Andaine, a small peninsula jutting out into the water near the village, is the best place on the bay to view Mont-St-Michel shimmering in the distance. Hikes or horseback rides across the bay at low tide (safe with a guide but very dangerous without one) can be arranged in Genêts (ask at any shop for a reliable guide) or at the café on the Bec d'Andaine. This café serves simple, inexpensive dishes and drinks on a small terrace in summer; there is also a tiny jazz club, the *Bec de Jazz,* that operates on the beach during the summer. The Grouin du Sud Peninsula south of Genêts (reached off D911 from the village of St-Léonard) is the best place in the area for viewing the dramatic incoming tides for which the bay is famous, especially during the period of a full moon or the spring and fall equinoxes. Ask for an *annuaire des marées* (tidal timetable) at any *maison de presse* (newsstand).

BEST EN ROUTE

Manoir de Brion This bed and breakfast in a medieval manor house in its own elegant park has 10 luxurious guestrooms, most with private baths. Open April to November. No credit cards accepted. Off D911, between Dragey and Genêts (phone: 33-70-82-36). Moderate.

AVRANCHES This town is best known for commanding a splendid view of Mont-St-Michel, especially at sunset in late spring or early fall. The Mont is most romantic by moonlight, when the great rock and its crowning glory, *La Merveille* (the Marvel), swim against a shimmering silver backdrop of sea and sand. The best spot for seeing it is from the viewing table on the terrace of the *Jardin des Plantes* (Botanical Gardens), on Place Carnot. It was a Bishop of Avranches, St. Aubert, who was initially responsible for establishing a place of worship on the nearby rocky islet in the bay, though only after some prodding, if legend is to be believed, by St. Michael the Archangel. Aubert's skull, with a dent in it where Michael zealously drove home his point, is one of the relics now housed in the *Basilique St-Gervais* (Pl. St-Gervais). This, together with other superb relics of the Middle Ages, can be seen by contacting the sacristan.

Manuscripts dating from the 8th to the 15th century, from or connected with Mont-St-Michel abbey, are some of the principal holdings of Avranches's museum (Pl. Jean de St-Avit; phone: 33-68-31-89). Among these are Abélard's famous *Sic et Non* (a collection of religious writings by the church hierarchy), an account by Abbot Robert de Torigni of the founding of Mont-St-Michel, and wonderful illuminated manuscripts. The museum also has rooms and artifacts illustrating the life and work of the people of rural Normandy, including the interior of a farm kitchen. The museum is closed Tuesdays and November through March; admission charge.

Avranches is the place where Henry II of England did his first public penance (in 1172) for the murder of Thomas à Becket. The scene took place at the old cathedral, which was destroyed in 1794; the stone where he knelt in repentance can still be seen; it's known as *La Plate-Forme* and is located near the police station, off Boulevard des Abrincates. Place Patton, near the center of town, has a monument to the American general, who was based here for a time during the Normandy invasion. An American cemetery is located south of Avranches near the village of Saint-James. From Avranches's airport (southwest of town via D456 and D556; phone: 33-58-02-91), you can arrange a flight in a small plane over Mont-St-Michel.

En Route from Avranches Head south on N175, turning right onto D75, which turns into D275. Whether you see Mont-St-Michel first from Granville, from the *Jardin des Plantes* in Avranches, or from any number of the side roads that extend toward it, it looks mystical, like something from a fairy tale or an ancient saga. The ideal—some would say requisite—approach is to walk across the causeway (slightly under a mile) from La Digue (13 miles/21 km from Avranches), the small mainland village opposite the rock. Stop first to look at the mount and its extraordinary assemblage of buildings from the bridge over the Couesnon River on the landward side of the causeway. There, when the tide is in, you can see Mont-St-Michel twice, as a jagged and formidable reality and as a shimmering, mysterious watery reflection. At first somewhat rocky, the causeway soon levels out so that one can concentrate on the shades and shadows as Mont-St-Michel comes more into focus, the vague gray shapes metamorphosing into precise forms and lines. (It's also possible to drive across the causeway; if you do, make sure to arrive before 8 AM to ensure a parking spot on high ground. As the tide comes in, improperly parked cars are sometimes inundated with salt water. High-tide warnings are always posted to advise visitors where, and for how long, they may park.)

MONT-ST-MICHEL At least a day is needed to take in Mont-St-Michel and its wonders. Turn left through the *Porte de l'Avancée,* the only opening through the ramparts; pass the guardhouse; and go through the *Porte du Roi* (King's Gate) onto the Grande-Rue. This narrow street of granite houses, some with mullioned windows and window boxes full of geraniums, is the secular heart of Mont-St-Michel. A proliferation of souvenir shops and restaurants has not destroyed the street's charm, although the summertime throng can be unnerving. The street climbs steeply past small garden plots nestling behind low stone walls to the medieval *Eglise St-Pierre,* the island's parish church. Well worth a stop, the church is dim and damp, with the smell of the sea permeating the solid stone walls. In the morning you may see pilgrims singing hymns in front of a burnished and bejeweled statue of St. Michael battling a dragon. The Grande-Rue passes more terraced lawns and rose gardens to the ramparts, where there is a fine view over the great tidal flats to the *Grand Degré* (Great Stair), which leads in turn to the only entrance to the abbey. Past the fortified gateway under the *châtelet* (small castle), steep stairs lead to the *Salles des Gardes* (Guards' Room), where a small entrance fee is paid. More steps lead up past the abbey lodgings, the cistern, and then finally reach Gautier's Leap. Just beyond is the *West Platform,* an open terrace with wonderful views south to La Digue and west to Brittany.

The labyrinthine interior of the abbey is navigable only to someone already familiar with the structure; if you're not, we strongly suggest taking an English-language guided tour, offered daily at 10:30 AM and 2:30 PM from the *West Platform* (schedules change often, so for exact times contact the tourist office at Bd. Avancée; phone: 33-60-14-30). The tour first leads into the abbey church, whose stained glass windows, ornaments, and furniture are gone; the mellow pink stone of the Romanesque arches in the nave and the spartan bareness of the Flamboyant Gothic choir, however, add up to an exceedingly graceful whole. In the traditional Norman Romanesque manner, the roof is supported not by vaults but by a timber ceiling. From one of the 16th-century chapels in the chancel— the second on the right—a doorway opens onto the *Escalier de Dentelle* (Lace Stairway), which leads up between elaborately carved stone balustrades to a gallery 394 feet above the sea, from which one can look across the sands and streamlets to the mainland over the heads of snarling gargoyles. The cloister, a favorite spot for many people, leads out of the church. Its garden-side perimeter is lined with two rows of columns along a low wall. On the enclosed side are sculpted flourishes of flowers, leaves, and vines occasionally enclosing figurines. The cloister's most interesting feature, however, is that it is constructed above the *Salle des Chevaliers* (Knights' Hall) on the level below and not, as the center garden might suggest, on rock.

Similarly, the adjacent refectory is built over the 13th-century *Salle des Hôtes* (Guests' Hall). About 50 slit windows in the refectory provide a memorable effect of suffused light. Descending to the old cloister on the next level, one can see where the seven-foot-thick walls meet the cold, damp rock. Also on this level is the catacomb-like *Chapelle de Notre-Dame-sous-Terre;* the *Chapelle de St-Martin,* with its spartan altar and simple crucifix; and the *Crypte des Gros Piliers,* directly underneath the chancel of the church. The two major rooms on the middle level are the *Salle des Hôtes* and the *Salle des Chevaliers.* Although the abbey closes at 11:30 AM for two hours, anyone wishing to remain for the noon mass may do so. If the number of visitors is not large, they are invited into the sanctuary for the service with the Benedictine monks and sisters.

Leaving the church by the *Grand Degré,* one passes a gate and a small souvenir shop, on the other side of which are the abbey gardens. The west end of the lower garden, above *St. Aubert's Oratory* (on a rock just above the beach), is the best spot from which to watch the incoming tide. It comes first as a trickle, then streamlets merge to become rivulets, pools join pools and become lagoons, until all the island except the causeway is surrounded by rippling water. Because of silting in the bay, only the highest tides of the year produce the spectacular effect for which the mount was long famous. The best times are in March, September, and sometimes October. Swimming in the bay and hiking across the bed of the bay at low tide to Mont-St-Michel can be very dangerous for the uninformed; high and low tides change fairly drastically from day to day, and there are treacherous currents and a strong undertow in the seemingly placid waters. The bay can be crossed at low tide on foot or horseback (a traditional pilgrimage), but should *always* be done with a guide; there are several based near the Bec d'Andaine or in Genêts.

The abbey is closed January 1, May 1, November 1 and 11, and *Christmas*. Additional summer hours (10 PM to midnight or 1 AM nightly except Sundays from mid-June through September) allow tourists to visit at night, when the abbey is illuminated. For more information, contact Mont-St-Michel's tourist office (see above). Also see *Memorable Museums and Monuments* in DIVERSIONS.

The handful of small guesthouses on Mont-St-Michel are delightful for an overnight stay, simply because the mount minus the daytime crowds is a completely different experience, but during the summer you are more likely to find a room in one of the large modern hotels on D976 leading to the mount's causeway.

BEST EN ROUTE

Mère Poulard With flagstone floors, a fireplace, and gleaming glassware, this restaurant lives up to its location on Mont-St-Michel, even if word is that the welcome can be indifferent. It is famous for its huge omelettes, which are actually more like soufflés—the most dramatic version, *à la Mère Poulard,* is flambéed for dessert. Another specialty is *agneau pré-salé* served with *flageolets* (beans). There also are 26 simple, comfortable rooms and one luxurious suite above the restaurant. Open daily. Reservations necessary. Major credit cards accepted (phone: 33-60-14-01; fax: 33-48-52-31). Expensive.

Saint-Pierre In the shadow of the mount's ramparts, this fine 21-room hotel occupies a converted half-timbered, 15th-century mansion. Its restaurant features seafood and local lamb. Closed December through mid-February. Grande-Rue (phone: 33-60-14-03; fax: 33-48-59-82). Expensive.

Le Manoir de la Roche Torrin In a lovely manor house near Mont-St-Michel's bay, this hotel has a large garden, 12 comfortable rooms, and a good restaurant serving traditional cuisine. Closed mid-November to mid-March. MasterCharge and Visa accepted. In Courtils, 6 miles (10 km) east of Mont-St-Michel (phone: 33-70-96-55; fax: 33-48-35-20). Moderate.

Terrasses Poulard With huge windows overlooking the bay, this modern place sometimes confuses visitors looking for the famous *Mère Poulard* (the restaurant also serves omelettes *à la Mère Poulard;* see above). There also are 30 comfortable rooms. Open daily. Reservations advised. Up Mont-St-Michel from *Mère Poulard,* on the Grande-Rue (phone: 33-60-14-09; fax: 33-60-37-31). Moderate.

Brittany

Surrounded on three sides by water, Brittany always has been an anomaly with respect to the rest of France. Something quiet and mysterious in the nature of the land itself—the dark mountains and the forests that once covered the inland sections, the sea that crashes on the shoreline boulders and cliffs—inspired a deep mysticism in the region's people as early as 3500 BC, when huge monuments of rough stone slabs weighing several tons each were erected. The population claims as ancestors the Gauls, who arrived in the 6th century BC and called the country Armor (Country by the Sea) and Argoat (Country of Wood); the Romans, who came at about the time of Christ; and the Celts, who fled the Angles and the Saxons in Britain in the 5th century. The Celts brought their keenly felt Catholicism, and with their saints and the seeds of a religious approach to life, found fertile ground in the Breton spirit. They also contributed their language, which immediately opposed itself to early French and reached its zenith in the wake of one Nominoé, who established a dynasty that controlled the area for a century.

Breton independence from the then-nascent French monarchy was guarded fiercely against further onslaughts for 400 tumultuous years, but in the end it was no match for the tremendous power of the throne. Anne of Brittany married two French kings, Charles VIII and his successor, Louis XII, but maintained control of the duchy for herself. Her daughter Claude, more interested in gardening than politics, married Anne's husband's successor, François d'Angoulême, and soon allowed the duchy to become part of the legacy of their son Henri II, the future King of France. Independent Brittany was lost.

Even when seen as a part of France, however, the province always stood apart. Habitually resistant to any central control, the Bretons banded together against the throne in the 18th century and fomented the Revolution in its early years; then, when the rest of France arose, they fought passionately on the other side; anti-Revolutionary Breton peasants known as the Chouans were engineering revolts as late as 1832. During World War II the Bretons again resisted control by outsiders, this time the Germans. But also during the war, young men left the province by the thousands; when they came back, they had a broader worldview that dimmed the clarity of the folk legends of Brittany's past. Young people began leaving their homes for the large cities at about the same time, further eroding the culture, and large-scale commercial fishing threatened the region's local fishermen. As inexpensive, manufactured clothing and furniture proliferated, the cost of traditional Breton goods rose. Thus the traditional eventually became a luxury. Nowadays travelers seldom see the classic lace headdresses known as *coiffes* except on important holidays, even in rural hamlets and villages.

Nonetheless, the legacy of the past remains. Most obvious to the first-time visitor are the Breton place names, comprising such Celtic words as *coat, goat, goët,* and *hoët,* all of which mean "wood" (as in Huelgoat, "High Wood," and Penhoët, "End of the Wood"); *ker,* which means "village" or "house" (as in Kermaria, "Mary's Village"); *loc,* which means "holy place" (as in Locmaria, "Mary's Place"); *pleu, plo, ploe,* and *plou,* which mean "parish"; *tre* and *tref,* which mean "parish subdivision"; and *ty,* which means "house." Breton loyalties remain strong, particularly concerning their language. Gradually supplanted by French, both through usage and government edict, the Breton dialect enjoyed a resurgence in the 1970s; it's now taught in schools, appears on sign posts, is heard on TV and radio stations, and is spoken by an estimated 800,000 people. Breton songs and dances have become popular again as well. Another sign of regional pride are the letters BZH (which stands for Breizh, or Brittany) on the license plates of local cars.

Then there are the legends, which the people nourish by the score. The story of Tristan and Iseult (Tristram and Isolde) is said to have taken place here. It was in the Forest of Brocéliande (now known as the Forest of Paimpont) that Christ's disciple Joseph of Arimathea is believed to have vanished with the Holy Grail. In the same forest the renowned Merlin is said to have met and been inflamed by love for the fairy Viviane, who enclosed him in a magic circle in order to keep him forever. Then there is the story of good King Gradlon, who reigned over a section of Brittany known as Cornouaille in a beautiful capital city, Is, which was protected from the sea by a dike. Seduced by the devil in the form of a suitor, his beautiful but dissolute daughter stole the key to the seawall and flooded the city. Gradlon escaped on horseback only after he tossed his offspring into the sea—but Is was lost, and Gradlon went to Quimper to rebuild his kingdom. His daughter turned into a mermaid and charmed sailors to their deaths.

Many of Brittany's churches and chapels are the scenes of great religious processions known as *pardons,* and they draw huge crowds for long walks, masses, and bonfires. The people's considerable religious fervor, which went hand in hand with their belief in legends, found an enduring expression in stone. Nine cathedrals, thousands of churches and chapels, and even greater numbers of calvaries and simple crosses at crossroads were erected throughout the province as expressions of thanks for prayers answered. The native building material, granite, was nearly impossible to cut, yet motivated by their faith, artisans wrought wonders with the substance. Some communities feature uniquely Breton parish closes from the 15th and 16th centuries. These comprise a church; a calvary carved with episodes from the Passion, a type of monument that harks back to the menhirs of Brittany's earliest inhabitants; a cemetery; a triumphal arch guarding its entrance; and adjoining the cemetery, a charnel house, used to store the bones that were exhumed when a cemetery became overcrowded.

A visitor sees Brittany's tapestry of fact, folkway, legend, and belief against the backdrop of one of the greatest landscapes in France. Fringing Brittany is a seacoast so notched, cliff-bound, gorge-riven, and sea-pounded that the simple word "rocky" does not do it justice. Inland, the woods that the Gauls called Argoat have been effectively decimated, but in a few spots it's possible to envision the dark mystery of the country that nourished the legends. The *bocage* (patchwork) of small fields and pastures separated by hedgerows lends a serenity to the place that makes for exceptionally refreshing touring.

The food also seems to have restorative powers. The ingredients here are so fine as to require little in the way of elaborate cooking. The lambs that graze on the salt meadows within sight of the sea and the fruits and vegetables that grow on the edge of the escarpments along the north coast draw an additional tang from the salt air. There are excellent lobsters: *homards,* similar to the Maine crustaceans, as well as langoustes, more like the creatures of the Pacific coast. *Huîtres* (oysters) are bred in the beds in the Golfe du Morbihan and elsewhere, then shipped for fattening to estuaries in other sections of Brittany, where they gain a distinctive flavor from the mix of food substances in the water. *Cotriade*—Brittany's answer to bouillabaisse—is about as elaborate as the local cuisine gets. Thin pancakes are served in almost every small town, and it's easy to make a meal of either *galettes,* which are made of buckwheat flour and usually filled with cheese or tomatoes or bacon, or more delicate crêpes, made of wheat flour and filled with butter and sugar or jam. Breton cider, which is mildly apple flavored, not very sweet, and gently alcoholic, is the perfect accompaniment. Breton butter is, as befits a maritime region, generally mildly salted, unlike butter elsewhere in France. The most typical pastry is the simple *far breton,* a sturdy cake-cum-flan made with plenty of milk, eggs, and prunes soaked in rum.

The route outlined below takes in fishing villages and inland market towns, sophisticated resorts and backwoods farming centers. With the exception of Nantes, which provides an introduction to the folk art of the past and to some of the more interesting periods in Breton history, the tour avoids big cities—such as Rennes and Brest—which are on the whole less rewarding for visitors than the countryside. We suggest that you use the route as an outline. Then, with a detailed map, follow the unnumbered byways to the *artisanats* (craft shops), *moulins* (mills), *chapelles* (chapels), or châteaux signposted off the main roads. In general, the smaller and more obscure the road, the more appealing the scenery, and detours help travelers avoid the congestion of primary routes at the height of the season.

The *TGV-Atlantique* high-speed train has reduced travel time from Paris to Rennes or Brest to just over two hours, and to just three and a half to Quimper—a good incentive to take a train to any of these cities and, on arrival, rent a car for touring the countryside. Major car rental companies have kiosks at or near the train stations. Brittany's extremely well organized regional tourist office, the *Comité Régional du Tourisme de Bretagne* (74 *bis* Rue de Paris, Rennes 35069; phone: 99-28-44-30; fax: 99-28-44-40), is a good source of information about private châteaux that accept guests; hotels with equestrian, golf, or other sports facilities; and spas, of which Brittany has some of the finest in France. Brochures in English are available.

It's also possible to tour Brittany by bicycle or on foot. Cyclists can write to the *Comité Départemental de Cyclotourisme* (5 Belle-Vue, St-Nolff 56250; phone: 97-45-46-25) for information about bicycles. Brittany is a paradise for hikers; there are nearly 1,600 miles (2,600 km) of hiking trails throughout the region. Contact the local *syndicats d'initiatives* (tourist offices) for maps and other information. (Also see *Freewheeling by Two-Wheeler* in DIVERSIONS.)

May and September are ideal times for visiting Brittany—the weather is fine and there are no crowds. From October through March increasing numbers of hotels and restaurants close, so it sometimes seems that whole communities have turned into ghost towns. However, there usually are a few tourist facilities open year-round in every town. In summer reserving hotel rooms and seatings at well-known restaurants far in advance is a must. No matter when you travel, expect to pay $100 or more (sometimes much more) per night for a double room in an expensive hostelry; from $70 to $100 in a moderate one; and under $65 at an inexpensive place. Almost all hotels on the coast require *demi-pension* (breakfast plus lunch or dinner) in summer. Unless otherwise noted, the hotels listed below accept major credit cards and are open year-round. Nearly all feature telephones, TV sets, and private baths in all of their rooms. However, some more rustic establishments may lack TV sets, and some may have private baths in only some of their rooms; it's a good idea when making a reservation to confirm whether your room has a private bath. Almost no hotels in Brittany have air conditioning; it's really unnecessary. A meal for two will run $100 and up in an expensive restaurant; $65 to $100 in a moderate one; and under $65 in an inexpensive one—including service but not wine or drinks. All restaurants below are open for lunch and dinner unless otherwise indicated. Hotels and restaurants are listed alphabetically by price category for each location.

NANTES Its outskirts now full of auto dealerships and apartment towers, Brittany's largest city (pop. 44,000) became a prosperous shipping center thanks to its location about 30 miles inland from where the Loire River flows into the ocean. During the 18th century, before the abolition of the lucrative slave trade between West Africa and the Antilles, and before tonnage increases made it impossible for ships to travel upstream as far as Nantes, the town laid out gracious boulevards edged by stately rows of trees, and wealthy merchants built themselves fine mansions. A walk along the Place du Pilori, the Place Royale, Rue Crébillon (Nantes's answer to Paris's exclusive shopping street, Rue du Faubourg-St-Honoré), the Place Graslin, the octagonal Place Mellinet (with its eight identical townhouses), and the *Cours Cambronne,* a smaller version of Paris's *Jardin du Luxembourg,* will take you past a number of these homes. You'll also pass scores of glossy shops. The 19th-century *Palais Dobrée* (Place Jean IV; phone: 40-69-76-08), now a museum filled with its wealthy builder's collections of prehistoric and medieval antiquities, religious relics, and paintings, is closed Tuesdays. The *Passage Pommeraye* is a mid-19th-century shopping arcade with polished wood floors, a glass roof, pedestrian bridges, and ornate cast ironwork. The area around the 17th-century *Eglise Ste-Croix* is a medieval district with narrow, winding streets and half-timbered houses.

In the center of the city on the Place St-Pierre is the *Cathédrale de St-Pierre et St-Paul,* a truly fabulous structure, from its elegantly carved façade to its soaring interior. Unlike most Breton cathedrals, which are built of granite, Nantes's is constructed of Vendée stone; its lightness allowed the vaults to soar to 120 feet, about twice the height of other cathedrals in Brittany and even higher than that of *Notre-Dame* in Paris. The softness of the stone permitted the sculptors to give sharp definition to every bit of Flamboyant Gothic ornamentation and to outline the slender ribs and groins with a crispness difficult to achieve in granite. And although it was built over many centuries (between 1434 and 1893), it is architecturally harmonious, its pure Gothic lines unadulterated by any hint of other building styles.

Inside is the fine tomb of François II and his second wife, Marguerite de Foix, a memorial ordered by Anne of Brittany for her father and carved by the Breton sculptor Michel Colombe between 1502 and 1507. Note its interesting statue of Prudence, depicted holding a mirror, which stands for the future and in which is reflected the visage of an old man, who represents the past (the idea being that sagacity comes from consulting the past before determining a course for the future). Also note the fine modern windows: One, 80 feet high and 17 feet wide, portrays various Breton saints in unusually intense hues of scarlet and gold; others, ingenious and surprisingly beautiful, are done in oddly shaped glass pieces from pale to dark gray, which give the scenes the appearance of Cubist paintings from the outside. To the right of the cathedral is the Place de la Psalette, a lovely garden surrounded by Renaissance houses.

A visit is recommended to the excellent *Musée des Beaux-Arts* (10 Rue Georges-Clemenceau; phone: 40-41-65-65), one of the best of its kind in the country. Closed Tuesdays; admission charge.

The cathedral and the museum are different from those one would find in Brittany's little harbor towns, but the city's attachment to its Breton identity is not as tenuous as first appearances might indicate. The 15th-century *Château des Ducs de Bretagne* (Pl. Marc-Elder; phone: 40-41-56-56), with round towers and a moat edged by graceful willows, makes this apparent.

One of the most important historic Breton structures, it was the birthplace of Anne of Brittany. Rebuilt in 1466 from a 9th- or 10th-century structure by her father, it was luxurious and full of intrigue, as ministers, majordomos, and other factotums danced attendance on him. Henri IV came here in 1598 to discuss the epochal Edict of Nantes, which granted freedom of worship to French Protestants. Today the château houses three museums. Most interesting as an introduction to a tour of Brittany is the one devoted to popular arts; *coiffes,* embroidered costumes, pottery, ironwork, and carved oak box beds and chests can be seen in numbers not encountered elsewhere in the province. Displays are organized by region to facilitate methodical study, but even a cursory perusal turns up dozens of interesting exhibits, such as the array of carved wooden marriage spoons and the bright yellow mourning costumes of the Bigouden area. Also on the premises are a decorative arts museum displaying modern textiles and a maritime museum. All are closed Tuesdays and holidays; admission charge.

The *Syndicat d'Initiative* on the Place du Change (phone: 40-47-04-51) has maps and a wealth of other material, including an inexpensive, liberally illustrated book of walking tours. It also can provide information on events such as the *Festival des Arts et Traditions Populaires,* which takes place during the first two weeks of July every year. The office is closed Sundays.

When it comes to eating, pike, a local specialty, is found on many Nantes menus, either poached or in quenelles (small dumplings) and often doused with *beurre blanc* sauce. The *Maison des Vins de Nantes* in Lattaye-Fouassière (phone: 40-36-90-10), a picturesque village 6 miles (10 km) east of Nantes on N149 and D359, offers tastings and a wide selection of muscadets, Britanny's only wine, which go well with local seafood. It's closed Tuesdays.

BEST EN ROUTE

Abbaye de Villeneuve This luxurious 21-room, three-suite hotel with a good restaurant is housed in a cluster of 18th-century buildings within a large park. There is a pool. Seven miles (11 km) south of Nantes via N137 and D178. Rte. des Sables d'Olonne, Sorinières (phone: 40-04-40-25; fax: 40-31-28-45). Expensive.

L'Atlantide The chef at this light, modern dining spot loves to experiment. Creations such as langoustines sautéed in aquavit and other fresh seafood dishes win resounding praise from the locals—as well as from Michelin, which awarded the place a star last year. Closed Saturday lunch, Sundays, and three weeks in August. Reservations advised. Major credit cards accepted. Centre de Salorges, 16 Quai E.-Renaud (phone: 40-73-23-23; fax: 40-73-76-46). Expensive.

Delphin "La Châtaigneraie" This family-run restaurant in the countryside has earned one Michelin star for such specialties as squab in pastry and sole with saffron. Closed Sunday dinner, Monday lunch except in summer, three weeks in January, and late July through early August. Reservations advised. Major credit cards accepted. Ten miles (16 km) north of Nantes via D69. 156 Rte. de Carquefou, Sucé-sur-Erdre (phone: 40-77-90-95). Expensive.

Le Domaine d'Orvault In an attractive residential area, this luxurious Relais & Châteaux member with 24 rooms and two suites is a logical choice for peace and quiet. Closed weekends in February. The restaurant, which merits a Michelin star, is also closed Monday lunch and the first two weeks in March. Ten minutes northwest of the city center via N137 and P42. Chemin des Marais-du-Cens (phone: 40-76-84-02; fax: 40-76-04-21). Expensive.

Torigaï The odd mix of a Japanese eatery in an ultramodern building in an ancient Breton city actually works at this restaurant, one of Nantes's most highly rated. Shigeo Torigaï produces such eclectic delicacies as *vinaigrette de Saint-Jacques à la mousseline de céleri-rave truffée* (sea scallops in a vinaigrette sauce with truffled celery-root purée). Closed Sundays and August 10 to 31. Reservations necessary. MasterCard and Visa accepted. On the tiny Ile de Versailles, in the Erdre River off Rue Sully (phone: 40-37-06-37). Expensive.

Auberge du Château The chef at this local favorite uses traditional recipes and the finest ingredients. Closed Sundays, Mondays, three weeks in August, and *Christmas*. Reservations advised. Major credit cards accepted. 5 Pl. Duchesse-Anne (phone: 40-74-05-51). Moderate.

La Cigale Chic Nantais throng to this warm, busy café-brasserie not so much for the simple food but for the sumptuous turn-of-the-century surroundings—heavy iron-edged doors filled with beveled glass, walls partially faced with turquoise tiles, and ceilings full of gilded plaster, rosy-cheeked cherubs, and buxom damsels with masses of hair and angelic robes. Open daily until 12:30 AM. Reservations advised. Major credit cards accepted. 4 Pl. Graslin (phone: 40-69-76-41; fax: 40-73-75-37). Moderate.

En Route from Nantes Take N165 and N171 to La Baule, 44 miles (70 km) to the west.

LA BAULE This full-blown middle class French resort boasts discos, a casino, a yacht harbor, villas perfumed with honeysuckle and jasmine, the pine forest known as the Bois d'Amour, and dozens of boutiques as sophisticated as those in the south of France. This short stretch of coast owes its fame to a wide, 3-mile-long crescent of white sandy beach that, protected from the wind by pines to the north, by the Pointe de Penchâteau to the east, and by the Pointe du Croisic to the west, is thronged in season with vacationers and jammed edge to edge with nearly identical white high-rise hotels. But away from this overly developed stretch are quiet village streets and a picturesque port. The *thalassothérapie* spa, *Thalgo* (phone: 40-24-44-88), is one of France's finest. A very good European film festival takes place here the first week of October, and top-level equestrian and sailing events are held throughout the year. Contact the tourist office for information on these and other activities (8 Pl. de la Victoire; phone: 40-24-34-44). For additional details on La Baule, its casino, and its nightlife, see *Casinos Royale* in DIVERSIONS.

BEST EN ROUTE

Castel Marie-Louise In a handsome villa complete with gables and towers, this stylish 29-room, two-suite hostelry strikes a note of Edwardian grace in the nondescript symphony of contemporary beachfront high-rises that flank it on either side. The one-Michelin-star restaurant's cuisine is elegant and inventive. Tennis, a saltwater pool, golf, and bicycling are available at this member of the Relais & Châteaux group. Closed January. Esplanade du Casino, 1 Av. Andrieu (phone: 40-11-48-38; fax: 40-11-48-35). Expensive.

L'Hermitage This imposing, palatial 221-room hotel has all the expected amenities, in addition to a health center, day-care facilities, and a good restaurant. Ask for a room with a sea view—truly magnificent! Closed November through March. Esplanade L.-Barrière (phone: 40-11-46-46; fax: 40-11-46-45). Expensive.

En Route from La Baule To see huge Breton cliffs, tiny new moons of beach, and sweeping ocean vistas, take super-scenic D45, which skirts the Grande Côte between the Pointe de Penchâteau and the Pointe du Croisic. Le Croisic, whose port shelters fishing boats and pleasure craft, has a colorful fish market, with action from about 7 to 10 AM. You can get a fine view of the coast and the *marais salants* (salt marshes) to the north from the top of Mont-Esprit, a hill constructed from ships' ballast.

From Le Croisic follow D774 through Guérande (famous for its sea salt) to La Roche-Bernard, an erstwhile shipbuilding center about 21 miles (34 km) north that overlooks the Vilaine River. Turn west on N165 for another 21 miles (34 km) toward Vannes to cross the river on a 160-foot-long suspension bridge that seems to leap out of the cliffsides.

BEST EN ROUTE

Domaine du Château de Rochevilaine This luxurious, recently renovated 27-room hostelry, a former estate, sprawls over a rocky nipple of land that thrusts into the Atlantic near the mouth of the Vilaine River. Each of the guestrooms is different; some are huge, with lofty ceilings, crystal chandeliers, velvet-covered furniture, tapestries, Oriental rugs, spacious bathrooms, and fantastic views; ask for a room facing the sea. The gracious, one-Michelin-star dining room features such specialties as veal with a light essence of morel mushrooms and fish braised in shellfish stock. Closed January to mid-February. Pointe de Pen-Lan, Billiers-Muzillac (phone: 97-41-61-61; fax: 97-41-44-85). Expensive.

QUESTEMBERT Zigzagging between *armor* (sea) and *argoat* (woodland), the traveler should next stop at this minuscule town about 16 miles (26 km) east of Vannes on N166 and D775. Questembert is full of buildings constructed of a steely gray granite that seems hard and implacable, even by Breton standards. The 16th-century covered market pavilion that dominates the town, crowded on all sides by more stores, is attractive inside; massive timbers support the steeply pitched roof that sweeps practically to the ground.

BEST EN ROUTE

Bretagne/Georges Paineau By the time a diner discovers that there are fewer than a thousand calories in the "dietetic" meals that chef Georges Paineau offers at this two-Michelin-star Relais & Châteaux establishment, he or she probably is ready to throw caution to the wind and gobble every bite, from the feather-light *galettes de pommes de terre aux épices* (spiced potato pancakes) to the barely cooked oysters. The old stone structure wrapped in a tight net of vines is sheer visual delight inside, with its tapestry-covered chairs, gleaming silver, and polished walnut paneling. The recently renovated 13 rooms and three suites overlooking a small garden evoke the term *tout confort* (every comfort) with their modern bathrooms and firm double beds. Hotel and restaurant closed January through mid-February; restaurant also closed Sunday dinner and Mondays. 13 Rue St-Michel (phone: 97-26-11-12; fax: 97-26-12-37). Expensive.

En Route from Questembert Take D5 and D776 northeast to Malestroit, about 12 miles (19 km) away.

MALESTROIT The small bridge over the River Oust on the fringes of town is the best introduction to this charming, decidedly untouristy village. From here the visitor sees a fine view of the stream, the *allées* of trees reflected in its still waters, and the town's mountain range of rooftops bristling with antennas, chimneys, and steeples. Curiously, in this land of gray granite, most of the town's buildings are of a stone that is vaguely rust-colored, streaked with shades of gray, green, and brown. Many structures along the narrow streets near the 12th- and 16th-century *Eglise St-Gilles* have beams adorned with folksy, if at times alarming, carvings. (Don't be shocked at the one in the Place du Bouffay of the bourgeois flailing his errant wife.)

En Route from Malestroit Take D764 and D4 to Josselin, 22 miles (35 km) northwest.

JOSSELIN The Rohan family has been a force in this attractive village for more than half a millennium. Their coat of arms can be seen in an intensely colored stained glass window in the *Basilique Notre-Dame-du-Roncier,* a simple but elegantly detailed structure in the center of town.

Towering over the Oust River nearby is the imposing fortress-mansion that has been the family seat for 600 years. Constructed in the 11th century as a palace, the château was fortified with nine perfectly cylindrical towers and 12-foot-thick walls in 1370 by Olivier de Clisson. The Rohans, the family of Clisson's wife, Marguerite, acquired it upon his death in 1407. In 1488 the castle was partially destroyed on the orders of François II, Duke of Brittany, after Jean II de Rohan fought against him on the side of the French crown in the struggle for national unification. Subsequently, François II's daughter Anne of Brittany (who had married the King of France) made funds available to her husband's Rohan supporter to restore the castle. It was then that the façade of the mansion inside the walls was endowed with its distinctive granite carvings, as ornate and profuse as if they had been worked in wood. Of Clisson's towers, only three survived the often bloody years since then. The satiny gloss to which the conical slate roofs have been burnished by the centuries, together with the exterior wedding-cake carvings and the regal interiors (seen on guided tours), are the chief attractions of the château. A great *pardon* takes place here annually on the second Sunday in September. The mansion is closed in winter (phone: 97-22-22-50).

En Route from Josselin Take D4 and N166 about 22 miles (35 km) south and southwest to the town of Elven to see the spectacular son-et-lumière show inspired by the legend of Tristan and Iseult (Isolde). It is presented on Friday and Saturday evenings from mid-July to September at the *Tours de Largoet* (Rue Robert-de-la-Noë; phone: 97-53-52-79). Admission charge.
Continue on N166 for 7½ miles (12 km) to Vannes.

VANNES This agricultural center (pop. 45,000) is worth visiting for its particularly handsome and extensive Old Quarter, which dates back to 200 BC, when it was known as Men-Gweur (Stone of the Goat). The Kings (later the Dukes) of Brittany headquartered here. The moss-walled *Cathédrale de St-Pierre,* an infelicitous architectural hodgepodge noted primarily for its soaring 16th-century Italian Renaissance chapel, is at the heart of the Old Quarter. Extending from the cathedral, the Old Quarter is edged on one side by the town ramparts and, at their base, by gardens full of sharply clipped hedges laid out with geometrical precision. One of the most intriguing sights in Vannes, seen from Rue Alexandre-Le-Pontois near the Porte Poterne, is the view of these gardens and a cluster of ramshackle old washhouses, their terra cotta tile roofs punctuated with chimneys and reflected in a placid little river, with the ramparts and the cathedral's steeple looming behind.

The Old Quarter proper, reached by crossing a narrow bridge just above the washhouses, is a labyrinth of narrow pedestrian streets crowded by half-timbered houses. Particularly attractive are Rue St-Guenhaël, which skirts the cathedral, Rue de la Monnaie, and the Place Henri-IV, an enclave of gabled 300-year-old houses. The *Musée de la Cohue* (from the Breton *cochug,* meaning "market") is housed in a mostly 17th-century former market complex opposite the cathedral on the Place St-Pierre. Its varied collection includes ancient Celtic art objects, silver serving dishes created in Vannes in the 18th century, and contemporary art. It is closed Sunday mornings and Tuesdays except in summer; admission charge (phone: 97-47-35-86). Also worth a visit is the *Aquarium Océanographique et Tropical de Vannes* (*Parc du Golfe;* phone: 97-40-67-40). It is open daily with a midday closing; admission charge. The *Musée d'Archéologie* in the 15th-century *Château Gaillard* (2 Rue Noé; phone: 97-42-59-80) displays items from the area's Paleolithic, Celtic, and Gallo-Roman pasts. Open 9:30 AM to noon and 2 to 5 PM (afternoons only, October through March); closed Sundays; admission charge. Summer events in Vannes include a *Festival de Jazz* held in early August (phone: 97-01-80-00).

BEST EN ROUTE

Le Pressoir This lovely one-Michelin-star restaurant offers friendly service and inventive dishes like warm oysters with quail eggs and roast lobster. Closed Sunday dinner, Mondays, March 3 to 12, the first week of July, and two weeks in October. Reservations necessary. Major credit cards accepted. 7 Rue Hôpital, 2½ miles (4 km) north of Vannes via D767 (phone: 97-60-87-63; fax: 97-44-59-15). Expensive.

Aquarium The big attraction of this ultramodern 48-room hotel is the view of the Golfe du Morbihan from every room. There's a restaurant on the premises. *Parc du Golfe,* near the aquarium (phone: 97-40-44-52; fax: 97-63-03-20). Moderate.

La Marébaudière Set back from the road a bit and therefore quieter than other town hostelries, this establishment is only a couple of decades old, but the pretty wallpaper, draperies, and brass or antique bedsteads in its 42 rooms give the place more character than others of its vintage. Straightforwardly prepared seafood is offered in the hotel's restaurant, *La Marée Bleue,* in its own building across the street (8 Pl. Bir-Hakeim; phone: 97-47-24-29). Restaurant closed Sunday dinner off-season. 4 Rue Aristide-Briand (phone: 97-47-34-29). Moderate.

Regis Mahé Low beams, stained glass windows, a carved stone fireplace, and Genoese velvet chairs evoke an air of luxury in keeping with the chef's one-Michelin-star menu of seafood, grills, and refined versions of Breton specialties, such as *filets de rouget* (red mullet filets) with white beans and olive paste, and *gâteau breton* (a pound cake). Closed Sunday dinner, Mondays (except holidays), two weeks in February, and November. Reservations necessary. Major credit cards accepted. Pl. de la Gare (phone: 97-42-61-41). Moderate.

GOLFE DU MORBIHAN This nearly circular body of water measures 12 miles across; it stretches 10 miles from Vannes, on the northern end, to Port Navalo, on the southern. The pretty area, flatter than an oyster shell, is known for its rosy sunsets, subtle light, oyster beds, and dozens of islands, some woodsy and natural, others immaculately landscaped.

The best way to experience the area is by boat. Pack a picnic lunch and hire a *sinagot,* a small sailing craft piloted by local seamen. Contact the *Office du Tourisme* (1 Rue Thiers, Vannes; phone: 97-47-24-34) for information. Or climb aboard one of the *Vedettes Vertes* boats at the *Gare Maritime* (phone: 97-63-79-99) in Vannes. These craft call at most of the major islands, like the 4-mile-long Ile-aux-Moines (Monks' Island), where dolmens guard heather moors and fishermen pedal home to thatch-roofed cottages along quiet roadways. *Navix* organizes dinner cruises through the gulf (*Parc du Golfe,* Vannes; phone: 97-46-60-60).

Skirting the shoreline by car, with glimpses of the sea here and there, is another alternative. South and east of Vannes a tour might take in St-Armel; St-Colombier; the grand, windswept ruins of the 14th-century Suscinio château, where the Dukes of Brittany once summered; and St-Gildas-de-Rhuys, the site of the abbey to which the 12th-century philosopher Pierre Abélard retired after his forced separation from his beloved Héloïse.

BEST EN ROUTE

L'Arlequin In the middle of a park, this restaurant offers traditional cuisine with a light touch, such as pheasant with juniper berries and sole with sherry vinegar. Closed Sunday dinner. Reservations advised. Major credit cards accepted. *Parc Botquelin,* Arradon (phone: 97-40-41-41). Expensive.

Les Vénètes White and modern, this simple 12-room hostelry is just a short walk along the base of the cliffs from the Pointe Arradon, where there are fine sunset views. There's a restaurant. Closed October through March. On the harbor in Arradon (phone: 97-44-03-11). Moderate.

En Route from Vannes Moving west from Vannes, several highways connect small roads that reach to the very tip of the points of land that notch the coast. In the Marais de Pen-en-Toul, a visitor might spot a lonely heron standing sentry over a sawtoothed patch of grass, and in harbors like the ones at Arradon and Larmor-Baden, a traveler might spy fishermen unloading their day's harvest in the dark blue twilight. Near Moustoir, where a handful of signs point to obscure villages along lanes more suited to bicycles than cars, cows being herded from field to barn often block the road. At Port-Blanc there are boats to the Ile-aux-Moines, and Larmor-Baden has service to the Gavrinis Tumulus, one of the most interesting megalithic monuments in Brittany due to the extent and preservation of its chambers. Continue west on N165 to Auray, 12 miles (19 km) from Vannes.

AURAY Much smaller than Vannes and far more manageable, Auray also has a charming Old Quarter. Occupying a point created by a bend in the Auray River and connected to the town proper on the opposite bank by a narrow bridge, it has cobbled streets compressed to one lane by shuttered 15th-century stucco and stone houses. The heart of the area is the Place St-Sauveur, which is full of brasseries and cafés on the river—especially charming for afternoon coffee. Also worth exploring is the quay in the square.

The basilica of *Ste-Anne-d'Auray,* a few miles north, is the setting not only for some of Brittany's most important *pardons* in late July but also for the more minor pilgrimages that take place from Monday through Thursday nearly weekly between *Easter* and October. The elaborate costumes of the faithful are as impressive as the fervor with which they undertake their journeys; some struggle up the *Scala Sancta,* a double staircase leading from the square to the church, on their knees.

En Route from Auray Take D768 to Carnac, 8 miles (13 km) southwest.

CARNAC Megalithic monuments may seem dull, but not at Carnac, which has a concentration of these rough-hewn stones that knows few equals in all of Europe. Here they stand, some 3,000 of them, aligned with the points of the compass or with stellar and solar trajectories—eerie mementos that vibrate with a piety that, however ancient, is fully the equal of that of the *Ste-Anne* pilgrims. To get a sense of the magnitude of force required to erect the megaliths, which typically weigh as much as 350 tons, consider that when the 220-ton Luxor obelisk was set up in the Place de la Concorde in 1836, Parisians hailed it as an extraordinary feat.

Some of the stones are impressive for their sheer size, such as the Tumulus St-Michel, which conceals several burial chambers (accessible near the *Tumulus* hotel, off N781). Others are formidable for their sheer quantity, as is the case with the Ménec Lines (on the left of D196 north of Carnac), where more than a thousand stones of varying height punctuate the fields of golden broom in several straight lines for about three-quarters of a mile. A visitor scarcely has time to absorb this sight before the Kermario Lines appear along the road. The Kercado Tumulus, off the beaten path on the grounds of a private château, is only a bit farther; take the long, straight, tree-lined lane shooting off to the right past the Kermario Lines, pay a small fee at the gatehouse, and pick up the key to the barrow's locked door, a flashlight, and an information sheet. The turnoff is not signposted, so the site is nearly always deserted and feels every bit the tomb that it probably once was. At the Kerlescan Lines farther along, the stones are reputedly even more mystically powerful.

The *Musée de Préhistoire* (in town, at 10 Pl. de la Chapelle; phone: 97-52-22-04) displays prehistoric findings from the excavations of the Carnac monuments—necklaces, ax heads, vases, and the like. The museum is open from 10 AM to noon and 2 to 5 PM; closed Tuesdays; admission charge. A more contemporary attraction is Carnac's seawater treatment spa, the *Centre* de Thalassothérapie (Av. l'Atlantique; phone: 97-52-53-48; fax: 97-52-53-55), with every facility to get you in shape in luxury. Local links of the Novotel and Ibis hotel chain are connected to the spa and can arrange accommodations. The center is open from February to December.

BEST EN ROUTE

Auberge de Kérank Here is a cozy eatery with a terrace facing the sea and the freshest seafood, including broiled lobster. Closed Sunday dinner, Mondays, mid-November to mid-December, and January to early February. Reservations advised. Major credit cards accepted. Two miles (3 km) northwest of Carnac on D781. Rte. de Quiberon, Plouharnel (phone: 97-52-35-36). Expensive.

Le Diana This modern 30-room hotel on the beach has great views, a restaurant, a tennis court, and a health center. Some rooms have balconies. Closed mid-April to mid-October and two weeks in November. 21 Bd. de la Plage (phone: 97-52-05-38; fax: 97-52-87-91). Expensive.

En Route from Carnac Take D781 and then D768 south for the 11 miles (18 km) to Quiberon.

QUIBERON This busy resort center, extending landward from its beach and harbor, is something of a carnival in season, sporting hotels, villas, a casino, bars, discos, tearooms, fishing-supply stores, and boutiques. What makes Quiberon particularly noteworthy is the surrounding coastline, which boasts some of the most spectacular sights in southern Brittany. Near town at the Pointe du Conguel, the waves hurl themselves onto low-lying rocks that afford a fine view of Belle-Ile (Beautiful Island; see below) and the islands of Houat and Hoëdic. North of town they crash upon tiny beaches at the base of tall cliffs. It is easy to understand why this stretch of shoreline was dubbed the Côte Sauvage (Wild Coast).

Much of the coast is visible from the road that twists and climbs through the cliff-top moors. For the best view, park your car and walk the 2 miles (3 km) of coast between Port-Pigeon, midway along the peninsula's west coast, and Portivy, just north of the Pointe du Percho on the north. *Note:* Strong currents make swimming here dangerous.

BEST EN ROUTE

Sofitel For every comfort, including a saltwater spa, a pool, and tennis courts, this modern 116-room hotel is a good bet, even if it lacks local charm. The in-house restaurant, *Le Thalassa,* has excellent seafood and classic dishes like veal with truffles. Closed January (phone: 97-50-20-00; 800-763-4835; fax: 97-50-07-34). Expensive.

Bellevue The 39 rooms in this modern hotel are bright and cheerful; most have sea views and many have balconies. Closed November to mid-March. Rue Tiviec (phone: 97-50-16-28; fax: 97-30-44-34). Moderate.

Gulf Stream This simple 24-room inn on the harbor gets its charm from the classic balustrades and window boxes splashed with color. The whole place seems to gleam. No restaurant. Closed mid-November to early February. 17 Bd. Chanard (phone: 97-50-16-96; fax: 97-50-35-64). Moderate.

BELLE-ILE Of all the islands off the Breton coast, Belle-Ile, once frequented by Sarah Bernhardt and Monet (not together!), is considered a must. It is accessible by steamer (phone: 97-31-80-01) from Port-Maria, which dominates 10-mile-distant Quiberon. The scenery—shoreline cliffs, deep valleys, verdant pastures, wheat and potato fields interspersed with patches of weeds and stately trees, and small complexes of whitewashed farmhouses—is impressive. From several of the villages one can walk to spots on the coastline where the sea has carved caverns and odd shapes out of the cliffs. Don't miss the Grotte de l'Apothicairerie (Apothecary Grotto), named for the nests cormorants used to line up along niches in the cave walls like bottles in a pharmacy. Especially in the late spring and early fall there is a delightful serenity to this island. Touring by bicycle is a lovely way to enjoy the remarkable scenery.

BEST EN ROUTE

Castel Clara Boasting bathrooms paved with marble and balconies opening onto the sea, this comfortable, gleaming-white, 43-room member of the Relais & Châteaux group occupies a secluded hillside on the peaceful west coast of the island. There also is a good restaurant, a heated saltwater pool, tennis facilities, and a state-of-the-art saltwater spa. Closed mid-December to mid-February. Port-Goulphar (phone: 97-31-84-21; fax: 97-31-51-69). Expensive.

La Désirade A collection of sparkling white stucco bungalows is set around a pool at this refreshingly simple 24-room establishment. There's no restaurant, but breakfast is available. Closed January and February. Near Bangor and Port Coton, on Rte. Port-Goulphar (phone: 97-31-70-70; fax: 97-31-89-63). Moderate.

Manoir de Goulphar Thanks to its fine views and chic decor, this posh white structure on the peaceful coast has far more character than its modern construction might suggest. There are 60 rooms, some with balconies overlooking the sea, and a restaurant. Closed November through March. Port-Goulphar (phone: 97-31-80-10; fax: 97-31-51-69). Moderate.

En Route from Quiberon Take D768 back toward Carnac. Take D781 northwest for 27 miles (43 km) to Hennebont, then follow D769 and D110 north for about 19 miles (30 km) to Kernascléden.

KERNASCLÉDEN The care with which pious Bretons decorated their simple churches immediately is apparent in the restored 15th-century, lichen-splotched house of worship that dominates this little town. The slender belfry is elegantly proportioned and finely embellished with small ornamental motifs, as are the tops of the buttresses. The archway above the front door is topped with layer upon layer of decorative grooves; the porch is lined with niches, each one edged with a wealth of lace-like details that frame realistic statues of the apostles.

Of particular interest inside this church are its frescoes—some depict angels and scenes from the life of Christ and the Virgin; others, underneath a beautiful rose window, show macabre images like the Dance of Death among skeletons and courtiers, and horned devils plunging anguished sinners into pots of boiling oil.

BEST EN ROUTE

Château de Locguénolé In this courtly castle are 34 recently renovated guestrooms and an excellent one-Michelin-star dining room; swimming, tennis, and golf are all possible. For additional details, see *Romantic French Hostelries* in DIVERSIONS. Hotel closed January to mid-February; restaurant also closed Monday lunch in the off-season. About 2½ miles (4 km) south of Hennebont, just off D781 (phone: 97-76-29-04; fax: 97-76-39-47). Expensive.

En Route from Kernascléden Retrace the route to Hennebont and then continue south for 7 miles (11 km) to Lorient.

LORIENT Originally spelled "L'Orient" (the Orient), this town was founded in 1666 as the home base of the Compagnie des Indes, a royal monopoly established by Louis XIV that dealt in spices and other Far East merchandise. The French Revolution put an end to this profitable enterprise, but Lorient survived as a fishing center and, from the 19th century, as a naval base. During World War II the city suffered heavy bombing of its port and ancient city center, which were replaced by modern buildings. But Lorient makes up for its lack of architectural charm by hosting one of the world's largest Celtic celebrations, the annual *Festival Interceltique,* held during the first two weeks of August. For a program of events, call the festival (2 Rue Paul-Bert; phone: 97-21-24-29) or contact the *Office de Tourisme* (*Maison de la Mer,* Quai de Rohan; phone: 97-21-07-84). For additional details, see *Festivals à la Française* in DIVERSIONS. The week before *Bastille Day* (July 14), Lorient also hosts the annual *Les Océanes,* a celebration complete with sea tales, sea chanteys, and plays with maritime themes. For information about the program, contact the *Office de Tourisme* or *Les Océanes* (phone: 97-65-63-01).

L'Amphitryon Stop in at this lovely restaurant to sample light renditions of classic cuisine with a focus on seafood, such as crab with tomato essence and rockfish with anchovies. Michelin has awarded it one star. Closed Saturday lunch, Sundays, and *Christmas Week*. 127 Rue du Colonel-Müller (phone: 97-83-34-04). Expensive.

Mercure All 58 guestrooms in this modern, airy establishment are regularly renovated, so everything is in nearly pristine condition. The cozy bar is the perfect spot in which to lounge and sip a cognac; there's no restaurant. 31 Pl. J.-Ferry (phone: 97-21-35-73; fax: 97-64-48-62). Expensive.

Le Jardin Gourmand In this excellent eatery with its own garden, the top-notch chef specializes in traditional Breton fare enhanced by fresh vegetables and seafood. Try the *cotriade,* the *blanquette de jarret de veau* (veal-shank stew in a cream sauce), or the *galette de pommes de terre à l'andouille de Guémené* (a potato pancake with tripe sausage from Guémené, a town in Brittany renowned for this delicacy). Loire Valley wines predominate; the white Savennières (an Anjou wine) and the inexpensive red Gamay de Touraine are excellent. Closed Sundays, September 6 to 23, and December 20 to January 5. Reservations necessary. Major credit cards accepted. 46 Rue J.-Simon (phone: 97-64-17-24). Moderate.

Victor-Hugo While the 30 guestrooms in this charmer may not be the epitome of luxury, they are extremely comfortable and cheery, and the management is unusually friendly and helpful. There's no restaurant. Conveniently located between the port and the town center, at 36 Rue Lazare-Carnot (phone: 97-21-16-24; fax: 97-84-95-13). Inexpensive.

En Route from Lorient Take D769 north to Le Faouët, about 26 miles (42 km) away.

LE FAOUËT This old town has a 16th-century covered market building similar to the one at Questembert, with a forest of pillars inside, and also is well worth visiting for the two fine chapels nearby and the beautiful countryside in between the Stêr-Laër and Ellé Rivers. The better known of the two chapels is the one devoted to the Irish hermit St. Fiacre, the patron saint of gardeners. Somewhat asymmetrical but nonetheless balanced on the outside, this rather simple structure set alongside a farm has a carved Gothic choir screen inside; its lifelike carvings, executed in a primitive style, demonstrate the heights of the Breton woodcarvers' skill. On the nave side note the thieves contorted on their crosses and, along the border, the crowd of curious faces. Facing the chancel, don't miss the pie-eyed peasant vomiting a fox (symbolizing drunkenness) and the man with the woman lifting her skirts flirtatiously (symbolizing lust).

The *Chapelle Ste-Barbe,* a few miles away on the other side of Le Faouët, is remarkable not so much for its small interior as for its site; it clings to the side of a cliff just beneath the crest of a hill whose summit overlooks the fields and forests of the Ellé Valley. To get to the chapel, walk through the woods for about 10 minutes up a switchbacked trail that begins immediately across the road from the *Café de l'Ellé.* There are two ways to go, one considerably steeper than the other, and the signs are no help; inquire before starting out. The trail ends at a finely proportioned Renaissance stairway that leads to the chapel. *Pardons* are held here on December 4 and on the last Sunday in June. Yet another chapel just outside town is the late-Gothic *Chapelle St-Nicolas,* on a lovely site surrounded by forest; the saint's life is depicted in nine sculpted panels.

En Route from Le Faouët Take D790 south for 13 miles (21 km) to Quimperlé.

QUIMPERLÉ This unprepossessing hill town is well known to the fishermen who come for the salmon and trout in the placid little Isole and Ellé rivers, which converge here. But the town is more interesting for its Romanesque *Eglise de Ste-Croix,* laid out not in the shape of the rectangular Latin cross but in that of the square Greek cross, like the *Holy Sepulcher* in Jerusalem. The round arches, barrel vaulting, small apse with vividly colored windows, and cool crypt supported by capitals carved with vaguely Celtic designs make this a memorable spot. *La Maison des Arches* contains a museum of Breton traditions (7 Rue Dom Morice; phone: 98-39-06-63).

Not far from the church, along Rue Brémond-d'Ars and narrow, alley-like Rue Dom-Morice, are some pretty half-timbered houses with walls that lurch and lean with the abandon of a drunkard.

BEST EN ROUTE

L'Hermitage Occupying an old manor house and several stone outbuildings, this 24-room, four-suite establishment is notable for its setting on the edge of a forest, its gardens full of rosebushes and hydrangeas, and the sounds of the wind rushing through the pines that crowd the complex and edge the small slate-terraced pool. The rooms are large with rustic furniture and adequate bathrooms. There's a restaurant. Closed January. On D49, Rte. du Pouldu, about a mile (1.6 km) south of Quimperlé (phone: 98-96-04-66; fax: 98-39-23-41). Moderate.

Ty Gwechall This friendly and very typical Breton *crêperie* serves every kind of main-dish buckwheat *galette* and dessert crêpe you can imagine. Closed Wednesdays and December through January except *Christmas Week.* Reservations unnecessary. MasterCard and Visa accepted. 4 Rue Mellac (phone: 98-96-30-63). Inexpensive.

En Route from Quimperlé Take D49 south of Quimperlé for 2 miles (3 km) to the Forêt de Carnoët (Forest of Carnoët).

FORÊT DE CARNOËT Legend has it that this nearly 2,000-acre preserve once was inhabited by the Count of Comorre, also known as Bluebeard, a fellow who, because of his fear of a prophecy that he would be murdered by his son, killed four wives as soon as they became pregnant and slaughtered the son of a clever fifth wife who had managed to bear her child. But the prophecy was nonetheless fulfilled: The dying St. Trémeur, as the son was later known, lived just long enough to toss a handful of dirt at the count's castle with a force that made the building collapse, burying Bluebeard in the rubble.

Today many Bretons walk along the footpaths that lead from the road into this forest of beautiful tall, straight trees. Popular hiking destinations include the ruins of the *Abbaye St-Maurice* (accessible via D224, off D49); the Rocher Royal, a ridge that overlooks the serene Laïta River (a little over a mile/l.6 km from D49 via a footpath); and the *Château de Comorre*. A *pardon,* called the *Fête des Oiseaux* (Festival of the Birds), is held in the hamlet of Toulfoën at the edge of the forest on *Pentecost Sunday.*

BEST EN ROUTE

Chez Jacky This is a seafood lover's paradise. Grilled lobster served with a creamy house sauce is the specialty, and Bélon oysters are available. Everything is perfectly matched to the muscadets on the wine list. Open from 10 AM to 10 PM. Closed Mondays and October through March. Reservations advised. Major credit cards accepted. Port de Bélon, Riec-sur-Bélon (phone: 98-06-90-32). Expensive.

Manoir de Kertalg This peaceful nine-room, one-suite hotel in the converted stables of an ancient manor house is surrounded by a huge park. No restaurant. Open *Easter* to mid-November. MasterCard and Visa accepted. Rte. de Riec-sur-Bélon (D24), 1½ miles (2 km) outside Moëlan-sur-Mer (phone: 98-39-77-77; fax: 98-39-72-07). Expensive.

Les Moulins du Duc A tiny lake, swans, white doves, a waterwheel velvety with moss, comfortable quarters in a handful of rustic houses, a pool, and a woodsy valley setting make this 22-room, five-suite establishment one of the most inviting in the province. The restaurant features local products, including seafood. Nearby cascades the Bélon River, famous for its oysters. Closed mid-January through February; restaurant also closed Wednesday lunch off-season. Near Moëlan, about 5 miles (8 km) from the southern edge of the forest (phone: 98-39-60-73; fax: 98-39-75-56). Expensive.

En Route from the Forêt de Carnoët Take D783 and D49 to Pont-Aven, about 6 miles (10 km) away.

PONT-AVEN It was in the simple *Chapelle Trémalo* that artist Paul Gauguin found the 16th-century wooden Christ on which he modeled his well-known *Yellow Christ.* Less than a mile from this pleasant little town, the chapel can be seen by following D24 and a climbing, twisting side road through cow pastures edged by lines of tall, straight trees. The celebrated carving is still there, but the real allure of the place is the granite structure itself, simple, asymmetrical, and seemingly at the top of the world. The scene is especially beautiful at dusk, when the light imbues it with a mystical quality.

In fact, it was this very quality of light that attracted Gauguin, along with Maurice Denis, Paul Sérusier, Emile Bernard, and other painters, who together formed the Pont-Aven School. The town was particularly picturesque then, with its valley setting, its little white houses, and its mills driven by the Aven River. It is no less charming today, although a little more worldly. There are several galleries plus the *Musée de Pont-Aven* (Pl. de l'Hôtel de Ville; phone: 98-06-14-43), where you can see works by artists from the Pont-Aven School and temporary exhibits of contemporary painters. The museum is open 10 AM to 12:30 PM and 2 to 7 PM, late April through December. A few shops sell the delicious butter cookies for which Pont-Aven is known, and there are some antiques shops and boutiques of more than usual interest. Even the simplest bars and *crêperies,* with their whitewashed stucco walls, beamed ceilings, and polished antique furnishings, have atmosphere to spare, with the sound of the rushing waters that once powered the mills still reverberating between the stone walls.

BEST EN ROUTE

Le Manoir du Ménec This hotel and leisure center installed in a gracious 15th-century stone manor has cozy individual cottages as well as 10 deluxe guestrooms. The restaurant, with ancient stone walls and elegant chandeliers, is in the oldest part of the manor, while the heated pool, Jacuzzi, sauna, and gym are in the newer addition. There also are facilities for small conferences. Closed two weeks in February; restaurant also closed Wednesday lunch, for lunch from mid-November through March, and Tuesdays from mid-September through May. Northeast of Pont-Aven via D76 in Bannalec (phone: 98-39-47-47; fax: 98-39-46-17). Expensive.

Moulin de Rosmadec The sounds of the stream that borders it on three sides are only one reason that this reconstructed 15th-century stone mill is such a delightful dining spot (meriting one Michelin star). Consider also the antiques scattered around the cozy dining rooms inside, and the profusion of honeysuckle, roses, and rhododendrons crowding the mill walls and edging the terrace outside. Then look at the menu itself, which offers a lemony *soupe de poisson* (fish soup), *palourdes farcies* (stuffed clams), *homard grillé à l'estragon* (grilled lobster flavored with tarragon), *pigeonneau sauce foie gras* (young squab in foie gras sauce), and more. There are also four guestrooms, all with views of the river. Closed Wednesdays, Sunday dinner except in summer, February, and the last two weeks in October. Reservations necessary. Major credit cards accepted. Near the center of town (phone: 98-06-00-22; fax: 98-06-18-00). Expensive.

La Taupinière Surrounded by a beautiful garden and coiffed with a straw roof, this restaurant serves giant crayfish grilled in the fireplace, tuna seviche, anglerfish in butter, farmers' cider, as well as fine wines, including many rare bordeaux. Michelin has awarded it one star. Closed Monday dinner, Tuesdays, late September to late October, and two weeks in March. Reservations advised. Major credit cards accepted. Rte. de Concarneau, 1½ miles (2 km) from Pont-Aven (phone: 98-06-03-12). Expensive.

En Route from Pont-Aven Take D783 to Concarneau, 9 miles (14 km) west.

CONCARNEAU This erstwhile fortress town wears two faces—one of a popular summer resort, with a long stretch of beach and a *ville close* (walled city), where cars usually are prohibited; the other of a fishing center whose boats, which can be seen in the *nouveau port* (new port) behind the *ville close,* haul in some of the biggest tuna catches in France. The *ville close* has narrow streets attractively crowded by high, shuttered houses, but it also has trinkets-filled souvenir shops and galleries where seascapes are the staple. When fishermen unload their catch by the basket and buyers scramble to bid for the best, even jaded travelers are fascinated. Because of the continual influx of sailors, the city's middle class aura is tempered by an appealing raunchiness.

Drive along Boulevard Katerine-Wily, which wends its way between a wall of nondescript apartment towers and a glorious postcard sweep of bay. Buy a ticket at the clock tower just over the bridge at the entrance to the *ville close* and climb the ramparts for another view of the harbor. Also explore the *Musée de la Pêche* (10 Rue Vauban; phone: 98-97-10-20) and its exhibits on commercial fishing. Open daily; closed lunch hours from mid-September through mid-June. The next-to-last Sunday in August each year brings the *Fêtes des Filets Bleus* (Festivals of the Blue Nets), featuring singers, dancers, and craftspeople who don traditional Breton dress, as well as concerts of Breton music.

BEST EN ROUTE

Ferme du Letty The Guilbault family has converted this ancient farmhouse into one of Brittany's finest restaurants. The chef's trademark—incredibly fresh seafood accompanied by inventive sauces—has earned one Michelin star. The mussels and sole with orange sauce and *Kouign-Amann,* a classic Breton cake, are exemplary. Closed Wednesdays (except for dinner in July and August), Thursday lunch, and mid-October through February. Reservations necessary. Major credit cards accepted. In Letty, about 1½ miles (2 km) southeast of the small village of Bénodet via D44 (phone: 98-57-01-27). Expensive.

Le Galion The velvet curtains, white linens, silver, and crystal contrast strikingly with the low, rough beams and rugged granite walls of this lovely one-Michelin-star establishment. But the food is the real draw—mainly seafood that seems to have come straight from the surf. The chef excels in such imaginative dishes as *civet de lotte* (monkfish stew), *fricassée de langoustine* (lobster stew), *coquilles St-Jacques grillé au cumin* (sea scallops grilled with cumin), and *turbot braisé avec champagne* (turbot with champagne). There are five guestrooms upstairs. Closed Sunday dinner and Mondays except in summer, mid-January to March, and two weeks in November. Reservations advised. Major credit cards accepted. In the *ville close,* at 15 Rue St-Guénolé (phone: 98-97-30-16; fax: 98-50-67-88). Expensive.

Les Sables Blancs This modern 48-room hotel has smallish but comfortable rooms, most with splendid sea views, and a restaurant that features simple seafood dishes. Closed November through March. Plage des Sables Blancs (phone: 98-97-01-39). Moderate.

Grand Of the various Concarneau hostelries, this old-fashioned, 33-room inn, on a busy corner overlooking the port bristling with ships, is convenient to the *ville close.* There's no dining room. Closed October to mid-April. 1 Av. Pierre-Guéguin (phone: 98-97-00-28). Inexpensive.

En Route from Concarneau Take N783 northwest for the 15 miles (24 km) to Quimper.

QUIMPER Sprawling though it is, there still is something of the sleepy Breton village to this city of 62,000, whose name in Breton ("junction") refers to the meeting point of the Odet and the placid Steir Rivers. Narrow streets that were miraculously spared damage during World War II angle between tall half-timbered houses whose second stories are cantilevered out over the street. Walk through the old section of the city, following Rue Elie-Fréron, the Place au Beurre, Rue du Sallé (with many restored structures), Rue de Kerguelen, Rue Valentin, the Place Mesgloaguen, Rue St-Nicolas, Rue des Gentilshommes, Rue des Boucheries, and Rue du Guéodet (distinguished by a house whose ground floor is guarded by caryatids in antique costumes). Fairly detailed maps and guided walking tours (in warm weather) are offered by the tourist office (Pl. Résistance; phone: 98-53-04-05). Quimper is Brittany's best regional shopping center outside the major cities, and the town is full of boutiques purveying carved wood, embroidered items, musical instruments, regional clothing, handwoven cloth, the region's world-famous faïence (see below), and more. The place to buy authentic fisherman's clothing, from pea jackets to striped sailor's sweaters, is *La Boutique de l'Authentique Pull et Tricot Marin* (2 Pl. au Beurre; phone: 98-64-29-30).

   At the heart of the town and only a block from the graceful tree-lined quais of the Odet and Rue Ste-Catherine, where one of a half-dozen bridges laces the riverbanks together, is the *Cathédrale St-Corentin,* awkwardly proportioned compared with the one in Nantes but worth seeing nonetheless. The structure is named for King Gradlon's famous spiritual adviser, who according to legend subsisted on the meat of a single perpetually regenerating fish. (He's one of a handful of Breton saints not recognized by Rome.) The church was erected between the 13th and 15th century except for its pair of 250-foot towers, which were built in 1856 with funds provided by some 600,000 diocesans—each paying one sou annually for five years. There are some richly colored stained glass windows. Sunday visitors are in for a treat: The organ is one of the best in Brittany, and during high mass the air vibrates with its chords. Extensive renovation and cleaning of the cathedral was completed in 1994.

Immediately adjacent, in the 16th-century bishop's palace, is the *Musée Départemental Breton* (1 Rue Roi-Gradlon; phone: 98-95-21-60), with displays of Breton pottery, musical instruments, embroidered regional dresses and starched *coiffes,* and furnishings of lower Brittany. The carvings on the furniture demonstrate the considerable skill attained by Breton woodworkers. The ornamentation on the 19th-century *coffre à blé* (wheat storage chest) near the entrance resembles that found in Great Britain and Ireland—evidence of Brittany's ties to Celtic culture. The similarity is uniquely appropriate to an institution based, as this one is, in the capital of the region named La Cornouaille by its original settlers, who came from Cornwall, England. Also interesting is the Quimper ceramics display, which shows the development of the art from the very crude to the extremely refined and illustrates the evolution of the *petits bretons* (little Bretons) that are present on almost every traditional plate from their debut in the 1880s to the present. The museum is closed October through March.

White ceramics, painted in blue and yellow with Breton figures, flowers, and fruits, have been one of the city's primary claims to fame since the 17th century, when artisans from Rouen and elsewhere came to work in the Quimper potteries; they are featured in nearly every prominent shop window in the older part of town. Guided tours of the factories that produce ceramics also are available. Contact the *Faïenceries de Quimper Henriot* (Rue Haut; phone: 98-90-09-36) or the *Faïenceries Keraluc* (71 Rue du Président-Sadat; phone: 98-53-04-50). *Henriot* is open daily year-round; *Keraluc* is closed Sundays. Both arrange shipments abroad. The *Musée de la Faïence* in the suburb of Locmaria (14 Rue J. B. Bousquet; phone: 98-90-12-72) has a 500-piece collection tracing the history of the craft. Closed Sundays and October to April.

The restored *Musée des Beaux-Arts* (40 Pl. St-Corentin; phone: 98-95-45-20) boasts one of the best collections of paintings in provincial France; works from the Italian, Spanish, Flemish, and Dutch schools hang next to paintings by members of the Pont-Aven School and others who took their inspiration primarily from Breton scenes. The museum is closed Tuesdays, holidays, and Sunday mornings from October through March; admission charge.

It's also pleasant to board a boat for the three-hour round trip down the forest- and cliff-edged Odet River as far as the resort of Bénodet at its mouth. The week ending with the fourth Sunday in July brings the important week-long *Festival de Cornouaille,* which has been preserving and promoting Breton music and dance since 1923.

BEST EN ROUTE

Le Capucin Gourmand This one-Michelin-star restaurant specializes in excellent, primarily seafood-based dishes like lobster with morel mushrooms. Closed Sundays, Saturday lunch, Saturday dinner in winter, two weeks in February, and the first two weeks in July. Reservations advised. Major credit cards accepted. 29 Rue Réguaires (phone: 98-95-43-12). Expensive.

Le Gradlon This quiet 24-room hotel has a courtyard-garden where you can have breakfast, but there is no restaurant. In the center of town, at 30 Rue Brest (phone: 98-95-04-39; fax: 98-95-61-25). Moderate.

Crêperie le Rozell A lovely *crêperie* housed in a 17th-century building. Closed Sundays and Mondays except in July and August. Reservations unnecessary. MasterCard and Visa accepted. 17 Rue du Châpeau Rouge (phone: 98-55-62-53). Inexpensive.

En Route from Quimper Take D785 southwest for 13 miles (21 km) to Pont-l'Abbé.

PONT-L'ABBÉ The area around this town (pop. 7,700) offers travelers the rare opportunity to see traditional Breton dress—the richly embroidered velvet skirts, lace aprons, and starched white *coiffes.* Not only do the older women here wear them to the town's *pardon* in mid-July, but they also don traditional attire to bicycle to town on market day and to trudge to mass on Sundays, their black velvet skirts swishing and their wondrously tall headdresses bobbing with their every movement. In the town's 14th- to 17th-century fortress-château (phone: 98-87-24-44) is a collection of historical versions of these colorful outfits. It's closed October to May; admission charge. *La Maison du Pays Bigouden* (at the edge of town; phone: 98-87-35-63) is an outdoor museum that is a reconstruction of a turn-of-the-century Bigouden farm. It's closed Sundays, holidays, and October through May; admission charge.

BEST EN ROUTE

Bretagne This longtime local favorite has 18 guestrooms with such tasteful details as flowered wallpaper and spacious bathrooms; some have kitchenettes. It's simple, but a real find. Closed mid-January to early February; restaurant also closed Mondays off-season. 24 Pl. de la République (phone: 98-87-17-22; fax: 98-82-39-31). Moderate.

Château de Kernuz Reached by a winding, tree-lined lane, this comfortable 16th-century establishment with 19 renovated rooms and a pool has wonderful salons full of antiques, with chandeliers, beamed ceilings with refined paneling, and massive hearths. Closed October through April. 1½ miles (2 km) from Pont-l'Abbé on N785, Rte. de Penmarch (phone: 98-66-02-36; fax: 98-87-30-63). Moderate.

Relais de Ty Boutic Light, fresh foods, such as *langoustines à la fondue de poireau* (Dublin Bay prawns with leek sauce), are offered by the innovative chef here. Closed Mondays, Tuesday dinner and Thursday lunch off-season, and early February to early March. Reservations advised. Major credit cards accepted. Two miles (3 km) from town on Rte. de Plomeur (phone: 98-87-03-90; fax: 98-87-30-63). Moderate.

En Route from Pont-l'Abbé Brittany's west coast offers a study in the many meanings of the word "shoreline." Guilvinec, an otherwise undistinguished fishing port, is worth a detour around 5 PM, when the sardine and tuna boats come into port and the fishermen unload their catch. There is no question that fishing is important throughout the area; that it has been so historically is evident in Penmarch, where the doorways of the 16th-century Flamboyant Gothic *Eglise Ste-Nonna* are embellished with reliefs of the ships of the wealthy merchants who built it. The Pointe de Penmarch, where low tides reveal a liberal scattering of smooth, sea-pounded rocks that once might have been cliffs, offers a vision of one type of coastline with which Breton sailors always have had to contend. Rising above it are two lighthouses that have been warning sailors to steer clear of these waters ever since the 19th century; one of them, the *Phare d'Eckmuhl,* often can be toured. From its 213-foot-high gallery it's possible to see nearly the length of the coastline in fine weather; half a dozen lighthouses can be discerned in a single glance.

From here D80 hugs the water's edge as far as the resort of St-Guénolé. At high tide, when the surf is beating against the boulders along the shore, it's easy to envision a great wave sweeping away a whole family, a tragedy that actually happened in 1870 and that is commemorated by an iron cross attached to one of the rocks. The road turns inward, and the sea becomes accessible only by spur roads until Pouldreuzic, where D40 turns westward to Penhors. Site of the annual *pardon* of *Notre-Dame-de-Penhors* on September 8, one of the largest in Cornouaille, the area becomes thronged with the faithful, who join a procession through the countryside to the shoreline for a blessing of the sea. The unnumbered northbound continuation of D40 passes through charming tiny villages like Keristenvet, Plozévet, and Ports-Poulan before turning inland again.

At Audierne, an attractive small fishing port at the base of a woodsy hillside on the Goyen River estuary, lovers of Breton folklore will want to head for the Quai Pelletan, not far from the beach. From the Quai Pelletan one can catch the 90-minute boat trip to the wild, bare, and rocky Ile de Sein (from the Breton *seiz hun,* or seven sleeps, the name reflects its past as a holy place for druids). The reclusive islanders are known for their steadfast patriotism: During World War II, when General de Gaulle, then in London, broadcast an appeal for volunteer French troops to join him in an assault on German forces in France, all 150 able-bodied men of the Ile de Sein (except for the mayor and the curé) left for England. When de Gaulle later gave a roll call of his 600 new volunteers, asking where each was from, 150 answered, "Ile de Sein." De Gaulle responded, *"Sein, est-il donc le quart de la France?"* (Does Sein make up a fourth of France?). There is at least one daily boat trip if the weather permits, with three trips daily during July and August.

BEST EN ROUTE

Le Goyen This 26-room, three-suite establishment (a member of the Relais & Châteaux group), recently redecorated with flowery wallpaper and pine furniture in the English style, is clean, well kept, and very comfortable. In front is a long porch brightened with pots of geraniums and plenty of white chairs on which to while away a summer afternoon. The hotel also boasts a one-Michelin-star restaurant offering such dishes as lobster sautéed with mushrooms or with truffles; the chef favors traditional sauces with most dishes. Closed mid-November to mid-December; restaurant also closed Monday and Tuesday lunch off-season. Right on the harbor, at Pl. Jean-Simon, Audierne (phone: 98-70-08-88; fax: 98-70-18-77). Expensive.

POINTE DU RAZ A common destination for travelers leaving Audierne is the Pointe du Raz, a mass of craggy, tumbled cliffs and rocks that resemble the fin of a prehistoric animal. It is habitually battered by the sea with a ferocity that prompted Baudelaire to exclaim, *"Nul n'a passé le Raz sans peur ou sans douleur"* ("No one has passed through the Raz without fear or pain"). The two good-size parking lots and the square full of souvenir shops only begin to suggest the spot's popularity. But even when there are no parking spaces and the guides are occupied leading walking tours along the footpaths that squiggle to the sea, the grandeur of the scene is undeniable. The Baie des Trépassés (Bay of the Dead), to the right of the headland, is believed to have been the point of embarkation for druids bound for the Ile de Sein to bury their dead. Legend has it that the town of Is (pronounced *Ees*), the beautiful capital of Cornouaille at the time of good King Gradlon, was offshore.

En Route from the Pointe du Raz There are equally scenic points at the end of the spur roads off D7 to Douarnenez (23 miles/37 km from the Pointe du Raz)—notably the Pointe du Van, less overwhelming than Raz and accessible only by a half-hour's walk, but a good deal more peaceful; and the Pointe de Brézellac, farther along, where the viewing area is close to the road.

DOUARNENEZ This businesslike town (pop. 18,000) with packing plants and efficient docks offers a respite from touristy Raz. The quays are lined with straightforward bars with names like *Le Voyageur* and *Le Navigateur,* intended for sailors. A stop at the New Port, which looks more industrial than nautical with its seawalls, ramps, and warehouses, offers a look at the seafaring life, while its jetty provides a broad view of the town's namesake bay. At the open-air market near the Place Gabriel-Péri, ladies in *coiffes* sometimes can be seen. Boat lovers should not miss the *Port Musée* (Pl. de l'Enfer; phone: 98-92-65-20), with its fascinating marine memorabilia. It's open daily from 10 AM to noon and 2 to 7 PM; admission charge.

Offering another view of the craggy coast to the west are harbor cruises (phone: 98-27-09-54 or 98-92-10-38), in operation from June through September. They visit the *Réserve de Cap Sizun,* a seabird refuge; pass by the Grottes de Lanvilo, hollowed out by the sea; and take in the Ile Tristan, the legendary setting of the palace of King Mark of Cornwall. His nephew, Prince Tristan, was sent to Ireland to fetch Mark's bride, Iseult (Isolde), but the couple accidentally consumed a love potion intended to cement the king's own union. Breton fancies embellish the end: Some people say that Tristan was murdered by Mark; others marry off Tristan and Iseult and let them live happily ever after.

BEST EN ROUTE

Auberge de Kervéoc'h On the fringes of decidedly workaday Douarnenez, this snug, attractive 14-room hostelry, hidden deep in a country where the only sound is the twittering of birds, comes as quite a surprise. The adaptation of an old stone farmhouse was executed in the best 20th-century style, juxtaposing the beauty of the stone walls, great beams, and massive fireplaces with the most up-to-date decor. Good firm beds are the frosting on the cake. There's a dining room. Closed mid-October to *Easter,* except for two weeks in November and *Christmas.* MasterCard and Visa accepted. 2½ miles (4 km) from Douarnenez on D765 (phone: 98-92-07-58). Moderate.

En Route from Douarnenez Take D7 6 miles (10 km) east to Locronan.

LOCRONAN Some visitors find this enchanting inland town too pretty to be real; others lament the number of tourists who clog its narrow lanes and tiny craft stores and boutiques throughout the high season. Nonetheless, if you have time to visit only one of Brittany's inland towns during your stay, it should be this one.

Locronan's perfectly preserved 16th- to 17th-century square is rimmed by old houses built of granite gone mossy with age, brightened with pots of geraniums and punctuated by a small old well. The 15th- to 16th-century

Eglise et Chapelle du Pénity strikes just the right note in the setting. Inside are several statues, some carved out of soft Kersanton granite in the 17th century, others made of wood. The most notable is the granite one adorning the tomb of St. Ronan, an Irish bishop who came to the area (and gave it his name) during the Viking invasions of the 9th century in search of a solitary monastic environment. Tradition has it that passing underneath the statue, which is supported by a sextet of yard-high figures also carved from granite, suppresses symptoms of arthritis. Note the paintings on the pulpit that tell the story of St. Ronan's arrival in the area, his conversion of a peasant, his persecution by neighbors and by the peasant's wife, his resurrection of a child from the dead, and his ultimate defeat of the devil. The fortunate traveler will arrive at the church when the rich, sonorous organ is being played.

Locronan owes its current appearance to the weaving business that flourished here between the 16th and 18th centuries. The architectural harmony of the main square and the richness of the ecclesiastical embellishments are the legacy of those prosperous times, when acres of sailcloth were shipped to England, Spain, and Holland, among other places. The preservation of the structures is mainly a result of the village's poverty in the following years; the town was so poor by the beginning of the 19th century that when the church steeple collapsed, after being struck by lightning, the villagers could not afford to rebuild it and had no recourse but to finish pulling it down. This abject poverty has been ameliorated by the influx of tourists, and many old homes and other granite structures now house shops whose merchandise—mainly handwovens, hand-knits, and various one-of-a-kind wares—is decidedly above average. These, together with a handful of studios where artisans can be seen at their looms and workbenches, are scattered on the perimeter of the main square and along the streets and narrow alleyways radiating from it.

Locronan is also the site of an elaborate *pardon,* during which pilgrims walk to the top of Locronan Mountain via the path once taken by barefoot and fasting St. Ronan. A minor *pardon* is held on the second Sunday in July most years, while the larger *Grande Troménie* is held in mid-July every six years (one is scheduled for 1995). For the *Grande Troménie,* the procession route is extended to 7 miles (11 km), broken up by 12 stops. Cars can drive up the mountain year-round. There's a small chapel with pretty stained glass windows and a fine view over the area at the top.

BEST EN ROUTE

Manoir de Moëllien This charming hotel, converted from a 17th-century manor house, is snugly situated in the peaceful countryside. All 10 finely furnished rooms look out upon bucolic settings, and the restaurant specializes in simple yet elegant seafood dishes. Closed January to mid-March; restaurant also closed Wednesdays off-season. Just outside Locronan via C10 to the northwest, in Plonévez-Porzay (phone: 98-92-50-40; fax: 98-92-55-21). Moderate.

Bois de Nevet With 33 rooms, this modern hotel is set in a large park at the edge of town, near the sea and an equestrian center. Closed January through March. Rte. du Bois de Nevet, Locronan (phone: 98-91-70-67; fax: 98-91-83-12). Inexpensive.

En Route from Locronan Follow D63 north to Plonévez-Porzay, then D61 2 miles (3 km) to Ste-Anne-la-Palud, whose 19th-century chapel peers out over the flattest of seaside meadows, gilded beautifully in summer by little yellow flowers. Every year on the last Sunday of August the area is the setting for a massive Breton *pardon,* which draws so many of the faithful that the narrow roads become nearly impassable. From here return inland to Plonévez-Porzay, then take D63 north to Ploeven. Turn back toward the sea on the tiny road through St-Sébastien to Lestrevet, the southernmost crossroads settlement along the Lieue de Grève (Place of the Seashore), where there is a remarkably long, wide, straight, and flat Atlantic-pounded strand on one side of the road and an expanse of green pasture on the other.

Take the coast road north toward St-Nic, traveling through the wide-open country patched with fields and strips of trees. At St-Nic take D108 for about 2 miles (3 km) and D887 for about a third of a mile in the direction of Châteaulin to the turnoff for steep D83, which ascends the Ménez-Hom; its utterly bald, windswept, 1,082-foot summit is one of the finest viewing points in the province. On cloudy days you won't see a thing; don't even bother to leave the main road. The rest of the time Locronan Mountain, Douarnenez, and the Points du Van are visible; a viewing table identifies them all.

BEST EN ROUTE

Hôtel de la Plage Embraced on one side by the gorgeous Lieue de Grève and nuzzled by a garden and a couple of handsome cypress trees, this charming white stucco hostelry (a Relais & Châteaux member) with 26 rooms and four suites is tranquil as can be. There's a pool, tennis, and sunsets to admire (right from your room if it faces west). The one-Michelin-star restaurant—serving such specialties as lamb with tarragon cream sauce, and frozen raspberry soufflé—is the bonus. Closed mid-October through March. On the beach in Ste-Anne-la-Palud (phone: 98-92-50-12; fax: 98-92-54-56). Expensive.

Relais de Porz-Morvan This hostelry, whose 12 clean and comfortable, if not particularly spacious, rooms are installed in a granite farmhouse and the neighboring stables, is a good reason to winnow your way into the rural countryside, where absolute quiet reigns. Tennis is available. The cozy *crêperie,* with a collection of Breton antiques, serves fine crêpes—try the ones filled with apples and flambéed with calvados. Closed mid-November to *Easter*. MasterCard and Visa accepted. 1¼ miles (2 km) east of Plomodiern via Rte. de Cast (phone: 98-81-53-23). Moderate.

CROZON PENINSULA Route D887, which races through sweeping fields and pastures full of cows, leads west onto this peninsula, another grand Breton meeting ground for sea and sky. Each rocky point—the most southerly, the Cap de la Chèvre (Headland of the Goat), which pushes across Douarnenez Bay toward the Pointe du Van and the Pointe de Brézellac on the Pointe du Raz; the somewhat more formidable Pointe de Dinan, which ends in a castle-like rock formation; and the most northerly, the Pointe des Espagnols, on the end of a peninsula that boasts shoreline roads with exceptional scenery—begs to be explored. Perhaps the most impressive is the Pointe de Penhir, where there are cliffs rising 229 feet above the sea. It is perpetually windy on these heights, the view is grand, and it would be easy to spend a couple of hours here clambering over the rocks or, on a weekday in the off-season, enjoying a picnic lunch.

Of the trio of small towns on the Crozon Peninsula, Camaret is most notable. It is known as one of France's most important lobster ports, a fact confirmed by the abundance of boats in the harbor, though a dramatic decline in the catch has been reported for the past few years, and the town is turning more and more to tourism for its livelihood. The castle-like, red stucco structure full of slits—constructed by the 17th-century military architect Vauban—now houses a naval museum. Nearby, the simple, yellowish *Chapelle de Notre-Dame de Roc'h-Amadour* is the venue for an annual *pardon,* held on the first Sunday in September. On the outskirts of town are the Lagatiar menhirs, megalithic stones erected in a semicircle. Despite their awkward location opposite some nondescript vacation houses, these boulders exert a deep Celtic power. A visit to the beaches at Toulinguet and Very'ach reveals particularly beautiful and unspoiled vistas.

En Route from the Crozon Peninsula Head back to D887 and then to D791. This fast road ribbons through the woods, crosses the Aulne River, follows the picturesque coast, and traverses tiny Le Faou, where you should watch for D42 in the direction of Rumengol, where a large *pardon* is held on the Sunday closest to June 6 every year. D42 then winds through the hilly Forêt de Cranou, whose oak and beech woods eventually give way to the great windswept plateaus of the *Parc Naturel Régional d'Armorique,* which preserves the Arrée Mountains. These are not high—only 1,200 feet at the most, their once lofty peaks ground down and eroded to hills by the ages— but they seem elevated enough thanks to their barren windswept summits and the wide-open vistas they provide when clouds are not swirling around them.

At Croas-ar-Go turn left onto D342 toward Sizun, whose parish church has an organ (1683–84) with a carved and gilded case that compares favorably with the most beautiful Baroque instruments in Central Europe. Go north on D764 as far as Lanviguer, then turn north in the direction of La Roche–Maurice. At La Martyre is another parish close, where *pardons* are held on the second Sunday in May and July. Note the angels carved on the archway, framing a Nativity scene. Next, turn right on D35 toward Ploudiry, whose parish close has a bizarre ossuary on whose façade a Dance of Death is carved in relief. Lampaul-Guimiliau is 6 miles (10 km) farther.

LAMPAUL-GUIMILIAU The parish close in this otherwise insignificant inland town is most notable for the incredible richness of the decoration inside the 16th- to 17th-century church. The idea seems to have been to cover every square inch of wall with ornamentation. Woodcarving covers both sides of an overhead beam, blankets the 18th-century pulpit, and overlays two panels flanking the altar. Particularly notable is an altarpiece divided into eight compartments, each featuring a Passion scene peopled with figures carved with such skill that they almost seem to move. At the front of the church are lively paintings portraying square faces, each distinctive enough to suggest that they were done from life. Take D111 to Guimiliau, a few miles away.

GUIMILIAU This former weaving center (pop. 800) is named for a pious 8th-century prince who was decapitated after seven years on the throne at the instigation of his evil brother. Its parish close, which includes a 16th-century church whose style foreshadows the Renaissance, is even more striking than that of Lampaul-Guimiliau. On the Renaissance porch the arch forming the entrance is articulated with three rows of figures representing angels and saints; the corners sprout curious gargoyles. Inside the porch both walls are lined with niches occupied by statues representing the 12 apostles; other figures, depicting scenes from the Old Testament, alternate with rose medallions in an ornamental frieze below.

The large 16th-century calvary is adorned by some 200 figures. Many depict scenes from Christ's life, but there also are local motifs, such as the story of Catell-Gollet, or Catherine la Perdue (Catherine the Lost), a servant who stole a consecrated host as a present for her lover, actually the devil in disguise, and subsequently was condemned to all manner of hellish tortures. Young women with flirtation on their minds were meant to take note. The images are arranged on two levels, each of which seems to have been sculpted by a different artist.

Be sure to note the late 17th-century baptismal font inside the church, one of the most exuberant pieces of carved oak anywhere in Brittany, embellished by garlands, leaves, vines, tiny birds pecking at berries, saints, evangelists, and angels. The organ and the pulpit, supported by a column comprised of four cherubs, are also elaborately ornamented. A visitor might find the same sumptuous carving in a great cathedral, but here, as at Lampaul-Guimiliau, the profusion of work is concentrated in a relatively limited space. Accordingly, a sense of the talent and energy of the artists who wrought the wonders is brought home all the more clearly.

En Route from Guimiliau Take D18 and D118 for 7½ miles (12 km) to St-Thégonnec.

ST-THÉGONNEC Another magnificent Breton parish close can be found in the center of this little town. Note the calvary, built in 1610; the Passion is depicted on the base. The figure in the niche underneath is of St. Thégonnec, who is portrayed with the cart to which he harnessed a wolf after his donkey was consumed by its fellows. The town's namesake also is portrayed over the porch of the church and in a niche above the pulpit inside. The figure bearing a trumpet atop the canopy is the Angel of Judgment.

The organ, ordered in 1670, was the subject of a pair of lawsuits—one by a local noblewoman, who insisted that her coat of arms be put on the organ case rather than on the bay window at the rear of the church; the other by the men of the church, who complained that the factory had not delivered a satisfactory instrument. The suits only increased its cost, and the organ had to be rebuilt by another factory before final installation in 1684. It was restored on a regular basis for the next two centuries. Far from harming the sound, these restorations only enhanced the original, so that now the instrument—declared a historic monument—has a sonority as rich as the gilded carvings that encase it. Lucky are the travelers who arrive when the organist or a student is playing. Note the images on the console—among them St. Cecilia, the patroness of musicians.

BEST EN ROUTE

L'Auberge St-Thégonnec *Mille-feuille de coquilles St-Jacques au safran* (scallops with saffron in puff pastry) and *homard à la crème* (lobster in cream sauce) are just two of the dishes that have established this restaurant's culinary reputation. There also are 19 guestrooms. Closed Sunday dinner, Mondays off-season, and December 20 to mid-January. Reservations necessary in summer. Major credit cards accepted (phone: 98-79-61-18; fax: 98-62-71-10). Moderate.

Chez Madame Kergadallan In this comfortable bed and breakfast establishment are three neatly appointed rooms but no restaurant. Closed one month in winter. Most major credit cards accepted. 20 Av. Kérizella, St-Thégonnec (phone: 98-79-63-86 or 98-79-65-30). Inexpensive.

Crêperie Steredenn Large photographs of Breton scenes decorate the stone walls here, while a fire crackles in the huge hearth and recorded Breton and Irish music plays. This neat, friendly establishment rates kudos as one of the most pleasant *crêperies* in the province. Particularly tasty is the *crêpe druidique,* slathered with bitter orange marmalade and almonds flavored with Grand Marnier. Closed Mondays and Tuesdays. Reservations advised. MasterCard and Visa accepted. Up a hill on the street leading from the parish close, at 6 Rue de la Gare Thégonnec (phone: 98-79-43-34). Inexpensive.

En Route from St-Thégonnec Take N12 west and then D230 and D30 north to the coast. In contrast to the wild shoreline terrain in southern Brittany, this area is fertile, with fields of fragrant cauliflower and artichoke. The unnumbered coast road takes in farm settlements such as Forban, Poulfoën, Kervaliou, Moguériec, and Santec. Even these insignificant hamlets seem to have their imposing granite churches whose perforated belfries shoot high into the horizon; even a slight rise in the road opens up a huge panorama. From Roscoff, an attractive resort center with shops selling *vêtements marins* (nautical clothes) and a pretty harbor, there is regular ferry service to the Ile de Batz, itself little more than a quaint, untouristed village with huge stretches of coastline. Ferry service to Cork, in the Irish Republic, and to Plymouth, England, also is available. Bonny Prince Charlie took refuge here in 1746, after his abortive attempt to gain the English crown. From Roscoff take D769 3 miles (5 km) south to St-Pol-de-Léon.

BEST EN ROUTE

Brittany The dining salon in this 17th-century hostelry has stone floors, walls made of huge granite blocks, and a baronial fireplace. It serves good traditional fare. The bar is done up with red tartans, and the crystal chandeliers add to the overall air of stateliness. The 23 rooms and two suites, in a tower in the back, have balconies with views. Among the 20th-century comforts are a heated indoor pool and a health center. The property adjoins a small pebbly beach. Closed mid-November through mid-March; restaurant also closed Monday lunch. Bd. Ste-Barbe, Roscoff (phone: 98-69-70-78; fax: 98-61-13-29). Expensive.

Le Temps de Vivre Featuring both seafood and fine products from inland Brittany, this restaurant is getting a reputation as one of the region's best. Try the many dishes based on *tourteau* (giant crab) and the *far breton* for dessert. Closed Sunday dinner and Mondays. Reservations advised. Major credit cards accepted. Pl. Lacaze-Duthiers, Roscoff (phone: 98-61-27-28). Expensive.

ST-POL-DE-LÉON Between January and September the modern market here bustles with activity, as vehicles of all descriptions haul in artichokes, cauliflowers, onions, potatoes, and other vegetables from the fertile fields that surround the town. This is France's largest wholesale vegetable market, and the commerce adds another dimension to what is already a very worthwhile place to visit.

The chief attractions of the town, which was named for a Celtic religious leader who came here from Britain in the 5th century, are two ecclesiastic structures. The *Cathédrale de St-Pol-de-Léon,* built between the 13th and the 16th century, is especially elegant, thanks to its fine proportions and Norman limestone, whose pale hue lends a lightness to the interior.

There is also a beautiful 15th-century rose window; its bright colors often enliven the sanctuary's polished wood floor. Note the wooden statue of Ste. Apolline, the patron saint of dentists, whose torturers pulled out all her teeth. In the rear of the sanctuary are a few rows of skulls, relics of the dead formerly buried in the cemetery; some are enclosed in boxes ornamented by heart-shaped perforations that reveal a bit of bone inside. The carved-oak bishops' stalls are also very fine. The organ dates from the 17th and 19th centuries.

The *Kreisker Chapel,* down the road a short distance and now part of a boys' school, is known for its tall belfry set at the transept crossing, made to seem even taller than its 246 feet by the vertical tracery articulating the windows. Inspired by *St. Peter's* in Caen, Normandy, which was destroyed during the war, it in turn was the inspiration for many other chapels. The tall steeple is stabilized by four bell towers; the whole structure is supported inside by a stone vault joining four massive uprights. The rest of the roof inside is of wood.

En Route from St-Pol-de-Léon The narrow roads that hug the coast, with their vistas of ocean and artichokes, are the most scenic way to travel southeast. Farm compounds and resort communities nudge each other like the black and white squares of a chessboard and add still more variety. Carantec, on a point well off the highways, is particularly delightful (although the lovely beaches here can become quite crowded in July and August). The roads that wind through the residential areas are almost too narrow for even a single tiny French vehicle. Houses crowded with hydrangeas are angled this way and that to maximize the minuscule amount of space. There are fine views, like the one from the Pointe de Pen-Lan.

Going south, D73 toward Locquénolé hugs the west shore of the Morlaix estuary, crossing gently rolling countryside occasionally patched with trees. Now and then you can see a boat sailing back to its moorings at Morlaix or out for a day at sea. By the time D73 joins D769, the estuary narrows to the dimensions of a stream. High cliffs line it on one side and a wooded slope plunges on the other. Morlaix is 12½ miles (20 km) south of St-Pol-de-Léon on D73.

BEST EN ROUTE

La Falaise The yachtsmen who often patronize this small stucco-and-brick hotel give the place a particularly relaxed air, as does the friendly proprietor. The 24 guestrooms are simple and clean, with high ceilings. There's no restaurant. Closed mid-September through March. No credit cards accepted. Set on a high cliff above the Bay of Morlaix, at Plage de Kélenn, Carantec (phone: 98-67-00-53). Inexpensive.

Pors-Pol This simple family hotel provides 30 rooms with sea views, a restaurant, and a small beach nearby. Closed October to *Easter* and three weeks in

May. MasterCard and Visa accepted. In a residential neighborhood, at 7 Rue Surcouf, Carantec (phone: 98-67-00-52). Inexpensive.

MORLAIX Typical of many towns of its size (pop. 20,000), this erstwhile port dominating the estuary of its namesake river boasts an extremely handsome Old Quarter with narrow, twisting streets and lanes, row upon row of houses dating from the days of half-timbers through the 19th century, and fashionable shops purveying shoes, faïence, clothing, and antiques. Especially noteworthy are the Grand'Rue, the Place Salvador-Allende, the Place des Jacobins, and the Place des Viarmes. The corbeled 16th-century *Maison de la Reine Anne,* whose overhanging half-timbered second story seems to be supported by caryatids carved in the form of saints, is on Rue de Mûr, which parallels the Grand'Rue.

What makes Morlaix special is its topography—its steep hills demand perpetual downshifting in the car. From the topmost of the city's tiers are fine views of the estuary and the Old Town not far away. Across the estuary is a mammoth two-story viaduct measuring 190 feet in height and 935 feet in length; it is visible from most open areas in the city.

One unusual attraction in Morlaix is Coreff, the local beer, which is a dark brew made in the old-fashioned way and sold in several cafés. The brewery, *Brasserie des Deux Rivières* (1 Pl. de la Madeleine; phone: 98-63-41-92), can be visited on Wednesdays and Thursdays year-round; call ahead for an appointment.

BEST EN ROUTE

Europe A traditional, renovated 66-room hotel, it has an elegant restaurant whose chef, Olivier Brignou, is considered a promising young talent. His *pot au feu de poisson* (fish casserole) is a delight. 1 Rue Aiguillon (phone: 98-62-11-99; fax: 98-88-83-38). Expensive.

Patrick Jeffroy The finest restaurant in the area has earned one Michelin star for such unusual dishes as sole in coconut milk, roast free-range chicken, and *oeufs à la neige* (meringues in egg custard sauce). There are three guestrooms upstairs. Closed Sunday dinner, Sundays and Mondays off-season, and two weeks each in February and October. MasterCard and Visa accepted. Twelve miles (19 km) east of Morlaix via speedy N12, in Plounérin (phone: 96-38-61-80). Expensive.

La Marée Bleue In this old stone building that has been renovated to reflect contemporary design, the food is fully the equal of the extremely gracious reception accorded guests. Seafood is presented either plain or with sauces that simply are not found in every Breton restaurant. The lengthy, detailed wine list is an education in its own right. Closed Mondays, Sunday dinner off-season, and February. MasterCard and Visa accepted. 3 Rampe St-Mélaine (phone: 98-63-24-21). Moderate.

En Route from Morlaix Take D769 south for 17 miles (27 km) to Huelgoat.

HUELGOAT Breton scenery lovers come here by the score to walk through the forests and to see the huge sandstone and granite boulders tumbled through the woods and along the little Argent River. They are arranged in ways that have suggested such names as Chaos du Moulin (Mill Rock Chaos), Grotte du Diable (Devil's Grotto), Ménage de la Vierge (Virgin's Household), and Roche Tremblante (Trembling Rock). The last-named, which weighs in at about a hundred tons, sways on its base if you push hard enough. Great old oaks, beeches, spruces, and pines tower over these landmarks, reachable by well-marked footpaths. There also is a little lake, where anglers try for carp and perch, and a handsome square, the Place Aristide-Briand. The whole area abounds in hiking trails that take in fine scenery, and it would be easy to spend more than the hour and a half most visitors allot to whiz in and out of Huelgoat.

In nearby Locmaria-Berrien (4¼ miles/7 km from Huelgoat at the intersection of D769 and the small road descending from the village), a pretty chapel is fronted by two immense oak trees, one completely hollow inside and bound together by rusting bands.

BEST EN ROUTE

Auberge de la Truite This comfortable inn has six pleasant rooms, a fine wine cellar, and a good restaurant, where the *truite maison* (house-style trout) comes with a *beurre blanc* sauce. Closed Sunday dinner, Mondays (except in July and August), and January to April. MasterCard and Visa accepted. Locmaria-Berrien (phone: 98-99-73-05). Moderate.

En Route from Huelgoat The fields and forest scenery of the Argoat are at their best to the east, especially off the main roads. Follow the signs along the swooping curves of D769 through Poullaouen; then head northeast along D154 about 5 miles (8 km) to beautiful St-Gildas, where there is a picturesquely situated chapel just at the base of a hill where the Romans once camped—ideal for picnics. Follow the signs south through Carnoët to D787, then turn north toward Callac. From there follow D28 2 miles (3 km) to St-Servais, then continue 3 miles (5 km) to the intersection with D31 at Ty-Bourg. Drive north on D31 to Burthulet, in whose lonely chapel the devil is said to have died of cold, and to Bulat-Pestivien, whose 15th- to 16th-century church is one of the oldest in the Renaissance style in Brittany.

Retrace your way along beautiful D31 as far as Ty-Bourg and on D28, then continue south on D31. At Croas-Tasset is a turnoff west on D20 for the Gorges du Corong. Large trees planted atop the hedgerows arch over the road to the south. Rostrenen is about 9 miles (14 km) farther south on D31, near the intersection with N164.

From here it's possible to follow many beautiful country roads eastward, turning this way and that, to skirt the massive impoundment of the Blavet River known as the Lac de Guerlédan. About 3 miles (5 km) past the village of Gouarec off N164 are the deep Gorges du Daoulas, some almost vertical, formed where the Daoulas River joins the Blavet. Both D15A and D15, which branch off of N164 near here, cross the woods and heath plateau country of the 6,916-acre Forêt de Quénécan. Just off N164 on D15A are the impressive ruins of the 12th-century *Abbaye de Bon Repos,* where the ivy grows thickly on the granite stones and ferns feather the broken tops of the walls. Back in Gouarec turn north onto D8 for more exploring in the Argoat. At the Gorges de Toul Goulic, about 8 miles (13 km) north, a rather steep footpath leads to the point at which the Blavet River totally disappears into a cleft. About 3 miles (5 km) farther the *Chapelle de Notre-Dame-de-Guiaudet* appears almost out of nowhere; its immense belfry crammed with bells is outlined against the sky. Accessible via a road lined on both sides with straight rows of trees, it occupies a piece of property that itself is laid out in a cruciform with the Stations of the Cross, a fountain, and a war monument.

From the chapel continue on D8 to Guingamp, 13 miles (21 km) from the chapel.

BEST EN ROUTE

Blavet For peace and quiet, this *auberge* on a sometimes busy highway is not ideal, but the 15 rooms have real charm, with old-fashioned wallpaper, Breton armoires, antique headboards, high ceilings, and modern bathrooms. Some of them are quite elaborate, with four-poster beds and such; one wishes that the soft mattresses were equally satisfactory. The dining room is elegant, as is the food, which includes *huîtres chaudes aux poireaux* (warm oysters with leeks) and tournedos topped with wild mushrooms. Meals are served on the garden terrace in summer. Closed a week at *Christmas* and the month of February; restaurant also closed Sunday dinner and Mondays off-season. MasterCard and Visa accepted. N164 *bis,* Gouarec (phone: 96-24-90-03). Moderate.

GUINGAMP This beautiful erstwhile feudal city has a tree-bordered square, a batch of half-timbered houses, and a wonderful tiered fountain ornamented with carved horses with goose wings, dragon tails, and goat faces. The *Basilique de Notre-Dame de Bon-Secours* (Basilica of Our Lady of Perpetual Help) is Gothic only on one side: When the south side collapsed in the 16th century, the town held a competition, awarding the commission to a young architect whose plans were in the Renaissance style. The best views are from the opposite side of the church from the one facing Rue Notre-Dame. The Black Virgin, the basilica's patroness, has a chapel of her own opening onto Rue Notre-Dame; her altar is always amassed with flowers. A *pardon* held annually on the second weekend in July attracts thousands.

BEST EN ROUTE

Le Relais du Roy Ensconced in an old house, this hostelry is reason enough for travelers to seek out Guingamp. The seven rooms, reached by climbing a 16th-century stone-walled stairwell, are decorated in the best of taste, with oh-so-French furnishings and wallpaper. The same is true of the small, intimate dining room, where several carefully conceived table d'hôte dinners usually are available. The cozy bar, all polished mahogany and brass, is a fine place for a quiet afternoon coffee. Note the Renaissance doorway in the courtyard, edged with carvings of many droll faces. Closed *Christmas* through mid-January; restaurant also closed Sundays from September to mid-June. On the main square, at 42 Pl. du Centre (phone: 96-43-76-62; fax: 96-44-08-01). Expensive.

En Route from Guingamp Lannion and the coast can be reached in a flash on D767, but it's far more pleasant to make the trip along meandering country roads. Take N12 to the turnoff to the Menez-Bré. Follow a narrow, bumpy road that climbs to lush meadows, where there is a simple stone chapel, like one a child might draw, and a fine view that stretches for miles. Return to N12, and turn right toward Gollot and Manaty. Then make your way to D11, following D31A, D31, and D30.

From D11 you can turn off to see the Kergrist castle, whose gardens may be toured. Farther along signs point to the moss-splotched *Chapelle de Kerfons,* on a rutted road opposite a stone barn, and to the ruined 15th-century *Château de Tonquédec,* a hulk of granite topping the crest of a precipitous hill and surrounded by beautiful woods.

Return to D11 and go on to Lannion (4½ miles/7 km from the château); from there take D65 for 5½ miles (9 km) to Trébeurden.

CÔTE DU GRANIT ROSE This stretch of shore between Morlaix and St-Brieuc is aptly named for the beautiful rosy hue of the rocks. We begin our exploration at Trébeurden.

From this little beach town to the larger resort city of Perros-Guirec, the ocean has chiseled the granite rocks offshore into fabulous shapes. Any drive in this area turns up a handful of signs pointing to boulders that only occasionally resemble the elephants, gnomes, rabbits, thimbles, turtles, whales, and such for which they are named; points like the high, windy Pointe de Bihit at Trébeurden provide a panorama of such rocks up and down the coast. In Trégastel are the Tire-Bouchon (Corkscrew), which looks much like a pile of cow dung, and an improbable Roi Gradlon (King Gradlon). The hour-long walk along the Grève Blanche (White Seashore), roughly between the beach at the end of Rue Grève-Blanche and the far end of the Plage de Coz-Pors (Coz-Pors Beach), skirts the coast, where imaginative travelers can make up their own names for the rock formations along the way. Still others—the Tête de Mort (Death's Head) and the Tas de Crêpes (Pile of Pancakes)—lie just beyond.

Ploumanac'h, a fishing port and seaside resort farther along, has its own spate of rock formations, which surround a lighthouse a few yards from the sea. A platform close to the top provides a bird's-eye view of the coast. Nearby, the rocky landscape has been preserved as a municipal park. The Pointe du Squewel shows off the sawtoothed, rock-piled shoreline at its best. Those with a penchant for walking can follow the celebrated Sentier des Douaniers (Customs Agents' Footpath) along the tops of the 100-foot-high red and black stone cliffs within sight of more of these bizarre formations all the way to Perros-Guirec (about two and a half hours round trip); sometimes there are berries to pick en route. Offshore are the Sept-Iles, a sanctuary for the auks, cormorants, gannets, gulls, guillemots, and puffins that nest on the island cliffs. Bird watchers interested in coming here should call the *Office du Tourisme* in Perros-Guirec (phone: 96-23-21-15) for more information.

Every rocky point along the shoreline offers similar scenery. Sometimes there are grand vistas from the road or from a viewing point with parking; other times a short walk is required. Adventure-minded travelers can follow their own whims, twisting through the crannied lanes of the residential neighborhoods that cluster near the shore. The long crescent of sand at Perros-Guirec, presided over by a casino that looks like a Moorish temple without minarets, is usually fairly crowded, but other beaches, quieter and less heavily endowed with such facilities as trampolines and changing tents, are not hard to find. In the area near Porz-Hir and the Pointe du Château, *homards* (lobsters) and *huîtres* (oysters) are sometimes for sale. The whole landscape is strewn with boulders, and often the houses are built right alongside them. On these roads it is impossible to hurry.

Tréguier, the site of an extravagant *pardon* on the third Sunday in May honoring Brittany's beloved St. Yves, is another pretty Breton town. The 12th-century *Cathédrale de St-Tugdual* here is unusual for its handsome cloister and relatively unspoiled vertical lines; inside, the walls are full of simple carved plaques thanking the saint for miraculous deeds.

Particularly beautiful among the area's rocky viewing spots is the Pointe de l'Arcouest, where the shoreline slopes gently to the sea with a jumble of rocks whose hollows are filled with little pools of water that sparkle like sequins in the sun. The view is of the Ile de Bréhat, one mile long and twice that in width, where there are parks, gardens, villas, fields crossed by footpaths, and lots more rocky, cove-notched coast. Beautiful, silent, and incredibly pastoral, it is well worth a trip. According to local legend, Christopher Columbus learned about the existence of the New World nearly a decade before his milestone voyage from a seafaring man from Bréhat, whose fellow fishermen had been traveling there for years.

South of Paimpol are the farm-ringed ruins of the 13th- to 14th-century *Abbaye de Beauport*, built of warm, rose-colored granite furred with ivy, ferns, and other greenery. The beautifully articulated rose window is worth noting, even though it has no stained glass.

Binic, once a cod fishing center, still has a serviceable jetty and a plethora of marine stores. Inland, the village of Notre-Dame-de-la-Cour, named for the small 15th-century chapel at its center, has harmonious proportions, elegant detailing, and a dollhouse quality that is particularly appealing. On D786 from here to St-Brieuc, 8 miles (13 km) away, tiny spur roads run down to the sea. There are no obvious stops, no musts except the sunrises over the Baie de St-Brieuc, which are well worth the trouble it takes to see them. The best way to experience this coast is to follow your hunches, to pick a road and follow it to the end just to see what's there.

BEST EN ROUTE

Le Barbu Many a beautiful point in Brittany has its hotel, but few are as pretty as this old-fashioned 19-room, one-suite establishment, with a panoramic restaurant above the sea, a small pool, a hydrangea hedge, and a chandeliered salon. Closed January. MasterCard and Visa accepted. On the Pointe de l'Arcouest, about 3½ miles (5½ km) from Paimpol (phone: 96-55-86-98; fax: 96-55-73-87). Expensive.

La Cotriade A former cook from New York City's famed *Lutèce* now holds forth in this tiny harbor establishment, named for Brittany's fish stew; he has elevated regional dishes to works of art. His *homard grillé* (grilled lobster) and *turbot au beurre rouge* (turbot in red butter) are just two of the specialties for which the restaurant has earned a Michelin star. Closed Monday dinner, Tuesdays, and mid-January to mid-February. Reservations necessary; ask for a table with a view of the sea. Major credit cards accepted. Port de Piégu, about a half mile (1 km) from Pléneuf-Val-André (phone: 96-72-20-26). Expensive.

Ker Moor With 28 rooms (some with terraces), this modern hotel has great views of the sea, a path to the beach, and a good restaurant serving simple seafood dishes. Closed December 20 through Janurary. 13 Rue P.-le-Sénécal. St-Quay Portrieux, 13 miles (21 km) north of St-Brieuc via D786 (phone: 96-70-52-22; fax: 96-70-50-49). Expensive.

Manoir de Lan-Kerellec A Relais & Châteaux member, this hotel in a handsome old stone building has tall, smartly squared hedges and 18 comfortable, spacious rooms and suites with ocean views. The dining salon of the fine restaurant, with its vaulted ceiling and baronial paneling, is especially striking. Closed mid-November to mid-March; restaurant also closed Monday lunch except in summer. Trébeurden (phone: 96-23-50-09; fax: 96-23-66-88). Expensive.

Relais Brenner This lovely inn, one of the finest in Brittany, was practically destroyed by fire in 1990 but has been lovingly rebuilt. It offers 18 large, luxurious rooms, a pool, a garden sloping to the sea, and a fine restaurant that features lobster prepared in many different—and innovative—ways. Closed November to March; restaurant also closed for lunch except on weekends. 2 miles (3 km) west of Paimpol on D786 (phone: 96-20-11-05; fax: 96-22-16-27). Expensive.

Ti al-Lannec Rarely in Brittany do you find a hostelry like this one, in which the conversion from bourgeois mansion to hotel has been executed with fine taste and attention to detail. Lively wallpapers add cheer to the 13 rooms and 16 suites, all with large baths and some with fine views; some have terraces. Guests can play recordings of Bach and enjoy after-dinner coffee and chocolate truffles over a game of cards in the salon. The restaurant's food is traditional, and excellent. Closed mid-November to mid-March. Allée de Mézo-guen, Trébeurden (phone: 96-23-57-26; fax: 96-23-62-14). Expensive.

La Vieille Tour At this highly regarded one-Michelin-star restaurant seafood is as innovatively prepared as it is fresh. Unusual sauces, lobster cooked with herbed oysters, and light dessert pastries with caramelized strawberries (in season) are among the culinary stars here. Closed Sunday dinner, Mondays, and one week each in September and May. Reservations necessary. Major credit cards accepted. 75 Rue de la Tour, Port de St-Brieuc-le-Légué, in Plérin-sous-la-Tour, about 2 miles (3 km) from St-Brieuc on D24 (phone: 96-33-10-30). Expensive.

France In a large park filled with pines, this stately 30-room hotel overlooks the sea. The regularly refurbished rooms are quite comfortable. The restaurant serves traditional cuisine. Closed mid-October to mid-April. 14 Rue Rouzig, Perros-Guirec (phone: 96-23-20-27; fax: 96-91-19-57). Moderate.

CÔTE D'EMERAUDE Reaching from St-Brieuc to Dinard, this 39½-mile (63-km) stretch of coastline with crescent-shaped bays, the "Emerald Coast," takes in a string of pretty resort and harbor towns along D786. At both points of every crescent are fine views and pleasant walks.

At Le Val-André, noted for its beautiful long beach, a visitor might stroll along the cliff path high above the Bay of St. Brieuc to the Pointe de Pléneuf, or one might walk on the Promenade de la Guette (Watchman's Walk), where there are still other sea views. At Erquy a cluster of beautiful little houses wrap around a huge bay where a small scallop-fishing fleet anchors at night, and an early-evening walk might lead along the harbor to watch the sunset through a grid of masts. There are beaches to explore at Sables-d'Or-les-Pins, which is full of hotels, and at Le Vieux Bourg.

Two particularly fine experiences are the drive to Cap Fréhel, on a road that skims the cliff tops along the fringes of the gold-tinged fields, then drops off to perfect little beaches; and a walk on the cape itself, across moors flecked with tiny golden flowers where the constant wind has bent the heather to its will. The cliffs are rocky and high, reaching to some 230 feet, and the panorama stretches from the Ile de Bréhat on the left to the Pointe de Grouin on the right. In clear weather it's possible to see all the way to the Channel Islands. The whole area is crossed by paths; be sure to view the sea gulls and cormorants crowded on the Fauconnière rocks just offshore. At dusk the light transforms the landscape into a study in pastels. Just to the east from this hefty notch of land, it's possible to see *Fort La Latte,* a massive 13th- to 14th-century stronghold—everyone's idea of a medieval fort. You can visit the fort (signs near Fréhel point the way), which is well worth the long walk from the parking lot to the drawbridge, for here the thick stone walls frame some of Brittany's most stunning sea views. Incredible as it may seem, sections of the structure still are inhabited.

Dinard, which marks the eastern end of the Côte d'Emeraude, is tame by comparison, but its own charms, representing the civilized side of the province, are considerable. High Victorian villas crane toward the view; narrow lanes and pines characterize the residential neighborhoods. There is also a large casino and spa, a beach pinned at one end by a ruined priory, and a glittering round of resort life to be enjoyed in dozens of hotels. Then take D766 south for 14 miles (22 km) to Dinan.

DINAN This rampart-bound medieval town (pop. 14,000) stands out as one of Brittany's prettiest. It is guarded by a handsome castle and laced by winding streets lined with scores of half-timbered houses. Allow at least a couple of hours to dally among the shops in the picturesque Old Quarter.

The best place to begin is the *Jardin Anglais,* which snuggles up against the ramparts and offers a fine view of the valley of the Rance River and the 250-foot Romanesque bridge that spans it. The Promenade de la Duchesse Anne, shaded by beautiful chestnut trees and punctuated with benches, skirts the ramparts, then descends to the street, which eventually leads to the 14th-century castle, a section of which contains a museum of local history. Yet another gracious walkway, the Promenade des Petits-Fossés (Walk of the Little Ditches), skirts the base of the castle.

From the statue of the great 14th-century Breton soldier Bertrand du Guesclin, which stands at the midpoint of the promenade, it's only a short walk via Rue Ste-Claire and Rue de l'Horloge into the charming Old Quarter. The Place des Merciers, the Place des Cordeliers, and Rue de la Lainerie and its extensions, Rue du Jerzual and Rue du Petit-Fort, bounded by shops where artisans usually can be seen at work (except Mondays), all evoke another age. The *Eglise St-Sauveur,* where Romanesque and Gothic are in gentle counterpoint, shelters the heart of du Guesclin, whose body was buried at *St-Denis,* near Paris.

Avaugour This pleasant 27-room hotel overlooks the square in front and a garden in the rear. The restaurant features traditional cuisine using local seafood. Restaurant closed Sunday dinner and Mondays except in July and August. 1 Pl. de Champs Clos (phone: 96-39-07-49; fax: 96-85-43-04). Expensive.

Manoir du Vaumadeuc Built of Breton granite and fitted out with objets d'art from around the world, this former manor house is surely one of Brittany's most sumptuous hostelries. Its site deep in the quietest country is only part of the attraction. There are 10 elegant rooms and two suites, each with a fireplace and some with massive overhead beams. The cuisine is classic and ambitious, with lobster gratiné keeping company on the menu with *quenelles de brochet Nantua* (pike dumplings with a lobster sauce). Closed January to *Easter;* restaurant also closed weekdays for lunch and Wednesdays in May. Pléven, near Plancoët, about 14½ miles (23 km) from Dinan (phone: 96-84-46-17; fax: 96-84-40-16). Expensive.

Chez la Mère Pourcel In this medieval mansion with a wonderful 16th-century staircase, the chef presents simply prepared fresh seafood and products from inland Brittany. Closed Sunday dinner and Mondays except in summer. Reservations advised. Major credit cards accepted. 3 Pl. Merciers (phone: 96-39-03-80). Moderate.

En Route from Dinan Take D766 for 18 miles (29 km) north to St-Malo.

ST-MALO This one-time privateering and shipbuilding center is characterized nowadays by a motley assortment of visitors, ranging from touring Americans to Britons who arrive on yachts or ferries from Portsmouth, Guernsey, Jersey, or Sark to seamen from the French Navy and merchant marine who tie up here periodically. The mix gives the *ville close* an air of festive good cheer. The bars, especially the one at *L'Univers* on the Place Chateaubriand, are gleaming studies in brass and wood, with photographs of famous racing yachts. The restaurants are comfortable, appealingly decorated, and seldom formal, and there are plenty of attractive shops in which to while away an afternoon or two. A small, narrow-gauge train makes a 30-minute tour of the city with commentary in English and French; it leaves from the Porte St-Vincent and operates in-season only (phone: 99-40-49-49).

The center of town is the Place Chateaubriand, named for the Romantic novelist who was born here. There is a museum devoted to St-Malois history in the *Château de St-Malo* (Esplanade de Félicité Lamennais; phone: 99-40-71-11). The exhibits include pirate paraphernalia such as treasure chests and cannon, as well as memorabilia of Chateaubriand and of the French explorer Jacques Cartier. Closed Tuesdays from September to *Easter.* Also worth visiting is the handsome *Cathédrale de St-Vincent,* which has a 12th-century nave and a set of stunning, almost fiery modern windows.

The town's rooftops and port are best viewed from the ramparts (reached via a stairway near the Place Chateaubriand), remnants of when St-Malo was a republic in its own right. Though St-Malo seems very old, the structures themselves are restorations, since the *ville close* was largely destroyed during World War II. The tourist office is on the Esplanade St-Vincent (phone: 99-56-64-48).

If there's time, take the 25-minute breezy walk out to the islets of Grand and Petit Bé, where Chateaubriand wished to be buried. (Check the tide tables; go at low tide, and plan to return before the tide rolls in again.)

BEST EN ROUTE

Grand Hôtel des Thermes This Art Deco hostelry, which features a good restaurant, *Le Cap Horn,* is next to the city's famous saltwater spa, the *Termes Marins de St-Malo.* The 189 guestrooms range from simple to luxurious, with prices to match; the rooms facing the sea, most recently renovated, have great views. Closed most of January. Facing the bay, at 100 Bd. Hébert (phone: 99-40-75-75; fax: 99-40-76-00). Expensive.

Valmarin Set in a converted 18th-century house, this lovely 12-room hotel has its own park and offers charm and peace. There's no restaurant. Closed mid-November to mid-February. At the southern edge of town, at 7 Rue Jean-XXIII (phone: 99-81-94-76; fax: 99-81-50-03). Expensive.

La Grève Local seafood stars in this suburban restaurant with views of sailboats gliding along the Rance River. Reservations advised. Major credit cards accepted. Closed Sunday dinner, Mondays except in summer, mid-January to early February, and two weeks in October. Overlooking the port in St-Suliac, 6 miles (10 km) south of St-Malo via N137 and D117 (phone: 99-58-33-83). Moderate.

La Korrigane A graceful 19th-century mansion has been transformed into an intimate, refined 10-room hotel. There's a garden, parking, and English-language cable TV but no restaurant. Closed mid-November to mid-December. At the south end of town, at 39 Rue le Pomellec (phone/fax: 99-81-65-85). Moderate.

En Route from St-Malo Don't miss the Pointe du Grouin, accessible from scenic D201, which squiggles along the coast eastward. Along with the Grouin du Sud (on the Normandy side of the bay near Avranches), this is considered the best spot for viewing the astonishingly high tides in Mont St-Michel Bay. The locals don't exaggerate when they swear that the tides here rise at the speed of a galloping horse during the spring and fall equinoxes. A chart listing dates, times, and levels of tides is available from any *maison de la presse* (newspaper and magazine shop) in the area. Cancale is about 9 miles (14 km) east of St-Malo.

CANCALE This port of 5,000 has been famous for its oysters for centuries. Though the native shellfish population was decimated by a mysterious disease, Cancale has maintained its claim by using the oyster equivalent of seedlings, spats, imported from the community of Auray in the south. The spats are shoveled into bags made of tough netting, taken out to sea, and left to grow for a couple of years before harvesting. Late in the afternoon visitors gather along the port to watch the boats come in and unload their huge sacks full of the delicacies, and shopkeepers display baskets of oysters in all shapes and varieties. There's no need for a picnic table: The oysters can be opened and consumed with a squeeze of lemon on the spot.

BEST EN ROUTE

Château Richeux/Le Coquillage The Roellingers recently opened this 11-room hotel/restaurant in a converted mansion near the beach. The rooms are elegantly decorated in the country-English style and some have views of the sea. There's a large garden and a taxi to convey guests to *Le Bricourt* (see below). The hotel is a member of the Relais & Châteaux group. *Le Coquillage* is a seafood bistro serving simply prepared, fresh fare. Reservations advised. Hotel and restaurant closed mid-November to mid-December; restaurant also closed Monday and Tuesday lunch. In St-Méloir-des-Ondes (phone: 99-89-25-25; fax: 99-89-88-47). Expensive.

Maison de Bricourt/Hôtel Les Rimains The perfect place to savor the sea's best bounty. Michelin has awarded it two stars, and it is a member of the Relais & Châteaux group. The Cancale-born chef, Olivier Roellinger, is considered one of the country's most inventive; he was named France's Chef of the Year for 1994 by the prestigious *Gault-Millau* magazine. For more details on the restaurant, see *Haute Gastronomie* in DIVERSIONS. Six luxurious rooms are available in the adjoining hotel, *Les Rimains*. *Maison de Bricourt* is closed Tuesdays and Wednesdays (except dinner in July and August), and mid-December through mid-March; *Les Rimains* is closed mid-November through mid-March. Reservations necessary well in advance. 1 Rue Duguesclin (phone: 99-89-64-76; fax: 99-89-88-47). Expensive.

The Atlantic Coast

The 350,000 residents of Charente and 500,000 residents of Charente-Maritime are quick to point out the distinctions between the two *départements*. They are, however, linked by a common thread: the 225-mile Charente River, which Henri IV once called "the most beautiful stream in my kingdom." Just across the Gironde estuary from Bordeaux, the area is accessible to travelers via A10 from Paris to Bordeaux, or by the *TGV*, which has cut travel time from Paris to La Rochelle to a mere three hours. The region attracts lovers of oysters, cognac, history, and pastoral beauty, as well as just plain lovers.

This route heads west from Angoulême to Royan, then north to La Rochelle and the Marais Poitevin (Marsh of Poitou). It passes open meadows, rolling hills covered by lush vineyards, fields of corn or cows, rocky coastlines, enticing beaches, and more than its fair share of charming towns that history has left in its wake. It was from this area that French pioneers set sail for Canada and America. Huguenot emigrants, departing from La Rochelle, settled north of New York City in a town they named Nouvelle (New) Rochelle. Settlers of what became known as Acadia (now Nova Scotia and part of New Brunswick) and Prince Edward Island also hailed from here.

Charente and Charente-Maritime share characteristics with neighboring Brittany and Bordeaux, particularly the fishing culture of the former and the vineyards of the latter. Wealth derives equally from land, sea, and the estuaries in between, and stately châteaux stand as monuments to the prosperity the region has enjoyed. The most outstanding among them are the 15th-century *Château de la Roche Courbon,* near Saintes, and the 12th-century and Renaissance *Château de la Rochefoucauld.* Other architectural reminders also speak of the region's history; good examples are the whimsical façade of Angoulême's *Cathédrale St-Pierre,* the amphitheater in Saintes, and the fairy-tale stone towers guarding the entrance to La Rochelle's little port.

The region's simple food relies on the finest products of land and sea, rather than on culinary sleight of hand. The famous oysters of Marennes and the Ile d'Oléron are eaten *au nature* or accompanied by small eels and escargots. Another specialty is *chaudrée,* a fish soup made with white wine and the fresh catch of the day. The rich pasturelands produce beef, pork, and succulent *pré-salé* lamb, named for the saltwater-washed feeding grounds that give the meat its special flavor. Charente butter is prized by purists for its delicate flavor.

And then there is cognac. A substantial 236,000 acres in Charente and Charente-Maritime produce the white grapes from which France's famous elixir is made. The highest-quality grapes come from the Grande

Champagne, the area immediately surrounding the towns of Cognac and Segonzac. Cognac is a brandy, but most brandy is not cognac and cannot bear the name unless it is from this region and has been distilled twice, then carefully aged in oak barrels. The industry began in the 17th century, and today more than 300 firms produce cognac (many of the larger ones offer free tours and tastings). Before tasting cognac, it is traditional to hold the bulb-shaped snifter in your palm for a few minutes to warm it and release the spirit's vapors; sniff and then sip. Another regional libation is *pineau,* a mixture of one-third cognac and two-thirds unfermented grape juice, with an alcohol content of 16% to 22%.

The Charente River is navigable from Angoulême to Rochefort, with 21 tide gates over the 100-mile stretch. From April through September tour boats leave Rochefort, St-Savinien, Saintes, Cognac, and Jarnac; from April through July they also depart from Angoulême and Châteauneuf-sur-Charente. For information, contact the tourist office in Angoulême (2 Pl. St-Pierre; phone: 45-95-16-84; fax: 45-95-91-76). Barges also can be hired for four- to seven-day cruises. For information, contact the *Maison Poitou-Charentes* (70 Rue du Cherche-Midi, Paris 75006; phone: 42-22-83-74).

The region also offers the visitor quite a few land activities. There are over a dozen golf courses in the area; add zoos, parks, aquariums, bird sanctuaries, peaceful islands, and Venice-like canals winding through marshlands, and there's more than enough to justify an extended visit here.

An indispensable map for this region is Michelin No. 71, which covers the entire area, except for Angoulême.

The *départements* of Charente and Charente-Maritime have a vast selection of good hotels and, to a lesser degree, good restaurants at reasonable prices. For a double room per night in a very expensive hotel, expect to pay $130 or more; in an expensive place, $65 to $125; in a moderate hotel, $45 to $65; and in an inexpensive one, less than $45. Unless otherwise indicated, all hotels accept major credit cards and are open year-round. Most feature telephones, TV sets, and private baths in all of their rooms. However, some less expensive ones may have private baths in only some rooms; it's a good idea when making a reservation to confirm whether your room has a private bath. Most hotels in the region, except some more expensive ones, do not have air conditioned rooms. For a meal for two with service (usually included in the bill) but without wine, expect to pay $140 or more in a very expensive restaurant; $75 to $140 in an expensive place; between $45 to $75 in a moderate restaurant; and less than $45 in an inexpensive one. Unless otherwise noted, all restaurants are open for lunch and dinner. For each location hotels and restaurants are listed alphabetically by price category.

ANGOULÊME Nicknamed "The City Built on a Balcony," Angoulême is perched on a rocky ridge overlooking the Charente Valley. The principal town and administrative center of Charente, as well as the heart of France's paper industry, it has a population of 43,000, with another 50,000 people living in the outlying area. Finding the center of town is easy: Just keep climbing until you can't go any higher. All the sites are well marked, and the tourist office has a handy location by the cathedral (2 Pl. St-Pierre; phone: 45-95-16-84; fax: 45-95-91-76). Each year the city holds an international comic-strip festival at the end of January (sponsored by the *Musée de la Bande Dessinée;* see below; contact the museum for details), an international jazz festival at the end of May, and the *Circuit des Remparts* car race in September. There is a large covered market every morning in the Place des Halles.

The crowning glory of Angoulême is the *Cathédrale St-Pierre,* just off Rue de Friedland. The fourth building on this site (the first was built about AD 413), it was consecrated in 1118. Its whimsical façade contains figures depicting the Last Supper, the Ascension of Christ, Samson and the lion, St. George slaying the dragon, and a scene from the *Chanson de Roland.*

The excellent *Musée des Beaux-Arts* (1 Rue de Friedland; phone: 45-95-07-69) has striking ceramics by Alfred Renoleau, a master potter from Charente during the late 19th and early 20th centuries. One gallery is devoted to the works of another Charente artist, Léonard Jarraud, and two other rooms display stunning art from west and central Africa and a number of Pacific islands. Not to be missed is a haunting painting by Pierre Vafflard, *Richard Young Burying His Daughter* (1804). The museum is closed lunch hours, Tuesdays, and holidays. Renoleau's work also can be viewed in a gallery, *Faïencerie d'Art d'Angoulême* (5 Rue Alfred-Renoleau; phone: 45-95-01-75), which is open daily.

The *Maison St-Simon,* dating from 1550, now houses the *FRAC (Fond Régional d'Art Contemporain;* 15 Rue de la Cloche-Verte; phone: 45-92-87-01), which displays the work of up-and-coming artists. It is closed mornings, Mondays, and Tuesdays. The *Atelier-Musée du Papier* (134 Rue de Bordeaux; phone: 45-92-73-43) is interesting for its exhibits on paper production. The *Musée Archéologique* (44 Rue de Montmoreau; phone: 45-38-45-17) is informative about the history of the Charente region. It's closed lunch hours and Tuesdays; no admission charge. Devoted to French comic strips, the *Musée de la Bande Dessinée* (121 Rue de Bordeaux; phone: 45-95-16-31) has, in addition to a permanent collection of over 8,000 original works, many excellent temporary exhibits. Closed mornings, Mondays, and Tuesdays. The city's theater is on Avenue des Maréchaux beside the tree-lined Place New-York (phone: 45-38-61-55).

Be sure not to miss the town's ramparts. The Charente River is sometimes hard to find, lost as it is in a maze of roads and trees, and the horizon from the ramparts too often presents a modern or industrial landscape. But two sides of the city walls—the west and the south—are worth the walk. Start near the post office at Place Francis-Louvel and head down Rue de Beaulieu.

For a sweet-tooth fix, go to *Pinoteau* (32 Rue St-Martial; phone: 45-95-06-20), a pâtisserie/*salon de thé* where you can savor a *gâteau ganage* (a small cake with chocolate icing and a layer of semisweet chocolate inside) or *Le 16* (a regional cake filled with cognac).

Several pleasant outings are possible from Angoulême. If you have a free afternoon and an insatiable interest in papermaking, take D674 south for 2 miles (3 km) to D104, and continue 2½ miles (4 km) to the tiny town of Puymoyen. Follow the signs to the Verger paper mill, *Moulin du Verger,* a short hop along a narrow, winding, forested road through the Eaux Claires Valley. (Alternately, bus No. 8 from Place du Champs-de-Mars in town will take you to within 1 mile/1.6 km of the mill.) The mill (phone: 45-61-10-38), in operation since 1539, sells its fine handmade paper to buyers all over the United States and Europe. Workers here produce in one year the same amount of paper it would take a machine to make in half an hour, but the product will last for at least 500 years. Tours of the mill and explanations (in English) of the process are given daily at no charge. It's closed lunch hours on weekdays and mornings on weekends and holidays. You can purchase the mill's paper at the on-premises shop. Another paper mill in the area, *Moulin de Fleurac* (phone: 45-91-50-69), on D699 west of the city near Nersac, has a museum with exhibits of old documents as well as an explanation of the history of paper and writing. It's closed lunch hours and Tuesdays.

Another worthwhile excursion is to the 15th-century *Château de l'Oisellerie* (3 miles/5 km southwest of Angoulême on N10 in La Couronne; phone: 45-67-10-04; fax: 45-67-29-55), where visitors can taste and buy *pineau* and cognac. Open by appointment only; closed weekends. A bit farther is the 11th- to 12th-century abbey of La Couronne and its *Eglise St-Jean-Baptiste;* an adjacent 18th-century building boasts a beautiful Louis XV ironwork door.

Yet another excellent day trip is to the thousand-year-old town of La Rochefoucauld (pop. 3,500), about 14 miles (22 km) northeast of Angoulême on N141. Its 9th-century château has a 12th-century keep, a 15th-century tower, and a 16th-century galleried staircase and chapel. The castle is open daily from June through September; open Sundays and holidays from October through May. In July and August, the garden is the site of a historical son-et-lumière show, during which some 500 costumed citizens, including 60 horseback riders and coachmen, relate 11 centuries of local history in 11 tableaux. The show is held on Friday and Saturday nights; admission charge.

The tourist office in La Rochefoucauld is in a 14th-century cloister (Rue des Halles; phone: 45-63-07-45). It's open daily from mid-June through mid-September. At 39 Grande-Rue, Jacques and Mady Brun run a *salon de thé* (phone: 45-63-00-26) that was started by M. Brun's father in the late 1940s. The elder Brun created delicious chocolate candies, unique to this town, called *pichottes,* and Jacques "invented" the *caline,* a dark chocolate made with cognac and wrapped in gold paper. The shop is closed lunch hours, Mondays, and Tuesdays.

Hostellerie du Moulin du Maine Brun Comfortable and chic, this Relais & Châteaux member has 20 rooms, a fine restaurant, a pool, and its own park. Closed January through March. Five miles (8 km) northwest of Angoulême via N141 and D120 in La Vigerie, near Hiersac (phone: 45-90-83-00; fax: 45-96-91-14). Expensive.

Le Mercure With a good view of the valley and an exquisite garden, this great old hotel has 90 rooms, a large terrace built on 12th- and 13th-century ramparts, a restaurant, and a garage. In the center of town, at 1 Pl. des Halles, Angoulême (phone: 45-95-47-95; 800-221-4542; fax: 45-92-02-70). Expensive.

Les Gourmandines Traditional regional dishes prepared with contemporary finesse make this a favorite among locals. A very appealing decor adds to the pleasurable experience of dining here. Closed Sundays. Reservations advised. MasterCard and Visa accepted. 25 Rue de Genève, Angoulême (phone: 45-92-58-98). Moderate.

Hôtel du Palais It has 49 rooms on three floors and a comfortable sitting room, but no dining room. This is a clean, quiet place in a great location. In the center of the Old Town, at 4 Pl. Francis-Louvel, Angoulême (phone: 45-92-54-11; fax: 45-92-01-83) Moderate.

La Ruelle Modern art and ancient stone walls illuminated by a blazing fire set the stage for original preparations of traditonal fare. There's a good, well-priced wine list, and you can order by the glass. Closed Saturday lunch, Sundays, two weeks around late February or early March, and the first three weeks of August. Reservations necessary. Major credit cards accepted. 6 Rue des Trois-Notre-Dame, Angoulême (phone: 45-95-15-19). Moderate.

Trois Piliers Convenient to both downtown and the train station, this pleasant property has 30 rooms, a bar, a terrace, and a garage, but no restaurant. 3 Bd. de Bury, Angoulême (phone: 45-92-42-11; fax: 45-95-77-07). Inexpensive.

ON THE ILE DE BOURGINES

An excellent municipal campground (phone: 45-92-83-22) on the Ile de Bourgines, a quick bus ride (No. 7) or half an hour's walk from downtown Angoulême, is open from late March through October. An open-air municipal pool is nearby. The island also has a very nice youth hostel (phone: 45-92-45-80; fax: 45-95-90-71); though there are only 16 rooms, it looks like a small motel. Ile de Bourgines offers canoeing, kayaking, and other sports.

En Route from Angoulême N141 leads west for 27 miles (43 km) to the town of Cognac. Along the way you may want to stop in at the headquarters of *Courvoisier* cognac (5 Pl. du Château, Jarnac; phone: 45-35-55-55), 18 miles (29 km) from Angoulême.

COGNAC This unassuming town (pop. 20,000) has the equivalent of millions of bottles of cognac aging in porous oak casks; the vapors from all that cognac may help to account for the softness of the light in the afternoons, so beautiful that even the busiest sightseers are bound to stop to admire it. However, the fumes are also responsible for the city's dingy aspect; the black fungus that lives on the vapors has turned many of the buildings gray.

Cognac was the birthplace, in 1494, of François I, whose image and name are almost as ubiquitous around town as the word "cognac." The town square features an equestrian statue of him; *Parc François-I,* the municipal park (which has indoor and outdoor pools and 25 acres of shaded walkways), is named after him; and one of the hotels in town bears his name (see *Best en Route*). François I was born in the *Château de Cognac,* which is now the home of the *Otard* cognac firm (see below; there also is a son-et-lumière show here). Nearby is the 15th-century *Porte St-Jacques,* all that's left of the town's old fortifications, and beyond it, the *Hennessy* company (see below), whose main building is a 17th-century abbey. The gate marks the entrance to the oldest part of town, which has dwellings from the 15th to the 18th centuries, many of them now restored. On the other side of town, on Place Jean-Monnet, you can buy regional drinks, glasses, and cognac-drenched chocolates from *La Cognathèque* (8 Allée Corderie; phone: 45-82-43-31). Try its "cigar-drink," a test tube with a tobacco leaf wrapped around it like a cigar, but with cognac inside.

Also on Place Jean-Monnet, the tourist office (16 Rue XIV-Juillet; phone: 45-82-10-71; fax: 45-82-34-47) has a map of the cognac firms and their tour hours. Most are open weekdays and, during summer, at least part of the weekend; some by appointment only. For more information about visiting the companies, contact the following:

Camus, 29 Rue Marguerite-de-Navarre, Cognac 16100 (phone: 45-32-28-28).
Courvoisier, 5 Pl. du Château, Jarnac 16200 (phone: 45-35-55-55; see *En Route from Angoulême,* above).
Hennessy, 8 Rue de la Richonne, Cognac 16100 (phone: 45-35-72-68).
Martell, Pl. Edouard-Martell, Cognac 16100 (phone: 45-36-33-33).
Otard, Château de Cognac, 127 Bd. Denfert-Rochereau, Cognac 16100 (phone: 45-82-40-00).
Rémy Martin, 20 Rue de la Société Vinicole, Cognac 16100 (phone: 45-35-76-66).
Renault Bisquit, Domaine de Lignères, Rouillac 16170 (phone: 45-21-88-88).

The *Eglise-St-Léger* (55 Rue Aristide-Briand) was begun about 1130; the façade, walls of the nave, and base of the bell tower are all that remain from the 12th century. The rose window, a pretty addition but one that destroyed the church's Romanesque character, dates from the 15th century. If you look closely at the outermost section of the sculpted doorway, you'll recognize the signs of the zodiac. Its bell tower makes *St-Léger* the tallest edifice in town. Cognac has a good museum, the *Musée Municipal* (*Parc François-I;* phone: 45-32-07-25), with exhibits of wine-making tools and regional ethnography. It's closed Tuesdays, lunch hours from June through September, and mornings from October through May. There's no admission charge.

The municipal theater (Pl. Robert-Schuman; phone: 45-82-17-24) hosts film festivals, classical concerts, and theatrical productions of classical and modern works. Concerts also are held at the *Château de Cognac.* The *Centre des Congrès* (Convention Center; in the same building as the tourist office, see above) has changing exhibitions; it's open daily, and there is no admission charge.

For nightlife, the *Pub Victor-Hugo* (13 Av. Victor-Hugo; phone: 45-32-28-11) has a piano bar and a welcoming ambience.

Cognac's grapes are among the last to be picked in France; the harvest usually begins around the middle of October. On the weekend of the *Salon des Vendanges* (Grape Harvest Show), the town's streets, closed to traffic, fill up with colorful floats, majorettes, and marching bands. There's an admission charge for the festival. In July a son-et-lumière show and a *Spectacle Historique* (Historical Pageant) are presented at the abbey of St-Brice (3 miles/5 km from Cognac; phone: 45-32-06-90).

BEST EN ROUTE

Château de Mirambeau This restored 17th-century château boasts two tennis courts, a nine-hole golf course, health club, indoor pool, restaurant, bar, and 48 rooms—six of them suites. Add to the picture extensive, peaceful grounds and gardens, and you'll agree that there's practically no reason to leave the premises. Closed January 3 through March. From Cognac take D732 14 miles (22 km) southwest to Pons, then N137 14 more miles (22 km) south to Mirambeau (phone: 46-70-71-77; fax: 46-70-71-10). Very expensive.

L'Echassier This 21-room hotel in a turn-of-the-century dwelling offers such amenities as a pool, a garden, and—best of all—a fine restaurant. The elegant dining room features rich local food that marries well with bordeaux wines. Restaurant closed Sundays. Reservations advised. Major credit cards accepted. 72 Rue de Bellevue, Cognac-Châteaubernard (phone: 45-35-01-09; fax: 45-32-22-43). Expensive.

Moulin de Cierzac Located at the water's edge in a park, this inn has 10 rooms in an 18th-century mill and a super restaurant featuring such specialties as *chaudrée de poissons au pineau des Charentes* (fish and *pineau* soup with braised cabbage). Closed mid-January through mid-February; restaurant also closed Monday lunch. Reservations advised. Major credit cards accepted. Eight miles (13 km) south of Cognac via D731, in St-Fort-sur-le-Né (phone: 45-83-01-32; fax: 45-83-03-59). Expensive.

Moulin de Marcouze Definitely worth the 25-minute drive south of Cognac is this charming old mill, now a first class, two-Michelin-star restaurant that specializes in elegant renditions of seafood dishes. There also are 10 rooms. Closed November through February, and Tuesdays and Wednesday lunch from September 15 through June 15. Reservations necessary. Major credit cards accepted. From Cognac take D732 southwest to Pons, then N137 south to St-Genis-de-Saintonge, and D146 to Mosnac (phone: 46-70-46-16; fax: 46-70-48-14). Expensive.

Les Pigeons Blancs In a lovely wooded setting, this excellent dining room in a château-hotel (seven rooms) of the same name offers nouvelle cuisine, including a good *filet de sole à la cotinière aux huîtres* (filet of sole with oysters). Don't miss cocktails on the terrace, overlooking the garden. Closed Sunday dinner. Reservations necessary. Major credit cards accepted. Follow D731 north a short distance toward Cherves. 110 Rue Jules-Brisson, Cognac (phone: 45-82-16-36; fax: 45-82-29-29). Expensive.

Le Valois It offers 45 rooms with mini-bars, a large bar, and parking, but no restaurant. Closed December 23 through January 2. Near the post office at 35 Rue du XIV-Juillet, Cognac (phone/fax: 45-82-76-00). Expensive.

L'Auberge A good place to sample such fine traditional fare as *magret de canard aux pêches* (breast of duck with peaches). Closed Friday dinner and Saturdays, except for groups. Reservations advised. Major credit cards accepted. On a quiet side street near Pl. François-I, at 13 Rue Plumejeau, Cognac (phone: 45-35-42-26). Moderate.

François I General de Gaulle slept in this historic hostelry, right on the town square. There are 30 rooms distributed among three floors. Ask for one facing the plaza. There's no restaurant. 3 Pl. François-I, Cognac (phone: 45-32-07-18; fax: 45-35-33-89). Moderate.

La Ribaudière A variety of grilled dishes and meats are served here; in nice weather eat on the terrace facing the Charente River. Closed Mondays. Reservations advised. Major credit cards accepted. Follow N141 east for 6 miles (10 km) to Bourg-Charente; the restaurant is on the left-hand side of the road (phone: 45-81-30-54; fax: 45-81-28-05). Moderate.

En Route from Cognac Take N141 west for 16 miles (26 km) to Saintes.

SAINTES This charming town is reminiscent of St-Emilion in the Bordeaux region, with its cathedral and houses with red tile roofs. Everything about Saintes has a gentle quality—the people, the curve of the river, the arch of the two bridges in the center of town, and the shape of the plane trees shading the sidewalks along Cours National. It's a perfect place in which to wander aimlessly: Turn almost any corner, and you're bound to happen upon a quaint street. The tourist office (*Villa Musso,* 62 Cours National; phone: 46-74-23-82; fax: 46-92-17-01) provides a map with a walking tour of the city. It is open daily in summer; otherwise closed the first Tuesday of each month. Saintes has its share of ancient landmarks, such as the 1st-century Roman arch (the *Votive Arch of Germanicus*) and a reasonably well-preserved amphitheater, the large green elliptical basin between two hills. It once comprised three stories; by some miracle part of the first remains. Until the middle of the last century residents made a habit of removing the unevenly cut stones to build their own homes. Much earlier as many as 20,000 spectators sat here, watching gladiator battle gladiator or beast. Follow the signs for *Parc des Arènes,* then from the parking lot follow the well-worn footpath to the amphitheater. (Note: The signs from the parking lot lead toward the park, not the amphitheater.) The amphitheater is open daily; no admission charge.

Saintes's *Cathédrale St-Pierre* has been rebuilt so many times that its origins have been lost to us. One tradition holds that fire destroyed the original church on this site in 1026, and archaeologists agree that the north and south walls of the bell tower's base resemble a pre-Romanesque style that antedates the present cathedral. The oldest parts of the cathedral that are dated with certainty—the southern part of the transept and its dome—were erected in the middle of the 12th century. Most of what remains today, however, is from a 15th-century reconstruction in the Ogival Gothic style, exemplified by the western portal at the base of the steeple, a beautiful piece of sculpture that deserves special attention. The 205-foot clock tower dates from the 17th century. Note also the Renaissance chapel, the old cloister next to the cathedral, and the altar, a gift from Napoleon.

On the east side of the Charente, just beyond the Roman arch, the *Abbaye aux Dames* (off Rue St-Pallais; phone: 46-97-48-48), a Romanesque church dating from the 12th century, was administered for seven centuries by abbesses from distinguished French families. Converted to a prison during the French Revolution, it was used as a barracks and stable until 1924; its reconstruction began some 50 years later. Today the abbey houses a vibrant, living church; modern tapestries hang on the walls, and medieval music concerts and other cultural events are held here in the summer. The central portal is intricately carved, and the bell tower is also worthy of note.

The remarkable *Eglise St-Eutrope* (Rue St-Eutrope, near the amphitheater) was built on the pilgrimage route to Santiago de Compostela (in Spain) on the supposed spot where St. Eutrope was martyred. The church was consecrated in 1096; the vast crypt, which contains St. Eutrope's tomb, is the most interesting part of the church. Its entrance is on the north side. The bell tower, whose spire is almost 200 feet high, was built in the late 1400s. Across the street is a small, inviting park, a good *salon de thé,* and the *Maison d'Actions Sociales et Culturelles* (15 Rue St-Eutrope; phone: 46-

93-71-12), a good source of information about out-of-the-mainstream "happenings."

Saintes boasts one of the best collections of French folklore anywhere, housed in the *Musée Municipal de Dupuy-Mestreau* (4 Rue Monconseil; phone: 46-93-36-71). It has excellent exhibits of clothing, lace, peasant and upper class headdresses, 18th- and 19th-century dolls, jewelry from the time of Marie-Antoinette, ceramics, furniture, and re-creations of a 19th-century bedroom and kitchen from a Saintongeais house. Closed Tuesdays and October through *Easter.* Admission charge.

The *Musée du Présidial* (28 Rue Victor-Hugo; phone: 46-93-03-94), in a restored 17th-century *hôtel particulier* (townhouse), is worth a visit if only for the building that houses it. Its collection includes pottery from the 16th to the 18th century—with some works by the famous 16th-century artisan Bernard Palissy—and an interesting framed fragment of a tapestry from the 17th century portraying St. Peter holding the keys to heaven. Nearby, the *Musée de l'Echevinage* (Rue Alsace-Lorraine; phone: 46-93-52-39) has a dozen noteworthy paintings from the 19th and 20th centuries as well as Sèvres china. Both museums are closed Tuesdays, and both charge admission in summer only.

Along the banks of the Charente is a pleasant public garden with a gazebo and large dovecote. The municipal library (phone: 46-93-25-39), in the old *Hôtel Martineau* at Rue des Jacobins and Rue Martineau, houses the extensive collection of Maurice Martineau, a wealthy cognac dealer and philanthropist who donated the *hôtel* and a third of the library's more than 75,000 volumes to the city. Notice the beautiful wood door; the entrance is through the courtyard. Closed Sundays and Mondays; Tuesday, Thursday, and Friday mornings; and the first two weeks in August.

Saintes is a grand place to shop; walk along the small pedestrian Rue St-Michel or the larger Rues Victor-Hugo and Rue Alsace-Lorraine—all in the area between Cours National and the *Cathédrale St-Pierre.* The prices for food and clothing are generally quite reasonable. There are plenty of markets to stroll through: One is held Wednesdays and Saturdays beside the cathedral; another on Tuesdays and Fridays at Cours Reverseaux and Rue St-Macoult; and one on Thursdays and Sundays near the *centre ville* (downtown) train station on Cours Reverseaux. The first Monday of each month Saintes's streets fill up with vendors from the surrounding areas; look for them particularly near the arch at the *Abbaye aux Dames.* For a drink and the sounds of American music, drop by *Le Vaudeville* (13 Quai de la République; phone: 46-93-11-91).

The local food specialty is the *galette charentaise,* a glazed sugar cookie usually the size of a small pizza. To sample *pineau* where it is produced, visit *Paul Bossuet* (2 Chemin Terrières, Chaniers, 4 miles/6 km from Saintes on N141 toward Cognac; phone: 46-91-51-90; fax: 46-91-56-19). If you want to take home samples of pottery from Saintes and Angoulême, visit *Danielle Bovet* (82 Rte. Burie, St-Porchaire, 8 miles/13 km northwest of Saintes on

N137; phone: 46-95-61-86); or try the *Poterie Alexiu* (128 Rue Nationale, La Chapelle-des-Pots, 5 miles/8 km east of Saintes on D131; phone: 46-91-51-04; fax: 46-91-54-25).

Only 10 miles (16 km) north of Saintes on N137 is *La Roche Courbon* (phone: 46-95-60-10), the most elegant of the handful of large châteaux in this region that are open to the public. With its two towers, manicured lawns, and large reflecting pool, it's a real beauty. The impressive structure was built during the 15th century and renovated two centuries later. There is a small museum of prehistory in the château, and within walking distance of it are prehistoric caves to be explored. The interior of the château is ornate and filled with furnishings from many periods; one room is full of 17th-century paintings on wood, and the Louis XIII room has noteworthy painted beams. The gardens are open daily. The château is closed lunch hours, Thursdays from mid-September through mid-June, and mid-February through mid-March.

The environs of Saintes are filled with tiny 15th- to 18th-century churches and chapels—usually off the main road, but the turnoffs are well marked. You can take potluck or follow D129 10 miles (16 km) south to Rioux, site of a tiny Romanesque church whose carvings make the detour worthwhile.

BEST EN ROUTE

Relais du Bois St-Georges This inn, reposing like a country estate at the end of a tree-lined drive, has 27 rooms and three suites, all delightful and tastefully decorated with antique furniture. The glass-walled restaurant has Oriental rugs and a fireplace faced by comfortable leather chairs, and each of its 20 tables has a view of the lawn. Bass and turbot dishes are the house specialties, vegetables come straight from the garden, and the wine selection is extensive. There's also a bar beside an indoor pool. One mile (1.6 km) outside Saintes on Rue de Royan and Cours Genêt (phone: 46-93-50-99; fax: 46-93-34-93). Expensive.

Logis Santon One of the best restaurants in the region, this place serves traditional specialties with creativity (especially the sauces) in a charming setting that accommodates only 20 guests. Closed Sunday dinner and Mondays. Reservations necessary. Major credit cards accepted. 54 Cours Genêt (phone: 46-74-20-14; fax: 46-74-49-79). Moderate.

France This cozy, 26-room hotel is a very pleasant place to stay. Request a room facing the garden. There is a seafood restaurant, *Le Chalet*, and in summer you can dine outside under the trees. Restaurant closed Fridays from December through *Easter*. Reservations unnecessary. Major credit cards accepted. Across from the train station, at 56 Rue Frédérique-Mestreau (phone: 46-93-01-16; fax: 46-74-37-90). Inexpensive.

Le Procopio At this large Italian eatery, the best seating is upstairs, in the garden, and on the enclosed terrace. Almost any dish on the menu is large enough

to be shared by two. Closed Sundays and Mondays. Near the cathedral, at
5 Rue de la Comédie (phone: 46-74-31-91). Inexpensive.

En Route from Saintes Route N150 leads to Royan, 25 miles (40 km) southwest.

ROYAN A resort town that has known better days, Royan (pop. 17,000) was
destroyed in World War II and has been completely rebuilt, leaving it with
a mishmash of buildings, streets glutted with traffic, and none of its former
charm.

The real must-see here is the *Eglise Notre-Dame,* designed by Guillaume
Gillet and built in the late 1950s. It's impossible to miss it, rising like the
hull of a great ship moored at the highest point in the city. To say simply
that it looks like a boat does not do justice to the church's architectural
genius. The ceiling soars high overhead, with nothing—neither column nor
arch—obstructing the inner space. But it is the walls that are most captivating, accented by thin, vertical strips of vivid stained glass. The beauty of
the glass is emphasized by the somber gray hues of the concrete building.
Climb the stairs and walk the periphery. In summer an organ festival is held
here. Signs point the way to the church from the center of town; the uphill
climb is but a small price to pay for what lies ahead.

Good maps of the Charente-Maritime region are available at the Royan
Office de Tourisme (138 Rond-Point de la Poste; phone: 46-05-04-71; fax:
46-06-67-76), in a building to your left just as you come into town from the
east. Regular ferries (phone: 46-38-35-15 or 56-09-60-84) travel from Royan
to Pointe de Grave, near the town of Le Verdon, where major roads can
be picked up either along the Atlantic coast or through the wine-producing region of the Médoc. To reach the ferry quay, follow the Quai de
l'Amiral-Meyer south (oceanward) and watch for signs for *BAC* (the ferry).

BEST EN ROUTE

Résidence de Rohan This elegant 19th-century manor house has been converted
into a tranquil 41-room country inn. There's no restaurant. Closed mid-
November through mid-March. Two miles (3 km) north of Royan, at Plage
de Nauzan (phone: 46-39-00-75; fax: 46-38-29-99). Expensive.

En Route from Royan Follow the coastal road, D25, for 20 miles (32 km)
to Marennes, the most important center for oyster cultivation in France.
Nine miles (14 km) outside Royan in La Palmyre is France's largest zoo
(phone: 46-22-46-06) whose 34 acres of hills and valleys are home to a
thousand birds and animals. It's closed lunch hours from October through
March; admission charge. Just beyond the zoo is Pointe de la Coubre;
stop here to admire the lighthouse and its spectacular view of the Ile
d'Oléron and the cliffs to the north. Just south of the lighthouse is a nude

beach, but be forewarned that the water can be treacherous here. North of the lighthouse stretches the Côte Sauvage (Savage Coast); the name alone should be enough to discourage a quick dip, no matter how refreshing it might seem.

MARENNES Try to time your stop here as close as possible to the outgoing tides in order to see the huge oyster beds where people gather these delicacies from the sea. Purportedly the finest oysters in France, those found here are green because of the algae in the water. Stop to enjoy fresh oysters, mussels, and other seafood in La Cayenne, the town's oyster-fishing harbor. There is an oyster museum in the 17th-century *Fort du Chapus,* which, at high tide, is accessible only by boat. It is open daily from June through mid-September only. On the north side of town is the elegant *Château de la Gataudière* (phone: 46-85-01-07), part of which is now a maritime museum; the architecture and furnishings remain as they were when the château was built in the mid-18th century by François Fresneau, known as the "father of the raincoat" for his discovery of the useful applications of the rubber tree. The château is closed lunch hours and from December through February.

En Route from Marennes Full of hairpin turns, D3 leads from Marennes 4½ miles (7 km) to Brouage, whose walls rise up out of the road like a medieval mirage.

BROUAGE Founded in 1555, Brouage was a port city until land encroached upon the sea and changed its history. Samuel de Champlain, the founder of Quebec, was born here in 1570, and it was from here that colonists set sail for the New World. The old ramparts, built in the 1630s by order of Cardinal Richelieu, still encircle the town, which seems to have fallen asleep several hundred years ago. Though crumbling in places, the walls, a mile of them punctuated with 17 watchtowers, are still beautiful. The best way to see the town and the surrounding area is to walk halfway around the ramparts; go up the stairs to the left of the tourist office (beside the northern entrance on the main street, Rue du Québec; phone: 46-85-19-16) and come back down when you again reach Rue du Québec, which passes by the town's early-17th-century church. Once you look out over the ramparts, it's easy to imagine the water that once lapped these walls, the workers loading salt for export onto waiting ships, and the tragic heroine Marie Mancini bidding farewell to Louis XIV, the lover she was never to see again, as he sailed south in 1659 to marry Maria Theresa for political reasons.

En Route from Brouage The 9 miles (14 km) of road, still D3, leading to Rochefort are pastoral and winding; on either side sea grass grows profusely, and cows are penned in by narrow moats rather than fences.

ROCHEFORT The friendliness of this bustling city and its 26,000 residents is apparent immediately. Founded in the 17th century as a military port, Rochefort contains one of the greatest pieces of architecture from the reign of Louis XIV: the *Corderie Royale,* a 1,227-foot-long arsenal that burned in 1944 but has been almost completely restored. The *Corderie* extends majestically along the Charente River, beginning at the *Jardin des Retours* (Garden of the River Bends) and ending at the boat basin. Today it is the *Centre International de la Mer,* a living museum to the seafaring life (phone: 46-87-01-90), complete with exhibits and videotapes. It's open daily.

Place Colbert, in the center of town, is an open, graceful plaza. A few blocks away is the tourist office (Av. Sadi-Carnot; phone: 46-99-08-60; fax: 46-99-52-64), which is closed Sundays (except afternoons in summer). Also nearby is the only store in the region where cameras with serious problems can be repaired, *Vidéophot* (111 Rue de la République; phone: 46-99-63-84), with reliable service and reasonable prices.

Rochefort boasts one of France's best-kept secrets—at least from outsiders: the *Maison de Pierre Loti* (141 Rue Pierre-Loti; phone: 46-99-16-88). The birthplace and home of the famous French writer, soldier, and adventurer who collected an impressive number of souvenirs in his travels, the house can best be described as a showcase of extravagant curiosities. It contains, among other things, a Gothic room, a Turkish room, a Renaissance room, and a mosque with a sunken floor, an exquisite ceiling, and marvelous tiles and Oriental rugs. These rooms were backdrops for Loti's lavish parties, to which guests came decked out in magnificent costumes, many of them provided by their host. The weapons randomly placed throughout the house are works of art in themselves. Closed lunch hours; Sunday mornings from July through September; Sundays, Tuesday mornings, and holidays from October through June; and mid-December through mid-January. Tours (in French only) are included in the admission charge.

In the *Conservatoire du Bégonia* (1 Rue Charles-Plumier; phone: 46-99-08-26) are countless varieties of begonias and hybrids—the only such collection in Europe. Really a research institution, the garden offers the public (limited) opportunities to admire the blooms. Open by appointment only, Tuesdays and Thursdays from 3 to 4 PM; open to groups by appointment only, Tuesday and Thursday mornings and Mondays, Wednesdays, and Fridays.

The *Musée de la Marine* (Pl. de la Galissonnière; phone: 46-99-86-57) pays homage to the sea, its vessels, and their crews. Downstairs are enormous models of ships from the 17th through the 19th century; upstairs a modern section includes replicas of an ocean liner, a submarine, and much more. On the ground floor, but with its own entrance, is the *Grand Salle,* which has an exhibit of 47 nautical knots. The museum is next to the *Porte du Soleil* (Sun Gate), the principal entrance to the ancient marine arsenal. Closed Tuesdays, most holidays, and from mid-October through mid-November.

In the *Musée d'Art et d'Histoire* (63 Av. Charles-de-Gaulle; phone: 46-99-83-99) are paintings and ethnographic collections from the 16th to the

20th century. The museum is closed mornings and, from September through June, Sundays and Mondays.

The city has a transporter bridge dating from 1900, the last of its kind in France. Service on the bridge was discontinued in 1966, when its duties were taken over by a new bridge that in turn was torn down in 1991 and replaced by the Viaduc de la Charente, which stands today alongside the old transporter.

The 18th-century *Théâtre de la Coupe d'Or* (101 Av. de la République; phone: 46-82-15-15) stages concerts, light opera, and the works of such playwrights as Pinter and Anouilh; in the summer it sponsors open-air concerts and in May there's a lyric poetry festival.

On Tuesday, Thursday, and Saturday mornings vendors of prepared foods, produce, hamsters, and chickens descend upon Avenue Charles-de-Gaulle and Avenue Lafayette, transforming the streets into one of the largest, liveliest, and most colorful markets in the region. Use it as a chance to sample a regional specialty, *tourteau fromagé,* a round bread made with cottage cheese.

Rochefort has gained a reputation in recent years for its thermal springs, sought out by those seeking relief from rheumatism, circulatory ailments, and skin problems. Visitors who come for treatment—some 5,000 a year—must make reservations well in advance. For more information, contact the *Thermes de Rochefort* (Av. Camille-Pelletan, Rochefort 17300; phone: 46-99-08-64).

BEST EN ROUTE

Corderie Royale Regally housed in a 17th-century building, this establishment offers 50 modern rooms (with amenities such as mini-bars), a mini-health club, and a restaurant. Rue Jean-Baptiste Audebert (phone: 46-99-35-35; fax: 46-99-78-72). Expensive.

Café "Le Flore" Snuggled between the boat basin and the *Corderie Royale,* this is the local spot for steaks with *frites* (French fries), seafood, a burger, or drinks. Weather permitting, you can sit on the porch in one of the rocking chairs. Closed Wednesdays from September through April, and mid-December through early January. Reservations advised in summer. Major credit cards accepted. 1 Rue Jean-Baptiste Audebert (phone: 46-87-21-06). Moderate.

Le Soubise In this comfortable hotel are 24 rooms and an outstanding restaurant that specializes in regional dishes. Hotel closed the first two weeks in January and three weeks in October. Restaurant also closed Sunday dinner and Mondays, except holidays, from September through June. Reservations necessary for the hotel in July and August and for the restaurant year-round. MasterCard accepted. In the little town of Soubise, 5 miles (8 km) southwest of Rochefort on D238E, at 62 Rue de la République (phone: 46-84-92-16 or 46-84-93-36; fax: 46-84-91-35). Moderate.

Le Tourne-Broche Meat is grilled over a wood fire here, but regional fish dishes are the real specialty. Closed late June through early July and Sunday dinner from September through June. Reservations advised. Major credit cards accepted. 56 Av. Charles-de-Gaulle (phone: 46-99-20-19; fax: 46-99-72-06). Moderate.

La Belle Poule An attractive hostelry, it has 21 rooms and a restaurant. On Rue Gabriel-Allaire, the Royan road into Rochefort (phone: 46-99-71-87; fax: 46-83-99-77). Inexpensive.

La Presqu'île This little inn with lace curtains on the windows is certainly *charmante*. It has only eight rooms, and there is a good, small restaurant serving regional specialties such as *entrecôte à l'ardoise* (steak cooked on slate). Just before the bridge on the road to Saintes, near the boat basin, at 2 Av. William-Ponty (phone: 46-99-01-88). Inexpensive.

Roca-Fortis Only a short walk from the boat basin and near the center of town, this spacious hotel has 17 rooms but no restaurant. Closed December 23 through January 7. 14 Rue de la République (phone: 46-99-26-32; fax: 46-83-93-45). Inexpensive.

En Route from Rochefort N137 leads north for 21 miles (34 km) to La Rochelle.

LA ROCHELLE Called the "City of Lights," like its grander sister, the capital, this is nonetheless a dazzling town, night or day, and it also is the cultural and administrative center of the Charente-Maritime *département*. La Rochelle developed in the 10th century as a fishing village between two points of land jutting into the Atlantic: Minimes Point and Pallice Point. Two commanding towers—*de St-Nicolas* and *de la Chaîne*—guard the entrance to the old port, as they have for six centuries, making any approach to this city of 72,000 all the more dramatic. The fortified port has existed since the 13th century, by which time La Rochelle had already established itself as a major trading center. The two towers once had a chain stretched between them to keep out unknown ships, and to keep others from leaving without paying taxes. The *Tour de la Chaîne* is connected by a rampart to yet another tower, the *Tour de la Lanterne* (Lantern Tower), which was used as a lighthouse as well as a prison and for defense. The names of former inmates still are visible, carved into its walls. The crews of 15 British ships were held here during the American Revolution, which accounts for the number of English-language etchings. Some of the graffiti are quite artistic, such as the ship sailing out between two towers and the train on the second floor; both are unquestionably images of escape. The *Tour de la Lanterne,* with its Gothic spire, offers an impressive view of the city and the harbor. All three towers are open for visits (phone: 46-45-31-27, *Tour de la Chaîne;* 46-41-74-13, *Tour de St-Nicolas;* 46-41-56-04, *Tour de la Lanterne*).

La Rochelle has the largest number of streets with covered sidewalks in France and many houses dating from the 15th century, several of them of Revival timber design. The city also has impressive high-rise condominiums and the largest pleasure boat basin in all of Europe. Free parking is available throughout La Rochelle. On weekend nights in the summer the main street of the port, Quai Duperre, is closed to traffic, making it even more pleasant to stroll and admire the beautifully lit sweep of buildings along the seafront. The tourist office is on Place de la Petite-Sirène, Le Gabut, at the port (phone: 46-41-14-68; fax: 46-41-99-85). It's open daily from June through September; closed Sundays and holidays, October through May. The medieval gate to the old town, the *Porte de la Grosse Horloge,* right in the center of the harbor, beckons wayfarers into the heart of the city. The music of the hundred-year-old carousel on Place Meyer fills the air, advertising a free ride for anyone in the mood. Bicycles are provided (with ID) at Place Meyer and the Esplanade des Parcs at no charge daily except Sundays, Mondays, and holidays; they are especially fun to take to *Parc Charruyer,* a mile-long, 660-foot-wide strip of green with a stream running through it.

Rue Dupaty leads to a small square where you will find the central post office and the *Hôtel de Ville* (Town Hall; Rue de l'Hôtel-de-Ville), a striking building with a Gothic surrounding wall dating from the 15th century. The main part of the building, dating from the 16th century, is very decorative; the façade and staircase are in the style of Henri IV. Throughout, visitors will see many mementos from the siege of 1628, which was initiated by Cardinal Richelieu to bring the then-independent city under French rule. Guided tours in French are given every 20 minutes daily in summer and during the *Easter* and *Christmas* holidays; weekend afternoons only in the off-season. English-language tours may be arranged through the tourist office (see above).

The aquarium (Port des Minimes; phone: 46-44-00-00), France's largest, is a must-visit. It presents fish and other marine animals from all over the world in striking habitats. It's open daily; admission charge.

The *Musée du Nouveau Monde* (10 Rue Fleuriau; phone: 46-41-46-50) is housed in the superbly restored 18th-century *Hôtel Fleuriau.* Among its attractions are seven period rooms with beautiful wainscoting and fireplaces, plus exhibits focusing on the opening of Louisiana by Louis XIV and the lives of the early French settlers there. Objects on display date from the 16th through the mid-19th century. One room is devoted to the American Indian, a subject of great interest in France. Closed lunch hours, Sunday mornings, and Tuesdays.

Among the sundry attractions of the *Musée d'Orbigny-Bernon* (2 Rue St-Côme; phone: 46-41-18-83) are an 18th-century apothecary and a carved, oval Oriental bed on the third floor. The museum is closed lunch hours, Sunday mornings, and Tuesdays.

The *Musée d'Histoire Naturelle* (28 Rue Albert-I; phone: 46-41-18-25) is a bit of a hike from the center of town, but it has a nice garden that rewards the tired visitor. The museum is closed Sunday mornings and Mondays. Finally, the *Musée des Beaux-Arts* (28 Rue Gargoulleau; phone: 46-41-64-65) exhibits paintings from the 16th through the 20th century. It's closed mornings and Tuesdays. A special ticket gains the holder admission to the *Beaux-Arts, Orbigny-Bernon, Nouveau Monde,* and *Histoire Naturelle* museums.

La Coursive (4 Rue St-Jean-du-Pérot, beside the old port; phone: 46-51-54-00) presents a full and ever-changing agenda of films, music, dance, art exhibitions, and theater, as does the *Carré Amelot* (Municipal Youth Center; 10 *bis* Rue Amelot; phone: 46-41-45-62). Both are closed Mondays.

There's more to do in La Rochelle at night than simply admire the famous city lights. *Le Crystal* (54 Cours des Dames; phone: 46-41-43-10), an Art Deco café and piano bar with a chartreuse interior, is next to the *Tour de la Chaîne.* It serves delightful cocktails, ice cream, and tea. *Le Café de la Paix* (54 Rue Chaudrier, Pl. de Verdun; phone: 46-41-39-79) sometimes has live jazz or classical music. A couple of local hangouts that tourists might not ordinarily happen upon are the intimate *Piano Pub* (12 Cours du Temple, just off Rue du Temple via Petite Rue du Temple; phone: 46-41-03-42) and the *Cave St-Nicolas* (12 Rue St-Nicolas; phone: 46-41-16-07), where a young clientele goes for music and perhaps a game of chess. In addition, nightclubs are scattered around the old harbor.

La Rochelle is a good city for shopping (especially for nautical togs) and dining, though prices often are high. For local pottery, there is the *Poterie de La Rochelle* (27 Quai Maubec; phone: 46-41-38-14). Gastronomic pleasures revolve around seafood, naturally, and regional specialties on most menus include *mouclade* (mussels in a curry cream sauce), *chaudrée* (fish chowder), and *cagouilles* (small snails). For scrumptious chocolates and other sweets, visit *Jeff de Bruges* (4 Rue du Temple; phone: 46-41-26-33).

There is a covered produce market on Wednesday and Saturday mornings in the Place du Marché and a Saturday flea market in the Quartier St-Nicolas. In late June and early July an international film festival takes place; July also brings *Francofolies,* a festival of French songs. In September there is a sailboat festival; in November, a car rally.

For a real bird's-eye view of the city and surrounding area, take a sightseeing trip in a small airplane. Planes also go to the Ile d'Oléron and Ile de Ré. The latter is an 18-mile-long treasure of tiny villages, small whitewashed cottages, beaches, and mostly uninhabited land except in summer (which brings the tourist migration); there is a bird sanctuary at the northern end of the island. Oléron, on the other hand, has become very populated in recent years and has lost much of its charm. For more information on planes, call the *Aéro-Club de la Charente-Maritime* (phone: 46-42-54-74) at the *Aérodrome de La Rochelle-Laleu* on N237, about 3 miles (5 km) northwest of town. You also can reach the Ile de Ré via the Pont l'Ile de Ré (Ile de Ré Bridge) at La Pallice Point. In the summer you can rent a bike near the bridge; bike paths are plentiful on the island.

WARNING

It is dangerous to swim in the inlet, called Fier d'Ars, at the northeast end of the Ile de Ré, but there are plenty of safe, well-marked beaches elsewhere along the coast.

BEST EN ROUTE

La Marmite Here the chef holds to traditional bourgeois cooking and does it well, with the accent on quality of preparation and richness of ingredients. The restaurant has earned one Michelin star. Closed Wednesdays off-season. Reservations advised. Major credit cards accepted. 14 Rue St-Jean-du-Pérot (phone: 46-41-17-03; fax: 46-41-43-15). Expensive.

Maybelle Iribe All of the five rooms and one suite in this bed and breakfast establishment have fireplaces, though none has a phone. Breakfast is included in the rate and served in the garden. The owner runs an on-premises cooking school, whose courses include excursions to oyster beds, local vineyards, and markets. The restaurant serves dinner only, but a picnic basket can be arranged for lunch on the beach. No credit cards accepted. 33 Rue Thiers (phone: 46-41-62-23; fax: 46-41-10-76). Expensive.

Le Mercure Here are 43 rooms and three suites overlooking either the port or a pool, which is enclosed by ivy-covered walls. Each room has a refrigerator, and there's also a restaurant, *Le Yachtman.* Facing the old port, at 23 Quai Valin (phone: 46-41-20-68; 800-221-4542; fax: 46-41-81-24). Expensive.

La Monnaie In a stately stone building that served as La Rochelle's mint (thus its name) in the 17th century, this hotel offers 32 plush, modern rooms, four suites, and proximity to both the sea and the old port. There's no restaurant, but room service can be arranged in advance for late arrivals. 3 Rue de la Monnaie (phone: 46-50-65-65; fax: 46-50-63-19). Expensive.

Richard Coutanceau With two Michelin stars, it has a view of the sea to accompany such specialties as *salade de langoustines rôties et d'huîtres au vinaigre* (roast prawn and oyster salad with vinegar) and *bar moucheté en feuilles vertes au fumet de St-Emilion* (bass in green leaves with St-Emilion wine). There is a pleasing dessert selection and myriad white wines from which to choose. A member of the prestigious Relais & Châteaux group. Closed Sundays and, from October through May, also on Mondays. Reservations necessary. Major credit cards accepted. Behind the *Tour de la Lanterne,* Plage de la Concurrence (phone: 46-41-48-19; fax: 46-41-99-45). Expensive.

St-Jean d'Acre This pleasant place with 70 rooms (some overlooking the port) is tucked behind the *Tour de la Chaîne.* Its good restaurant, *Au Vieux Port,* has a terrace on the wharf and serves such regional specialties as grilled lobster, salmon, and turbot. Reservations advised. Major credit cards accepted. 4 Pl. de la Chaîne (phone: 46-41-73-33; fax: 46-41-10-01). Expensive.

St-Nicolas Quiet, yet only a few blocks from the flow of traffic and activity, this 79-room establishment is decidedly ultramodern, but the friendly staff makes staying here seem more like being in a home than in a hotel. There's a garage but no restaurant. 13 Rue Sardinerie (phone: 46-41-71-55; fax: 46-41-70-46). Expensive.

Chez Serge This well-known restaurant is surprisingly small and cozy, with lace curtains on the windows. In the summer request a table outside, beneath the towers. Seafood delights include lobster, crab, prawn pâté, and oysters on the half shell. Everything is served *à la charentaise* (accompanied by mayonnaise and butter). Open daily. Reservations necessary. Major credit cards accepted. Facing the old port, at 46 Cours des Dames (phone: 46-41-18-80; fax: 46-41-95-76). Moderate.

La Maison des Mouettes In summer grab a table on the terrace and order *langoustines au court-bouillon d'algues* (prawns in thick seaweed broth) or *l'effilage de volaille au crabe* (strips of poultry with crab). The selection is as expansive as the seaside view. Closed Mondays, except holidays, from September through June. Reservations advised. Major credit cards accepted. Route de la Plage, Aytré, 3 miles (5 km) south of La Rochelle via D937 (phone: 46-44-29-12; fax: 46-34-66-01). Moderate.

En Route from La Rochelle N11 leads to the Marais Poitevin, the "Green Venice," 15 miles (24 km) to the northeast.

MARAIS POITEVIN The Marais Poitevin comprises 177,000 acres, some 40,000 of them filled with canals and islands, flooded areas interspersed with clumps of forest, houses with thatch roofs, and friendly country people. Because of development in recent decades, the marshland has been disappearing at a phenomenal rate, but the French government has begun to take steps to preserve this unique habitat. The *Parc Naturel Régional du Marais Poitevin* is a protected area, and within it lie almost 45 miles of hiking trails, a 62-acre "zoorama" containing 600 animals (in Chizé Forest, 15 miles/24 km south of Niort), ethnography museums, châteaux, and abbeys. The old *Abbey of Maillezais,* now in ruins and lost in the moors, was the home of the writer Rabelais from 1523 to 1527. Only a flat-bottom boat can maneuver deep into the Marais, where lime-green algae blankets the water and trees intertwine overhead. For more details, call park information (phone: 46-27-82-44; fax: 46-27-83-45) or the tourist offices in Marans (phone: 46-01-12-87), Maillezais (phone: 51-87-23-01), Coulon (phone: 49-35-99-29), or Niort (phone: 49-24-18-79).

Bordeaux and the Médoc

The Bordeaux region in southwest France stretches from the tip of the Médoc peninsula—located between the Gironde River and the Atlantic Ocean—east to the border of neighboring Périgord and south to the splendid Arcachon Basin and the forests of the Landes. It contains the Médoc, some of the richest wine country in the world; glorious unsung beaches; two large lakes; the Arcachon Basin; nearly one million acres of serene, trail-covered pine forest; and seaside towns and tiny fishing villages that entice even the most blasé travelers. The best part is that all this is only an hour or less from Bordeaux, by any route. For additional information on the region, contact the *Comité Régional du Tourisme d'Aquitaine* (2 Rue René-Cassin, Bordeaux 33000; phone: 56-39-88-88; fax: 56-43-07-63).

Our suggested driving route first takes you north through the world-famous wine-producing region of the Médoc. While its flat terrain may not be particularly interesting, many find beauty in the elegant precision of its rows of burgeoning vines, every plant trimmed to identical height. The greenness is punctuated by red roses at the roadside ends of the rows; these traditionally served as an early warning system against fungus attacks on the grapevines, since the weaker roses would be the first to succumb. The villages along the Route des Châteaux (D2) derive their sustenance from wine: Joiners assemble wine cases in workshops around town squares while vineyard workers bicycle from their cottages to the fields. Even the printing of wine labels is an important subsidiary trade. Although the wines of the Médoc make up only about 13% of those produced in the Bordeaux region, these thoroughbreds set the standard to which the remaining 87% aspire.

In most wine making districts, the cellar master will invite you into a cool, low-ceilinged *cave* (cellar), but in Bordeaux, where the soil is sand and the water table is high, traditional wine cellars have been supplanted by the *chai,* a long shed with a sloping roof of sunbaked terra cotta tiles.

The terms first *cru* (growth), second *cru,* third *cru,* and so on refer to a system of ranking the top wines of the Médoc that was formulated almost 150 years ago, a system that has since been extended to other regions. In 1855, Napoleon III ordered a list of Bordeaux wines for the *Exposition Universelle de Paris,* a world's fair. The Bordeaux Chamber of Commerce in turn asked a group of wine brokers to prepare the list. Although the *Crus Classés de la Gironde* (Classified Wines of the Gironde) list compiled by the brokers was intended only as a compilation of names, people interpreted it as a rating system. This classification still is used, and although it remains accurate in its assessment of the very top of the *grand crus* (great growths), there are many who argue that some wines deserve to be upgraded in rank and others lowered.

There is no great mystery to tasting wines. You'll find the people who work with wine completely free of the jargon and pretension that wine snobs like to invoke to intimidate lesser mortals. Just hold the glass by the stem or the base and raise it to the light. The wine should be a rich, vibrant red, perfectly clear and limpid. Swirl it gently in the glass, then smell it. Take a small sip and hold the liquid in your mouth. Let the wine tumble about the tip and sides of your tongue while you assess the taste. Then spit it out, especially if you're trying several different wines. This may be embarrassing at first, but it is a common practice. Some châteaux provide sawdust-filled tubs for spitting; at others, use the floor as professionals do, but remember to turn your head to the side. Even the best-brought-up tyro soon will be spitting with the rest.

From the Médoc, our route next takes you back south along the coast, toward Bordeaux, passing along the way a string of unsung beaches lazing in the French sunshine. The stretch of Atlantic from Soulac-sur-Mer, just below the mouth of the Gironde River, to Cap-Ferret, at the entrance to the Arcachon Basin—71 miles (115 km) of beautiful coastline backed by towering pine trees—has long been enjoyed by vacationers. (For additional details, see *Best Beaches* in DIVERSIONS.) Though certainly popular, these beaches are not as crowded as those along the southern expanse of the Côte d'Argent, and they rub elbows with two large lakes that offer boating, sailing, and swimming, with no waves or undertow to battle. Keep in mind that the beaches in this area have a strong undertow; be especially attuned to flags posted to indicate the safety of the water on any given day. A green flag means that swimming is safe and a lifeguard is on duty; a yellow flag is a warning to proceed with caution; and a red flag means bathing is prohibited. Sunbathing and reading are always possibilities when the waves are off-limits, but don't expect to collect shells; you'll usually find only smooth stones and pebbles, and occasionally ravenously hungry insects (bring repellent). Some beaches are designated *naturiste,* meaning that bathers *must* be nude. However, swimming and sunning in the buff occur openly at most places; in France, topless bathing is common wherever sand and water exist in tandem.

Finally, we suggest a trip southwest of Bordeaux to the tidy triangle called the Arcachon Basin. It's a popular weekend destination for Bordeaux residents, a mooring spot for thousands of sailboats, a breeding ground for several varieties of oysters, a source of livelihood for a handful of small fishing villages and beach communities, and an exquisite backdrop for the resort town of Arcachon, which still bears vestiges of the Belle Epoque days when it was a favorite of English gentry and French artists alike. A few miles south of Arcachon, at Pyla-sur-Mer, sprawls Pilat Dune, the largest sand dune in Europe. Scale its 375-foot (and still growing!) height for the best view of the region's odd juxtaposition of pine trees, sea, and dunes.

In the Médoc, along the coast, and around the Arcachon Basin, expect to pay $200 or more per night for a double room in a hotel in the very expensive category; $100 to $200 in an expensive place; $65 to $100 in a moderate one; and less than $65 in an inexpensive place. Most hotels listed below feature telephones, TV sets, and private baths in all of their rooms. However, some less expensive hotels may have private baths in only some of their rooms; it's a good idea to confirm whether your room has a private bath when making a reservation. For the most part, only very expensive hotels in this coastal area have air conditioned rooms. All hotels accept major credit cards and are open year-round, unless otherwise noted.

For a meal for two, with service (usually included in the bill), but not wine or drinks, expect to pay $110 or more in an expensive restaurant, between $75 and $110 in a moderate one, and less than $75 in an inexpensive one. Unless otherwise noted, all restaurants listed below are open for lunch and dinner. For each location, hotels and restaurants are listed alphabetically by price category.

THE MÉDOC

Most of the châteaux in the Médoc have an informed representative on hand to greet visitors, take them on a tour of the *chais* (wine storehouses), explain the wine making processes, and perhaps invite them to taste the most recent vintage from the barrel (there is a fee for some tastings). An appointment usually is necessary. Tours generally include visits to the *chais* only, not to the châteaux themselves. (Be forewarned that the *maître de chai* probably won't speak English, although your tour guide may, and that most châteaux do not allow visits during the grape harvest.) Contact a French Government Tourist Office in any major US city (for addresses, see GETTING READY TO GO) before leaving for France and ask for the brochure *Découverte Médoc,* an excellent guide to châteaux and accommodations in the region. Or drop by the *Maison du Vin* in Bordeaux (1 Cours du 30-Juillet; phone: 56-00-22-88 or 56-00-22-66; fax: 56-00-22-77) weekdays for a copy. The guide lists the châteaux that are open to the public and indicates whether they have English-speaking guides.

Bottles or cases of recent vintages usually are sold at the châteaux, but if you intend to make a substantial purchase, it's wise to get an idea of the best buys ahead of time by consulting reliable vintage charts and asking the advice of a respected wine dealer. If you are interested in buying wine, also visit the *Maison du Tourisme et du Vin de Médoc* in Pauillac (see *Pauillac,* below).

BORDEAUX For a complete description of the city and its sights, hotels, and restaurants, see *Bordeaux* in THE CITIES.

En Route from Bordeaux Despite its importance to the city, the Médoc is poorly marked from Bordeaux. Follow the signs for Le Verdon or the Barrière du Médoc. The Route des Châteaux, D2, branches off to the right about 2 miles (3 km) beyond the turnoff for the Paris autoroute. At this point, follow the signs that indicate Route Touristique du Médoc Nord (or Sud). All the châteaux are marked, right along with the towns.

Château Cantemerle The handsome stone manor house of Château Cantemerle nestles deep amid grand old trees in a beautiful parkland setting. The fifth-*cru* wine of this château enjoys continuing popularity. Closed August, weekends, and at harvest time; open by appointment only. Macau (phone: 57-97-02-82; fax: 57-97-02-84).

MARGAUX Seventeen miles (27 km) from Bordeaux are the more than 3,000 vineyard acres of Margaux. Each year about seven million bottles of wine are produced here, some 75% to 80% of which is exported to eager foreign buyers. Margaux boasts the deepest beds of pebbled earth in the Médoc. For more information, visit the *Maison du Vin de Margaux* (Pl. la Trémoille; phone: 57-88-70-82; fax: 57-88-38-27); closed Sundays and Monday mornings.

Château Giscours At the end of World War II, this third-*cru* château—along with many other Bordeaux properties—lay in virtual desolation from the German occupation. Under the supervision of the father-son team that owns the property, the vineyards have been restored to full production, and the quality of the wine has been restored. Land unsuitable for viticulture has been planted with many varieties of rhododendrons, which make for a magnificent blooming display in the parkland behind the château. Open daily; closed lunch hours. English is spoken. Labarde (phone: 57-97-09-20; fax: 57-97-09-00).

Château Prieuré-Lichine At Cantenac, where the Route des Châteaux bends, you'll catch your first sight of this fourth-*cru* château, whose late owner, American Alexis Lichine, was the author of the informative *Guide to the Wines and Vineyards of France*. For a detailed description, see *Most Visitable Vineyards* in DIVERSIONS. Open daily. Cantenac (phone: 57-88-36-28; fax: 57-88-78-93).

Château d'Issan A stroll from *Château Prieuré-Lichine* along a grassy avenue of stately plane trees leads to this 17th-century château, which, with its pepperbox turrets and moat, looks like a fairy-tale castle. In the spring, the grounds are carpeted with wildflowers. One of the *chais* is so magnificent that it has been designated a historic monument; it's not to be missed. Closed weekends; call a few days in advance to arrange a visit. Cantenac (phone: 57-88-35-91 mid-June through mid-September; 57-88-35-91 the rest of the year).

Château Palmer This compact, attractive château is situated on the right side of the Route des Châteaux. For a detailed description, see *Most Visitable Vineyards* in DIVERSIONS. Closed weekends. Cantenac (phone: 57-88-72-72; fax: 57-88-37-16).

Château Margaux Take the Route des Châteaux about half a mile (1 km) farther to the marked turnoff to *Château Margaux*, which, along with its *chai* and grounds, has been designated a historic monument. The grand house, with its Ionic columns, was built in 1802; it's considered a perfect example of the Empire style. An intensive program of restoration of the house and modernization of the vineyards and wine making areas has been under way since 1977, when the first-*cru* property was bought by a couple who headed one of France's largest supermarket chains.

Château Margaux is one of the few places whose wine production is large enough to justify making its barrels in the property's own cooperage. Daylight streams through the clerestory windows of this vast room, with walls of the pale gold stone of the region and an enormous fireplace where flames leap from crackling vine clippings. Before the fire, burly coopers wrestle the hoops down over the barrel staves in a scene like something in a medieval woodcut.

The château is not open to visitors, but an English-speaking guide will take you through the *chai;* an appointment is required. Closed weekends, August, and at harvest time. Margaux (phone: 57-88-70-28; fax: 57-88-31-32).

BEST EN ROUTE

Le Relais de Margaux Luxury is the key in the 28 rooms and three suites of this hotel, well-equipped with tennis courts, a pool, and a beautiful, serene park. Its restaurant offers such specialties as asparagus with truffles and fish filet with herbs. Restaurant open daily mid-May through October; closed Sunday dinner and Mondays November through late December and March through mid-May. Hotel and restaurant closed late December through February. Reservations advised. Major credit cards accepted. About 1 mile (1.6 km) north of Margaux, on Chemin d'Ile-Vincent (phone: 57-88-38-30; fax: 57-88-31-73). Very expensive.

Le Lion d'Or A lively, rustic bistro where many local wine producers congregate for friendly lunches. You may bring your own wine. Closed Sunday dinner, Mondays, and one week in January. Reservations advised. American Express accepted. From Margaux, take D2 north for 4 miles (6 km) to Arcins. Pl. de la République (phone: 56-58-96-79). Inexpensive.

Le Savoie This inn serves straightforward cooking, complemented by a wide variety of local wines. Eat in the garden in season. Closed Sundays and holidays. Reservations unnecessary. No credit cards accepted. 1 Pl. de la Trémoille, Margaux (phone: 57-88-31-76). Inexpensive.

En Route from Margaux Although D2 is the main Route des Châteaux, many smaller roads also will take you to châteaux that produce sound, reliable wines often equalling those of the lesser great vineyards. In a few cases, the wines are truly distinguished. A few miles northwest of Margaux via D5 is Moulis, the site of two worthy châteaux. *Château Maucaillou* (phone: 56-58-01-23; fax: 56-58-00-88) features a *Musée des Arts et des Métiers de la Vigne et du Vin.* Dedicated to wine and the art of viticulture, the museum is open daily; there is a fee for tastings. Also in Moulis is *Château Chasse-Spleen* (phone: 56-58-02-37; fax: 56-58-05-70), whose name means "banish the blues." Other noteworthy *crus bourgeois* châteaux in the area are *Château Lanessan* (in Cussac-Fort-Médoc, farther north on D2; phone: 56-58-94-80; fax: 56-58-93-10) and *Château d'Angludet* (in Cantenac; phone: 57-88-71-41). Their wines are less expensive than those of the *grands châteaux,* and the welcome is often more sincere.

As you continue on the Route des Châteaux toward St-Julien, note the contrast between low-lying fields of rich, loamy soil, where fat dairy cows amble about the pasture, and the raised vineyard plantations, where the fast-draining, pebbly soil fosters a king's ransom in wines but could hardly feed a cow for a week.

ST-JULIEN Here, about 10 miles (16 km) from Margaux, 2,075 acres produce about five million bottles of wine every year.

Château Beychevelle The first vineyard in St-Julien, this is a fourth *cru,* though ranked higher by professionals. Once a monastery, it was rebuilt in 1757, and the long, low, elegant château is considered a particularly lovely example of the Chartreuse style. At the end of the 16th century, the property belonged to the Grand Admiral of France. Mariners plying the river saluted him by dipping their sails, and the name Beychevelle (for *baisse-voile,* meaning "lower the sail") commemorates that salute. In July and August, guided English-language tours of the *chais* and park-like gardens are given. Closed lunch hours and weekends; visits by appointment only (phone: 56-59-23-00; fax: 56-59-29-00).

Château Ducru-Beaucaillou The vineyards of this château, a second *cru,* adjoin those of Beychevelle. The name *beau caillou* (beautiful pebble) refers to the soil on which the life of the château depends. The *chais* have a cool, damp atmosphere especially conducive to the preservation of old wines. (In surroundings that are too dry, corks will desiccate and crumble, allowing air to enter the bottle, so that the wine oxidizes and begins to evaporate.) Closed August and at harvest time; visits by appointment only. English is spoken (phone: 56-59-05-20; fax: 56-59-27-37).

BEST EN ROUTE

Relais du Médoc In addition to seven simple rooms, this place has good, Bordeaux-style home cooking. Restaurant closed Wednesday dinner and Mondays. Reservations advised. Major credit cards accepted. 70 Rue Principale, Lamarque (phone: 56-58-92-27; fax: 56-58-95-67). Inexpensive.

PAUILLAC This quiet, attractive little town (pronounced more or less *Po*-yak) is one of the oldest in the Médoc. Pauillac has several things going for it, among them the *Maison du Tourisme et du Vin de Médoc* (Quai Léon-Perrier at *La Verrerie;* phone: 56-59-03-08; fax: 56-59-23-38), the only place in the region where Médoc wines can be purchased at just over wholesale prices. The *maison's* list includes over 180 choices; be aware, however, that there are no tastings, and they do not ship wine overseas. It is open daily. Pauillac's *maison de la presse,* or newsstand (9 Quai Léon-Perrier; 56-59-07-08), sells a number of English-language newspapers, as well as good maps and postcards; there's a handy camera store, *Photo Véran* (phone: 56-59-02-44), right next door.

An annual marathon that winds through the Médoc begins and ends in Pauillac; it is held the second Saturday in September. For more information, consult the *Maison du Tourisme* (see above).

Stroll along the promenade by the river or out onto the piers, admire the pleasure boats, go for a swim at the town's indoor pool (phone: 56-59-05-06). And, of course, visit some of the most famous châteaux in the world, where 2,643 acres produce close to seven million bottles of wine a year.

Château Latour This great first-*cru* château, surprisingly modest in appearance, straddles the boundary of St-Julien and Pauillac. The fortress that once stood on the site was built to repulse the river pirates and bands of pillaging mercenaries who roamed Europe in the wake of medieval wars. By the end of the Hundred Years' War, which pitted England and France against each other until 1453, the fort was little more than a heap of rubble. The sole vestige is *la tour* (the tower), which stands today like a sentinel keeping watch over the vineyards. Open year-round; visits by appointment only. English is spoken (phone: 56-59-00-51; fax: 56-59-23-49).

Château Mouton-Rothschild Classed as a second *cru* in 1855, this has been ranked with the first *crus* of the Médoc since 1973, thanks to the unremitting efforts of the late owner, Baron Philippe de Rothschild. The grounds here are kept meticulously, and the château is surprisingly small, because it was the last of the existing buildings to be added and there wasn't much room left. In the *Musée du Vin,* housed in former wine cellars, paintings, tapestries, finely wrought silver, and all manner of antique and contemporary art celebrate the history and pleasures of wine. In the *chais,* rows of barrels extend for about 3,000 feet. Closed during lunch hours, on weekends, and after 5 PM. Visits are by appointment only, and they're difficult to get. English is spoken (phone: 56-59-22-22).

Château Pontet-Canet Right across the road from *Château Mouton-Rothschild* is the Médoc's largest vineyard, at 170 acres, and one of its loveliest: A narrow driveway leads through shade trees to the simple 18th-century stone château, with its white shutters and clean lines. The rose garden and gray, vine-covered outbuildings with claret-colored shutters add to the beauty of the place. Unlike most châteaux in the region, this one is lived in year-round. Many believe that the wine produced here deserves far better than its fifth-*cru* status. Open daily in summer; closed lunch hours; closed weekends the rest of the year. English is spoken (phone: 56-59-04-04; fax: 56-59-26-63).

Château Lafite Rothschild The word "Lafite" supposedly is a corruption of the local dialect term *la hite* (the height), referring to the elevation on which the château, with its medieval tower, is built. The cousins of Baron Philippe de Rothschild have owned the property since 1868, but its reputation predates the Rothschilds by far. Wine making has been carried on here for at least 800 years, by some accounts. The wine of Château Lafite is said to have been the favorite of two mistresses of Louis XV: the Marquise de Pompadour and the Comtesse du Barry. During World War II, the Nazi field marshal Hermann Göring declared his intention of taking the first-*cru* Lafite, with its exquisite vaulted *chais,* as his share of the spoils of France after Germany's victory, which he considered inevitable. Closed mornings and Fridays through Mondays; visits by appointment only and limited to six people at a time for tastings. English is spoken (phone: 42-56-33-50 in Paris; fax: 56-59-26-83).

BEST EN ROUTE

Château Cordeillan-Bages This 17th-century château now does service as a deluxe 25-room hotel, a member of the Relais & Châteaux group. The *Ecole du Bordeaux,* based here, offers weekend and short-term wine making and tasting sessions for professionals and novices. There also is a restaurant known for specialties such as *agneau de Pauillac rôti au thym frais* (roasted Pauillac lamb with fresh thyme) and *bar au cerfeuil, fenouil, et jus poivré* (bass with chervil, fennel, and pepper sauce). Hotel and restaurant closed December 1 through January 2; restaurant closed Monday lunch and Sundays as well. Reservations necessary. Major credit cards accepted. 61 Rue Vignerons (phone: 56-59-24-24; fax: 56-59-01-89). Hotel: expensive; restaurant: moderate.

Hôtel de France et d'Angleterre This modern 29-room hotel is an excellent bargain; English-speaking staff is an added attraction. The restaurant specializes in the famous Pauillac lamb. Closed December 21 through January 9. 3 Quai Albert-Pichon (phone: 56-59-01-20; fax: 56-59-02-31). Inexpensive.

Hôtel de la Renaissance The views from this modern, 10-room hotel make it worth a stop. Its restaurant, which serves traditional fare, is closed Sundays. 43 Av. Général-de-Gaulle, St-Laurent-de-Médoc, 11 miles (7 km) southwest of Pauillac on D206 (phone/fax: 56-59-40-29). Inexpensive.

Relais du Manoir Set in an old manor house, the kitchen prepares regional foods in original ways; try the assortment of salads with foie gras. There are also eight reasonably priced rooms. Restaurant closed Sunday evenings.

Reservations advised. Major credit cards accepted. Just outside Pauillac, on Rte. de la Shell (phone: 56-59-05-47). Inexpensive.

La Salamandre The price is right and the food's good at this little brasserie. Open daily June through August; closed weekdays for dinner September through May. Reservations advised. Major credit cards accepted. 16 Quai Léon-Perrier (phone: 56-59-24-87). Inexpensive.

ST-ESTÈPHE Some 7.9 million bottles of wine are produced on 2,940 acres yearly in this tiny village about 5 miles (8 km) from Pauillac, although less than 20% percent of the total is from classified growths. The soil of St-Estèphe has the least gravel in the Médoc, and its moisture-retaining clay imparts a somewhat "heavier" quality to the wine. The *Maison du Vin de St-Estèphe* (phone: 56-59-30-59) sells all the wines from the region and presents an audiovisual show; it also exhibits a collection of old wine cellar tools. It's closed Sunday mornings July through September, lunch hours and Sundays March through June and October through December, and January and February.

Château Cos d'Estournel While the second-*cru* wine produced here is unquestionably first class, you're more likely to remember Cos d'Estournel for its bizarre architecture. The château, whose first owner traveled in the Far East, was built in the 19th century with such incongruous details as pagoda towers and massive, carved wooden doors from the palace of the sultan of Zanzibar. Of all the châteaux, it casts the most exotic outline against the already dramatic Médoc sky. Tours are available in English, and an audiovisual show is presented. This château is very popular in season, and it's open by appointment only (phone: 56-73-15-55; fax: 56-59-72-59).

Château Calon-Ségur A third *cru,* this is the northernmost grand *cru* of the Médoc. "Calon" refers to the small boats that were once used extensively to ferry timber across the Gironde from the heavy forests of St-Estèphe; the name Ségur is that of an 18th-century proprietor, who also owned Château Lafite and Château Latour. The heart design on Calon-Ségur's label symbolizes Ségur's great love for this vineyard, and the motto carved in stone at the arched entrance to the château echoes this sentiment: "I make wine at Lafite and Latour, but my heart is at Calon." The underground *cave,* unusual for the region, is particularly noteworthy. The château is open by appointment only. Tours are in French (phone: 56-59-30-08 or 56-59-30-27).

En Route from the Médoc After looking at nothing but straight vine rows along most of the Route des Châteaux, travelers may find its northern end a surprising, perhaps welcome, change. The flatness of the lower reaches gives way to wooded slopes and fields of more conventional farm crops, such as corn, and grazing land. A salty breeze is a reminder that this last stretch of the Gironde is the estuary where fresh water meets the Atlantic.

From St-Estèphe, take D204E and D204 to Lesparre and then N215
toward Soulac, 18 miles (29 km) farther along.

BEST EN ROUTE

Château Layauga An 18th-century château, it has been converted into a luxury
hotel with seven rooms, decorated in Louis XV style. Its one-Michelin-star
restaurant serves updated French classics, accompanied by an excellent
range of wines. Reservations necessary. MasterCard and Visa accepted.
Just north of Lesparre on N215, in Gaillan (phone: 56-41-26-83; fax: 56-
41-19-52). Moderate.

Vieux Acacias This pleasant hotel offers 20 rooms and three suites (with no TV
sets) amid a peaceful park and gardens. It provides a good stopping point
between the vineyards of the Médoc and the Atlantic Coast. There's no
restaurant, but breakfast is served (don't miss the melon jam). Closed
December 21 through January 31. Take the Queyrac turnoff, 4 miles (6
km) north of Lesparre on N215 (phone: 56-59-80-63). Inexpensive.

THE COAST

The opposite side of the Bordeaux peninsula from the Médoc, and the
northern third of the increasingly popular Côte d'Argent (also known here
as the Côte d'Aquitaine), this string of beaches is still refreshingly under-
populated. Small coast roads, often *routes forestières* (one-lane, unmarked
dirt roads), link the beaches of Montalivet-les-Bains with Hourtin Beach,
and Carcans Beach with Lacanau-Océan, but it's most often necessary (and
faster) to take the more inland route, D101, from Soulac as far as Hourtin
and then D3. This route passes just east of two large lakes, Lac d'Hourtin-
Carcans and Lac de Lacanau, linking the forested towns of Soulac, Vendays-
Montalivet, Hourtin, Carcans, Lacanau, Le Porge, and Lège-Cap Ferret,
where it splits around the Arcachon Basin; roads connect the towns to their
respective beaches.

SOULAC-SUR-MER The largest town along this part of France's Atlantic coast,
Soulac is a tidy, bustling place with brick houses that have especially colorful shutters and trim. In summer, its population grows from 2,800 to as
many as 60,000. The *Fondation Soulac-Médoc* (Rue Ausone; phone: 56-09-
83-99) features the paintings, drawings, and sculpture of more than 100
Aquitaine artists. It's open daily from 5 to 7:30 PM from June through
September (and again from 9 to 11:30 PM in July and August). There also
is the *Musée d'Archéologie* (28 Rue Victor-Hugo; phone: 56-09-90-50),
which includes prehistoric, protohistoric, and Gallo-Roman pieces. It's
open daily; closed lunch hours and September through June. But the town's
crowning attraction is the *Basilique Notre-Dame-de-la-Fin-des-Terres* (29
Rue Ausone; phone: 56-09-81-02), a splendid 12th-century Romanesque
church that had been completely covered by sand by the 18th century and

was not unearthed until 1860. In July and August, a music festival takes place in the church.

Soulac has a municipal pool (phone: 56-09-81-60), which is open daily July and August; closed the rest of the year. It also has 21 tennis courts, two of them covered; a gym; a cinema; and a casino (Bd. Charcot; phone: 56-09-82-74), which is open June through August. Visitors can rent horses at the *Club Hippique* (phone: 56-09-71-93), and adventurous travelers can try parachuting with the *Centre Départemental de Parachutisme Sportif de la Gironde* (*Aérodrome de Soulac;* phone: 56-09-84-50). The nearby beach at L'Amélie-sur-Mer, just south of Soulac, is especially striking, with its black rock formations and dunes. Soulac also has two nightclubs, *Memphis* (in the casino; see above) and *Le Koala* (Chemin de la Briquetterie; phone: 56-09-94-49).

Soulac is only 3½ miles (6 km) south of Le Verdon, where ferries (phone: 56-09-60-84 in Le Verdon; 46-38-35-15 in Royan) depart for Royan every half hour or hour, depending on the time of day, from late June through August, and every hour to two-and-a-half hours the rest of the year. For more information on the attractions listed above or the coastal resort towns, drop by the tourist office (Rue de la Plage, near the basilica; phone: 56-09-86-61; fax: 56-73-63-76). It's open daily.

BEST EN ROUTE

Des Pins About 100 feet from the beach, the hotel has 34 rooms and a restaurant (with a terrace) specializing in seafood and the foie gras and *magret de canard* of the Dordogne region. Closed mid-November through mid-March. Reservations advised in summer for both hotel and restaurant. In L'Amélie-sur-Mer, 2 miles (3 km) south of Soulac (phone: 56-09-80-01; fax: 56-73-60-39). Moderate.

Dame de Coeur In the heart of town (though far from the beach), here are 16 rooms, all with private baths; the restaurant serves hearty fare. Reservations advised in summer for both hotel and restaurant. 103 Rue de la Plage, Pl. de l'Eglise (phone: 56-09-80-80; fax: 56-09-97-47). Inexpensive.

L'Hacienda With its lush garden and terraces, this hotel looks as though it were transported intact from Spain. It has 11 rooms, plus a restaurant under separate management—the *NovioMagus,* which serves traditional cuisine. Restaurant closed Sunday dinner and Monday lunch. Hotel reservations advised in summer. 4 Rue Pérrier-de-Larsan, Soulac-sur-Mer (phone: 56-09-81-34, hotel; 56-09-99-45, restaurant). Inexpensive.

Lescorce This comfortable, 18-room hotel has a gameroom for table tennis and billiards, a tennis court (book court time in the hotel bar; you don't have to be a guest to play), a TV room, a restaurant, and a homey ambience. The owner speaks English. Closed October 15 through *Easter.* 36 Rue Trouche (phone: 56-09-84-13). Inexpensive.

En Route from Soulac The first 19 miles (30 km) of the drive south from Soulac on D101, along the backside of beaches masquerading as farmland, are especially pastoral and pleasant.

At Vendays-Montalivet, take D102 west to the beach at Montalivet-les-Bains.

MONTALIVET-LES-BAINS This long stretch of beach is officially designated *naturiste* (nude). Large enough to afford plenty of privacy, it is frequented mostly by young couples with children. Simply park by the side of the road and walk across the dunes. Take along insect repellent, and carry your valuables with you; it's not safe to leave them in the car.

BEST EN ROUTE

La Clef des Champs Elegant and off the beaten track, this restaurant-farm is managed by a mother-and-daughter team. The menu offers whatever game and vegetables are in season. Closed occasionally in winter; call ahead to check. Reservations necessary. Major credit cards accepted. Three miles (5 km) from Montalivet off D102, between Vendays-Montalivet and Montalivet-les-Bains; watch for signs (phone: 56-41-71-11). Moderate.

En Route from Montalivet Take D101 and D3 south from Vendays for 20 miles (32 km) to Carcans.

CARCANS The streets in this small town end at a 20-foot sand dune, which you have to climb over to get to the ocean. This beach is more crowded—and more conservative—than Montalivet. The town also has a small *Musée des Arts et Traditions Populaires* (phone: 56-03-36-65), featuring local crafts, furniture, and clothing. It's open daily from mid-June through mid-September; closed mornings; open other times by appointment only. For additional information, contact the *Office de Tourisme Carcans-Maubuisson* (127 Av. de Maubuisson; phone: 56-03-34-94; fax: 56-03-43-76). It's open daily *Easter* through mid-October, and during school vacations in spring and winter; closed Sundays the rest of the year.

En Route from Carcans If at this point you've had enough sun and salt water and want a break, visit Lac d'Hourtin-Carcans, a pebble's throw away on D3. Maubuisson, a tiny resort town on the lake's southern shore, reached by D207 from Carcans, has a couple of decent hotels and restaurants. The lakeside resort complex of Bombannes, about 1 mile (1.6 km) north of Maubuisson, is a must for the sports-minded. Facilities include four indoor and 22 outdoor tennis courts, two pools, a gym, and picnic areas, and the ocean is a short drive away. The complex is open daily (phone: 56-03-31-01; fax: 56-03-42-46). There are apartments available in the complex, but only for rental by the week; for information, contact *Les Dunes* (phone: 56-03-95-00).

Head south of Carcans on D3 for 7 miles (11 km) to Lacanau, and from there to Lacanau-Océan, another 8 miles (13 km) west on D6.

LACANAU-OCÉAN The cleanest of all the beaches and the one best equipped for demanding travelers, Lacanau-Océan has a couple of large, seafront hotels. The brick dwellings look like gingerbread houses, sculpted dunes adorn the beach, and a sandy promenade runs parallel to the ocean. The tourist office (438 Pl. de l'Europe; phone: 56-03-21-01; fax: 56-03-11-89) is open daily.

Activity-inclined vacationers can rent surfboards, windsurfers, and Hobie Cats from *Lacanau Lou* (*Résidence Casino A;* phone: 56-26-36-74); take surfing lessons at the *Lacanau Surf-Club* (17 Bd. de la Plage, phone: 56-26-38-84, fax: 56-26-38-85; or in Lacanau at 10 Av. Général-Leclerc, phone: 56-26-36-10); learn windsurfing at the surf club or the *Club de Voile Lacanau-Guyenne* (*Club House de la Grande Escoure,* 24 Allée Club-de-Voile, Lacanau; phone: 56-03-05-11; fax: 56-26-23-34); go horseback riding at the *Club Hippique de Lacanau-Lac* (Marina de Talaris; phone: 56-03-52-74); or take a five-day tennis course at the *Tennis Club Ardilouse* (between Lac Lacanau and Lacanau-Océan; phone: 56-03-24-91; fax: 57-70-00-68). Lac Lacanau is nearby, and there's an excellent 27-hole golf course, *Golf de Lacanau* (phone: 56-03-25-60).

June brings the *24 Heures de Planche à Voile,* a spectacular, one-day windsurfing regatta. There's an international tennis tournament and a dance festival in July; and the *Pro de Surf* international surfing competition takes place in mid- to late August.

BEST EN ROUTE

Hôtel du Golf A modern hostelry surrounded by trees at the edge of *Golf de Lacanau* (see above), it offers 50 comfortable rooms and apartments with terraces overlooking the greens. There's also a pool and a restaurant. Closed January and February. A 10-minute stroll from the ocean, in Domaine de l'Ardilouse (phone: 56-03-23-15; fax: 56-26-30-57). Moderate.

L'Etoile d'Argent Right by the water, this impressive property has 14 rooms facing the beach, plus a dining room. Closed December through mid-January. Pl. de l'Europe, Lacanau-Océan (phone: 56-03-21-07). Inexpensive.

La Taverne de Neptune Sit inside by the glow of candlelight or out on the porch by the glow of your fondue flame. Service is slow, but the food is delicious. English is spoken, and the menu is translated for you. Open daily for dinner only; closed October through mid-March. Reservations advised. No credit cards accepted. 11 Av. de l'Europe, Lacanau-Océan (phone: 56-03-21-33). Inexpensive.

En Route from Lacanau-Océan Take the inland road, D3, south; from Le Porge, drive west along D107 to lovely Le Porge-Océan. This way, you can truly appreciate the stately, dense pine forest and get a good sense of the peaceful solemnity it imparts. The drive to the beach may be the most serene 7 miles (11 km) of your trip, especially if you go in the morning when the mist still hovers in the forest. Near Le Porge-Océan is a well-kept 114-acre municipal campground (phone: 56-26-54-88) and a nudist colony called *La Jenny* (Rte. de Lauros; phone: 56-26-56-90; fax: 56-26-56-51).

Continue south from Le Porge on D3 for about 7 miles (11 km) to Lège-Cap-Ferret and the Arcachon Basin. From here, D106 leads to the west around the basin to Cap-Ferret, and D3 continues around to the east for 15 miles (23 km) before it meets N250, the direct route from Bordeaux. Le Teich is a few miles west on N250.

THE ARCACHON BASIN

The most popular close destination for Bordelais who have their hearts set on sunning, swimming, and sailing is the Arcachon Basin. A road loops 112 miles (180 km) around the triangular basin, connecting a baker's dozen of communities. The most appealing spots, however, all fall along the base (or southern part) of the triangle, on D650, from Le Teich to Arcachon. Cap-Ferret, across the channel from Arcachon, is a boat ride away and a pleasant day trip. No cars are allowed on the boats, so those who insist on four wheels can get there only by making the tedious, traffic-riddled trip around the Basin.

LE TEICH In the southeast corner of the Arcachon Basin, Le Teich is the site of the *Parc Ornithologique,* a bird sanctuary (Rue du Port; phone: 56-22-84-89 or 56-22-80-93; fax: 56-22-69-43). It comprises 296 acres, 198 of which contain still, brackish water used as a fish preserve. In winter, more than 25,000 birds inhabit the park, and ducks, geese, swans, herons, storks, and flamingos are among the 260 species to be found here over the course of a year. Two hiking trails offer a one- or two-hour diversion, but the longer one, which follows a flat course with no shade trees, is of interest only to committed bird watchers, who visit in winter. Buy a small bag of grain at the entrance to placate the ducks waddling in your wake. The paths are gravelly, so don't wear sandals. The plentiful observation booths contain useful information in French about yearly migrations (for non–French speakers, the maps are still helpful). The park is open daily from March through September; closed weekdays (except holidays) from October through February. Plan to arrive before 4 PM or you may not be allowed to enter. There's an admission charge.

En Route from Le Teich Just 1 mile (1.6 km) west on D650 is *Ker Helen* (phone: 56-66-03-79; fax: 56-66-51-59), a lovely campground dotted with roses and striped with grapevines. The proprietors are especially helpful to visitors. Continue west for 3 miles (5 km) to Gujan-Mestras.

GUJAN-MESTRAS Nicknamed "the oyster capital," this tiny village contains no less than seven ports. The small tourist office (41 Av. Mal.-de-Lattre-de-Tassigny; phone: 55-66-12-65; fax: 56-66-94-44) is open daily; closed afternoons. Look for it on the Basin side of the road. If you want to taste some of the local oysters, visit Marc Druart (Port de Larros; phone: 56-66-72-04), Roger Druart (11 Rue Jules-Barat; phone: 56-66-00-11), or one of the seemingly innumerable members of the Castaing family, all of whom sell oysters directly from their shops at Port de Meyran.

BEST EN ROUTE

La Coquille Try the oysters at this restaurant with a cheerful black and white tile floor and tables covered with crisp white cloths. Other specialties include stuffed mussels and fish soup. Closed Sunday dinner; also closed Mondays in the off-season. Reservations unnecessary. Major credit cards accepted. 55 Cours de Verdun (phone: 56-66-08-60; fax: 56-66-09-09). Moderate.

En Route from Gujan-Mestras Continue west toward Arcachon, 9 miles (15 km) away. If it's the summertime, you may want to stop at La Hume, 2 miles (3 km) along the way. Every day from mid-June through mid-September, the restored medieval village here comes alive with craftspeople—50 in all—dressed in period costume (phone: 56-66-16-76). Follow the signs marked "Artisans d'Art." Two miles (3 km) south of La Hume on D652, just off N250, is *Aquacity: Aquatic Jungle Parc* (phone: 56-66-39-39), which offers swimming and amusements. It's open daily from June through early September; there's an admission charge.

ARCACHON This seaside resort, once sought out for its curative waters, enjoyed its heyday in the mid- to late 1800s, when European high society filled its streets, cafés, casino, hotels, and beaches. Arcachon also lured artists such as Manet and Toulouse-Lautrec and the composer Debussy. Today it enjoys continued popularity, primarily among the Bordelais and Germans. Especially appealing are the old beachfront hotels, sidewalk cafés, the tamarisk-lined promenade, and the beach.

The tourist office (Pl. Roosevelt; phone: 56-83-01-69; fax: 57-52-22-10) is open daily in season; closed weekends the rest of the year. The casino (163 Bd. de la Plage; phone: 56-83-41-44), a white, castle-like building complete with turrets, is open afternoons and evenings in season; off-season it is open Friday and Saturday evenings and Sunday afternoons and evenings. The aquarium (2 Rue du Professeur-Jolyet; phone: 56-83-10-22) has an exhibit on oyster cultivation, plus a number of tropical and local fish. It is open daily; closed November 2 through March 20. Admission charge.

The Ville d'Hiver (Winter City), behind the tourist office in the opposite direction from the Arcachon Basin, is Arcachon's Old Town. It is a jumble of winding streets (laid out this way for protection from the wind) filled with 19th-century villas and chalets; Allées Alexandre-Dumas, Pasteur, Faust, Pereire, Brémontier, Velpeau, Docteur-Lalesque, and Avenue Victor-Hugo are notable. A walking-tour guide of the Ville d'Hiver can be purchased at the tourist office in Bordeaux; in season, the tourist office in Arcachon offers walking tours of the town. Boat trips are available to Cap-Ferret (see below), to nearby Ile aux Oiseaux (Bird Island), to an oyster park, and for deep-sea fishing excursions. For information, contact the tourist office or, for groups, *Union des Bateliers Arcachonnais* (phone: 56-54-83-01).

BEST EN ROUTE

Grand Hôtel Richelieu This impressive establishment overlooking the Arcachon Basin and the Quai Thiers offers direct access to the beach. It has 43 rooms, a tearoom, a bar, and free parking. It has no dining room of its own, but is surrounded by restaurants. Closed November through mid-March. Centrally located, at 185 Bd. de la Plage, Arcachon (phone: 56-83-16-50; fax: 56-83-47-78). Moderate.

Roc Cheerful brown-and-white-striped awnings adorn this hostelry, which has 33 modern, comfortable rooms and a restaurant. Near the casino, at 200 Bd. de la Plage, Arcachon (phone: 56-83-07-43; fax: 56-83-22-76). Moderate.

Chez Yvette Exceedingly popular throughout the region, this old inn takes pride in its *lamproie à la bordelaise* (lamprey eel in red wine sauce); for the less adventuresome, the menu also offers more traditional fare. The bread, ice cream, and sorbets are homemade. Open daily. Reservations advised. Major credit cards accepted. Across from the tourist office, at 59 Bd. Général-Leclerc, Arcachon (phone: 56-83-05-11; fax: 56-22-51-62). Inexpensive.

Les Ormes A pleasant, modern hotel with 28 rooms, 12 overlooking the Arcachon Basin, and a restaurant with a summer terrace on the beach. Reservations necessary in July and August for both hotel and restaurant. A short distance from the center of town, at 77 Bd. de la Plage (phone: 56-83-09-27; fax: 56-54-97-10). Inexpensive.

Excursion from Arcachon *Pinasses* (small flat-bottomed boats) make regular trips across the Teychan Channel between Arcachon and the seaside community of Cap-Ferret each day (for an alternate route by land, see *En Route from Lacanau-Océan*, above).

CAP-FERRET This beach town has two beaches, one facing the ocean, the other facing the still, safe waters of the Basin. A small train trundles tourists from the town to the ocean, though the channel-side beach is better by far because it is both safer and cleaner. From June 15 through September 15, a second tourist office is opened at 12 Avenue de l'Océan in the *Panier Fleuri* building (phone: 56-60-63-26). The year-round office is harder to find; it's in the

Hôtel de Ville (Town Hall) in the community of Le Canon, north of Cap-Ferret (phone: 56-60-86-43; fax: 56-60-94-54). In fact, none of the streets here is clearly marked, so expect to be lost most of the time, whether you are on foot or wheels.

There is a splendid view from the *Phare du Cap-Ferret* (Cap-Ferret Lighthouse; phone: 56-60-62-76), whose 258 steps climb to a height of 175 feet. It is closed mornings the first two weeks in June and the last two weeks in September, and lunch hours mid-June to mid-September; open by request only October through May. Bikes can be rented from Mme. Goffre (47 Av. de l'Océan; phone: 56-60-62-16) or from M. Charbonnier (51 Av. de l'Océan; phone: 56-60-61-87); sailboats, from *Evasion Nautique* (22 Av. de Bordeaux; phone: 56-60-44-18); jet skis, from *Centre Marin* (37 Av. de l'Atlantique; phone: 56-60-63-56). Ocean conditions are given daily in the regional newspaper *Sud-Ouest*.

En Route from Arcachon Those who live in the area praise the stretch of beaches south to Biscarrosse-Plage. Take D218 south, stopping along the way at Pilat-Plage to be awed by the Pilat Dune. Like a gigantic glacier made of sand, this dune—6½ miles long and about 375 feet high, and still growing—encroaches on forest, town, and beach. Rugged beach buffs hike over it to get to the water; others take the stairs.

To return to Bordeaux from Arcachon, follow N250 east for 38 miles (61 km).

Périgord

Wedged neatly between the high plateau and volcanic formations of the Massif Central, the plains of the Guyenne, and the sun-soaked lands of the Midi is the lush green province of Périgord, corresponding approximately to the modern *département* of the Dordogne (the second-largest in France). One of France's richest areas of natural and manmade treasures, the region remains, if no longer undiscovered, at least still relatively unspoiled.

Coming into the Dordogne from the north, one notices a gradual change, not only in the terrain, but also in the tempo of life. The autoroute gives way to tiny roads that wind through deep, cool, fern-carpeted forests, rolling hills, opulent valleys strewn with wildflowers, and tall white limestone cliffs that drop dramatically into deep river gorges. Except in July and August, when increasing numbers of tourists descend on the region, you can drive for miles on the smaller, picturesque roads without passing another soul— the only signs of life being an occasional group of grazing cows or a stray goose.

The region owes much of its beauty to the Dronne, Isle, Auvézère, and Vézère Rivers, all flowing into the majestic Dordogne, considered by many to be the most beautiful river in France. The river valleys are dotted with charming towns of stone churches and medieval houses. Firmly entrenched on the heights are the châteaux, with their proud military bearing, in sharp contrast to the elegance of the Loire Valley palaces and reflecting a troubled, war-torn past.

Some 40,000 years ago a prehistoric race walked these valleys, as testified to by the region's many awesome cliff shelters and caves that have walls decorated with beautiful enigmatic symbols and paintings. Carbon dating places the majority of these sophisticated works in the Magdalenian era of the Upper (late) Paleolithic period. Discovered only about a century ago, a wealth of prehistoric sites in and around Les Eyzies, in the heart of Périgord, continues to draw anthropologists from around the world.

About 35,000 years after Paleolithic times, the Romans settled here, even before Julius Caesar forced the Gauls to capitulate. The vestiges of their arenas, baths, and temples are signs of the prosperity of the Roman predecessors of Périgueux and the other principal cities. The province was in turn conquered by the Visigoths and then taken by Clovis. These serene valleys were turned into battlefields during the Middle Ages, thanks in large part to Eleanor of Aquitaine, whose divorce from Prince Louis, son of the King of France, freed her to marry Henry Plantagenet, who ascended to the throne of England two years later, in 1154. Eleanor brought her precious dowry, the ancient Duchy of Aquitaine, to the British crown, thereby upsetting the already tenuous balance of power between France and England and launching a bitter war for possession of the region that lasted for 300 years. During much of that period Périgord suffered incredible devastation; it wasn't until the end of the Hundred Years War in 1453, that the area reverted to French hands.

In the 16th century the Wars of Religion brought more conflict. Périgueux was a Protestant stronghold between 1515 and 1581, after being taken by Geoffroi de Vivance, the Huguenot leader. Neighboring Bergerac, once the headquarters of the Reformed church, was taken by Catholics in 1562, then lost, and finally recaptured. The political situation stabilized in the 17th century, and from the reign of Louis XIV on the history of Périgord pretty much parallels that of the rest of France.

The area is almost as rich in architecture as it is in natural beauty. Most of its churches are in the Romanesque style, since the turbulence of the Hundred Years War discouraged the building of anything more elaborate or less practical than fortified castles and *bastides,* the defensive towns constructed under orders of the opposing Kings of France and England. Some of the humbler structures include *bories* (low, conical huts composed entirely of stones), and *pigeonniers* (small, square buildings perched on stilts with holes carved in the walls for nesting birds). The region also is home to about 1,500 châteaux, many of them incorporating several architectural styles, having been added to, embellished, and in some cases almost entirely rebuilt during various periods.

Périgord's rich gastronomic traditions are in themselves reason enough for a visit. This is the land of foie gras, *confit d'oie* (preserved goose), *magret de canard* (sliced duck breast), truffles and *cèpes* (wild boletus mushrooms), walnut cakes, liqueurs, and oil, fresh river trout, beef *à la périgourdine* (in a red-wine sauce similar to *à la bordelaise*), the hearty red wines of Cahors and Bergerac, and sweet white Monbazillac, drunk chilled as an accompaniment to foie gras. Nouvelle cuisine has made few inroads here, and the prices often match the down-home fare. For more information on the region, contact the *Maison du Périgord* (6 Rue Gomboust, Paris 75001; phone: 42-60-38-77) or the *Office Départemental du Tourisme de la Dordogne* (16 Rue Wilson, Périgueux 24009; phone: 53-53-44-35; fax: 53-09-51-41).

Our tour route starts in Limoges, then curves southwest to Brantôme and Périgueux before turning into the heart of the region, where most of the grottoes and prehistoric sites are found. Just a little to the east are the two most heavily visited towns, Sarlat and Rocamadour. The route then sweeps south to Cahors and the nearby grotto of Pech-Merle, then follows the wine route west of Cahors before turning north again, up to Bergerac and eventually back to Limoges.

For a double room per night, expect to pay $130 or more in a very expensive hotel; $90 to $130 in an expensive place; between $50 and $90 in a moderate establishment; and less than $50 in an inexpensive one. Unless otherwise indicated, all hotels accept major credit cards and are open year-round. Most hotels in this region are cozy, comfortable, and traditional. For the most part, it's not an area for those who insist upon such modern conveniences as air conditioning and overnight dry-cleaning service, though most hotels do feature telephones, private baths, and, more rarely, TV sets in their rooms. Some less expensive hotels may have private baths in only some of their rooms; it's a good idea to confirm whether your room has a private bath when making a reservation. Be forewarned that in July and August, many hotels with restaurants require that guests take breakfast and one more meal there each day (a practice called *demi-pension,* or half board). A meal for two in a very expensive restaurant will cost $110 or more; in an expensive restaurant, between $80 and $110; in a moderate one, between $50 and $80; and in an inexpensive place, less than $50. Prices include service but not wine or drinks. All restaurants are open for lunch and dinner unless otherwise noted. For each location hotels and restaurants are listed alphabetically by price category.

LIMOGES There is a special appeal to this busy city (pop. 150,000), which straddles the Vienne River on the site of the Gallo-Roman town of Augustoritum. It owes much of its modern strength and the title "City of Art" to its world-renowned porcelain factories and enamel works. Porcelain has been produced here since the end of the 18th century, when kaolin, the pure white clay from which it is made, was discovered 38 miles (61 km) south of the city, in St-Yrieix. (The Impressionist painter Auguste Renoir worked for a time in his native Limoges as a porcelain decorator.) Today more than 50% of all French porcelain is made in the factories here.

Don't expect to save money when buying porcelain here—most major firms sell no china at their factories, but simply refer purchasers to nearby retail stores, which follow the same price lists as the shops in Paris and other cities. From July through September, however, Limoges holds a large free exhibition of porcelain in the *Pavillon du Verdurier* (Pl. St-Pierre); lists of the many stores in town selling the porcelain are available at the door. The best ones—*Prestige de Limoges* and *Charme du Logis*—are on Boulevard Louis-Blanc.

Limoges also offers the visitor a chance to view the manufacture of porcelain in all stages, from the blending of the paste from feldspar, quartz, and kaolin through its molding into a multitude of forms and its elaborate decoration, much of it still done by hand. *Le Pavillon de la Porcelaine (Z. I. Magré,* Rte. de Toulouse; phone: 55-30-21-86), which offers the city's most complete exhibition, reserves a special welcome for Americans as the firm was founded by an American and always has had a large proportion of Americans among its clientele. Free demonstrations are conducted daily year-round, except Sundays from November to *Easter,* from 8:30 AM to 7:30 PM. *La Maison de la Porcelaine* also provides visitors with a complete view of the manufacturing process. In Aixe-sur-Vienne, 8 miles (13 km) southwest of Limoges on N21 toward Périgueux, the factory (14 Av. du Président-Wilson; phone: 55-70-14-68) offers free guided tours weekdays at 10 AM and 3 PM; from July through September there are tours every hour from 10 AM to 5 PM except during lunchtime. The outlet on the premises sells first- and second-quality merchandise. Although its porcelain-making process is not viewable, *Pastaud* (36 Rue Jules-Noriac; phone: 55-77-44-18) offers a close look as its workers embellish the pieces—carefully applying intricate decals and painting with amazingly precise brushstrokes. The 19th-century kilns, which have been replaced by modern electric ones, and some of *Pastaud*'s past work, including a gold-decorated dinner plate made for Franklin D. Roosevelt, are also on display. Appointments are required.

The art of *émaux* (enameling) has been practiced since antiquity, but it wasn't until the 12th century that Limoges's enamelers perfected their craft, using the lead silicates and oxides of rare metals, including gold, silver, and cobalt, found in the primary faults of the area. Enamels still are made in tiny kilns at the rear of each workshop. Several of these shops are clustered around Place Wilson and in the old part of the city; visitors are welcome to wander in and observe the process. For an enlightening discussion on the current state of the art, stop in at 19 Rue des Tanneries, where Boris Veisbrot creates striking contemporary pieces. Two interesting shops for modern enamel are *René Restoueix* (2 Rue Haute Cité) and *Vincent Pécaud* (23 Rue Elie-Berthet).

The *Musée National Adrien-Dubouché* (Pl. Winston-Churchill; phone: 55-77-45-58) has more than 10,000 pieces of pottery and porcelain which trace the evolution of china making from antiquity to the present. For addi- tional details on the museum, which is closed during lunch hours and Tuesdays, see *Memorable Museums and Monuments* in DIVERSIONS. The *Musée Municipal* (Mairie de Limoges; phone: 55-45-60-00), housed in a beautiful 18th-century building that once was the *Palais de l'Evêché* (Bishop's Palace), has a wonderful collection of enamels dating from the 12th cen- tury to the present. It includes many pieces by Léonard Limousin, enam- eler to the kings of France in the 16th century, and a fine group of Postimpressionist paintings. It is open from 10 AM to noon and 2 to 5 PM; closed Tuesdays. There is an admission charge for each museum.

A short walk from the municipal museum is Limoges's striking *Cathédrale St-Etienne,* begun in 1273 on the site of a Romanesque church, part of whose crypt and belfry remain. The cathedral is the only one in the Limousin region constructed completely in the Gothic style. Of particular interest are the Flamboyant Gothic St. John doorway, the delicately chiseled lime- stone screen inside at the end of the nave, and the three tombs flanking the chancel. The expansive gardens behind the cathedral are magnificent as well. Directly north of the cathedral entrance are the crooked streets of Vieux (Old) Limoges; especially charming is Rue de la Boucherie, lined with half-timbered houses where the city's butchers have lived since the 10th century. Don't miss the 13th-century St-Etienne Bridge, with eight elegant arches.

Also of interest are the *Orsay Gardens,* where the ruins of a Gallo-Roman arena were discovered during excavations in 1966. Near the tree-shaded Place de la République are two other churches, *St-Michel-des-Lions,* begun in 1364, and *St-Pierre-du-Queyroix,* its Flamboyant façade built in 1534. It was here, under the Place de la République, that the crypt of the former *Abbaye St-Martial,* dating from the 4th century, was found during excavations in 1960. Inside the abbey is the sarcophagus of St. Martial, the Limousin apostle who came to the area to convert people to Christianity in about AD 250. The abbey, destroyed in 1791, once was an important stop for pilgrims en route to Santiago de Compostela in Spain. The tourist office is on Boulevard Fleurus (phone: 55-34-46-87).

BEST EN ROUTE

La Chapelle St-Martin Surrounded by a park with tennis courts, a pool, and peaceful *étangs* (ponds) is this elegant inn, a Relais & Châteaux member and formerly a 19th-century home. There also are 10 rooms and three suites, furnished with lovely antiques, paintings, and porcelain. Everything served in the one-Michelin-star restaurant is excellent and original, including the *bar à la vinaigrette aux herbes* (bass in vinaigrette sauce) and *carré d'agneau du Limousin à l'aïl confit* (rack of lamb with preserved garlic). Closed January and February; restaurant also closed Monday dinner. Reservations advised. MasterCard and Visa accepted. Six miles (10 km) northwest of Limoges in St-Martin-du-Fault, near Nieul, via N147 and D35 (phone: 55-75-80-17; fax: 55-75-89-50). Very expensive.

Moulin de la Gorce Lost in the countryside, this lovely former mill has nine rooms, one suite, and a two-Michelin-star dining room. For additional details, see *Romantic French Hostelries* in DIVERSIONS. Hotel closed January through early February; restaurant also closed Sunday dinner and Mondays from mid-September through April. In La-Roche-l'Abeille, 17 miles (27 km) south of Limoges on D704 (phone: 55-00-70-66; fax: 55-00-76-57). Very expensive.

Le Champlevé This eatery serves traditional cuisine presented on elegant porcelain. Closed Saturday lunch, Sundays, and January through mid-February. Reservations advised. Major credit cards accepted. Pl. Wilson (phone: 54-34-43-34). Expensive.

Royal Limousin A comfortable, modern hotel, it has 75 spacious rooms but no restaurant. Pl. de la République (phone: 55-34-65-30; fax: 55-34-55-21). Expensive.

L'Amphitryon Set in an ancient house on a tiny street, this lovely restaurant features contemporary versions of such regional classics as lamb lasagna and sautéed quail breast. Closed Sundays, Monday lunch, and two weeks each in August and February. Reservations advised. Major credit cards accepted. 26 Rue de la Boucherie (phone: 55-33-36-39). Moderate.

Caravelle Recently remodeled, this 37-room hotel has its own bar but no restaurant; some of the rooms overlook a large park. 21 Rue A.-Barbès (phone: 55-77-75-29; fax: 55-79-27-60). Moderate.

La Meule A modest 10-room hostelry, it boasts a rustic restaurant serving generous meals, including hearty breakfasts, that have earned the place a star from Michelin. Closed three weeks in January; restaurant also closed Tuesdays off-season. In Séreilhac, 10 miles (16 km) southeast of Limoges on N21 (phone: 55-39-10-08; fax: 55-39-19-66). Moderate.

En Route from Limoges Head south on D704, turning west onto D78 at St-Yrieix-la-Perche to reach *Jumilhac-le-Grand,* 36 miles (58 km) from Limoges, a romantic, turreted château on the rocks overlooking the Isle River. The core of the château was built during the 14th century; the two lateral wings were added in the 17th century. Inside one of the wings is a great hall with wood carvings and a Louis XIV fireplace. Legend has it that a mistress of the castle, Louise de Hautefort, nicknamed "La Fileuse" (The Spinner), was locked up in the tower for life after her husband found her with a lover. Today you can visit the room where she is said to have sat spinning wool, making decorations, and painting her portrait on the door.

From Jumilhac continue west on D78 for about 15 miles (24 km) to St-Jean-de-Cole, one of the most beautiful villages in France. Half-timbered and ochre-tinted houses crowd around its charming central square; an 11th-century church, a medieval bridge, and a rustic covered market are located right in the middle of the village. Contact the *Syndicat d'Initiative* (phone: 53-62-14-15) for further information.

Follow D78 for 12 more miles (19 km) to Brantôme.

BRANTÔME This peaceful little town on the Dronne River is dominated by its Benedictine abbey, founded by Charlemagne in 769. Sacked by the Normans and rebuilt in the 11th, 14th, 18th, and 19th centuries, the abbey once was presided over by Pierre de Bourdeille. Better known as Brantôme, this chronicler's literary fame derives mainly from his witty and often cynical accounts of the lives of the *grands capitaines* and *dames galantes* of the late 16th century, an era rich in scandal.

Of particular interest here is the gabled Romanesque belfry, the oldest of its kind in the Limousin, erected in the 11th century. It stands apart from the abbey church on a 40-foot-high rock. Behind the abbey, in the caves that housed the monks' bakery and wine cellar, are huge 16th-century carvings of the Last Judgment and the Crucifixion. Every year an exhibition of classical dance is held in these caves. Also noteworthy are the monastery buildings, with two 18th-century wings and a beautiful 17th-century staircase. The buildings house the *Hôtel de Ville* (Town Hall), schools, and the

Musée Fernand-Desmoulin (phone: 53-05-80-63), which has many prehistoric artifacts found in the area and the bizarre paintings of Desmoulin, produced while this 19th-century Périgord artist was under the influence of a medium. The museum is closed Tuesdays; there is an admission charge. The real pleasure of Brantôme lies in its serene storybook setting. Stroll among the willows on the banks of the Dronne, cloaked with white water hyacinths and spanned by asymmetrical stone bridges. Don't miss the Friday morning open-air food market, held in the central square near the abbey church.

A worthwhile side trip from Brantôme is to Bourdeilles, 6 miles (10 km) southwest on D78. One of the four feudal seats of old Périgord (Biron, Beynac, and Mareuil were the other three), this small town and its towering castle on a cliff over the Dronne are perhaps more interesting than Brantôme. What makes the castle here particularly intriguing is that it actually is comprised of two adjacent châteaux: a massive fortress started in the 13th century and an airy, festive palace filled with wonderful pieces dating from the 15th to the 17th century. In the palace are Flemish and Aubusson tapestries, Italian paintings and porcelain, and Spanish furniture inlaid with gold and ivory. The palace was begun in the 16th century by Jacquette de Montbron, a sister-in-law of Pierre de Bourdeille (the famous Brantôme), in anticipation of a visit by Catherine de Médicis. Catherine never arrived, and the palace remained incomplete. One of its most magnificent features is the *Golden Room,* decorated by Ambroise Le Noble, one of the painters of Fontainebleau. The castle is closed Tuesdays except in July and August; there is an admission charge (phone: 53-03-73-36).

BEST EN ROUTE

Château de Vieux-Mareuil Perched on a hill, this lovely 15th-century château has 12 elegant rooms and two suites, all with modern comforts and splendid views. There is a pool. The restaurant serves highly rated traditional cuisine, such as salmon in potato crust and warm foie gras. Closed mid-January to March; restaurant also closed Sunday dinner and Mondays in winter. About 7 miles (11 km) northwest of Brantôme via D939 (phone: 53-60-77-15; fax: 53-56-49-33). Very expensive.

Moulin de l'Abbaye What used to be an old mill on a gentle bend in the Dronne is now one of the region's most delightful hostelries. Its 16 rooms and four suites (elegantly furnished and decorated with French provincial fabrics) and the Louis XIII dining room, which opens onto a tree-shaded riverside terrace, contribute to the genteel luxury that characterizes this member of the Relais & Châteaux group. The menu—Michelin has awarded it one star—is an adroit blend of such up-to-date dishes as *dodine de barbue* (cold terrine of brill) and more traditional Périgord fare. Closed late October through April; restaurant also closed Monday lunch. 2 Bd. Charlemagne, Brantôme (phone: 53-05-80-22; fax: 53-05-75-27). Very expensive.

Chabrol This refined, comfortable hostelry overlooking the Dronne has 19 small-ish, recently redecorated rooms, some with river views. The restaurant offers a satisfying three-course meal in a wonderfully appointed dining room, also with a river view. Try the scallops with truffles, the squab, and for dessert, sweet Dordogne strawberries marinated in champagne. Closed February and mid-November to mid-December; restaurant also closed Sunday dinner and Mondays from October through June. 57 Rue Gambetta, Brantôme (phone: 53-05-70-15; fax: 53-05-71-85). Expensive.

Moulin du Roc On the verdant banks of the Dronne, this 17th-century walnut mill has been converted into a romantic, peaceful inn. The 10 guestrooms and four suites are furnished with period pieces and mini-bars. The cozy but elegant dining room and public rooms are decorated with antiques and objects from the old mill; there are two terraces for dining and lounging. Such imaginative specialties as warm foie gras in cabbage leaves and *pommes de terre aux truffes* (potatoes with truffles) have earned the place one Michelin star. The wine list features an extensive selection of fine Bordeaux. Closed mid-January to mid-February, and mid-November to mid-December; restaurant also closed Tuesdays. About 3½ miles (6 km) northeast of Brantôme, in Champagnac-de-Bélair (phone: 53-54-80-36; fax: 53-54-21-31). Expensive.

En Route from Brantôme Take D939 south for 16 miles (26 km) to Périgueux.

PÉRIGUEUX The capital of the Dordogne, this modern town in the center of the fertile Isle Valley is one of the oldest settlements in France. It retains ample evidence of its long and eventful history. During Gallo-Roman times Vesunna, as it was then called, was one of the most prosperous towns in Aquitaine. Remnants of the *Tour de Vésone*—a round temple dedicated to the deity for whom the settlement was named—and the ruins of the 20,000-capacity elliptical amphitheater can still be seen today. Vesunna was sacked by the Alemans in the 3rd century. During the Middle Ages the site was shared by two rival cities—Puy St-Front, a commercial and monastic center on the hill, and the nearby Cité, where the aristocrats lived. The two were reluctantly united under the name Périgueux in 1251, but it was some time before these bitter rivals reconciled their differences, coming together for the good of the country only during the Hundred Years War.

A good example of the early Périgord-Romanesque style is the *Eglise St-Etienne de la Cité* (Rue de la Cité), built in the 12th century and topped with four domes (two of which were destroyed during the Wars of Religion). The town's most arresting and curious sight, however, is the *Cathédrale St-Front* (12 Rue du Phantier), a sprawling Byzantine structure built in the shape of a Greek cross and crowned with five cupolas similar to those of *St. Mark's* in Venice. The church was completed in 1173. Visitors can see the cloisters (half Romanesque and half Gothic), the crypt, and confessionals. In summer you can walk around the domes of the cathedral roof, which affords an excellent view of the Puy-St-Front district (the Old Quarter). Back on ground level wander through the streets of Puy-St-Front to discover ruins of Renaissance mansions. One of the most appealing streets is Rue Limogeanne, where 15th- and 16th-century houses have been renovated by their owners. Other picturesque streets are Rue de la Clarté, Rue de la Sagesse, and those of the Quartier Sauvegard.

Well worth a leisurely visit is the *Musée du Périgord* (22 Cours Tourny; phone: 53-53-16-42). Its impressive collection features prehistoric objects from all over the world, including some found in the area. There are tools from the Paleolithic era, the skeleton of Chancelade man (late Paleolithic), and engraved bones and mammoth tusks. A Gallo-Roman gallery on the main floor displays pieces found during the excavation of the arena and the *Tour de Vésone,* including mosaic floors that once flanked an altar on which bulls were sacrificed. Other sections of the museum are devoted to the paintings and arts of the region, such as enamels. The museum is open from 10 AM to noon and 2 to 5 PM; closed Tuesdays; there is an admission charge.

There's a colorful local market Wednesday mornings in front of the cathedral and the public market at Place Coderc can be of interest on a busy day. Near the markets are plenty of unpretentious little restaurants in which to sample regional specialties. The city's tourist office is at 26 Pl. Francheville (phone: 53-53-10-63). Périgueux's regional tourist office, the *Comité Départemental du Tourisme* (16 Rue Wilson; phone: 53-53-44-35), organizes cooking classes and wine tastings (in French) from September through June, providing a real introduction to local tastes.

Two worthwhile side trips are possible from Périgueux. Follow D5 for 24 miles (38 km) northeast to the fine 17th-century palace at Hautefort, possibly the most handsome in Périgord. The château that stood on this spot in the 12th century belonged to the Born family, whose two sons, Bertran (of troubadour-knight fame) and Constantin, fought over the building. Though he had the support of Henry II of England, Bertran eventually lost the château to Constantin, whose ally was Richard the Lion-Hearted. Years later the property passed into the hands of the Gontaut family, who took the Hautefort name and crest and rebuilt the château during the early 1600s. Today it looks much as it did more than 350 years ago. Several important pieces—including 16th- and 17th-century tapestries and urns by the sculptor Torod—are on view. In the guard tower is a small museum dedicated to Eugène Le Roy, one of France's most respected authors, born here in 1836. The chapel contains 16th-century paintings on leather, the altar at which Charles X was crowned, and other noteworthy objects. The château is open daily; closed late November through mid-January. There is an admission charge (phone: 53-50-51-23). The château is surrounded by neatly manicured gardens and a 99-acre park. Down below, in the town, is a charity hospital and church built in the same style as the restored château. A gift to the village from the Marquis d'Hautefort, it was designed to house 33 sick people, one for every year of Christ's life.

Truffle fanatics will appreciate the *Ecomusée de la Truffe*, a small museum in Sorges (14 miles/22 km outside Périgueux) with exhibits lauding the prized black fungus. The museum is run by the *Syndicat d'Initiative*, which organizes truffle classes and walks to areas where the elusive delicacy can be found. The museum is closed during lunch hours, Mondays from September through May, the first two weeks of February, and holidays (phone: 53-05-90-11).

BEST EN ROUTE

Château de Lalande A magnificent 18th-century château in a large park. The 22 spacious rooms are tastefully appointed and comfortable, and the restaurant serves excellent regional cuisine. Closed mid-November through mid-March; restaurant also closed Wednesday lunch except in July and August. Six miles (10 km) southwest of Périgueux via N89, then D3E and D3 from Razac-sur-L'Isle (phone: 53-54-52-30; fax: 53-07-46-67). Expensive.

Château des Reynats This creamy-white, turreted château in its own park has 37 rooms, a restaurant, tennis courts, and a pool. It's also near the 18-hole *Golf Public du Périgord*. Restaurant closed Sunday dinner from October through March. In Chancelade, a few minutes out of town on D710 and D1 (phone: 53-03-53-59; fax: 53-03-44-84). Expensive.

L'Oison A one-Michelin-star dining room fills this old hosiery workroom near the cathedral. Specialties include fish grilled in olive oil and casserole-roasted veal. Closed Sunday dinner, Mondays, and two weeks each in February and July. Reservations advised. Major credit cards accepted. 31 Rue St-Front (phone: 53-09-84-02; fax: 53-03-27-94). Expensive.

Hôtel du Périgord Part of the Logis de France chain, this property has 20 rooms and a flower garden with a fish-stocked pond. Its restaurant specializes in regional and Spanish fare. Closed two weeks in February and late October through early November; from October through February the hotel is closed Fridays, and the restaurant is closed Sunday dinner and Saturdays. 74 Rue Victor-Hugo (phone: 53-53-33-63). Moderate.

Le Tournepiche In front of the cathedral, this 18th-century structure houses a rustic restaurant that serves regional fare under vaulted stone arches. Closed Sundays, Monday dinner, and the first week of January. Reservations advised. Major credit cards accepted. 2 Rue de la Nation (phone: 53-08-09-76). Moderate.

En Route from Périgueux Take D710 and D47 to Les Eyzies, 27 miles (43 km) southeast.

LES EYZIES-DE-TAYAC It was in the caves near this sleepy little village at the meeting of the Vézère and the Beune Valleys that evidence of one of man's most distant ancestors was found. There are at least a dozen grottoes and prehistoric sites in the vicinity of Les Eyzies, without question one of the areas in the world richest in vestiges of prehistory. Several of the caves, with their remarkable Paleolithic paintings, can be visited, but the number of visitors is strictly limited. For details on Les Eyzies, see *Memorable Museums and Monuments* in DIVERSIONS and call the tourist office (Pl. Mairie; phone: 53-06-97-05). The most interesting caves are usually closed Tuesdays and from mid-November to *Christmas*; there is an admission charge.

The *Musée National de la Préhistoire* (phone: 53-06-97-03), in the restored medieval castle of Tayac halfway up a cliff near Les Eyzies's main street, houses one of the world's most important collections of prehistoric tools and weapons, tombs, ornaments, and Cro-Magnon skeletons—with enough models and explanations to help you understand what you saw in the caves. It is open from 9:30 AM to noon and 2 to 5 PM from December through March; to 6 PM from April through November (with no lunchtime closing in July and August); closed Tuesdays year-round. There is an admission charge.

For an equine excursion, visit the *Equestre de la Baronie* (on D706 in nearby Tursac; phone: 53-06-93-83), a small family-run operation that arranges rides through the lovely countryside year-round. The horses and ponies are so gentle that even the most skittish rider will feel safe. Picnic lunches are provided for day trips.

BEST EN ROUTE

Le Centenaire At one end of the short main street is this sparkling member of the Relais & Châteaux group with 19 rooms and five suites. Amenities include a pool, sauna, and gym. The chef, Roland Mazère, also rents rooms in his own house high on a hill near the restaurant; his resolutely modern approach to cooking has won the place two stars from Michelin. Closed November through March; restaurant also closed Tuesday lunch (phone: 53-06-97-18; fax: 53-06-92-41). Very expensive.

Cro-Magnon It is speculated that this wonderful vine-covered inn stands where the Cro-Magnon skeletons were discovered in the 1860s. It clings to the side of massive, overhanging rocks and provides modern luxury and efficiency without forfeiting somnolent charm. There are 18 rooms and four suites, a pool, and extensive grounds. The one-Michelin-star kitchen can be counted on for classic traditional fare plus more adventurous dishes, such as *foie gras de canard au poivre* (duck foie gras with pepper) and a whole truffle baked in pastry. Closed mid-October through April; restaurant also closed Wednesday lunch except on holidays (phone: 53-06-97-06; fax: 53-06-95-45). Expensive.

En Route from Les Eyzies Take D706 north for 15 miles (24 km) to Montignac, above which are located the famous Lascaux Caves.

LASCAUX CAVES One of the greatest prehistoric finds in Europe, these caves contain magnificent friezes of bulls, horses, deer, and unicorn-like creatures, some larger than life and delicately shaded with black and red. The Paleolithic drawings are remarkable not only for their quantity but for their grace and lifelike quality. Carbon dating indicates that the caves were occupied about 15000 to 13000 BC, and it is thought that they were used for primitive rites and magic. The caves were discovered in the 1940s by four children attempting to rescue a dog that had fallen into a hole. They were open to the public for about 20 years, until it was realized that the atmospheric imbalance created in the small space by the carbon dioxide being exhaled by large numbers of visitors was causing bacteria to grow, which were gradually destroying the paintings. As a result, Lascaux was closed to the general public in 1963.

However, *Lascaux II,* an exact replica of the most interesting sections of the original, was created by artists from the *Ecole des Beaux-Arts* in Paris, who, inch by inch, copied the many hundreds of paintings occupying four chambers using the same vegetable dyes and oxides the original artists must have used. *Lascaux II* (phone: 53-53-44-35) is open daily from 9:30 AM to 7 PM in July and August; from 10 AM to noon and 2 to 5:30 PM except Mondays from September through December and February through June; closed January. Because of heavy visitor volume in July and August, tickets are sold at the "Point Information" booth in Montignac; follow the many signs marked *billets* or contact Montignac's *Syndicat d'Initiative* (Pl. Léo-Magne; phone: 53-51-82-60) for information. It's best to buy tickets early in the day. In the winter tickets are sold at the entrance to the cave. Entry price includes admission to *Le Thot,* in nearby Thonac, which offers a video presentation on prehistoric people and an exhibit on the construction and painting of *Lascaux II.*

BEST EN ROUTE

Château de Puy Robert A turreted storybook château in a wooded park, it has been converted into a deluxe hotel with 33 rooms and five suites, a pool, and a one-Michelin-star restaurant serving regional cuisine. The hotel is a member of the Relais & Châteaux group. Closed mid-October through early May; restaurant also closed Wednesday lunch. One mile (1.6 km) south of Montignac via D65 (phone: 53-51-92-13; fax: 53-51-80-11). Very expensive.

Soleil d'Or Set in a wonderful park, this hotel has 28 spacious rooms, four suites, a pool, and a restaurant (open to hotel guests only) that features *cuisine bourgeoise.* Closed Mondays, Sundays off-season, and mid-January to mid-February. 16 Rue du 4 Septembre, Montignac (phone: 53-51-80-22; fax: 53-50-27-54). Expensive.

En Route from the Lascaux Caves Take D704 south for about 15 miles (24 km) to Sarlat-la-Canéda, capital of Périgord-Noir.

SARLAT-LA-CANÉDA One of the best-preserved medieval and Renaissance towns in France, the city was a religious center from the 14th to the 18th century, which accounts in part for its fine architecture. Many of the old buildings are still standing, thanks to the efforts of Prosper Mérimée, an inspector of historic monuments during the last century. In recent years a plan to restore and safeguard Vieux (Old) Sarlat has been adopted by the city.

Rue de la République, a road lined with modern shops, unfortunately cuts right through the center of Vieux Sarlat. To enjoy the city to its fullest, park your car and then wander through the maze of curving streets and passageways. Start at the *Maison de La Boétie* (Pl. du Peyrou), the lovely Renaissance house in which Etienne de La Boétie, magistrate, poet, and close friend of the writer Montaigne, was born. Across the street is the 16th-century *Cathédrale St-Sacerdos,* which weds Romanesque and Gothic elements. Behind the cathedral, past the terraced garden, is the curious *Lanterne des Morts* (Lantern of the Dead), a 12th-century tower with a cone-shaped roof commemorating a miraculous healing performed here by St. Bernard in 1147. To the north on Rue Landry is the *Présidial* and its gardens; farther on are Rue de la Salamandre and the Place de la Liberté, which during July and August are transformed into open-air theaters where plays by Molière and Shakespeare are performed. On Rue des Consuls is the magnificent *Maison des Consuls,* built between the 14th and 17th centuries and now a restaurant. Colorful Wednesday and Saturday morning markets are held in the Place des Oies (also called the Place du Marché) and Place de la Liberté; there also are a number of shops selling foie gras, walnut oils, *cèpes,* and other Périgord delicacies.

The *Moulin de la Tour* in Sainte-Nathalène, 6 miles (10 km) northeast of Sarlat via D47, is a family-owned mill producing wonderful walnut and hazelnut oils (which should be refrigerated after opening); it is closed Sundays. Several foie gras factories can be visited in Sarlat, one of which offers a tasting. For details, consult the tourist office (Pl. de la Liberté; phone: 53-59-27-67), which is open from 9:30 AM to noon and 2 to 6:30 PM (to 5:30 PM in winter); closed Sundays. In the summer guided walking tours of Vieux Sarlat start at the Place de la Liberté (next to the tourist office) at 10:30 AM and 10 PM weekdays (check with the tourist office for hours of weekend tours).

From Sarlat take a short detour on D57 south to Beynac-et-Cazenac, another of the four feudal seats of the Périgord. The château here looms magnificently some 500 feet above the Dordogne, like an extension of the rock on which it was built. In the 12th century, during the continuing struggle between the Plantagenets and Capetians, Richard the Lion-Hearted gave the fortress on this site to his defender, the bloodthirsty Mercadier.

In 1214 it was demolished by the crusader Simon de Montfort, who over-ran much of the south of France. The castle was rebuilt by the Barons of Beynac in the early 13th century and added to from the 14th to the 17th century. Especially interesting are the 14th-century frescoes in a small ora-tory off the impressive state hall, where the nobility of the four baronies of Périgord met once a year. The panorama from the terrace here is superb: The sinuous course of the Dordogne seen below marked the dividing line in the struggles between the British and the French during the Hundred Years War. The restored château is open from March to mid-November; there is an admission charge (phone: 53-29-50-40).

On the river's opposite bank are *Fayrac Castle* (privately owned) and, beyond, the 12th-century *Château de Castelnaud,* once occupied by the English. *Castelnaud,* which is open to visitors, has been partly restored and offers a superb view of the Dordogne Valley far below. It is closed Saturdays from November through March (phone: 53-29-57-08).

A few miles southeast of Beynac and worth another detour is Domme, a well-preserved *bastide* (fortified town) on a rocky cliff with a panoramic view of the Dordogne Valley. Don't miss the well-preserved covered mar-ket and another spectacular view from the *Terrasse de la Barre.*

The *Manoir d'Eyrignac* (near Salignac, 8 miles/13 km northeast of Sarlat off D47; phone: 53-28-99-71) offers a splendid example of 18th-century French garden style. Completely restored to their original state by the cur-rent owners, the gardens are considered among the most beautiful in France. It is open daily; closed 12:30 to 2 PM from October through June; there is an admission charge.

BEST EN ROUTE

Domaine de Rochebois In a restored 19th-century house, this lovely new hotel has a great view of the countryside. The 34 spacious rooms and six suites are luxuriously decorated in traditional style; there is a health center and sauna. Ask for a room overlooking the park. The restaurant serves regional cui-sine. Closed December through March. In Vitrac, 6 miles (10 km) south of Sarlat via D46 (phone: 53-31-52-52; fax: 53-29-36-88). Very expensive.

Hostellerie Meysset An ivy-covered manor house, it has 23 rooms, three suites, and a fine restaurant serving many duck dishes. Closed mid-October through April; restaurant also closed Wednesday lunch. North of Sarlat on Rte. des Eyzies in Argentouleau (phone: 53-59-08-29; fax: 53-28-47-61). Expensive.

La Hoirie This pleasant 15-room hotel occupies a Périgourdine house in a garden. It has a pool and a restaurant. Closed mid-November to mid-March. About 1½ miles (2 km) south of Sarlat on C1 (phone: 53-59-05-62; fax: 53-31-13-90). Moderate.

La Madeleine All 23 rooms in this distinguished and traditional hostelry are air conditioned. Among the well-prepared and -presented classic dishes served in the dining room are *magret à la bordelaise* (sliced duck breast, Bordeaux-style) and *confit de canard en pot au feu* (preserved duck). Make sure to leave room for the walnut cake. In high season guests are required to take breakfast and dinner at the hotel. Closed mid-November to mid-March; restaurant also closed Monday lunch. In Vieux Sarlat, at 1 Pl. Petite-Rigaudie (phone: 53-59-10-41; fax: 53-31-03-62). Moderate.

Le Relais Moussidière Designed to resemble an old stone farmhouse, this hotel has 35 quiet and comfortable rooms, a welcoming fireplace, a large pool, a patio, a breakfast room, and a restaurant that serves dinner only. Two miles (3 km) south of Sarlat via D46 and D57 toward Bergerac (phone: 53-28-28-74; fax: 53-28-25-11). Moderate.

En Route from Sarlat Seventeen miles (27 km) to the east via D704 and D703 is Souillac.

SOUILLAC Less sensational than Sarlat, Souillac grew up around a 12th-century Benedictine abbey. The monastery was sacked by the English during the Hundred Years War and by the Protestants during the Wars of Religion, then destroyed by fire in 1572. The surviving abbey church (Pl. de l'Abbaye) remains the town's main attraction. Its domed Romanesque-Byzantine style is similar, though on a much smaller scale, to that of the cathedral in Périgueux. Inside, the bas-reliefs of the prophet Isaiah and St. Joseph on either side of the doorway are noteworthy for their detail and sense of motion. Equally well executed is the bas-relief over the doorway, in which delicately chiseled scenes from the life of the monk Theophilus are framed by carvings of St. Peter and St. Benedict.

BEST EN ROUTE

La Vieille Auberge One of the nicest of several traditional inns near the center of old Souillac, it has 20 simply decorated rooms in the original building and 25 more down the street in an annex with a pool. In the kitchen, Robert Véril adds a delicate touch to such local classics as *émincé de pigeonneau aux figues* (squab with figs), *farandole de poissons* (an array of fish), and *chausson du "diamant noire"* (a truffle wrapped in foie gras and ham and baked in puff pastry). Closed Monday dinner and Tuesdays from November to *Easter*. Pl. de la Minoterie (phone: 65-32-79-43; fax: 65-32-65-19). Moderate.

En Route from Souillac Take D23 southeast for 6 miles (10 km) to the caves at Lacave. Though less impressive in size and grandeur than those at the Gouffre de Padirac (see below), the stalagmites and stalactites here have a more delicate beauty. It doesn't take much imagination to see the shapes of small people and animals in these fine crystalline deposits. Most intriguing is the *Salle du Lac* (Lake Chamber), which is suffused with the natural, dim, purple-white fluorescence of the still-growing formations.

BEST EN ROUTE

Château de la Treyne In a lovely 17th-century château, this luxurious inn, with 12 beautifully furnished rooms and one suite, sits on the edge of a cliff, attached to a 120-acre private park with a pool, tennis courts, and a sauna. The restaurant, which has a terrace garden, features such classic dishes as *magret de canard au vin* (duck breast cooked in wine). Closed mid-November to *Easter;* restaurant also closed Tuesday and Wednesday lunch. Two miles (3 km) west of Lacave via D43 (phone: 65-32-66-66; fax: 65-37-06-57). Very expensive.

Le Pont de l'Ouysse Close to the *Château de la Treyne* (above), this establishment offers 12 cheerfully decorated rooms and one suite, with breakfast served in the garden if weather permits. The one-Michelin-star restaurant features a good but pricey à la carte menu. Specialties include foie gras and *magret de canard.* Closed January and February; restaurant also closed Mondays except for dinner in summer. Lacave (phone: 65-37-87-04; fax: 65-32-77-41). Very expensive.

En Route from Lacave Continue southeast to Rocamadour, 7 miles (11 km) farther on D247.

ROCAMADOUR The first glimpse of Rocamadour from the L'Hospitalet road across the Alzou Canyon is unforgettable, particularly if you arrive in the morning, when the sun shines on the rugged face of the cliff to which this village of medieval dwellings, towers, chapels, and ramparts clings. Rocamadour has steadfastly occupied this rock for centuries, having been an important pilgrimage site for more than 800 years. For a detailed description of the village, see *Memorable Museums and Monuments* in DIVERSIONS. A well-known market featuring mainly goat cheese is held annually on *Pentecost Sunday* in the center of town.

BEST EN ROUTE

Château de Roumégouse This lovely Gothic-Renaissance château, a member of the Relais & Châteaux group, has 14 luxurious rooms, two suites, and a restaurant. Ideal for those who appreciate elegance and isolation, it's in a wooded park and provides magnificent views of the Causse foothills. Closed November through mid-April; restaurant also closed Tuesday lunch. Off N140 in Rignac, 9 miles (14 km) from Rocamadour (phone: 65-33-63-81; fax: 65-33-71-18). Very expensive.

Domaine de la Rhue In the former outbuildings of a private château, this luxurious hotel has huge rooms with beamed ceilings, a pool, and its own park.

There is no restaurant. Closed November to *Easter*. MasterCard and Visa accepted. Off N140, 4 miles (6 km) north of Rocamadour (phone: 65-33-71-50; fax: 65-33-72-48). Expensive.

Beau Site et Notre-Dame Wedged between souvenir stands on the sloping main street, the distinguished façade of this venerable 42-room, two-suite establishment offers a warm welcome to the modern pilgrim. The restaurant, *Jehan de Valon,* features a terrace with a beautiful view. Closed mid-November to mid-February and the last two weeks of March. Rue Roland-le-Preux (phone: 65-33-63-08; fax: 65-33-65-23). Moderate.

En Route from Rocamadour Take D673 and D90 northeast for 9 miles (14 km) to the famous Gouffre de Padirac.

GOUFFRE DE PADIRAC (PADIRAC CHASM) One of nature's more dramatic feats in the region, this series of underground caverns dug out over the centuries by an underground river is adorned with fascinating limestone concretions. Start your journey by descending into the gaping hole 325 feet across and 328 feet deep, the natural entrance to this surreal belowground world. Part of the journey is accomplished by boat on the cool, clear river, part on foot up, down, and around the intriguing stalagmites and stalactites. Note that the tour is 1¼ miles (2 km) long—only a third by boat—and that the climbing is at times strenuous. The most impressive features of the chasm are the *Grande Pendeloque* (Great Pendant), a giant stalactite overhanging and nearly touching the river's surface, and the *Salle du Grande Dome* (Hall of the Great Dome), which, at 250 feet high, is the largest and most beautiful of Padirac's chambers.

Superstition surrounds this awesome natural phenomenon. According to legend, the great gaping hole in the earth was the work of the devil: It's said to have been the site of a showdown between St. Martin, returning from an excursion in search of souls to save, and Satan, who was toting a sack of souls condemned to hell. Satan offered St. Martin a deal: He would surrender the doomed souls if the holy man could make his reluctant mule cross an obstacle created by the devil. An agreement was struck, the devil stamped the earth with his hoof, and the great chasm yawned open. When St. Martin's mule heroically jumped clear of the hole, Satan was forced to give up the souls. He retreated to hell through the mouth of the chasm.

En Route from Padirac Head back on D90 and D673 to N140 and follow it southeast to Figeac, 26 miles (42 km) from the intersection of D673 with N140. Figeac is the site of one of the region's newer museums, the *Musée Champollion* (Impasse Champollion; phone: 65-34-66-18). Containing Egyptian artifacts, it is in the house where the French Egyptologist Jean-François Champollion was born. The museum is closed Mondays; there is an admission charge.

From Figeac, Cahors is 43 miles (69 km) west via D13 and D653.

CAHORS South of the Dordogne Valley in a deep loop of the Lot River is Cahors, one of the main gateways to southern France. It is most famous for the red wine made from the grapes grown on the hills along the Lot, west of the city. For more details on the wine of Cahors, see *Most Visitable Vineyards* in DIVERSIONS.

First known as Divona Cadurcorum and later Cadurca, the city grew prosperous under the Gauls and the Romans, acquiring the requisite forum, theater, baths, and temples. By the early Middle Ages Cahors was an important commercial and university center, but it reached its zenith in the 13th century, when an influx of Lombard merchants and bankers earned it a reputation as the first banking city in Europe. The Lombard firms, known for their business acumen and their usurious lending habits, soon made Cahors world famous. The city's fortunes fell during the Hundred Years War, however, and eventually wine production replaced banking as its chief industry.

Cahors's two most compelling sights are the Pont Valentré and the Romanesque *Cathédrale St-Etienne*. The first, one of the few surviving examples of a medieval fortified bridge, is still used. Its three crenelated towers rise to 130 feet; its narrow gateways allow only one vehicle to pass at a time. The best view of this proud, unusual structure is from the right bank of the Lot, slightly upstream. It is particularly impressive when lighted at night. The *Cathédrale St-Etienne,* in the old part of town, dates from the 11th century, when Bishop Géraud of Cardaillac began building here on the site of a 6th-century church. Particularly noteworthy is the north door, an intricate, Romanesque carving of the Ascension executed about 1140.

The Cahors tourist office (Pl. A.-Briand; phone: 65-35-09-56) provides a map that outlines a pleasant walking tour of the old part of the city. It takes visitors past such medieval and Renaissance structures as the late-15th-century *Roaldès Mansion* (Quai Champollion), with crooked timberwork on one side and a rose window and mullioned doors and windows on the other. The mansion is open in July and August only. Also of interest is the *Musée Municipal* (Rue Emile-Zola; phone: 65-30-15-13); housed in a former episcopal palace, its collection includes a Roman sarcophagus, 15th- and 16th-century sculpture, and mementos of Cahors's most famous sons, including Pope John XXII, French magistrate Léon Gambetta, and the 16th-century writer Clément Marot. For details on closing dates, contact the tourist office (see above); there is an admission charge. A wonderful foie gras and truffle market is held on Saturday mornings from November to March in the Allées Fénelon.

BEST EN ROUTE

Château de Mercuès In a turreted 12th-century castle perched above the Lot River, this member of the Relais & Châteaux group has 25 rooms, six luxury suites, tennis courts, and a pool. The excellent (albeit overpriced) restaurant offers commanding views. Closed November through March. Six miles (10 km) north of Cahors via N20 and D911, in Mercuès (phone: 65-20-00-01; fax: 65-20-05-72). Very expensive.

Marco In an old vine-covered house, this one-Michelin-star restaurant serves local cuisine, with a focus on foie gras and truffles. The wine list is something to write home about, boasting everything from a rare Cahors to a superb 1983 Domaine Eugénie. As we went to press, guestrooms are being constructed around the new swimming pool located next to the restaurant. Closed Sunday dinner and Mondays off-season, January through early March, and late October through early November. Reservations necessary. Major credit cards accepted. Five miles (8 km) from Cahors via D653, in Lamagdelaine (phone: 65-35-30-64). Expensive.

Terminus With lovely stained glass windows dating from the early part of this century, this traditional hotel has 31 clean, bright rooms. The restaurant, *Le Balandre*, is one of the best in town; it serves nouvelle fare, and its cellar is well stocked with fine Cahors wines. The owners are particularly friendly and helpful. Restaurant closed Sunday dinner and Mondays (except in summer), two weeks in January, and the first two weeks of July. Across from the train station, at 5 Av. Charles-de-Freycinet (phone: 65-35-24-50; fax: 65-22-06-40). Moderate.

En Route from Cahors Wander along the course of the Lot River east of Cahors via D653 and D662 to St-Cirq-Lapopie, 18 miles (29 km) away.

ST-CIRQ-LAPOPIE Dominated by a 15th-century church, this picturesque village (pop. 200) sits precariously atop a rocky escarpment, high above the meandering river. Though tiny, the village is not short on historical interest. This cliff site, a natural stronghold for the valleys below, was long a source of strife. In the 8th century it was the site of the Duke of Aquitaine's last stand against Pepin the Short; in 1198 Richard the Lion-Hearted unsuccessfully attempted to seize it. St-Cirq was contested fiercely by the British and French during the Hundred Years War and by the Huguenots during the Wars of Religion, and both Louis XI (in 1471) and Henri de Navarre (1580) ordered the strategic castle destroyed. What remains of it sits at the highest point of the cliff (accessible by a dirt path), from which there is an inspiring view of the surrounding terrain. Many of the half-timbered and stone houses of the village, located on steep lanes (which are closed to traffic during the summer months), are inhabited by artisans.

BEST EN ROUTE

Auberge du Sombral In this comfortable little inn are eight rooms furnished in a delightful country style. The restaurant features regional cuisine. Closed mid-November through March; restaurant also closed Tuesdays and

Wednesdays. MasterCard and Visa accepted. On one corner of the sleepy central square (phone: 65-31-26-08). Moderate.

La Pélissaria This lovely 13th-century house has five rooms and two suites with whitewashed walls, exposed beams, and hand-turned wooden furniture. All rooms (including the restaurant) have views of the garden, the village, or the Lot with its limestone cliffs. The restaurant (open for dinner only) serves good regional fare. Closed mid-November to mid-April; restaurant also closed Thursdays. MasterCard and Visa accepted (phone: 65-31-25-14). Moderate.

En Route from St-Cirq-Lapopie A well-marked route on tiny back roads leads to the vast underground cave at Pech-Merle, a few minutes away.

GROTTE DU PECH-MERLE Near the village of Cabrerets, these grottoes were inhabited by a prehistoric people some 20,000 years ago. They were discovered in 1922, when two boys happened to venture into the huge chambers. They found what you still can see today: marvelous and mysterious prehistoric paintings and weirdly beautiful stalagmites and stalactites. In the *Galerie des Peintures* are stunning spotted horses and silhouetted handprints; in the *Salles des Hiéroglyphes,* the outlines of feminine forms are vaguely visible on the cave's low clay roof. Nearby are the footprints of primitive humans, petrified in the calcite-rich clay of the cave floor. The *Salle des Disques* contains strange, slanted disk-shaped formations whose origins remain a mystery to scientists. In the *Salle de la Colonne Brisée* (Hall of the Broken Column) is a frieze of mammoths and bison believed to date from the Aurignacian age. The price of admission to this, one of the most intriguing of France's many grottoes, entitles the visitor to view a film before entering the cave and to visit the adjoining *Musée de Préhistoire Abbé-Lemozi* (phone: 65-31-27-05), where more prehistoric artifacts are on view. Open daily from April through November.

En Route from the Grotte du Pech-Merle Return to Cahors; then drive west along the picturesque wine route (marked "La Route du Vin de Cahors") and north on D710. Scattered through this area south of Bergerac are a number of *bastides,* small feudal fortress towns constructed in the 13th century by the French and the English when both countries claimed sovereignty over the region. Monpazier, on D660, is perhaps the best-preserved *bastide* in France. Built by the English in 1284, it features a layout common to most *bastides,* with streets arranged in a grid and alleys between the houses to form firebreaks. The central square and covered market are flanked by vaulted arcades and surrounded by houses, some with lovely Gothic bays. Nearby is the *Eglise St-Dominique* and the 13th-century *Maison du Chapitre* (Chapter House). Three of the six gates to the village remain, protected by towers set in the ramparts. Other *bastides* of interest are at

Lalinde, Villeneuve-sur-Lot, Villeréal, Puylaroque, Sauveterre de Guyenne, Domme, and Villefranche-du-Périgord.

From Monpazier, continue on D660 to Bergerac, 27 miles (43 km) to the northwest.

BERGERAC The name of this viticultural and tobacco center will be familiar to lovers of wine and literature. The hills nearby produce fine dry Bergerac reds and a sweet, white Monbazillac, a perfect companion to foie gras. On the Place de la Myrpe a statue of playwright Edmond Rostand's immortal hero, Cyrano de Bergerac, marks the town's literary connection.

Tobacco has helped make Bergerac prosperous, so it's fitting that it should have the only tobacco museum in France. In the old part of town, the *Musée du Tabac* (10 Rue Ancien Pont; phone: 53-63-04-13) has several displays and exhibits on the history of the plant, how it's produced, and how it's consumed. The museum is open from 10 AM to noon and 2 to 6 PM; closed Mondays; there is an admission charge. Next door is a small municipal museum with prehistoric items, the works of Bergerac painters, and a section on local history.

Near the tobacco museum is the *Couvent des Récollets* (Monastery of the Recollects), a cloister built between the 12th and 17th centuries. A few doors away is the *Maison du Vin* (2 Pl. du Docteur-Cayla; phone: 53-57-12-57), a small museum with exhibits on the region's wines. The museum is open 10 AM to noon and 2 to 5:30 PM, Tuesdays through Fridays; 10 AM to noon on Saturdays; and 2 to 6:30 PM on Sundays. It is closed Mondays; there is no admission charge.

The *Eglise Notre-Dame,* built in the 19th century in imitation Gothic style, has two Italian paintings from the early Renaissance and an immense Aubusson tapestry depicting the Bergerac coat of arms.

BEST EN ROUTE

Auberge de la Devinière This quiet inn in a large park has seven rooms and one suite, a pool, and a restaurant featuring regional cuisine. Closed the first two weeks in March and the last two in October; restaurant also closed November through March and Sunday dinner and Mondays except in summer. In Mussidan, 7 miles (11 km) north of Bergerac via D709 and D15 (phone: 53-81-66-43; fax: 53-81-54-44). Expensive.

Manoir Le Grand Vignoble An elegant, quiet establishment whose 44 rooms are exquisitely appointed (except those in the thoroughly modern annex). Horseback riding, tennis courts, a heated pool, and a putting green are on the premises, along with a restaurant. An equestrian camp for children and teenagers is held here in July and August. Closed late December to mid-January; restaurant also closed Sunday dinner and Mondays from November through March. Seven miles (11 km) north of Bergerac via N21 and D107, in St-Julien-de-Crempse (phone: 53-24-23-18; fax: 53-24-20-89). Expensive.

Le Cyrano In this charming spot are 11 simple guestrooms. The restaurant focuses on classics of the area like *escalope de foie chaud de canard grillotin* (slices of hot duck liver) and, for dessert, *gratin de fruits rouges au sabayon de Monbazillac* (baked fruit in a warm custard sauce made with Monbazillac wine). Closed two weeks in June and one in December; restaurant also closed Sunday dinner and Mondays off-season. 2 Bd. Montaigne (phone: 53-57-02-76; fax: 53-57-78-15). Moderate.

En Route from Bergerac Take the scenic Route du Tabac (Tobacco Route; D13) for a 4-mile (6-km) detour south to the lovely *Château de Monbazillac* and vineyard.

CHÂTEAU DE MONBAZILLAC AND VINEYARD The reputation of Monbazillac wine goes back centuries: Legend has it that when a group from Bergerac made a pilgrimage to Rome in the Middle Ages, they were asked by the pope where their home was. "Near Monbazillac" was the reply, to which the pope is said to have responded with the benediction *"Bonum vinum."*

Built in about 1550, the small, gray stone château is a pleasing amalgam of fortified castle and Renaissance palace. The surrounding grounds are well kept, and the view of the Bergerac Valley below is superb. Today the nobly decorated château is owned by the Monbazillac wine cooperative. Following a tour, guests are invited to visit the 17th-century wine cellar, now a tasting room, to sample (and, if they wish, purchase) Bergerac and Monbazillac wines. Open weekdays year-round; there is an admission charge (phone: 53-57-06-38; fax: 53-63-01-62). The cooperative will ship cases of wine overseas. It also runs a small restaurant (open for lunch only) in what were once the stables.

BEST EN ROUTE

Château des Vigiers Elegance is the key at this château in a large park with 25 rooms, a pool, fly-fishing facilities, and a very good restaurant with inventive modern cuisine. Closed mid-November through March; restaurant also closed weekday lunch except on holidays. In Monestier, 16 miles (26 km) southwest of Bergerac via D936 and D4 (phone: 53-61-50-00; fax: 53-61-50-20). Expensive.

Hôtel du Château A pleasant seven-room hotel and restaurant has been created from a former prison, which you'd never guess given the elegant decor. The traditional restaurant has an excellent wine list; several guestrooms have stunning views of the Dordogne. There is a pool. Closed December through February; restaurant also closed Fridays. Fourteen miles (22 km) east of Bergerac via D660 and D703, Rue de la Tour, Lalinde (phone: 53-61-01-82). Expensive.

En Route from Monbazillac Follow the Dordogne along D660 east, D703 north, and D30 south for about 20 miles (32 km). Right outside Trémolat, at the crest of a hill, is a particularly arresting view of the Cingle de Trémolat, a wide loop in the Dordogne River that encircles a resplendent valley of walnut orchards and soft, flat fields sprinkled with flowers.

BEST EN ROUTE

Le Vieux Logis With 19 cozy rooms and five luxurious suites, this wonderful hotel with a one-Michelin-star restaurant really knows how to pamper its guests. For additional details, see *Romantic French Hostelries* in DIVERSIONS. Closed January through early February; restaurant also closed Wednesday lunch and Tuesdays off-season. Trémolat (phone: 53-22-80-06; fax: 53-22-84-89). Very expensive.

Gascony

Any reference to the province of Gascony—the land of d'Artagnan and the musketeers, Henri IV, the troubadours, and Blaise de Monluc—is likely to conjure up vivid and romantic images. It was part of the province of Aquitaine, which was keenly contested and controlled alternately by the French and the English during the Middle Ages. Gascony also is the source of some of France's best-loved dishes, including cassoulet (a casserole of beans and meat); foie gras; *garbure* (a thick vegetable soup); *tourin* (garlic soup); duck and goose prepared in a variety of ways, including *confit* (preserved) and *magret* (sliced and grilled); and succulent game birds in heady dark sauces. And to add the finishing touch to a Gascon meal, there's armagnac, the fiery brandy dubbed "the soul of Gascony."

In the heart of France's southwest, Gascony, a historical rather than an official appellation, today does not have strict boundaries. It generally is considered to take up the modern *départements* of the Gers and the Landes, bordered to the north by the mighty Garonne River and to the east by Toulouse, extending south into the foothills of the Pyrénées and west to the Golfe de Gascogne (Bay of Biscay) on the Atlantic coast.

The region is one of physical contrasts: The Gers is characterized by scenic rolling hills dotted with villages, vineyards, and neat fields of sunflowers and wheat. The Landes, to the west and northwest, is a flat, sandy expanse of sparsely settled land, a full two thirds of it a vast manmade forest. The two *départements* meet in an area abundant in agricultural produce.

When Roman armies penetrated these areas half a century before Christ, they found a number of independent settlements whose inhabitants shared physical characteristics and a language more closely related to those of the Basques in the Pyrénées than to those of the peoples in the rest of Gaul. The region prospered under Roman rule, as evidenced by remnants of Gallo-Roman villas, particularly those unearthed in Séviac, near Montréal.

The Vandals invaded in the early 5th century, and the Visigoths moved in around 418, only to be superseded after 507 by the Franks. Around the beginning of the 7th century the Basques moved north from their base in the Spanish Pyrénées, penetrating Gascony and reinforcing cultural similarities.

By the 10th century Gascony had become almost totally independent, but in 1052 the Count of Armagnac was forced to cede his realm to the Duke of Aquitaine. One hundred years later Gascony was included in the dowry that Eleanor of Aquitaine presented to her second husband, Henry Plantagenet, heir to the English crown, and in 1154, when he ascended to the throne, Gascony became part of England. For the next 300 years Gascony and its neighbors to the north and west suffered continuous turmoil as the

French and English battled for sovereignty. Several *bastides* (fortified villages) constructed by the opposing kings during this period still stand; particularly interesting are the remnants of these fortifications at Fourcès (near Montréal), Beaumarchés, Marciac, and Bassoues (near Plaisance). Around the middle of the 14th century the Counts of Armagnac regained control of their lands, and for a time, under Bernard VII, Gascony's soldiers controlled almost the whole of France. But the area once again was plunged into bitter conflict during the Wars of Religion. Thanks to Jeanne d'Albret, mother of Henri de Navarre (the future King Henri IV), Nérac, in the north of Gascony, became an important Protestant stronghold and a frequent target of the Catholics. (She, and later her son, held court there.) It was only in 1589, when Henri ascended to the French throne, that peace returned to the area, and in 1607 the lands of the Counts of Armagnac were incorporated into the royal domain under Henri's rule.

The Gascons did not, however, forfeit their independent spirit to the French kingdom. The region's individuality lives on today, embodied by the legendary d'Artagnan, certainly Gascony's most famous native son. Born Charles de Batz around 1615 near Auch, d'Artagnan (who assumed his mother's family name) gained the confidence of Louis XIII, eventually winning appointment, under Louis XIV, as the first marshal of the king's company of musketeers, that gallant band of men whose swashbuckling exploits were immortalized (and certainly embellished) by Alexandre Dumas in *The Three Musketeers.*

Though Gascony frequently is overlooked by both travel guides and tourists, the region has a serendipitous appeal. Its subtle attractions—narrow, tree-lined roads winding through sunflower-dotted landscapes; calm, inviting lakes; crumbling stone fortifications; and arcaded town squares—seem to exist in a land forgotten by time.

Gascon cuisine also is reminiscent of another time, when portions were generous, food hearty and satisfying, and prices reasonable. The region is rich in family-run inns, where the quality of food is outdone only by the characteristic warmth of the Gascon welcome. The Gascons are serious about their food, a fact exemplified by an organization of chefs, *La Ronde des Mousquetaires,* whose members meet frequently at each other's establishments to share ideas, camaraderie, and—most important—fine cuisine. Food lovers will find guidance in a small paperback entitled *Le Guide Gascogne* (The Gascony Guide), available in most bookshops in the region; it lists undiscovered, out-of-the-way places of particularly good value.

This tour route starts in Auch, at the heart of the Gers; it then moves north to Lectoure and on to Condom, the center of armagnac production. It continues west through the southern edge of the pine forests of the Landes, then over to the Golfe du Gascogne and the seaside resorts of Hossegor and Capbreton.

Accommodations in Gascony range from the very expensive, where rooms are $120 or more a night for two; to expensive, about $85 to $120;

to moderate, from $45 to $85; to the bargain inns, where an inexpensive room is less than $45. Unless otherwise indicated, all hotels accept major credit cards and are open year-round. Most hotels feature telephones, private baths, and (less frequently) TV sets in their rooms. Some less expensive hotels may have private baths in only some of their rooms; it's a good idea to confirm whether your room has a private bath when making a reservation. Very few hotels in the region have air conditioning. Dinner for two with service (usually already included in the bill) at a very expensive restaurant will cost more than $150; at an expensive restaurant, from $85 to $150; at a moderate place, $55 to $85; and at an inexpensive spot, less than $55. Prices do not include wine or drinks. Unless otherwise noted, all restaurants listed below are open for lunch and dinner. For each location, hotels and restaurants are listed alphabetically by price category.

AUCH (pronounced *Osh*) The administrative capital of the Gers, Auch is a lively market center on the banks of the Gers River. Its Vieille Ville (Old Town) sits on a hill, grouped around the majestic, 15th- to 17th-century pale ocher cathedral that dominates the horizon for miles around.

People lived on this hill long before the arrival of Roman troops in the middle of the 1st century BC. It became an important Roman town called Augusta Auscorum, a crossroads on the busy route from Toulouse to the Atlantic, and has continued to play a key role in the life and commerce of the region.

Auch is d'Artagnan's hometown, and it pays homage to its valiant musketeer with a swashbuckling statue perched midway up the monumental 370-step staircase that connects the lower, newer town to the high ground on which the Old Town sits. At the top of the staircase is the serene, tree-shaded Place Salinis, overlooking the valley of the Gers and the rooftops of the ever-expanding modern part of town. Nearby rises the 14th-century *Tour d'Armagnac,* formerly a prison; it's not open to the public. In the same vicinity picturesque narrow lanes wind steeply down the hill to the Gers past crooked structures dating from the Middle Ages.

More antiquities, such as the intriguing 15th-century structure that houses the tourist office (Pl. Cathédrale, phone: 62-05-22-89; fax: 62-05-92-04), line Rue Dessoles, a lively pedestrian street that begins at Place Cathédral. On Saturday mornings this square is transformed into a colorful open-air market. On the north side of the square is the prefecture, housed in a superb yellow brick, 18th-century structure that once was the archbishop's residence (it's not open to the public). Also of interest is the *Musée des Jacobins* (Pl. Louis-Blanc; phone: 62-05-74-79), a former priory now housing a somewhat eclectic collection that includes Gascon furniture, old porcelain, a sizable grouping of pre-Columbian pieces, and the haunting works of a local turn-of-the-century painter, Jean-Louis Rouméguère. It's closed during lunch hours, Mondays, and holidays. The *Maison de Gascogne* (Pl. Jean-David; phone: 62-05-12-08) exhibits and sells regional foods and drinks, art, and crafts. It's open daily (closed lunch hours) in July and August; hours vary depending on individual exhibitions the rest of the year.

Auch's most precious treasures, however, are found inside the *Cathédrale Ste-Marie*. Construction of this magnificent work was started in 1489 but was not completed until the 17th century. The Renaissance windows of the Gascon painter Arnaud de Moles are remarkable for their vivid colors and the strikingly expressive, caricature-like faces of the elaborately clothed figures. Equally awesome are the 113 intricately carved choir stalls bearing more than 1,500 different figures.

The city's annual *Festival de Musique* includes classical concerts performed in the cathedral in June. The cathedral is also the location for *Les Lumières du Ciel,* a son-et-lumière performance shown Wednesday and Saturday evenings at 9:30 during July and August. *Gascogne Expo,* a three-day agricultural fair, takes place the last week of September.

BEST EN ROUTE

France The domain of the Daguin family since 1884, this venerable hostelry, a member of the Relais & Châteaux group, sits like a duchess surveying the activity of the square below. It is a lively meeting place for those drawn by the renown of its superb restaurant, *André Daquin,* perhaps the best reason for an extended stay. The eponymous owner of this restaurant and founder of *La Ronde des Mousquetaires* is one of Gascony's most beloved and lauded chefs. His two Michelin stars are well earned, though there have been complaints that, though undeniably excellent, the food is no longer up to its former dazzling perfection. Dinner in the lush dining room, at once grand and homey, is a memorable experience, as is the array of culinary delights, such as *gratin d'huîtres au magret fumé* (breaded oysters with smoked duck breast) and inventive creations using foie gras. The hotel's 27 rooms and two suites, each individually decorated, have old-fashioned charm. Closed the first two weeks in January; restaurant also closed Sunday dinner and Mondays, except from mid-July through mid-September. 2 Pl. de la Libération (phone: 62-61-71-84; fax: 62-61-71-81). Very expensive.

Château de Larroque Set in a park, this stately member of the Relais & Châteaux group has 15 pleasant rooms, a nine-hole golf course, tennis courts, a pool, a serene terrace overlooking the gentle hills of Gascony, and a well-regarded restaurant. Closed late January to late February. Fifteen miles (24 km) east of Auch via N124, Rte. de Toulouse, in Gimont (phone: 62-67-77-44; fax: 62-67-88-90). Expensive.

Claude Laffitte This cozy restaurant offers regional character and a fine selection of well-prepared Gascon specialties such as *salmis de palombes* (pigeon stew) and an exceptional *croustade du Bas-Armagnac* (thin pastry laced with prunes and armagnac). Dine downstairs in the bistro atmosphere or upstairs amid wooden beams and flowers. Closed Sunday dinner and Mondays. Reservations advised. Major credit cards accepted. Near the cathedral, at 38 Rue Dessoles (phone: 62-05-04-18; fax: 62-05-93-83). Moderate.

Relais de Gascogne A modern hotel in the lower town, it has 38 comfortable rooms. There also is a restaurant and parking. Closed late December through January. 5 Av. de la Marne (phone: 62-05-26-81; fax: 62-63-30-22). Moderate.

En Route from Auch To get the flavor of the Gascon countryside, take N124 west toward Condom; after about 3 miles (5 km), take D930 north, a pleasant tree-lined route that winds over verdant hills and dales on the way to Castéra-Verduzan.

CASTÉRA-VERDUZAN The therapeutic properties of this town's two natural mineral springs were appreciated even in Roman times: The 4th-century author Flavius Vegetius Renatus wrote about the Roman camp here called Castéra-Vivant. The Counts of Armagnac and French royalty also came to take the cure, but today this quaint village (pop. 800) seems to have been passed up for more dramatic attractions. It's worth a stop, if only to take the waters; a visit to the pavilion housing *Les Thermes* (Rue Principale; phone: 62-68-13-41) provides a glimpse of what the world of spas is all about in France. The spa is closed during lunch hours and from November through May; only visitors taking the waters—that is, no sightseers—are allowed during the morning. There's no admission charge.

BEST EN ROUTE

Le Florida The dining rooms and shaded terrace are full of provincial charm, and the chef serves a wonderful combination of homey, traditional fare and dishes featuring his own contemporary style. Try the foie-gras-and-*confit*-laced Gascon salad or the impeccable *croustade de confit de canard à l'oignon* (sliced preserved duck with onions). Closed Sunday dinner and Mondays from October through March and Wednesdays from April through September. Reservations advised. Major credit cards accepted. Rue du Lac (phone: 62-68-13-22; fax: 62-68-10-44). Moderate.

Ténarèze Here are 24 modern, simple rooms. There's a bar but no restaurant, though *Le Florida* (see above) is run by the same family. Closed February. Av. de la Ténarèze (phone: 62-68-10-22; fax: 62-68-14-69). Inexpensive.

En Route from Castéra-Verduzan Take vineyard-flanked D42 north for 5 miles (8 km) to St-Puy, a tiny hillside village at the foot of *Château Monluc*.

This hill was lost and regained by the French four times during their battles with the English, and the châteaux that stood here were repeatedly destroyed and rebuilt. What remains today dates mostly from the 15th and 18th centuries, though part of the crumbling stone walls around it date from the 12th century. In the mid-16th century the château was the property of Blaise de Monluc, who fought fiercely against the Protestants during the Wars of Religion and later recorded his regret at having done so in his famous 1592 memoirs, *Commentaires*. Only part of *Château Monluc* is open to visitors, as it is now the home of M. and Mme. Lassus, producers of Monluc, a dry sparkling wine that is the base for the most Gascon of aperitifs, the *pousse-rapière* (sword's thrust), a mixture of sparkling wine and armagnac. The château is closed during lunch hours and on Sundays (phone: 62-28-55-02; fax: 62-28-55-70). The tour includes a visit to the cellars, where the wine is aged under the old vaulting of an earlier château, and a tasting of the wine and the *pousse-rapière*.

Continue on D42 about 12 miles (19 km) to Lectoure.

LECTOURE Even in this region so abundant in lofty villages, Lectoure (pop. 4,000) is noted for the stunning vistas it affords of the Gers Valley. On a clear day the Pyrénées can be seen in the distance from the lovely tree-shaded Promenade du Bastion, near the gardens of the *Hôtel de Ville* (Town Hall) and the tourist office (phone: 62-68-76-98; fax: 62-68-79-30), both on Place Hôtel de Ville. This town was the home of the Counts of Armagnac (a hospital now stands on the ramparts of their château), and it later became an important episcopal seat. Numerous *hôtels particuliers* and religious structures in the region's characteristic pale yellow stone line the old streets; their scars bear witness to the town's stormy past. This was the site in 1473 of a terrible battle between the troops of Louis XI and those of Count Jean V, in which the latter was killed. The old cathedral, badly damaged during that siege, suffered more abuse during the Wars of Religion, and the remnants of the original spire were torn down in 1782. The oldest parts of the present cathedral, built in the Gothic style of the southwest, date from the 16th century.

Also of interest here is the *Musée Lapidaire Gallo-Romain* (Pl. Hôtel-de-Ville; phone: 62-68-76-98), which houses a famous collection of *tauroboles* (sacrificial altars emblazoned with bulls' heads and inscriptions), relics of the cult of Mithra. The Mesopotamian cult was adopted by the Greeks and the Romans some 2,300 years ago; these marble altars, on which bulls were sacrificed, are subsequent Roman imports to Gaul. Twenty of the 40 *tauroboles* known to exist in France are assembled here. The museum is open daily.

En Route from Lectoure Take D7 west for 15 miles (24 km) to Condom.

CONDOM Set on a hill above the Baïse River, Condom (pop. 7,800) is the capital of the Ténarèze, one of the three armagnac-producing areas in Gascony.

Among Condom's noteworthy structures is the 18th-century *Hôtel de Cugnac* (36 Rue Jean-Jaurès; phone: 62-28-08-08; fax: 62-28-16-42). Since 1905 it has been home to the *Maison Ryst-Dupeyron,* an armagnac producer that allows free visits to the *chai* (the storehouse for the armagnac) and acts as a local welcoming committee by arranging bus excursions for groups (individuals and couples should inquire anyway; there may be empty seats). The riverside quays here, in times past crowded with boats carrying armagnac to market in Bordeaux, are pleasant for a leisurely stroll, but the chief sight is the *Cathédrale St-Pierre.* Begun in the 14th century and rebuilt between 1507 and 1531, it is one of the most stunning examples of Flamboyant Gothic architecture in the French southwest. Particularly beautiful but badly eroded is the elaborate south doorway, with 24 statuettes; take a look, too, at the neo-Gothic choir enclosure, adorned in 1844 with magnificently delicate, almost lacy terra cotta figures of saints and angels. The tourist office is across the street from the cathedral (Pl. Bossuet; phone/fax: 62-28-00-80).

Also interesting is the *Musée de l'Armagnac* (2 Rue Jules-Ferry; phone: 62-28-31-41), which displays antique tools and equipment used in the production of the brandy. It's open daily (except during lunch hours) from June through August; the rest of the year by appointment only. There's an admission charge.

Condom is an excellent base for excursions into the surrounding countryside, particularly rich in antiquities. Five miles (8 km) south of town on D930 is the 12th-century Cistercian *Abbaye de Flaran.* Set back from the road in an isolated, tranquil spot near the confluence of the Baïse and Auloue Rivers, the abbey is an important testament to the intense religious activity in the region in the 12th and 13th centuries. The complex consists of a predominantly Romanesque church of warm ocher stone, a small, elegant 14th-century cloister, and an adjoining renovated 18th-century refectory. The cloister houses an exhibit on the pilgrimage routes to Santiago de Compostela, Spain, which, in passing through Gascony, included a stop here. Special changing exhibits are mounted in the refectory. Particularly lovely is the small chapel beside the cloister; it has a low, vaulted ceiling and columns of the black, red, and white marble of the Pyrénées. Damaged during the Wars of Religion, the abbey is now owned by the *département* of the Gers, which has made it the best-preserved in southwest France. The abbey is open daily in the summer; closed Tuesdays from September through June (phone: 62-28-50-19).

From the abbey, take D142 northwest for about 2 miles (3 km) to *Château Cassaigne,* once the retreat of the Bishops of Condom. Life in the Condom area revolves around increasingly popular armagnac, and this château is one of the most congenial places in which to taste and learn about it. First built in 1247, the original structure was renovated at various periods, and it retains architectural features of each. The thick-walled stone *cave* (cellar) where the armagnac is aged dates from the 13th century; the intriguing kitchen, whose vaulted ceiling was constructed like a bread oven, is from the 16th century; and the classic Renaissance façade is from the 18th century. The Gascon warrior Blaise de Monluc (from nearby *Château Monluc*) secured the Bishopric of Condom—and with it *Château Cassaigne*—for his son after the latter's heroism during the siege of Malta. Monluc came to his son's château to recuperate and write his memoirs after being injured in the Siege of Rabastens. One room is devoted to old documents of the bishops and other residents of the château, another to the explanation of local viticulture. If you are lucky enough to see Henri Faget, an armagnac producer and the present owner of the château, your visit will be enriched by this lively Gascon's evocative account of the history of the region and of the brandy. The château is open daily, except during lunch hours (phone: 62-28-04-02; fax: 62-28-41-43).

Return to Condom on D208 and D931.

BEST EN ROUTE

Trois Lys In this 18th-century mansion are 10 rooms, each individually decorated in keeping with that period. There's also a pool, a bar, a terrace, and parking. The brasserie menu changes daily, or, if you request in advance, the proprietors will arrange for you to dine with them (at separate tables). In the heart of Condom, at 38 Rue Gambetta (phone: 62-28-33-33; fax: 62-28-41-85). Expensive.

La Ferme de Flaran A former farm, this 15-room provincial inn offers a pool, a terrace, and a comfortable, rustic dining room serving regional cuisine. Closed January 9 through February 6; restaurant also closed Sunday dinner and Mondays from September through March. Five miles (8 km) south of Condom on D930, in Valence-sur-Baïse (phone: 62-28-58-22; fax: 62-28-56-89). Moderate.

Logis des Cordeliers A modern hotel with 21 simple rooms, 11 of them overlooking the pool and a serene walled garden. There's no restaurant, but breakfast is served. Closed January. 2 *bis* Rue de la Paix, just off Rue des Cordeliers (phone: 62-28-03-68; fax: 62-68-29-03). Moderate.

En Route from Condom Take D15 west for 3 miles (5 km) to Larressingle, perhaps the smallest fortified town in France. This dreamy, moat-encircled, 13th-century fortress overhanging the Osse Valley is another legacy of the Bishops of Condom, who built it as a lookout and haven for the barons of Armagnac traveling through the region. Inside its stone walls and arched gateway is a Romanesque church, an inn, a flower-filled courtyard, and pretty little houses that still are inhabited. The square-towered château affords a commanding view (it's not open to the public). The tourist office (phone: 62-28-33-76) is open in the summer only.

Continue another 6 miles (10 km) on D15 to Montréal.

MONTRÉAL One of the first *bastides* (fortified villages) in Gascony, Montréal was completed in 1289 by order of King Edward I of England. The *bastide* was almost completely destroyed during the French Revolution; today only the ruins of the *Eglise St-Pierre-de-Genens,* the ramparts, and one fortified gate remain.

Montréal makes an ideal base for several interesting side trips. Take D29 southwest toward Eauze; turn right at the sign for Séviac, the site of an important Gallo-Roman settlement that stood on this plateau some 18 centuries ago. Séviac's real treasures—its colorful, detailed mosaics—were discovered in 1868; in 1911 further digs unearthed marble columns and the remnants of luxurious public baths. Today you can walk through the ruins, tracing the layout of an opulent villa from its vast inner courtyard to the residential apartments, which reveal vestiges of an underground heating system, and on to the public areas and pools. Throughout, you'll see rich and varied mosaic designs. Tours of the ruins can be arranged in Montréal through the tourist office, which is open daily in summer (phone: 62-29-42-85), or the *mairie* (Town Hall; phone: 62-29-43-10); both are on the Place de l'Hôtel de Ville.

Only 3 miles (5 km) north of Montréal, along the Auzoue River, is Fourcès, another English *bastide.* It was founded in the mid-1200s by English King Edward I as a small and sturdy defense against the attempts of the French to regain their lost territory. All but forgotten in past decades and threatened with destruction by modern developers, Fourcès is now undergoing renovation. In addition to the lovely circular core, flanked by stone and typical split-timbered houses, there is a late 15th- to early 16th-century château (not open to the public) and a Gothic bridge.

BEST EN ROUTE

A La Belle Gasconne In the tiny town of Poudenas food lovers will find one of France's favorite chefs, Marie-Claude Gracia, at the stove of this quaint former wine cellar next to a mill. Such specialties as *salade de foie gras de canard chaud au vinaigre de prune* (salad of warm duck foie gras with plum sauce) and *civet de canard au Buzet* (duck stewed in the wine of nearby Buzet) have earned the place one Michelin star. The small mill next door contains six individually decorated rooms and one suite; there's also a pool. Closed the second week of December and January 2 through 31. Go north of Fourcès for about 5 miles (8 km) to Mézin, then west on D656 for about 2 miles (3 km) to Poudenas (phone: 53-65-71-58; fax: 53-65-87-39). Expensive.

La Gare Old railroad posters and train schedules adorn this delightful restaurant, ensconced in Montréal's old train station. It's a warm, amusing setting for such homey specialties as *garbure, tête de veau vinaigrette* (braised calf's head with vinaigrette sauce), and *poulet grillé à l'échalote* (grilled chicken with shallots). There also are five simple rooms, four in the station and one in the lampman's house. Closed Fridays. Two miles (3 km) south of town; take D29 and turn right at the railroad trestle (phone: 62-29-43-37; fax: 62-29-49-82). Inexpensive.

En Route from Montréal Take D29 south 9 miles (14 km) to Eauze, then D931 and N124 to Aire-sur-l'Adour, another 24 miles (38 km) away. This route skirts the northwest border of the Gers. For those who are *bastide* buffs, some of the region's finest examples lie to the southeast at Beaumarchés and Marciac (both along D935 and D3, between 20 miles/32 km and 27 miles/43 km east of Aire-sur-l'Adour) and at Bassoues (along D935, D3, then east on D946 at Beaumarchés, about 29 miles/46 km from Aire-sur-l'Adour). An international jazz festival is held in tiny Marciac during the second week of August. From Aire-sur-l'Adour take D2 southwest, then D11 north for 12 miles (19 km) to Eugénie-les-Bains, one of France's most famous spas.

EUGÉNIE-LES-BAINS This tiny village was named for Empress Eugénie, consort of Napoleon III, who came here frequently to take the waters. Its name has become world famous ever since Michel and Christine Guérard opened their elegant spa, *Les Prés d'Eugénie* (see *Best En Route,* below), here. There is not much of interest in the town itself, centered as it is around a short main street with only a few cafés and shops. The Guérards' *Les Prés,* however, is a destination in itself. More than any other in the area (and perhaps more than any in France), this establishment conforms to the American idea of a spa, offering not only therapeutic hot springs treatments but also a full range of modern amenities, including saunas, exercise equipment, mud baths, massages, weight-loss programs, and beauty treatments. The experience is definitely for those who like deluxe treatment and don't mind paying for it.

BEST EN ROUTE

Les Prés d'Eugénie This white Second Empire mansion with a Baroque lounge and a tranquil, arcaded terrace sits back from the road; it is graced by a lush tropical garden and flanked by two newer annexes that house the spa facilities. The 40 rooms are large, modern, and elegantly furnished with a pleasing mix of antique and contemporary pieces. In addition to the spa, there are tennis courts, a pool, a bocci court, and a billiard room. The main attraction, however, remains the three-Michelin-star restaurant, presided over by culinary celebrity Michel Guérard. (For a detailed description of the restaurant, see *Haute Gastronomie* in DIVERSIONS.) The hotel also offers seven different thematic-week packages, including a cooking-school week learning from Guérard's chefs, a golf week, and a wine studying week, among others. Closed early December through mid-February; restaurant also closed Wednesdays and Thursday lunch, except from mid-July through mid-September and holidays (phone: 58-05-06-07; fax: 58-51-13-59). Very expensive.

En Route from Eugénie-les-Bains Travel north along D11 and N124 to Mont-de-Marsan, the starting point for a visit to the vast pine forests of the Landes.

PARC NATUREL RÉGIONAL DES LANDES DE GASCOGNE *Lande* means "moor," and until the end of the 18th century the region was just that: desolate, inhospitable land, sandy at the coast and swampy inland. Swept progressively farther east by the Atlantic winds, the dunes of the coast threatened to turn the region into a desert until 1788, when a clever engineer named Nicolas Brémontier came up with a solution to stop the annual encroachment of the sands. After barricading the dunes with wooden planks, he planted them with hardy, strong-rooted ground cover. With the sands no longer a problem, the marshy areas inland could be drained and planted with pine groves, and this poor, barren region became the richest source of France's timber and resin for turpentine and varnish. Today the 510,000-acre regional park remains sparsely populated, dotted with tiny isolated villages, sawmills, and furniture factories.

The most dramatic attraction here is the forest itself, which is open to the public. Fire has proved a serious hazard; from 1944 to 1949 it wiped out more than a third of the forest, which has since been replanted. Needless to say, campsites are regulated carefully. For more information about the park, contact *Informations Touristiques Permanentes,* Belin-Beliet 33830 (phone: 58-88-06-06).

If you are smitten with the forest, you can wander leisurely through the region above Mont-de-Marsan. From Mont-de-Marsan take N134 northwest for 22 miles (35 km) to Sabres. Leave your car there and take a small train 2 miles (3 km) farther to the open-air *Ecomusée de Marquèze,* a functioning 19th-century–style community, where fashion, tools, and the rhythm of life are frozen in time. On Tuesdays sap is drained from the pines; on Wednesdays the old locomotive is brought out for a spin; Thursdays are reserved for milling; and the outdoor bread oven is in operation all the time. Visitors can help shear the sheep in late May or harvest the crops in mid-September. The museum is open daily, June through September; weekends, holidays, and by appointment *Palm Sunday* through May and in October; closed November to *Palm Sunday* (phone: 58-07-52-70). Those who want to extend their stay can try the 26-room inn in Sabres, *L'Auberge des Pins* (phone: 58-07-50-47; fax: 58-07-56-74), which has a restaurant and is closed January.

En Route from the Parc Naturel Régional des Landes de Gascogne The quickest way from Mont-de-Marsan to the coast is via N124, passing the town of Dax, 32 miles (51 km) away, on the Adour River. Boasting thermal springs that used to ease the aches and pains of the Romans, modern-day Dax now sports a casino, a good assortment of hotels and restaurants, and the lovely *Parc Théodore-Denis,* where vestiges from Roman days still can be seen. Continue along N124 and A63; the coastal resorts of Hossegor and Capbreton lie just a couple of miles off A63 via D33 and D28, respectively.

HOSSEGOR The pine forests of the Landes meet the wide sandy beaches of the sea beside a tranquil blue lake fed by the tide through a canal built in 1886. Although both Hossegor and nearby Capbreton lack some of the cachet of the larger Atlantic resorts of Biarritz and St-Jean-de-Luz to the south, their beaches are cleaner and less crowded, the towns have a provincial charm, their hotels are more reasonably priced, and their surroundings are wild and unspoiled. Until the turn of the century, the area around Hossegor's marine lake was little more than a sweep of desolate sand dunes, like much of the Landes coastline. It grew up somewhat haphazardly through the 1930s, its pleasing climate and recreational potential attracting a following of writers, artists, composers, and—no surprise—nature lovers and sports enthusiasts.

Hossegor's town center, clean, white, and planted with flowers, lies between the lake and the ocean. Pretty little villas and quaint Basque hotels speckle the lakefront and nestle in the deep pine groves that stretch east from the beach and the lake. This place is ideal for those interested in sailing, windsurfing, golf, tennis, hiking or horseback riding through the forests, or just basking in the sun.

Hossegor's casino, the *Complexe du Sporting Casino* (Av. de Gaujacq; phone: 58-43-50-10 or 58-43-96-47) has a saltwater pool, five tennis courts, and a miniature golf facility. The town also has a *pelote* (jai alai) arena (at the casino; phone: 58-43-54-12), a yacht club (*Yacht Club Landais;* Av. du Touring Club; phone: 58-43-96-48), and a golf course (on the southeastern edge of town; phone: 58-43-56-99). Surfing gear is available at *Hossegor Surf Patrol* (Av. Paul-Lahary; phone: 58-43-74-58) and *Body Surf Club Hossegor* (Pl. des Landais; phone: 58-43-02-54); there is also a private surfing club which sponsors a surfing championship, the *Rip Curl Pro Landes Championship,* each August. Each Wednesday in July and August there is a bloodless bullfight, with a wild cow playing the main role. The tourist office, in the center of town (Pl. Louis-Pasteur; phone: 58-41-79-00; fax: 58-41-70-15), is closed Sundays in winter.

CAPBRETON Just a couple of miles south of Hossegor, Capbreton seems almost an extension of its neighbor. Its past is a bit more colorful, though: Once at the mouth of the Adour River, the town grew into a lucrative fishing port and maritime city between the 10th and 16th centuries, until the river changed its course and the harbor filled with silt. The 16th-century tower that guided navigators and fishermen still stands witness to this prosperous past. It was from Capbreton that seafarers set off for their new home on Cape Breton Island, in northeastern Nova Scotia (the island was a French possession from 1627 to 1763). The waves on this beach are particularly gentle and pleasant for bathing. Capbreton's tourist office (Av. Georges-Pompidou; phone: 58-72-12-11; fax: 58-41-00-29) is closed Sundays in winter. The season in the resorts of Capbreton and Hossegor begins in June and runs through September 15, although a few hotels and restaurants stay open year-round.

BEST EN ROUTE

La Sardinière This modern restaurant with seafaring motifs and an outdoor terrace facing the marina serves a good rendition of *ttoro,* a rich fish soup that is the Atlantic coast's version of bouillabaisse. It also prepares plentiful seafood platters and a wide choice of other fish and meat dishes. Closed Monday dinner, Tuesdays, and mid-November through mid-December. Reservations advised. MasterCard and Visa accepted. 87-89 Av. Georges-Pompidou (phone/fax: 58-72-10-49). Expensive.

L'Océan A neat white hotel rimmed with balconies, it looks like a small ocean liner moored on the quay facing the colorful marina. Its 47 rooms, many of which overlook the marina, are simple and comfortable; the management is congenial; and there's a restaurant. Closed mid-October through mid-March. 85 Av. Georges-Pompidou (phone: 58-72-10-22; fax: 58-72-08-43). Moderate.

Le Régalty A pleasant port-side restaurant with a dining terrace, where good Landes-style cuisine is prepared with a nouvelle touch. Closed Mondays and two weeks each in January and November. Reservations advised. Major credit cards accepted. Quai Pêcherie (phone: 58-72-22-80). Moderate.

The Pyrénées

The Pyrénées Mountains stretch from the rocky shores and sandy beaches of the western Atlantic coast to the lush Côte Vermeille (Vermilion Coast) of the Mediterranean in the east, forming a natural frontier between France and Spain and offering the most varied and enchanting panoply of scenery, culture, and history imaginable. Legend has it that the goddess Pyrene, the lover of Hercules, is buried somewhere in this range—whence, presumably, it derives its name.

The range extends some 275 miles from west to east, its highest peaks reaching about 10,500 feet, only slightly lower than those of the French Alps. Their relative isolation from Paris, 800 miles (1,280 km) away, has left them pristine, allowing their peoples to preserve the languages, customs, cuisines, architectural styles, and independence of their ancestors.

The Pyrénées can be divided into three groups. The western Pyrénées are characterized by verdant hills rising inland from the ocean in roller-coaster fashion and growing into high, forested slopes. The rugged central Pyrénées, the highest peaks in the range and the most dramatic, overlook glacial valleys that snake between the heights. The eastern Pyrénées ease into the heavily wooded slopes and the chalky cliffs and gorges of the Ariège Valley, eventually giving way again to gentler terrain and tumbling down to the lush, semitropical vegetation of the Roussillon's red, baked soil.

Equally varied are the culture and history of these areas. To the west is the Pays Basque (Basque Country), dotted with tiny villages of split-timbered houses. The origins of the highly individualistic Basque people, who share a language (Euskara), traditions, and physical characteristics with their neighbors on the Spanish side of the border, are still a mystery. According to some theories, their civilization goes back 25 centuries, starting with *Homo pyreneus,* a contemporary of Cro-Magnon man. But an abundance of caves in the Pyrénées also gave shelter to even earlier inhabitants, whose traces were found—in the form of a human jaw 300,000 to 400,000 years old—near Montmaurin in 1949. The Basque are a proud people who, along with their Spanish cousins, continue to fight for self-determination. Their rustic, flower-bedecked inns are perfect Pyrenean retreats, and their hearty cuisine is the most distinctive of the region.

The central and eastern Pyrénées are a mix of modern ski resorts and lazy sun-warmed thermal spas, whose springs have been popular since Roman times. The impenetrable peaks behind these valleys protected them from attack from the south and allowed them to develop into strong, independent states during the Middle Ages, ruled over by the Counts of Béarn, Bigorre, and Foix and later by the Kings of Navarre. Their strong stone châteaux still stand proudly on the heights.

In 72 BC the Romans founded Lugdunum Convenarum, a trading post and small fortress that later became St-Bertrand-de-Comminges. Sixteen years later Crassus, Julius Caesar's lieutenant, conquered this area, establishing thriving settlements and the first spas, whose remnants can be seen at Montmaurin and St-Bertrand-de-Comminges. In the 3rd century the region was invaded by Germanic tribes, who were followed by the Normans in the 9th century.

During the Middle Ages the area was marked by keen religious activity. Scores of religious pilgrims from all over Europe regularly converged on St-Jean-Pied-de-Port and Sare in the Pays Basque on their way to the important shrine of Santiago de Compostela in Spain. At about the same time Romanesque churches and cathedrals were being erected in the central area, while farther east the papacy and the ruling Capetians waged war on the Cathari (or Albigensians), religious dissenters who shunned the evils of earthly life and attacked the worldly ways of the established church. At least four hilltop châteaux in which the Cathari sought refuge, before being wiped out by the Inquisition in the mid-14th century, still can be seen around Foix. England gained control of the area in 1360, during the Hundred Years' War, and France won it back in 1463.

It wasn't until 1659 that much of the Pyrénées came under French dominion, when the mountain range was established as the official boundary between France and Spain with the signing of the Peace of the Pyrénées by Louis XIV and Philip IV of Spain. But three centuries of French rule have not erased the strong regional identity of the Pyrenean people. Indeed, many of these citizens consider themselves to be first Basque, Béarnais, or, to the far east, Catalan, placing secondary emphasis on their membership in the French republic.

To appreciate fully the distinct charms of each area and the depth of its incredible natural beauty, a good pair of sturdy walking or hiking shoes is mandatory. Recreational possibilities in this region include camping, hiking, climbing, horseback riding, skiing, and fishing in clear mountain streams. If you happen to be in Paris first, stop at the *Maison des Pyrénées* (15 Rue St-Augustin; phone: 42-86-51-86; fax: 42-86-51-65), where helpful English-speaking employees can fill you in on upcoming events and sites of particular interest in the central and eastern Pyrénées. They also can arrange package tours, such as three- to seven-day hiking itineraries that include hotels and luggage transportation from one destination to the next. For information on the Basque area, contact the *Agence de Tourisme du Pays Basque* (1 Rue Donzac, Bayonne; phone: 59-59-28-77; fax: 59-25-48-90). It provides enticing literature on the western end of the Pyrénées, including an excellent free booklet in English.

This driving route starts at Bayonne, the gateway to the Pays Basque, then follows the coastline south to St-Jean-de-Luz before turning inland and climbing into the heart of the Pays Basque. After a short detour north to Pau, the region's cultural capital, it climbs into the high Pyrénées, zigzagging from mountain ski resort to thermal spa, including stops at Lourdes and Cauterets. Then it picks up the Route des Pyrénées, crossing three mountain passes before Luchon and then continuing into the lovely Ariège Valley and the romantic lands of the Counts of Foix. Finally, the tour wends its way to the Mediterranean, where the beautiful beach resorts of the Côte Vermeille await the weary traveler.

As in many of the "undiscovered" regions of France, most of the hotels here fall into moderate or inexpensive price ranges. In a few such modern comforts as air conditioning, TV sets, and room service are lacking (private baths, however, are standard), but they are compensated for by the rustic charm of flower-bedecked balconies, antique armoires, and down quilts. For a double room per night in an expensive hotel, expect to pay $100 or more; in a moderate place, $70 to $100; and in an inexpensive place, less than $70. Hotels accept major credit cards and are open year-round unless otherwise indicated. Dinner for two with service (usually included in the bill) in an expensive restaurant will cost $100 or more; in a moderate place, between $50 and $100; and in an inexpensive one, less than $50. Prices do not include wine or drinks. Unless otherwise noted, all restaurants listed below are open for lunch and dinner. For each location hotels and restaurants are listed alphabetically by price category.

BAYONNE This lively port 4½ miles (7 km) inland from the white beaches and rocky precipices of Biarritz manages to combine a busy commercial life with a lighthearted holiday spirit. It is the meeting point of Gascony and the Pays Basque, and it exhibits the characteristics of both cultures, while its proximity to Spain adds yet another dimension.

Bayonne was inhabited by the Romans, who called it Lapurdum, from which the coastal Basque region of Labourd takes its name. As part of the province of Aquitaine, the town passed into English hands in 1152, when Eleanor wed the British monarch Henry Plantagenet.

The city fared badly after the resumption of French rule in 1451, but in 1578, under Charles IX, canals were dug that reopened the city's silted-up port to the sea. In 1784 Bayonne was declared a free port and its already healthy trade tripled, enjoying brisk commerce between Europe and the West Indies, while its fishing fleet brought in plentiful cod from the waters near Newfoundland. Cocoa beans first entered France through the port here, and the city still is famous for its fine chocolate, as well as for its smoked hams, which resemble those from Italy's Parma. Bayonne also was known for its ironworkers and gunsmiths, who are credited with inventing the bayonet in the 17th century.

During the Revolution Bayonne's free-port status was preempted, and the blockade put an end to the city's trade with the British. In 1813, during the Napoleonic Wars, the Duke of Wellington trekked over the Pyrénées from Spain, dispatching a division of his army to take Bayonne, but the city's garrison held out, capturing the English general. The garrison repelled another siege by combined English, Portuguese, and Spanish forces in 1814.

Bayonne did not return to its former position of glory until this century, when oil and natural gas were discovered at Lacq, 75 miles (120 km) to the east. By 1990 the port's traffic had passed the 3.5-million-ton mark, almost five times its volume in 1960.

One of the best reasons to visit this city is the *Musée Bonnat* (in Petit Bayonne, the area between the Nive and the Adour Rivers, at 5 Rue Jacques-Lafitte; phone: 59-59-08-52), built around the private collection of the painter Léon Bonnat, who willed it to his native city upon his death in 1922. One of the finest and richest art museums in France, it includes works by Van Dyck, El Greco, Goya, Degas, Leonardo, Raphael, Dürer, Rubens, Rembrandt, Fragonard, and Delacroix. The museum is closed Tuesdays; admission charge. Unfortunately, the *Musée Basque* (Rue Marengo; phone: 59-59-08-98) is closed for renovations and will not reopen until 1996 at the earliest.

On the opposite side of the Nive are the active pedestrian streets of the old city and, nearby, on Rue des Gouverneurs, the Gothic *Cathédrale Ste-Marie,* whose delicate spires dominate the horizon. The cathedral was begun in the 13th century but wasn't completed until the 16th. It has a 14th-century cloister, lovely Renaissance windows, and, in one chapel, a curious plaque commemorating the "Miracle of Bayonne," when a strange white light is said to have appeared in the sky. It was considered a portent of the imminent surrender of the English in 1451.

Also on Rue des Gouverneurs is the *Château Vieux* (Old Castle), a massive, square fortress with round towers; it's not open to the public. Before leaving town, walk down the pedestrian Rue du Pont-Neuf and drink thick hot chocolate under the arcades, where the city's famous confectioners have been making their sweet delicacies for more than 300 years. Continue on to the animated Place de la Liberté and nearby public gardens (half of the area has been turned into a parking lot) and then to the *Hôtel de Ville* (Town Hall) and the municipal theater; both are in the same building as the tourist office (Pl. des Basques; phone: 59-46-01-46).

Each year at the beginning of August, the city holds a colorful week-long festival that includes bullfights, dancing, singing, and *pelote* games. The rest of the year rugby games are held on Sundays at the *Stade de Bayonne* in the *Parc des Sports* (phone: 59-63-32-54).

BEST EN ROUTE

Le Grand–Best Western This graceful establishment flanked by the sidewalk cafés and shops of the main commercial street has 54 unassuming but comfortable rooms, a cozy little lounge, and a fine restaurant, *Les Carmes.* 21 Rue Thiers (phone: 59-59-14-61; 800-528-1234; fax: 59-25-61-70). Expensive.

Cheval Blanc Regional and fish dishes are offered at this eatery, housed in a half-timbered Basque house (ca. 1710). The wine cellar is well stocked with local varieties. Closed Sunday dinner and Mondays (except in July and August) and the last three weeks of February. Reservations necessary. Major credit cards accepted. In the old city, at 68 Rue Bourgneuf (phone: 59-59-01-33). Moderate.

Euskalunda The decor and ambience at this cozy bistro are as typically Basque as its name. A meal of authentic fare here—try the cuttlefish in its own sauce—is a perfect preface to an excursion into the Pays Basque. Closed Sundays, Mondays, the last two weeks in May, and the last two weeks in October. Reservations unnecessary. MasterCard and Visa accepted. On a narrow street in Petit Bayonne, at 61 Rue Pannecau (phone: 59-59-28-02). Moderate.

Mercure An ultramodern, almost high-tech hotel, it seems out of place in this old city. Nonetheless, it provides modern conveniences in its 108 comfortable, contemporary rooms. There's a restaurant. On the edge of the old city, on Av. J.-Rostand (phone: 59-63-30-90; fax: 59-42-06-64). Moderate.

En Route from Bayonne Just a quick hop to the Atlantic via D260 leads to the bright lights, lovely beaches, and beckoning waves of Biarritz.

BIARRITZ For a detailed report on this city—known as the "Queen of Beaches"—its sights, hotels, and restaurants, see *Biarritz* in THE CITIES.

En Route from Biarritz Route N10 leads south for 10 miles (16 km) to St-Jean-de-Luz.

ST-JEAN-DE-LUZ If Biarritz is the "Queen of Beaches," then St-Jean-de-Luz certainly is the crown princess, whose casual, impulsive character is in many ways more appealing than the distinguished charm of Her Majesty.

The biggest attraction here is the expansive, gracefully curving stretch of white sand. Usually very crowded, the beach is in a naturally protected horseshoe-shaped bay between the sea and the mouth of the Nivelle River. The sunsets here are superb. In addition to being one of the most popular resorts on France's Atlantic Coast, St-Jean-de-Luz also is the principal fishing port of the Basque coast, and its restaurants always are supplied with an abundance of fine, fresh seafood. Like Biarritz, St-Jean-de-Luz was an important whaling center by the 9th century. When the whales disappeared from this area, the fishermen turned to cod; today the big catch includes tuna, sardines, and anchovies.

St. Jean's proximity to the Iberian border made it a frequent target of the Spanish, who burned it to the ground in 1558 and again in 1635, which accounts for the paucity of ancient structures in town. The city's finest hour came on June 9, 1660, when it was the site of the marriage of Louis XIV and Maria Theresa, the daughter of King Philip IV of Spain. Today you can visit the *Maison Lohobiague* (Pl. Louis-XIV; no phone), where the Sun

King stayed for 30 days before the wedding. Formerly the home of a wealthy shipbuilder, it is filled with ornate furnishings and intriguing souvenirs of the king's stay. The guided tour is in French, so ask for the English crib sheet to take along. The *Maison Lohobiague* is open Saturdays at 3 PM only; there's no admission charge.

The marriage ceremony was held in the *Eglise St-Jean-Baptiste* (Church of St. John the Baptist), not far from Place Louis-XIV, and the door through which the royal couple passed after the elaborate street processional was permanently walled over after the ceremony so that no other human would again cross the threshold. The church's interior is typically Basque, its walls stacked with three tiers of wooden galleries accessible only to the men of the congregation. Rebuilt after the fire in 1558 destroyed the original 13th-century structure, this is perhaps the most sumptuous Basque church. Its magnificent retable, which dates from about 1670, contains large gilt statues of the popular saints of the Pays Basque.

Also of architectural interest is the gracious brick-and-stone *Maison de l'Infante* (not open to the public), where Maria Theresa stayed before the wedding, and, across the river in Cibourne, at 12 Quai Ravel, the 17th-century house in which the composer Maurice Ravel was born in 1875.

Explore Rue de la République and Rue Gambetta behind the port, and stop for a drink at one of the cafés on lively Place Louis-XIV, where, on Sundays in summer, Basque music and dancing take place. For more information, contact the tourist office (Pl. du Maréchal-Foch; phone: 59-26-03-16; fax: 59-26-21-47).

For a rewarding side trip, follow D912 around the bay to Socoa, along the Corniche Basque, with its 16th-century fortress and magnificent vistas, and then south to Hendaye, another popular resort, on the Spanish border. According to some, the beaches here are the French coast's most beautiful.

BEST EN ROUTE

Chantaco In this genteel turn-of-the-century Basque mansion, graced by archways and quiet gardens, are 24 tranquil, pleasingly furnished rooms and a restaurant that matches the quality of the hotel. There's also a pool, and a golf course is right across the street. Closed November through *Easter*. Book well in advance. One mile (1.6 km) or so south of town via D918 (phone: 59-26-14-76; fax: 59-26-35-97). Expensive.

Grand An original ambience and such nouvelle-inspired cuisine as *langoustines rôties aux graines de sésame* (prawns roasted with sesame seeds) distinguish this restaurant, which has been awarded a star from Michelin. There are also 44 guestrooms. Closed mid-January through mid-February. Reservations advised. Major credit cards accepted. 43 Bd. Thiers (phone: 59-26-35-36). Expensive.

L'Hélianthal An ultramodern 100-room property, it's most popular for its *thalassothérapie* (seawater therapy) treatments and its fine restaurant. Closed the last two weeks of January. Near the beach, at Pl. M.-Ravel (phone: 59-51-51-60; fax: 59-51-51-54). Expensive.

Le Madison This pleasant hotel has 25 attractive rooms, a sauna, gym, and very congenial management. There's no restaurant. Conveniently located at 25 Bd. Thiers (phone: 59-26-35-02; fax: 59-51-14-76). Expensive.

Chez Margot On the opposite side of the bay, in front of the harbor and below the fortress of Socoa, this rustic restaurant-bar offers a variety of simple Basque food, especially fish. Closed Wednesday and Friday dinner and October. Reservations advised. Major credit cards accepted. Port de Socoa (phone: 59-47-18-30). Moderate.

La Plage This homey, Basque-style family establishment has 25 simple rooms and a restaurant. During the summer half or full board is required. Closed mid-October through *Easter*. MasterCard and Visa accepted. Just a few steps from the beach, at 33 Rue Garat (phone: 59-51-03-44; fax: 59-51-03-48). Moderate.

La Taverne Basque Seafood and tasty sheep's-milk cheese are the featured fare here, accompanied by delicious light local wines. Closed Wednesday lunch and Thursdays off-season and mid-January through March. Reservations unnecessary. Major credit cards accepted. In the center of town, at 5 Rue de la République (phone: 59-26-01-26). Moderate.

Prado A small, family-run place in which six of the 38 rooms overlook the beach. There is also a restaurant. Pl. M.-Ravel (phone: 59-51-03-71; fax: 59-26-27-61). Inexpensive.

En Route from St-Jean-de-Luz Route D918 leads southeast from St-Jean-de-Luz toward St-Jean-Pied-de-Port, 39 miles (62 km) away. The road follows the Nivelle River into the heart of Basque country through tiny villages of split-timbered houses with rust-colored shutters and wooden balconies. Every town, no matter how small, has a *pelote* court where the sport is played by young and old. If you are lucky enough to visit on a Sunday, you'll see the Basques dancing the fandango. For a picturesque detour, turn onto D4 just 4 miles (6 km) outside St-Jean-de-Luz, and drive through Ascain. Continue on this curving route south to Sare, a storybook village huddled in the climbing hills that announce the ascent of the Pyrénées. Just a couple of miles before this town is a curious little train that runs up a steep hillside; in summer it takes visitors on a 3-mile (4-km) ride up to the summit of La Rhune for an awesome view of the coast, including the beautiful Bay of San Sebastián, in Spain. Sare was a stopover for the 12th-century pilgrims who made the trek from all over Europe to Santiago de

Compostela. The town, with its friendly hostelries, still maintains the tradition of welcoming visitors.

BEST EN ROUTE

Arraya Wooden beams, stucco, and colorful fabrics characterize this inn, which has a refinement and plushness rare in this out-of-the-way province. The one suite and 20 rooms, most facing an interior garden, are luxurious. The hotel's hearth-warmed dining room is particularly well known for its preparation of game birds in the fall; the Basque specialties also are very tasty. Closed mid-November through April. Sare (phone: 59-54-20-46; fax: 59-54-27-04). Expensive.

ST-JEAN-PIED-DE-PORT Today's traveler wouldn't be at all surprised to see a bent, gray-cloaked, 12th-century pilgrim, staff in hand, emerge from behind the ramparts here, so convincing is the ambience of this Basque village, the last stop along the ancient road to the Spanish border. Its location required heavy fortification, and the old part of the village, the Ville Haute (Upper Town), is encircled by 15th-century stone ramparts that climb up the hill to the 13th-century citadel, built by the King of Navarre. Inside the Ville Haute are steep, narrow stone streets, a church built into the ramparts, and Basque houses, their rickety, flower-entwined balconies overhanging the Nive River. Wander through the old streets, climb up to the citadel, and let your imagination take wing.

Just outside the gates of the Ville Haute is the modern town, the capital and market center of the Basse-Navarre, one of the three French Basque provinces. On Mondays the sloping main street, with lively Basque cafés and *auberges* (inns), turns into a bazaar where vendors sell food, clothing, books, and just about everything else. Many of the shops here specialize in colorful Basque linens.

For a glimpse of Basque camaraderie, stop at the *Etche Ona* (Pl. Floquet; phone: 59-37-01-14), a provincial *auberge* in the Ville Haute where bereted, ruddy-cheeked locals take animated afternoon breaks. St-Jean-Pied-de-Port is an excellent point of departure for several excursions—north to the grottoes of Isturits and Oxocelhaya, with their prehistoric carvings, and south to the Iraty Forest, one of the most lush in the Pyrénées.

BEST EN ROUTE

Arcé This is a perfect Pyrenean retreat—with 19 rooms, six suites, a pool, and a tennis court—secluded on the banks of a clear mountain stream. In the summer guests dine on the garden terrace that overhangs the stream, the source of the delicious fresh trout served. Closed mid-November through mid-March. About 7 miles (11 km) west on D15, in St-Etienne-de-Baïgorry (phone: 59-37-40-14; fax: 59-37-40-27). Expensive.

Pyrénées This white stucco house has neat flower-bedecked balconies and a pleasing tree-shaded dining terrace overlooking the main street and the city's ramparts. A member of the Relais & Châteaux group, it has two suites and 18 simply decorated, comfortable rooms, and a fine restaurant whose two Michelin stars are well deserved. A meal on the terrace can be memorable, whether you order a traditional Basque fish soup or a more unusual creation, like roast squab with wild-mushroom ravioli or cod-stuffed peppers. Try the Irouléguy wines from the vineyards nearby. Closed the last three weeks of January and mid-November through mid-December; restaurant also closed Monday dinner from January through March and Tuesdays from mid-September through June (except holidays). Pl. Général-de-Gaulle (phone: 59-37-01-01; fax: 59-37-18-97). Expensive.

En Route from St-Jean-Pied-de-Port Leave by D933 north, turning east onto D918 and crossing the Col d'Osquich pass before reaching the charming little town of Mauléon Licharre, whose small, early 17th-century *Château d'Andurain* is worth seeing. It's closed during lunch hours, on Thursdays, Sunday mornings, and from mid-September through June (phone: 59-27-55-21 or 59-28-00-24). The town also is France's largest producer of espadrilles, those comfortable rope-soled canvas shoes. Continue on to Oloron-Ste-Marie via D24 and D25 east and D936 southeast. Beret lovers might recognize the name of this town at the junction of two swift mountain streams as that stamped inside most of the world's authentic Basque caps. Other than to buy a beret, you should stop here to visit the *Cathédrale Ste-Marie* (Rue Cathédrale), a 13th-century church with an impressive Romanesque façade. Carved of Pyrenean marble that has mellowed to an ivory-like patina, its portal is peopled by scores of curious, intricately detailed creatures. Oloron is a lively, attractive town of 11,000, the capital of the Haut-Béarn. During the last week of July and the first two weeks of August in even-numbered years, it hosts the big *Festival International des Pyrénées,* which brings together top folk-dance companies from all over the world. (In odd-numbered years the festival is held in Jaca, on the other side of the Pyrénées in Spain.) For details, contact the festival office (1 Rue Camou, Oloron-Ste-Marie 64400; phone: 59-39-37-36; fax: 59-39-18-83). Route N134 leads from Oloron-Ste-Marie to Pau, 59 miles (98 km) from St-Jean-Pied-de-Port.

PAU The largest and most cosmopolitan city of the western Pyrénées and the capital of the Pyrénées-Atlantiques *département,* Pau combines all the advantages of a metropolitan area with the genteel atmosphere of a mountain resort. Its graceful Boulevard des Pyrénées, the work of Napoleon, offers magnificent vistas of the surrounding hills and the peaks of the high Pyrénées. To the east lies 9,504-foot Midi de Bigorée; to the south, slightly higher Midi d'Ossau. The peaks are especially spectacular on summer mornings and at sunset.

Pau once was the capital of the historical Béarn region, land of the kings of Navarre and of Henri IV, one of France's most colorful and best-loved monarchs. The best introduction to the history of the Béarn and to the fascinating lore surrounding Henri is found in the magnificent château where he was born in the mid-16th century. Set on high ground at the end of Boulevard des Pyrénées and overlooking the River Gave de Pau, it is surrounded by the narrow buildings and streets of the old town. The château has a wonderfully ornate Renaissance style, having been renovated in the 16th century by Marguerite of Angoulême, the beautiful and celebrated wife of Henri d'Albret, King of Navarre, who wrote the *Heptameron,* a collection of tales modeled after Boccaccio's. (The château also was embellished in the 19th century by both Louis-Philippe and Napoleon III.) Marguerite and Henri's daughter, Jeanne d'Albret, gave birth to Henri IV here on December 13, 1553, and the curious tortoiseshell cradle in which the infant slept is on display. Other treasures here include richly carved Renaissance furniture, priceless artwork, and, most awesome of all, the world's most precious collection of Gobelin and Flemish tapestries. On the third floor is a fascinating exhibit on the history and culture of the Béarn. The curator gladly will explain the furnishings, art, models, and any other parts of the exhibit that interest you. The château is open daily, except during lunch hours (phone: 59-82-38-00).

The massive square stone tower at the entrance to the château was built by the legendary Gaston III of Béarn, who modestly dubbed himself *"fébus"* ("brilliant"). This hunter, poet, and military strategist built the Béarn into a strong and independent state in the 14th century, and many of his castles still can be seen throughout the area. The tower, which is open daily, is all that remains of the militaristic medieval structure that once stood here; there's no admission charge.

At the opposite end of Boulevard des Pyrénées is *Parc Beaumont,* a graceful, verdant city park with a small lake and a tawdry casino. Nearby, on Rue Mathieu-Lalanne, the *Musée des Beaux-Arts* has important Italian, Dutch, Flemish, Spanish, and French works dating from the 17th to the 20th century. The museum is closed Tuesdays; there's an admission charge (phone: 59-27-33-02). The *Musée Bernadotte* (Rue Tran; phone: 59-27-48-42) is housed in the birthplace of, and is devoted to, Marshall Jean-Baptiste Jules Bernadotte (1764–1844), who in 1818 became King Charles XIV of Sweden after being adopted as heir by Charles XIII. The museum is closed Mondays; there's an admission charge. The tourist office is in the *Hôtel de Ville* (Pl. Royale; phone: 59-27-27-08; fax: 59-27-03-21).

The city's benign climate made it a favorite destination of the British, who at one point constituted almost 15% of the town's population. Though the English left with the World Wars, some of their customs, such as afternoon tea, remain. *L'Isle au Jasmin* (28 Bd. de Pyrénées) is a charming place to enjoy one of more than a dozen varieties of tea and half a dozen coffees. In May is the *Grand Prix de Pau* car race, and in June and early July Pau's streets come alive with music, dance, and theater festivals, many of the performances free.

BEST EN ROUTE

Pierre Considered Pau's finest for classic cuisine, service, and appointments, it has one Michelin star. Closed Saturday lunch and Sundays (except holidays). Reservations necessary. Major credit cards accepted. 16 Rue L.-Barthou (phone: 59-27-76-86). Expensive.

Continental A grand old establishment with 80 rooms, most of which have been renovated with a modern functional decor. Ask for one of the four less modern, more charming rooms in the rotunda. There's a restaurant. In the heart of Pau, at 2 Rue Maréchal-Foch (phone: 59-27-69-31; fax: 59-27-99-84). Moderate.

La Goulue A tiny, curious little café whose walls are plastered with art and theater posters. The menu includes such southwestern French specialties as *magret* (grilled duck breast) and *confit* (preserved duck or goose simmered in its own fat and aromatic spices). Try the Jurançon wines produced near Pau. Closed Saturday lunch. Reservations unnecessary. MasterCard and Visa accepted. Near the château, at 13 Rue Henri-IV (phone: 59-27-44-44). Moderate.

Gramont This quiet, traditional hotel has 36 simple, spacious rooms and a breakfast room but no restaurant. The staff is friendly. 3 Pl. de Gramont (phone: 59-27-84-04; fax: 59-27-62-23). Moderate.

En Route from Pau Take D937 for 26 miles (42 km) to Lourdes. Along the way, just past the village of Lestelle-Bétharram, 16 miles (26 km) outside Pau, is the curious *Eglise Notre-Dame-de-Bétharram* (Church of Our Lady of Bétharram), constructed in 1661 on the spot where several miracles are said to have occurred, particularly between 1620 and 1640. Once an important pilgrimage site, it was overshadowed in the 19th century by nearby Lourdes. Most intriguing is the painted ceiling under the organ loft, depicting the ancestors of Christ according to the Gospel of St. Matthew.

Be sure to stop 3 miles (5 km) farther on at the Grottes (Grottoes) de Bétharram. A rickety aerial tram takes visitors up over a giant hill and down to the entrance of these stalactite- and stalagmite-filled caves, where one can travel almost 2 miles by boat, foot, and train past nature's awesome work.

LOURDES On February 11, 1858, Bernadette Soubirous, the 14-year-old daughter of an impoverished Lourdes miller, claimed to have seen a vision of the Virgin Mary in a rocky grotto surrounded by woods near the Gave de Pau. In all, the girl had 18 such visions, and one was accompanied by the spouting of a spring when Bernadette scratched the dry ground with her fingers. The spring's waters were believed to possess healing powers to which miracles were attributed; word spread, and pilgrims flocked here. In 1862 the church officially recognized this as a holy place, constructing a sanctuary at the grotto, and in 1933 Bernadette was canonized. Today the small grotto chapel by the mountain stream is overshadowed by a monstrous double-decker basilica whose monumental semicircular staircase leads to the upper church and embraces a large open plaza. For additional details on the shrine of Lourdes, see *Memorable Museums and Monuments* in DIVERSIONS.

Each year, nearly five million pilgrims, many of them sick and disabled, come here to bathe in the waters of the spring with the hope of being cured. The pilgrims support this not-so-appealing town of just over 16,000, which seems to consist only of hotels and saintly souvenir shops selling blue-and-white plastic bottles in the shape of the Virgin (people fill them with water from the central fountain). There are more than 400 hotels here, modern structures stacked one next to the other on the hilly streets like so many pastel matchboxes. In fact, Lourdes has the largest number of hotel rooms of any French city besides Paris. Despite that, don't try to get a room around August 15, the most important of six annual pilgrimage dates.

If you do stop, see the fortified pre-miracle château high on a hill above the town. It is an impressive example of medieval architecture that served as a state prison in the 17th and 18th centuries, and it contains an interesting museum on the culture and traditions of the Pyrénées. The château is open daily, April through September; there's an admission charge (phone: 62-94-02-04). You also can visit the *Moulin de Boly* (12 Rue Bernadette-Soubirous), the house where Bernadette was born, and see a film on her life. It's open daily; no admission charge. On Sunday afternoons watch a rugby match at the *Stade Municipal* (Av. Antoine-Béguin; phone: 62-94-14-24 or 62-94-21-18); the local club is one of the best in France.

Though there are plenty of hotels from which to choose, you might do well to leave the city via N21 south and drive for 8 miles (13 km) into the nearby valley, where there are many pleasing rural hotels near Argelès-Gazost.

BEST EN ROUTE

Le Relais de Saux This charming 17th-century hostelry with seven rooms and a restaurant offers a splendid view of the mountains. The owners make their guests feel very welcome. About 1½ miles (3 km) north of the city via D914, at Hameau de Saux (phone: 62-94-29-61; fax: 62-42-12-64). Expensive.

En Route from Lourdes Continue south on N21, followed by D920, driving to where the flat valley suddenly climbs into the mountains to the resort of Cauterets, about 19 miles (30 km) from Lourdes.

CAUTERETS This small, appealing resort, compactly arranged at the feet of sharply rising peaks, serves double duty as a ski resort and a health spa, and is as lively in the summer as in the winter. Its large thermal establishment attracts "curists" with respiratory ailments. (The waters also are said to benefit infertile women.)

The town is a pleasant base for excursions into the *Parc National des Pyrénées* (National Park of the Pyrénées), which begins a couple of miles beyond Cauterets. To reach the park, drive along scenically winding and climbing D920 to the Pont d'Espagne, where there is a magnificent waterfall. The road ends here, so either continue on foot into the forest or take a chair lift to the lovely, clear lake of Gaube, about 6 miles (10 km) away. To reach another sublime work of nature, take D920 back from Cauterets to where it meets D921, and take D921 up to Luz-St-Sauveur. From here continue as the road narrows to the town of Gavarnie; from there you can walk or take ponies to the Cirque de Gavarnie, a superb semicircular formation of mountains with tall, awesome waterfalls—the product of glacial erosion.

BEST EN ROUTE

Etche Ona A friendly Basque hotel between the slopes and the spa, with 33 modern and comfortable rooms. The dining room and lounge are pleasant, and the homey food with an occasional Basque accent also is quite good. Closed May, October, and November. Rue Richelieu (phone: 62-92-51-43; fax: 62-92-54-99). Inexpensive.

La Fruitière This little eight-room *auberge* in the mountains is the choice of regulars for creative, well-prepared fare. Closed mid-October through mid-May; restaurant also closed Sundays. No credit cards accepted. Four miles (6 km) south of Cauterets on D920, the road to the Pont d'Espagne (phone: 62-92-52-04). Inexpensive.

En Route from Cauterets Take D20 and D921 to Luz-St-Sauveur and pick up the Route des Pyrénées (D918, then D618) again and follow its breathtakingly scenic path to Bagnères-de-Luchon (71 miles/114 km from Cauterets), crossing three great mountain passes. These are in the high Pyrénées, ruggedly beautiful and dotted with quaint old spas and modern ski resorts. Cross the dizzying Col de Tourmalet (*col* means "pass"), south of 9,455-foot Pic du Midi de Bigorre. Farther down the sinuous route is the Col d'Aspin, and finally you'll cross the Col de Peyresourde before reaching Bagnères-de-Luchon. This stretch is one of the most important stages of the *Tour de France* bicycle race that takes place each July, and the victor of this section traditionally wins the entire event.

BAGNÈRES-DE-LUCHON Though it's billed as the premier spa of the French Pyrénées, this quiet resort in a lush, flat valley shadowed by the highest of Pyrenean peaks seems to have lost some of its cachet in recent years. Evidence of the town's former status remains in the form of the park-encircled thermal establishment, its dimensions and façade reminiscent of a theater or opera house, and the elegant tree-lined main street with its smart shops and cafés. The sulfur springs, named Ilixo by the Romans, are said to be particularly therapeutic for respiratory and throat problems. In winter Bagnères-de-Luchon welcomes skiers drawn to the steep, snowy slopes of the nearby *Superbagnères* ski area. If the weather is clear, Luchon affords a magnificent view of the surrounding valleys and the Maladetta range at the Spanish border.

BEST EN ROUTE

Corneille A gracious old white mansion surrounded by gardens, it provides four suites and 52 cozy rooms, each individually decorated. The staff is extremely personable, and the food in the provincial dining room is good. Closed November through March. 5 Av. Alexandre-Dumas (phone: 61-79-36-22; fax: 61-79-81-11). Expensive.

Grand Hôtel des Bains This traditional turn-of-the-century hotel has 50 spacious rooms with high ceilings and wrought-iron balconies and three restaurants—Italian, Spanish, and French. Closed November through *Christmas*. 75 Allées Etigny (phone: 61-79-00-58; fax: 61-79-18-18). Moderate.

En Route from Bagnères-de-Luchon Take D125 north, which becomes N125, then tiny D26 to St-Bertrand-de-Comminges, 20 miles (32 km) away. Not far out of town, an immense stone cathedral surrounded by ramparts rises high on a hill in the distance, dominating the flat valley below.

ST-BERTRAND-DE-COMMINGES This practically deserted, walled village of no more than 20 or 30 residents and the town on the plain below (inhabited by another 200) were much livelier 2,000 years ago. Founded in 72 BC by Pompey on his return from a Spanish campaign, it was called Lugdunum Convenarum in its earlier life. Because it was on the busy route from Toulouse to the popular baths at Bagnères-de-Luchon, the town grew rapidly, claiming by the end of the 1st century about 60,000 inhabitants. (According to the Jewish historian Flavius Josephus, it was here that Herod and his wife, murderers of St. John the Baptist, later lived in exile.)

The city was wiped out in the 6th century—by barbarians, according to some chroniclers; by the plague, according to others. The Roman city silted over, and archaeological digs have only recently unearthed remains of the old forum and some public monuments. The plain and the hillside apparently remained uninhabited until the 12th century, when Bertrand, Bishop of Comminges and later St. Bertrand, decided the magnificent acropolis was an ideal site for a cathedral, which he began building in 1120. At the end of the 13th century Bertrand de Got, the future Clement V, first Pope to reside in Avignon, began to enlarge the cathedral, completing the work in 1352. The lovely Romanesque cloister, part of which was added in the

15th century, provides a stunning view of the river and valley below. The cathedral's interior, embellished during various periods, is a fascinating lesson in ecclesiastical architecture, featuring pure examples of Romanesque, Gothic, Renaissance, and Baroque design. Perhaps its most beautiful treasures are the magnificent, intricately carved 16th-century wood choir stalls that tell the story of the Redemption. Behind the altar is the frescoed stone tomb of St. Bertrand. There also is an exhibit of religious antiquities, such as richly embroidered bishops' capes dating from the 13th century.

Before leaving this lovely site, wander through the steep, curving stone streets of the walled village surrounding the cathedral. The tourist office is at Les Olivetains (phone: 61-95-44-44).

En Route from St-Bertrand-de-Comminges Rejoin N125 going north, and at Montréjeau travel east along N117, which briefly splits off to N127 before meeting D117 southeast toward Foix. In the valley a mile (1.6 km) north of St-Bertrand, where the road rejoins N125 at Valcabrère, is the 11th-century *Basilique St-Just*. A graceful yellow stone example of early Romanesque design, it sits serenely in a cemetery surrounded by cypresses.

An interesting side trip takes in the well-preserved remains of an opulent Gallo-Roman villa at Montmaurin. To reach it, follow N125 and N117 to D633 north, then take D69C; Montmaurin is about 13 miles (21 km) from the intersection with D633. Also, near Montréjeau, are the Grottes (Grottoes) de Gargas, a cave inhabited by Aurignacian man, whose mysterious engravings of more than 230 mutilated hands, perhaps associated with some cult or ritual, have earned it the title "Cave of the Cut Hands." The grottoes are located a little over 4 miles (6 km) southwest of Montréjeau via D71; at Aventignan turn left to the grottoes.

Traveling east on N117, then turning southeast on D117 (after the brief right fork onto N127), the route soon passes into the department of the Ariège, the former domain of the Counts of Foix, an area whose romantic and colorful past is nearly eclipsed by the natural beauty of its glacial valley. This splendid wooded country is punctuated by chalky cliffs and commanding green mountains topped with the ruins of the medieval fortresses and stone strongholds of the 12th-century Cathari (or Albigensians), the heretical sect who criticized the established church and were wiped out during the Albigensian Crusade.

The area also is rich in natural caves, where prehistoric man lived and left mystical clues to his activities, in the form of drawings and engravings on the porous rock surfaces. One such cave is the Grotte du Mas-d'Azil, north on D119 just past the village of St-Girons. This curious tunnel-like grotto, 1,400 feet long and 165 feet wide, was carved out by the Arize River under the Plantaurel range. Inhabited by prehistoric man from 40,000 to 8,000 BC, it bears graceful, scratched images of bison and horses. Digs have turned up a wealth of implements used by Magdalenian man. Later the early Christians hid here, followed in the 12th and early 13th centuries by the Cathari and, four centuries later, by the Huguenots. You still can see the *Salle du Temple,* the hiding place where the latter sought refuge in 1625 from the fierce attacks of Cardinal Richelieu.

Return to D117 and travel east about 22 miles (35 km) to Foix.

FOIX The unassuming capital of the *département* of the Ariège is notable for the 11th-century château of the Counts of Foix , set commandingly on a rock high above the town. In 1002 Roger le Vieux, Count of Carcassonne, to the north, bequeathed this part of his realm to his son, who took the title Count of Foix, the first in an illustrious line. A famous battle took place here in 1272, when one of the counts refused to recognize the sovereignty of the King of France, Philip the Bold, who in turn mounted a dramatic and successful attack against the château. When the Counts of Foix acquired the Béarn in 1290, they lost interest in Foix and its château, which came under French jurisdiction in 1607, during the reign of Henri IV. What remains of the château today—the central tower and core of the original structure, flanked by two separate stone towers added later—is only a small part of the fortress that once stood here. The three towers nevertheless form a romantic silhouette. During the 19th century the towers were used as a prison, and the graffiti of political prisoners still can be seen on the walls of the round tower. Today the three floors of the tower house collections of prehistoric, Gallo-Roman, and medieval artifacts found in the region. The central structure has an exhibit of the arts and traditions of the Ariège. The château is open daily; there's an admission charge (phone: 61-65-56-05).

The *Journées Médiévales Gaston Fébus,* a festival held during the second week of July, features parades of citizens in medieval garb, street fairs, and other activities. Son-et-lumière displays take place in an open-air theater in July, August, and September. For details, visit the Foix tourist office (45 Cours G.-Fauré; phone: 61-65-12-12) or the regional tourist office (*Hôtel du Département,* Rue Cap-de-la-Ville; phone: 61-02-09-70).

En Route from Foix The potential for side trips, detours, and unexpected adventures is great along the winding roads between Foix and Céret. First take N20 south and D8 from Tarascon to the Grotte de Niaux, one of the most superb repositories of prehistoric painting in France. Lining the walls are graceful bison, horses, and deer-like animals colored with oxides and manganese; dating from 12,000 BC, they represent the height of Magdalenian art. In recent years authorities have regulated the number of visitors to prevent the deterioration of these treasures. The caves are open daily (except lunch hours) from July through September only. Visits are restricted to groups of 20 people every 45 minutes, so reservations are strongly advised (phone: 61-05-88-37).

Back on D117 east, turn south on D9 to Montségur (about 19 miles/30 km from Foix), the last stronghold of the Cathari, who were destroyed by Pope Innocent III's vicious crusade against them. The infamous warrior

Simon de Montfort, bent on eradicating the sect in the name of his church and country, pursued them mercilessly, leaving a path of death and destruction from Toulouse to Montpellier and south to the Pyrénées. In 1244 the last 207 leaders of the cult were forced to seek refuge from a Catholic army of almost 10,000 men in this high fortress on a seemingly impregnable mount. The final showdown took place in March, when, according to some chroniclers, the fortress was set ablaze and the 207 Cathari were burned alive. (Other accounts hold that they finally came out and surrendered.) Only the ruined stone walls and part of the square dungeon remain today. The ruins sit above the small village of Montségur, where there is a Catharist museum. Though you can drive up to the pass, you have to climb the final slope on foot—no small task, as the trail is steep and rugged; it takes about 45 minutes to reach the château. Those who do make the climb will be rewarded with a marvelous view of the surrounding valleys and mountains. The fortress and museum are closed December through March; there's an admission charge (phone: 61-01-06-94). There are two other Catharist châteaux in the area, one at nearby Roquefixade (follow D9 north of D117), also set on a rocky hilltop; the other at Puivert (12 miles/19 km east of the nearby village of Lavelanet on D117).

Follow D117 east from Lavelanet to pick up D613 southwest just before Quillan. At Ax-les-Thermes the road runs into N20, which follows the course of the Ariège River south into ruggedly beautiful mountain terrain, across the high Col de Puymorens (closed in bad winter weather), which serves as the grand gateway to the Cerdagne, the ancestral home of the Catalan people. Here, during the Middle Ages, they gained renown for their top-secret iron-smelting and -forging techniques, which produced the strongest iron in Europe—much in demand in that bellicose period. The Catalan Counts of Cerdagne went on to become Counts of Barcelona and Roussillon and Kings of Aragon.

Take N20 from the Col de Puymorens to Bourg-Madame on the Spanish frontier, then N116 northeast through the high mountain plain of the Cerdagne past a string of ski resorts. This area has more sunny days than any other in France, hence the French government's solar energy program at Font-Romeu and Odeillo, 6 miles (10 km) east of Mont-Louis off N16 via D618, where the *Four Solaire,* a huge solar oven with 2,000 square yards of mirrors, is the largest in Europe.

Farther down N116 is the region called the Conflent, so named because it is at the confluence of several small rivers. Villefranche-de-Conflent is a thousand-year-old walled town that was massively fortified by Marshal Vauban, Louis XIV's military architect, in the 17th century when Roussillon was incorporated into France. The *Association Culturelle* (Rue St-Jean; phone: 68-96-25-64) schedules a rich program of historical tours and musical events in the summer.

From Villefranche-de-Conflent take a 4-mile (6-km) detour south on D116 to the faded spa town of Vernet-les-Bains, where an unobscured view of majestic Pic du Canigou, the symbol of the Catalan people, greets you. It is snow-covered into May in most years. Continue on the small, winding road south to the magnificent 11th-century *Abbaye de Saint-Martin-du-Canigou* (Abbey of St. Martin of Canigou; phone: 68-05-50-03), renowned for the grace and harmony of its church and cloister as well as for its commanding view—thanks to its magnificent location on the slopes of towering Canigou. The abbey itself is not accessible by car. Hikers can reach it by steep, rugged trails from the village of Casteil, a two-hour round trip. The *Garage Villacèque* (phone: 68-05-51-14) in Vernet-les-Bains can arrange for a jeep to take visitors up.

Prades, 4 miles (6 km) from Villefranche-de-Conflent along N116, is the main town of the sunny, fruit-growing valley of the Conflent. Pablo Casals, the Catalan cellist, put Prades on the map in the 1950s when, in exile from his native Spain, he settled here and started the prestigious classical music festival that bears his name. It is still held annually from late July through mid-August. For details, contact the *Office de Tourisme* (Rue Victor-Hugo; phone: 68-96-27-58; fax: 68-96-50-95). The principal site of the concerts is the *Abbaye de Saint-Michel-de-Cuxa* (Abbey of St. Michael of Cuxa). Travelers familiar with the *Cloisters* of the *Metropolitan Museum of Art* in New York City will be especially interested in seeing the lovely 10th-century Romanesque abbey where many of the American museum's sculpted marble capitals originated—before they were transported to their new home in *Fort Tryon Park*. Concerts are also held in the *Eglise St-Pierre* in the center of otherwise uninteresting Prades. It has a huge elaborately hand-carved and gilded altarpiece by Catalan artisan Joseph Sunyer. Completed in 1699, this glorification of St. Peter has been called a "sculpted opera."

From Prades drive east on N116 about 9 miles (14 km) to pick up D618, which winds slowly and picturesquely southeast to Amélie-les-Bains-Palalda. About 5 miles (8 km) after the turnoff from N116, keep an eye out on your right for the little twisting drive to the *Prieuré de Serrabone,* the oldest Augustinan priory in Europe, founded in 1082. The austerity of its gray schist exterior masks one of the high points of Catalan Romanesque art inside—rose marble columns bearing a dazzlingly imaginative ensemble of sculpted capitals representing beasts and monsters from the Book of the Apocalypse. The priory also has a large botanical garden of Mediterranean plants and, as from many points in the area, a great view of Canigou, only 10 miles (16 km) to the west.

Continue south on D618 to Amélie-les-Bains-Palalda, whose thermal springs have attracted people with respiratory and muscular ailments from Roman times to the present day. This is the perfect starting point for some pleasant walks; a 30-minute stroll due south, for instance, leads to the impressive Gorges du Mondony.

Only 5 miles (8 km) away, due east on D115, is Céret, a little Catalan town that once attracted the likes of Picasso and Braque, among others.

Château de Riell Formerly a private mansion, this Relais and Châteaux member has 19 romantic guestrooms and three suites, complete with lovely antiques and roaring fireplaces. The hotel also has two pools and two tennis courts on its 60 acres of wooded private park, with a view of Pic du Canigou. On request the hotel will set up a program of thermal treatments at the Molitg-les-Bains spa. The one-Michelin-star restaurant excels in Catalan-French fare such as anchovy puff pastry, roast lamb with thyme and pimientos, filet of sole with poached oysters and caviar, and ice cream with fresh apricots and figs. Closed November through March. Molitg-les-Bains, 4 miles (6 km) north of Prades via D14 (phone: 68-05-04-40; fax: 68-05-04-37). Expensive.

CÉRET With a population of only 7,300 people, Céret, called the "Mecca of Cubism," is best known for the artists who used to live and work here and for its *Musée d'Art Moderne* (8 Bd. Maréchal-Joffre; phone: 68-87-27-73; fax: 68-87-31-92), filled with their paintings and sculpture. Enlarged and renovated in 1992, it is one of the most attractive art museums in France, with a collection that includes works by Matisse, Chagall, Juan Gris, Miró, Dalí, Maillol, and Manolo, the sculptor credited with luring the other artists here in the first place. There are also outstanding contemporary works by Tapiès, Viallat, and the Capdevilles, to name just a few. The museum has 53 pieces by Picasso, including a series of 28 delightful ceramic bowls that depict bull-fighting scenes. The museum is closed Tuesdays from October through June; there's an admission charge.

Not surprisingly, there is a plaza named after Picasso in the old part of Céret, as well as a monument to this well-loved "adopted" son. Be sure to see the restored 14th-century Pont du Diable (Devil's Bridge), which rises 73 feet over the Tech River in a single arch. The tourist office is at 1 Av. G.-Clemenceau (phone: 68-87-00-53).

Les Feuillants A rare find in this out-of-the-way region, this harmoniously decorated restaurant in an Art Nouveau mansion, under the huge plane trees of old Céret, offers the sophisticated Catalan-Mediterranean cuisine of Didier Banyols. Marie-Louise Banyols, one of Roussillon's top sommeliers, complements her husband's cooking with an outstanding selection of regional wines. Their efforts have earned them one Michelin star. The prix fixe lunch menu on weekdays is a good value. There are also three guestrooms. Closed Mondays (except in July and August) and Sunday dinner. Reservations advised. Major credit cards accepted. 1 Bd. La Fayette (phone: 68-78-37-88; fax: 68-87-44-68). Expensive.

Terrasse au Soleil This charming old Catalan farmhouse with a modern hotel annex sits in the hills covered with cherry orchards above Céret and offers yet another fine view of lofty Pic du Canigou. A member of the Relais de Silence group of hotels, it has 27 sunny rooms, a large swimming pool, a tennis court, a golf practice lawn, and a restaurant with good, basic cuisine of the region, such as *magret de canard aux cerises* (duck breast with cherries). The attractive young owners, Pascal and Brigitte Levielle-Nizerolle, have both worked in the United States. Closed January 2 through the first week of March. A mile (1.6 km) west of the village on D13F, Rte. de Fontfrède (phone: 68-87-01-94; fax: 68-87-39-24). Expensive.

En Route from Céret Continue east on D618 through the cherry orchards of the Tech Valley and, via N114, south to the resorts of the Côte Vermeille (Vermilion Coast). Collioure is 20 miles (32 km) from Céret.

COLLIOURE This tiny fishing port 15 miles (24 km) north of the Spanish border has been called the "Pearl of the Côte Vermeille"; it is certainly one of the most picturesque and pleasant bathing resorts on the Roussillon coast. The tranquil beauty of the spot, with its two tiny bays separated by an impressive fortified château, became a favorite subject for such turn-of-the-century artists as Matisse, Derain, Dufy, Picasso, and Braque. Collioure is considered the birthplace of the Fauvist movement, a precursor of Cubism.

Collioure was a port for Phoenician and then Roman merchants, and continued to be an important center of commerce during the Middle Ages, when the Catalonian coast dominated Mediterranean trade. However, it lost commercial importance in the mid-17th century, when Marshal Vauban destroyed almost half of the city and gave it its present look.

The sprawling brick château here was the summer home of the kings of Majorca during their short but remarkable reign (ca. 1276–1344) over Perpignan and Roussillon. The château has changing exhibits and is open daily; there's an admission charge. The 17th-century *Eglise Notre-Dame-des-Anges,* set at the edge of the old port near the beach, has a magnificent gilded retable crafted in 1698 by Joseph Sunyer. The church's tower once served as the port's lighthouse.

Aside from these historical points of interest, the town's principal attractions are sandy beaches, albeit relatively small and crowded, and the charm of its tiny streets, lined with inviting little outdoor restaurants serving such simple pleasures as fresh anchovies and great iced platters of fresh seafood, accompanied by the wines of neighboring vineyards.

BEST EN ROUTE

Casa Païral A century-old Catalan mansion is now a 26-room luxury hotel, a Relais de Silence member. It sits in its own private park with flower gardens, palm trees, and a pool, only 125 yards from the beach. There's no restaurant. Impasse des Palmiers (phone: 68-82-05-81; fax: 68-82-52-10). Expensive.

Relais des Trois Mas This elegant hotel in a converted private house offers 19 rooms and four suites, each decorated in the style of one of the painters who frequented the region; all rooms have Jacuzzis and views of the sea. The restaurant, *La Balette,* serves well-prepared local specialties (try the fresh anchovies); there's also a pool and fitness center. Closed mid-November through mid-December (phone: 68-82-05-07; fax: 68-82-38-08). Expensive.

Hostellerie des Templiers This lively hotel-bar-restaurant near the port was once the gathering place for the Fauves who lived and worked here in the early years of this century. The walls of its charmingly cluttered bar are lined with their sketches and paintings. The dining room, on the other hand, is strictly contemporary, with a fresco by Claude Viallat along one whole wall; there's also a terrace for outdoor dining facing the port and the château. Fresh local fish is the specialty of the house. The 52 simple rooms in the inn and its nearby annex were recently tastefully renovated. Closed January; restaurant also closed Sunday dinner and Mondays. Quai de l'Amirauté (phone: 68-98-31-10; fax: 68-98-01-24). Moderate.

San Vicens et Vieux Remparts One of a number of simple, outdoor café-restaurants overlooking the beach, this place offers fresh anchovies, salads, and copious platters of fresh seafood. Open daily. Reservations unnecessary. MasterCard and Visa accepted. Av. Boramar (phone: 68-82-05-12). Inexpensive.

En Route from Collioure The winding coast road that leads south from Collioure toward Spain is magnificently scenic, flanked on one side by the vine-covered slopes that produce the famous, sweet Banyuls wine, on the other by a breathtaking expanse of clear blue sea. Port-Vendres and Banyuls-sur-Mer (the birthplace of the sculptor Aristide Maillol), both only a few miles from Collioure, are extremely enjoyable places in which to soak up the Mediterranean sun and relax after a trek through the Pyrénées.

The Languedoc

Even the name of this large, infinitely diverse, and colorful region in France's sunny southwest promises a certain magic. Languedoc literally means "language of *oc*," *oc* meaning "yes" in the southern dialect, which long ago gave way to the official language of the north and its affirmative *oïl* (which became *oui*). But even if the province today submits to the language of the north, its heart and soul remain proudly independent. This is the deep south—a Mediterranean province blessed with sun, a beautiful coastline of sandy beaches, lush valleys resplendent with vineyards and orchards, and to the north, the rugged, mysterious terrain of the Causses and the Cévennes Mountains, some of the wildest and most beautiful country in all of France.

The regional boundaries of the Languedoc, as much a historical as an official entity, are not distinct, but are considered to take in the *départements* of Lozère, Gard, Hérault, Aude, Pyrénées-Orientales, and historically, parts of Tarn and Haute-Garonne. At one time the language of *oc* was spoken in nearly all the areas south of what might be considered the French Mason-Dixon Line, starting at the confluence of the Garonne and Dordogne Rivers in the west and curving up to Angoulême, across to Vichy, St-Etienne, and the Italian border in the east. Physically cut off from the north by the Massif Central, this region had reached a more advanced level of art and culture by the 9th and 10th centuries than the barbarian north. The seeds of this early development were planted by the Phoenicians, who colonized the Mediterranean coast circa 600 BC. They were followed in the 1st century BC by the Romans, who settled in the Bas Languedoc around Narbonne, making it the capital of the rich province of Gaule Narbonnaise. The remnants of their stay here are most visible in Nîmes, which boasts one of the world's best-preserved Roman temples.

The Visigoths held sway over this territory from the 5th century until their defeat in the 8th century by Charles Martel. The 9th century saw the establishment of the Counts of Toulouse, who controlled much of the Languedoc until the Albigensian Crusade, combined with the assaults of the jealous Capetian rulers in the north, brought their dynasty to an end in the 13th century and marked the beginning of the north's preeminence. The short but terrifying crusade against the Albigensians, religious dissenters who took their name from the city of Albi, where they found refuge early in their movement, left deep scars in the area. When the crusaders reached Béziers in 1209, the Catholics were invited to leave the city before the siege began, but they refused; in the end, the town's entire population, Catholics, Jews, and heretics alike, was massacred.

Farther south the Roussillon, the southern coastal area that, along with the adjacent northeast corner of Spain, forms Catalonia, was alternately under the jurisdiction of France and Spain during this period. Perpignan's formidable *Palais des Rois de Majorque* (Palace of the Kings of Majorca) bears witness to the glory of that dynasty. It wasn't until the Treaty of the Pyrénées in 1659 that this area came permanently under French rule. The official incorporation of the Languedoc and the rest of the southern part of the country into France started with Louis XIV in the late 17th century and was reinforced by Napoleon during the 19th century. Today an undercurrent of dissension against authority and northern rule still seems to exist here, occasionally erupting in vague separatist movements for a free Occitan state or, in Roussillon, a united Catalan state. There also has been a resurgence in the use of Languedoc's regional language, which is taught in the area's schools.

The Languedoc offers a range of cuisine: the much-heralded cassoulets of Toulouse, Carcassonne, and Castelnaudary; the traditional *cargolada* feast of Catalonia; bouillabaisse and a wealth of seafood along the coast; and rich, flavorful cheeses, including the famous Roquefort, from the Causses range. The region's most important product is the grape—one *département* alone, Hérault, produces almost one-fifth of all the wines of France—and a visit would not be complete without tasting some of the many local wines.

Besides delicious food, the region offers interesting historical sites and wonderfully diverse and dramatic countryside, the highlight of which is the 30-mile-long Gorges du Tarn. There also are darkly wooded mountains, the arid plateau of the limestone Causses, the wild Cévennes range rolling down into rugged, brush-covered areas, and the long Mediterranean coastline, backed by sunbaked vineyards. For more information on the area, contact the *Comité Régional du Tourisme* (12 Rue Salambo, Toulouse 31200; phone: 61-47-11-12).

This tour starts at Toulouse, the ancient capital of the Languedoc, and moves east to the great walled city of Carcassonne, then loops north to Albi, with a side trip to Cordes. From Albi it continues east to the rugged Causses Mountains, through the Gorges du Tarn and down the southern slopes of the Cévennes range to Nîmes, on the eastern border of the Languedoc. From Nîmes and its nearby Pont du Gard—a 1st-century Roman bridge—it curves down to Montpellier. From there a side trip to the Camargue area is possible; afterward the route follows the Mediterranean coast to Perpignan.

Though this area hardly can be considered undiscovered, it is less crowded than the neighboring Côte d'Azur, and its hotels and restaurants are relatively reasonable. For a double room per night, expect to pay $150 or more at a very expensive hotel, $100 to $150 at an expensive place, between $50 and $100 at a moderate hotel, and less than $50 in an inexpensive one. Unless otherwise indicated, all hotels accept major credit cards and are open year-round. Note that in July and August most hotels with restaurants require *demi-pension* (a higher rate that includes breakfast and either lunch or dinner). With very few exceptions the places listed below feature telephones, TV sets, and private baths in all of their rooms. However, some less expensive hotels may have private baths in only some rooms; it's a good idea when making a reservation to confirm whether your room has a private bath. Many hotels, even expensive ones, do not have air conditioning (although all truly deluxe establishments do). For a dinner for two with service (usually included in the bill) but not wine or drinks, expect to pay more than $100 in an expensive restaurant; $60 to $100 in a moderate place; and less than $60 in an inexpensive eatery. Unless otherwise noted, all restaurants listed below are open for lunch and dinner. For each location hotels and restaurants are listed alphabetically by price category.

TOULOUSE Someone once described Toulouse as "a city pink at dawn, red at midday, and mauve at dusk," a characterization that aptly captures the face of this warm, animated metropolis. Toulouse owes much of its visual charm to terra cotta brick, red roof tiles, the Garonne River, and the southern sun which, set in a translucent sky, plays off them all. The old capital of the Languedoc, it is today the fourth-largest city in France, a cultural capital and university center, and the heart of the nation's aerospace and electronics industries (the *Concorde* and the *Airbus* are built here, and their current financial difficulties may hurt the city's economy). It is also one of France's most appealing *villes d'art*.

This spot at a ford in the Garonne River was settled even before Rome; its early inhabitants were a tribe called the Volques-Tectosages. Later colonized by the Romans, it grew to become the third largest city in Gaul by the 3rd century. Around this time the evangelist St-Sernin arrived, converting much of the populace to Christianity. The Visigoths invaded in 410, making this the capital of their vast territory. Next came the Franks and a period of chaos. Order returned in 778 under Charlemagne, who created the Kingdom of Aquitaine. When Louis le Pieux (the Pious) became King of Aquitaine, he designated advisers from his family to oversee the city, thereby starting the line of the great Counts of Toulouse. For centuries these counts, whose lands spread from the Pyrénées to Auvergne, ruled over one of the liveliest courts in Europe. The city itself was governed by *capitouls* (consuls), who advised the counts on matters of defense and negotiation with vassals. This brilliant court was brought to its knees in the early 13th century during the bitter conflicts between the north and the south over the Cathari, or Albigensians, religious heretics against whom Pope Innocent III and the ruling Capetians of the north mounted a fierce crusade, led by the notorious Simon de Montfort. Count Raymond VI of Toulouse, accused of complicity with the heretics, fought to defend his city against the attacks of Montfort, who was killed here in 1218. In 1229 Raymond VII, demoralized by continued attacks from the north, agreed to abide by the Peace of Paris, which marked the beginning of the gradual incorporation of this area into the royal domain.

Meanwhile, Toulouse remained an important cultural center; this was the home of the troubadours, who around the year 1323 founded France's first literary society, the Académie des Jeux Floraux, to preserve *la langue d'oc.* Following the Albigensian Crusade and the devastation of the Hundred Years War, Toulouse experienced an economic renaissance thanks to a small plant called *coquanhas,* which yielded a popular blue dye whose production brought great fortunes to the city. Many of the palaces built by the newly rich *pastel* (dye) merchants in the early 16th century still remain.

Toulouse's old districts abound in architectural gems, from 11th-century stone dwellings to Renaissance *hôtels particuliers.* Near the heart of town and Rue d'Alsace-Lorraine, Toulouse's main commercial street, is the *Hôtel de Ville* (Town Hall), a marble-pillared Baroque marvel dominating the immense Place du Capitole. Next door is the tourist office (in the historic *Donjon du Capitole,* Rue Lafayette; phone: 61-11-02-22). Nearby are two of the city's loveliest Renaissance structures: the *Hôtel de Bernuy,* at 1 Rue Gambetta, and farther south, off the broad Rue de Metz, the *Hôtel d'Assézat.* The latter was built in the 1550s by Toulouse's greatest Renaissance architect, Nicolas Bachelier, for one of the city's *pastel* merchants. On Rue Lakanal are the church, cloister, and convent of *Les Jacobins.* The church, an example of the unusual Gothic style of the region, features four single rows of tall supporting pillars across the middle of the nave; the play of light and color in its spacious polychrome interior is wonderful. There is also a reliquary containing the remains of St. Thomas Aquinas.

On Rue du Taur (Bull Street) is the *Eglise Notre-Dame-du-Taur,* said to have been constructed on the spot where, in 250, the body of the martyred St. Sernin was left after he had been dragged through the streets by a bull until he died. At the end of Rue du Taur is Toulouse's gem, the magnificent *Basilique St-Sernin,* the largest and considered to be the most beautiful Romanesque church in the south of France. Begun in 1080 on the foundation of a 4th-century basilica, consecrated in 1096, and completed in the middle of the 14th century, it is laid out in the form of a Latin cross. Notice the nine chapels surrounding the apse, the superb 12th-century five-story bell tower, and the Renaissance *Porte Miégeville* (Miégeville Gate) with its magnificently carved marble figures.

Another of Toulouse's old districts is centered around the *Cathédrale St-Etienne* (Pl. St-Etienne, off Allée François-Verdier), a structure that, in comparison with the exquisitely harmonious *St-Sernin,* appears jarringly lopsided and disparate. Not to be missed is the *Musée des Augustins* (21 Rue de Metz; phone: 61-22-21-82). It is filled with paintings and sculpture from all periods, including the richest collection of chiseled stonework in France, all in the pleasing medieval setting of an old Augustinian convent. The *Notre-Dame-de-Grâce* here is one of the most celebrated medieval sculptures of the Virgin and Child. The museum is closed Tuesdays; there's an admission charge. The *Musée Paul-Dupuy* (13 Rue de la Pleau; phone: 61-22-21-83) is devoted to applied arts from the Middle Ages to the present; the displays include clocks, coins, metalwork, and stamps. It is closed Tuesdays and Sunday mornings; there's an admission charge. The *Musée du Vieux-Toulouse* (7 Rue du May, off Rue St-Rome; no phone) contains regional art and displays on the history and traditions of the city. It is closed mornings, Sundays, and in winter on Thursdays; there's an admission charge. The *Musée d'Histoire Naturelle* (35 Allées Jules-Guesde; phone: 61-52-00-14) has a significant prehistoric collection. It is closed Tuesdays; admission charge. Down the street are the law courts (12 Allées Jules-Guesde).

Also in this district are the *Palais de Justice* (Pl. du Salin), on the site of the former residence of the Counts of Toulouse; the *Eglise Notre-Dame-de-la-Daurade* (Quai de la Daurade), which has a lovely Renaissance doorway; and the *Hôtel de Clary* (Rue de la Dalbade), with its 17th-century stone façade. At the end of Pont Neuf is the *Château d'Eau,* an 1822 water tower that is now a museum and photography gallery. The museum is closed Tuesdays; there's an admission charge (phone: 61-42-61-72).

Don't leave Toulouse without strolling through one of its many delightful small parks or tasting its cassoulet, the hardy white bean, duck (or goose), and sausage dish that the city claims as its own. Duck products are sold at *Ducs de Gascogne* (60 Bd. Carnot; phone: 61-62-28-00), a link in the nationwide chain that specializes in foie gras, *magret,* and *confit de canard.* Oenophiles might be interested in *Domaine de Lastours* (44 Rue de Languedoc; phone: 61-52-05-20), the oldest wine merchant in town, which carries more than 3,000 different varieties. *Mélomanes* (music lovers) may want to check out Toulouse's world class orchestra, which makes its home in the *Théâtre du Capitole* (Pl. du Capitole; phone: 61-23-21-35); for additional details, see *The Liveliest Arts: Theater, Opera, and Music* in DIVERSIONS. And one of the biggest and best antiques fairs in France, the *Salon des Antiquaires Languedoc-Midi-Pyrénées,* is held here around the second week in November at the *Parc des Expositions.*

BEST EN ROUTE

Grand Hôtel de l'Opéra This gracious 17th-century edifice, once a convent, has been completely transformed into one of the most charming and comfortable hostelries in town. Its entrance is secluded in a tranquil courtyard, and in addition to its nine suites and 42 contemporary rooms, there are a pool, a fitness center, and an excellent two-Michelin-star restaurant, *Les Jardins de l'Opéra.* Here, Dominique Toulousy, one of France's most promising young chefs, concocts such heavenly specialties as *raviolis de foie gras frais* (ravioli filled with fresh foie gras) and *poularde truffée* (young chicken with truffles), which are served in lovely flower-filled garden dining rooms. Restaurant closed Sundays, holidays, and three weeks in August. Reservations necessary. Major credit cards accepted. 1 Pl. du Capitole (phone: 61-21-82-66, hotel; 61-23-07-76, restaurant; fax: 61-23-41-04). Hotel, very expensive; restaurant, expensive.

Grand Hôtel Capoul Right in the center of town, this 133-room, seven-suite hotel features large rooms and a good brasserie-style restaurant. 13 Place du Président-Wilson (phone: 61-10-70-70; fax: 61-21-96-70). Expensive.

Vanel At this one-Michelin-star restaurant, Gascon specialties dominate. The surroundings are modern, refined, and pleasingly relaxed. Closed Sundays, holidays, and the first two weeks in August. Reservations advised. Major credit cards accepted. 22 Rue Maurice-Fontvieille (phone: 61-21-51-82; fax: 61-23-69-04). Expensive.

Des Beaux-Arts In a lovingly remodeled building, this 20-room hotel contains a Parisian-style brasserie. Near the edge of the Garonne and the *Ecole des Beaux-Arts,* at 1 Pl. du Pont Neuf (phone: 61-23-40-50; fax: 61-22-02-27). Moderate.

Colombier A pleasingly unpretentious restaurant, it is reputed to serve the best cassoulet in town; the *magret aux cèpes* (duck breast with wild mushrooms) is also good. Closed Saturday lunch, Sundays, *Easter,* three weeks in August, and *Christmas* week. Reservations advised. Major credit cards accepted. Near the train station, at 14 Rue Bayard (phone: 61-62-40-05). Moderate.

En Route from Toulouse Paralleling A61 to Carcassonne is France's engineering masterpiece from the era of Louis XIV—the Canal du Midi. Completed in 1680, the 150-mile waterway linking Toulouse and Sète was once the main connection between the Atlantic Ocean and the Mediterranean Sea. Boats transported wine, wheat, lumber, and passengers until the canal was supplanted by the railroad in the late 19th century. Today vacation houseboats and wine barges ply the waters. A61 continues southeast to the great fortified city of Carcassonne, 58 miles (93 km) from Toulouse, passing Castelnaudary on the way. Both cities, like Toulouse, lay claim to the quintessential cassoulet, so if you're one to make gastronomic comparisons, a lunchtime stop at Castelnaudary is a must. *Mapotel Les Palmes* (10 Rue Maréchal-Foch; phone: 68-83-17-10) and the *Grand Hôtel Fourcade* (14 Rue des Carmes; phone: 68-23-02-08) are hotels with restaurants that come highly recommended for their cassoulet; both accept major credit cards.

CARCASSONNE One of the largest fortified cities in Europe, Carcassonne stands like a turreted fairy-tale creation high on a plateau overlooking the Aude River. Its imposing ramparts are even more impressive at night when illuminated. The city is made up of two parts: the Ville Nouvelle (New City), established by Louis IX in the 13th century on the river's left bank, and La Cité, the older fortified city, on top of a 1,500-foot hill on the right bank. Leave your car in the lot on the city's east side and walk through the lovely *Porte Narbonnaise* (Narbonne Gate) and across the drawbridge into the older part of the city. Souvenir stalls abound, but the city's curving streets and half-timbered and stone dwellings retain enough charm to allow one to drift back to the time of Raymond-Roger Trencavel, Viscount of Carcassonne, under whose dynasty many of its grandest monuments, including the walled *Château Comtal* and the *Basilique St-Nazaire,* were constructed. Long before the Trencavels, the Romans fortified this spot in the 1st century, and in the 5th century the Visigoths added their share of stones to the strategic ramparts, for centuries the border between France and Spain.

Charlemagne besieged the city for five years in the 9th century; according to legend he eventually was outwitted by Dame Carcas, a clever townswoman who tossed the city's last remaining pig, stuffed with the last rations of wheat, over the ramparts, thereby giving him the impression that their larders were well stocked and their spirits unbroken. Discouraged, Charlemagne retreated, his departure announced by Dame Carcas's trumpet call and the townspeople's jubilant cries of "Carcas sonne" ("Carcas sounds the horn").

During the Albigensian Crusade of the 13th century, the Trencavel dynasty and the city fell to Simon de Montfort, who then established this fort as his base in the south. Later, Louis IX (St. Louis) and then his son Philip III (the Bold) further strengthened the city with a second series of ramparts encircling the first. The strength of this double-walled system was never tested, however, because the city lost its strategic importance when the 1659 Treaty of the Pyrénées established that mountain range as the boundary between France and Spain. The new city became a major textile manufacturing center, and the fortress was neglected until 1844, when, at the behest of the French government, architect Eugène Viollet-le-Duc was commissioned to restore it. His ambitious project resulted in a largely accurate vision of how Carcassonne must have looked during the Middle Ages, though there is debate to this day about how far such restorations should go to reconstruct missing elements of historical treasures based solely on the educated guesses of contemporary scholarship.

A tour of the 12th-century *Château Comtal,* its museum, and the surrounding ramparts is a must. The château is closed on holidays; there's an admission charge (phone: 68-25-01-66). Also make sure to visit the *Basilique St-Nazaire* (also in La Cité), with its lovely Gothic windows, considered among the finest in the Midi. The city's winding streets are alive with cafés and pleasant restaurants, many featuring cassoulet. In summer there are frequent concerts in the open-air amphitheater, the *Grand Théâtre.* The city is particularly spectacular on *Bastille Day* (July 14); for details, see *Festivals à la Française* in DIVERSIONS. For two weeks in August the city presents various shows on medieval life. For information, contact the main tourist office (15 Boulevard Camille-Pelletan; phone: 68-25-07-04) or its branch (*Porte Narbonnaise;* phone: 68-25-68-81); the latter is open from *Easter* through October only.

Château St-Martin ("Logis de Trencavel") A member of the Relais & Châteaux group, this elegant restaurant, set in a château in its own park, is worth the short trip from town. Boasting one Michelin star, it is reputed to serve the best cassoulet in town; a wide array of other tempting, creative specialties rounds out the menu. Closed Wednesdays and a week at *Easter.* Reservations necessary. Major credit cards accepted. About 3 miles (5 km) northeast of the ramparts of La Cité, via Rue A.-Marty, in the suburb of Montredon (phone: 68-71-09-53). Expensive.

La Cité This elegant former pope's palace within the ramparts sustains the medieval mood with appropriately heavy and grand decor. Its 23 large, renovated rooms and three suites, with high ceilings and balconies, are luxurious; there is also a pool and lovely terrace. Its restaurant, *La Barbacane,* features Provençal cuisine with touches of the southwest; considered one of the best dining spots in town, it has earned one Michelin star. Specialties include excellent cassoulet, fresh tomato tart with fried basil leaves, and *beignets de fruit* (fruit fritters) for dessert. Hotel closed mid-January through mid-February; restaurant also closed Sunday dinner and Mondays. Reservations necessary. Major credit cards accepted. Pl. de l'Eglise (phone: 68-25-03-34, hotel; 68-71-60-60, restaurant; fax: 68-71-50-15). Expensive.

Domaine D'Auriac One of the best restaurants in the region, with one Michelin star, this is the place to try foie gras done in salt and the more esoteric cow's cheek with pig's ear *à la carcassonnaise.* There are also 23 guestrooms at this Relais & Châteaux member. Closed Sunday dinner and Monday lunch from November through *Easter,* and three weeks in January. Reservations necessary. Major credit cards accepted. Two and a half miles (4 km) south of Carcassonne, on the Rte. de St-Hilaire, in Auriac (phone: 68-25-72-22; fax: 68-47-35-54). Expensive.

Donjon This small hotel has a pleasing, airy mood and 36 simply decorated rooms, some with small balconies. There's a nice garden restaurant, open to hotel guests only. In the heart of La Cité, at 2 Rue du Comte-Roger (phone: 68-71-08-80; fax: 68-25-06-60). Expensive.

Auberge du Pont-Levis-Pautard An elegant family-run restaurant with a flower-filled terrace at one of the entrances to La Cité, it focuses on regional dishes and local wines. Closed Sunday dinner, Mondays, three weeks in January, and two weeks in September. Reservations advised. Major credit cards accepted. At the Pont Levis, near the *Porte Narbonnaise* (phone: 68-25-55-23; fax: 68-47-32-29). Moderate.

Mercure La Vicomté This modern hotel with 58 rooms and three suites also has an excellent view of the ramparts and a big swimming pool. There's no restaurant. 18 Rue C.-Saint-Saens, *Porte Narbonnaise* (phone: 68-71-45-45; 800-221-4542; fax: 68-71-11-45). Moderate.

Pont Vieux There are 20 rooms in this charming hotel but no restaurant. Closed two weeks in January. Between the Pont Vieux and the walls of La Cité, at 32 Rue Trivalle (phone: 68-25-24-99; fax: 68-47-62-71). Moderate.

En Route from Carcassonne Take D118 north into the Montagne Noire (Black Mountains), a gentle range that marks the extreme southeastern limit of the Massif Central. The southern slopes of these mountains are arid, but on the northern side, where rainfall is heavy, they are cloaked with lush forests whose thick darkness has given the range its name. The highest peak is 3,699-foot Pic de Nore. Its northern slopes roll down into the *Parc Régional du Haut Languedoc,* an area dotted with lakes and beautiful scenery too often overlooked by visitors. The nature lover will want to make a small circuit of the small, often unnumbered roads of the Montagne Noire and the park. The town of Mazamet, the regional center of France's wool industry since the 18th century, makes a convenient base for excursions. For information, stop at the tourist office (Rue des Casernes; phone: 63-61-27-07).

Head northwest for 11 miles (18 km) on N112 to Castres, the birthplace of the socialist leader Jean Jaurès. In town is the *Musée Jean-Jaurès* (Pl. Pelisson; phone: 63-72-01-01), which is closed Mondays except in July and August; there's an admission charge. The *Hôtel de Ville* (Town Hall; Rue de l'Hôtel de Ville), formerly a bishop's palace, has an elegant sculpted garden, the *Jardin de l'Evêché,* the work of André Lenôtre, landscaper of the gardens of Versailles. And don't miss the *Musée Goya* (Rue de l'Hôtel de Ville; phone: 63-71-59-30), with a collection of paintings spanning 50 years of the artist's life. The museum is closed Mondays except in July and August; there's an admission charge. For additional details, contact the tourist office (Pl. de la République; phone: 65-59-92-44).

From Castres take a short detour east on D622 to the Sidobre, a granite plateau with strange, fascinating rock formations. Cut with grottoes and the deep gorges of the Agout and Durenque Rivers, the site also features gigantic granite quarries. Although the great round boulders piled precariously on top of one another seem to be human creations, the picturesque curiosities, with names like "Rock of the Goose," "Trembling Rock," and "Three Cheeses," are the work of nature. Back in Castres continue north on N112 to Albi, 25 miles (40 km) away.

BEST EN ROUTE

Château de Montlédier This medieval structure converted to a comfortable hotel features 10 spacious rooms overlooking the gorges of the Arn, plus a restaurant. Closed January. Near the Pont de l'Arn, about 3 miles (5 km) east of Mazamet via D109 and D54 (phone: 63-61-20-54; fax: 63-98-22-51). Expensive.

La Métairie Neuve Set in a converted farmhouse, this charming hotel has 11 rooms, a pool, and a restaurant. Closed mid-December through mid-January. In Bout-du-Pont-de-Larn, 1 mile (1.6 km) outside Mazamet via D54 (phone: 63-61-23-31; fax: 63-61-94-75). Moderate.

ALBI This enchanting pink city is somewhat off the tourist track, but a glimpse of the powerful brick cathedral, towering above the Tarn River, will make you glad you came. Like Toulouse, Albi la Rouge, as it is called, is built of terra cotta brick and red roof tiles, and the tones and moods of the city change with the movement of the sun.

Albi was an important religious center during the 12th and 13th centuries, not only for the Catholic church but also for the Cathari, or Albigensians, a sect that found refuge and gathered strength in this city. They were later chased south by Simon de Montfort, the warrior who led Pope Innocent III's fierce crusade against them. Albi's great *Cathédrale Ste-Cécile* (Pl. Ste-Cécile) was built at the end of the 13th century after the martyrdom of the last of the Cathari, a symbol of the restored strength and irrefutability of the Catholic church's dominance. For additional details on the cathedral, see *Celebrated Châteaux and Cathedrals* in DIVERSIONS. Next door is the 13th-century *Palais de la Berbie,* formerly the archbishop's palace and now the *Musée Toulouse-Lautrec* (phone: 63-54-14-09), which has the most important collection anywhere of the Albi-born artist's work. For additional details on this extraordinary museum, which is closed Tuesdays in off-season, see *Memorable Museums and Monuments* in DIVERSIONS.

You can visit some of the rooms in Toulouse-Lautrec's birthplace, now the *Hôtel du Bosc* (14 Rue Toulouse-Lautrec; phone: 63-69-20-83) in Vieil Albi (Old Albi). The home is open daily; admission charge. This section of town is filled with charmingly lopsided, half-timbered houses, artisans' workshops, and cozy little restaurants. The plaques of the Circuit Pourpré (Crimson Circuit) mark a self-guided tour of Vieil Albi, which passes by the beautiful *Eglise* and *Cloître St-Salvy* (Rue Ste-Cécile), created in several styles from the 12th through the 15th century. In July and August, the tourist office (19 Pl. Ste-Cécile; phone: 63-54-22-30) operates a small sightseeing train. It operates daily (on weekends, afternoons only), leaving every 45 minutes from the Place Ste-Cécile in front of the tourist office; there's an admission charge. During the summer Albi holds several festivals, including the *Festival de Musique* in August, and the town's *Bastille Day* fireworks, bursting over the placid Tarn with the illuminated cathedral as a backdrop, are breathtaking. Consult the tourist office for information and schedules; it's open daily.

BEST EN ROUTE

La Réserve A plush Relais & Châteaux member, it has 20 rooms and four suites, plus a pool, tennis courts, and a fine restaurant. Closed November through

April. Reservations essential for hotel and restaurant. Two miles (3 km) outside town at the edge of the Gorges du Tarn via D600, Rte. de Cordes (phone: 63-47-60-22; fax: 63-47-63-60). Very expensive.

Hostellerie St-Antoine Founded in 1739, this establishment was rebuilt in the 1960s, so it looks relatively modern. The lobby is decorated with antiques and flowers, the tranquil breakfast garden is lovely, the 42 rooms and eight suites are pleasant and comfortable, and the restaurant is very good. Guests may use the pool and tennis facilities of *La Réserve* (above). Half hidden on a quiet street near the center of Albi, at 17 Rue St-Antoine (phone: 63-54-04-04; fax: 63-47-10-47). Expensive.

Hostellerie du Vigan This comfortable, well-maintained hotel has 40 rooms and a terrace restaurant with a great view of the old city. 16 Pl. Vigan (phone: 63-54-01-23; fax: 63-47-05-42). Moderate.

Le Jardin des Quatre Saisons The chef here favors seasonal specialties with a light touch, such as crab and eggplant cannelloni; the wine list is outstanding. Closed Mondays. Reservations advised. Major credit cards accepted. 19 Bd. Strasbourg (phone: 63-60-77-76). Moderate.

Mercure-Altéa Albi Bastide In what was once a mill are 56 smallish but charming rooms with modern amenities, such as mini-bars, and spectacular views of the city; those facing the cathedral are quieter than those overlooking the Tarn. There's a restaurant. 41 *bis* Rue Porta (phone: 63-47-66-66; 800-221-4542; fax: 63-46-18-40). Moderate.

Moulin de La Mothe In a converted mill with a lovely terrace on the banks of the Tarn, this restaurant features local specialties such as squab with wild mushrooms. Guestrooms also should be available beginning this year. Closed Wednesdays, Sunday dinner except in July and August, and two weeks each in February and November. Reservations advised. Major credit cards accepted. Rue Lamothe (phone: 63-60-38-15; fax: 63-47-68-84). Moderate.

En Route from Albi Travel 16 miles (26 km) northwest on D600 through pastoral countryside to the medieval town of Cordes.

CORDES This town also is called Cordes-sur-Ciel (Cordes on the Sky), because of its dramatic location on the crest of a steep hill, and La Dame en Pierre (The Woman in Stone), because of the lovely stone structures that line its steep, narrow streets and the five sets of protective walls that surround them. The Counts of Toulouse built their hunting lodges on this hill in the early 13th century. Later, Count Raymond VII fortified the town, making it a Catharist refuge and a stronghold against the advances of Simon de Montfort. After the Albigensian Crusade the city grew into a prosperous center for leatherwork and weaving. During the 16th century it again offered refuge, this time to Catholics, who in 1568 were attacked by the Protestants here. As a result of the bubonic plague and several wars, in later centuries the town was virtually abandoned, until Prosper Mérimée, the inspector of historical monuments under Louis-Philippe, ordered its restoration.

Cordes boasts some of the finest examples of Gothic civic architecture in France. Particularly beautiful are the old hunting lodges and the grand façades of homes built during the city's heyday. Today a handful of artists and craftspeople have boutiques here, and there are pleasant cafés and hotels. Although you can drive into Cordes, the streets are very narrow; it's best to leave your car in a lot near the city entrance and explore on foot. For information, stop by the tourist office (*Hôtel de Ville;* phone: 63-56-00-52), which is closed from mid-September through *Easter.*

BEST EN ROUTE

Le Grand Ecuyer The former hunting lodge of Count Raymond VII of Toulouse, this magnificent medieval edifice has 12 large, elegant rooms, some with fireplaces and all furnished with antiques. The welcoming restaurant, with its warmly lighted lounge, serves creative cuisine that has earned a star from Michelin. Closed mid-October through March; restaurant also closed Mondays except in July and August. On the tiny, unnamed, cobblestone main street (phone: 63-56-01-03; fax: 63-56-16-99). Expensive.

Hostellerie du Vieux Cordes Of the 21 lovely rooms here, ask for one with a view of the valley, which is spectacular. There's also a good restaurant, with a pleasant vine-festooned terrace overlooking the valley; the quirky menu proudly celebrates the virtues of salmon and duck and offers a surprisingly varied array of dishes featuring one or the other. Closed January. In the center of town, on a tiny unnamed street (phone: 63-56-00-12). Moderate.

En Route from Cordes Return to Albi and take D999 toward Millau, 68 miles (109 km) to the east. You'll notice a gradual change in the scenery as you move into the range known as Les Causses, roughly translated as "The Chalky Lands." Here the land was pushed up by the same cataclysmic shifting of continents that produced the Pyrénées, forming great plateaus resembling those in Arizona and New Mexico. Les Causses dominate the landscape, rising dramatically above the surrounding valleys and gorges. There are many caves here where prehistoric peoples once lived, but now the arid limestone plateaus are largely uninhabited, except for herds of about a million sheep. Their rich milk produces such flavorful cheeses as roquefort, made in Roquefort-sur-Soulzon (14 miles/22 km outside of Millau). The tour there of the roquefort cheese operation (phone: 65-58-58-58), however, is crowded and uninteresting.

MILLAU Sitting placidly at the confluence of the Tarn and the Dourbie Rivers, in a rich green valley rimmed with the limestone walls and forested slopes, Millau is the largest city in the Causses and the western gateway to the magnificent Gorges du Tarn. The Romans settled here in 121 BC near a rich bed of fine clay that ancient craftspeople fashioned into the pottery known as Graufesenque, famous throughout the Roman world. Digs in the area have turned up many examples of this glazed red pottery, which also has been found in Italy (near Pompeii), Germany, and Scotland. Since the 12th century Millau has been known for fine leatherwork, particularly gloves made from the skins of the mountain sheep that produce the region's cheeses. The city still produces about a third of the gloves made in France plus a vast array of other leather goods that can be purchased in the shops lining the commercial streets. Although there are some sites of interest—the *Eglise Notre-Dame,* the 12th-century Gothic belfry, the archaeological museum with a collection of Graufesenque pottery (all on Place Foch), and the quaint old section of town—Millau's real appeal is its scenic location, its pleasant arcaded squares, and its unhurried pace of life. For more information, contact the tourist office (1 Av. Alfred-Merle; phone: 65-60-02-42).

BEST EN ROUTE

La Musardière This 120-year-old hotel, a former *hôtel particulier,* retains the atmosphere of an elegant private home, with a grand stairway and 12 large, individually furnished bedrooms. The lively patroness cultivates a homey feeling; her plush dining room offers traditional fare. Closed from November through *Easter.* 34 Av. de la République (phone: 65-60-20-63; fax: 65-61-02-05). Expensive.

Château de Creissels Set on a hill overlooking Millau is this old château with a crenelated tower, 33 simply furnished yet comfortable rooms, and a breakfast garden. The dining room is under the warm stone vaulting of the oldest part of the castle, which dates from the 8th century. Closed late December through mid-February. About a mile (1.6 km) west of town via D992, Rte. St-Affrique, in Creissels (phone: 65-60-16-59; fax: 65-61-24-63). Moderate.

International Although this establishment has 110 rooms, service is very personalized. The rooms on higher floors have breathtaking views. The restaurant features typically French dishes. 1 Pl. de la Tine (phone: 65-60-20-66; fax: 65-59-11-78). Moderate.

Relais du Bois du Four This rustic, 27-room hotel has comfortable rooms overlooking a large park. There's also a simple restaurant. Hotel closed December through mid-March; restaurant also closed Wednesdays except from July through September. In St-Léons, 12 miles (19 km) northeast of Millau via D911 and D529 (phone: 65-61-86-17). Inexpensive.

En Route from Millau Follow D110 northeast for 6 miles (10 km) to the Chaos de Montpellier-le-Vieux, an extraordinary group of bizarre rock formations built up over centuries by the slow dripping of water on the surface of the Causse Noir. This rock forest in the middle of nowhere looks, from a distance, somewhat like a city in ruins; it once was feared by the inhabitants of the area as a cursed place haunted by the devil. Signs for the Chaos lead from the main road to the *Auberge du Maubert,* in a clearing, where one can purchase tickets before driving 2 miles (3 km) farther to a parking lot at the entrance. A walk through this rock labyrinth, which is open daily from mid-March through October only, takes about one and a half hours. Signposts guide you past masses of tall rocks shaped like bears, sphinxes, and other creatures; one is even labeled Queen Victoria, although the resemblance is scant.

Continue northeast on D110, then D29 to Le Rozier (13 miles/21 km from Millau); from there pick up D907 north, which for the next 30 miles (48 km) or so winds its way through the Gorges du Tarn, one of the most extraordinarily scenic stretches of country in all of France.

GORGES DU TARN Like the Causses, these limestone gorges at the southern extreme of the Massif Central probably were formed at the same time as the Pyrénées. The Tarn River, flowing down from Mont-Lozère in the Cévennes range, ran into the giant fissure, carving its deep, dramatic path through these canyons over millions of years. The road snakes along the Tarn in the shadow of sheer limestone cliffs and magnificent rock formations towering high above the riverbed. A number of quaint villages are nestled amid these canyons, with rustic *auberges* and cozy restaurants. Some of the most beautiful rock formations are found around Les Vignes, one of the first villages along the way. For a magnificent vista of the gorges, take the small side road at Les Vignes up a hill to Point Sublime, some 1,320 feet above the river. A little farther is the town of La Malène, the starting point for one of several boat trips through the gorges; this one leads through the beautiful *détroits* (straits) and the Cirque des Baumes, a circular rock formation inaccessible by car. A few miles past La Malène on D907 is one of the loveliest hotels in the gorges, the *Château de la Caze* (see *Best en Route*), worth a look even if you don't plan to spend the night.

At a northern loop in the river a bit farther along D907 is the medieval village of Ste-Enimie, a picturesque place with lively cafés and shops. The ancient convent with the Romanesque chapel is said to have been built by St. Enimie herself, a young noblewoman who was cured of leprosy at this spot and thereafter devoted her life to God. See also the *Fontaine de Burle* (Burle Fountain), whose waters are purported to have cured the saint, and the grotto chapel in the rocks above the village.

From Ste-Enimie a southern detour of 16 miles (26 km) via D986 leads to the grottoes of Aven Armand, whose stalagmites, reaching to nearly 100 feet, are considered some of the most magnificent in the area. Return to Ste-Enimie. Follow the windings of the river along D907, then take N106 south to Florac, the eastern gateway to the gorges. From here take sinu-

ous N106 southeast through the beautiful, wild, green mountains of the
Cévennes range to Nîmes, about 60 miles (96 km) away.

BEST EN ROUTE

Château de la Caze This wonderful pale stone château, built in the 15th century,
sits in a low meadow on the banks of the Tarn under the shadow of a tremendous looming rock. The mood is late-medieval and tranquil, the 12 large
rooms and, in an annex, six suites are decorated with antiques, and the
restaurant's food is very good. Closed November through April; restaurant
also closed Tuesdays and for lunch except on weekends and holidays. Four
miles (6 km) northeast of La Malène (phone: 66-48-51-01; fax: 66-48-55-
75). Expensive.

Manoir de Montesquiou This hotel in a 15th-century converted manor house has
10 rooms and two suites. Some of the spacious rooms have canopy beds;
ask for one with a view of the gorge. The restaurant offers inventive cuisine with a light touch, like trout cooked with local ham. Closed November
through March. Reservations necessary. MasterCard and Visa accepted.
La Malène (phone: 66-48-51-12; fax: 66-48-50-47). Expensive.

NÎMES Although this appealing southern city lies in the Languedoc, its mood is
much like that of neighboring Provence. There is a certain sweetness of life
here, heightened by the physical beauty of the city, with its wide tree-lined
boulevards and its remarkable monuments. Nîmes often is called the French
Rome, and for good reason: Two Roman emperors were born here, and
the city is generously endowed with magnificent remnants of the prosperous Roman settlement that grew up around a sacred spring here a century
before Christ. This spring was said to have been frequented by the god
Nemausus, who gave the city its name.

The first glimpse of Nîmes's double-arched stone amphitheater in the
center of town is arresting, evoking chariot races and gladiatorial combat.
Built early in the 1st century, it looks very much like a smaller version of
the *Colosseum* in Rome. For additional details on the amphitheater, see
Memorable Museums and Monuments in DIVERSIONS.

Equally well preserved is that other jewel of Nîmes, the *Maison Carrée*
(Pl. de la Comédie; no phone), a temple from the 1st century that looks as
if it belongs on the Acropolis. It now is a museum containing Roman artifacts, including a statue of Apollo found during excavations of the area. The
temple is open daily; there's no admission charge. Renovation of the square
around the *Maison Carrée* and of the surrounding area has yielded new
Roman and post-Roman artifacts buried under layers of history. Less well
preserved but no less evocative of Roman times is the *Temple de Diane*
(Temple of Diana), in the beautiful *Jardin de la Fontaine* (Fountain Garden;
Quai de la Fontaine). The name of this crumbling remnant of what was once

a much larger structure is unfounded, as there is no proof it was dedicated to Diana or even that it was used as a temple. Many scholars believe it was part of the city's public baths, which feature some interestingly graphic 17th- and 18th-century stone carvings high up on the walls. To the north is the *Tour Magne*, a watchtower, on Mont-Cavalier; climbing the 140 steps to the top offers a good workout and a splendid view of the city and its environs. The largest of the towers built into the walls surrounding the Roman city, it dates from about the 1st century BC. It's closed lunch hours and some holidays; there's an admission charge. The *Porte d'Auguste* (Gate of Augustus), also called the *Porte d'Arles,* and other remnants of the old ramparts—the longest in Gaul, extending more than 4 miles—are visible around the city. The *Castellum* (Roman water tower), which received the town's water supply via an aqueduct from Uzès, is on Rue Lampèze, east of Mont-Cavalier.

Nîmes also has a number of more modern monuments: the *Eglise St-Perpétue* (Bd. de Prague); the *Palais de Justice* (Bd. des Arènes), built by Gaston Bourbon and closed to the public; and the *Esplanade* (near Bd. des Arènes), with a fountain designed by Jacques Pradier. All date from around the mid-19th century. In the 18th and 19th centuries Nîmes was famous for its textile production, including its "bleu de Nîmes," a sturdy cloth that has preserved the name "denim." Nîmes also has some interesting museums, including a new museum of contemporary art, the *Carré d'Art* (Place de la Maison Carrée; phone: 66-76-35-35). Opened in 1993, the museum recalls Roman architecture in its portico and columns; several stories were built underground in order to remain in keeping with the scale of the surrounding historic area. The museum is closed Mondays; there's an admission charge. The *Musée Archéologique* (13 Bd. Amiral-Courbet; phone: 66-67-25-57) is closed Mondays and some holidays; there's an admission charge. The *Musée du Vieux-Nîmes* (Pl. aux Herbes; phone: 66-36-00-64), formerly the episcopal palace, has a fine collection of 17th- and 18th-century furniture. It's open daily, and there's an admission charge.

Colorful parades, dancing in the streets, and corridas (bullfights) take place in May and September during the city's spring and harvest festivals (reserve a hotel room well in advance at these times), and in July there are opera and jazz festivals. A *Festival des Santons* (the quaint clay figurines of Provence used in *Christmas* crèches) takes place during the second and third weeks of November in the nearby town of Garons. For information, contact the Nîmes tourist office (6 Rue Auguste; phone: 66-67-29-11; fax: 66-21-81-04); it's closed for lunch on Saturdays and Sunday afternoons, except in July and August. There's also the *Comité Départemental du Tourisme du Gard* (3 Pl. des Arènes; phone: 66-21-02-51).

BEST EN ROUTE

Impérator-Concorde An elegant dowager renovated in 1994, it has two suites and 60 large rooms, a gracious lobby, and a delightful garden where guests may dine in the summer. Its restaurant, *L'Enclos de la Fontaine,* one of the city's best, serves fine inventive fare, such as sole with fresh coriander, in plush surroundings. Facing the *Jardin de la Fontaine,* Quai de la Fontaine (phone: 66-21-90-30; fax: 66-67-70-25). Very expensive.

Le Cheval Blanc With 18 rooms and eight suites, this venerable hotel where Cocteau and Picasso once stayed recently has been completely renovated, and now contemporary furniture contrasts strikingly with its ancient stone walls. There's a restaurant with a pleasant shrub-enclosed dining terrace facing the Roman amphitheater. The one-Michelin-star menu includes creatively prepared regional specialties; the chef grows his own herbs and uses them lavishly. 1 Pl. des Arènes (phone: 66-67-32-32; fax: 66-76-32-33). Expensive.

En Route from Nîmes Take a short northeastern detour (14 miles/22 km) on N86 to the Pont du Gard aqueduct, near Remoulins (for a detailed description, see *Memorable Museums and Monuments* in DIVERSIONS), then proceed to the beautiful medieval town of Uzès, about 9 miles (14 km) northwest of the aqueduct.

BEST EN ROUTE

Le Vieux Castillon This member of the Relais & Châteaux group offers 33 splendid guestrooms and two suites in a medieval setting, overlooking the impressive Pont du Gard. Its dining room, which has earned a star from Michelin, serves such first-rate fare as roast lamb with garlic. On the premises are a pool, tennis courts, and a beauty salon; golf facilities are nearby. Closed January through early March. Three miles (5 km) northeast of the Pont du Gard, in Castillon-du-Gard (phone: 66-37-00-77). Very expensive.

UZÈS For generations a powerful religious center, Uzès is filled with architectural treasures in stone. Most spectacular among these is the *Duché* (Pl. du Duché; no phone), a feudal fortress built over centuries by the Dukes of Uzès. It includes the 14th-century *Tour Vicomté,* the 11th-century rectangular *Tour Bermonde,* a spectacular 16th-century façade, and various elaborately decorated apartments within. The *Duché* is open daily year-round; there's an admission charge. The 17th-century *Cathédrale St-Théodorit* (Pl. de la Cathédrale) contains a well-preserved 18th-century organ; next to the cathedral is the remarkable 12th-century *Tour Fenestrelle,* all that remains of a Romanesque church destroyed during the religious wars that devastated the Languedoc for centuries. The rounded tower, the only one of its kind in France, contains many windows, giving it an airy look. The interior is closed to the public. Promenade Jean-Racine, named for the playwright, who studied here in the 17th century, begins to the right of the cathedral's entrance; it offers spectacular views of the countryside. The Place aux Herbes (also known as the Place de la République) is one of Uzès's most beautiful features. Stroll across the cobblestones beneath curved stone arcades backed by several 17th-century houses; the best time to come here is on Saturdays, when a lively food market takes place. Farmers from throughout the area come here to sell their best braided strands at the *Fête de l'Ail* (Garlic Festival) during the third week of June. For quintessentially Provençal fabrics and lovely ceramic dishes, go to the *Céramique d'Uzès-Pichon* (6 Rue St-Etienne; phone: 66-22-36-31), which is closed Mondays and mornings except Saturdays. The Uzès *Office de Tourisme* (Av. de la Libération; phone: 66-22-68-88) is efficient and helpful.

BEST EN ROUTE

D'Entraigues A 15th-century house converted into a sumptuous 19-room hotel, this is definitely the best lodging place in town. For a great view, ask for a room on the third floor. The restaurant, *Les Jardins de Castille,* has a flower-filled terrace and serves dishes with a nouvelle accent, such as oyster consommé with truffle juice. There is also a heated pool. Restaurant closed Tuesday and Wednesday lunch from September through June; open for dinner only in July and August. 8 Rue Calade (phone: 66-22-32-68; fax: 66-22-57-01). Expensive.

Hôtel Marie d'Agoult This hotel set in an 18th-century château has 26 rooms and one suite; there's also a huge swimming pool, a tennis court, and a restaurant for hotel guests only. Closed mid-November through mid-March. *Château d'Arpaillargues,* 3 miles (5 km) west of Uzès via D982 (phone: 66-22-14-48; fax: 66-22-56-10). Expensive.

En Route from Uzès Return to Nîmes and take A9 to Montpellier, 32 miles (51 km) southeast.

MONTPELLIER The capital of Bas Languedoc and an important university town, Montpellier is a busy and animated metropolis, one of the fastest-growing cities in France, whose wide avenues, tree-lined promenades, and superb 17th-century public monuments give it a grace and charm unmatched by other cities in the region. In recent years ultramodern structures such as the *Polygone* shopping center (Pl. de la Comédie) have added a new dimension. The area was settled in the 9th and 10th centuries by spice merchants engaged in trade with the East, and it remained a dominant Mediterranean trading center until Provence, with its major port of Marseilles, became part of France in 1481. It was in Montpellier, around the beginning of the 13th century, that France's first medical school (Rue de l'Université) was established, an outgrowth of the herb and spice trade, whose merchants were aware of the therapeutic qualities of their goods. One of the school's most famous graduates was François Rabelais, who studied here in the 1530s. Some of the original buildings, dating from the 14th century, are still in use.

The university area is the oldest section of town, and its crooked streets are lined with ancient stone dwellings and elaborately decorated *hôtels particuliers,* once the residences of wealthy 17th- and 18th-century merchants. Near the medical school is the former chapel, now the *Cathédrale St-Pierre* (Rue de Candolle), the only church in Montpellier not completely demolished during the devastating Wars of Religion of the 16th century. The cathedral was built in 1364; restored in the 17th and 19th centuries, it retains a fortress-like façade, with romantic stone towers and a vaulted entrance.

Across the street from the cathedral is the *Jardin des Plantes,* France's first botanical garden, founded in 1593. The boulevard leads south to the *Promenade du Peyrou,* the exquisite 17th-century public garden and promenade at the crest of the hill on which the city was built. At one end is the *Arc de Triomphe,* built in 1691 to honor Louis XIV; an equestrian statue of the Sun King stands in the center of the gardens. At the opposite end is the Corinthian-columned *Château d'Eau de Peyron,* a superb decorative structure perched on the highest point of the promenade and cleverly concealing the tank in which the city's water supply once was stored after being transported via an aqueduct from a spring 9 miles (14 km) away. From this point the view of Montpellier and the surrounding area is superb; on a clear day the sparkling Mediterranean coast is visible. Tuesdays bring a colorful flower market to the area under the arches of the aqueduct, beside the *Promenade du Peyrou.*

The town's center of activity is the Place de la Comédie, a giant marble plaza. Nearby is the tree-lined Esplanade and the *Musée Fabre* (13 Rue Montpellier; phone: 67-14-83-00), with a rich collection of painting and sculpture, including works by Ingres, David, Delacroix, Courbet, Houdon, and Barye. The museum is closed Mondays; admission charge. Among the many beautiful *hôtels particuliers* studding the old sections of town are the 18th-century *Hôtel de Rodez-Bénavent* (Rue des Trésoriers de la Bourse) and the *Hôtel Varenne* (Pl. Pétrarque; phone: 67-66-02-94), which contains the *Musée du Vieux Montpellier.* The latter is closed Sundays; there's no admission charge. A five-minute walk from the Place de la Comédie brings you to *Antigone,* a 60-acre residential and commercial metropolis designed by Spanish architect Ricardo Bofill in somewhat oversized classical architectural style, using modern materials. The last sections are scheduled for completion in the year 2000, when *Antigone* will also house various cultural institutions. For more information on the city's sights, contact the main tourist office in the *Triangle* building on the Place de la Comédie (phone: 67-58-67-58) or one of the three branch offices, including one near *Antigone* (78 Av. Pirée; phone: 67-22-06-16).

Several beaches lie within a couple of miles of town, and sparkling new resorts are just a short drive east, although the coast here becomes extremely crowded in July and August. Worth an excursion is Pic St-Loup (14 miles/22 km north via D986 and D113), rising 2,171 feet at the end of a long, stark ridge and providing a stunning panorama of the area. The Grotte des

Demoiselles (Grotto of the Damsels; 12 miles/19 km farther along D986), discovered in 1770, is filled with white calcite stalactites and stalagmites. The largest cavern is cathedral-like in size, with a ceiling that soars 165 feet overhead. The cave is open daily; admission charge.

For another fascinating side trip from Montpellier, travel west on N109, then north on D32 at Guignac and west on D27 at Aniane (about 21 miles/34 km) to St-Guilhem-le-Désert, a small village of warm yellow stone houses and narrow streets curiously wedged into the mouth of the Gorges de l'Hérault. Home to many artists and somewhat reminiscent of Les Baux-de-Provence, the town is arranged around a beautiful old abbey, part of whose cloisters were dismantled by the American sculptor George Grey Barnard in 1906 and re-created as the *Cloisters,* a branch of the *Metropolitan Museum of Art* in New York City. Along the way, just 2 miles (3 km) before the village, off D27, is the Grotte de Clamouse, with its dramatically lighted interior.

BEST EN ROUTE

Alliance-Métropole This 80-room hotel, furnished with lovely antiques, is conveniently located in the center of town. Its interior garden is a delight, and the restaurant, *La Closerie,* features local seafood and fine regional wines. 3 Rue Clos-René (phone: 67-58-11-22; fax: 67-92-13-02). Expensive.

Chandelier This one-Michelin-star restaurant has been a local favorite for years. Its inventive cuisine includes crayfish *beignets* (fritters) and various other seafood dishes. Closed Sundays and Monday lunch. Reservations advised. Major credit cards accepted. 3 Rue Leenhardt (phone: 67-92-61-62). Expensive.

Demeure des Brousses Ensconced in an 18th-century house surrounded by a private park are 17 comfortable guestrooms and a restaurant. Closed mid-December through February. Three miles (5 km) east of the city center via D24 and D172E, on Rte. de Vaugières (phone: 67-65-77-66 or 67-22-22-17). Expensive.

Le Jardin des Sens The city's best, this two-Michelin-star dining place is decorated in a contemporary style that fits the nouvelle touches of the cuisine. Filets of sole rolled around truffle purée, and mackerel tart (made only from October through February, when the fish are running) are among the specialties. Closed Sundays, two weeks in January, and the first two weeks in August. Reservations necessary. Major credit cards accepted. 11 Av. St-Lazare (phone: 67-79-63-38; fax: 67-72-13-05). Expensive.

Résidentiale In a quiet, residential area near the Antigone complex, this 78-room hotel has a pool and tennis court. Ask for a room overlooking the garden. There's no restaurant. 70-72 Av. Pont-Juvénal (phone: 67-22-74-74; fax: 67-22-74-75). Expensive.

Noailles This romantic hostelry, a former 17th-century *hôtel particulier,* is a treasure for its vaulted stone lobby, its lounge, and its 30 delightfully furnished rooms (some overlooking the Esplanade). There's no restaurant. Closed December 22 through January 18. 2 Rue des Ecoles-Centrales, Vieux Montpellier (phone: 67-60-49-80; fax: 67-66-08-26). Moderate.

L'Olivier Another one-Michelin-star place, this one offers such a friendly welcome that you feel as if you're in someone's home. The chef prefers local products and regional wines for such dishes as sweetbreads cooked in sweet Banyuls wine. Closed Sundays, Mondays, holidays, and the last two weeks of August. Reservations advised. Major credit cards accepted. 12 Rue A.-Ollivier (phone: 67-92-86-28). Moderate.

En Route from Montpellier Before traveling south along the Languedoc coast, we suggest a detour east via D21 and D62 to the lagoon-studded area known as the Camargue.

THE CAMARGUE Most of this region was mosquito-infested swampland until the 1960s, when the government, hoping to reduce pressure on the overcrowded Riviera, dredged the lagoons and created eight resorts at its southwest corner. La Grande-Motte, 12 miles (19 km) from Montpellier, is the most famous of these developments; its beaches are lined with the futuristic pyramidal hotels and apartment buildings that have come to symbolize the project. Although the architecture is somewhat jarring, the beaches here are wide and sandy—and very crowded in July and August.

The Camargue comprises almost 200,000 acres of swamps, shallow lakes, sand dunes, and natural and artificial canals. Despite the summer onslaught of human visitors, various wildlife—pink flamingos, wild horses, Camargue bulls, birds, and fish—still manages to thrive here. Two cities dominate the area: Aigues-Mortes in the southwestern corner and Stes-Maries-de-la-Mer in the south. Six miles (10 km) past La Grande-Motte along D62 is Aigues-Mortes, a medieval town that stands in sharp contrast to its ultramodern neighbor. Visitors can walk around the massive ramparts and towers of this fortified city founded by Louis IX (St. Louis), who set off on his first crusade in 1248 from the port. Up to the middle of the 14th century, the city rivaled nearby Marseilles, but the receding sea and development of Sète Port relegated Aigues-Mortes to the status of a local agricultural center. Having escaped the destruction of war, it is one of the most authentic remnants of the Middle Ages in the region. Its largest tower, the *Tour de Constance,* was used as a prison. The ramparts and towers are closed some holidays and lunch hours from October through May. There's an admission charge (phone: 66-53-61-55).

In Stes-Maries-de-la-Mer, 20 miles (32 km) farther on D58 and D38C west and D570 south, Gypsies from all over Europe gather twice a year—at the end of May and the end of October—to pay homage to Sarah, their patron saint. (For additional details on the *Grand Pèlerinage de Mai,* as the festival is called, see *Festivals à la Française* in DIVERSIONS.) The Stes-Maries-de-la-Mer tourist office (5 Avenue Van-Gogh; phone: 90-97-82-55) can provide information on the festival and other attractions in the region.

En Route from the Camargue Return to Montpellier, then take A9 for 18 miles (29 km) south, turning off at D2 for Sète.

SÈTE Curiously set on and around Mont St-Clair and lined with canals, this delightful port once provided Montpellier's access to the sea. Granted free trade status by Louis XIV in the 17th century, Sète prospered as France's fifth most important port until the mid-19th century. Today the town, located on a spit of land reached by a narrow causeway, is an important port for car-ferry crossings to North Africa, as well as a fishing center. It's definitely worth a stop for some of its famous seafood. Order a plate of oysters in any of the simple outdoor restaurants lining the Quai de Bosc.

BEST EN ROUTE

Le Grand Hôtel This refurbished, turn-of-the-century hotel has 43 rooms and four suites with spectacular views of Sète from the upper floors. There's a simple restaurant. Closed December 24 through January 3. 17 Quai Maréchal-de-Lattre-de-Tassigny (phone: 67-74-71-77; fax: 67-74-29-27). Moderate.

Palangrotte For an elaborate presentation of the area's renowned oysters, we recommend this seafood restaurant. Closed mid-January through mid-February, one week in November, and Sunday dinner and Mondays from October through June. Reservations advised. Major credit cards accepted. 1 Rampe Paul-Valéry (phone: 67-74-80-35). Moderate.

En Route from Sète Take A9 south for about 38 miles (61 km) to Narbonne.

NARBONNE In Roman times this peaceful, slow-paced city was a key Mediterranean port and the capital of Gallia Narbonensis, a large and flourishing Roman province that stretched all along the coast and inland toward Carcassonne. Later it served as a base for the Visigoth kings. When its port silted up in the 14th century, the city's fortunes waned, but it remained an important religious center, evidenced by its beautiful cathedral and archbishop's palace. The *Cathédrale St-Just* (Pl. R.-Salengro), Narbonne's most impressive monument, was begun in 1272, but the interior never was completed. Nonetheless, its Gothic choir is, at 135 feet, one of the tallest in France, surpassed only by those in the cathedrals in Amiens and Beauvais. A 14th-century cloister connects the cathedral to the archbishop's palace (Place de l'Hôtel-de-Ville; phone: 68-90-30-30), which contains two museums—one of art and history, the other of archaeology—as well as the *Hôtel de Ville,* which was rebuilt by Viollet-le-Duc in 1840. The beautifully ornamented palace was built between the 10th and the 17th century. The museums are closed Mondays from October through April, and during lunch hours. There's an admission charge, which includes entrance to the nearby *Horreum,* the excavated ruins of a Roman warehouse, and during the summer only, to the *Musée Lapidaire.* The *Musée Lapidaire* (Lapidary Museum; Pl. Lamourguier) contains an interesting collection of carved stone—including ancient inscriptions, steles, lintels, busts, sarcophagi—much of it originally from the town's ramparts. Stop at the tourist office (Pl. R.-Salengro; phone: 68-65-15-60) for more information.

Narbonne vies with nearby Béziers as a center of the region's flourishing wine trade; the *Poudrière,* a former Dominican church near the cathedral, has regular exhibits on wine production. Finally, the wide boulevards, pleasant parks, and Mediterranean mood are attractions in themselves. Narbonne-Plage, a sandy beach lined with small hotels and holiday homes, is 8 miles (13 km) east via D168 through the rugged hills of the coast.

Take N113 west and D613 south, then a small unmarked road to the left just before the tiny village of St-Julien to reach the solitary, late 11th-century Cistercian abbey of Fontfroide, about 9 miles (14 km) from Narbonne. This harmonious ensemble of Romanesque church, beautiful cloister, and stone abbey is hidden away in a grove of cypresses and poplars surrounded by a wild, deserted valley. The stained glass windows are a modern addition.

BEST EN ROUTE

Relais du Val d'Orbieu A charming country inn set in a restored mill has 15 rooms and five suites; some of the rooms have terraces and all have mini-bars. It also boasts a fine restaurant, a pool, and a tennis court. Closed late December through February. In Ornaisons, 9 miles (14 km) outside Narbonne via N113 and D24 (phone: 68-27-10-27; fax: 68-27-52-44). Expensive.

L'Olibo With a new chef, this restaurant has become one of the city's best. Local products and regional wines are featured. Closed Sundays and Wednesday dinner. Reservations advised. Major credit cards accepted. 51 Rue Parerie (phone: 68-41-74-47; fax: 68-42-84-90). Moderate.

En Route from Narbonne A9 continues south from Narbonne for 40 miles (64 km) to Perpignan. Along the way, near the town of Sigean, is the *Réserve Africaine de Sigean,* a drive-in wildlife park with Tibetan bears, white rhinoceroses, lions, birds, and other animals living on the edge of a saltwater lagoon. It's open daily; there's an admission charge (phone: 68-48-20-20).

PERPIGNAN The last important metropolis before the Spanish border, Perpignan is a city whose heart, soul, and history are divided. Culturally, linguistically, and to a certain extent commercially, it is tied to Catalonia, the region that encompasses both sides of the border from Perpignan to Barcelona. Perpignan and the surrounding Roussillon territory, of which it was once the fortified capital, bounced back and forth between France and Spain for hundreds of years; it wasn't until the Peace of the Pyrénées, signed by Louis XIV in 1659, that they shifted permanently into the French domain.

The 20th century has brought prosperity to this once poor and war-torn area. Since 1914 Perpignan has almost tripled in population (now 106,000). Its economic vitality comes chiefly from the orchards and vineyards of the surrounding plains and coastal area, which produce a significant share of France's table wines and fruit. During the past few decades local cooperatives have made great strides in dispelling their image as producers of "plonk" by making wines of considerable quality.

Throughout Perpignan the Spanish influence is apparent, from the orange-and-yellow Catalan flag that flies proudly throughout the city to the clean white stucco dwellings with bougainvillea-laced wrought-iron balconies. But the most stunning souvenir of Spanish rule is the immense *Palais des Rois de Majorque* (Palace of the Kings of Majorca) off the Rue des Archers on the right bank of the River Têt. A tour of the city might well start at this formidable Gothic fortress, enclosed by ramparts. A long, curving ramp under brick vaulting leads to the upper level, where a lovely garden and an elegant arcaded inner courtyard are surrounded by great meeting halls and two Gothic chapels. The top of the palace keep commands a lovely view of the city. It's open daily; there's an admission charge (phone: 68-34-48-29).

From the palace it's a short walk north to the heart of the Old City. The tourist office offers a walking tour of this area every afternoon from June through August, starting from the office in the *Palais des Congrès* (Pl. A.-Lanoux; phone: 68-66-30-30); tours are available in French, English, Spanish, and German. The first stop is the *Castillet* on the Place Verdun, an elegant red brick, fort-like château built in 1368, originally the gateway to the town and later a prison. Today it houses the *Casa Païral* (phone: 68-35-42-05), a museum devoted to the arts and traditions of Catalan culture. It is closed Tuesdays and most holidays; there's no admission charge. Nearby is the paved pink marble Place de la Loge, the animated center of the Old City, still a favored meeting place, where on summer nights residents dance the traditional Catalan *sardana.* Here also is the lovely 14th-century Gothic *Loge de Mer;* once the trade exchange, it now houses a lively café. Next door is the *Hôtel de Ville* (Town Hall), a beautiful 18th-century edifice (sections date from the 14th and 16th centuries) whose courtyard shelters Aristide Maillol's graceful bronze statue *The Mediterranean.* Ask the concierge for permission to see the marriage hall, with its magnificent 15th-century Moorish wood ceiling and 19th-century wall paintings. See also the façade of the small 15th-century *Palais de la Députation,* next to the *Hôtel de Ville.* On a small back street nearby, at 2 Rue des Fabriques d'En Nabot, is the *Maison Julia,* an exquisite private residence with a courtyard encircled by 14th-century Gothic arches and a gallery. The interior is open to the public only by special arrangement with the tourist office (see above).

Take Rue St-Jean to Place Gambetta and the *Cathédrale St-Jean,* founded in 1324 by Sanche, the second king of Majorca. Particularly noteworthy here, in a small chapel near the right entrance, is the *Devout Christ,* a haunting wood carving of Christ on the cross, believed to have been made in Germany in the 14th century and brought here two centuries later. In this poignant work, Christ's head hangs very near his shoulder and is said to move infinitesimally closer each year. According to legend, when the head touches his shoulder, the world will come to an end.

Perpignan's *Musée d'Histoire Naturelle* (Museum of Natural History; 12 Pl. de la Fontaine-Neuve; phone: 68-35-50-87) is closed Tuesdays; there's no admission charge. The *Musée Hyacinthe-Rigaud,* a block southeast of Place Arago (16 Rue de l'Ange; phone: 68-35-43-40), exhibits paintings by early Catalan and Spanish masters from the 14th, 15th, and 16th centuries as well as several works by Perpignan-born Rigaud, who was an official court painter to Louis XIV and Louis XV. The museum is closed Tuesdays; there's no admission charge.

Spring and summer are lively in Perpignan; especially colorful are the procession of *Pénitents de la Sanch* on *Good Friday* and the annual modern dance festival in July.

The best way to see the surrounding vineyards is by car, driving into the valleys of the Têt, Tech, and Agley Rivers. These lush areas of gently rolling, vine-covered hills are among the loveliest sights in the Languedoc.

BEST EN ROUTE

Park A modern 67-room hotel, it offers comfort and hospitality. The one-Michelin-star restaurant here, *Le Chapon Fin,* features a noisy Mediterranean atmosphere and inventive French and Catalan dishes; the newer, more casual *Le Bistrot* features seafood. Both restaurants are closed Sundays; *Le Chapon Fin* is also closed Monday lunch, the first two weeks in January, the last two weeks in August, and the first week of September. 18 Bd. J.-Bourrat (phone: 68-35-14-14; fax: 68-35-48-18). Expensive.

Villa Duflot Set in a private park, this luxurious 25-room villa has become the city's top-ranked hotel. There is a restaurant and a pool. Right outside the city via N9, at 109 Av. V.-d'Albiez (phone: 68-56-67-67; fax: 68-56-54-05). Expensive.

Festin de Pierre A bright eatery whose chef favors local products. The wine list is a treasure trove of regional varieties. Closed Tuesday dinner, Wednesdays, two weeks in February, and June 13 to 30. Reservations advised. Major credit cards accepted. 7 Rue du Théâtre (phone: 68-51-28-74). Moderate.

L'Hostal This bucolic restaurant is located in a walled hilltop outpost, surrounded by the wild, romantic Roussillon landscape. The food is as authentically Catalan as you'll find in France, featuring the traditional *cargolade* (snails, local sausages, and lamb chops), grilled outside over aromatic vine branches.

After lunch wander through the winding, p[...] village, an unspoiled treasure. Closed Mondays, W[...] and February. Reservations necessary. No credit car[...] miles (19 km) southwest of town via D612 toward Thuir and [...] ing D48, in Castelnou (phone: 68-53-45-42). Moderate.

Windsor This modern hotel with 50 rooms and five suites faces the flower m[...] ket. There's no restaurant, but a cold menu is available through room service. 8 Bd. Wilson (phone: 68-51-18-65; fax: 68-51-01-00). Moderate.

, temperament, and culture, the essence of
most region of France, bordering Italy, is more
than that of the rest of France. Some geographers
ts of the Mediterranean region by the latitude at
growing, and certainly silver-leaved, gnarled olive
features of the Provençal landscape. So, too, are
d cypresses; almond groves and shady *micocoulier de*
neyards; arid but fragrant scrubland of wild lavender,
thyme, rosemary, and other familiar *herbes de Provence;* stone buildings;
pastel colors, and Roman tiles. Another distinct feature of Provence is
the mistral, the famous northerly wind, which keeps the skies blue and
forces farmers to grow cypress ash hedges to protect their fruit trees and
vegetable gardens.

Due—or so it seems—to the region's sunny weather, brilliant blue skies,
siesta-inducing afternoons, and mellow evenings, Provence residents are
easygoing folk whose leisurely, lilting accent is imbued with the warmth of
the climate. Provence owes much of its Mediterranean flavor to the Romans.
While the Celts and Germanic tribes were settling the rest of France, Rome
colonized Provence (Provincia Romana) in 125 BC, after Marseilles, then
a Greek port, had asked for help against Ligurian pirates and Gallic tribes
in its hinterland. With the first Roman foothold at Aix (Aquae Sextiae),
Provence became a vital communications link between Rome's Spanish
possessions and Italy. Emperor Augustus intensified the Roman presence
by giving the town of Nîmes to the war veterans who had defeated Antony
and Cleopatra. Orange was a center of Roman commercial prosperity, and
Emperor Constantine made Arles his home.

Something of a backwater in the Middle Ages, Provence reemerged in
the 14th century as an alternative home for the popes, who had fled the
turmoil of Italy to set up headquarters at Avignon. While the French kingdom acquired most of the region in 1486, Avignon and the papal lands of
the Comtat Venaissin (including Apt, Carpentras, and Cavaillon) remained
independent until the French Revolution. During World War II Provence
was part of the *zone libre* (unoccupied zone) until the end of 1942, when
the Germans invaded.

The dazzling Provençal light, which drives sane locals into the shade,
was the inspiration for Paul Cézanne's most mature work. Disgusted with
the Parisian art world, he returned to his native Aix-en-Provence and found
in the surrounding countryside the inspiration for the intense colors of his
greatest landscapes. For the modern visitor, there's a special joy in seeking out the locations depicted on those canvases, most notably around the
Montagne Ste-Victoire area east of Aix.

At the same time, over in Arles, the sun was having its effect on Vincent van Gogh, for whom the contrast with the cooler light of his native Holland was creatively explosive. In his work light bursts all over the streets and squares of Arles, the fields outside of town, and the country road to Tarascon.

Away from the main roads, the most characteristic Provençal landscapes abound around the lovely Luberon hill villages east and southeast of Avignon and the spectacular springs of Fontaine-de-Vaucluse. South of St-Rémy the terrain becomes wilder and more rugged, with stark outcroppings reminiscent of Arizona or New Mexico. These are the last splutterings of the Alpilles, the western end of the Alpine mountain range.

While driving around Provence, it's easy to imagine what the Roman Empire must have looked like in its heyday. In fact, many Roman ruins—the magnificent theater and triumphal arch at Orange, the grand arena of Arles, the gigantic aqueduct at Pont du Gard, and the ruined houses of Vaison-la-Romaine and St-Rémy—are better preserved here than in Italy. Every now and again you will find yourself trundling along a stretch of original paving from the Via Aurelia, the ancient precursor of a freeway linking Rome and Arles via Genoa, Nice, Aix, and farther west toward Spain.

Summer in Provence is a celebration of modern culture, attracting top international stars to the tiniest villages. Apart from the great theater and music festivals in Avignon and Aix, opera, ballet, and choral works are performed in Carpentras, in the amphitheaters of Orange and Vaison, and in the arena at Arles. The settings and the atmosphere of a balmy Provençal evening lend a particular magic to these experiences. Most of the festivals are held in July and early August. For the best seats, book tickets (and hotel rooms) by early March.

The region's cuisine is adapted admirably to the sunny, outdoor life here, with enough "temples" of gastronomy and examples of innovative culinary arts to satisfy even the most demanding palate. At almost every table sweet garlic and young onions dominate, joined by tomatoes, green peppers, zucchini, eggplant, and the ubiquitous olives, all marvelously enhanced by the aromatic local herbs. Ratatouille is a stew of the whole kit and caboodle. Salads are heavenly here, and the whole of France swears by the melons of Cavaillon. Fig jam makes a wonderful spread on a breakfast brioche. The region's fresh seafood includes *daurade* (sea bream), delicate *rouget* (red mullet), *loup de mer* (sea bass) served with fennel, and sardines. Lamb, with the local rosemary, takes pride of place over beef.

The region's wines have none of the aristocratic pretensions of burgundy or bordeaux, but as you travel down the Rhône Valley, you'll come across some great Crozes-Hermitage and Châteauneuf-du-Pape reds and some refreshing tavel rosés. In Provence proper beware of the punch of the splendid Gigondas reds.

The itinerary we recommend starts just south of Lyons at Valence, then heads 21 miles (34 km) down the west bank of the Rhône to Baix, before taking the aptly named Autoroute du Soleil (A7) to the Provençal gateway town of Orange (with perhaps a stop to see the Roman ruins and enchanting medieval town at Vaison-la-Romaine). From there the route heads south to Fontaine-de-Vaucluse, then across to the Lubéron and a circuit covering a couple of hundred miles or so, around Avignon, St-Rémy, the Alpilles, and Les Baux-de-Provence, southwest to Arles, and then southeast again via Salon-de-Provence to end up at Aix.

For a double room per night, expect to pay $150 and up in a very expensive hotel; $100 to $150 in an expensive place; $50 to $100 in a moderate hotel; and less than $50 in an inexpensive one. Unless otherwise indicated, all hotels accept major credit cards and are open year-round. Most hotels listed below feature telephones, TV sets, and private baths in their rooms. However, some less expensive ones may have private baths in only some of their rooms; it's a good idea when making a reservation to confirm whether your room has a private bath. Also, many of these often centuries-old hostelries—even the pricier establishments—do not have air conditioning, but generally the combination of fresh country air and a charm undisturbed by modern conveniences makes it a negligible, or even welcome, omission. A few of these same hotels lack TV sets, but again they'll hardly be missed by visitors whose express wish is to escape such contemporary intrusions. Dinner for two, with service (usually included in the bill) and a good local wine, in a very expensive restaurant will cost $150 or more; in an expensive place, $100 to $150; in a moderate spot, $50 to $100; and in an inexpensive eatery, under $50. Unless otherwise noted, all restaurants are open for lunch and dinner. For each location hotels and restaurants are listed alphabetically by price category.

VALENCE This market town is the distribution point for the great fruit and vegetables of the Rhône Valley. François Rabelais spent his student days here in the 15th century, and Valence today pays fitting homage to the gargantuan appetites celebrated in his lusty writings with a much revered gastronomic shrine, *Pic* (see *Best en Route*).

The esplanade of the Champ de Mars commands a fine view across the Rhône River to a ruined château atop the white stone Mont Crussol, a challenge to any climber—not least of all Napoleon Bonaparte, who is said to have scaled it in 1785, when he was a cadet at the *Ecole d'Artillerie* (Artillery School). Valence is also the home of the *Arsenal,* one of France's oldest gunpowder factories.

In the *Musée des Beaux-Arts* (4 Pl. des Armeaux; phone: 75-79-20-80), south of the austere and over-restored cathedral, is a fine collection of 18th-century *sanguines* (red chalk drawings) by Hubert Robert, whose studies of Rome's ancient ruins evoke something of the wistfulness of Provence's imperial monuments. The museum is open daily; admission charge.

Chabran In an age when fanciful sauces supersede the simple joy of a good meal prepared with finesse, this small establishment deserves hearty praise. Chef Michel Chabran has earned two Michelin stars for his artful renditions of mouth-watering lobster salad, duck braised in wine, and terrine of foie gras accompanied by artichokes and zucchini. The wine list is creditable. There are also 12 guestrooms. Closed Sunday dinner. Reservations necessary. Major credit cards accepted. Six miles (10 km) north of Valence by N7, on Av. du 45e Parallèle, Pont-de-l'Isère (phone: 75-84-60-09; fax: 75-84-59-65). Very expensive.

Pic For many it's the only reason for making a trip to Valence. If you can't get a table in the charming shady garden, the dining room is elegant without being overdone, just as Jacques Pic's three-Michelin-star cuisine manages to be sumptuous without losing its subtlety. Langouste salad, sea bass, veal sweetbreads, and ingenious desserts are some of the triumphs of his repertoire. The local Côtes du Rhône wines are excellent. If you're staying overnight at this Relais & Châteaux member, risk indulging in the cornucopia of the *menu Rabelais*. Reserve a month or two in advance to stay in one of the house's two beautiful bedrooms or two suites. Closed Sunday dinner, Wednesdays, February, and August. Reservations necessary. Major credit cards accepted. 285 Av. Victor-Hugo, Valence (phone 75-44-15-32; fax: 75-40-96-03). Very expensive.

Château d'Urbilhac It's worth the drive to reach this pretty, romantic hideaway that exudes a somewhat faded Provençal charm. All 13 guestrooms are tastefully appointed and unusually cozy, and there is a pool and access to nearby tennis courts. There's also a restaurant. Take D533 for 21 miles (34 km) northwest of Valence, then go southeast 1 mile (1.6 km) on Rte. de Vernoux-en-Vivarais (D2) to Lamastre (phone: 75-06-42-11; fax: 75-06-52-75). Expensive.

Hôtel 2000 Efficiency wins out over charm at this modern and clean establishment. Among its other assets are a quiet location and breakfast served in the garden. It has 31 rooms, good service, and a restaurant. Av. de Romans, Valence (phone: 75-43-73-01; fax: 75-55-00-95). Moderate.

En Route from Valence Take N532 west over the river to winding D279 and D479, and connect with D232 west, then D266 and finally D21, which rejoins N86; continue south past orchards of apricot, pear, and peach trees to the pretty little village of Baix. From there backtrack north for 4 miles (6 km) to the Autoroute du Soleil (A7), near Le Pouzin, for the 45-minute drive to Orange.

La Cardinale et Sa Résidence This charming hotel, a member of the Relais & Châteaux group, offers five comfortable rooms in the 17th-century manor house, plus 10 secluded rooms and a pool at an attractive property in the hills 2 miles (3 km) from Baix up N86. The flowery waterside terrace affords a delightful Rhône River view; it's also the place to savor the restaurant's specialties of *cassolette d'escargots* (stewed snails), *lotte* (monkfish) *à l'orange,* and chicken fricassee in tarragon. Restaurant and hotel closed from November through mid-March. Reservations necessary. Major credit cards accepted. Quai du Rhône, Baix (phone: 75-85-80-40; fax: 75-85-82-07). Expensive.

La Beaugravière An unpretentious haven for regional cooking, over which Guy Jullien presides. All of the fine fare prepared here is based on classic Provençal recipes, such as *pieds et paquets* (lambs' feet and tripe stuffed with pork, garlic, and parsley) and lamb stew steeped in wine, accompanied by anchovies, capers, and *cornichons.* Jullien's pride is his fine collection of reasonably priced Rhône wines. Closed Sunday dinner, Monday dinner from October through *Easter,* and two weeks in September. Reservations advised. Major credit cards accepted. Rte. Nationale, 10 miles (16 km) north of Orange, in Mondragon (phone: 90-40-82-54). Moderate.

ORANGE Although this town was (and still is) an important agricultural center, and while there are a few orange trees in its gardens, its name has nothing at all to do with that bright citrus fruit. The current name is a corruption of Arausio, the town's original Celtic name. Orange is a cheerful yet charmingly sleepy town today. Its magnificently preserved monuments recall its ancient role as a major center of Roman trade. For a panoramic view, drive up the Colline St-Eutrope south of town to the park where first Celtic, then Roman, armies had encampments.

On the northern side of town, the *Arc de Triomphe* dates from 20 BC. Its sculpted reliefs from AD 26–27 on the northern façade commemorate Roman Emperor Tiberius's victories over local Gallic tribes and the Greek merchant ships of Marseilles. It stands astride the old Via Agrippa (what is now N7), once the link between Arles and Rome's Gallic capital at Lyons.

At the foot of the hill, the *Théâtre Antique* (Amphitheater) is a few decades older than the arch. Revered by scholars as the most handsome and best preserved of its kind in the former empire, it is the only one with its monumental scenic wall still standing, complete with a heroic statue of Augustus Caesar at its center. Today it offers opera lovers a magical backdrop and stunning acoustics for the summer festival, usually held the second week of July, which attracts the world's greatest singers. Reservations for the festival can be made as early as January, and tickets are often gone by May. Get details and ticket order forms from *Chorégies d'Orange* (Pl.

Frères-Mounet; phone: 90-34-24-24) or the tourist office (Cours A.-Briand; phone: 90-34-70-88).

BEST EN ROUTE

Château de Rochegude This former castle was remodeled in the 18th century; today it is a member of the Relais & Châteaux group. It has 25 rooms, four suites, a park, a tennis court, and a pool. Its one-Michelin-star restaurant offers regional fare emphasizing local herbs as well as Rhône wines. Closed January and February. Nine miles (14 km) from town via D976, D11, and D117, in Rochegude (phone: 75-04-81-88; fax: 75-04-89-87). Expensive.

Arène It's miraculously quiet for its location, and most of the 30 comfortable little rooms have balconies. The service is intelligent and considerate. There's no restaurant. Closed November through mid-December. In the center of town, on Pl. de Langes, Orange (phone: 90-34-10-95; fax: 90-34-91-62). Moderate.

En Route from Orange Archaeology buffs should head 20 miles (32 km) northeast on D975 to Vaison-la-Romaine.

VAISON-LA-ROMAINE While the ruins here do not have the dramatic impact of the great monuments of Orange or Arles, the excavated sites do resemble the layout of a Roman town. You'll see its houses and streets, together with a little museum where the more valuable finds are displayed and an explanation of the ruins given (in French). Concerts and operas are held during the summer months in the amphitheater. For information, contact the tourist office (Pl. Abbé-Sautel; phone: 90-36-02-11).

Vaison is worth a visit just for the cobblestone Haute Ville, the medieval quarter huddled around a 12th-century fortress atop the hill above the little Ouvèze River. A 2,000-year-old Roman bridge connects it to the rest of the town. The *Galerie du Vieux Marché* (Haute Ville; phone: 90-36-16-05) sells superb olivewood kitchenware and sculpture (it's closed from mid-November through February).

BEST EN ROUTE

Hostellerie de Crillon le Brave At this remote, romantic inn overlooking the Mont Ventoux vineyards, the 15 rooms and five suites feature stone walls, wood beams, and terra cotta tile floors, and there's a pool. *Bourride* (Provençal fish stew) is a specialty of the dining room, which has a terrace for outdoor dining. Closed January through March. Sixteen miles (26 km) southeast of Vaison-la-Romaine via D938, on Pl. de l'Eglise, Crillon-le-Brave (phone: 90-65-61-61; fax: 90-65-62-86). Very expensive.

Domaine de Cabasse While the 12 lovely guestrooms of this appealing little inn are comfortable, the dining room is considered the main attraction. Nadine

Latour prepares succulent selections ranging from the classic *bouef en daube* to boiled chicken served with escargots, salted cod, and garlic aïoli. The inn also has a pool. Restaurant closed Mondays, except in July and August. Reservations necessary. Major credit cards accepted. Rte. de Sablet, 6 miles (10 km) out of Vaison-la-Romaine by D977 and D88, in Séguret (phone: 90-46-91-12; fax: 90-46-94-01). Moderate.

La Table du Comtat In a fairy-tale setting amid medieval stone houses set high on a hill, this tiny establishment offers eight prettily furnished rooms and a one-Michelin-star restaurant. Among the finer selections on the menu are pheasant eggs with truffles, and filet mignon and lamb with peppercorns. Hotel closed from late November through early December; restaurant also closed Tuesdays and Wednesdays in the off-season. Reservations necessary. Major credit cards accepted. Le Village, Séguret (phone: 90-46-91-49; fax: 90-46-94-27). Moderate.

En Route from Vaison-la-Romaine Take D938 17 miles (27 km) south to Carpentras, home of France's oldest synagogue (signposted near the *Hôtel de Ville*). The 14th-century structure still has the ritual *mikvah* (bath) in its basement, a baking oven for matzos on the ground floor, and a fine paneled hall of worship upstairs. Before the French Revolution 20% of the town's population was Jewish; at that time they lived in a walled ghetto and were forced to wear yellow hats to identify themselves. Continue for 13 miles (21 km) to Fontaine-de-Vaucluse.

FONTAINE-DE-VAUCLUSE The gushing springs for which this town is named are among those beautiful natural wonders that are so popular that they really can be enjoyed only out of season. If possible, visit during the spring or winter, when the waters are higher and more spectacular. Among lush trees, they pour out of a great cavern at the base of a 750-foot cliff in marvelous, emerald green cascades at a rate of up to 7,000 cubic feet per second. The site is a 15-minute walk from the parking lot along the river, which unfortunately is cluttered by a rather ugly collection of restaurants. The Italian poet Petrarch (Francesco Petrarca) lived in the valley on and off for 25 years, and it was here that he wrote of his love for Laura, who came from nearby Avignon.

Nearby, west of town, is L'Isle-sur-la-Sorgue, an island village in the middle of the Sorgue River, noteworthy for its picturesque location and its flea market/antiques fair, which takes place along the western bank every Sunday (in season).

BEST EN ROUTE

Mas de Cure Bourse In a converted farmhouse, Françoise Donzé serves up such tasty fare as grouper in a red wine sauce, eggplant with tomato *coulis,* and a delectable pear tart. There are also 13 guestrooms and a pool. Closed

Sunday dinner and Mondays. Reservations advised. Major credit cards accepted. Carrefour de Velorgues, L'Isle-sur-la-Sorgue (phone: 90-38-16-58; fax: 90-38-52-31). Expensive.

La Maison aux Fruits Each of the four rooms in this cozy inn has murals that were painted by the owner. There's no restaurant. No credit cards accepted. Fontaine-de-Vaucluse (phone: 90-20-39-15). Inexpensive.

En Route from Fontaine-de-Vaucluse Continue south on D938 for 10 miles (16 km) toward Cavaillon. The rugged mountains at the southern end of the Vaucluse plateau, the villages with their pretty gardens and tasteful boutiques, and the surrounding countryside of fragrant heathland blend to form the classic Provençal landscape, an area where visitors should get out of the car and walk whenever the impulse strikes (which it may often). Stock up on melons and other picnic goodies at Cavaillon's street market before heading east on D2 to Gordes, 10 miles (16 km) away.

GORDES Spotless houses, solid *bastides,* and *bories* (stone huts) characterize this town, best known for its hilltop medieval and Renaissance château. In it is the *Musée Vasarely*, featuring five rooms of works by the Hungarian artist. It's closed Tuesdays in July and August, and on holidays. Nearby, the *Musée du Vitrail* (Rte. de St-Pantaléon; phone: 90-72-22-11) is devoted to stained glass, particularly from the Middle East. It's open daily; closed during lunch hours. There's an admission charge.

BEST EN ROUTE

Domaine de l'Enclos Really a collection of houses clustered around a restaurant, this luxurious hotel has nine rooms and five suites, all airy, brightly furnished, and each with its own little garden. The view over the Lubéron mountains alone is worth the price. The restaurant serves a sophisticated cuisine using classic Provençal ingredients, including those from the nearby sea. There's also a tennis court and pool. On the northern outskirts of Gordes, on the Rte. de Sénanque (phone: 90-72-08-22; fax: 90-72-03-03). Very expensive.

Les Bories This tiny and utterly delightful stone-walled inn with 18 rooms has an outdoor terrace with a view that allows for languid lunching in the shade of olive trees while stray shafts of sunlight glow through a bottle of rosé. The restaurant serves excellent Provençal specialties; try the feather-light *salade folle* (crazy salad) with duck and crayfish, or the lamb grilled on an open wood fire. Closed December through mid-January. Reservations necessary. Major credit cards accepted. A mile (1.6 km) northwest of town by the Rte. de Sénanques (phone: 90-72-00-51; fax: 90-72-01-22). Expensive.

Mas des Herbes Blanches Set between the Lubéron and Ventoux mountain ranges, this traditional stone house (a member of the Relais & Châteaux group) has 16 rooms and two suites, a pool, tennis courts, and a delightful restaurant that offers nouvelle and classic cuisines. Closed January through early March. Reservations necessary. Major credit cards accepted. Four miles (6 km) east of Gordes on D102A, Rte. de Murs, in Joucas (phone: 90-05-79-79; fax: 90-05-71-96). Expensive.

En Route from Gordes Drive 2 to 3 miles (4 km) north along winding D177 to the *Parc du Lubéron,* a protected national park, and the exquisitely restored 12th-century Cistercian *Abbaye de Sénanques* (phone: 90-72-02-05). The abbey is a striking setting for two permanent exhibitions, one on symbolism and architecture, the other on the desert and humankind. The abbey is closed Sunday mornings; admission charge.

Back on D2, go 7 miles (11 km) east to Roussillon, a provocation for any painter as it rises rust-colored from its wreath of ocher quarries and red cliffs dotted with Mediterranean pines and green oaks. The little D149 heads south 7 miles (11 km) across a main road to Bonnieux, perched on a hill with a terrace behind the *Hôtel de Ville* (Town Hall) that affords a panoramic view across to Roussillon and Gordes. For a good view back at Bonnieux itself, take D3 west toward the 15th-century hilltop citadel of Ménerbes (with a pretty 14th-century church on its outskirts), then continue on to the strange but beautiful ruined village of Oppède-le-Vieux, abandoned at the turn of the century but gradually being restored by painters. Writers come here from all over France for a little peace of mind; the dilapidated 12th-century castle is a melancholy poem in itself.

N100 continues 21 miles (34 km) west to Avignon (for a detailed report on the city, its sights, its hotels, and its restaurants, see *Avignon* in THE CITIES). From there St-Rémy is only 12 miles (19 km) south via D571.

BEST EN ROUTE

Mas de Garrigon This inn has nine small, comfortable rooms, charmingly decorated in traditional Provençal style. The big fireplace in the lounge creates the ambience of a large country house. Other features: a pool, horseback riding, a library, a good restaurant, and a lovely view of the countryside from the terrace. Restaurant closed Sunday dinner, Mondays, and mid-November through December. Reservations necessary. Major credit cards accepted. Rte. de St-Saturnin-d'Apt, 2 miles (3 km) north of Roussillon via C7 and D2 (phone: 90-05-63-22; fax: 90-05-70-01). Expensive.

La Tarasque A pleasant bistro with an accent on herb-scented Provençal dishes. Closed Wednesdays and mid-February through mid-March. Reservations necessary on weekdays in winter. Major credit cards accepted. Rue Richard-Casteau, Roussillon (phone: 90-05-63-86). Expensive.

ST-RÉMY-DE-PROVENCE One of those Provençal market towns with great charm and interesting Roman ruins nearby, St-Rémy has become a magnet for celebrities and international royalty, who frequently vacation here. You'll need at least a couple of days to soak up the atmosphere of the carefree daily life, watching the world go by over a coffee or *pastis* at the *Brasserie du Commerce* (Pl. de la République); checking out the local goat cheeses, olives, almonds, and fresh fruits and vegetables at the market; and tossing a *boule* or two in a game of *pétanque* with the locals. The town's annual *Festival de Musique* runs from mid-July through September; for details, contact the tourist office (Pl. Jaurès; phone: 90-92-05-22).

On the southern outskirts of town, down D5, is the ruined Greco-Roman city of Glanum (signposted as Les Antiques), which dates back to the town's colonization by the Greek merchants of Marseilles in the 3rd century BC. Buildings in the town were constructed with perfectly chiseled stones that were held together by their fit, rather than by mortar. The city was destroyed by Germanic tribes 600 years later. Its two most important monuments are the mausoleum erected to the memory of Augustus Caesar's grandson and an older, more dilapidated (but still impressive) triumphal arch from the end of the 1st century BC. The rest of the site shows the layout of the town— houses, forum, fountains, and bathhouse. Glanum became St-Rémy after Frankish kings gave it to a monastery, *St-Remi de Reims,* as a token of appreciation for the Catholic church's help in obtaining Provence in the 9th century. Near the ruins look for the medieval monastery of *St-Paul-de-Mausole,* now converted into a sanatorium; self-confined Vincent van Gogh was its most celebrated patient. Visit the graceful Romanesque cloister for a contemplative moment out of the sun.

Back in St-Rémy, in the *Hôtel de Sade* on Rue du Parage, a museum (phone: 90-92-13-07) houses the town's sculptural treasures and an archaeological account of Glanum's daily life. The museum is closed January through March; the rest of the year tours (in French) are offered on the hour from 10 AM to 4 PM (except for 1 PM) and at 5:30 PM; there is an admission charge. The famous astrologer and physician Michel de Nostredame (better known as Nostradamus) was born here in 1503.

BEST EN ROUTE

Hostellerie du Vallon de Valrugues Lush, vibrant, and lavishly decorated, this 53-room hotel, a member of the Concorde group, has become the choice for well-heeled visitors. The one-Michelin-star restaurant features Joël Guillet's celebrated cooking, including lamb with Provençal artichokes, and *aubergine* (eggplant) cannelloni, served in a sublime setting. There's also a pool, a fitness center, and two tennis courts. Open daily. Reservations necessary. Major credit cards accepted. A few minutes' walk from the town's center, on Chemin Canto Cigalo (phone: 90-92-04-40; 800-888-4747; fax: 90-92-44-01). Very expensive.

Château des Alpilles Here you'll find the peace and quiet of a modernized 19th-century country manor on tree-shaded grounds offering 16 rooms and two suites, as well as tennis courts, a pool and barbecue, a sauna, and a restaurant. Closed mid-January through mid-March and mid-November through December 21. Five minutes west of town on D31 (phone: 90-92-03-33; fax: 90-92-45-17). Expensive.

Le Bistrot des Alpilles No relation to the *Château des Alpilles* (see above), this unpretentious, old-style eatery offers the best of simple Provençal cuisine, with top honors going to that pungent celebration of garlic, the *brandade de morue*—a purée of cod cooked in olive oil and garlic. The grilled salmon and the calf's liver with raisins are also excellent. There is live jazz on Friday and Saturday nights. Closed Sundays. Reservations advised. Major credit cards accepted. 15 Bd. Mirabeau, St-Rémy-de-Provence (phone: 90-92-09-17). Moderate.

Café des Arts Not at all fancy, this is a lively local rendezvous for the town's artistic community. Its walls are decorated with the works of local artists (which are for sale). Stick to the steaks, chops, salads, and omelettes. There are 17 serviceable rooms upstairs. Closed Wednesdays, February, and the first two weeks of November. Reservations unnecessary. Major credit cards accepted. 30 Bd. Victor-Hugo, St-Rémy-de-Provence (phone: 90-92-08-50). Moderate.

Le Castelet des Alpilles Related to neither the *Château* nor the *Bistrot* (see above), this old, formerly private mansion is a stone's throw from the central square but seems in a world of its own, thanks to 18 tranquil rooms overlooking the soothing garden. There's a restaurant. Hotel closed November through March. Pl. Mireille, St-Rémy-de-Provence (phone: 90-92-07-21; fax: 90-92-52-03). Moderate.

En Route from St-Rémy-de-Provence Drive 6 miles (10 km) south along winding D5 to Les Baux-de-Provence; for a magnificent view of the mountains and the Camargue plain west of Marseilles, take a little detour east to the observation point of La Caume (near the TV relay station).

LES BAUX-DE-PROVENCE This ruined medieval citadel occupies a spectacular position high on a promontory of sheer rock ravines, overlooking the Provençal plain and the Val d'Enfer (Valley of Hell). The caves here were first inhabited in 3,000 BC, and the site—much like Fontaine-de-Vaucluse—is a tiresome crush in midsummer. But don't hesitate to visit in spring, autumn, or especially winter, when it is even more desolate.

This splendid feudal redoubt was defended for centuries by robber barons against French kings and the Avignon popes. As the star of Christ's Nativity on their coat of arms indicates, the original Lords of Les Baux claimed descent from Balthazar, one of the three kings who traveled to Bethlehem. From the 11th to the 15th century they ruled more than 80 Provençal townships, and their court was a center of medieval chivalry.

When it became a focus of rebellion for the region's Protestants in the 17th century, Cardinal Richelieu, head of Louis XIII's government council, decided to do away with the citadel, making the residents pay for its demolition. The job, however, was never completed; today large sections of the baron's 13th-century castle and its chapels are still visible outside the main village, in what is known as the Ville Morte (Dead Town). Each structure affords superb vantage points overlooking the Val d'Enfer to the east or the Vallon de la Fontaine to the west. The hill on which the fortress stands contains the bauxite mineral to which the town gave its name. The bottom slopes on the southern side are covered with thousands of olive trees, some planted by the Greeks and Romans; the oil they produce is considered the best in France.

BEST EN ROUTE

Oustaù de Baumanière A must stop on any affluent itinerary is this hostelry, tucked into the rocky crags of the gleaming Alpilles foothills. There are 11 rooms, 13 suites, plus one of the best restaurants in Provence, which boasts two Michelin stars. (For more details about the hotel and restaurant, see *Romantic French Hostelries* and *Haute Gastronomie,* respectively, in DIVERSIONS.) Closed mid-January through early March; restaurant also closed Wednesdays and Thursday lunch from November through March. Reservations necessary. Major credit cards accepted. In the Vallon de la Fontaine (phone: 90-54-33-07; fax: 90-54-40-46). Very expensive.

La Benvengudo A respectable alternative to the *Cabro d'Or* (see below), this classic Provençal country house offers 17 traditionally furnished rooms and three suites with nice big bathrooms. The restaurant does an admirable job with regional products on a rich and varied menu—the bass with *cèpe* mushrooms is a special treat. Restaurant closed Sunday dinner and from November through January. Reservations necessary. Major credit cards accepted. In a superb secluded setting, 1 mile (1.6 km) southwest of town on D78F (phone: 90-54-32-54; fax: 90-54-42-58). Expensive.

Cabro d'Or Despite its fairy-tale setting at the foot of the old city, this member of the Relais & Châteaux group offers modern amenities in each of its 22 rooms. It also has a one-Michelin-star restaurant; for details, see *Haute Gastronomie* in DIVERSIONS. Closed mid-November through mid-December; restaurant also closed Mondays and Tuesday lunch. Reservations necessary. Major credit cards accepted. Less than a mile (1.6 km) southwest of town by D78F (phone: 90-54-33-21; fax: 90-54-45-98). Expensive.

Bautezar If the town is not overcrowded, try this attractive little place, which boasts 10 comfortable rooms and a stupendous dining room view past the terrace to the Val d'Enfer and the Vallon de la Fontaine. Closed January and February. Grande-Rue Frédéric-Mistral, Les Baux-de-Provence (phone: 90-54-32-09). Moderate.

Le Bistro du Paradou The Pons family has transformed this white house into a genuine country bistro/café that features a set daily menu, accompanied by a
single wine. Daily specials include *lapin à l'ail nouveau* (rabbit with fresh
garlic) and *gigot d'agneau* with *gratin de pommes de terre* (leg of lamb with
potatoes au gratin). Closed Sundays. Reservations necessary. MasterCard
and Visa accepted. A short drive from Les Baux-de-Provence east on D17,
in Le Paradou (phone: 90-54-32-70). Moderate.

En Route from Les Baux-de-Provence Continue southwest on D17 for 11
miles (18 km) to Arles.

ARLES A major link in Rome's chain of communications with its Spanish colonies,
Arles today uses its imposing ancient arena (capacity 26,000) for colorful
bullfights. If you don't visit during the summer bullfight season, be sure to
climb the tower beside the arena's entrance for a walk along the roofs of
the arches.

Southwest of the arena and a century older, the amphitheater is less
well preserved than the one at Orange, since it was in great part dismantled in the Middle Ages to build the city's churches. But it still serves as a
striking setting for open-air theater, an international photography festival
at the beginning of July (when there also are outdoor slide presentations
in the Place du Forum), and dance and folklore festivals in the summer.

There is a rare jewel of Provençal Romanesque architecture in the *Eglise
de St-Trophime* (Pl. de la République), with its beautifully sculpted portal
depicting the Last Judgment. Don't miss the church's cloister and the richly
carved pillars of the arcade, especially those on the northwest and northeast corners.

Arles was the home of Vincent van Gogh in the late 1880s. The artist's
house has disappeared, but one of his subjects remains: the melancholy
alley of sarcophagi at the Roman cemetery of *Les Alyscamps,* in the southwest corner of town. Picasso loved the town so much that he gave it 57
drawings, which are now housed in the *Musée Réattu* (10 Rue du Grand
Trieuré; phone: 90-96-37-68). The view of the Rhône River from the
museum's windows is breathtaking, particularly when the strong mistral
is blowing. The museum is open daily; admission charge. Perhaps the
most pleasant place in Arles is the Place du Forum, a perfect spot to start
the day with morning coffee, to have a light lunch, to sip a predinner drink,
or to enjoy a nightcap. *Tout* Arles comes here to observe life from a table
at one of the cafés, under the heavy shade of century-old plane trees. For
more information on activities in Arles, stop by the tourist office
(Esplanade des Lices; phone: 90-18-41-20; fax: 90-93-17-17); it's closed
Sunday afternoons from April through October and all day Sundays the
rest of the year.

For a worthwhile side trip, head south of Arles on D570 to the *Réserve
Nationale de la Camargue* (Camargue National Park), one of Europe's most

important wildlife preserves. For additional information on the Camargue, see *The Languedoc* in DIRECTIONS.

BEST EN ROUTE

D'Arlatan Amazingly quiet for their location in the busy center of town, this 15th-century building, for centuries the home of the Counts of Arlatan, offers 34 exquisitely furnished rooms and seven suites. The rooms overlook either a lovely garden or the pool, and larger rooms, sleeping three or four, are available at the same rate as regular doubles, making this a good choice for families. Roman artifacts unearthed during the installation of an elevator are displayed in the lobby. There's no restaurant. Reserve well in advance for the summer festival season. 26 Rue du Sauvage (phone: 90-93-56-66; fax: 90-49-68-45). Expensive.

Grand Hôtel Nord-Pinus This landmark, which used to host the toreadors who performed at the arena, is still a focal point of bullfighting fans, as attested to by the formidable collection of posters gracing its walls. The hotel has 23 rooms, each with old-fashioned, atmospheric flair, and a brasserie. Closed mid-November through February. Pl. du Forum, Arles (phone: 90-93-44-44; fax: 90-93-34-00). Expensive.

Jules César Converted from a 17th-century convent—complete with a Baroque chapel—this 49-room, three-suite hotel, a Relais & Châteaux member, makes for a comfortable stop. The best rooms (besides the suite that was once the Mother Superior's quarters) are those overlooking the cloister. The restaurant, *Lou Marquès,* does a fine job of scrambled eggs with anchovy-and-olive *tapenade,* and leg of baby lamb. There's also a pool. Closed November through December 22. Near the center of town, on Bd. des Lices (phone: 90-93-43-20; fax: 90-93-33-47). Expensive.

L'Olivier A good range of cheeses, a creditable wine list, and excellent service characterize this small eatery, whose daily menu might include roast salmon or—in season—*mousseline d'asperges* (asparagus with a frothy hollandaise-style sauce). Closed Sundays and Mondays. Reservations advised. MasterCard and Visa accepted. 1 *bis* Rue Réattu, Arles (phone/fax: 90-49-64-88). Expensive.

Les Vaccarés Picturesque views overlooking a charming square, a statue of native poet Frédéric Mistral, and a row of stalwart plane trees are some of the delights of this intimate establishment. Classic dishes such as lamb with garlic and basil and guinea hen with new potatoes crown the menu, and the reasonably priced wine list enhances the bill of fare. Closed Sundays. Reservations advised. Major credit cards accepted. Pl. du Forum, Arles (phone: 90-96-06-17; fax: 90-96-24-52). Moderate.

Le Cloître This modest little place is quiet, comfortable, and clean. Several of the 33 rooms face the *Cloître* (Cloisters) *de St-Trophime*. There's no restaurant.

Centrally located, at 18 Rue du Cloître, Arles (phone: 90-96-29-50; fax: 90-96-02-88). Inexpensive.

En Route from Arles Head east toward Aix on N113 to the autoroute, and stop at Salon-de-Provence. The town is noteworthy for its ingenious use of the region's handsome ocher sandstone, which blends the modern architecture of its boutiques, cafés, and apartments with the old castle towering above them. The castle, *Château Empéri* (no phone), was first built in the 10th century and rebuilt several times up to the 19th century to incorporate each era's architectural style. Military buffs will want to visit the castle's museum, which houses a collection of French army uniforms and weapons from the 17th century to World War I. The castle is closed Tuesdays; admission charge. Nostradamus, who lived and wrote *Centuries* here, is buried at the *Eglise St-Laurent* (Bd. David). Drink a fresh fruit milk shake on the terrace of the *St-Michel* brasserie (Pl. de la Salomenque).

BEST EN ROUTE

Abbaye de Sainte-Croix A 12th-century Romanesque abbey converted, with considerable taste, into a luxury hostelry—a member of the Relais & Châteaux group—with a grand view over the Salon plain. Its 24 rooms and suites are named after saints, but the comfort is far from monastic. The hotel has a great pool set among wild shrubs in the hillside, and it can arrange temporary membership in the exclusive tennis club just down the road. The one-Michelin-star terrace restaurant serves regional cuisine prepared with great subtlety, notably bass with basil, and purées of garlicked zucchini and pumpkin. Côtes de Provence and Palette wines accompany. The chef could lay claim to the best apple pie in Provence. Closed October through mid-March; restaurant also closed Monday lunch. Three miles (5 km) northeast of Salon-de-Provence by D17, then D16, Rte. du Val de Cuech (phone: 90-56-24-55; fax: 90-56-31-12). Expensive.

En Route from Salon-de-Provence Take the autoroute for 23 miles (37 km) to Aix-en-Provence, the perfect climax to a Provençal peregrination. For a detailed report on the city, its sights, its hotels, and its restaurants, see *Aix-en-Provence* in THE CITIES.

The Côte d'Azur

The term "Côte d'Azur" can be confusing. Not an official administrative *département,* it usually describes that privileged part of the Mediterranean coastline from Menton in the east to just beyond St-Tropez in the west, embracing part of the Riviera (which extends from La Spezia in Italy to Cannes in France) and forming part of the ancient province of Provence. It is an area of spectacular beauty, with dazzling white or red cliffs rising from the soothing blue sea, gracefully curved bays, and rich varieties of conifer trees. The translucent quality of light gives a special spark to the colors, and the smells of the salt water, flowers, and pine trees only add to the area's splendor.

The Côte d'Azur is a place for sunning, swimming, gambling, eating, and nightclubbing. It is also home to some of the finest collections of modern paintings in France, since many of the most prominent figures in 20th-century art, drawn by the beauty of the terrain and the extraordinary quality of the light, lived here at one time or another. The past dozen years or so have seen the urbanization of most of the coastline; except for parts of the bottom slopes of the Massif de l'Esterel, east of Cannes, it is difficult to find spots that are not filled with vacation retreats. These include some of the most luxurious and palatial hotels in the world. Besides the intensive development along the sea (the landscape becomes wilder as you move up into the mountains above the coast towns), another plague has hit the Côte: the summer forest fire. Nearly every year from May to September, hundreds of fires burn thousands of acres of forest. In 1990, for example, half of the Massif des Maures, the spectacular forest behind St-Tropez, was destroyed.

The statues of Queen Victoria in Menton and of Lord Brougham (a Victorian aristocrat and politician) in Cannes are reminders that the Côte d'Azur was developed by upper-crust English during the last part of the 19th century. In those days it was the exclusive resort of the rich and leisured, who were attracted by the mild climate. For many years no self-respecting monarch, cabinet minister, or business tycoon would miss spending a part of the winter in one of the elegant, wedding-cake hotels of Menton, Monte Carlo, or Nice, or in an Edwardian villa tucked away behind the bougainvillea and frangipani along the splendid Cap d'Antibes.

More recently visitors have begun to forsake the sedateness of these towns for the frivolity and frenzy of St-Tropez and Cannes. Though the coast is lively year-round, nowadays the high season is July through August, when people from all over the world—including France—flock here for vacation. Indeed, the mass influx of people can be something of a nightmare; in summer the traffic in St-Tropez becomes so congested that entering the town by automobile is virtually impossible, and bumper-to-bumper traffic is the norm in Nice and Cannes.

Many of the Côte d'Azur's beaches are rocky or pebbly, but there are plenty of sandy swaths, especially between Antibes and St-Tropez. Some beaches are public and free of charge; others are "private," which usually means they belong to a restaurant or hotel. Topless sunbathing, said to have originated at La Ramatuelle near St-Tropez in the early 1970s, is ubiquitous but hardly the rule: One of the great delights of the Côte d'Azur is that everyone does his or her own thing.

Of course, there's more to do than just sit on the beach. If you feel the need to escape wall-to-wall people, take a day trip to Grasse, the famous perfume center, or to any of the other villages in the mountains. Or indulge in some lazy people watching: Seek out the heart of any Provençal village and its charming central square, which usually is graced by a fountain, shaded by plane trees, and often edged by small cafés. At the end of the afternoon, sit on a café terrace with a deliciously cooling *kir* (white wine with a dash of black currant liqueur) or a *pastis* (a potent anise-flavored drink), and watch the residents play *boules* (lawn bowling). Or, if you're feeling energetic, visit one of the abundant fruit, vegetable, or flower markets or perhaps an art museum. Admission charges to museums tend to be low, despite the generally high cost of just about everything on this gold coast. The work of the modern masters—Renoir, Matisse, Picasso—is exhibited in delightful settings throughout the region. Note that some museums and other attractions close one day a week, usually Monday or Tuesday, and many close daily from noon to 2 PM.

There are gastronomic masterpieces to sample as well: bouillabaisse, the classic fish stew made with onions, tomatoes, garlic, olive oil, and saffron; *rouille,* a fiery mayonnaise made with red chili pepper; aioli, a mayonnaise based on olive oil and garlic; and *pissaladière,* a pizza topped with onions, anchovies, and black olives. Provence is not one of France's greatest wine regions, but there are several local vintages; try the dry whites from Cassis, the Bandol reds, or the Bellet reds or whites. Light and fruity Côtes de Provence rosés can be enjoyed with most fish or meat dishes.

In an effort to provide the quintessential Provençal experience, we have suggested three tour routes that can be followed separately or combined, depending on the amount of time available. Motorists should buy the Michelin green map No. 195 (*Côte d'Azur–Alpes Maritimes*) or the Michelin yellow map No. 245 (*Provence–Côte d'Azur*), which extends slightly farther west. Our first route, covering a distance of 17 miles (27 km), explores Les Corniches (the coast roads, known as Inférieure, Moyenne, and Grande—or lower, middle, and upper) between Nice and Menton. These three roads roughly follow the outline of the coast and, when they climb high into the crags of the maritime Alps and through the villages perched there, they provide spectacular views of the sea and mountains. The second route is a Nice-Cannes round trip that ventures slightly inland to Grasse and to St-

Paul and Vence and calls at Antibes, on the coast. Our third route, a Cannes-St-Tropez round trip (a distance of 47 miles/75 km), takes in St-Raphaël, Ste-Maxime, Port Grimaud, and other beach resorts.

Despite the Côte d'Azur's extravagant reputation, there is a wide range of accommodations at various prices (except in Monaco, which caters mostly to the well-heeled tourist). For a double room in a very expensive hotel, expect to pay $200 and way up per night; in an expensive one, from $100 to $200; in a moderate place, from $60 to $100; and in an inexpensive hotel, under $60. Unless otherwise indicated, all hotels accept major credit cards and are open year-round. Most hotels feature telephones and private baths in all of their rooms. However, some less expensive ones may have private baths in only some rooms; it's a good idea to confirm whether your room has a private bath when making a reservation. Also, quite a few hotels on this balmy coastline, even in the pricier range, do not have air conditioning; some do not have TV sets in the rooms. For July and August, reserve rooms well in advance. The tab for dinner for two will be $200 or more in a very expensive restaurant; from $100 to $200 in an expensive place; from $50 to $100 in a moderate one; and under $50 in an inexpensive restaurant. A few last caveats: The above prices do not include wine or drinks (though service usually is included); prix fixe menus are always more economical than ordering à la carte; and in high season you may be required to have lunch and/or dinner at your hotel in order to get a room, an obligation called *pension complète* for both meals and *demi-pension* for just one (plus breakfast in both cases). All restaurants listed below are open for lunch and dinner unless otherwise noted. For each location hotels and restaurants are listed alphabetically by price category.

LES CORNICHES

NICE For a detailed report on the city, its sights, its hotels, and its restaurants, see *Nice* in THE CITIES.

En Route from Nice Drive east along the Corniche Inférieure (the ancient Via Aurelia, built by the Romans, which hugged the coast all the way to Rome), which offers grand views of the sea. Villefranche-sur-Mer is 4 miles (6 km) away.

VILLEFRANCHE-SUR-MER Full of steep, old streets (be sure to walk the Rue Obscure, dating from the 13th century), with a magnificent backdrop of soaring mountains, this town offers a respite from the often-frenzied pace of nearby Nice. Its deep harbor is a safe anchorage for fleets of oceangoing cruise ships and naval warships that frequently arrive on courtesy visits, and you're quite likely to rub shoulders with sailors from the giant US carriers *Nimitz* and *Kennedy* in the town's bars and restaurants. Not to be missed is the 16th-century *Citadelle Ste-Elme,* which was used by the military until 1965, and the *Chapelle St-Pierre,* which was decorated in 1957 by Jean Cocteau, the French writer, filmmaker, and painter.

BEST EN ROUTE

Les Olivettes Surrounded by greenery, this renovated 21-room hotel affords guests a spectacular view of the old city and Cap Ferrat. There's a pool and a restaurant, which is open only to hotel guests. 17 Av. Léopold-II (phone: 93-01-03-69; fax: 93-76-67-25). Very expensive.

La Mère Germaine Seafood is the specialty at this harborside eatery, which has been run by the same family for more than half a century. We especially recommend the bouillabaisse, the *salade niçoise,* and the lemon meringue tart for dessert. Closed November 22 through December and Wednesdays from October through March. Reservations advised. Major credit cards accepted. 7 Quai Courbet (phone: 93-01-71-39; fax: 93-76-94-28). Expensive.

Welcome Jean Cocteau often stayed in this hotel, whose seaside terrace restaurant serves food prepared in the tradition of lauded local chef Georges Escoffier (1846–1935). Escoffier created, among other things, peach Melba and "introduced the frying pan to the English, who only knew how to boil," according to one staff member. Most of the 32 comfortable rooms overlook the port; parking is available. Closed November 20 through December 20; restaurant also closed Mondays from September through May and for lunch in summer. Across from the *Chapelle St-Pierre,* at 1 Quai Courbet (phone: 93-76-76-93; fax: 93-01-88-81). Expensive.

En Route from Villefranche Turn right onto D25 to the wooded peninsula of St-Jean-Cap-Ferrat.

ST-JEAN-CAP-FERRAT This old fishing port, now taken over by pleasure craft, is worth visiting for a look at the *Villa Ephrussi de Rothschild* (Bd. Denis-Semeria; phone: 93-01-33-09), now an eclectic museum on the former property of the late King Leopold II of Belgium. It contains Mme. Rothschild's collection of paintings, china, tapestries, and furniture. It is closed Sunday mornings, Mondays, and November; there's an admission charge. Also notable are the botanic garden and the *sentier touristique* (walking trail) that circles the peninsula and offers spectacular views of the sea and coast. The ceiling in the marriage room of the *Mairie* (Town Hall) was decorated by Cocteau.

BEST EN ROUTE

Grand Hôtel du Cap-Ferrat Arguably the finest hostelry on the entire Riviera, with 48 rooms and 11 suites situated on gorgeous grounds, a beach, a spectacular pool, tennis, and a one-Michelin-star restaurant. Closed mid-January through mid-February. For additional details, see *Romantic French Hostelries* in DIVERSIONS. Bd. du Général-de-Gaulle (phone: 93-76-50-50; fax: 93-76-04-52). Very expensive.

Royal Riviera This turn-of-the-century palace has regained its former glory under new management. Most of the 72 rooms and five suites have views over a large park. There is a superb pool and a private beach, as well as a good restaurant with an inventive young chef. Closed mid-November to December 23. 3 Ave. J.-Monnet (phone: 93-01-20-20; fax: 93-01-23-07). Very expensive.

Voile d'Or This elegant (some would say stuffy) 50-room, five-suite property has a heated pool and superb views of the port. The one-Michelin-star dining room features fish specialties. Closed November through mid-March. On the harbor, at Port de St-Jean (phone: 93-01-13-13; fax: 93-76-11-17). Very expensive.

Le Provençal/Jean-Jacques Jouteux The specialties of this beautiful dining spot—which has been awarded a star from Michelin and is now named for its chef—are light *nouvelle* dishes such as squid sautéed with vegetables and garlic. Closed November, December, mid-January through February, Sunday dinner, and Mondays in the off-season. Reservations necessary. MasterCard and Visa accepted. 2 Av. D.-Sémeria (phone: 93-76-03-97). Expensive.

En Route from St-Jean-Cap-Ferrat D25 will take you right into adjacent Beaulieu.

BEAULIEU-SUR-MER Protected from cold north winds by the surrounding hills, Beaulieu (whose name means, accurately, "Beautiful Place") is one of the warmest spots on the Riviera. Among the many glamorous homes built here by wealthy visitors is the *Villa Kerylod,* a beautiful reconstruction of an ancient Greek dwelling. It also houses a small sculpture museum. On a promontory overlooking the Baie des Fournis on Rue Gustave-Eiffel, the villa offers magnificent views of Cap-Ferrat, Eze, and Cap-d'Ail. It is closed Mondays and November; admission charge (phone: 93-01-01-44).

BEST EN ROUTE

Le Métropole Reminiscent of an Italian palazzo, this luxurious 50-room, three-suite Relais & Châteaux member has a heated pool, an excellent one-Michelin-star restaurant, and a private helicopter pad. Closed October 20 through December 20. 15 Bd. Maréchal-Leclerc (phone: 93-01-00-08; fax: 93-01-18-51). Very expensive.

La Réserve de Beaulieu Under new management, this 37-room, three-suite property seems to have regained much of its former status as one of France's top luxury hotels. Dining in the sleek salon feels a little like sitting at the captain's table on an old-fashioned luxury liner, with the blue sea and bluer-than-blue sky stretching away just beyond the chandeliers. One level down is a handsome pool, and a notch below that, a stony beach and an amply stocked yacht basin. The grounds are enthralling. On the sea, at 5 Bd. Maréchal-Leclerc (phone: 93-01-00-01; fax: 93-01-28-99). Very expensive.

Frisia This 35-room hotel has been run by the same family for almost a century, and the service is particularly friendly. Ask for a room with a balcony overlooking the water. There's no restaurant. Closed November through December 22. Overlooking the yacht basin, on Bd. Maréchal-Leclerc (phone: 93-01-01-04; fax: 93-01-32-92). Expensive.

La Résidence Carlton Most of the 27 rooms in this luxurious establishment have balconies overlooking the pretty private garden. Closed October through *Easter*. No restaurant. Av. Albert I (phone: 93-01-06-02; fax: 93-01-29-62). Expensive.

En Route from Beaulieu Take N98 about 7 miles (11 km) to Monaco.

MONACO For a complete report on the principality, its sights, its hotels, and its restaurants, see *Monaco (and Monte Carlo)* in THE CITIES.

En Route from Monaco Take N7, following the signs to Cap-Martin. The road climbs gently, the mountainside becomes more densely wooded, and it's worth stopping for a moment at one of the bends to look back for some marvelous views of Monaco and the bay to Cap-d'Ail. Around the cape the road is flanked by handsome villas with luxuriant gardens of pines, palms, and olive trees. There are fine views of the Bay of Menton on your right as you swing toward Roquebrune, a total of about 4 miles (6 km) from Monte Carlo.

ROQUEBRUNE This town and its peninsula, Cap-Martin, merge into Menton as you follow D52 along the beachfront. Roquebrune and Menton are also linked historically: Dating from about the 10th century, they were held successively by the Counts of Provence, the Republic of Genoa, and the Grimaldis of Monaco until 1793, when they elected to become part of France after the French Revolution. Under the 1814 Treaty of Paris, the two towns reverted to the Princes of Monaco; they finally joined France in 1861. The medieval village of Roquebrune is particularly worth a visit, with its steep, narrow passageways and carefully restored 15th-century castle. At Rue de la Fontaine and Route de Menton, about 200 yards from the village, is a thousand-year-old olive tree; it's said to be one of the oldest trees in the world. In 1467 survivors of the bubonic plague held performances of a Passion Play here, and the town continues that tradition on its esplanade every August 5.

BEST EN ROUTE

Vista Palace Beautifully set on a cliff, this luxurious 63-room, five-suite hotel affords exceptional views of Roquebrune and the French and Italian coasts.

A fine restaurant, a pool, gardens, a health center, and parking complete the amenities. In addition, some of the suites have private pools. Open year-round. More than two miles (3 km) from the center of Roquebrune on the Grande Corniche (phone: 93-10-40-20; fax: 93-35-18-94). Very expensive.

Alexandra Its wonderful view of the mountains and sea stretching all the way to Italy makes this quiet 40-room hotel one of the best in town. Early risers will be rewarded by the extraordinary sunrises. No restaurant. Closed mid-November through mid-December. At the entrance to the Cap-Martin Peninsula, at 93 Av. Sir-Winston-Churchill, Roquebrune–Cap-Martin (phone: 93-35-65-45; fax: 93-57-96-51). Moderate.

La Dame Jeanne A real dining find on the over-touristed coast is this cozy, authentic restaurant where the chef herself recites the menu to patrons. Try the risotto with wild mushrooms or the chicken breast with *pistou* (a Provençal version of pesto). Closed Sunday dinner except in summer. Reservations necessary. No credit cards accepted. 1 Chemin Ste-Lucie, Roquebrune (phone: 93-35-10-20). Moderate.

Reine d'Azur A good, simple hotel with 32 rooms; guests who take their meals here are in for a bargain. Closed November 10 through early December. 29 Promenade Cap-Martin, Roquebrune–Cap-Martin (phone: 93-35-76-84; fax: 93-28-02-91). Moderate.

MENTON Like Beaulieu, Menton (pop. 28,000) is protected from the cold northern winds by mountains. As a result, it has the mildest climate on the Côte d'Azur, and its nearly perpetually warm and sunny weather is responsible for the region's famous profusion of flowers and citrus fruit, especially lemons. The delicate lemon tree produces fruit year-round, a fecundity celebrated in the charming *Fêtes du Citron* during late February and early March.

Also due to its mild weather, Menton for many years was considered the traditional winter resort for older people; although the character of the town has changed somewhat, it's still a good deal more sedate than Cannes and Nice. The town is also something of a cultural center, hosting a *Chamber Music Festival* in August.

Take a stroll along the Promenade du Soleil, which runs along the beaches and is lined with hotels. At the end of the promenade is the *Musée Cocteau,* featuring drawings, paintings, and stage sets by the artist. It is closed Mondays and Tuesdays; there's an admission charge (phone: 93-57-72-30). Continue past the museum along the Quai Napoléon-III for a magnificent view of the Vieille Ville (Old Town). *L'Hippocampe* (phone: 93-35-51-72), a tourist excursion boat, sets off from the quay daily from May through October for a short trip along the coast. In the heart of the Vieille Ville is the 17th-century *Eglise St-Michel,* the finest Baroque church in the region, with a beautiful Italianate square in front.

The Rue St-Michel leads into the pedestrian precinct, just behind the Promenade du Soleil. Close by is the *Hôtel de Ville* (Town Hall), which has a marriage room decorated with murals by Cocteau. The ticket for this includes admission to the *Musée Cocteau* (see above). Also not to be missed is the indoor market, housed in an old wrought-iron building reminiscent of a Victorian train station.

The centerpiece of the modern town is the impressive turn-of-the-century *Jardin Biovès,* best viewed with one's back to the *Casino Municipal.* The garden is bordered with plane and palm trees, interspersed with lemon trees. Among the fountains and statues is a memorial commemorating the annexation of Menton and Roquebrune by France in 1793. On the right is the vast *Palais d'Europe,* which houses the tourist office (phone: 93-57-57-00) and is the center of the town's many cultural activities.

BEST EN ROUTE

Napoléon Each of this hotel's 40 soundproofed rooms has a view of the mountains or the sea. The restaurant has a stunning view of the coastline. Closed November through mid-December. 29 Porte de France (phone: 93-35-89-50; fax: 93-35-49-22). Moderate.

Piccolo Mondo This genuine Italian trattoria, a branch of a popular restaurant in nearby San Remo, Italy, has won a local following for its herb ravioli and light zucchini tart. Closed Monday dinner and Tuesdays. Reservations advised. MasterCard and Visa accepted. 10 Rue Trenca (phone: 93-57-53-11). Moderate.

En Route from Menton Take D22 north, following the signs to Ste-Agnès. The road climbs rapidly and tortuously, offering a magnificent view of the valley. From higher still you'll see the whole of the Bay of Menton spread out below. After 9 miles (14 km) of this serpentine ascent, you'll enter Ste-Agnès.

STE-AGNÈS Clinging precariously to the mountainside at an altitude of 2,262 feet, this medieval village claims to be the highest coastal town in Europe. Ste-Agnès is one of the most unaffected places on the Côte d'Azur, and its steep, cobbled streets contain many shops in which genuine bargains in woolens, ceramics, leather goods, and locally distilled essences of lemon and lavender may be found. Like those in St-Jean-Cap-Ferrat and Menton, Ste-Agnès's *Mairie* (Town Hall) has a marriage room decorated by Jean Cocteau. Also worth visiting in the town's 16th-century *Eglise Notre-Dame des Neiges.*

En Route from Ste-Agnès Continue on D22. As the tortuous road winds up to an elevation of 2,600 feet at the Col de la Madone, you'll often have to stop to let other cars pass. Turn right at D53 into Peille, a quiet town worth visiting for its 11th-century ramparts and two chapels, *St-Joseph* and *St-Antoine*. Far off the usual tourist track, Peille has its own language, *pelhasc,* which is related to the old Niçois tongue. The village's traditions are the subject of the tiny *Musée du Terroir* (Museum of Local Culture), which is open Sunday afternoons only except in July and August, when it's open Wednesday and Saturday afternoons as well; admission charge (no phone).

About 3 miles (5 km) down the hill toward Nice on D53 is another "perched" village, perhaps the most beautiful and best-preserved: Peillon. Take the time to wander up and down the village's alleyways.

Return on D53 to Peille, then continue south on D53 to La Turbie.

BEST EN ROUTE

Auberge de la Madone Ideal for a romantic weekend, this luxurious 17-room, three-suite inn is hidden away in the countryside. Its excellent restaurant features Provençal dishes with creative touches, like *lapereau aux pâtes fraîches* (young rabbit with fresh pasta) in a sauce made with dark beer. Closed three weeks in January and late October through December 20; restaurant also closed Wednesdays. Peillon (phone: 93-79-91-17; fax: 93-79-99-36). Expensive.

Belvédère Hôtel Not to be missed, with five small, very simple, clean rooms with views of surrounding cliffs, and a restaurant that offers copious prix-fixe menus featuring family-style Provençal specialties. Closing dates vary; call ahead to confirm. Reservations for the rooms must be made *in writing* well in advance. Reservations at the restaurant advised in summer. No credit cards accepted. Peille 06440 (phone: 93-79-90-45). Inexpensive.

LA TURBIE At 1,575 feet, this town is best known for its Roman relic, the *Trophée des Alpes,* built in 6 BC to commemorate Augustus Caesar's victory over the Gallic tribes of the region. There are only two structures of this kind still standing (the other is in Romania). The round pillar originally stood 160 feet high, and on the base was engraved a list of the 44 conquered tribes. Above, between Doric columns, were statues of the generals who took part in the campaign. The top was surmounted by a statue of Augustus himself, flanked by two prisoners. A large part of the monument was destroyed by the Lombards in the 6th century, and villagers took much of the fallen stone for their houses. From the ruins—signposts direct you to them from the village—you can catch some spectacular views (particularly at night) of Monaco and down the coast as far as Bordighera in Italy. The adjacent *Trophée des Alpes* museum has interesting photographs of the restoration of the area, done some 40 years ago. The monument and museum are closed Tuesdays and holidays; admission charge (phone: 93-41-10-11 for both).

On the side of the mountain below the Old City is an image of a dog's head; from there a once spectacular view of the Riviera has been marred by blackened tree trunks from perennial summer fires. In January the final stages of the *Monte Carlo Rally* twist around La Turbie's treacherous roads.

BEST EN ROUTE

Le Napoléon A comfortable, modernized hotel with 24 rooms, a bar, a restaurant, and a flowered terrace. Hotel open year-round. Restaurant closed Tuesdays from October through March. 7 Av. de la Victoire (phone: 93-41-00-54). Moderate.

En Route from La Turbie Follow the signs to the Moyenne Corniche and the village of Eze, 3 miles (5 km) away.

EZE Perched more than 1,300 feet above the sea, Eze-Village is an ancient, walled town of golden stone set off by geraniums and flowering vines. Famous for its vertiginous views of the sea (on a clear day you may see Corsica) and artisans' boutiques, it has become the dropping-off point for many a tour bus, yet it is still an enticing place. Aside from the breathtaking setting, Eze is notable for its 14th-century *Chapelle des Pénitents-Blancs,* which contains a fine Catalan crucifix dating from 1258 and several paintings and enamels of the crucifixion. The *Jardin Exotique* (Exotic Garden) has a rich collection of cacti. For fit walkers, a (mostly) paved footpath connects high-up Eze-Village with Eze-Bord-de-Mer (Eze-by-the-Sea, where the train station is) via the Sentier Nietzsche (Nietzsche Pass); the descent takes one-and-a-half to two hot, dusty hours, but affords many a sweeping view over the landscape.

BEST EN ROUTE

Cap Estel Perched on a promontory with a sea view from each of the 43 rooms and seven suites, and everything covered in flowers, this luxurious hotel seems like a Hollywood stage set. There's a restaurant. Closed late October through March. Eze-Bord-de-Mer (phone: 93-01-50-44; fax: 93-01-55-20). Very expensive.

Château de la Chèvre d'Or A member of the Relais & Châteaux group, with 15 rooms (six of them in a separate building perched on the edge of the cliff), three suites, plus a one-Michelin-star dining room. For additional details, see *Romantic French Hostelries* in DIVERSIONS. Closed December through February; restaurant also closed Wednesdays in March. Rue du Barri, Eze-Village (phone: 93-41-12-12; fax: 93-41-06-72). Very expensive.

Château Eza Once the residence of Prince William of Sweden, this five-room, three-suite (two with fireplaces) hostelry offers splendid views from high over the Mediterranean. (The double beds seem diminutive compared with their American counterparts.) The restaurant, which is under the tenure of a new chef, has one Michelin star; the wine list is excellent, too. Closed November through March. Rue du Barri, Eze-Village (phone: 93-41-12-24; fax: 93-41-16-64). Very expensive.

En Route from Eze Turn right on D46, which winds up the mountain to rejoin the Grande Corniche; from here you can descend back into Nice, a 7-mile (11-km) drive from Eze.

NICE-CANNES ROUND TRIP

En Route from Nice Leave Nice by the Promenade des Anglais; follow the coast road (N98) west for 8 miles (13 km), past the airport and *Cap 3000,* a vast shopping center that is worth a visit, to Cros-de-Cagnes. Follow the signs through Cagnes-Ville (the modern town) to Haut-de-Cagnes, all part of Cagnes-sur-Mer.

CAGNES-SUR-MER This includes the medieval village of Haut-de-Cagnes, perched on a hillside covered with olive, citrus, cypress, and palm trees, a mile back from the sea; Cros-de-Cagnes, the somewhat tacky coastal strip; and Cagnes-Ville, the mundane modern neighborhood.

Head straight for the castle in Haut-de-Cagnes, which dates from the early 14th century and whose history has been dominated by the ubiquitous Grimaldi family. The *Château Musée,* a fortress once owned by the Grimaldis, contains three museums, one devoted to the olive, another a collection of terrible portraits of the French nightclub singer Suzy Solidor, and the third, the *Musée d'Art Moderne Méditerranéen,* which includes paintings by 20th-century artists who lived near the Mediterranean, including Marc Chagall and Raoul Dufy. The former reception hall of the fortress has a trompe l'oeil ceiling fresco of the *Fall of Phaeton* by Carlone. The museums are closed Tuesdays (except July through September) and October 15 through November 15. There's an admission charge (phone: 93-20-85-57). The *Musée d'Art Moderne Méditerranéen* also is the home of the *Cagnes International Festival of Painting,* held during July, August, and September. In the castle precincts are a number of bars and restaurants, one of which, *Jimmy's,* is a good place to stop for a refreshing drink or snack. Haut-de-Cagnes also has some interesting nightclubs (gay and straight).

Les Collettes, the house where Pierre-Auguste Renoir lived for the last 12 years of his life, is on Avenue des Collettes in Cagnes-Ville (phone: 93-20-61-07). His first-floor studio has been left just as it was; in the garden is his magnificent bronze statue of Venus. On the grounds are more than six acres of olive trees, mimosa, and flower gardens. *Les Collettes* is closed Tuesday mornings except June through mid-October; closed mid-October through mid-November; admission charge. The racetrack, *Hippodrome de la Côte d'Azur* (near the sea, on Bd. Kennedy, Cagnes-sur-Mer; phone: 93-20-30-30), is open December through February and August through

September. Six miles (10 km) south of Cagnes is Villeneuve-Loubet, the birthplace of Georges Auguste Escoffier, one of France's great *cuisiniers,* inducted into the French Legion of Honor. His former childhood home now houses a museum of culinary art (3 Rue Escoffier; phone: 93-20-80-51). The museum is closed Mondays, November, and official holidays; admission charge.

BEST EN ROUTE

Le Cagnard In a picturesque part of the city, this Relais & Châteaux establishment has 18 rooms and 10 suites, each with a mini-bar and some with terraces. The place's biggest draw is its one-Michelin-star restaurant, which specializes in such dishes as *chaud-froid de foie gras* (foie gras in aspic) and *filet de turbot aux palourdes* (filet of turbot with clams). Closed from early November through December 21; restaurant also closed Thursday lunch. Major credit cards accepted. In the Vieille Ville (Old Town), on Rue Sousbarri, Cagnes-sur-Mer (phone: 93-20-73-21; fax: 93-22-06-39). Very expensive.

En Route from Cagnes-sur-Mer Follow D36 and D2 for 4 miles (6 km) to St-Paul-de-Vence.

ST-PAUL-DE-VENCE Set in olive groves with splendid views on all sides—the Alps to the north, the Mediterranean and Cap-d'Antibes to the south—the town is enclosed by massive ramparts arranged in the form of an acropolis. A single cannon known as the *Lacan,* which guards the entrance, dates from the 1544 Battle of Cerisilles.

Something of an artists' colony (Modigliani, Bonnard, Soutine, and Chagall lived here), the town is filled with studios, boutiques, and galleries. Don't miss the *Fondation Maeght,* a museum in the center of town that houses one of the finest collections of modern art in France. Within the house, courtyard, and garden are beautifully displayed works by Braque, Chagall, Kandinsky, Miró, Giacometti, Bonnard, Derain, Matisse, Bazaine, and many other artists. Special exhibitions featuring contemporary artists, films, ballet performances, and poetry readings are presented throughout the year. Closed mid-November through mid-December; admission charge (phone: 93-32-81-63).

Also worth a stop is the *Eglise St-Paul-de-Vence,* a 12th- and 13th-century church whose collection includes such treasures as a painting of St. Catherine of Alexandria attributed to Tintoretto and a 16th-century alabaster Madonna. St-Paul-de-Vence's tourist office is on Rue Grande (phone: 93-32-86-95).

La Colombe d'Or This place owes its fame to its remarkable Postimpressionist art collection—Matisse and other artists sometimes paid their bills during the 1920s and 1930s with the paintings that now decorate the walls. The sumptuous hotel, which has 16 rooms, nine suites, plus a heated pool, is regularly refurbished. The restaurant specializes in grills and roasts, and in summer its terrace affords a lovely view. Closed mid-November through mid-December. 1 Pl. du Général-de-Gaulle, (phone: 93-32-80-02; fax: 93-32-77-78). Very expensive.

Mas d'Artigny A Relais & Châteaux member, this modern establishment has 53 balconied bedrooms and 29 villas, each of the latter with its own private patio and pool; it also has a fine one-Michelin-star restaurant. For additional details, see *Romantic French Hostelries* in DIVERSIONS. Rte. des Hauts de St-Paul (phone: 93-32-84-54; fax: 93-32-95-36). Very expensive.

Le Hameau A garden setting enhances this pleasant hostelry with 13 rooms, many with views of the sea; there are also three suites. There is no restaurant. Closed mid-November through mid-December and mid-January through mid-February. On D7 (phone: 93-32-80-24; fax: 93-32-55-75). Expensive.

Marc-Hély All of the 13 rooms in this comfortable hotel have terraces overlooking St-Paul. There is a flower-filled garden; no restaurant. Closed mid-November through mid December. Rte. de Cagnes, La Colle-sur-Loup (phone: 93-22-64-10; fax: 93-22-93-84). Moderate.

En Route from St-Paul-de-Vence Continue for about 2 miles (3 km) to Vence.

VENCE On a 1,400-foot plateau and separated from the sea by low, wooded hills, this picturesque town has fine views of the surrounding mountains. Unlike St-Paul, Vence has spread out into a complex tangle of suburbs, but don't be put off: Head straight for the walled Vieille Ville (Old Town), one of the most important religious centers in southern France until the French Revolution. Take note of the 10th-century *Cathédrale de Notre-Dame de la Nativité*, with a 19th-century rococo façade, handsomely carved choir stalls, and a Chagall mosaic of Moses parting the waters; the urn-shaped fountain in Place du Peyra, on the site of the old Roman forum; and the *Chapelle du Rosaire,* designed by Matisse in such a way that the sunlight streaming through the luminous stained glass windows creates striking patterns on the walls. The chapel is open Tuesdays and Thursdays; closed November through mid-December (phone: 93-58-03-26). For information, stop in at the tourist office on Place Grand-Jardin (phone: 93-58-06-38).

Château du Domaine St-Martin A typically posh Relais & Châteaux member filled with antique furniture and tapestries, with 17 rooms, 10 villas in a huge garden, and a one-Michelin-star restaurant. There is also a heated pool. For additional details, see *Romantic French Hostelries* in DIVERSIONS. Closed mid-November through mid-March; restaurant also closed Wednesdays in off-season, except to hotel guests. Rte. de Coursegoules (phone: 93-58-02-02; fax: 93-24-08-91). Hotel, very expensive; restaurant, expensive.

Relais Cantemerle Quiet and comfort are assured in this lovely inn lost in the countryside. The inn is appointed in Art Deco style; the restaurant features traditional French food, as interpreted in Provence; and the 20 split-level suites overlook the pool and garden. Closed mid-October through mid-March; restaurant also closed Wednesdays except in summer. 258 Chemin Cantemerle (phone: 93-58-08-18; fax: 93-58-32-89). Expensive.

Le Vieux Couvent This restaurant in a former convent built in the 17th century has won a local following for its inventive variations on Provençal specialties. Closed Wednesdays and January. Reservations advised. Major credit cards accepted. 68 Av. Générale Leclerc (phone: 93-58-78-58). Expensive.

La Farigoule All the charm of Provence is on display in this cozy restaurant, from the Soleiado tablecloths to such featured dishes as the *farandole des tarraïettes,* an appetizer assortment. Closed Friday, Saturday lunch, and mid-November through mid-December. Reservations necessary. No credit cards accepted. 15 Rue H. Isnard (phone: 93-58-01-27). Moderate.

Miramar The 17 rooms in this quiet hotel are elegantly simple; most look out over the sea. No restaurant. Closed November through February. Plateau St-Michel (phone: 93-58-01-32). Moderate.

La Roseraie At this restored 12-room manor house, comfortably furnished in Provençal style, you will find gardens, a pool, and a restaurant (for hotel guests only) featuring the cuisine of southwest France. Restaurant closed Tuesdays, Wednesday lunch, and January. Rte. de Coursegoules (phone: 93-58-02-20; fax: 93-58-99-31). Moderate.

En Route from Vence Take D2210, which winds west through lushly wooded countryside with views of the Gorges du Loup unfolding on your right. Stop at the medieval village of Tourrette-sur-Loup to visit the 15th-century church, with a triptych by Bréa, and the *Chapelle St-Jean,* for its naive frescoes by Ralph Soupault. As you approach Pont-du-Loup, there's a fabulous view of the waterfalls streaming from the heart of the mountain hundreds of feet above. Out of Pont-du-Loup the road climbs past the ruins of the old railroad viaduct, which was destroyed in 1944. Two miles (3 km) farther is the village of Le Bar-sur-Loup, set among the orange terraces and jasmine and violet fields that supply ingredients for the perfume factory on the right. Le Bar-sur-Loup also is interesting for its 14th-century dungeon. A fine view of the Gorges du Loup and the hills behind Vence can be seen from the porch of the *Eglise St-Jacques.* At Le Pré du Lac, at the junction of D2210 and D2085, turn right for Grasse, 4 miles (6 km) down the road.

GRASSE Since the 17th century the very name of this city has been synonymous with perfume: Today three out of four bottles of perfume sold in the world contain essences distilled here. Ten thousand tons of jasmine, mimosa, and lavender flowers are used every year by the three major manufacturers, *Fragonard, Galimard,* and *Molinard.* And in small plots, neighborhood farmers cultivate jasmine and roses (a half dozen tons of petals are required to produce just a quart of essence).

The laboratories of *Fragonard* (20 Bd. Fragonard; phone: 93-36-44-65), *Galimard* (Esplanade du Cours; phone: 93-09-20-00), and *Molinard* (60 Bd. Victor-Hugo; phone: 93-36-01-62) give free tours. During a typical tour guides (some English-speaking) explain how the essences are extracted and distilled; try to catch the master perfumer (usually called *le nez*—the nose) at work, blending essences. The salesrooms in which the tours end are full of pretty souvenirs: scented candles, soaps, sachets of lavender and potpourri, and dozens of bottles of fragrances. Each *parfumerie* sells only its own creations, not only the brands associated with it but also many with unfamiliar names that are imitations of the popular scents of other houses (such as YSL's Opium). Discounts of about 5% are usually available, and many of the virtually unknown scents are very inexpensive. Grasse's *Musée International de la Parfumerie* (8 Pl. du Cours; phone: 93-36-80-20) offers a fascinating look into the production of the aromatic liquid. Closed Mondays and Tuesdays in winter and on holidays; admission charge.

Also of interest is the Vieille Ville (Old Town), hardly changed since the 18th century. The 12th-century *Cathédrale Notre-Dame-du-Puy* contains paintings by Rubens and a fine tryptych by Louis Bréa. The *Fragonard Villa* is a museum honoring the painter Jean-Honoré Fragonard. It's closed Mondays, the second and third Sunday of each month, and the month of November (phone: 93-36-01-61 or 93-36-02-71). The *Musée d'Art et d'Histoire de Provence* has exhibits on the art and history of the area from prehistory to the end of the 19th century. It's closed the same days as the *Fragonard Villa;* one ticket grants admission to both (phone: 93-36-01-61). The *Musée de la Marine (Hôtel Particulier Pontèves-Morel,* Bd. du Jeu-de-Ballon; phone: 93-09-10-71) has an interesting collection of 18th-century model boats. It is closed Saturdays, Sundays, and November; admission charge.

Additional details on Grasse and its perfumeries are available from the tourist office (Pl. de la Foux, on the right as you enter town; phone: 93-36-03-56).

Hôtel des Parfums This modern luxury property has 71 comfortable rooms and suites, each with a terrace, as well as a health center and a restaurant. The suites have kitchen facilities. Hotel and restaurant closed January; restaurant also closed Sunday dinner. Bd. E.-Charabot (phone: 93-36-10-10; fax: 93-36-35-48). Expensive.

Pierre Baltus This tiny, cozy restaurant features local foods and wines. Try the sole with herbs or the duck with green peppercorns. Closed Mondays and mid-February through mid-March. Reservations necessary. MasterCard and Visa accepted. 15 Rue Fontette (phone: 93-36-32-90). Inexpensive.

En Route from Grasse Six miles (10 km) south is Mougins.

MOUGINS This quiet hilltop village (pop. 12,000) retains little of its early fortifications except a 15th-century gate. During medieval times it was an important agricultural center. At nearby *Notre-Dame-de-Vie* is the house where Picasso spent his last years. Mougins is known mostly for its fine restaurants, so it's the place to stop if you've a taste for some rich or elaborate food. Three miles (5 km) from Mougins on the road to Cannes (N85) is an interesting vintage car museum, *Musée de l'Automobile* (722 Chemin de Font-de-Currault; phone: 93-69-27-80). It's open daily; no admission charge for children under 12. Two interesting shops in Mougins are the *Boutique du Moulin* (Pl. du Commandant-Lamy; phone: 93-90-19-18), which sells Provençal antiques and oils and mustards and jams made by the owner's husband, master chef Roger Vergé of the restaurant *Moulin de Mougins* (see below); and *Ombres et Soleil* (21 Ave. de Tournamy; phone: 93-75-39-18), which features hand-embroidered table linens, bedspreads, and locally made tableware.

BEST EN ROUTE

Mas Candille Of the many fine hotels in Mougins, this is considered the best. The 21 spacious, recently redecorated rooms open onto a vast park, and amenities include a restaurant, a pool, and tennis courts. Closed November through early December; restaurant closed Wednesdays, Thursday lunch, and mid-December to April. Bd. Rebuffel (phone: 93-90-00-85; fax: 92-92-85-56). Very expensive.

Le Moulin de Mougins Set in a 16th-century olive-oil mill, with exotic plants outside and paintings within, this is one of the most famous restaurants in France, boasting two Michelin stars. However, a definite decline has been reported lately. To draw customers back again, prices have been lowered, but the quality of the once-celestial cuisine remains uneven. For additional details, see *Cannes* in THE CITIES. Closed Mondays in off-season, Thursday lunch, and late January through March. Reservations necessary. Major credit cards accepted. Notre-Dame-de-Vie, 1 mile (1.6 km) southeast of Mougins via D3 (phone: 93-75-78-24; fax: 93-90-18-55). Very expensive.

L'Amandier de Mougins Roger Vergé's "other" restaurant, which serves simpler food, is in another former olive-oil mill. The seasonal brasserie fare includes various fish and meat dishes. Above the restaurant is Vergé's famous cooking school; for additional details, see *Learning the Culinary Arts* in DIVERSIONS. Closed Wednesdays and Saturday lunch. Reservations necessary. Major credit cards accepted. Pl. du Commandant-Lamy (phone: 93-90-00-91; fax: 93-90-18-55). Expensive.

Les Muscadins There are seven guestrooms and one suite at this elegant place, one of the best in the area. The enticing hotel restaurant, with a terrace overlooking the coast and a fireplace, offers excellent cuisine centered on fresh local products. Hotel and restaurant closed February; restaurant also closed Tuesdays and Wednesday lunch. Reservations advised. 18 Bd. Courteline (phone: 93-90-00-43; fax: 93-92-88-23). Hotel, expensive; restaurant, moderate.

Le Relais à Mougins Given the wavering quality at *Le Moulin* (see above), many feel this is now the finest restaurant in Mougins. Try the *dindonneau* (young turkey) braised in sweet Banyuls wine. Closed Mondays and Tuesday lunch. Reservations advised. Major credit cards accepted. Place de la Mairie (phone: 93-90-03-47; fax: 93-75-72-83). Expensive.

En Route from Mougins Take N85 4 miles (6 km) south to Cannes.

CANNES For a detailed report on the city, its sights, its hotels, and its restaurants, see *Cannes* in THE CITIES.

En Route from Cannes Take D803 to Vallauris, a pottery center and the home of the *Biennial International Festival of Ceramic Art* (for details on the festival, contact the tourist office at Pl. 8 Mai, phone: 93-63-82-58; or the *Palais des Festivals et des Congrès,* phone: 93-39-24-53). Picasso spent several years here working in clay, and in 1952 he was asked by the town council to decorate the chapel of the local priory. The resulting fresco, called *War and Peace,* can be seen at the *Musée National Picasso,* which is closed Tuesdays. There's an admission charge (phone: 93-64-18-05). Along Avenue Georges-Clemenceau are a number of pottery shops. Some of the best are *Foucard Jourdan* (65 *bis* Av. Georges-Clemenceau; phone: 93-64-66-38) and *Madoura,* which still sells some of Picasso's ceramics.

From Vallauris follow D135 for 1 mile (1.6 km) to the old fishing port of Golfe-Juan, given over to pleasure craft and popular for water sports of all kinds. It has good, sandy beaches; there's a sailing school and club that holds regular regattas; and wind surfing and water skiing are easily arranged. The town has historical as well as sporting associations: A 1932 plaque on the quayside commemorates Napoleon's landing here on March 1, 1815.

He chose this spot for his return from exile on Elba because Cap d'Antibes and the headland of the Croisette provided protection from the guns of the forts of Antibes and Cannes. The south of France was Royalist territory, so Napoleon quickly headed north, on what later became known as the famous Route Napoléon, with his small army of 1,200 men. Along the seafront Golfe-Juan merges imperceptibly into Juan-les-Pins, which comes alive in the summer, its cafés and discos throbbing with activity and young people. The nightlife centers mostly around the *Eden Beach* casino (phone: 92-93-71-71), set in a cool garden set back from the sea. (For additional details, see *Casinos Royale* in DIVERSIONS.) Restaurants and cafés line the seafront, each with its own section of beach. In July a *World Jazz Festival* is held in Juan-les-Pins's *Palais des Congrès* and outside among the pine trees. For details on this and other events, contact the tourist office (51 Bd. Guillaumont; phone: 93-61-04-98).

BEST EN ROUTE

Belles Rives F. Scott Fitzgerald often stayed in this palatial 41-room, two-suite hotel, recently extensively remodeled. A splendid view of the bay, Art Deco furniture, and a fine restaurant that serves original dishes like shrimp with almonds and pine nuts are the attractions here. The view more than makes up for the somewhat small rooms. Closed mid-October through mid-April. Bd. du Littoral, Juan-les-Pins (phone: 93-61-02-79; fax: 93-67-43-51). Very expensive.

Juana Its excellent location—only 100 yards from the beach—affords most of the 45 rooms and five suites of this elegant hotel lovely sea views. There's also a heated pool, a private beach, and two bars. Its restaurant, *La Terrasse,* has two Michelin stars. The hotel and restaurant are closed from November until 10 days before *Easter;* the restaurant is also closed Wednesdays (except in July and August, when it's closed daily for lunch). Reservations advised. No credit cards accepted. Av. G.-Gallice, Juan-les-Pins (phone: 93-61-08-70; fax: 93-61-20-37). Very expensive.

Astoria This renovated, comfortable 55-room hotel right near the shore is one of only a handful that are open year-round. 15 Av. Maréchal-Joffre, Juan-les-Pins (phone: 93-61-23-65; fax: 93-67-10-40). Expensive.

Les Mimosas A pleasant hostelry in a garden setting, it has 34 rooms with balconies, a pool, and parking, but no restaurant. Closed November through March. MasterCard and Visa accepted. Rue Pauline, Juan-les-Pins (phone: 93-61-04-16; fax: 93-93-06-46). Expensive.

Le Pré Catalan This peaceful 18-room hotel near the sea has its own restaurant and a private beach, and is one of the few that is open all year. 22 Av. Lauriers, Juan-les-Pins (phone: 93-61-05-11; fax: 93-67-83-11). Expensive.

Tétou Grilled lobster and bouillabaisse are good choices at this one-Michelin-star eatery. Closed Wednesdays, mid-October through December 20, and for dinner from December 20 through March. Reservations advised. No credit cards accepted. Bd. des Frères-Roustan, on the beach in Golfe-Juan (phone: 93-63-71-16). Expensive.

Bijou-Plage This bright restaurant overlooking the beach (ask for a table on the terrace) serves fresh seafood and such inventive dishes as risotto with truffle butter. Closed one month in winter (dates vary; call for updated information). Reservations advised. Major credit cards accepted. Bd. Guillamont, Juan-les-Pins (phone: 93-67-81-78). Moderate.

En Route from Juan-les-Pins Follow D2559 around the cape, ignoring the "Direct to Antibes" signs. Lovely villas line the approach to adjacent Cap d'Antibes.

CAP D'ANTIBES This peninsula is one of the most exclusive spots on the Côte d'Azur, where the sun is worshiped in high style. The ultimate Antibes stopping place is the luxury-soaked, seaside *Hôtel du Cap–Eden Roc* (see *Best en Route*); a stay there will convince you that Cap d'Antibes deserves its romantic reputation. After your feet touch the ground again, the *Musée Naval et Napoléonien* (Batterie du Grillon; phone: 93-61-45-32) is worth a look for its memorabilia of Napoleon's landing at Golfe-Juan. Closed Saturday afternoons, Sundays, and October; admission charge. Also interesting is the *Jardin Thuret,* a 10-acre botanical garden established in 1856 to introduce tropical vegetation to the surrounding area.

BEST EN ROUTE

Don César Overlooking the sea, this luxury hotel has a pool; all 19 units have private balconies. Closed mid-November through March. 40 Bd. Garoupe (phone: 93-67-15-30). Very expensive.

Hôtel du Cap–Eden Roc This truly grand hotel has 130 handsome guestrooms. For additional details, see *Romantic French Hostelries* in DIVERSIONS. Closed October through mid-April. No credit cards accepted. Bd. Kennedy (phone: 93-61-39-01; fax: 93-67-76-04). Very expensive.

Bacon Here on a terrace overlooking the sea, diners may choose bouillabaisse or excellent fresh fish from a one-Michelin-star menu. Closed Mondays and November through January. Reservations necessary. Major credit cards accepted. Bd. Bacon, on the northeastern point of the cape as you approach the town of Antibes (phone: 93-61-50-02; fax: 93-61-65-19). Expensive.

La Gardiole This simple, quiet hostelry set among the pines has 21 rooms, some of which face the sea, as well as a charming wisteria-draped terrace and a fine restaurant. Closed November 5 through February. Chemin de la Garoupe (phone: 93-61-35-03; fax: 93-67-61-87). Moderate.

ANTIBES One of the oldest settlements on the Côte d'Azur, Antibes was founded by the Greeks in the 5th century BC. It quickly became a chief port of trade between Marseilles and Italy and an important stop on the Via Aurelia, which once extended from Rome to Spain. Several centuries later Antibes's strategic military position—on the border of Savoy—proved valuable to the Kings of France, who from the 15th to the 17th century built and rebuilt the town's fortifications. Of these efforts, only *Fort Carré,* north of the harbor, and some of the ramparts along the seafront remain. During the French Revolution the city served as Napoleon's base.

Nowadays, Antibes has a more tranquil reputation as a center for commercial flower production, primarily roses and carnations. The town also is notable for its excellent *Musée Picasso,* a collection of some of the artist's best later paintings, drawings, and ceramics. The museum is in the Vieille Ville (Old City), housed in the *Château Grimaldi,* built in the 12th century and rebuilt in the 16th. It's closed Tuesdays and November; no admission charge on Wednesdays (phone: 93-34-91-91). For additional details, see *Memorable Museums and Monuments* in DIVERSIONS.

Behind the château on Cours Masséna is the marketplace; a walk through here and the Vieille Ville, which buzzes with activity all year, and along the city ramparts is a must. A delightful flea market takes place on Place Aubertini on Thursdays and Saturdays. Antibes's tourist office is at 11 Pl. Général-de-Gaulle (phone: 93-34-91-91.)

BEST EN ROUTE

Chez Paul le Pêcheur Possibly the best fish soup on the Côte d'Azur is served here; the owner sometimes goes all the way to Marseilles to get the freshest possible delicacies from the sea. His grilled and fried fish also are delicious; the portions, copious. Closed Wednesdays off-season. Reservations necessary. Major credit cards accepted. 42 Bd. d'Aiguillon (phone: 93-34-59-42). Expensive.

Mas Djoliba This small, quiet hotel with 13 rooms and a pool is set in a beautiful park. The dining room is open to guests only. In the center of town, at 29 Av. de Provence (phone: 93-34-02-48; fax: 93-34-05-81). Expensive.

La Bonne Auberge This landmark establishment where the late Jo Rostang garnered three Michelin stars has been completely overhauled by his son Philippe. While the stars were stripped away, the decor is brighter and more modern than before, and the menu focuses on inventive versions of Mediterranean cuisine, such as spinach ravioli and veal marengo. Closed Mondays year-round, Sunday dinner and Tuesday lunch from October through May. Reservations necessary. Major credit cards accepted. On the left-hand side of N7, en route to Nice, in La Brague (phone: 93-33-36-65; fax: 93-33-48-52). Moderate.

L'Oursin A popular little eatery with mahogany woodwork and a spare nautical motif, it has the best seafood in the downtown area. Closed Sunday dinner, Mondays, and July 23 to August 26. Reservations necessary. MasterCard and Visa accepted. 16 Rue de la République (phone: 93-34-13-46). Moderate.

Les Vieux Murs The perfect spot for lunch, with a great view of the water. The spic-and-span blue-and-white dining room serves first class seafood. Open daily. Reservations advised. Major credit cards accepted. Promenade Amiral-de-Grasse (phone: 93-34-06-73; fax: 93-34-81-08). Moderate.

En Route from Antibes A few miles along the coast (N7 or N98), perched on a hilltop, is Biot, a village renowned for its ceramics. Founded by Greeks and Romans, it was fortified by Templars in the 13th century. At the *Verrerie de Biot* (Biot Glassworks; phone: 93-65-03-00), reached via D4, visitors can watch glass being blown or buy the finished product. *Fenouil* (phone: 93-65-09-46), at the edge of the Golfe de Biot, sells *barbotine,* a local pottery with clay bas-reliefs fired onto it. Off D4 and well worth visiting is the *Musée Fernand Léger,* devoted exclusively to the post-Cubist artist's paintings, mosaics, and sculptures. It's closed Tuesdays; admission charge (phone: 93-65-09-46). Route N98 will take you the 14 miles (22 km) back to Nice via the coast.

CANNES–ST-TROPEZ ROUND TRIP

En Route from Cannes Take A8, the autoroute, west for 45 miles (72 km) to exit at Le Cannet des Maures, then go south for 11 miles (18 km) on D558, which will climb up the steep mountains to La Garde-Freinet.

LA GARDE-FREINET Surrounded by cork-producing forests and perched on the crest of the Massif des Maures, this little town is notable for its ruined "Saracen" castle, built to protect against Saracen invasions but abandoned in the 10th century. From here there's a fine view out to sea.

BEST EN ROUTE

La Faùcado This attractive terrace restaurant has a magnificent view of the wooded valley below. Classic dishes are the focus here; there's a fine prix fixe menu at lunchtime. Closed mid-January to mid-March and Tuesday lunch. Reservations advised. Major credit cards accepted. 31 Bd. de l'Esplanade (phone: 94-43-60-41). Moderate.

En Route from La Garde-Freinet Take D558 (through the village of Grimaud) and N98, which wind down the 12 miles (19 km) to St-Tropez.

Giraglia A comfortable 48-room lodging in a seaside setting, it has a private beach and a fine restaurant, recently enhanced by the addition of a terrace overlooking the sea. Closed mid-October through *Easter*. Pl. du 14-Juin, Port-Grimaud (phone: 94-56-31-33; fax: 94-56-33-77). Hotel, very expensive; restaurant, expensive.

ST-TROPEZ For a detailed report on the city, its sights, its hotels, and its restaurants, see *St-Tropez* in THE CITIES.

Although the "real" Côte d'Azur more or less ends at St-Tropez, the scenery farther west is still quite dazzling. Before you start back to Cannes, we suggest a short detour west along the coast road. Drive west on N98 and D559 toward Cavalaire-sur-Mer for a view of its dramatic high cliffs and expansive seascapes. Farther west on D559 is Le Lavandou, a former fishing village that is now a resort with fine sandy beaches. From here you can take a boat to the Iles d'Hyères—Porquerolles, Port-Cros, and Levant—where you may swim, sunbathe, picnic, bicycle, or walk among the fragrant pine and eucalyptus trees. (For ferry schedules from Le Lavandou, call 94-71-01-02. Other boats leave from the Hyères peninsula of Giens, at *La Tour Fondue,* phone: 94-58-21-81; and Toulon, phone: 94-92-96-82.) Still farther west, via D559 and D41, is Bormes-les-Mimosas, a charming old village set on a steep hill among pines and mimosas and overlooking the sea, with sandy beaches and a marina. From D41 turn right on the mountain road, N98, to return to St-Tropez.

Mas du Langoustier One of the most exclusive on the Côte d'Azur, this 57-room, four-suite hotel has an excellent one-Michelin-star restaurant. For additional details, see *Romantic French Hostelries* in DIVERSIONS. Ferries to the island leave from Le Lavandou and Hyères (see above). Reserve well in advance. Closed November through April. Ile de Porquerolles (phone: 94-58-30-09; fax: 94-58-36-02). Very expensive.

Le Manoir Quiet is assured in the only hotel on Port-Cros island, which is primarily a nature preserve. (See ferry information above.) Some of the 23 spacious rooms have balconies, and there is a restaurant serving Provençal specialties. Closed October through May. MasterCard and Visa accepted. At the port, Ile de Port-Cros (phone: 94-05-90-52; fax: 94-05-90-89). Expensive.

En Route from St-Tropez Take N98 9 miles (14 km) east along the coast to Ste-Maxime.

STE-MAXIME A quiet seaside resort popular with young families, Ste-Maxime has a 16th-century fortress and a fine sand beach, plenty of water sports, and a bustling marina. Follow the signs 1 mile (1.6 km) north (via Bd. Bellevue) to the *Sémaphore,* at an altitude of 400 feet, for a sensational view of the coast and the mountains. East of Ste-Maxime, past Cap des Sardinaux, is La Nartelle, where the Allies landed in August 1944. From here to St-Aygulf are a number of small beach resorts, including Val d'Esquières, San Peïre, Les Calanques, and Les Issambres.

BEST EN ROUTE

Hostellerie de la Belle Aurore The view of the Golfe de St-Tropez is magnificent from most of the 17 rooms (ask for a sea view), the pool, and the very good restaurant, which specializes in seafood. Closed October through mid-March. 1 Bd. Jean-Moulin (phone: 94-96-02-45; fax: 94-96-63-87). Very expensive.

Playamaxime This recently opened hotel offers 126 luxury rooms (ask for a beach view) and a pool; it's one of the few in the vicinity to remain open year-round. There's a restaurant. In the suburb of Les Myrtes, on N98 leading from St-Tropez (phone: 94-96-56-50; fax: 94-43-94-42). Very expensive.

Calidianus A simple, modern property with 33 comfortable rooms, a beach, tennis courts, two pools, but no restaurant. Closed January through early February. Most major credit cards accepted. Bd. Jean-Moulin (phone: 94-96-23-21; fax: 94-49-12-10). Expensive.

La Gruppi Excellently prepared seafood dishes and friendly service are highlights here. Closed Mondays in off-season and major holidays. Reservations advised. Most major credit cards accepted. Av. Charles-de-Gaulle (phone: 94-96-03-61). Expensive.

En Route from Ste-Maxime Continue on the coastal road for 12 miles (19 km) to Fréjus.

FRÉJUS Founded by Julius Caesar in 49 BC as Forum Julii, Fréjus was an important Roman naval base, with a population of 40,000 and a large inland harbor connected to the sea by canal. By the Middle Ages the port had declined in importance and gradually became occluded from the sea. Outbreaks of plague in the 14th century and endemic malaria drove the inhabitants from the Roman site, and by 1780 the population had declined to 2,000. Today Fréjus consists of two entities: Fréjus Plage, 3 miles of magnificent sandy beach that blend into that of St-Raphaël; and the Vieille Ville (Old Town), now about a mile from the sea and a treasure trove of Roman remains and medieval buildings, all of which can be visited. Among the Roman ruins are fortifications, houses, baths, and the huge *Amphithéâtre* accommodating 10,000 people; it now is the venue for bullfights in July and August (closed Tuesdays). Also noteworthy is the Episcopal quarter, built in the Middle Ages on a small area of the Roman site; it consists of a cathedral with a 5th-century baptistry (one of the oldest ecclesiastical buildings in France) and magnificent 12th-century cloisters. Behind the cloisters the *Museé Archéologique* contains some splendid Roman mosaics, a marble statue of the god Hermes, and a 1st-century BC bust of Jupiter. For details on hours and tours, contact the tourist office on Place Calvini in Fréjus-Ville (phone: 94-51-53-87) in season or the one at 325 Rue Jean-Jaurès (phone: 94-53-82-85) in the off-season.

BEST EN ROUTE

Les Résidences du Colombier This modern, quiet hotel has 60 rooms in individual Provence-style bungalows (each with a private garden and terrace) set among pine trees in a private eight-acre park. It has a restaurant, a pool, and tennis facilities. Rte. de Bagnols (phone: 94-51-45-92; fax: 94-53-82-85). Expensive.

ST-RAPHAËL The sister town to Fréjus, it also was founded by the Romans, although no ruins from their occupation remain. A pyramid on the harbor (Av. Commandant-Guilbaud) commemorates Napoleon's return to France from his Egyptian campaign; he landed here in 1799, and it was from here that he was dispatched to exile on Elba in 1814. The town was a favorite vacation spot for Berlioz, Alexandre Dumas, Maupassant, and many others during the late 19th century. From the promenade along the water you can see the reddish offshore twin rocks called Lion de Terre (Land Lion) and Lion de Mer (Sea Lion).

St-Raphaël is a very pretty and popular resort. In addition to its splendid beach and marina, the town has a full and varied program of cultural and sports events from February right through to November. Visit the tourist office near the train station for details (Rue Rousseau; phone: 94-95-19-70). The *Musée d'Archéologie Sous-Marine* (Museum of Underwater Archaeology; Av. de Valescure; phone: 94-19-25-75) has an important collection of amphorae (ancient Greek jars) found in the sea, but is closed indefinitely for renovation. Some of the city's finest hotels, northeast of the town center via D37 and the Route Golf, are especially appealing to golfers. One of the best layouts in the area, the Robert Trent Jones Sr.–designed *Golf de l'Estérel* (Av. Golf; phone: 94-82-47-88), is on the grounds of the *Latitudes* hotel (see *Best en Route*, below); for additional details on the links, see *Great French Golf* in DIVERSIONS.

BEST EN ROUTE

Hôtel Golf de Valescure A favorite among golfers, this modern place has 40 spacious rooms, many of which have views over the *Golf de Valescure* course. There also is a restaurant, a pool, and tennis courts. Closed mid-November through December 22 and three weeks in January. Rte. de Golf de Valescure, just outside St-Raphaël (phone: 94-82-40-31; fax: 94-82-41-88). Expensive.

Latitudes An 89-room luxury hotel, it boasts the *Golf de l'Estérel* course, which is free for hotel guests. There's also a pool, tennis courts, and a restaurant. Av. Golf (phone: 94-82-42-42; fax: 94-44-61-37). Expensive.

La Potinière Set in a garden, this quiet, modern place has four suites and 25 rooms with balconies, a pool, and a tennis court. Restaurant closed Thursday lunch during the off-season. Near the beach in Boulouris, 3 miles (5 km) along N98 toward Cannes (phone: 94-95-21-43; fax: 94-95-29-10). Expensive.

San Pedro This hotel occupies a slightly too formal-looking modern building surrounded by its own garden, but the 28 rooms are very comfortable, and there are many facilities for fitness buffs, including a saltwater spa. The restaurant, with a lovely flower-filled terrace, features *nouvelle*-inspired dishes. Closed late January through mid-February; restaurant also closed Sunday dinner and, from mid-September through mid-June, on Mondays. Av. Col.-Brooke (phone: 94-83-65-69; fax: 94-40-57-20). Expensive.

Pastorel Considered by most to be the best in St-Raphaël, this charming dining place has consistently good food, nice wines, and great service. Closed Sunday dinner, Mondays, mid-February to mid-March, mid-November to mid-December, and for lunch during August. Reservations advised. Major credit cards accepted. 54 Rue de la Liberté (phone: 94-95-02-36; fax: 94-95-64-07). Moderate.

En Route from St-Raphaël This last leg east along the Corniche de l'Estérel to Cannes (some 27 miles/43 km) offers breathtaking views, so drive slowly. You'll pass through the resort towns of Boulouris, Camp Long, Le Dramont, Agay, Anthéor, Le Trayas, Miramar, Théoule, and La Napoule, all with marvelous sand beaches. You even might discover some tiny hidden strands if you scramble down the rocky cliffs from the road. As you pass the Pointe de l'Aiguille, just before Théoule, the coastline softens into the magnificent Golfe de Napoule, with Cannes to the northeast.

BEST EN ROUTE

L'Oasis Practically a Côte d'Azur landmark, this two-Michelin-star restaurant remains near the top of the area's best dining establishments. Mediterranean decor has replaced the extremely formal Louis XV furnishings, and the new chef has produced an inventive menu featuring some vaguely Oriental (especially Thai) touches, evidenced in the *langouste aux herbes thaï* (rock lobster with Thai herbs), along with classic dishes like seafood risotto, and kidneys in sherry vinegar. Closed Sunday dinner, Mondays, the first half of March, and mid-November through early December. Reservations necessary. Major credit cards accepted. Rue Jean-Honoré-Carle, La Napoule (phone: 93-49-95-52; fax: 93-49-64-13). Very expensive.

Royal Hôtel Casino A luxury 196-room, 15-suite establishment right on the beach, it has a heated pool, an impressive casino, and a good restaurant done up as a yacht. Request a room facing the beach; those overlooking the road are somewhat noisy. Bd. Henri-Clews, La Napoule (phone: 93-97-70-00; fax: 93-49-51-50). Very expensive.

Miramar Beach Isolated among pine trees and red rocks on the Corniche de l'Esterel, this modern hostelry (formerly the *St-Christophe*) offers a seafood restaurant, a private beach, a small pool, and a spectacular view. Each of the 51 rooms and nine suites has a balcony or terrace, with a garden or sea view. Four miles (6 km) from Miramar and Théoule-sur-Mer via N98, at 47 Av. de Miramar, Miramar (phone: 93-75-41-36; fax: 93-75-44-83). Expensive.

Les Flots Bleus This is the place to go when you crave excellent seafood and fish soup with fiery *rouille* but don't feel in the mood for formal dining. The terrace of this gleaming restaurant, whose name means "Blue Waves," is perched above a small beach; the red-rock coastline is spectacular. There are 19 simple hotel rooms upstairs. Closed mid-November through February. Reservations advised. MasterCard and Visa accepted. On N98 in Anthéor (phone: 94-44-80-21). Moderate.

La Maison de Bruno et Judy Bruno is French, Judy is Australian, and the menu in this friendly restaurant is eclectic, with lamb curry, osso buco, and many fine seafood dishes. Wines from all over the world are on the list. The prix fixe menu is a bargain. Closed Tuesdays in the off season and November through December 20. Reservations advised. MasterCard and Visa accepted. Pl. du Château, La Napoule (phone: 93-49-95-15). Moderate.

The Alps

Waterfalls crashing over rocks, glacial streams racing through valleys surrounded by snow-capped mountains, pine forests alluring as sirens, meadows of gentian and edelweiss, a dizzying array of breathtaking vistas and of pass after vertiginous pass—open those eyes and fasten those seat belts, you're in the Alps.

For most travelers to the Alps, goggling at the magnificent scenery, skiing, fishing, and swimming usually replace any preoccupation with Roman ruins, medieval ramparts, and the like. However, there is more to this region than just wildflowers and resorts, even if it is known to most people as the home of Mont-Blanc, Western Europe's highest peak at 15,771 feet.

Composed of two ancient provinces, Dauphiné and Savoy, the French Alps are bordered by Italy, Switzerland, and, to the north and west for about 200 miles, the Rhône River. The Dauphiné, occupying the southern half of the high Alps and taking in the official *départements* of Hautes-Alpes, Isère, and Drôme, belonged first to the Kingdoms of Provence and Arles, then to the Holy Roman Empire. It came under French control without violence fairly early, in 1349, when it was sold by pious but profligate King Humbert II of the Dauphiné. On the other hand Savoy was the object of repeated assaults by countries seeking control of its mountain passes, strategically important from both a military and commercial standpoint. Ruled first by the Kingdom of Burgundy, then Arles, then as part of the Holy Roman Empire, in the 11th century Savoy was consolidated with other fiefdoms under Humbert the White-Handed, who founded the House of Savoie. Over the years Savoy became a powerful duchy that governed parts of France, Italy, and Switzerland. In the 16th century the ducal seat was moved to Turin, making Savoy Italian rather than French, and in the 18th century it became part of the Kingdom of Sardinia. The 1860 Treaty of Turin ceded the region to France.

Today the French Alps have a character all their own. The people are feisty, industrious, and laconic—the Gallic equivalent of New Englanders. You might still hear the older generation speak the regional patois, pronouncing words ending in *oz* or *az* as if the last two letters didn't exist; for example, Sierroz becomes *Sierre* and Clusaz is pronounced *Cluse.*

Alpine cuisine is straightforward, hearty, and healthy. Regional menus feature freshwater fish (trout, pike, carp), ham, sausage, and wild game. Crayfish and *morilles* (morel mushrooms) are two favorite delicacies. Among the excellent cheeses of the area are *chèvre* (goat cheese); *reblochon,* a mild creamy cheese; *tomme de Savoie,* also mild; and *beaufort,* a type of gruyère. The wines of the region marry well with the cuisine; sparkling white Seyssel is considered one of the best. The region's liqueurs—gentian (flavored with the flower) and the famous Chartreuse—are interesting finales to dinner;

also try the local *marc de Savoie,* a brandy made from the residue that remains after wine is pressed.

In both summer and winter thousands of tourists come to enjoy the beauty and majesty of the Alps. Winter is not a time for touring but rather for skiing, hiking, and taking part in other sports. The major mountain passes generally are closed, the weather is unpredictable, and the roads can be treacherous, although those in Savoie's Tarentaise Valley were improved to facilitate access to the 1992 *Winter Olympics* sites. While the tour that we suggest is designed for when most of the highest roads are open, we have included some winter highlights as well.

Before embarking on a driving tour of this region, make sure to check your car's tire pressure and suspension. The winding mountain roads require special attention and careful driving. Be aware also of the peculiar French habit of occasionally ignoring center lines in taking hairpin curves. One more caveat: The region's growing popularity has been known to produce bumper-to-bumper traffic.

Our tour of the French Alps forms an extended oval, starting in the extreme north at Lake Geneva (Lac Leman in French), going through the eastern side of the Alps, and passing along the southern part of the Dauphiné through Gap. It then moves back up the western ridge of the Alps, through the parks of Vercors and Chartreuse, through Grenoble, and ends up in the idyllic lakeside city of Annecy. Lovely villages and spectacular views are so abundant that it is impossible to begin to capture them all; if you take an alternate route, you can hardly go wrong.

In a way, the Alps are too beautiful. They attract hordes of tourists, and during the high season it is easy to be put off by the disappointing lack of tranquillity and by the sheer volume of people. The best way to deal with this is to visit off-season or to seek out lesser-known areas. Vercors, for instance, on the western side of the Alps, is not as famous as Chamonix or Val-d'Isère, but it is spectacular in its own right. For more general information on the region, contact the *Comité Départemental du Tourisme des Hautes-Alpes* (BP 46, Gap 05002; phone: 92-53-62-00) or, in Paris, the *Maison des Hautes-Alpes* (4 Av. de l'Opéra, Paris 75001; phone: 42-96-05-08; fax: 40-15-04-82). In the US, the *French Alps Tourism and Trade Commission* (610 Fifth Ave., New York, NY 10020; phone: 212-582-3439) can provide helpful information for planning a trip to the area. They offer the annually published *French Alps Guide* free of charge; it is also available from the "France on Call" hotline (phone: 900-990-0040).

The Alps have been heavily developed for the tourist trade, which means there's a plethora of hotel rooms in every price range. For a double room per night, expect to pay more than $300 in a very expensive hotel; between $180 and $300 in an expensive place; from $100 to $180 in a moderate one; and less than $100 in an inexpensive one. All hotels accept major credit cards and are open year-round unless otherwise noted. Most hotels feature telephones, private baths, and TV sets (less frequently in inexpensive hotels) in their rooms. Some less expensive hotels may have private baths in only some rooms; it's a good idea to confirm whether your room has a private bath when making a reservation. Very few hotels in these predominantly winter resort towns have air conditioning. Dinner for two with wine and service (usually already included in the bill) in a very expensive restaurant will cost $220 or more; in an expensive one, from $150 to $220; in a moderate one, from $100 to $150; and in an inexpensive one, less than $100. Unless otherwise indicated, all restaurants listed below are open for lunch and dinner. For each location hotels and restaurants are listed alphabetically by price category.

EVIAN-LES-BAINS About two-thirds of the southern coast of Lake Geneva belongs to France. Evian-les-Bains, on the lakeshore, has a familiar name because of the spring water that takes its name from the town. Until the 19th century, when the health-restoring properties of its waters were discovered, Evian-les-Bains was a tiny fortified city. While traces of the pre-spa city remain (three towers, remnants of the city walls, and a few old buildings), what Evian really has to offer is Belle Epoque grandeur. Though no longer only for the very rich, it looks as if it were, with opulent hotels, exquisitely manicured gardens, a long lakefront promenade, and an elegant casino (for a detailed description, see *Casinos Royale* in DIVERSIONS). Every May the casino hosts the well-known *Rencontres Musicales d'Evian* (phone: 44-35-26-90 in Paris), which includes a competition for string quartets and features world-renowned soloists and conductors.

Stroll along the boulevards and the promenade, and drift into Marcel Proust's world of idleness and wealth. Proust stayed at the now-defunct *Splendid* hotel at the turn of the century and fashioned his "Balbec baths" after Evian's. If fitness, health, and beauty rank high among your preoccupations, indulge in some à la carte spa treatment. For more information, contact the tourist office (Pl. d'Allinges; phone: 50-75-04-26; fax: 70-75-61-08) or *L'Espace Thermal* (phone: 50-75-02-30; fax: 50-75-65-99).

Evian makes an excellent base for a number of short outings. Thonon-les-Bains, some 5½ miles (9 km) west, also is a spa, but more bustling and modern; it's a good place for shopping. About a mile (1.6 km) north of Thonon is the *Château de Ripaille,* which Savoyard King Amadeus VIII made his home two times in the 15th century. The château is closed mornings during the last two weeks of February, in March, and during the first two weeks of November; lunch hours from April through October; and from mid-November through mid-February (except by special arrangement). There's an admission charge (phone: 50-26-64-44). Lake Geneva, shaped like a giant boomerang, lends itself to innumerable boat trips. A tour of the entire lake takes about 10 hours; an alternative is to take a 35-minute boat trip into Switzerland, to the lakeside cities of Lausanne-Ouchy (directly across the lake) or Montreux (23 miles/37 km to the east), the latter the site of the *Château de Chillon*, a 13th-century medieval fortress virtually built on the lake. Lord Byron, while visiting his friend Percy Bysshe Shelley's home on the lake, based his poem "The Prisoner of Chillon" on the imposing structure.

BEST EN ROUTE

Le Royal Built in 1907 for King Edward VII of England, this "palace" offers refinement and modern comforts in its 156 rooms and spa facilities. For additional details, see *Romantic French Hostelries* in DIVERSIONS. Closed December and January. Rte. du Mateirons (phone: 50-26-85-00; fax: 50-75-61-00). Very expensive.

Bourgogne Of the fine traditional fare served in this one-Michelin-star establishment, the *omble-chevalier* (charfish) is especially good. Other specialties include duck foie gras and dishes featuring fresh fish from Lake Geneva. There are also 31 comfortable rooms. Closed November and Sunday dinner and Mondays from mid-September through July. Reservations necessary. Major credit cards accepted. 73 Rue Nationale (phone: 50-75-01-05; fax: 50-75-04-05). Expensive.

Toque Royale This one-Michelin-star restaurant's extensive menu features specialties such as crusty filet of pike and veal sweetbreads with mushrooms. It's easy to spend any money left after the meal, since the restaurant is in the casino. Open daily. Reservations advised. Major credit cards accepted (phone: 50-75-03-78; fax: 50-75-48-40). Expensive.

La Verniaz et Ses Chalets Set in gardens overlooking Lake Geneva, this elegant member of the Relais & Châteaux group has 35 rooms and five private chalets, plus a pool, tennis courts, and a first class restaurant. Closed December and January. Rte. Abondance (phone: 50-75-04-90; fax: 50-70-78-92). Expensive.

Terrasse An attractive hostelry with 29 rooms, a restaurant, and a private garden. 10 Rue B.-Moutardier (phone: 50-75-00-67; fax: 50-75-68-07). Moderate.

En Route from Evian-les-Bains Head east on N5 along the lake to the French border town of St-Gingolph, then south on Route 21 through the Swiss towns of Vouvry and Monthey. At Martigny, you may want to visit the *Musée de l'Automobile* (59 Rue du Forum; phone: 026-22-39-78 in Switzerland; from France, dial 19-41-26-22-39-78). It's open daily. Then take the Col de la Forclaz back into France; the border town is Vallorcine. Route N506 leads to Chamonix, a total of 65 miles (104 km) from Evian.

CHAMONIX At the base of 15,771-foot Mont-Blanc, Chamonix is probably Europe's most important center for serious alpinism. Compared with nearby Megève and Val-d'Isère (see below), it's a no-frills town: In its hyperactive center,

Chalet du Mont d'Arbois A splendid 20-room Relais & Châteaux member, located in a tranquil setting. For additional details, see *Romantic French Hostelries* in DIVERSIONS. Closed April through mid-June and November. Three miles (5 km) up the road on Rte. du Mont-d'Arbois (phone: 50-21-25-03; fax: 50-21-24-79). Very expensive.

Parc des Loges This luxury hotel, decorated in Art Deco style, has 53 rooms, suites, and apartments, many with fireplaces. There are two restaurants, an outdoor pool, a Jacuzzi, a sauna, and a solarium. 100 Rte. d'Arly (phone: 50-93-05-03; fax: 50-93-09-52). Very expensive.

Au Coin du Feu Run by the same folks who own *Les Fermes de Marie* (see below), this gem has 23 cozy rooms furnished with 19th-century antiques. The small restaurant proffers fine traditional fare. Closed April through mid-July and September through mid-December. Rte. de Rochebrune (phone: 50-21-04-94; fax: 50-21-20-15). Expensive.

Les Fermes de Marie Several old farmhouses were brought here in pieces, then reassembled in what looks like its own little village, with 42 luxurious rooms, a restaurant, a pool, a fitness center, and Turkish baths. Closed mid-April through mid-June and mid-September through mid-December. Chemin de Riante-Colline (phone: 50-93-03-10; fax: 50-93-09-84). Expensive.

Auberge Les Griottes This fine restaurant features a good choice of fish dishes. The terrace is open in summer. Closed Sunday dinner, Mondays (except during school holidays), and mid-November through mid-December. Reservations advised. Major credit cards accepted. Rte. Nationale (phone: 50-93-05-94). Moderate.

Le Chamois Its renditions of such regional fare as fondue, raclette, and smoked ham have made this a popular dining spot. Open daily. Reservations advised. MasterCard and Visa accepted. In the center of Megève, at Pl. de l'Eglise (phone: 50-21-25-01). Moderate.

Ferme Hôtel Duvillard At the bottom of the ski slopes, this 19-room chalet is decorated with beautifully painted rustic furniture. Facilities include a restaurant, a sauna, a pool, and conference rooms. Closed mid-April through mid-June and mid-October through mid-December. Plateau du Mont-d'Arbois (phone: 50-21-14-62; fax: 50-21-42-82). Moderate.

Les Sapins Here are 19 rooms, a garden, and a pool. The restaurant has a terrace for outdoor dining. Closed late April through mid-June and mid-September through mid-December. Rte. de Rochebrune (phone: 50-21-02-79; fax: 50-93-07-54). Inexpensive.

En Route from Megève Head southwest on N212 toward Flumet, Ugine, and Albertville, the main site of the 1992 *Winter Olympics*. You might want to take a quick detour across the river from Albertville to the restored walled village of Conflans, many of whose buildings date back to the 14th century. From Albertville go south on N90 to D915A south (which becomes D117) to St-Martin-de-Belleville, 28 miles (45 km) away.

BEST EN ROUTE .

Million This 29-room hotel, a member of the Relais & Châteaux group, has one of the best kitchens in Savoie, rating two Michelin stars. Its bill of fare includes seafood platters, stuffed Bresse chicken, *galettes de langoustines poêlées* (pan-fried crayfish cakes), and many other Savoie specialties. The restaurant is closed Sunday evenings, Mondays, the last week of April, the first week of May, and the first two weeks of July. 8 Pl. Liberté, Albertville (phone: 79-32-25-15; fax: 79-32-25-36). Expensive.

Le Roma This comfortable hotel has 150 modern rooms and suites plus an outdoor pool and tennis courts. Its restaurant, *La Montgolfière,* is an excellent value. Rte. de Chambéry, Albertville (phone: 79-37-15-56; fax: 79-37-01-31). Inexpensive.

ST-MARTIN-DE-BELLEVILLE This picturesque town of 2,340 people and 2,000 goats offers vacationers a Savoy farm village—complete with traditional homes made of stone, wood, and slate and narrow, steep streets—and access to the ski slopes. Though not as high as the other resorts in the Belleville Valley, St-Martin has lifts that carry skiers up to the slopes of Les Trois Vallées. Its tourist office (phone: 79-08-93-09; fax: 79-08-91-71) is near the *Alp* hotel (see *Best en Route*).

BEST EN ROUTE

Alp This inn offers quiet relaxation and, right outside, a ski lift to the summit of La Masse. All 30 rooms have balconies with spectacular views. There is a restaurant, sauna, Jacuzzi, and solarium. Closed mid-April through mid-December. (phone: 79-08-92-82; fax: 79-08-94-61). Inexpensive.

En Route from St-Martin-de-Belleville Take D117 south for 10 miles (16 km) to Les Menuires. Along the way, be sure to stop at the 17th-century Baroque *Chapelle Notre-Dame-de-la-Vie.*

LES MENUIRES Although it isn't as developed as Val-Thorens, Les Menuires offers quite good skiing on its numerous downhill and cross-country trails—it's the training ground for the French national ski teams. Summertime here is ideal for families: Tennis, mountain biking, swimming, horseback riding, hang gliding, parasailing, whitewater rafting, and trout fishing are all possible, and accommodations in residences and condominiums are easily found. There also are a few hotels. The tourist office is next to the stadium (phone: 79-00-73-00; fax: 79-00-75-06).

BEST EN ROUTE

Latitudes All 95 rooms in this hotel have balconies and views of the Belleville Valley. There are two restaurants, and the community pool and skating rink next door are free to guests. The bar features live jazz nightly. Half or full board is required. Closed mid-April through mid-December. Reberty, Les Menuires (phone: 79-00-75-10; fax: 79-00-70-70). Moderate.

La Marmite de Géant A good place to sample typical Savoyard fare, including *salade campagnarde* (with tomatoes, eggs, croutons, and ham), raclette, and *fondue bourguignonne*. Open daily. Reservations necessary. Major credit cards accepted. Next to the *Latitudes* hotel in Reberty, Les Menuires (phone: 79-00-74-75). Moderate.

L'Ours Blanc Each of the 47 rooms (including two suites and two apartments) has a balcony. The hotel faces the peak of La Masse, and after a day on the slopes (right outside), skiers can enjoy the steambath and solarium. There's a day-care center run by an English nanny, a restaurant, a bar, and meeting rooms. Closed May through early December. Reberty, Les Menuires (phone: 79-00-61-66; fax: 79-00-63-67). Moderate.

En Route from Les Menuires Continue on D117 for 6 miles (10 km) to Val-Thorens.

VAL-THORENS The first thing the visitor notices on approaching Val-Thorens is its breathtaking stark landscape. It is one of the resorts of Les Trois Vallées, one of the largest ski areas in the world. Because it is the highest resort in Western Europe, Val-Thorens is colder than most other places along this route, and even when there is little snow in other parts of the Alps, one always can count on fine skiing on the north slopes. For additional details on skiing here, see *Sensational French Skiing* in DIVERSIONS.

No parking is allowed within the resort during high season. After being greeted at the 24-hour welcome booths by tourist office staff, visitors park in garages at the resort's entrance and then take free shuttle buses to their lodgings. The tourist office (*Maison de Val-Thorens;* phone: 79-00-01-08; fax: 79-00-08-41) has information on activities. Those interested in athletic endeavors other than skiing should head over to the huge *Centre Sportif* (*Galerie Caron;* phone: 79-00-00-76), which is open daily. It offers tennis, squash, golf simulators, badminton, Ping-Pong, volleyball, a pool, a sauna, a whirlpool, and a gym with weight-training equipment and aerobics and dance classes.

Fitz Roy An indoor glass elevator carries guests to the 33 rooms (with balconies) and three suites (with balconies and fireplaces) of this exquisite Relais & Châteaux member. There is a restaurant serving truly haute cuisine plus a tearoom, bar, pool, fitness center, sauna, Jacuzzi, and meeting room. The hair salon and beauty treatment center is the only one in Val-Thorens. Closed mid-May through November. In the center of Val-Thorens (phone: 79-00-04-78; fax: 79-00-06-11). Expensive.

Le Val Thorens All 81 rooms surround an interior courtyard; most have views of the slopes (some from balconies). There's also a restaurant, fitness center, bar, and ski shop. Closed May through November (phone: 79-00-04-33; fax: 79-00-09-40). Expensive.

La Marmotte This modern hotel offers 22 rooms right at the foot of the slopes, a restaurant, and a fitness center. Half board is required. Closed mid-May through June and September through mid-December. MasterCard and Visa accepted. Conveniently located at the bottom of the slopes (phone: 79-00-00-07; fax: 79-00-00-14). Moderate.

Trois Vallées A good address for families, this modern 28-room hostelry has rooms large enough to sleep four; the restaurant offers a special children's menu. Closed mid-May through June and September through mid-October. MasterCard and Visa accepted (phone: 79-00-01-86; fax: 79-00-04-08). Moderate.

En Route from Val-Thorens Return along D117 northwest to Moûtiers. Then follow D915 east and D90 south to attractive Méribel, a drive of about 9 miles (14 km).

MÉRIBEL After the German invasion of Austria in 1938, the British needed a new place to ski, and they chose Méribel. First a pastoral village, it was built up slowly over the years; now it covers five distinct areas. Méribel's strict zoning code requires that everything be constructed according to Alpine architectural design: double-slanted roofs atop chalets with wood and stone façades and balconies.

Méribel's east-west exposure affords the resort lots of sunshine, making it an ideal place to ski. In addition to hotels, construction for the 1992 *Olympics* included a sports complex with a skating rink and a café where concerts are held nightly in winter and weekly in summer. When the snow melts, families often come here for a variety of summer sports—tennis, mountain biking, hiking, rock climbing, swimming, rafting, and golfing at an 18-hole course. Cultural events include the *Festival de Musique et d'Art Baroque Tarentaise* every August. Méribel's tourist office is in the center of the resort (phone: 79-08-60-01; fax: 79-00-59-61).

Le Chalet In this hotel are 34 beautifully decorated rooms (including six suites). Sports oriented, it is right next to the cable cars and close to a golf course; there's a Jacuzzi, a steamroom, a sauna, an indoor/outdoor pool, and fitness equipment. The restaurant has an open grill, and the bar is complete with a piano and fireplace. A meeting room, playroom, and garage are also on the premises. Closed mid-April through mid-December. Le Belvédère (phone: 79-23-28-23; fax: 79-00-56-22). Very expensive.

Allodis Each of this hotel's 43 rooms (including 12 suites) is decorated in a different style. All three of its restaurants face the slopes; there is also a fitness center, pool, sauna, and conference room. Closed May, June, and mid-September through mid-December. Le Belvédère (phone: 79-00-56-00; fax: 79-00-59-28). Expensive.

Le Grand Coeur The oldest hotel in the resort, this member of the Relais & Châteaux group has 45 rooms—all with balconies—and direct access to the slopes. There is a restaurant, piano bar, gameroom, fitness center, sauna, and steamroom. Half or full board required. Closed mid-April through mid-December (phone: 79-08-60-03; fax: 79-08-58-38). Expensive.

Orée du Bois Surrounded by pine trees, this hotel has 37 rooms with cable TV, plus a restaurant, a Jacuzzi, a ski shop, and an outdoor pool open in summer. Closed September through *Christmas* and *Easter* through June. Rond-Point des Pistes (phone: 79-00-50-30; fax: 79-08-57-52). Moderate.

En Route from Méribel Head back toward Moûtiers, but at D915 go east instead of west. Then follow D91 south for 17 miles (27 km) to the ritzy resort of Courchevel.

COURCHEVEL One of France's first ski resorts, Courchevel is well known for its luxury hotels and as a favored destination of royalty (including the Aga Khan, the King of Spain, and Princess Caroline of Monaco) and French celebrities. Courchevel's prices are much higher than other areas in Savoy, although it was originally conceived as a working class resort back in the 1940s. For details on skiing in Courchevel, see *Sensational French Skiing* in DIVERSIONS.

Courchevel offers a wide array of activities besides skiing—including skating, mountain biking, golf, tennis, swimming, hang gliding, hiking, canoeing, concerts, and language courses. The resort's sports complex, the *Forum* (located at *Courchevel 1850,* one of the four ski areas that make up the resort) is the place to go for many of these pursuits. The tourist office (also at *Courchevel 1850*, on La Croisette; phone: 79-08-00-29; fax: 79-08-33-54) can provide details about activities.

Les Airelles In the lobby of this renovated hostelry, a heated pillar surrounded by seats offers immediate warmth from a day on the slopes right outside. Such royal vacationers as Princess Anne of England and the Queen of Norway have stayed here, and France's high society makes it their home away from home. And it's no wonder—the 56 luxurious rooms (including suites and apartments) are decorated with hand-painted tiles and feature amenities such as mini-bars, cable TV, VCRs, and heated towel racks. There is a restaurant, a piano bar, a pool, a fitness center, a Jacuzzi, a steamroom, tanning beds, a beauty salon, and three meeting rooms. Half or full board required. Closed May through mid-December. *Jardin Alpin, Courchevel 1850* (phone: 79-09-38-38; 800-223-6800; fax: 79-08-38-69). Very expensive.

Bellecôte Decorated with a mixture of traditional regional furniture and antiques from Afghanistan (note the 17th-century carved doors), this 53-room hotel (plus two suites and one apartment) is directly on the slopes. It has a restaurant, a piano bar, meeting rooms, a pool, a fitness center, a sauna, a Jacuzzi, and a hair salon. All rooms have balconies. Half or full board required. Closed May through November. *Courchevel 1850* (phone: 79-08-10-19; fax: 79-08-17-16). Very expensive.

Byblos des Neiges Like its sister hotel in St-Tropez, the oldest hostelry in Courchevel was built with lavishness in mind. The 75 elegant rooms and suites all face south (the best view of the slopes) and have cable TV and mini-bars. There are two restaurants (one specializing in seafood), a bar, a pool, a fitness center, a sauna, boutiques, and a hair salon. Half or full board required. Closed mid-April through mid-December. *Jardin Alpin, Courchevel 1850* (phone: 79-08-12-12; fax: 79-08-19-38). Very expensive.

Le Chabichou Here is one of the best tables in Courchevel (Michelin has awarded it two stars). The chef specializes in an idiosyncratic interpretation of traditional bourgeois cuisine, creating such dishes as potato stew with truffles. There also are 40 guestrooms. Closed mid-May through mid-June and the first week of November. Reservations necessary. Major credit cards accepted. *Courchevel 1850* (phone: 79-08-00-55; fax: 79-08-33-58). Very expensive.

Le Bateau Ivre Another two-Michelin-star winner, this restaurant has a panoramic view of the Vanoise Mountains. Specialties include lobster tails in herb butter and chocolate mousse soufflé with orange ice cream. Closed mid-April through mid-December. Reservations advised. Major credit cards accepted. In the *Pomme de Pin Hotel, Courchevel 1850* (phone: 79-08-36-88; fax: 79-08-38-72). Expensive.

La Cendrée If you're tired of fondue and raclette, this fine Italian restaurant is the place to go. The fare ranges from brick-oven pizza to such pasta dishes as spaghetti alla carbonara and penne alla foie gras to various meat and fish dishes. It is frequented by Courchevel's jet set, perhaps because of its extensive wine selection. Closed May through July. Reservations necessary. Major credit cards accepted. *Courchevel 1850* (phone: 79-08-29-38 or 79-08-34-36). Expensive.

Le Chamois Each of the 30 rooms has a mini-bar, and breakfast is included in the price. There are also eight studios with kitchenettes but no restaurant. Closed mid-April through mid-December. *Courchevel 1850* (phone: 79-08-01-56; fax: 79-08-34-23). Expensive.

Les Grandes Alpes All 37 renovated rooms in this hotel have balconies. There is a restaurant, American bar (with a full range of liquors), garage, pool, fitness center, steamroom, and Jacuzzi (the suites and the VIP room have their own). Unlike other Courchevel hotels, it is open all summer. Closed the last two weeks in May and September through November. *Courchevel 1850* (phone: 79-08-03-35; fax: 79-08-12-52). Expensive.

La Sivolière Quaint, cozy, and exquisitely kept, this hotel has 30 rooms and a good restaurant. Visitors can munch on succulent pastries in front of the fireplace at teatime after a long day of schussing down the mountainside. Closed mid-May through mid-November. *Courchevel 1850* (phone: 79-08-08-33; fax: 79-08-15-73). Expensive.

La Bergerie This rustic eatery is in a former shepherd's dwelling, the oldest house in Courchevel. Choose from typical Savoyard fare—raclette or *fondue bourguignonne*—or such traditional French dishes as salmon filet with vegetables. At night the first floor becomes a disco. Closed June through mid-December. Reservations necessary for dinner. American Express accepted. *Jardin Alpin, Courchevel 1850* (phone: 79-08-24-70; fax: 79-08-08-29). Moderate.

En Route from Courchevel Head back to D915. Before returning west to Moûtiers, you might want to detour east to Pralognan-la-Vanoise, one of the gateways to the *Vanoise,* France's first national park (created in 1963). With its outlying areas, this wonderland for hikers and campers encompasses some 80,000 acres of spectacular mountains and meadows. Automobile traffic is barred in the park itself, and indigenous mountain animals such as the ibex and chamois roam unthreatened.

For an alternative route to the *Vanoise,* follow the road back from Pralognan to where it branches off toward Champagny-en-Vanoise; then take it through the village to its very end, crossing a lovely high valley to reach a much less populated jumping-off point for the park. For a breathtaking bit of shunpiking (taking side roads) on the way back toward Moûtiers from Champagny-en-Vanoise, at Bozel pick up D89, the serpentine back road that becomes D89E and leads up to Feissons-sur-Salins. This is the real Savoy: tiny tourist-empty hamlets clinging to the sides of steep hills, and successions of spectacular views. Returning to D89 and continuing to D90 and from there back to D915, go west to Moûtiers.

Back in Moûtiers, pick up N90 northeast toward the sports center of Bourg-St-Maurice, then follow lovely, winding D902 south (and up) to the remarkable resort of Tignes, a total drive of about 48 miles (77 km) direct from Courchevel (without the scenic detours).

BEST EN ROUTE

Petite Auberge An appealing inn slightly off the main road, it offers 15 comfortable rooms, a pleasant terrace restaurant, and a family atmosphere. Closed the last week of September and mid-December through mid-January; restaurant also closed Sunday dinner, Mondays, and, Wednesdays from September through May. MasterCard and Visa accepted. Rte. de Moûtiers, Le Reverset, on the outskirts of Bourg-St-Maurice (phone: 79-07-05-86). Inexpensive.

TIGNES With the construction of a hydroelectric dam in the 1950s, the old village of Tignes was displaced and reestablished some thousand feet higher, by a small natural lake. You'll know you've reached the resort when you come upon a painting of Hercules, painted on the wall of the dam. Said to be the largest mural in the world, it represents both the strength of the ancient world and the energy of the modern one. The new town (Tignes is actually three villages) is an anomaly in France—even the oldest buildings date back only 40 years. Apartments, boutiques, and restaurants verging on the futuristic are strung together in an oddly mechanical, modern style that, while undeniably unattractive, manages somehow to blend in perfectly with the imposing moon-like landscape.

With 90 miles of runs, Tignes is the venue for some superb skiing (for details, see *Sensational French Skiing* in DIVERSIONS). Tignes also offers 32 miles of summer skiing, access to the *Vanoise*, water sports on the lake, an 18-hole golf course (the highest in Europe), tennis, and a variety of other activities. The local tourist office (on the lake; phone: 79-06-15-55; fax: 79-06-45-44) can provide details.

BEST EN ROUTE

Ski d'Or At this pleasant member of the Relais & Châteaux group, there are 22 inviting rooms, a good restaurant, a fitness center, a Jacuzzi, and a meeting room. In December, January, and April, a ski pass is included with a six-day minimum stay. Half or full board required. Closed May through November. Val-Claret, 1 mile (1.6 km) southwest of Tignes via D87 (phone: 79-06-51-60; fax: 79-06-45-49). Expensive.

Curling All 35 rooms in this hostelry near the *Olympic* stadium have balconies. There is a breakfast room, bar, meeting room, but no restaurant. Breakfast is included in the rate. Closed May, June, September, and October. Val-Claret, 1 mile (1.6 km) southwest of Tignes via D87 (phone: 79-06-34-34; fax: 79-06-46-14). Moderate.

La Troïka The delicious fish soup here is served *à la marseillaise* (with garlic mayonnaise, cheese, and croutons). There also is brick-oven pizza plus many traditional French dishes. Open daily, December through May; closed Sundays the rest of the year. Reservations advised. Major credit cards accepted. Rue de la Poste, Tignes-le-Lac (phone/fax: 79-06-30-24). Moderate.

Campanules Each of the 36 rooms in this comfortable hostelry has a view of the mountains; there is a restaurant. Closed *Easter* through June and September through mid-November. Visa accepted. Tignes-le-Lac (phone: 79-06-34-36; fax: 79-06-35-78). Inexpensive.

En Route from Tignes Continue on D902 south for 8 miles (13 km) to Val-d'Isère.

VAL-D'ISÈRE This town is not as picturesque as Megève or as imposing as Chamonix, but its nightlife is renowned, and the surrounding landscapes provide their own magic. Unlike Tignes, Val-d'Isère is a centralized resort, and some are of the opinion that it offers the best skiing in the world—many of the skiing events in the 1992 *Olympics* took place here. (For details, see *Sensational French Skiing* in DIVERSIONS.)

From morning, when the streets are clogged with skiers and village buses shuttling to the lift base, until late at night, when the little avenue rings with the cries of merrymakers going from one bar or disco to the next, Val-d'Isère is a glamorous, busy place. In addition to almost 200 miles of runs, Val-d'Isère offers parasailing, gliding, snowshoeing, husky sleighing, and the *Group Audhoui* school (*Salon de 4 x 4,* Plaine de la Daille; phone: 79-06-21-40), where you can learn how to drive a car on ice and snow (very useful here). Stroll around the old village to look at the small stone houses and the 11th-century church. For après-ski, check out the *Sofitel*'s fitness center (see *Best En Route*).

Popular places to experience Val-d'Isère's nonstop nightlife include pubs such as the *Lodge* (phone: 79-06-04-03), where tropical cocktails and atmospheric music are the draws, and *Club 21* in the *Park* hotel (phone: 79-06-04-03), where the dancing doesn't get started until midnight.

Summer brings a wide variety of outdoor activities, including "grass skiing." We recommend taking a cable car ride to the Rocher de Bellevarde or hiking up to the Tête du Solaise. In August the resort hosts the *Salon International de 4 x 4 et Tout Terrain* (International Four-Wheel-Drive and All-Terrain Motor Show). For more information, consult the tourist office (close to the town center in the *Maison de Val-d'Isère;* phone: 79-06-06-60; fax: 79-06-04-56).

Christiania This comfortable hostelry has a restaurant, bar, fitness center, indoor pool, and, in the lobby, a circular fireplace. Each of the 68 rooms (including 10 suites) has a balcony. Breakfast is included in the rate. Closed May through November. Visa accepted (phone: 79-06-08-25; fax: 79-41-11-10). Very expensive.

Sofitel Its *Centre de Balnéothérapie* (Health and Fitness Center), which offers many activities, including an indoor/outdoor pool, is the main draw of this 53-room modern establishment. There are two restaurants (one buffet-style) and a lovely bar in the lobby. Closed May through June and September through November (phone: 79-06-08-30; 800-763-4835; fax: 79-06-04-41). Very expensive.

Altitude This 41-room hotel, which boasts a restaurant, terrace, bar, and outdoor pool, is particularly quiet. Closed early May through June and September through November (phone: 79-06-12-55; fax: 79-41-11-09). Moderate.

La Pedrix Blanche Bountiful portions of shellfish are served at this casual restaurant. The wine list is excellent. Closed May through November. Reservations unnecessary. MasterCard and Visa accepted (phone: 79-06-12-09). Moderate.

Kern Antiques abound in this charming inn, which has 20 rooms and a restaurant. Closed May through November (phone: 79-06-06-06; fax: 79-06-26-31). Inexpensive.

En Route from Val-d'Isère Head south to Briançon, 98 miles (157 km) away, taking D902 to N6, to D902 again, then to N91.

For those who love the high, high Alps, this leg of the route offers everything one could hope for, including two unbelievably beautiful mountain passes. The first is the Col de l'Iseran, whose summit is about 9,000 feet above sea level. Historically, it was so hard to get there that, until the mid-19th century, cartographers simply guessed at its location. It was only in 1937 that the first road over the pass was opened. As might be expected, the air here is bracing, the views spectacular, and the road, with its intermittent railings, cause for occasional heart palpitations. Climbers who are properly equipped and experienced (this trail is *not* for the inexperienced or easily frightened) can hike from the summit of the Col de l'Iseran to the Pointe des Lessières, about 1,000 feet higher, for a magnificent Alpine panorama. Before setting out, make sure conditions are favorable.

The Col de l'Iseran descends into the Maurienne Valley, through which the Arc River courses. This somewhat industrial yet nonetheless pleasant route goes through the towns of Bonneval-sur-Arc, Lanslevillard, Termignon, Modane, and St-Michel-de-Maurienne. Bonneval is particularly attractive;

its ambience is due primarily to the delightfully unpretentious Alpine architecture of its buildings. Another especially pleasing village, about 22 miles (35 km) farther, is Aussois, off N6 at Modane via D215. In addition to the attractions of the town itself, there are a couple of interesting sites in the immediate vicinity: Two miles (3 km) northeast of the village is the Monolithe de Sardières, a spectacular isolated rock face first scaled in 1960, and between Aussois and the village of Avrieux (take a left before the church in Aussois) are the massive *Forts de l'Esseillon,* which were constructed at great labor and expense in 1815 by the Sardinian regime to protect against a French invasion and then never used.

After St-Michel-de-Maurienne the road climbs steeply; the Col du Télégraphe is some 2,500 feet above St-Michel. The second great pass of this section of the route is the Col du Galibier, which takes you from the Maurienne to the Briançonnais, the area surrounding the town of Briançon. Rising to 8,500 feet above sea level, the Col du Galibier is just as spectacular as the Col de l'Iseran. A magnificent view awaits those who leave their car at the road's high point and climb to the viewing station.

Taking on the Col de l'Iseran and the Col du Galibier in a single day is possible but taxing; fortunately, there are a number of attractive lodging places along the way. If you decide to press on, there is a splendid stopover just south of the Col du Galibier.

BEST EN ROUTE

Auberge du Choucas In this completely renovated 1770 farmhouse are eight rooms, four independent studios, and a restaurant. The *Parc National des Ecrins* and the skiing area of Serre-Chevalier, 500 yards away, are easily accessible from here. Closed November through mid-December. Visa accepted. Nestled in an Alpine village just beyond the Col du Galibier, in Le Monêtier-les-Bains (phone: 92-24-42-73; fax: 92-24-51-60). Moderate.

Club Les Carrettes Here you'll find 30 modern, comfortable rooms, a restaurant, a pool, and an owner who doubles as a nightclub performer in his hotel. Closed mid-April through July and September through mid-December. MasterCard and Visa accepted. Valloire (phone: 79-59-00-99; fax: 79-59-05-60). Moderate.

Le Choucas Twenty-eight comfortable, simple rooms are available here. There is a perfectly tended little garden and an outdoor terrace for dining. Closed May, October, and November. MasterCard and Visa accepted. Aussois (phone: 79-20-32-77). Inexpensive.

La Marmotte Attractively situated, it offers 28 rooms and a dining room. Closed May through mid-June and October through mid-December. MasterCard and Visa accepted. Bonneval-sur-Arc (phone: 79-05-94-82; fax: 79-05-90-08). Inexpensive.

BRIANÇON Poised at an entry point into Italy and at the foot of several mountain passes, Briançon has long been important militarily and commercially. Today its glorious climate (it is one of Europe's most important healing centers for asthma and also has an international center for sports training in high altitudes) and beautiful location (at 4,333 feet, it is one of the highest towns in Europe) make it a major tourist draw. Unlike many ski-based Alpine resort villages, however, Briançon has a rich historical foundation. The real highlight is the Ville Haute (Upper Town), also called Briançon-Vauban, for the engineer who controlled its reconstruction in the late 17th and 18th centuries after a fire destroyed the village. With no traffic and surrounded by ramparts, cute but not kitschy, the Ville Haute invites the visitor to stroll, explore, and relax. Leave your car at the *Champ-de-Mars* and enter by the *Porte de Pignerol* (Pignerol Gate), next to the tourist office (phone: 92-21-08-50; fax: 92-20-56-45). Grande-Rue is relatively broad and bustling, and each of its many side streets has its own special charm. The graceful, twin-towered *Eglise Notre-Dame,* built by Vauban from 1703 to 1718, is just off Grande-Rue, and beyond it is a lovely view. The citadel above the Ville Haute commands an excellent panorama of the surrounding peaks and the Durance Valley. The Pont d'Asfeld, constructed in 1754, arcs audaciously over the river gorge at a height of 17 feet; those who can get to the bridge (by footpath) are welcome to walk across.

BEST EN ROUTE

Le Péché Gourmand Poultry and fish dishes with exquisite sauces are the specialties here. Be sure to save room for the wonderful desserts. Closed Sunday dinner and Mondays (except in July and August) and mid-September through early December. Reservations advised. Major credit cards accepted. 2 Rte. de Gap (phone: 92-20-11-02). Moderate.

Vauban There are 44 very comfortable rooms in this hostelry with a garden. The restaurant has an excellent, reasonably priced menu. Closed November through mid-December. MasterCard and Visa accepted. 13 Av. Général-de-Gaulle (phone: 92-21-12-11; fax: 92-20-58-20). Inexpensive.

En Route from Briançon Those who wish to stay in the most "Alpine" part of the Alps should head back up to the Col du Lautaret, via N91, and continue on to Grenoble, 73 miles (117 km) away. Consider stopping at a major ski resort such as Les Deux-Alpes or L'Alpe d'Huez. For information on skiing in L'Alpe d'Huez, see *Sensational French Skiing* in DIVERSIONS.

The winding southern route to Grenoble is much more circuitous than the one described above, covering well over 200 miles (320 km). It is worth the detour, however, and in no case should the spectacular *Parc Régional du Vercors* be missed, be it along this route or as a day trip from Grenoble. One really should follow this route in a leisurely fashion over a few days.

South of Briançon you can take N94 or slower D902, which leads through the *Parc Régional du Queyras* and rejoins N94 22 miles (35 km) farther, at Guillestre. *Queyras* benefits from excellent weather and a wide variety of flora and fauna; at its heart, off D902 on D947, is *Château-Queyras,* a 13th-century fortress. Guided tours are given daily from June through September (phone: 92-46-76-18). Guillestre is a lively market and resort town; about 2 miles (3 km) west of there pick up N94, which now winds through the Durance Valley. About 12 miles (19 km) down N94, just before the 7,410-acre artificial lake of Serre-Ponçon, is the town of Embrun. Eburodunum under the Romans, then a major ecclesiastical center, Embrun was for many years of major importance. Now it is little more than a village with a lovely church, the *Cathédrale Notre-Dame,* well worth visiting, and a commanding view of the valley.

Continue west for 24 miles (38 km) to Gap, a bustling commercial center with an attractive downtown area. From Gap some serious trout, perch, chub, and barbel fishing is possible. For information about the area's mountain streams and lakes or for more general information, write to the *Comité Départemental du Tourisme des Hautes-Alpes* (BP 46, Gap 05002) or contact the tourist office (12 Rue Faure du Serre; phone: 92-51-57-03; fax: 92-53-63-29).

From Gap take the famous and much-traveled Route Napoléon (N85) north for 25 miles (40 km) to Corps, a comely little town perched above Lac du Sautet. To reach the *Parc Régional du Vercors,* leave N85 at Corps to travel on back roads through the villages of La Croix-de-la-Pigne, Mens (D66 west of Corps), Lavars (D34A off D34), and Clelles (D526 west of Mens). Far more bucolic than the high Alps, the scenery—pastures, rock faces, and pine forests—is nonetheless splendid in its own right.

Clelles is at the edge of *Vercors,* a marvelous agglomeration of buttes, boulders, and ravines reminiscent of the American Southwest. By heading from Clelles to Châtillon-en-Diois on D7 and D120 and then to the town of Die (pronounced *Dee*) on D539 and D93, one gets not only a beautiful tour through *Vercors* but also a glimpse of the narrow, lavender-planted valley of the Drôme. Lovely Die is renowned for its bubbly white wine, Clairette de Die. The main road back into *Vercors* from Die, D518, scales the Col de Rousset and passes through the resort towns of St-Aignan-en-Vercors and Ste-Eulalie-en-Royans, where D54, followed by D531 leads east to yet another resort, Villard-de-Lans; the town's tourist office is on the Place Mure-Ravaud (phone: 76-95-10-38; fax: 76-95-98-39). From there Grenoble is 21 miles (34 km) northeast on D531.

BEST EN ROUTE

Eterlou There are 24 rooms in this pleasant hostelry, which also has a restaurant, an outdoor pool, and tennis courts. Closed September through November.

In the northern part of Villard-de-Lans (phone: 76-95-17-65; fax: 76-95-91-41). *Expensive.*

Grand Hôtel de Paris A stately old hotel, it is in an attractive private park of its own. There is something pleasingly anachronistic about the place, which has 64 rooms, a small dining room, a tennis court, and a pool. Closed April and November. MasterCard and Visa accepted. In the *Parc Régional du Vercors,* Villard-de-Lans (phone: 76-95-10-06; fax: 76-95-10-02). *Moderate.*

La Poste A popular eatery with a terrace, it offers well-prepared meals that are an excellent value. There also are 20 guestrooms. Closed December through January. Reservations necessary. MasterCard and Visa accepted. Bordering Rte. Napoléon in Corps (phone: 76-30-00-03; fax: 76-30-02-73). *Moderate.*

Les Barnières I and II These two hotels have a total of 82 rooms furnished with modern amenities (only the rooms in *Les Barnières II* have TV sets). They also offer tennis, a pool, and a superb view of the Durance Valley. Full board required during July and August. *Les Barnières I* is closed October through May; *Les Barnières II* is closed mid-October through mid-December. Guillestre (phone: 92-45-04-87 or 92-45-05-07; fax: 92-45-28-74). *Inexpensive.*

La Petite Auberge Good regional cooking for the price; there are 11 rooms as well. Closed Sunday dinner, Wednesdays, Mondays in July and August, and mid-December through mid-January. Reservations advised. MasterCard and Visa accepted. Across from the train station, on Av. Sadi-Carnot, Die (phone: 75-22-05-91). *Inexpensive.*

GRENOBLE The city of Grenoble (pop. 400,000), which has been around since the year 1 BC, today is the French Alps' major urban center, with a thriving commercial and intellectual life. The *University of Grenoble,* founded in 1339, has a student body of some 40,000.

Walk through the bustling downtown area, with its elegant squares, well-designed parks, and old buildings; a map is available at the tourist office (14 Rue de la République; phone: 76-42-41-41; fax: 76-51-28-69). For a bird's-eye view, take the little *téléphérique* at Quai Stéphane-Jay across the Isère River to the *Fort de la Bastille.* From the fort it's possible to explore the neighboring *Parc Guy-Pape* and the *Jardin des Dauphins,* sip a cup of coffee or have a bite to eat, and gaze at the city and mountain spires (on clear days, Mont-Blanc included).

Grenoble has a number of interesting museums, foremost among them the *Musée de Grenoble* (Pl. Lavalette; phone: 76-63-44-44). Considered one of France's best outside Paris, it has been completely renovated and enlarged, reopening last year. The museum has an excellent collection of paintings, including works by Corot, Renoir, Monet, Picasso, Modigliani, and Tanguy, as well as impressive Egyptian holdings. It is closed Tuesdays; there's an admission charge. The *Musée Stendhal* (in the old *Hôtel de Ville,*

1 Rue Hector-Berlioz; phone: 76-54-44-14) contains memorabilia pertaining to Stendhal (the nom de plume of Marie-Henri Beyle), author of *Le Rouge et le Noir* (The Red and the Black) and *La Chartreuse de Parme* (The Charterhouse of Parma), who was born in Grenoble in 1783. The museum is closed mornings and Mondays; there's no admission charge. The *Centre National d'Art Contemporain* (*Le Magasin,* 155 Cours Berriat; phone: 76-21-95-84), a contemporary art museum, is housed in a former factory. It's closed Mondays; there's an admission charge. The small *Musée de la Résistance et de la Déportation* (Museum of the Resistance and Deportation; 14 Rue Jean-Jacques-Rousseau; phone: 76-44-51-81) is a moving tribute to the heroes of World War II; it was built on the site of Stendhal's birthplace. It's closed Sundays and Tuesdays; there's no admission charge.

Grenoble is a clean, modern city that has seen tremendous growth in the last few decades, but historic enclaves remain amid the proliferating new buildings. Make your way to the Place Grenette in the old part of town, and wander among the streets and gardens around it. Across the river, on Quai Xavier-Jouvin, is the *Eglise St-Laurent,* which contains one of the oldest crypts in France.

The Dauphiné may be best known for its skiing, but it also is a great area for fishing. For specific information, contact the *Fédération de la Pêche de l'Isère* (Rue du Palais, Grenoble 38000; phone: 76-44-28-39). Grenoble is also home to one of France's most highly regarded theater groups, the *Centre Dramatique National des Alpes* (4 Rue Paul-Claudel; phone: 76-25-54-14); for details, see *The Liveliest Arts: Theater, Opera, and Music* in DIVERSIONS. One of France's top antiques salons, the *Salon Européen des Antiquaires,* is held here at *Alpexpo* in late January or early February.

BEST EN ROUTE

Park This hotel has 50 cheerful rooms and a cozy, wood-paneled lobby and restaurant. Closed the first three weeks in August and December 23 through *New Year's Day.* Conveniently situated downtown, at 10 Pl. Paul-Mistral (phone: 76-87-29-11; fax: 76-46-49-88). Very expensive.

Chavant One of the area's more elegant restaurants, with good service and a vast menu featuring both traditional and more creative fare. There also are seven guestrooms and an outdoor pool in a shaded garden. Closed Sunday lunch, Mondays, and *Christmas* through *New Year's Eve.* Reservations advised. Major credit cards accepted. A few miles south of Grenoble via D264, in Bresson (phone: 76-25-15-14; fax: 76-62-06-55). Expensive.

L'Epicurien Ham cooked in hay is the surprisingly refined specialty of this dining spot. Closed Sundays and Saturday and Monday lunch. Reservations advised. Major credit cards accepted. 1 Pl. aux Herbes (phone: 76-51-96-06). Moderate.

Lesdiguières Located in a park, this 36-room hotel is very comfortable. Perhaps because it is also a hotel school, the staff is particularly attentive. There's a restaurant. Closed August and at *Christmastime.* 122 Cours de la Libération (phone: 76-96-55-36; fax: 76-48-10-13). Moderate.

Les Oiseaux In an especially appealing setting are 18 pleasant rooms, a dining room, and a pool. Closed January. Six miles (10 km) south of Grenoble via A480, exit 9, at 8 Rue des Perouses, Claix (phone: 76-98-07-74; fax: 76-98-82-33). Moderate.

Poularde Bressane Specialties at this dining spot include both fresh and smoked salmon. Closed Saturday lunch, Sundays, and mid-July through mid-August. Reservations advised. Major credit cards accepted. 12 Pl. Paul-Mistral (phone: 76-87-08-90). Moderate.

Le Petit Vatel A first-rate, if simple, bistro, it takes its name from a famous French chef who committed suicide when a fish dish turned out to be a failure. Closed Sunday dinner and Mondays. Reservations advised. MasterCard and Visa accepted. 3 Pl. des Gordes (phone: 76-44-68-26). Inexpensive.

Skieurs This hostelry has 18 clean, simple rooms, a restaurant, and a pool. Closed April, November, and December. In Le Sappey-en-Chartreuse, a pleasant little village 10 miles (16 km) north of Grenoble via D512 (phone: 76-88-80-15; fax: 76-88-85-76). Inexpensive.

En Route from Grenoble To go directly to Chambéry, 34 miles (54 km) to the north, follow the autoroute (A41). However, we suggest a more circuitous route—one that takes in the Chartreuse mountain range, one of the highest in France. One of its tranquil valleys harbors a unique history: In 1084 St. Bruno and seven followers bushwhacked their way 16 miles into these unruly hills to found the Carthusian order of monks, which has been based here ever since (with the exception of the years 1903 to 1941, when they were expelled). For the past several hundred years the monks, who are isolated not only from the world but most of the time from each other as well, have been making well-known and exceptionally high-proof green and yellow liqueurs, both named Chartreuse, whose formulas always have remained a secret to all but three of them at a time. From Grenoble head into the thick of the forest via D512 over the Col de Porte. The charterhouse of the monks, *La Grande Chartreuse,* is not open to the public, though an outbuilding about a mile away off D520B houses a small museum devoted to the daily life of these recluses. Called *La Correrie,* it is closed during lunch hours and November through early March; there's an admission charge (phone: 76-88-60-45). The proceeds from the million bottles of Chartreuse sold annually, half of them to the French, support 460 Carthusian monks in 24 monasteries worldwide.

Continue on D520B west to St-Laurent-du-Pont; then take D520 and N6 to Chambéry.

CHAMBÉRY An appealing little city (pop. 54,000), the namesake of a pale vermouth, and the capital of Savoie from the 13th to the 17th century, it exists today as a compact assemblage of squares, boulevards, arcades, and alleyways. In the dead center of town is the *Fontaine des Eléphants*, commemorating a trip to India that the Count of Boigne, a local hero and benefactor, once made. Ensconced where Rue de Boigne and Boulevard de la Colonne merge, the four bronze behemoths date from 1838. Rue de Boigne and Rue Juiverie lead pleasantly to the old château of the Dukes of Savoy; the large, oblong Place St-Léger, filled with fountains and lampposts, is nearby. At the other end of the Boulevard de la Colonne from the *Fontaine des Eléphants* is the tourist office (24 Bd. de la Colonne; phone: 79-33-42-47; fax: 79-85-71-39); it can provide information on guided tours of the city and its environs. About a mile (1.6 km) south of town via D4 is *Les Charmettes* (phone: 79-33-39-44), the house in which Jean-Jacques Rousseau lived blissfully with Madame de Warens for six years. Today it is filled with Rousseau memorabilia. It's closed Tuesdays; there's an admission charge. Try to taste some of the luscious wild raspberries and strawberries that grow on the surrounding mountainsides.

BEST EN ROUTE

Château de Trivier Now a lovely 30-room hotel, the ancestral home of the Seigneurs de Trivier is a pocket of tranquillity, surrounded by a small park complete with its own pond. There is a restaurant. Closed the last week of April and the first week of November; restaurant also closed Sunday dinner and Wednesdays off-season. Four miles (6 km) east of Chambéry via N6, in Challes-les-Eaux (phone/fax: 79-72-82-87). Moderate.

Hôtel du Château The former 15th-century home of the Counts of Challes is today a 60-room link in the Best Western chain. On the grounds are a restaurant serving regional fare, tennis courts, a pool, a casino, and meeting facilities. Four miles (6 km) east of Chambéry via N6, in Challes-les-Eaux (phone: 79-72-86-71; 800-528-1234; fax: 79-72-83-83). Moderate.

Les Princes A comfortable 45-room hotel whose adjoining eatery specializes in seafood. In the center of town, at 4 Rue Boigne (phone: 79-33-45-36; fax: 79-70-31-47). Moderate.

En Route from Chambéry A lovely road, D912, heads north for 12 miles (19 km) toward St-Jean-d'Arvey. A little farther on take D913 west through La Féclaz, a winter sports center, and over Mont-Revard to Aix-les-Bains, a grand old spa well sited on Lac du Bourget. A stroll through Aix's elegant streets or on its long, handsome promenade is well worth the trip. Across the lake is the *Abbaye de Hautecombe,* which deserves a visit, either by boat from Aix (a two-hour trip one way) or by car. On Sundays at 9:15 AM and weekdays at 9:30 AM, mass includes Gregorian chants. If you're in town at night, try your luck at one of Aix's two casinos (for details, see *Casinos Royale* in DIVERSIONS). From Aix you can pick up A41, which takes you north for 20 miles (33 km) to Annecy. If you have chosen to bypass Aix, take N201 from Chambéry to pick up A41 northeast for the 30 miles (48 km) to Annecy.

BEST EN ROUTE

Ombremont A member of the Relais & Châteaux group, this secluded hotel has 19 rooms, including six suites. It's ideally located in a park on Lac du Bourget, the lake that inspired the romantic poet Lamartine's tragic lament "Le Lac." On the premises are a pool and a good restaurant whose specialties include salad of duck and foie gras and fish filets in sorrel sauce. Closed November through April. American Express and Visa accepted. Nine miles (14 km) north of Chambéry via N504, in Le Bourget-du-Lac (phone: 79-25-00-23; fax: 79-25-25-77). Very expensive.

Le Bateau Ivre Set in a 17th-century barn and now surrounded by a garden full of flowers, this two-Michelin-star restaurant, a member of the Relais & Châteaux group, specializes in fish and luscious desserts (try the *tarte tatin aux pêches,* a caramelized peach tart). Closed November through April. Reservations necessary. Major credit cards accepted. Eight miles (13 km) north of Chambéry via N504, La Croix Verte, Le Bourget-du-Lac (phone: 79-25-02-66; fax: 79-25-25-03). Expensive.

L'Orée du Lac This 12-room jewel of a hotel offers a restaurant (for guests only), its own park, a pool, and tennis courts. Closed mid-November through mid-January. Eight miles (13 km) north of Chambéry via N504, La Croix Verte, Le Bourget-du-Lac (phone: 79-25-24-19; fax: 79-25-08-51). Expensive.

Park Hotel du Casino This beautiful hotel has 92 rooms, indoor and outdoor pools, and a restaurant. Set in a park, on Av. Général-de-Gaulle, Aix-les-Bains (phone: 79-34-19-19; fax: 79-88-11-49). Expensive.

Auberge Lamartine Named after the poet, this one-Michelin-star dining spot overlooking the lake specializes in game in season (mid-September through mid-December). At other times try the roasted foie gras. Closed Sunday dinner, Mondays, January, and December. Reservations necessary. MasterCard and Visa accepted. Ten miles (16 km) north of Chambéry via N504, near Le Bourget-du-Lac (phone: 79-25-01-03). Moderate.

ANNECY Annecy has boomed into a major urban center in the last 20 years for several reasons, not the least of which is a sage town government that has encouraged industry while recognizing the importance of the city's physical setting. Its tourist office is housed in the ultramodern shopping mall

Centre Bonlieu (1 Rue Jean-Jaurès; phone: 50-45-00-33; fax: 50-51-87-20).

Annecy was the home of St-François de Sales (1567–1622), a nobleman, missionary, and writer who was canonized in 1665, and the town also played an important part in the life of Jean-Jacques Rousseau, who lost his heart to Madame de Warens here. Today the Old City is charming and well preserved, with a number of attractive churches, including the *Eglise St-Maurice* (Pl. St-Maurice) and the *Eglise St-François* (Pl. St-François). The château (Pl. du Château; phone: 50-45-29-66), the former residence of the Counts of Geneva and the Dukes of Savoie-Nemours, also deserves a visit. It is closed Tuesdays except in July and August; there's an admission charge.

If you are in Annecy the last Saturday of any month, stop at the flea and antiques market that takes place on the streets of the Old City. At other times try the *Atelier du Sarvan* (7 Rue Perrière; phone: 50-45-75-68) and *Art-Chipel* (24 Pl. Ste-Claire; phone: 50-45-65-25) for local handicrafts, crystals, and stones.

The lakefront at Annecy is popular, crowded, and active; the relatively new casino offers traditional and newer games (for details, see *Casinos Royale* in DIVERSIONS). If you want to get away from it all, however, follow the east coast of the lake to Talloires. This little village, nestled behind a point and across from the striking (and privately owned) *Château de Duingt* at the foot of the Aravis Mountains, is a model of elegance, tranquillity, and taste. A picnic lunch at the lakeside here is a pleasure, as is the water, ideal for swimming. A few miles beyond the south end of the lake on N508 is the village of Faverges, a good starting point for some pleasant meandering; take D12 to the right at the junction here and head toward Tertenoz and perhaps beyond for a sense of the real Savoyard countryside, an enticing blend of gently rolling pastures and soul-stirring Alpine vistas.

BEST EN ROUTE

Auberge de l'Eridan Located in a lovely, lavender-blue house, this two-Michelin-star place—a favorite of François Mitterrand—sets one of the best tables in the French Alps. The chef seasons his fare with fresh herbs, roots, and flowers that he picks himself. Those who savor unusual and innovative dishes will want to try this member of the Relais & Châteaux group, which also offers 11 guestrooms. Closed Sunday dinner and Wednesdays. Reservations necessary. Major credit cards accepted. 13 Vieille Rte. des Pensières, Veyrier-du-Lac, 3 miles (5 km) south of Annecy along the eastern shore of the lake (phone: 50-60-24-00; fax: 50-60-23-63). Very expensive.

Auberge du Père Bise The quality and richness of its cuisine have made this two-Michelin-star eatery famous throughout France. Twenty rooms and seven suites also are available at this Relais & Châteaux member. For additional details, see *Haute Gastronomie* in DIVERSIONS. Closed mid-November through mid-February. Reservations necessary. Major credit cards accepted. On the eastern shore of Lac Annecy on Rte. du Port in Talloires, 7 miles (11 km) south of Annecy (phone: 50-60-72-01; fax: 50-60-73-05). Very expensive.

L'Impérial Palace A Belle Epoque palace hotel, this enchanting establishment occupies an ideal location on the Annecy lakeshore and commands truly extraordinary mountain views. All 91 rooms and eight suites are meticulously appointed. There are tennis courts, a private beach, three restaurants (try the sliced smoked salmon with dill and goat cheese for a sumptuous breakfast), a casino, and conference facilities. Special "fitness weekend" rates are available. 32 Av. d'Albigny, Annecy (phone: 50-09-30-00; fax: 50-09-33-33). Very expensive.

Abbaye A member of the Relais & Châteaux group, this former 17th-century Benedictine abbey (more recently the refuge of Haïti's Jean-Claude "Baby Doc" Duvalier) boasts a shaded garden, terrace, pool, and fitness center. The 30 rooms and three suites, monks' cells at one time, are decorated in a modern style that is far from spartan. Closed mid-December through mid-March. On the east side of Lac Annecy in Talloires, 7 miles (11 km) south of Annecy (phone: 50-60-77-33; fax: 50-60-78-81). Expensive.

Beau Site The main hotel has 29 well-appointed rooms and a private beach and tennis court that overlook Lac Annecy. A charming canopy of century-old trees graces the property. The lakefront setting of its luxurious 12-room annex is another appealing feature. Main hotel closed mid-October through mid-May; annex closed November through mid-February. Seven miles (11 km) south of Annecy in Talloires (phone: 50-60-71-04; fax: 50-60-79-22). Expensive.

L'Amandier Its renditions of traditional Savoyard fare have won this restaurant a Michelin star. Closed Sundays from October through *Easter* and Sunday dinner from *Easter* through mid-June. Reservations necessary. Major credit cards accepted. 91 Rte. d'Annecy, Chavoires, 2 miles (3 km) south of Annecy along the eastern lakeshore (phone: 50-60-01-22; fax: 50-60-03-25). Moderate.

Marceau Perched on a hilltop, this 16-room hostelry is quiet and restful. It has a restaurant, tennis court, and garden. Closed mid-October through January. Fourteen miles (22 km) south of Annecy, past Lac Annecy's southern shore, at 115 Chemin de la Chapellière, Marceau-Dessus, Doussard (phone: 50-44-30-11; fax: 50-44-39-44). Moderate.

Gay Séjour This family-run enterprise off the beaten track offers 12 rooms with lovely mountain views and a restaurant. Closed Mondays and January; restaurant also closed Sunday dinner. In Tertenoz; from Faverges take D12 south for 2 miles (3 km) toward the Col de Tamie (phone: 50-44-52-52; fax: 50-44-49-52). Inexpensive.

Hôtel du Nord A 35-room property with appealing modern decor. The friendly staff speaks English. There's no restaurant. In the center of Annecy, at 24 Rue Sommeiller (phone: 50-45-08-78; fax: 50-51-22-04). Inexpensive.

Burgundy

When most people hear the word "Burgundy," they think of wine. But France's Burgundy region offers visitors much more than just the pleasures of its famous vintages. Stretching from the Seine and the border of the Champagne region in the north down through the Beaujolais country just north of Lyons, Burgundy's countryside is remarkably varied, ranging from the bucolic rolling pastures of Aix-en-Othe to the rough and striking hill country around Cluny to the lakes and forests of the Morvan.

Burgundian villages seem to be caught in an enchanting time warp: Driving along a pleasant, winding country road, visitors suddenly find themselves among beflowered stone buildings that date from the 16th century. Burgundy's unchanging, timeless quality applies also to its people, who are profoundly conservative, rooted to their land, and suspicious of the city and modern ways. Though Paris is only a few hours' drive away on the autoroute, it is a trip that though not a few Burgundians have made only once, if at all.

Burgundy's story is as long as it is rich. At Solutré, a village at the foot of an imposing precipice in the Mâconnais region, archaeologists came upon the skeletons of 100,000 horses. One theory is that, about 15,000 years ago, early Burgundian hunters herded the horses together, probably using firebrands, and then drove them over the cliff. (An alternate theory has it that the hunters simply killed them as they migrated past the base of the cliff.) Later, Burgundy became a center of Celtic civilization, and then of Celtic resistance to Rome's northern expansion. It was at the center of the tribal domain of Bibracte, the present Autun, that the Gallic chief Vercingétorix held a war council of tribes committed to contest Rome's drive into Burgundy; at Alésia (Alise Ste-Reine), Vercingétorix and his 250,000 troops were defeated at the hands of Julius Caesar.

With the fall of the Roman Empire, the area changed in character and acquired its present name. The Burgund tribe, originally from the Baltic Sea, gradually emigrated south and west, and in the fifth century, Aetius, a general charged with defending the crumbling Roman Empire, invited them to settle in Sapaudia (Savoy). The Burgundians extended their hegemony to west of the Saône, and the kingdom of Burgundy was born.

It was not until the 14th century that Burgundy's halcyon days began. Philip the Bold, John the Fearless, Philip the Good, and Charles the Bold marked a succession of dukes with enough power to challenge that of the Kings of France. Palace life in Dijon, the seat of the dukes' vast holdings, was opulent, and the Burgundian Renaissance preceded the French one by several decades. During the 1470s the dukes' power was sharply reduced; Burgundy itself was annexed by Louis XI, while the remaining provinces of Flanders, Artois, and Franche-Comté were handed over to Austria by marriage. By then, however, Burgundy's legacy already had been established; the century of glory conveyed on the region a luxurious and lasting sheen of royalty.

Food was a central luxury in the life of the grand Dukes of Burgundy, and today Dijon still enjoys a reputation as a gastronomic capital. Burgundian dishes are hearty and based on the region's produce, including poultry from Bresse, lean beef from Charolais, and freshwater fish from the Saône and Rhône rivers. Four universally recognized Burgundian specialties are *coq au vin* (chicken in wine sauce), *escargots* (snails) cooked with garlic butter, *oeufs en meurette* (poached eggs in red wine sauce), and *boeuf bourguignon* (beef in red wine sauce). Cassis, the local liqueur made from black currants, is well worth sampling; try a *kir* (*aligoté*, a dry white wine, with cassis), a *kir royal* (made with champagne), or the sweeter *suze cassis* (a combination of cassis and suze, the gentian-derived liqueur). Every visitor should sample the famous Burgundian wines, which include the dry white made in Chablis, the full-bodied, aromatic reds and whites produced along the Côte d'Or south of Dijon, and the light, fruity reds made in the Beaujolais. Burgundian wine lists are a pleasure to the connoisseur and novice alike, although the latter may find the *vins de table* far less expensive and eminently satisfactory.

The driving route below starts in the Pays d'Othe, in the northern tip of Burgundy, and works its way south, culminating with visits to Beaune, home of the *Hôtel-Dieu,* and to Cluny, the seat of the ancient abbey. For those who seek a change of pace, there is an alternative to the automobile—the boat. Burgundy is crossed with more than 600 miles of navigable canals, and you can tour them on day cruises; on boats you rent and pilot yourself; or on luxurious barge "hotels," floating cruise craft that generally operate April through October. You can make reservations for the floating hotels through *Bateaux de Bourgogne* (1-2 Quai de la République, Auxerre 89000; phone: 86-51-12-05), a central reservations office for 12 boat companies, or *Continental Waterways/Abercrombie and Kent* (1520 Kensington Rd., Ste. 212, Oak Brook, Illinois 60521; phone: 800-323-7308; 708-954-2944 in Illinois; fax: 708-954-3324). The *Comité Régional du Tourisme de Bourgogne* (BP 1602, Dijon 21035; phone: 80-50-10-20; fax: 80-30-59-45) offers *Boating Holidays in Burgundy,* a brochure detailing a variety of regional cruising possibilities. (Also see *Boating: France's Wonderful Waterways* in DIVERSIONS and the list of inland waterway cruise companies in GETTING READY TO GO.) In addition, some of France's most elegant hot-air balloon rides are available in Burgundy, where a wine tasting is usually organized wherever you touch down. Contact *Buddy Bombard's Balloon Adventures* (*Château Laborde,* Meursanges 21200; phone: 80-26-63-30) or *Air Escargot* (Remigny, Chagny 71150; phone: 85-87-12-30; fax: 85-87-08-84). Both companies operate May through October.

For a double room in this region, expect to pay $125 or more in a very expensive hotel; $90 to $125 in an expensive one; $60 to $90 in a moderate one; and less than $60 in an inexpensive place. Unless otherwise indicated, all hotels accept major credit cards and are open year-round. Most hotels, except very expensive ones, do not have air conditioning, but it's unnecessary as a rule in this pleasantly temperate region. Hotels almost always have private baths and telephones in the rooms, though in a moderate or inexpensive establishment, it's a good idea to confirm that your room has a private bath when making a reservation. You'll find few TV sets in the less expensive country inns. Dinner for two, including service (usually added to the bill) but not wine, will cost $150 or more in a very expensive restaurant; $100 to $150 in an expensive one; from $75 to $100 in a moderate place; and less than $75 in an inexpensive one. Unless otherwise noted, all restaurants are open for lunch and dinner. For each location, hotels and restaurants are listed alphabetically by price category.

SENS Originally called Agendicum, this was one of the most important towns in Roman Gaul. It became a regional capital in AD 395, and soon after, the boundaries of its domain were adopted by the Catholic church, transforming the town into a major archbishopric. It was split up in 1622, after which Sens began its slow decline to its present status as a modest provincial town.

Sens's centerpiece is the *Cathédrale St-Etienne* (Pl. de la Cathédrale; no phone); located in the middle of the Old Town, it is a prime example of early Gothic architecture. Particularly noteworthy are the stained glass windows, constructed between the 12th and 17th centuries. Be sure to visit the *Trésor* (Treasury), one of the richest in France; it offers a collection of fabrics, liturgical vestments, shrouds, tapestries, and reliquaries. The *Palais Synodal* (phone: 86-64-15-27), at the cathedral, was the seat of the Officialité, a major ecclesiastical tribunal. Architecturally elegant, it is historically grisly: The tour, which is available for a small fee, includes a visit to the dungeon where heretics and sinners awaited trial. The *Palais Synodal* was restored in the 19th century by the famous Eugène Viollet-le-Duc, the architect who renovated many of Burgundy's cathedrals. Closed lunch hours; Monday, Thursday, and Friday mornings; Tuesdays; and from October through April. Admission charge.

A stroll through Sens is imperative if you want a real sense of the town. Look for the two interesting old buildings, called *Maison d'Abraham* (Abraham's House) and the *Maison du Pillier* (House of the Pillar), which sit beside each other at the intersection of Rue de la République and Rue Jean-Cousin. Neither is open to the public.

BEST EN ROUTE

Hostellerie du Castel Boname This lovely brick house in the countryside is a comfortable, quiet hotel with 14 rooms, a pool, a tennis court, and a pleasant restaurant. Closed Sundays and Mondays in the off-season and mid-January through late February. In Villeneuve-la-Dondagre, 7 miles (11 km) southwest of Sens by N60 and D63 (phone: 86-86-04-10; fax: 86-86-08-80). Expensive.

Hôtel de Paris et de la Poste Recently completely renovated, this bourgeois (in the best sense) inn offers flowery wallpaper in its 30 cozy rooms and suites and classic Burgundian cuisine in the rustic dining room. 97 Rue de la République, Sens (phone: 86-65-17-43; 800-528-1234; fax: 86-64-48-45; 602-957-5895 in the US). Expensive.

En Route from Sens Head south on N6 to Joigny (19 miles/30 km from Sens), worth a stop for its restaurant, *La Côte St-Jacques* (see *Best en Route*, below), as well as for its streets lined with half-timbered houses and two picturesque churches, *St-Thibault*, on Place St-Thibault, and *St-Jean*, on Place St-Jean (no phone for either).

Leave Joigny via D943 traveling east, then turn south to Tonnerre via D905 toward château country to visit two indisputably fine châteaux, *Tanlay* and *Ancy-le-Franc*. *Tanlay*, on D965 4 miles (6 km) east of Tonnerre, was built in the 16th century, and its stately elegance reflects the spirit of Louis XIII. The *Petit Château*, as it is called, is most notable for its frescoes, but a tour of the interior reveals a fine display of antique furniture as well. *Tanlay* is closed Tuesdays; admission charge (phone: 86-75-70-61). A few miles farther east via D965, on Rue du Bourg in the town of Châtillon-sur-Seine, is the *Musée Archéologique*, a fine museum with exhibits from the *Trésor de Vix* (Treasure of Vix), a sepulcher dating from the 6th century BC. Among the most striking of many impressive artifacts is an enormous bronze vase—almost five-and-a-half feet tall and weighing well over 400 pounds. The museum is closed Tuesdays; admission charge (phone: 80-91-24-67).

The château of *Ancy-le-Franc*, which can be reached from *Tanlay* by taking D965, then tiny D12 at Pimelles, was built a few years before *Tanlay* by Antoine de Clermont, Earl of Tonnerre, according to plans drawn up by the famed Italian architect Sebastiano Serlio. Among the many impressive rooms in the palace, the most striking is the *Guards Hall*, an immense space of almost 3,000 square feet. *Ancy* is open daily; closed mid-November through February. Admission charge (phone: 86-75-14-63).

From *Ancy-le-Franc*, take D905 through Tonnerre, then D965, for 32 miles (51 km) to Auxerre; along the way you'll pass through Chablis, home of the famous wine. Cellars in the area usually allow visitors, so ask around if you're interested in wine tasting.

BEST EN ROUTE

L'Abbaye Saint-Michel Joan of Arc, who stopped here in 1429, would be amazed at the transformation of this 10th-century Benedictine abbey into a luxurious inn, today a member of the Relais & Châteaux group. The nine rooms and five suites are divided between two wings, one old and the other modern. The two-Michelin-star restaurant (for a detailed description, see *Haute Gastronomie* in DIVERSIONS) features inventive cuisine such as puff pastry with foie gras or rhubarb. Hotel closed January through early February; restaurant also closed Tuesday lunch, and Mondays from November through April. Reservations advised. Rue St-Michel, Tonnerre (phone: 86-55-05-99; fax: 86-55-00-10). Very expensive.

La Côte St-Jacques An 18th-century former *maison bourgeoise,* this is the weekend destination of connoisseurs from Paris and beyond, who come to savor three-Michelin-star cuisine and stay in the hotel's 29 guestrooms. For detailed descriptions of the hotel and restaurant, respectively, see *Romantic French Hostelries* and *Haute Gastronomie* in DIVERSIONS. Closed early January through early February. Reservations advised. 14 Faubourg de Paris, Joigny (phone: 86-62-09-70; fax: 86-91-49-70). Very expensive.

Hostellerie des Clos This peaceful inn comprises 26 comfortable rooms, decorated in a modern style, and an excellent one-Michelin-star restaurant that features Burgundian specialties. Hotel closed early December through early January; restaurant also closed Thursday lunch (except in July and August) and Wednesdays. 18 Rue J.-Rathier, Chablis (phone: 86-42-10-63; fax: 86-42-17-11). Expensive.

La Vaudeurinoise A 10-room hostelry, recommended for the tranquillity of its surroundings and its tradition of gracious service and excellent cuisine. Nearby are tennis courts and horseback riding. Closed two weeks each in January and February; restaurant also closed Tuesday dinner and Wednesdays, except in July and August. Restaurant reservations unnecessary. MasterCard and Visa accepted. Rte. de Grange-Sèche, Vaudeurs, about 20 miles (32 km) northwest of Joigny (phone: 86-96-28-00; fax: 86-96-28-03). Moderate.

AUXERRE This attractive, bustling city on the left bank of the Yonne River has been the home of a number of French celebrities, including Germain, the famed fifth-century bishop, and Marie-Noël, the 20th-century "poetess of love."

With its sculpted portals and elegant nave, the *Cathédrale St-Etienne* (Pl. St-Etienne; no phone) is a first class example of 13th-century Flamboyant Gothic architecture. Be sure to visit the Romanesque crypt; hauntingly beautiful, it features a rare and remarkable 11th-century fresco entitled *Christ on Horseback.* Also impressive are the frescoes in the crypts of the *Abbaye St-Germain* (at the other end of Rue Cochois, on Pl. St-Germain), which was established in the sixth century by Queen Clothilde on the spot where that saint was buried in AD 448. Numerous old houses are notable, including the *Coche d'Eau* at the foot of the *Abbaye St-Germain* in the Marine Quarter, and the buildings at 16-18 Place de l'Hôtel, 3-5 Place Charles-Surugue, 14-16 Rue Sous-Murs, and 21 Rue de Paris. Guided visits of the abbey are available every half hour, starting at the *Coche d'Eau;* the abbey is closed lunch hours, Tuesdays and holidays. There's an admission charge (phone: 86-51-09-74).

BEST EN ROUTE

La Chamaille An old manor house on the edge of a little stream, where the one-Michelin-star cooking is traditional Burgundian (a meat terrine is brought to your table while you are reading the menu). The hosts are friendly, and the chablis and other local wines are superb. Closed Mondays, Tuesdays, mid-January through mid-February, one week in September, and *Christmas.* Reservations advised. Major credit cards accepted. Five miles (8 km) southwest of Auxerre via N151 and D1 at 4 Rte. de Boiloup, Chevannes (phone: 86-41-24-80). Moderate.

Jean-Luc Barnabet An old building on the quay, fitted out in post-modern decor, this is a favorite among local *becs fins.* One-Michelin-star specialties include *meurette d'oeufs pochés aux escargots* (poached eggs and snails in red Burgundy sauce) and *ris de veau poêlés aux champignons de bois* (veal sweetbreads sautéed with wild mushrooms). Closed Sunday dinner, Mondays, and December 20 through mid-January. Reservations advised. Major credit cards accepted. 14 Quai de la République (phone: 86-51-68-88; fax: 86-52-96-85). Moderate.

En Route from Auxerre Head southeast toward Noyers-sur-Serein via St-Bris-le-Vineux and D956. (Incidentally, although the wine of St-Bris-le-Vineux is less well known than that of Chablis, it's thought by many Burgundians to be superior.) Noyers is a special treat: It's a well-preserved little medieval town that sees surprisingly few tourists.

Not far away, via D86 and D11 south and D957 west, is another pretty medieval town; at the crest of the hill on which it sits is a small 12th-century church, *Eglise de Montréal* (Pl. de l'Eglise; no phone). The church, like the *Palais Synodal* in Sens, is one of Viollet-le-Duc's 19th-century restorations; a superb panorama of the surrounding countryside can be seen from the terrace at its rear.

From Noyers, Avallon is about 12 miles (19 km) south via D86. (To get there from Montréal, just follow D957 southwest.)

AVALLON High on a hill above the Vallée du Cousin, Avallon was a major stronghold during the Middle Ages. As weaponry became more sophisticated, however, its military significance declined. Today, Avallon is resigned to playing touristic second fiddle to its near neighbor, Vézelay, whose cathedral is considered by many the gem of Burgundy. Nonetheless, Avallon has much to offer, including the fourth-century *Eglise St-Lazare* (Pl. de la Collégiale; no phone). Around AD 1000, the church received a relic of St. Lazarus, the patron saint of lepers, and pilgrimages to the church by lepers began en masse. Over the following centuries, the small church was expanded a number of times to accommodate these pilgrims; its most interesting features are the two Romanesque portals, with varied sculptures showing musicians of the Apocalypse, signs of the zodiac, wine, acanthus leaves, and more. No visit to Avallon is complete without a leisurely stroll along the ramparts and a look at the 15th-century clock tower on the *Porte de la Boucherie* (Butcher's Gate).

BEST EN ROUTE

Hostellerie de la Poste An atmospheric little inn with only 23 rooms, this former posting house, built in 1707, dispenses consistently fine food and wines. Closed mid-November through March. 19 Pl. Vauban, Avallon (phone: 86-34-06-12; 800-332-5332; 310-645-3070 in the US; fax: 86-34-47-11; 310-645-1947 in the US). Expensive.

Le Relais Fleuri Modern amenities, including three tennis courts and a pool, are a plus for this well-managed 48-room hotel in a pleasant setting. Another draw is its good restaurant. Reservations advised. On the edge of Avallon, just off A6 on D944, Rte. de Saulieu (phone: 86-34-02-85; fax: 86-34-09-98). Moderate.

En Route from Avallon Head 9 miles (14 km) southwest to Vézelay via the Vallée du Cousin, on a lovely, shaded section of D957 that wends its way beside the Cousin River. There are numerous places to pull off the road for an undisturbed, feet-in-the-water picnic. At Pontaubert, turn left and follow D957 into Vézelay. For an exotic side trip, pick up N6 out of Avallon or after the Vallée du Cousin and head for the *Grottes d'Arcy-sur-Cure,* some 12 miles (19 km) north of Vézelay. This fantastic underground world of stalactites, stalagmites, and lakes comprises approximately 1½ miles of subterranean grottoes, about half of which can be explored.

BEST EN ROUTE

Château de Vault de Lugny Surrounded by a moat in a bucolic setting, this 16th-century château has 11 charmingly appointed rooms. Also on the premises are a tennis court and a small dining room, which is open only to hotel guests. Closed mid-November through mid-March. Three miles (5 km) outside of Avallon, via D957 and D142, in Vault de Lugny (phone: 86-34-07-86; fax: 86-34-16-36). Very expensive.

Le Moulin des Ruats This converted mill on the banks of the Cousin River has 26 simply decorated rooms and one suite. It's a soothing place to sojourn, with the stillness of the surrounding glade disturbed only by the rush of water through the millrace. The restaurant concentrates on Burgundian cuisine. Hotel closed mid-November through mid-February and October through

May; restaurant also closed Monday lunch and Tuesdays. About 2 miles (3.5 km) outside Avallon on D427 in Vallée du Cousin (phone: 86-34-07-14; fax: 86-31-65-47). Expensive.

Le Moulin des Templiers Well managed and tiny (14 rooms), this place has an eccentric country charm—its owner keeps a small menagerie of goats, turkeys, and other animals across the road. There's no restaurant, but breakfast is served on a terrace next to the Cousin River. Closed November through mid-March. No credit cards accepted. Vallée du Cousin, Pontaubert (phone: 86-34-10-80). Moderate.

VÉZELAY This town owes its fame to that jewel of Romanesque architecture, the *Basilique Ste-Madeleine* (Rue St-Pierre; phone: 86-33-24-36). The basilica is part of the *Abbaye de Vézelay,* which was founded in the ninth century, according to popular memory, by the legendary Girart de Roussillon, an early Count of Burgundy, and consecrated by Pope John VIII in AD 878. In the 11th century, the abbey was taken over by the powerful *Abbaye de Cluny.* A multitude of miracles were reported to have taken place here thanks to the relics of Mary Magdalene that the basilica housed, and so began an onslaught of pilgrimages to the church. This precipitated a disaster in 1122, when a massive fire broke out and the church collapsed, burying thousands of pilgrims alive. But the church soon was rebuilt, this time with a narthex (a vestibule leading to the nave), added to provide overnight lodging for the many pilgrims. Some years later, other relics of the saint were found in Provence, a discovery that cut into Vézelay's appeal. The basilica, which suffered destruction during the religious wars and then the French Revolution, went into decline until 1840, when its beauty was "discovered" by the writer Prosper Mérimée, working in his capacity as inspector of historical monuments. An immense restoration of the building took place, a project in which Viollet-le-Duc played a leading role.

Today, the church is a masterpiece of light and space. Note particularly the tympanum over the central entryway and the sculpted details of the interior columns. Energetic visitors should undertake a hike to the top of the tower, which commands a magnificent view of the surrounding countryside.

BEST EN ROUTE

L'Espérance A quintessentially elegant hotel, it boasts 34 rooms and six suites, plus a superlative restaurant that has earned three Michelin stars. For additional details, see *Romantic French Hostelries* in DIVERSIONS. Closed late January through early March; restaurant also closed Wednesday lunch in the off-season and Tuesdays. Reservations necessary. St-Père-sous-Vézelay (phone: 86-33-20-45; fax: 86-33-26-15). Very expensive.

Le Pontot This 15th-century residence offers seven rooms and three suites, each uniquely appointed. A large Louis XVI–style room has canopy beds, a fireplace, and a dressing room; another apartment has stone floors, a 16th-century beamed ceiling, and antique peasant furniture. All have modern baths. Breakfast is served in the paneled *Salon Louis XVI* or in a walled garden. There's no restaurant, but *L'Espérance* (see above) is nearby. Boat trips and balloon rides can be arranged. Closed from November through *Easter*. Pl. de l'Hôtel de Ville, Vézelay (phone: 86-33-24-40). Expensive.

En Route from Vézelay Head south for about 60 miles (96 km) to Autun through the Morvan, the northern reaches of France's Massif Central and of Burgundy's hill country. Derived from the Celtic for "black mountain," the word *morvan* captures the spirit of the region. Less prosperous and less pastoral than the rest of Burgundy, it is nevertheless a regional center for sports lovers and a popular weekend spot for Parisians.

Each of the seemingly infinite ways to cut through the Morvan yields a host of striking vistas. A good midway point is Château-Chinon, the capital of the area, whose Calvary hill affords an excellent view of the surrounding landscape. South of Château-Chinon is the High Morvan, the more mountainous part of the region. Take D27 through the *Forêt de la Gravelle,* then head toward St-Léger on the D18. Five miles (8 km) to the west of St-Léger is Mont-Beuvray, where, on clear days, one can see east as far as Mont-Blanc.

AUTUN Originally called Augustodunum (for Augustus Caesar), this city was a major Roman garrison, serving as a base of operations for the destruction of the Bibracte. In Gallo-Roman times, it became an important commercial center on the route between Lyons and Boulogne. Autun's prominence, however, made it a popular military target, and after many invasions, the city went into decline. Autun enjoyed a renaissance in the 15th century, thanks largely to the efforts of Nicolas Rolin, Philip the Good's chancellor and a native of Autun, and his son, the Cardinal Rolin, who made Autun a major church center.

Today, Autun is a thriving provincial town (pop. 20,000) with several sights of interest. The *Cathédrale St-Lazare* (Rue des Bancs; no phone), built between 1120 and 1146, is most celebrated for the tympanum over the central portal. Rendered by the sculptor Gislebertus, it portrays the Last Judgment and is less gloomy than many such depictions; heaven occupies the greatest portion of the tympanum, with hell confined to a small corner on the right.

Just a few steps away is the *Musée Rolin* (3-5 Rue des Bancs; phone: 85-52-09-76), in a house built for Nicolas Rolin; it has a fine collection of Gallo-Roman artifacts and 14th- and 15th-century sculpture and paintings, as well as 19th- and 20th-century works. In the collection are two depictions of Old Autun that combine the qualities of map and painting, providing the viewer with a good picture of what the city was like. The museum is closed lunch hours, Tuesdays, and some holidays; there's an admission charge.

La Porte St-André (St. Andrew's Gate), on the north side of town, is a remnant of the Roman walls that used to surround Autun. This great edifice has two large arches through which vehicles may pass and two smaller ones for pedestrians. Between June and August every year, Autun celebrates its Roman past with a festival in which 600 costumed Autun citizens take part. Consult the city's tourism office (3 Av. Charles-de-Gaulle; phone: 85-52-20-34) for details. The office is open daily.

About 1½ miles (2 km) south of Autun via D256 is *La Cascade de Brisecou* (Breakneck Waterfall). To get there, leave your car at the church at the town of Couhard and follow the signs on foot for about 20 minutes. On the walk back, note the odd, pyramidal *Pierre de Couhard* (Couhard Stone), believed to date from Roman times.

BEST EN ROUTE

Hôtel des Ursulines A former convent, it offers 32 comfortable and (as one might imagine) quiet rooms and five suites surrounding a well-manicured garden. In fine weather you can dine on the restaurant's terrace, which overlooks the city. Reservations advised. 14 Rue de Rivault (phone: 85-52-68-00; fax: 85-86-23-07). Expensive.

En Route from Autun The town of Saulieu, about 25 miles (40 km) north of Autun by D980, hosts an annual event food lovers should put on their calendars. At the gastronomic fair, the *Journées Gourmandes du Grand Morvan,* producers of edibles from wine to cheese put their wares on display in late April or early May. For more details, contact the tourist office in Saulieu; it's open daily (phone: 80-64-00-21).

Continue north on D980 for about 19 miles (30 km) to the lovely town of Semur-en-Auxois.

BEST EN ROUTE

Château de Chailly A Renaissance castle in the midst of calm and greenery, this elegant structure is now a 36-room, nine-suite hostelry. On the grounds are an 18-hole golf course, a heated pool, and four tennis courts. The accommodations rank among the most luxurious in the region—there is even a Zen meditation room in one tower. The restaurant, *L'Armançon,* with an ambitious new chef who has won it a Michelin star, focuses on traditional cuisine, and the wine list is strong on regional vintages. Closed December 23 through January. Reservations advised. About 15 miles (25 km) from Saulieu, via N6 south and D977 bis east, on N81 in Chailly-sur-Armançon (phone: 80-90-30-30; 800-888-1199; fax: 80-90-30-00). Hotel: Very expensive. Restaurant: Expensive.

La Côte d'Or This 16-room, four-suite hostelry—a member of the Relais & Châteaux group—has two sections: one dating from the 19th century, and the other, whose rooms have garden views, from the 20th century. Rumor has it that this is a favorite stopover for François Mitterrand. The dining room, which has garnered three Michelin stars, is celestial (for details, see *Haute Gastronomie* in DIVERSIONS). Restaurant closed Mondays from November through March and Tuesday lunch. Halfway to Semur from Autun on the D980 at 2 Rue d'Argentine, Saulieu (phone: 80-64-07-66; 800-FRANCOISE or 212-757-0874 in the US; fax: 80-64-08-92; 212-757-1377 in the US). Very expensive.

SEMUR-EN-AUXOIS During the Middle Ages, this town enjoyed a reputation as a virtually impregnable fortress, and it still has all the lineaments of its past might. The approach to Semur via the flower-lined Pont Joly gives the visitor a striking first glimpse, although a walking tour is the best way to enjoy this medieval town. Stroll along the ramparts for a look at the many attractive old buildings and a view of the surrounding countryside, or stop in at *Eglise Notre-Dame* (Pl. Notre-Dame, in the center of town; no phone), originally built in the 11th century but containing elements added from the 13th to the 16th century. The church also underwent restoration under the direction of the 19th-century architect Viollet-le-Duc.

Not far from Semur, and within a few miles of each other, are a number of unusually interesting places. Some 12 miles (19 km) east via D954 and D9 is Flavigny-sur-Ozerain, a medieval walled hilltop city surrounded on three sides by water. It's appealing for its sleepy, scarcely trafficked streets; pretty, old houses; and ancient ramparts. Flavigny was a fortification of some significance during the Middle Ages, but it's mostly notable these days for the popular lozenges produced by a nearby abbey.

About 4½ miles (7 km) from Flavigny via D29 is the town of Alise-Ste-Reine, the site of ancient Alésia, where the 250,000-strong army of Vercingétorix succumbed to the siege of the amassed Roman legions in 52 BC. The saga of Vercingétorix's defeat is tragic: He was taken as a prisoner to Rome, kept there for six years, forced to participate in Caesar's triumphal march, and, after that humiliation, summarily executed. In the 19th century, Napoleon III had an enormous statue of Vercingétorix built at the site of ancient Alésia, where it still stands in all its kitschy glory.

A few miles down D954 from Alise-Ste-Reine is the *Château de Bussy-Rabutin,* small (by château standards), handsome, and bubbling over with effrontery. The château reflects the spirit of its irrepressible owner, the soldier and writer Roger de Rabutin, Comte de Bussy, whose barbed verses incurred the wrath of Louis XIV. He was sent into exile at Bussy-Rabutin, where he wrote *Une Histoire Amoureuse des Gaules* (An Amorous History of the Gauls). For this effort, which mocked members of Louis's court, de Rabutin landed in the Bastille. The *Château de Bussy-Rabutin* was known to contemporaries of the count as the Temple of Impertinence, and it deserved the title. A typically irreverent touch is the series of moons at the entrance, a not-so-subtle counterpoint to that glorious symbol so often used to represent the Sun King, Louis XIV, in Paris. The château is open daily; closed Tuesdays and Wednesdays from October through March. Admission charge (phone: 80-96-00-03).

A different experience is found at the famous *Abbaye de Fontenay.* To get here from Semur-en-Auxois, head north of *Bussy-Rabutin* via D954, then follow D905 toward Montbard. This 12th-century Cistercian monastery has gone through a number of changes since its heyday. It first was abused by avaricious abbots, then converted into a paper factory after the French Revolution. Most of the buildings are intact, and a visit to the tranquil, elegant site gives a fine sense of the monastic life of 800 years ago. Closed lunch hours; admission charge (phone: 80-92-15-00).

Three miles (5 km) south of Semur-en-Auxois on D103 is the Lac de Pont, a large artificial lake with a sandy beach surrounded by a forest. A lovely hiking trail circles the lake, making this a perfect place to picnic or swim.

West of Semur on D954 is the sleepy town of Epoisses, whose château, owned by the same family since the 17th century, has welcomed such noble visitors as Henri IV, Madame de Sévigné, and Chateaubriand. Built over several centuries, the château has the remains of a seventh-century moat, a 13th-century church and tower, a lovely 15th-century *pigeonnier* (pigeon tower), and a Renaissance well. The château's gardens are open daily; closed September through *Easter.* The interior of the château is open in July and August only; closed lunch hours and Tuesdays. There's an admission charge (phone: 80-96-40-56 or 80-96-42-65). In spite of its noble past, Epoisses is now known primarily for its local cheese, a tangy cow's milk cheese bathed in *marc de Bourgogne* (grape eau-de-vie) as it ages.

BEST EN ROUTE

Le Moulin de Lamargelle An appealing *ferme auberge* (farm open to the public serving simple meals) with four rustic rooms. Guests dine in a stone enclave built around an old mill. Freshly fished trout and many farm-raised products figure prominently on the menu. Inn and restaurant closed November through March. Restaurant open daily in July and August; weekends only the rest of the year. Reservations necessary. No credit cards accepted. Twenty-one miles (34 km) east of Semur at the crossing of D6 and D16 at Lamargelle (phone: 80-35-15-06). Inexpensive.

En Route from Semur-en-Auxois Head back south to Saulieu; from there, pick up D977 east, which leads to the autoroute to Dijon (44 miles/70 km from Saulieu), the true heart of Burgundy.

DIJON For a detailed report on the city, its sights, its hotels, and its restaurants, see *Dijon* in THE CITIES.

En Route from Dijon South of Dijon is the part of Burgundy with which most people are familiar—the famed Côte d'Or (Gold Coast). Take D122 (known as the Route des Grands Crus) south until it joins N74 at Vougeot; follow this road to Beaune, 26 miles (42 km) from Dijon. Along the way are some of the great wine producing villages, among them Gevrey-Chambertin, Morey-St-Denis, Chambolle-Musigny, Vougeot, Vosne-Romanée, Nuits-St-Georges, Pernand-Vergelesses, Aloxe-Corton, Savigny-les-Beaune, Pommard, Volnay, Meursault, Puligny-Montrachet, Chassagne-Montrachet, and Santenay; you might stop to visit their vineyards. The people at *Morin et Fils* in Nuits-St-Georges are particularly friendly, and offer a broad selection of wines for tasting (phone: 80-61-19-51).

One highly recommended stop on the Côte d'Or, along N74, is the *Château du Clos de Vougeot.* Surrounded by priceless vineyards, this old building houses the *Confrérie des Chevaliers du Tastevin,* the Burgundian wine tasting society. Tours of the château, along with descriptions of the activities of the somewhat Elk-ish *Confrérie* (which include the promotion of Burgundy's wines), are given on a regular basis. The tour also takes the visitor through rooms full of fascinating old wine making apparatus. The château is open daily; closed lunch hours. There's an admission charge (phone: 80-62-86-09).

BEST EN ROUTE

Château de Gilly At the edge of the Citeaux forest, this palatial 14th-century abbey, opulently remodeled in the 17th century into an aristocratic family's residence, has been once again transformed, this time into a luxurious 39-room, eight-suite hostelry, a member of the prestigious Relais & Châteaux group. The romantic complex has vaulted hallways, Gothic dining rooms, elaborately painted beams, and Louis XV bedrooms, as well as more contemporary amenities, such as conference facilities for up to 100. Louis XIV visited the formal gardens. The restaurant features Burgundian cuisine and wines. Closed February through mid-March. Around 4 miles (6 km) northeast of Nuits-St-Georges via D25, in Gilly-lès-Citeaux (phone: 80-62-89-98; fax: 80-62-82-34). Hotel: very expensive. Restaurant: expensive.

Domaine de Loisy A spirited countess welcomes overnight guests into this privileged world, a dignified manor house with four rooms, set among vineyards. A certified oenologist, the *comtesse* offers weekend wine tasting seminars. There's no restaurant. Reserve well in advance. No credit cards accepted. 28 Rue Général-de-Gaulle, Nuits-St-Georges (phone: 80-61-02-72; fax: 80-61-36-14). Expensive.

La Rôtisserie du Chambertin The quaint town of Gevrey-Chambertin is famous for its powerful red wine and its semisoft cow's milk cheese, and this is the place to try them, as well as a quintessential *coq au vin* and a less familiar *fricassée des grenouilles et escargots* (fricassee of frogs and snails). The wine list is extraordinary. Closed Sunday dinner, Mondays, February, and one week in August. Reservations necessary. Major credit cards accepted. Seven miles (11 km) south of Dijon on N74 in Gevrey-Chambertin (phone: 80-34-33-20; fax: 80-34-12-30). Expensive.

BEAUNE This thriving city (pop. 20,000) is renowned not only for being the heart of Burgundy's wine country but also for its many fine treasures of art and architecture. Beaune's most famous structure is the *Hôtel-Dieu* (Rue de l'Hôtel-Dieu; phone: 80-24-45-00), built in the 15th century by the Chancellor (and tax collector) of Burgundy, Nicolas Rolin, to provide care and comfort for the poor, sick, and aged. This striking example of Flemish-Burgundian architecture, somewhat somber overall, is topped by an eye-catching roof of colorful ceramic tiles laid out in an intricate geometric pattern. (The duchy of Burgundy at one time included much of present-day Holland and Belgium, which accounts for the distinct Flemish influence in Burgundian architecture.) The structure functioned as a hospital right up through 1971, when it was converted to a home for the elderly. A tour of the *Hôtel-Dieu* includes a visit to its museum, which contains some beautiful tapestries and a remarkable polyptych of *The Last Judgment,* painted by the 15th-century Flemish artist Roger van der Weyden. A son-et-lumière show is held in the courtyard during the summer. Open daily; closed lunch from October through April. Admission charge.

Nicolas Rolin also bequeathed to the hospital his vineyards, wine from which is sold at the annual auction held at Beaune's marketplace. Although these wines frequently command a high price because the proceeds go to the hospital and other charities, they also usually set the trend for the sale of other Burgundian wines. The auction, held during a three-day festival ("*Les Trois Glorieuses*") that takes place the third Saturday, Sunday, and Monday in November, draws buyers and oenophiles from all over the world. (For additional details on the event, see *Festivals à la Française* in DIVERSIONS.)

Near the *Hôtel-Dieu* is the *Musée du Vin de Bourgogne* (Rue d'Enfer; phone: 80-22-08-19), in the old mansion of the Dukes of Burgundy, which documents the history of viticulture and wine making. Guided tours in English are given every hour. It's closed lunch hours, Tuesdays, and holidays; there's an admission charge.

The *Marché aux Vins* (Rue Nicolas-Rolin; phone: 80-22-27-69) has one of the most instructive independent wine-tasting setups around. About 40 wines are set out on barrels (less expensive ones in a *cave* and others on the main floor); visitors buy a small wine glass and wander around tasting at their discretion, marking their responses on a card listing all the wines on display. (Tasters spit out the wine into the small wooden buckets on the floor next to the barrels.) The choice of wines usually includes most of the main burgundies, or various vintages. The idea is that visitors will buy a bottle or case of their favorite at the end of the tour, but there is no pressure from the staff to do so. Closed lunch hours and mid-December through late January.

Several organizations offer informative presentations and free *dégustations* (tastings). *L'Ambassade du Vin* (20-22 Rue du Faubourg-Madeleine; phone: 80-21-53-72; fax: 80-21-51-10) supplements tastings with a wine expert's commentary (usually in French, though there are some commentaries in English). Reservations for tastings here are required, and there is an admission charge. The *Caves des Cordeliers* (Couvent des Cordeliers; 6 Rue de l'Hôtel-Dieu; phone: 80-22-14-25) offers free tastings (in English if requested); reservations are required for groups only. The venerable house of *Patriarche Père et Fils* (7 Rue du Collège; phone: 80-24-53-78; fax: 80-24-53-03), founded in 1780 and Burgundy's foremost wine *négociant* (dealer), has around 20 wines in its *dégustation,* for which no reservations are required; there is an admission charge. All three of the above are open daily. *Caves du Chancelier* (1 Rue Ziem; phone: 80-24-05-88) and *La Reine Pédauque* (2 Rue Faubourg St-Nicolas; phone: 80-22-23-11; fax: 80-26-42-00) are also good choices. Both are open daily and do not require reservations; both charge admission.

A source of *grands vins* from many different houses is *La Vinothèque* (4 Rue Pasumot; phone: 80-22-86-35), near the *Hôtel-Dieu,* which also handles shipments of large orders; also good is *Denis Perret* (corner of Rue Carnot and Pl. Carnot; phone: 80-22-35-47; fax: 80-22-57-33), the official distributor in Beaune for various fine wine houses including Bouchard Père et Fils, Louis Latour, Louis Jadot, and Joseph Drouhin. A source for *tastevins* (the flat silver cups used by sommeliers to taste wine) and other typical Burgundian objects is *Beaune Choses* (Pl. Carnot; phone: 80-22-11-56); they speak English, have a tax-free discount, and handle shipment abroad. *Athenaeum* (7 Rue de l'Hôtel-Dieu; phone: 80-22-12-00) is a distinctive bookshop that also sells wines from *Patriarche Père et Fils* (see above), either by the bottle or by the glass in the small in-store wine bar. Browse through the shop's extensive collection of books on wine, food, and travel, many in English; excellent maps of Burgundy's wine routes also are sold here.

Of interest to summer visitors is Beaune's annual music festival, held during the last week of June and the first three weeks of July, and a parade and fair to mark the *Fêtes Internationales de la Vigne* (International Celebration of the Grapevine), held on the second Saturday in September. The *Office du Tourisme de Beaune* (Rue de l'Hôtel-Dieu; phone: 80-22-24-51; fax: 80-24-06-85), one of Burgundy's most active and efficient, will provide information on any special events, as well as a wide assortment of brochures on Beaune's attractions and a list of *caves* offering *dégustations* in Beaune and the surrounding area; it's open daily. Golfers who would like to tee up in the lush countryside should visit the 18-hole *Golf de Beaune* (phone: 80-24-10-29) in the nearby village of Levernois, 2 miles (3 km) southeast of Beaune on D970; it's open year-round.

For a taste of the glories of medieval Burgundy, take D973 southwest for 8 miles (13 km) to the *Château de la Rochepot*, built between the 13th and 15th centuries. Its creamy white walls and pointed turrets might remind you of the châteaux of the Loire Valley, but the multicolored tiles of the roofs are unmistakably Burgundian. The château was owned in the 15th century by two Knights of the Golden Fleece (Régnier and Philippe Pot). Almost destroyed during the Revolution, it was rebuilt in the 19th century. The most notable features are the 12th-century chapel, a colorful guard's room, a huge medieval kitchen, and apartments furnished in medieval or Renaissance style. The château is closed Tuesdays and November through March. Admission charge (phone: 80-21-71-37; fax: 80-21-83-33).

BEST EN ROUTE

Hostellerie de Levernois Set in a 10-acre park, this gracious Relais & Châteaux member has 16 spacious, comfortable rooms. The inviting, terraced dining room, *Jean Crotet,* specializes in regional fare and has earned two Michelin stars. Hotel closed from December 20 through January 10; restaurant also closed Tuesdays from December through March and Wednesday lunch. Reservations necessary. Two miles (3 km) southeast of Beaune by D970, then D911 (Rte. de Combertault) in Levernois (phone: 80-24-73-58; fax: 80-22-78-00). Very expensive.

Le Cep With 49 luxurious rooms and three suites in a converted Renaissance building, this is one of the best hotels in town. Lyons-trained chef Bernard Morillon offers light traditional *bourguignon* fare—with a heavy accent on fish—in his self-named restaurant, which has won a star from Michelin. Guests dine in a covered outdoor garden. Hotel and restaurant closed two weeks in February and a week in August; restaurant also closed Tuesdays for lunch and Mondays. Reservations advised. 27-29 and 31 Rue Maufoux (phone: 80-22-35-48 for the hotel; 80-24-12-06 for the restaurant; 800-927-4765 for both; 212-689-5400 in the US; fax: 80-22-76-80 for the hotel; 80-22-66-22 for the restaurant; 212-689-5435 in the US). Expensive.

Hostellerie du Vieux Moulin There are 25 rooms and two suites in this inn, which also boasts a one-Michelin-star restaurant. The restaurant has been redecorated in contemporary style, which, some speculate, may have contributed to its loss of a second Michelin star last year; the food remains outstanding. Chef Jean-Pierre Silva creates such delights as *bar rôti au jus de homard* (roasted sea bass with lobster essence) and *pigeonneau rôti dans son jus* (young squab roasted in its juices). Hotel closed three weeks in January; restaurant also closed Thursdays for lunch and Wednesdays (except holidays). Ten miles (16 km) outside of Beaune on D2, in Bouilland (phone: 80-21-51-16; fax: 80-21-59-90). Expensive.

Hôtel Belena Located at the edge of Beaune, this contemporary hotel has 40 spacious and amenity-laden rooms. The restaurant, *Jacques Lainé*, serves a sumptuous brunch in addition to classic Burgundian cuisine. Restaurant closed Wednesday lunch, Tuesdays, and the last two weeks of February. 10-12 Bd. Foch (phone: 80-24-01-01; fax: 80-22-77-78). Expensive.

Hôtel de la Poste At this old favorite, with 21 comfortable rooms and nine suites offering a view of the vineyards and Beaune's ramparts, travelers will find tasty regional cuisine and a good list of local wines. Restaurant closed Thursday lunch and Wednesdays. 1 Bd. Clemenceau (phone: 80-22-08-11; 800-221-4542; 914-472-0370 in the US; fax: 80-24-19-71; 914-472-0451). Moderate.

En Route from Beaune Although the Côte d'Or ends at Chagny, 9 miles (14 km) south on N74, this is not the end of Burgundy's wine country. Between Chagny and Chalon-sur-Saône is the area known as the Chalonnais, which has four more wine villages—Rully (where a popular fruity Rully *blanc* is produced), Mercurey, Givry, and Montagny. South of Chalon is the Mâconnais wine country; still farther south is the Beaujolais. Continue south on A6 for about 31 miles (50 km) to Tournus.

BEST EN ROUTE

Lameloise At this atmospheric, 15th-century country mansion, which has been awarded three Michelin stars, Burgundian cooking is raised to a high art. There are 20 rooms, in case you need to sleep off the heady gustatory experience of dining here. A member of the Relais & Châteaux group. Closed mid-December through late January; restaurant also closed Wednesdays and Thursday lunch. Reservations advised. Major credit cards accepted. 36 Pl. d'Armes, Chagny (phone: 85-87-08-85; fax: 85-87-03-57). Very expensive.

Moulin d'Hauterive A restored mill turned inn, it's off the beaten path on the edge of a sleepy stream. The isolated setting and tranquil surroundings enhance the kitchen's fine renditions of nouvelle cuisine. The 22 rooms (11 of them suites) have beamed ceilings and cozy furnishings; there is a fitness center, too. Hotel closed December through February; restaurant also closed Tuesday lunch and Mondays. Take D62 from Chagny to Chaublanc, and follow signs to the tiny hamlet of St-Gervais-en-Vallière (phone: 85-91-55-56; fax: 85-91-89-65). Expensive.

TOURNUS At the northern edge of the Mâconnais on the banks of the Saône is Tournus, the home of the old *Eglise St-Philibert* and its abbey (Pl. des

Arts; no phone). The abbey was built on the spot where Valerian, an early Christian, was martyred in the second century. Construction was begun in the 10th century, and continued over the next several centuries. The church is a marvel of Romanesque architecture, as exemplified by its plain façade and simple, heavy narthex. Its nave, devoid of decoration, is handsome and uplifting, suffused with light from high windows toward which reach tall, slender columns made of beautiful rosy stone quarried in nearby Préty.

BEST EN ROUTE

Greuze Fine, traditional Burgundian food and beaujolais are offered at this charming restaurant. Jean Ducloux's opulent, traditional cuisine—try the tender *rognon à la dijonnaise* (kidney with mustard sauce)—has earned the place two Michelin stars. Closed the first 10 days of December. Reservations necessary. Major credit cards accepted. 1 Rue Thibaudet, Tournus (phone: 85-51-13-52; fax: 85-40-75-40). Expensive.

En Route from Tournus Take A6 south for 18 miles (29 km) to the village of Mâcon, also on the Saône.

BEST EN ROUTE

Château de Fleurville This quiet 15-room hotel and its restaurant are part of a group of fortified buildings that were built by the Counts of Fleurville and later belonged to the Counts of Talleyrand-Périgord. Closed the month of February and mid-November through mid-December; restaurant also closed Monday lunch. Eight miles (13 km) south of Tournus via N6 in Fleurville (phone: 85-33-12-17). Expensive.

MÂCON The city's famous native son is Alphonse de Lamartine, the 19th-century Romantic poet. Among his several volumes of poetry, Lamartine's most successful was *Méditations Poétiques.* To learn more about his life, visit the *Musée Lamartine* (Rue Sigorgne, *Hôtel Senecé;* phone: 85-38-96-19), which is closed lunch hours, Sundays, some holidays, and the months of January and February. The *Circuit Lamartine,* a 40-mile (64-km) drive through the environs of Mâconnais, takes in the *Château de Monceau,* one of Lamartine's favorite residences and now a retirement home, and Milly-Lamartine, the town where Lamartine lived as a child. For information on this route, contact Mâcon's *Office du Tourisme* (187 Rue Carnot; phone: 85-39-71-37); it's open daily.

Wine lovers also will find things of interest in the area. The *Maison Mâconnaise des Vins* (Av. M.-de-Lattre-Tassigny; phone: 85-38-36-78), a center promoting local wines, hosts tastings, exhibits, and more. And the vineyards of the Mâconnais region extend south past Mâcon to the northern reaches of the Beaujolais. Perhaps the best known of the Mâconnais wines is the pouilly-fuissé, produced in the villages of Solutré-Pouilly, Davayé, and Fuissé. All three are in the lovely hills west of Mâcon, in the general direction of the Roche de Solutré and the Roche de Vergisson, two of the rocky hills jutting up from the flat countryside. After a visit to these vineyards, head up from the village of Vergisson to Solutré for a look at the precipice over which thousands of wild horses are believed to have been stampeded 15,000 years ago.

The region between Mâcon and Villefranche-sur-Saône, 25 miles (40 km) south, is known as the Beaujolais, and vineyards are found in many of the villages here. Those that consistently produce first class wines are known as the Beaujolais-Villages, and the very finest vineyard sites go by their own *appellations*—St-Amour, Juliénas, Chénas, Moulin-à-Vent, Fleurie, Chiroubles, Morgon, Brouilly, Côtes de Brouilly, and Regnié, the latest *cru* to be promoted to this status. *Le Hameau du Vin* is a wine museum and boutique, and a tasting center recently opened in the former train station of Romanèche-Thorins, south of Mâcon via N6. Georges Duboeuf, a *négociant* and wine producer who is known in France as "Monsieur Beaujolais" for his efforts to promote the wine, is the guiding spirit behind the museum. Open daily; closed most of January. Admission charge (phone: 85-35-22-22; fax: 85-35-21-18).

BEST EN ROUTE

Georges Blanc Occupying the same premises since 1872, this superb three-Michelin-star restaurant is also a 24-room hotel. It is a member of the Relais & Châteaux group. (For details, see *Haute Gastronomie* in DIVERSIONS.) Closed Wednesdays, Thursdays (except for dinner in summer), and January through mid-February. Reservations necessary. Major credit cards accepted. Twelve miles (19 km) east of Mâcon via N79 and D269, on the bank of the Veyle River in Vonnas (phone: 74-50-00-10; fax: 74-50-08-80). Very expensive.

Auberge du Cep In this two-Michelin-star gastronomic temple with the feel of a country inn, try the *cuisses de grenouilles rôties* (roasted frogs' legs) or the *queues d'écrevisses en petit ragoût* (stew of crayfish tails). There have been grumblings recently that the quality is not as high as the prices, but this is still an institution to be reckoned with. As one would expect, the wine list concentrates on regional vintages, with an emphasis on beaujolais (try the white). Closed Sunday dinner, Mondays, and mid-December through mid-January. Reservations necessary. Major credit cards accepted. Thirteen miles (21 km) south of Mâcon on Pl. Eglise, Fleurie (phone: 74-04-10-77; fax: 74-04-10-28). Expensive.

En Route from Mâcon Sixteen miles (26 km) northwest of Mâcon via N79 and D980 is the ancient city of Cluny. The trip, which takes you through surprisingly rough hill country, is quite enjoyable; you might stop at a goatherd's hut along the way to pick up some homemade *chèvre* (goat cheese).

CLUNY This town is home to the once powerful *Abbaye de Cluny,* set in the center of town. Founded in 910, the Cluniac order was unique in that its constitution provided for freedom from secular supervision as well as from that of the local bishop. As a result, the abbey became a wellspring of spiritual influence and religious reform throughout Europe. Numerous small priories were opened, with as many as 10,000 monks in different countries under the authority of Cluny's abbot. During the 14th century, the power of the order began to decline, and after the French Revolution many of the abbey's buildings here were torn down—including a magnificent cathedral, which, until the construction of *St. Peter's* in Rome, was the largest in the world. Today, only the south part of the transept remains; a tour of it, included in the admission charge, is stimulating. The abbey is open daily; the museum, with fascinating exhibits on the abbey's early days, is closed Tuesdays. There is an admission charge for both (phone: 85-59-12-79).

BEST EN ROUTE

Château d'Igé An enchanting 13th-century château set in its own park, this Relais & Châteaux member has seven luxurious rooms, six suites, and excellent service. The restaurant offers traditional Burgundian cuisine in elegant surroundings. Hotel closed December through February; restaurant closed December 20 through January 20. Eight miles (13 km) southeast of Cluny via D134 in Igé (phone: 85-33-33-99; fax: 85-33-41-41). Very expensive.

Hôtel de Bourgogne This inn has 12 comfortable rooms, three suites, and a very good dining room. Closed mid-November through mid-February; restaurant also closed Wednesday lunch and Tuesdays. Near the abbey, on Pl. de l'Abbaye, Cluny (phone: 85-59-00-58; fax: 85-59-03-73). Expensive.

Potin Gourmand A rustic local favorite for fresh and inspired *cuisine marché* (the chef uses products bought at the market that day). Closed Sunday dinner, Mondays, and January through early February. Reservations advised. Major credit cards accepted. 4 Pl. du Champs de Foire, Cluny (phone: 85-59-02-06; fax: 85-59-22-58). Moderate.

En Route from Cluny About 25 miles (40 km) west on N79 is Paray-le-Monial, worth a stop for its *Basilique du Sacré-Coeur* (Av. Jean-Paul-II; no phone). Modeled after the (no longer extant) cathedral in Cluny, it is a fine example of Romanesque architecture. Simple yet elegant, the church has two square towers over the narthex and an octagonal tower over the transept. The interior is striking for its height and simplicity.

Next door, in the former priory, is a museum devoted to the faïence of Charolais (Av. Jean-Paul-II; phone: 85-88-32-47), a decorative earthenware made in the region. In addition to a collection of over 2,000 pieces, the oldest of which date from 1836, the museum contains a section focusing on pottery-making tools and an archive of designs used for the faïence. The museum is closed mornings, Thursdays, and October 20 to March 20; there's an admission charge.

Alsace

So much of the green, hilly strip that is Alsace is covered with vineyards and orchards that Louis XIV is reported to have exclaimed, "What a beautiful garden!" upon first seeing it. The region lies between the Rhine Valley and the Vosges Mountains, which act as umbrellas, protecting the vine-covered hillsides from too much rain and providing ideal growing conditions—principally in the area from Marlenheim to Thann, in the valleys of the Thur and Bruche Rivers—for many varieties of grapes and other fruit. The fruits are used to make the prized Alsatian eaux-de-vie (dry, colorless, fruit-flavored alcohols), while the grapes are turned into fresh, fruity, mostly white wines.

The Celts first settled this area in the 8th century BC. Like most of Europe, Alsace later was annexed by the Romans, who were thrown out in the beginning of the 5th century. In the 7th century, under the Merovingian kings, Alsace became a free duchy and then part of Charlemagne's empire. It was officially annexed to France under the terms of the Treaty of Westphalia, in 1648, but was then annexed by Germany after the Franco-Prussian War, in 1871. The desire to reclaim Alsace became part of the growing French nationalism prior to World War I, and it was a joyful day for the entire country when, in 1918, the region was returned to France. During World War II Alsace was occupied by Germany.

Today the relationship between this very singular region and France and Germany is still complex. Perhaps because of its seesaw history, Alsace has clung ferociously to its own mixed culture, architecture, and traditions. Some of its villages, wines, and people have German names, and until 1945 most of the street names were in German. Much Alsatian architecture—white, geranium-trimmed, half-timbered houses with steeply pitched roofs—is reminiscent of that found in northern European Rhenish villages. But in certain cultural aspects—art, music, and hospitality—Alsace is most resolutely French. This dichotomy of history and culture is partly responsible for the region's quirky charm.

To preserve its natural parks and villages while allowing for 20th-century advances, the Alsatians have organized several preservation groups. Entire sections of Strasbourg and Colmar, two of the region's major cities, have been restored to their original condition and closed to automobile traffic. And Alsace is well organized for tourism, with *Offices de Tourisme* and *Syndicats d'Initiative* in most towns offering a seemingly infinite supply of maps and brochures, most available in English.

Alsace comprises two *départements,* the Bas-Rhin and the Haut-Rhin, which are bordered by Germany and Switzerland as well as the Rhine River. The Bas-Rhin is appealing for its forests and national parks, which have a complex pattern of meticulously marked hiking trails. The Haut-Rhin gave birth to the idea of *fermes auberges*—farms that give the adventurous tourist an alternative to traditional restaurants. Travelers can dine with families of the many *fermes auberges* scattered throughout the region, a great many located in the Vosges Mountains; some of them also rent rooms. For information about the Bas-Rhin, contact the *Office Départemental du Tourisme du Bas-Rhin* (9 Rue du Dôme, Strasbourg 67000; phone: 88-22-01-02; fax: 88-75-67-64); for Haut-Rhin information, contact the *Association Départementale du Tourisme du Haut-Rhin* (*Hôtel du Département,* Colmar 68006 CEDEX; phone: 89-20-10-68; fax: 89-23-33-91).

Like other French regions, Alsace has its own style of cooking, which borrows from its German and Swiss neighbors. Its basic character is homey, simple, and lusty, with a preponderance of pork, goose, potatoes, and cabbage. The best-known local dish is *choucroute,* sauerkraut cooked in wine and served with a variety of sausages and hams. Among Alsace's other gastronomic specialties are *tarte à l'oignon* (onion tart) and *tarte flambée* (a type of thin pizza topped with cream, cheese, onion, and bacon). *Coq au riesling* is chicken cooked in a regional white wine; *schiefala* (smoked pork shoulder) often is served with warm potato salad. *Baeckeoffe,* a stew of pork, lamb, and veal with onions and potatoes, frequently must be ordered in advance. Desserts include simple fruit tarts, light *tarte au fromage* (cheese tart), and *kugelhopf,* a sweet yeast bread studded with raisins and dusted with sugar and almonds.

Alsatian wines, primarily white, constitute almost 20% of the *appellation controlée* white wine produced in France, and are a source of great regional pride. Wines here take their names from the grape variety that goes into them, unlike the rest of France, where wines are named after the regions where they are produced. The best-known Alsatian wine, riesling, gets better with age and is very dry, with a delicate bouquet. Sylvaner is fresh, light, and dry; pinot blanc is dry and supple. The heady, full-bodied tokay pinot gris is an excellent accompaniment to fowl or game. Gewürztraminer is a spicy, fruity wine, to be drunk with rich foods; it's a good choice with foie gras, the fattened goose livers that are another prized regional specialty. Pinot noir is the Alsatian red or rosé wine, lightweight but fruity. Muscat is a dry, very fruity white wine, usually served as an aperitif or with pastries.

Our suggested driving route is divided into two parts, each about 75 miles (120 km) long. The first itinerary begins in the cosmopolitan city of Strasbourg, making a circle through the northernmost countryside of Alsace and giving the traveler a look at the region's natural parks and forests and its many lovely villages. The second itinerary, the Route du Vin (Wine Road), extends from Marlenheim to Mulhouse, near the Swiss border, and includes a number of typical villages whose well-ordered fields produce the popular Alsatian wines. This trip also includes Colmar, noted for its architectural beauty. The entire Alsatian route is covered by Michelin map No. 87.

Although this area generally has not been discovered by Americans, it does see a fair amount of tourism, and reservations are advised in high season (summer). Expect to pay more than $130 per night for a double room with bath at a very expensive hotel; from $95 to $130 at an expensive one; from $65 to $95 at a moderate place; and less than $65 at an inexpensive one. Unless otherwise indicated, all hotels accept major credit cards and are open year-round. For a meal for two, expect to pay more than $95 at an expensive restaurant; from $65 to $95 at a moderate place; and less than $65 at an inexpensive one. Prices do not include wine or drinks but usually service. Good restaurants often are full even in the off-season, so make reservations when you can. Unless otherwise noted, all are open for lunch and dinner. For each location hotels and restaurants are listed alphabetically by price category.

NORTHERN ALSACE ROUTE

STRASBOURG For a detailed report on the city, its sights, its hotels, and its restaurants, see *Strasbourg* in THE CITIES.

En Route from Strasbourg Take D41 northwest for 23 miles (37 km) to Saverne.

SAVERNE A small town perched on a hill, Saverne boasts the enormous and elegant 18th-century *Château des Rohan,* named after the powerful family of princes and bishops. Its pink sandstone façade overlooks the Canal de la Marne au Rhin; inside are two small museums, one of archaeology and the other of history. The museums are open Wednesday through Monday afternoons from June through September; closed the rest of the year. One charge covers admission to both. Other local attractions include a nearby outdoor market that bustles on Thursday mornings on the Place du Général-de-Gaulle. On Grand' Rue, the main pedestrian street, is the *Hôtel de Ville* (Town Hall), flanked by the *Maison Katz,* dating from 1605, with its lovely mullioned windows. *Muller Oberling* (66-68 Grand' Rue) is a good tearoom.

While in the area, take D171 south 2½ miles (4 km) from Saverne to visit the Romanesque chapel and ruins of the 12th-century *Château du Haut-Barr.*

BEST EN ROUTE

Auberge de Kochersberg This spot does double duty as a lunchtime canteen for employees of the nearby Adidas sneaker factory and as a highly respected one-Michelin-star restaurant that opens to the public for lunch (after the Adidas folks leave, at 12:30 PM) and dinner. Closed Sunday dinner, Mondays, one week in late February, and late July to mid-August. Reservations necessary. Major credit cards accepted. Eight miles (13 km) from Saverne on D41 in Landersheim (phone: 88-69-91-58; fax: 88-69-91-42). Expensive.

Chez Jean Here you'll find 24 clean, rustic rooms and a restaurant that serves hearty food, including immense portions of *choucroute* and good steaks, and Alsatian wines by the carafe. There is a *winstub* next door. Restaurant closed Sunday dinner, Mondays, and December 22 through January 10. 3 Rue de la Gare, Saverne (phone: 88-91-10-19; fax: 88-91-27-45). Moderate.

En Route from Saverne Follow the signs to the Col de Saverne. Along the way is *La Roseraie* (phone: 88-71-83-33), a four-acre rose garden with 7,500 rose bushes of 450 varieties. Open June through September. The forest here, filled with footpaths and picnic tables, is a tempting place to stop for lunch.

Take D122, D133, and D178 to La Petite-Pierre, where a castle and fortified village dominate the mountaintop. From La Petite-Pierre D7 leads east to Weiterswiller and Bouxwiller, pretty Alsatian villages notable for their 17th-century houses with exposed beams. Continue north on D7 and D6 to Ingwiller and D28 northeast to Niederbronn-les-Bains, and enjoy the gorgeous scenery, rolling hills, and tiny villages of the *Parc Naturel Régional des Vosges du Nord.* Niederbronn is a spa, prized for its mountain waters used in the treatment of arthritis and rheumatism. The town's archaeological museum (44 Av. Foch; phone: 88-80-36-37) has a small collection of medieval artifacts. It's closed Tuesdays; admission charge.

In the area surrounding Niederbronn are many ruins of centuries-old châteaux. North of Niederbronn, on D653 and then left on D53, are the *Châteaux de Windstein,* two castles built in 1212 and 1340, right next to each other. The ruins can be reached only on foot.

Back on N62, go northwest to the *Château de Falkenstein,* which was founded in 1128 and destroyed in 1564; only ruins remain. It also may be reached only by foot. From the ruins one has a view of the northern Vosges. Continue on small N62 to Etang de Hanau; from there link up with D3 to travel east through Obersteinbach and on to the *Château de Fleckenstein.* This stretch passes a large, curious, and beautiful Alsatian farm, with crooked rooftops and windows crazily askew. The château, another ruin but accessible by car, overlooks the German border. Inside, the rooms are cut directly from the rock. From the *Château de Fleckenstein* continue on D3 to Wissembourg, about 11 miles (18 km) away.

BEST EN ROUTE

La Clairière This modern, chalet-style country resort has 50 cheerful rooms with direct-dial phones, satellite color TV, mini-bars, and views of the wooded countryside. Other amenities include a heated indoor pool, a gym, a sauna, a solarium, and six conference rooms. The restaurant serves a first-rate selection of typically French fare, in addition to Alsatian dishes. 63 Rte. d'Ingwiller, La Petite-Pierre (phone: 88-70-47-76; fax: 88-70-41-08). Expensive to moderate.

Aux Trois Roses A fine view, an indoor pool, and a tennis court enhance this 43-room hotel. There is a restaurant. Hotel open year-round; restaurant closed Sunday and Monday dinner. 19 Rue Principale, La Petite-Pierre (phone: 88-89-89-00; fax: 88-70-41-28). Moderate.

Auberge d'Imsthal In a calm setting next to a large pond, this 23-room hotel has a fitness center with a Jacuzzi, a sauna, a steambath, and a solarium. The restaurant serves ham, game, and pot-au-feu (a hearty meat and vegetable stew). Restaurant open daily. Rte. Forestière, La Petite-Pierre (phone: 88-70-45-21; fax: 88-70-40-26). Moderate to inexpensive.

Les Acacias A rustic restaurant in the woods serving Alsatian cuisine, it offers outdoor dining on the terrace in the summer. A year-round specialty is *papillote de sandre au foie gras* (a perch-like local fish cooked in parchment and served with foie gras). Local game and wildfowl are featured in the winter. Closed Fridays, late January to mid-February, and the first two weeks of September. Reservations advised. Major credit cards accepted. 35 Rue des Acacias, Niederbronn-les-Bains (phone: 88-09-00-47). Inexpensive.

WISSEMBOURG The doorway between France and Germany during the last two wars, this town fortunately remains beautifully preserved. The main square, the Place de la République, is the site of an outdoor market on Saturday mornings. On the Rue de la République is the 18th-century *Hôtel de Ville* (Town Hall). A tiny street leads to the Lauter River, with its small bridge and view of the old houses along it.

The *Eglise St-Pierre et St-Paul,* built in the 13th century, is Alsace's largest Gothic church after Strasbourg's cathedral. It has an ornate interior of pink stone, with vestiges of frescoes (the 40-foot-tall *St. Christopher,* near the apse, is the largest portrait in Europe) and 13th-century stained glass windows. Across the river, on Quai Anselman, is a richly decorated house that dates from 1540.

Five miles (8 km) west of Wissembourg on D3, near the town of Lembach, are the Maginot Line fortifications built by the French between the world wars to protect their northeastern border with Germany. *Le Four à Chaux,* a vast subterranean fortress, is open to visitors from mid-March to mid-November. For information, contact the Lembach *Office de Tourisme* (phone: 88-94-43-16; fax: 88-94-20-04).

BEST EN ROUTE

L'Ange In a 16th-century house, this restaurant is more picturesque outside than in. There are several prix fixe menus as well as many à la carte selections. Closed Tuesday dinner, Wednesdays, and the first two weeks in August. Reservations advised. Major credit cards accepted. 2 Rue de la République, Wissembourg (phone: 88-94-12-11). Moderate.

Au Cygne The main hotel has 11 modest rooms, and there are five pretty rooms in the annex next door. There's also a restaurant. Hotel closed February and the first two weeks of July; restaurant closed only Wednesdays and Thursday lunch. 3 Rue du Sel, Wissembourg (phone: 88-94-00-16; fax: 88-54-38-28). Inexpensive.

En Route from Wissembourg Follow village-dotted D263 south toward Haguenau. Halfway there you can detour onto D243 to visit Betschdorf, known for its handsome dark blue-and-gray stoneware. The village has a pottery museum (4 Rue de Kuhlendorf; phone: 88-54-48-07), which is open daily from *Easter* through October, and several shops sell the stoneware.

Six miles (10 km) southeast through Haguenau Forest on D344 is Soufflenheim, Alsace's other great pottery center, famed for its brown-and-yellow earthenware baking and serving dishes. The local *Office de Tourisme* (phone: 88-86-74-90) organizes visits to the many potters' workshops daily, year-round. From Soufflenheim take N63 9 miles (14 km) west to Haguenau.

HAGUENAU The city itself is of interest mainly for its museums and church. In a restored 15th-century building, the *Musée Alsacien* (1 Pl. Joseph-Thierry; phone: 88-73-30-41) has beautiful furniture collections and pottery and metal household objects on the first floor, and a re-created potter's studio and some examples of Betschdorf pottery upstairs. The museum is closed Saturdays, Sundays, and Tuesday mornings. There's also the *Musée Historique* (9 Rue du Maréchal-Foch; phone: 88-93-79-22; fax: 88-93-48-12), whose archaeological collections include items from Bronze and Iron Age tombs in the Haguenau Forest, Roman-era bronze objects, books printed in the 15th and 16th centuries, and an exhibit devoted to the history of the town. It's closed Saturday and Sunday mornings year-round, Tuesdays from September through June, and Tuesday mornings in July and August.

The Romanesque/Gothic *Eglise St-Nicolas* boasts magnificent 18th-century woodwork on the organ and choir stalls; the chapels have several intriguing woodcarvings of religious subjects.

BEST EN ROUTE

Barberousse Robust regional cuisine—meat dishes like *salade de langue et cervelle de veau* (salad of veal tongue and brains) and *tête de veau ravigote* (calf's head in a vinaigrette dressing)—as well as fresh fish from the local market characterize this family-run restaurant. Dine on the outdoor terrace during the warmer months. Closed Sunday dinner, Mondays, the last week in July, and the first two weeks in August. Reservations advised. Major credit cards accepted. 8 Pl. Barberousse, Haguenau (phone: 88-73-31-09; fax: 88-73-45-14). Inexpensive.

En Route from Haguenau Take N63 18 miles (29 km) to return to Strasbourg.

ROUTE DU VIN

STRASBOURG For a detailed report on the city, its sights, its hotels, and its restaurants, see *Strasbourg* in THE CITIES.

En Route from Strasbourg Take N4 west for 12 miles (19 km) to Marlenheim, where the Route du Vin (Wine Road) begins. The scenery changes as the road nears, then veers from, the mountains. The villages along the way are characterized by structures with half-timbered façades and quirky roofs. The well-marked road winds south, zigzagging back and forth across N422.

Alsace's wine villages are completely hidden from these main arteries. The vineyards of this region bear little resemblance to France's other wine-producing regions, primarily because the area is so mountainous. The wineries welcome visitors, and all along the road stands offer free tastings and sell bottled wines to travelers.

From Marlenheim, before rejoining D422 south, take a brief detour via D142 west and D625 east through Wangen and Westhoffen to Molsheim. These are typical wine villages, with old houses and winding, narrow streets that climb the hillsides.

BEST EN ROUTE

Hostellerie Le Cerf This comfortable 15-room hotel has a fine two-Michelin-star restaurant serving imaginative adaptations of many regional favorites, including game, foie gras, and several stews of fish and fowl. Restaurant closed Tuesdays and Wednesdays. 30 Rue du Général-de-Gaulle, Marlenheim (phone: 88-87-73-73; fax: 88-87-68-08). Expensive to moderate.

MOLSHEIM A lovely town, it clings to the left bank of the Bruche River, at the foot of the Vosges. Visit the *Metzig,* a Renaissance building on Place de l'Hôtel-de-Ville with the steeply pitched roof and dormer windows typical of Rhenish architecture; a double staircase leads to a central door surmounted by a fanciful clock tower. Built in the 16th century by the local butchers' corporation, it now houses a restaurant. On the Place de l'Eglise is a former Jesuit seminary, built in 1618; inside are elaborate stucco decorations and a richly sculpted pulpit. Lovely houses line the Rue de Strasbourg: One is decorated with sculpted heads of people and animals.

BEST EN ROUTE

Père Benoît At this family-run 60-room hotel on the site of an 18th-century farmhouse, Alsatian specialties such as *tarte flambée* are served in front of a log fire under the vaulted ceiling of what used to be the cellar. Closed *Christmas* through *New Year's;* restaurant also closed the first two weeks of July, Monday and Saturday lunch, and Sundays. MasterCard and Visa accepted. East of Molsheim via A352, and five minutes from the Strasbourg airport, at 34 Rte. de Strasbourg, Entzheim (phone: 88-68-98-00; fax: 88-68-64-56). Moderate to inexpensive.

En Route from Molsheim Take D422 and D35 for 4½ miles (7 km) to Rosheim.

ROSHEIM This Romanesque town nestles in a verdant, sweeping valley. On Rue du Général-de-Gaulle are some of Alsace's oldest houses, made of gray stone with curious, tiny windows; the oldest house, nicknamed "House of the Heathen," dates from around 1170. The 12th-century *Eglise St-Pierre et St-Paul* is a masterpiece of Romanesque church architecture, with remarkable sculptures. It is normally locked to prevent vandalism, but you can get the key from the baker across the street. The ancient gateways to the town remain, as do some of the ramparts. The town also produces rouge d'Ottrott, one of Alsace's few red wines. The Rosheim *Office de Tourisme* is in the *Hôtel de Ville* (Town Hall) on the Place de la République (phone: 88-50-75-38).

En Route from Rosheim Continue south for 4 miles (6 km) to Obernai.

OBERNAI This completely preserved town is the most beautiful on this part of the Route du Vin. The ramparts and towers date from the Middle Ages, the *Hôtel de Ville* (Town Hall) and belfry from the Renaissance. The *Hôtel de Ville,* built of golden local stone, marks the beginning of a passageway lined with galleries. The old *Halle aux Blés* (Wheat Market) is topped by a huge stork's nest. *Urban,* a pastry shop on the Place du Marché, has windows full of *kugelhopf,* the buttery circular cake so popular in this region. About 300 feet down Route du Général-Gouraud is *Gross,* another fine pastry shop. Local celebrations include the *Obernai C'est la Fête,* an annual folkloric festival held the third weekend of July, and the yearly harvest festival that takes place the third weekend of October. Every year on December 13, the *Feast of St. Odilia,* the patron saint of Alsace, attracts pilgrims to nearby Mont Sainte Odile from all over the region.

BEST EN ROUTE

Cour d'Alsace This elegant, 43-room country hotel is housed in an ensemble of 16th- and 17th-century antiques-filled structures. Restaurant closed Sunday dinner. 3 Rue de Gail, Obernai (phone: 88-95-07-00; fax: 88-95-19-21). Expensive.

Le Parc Fifty spacious rooms, saunas, a gymnasium, and indoor and outdoor pools are offered at this hostelry. Try the restaurant's sumptuous lunch buffet on

Sunday, or one of its many updated Alsatian specialties and its peerless selection of eaux-de-vie any day. Closed December; restaurant also closed Sunday dinner and Mondays. 169 Route d'Ottrott, Obernai (phone: 88-95-50-08; fax: 88-95-37-29). Expensive to moderate.

La Halle aux Blés Perhaps the prettiest restaurant in town, it has a brasserie on the main floor and a more elegant room upstairs. Reservations unnecessary. MasterCard and Visa accepted. In the old *Halle aux Blés* on Pl. du Marché, Obernai (phone: 88-95-56-09; fax: 88-95-27-70). Moderate to inexpensive.

Les Vosges This small place offers 20 convenient and clean, if modest, rooms. Restaurant closed the last three weeks in January, the last two weeks in June, and Sunday dinner and Mondays off-season. MasterCard and Visa accepted. 5 Pl. de la Gare, Obernai (phone: 88-95-53-78; fax: 88-49-92-65). Inexpensive.

En Route from Obernai Proceed south on the Route du Vin for 18 miles (29 km) toward Sélestat, stopping off at Barr, where an annual wine fair is held in mid-July and a harvest fair in early October. For information, inquire at the *Office de Tourisme* (Pl. Hôtel-de-Ville; phone: 88-08-66-65; fax: 88-08-57-27). Also stop off at Andlau, whose mostly 12th-century abbey is sculpted with fantastical figures.

Aficionados of eaux-de-vie might want to stop at one of the region's many distilleries. The most prestigious are around the town of Villé, about 10 miles (16 km) west of the Route du Vin on D424 between Barr and Sélestat. Villé's tourist office (Pl. du Marché; phone: 88-57-11-69) will supply a list of distilleries. *Meyblum* (1 mile/1.6 km from Villé in Albé; phone: 88-57-12-71; fax: 88-57-26-28) and *Nusbaumer* (4 miles/6 km from Villé in Steige; phone: 88-57-16-53; fax: 88-57-05-79) offer visits with free tastings daily throughout the year. From Villé D424 east leads to Sélestat.

BEST EN ROUTE

Hostellerie La Cheneaudière This Relais & Châteaux member is the epitome of rural luxury; the 25 elegant rooms and seven suites all have picture windows with magnificent views of the pine-covered Vosges Mountains. The one-Michelin-star restaurant features a remarkable wine list. The beautiful pool complex has a wood-beamed cathedral ceiling and a whirlpool bath. Closed January and February. In the tiny hilltop village of Colroy-la-Roche, west of Villé on hilly D424 (phone: 88-97-61-64; fax: 88-47-21-73). Very expensive to expensive.

Arnold An appealing, Tudor-style, 28-room inn with antique furnishings and a good restaurant, it's set beautifully in the middle of vineyards. The hotel has recently been refurbished, but the lovely antiques have been retained.

Restaurant closed Sunday dinner and Mondays. About halfway between Obernai and Sélestat on Route D335, 1 mile (1.6 km) west of D422, in Itterswiller (phone: 88-85-50-58; fax: 88-85-55-54). Expensive to moderate.

SÉLESTAT A mostly modern town on the left bank of the Ill River, Sélestat has two lovely churches. The 12th-century pink sandstone *Eglise Ste-Foy,* in the center of town, is considered one of the best examples of Romanesque churches in Alsace. Next to it is the *Eglise St-Georges* (dating from the 13th to the 15th century), with stained glass windows executed by Max Ingrand. Sélestat was once the seat of a flourishing university, and the *Bibliothèque Humaniste* (Humanities Library; phone: 88-92-03-24), founded in 1452, is rich in rare manuscripts. Among the library's treasures are a seventh-century Merovingian dictionary, some 2,000 15th-century Humanist works, and the *Cosmographiae Introductio,* a document drawn up in 1507 in the Alsatian town of St-Dié, in which the word "America" was first used in print to identify the Western Hemisphere. The library is open year-round.

Eight miles (13 km) west of Sélestat on D159 is the *Château du Haut-Koenigsbourg* (phone: 88-82-50-60), one of the most visited castles in France. The road climbs through two parks: *Monkey Mountain* and *Eagle's Park.* The château, which belonged to a family of Swiss counts, dates from feudal times, but it was completely restored in 1908 by Kaiser Wilhelm II, who used a rather heavy hand. As a result, the present architecture suggests the early 20th century rather than the Middle Ages. The castle sits high—some 2,000 feet—above the Rhine plain on a rocky outcrop, thus commanding a fine view of the surrounding vineyards and neighboring Germany. It is open year-round.

BEST EN ROUTE

Abbaye de la Pommeraie This Relais & Châteaux member, owned and managed by the François family, is an 18th-century Cistercian abbey converted to a charming and elegant, antiques-filled hotel with 10 rooms and four suites. The restaurant is also fine. Restaurant closed Sunday dinner. 8 Av. Foch, Sélestat (phone: 88-92-07-84; fax: 88-92-08-71). Very expensive.

La Vieille Tour In a lovely old half-timbered house, this restaurant has warmth and good old-fashioned Alsatian cuisine. Closed Mondays and mid-February through the first week of March. Reservations advised. MasterCard and Visa accepted. 8 Rue de la Jauge, Sélestat (phone: 88-92-15-02; fax: 88-92-19-42). Moderate to inexpensive.

En Route from Sélestat Leave the Route du Vin by crossing the Ill River on D424. Then head 9 miles (14 km) southeast to Marckolsheim, where the *Mémorial-Musée de la Ligne Maginot du Rhin* (Memorial Museum of the Maginot Line; Rte. du Rhin; phone: 88-92-57-79) is installed in a World War II bunker. Among the exhibits here are a Sherman tank, French and German arms, and maps of the area showing the French defense strategy. The museum is closed mid-November through mid-March and lunch hours from mid-June through mid-September; open Sundays and national holidays only from mid-March through mid-June and from mid-September through mid-November.

To rejoin the Route du Vin, head west on D10 and D106 to Ribeauvillé.

RIBEAUVILLÉ This bustling town is a center for wine making, as the statue of a vintner at its entrance suggests. Leave your car here and explore the Grand' Rue, the main street, which is lined with old buildings. One house, inscribed "Ave Maria," has a central oriel window flanked by two caryatids, one representing an angel, the other representing the Virgin Mary, together portraying the Annunciation.

The *Chapelle de l'Hôpital* dates from the 14th century. The *Halle aux Blés* (Wheat Market), a 16th-century Gothic building with two arches, leads to the tiny Rue des Tanneurs, bordered with lovely houses. At No. 9 is the eau-de-vie distillery of Jean-Paul Metté (phone: 89-73-65-88), who welcomes visitors weekday afternoons. *John,* a pastry shop (58 Grand' Rue), sells *kugelhopf* by the slice. Don't miss the outlet store of the *Manufacture d'Impression sur Etoffes* (19 Rte. de Ste-Marie-aux-Mines; phone: 89-73-74-74), which produces extraordinarily beautiful fabrics. The street widens at the *Hôtel de Ville* (Town Hall), a lovely 18th-century structure. Opposite is the *Eglise des Augustins,* with its multicolored tile roof. At the square's edge is the *Tour des Bouchers,* a 13th-century belfry. The street and the town end at the Place de la République, with a Renaissance fountain bearing the coat of arms of Ribeauvillé. *Pfifferday* (Pipers Day), a folklore festival, is held the first Sunday in September; there's also a wine festival on the next to last Sunday in July.

BEST EN ROUTE

Clos St-Vincent A lovely place with 15 units and a restaurant, it is set in the vineyards above Ribeauvillé. Closed mid-November to mid-March; restaurant also closed Tuesdays and Wednesdays. MasterCard and Visa accepted. Rte. de Bergheim (phone: 89-73-67-65; fax: 89-73-32-20). Very expensive.

Auberge de l'Ill On the bank of the Ill, with a sweeping green lawn bordered by feathery willow trees, this ambrosial three-Michelin-star restaurant is a romantic spot indeed—book well in advance. Closed Mondays (except lunch April through October), Tuesdays, and the month of February. Reservations necessary. Major credit cards accepted. For additional details, see *Haute Gastronomie* in DIVERSIONS. Rue de Collonges, Illhaeusern (phone: 89-71-83-23; fax: 89-71-82-83). Expensive.

Les Vosges Clean and modern, this restaurant (with one Michelin star) features an extensive menu of traditional regional cuisine with a three-course fixed-price meal. There also are 18 modest but comfortable guestrooms. Closed February; restaurant also closed Mondays and Tuesday lunch. Reservations necessary. Major credit cards accepted. 2 Grand' Rue (phone: 89-73-61-39; fax: 89-73-34-21). Restaurant expensive; hotel moderate.

Le Ménestrel Alsace's gently sloping vineyards surround this modern, flower-studded, 28-room inn. There's no restaurant. Closed February to mid-March. Just outside town, at 27 Av. du Général-de-Gaulle (phone: 89-73-80-52; fax: 89-73-32-39). Moderate.

La Tour Run by a wine-making family, this charming 35-room hotel occupies what used to be a winery. There's no restaurant. Closed January to mid-March. 1 Rue de la Mairie (phone: 89-73-72-73; fax: 89-73-38-74). Inexpensive.

Zum Pfifferhüs An appealing *winstub* in a landmark 16th-century building, it serves excellent *choucroute*. Closed Wednesdays, Thursdays, the first three weeks in March, the first two weeks in July, *Christmas,* and *New Year's Day*. Reservations unnecessary. MasterCard and Visa accepted. 14 Grand' Rue (phone: 89-73-62-28). Inexpensive.

En Route from Ribeauvillé Take D3 south for 2 miles (3 km) to Riquewihr. This road, and beyond it as far as Kaysersberg, was the scene of intense fighting during World War II, which accounts for the abundance of memorials and graves. On the way you'll pass a stork preserve, part of a program to restock the area with these harbingers of good fortune. Generally regarded as the symbol of Alsace, the stork has been threatened with extinction due to the disappearance of the marshes, its natural habitat.

RIQUEWIHR This entire picture-postcard village is a historical monument, and Riquewihr's *Société d'Archéologie* publishes an excellent map showing 33 buildings of interest; ask for it at the tourist office (2 Rue de la Première Armée; phone: 89-47-80-80; fax: 89-49-04-40) or at any bookstore or hotel. At the beginning of the cobblestone main street, the Grand' Rue, is the *Musée des Postes et Télécommunications*. Formerly the castle of the Dukes of Wurtemberg-Montbéliard, it features an exhibit explaining how the mail system was created by Roman Emperor Augustus to transmit his orders throughout the empire, which included Alsace. Beautiful wrought-iron signs, old wagons, telephones, and mailmen's uniforms are among the other attractions. The museum is closed mid-November through the first week of April (phone: 89-47-93-80).

The Grand' Rue is lined with extraordinary houses, completely preserved; many are now restaurants and tearooms. No. 18, dating from 1535, has a courtyard surrounded by a sculpted balcony. Vaulted passageways lead to tiny streets and hidden courtyards. In the Cour des Vignerons the *Maison Ancienne de Vignerons* (Old Wine Makers' Guildhall) is decorated with a dazzling array of window boxes brimming with flowers. The Rue des Cerfs, marked by a stag's head, has many signs welcoming guests to bed and breakfast accommodations.

The *Dolder,* a 13th-century guard tower set into the city walls, houses a museum of old money and arms (phone: 89-47-80-80). The walls themselves formed a double ring of protection for the town, and the old gates and iron doors are perfectly preserved.

Among the town's many wineries open for tastings is *Hugel et Fils* (phone: 89-47-92-15; fax: 89-49-00-10), a highly respected producer of riesling and gewürztraminer (for additional details on the *caves,* see *Most Visitable Vineyards* in DIVERSIONS). Because Riquewihr attracts so many tourists, avoid it during the summer, except in the early morning and late afternoon. August is a particularly bad time for a visit, as nearly everything is closed.

BEST EN ROUTE

Auberge du Schoenenbourg Enjoy one-Michelin-star Alsatian food with nouvelle cuisine touches and gaze out at the vineyard stretching behind the restaurant. The wines served are made from grapes grown here. Closed Tuesday lunch, Wednesdays, Thursday lunch off-season, and mid-January to mid-February. Reservations necessary. MasterCard and Visa accepted. 2 Rue de la Piscine, Riquewihr (phone: 89-47-92-28; fax: 89-47-89-84). Expensive to moderate.

St. Nicolas Once a private residence, it is now a comfortable 34-room hotel, complete with a restaurant. 2 Rue St-Nicolas, Riquewihr (phone: 89-49-01-51; fax: 89-49-04-36). Inexpensive.

Au Tire Bouchon Hearty local food is served amid lovely decor. Closed late February to mid-March. Reservations advised, Major credit cards accepted. 29 Rue du Général-de-Gaulle, Riquewihr (phone: 89-47-91-61; fax: 89-47-99-39). Inexpensive.

En Route from Riquewihr Continue south on D3 and D10 and then west to Kaysersberg, 7 miles (11 km) away. The road, which climbs into the hillier vineyards, is marked with military cemeteries and memorials to the two world wars. In Mittelwihr the *Mur des Fleurs* (a flower-decked wall at the entrance to the town) was covered in red, white, and blue flowers during the Occupation as a symbol of Alsatian fidelity to France. The *Nécropole Nationale* (National Cemetery) at Sigolsheim, which looks out over the vine-covered hills, is a burial ground for French soldiers who died in World War II.

KAYSERSBERG Known mainly as the birthplace of Albert Schweitzer (in 1875), this is a delightful wine village, filled with medieval houses and bustling farm activity. The southern bank of the meandering Weiss River affords a good view of the ruins of the ancient castle perched above the town, the elegant 16th-century *Hôtel de Ville* (Town Hall), and the Romanesque *Eglise de la Ste-Croix,* hugged by tiny streets (Rues Eglise, Hôpital, Gendarmerie) bordered with ancient houses. Rue du Général-de-Gaulle, also called the Grand' Rue, has its fair share of lovely old houses as well. The quirky architecture here is silhouetted against a pine forest. Cross over on the fortified bridge, which dates from 1511 and incorporates a minuscule chapel.

The tourist office is at 37 Rue du Général-de-Gaulle (phone: 89-78-22-78), right behind *Ste-Croix.* Next door is the tiny *Chapelle St-Michel,* which dates from 1463. To visit, knock on the door of house No. 43, to the left of the chapel; once inside make a point of seeing the interesting 14th-century crucifix in the choir. Local festivals include the *Fête du Vin* (Wine Festival), held the last weekend in September, and *Noël à Kaysersberg,* the annual *Christmas* fête, held four weekends before December 25.

Schweitzer's birthplace (126 Rue du Général-de-Gaulle; phone: 89-47-36-55) is now a cultural center in his honor; it is closed November through April. The *Musée Historique* (64 Rue du Général-de-Gaulle; phone: 89-47-10-16) features some notable works of religious art, regional archaeological finds, and documents of Kaysersberg's famous sons, including Jean Geiler and Mathias Zell. It is open daily in July and August; open weekends only in June, September, and October; closed the rest of the year.

In Lapoutroie, west of Kaysersberg on N415, is a museum dedicated to the fiery Alsatian liquor. The *Musée des Eaux de Vie* (85 Rue du Général-Dufieux; phone: 89-47-50-26) is open daily; closed lunch hours.

BEST EN ROUTE

Résidence Chambard A comfortable, modern 20-room hotel, it has conveniences that include direct-dial telephones. Its gracious one-Michelin-star dining room offers specialties such as foie gras cooked in cabbage leaves. Closed most of March; restaurant also closed Mondays and Tuesday lunch. 9-13 Rue du Général-de-Gaulle, Kaysersberg (phone: 89-47-10-17; fax: 89-47-35-03). Expensive.

Château This simple but acceptable eight-room lodging has a restaurant. Closed mid-February through mid-March, Thursdays, and the first two weeks of July. MasterCard and Visa accepted. 38 Rue du Général-de-Gaulle, Kaysersberg (phone: 89-78-24-33). Inexpensive.

En Route from Kaysersberg Through Ammerschwihr and Niedermorschwihr, the Route du Vin overlooks the entire plain of Alsace. The *Caveau Morakopf* is a fine *winstub* in Niedermorschwihr. Nearby, also in Niedermorschwihr, the *Maison Ferber* pastry shop (18 Rue des Epis; phone: 89-27-05-69) has probably the best *kugelhopf* in Alsace.

In the town of Turckheim, a few miles farther south, a watchman in Renaissance dress patrols the streets in summer, sword in one hand, lantern in the other. The three ancient entries into town remain: *Brand Gate* straddles Rue des Vignerons, while *Munster Gate* and *France Gate,* with its huge tower, are both just off the quay beside the Fecht River.

Take D10 west to Munster, where the famous cheese is made. Scattered nearby are *fermes auberges,* farms open to the public that serve simple meals for low prices. An excellent guide to the Vallée de Munster is available free at most tourist offices in the area. From Munster take D417 12 miles (19 km) to Colmar.

BEST EN ROUTE

Aux Armes de France This restaurant's traditional French cuisine has earned it one Michelin star; don't miss the outstanding foie gras. There also are 10 moderately priced rooms. Restaurant closed Wednesdays and Thursday lunch. Reservations necessary. American Express, Diners Club, and Visa accepted. 1 Grand' Rue, Ammerschwihr (phone: 89-47-10-12; fax: 89-47-38-12). Expensive.

COLMAR Alsace's most beautiful city, now lovingly restored, Colmar was once the royal residence of Charlemagne. Since the Middle Ages it has housed artists and artisans, and its graceful streets and often spectacular architecture still reflect this past.

Begin at La Petite Venise (Little Venice), a restored neighborhood of half-timbered houses, shops, and artist's studios perched along the banks of the Lauch River. Pont St-Pierre overlooks the tranquil scene. Wander along any of the picturesque streets toward the *Ancienne Douane* (Old Customs House), a large, 15th-century arcaded building with a roof tiled in a colorful diamond pattern; also known as the *Koifhus,* this landmark now is a conference center.

Directly north is the Quartier des Tanneurs, where leatherworkers once labored; the entire neighborhood has been restored and converted to a pedestrian zone, as has most of Old Colmar. Many distinguished buildings are crammed into the tiny streets, and all are well marked in French and German. The *Office de Tourisme* (4 Rue Unterlinden; phone: 89-20-68-92; fax: 89-41-34-13) and bookshops can provide excellent maps and guides in English. From mid-April to mid-October the tourist office sponsors a mini-train that travels a 50-minute route to the city's main attractions. It leaves several times a day from the Quai de la Sinn, in front of the *Musée d'Unterlinden* (see below).

The *Maison Pfister,* built midway along the lovely Rue des Marchands in 1537 and restored in 1971, displays an imaginatively painted exterior of emperors, allegorical figures, and animals. Five swooping arches grace the ground level, and a spiral staircase leads to the upper floors. A large oriel window overlooks the outdoor café in the plaza below, and the third-floor balcony overflows with pink, purple, and red impatiens. A jaunty green turret caps the impressive creation. Across the street is the *Maison Schongauer;* the house once belonged to the family of the 15th-century artist Martin Schongauer.

The *Eglise des Dominicains,* built in the 14th century of warm, golden stone, houses a magnificent altar painting by Schongauer, *The Virgin in the Rose Bush* (1473); the stained glass windows deserve special attention as well (open mid-March to mid-November). The restored 14th-century *Eglise St-Martin* has a pink stone exterior with an intricately sculpted portal depicting the Last Judgment.

Entire books have been written on Colmar's *Musée d'Unterlinden* (Pl. de la Sinn; phone: 89-20-15-25), the most visited museum in France outside of those in Paris. Its two major treasures are the *Issenheim Altarpiece* by Matthias Grünewald and the 24-panel Passion series by Schongauer. The altar is an artistic curiosity, its paintings alternately expressionist and surrealist. Chamber pots and dirty linen are depicted next to angels and virgins. The altar's central panel is flanked by side panels that open in an intricate design; a *maquette* (model) in the gallery demonstrates how the work looks both open and closed. The museum, in a 13th-century convent with a vine-covered cloister, has a delightful collection of Alsatian folk art—paintings of peasant scenes, folk costumes, unique musical instruments, arms, and ceramics—on the second floor. Ask the guard to turn on the sophisticated animated toys. The museum is open daily, April through October; closed lunch hours and Tuesdays, November through March, and on major holidays. There's an admission charge (phone: 89-41-89-23).

Scattered throughout Colmar's squares are statues by Auguste Bartholdi, the sculptor of the *Statue of Liberty,* who was born here in 1834. A museum in his family's home (30 Rue des Marchands; phone: 89-41-90-60) displays many of his works. Closed lunch hours in April, Tuesdays in January and February. There's an admission charge.

Every year Colmar holds a week-long wine festival that encompasses the *Feast of the Assumption* (August 15). A newer annual tradition is the *Festival International de Musique de Colmar,* held for 15 days in early July and featuring a week of classical concerts by world-class visiting groups and soloists. Colmar's *Festiga,* an international festival of gastronomy, is held in March in even-numbered years; it hosts chefs and participants from all over France and other countries. For information on special events, contact the *Office de Tourisme* (see above).

Shopping in Colmar can be a distinct pleasure, especially if you're in the market for local comestibles. The Rue des Boulangers has the greatest concentration of food shops, including *Glasser* (No. 18) and *Sigmann* (No. 6), both charcuteries, and *Alou* (No. 16), which carries fresh produce,

Alsatian wines, and eaux-de-vie. On nearby Rue des Têtes are *La Ferme* (No. 34), a cheese shop, and *Au Bon Nègre* (No. 9), which stocks exotic coffees and teas, along with their appropriate pots and cups.

BEST EN ROUTE

Au Fer Rouge Tucked into a charming house, this restaurant has been awarded a Michelin star. It has an inventive young chef, a good wine list, and a luxurious yet cozy atmosphere. Closed Sunday dinner, Mondays, and the first two weeks of January. Reservations necessary. Major credit cards accepted. In the center of town, at 52 Grand' Rue, Colmar (phone: 89-41-37-24; fax: 84-23-82-24). Expensive.

Le Maréchal At the water's edge, this sprawling collection of half-timbered houses with flower-strewn balconies and crooked stairways has a quirky charm. Its 30 rooms, which have been remodeled, are named for classical composers, and each is decorated differently. The paneled, candlelit restaurant overlooks the water. In La Petite Venise, at 4-6 Pl. des Six-Montagnes-Noires, Colmar (phone: 89-41-60-32; fax: 89-24-59-40). Expensive.

Schillinger Caring service and regional specialties and game dishes, such as partridge on a bed of *choucroute,* foie gras, and sumptuous desserts, have earned this restaurant two Michelin stars. Closed Sunday dinner, Mondays, late January to early February, and July. Reservations advised. Major credit cards accepted. 16 Rue Stanislas, Colmar (phone: 89-41-43-17; fax: 89-24-28-87). Expensive.

Maison des Têtes At this simple restaurant in an extraordinary 17th-century landmark building, dozens of tiny carved heads of people and mythical animals adorn the façade, imploring you to enter. Closed Sunday dinner and Mondays. Reservations necessary. Major credit cards accepted. 19 Rue des Têtes, Colmar (phone: 89-24-43-43; fax: 89-24-58-34). Expensive to moderate.

Terminus-Bristol This old-fashioned hotel has 70 remodeled rooms; ask for a deluxe room to experience the best of these high-style *chambres.* The restaurant, *Rendez-vous de Chasse,* offers one of the town's most refined and inventive menus. (A second, less formal restaurant next door, *L'Auberge,* serves traditional fare.) 7 Pl. de la Gare, Colmar (phone: 89-23-59-59; 89-41-10-10, restaurant; fax: 89-23-92-26). Expensive to moderate.

Chez Hansi Alsatian specialties, including the best *choucroute* in Colmar, form the mainstay of the menu here. The ambience rounds out the experience, right down to the waitresses' uniforms, which include an elephantine headdress called a *Schlupkapp.* Closed Wednesday dinner, Thursdays, and January through mid-February. Reservations advised. MasterCard and Visa accepted. 23 Rue des Marchands, Colmar (phone: 89-41-37-84). Moderate.

St-Martin With its superb Renaissance staircase, this inn has 12 modern rooms and 12 older, simple but comfortable *chambres* from which to choose. There's no restaurant. Closed January and February. In the center of the old town, at 38 Grand' Rue, Colmar (phone: 89-24-11-51; fax: 89-23-47-78). Moderate.

Caveau St-Pierre At this *winstub* you can admire the scenery, fill up on hearty fare, and imbibe at leisure. Closed Sunday dinner and Mondays, *Christmas* through *New Year's,* late February to early March, and the first two weeks of July. Reservations unnecessary. MasterCard and Visa accepted. Smack on the water in La Petite Venise, at 24 Rue de la Herse, Colmar (phone: 89-41-99-33; fax: 89-23-94-33). Moderate to inexpensive.

S'Parisser Stewwele The most atmospheric *winstub* in town, decorated with etchings by Hansi, the Norman Rockwell of Alsace. A lively crowd of upscale locals comes to drink or indulge in Alsatian classics and such dishes as *bibeleskäs,* an herbed cheese. Closed Tuesdays, three weeks in February, the last week in June, and the third week in November. Reservations unnecessary. No credit cards accepted. 4 Pl. Jeanne-d'Arc, Colmar (phone: 89-41-42-33; fax: 89-41-37-99). Moderate to inexpensive.

Unterlinden A classic menu of typically Alsatian dishes—including *tarte à l'oignon* and hot munster cheese—is prepared under the careful guidance of Madame Stockel. Closed Sunday dinner, Tuesdays, and the last two weeks in January. Reservations unnecessary. MasterCard and Visa accepted. Across from the *Musée d'Unterlinden,* at 2 Rue Unterlinden (phone: 89-41-18-73). Moderate to inexpensive.

En Route from Colmar Take the Route du Vin from Wintzenheim (west of Colmar) and Wettolsheim to Eguisheim, another perfectly preserved wine village set into the vine-crested hills. The main square, with a lovely Renaissance fountain, is the center of a web of circular streets and alleys crammed full of old houses. The imposing pink sandstone towers, ruins of the castle built seven centuries ago, dominate the hill. Shops line the main square; the best buys are in cookware, especially copper utensils and pottery. *Léon Beyer* (phone: 89-41-41-05; fax: 89-23-93-63), a name that evokes some of the region's most beloved wines, has a tasting room in town (for additional details, see *Most Visitable Vineyards* in DIVERSIONS).

The village of Husseren-les-Châteaux, the highest point on the Route du Vin, commands an excellent view of the entire valley and of Eguisheim, to the north. Hattstatt, once a fortified town, has an interesting church that comprises Romanesque, Renaissance, and Baroque styles.

Continue south for 9 miles (14 km), through Gueberschwihr and Pfaffenheim, to Rouffach.

Caveau d'Eguisheim Renowned for its *choucroute,* frogs' legs, *tarte à l'oignon, kugel-hopf,* and other regional specialties, this homey dining place is especially welcoming to visitors. It also features wines of the village, including those from *Léon Beyer.* The building dates from 1603. Open daily, July through October; closed January and February; closed Wednesdays the rest of the year. Reservations necessary. Major credit cards accepted. 3 Pl. du Château-St-Léon, Eguisheim (phone: 89-41-08-89; fax: 89-23-79-99). Expensive to moderate.

ROUFFACH The *Eglise Notre-Dame de l'Assomption,* begun in the Romanesque style in the 11th century and completed several centuries later, was built in the same pink stone as Strasbourg's *Cathédrale Notre-Dame.* Plan to visit at the end of the day, when the sunlight filters through its lovely rose window. On the square outside the church is the 16th-century *Halle aux Blés* (Wheat Market) and an old *Hôtel de Ville* (Town Hall) with a charming Renaissance façade. The crenelated 13th-century *Tour des Sorcières* (Witches' Tower) wears a stork's nest headdress.

BEST EN ROUTE

Château d'Isenbourg This luxurious, spacious, and utterly hospitable Relais & Châteaux inn sits above the village in the midst of a gracefully landscaped vineyard. Its 37 rooms and three suites are decorated with antiques, and some offer a view of the valley. Amenities include a pool, tennis courts, and a fine, one-Michelin-star restaurant in a vaulted room dating from the 13th century. Closed mid-January to mid-March. MasterCard and Visa accepted. Rouffach (phone: 89-49-63-53; fax: 89-78-53-70). Very expensive.

En Route from Rouffach Take N83 south for 6 miles (10 km) to Guebwiller.

GUEBWILLER Many remarkable old Alsatian houses grace this town, which is the gateway to the Florival, the flower-filled Lauch River Valley. Don't miss 107 Rue Théodore-Deck, with its three-story oriel window. The *Hôtel de Ville* (Town Hall) has a lovely protruding window with geraniums cascading from it, as well as a 16th-century carved Virgin. Note the outstanding Art Nouveau building with winding plant motifs next door.

The triple-towered *Eglise St-Léger,* just off the Rue de la République, was built during the 12th and 13th centuries. Its elegant portal features ribbed arches and bays, and the choir is carved ornately in wood.

En Route from Guebwiller D430 and D431 lead in a roundabout fashion from Guebwiller into the mountains past the Grand Ballon peak to Cernay. Called the Route des Crêtes (roughly, Crest of Ridge Road), this is perhaps the loveliest part of the trip: steep, forested, and spectacularly colored in autumn.

East of Cernay, across N83 via D44, lies Ungersheim. Close to the village is the *Ecomusée* (phone: 89-74-44-74). This open-air museum includes old farms, peasant houses, and other examples of Alsatian architecture that were destined for demolition until a group of students got the idea of dismantling, moving, and carefully reassembling them here. It's open from 9 AM to 7 PM in summer and from 11 AM to 5 PM the rest of the year; closed January and February.

Back in Cernay, take N66 4 miles (6 km) west to Thann.

THANN This village marks the southern end of the Route du Vin. The soaring yellow stone *Collégiale St-Thiébault* (Collegiate Church of St. Theobald) dominates the town, its elegant spire piercing the sky. It was built in stages from 1351 to the end of the 15th century and was restored in 1989. Although the exterior is obscured by scaffolding, this remains the most beautiful Gothic structure in all of Alsace. Inside, the vaults are joined by painted keys. The extraordinary carved wooden choir stalls display sculptures of monsters and humans in minute detail. Small angels peer from the ceiling, painted at the cross of the vaults' ribs.

En Route from Thann Take N66 east for 12 miles (19 km) to Mulhouse, almost at the Swiss border.

MULHOUSE (pronounced Mu-*looze*) Compared to the delightful wine villages and the seductive architecture of Colmar, this is an ugly, predominantly modern city, principally a border town with thriving chemical plants. Yet travelers may prefer to stay here rather than next door, in pricier Switzerland.

Mulhouse does boast five noteworthy museums—of automobiles, history, fine arts, textiles, and railroad cars. The Mulhouse *Office de Tourisme* is at 9 Avenue Maréchal-Foch (phone: 89-45-68-31; fax: 89-45-66-16).

At the edge of town, the *Musée National de l'Automobile* (192 Av. de Colmar; phone: 89-42-29-17) is perhaps Mulhouse's greatest attraction. The former private collection of two Swiss industrialists, the many vintage cars were claimed by the French government in payment of taxes and are now packed into this vast building. For additional details, see *Memorable Museums and Monuments* in DIVERSIONS. The museum is closed Tuesdays in winter.

The *Musée Historique* (Pl. de la Réunion; phone: 89-32-59-46), in the beautifully restored 16th-century *Hôtel de Ville* (Town Hall) is a charming blend of the past and present. The museum is filled with costumes, musical instruments, a postcard collection, playing cards, dolls, toy soldiers, and *kugelhopf* molds. Several rooms depicting late 19th-century bourgeois living are furnished with household utensils. The entrance is at ground level to the right of the stairs; admission includes access to the other parts of the *Hôtel de Ville*. The museum is closed Tuesdays and during lunch hour.

In the *Musée des Beaux Arts* (4 Pl. Guillaume-Tell; phone: 89-32-58-46) are 15th-century religious paintings; early Protestant art; works by the School of Cranach, Brueghel the Younger, and Boucher; 19th-century landscapes; academic paintings from local private collections; and contemporary paintings and sculpture. The museum is closed Tuesdays and during lunch hour.

The *Musée de l'Impression des Etoffes* (3 Rue des Bonnes-Gens; phone: 89-45-51-20) is devoted to the art of fabric printing. In summer several Rube Goldbergesque presses demonstrate various printing techniques. The archives, which contain some four million samples of fabric and original designs, are an important reference point for designers and couturiers. There's also an outstanding collection of handkerchiefs, of which the gift shop sells copies. The museum is closed mid-September through December and Tuesdays from January through May. Nearby, at the corner of the Rue du Sauvage and Rue de Sinne, the *Charcuterie Alsacienne* beckons museumgoers with a dozen varieties of homemade sausage.

A huge train station houses the *Musée Français du Chemin de Fer* (on the edge of town, at 2 Rue Alfred-de-Glehn; phone: 89-42-25-67), in which old locomotives rest on six tracks. All the railroad cars, some dating from the 1800s, have been beautifully restored and painted. On display are three kinds of steam engines and the first electric train, from 1900. One car, from the prestigious *Train Bleu*, has gleaming brass and crystal figures. Another, from 1856, was used by Napoleon III's aides and was decorated by the architect Viollet-le-Duc. The museum is open daily.

BEST EN ROUTE

Parc This splendid Art Deco establishment offers luxurious surroundings and attentive service. Many of the 73 nicely appointed guestrooms overlook *Parc Steinbach. Charlie's Bar* attracts a lively crowd of locals; there is also a restaurant, *Le Park's,* that serves classic regional French cooking. Downtown, at 26 Rue de la Sinne, Mulhouse (phone: 89-66-12-22; fax: 89-66-42-44). Very expensive.

Poste This fine, one-Michelin-star restaurant features traditional Alsatian ingredients prepared with a twist, as in *tartar d'anguille fumée, petits blinis,* and *pyramide de choucroute tiède émulsion à la moutarde* (smoked eel tartare, *blinis,* and a warm sauerkraut pyramid with mustard sauce). Closed Sunday dinner, Mondays, and three weeks in August. Reservations advised. Most major credit cards accepted. Just outside Mulhouse at 7 Rue Géneral-de-Gaulle, Riedisheim (phone: 89-44-07-71; fax: 89-64-32-79). Expensive.

Auberge de la Tonnelle The classic French cuisine at this establishment has earned a Michelin star. Closed Wednesdays and for a week in August. Reservations advised. Visa accepted. Just outside Mulhouse at 61 Rue du Maréchal-Joffre, Riedisheim (phone: 89-54-25-77; fax: 89-64-29-85). Expensive.

Novotel Mulhouse-Sausheim In this contemporary 77-room hotel are a grill-type restaurant, a buffet breakfast room, a bar, and an especially pleasant outdoor pool. In Sausheim, 3 miles (5 km) northeast of Mulhouse, on Rue de l'Ile-Napoléon (phone: 89-61-84-84; 800-221-4542; fax: 89-61-77-99). Moderate.

Auberge de Froeningen This quiet, seven-room inn is lovingly run; its homey touches include cheery flower arrangements, an herb garden, and a restaurant that serves one of the most succulent and ample breakfasts in the area. Closed three weeks in January and the last two weeks in August. Four miles (6 km) southwest of Mulhouse, at 2 Rte. d'Illfurth, Froeningen (phone: 89-25-48-48; fax: 89-25-57-33). Moderate to inexpensive.

Winstub Henriette Here is an oasis of Alsatian tradition. Warm wood walls and furnishings provide a charming backdrop for hearty servings of *choucroute* and other regional specialties. More adventurous folks can try the *tête de veau vinaigrette* (calf's head accompanied by a vinaigrette dressing). Closed Saturday dinner, Sundays, and holidays. Reservations unnecessary. Major credit cards accepted. 9 Rue Henriette, Mulhouse (phone: 89-46-27-83; fax: 89-52-51-70). Moderate to inexpensive.

Auberge du Vieux Mulhouse This well-located place offers a variety of prix fixe menus. Closed Sundays. Reservations unnecessary. Major credit cards accepted. Pl. de la Réunion, Mulhouse (phone: 89-45-84-18; fax: 89-45-29-80). Inexpensive.

Lorraine

Although Lorraine has a historical and artistic unity, it is a region of enormous diversity. A land of quiche, quetsch (a variety of plum), and crystal, it contains forests and farms, factories and shops, and two proud, prominent cities: Metz and Nancy. While Lorraine is inextricably linked in people's minds with Alsace, its sister province, it is profoundly different in its geography, architecture, cuisine, and temperament. Indeed, the many parts of Lorraine are strikingly different from one another.

The region is by no means a popular destination for tourists from abroad. The northeastern corner, with its severely depressed mining and steel industries, often is bleak. But Lorraine does have some points of interest and beauty. French campers head for sites in forests and by rivers and lakes throughout the region. In the southeast the countryside of predominantly gently rolling hills rises to the Vosges Mountains, where winter and summer resorts attract French vacationers. The health spas in the south—particularly Vittel and Contrexéville—also have a strong French following. Remnants of Lorraine's rich history, from Roman times through the world wars, provide attractions in the form of churches, châteaux, artworks, and war memorials, and its splendid chief cities merit attention.

A longtime European crossroads, Lorraine first came into prominence as a center of trade and communication between the Mediterranean and northern Europe after the conquest of Gaul by the Romans. The region is bordered on the north by Belgium and Luxembourg and on the northeast by Germany; Switzerland is not far from its southeastern corner. Alsace is to the east, Champagne to the west, and Burgundy just a short way across the tip of Champagne to the south. Today Lorraine's excellent highway system and its railroad lines serve as trunk routes to the east and west of Europe.

Lorraine's name dates from the ninth century. In 843 the Treaty of Verdun divided Charlemagne's huge empire among his three grandsons, one of whom, Lothair, received a section that was named Lotharingia; the word in due course metamorphosed into Lorraine. In addition to Lorraine, Lothair's original allotment included the present Netherlands, Belgium, Luxembourg, Alsace, and parts of Germany.

During the Middle Ages, as the fates of the German ruling families in the area rose and fell, a much-reduced entity known as the Duchy of Lorraine emerged, pockmarked by various independent fiefs—such as the Duchy of Bar and the three bishoprics of Metz, Toul, and Verdun—which the dukes were unable to control.

The French domination of Lorraine dates only from the 16th century, and the formal annexation of Lorraine to France did not take place until 1766. A century later, after the French defeat in the Franco-Prussian War of 1870–71, part of Lorraine passed to Germany with Alsace; it was returned to France after the German defeat in World War I. Except during four years of Nazi occupation, the province has remained French ever since. Throughout these vicissitudes, the sympathies of the people have tended strictly toward Paris (it's no accident that two of the most potent symbols of French patriotism—Joan of Arc and the Cross of Lorraine—are native to the region). German rule caused many Lorrainers to resettle in more western areas of France; and in their place workers from Mediterranean and North African countries came to take advantage of the post–World War II industrial boom.

The route outlined below begins in Verdun, taking in the World War I battlefields and war memorials surrounding the town. From Verdun the route heads east to Metz, although you may choose to take a side trip to Bar-le-Duc first. The hour-long drive to Metz via A4, the toll road, passes through the farmland and forests of the huge *Parc Naturel Régional de Lorraine.* Should you choose the slower D903 to Metz, however, you can take in a few towns and a few more glimpses of the countryside. Then it's south to Nancy, an elegant commercial and intellectual center and the base for side trips to the old town of Toul; the birthplace of Joan of Arc in Domrémy-la-Pucelle; Lunéville, the town famous for its small-scale version of Versailles; and Baccarat, whose name is synonymous with crystal. The final leg of the tour takes you farther south, to Vittel and Contrexéville, and east, to Gérardmer, a lake resort on the western slopes of the Vosges. In Gérardmer you are merely a mountain's crest away from Alsace. Michelin maps No. 57 and No. 62 include the areas covered in this route.

Though Lorraine claims no world class restaurants, you'll find lots of good ones, and there will be plenty of opportunities to taste the local specialties, including quiche. For dessert, there are the famous *madeleines* of Commercy, the macaroons of Boulay and Nancy, and many fresh fruits and berries, including quetsch plums and *mirabelles,* the small yellow plums that are a Metz specialty. The same fruits are distilled into a potent eau-de-vie, the *digestif* of the region. For those who like their fruits sweet and without alcohol, there are the special jams of Bar-le-Duc, made of local *groseilles* (currants).

For a double room per night, with bath but without breakfast, expect to pay $100 or more at an expensive hotel; $75 to $100 at a moderate one; and less than $75 at an inexpensive place. Unless otherwise indicated, all hotels accept major credit cards and are open year-round. Most hotels in the region feature telephones, TV sets, and private baths in all of their rooms. However, some less expensive hotels may have private baths in only some of their rooms; it's a good idea to confirm when making a reservation whether your room has a private bath. Very few hotels, except more modern ones, have air conditioned rooms. Dinner for two will run $100 or more in an expensive restaurant; $70 to $100 in a moderate one; and less than $70 in an inexpensive place. Prices include service but not drinks or tip. Unless otherwise noted, restaurants are open for lunch and dinner. For each location hotels and restaurants are listed alphabetically by price category.

VERDUN Built on the banks of the Meuse River, this former fortified town has played a strategic role in French history. Approached from the west of France, it is the gateway to Lorraine and to the areas of Germany, Luxembourg, and Alsace that lie beyond. Invaders, however, historically have approached Verdun from the east, seeing it as a gateway of a different sort. Verdun was already a fortress in Gallic and Roman times, and it has a huge underground citadel from the reign of Louis XIV. It was only in reaction to a siege by the Prussians in 1870 that a string of forts was built around the town.

In 1916 Verdun became the site of the longest and perhaps the bloodiest battle of World War I. The Battle of Verdun began in February with a massive German assault along an 8-mile front to the north and east of town. The first of the outlying forts fell almost instantly, but General Pétain organized the French to the cry of "They shall not pass!" (which became the French slogan for the rest of the war), and brutal fighting, characterized by the use of poison gas and flamethrowers, went on for 11 months. By December Verdun's defenders had recovered most of the territory lost, and the Germans had been driven back to about the same positions they had held before the attack. In the meantime the city had been destroyed, nearly 350,000 French soldiers and an almost equal number of Germans had lost their lives, and Verdun had become a symbol of the most horrific and pointless aspects of war.

Despite further heavy damage in 1944, Verdun (pop. 24,000) is today a pleasant administrative center, busy and modern, with more than a few architectural hints of its past. The Meuse divides the city into a lower town of residential and commercial areas and an upper town, which contains the restored *Cathédrale Notre-Dame* and the *Citadelle Souterraine,* both worth a visit. The cathedral, built on the highest spot in town, is an interesting blend of Romanesque and Gothic styles; it dates back largely to the 11th and 12th centuries, and its cloister dates from the 14th to the 16th century. Not far away, the 17th-century citadel contains several miles of subterranean galleries in which troops defending the city were fed and housed. The citadel is open year-round and offers a 30-minute audiovisual presentation in six languages, including English. The tourist office is near the river on Pl. de la Nation (phone: 29-84-18-85 or 29-86-14-18).

What really makes Verdun a place of pilgrimage is its surrounding countryside. A visit to the right bank of the Meuse, with its battlefields and commemorative monuments, is a must. For the approximately 20-mile (32-km) drive, take N3 out of Verdun toward Etain, passing the 5,000 graves of the

Cimetière National du Faubourg-Pavé. Farther along take the turnoff (left onto D913, then right onto D913A) for the *Fort de Vaux.* The Germans laid siege to this fort on March 9, 1916, but did not overcome a heroic defense by the garrison until June 7. Five months later the fort was recaptured. Guided tours take visitors through the fort, whose top commands an impressive panorama of the surrounding landscape and war memorials; tours are offered year-round. Return to D913, following it toward Douaumont. The *Mémorial-Musée de la Bataille de Verdun* is on the site on which the village of Fleury once stood; it's closed from mid-December to mid-January (phone: 29-84-35-34).

Farther along D913 the *Ossuaire de Douaumont* is the most important French memorial to the dead of 1914–18. The remains of 100,000 unidentified soldiers lie in this long, low necropolis; in the *Cimetière National* in front of it, 15,000 crosses on a carpet of green mark additional graves. In the center of the ossuary is a Catholic chapel; at the top of the tower rising above it, orientation tables pick out the various sectors of the battlefield. The ossuary is open from March through December. The nearby *Fort de Douaumont* fell on February 25, 1916, and was not retaken until late in October. It's open year-round; guided tours take place daily. From the heights of this multilevel fortification is a full view of the battlefield, surrounding forest, and ossuary.

To reach the next monument, the *Tranchée des Baïonnettes* (Trench of Bayonets), where an infantry section was buried alive following violent bombing on June 10, 1916, go back toward the ossuary and follow the signs. From the *Tranchée* follow the winding road down the *Ravin de la Mort* (Ravine of Death) to Bras, and then take D964 to return to Verdun.

BEST EN ROUTE

Hostellerie Coq Hardi There are 40 rooms and three apartments in this comfortable house, old-fashioned but for color TV sets. In its opulent, family-run dining room, the chef turns out superb sauces and a light cuisine that has earned one Michelin star. It can be tasted to maximum effect in such dishes as *salade Coq Hardi* (various types of lettuce with crayfish, foie gras, green beans, and green mustard), foie gras with fresh noodles, and wild salmon with parsley and flambéed *mirabelles.* Hotel closed January; restaurant also closed Fridays. Near the center of town, at 8 Av. de la Victoire, Verdun (phone: 29-86-36-36; fax: 29-86-09-21). Expensive to moderate.

Bellevue Operated by the owners of the *Hostellerie Coq Hardi,* it has 72 rooms with color TV sets, some with lovely views of Verdun's *Botanical Garden.* There is a restaurant, a garage, and a nice garden in back. Closed November through March. 1 Rond-Point du Lattre-de-Tassigny, Verdun (phone: 29-84-39-41; fax: 29-86-09-21). Moderate.

En Route from Verdun From here you can take either A4 directly to Metz, 48 miles (77 km) to the east (see below), or N35 southwest to Bar-le-Duc. The 35-mile (56-km) stretch of road between Verdun and Bar-le-Duc is known as the Voie Sacrée (Sacred Way), because it was the crucial supply route for men and matériel coming to bolster the defense of Verdun following the surprise German attack of 1916.

BAR-LE-DUC This busy commercial center (pop. 17,500) was once the capital of the important Duchy of Bar, which was united to the Duchy of Lorraine late in the 15th century. Occupying a picturesque spot on the Ornain River, the town contains a remarkable group of 16th- to 18th-century houses, as well as the 15th-century Gothic *Eglise St-Etienne*. The church is best known for *Le Squelette* (The Skeleton), a decidedly macabre statue by Ligier Richier, a distinguished regional artist of the 16th century. The work is a likeness of René de Châlon, Prince of Orange, who was depicted—according to his wishes—as he would appear after death. Another work by Richier, a wooden statue of Christ, is in the town's *Eglise Notre-Dame*.

Bar-le-Duc is known for its *confitures de groseilles* (currant preserves); their production has been a flourishing local industry for centuries. If you come to town in early September, you can witness an old-fashioned country fair and antiques show that celebrates the Barisien delicacy. Bar-le-Duc's tourist office is at 5 Rue Jeanne d'Arc (phone: 29-79-11-13).

BEST EN ROUTE

La Meuse Gourmande This popular restaurant in a former convent serves good regional cuisine—mushrooms, snails, eels, blood sausage—and creditable local wines, particularly the Côtes-de-Meuse. Avoid any nouvelle dishes. Closed Sunday dinner and Wednesdays. Reservations advised. Major credit cards accepted. 1 Rue François-de-Guise, Bar-le-Duc (phone: 29-79-28-40). Moderate to inexpensive.

En Route from Bar-le-Duc Take N35 and D901 55 miles (88 km) to Metz.

METZ (pronounced *Mess*) At the confluence of the Seille and Moselle Rivers, Metz (pop. 120,000) is a thriving regional administrative, commercial, economic, and cultural center. The city is especially well known for its orchestra, the Orchestre Philharmonie de Lorraine, which makes its home in the 19th-century concert hall, L'Arsenal (Av. Ney; phone: 87-39-92-00). For additional details on the orchestra, see The Liveliest Arts: Theater, Opera, and Music in diversions.

Metz is an attractive blend of old and new architecture. Streets in the heart of town have been turned into appealing pedestrian shopping malls; riverside parks and an esplanade are filled with flowers, terraces, and recreational facilities; and sailing and other boating activities are popular along the Moselle.

Metz was an important city of Roman Gaul from the time of Julius Caesar to that of the Frankish King Clovis. Later, during the reign of Charlemagne (768–814), it became the intellectual cradle of the Carolingian Empire. In the 12th century it became a free city, a rival to the great Flemish, German, and Italian cities of the time and strong enough to repel the frequent attempts of the Dukes of Lorraine to annex it. Instead, along with the other two independent bishoprics of Verdun and Toul, it was captured by Henri II of France in 1552; its status as part of France was confirmed in 1648 by the Treaty of Westphalia.

The city's one touristic "must" is the soaring Gothic *Cathédrale St-Etienne*, mostly built from the mid-13th to the early 16th century on the site of two previous adjoining churches, one of them an oratory dedicated to St. Stephen that miraculously escaped the devastation of Attila and the Huns in the fifth century. The height of *St-Etienne*'s nave (131 feet) and aisles (44 feet) makes it one of the loftiest cathedrals in France; at 372 feet, it also is one of the longest. It is most noted, however, for its sublime stained glass windows. The rose window above the central doorway is the work of Hermann of Munster (1384–92); the window of the left transept in Flamboyant Gothic, that of Theobald of Lyxheim (1504); the window of the right transept in Renaissance style, that of Valentin Bousch (1521–27). The latter two windows, said to be the largest in the world (each covers about 4,140 square feet), bathe the transepts in a glorious symphony of colored light. Some of the cathedral's other stained glass was lost during World War II, but there are splendid modern windows, including those done in the 1960s by Marc Chagall.

The city's exemplary *Musée de La Cour d'Or* (2 Rue du Haut-Poirier; phone: 87-75-10-18) also merits a visit. Its contents, covering 1,700 years of history, are housed in ancient structural remains ranging from the marble-covered sandstone walls of Roman baths to the façade of a Renaissance mansion. Exhibits include a collection of Merovingian artifacts excavated in Metz over the last 150 years and, particularly interesting, objects belonging to Charlemagne. Incorporated in the museum is a five-story, 15th-century granary, the only one of its kind in Europe, which houses an extensive Gothic collection and ambitious programs of Gothic art and artisanship, such as glassware workshops. The museum is closed lunch hours.

Among Metz's other notable buildings are the enormous train station, built from 1905 to 1908 in the massive Roman Rhenan style; across from it, the post office, built in the same style in 1911 of red Vosges sandstone; the large 18th-century *Hôtel de Ville* (Town Hall) in the Place d'Armes; the *Porte des Allemands,* a 13th-century château-fort on the Seille River; and the *Eglise St-Pierre-aux-Nonnains* on Avenue Ney, next to the *Jardin de l'Esplanade.* Dating from the 4th century, the *Eglise* is reportedly the oldest church in France, but it is closed to visitors. Useful English-language information on Metz may be found at the *Office du Tourisme* (Pl. d'Armes; phone: 87-55-53-76).

La Dinanderie This fine restaurant has a contemporary and elegant setting. Expect fine produce and diverse fare with light sauces that show off the chef's masterful touch. The fish dishes are especially good. Closed Sundays, Mondays, the last week of February, and the last three weeks of August. Reservations advised. Major credit cards accepted. 2 Rue de Paris, Metz (phone: 87-30-14-40; fax: 87-32-44-23). Expensive.

Royal-Concorde A turn-of-the-century place, with 63 large and comfortable rooms and a restaurant. In the residential area near the train station, at 23 Av. Foch, Metz (phone: 87-66-81-11; fax: 87-56-13-16). Expensive.

Le Crinouc A trendy, one-Michelin-star restaurant whose cuisine is a successful blend of tradition and innovation. The sauces are perfection. Closed Sunday dinner, Mondays, and the first two weeks of January. Reservations advised. Major credit cards accepted. 79 Rue du Général-Metman, Metz (phone: 87-74-12-46; fax: 87-36-96-92). Expensive to moderate.

A La Ville de Lyon The regional cuisine is consistently good at this place, a favorite with locals. Closed Sunday dinner, Mondays, the last week of February, and August. Reservations advised. Major credit cards accepted. 7 Rue des Piques, Metz (phone: 87-36-07-01; fax: 87-74-47-17). Expensive to moderate.

Mercure Altéa St-Thiébault This modern hotel has 110 large, well-equipped rooms and a dining room. On a beautiful square near the city center, at 29 Pl. St-Thiébault, Metz (phone: 87-38-50-50; fax: 87-75-48-18). Moderate.

Novotel Metz Centre Here are 120 comfortable, air conditioned rooms, a piano bar, an outdoor pool, and a restaurant. The hotel is conveniently located downtown, near the main shopping area and the heart of the St-Jacques commercial center. Pl. des Paraiges, Metz (phone: 87-37-38-39; 800-221-4542; fax: 87-36-10-00). Moderate.

Cécil A small, undistinguished hotel in an old building, it has 39 modern, functional rooms. There's no restaurant. Near the train station, at 14 Rue Pasteur, Metz (phone: 87-66-66-13; fax: 87-56-96-02). Inexpensive.

Foch This pretty 1920s building now houses an old-style hostelry offering 38 comfortable rooms with modern baths and TV sets, but no restaurant. Between the town center and the train station at 8 Pl. R.-Mondon, Metz (phone: 87-74-40-75; fax: 87-74-49-90). Inexpensive.

En Route from Metz Continue 35 miles (56 km) south to Nancy.

NANCY This city (pop. 100,000) is a regional hub of government and commerce; a center of finance, mining, metallurgy, and engineering; and the seat of the third largest scientific university in France. It also is a city of classic

French culture and elegance, with an astonishing group of 18th-century buildings at its core that testify to a notable past.

As the capital of the Duchy of Lorraine from the 12th to the 18th century, the city was the creation of its dukes—particularly of the last, who was not French but Polish. By an arrangement that ended the War of the Polish Succession, François III, Duke of Lorraine, exchanged his duchy for that of Tuscany. In his place Louis XV installed Stanislas Leszczynski, his own father-in-law and the deposed King of Poland, on the throne of Nancy in 1737. On Leszczynski's death (in 1766), Nancy and Lorraine became part of France.

During his reign, Leszczynski set about beautifying and developing the city, and the large, regal square now named Place Stanislas was his showplace. The work of architect Emmanuel Héré and ironmaster Jean Lamour, this beautifully proportioned ensemble of palaces and gilded wrought-iron grillwork—in gateways, fountains, railings, and balconies—is considered a supreme achievement of 18th-century art. The largest building on the square, now the *Hôtel de Ville* (Town Hall), contains a magnificent wrought-iron staircase leading to salons from which Stanislas's entire urban plan is visible in all its refined harmony. Buildings ornamented with imposing arcades flank the *Hôtel de Ville;* directly in front of it is the *Arc de Triomphe,* which honors Louis XV. Behind that is the Place de la Carrière, which dates from the 16th and 17th centuries but was transformed by Héré. This long rectangle is surrounded by 18th-century townhouses, embellished by more fountains and grillwork, and closed off at its far end by a colonnade and the *Palais du Gouvernement,* once the residence of the Governors of Lorraine.

Pass to the left of the *Palais du Gouvernement* and take the Grand' Rue to the *Palais Ducal,* the palace where the dukes and their courts once resided. Built principally by Duke Antoine in the 16th century, the structure was restored considerably following damage in the 19th century. Of particular interest is the famous *Porterie,* an elaborate doorway in the Grand' Rue façade surmounted by an equestrian statue of Duke Antoine topped with a Flamboyant Gothic gable. Housed in the *Palais Ducal* is the *Musée Historique Lorrain* (phone: 83-32-18-74), which contains a rich collection pertaining to the history of Nancy and the region. An archaeological garden displays Celtic, Gallo-Roman, and Frankish artifacts; there's also an almost complete collection of the engravings of Jacques Callot (a native of Nancy), a sampling of paintings by Georges de la Tour (a native of Lorraine), a floor full of the furniture and folk art of the area, Judaica, and a museum of pharmacology. Closed lunch hours in summer and Tuesdays year-round.

Adjoining the ducal palace is the *Eglise des Cordeliers.* The church contains numerous ducal tombs, including the notable 16th-century tombs of René II and his wife, Philippa de Gueldre, the tomb of the latter a work of Ligier Richier. The church is closed lunch hours in summer and Mondays year-round.

The *Musée des Beaux-Arts,* in one of the palaces on Place Stanislas (at No. 3; phone: 83-85-30-72), is devoted to European paintings from the 14th century to modern times, including works by Perugino, Tintoretto, Rubens, Delacroix, Manet, Bonnard, Utrillo, and Modigliani, among others. It is closed lunch hours, Monday mornings, and Tuesdays. Southwest of the city's center, another point of interest is the *Musée de l'Ecole de Nancy* (36-38 Rue Sergent-Blandan; phone: 83-40-14-86), with furniture, glassware, and ceramics by artists of Nancy's own Art Nouveau school, including objects from the workshop of Emile Gallé, who was its inspiration. It's closed lunch hours in summer and Tuesdays year-round.

Nancy is a fine city for walking. There are shop-lined streets and shopping arcades, university areas, pleasant squares with fountains, and numerous parks for sitting and strolling, notably the large *Parc de la Pépinière* off Place de la Carrière. The best people watching spot is at the *Grand Café Foy* (1 Pl. Stanislas; phone: 83-32-15-97). A short walk from Place Stanislas is the factory and showroom of *Daum* (17 Rue des Cristalleries; phone: 83-32-14-55), a fine French crystal less well known than Baccarat. *Daum*'s workrooms can be visited Monday through Saturday mornings and Saturday afternoons. Nancy's *Office du Tourisme* is at 14 Place Stanislas (phone: 83-35-22-41).

BEST EN ROUTE

Le Capucin Gourmand There's delicious food here, and the decor features some shining examples of Nancy's Art Nouveau. Traditional cuisine is limited to a few outstanding choices (try the fresh foie gras), supplemented by a half dozen or so specials (notable are the *feuilleté* of oysters and the pigeon *kefta*). The cheese tray is outstanding; the desserts, such as apple *galette* perfumed with *bergamote*—the local bonbon—are unusual. Closed Sundays, Mondays, two weeks in January, and August. Reservations advised. MasterCard and Visa accepted. 31 Rue Gambetta, Nancy (phone: 83-35-26-98; fax: 83-35-75-32). Expensive.

Le Goéland The only place in town with a really luxurious, contemporary dining room (it's been awarded one Michelin star). The specialty is seafood, prepared with inventiveness and subtlety, and there's a nice wine list. Closed Sundays, Mondays, holidays, and the first two weeks in August. Reservations advised. Major credit cards accepted. 27 Rue des Ponts, Nancy (phone: 83-35-17-25; fax: 83-35-72-49). Expensive.

Grand Hôtel de la Reine A fine hotel (a member of the Relais & Châteaux group) in a landmark 18th-century building whose 50 rooms have modern conveniences, including color TV sets. There's also a one-Michelin-star restaurant, *Stanislas,* with a wonderful fixed-price menu. 2 Pl. Stanislas, Nancy (phone: 83-35-03-01; fax: 83-32-86-04). Expensive.

Altéa Thiers The 185 rooms in this link in the reliable chain are comfortable (with TV sets and air conditioning) and well decorated; there's a good restaurant and bar as well. Near Pl. Stanislas, at 11 Rue Raymond-Poincaré, Nancy (phone: 83-39-75-75; fax: 83-32-78-17). Expensive to moderate.

Albert I–Astoria A quiet, comfortable place with 126 rooms, it has been renovated to include conference rooms and other conveniences. There's no restaurant. Near the train station, at 3 Rue de l'Armée-Patton, Nancy (phone: 83-40-31-24; fax: 83-28-47-78). Moderate.

Excelsior A classic Art Nouveau brasserie with high, ornate ceilings, leaded stained glass, graceful fixtures, and a varied choice of reasonably priced specialties. The service can be slow. Open daily, with drinks and snacks served between meal times. Reservations advised. Major credit cards accepted. 50 Rue Henri-Poincaré, Nancy (phone: 83-35-24-57). Moderate.

La Gentilhommière This charming provincial place serves excellent meat and poultry dishes with refined sauces. Closed Saturday lunch, Sundays, the first week of February, and most of August. Reservations advised. Major credit cards accepted. 29 Rue des Maréchaux, Nancy (phone: 83-32-26-44). Moderate.

Le Comptoir du Gastrolatre A pleasant bistro offering simple, delicious country food. Closed Sundays, Monday lunch, *Easter* week, and the last two weeks of August. Reservations advised. No credit cards accepted. Pl. Vaudemont, Nancy (phone: 83-35-51-94). Inexpensive.

Excursions from Nancy Nancy makes a perfect base for side trips to several points of interest. Domrémy-la-Pucelle, the birthplace of Joan of Arc, is southwest of the city via Toul, once an important town and worth an excursion in its own right. Southeast of Nancy is a splendid 18th-century château at Lunéville; after a visit there fanciers of fine crystal often proceed to Baccarat. Directly south of Nancy are the spa towns of Vittel and Contrexéville; farther east, the resort of Gérardmer.

TOUL Take A31 west from Nancy for 14 miles (22 km). Along with Metz and Verdun, Toul was one of the three bishoprics that emerged as independent cities during the Middle Ages and remained free until the mid-16th century, when they were captured for France by Henri II. Much damaged during World War II, the town is the site of the battered yet still fascinating *Cathédrale St-Etienne,* built from the 13th to the 16th century. The church has a magnificent Flamboyant Gothic façade and a beautiful cloister.

DOMRÉMY-LA-PUCELLE From Toul it's 24 miles (38 km), south on N74 and then west on D19, to Domrémy-la-Pucelle (Domrémy-the-Maid), as the village was renamed in honor of its most famous daughter. In 1411 or 1412 Joan of Arc was born to two pious peasants in a starkly simple house here. Next to the house is a small museum devoted to her life. The house and museum (phone: 29-06-95-86 for both) are open daily from April through mid-

September; closed Tuesdays in winter. The local church in which Joan was baptized is much changed, but it contains a few objects from her time, including the baptismal font.

LUNÉVILLE Twenty-two miles (35 km) southeast of Nancy via N4 is this town, where the center of attraction is a château known as *Petit Versailles*. Lunéville was the favorite residence of Léopold, Duke of Lorraine, who commissioned the château as a modest replica of the great palace in 1703. Designed by Germain Boffrand (a student of Jules Hardouin-Mansart, the architect of Louis XIV's royal buildings), the château has a huge, majestic court on the west side, two small wings separated from the great halls by porticoes, and a chapel modeled on that at Versailles. It became the favorite residence of Stanislas Leszczynski, the last duke of Lorraine, who died here. Stanislas was instrumental in decorating the château and in laying out the beautiful gardens of the adjoining *Parc des Bosquets* (now the setting for a summer son-et-lumière show), and he entertained an array of notable guests here, including Voltaire and Diderot. A small museum displays furniture, engravings, historical documents, and a distinguished collection of Lunéville faïences. The museum is closed lunch hours and Tuesdays (phone: 83-76-23-57).

BACCARAT Southeast of Lunéville down N59, it's 15 miles (24 km) to Baccarat, a name synonymous with fine crystal since the founding of its factory in 1764. During the summer tourists throng the small town to marvel at antique and modern works in the *Musée du Cristal* (Rue des Cristalleries; phone: 83-76-60-06 for information on hours). From there visitors go on to acquire souvenirs in glass—at decent prices—in any number of accommodating shops along the main street. The best is *Baccarat–Magasin de Vente* (Rue des Cristalleries; phone: 83-76-60-01), which ships all over the world. It's open daily; closed lunch hours. The crystal decorations in the little town church, built in 1957, also are worth a look.

BEST EN ROUTE

Château d'Adomenil This delightful mansion (a member of the Relais & Châteaux group) and its well-tended park are in a lovely country setting. The one-Michelin-star menu features seasonal fish and game specialties, and the service is excellent. Also on the premises are seven rooms and one suite. Closed Monday and Tuesday lunch, February through October, and Sunday dinner and Mondays November through January. Reservations necessary. Major credit cards accepted. Three miles (5 km) south of Lunéville, in Réhainviller-à-Doménil (phone: 83-74-04-81; fax: 83-74-21-78). Expensive.

En Route from Nancy South of Nancy in the woods of southern Lorraine is an area known for its mineral and thermal springs and consequently for its spa resorts. Vittel, 43 miles (69 km) from Nancy via D413, is the largest and one of the best known of these spa towns.

VITTEL Its cold-water springs were familiar to the Romans, then forgotten, then rediscovered in the mid-19th century. Today Vittel water at its source is used internally and externally to treat a variety of illnesses (including liver and kidney diseases, gout, and rheumatism), and bottled Vittel water is much more likely to be found on French tables than Perrier. Besides the springs, located in a large park, this low-key town has a number of other attractions that draw health-conscious visitors. Golf, tennis, swimming, and riding facilities are in good supply, and there's even a casino. The *Office de Tourisme* is on Avenue Bouloumié (phone: 29-08-08-88).

En Route from Vittel Take D429 3 miles (5 km) west to Contrexéville.

CONTREXÉVILLE Like Vittel, its neighbor is known for its mineral water, which also springs cold from its source and is bottled and popular all over France. Also like Vittel, it's a low-key place complete with a casino, but Contrexéville is the smaller of the two and has the nicer accommodations. The *Office de Tourisme* is on Rue du Shah-de-Perse (phone: 29-08-08-68).

BEST EN ROUTE

L'Aubergade A warm welcome greets all who enter this lovely, small dining room. Specialties include salmon in puff pastry, steaks with mushrooms, and a few daring but successful dishes. The homemade desserts, which use such local fruits as peaches and *mirabelles,* are delicious. Adjoining is a nine-room hotel. Restaurant closed Sunday dinner and Mondays, except in July and August. Reservations advised. Major credit cards accepted. 265 Av. des Tilleuls, Vittel (phone: 29-08-04-39). Expensive to moderate.

Cosmos In a lovely, quiet park, this hotel has 81 beautifully furnished rooms and a restaurant. Closed late October through April. 13 Rue de Metz, Contrexéville (phone: 29-07-61-61; fax: 29-08-68-67). Moderate.

Grand Hôtel Etablissement A charming old hotel on the park, it has 39 rooms and a restaurant. Closed October through March. Cour d'Honneur, Contrexéville (phone: 29-08-17-30; fax: 29-08-68-67). Moderate.

En Route from Vittel/Contrexéville Take D434 northeast and D63 south, through the lovely forest of Darney, to the nearby hot-water spas of Bains-les-Bains and Plombières-les-Bains, both in use since Roman times. From Plombières it is 26 miles (42 km) to Gérardmer, the main resort of the Vosges Mountains. Follow D63 south for 2 miles (3 km) and then take N57 northeast.

GÉRARDMER This popular resort occupies a magnificent site in the midst of ever-green forests, on the western slopes of the Vosges and at the eastern end of the largest of the range's many lakes, Lac de Gérardmer. It is an excellent spot for skiing and skating in winter and for swimming, boating, fishing, and hiking in summer. Sightseeing possibilities include a look at the local church, made of Vosges sandstone; a circuit of the lake, which can be done by motorboat or by car (the 4-mile/6-km drive sometimes winds through forest and sometimes opens up to views of water and encircling mountains); and any number of excursions to neighboring slopes or to Lac de Longemer and Lac de Retournemer. The town is well equipped for visitors, with hotels, restaurants, a casino, and the oldest tourist office in France (Pl. Déportes; phone: 29-63-08-74).

BEST EN ROUTE

Grand Hotel Bragard This nicely furnished hotel has 48 rooms, 12 suites, a pool, a sauna, and an exercise room. Its restaurant, *Au Grand Cerf,* offers fine traditional local dishes and nouvelle cuisine. In town, on Pl. Tilleul, Gérardmer (phone: 29-63-06-31; fax: 29-63-46-81). Expensive to moderate.

Hostellerie Bas-Rupts A modern, chalet-style, 32-room hostelry on a quiet mountainside. There are tennis courts with instruction and a pool, and the hotel is only a short distance from ski resorts. The luxurious restaurant, *Les Bas-Rupts,* is done in rustic Louis XIII decor. It boasts a masterful chef, exquisite service, and a refined menu of light, delicious dishes that merits one Michelin star. In good weather you can eat outdoors on the terrace. Two miles (3 km) south of Gérardmer via D486, in Bas-Rupts (phone: 29-63-09-25; fax: 29-63-00-40). Expensive to moderate.

Champagne

Champagne. The word is as charged with rich associations as the bottles of sparkling wine that bear it on their labels. The world's most famous wine takes its name from the region 90 miles (144 km) east of Paris that produces it, though the region is less known outside France than the celebrated bubbly product.

An elongated oval stretching a hundred miles from north to south, Champagne offers visitors a surprising wealth of sights. Foremost among them are its glorious Romanesque and Gothic churches, including the incomparable *Cathédrale Notre-Dame* in Reims; its great champagne houses, with miles of cellars housing millions of bottles of champagne; and the vineyards themselves, more than 75,000 fertile acres spread across the landscape. Perhaps the greatest charm of the region lies in the villages scattered throughout the countryside. Beyond the often uninteresting, even bleak views afforded by the region's highways, it is possible to sample French provincial life, to step back into the 19th century in villages crowded around medieval churches, and to drive along narrow, nearly deserted roads through fields and vineyards seemingly bypassed by modernization.

The word "champagne" comes from the Latin *campania,* meaning "open, level, unforested land," and indeed, the entire area is a plateau seldom exceeding 600 feet in altitude, a topographical fact that, combined with the region's location, shaped its destiny. Inhabited since the Neolithic era, Champagne has been a crossroads of Europe, a route of invasion, and a battlefield for 2,000 years. It has been ravaged repeatedly—Epernay alone was destroyed close to two dozen times.

Julius Caesar brought his Roman legions to Champagne when he conquered Gaul between 58 and 51 BC. Under the Roman occupation the region flourished, with Reims, then a city of over 80,000 inhabitants, far exceeding Paris in size and importance. In AD 451 Attila the Hun and half a million barbarian soldiers stormed Roman Gaul, making their camp on the plains of Champagne. What ensued was one of the fiercest and bloodiest battles in history, a monumental encounter between Orient and Occident in which one million soldiers fought, 200,000 died, and Attila was defeated. But war in the region continued: By the end of the 10th century Champagne had been the scene of numerous invasions and annexations, and Reims had been razed to the ground seven times. A few centuries of peace and prosperity followed. Champagne became a center of commerce between the textile regions of the north and the Mediterranean, and the great Champagne fairs of the Middle Ages attracted merchants from all over Europe. Prosperity led to a flowering of culture, which culminated in the poetry of Chrétien de Troyes and in the cathedral at Reims. This peaceful interlude was only temporary, however: Champagne was one of the principal battlegrounds of the bloody Hundred Years War (1337–1453) and the site of conflicts during the French Revolution, the Napoleonic Wars of the late 18th and early 19th centuries, and the Franco-Prussian War of 1870–71.

During World War I the Champagne region was the scene of the nightmare Battles of the Marne (1914 and 1918). In 1914—at the onset of more than a thousand days of bombardment—the Germans shelled Reims's cathedral, an outrage never forgotten by the people of Champagne. Throughout the war fighting took place in the vineyards; by the war's end the countryside was scorched and the large towns heavily damaged. The Champenois fared little better during World War II: In 1940 Nazi tanks stormed into France via Champagne, and during the next five years only Normandy suffered greater devastation in France. Afterward reports emerged of the powerful underground resistance movement that had operated in German-occupied Champagne—accounts of walled-off champagne cellars hiding precious stocks from the Germans, of rerouted trains, of remarkable individual heroics. Today the two wars are part of the Champenois soul, and monuments, cemeteries, and rebuilt towns throughout the region are poignant reminders of its ordeals.

Since champagne is the region's lifeblood, a brief introduction to the king of wines (and the wine of kings) is indispensable. Ever since the Romans planted vines in the 1st century, Champagne has been known for its wine. By the Middle Ages the wine was being exported, but it was not the sparkling variety; the techniques that gave birth to the effervescent wine were developed only at the end of the 17th century. In the next century the sparkling wine became supreme, welcomed and praised widely at all the best tables. This in turn led to the mystique of champagne, to the industry's expansion, and to the exportation of the wine in the 19th and 20th centuries. Meanwhile a significant change in the character of the wine was occurring. At first the sparkling wine was sweet, but as tastes changed, particularly in this century, most champagne was made drier. Today 85% of the approximately 200 million bottles produced annually are brut (dry). After years of economic hardship caused by declining markets in the United States and the United Kingdom, along with high grape prices and the unavoidable expenses of the champagne process, the champagne industry began an upturn in early 1994, following a reduction in grape prices and stepped-up buying abroad.

Champagne's northern climate; its chalky soil; the type, characteristics, and quality of the grapes used (by law, only chardonnay, pinot noir, and pinot meunier may be used); the time-honored and meticulous techniques of vine cultivation; and the highly regulated wine-making process all guarantee the distinctive quality of the most imitated wine in the world. Champagne is a blend of many wines that have been caused to ferment a second time in a stoppered bottle. The grapes, which come from 250 villages, are pressed according to rigorous standards; they are then fermented in vats into still wines at the region's 110 champagne houses. The still wines are next married to wines from other vine stocks, other sources, and even other years, according to the taste of the cellar master, resulting in a blend known as the *cuvée*. Champagnes containing wines from several years—the most common type—are classified as nonvintage; if the wines are all from the same year, the champagne will be vintage and will bear the year on its label.

At this point the white wine is bottled, and yeasts and a small quantity of sugar are added to cause a second fermentation, which takes place in the champagne house's labyrinthine chalk cellars, where the wines are left to mature, usually for three to five years. The sediment thrown off by the second fermentation is eliminated by tilting the bottle neck downward and rotating it frequently; the sediment thus collects on the cork. This process, usually done by hand, is known as riddling, or *remuage*. The *dégorgement* process follows, whereby the neck is frozen and the cork is removed, allowing the pressure in the bottle to expel the ice pellet with the sediment. The bottle is then topped off with the *dosage,* a reserve wine with cane sugar added to establish the desired sweetness, and recorked.

From north to south the Champagne region has four vine-growing areas—the Montagne de Reims (Mountain of Reims), the Vallée de la Marne (Valley of the Marne), the Côte des Blancs (Slope of the Whites), and the region of the Aube—and the three centers of Reims, Epernay, and Troyes. The route we suggest begins in the city of Reims and circles south through the hilly vineyards and small villages of the Montagne de Reims before reaching Epernay. Next it follows the Vallée de la Marne, which stretches east and west of Epernay, then turns south through the villages and vineyards of the Côte des Blancs. After a visit to the historic town of Châlons-sur-Marne, it continues south to Troyes, the former capital of Champagne as well as an art center. From there it proceeds southeast through the remaining Aube vineyard area, to end at the threshold of yet another famous wine region, Burgundy. All along are small champagne houses, most of which can be visited informally. Michelin map No. 56 covers the entire champagne area (and the northern leg of our route); No. 61 covers the area beyond Châlons-sur-Marne.

Since many noteworthy sites and sights lie in and around Reims and Epernay, which are only 16 miles (26 km) apart (by the direct, not the scenic, route), doubling back to hotels, restaurants, villages, and other sites presents little inconvenience. If you hope to stay in a small hotel or to visit during the harvest (which usually begins during the second half of September and lasts two to three weeks) or in the peak tourist months of July and August, make reservations in advance. For a double room per night without breakfast, expect to pay $175 or more at a very expensive hotel; $125 to $175 at an expensive establishment; $75 to $125 at a moderate hotel; and less than $75 at an inexpensive place. All hotels accept major credit cards and are open year-round unless otherwise noted. Most hotels feature telephones, TV sets, and private baths in all their rooms. However, some less expensive hotels may have private baths in only some rooms; it's a good idea to confirm whether your room has a private bath when making a reservation. Very few hotels in the region have air conditioning. A full meal for two, excluding wine and drinks but with service usually included in the bill, will run $175 or more in a very expensive restaurant; $125 to $175 in an expensive restaurant; $75 to $125 in a moderate one; and less than $75 in an inexpensive one. Unless otherwise indicated, all restaurants are open for lunch and dinner. For each location hotels and restaurants are listed alphabetically by price category.

REIMS For a detailed report on the city, its sights, its hotels, and its restaurants, see *Reims* in THE CITIES.

En Route from Reims The Montagne de Reims, the first of Champagne's wine-growing areas, is a gentle, wooded, hilly area rising between Reims and the valleys of the Vesle and the Ardre to the north and Epernay and the Vallée de la Marne to the south. N51 cuts across it from north to south—between what is known as the *petite montagne* to the west and the *grande montagne* to the east—and connects Reims and Epernay somewhat as the crow flies. The vineyards and wine villages, however, which lie against the slopes, lead from one city to the other by a more circuitous route.

Take N380 from Reims toward Château-Thierry, then turn left onto D26 to follow the flank of the *petite montagne,* whose vineyards produce the most acidic grapes in the region. Leave the road briefly to see the beautiful church with a square steeple and lovely interior in Ville-Dommange and, nearby, the small 12th- to 16th-century *Chapelle de St-Lié,* surrounded by a quiet cemetery marked with two World War I casemates (bombproof shelters). Pause for a view of Reims and its cathedral, the Reims plain, and the Tardenois woods, then drive on to Sacy, which has a beautiful 12th-century church, and follow D26 through Ecueil, Chamery, and Sermiers (there's a nice statue-fountain dated 1900 near its church) to Montchenot, 7 miles (11 km) south of Reims.

BEST EN ROUTE

Auberge du Grand Cerf With one Michelin star, this restaurant is one of the best in the area. The chef favors such inventive nouvelle dishes as warm oysters or scallops in puff pastry, both perfect with champagne; there is also a good selection of traditional dishes. Also recommended: any fish dish, the beautiful salads (for example, lobster and mango) made from fresh market produce, and the remarkable lobster risotto. The prix fixe menus give a good sampling. There is a terrace for summer dining. Closed Sunday dinner, Wednesdays, and two weeks each in January and August. Reservations advised. Major credit cards accepted. On N51 in Montchenot (phone: 26-97-60-07; fax: 26-97-64-24). Expensive.

En Route from Montchenot After crossing N51, D26 follows the flank of the *grande montagne.* Villers-Allerand, which has a church dating from the 13th and 14th centuries, is the first village down the road; next is Rilly-la-Montagne, which counts a number of champagne producers among its thousand inhabitants. Fittingly, the town's church has sculptured stalls depicting *vignerons* (vine growers). Rilly is the starting point for walks on 900-foot-high Mont-Joli, one of the few places where the Montagne de Reims comes to a point and thus affords a wonderful panorama of the Reims plain.

Next on D26 is Chigny-les-Roses, whose church's sanctuary has an interesting Renaissance door, and Ludes, whose 15th- to 16th-century church has a statue of the Virgin and Child holding a bunch of grapes. Ludes also houses the champagne cellars of *Canard-Duchêne* (1 Rue Edmond Canard; phone: 26-61-10-96; fax: 26-61-13-90). These beautiful, long, scrupulously clean chalk cellars are open weekdays from 10 AM to noon and 2 to 4 PM; closed August and holidays; there is an admission charge. To arrange English-language tours, call or fax some weeks ahead.

An area of first-rate vineyards begins at Mailly-Champagne, where you can visit the champagne cellar of the village's cooperative *Société des Producteurs* (28 Rue de la Libération; phone: 26-49-41-10). It is open year-round, weekdays from 9 AM to noon and 2 to 5 PM; Saturdays from 9 to 11 AM and 3 to 5:30 PM; and Sundays from 3 to 5:30 PM. There is a charge for the visit and tasting. The vineyards of Verzenay, about 2 miles (3 km) away, produce exceptional wine. The town also is well known for its old windmill, probably the only one left in Champagne, which was used as an observation tower during World War I. In nearby Verzy follow the road on the right (D34) into the forest, leave your car in the parking lot, and walk to the observatory of Mont-Sinaï. From this panoramic spot, the highest in the Montagne de Reims (928 feet), General Gouraud watched the progress of the Battle of Reims in 1918.

For an unusual sight, take the forest road to the left of the modern chapel of St-Basles on D34 to reach the Faux de Verzy, a bizarre landscape of twisted beech trees with corkscrew-like branches. Beyond Verzy is Villers-Marmery, where you can detour 3 miles (5 km) off D26—crossing A4, N44, and the village of Les Petites Loges—to Sept-Saulx, the site of the *Cheval Blanc,* a fine restaurant and hotel (see below).

Continuing on D26, you come to Trépail, whose small church has columns decorated with sculptured animals. Beyond is a string of villages known for their fruity red wines. One of these, Ambonnay, is picturesquely set amid the vines, with a church that has an elegant Romanesque steeple and a pure, well-preserved interior. Another, Bouzy—reached by switching from D26 to D19 at Ambonnay—is famous for its non-sparkling red wine. Just northwest of Bouzy is Louvois, with a 12th-century church. Here, where the vineyards end, you can look through 18th-century wrought-iron gates to see an impressive château standing in the midst of a vast park. Much of *Château Louvois,* which belonged to a chancellor of France and the father of one of Louis XIV's ministers, was destroyed during the French Revolution, so except for its outbuildings, most of what you see dates from postrevolutionary days.

The drive from Louvois to Epernay (8 miles/13 km from Montchenot) on D9 goes through farmland, woods, and the villages of Tauxières, Mutry, Fontaine-sur-Ay, and Avenay-Val-d'Or. This last is worth a stop to see the Flamboyant Gothic portal and rich interior of *St-Trésain,* a beautiful church built in the 12th and 16th centuries, and to visit the *caves* (cellars) of *Ricciuti-Révolte* (18 Rue Lieutenant de Vaisseau; phone: 26-52-30-27); for additional details on the vineyards and cellars, see *Most Visitable Vineyards* in DIVERSIONS. D9, D1, and D201 will take you to Ay, a small town that is the home of champagne houses, and then Epernay, with even more champagne houses. Since Ay is an appropriate starting place for a tour of the villages and vineyards of the Marne, stretching east and west of here, we recommend visiting Epernay first and returning to Ay later.

BEST EN ROUTE

Cheval Blanc In the middle of a quiet village, this charming, vine-covered inn offers views of a park and of the Vesle River. There are four suites and 21 well-equipped rooms (all with color TV sets and decorated with antique furniture) and a tennis court. The large, comfortable dining room has an elegant country look and a fireplace where meat is broiled over an open flame. The atmosphere is friendly and cordial, the service attentive, the wine list exemplary, and the food excellent. Try the fish dishes or the lamb with fresh mint. Closed mid-January through mid-February. Demi-pension required in high season (July and August). Rue du Mullion, Sept-Saulx (phone: 26-03-90-27; fax: 26-03-97-09). Expensive.

EPERNAY In the heart of the vineyards, strongly provincial in character, and dotted with parks and gardens, Epernay rivals Reims as the capital of the king of wines. It is small (pop. 30,000) compared with Reims, and it lacks the other city's architectural richness; the great champagne firms established here are its main attractions. Miles and miles of *caves,* where millions of bottles of bubbly age, have been hewn out of the chalky soil under Epernay, and the major champagne houses offer tours of their facilities. The *Office du Tourisme* (7 Av. de Champagne; phone: 26-55-33-00; fax: 26-51-95-22) distributes a brochure giving the firms' hours; several of the most famous are on the Avenue de Champagne. Remember that the cellars have a constant temperature of 45F to 50F, so bring a jacket or warm sweater. Comfortable, rubber-soled shoes also are recommended, in part because some cellars are damp and may be slippery, and because the tours usually involve a bit of walking underground, occasionally in dark surroundings. Most tours charge admission, and it is not unusual for them to end with a taste of the product. Tours in English are offered by most firms, but if you are traveling in the off-season, call ahead to make sure a guide is available.

Of the major houses open to the public in Epernay, *Moët & Chandon* (20 Av. de Champagne; phone: 26-54-71-11) is the largest, with 17 miles of cellar galleries. This is one of the most popular tourist spots in France, and *Moët*'s explanation of champagne making is extremely good. The *caves* are open daily (except during lunch hours), April through October; closed weekends, November through March. Nearby, *Mercier* (70 Av. de Champagne; phone: 26-54-75-26) conducts tours in English of its 11 miles of cellars aboard an electric train. The cellars are open Mondays through Saturdays from 9:30 to 11:30 AM and 2 to 4:30 PM; Sundays and holidays to 5:30 PM; closed Tuesdays and Wednesdays, December through February. Neither *Moët & Chandon* nor *Mercier* requires an appointment, but *Perrier-Jouët* (26 Av. de Champagne; phone: 26-55-20-53) does. Its 6 miles of *caves* are open weekdays from 9 AM to noon and 2 to 5 PM, May to mid-September only. The 6 miles of cellars at *De Castellane* (57 Rue de Verdun; phone: 26-55-15-33) are open daily from 10 AM to noon and 2 to 6 PM from May to November; in winter by appointment only. The dark, spacious cellars of *Pol Roger* (1 Rue Henri-Lelarge; phone: 26-59-58-00) are open weekdays except in August, when it's by appointment only.

Other points of interest in Epernay include the colorful *Musée de Préhistoire et d'Archéologie Régionale et Musée du Vin de Champagne* (13 Av. de Champagne; phone: 26-51-90-31). Set up in the 19th-century *Château Perrier,* the museum contains maps of the region, agricultural tools, wine presses, labels, and old bottles. It is open Mondays through Saturdays (except Tuesdays) from 10 AM to noon and 2 to 6 PM; Sundays to 5 PM; closed December through February. There's an admission charge. The *Hôtel de Ville* (Town Hall), at the Place de la République end of Avenue de Champagne, is an imposing building in the center of a 19th-century garden. The Renaissance stained glass windows in the *Eglise Notre-Dame* (Pl. Mendès-France) are worth a look too. *INOKADO* (Zone Industrielle de Mardeuïl; phone: 26-51-96-00), a division of the *Institut Oenologique de Champagne,* offers a variety of gift items related to wine and the art of serving it. It's open weekdays only.

A pleasant way to view the surrounding countryside is to take a short cruise on the Marne River. Boats leave from Cumières, 2 miles (3 km) north of Epernay. Cruise on the *Champagne Vallée* (phone: 26-54-49-51) or *Le Coche d'Eau* (phone: 26-72-68-27), both of which offer meals and music from May through August. A tour of the city and surrounding vineyards by narrow-gauge train can be arranged through *Sparna Conseil* (142 Av. Foch; phone: 26-51-76-81).

For those with a serious interest in learning more about champagne, courses and well-organized tastings are offered at *Les Celliers de Pierry* in the village of Pierry, a suburb of Epernay (phone: 26-54-81-75).

BEST EN ROUTE

Petit Comptoir Superchef Gérard Boyer's bistro is housed in a picturesque converted barn. Inventive specialties include warm duck pâté and goat-cheese ravioli. Closed Saturday lunch, Sundays, two weeks in August, and December 22 to 31. Reservations advised. Major credit cards accepted. 3 Rue du Docteur-Rousseau (phone: 26-51-53-53). Moderate.

Le Théâtr' Gourmand An authentic bistro with turn-of-the-century decor, this eatery serves simple classics like calf kidneys in wine sauce. Closed Mondays and two weeks each in August and February. Reservations advised. MasterCard and Visa accepted. 10 Pl. Mendès-France (phone: 26-51-77-77). Moderate.

Champagne This small hotel has 35 modern, functional rooms. No restaurant, but parking is available. Near the center of town, at 30 Rue Eugène-Mercier (phone: 26-55-30-22; fax: 26-51-94-63). Inexpensive.

En Route from Epernay You can tour the vine-laden slopes and graceful landscapes of the Vallée de la Marne by taking D201 for a few miles directly into Ay, crossing the Marne and the canal that runs along it. For a more comprehensive trip, take N3 east, crossing the Marne some miles down the road via D19 into Tours-sur-Marne and returning west toward Ay via D1. The more circuitous route takes you through Tours-sur-Marne, a town with an old priory and, near the tree-lined canal, the headquarters of *Laurent-Perrier* (phone: 26-58-91-22), whose old cellars and collection of rare, large champagne bottles are open weekdays, except in August, by appointment. Also on the detour is Bisseuil, famous for its red wines. In the center of the village is its church, worth visiting for the beauty of its vaults and fine columns (ask for the key at the house next door). The longer route further takes in Mareuil-sur-Ay, which offers a good view of the vineyards, a 12th-century church, and the headquarters of *Philipponnat* (phone: 26-52-60-43), whose cellars can be visited weekdays, except in August, by appointment.

AY (pronounced Ah-ee) This quiet town (pop. 5,000) stands on the banks of the canal across the Marne. Because the area's vineyards are felicitously sited on slopes of undulating ground, its wine has been renowned for centuries, enjoyed at times by the Kings of France and England and a Renaissance pope. Ay suffered serious damage during both World Wars, but it still has some preserved 15th- and 16th-century churches and several half-timbered houses, including a wood-paneled one on Rue St-Vincent that is said to have been the press house of Henri IV. The champagne cellars of *Bollinger* (4 Bd. Maréchal-de-Lattre; phone: 26-55-21-31; fax: 26-54-85-59) and *Ayala*

(2 Bd. du Nord; phone: 26-55-15-44) can be visited by appointment on weekdays only. There also is a museum containing a collection of tools relating to the cultivation of the vine.

En Route from Ay As you head west on D1, celebrated vineyards are on your right; the left is dominated by a developing suburb of Epernay. In Dizy turn right onto N51 and drive up the rising road to Champillon. Here, amid hilly landscape, is a splendid, not-to-be-missed panorama of the Vallée de la Marne vineyards. Hautvillers, about 6 miles (10 km) from Ay, can be reached directly from D1 back at Dizy via N386 or through the tiniest of back roads from Champillon.

BEST EN ROUTE

Royal Champagne Set high in the countryside, this outstanding hotel (a Relais & Châteaux member) looks down on the vineyards, the Vallée de la Marne, and Epernay, 3½ miles (6 km) away. Its 27 rooms and three suites, set off from the main building—formerly an 18th-century coach house—are beautifully furnished, and most of them have terraces with vineyard views. Its celebrated one-Michelin-star restaurant offers traditional and nouvelle dishes, including several fish offerings that go splendidly with champagne, and Bresse poultry and truffles with cabbage. There is a nice selection of local cheeses and an extensive wine list, from which a friendly sommelier will help you select a champagne or local still wine not normally found outside France. Closed three weeks in January. Book ahead, especially for summer and harvest time. On N2051 in Champillon (phone: 26-52-87-11; fax: 26-52-89-69). Very expensive.

HAUTVILLERS This tiny hilltop village has old, half-timbered houses with arched doorways and interesting wrought-iron signs depicting the various tasks of the *vigneron* (vine grower), but it is the *Abbaye de St-Pierre d'Hautvillers* that always has been the focus for travelers. Of all the medieval abbeys in Champagne, none was better known than this, which for nearly 12 centuries from the time of its founding in 660 was one of the most famous in France. The continuing fame of the abbey (though not much of it remains) is due to the Benedictine monk Pierre Pérignon, its cellar master from the late 1660s to 1715. Dom Pérignon revolutionized local wine making by, among other innovations, developing the technique of the second fermentation in the bottle that gives champagne its sparkle and by creating the *cuvée* (blend) that in part is champagne's guarantee of quality and consistency. He is said to have exclaimed to his fellow monks, "Come quickly! I am drinking stars!" on the occasion of the world's first champagne tasting.

The abbey site, above the village, is owned by *Moët & Chandon,* whose attractive *Musée Dom Pérignon* (phone: 26-59-62-67) is filled with historic documents and artifacts relating to champagne making. The museum is open weekdays from March through October by appointment only. Not to be missed is the spectacular view from the abbey's broad stone terrace. Then visit the little church where Dom Pérignon is buried, with its fine woodcarvings and organ.

En Route from Hautvillers Return to D1 and turn right to reach Cumières, a village known for its delicate red wine. The picturesque road continues along the right bank of the Marne through Damery, which has a fine 12th- to 16th-century church, and then through Venteuil, Reuil, and Binson, which has an old priory with a restored 12th-century chapel. A little farther west and just off D1 is Châtillon-sur-Marne, with a large statue of Pope Urban II, the remains of a castle, and a good view of the Marne. Go through Verneuil and Vincelles—the limit of the Marne *département*—and cross the river to Dormans, a picturesque old town considerably damaged during both World Wars, particularly the first, but still endowed with a beautiful 13th-century church, a 17th-century château, and a working windmill. The *Chapelle de la Reconnaissance* (Chapel of Gratitude), built in the middle of a large park to commemorate the Battles of the Marne, commands a fine view over the valley.

Dormans is the turnaround point for the stretch of the Champagne route leading through the vineyards of the Vallée de la Marne. You can return to Epernay along the southern side of the river by staying on N3 the whole way or, for a better view from a higher road, by going part of the way on D222 (reached by taking D226 uphill out of Port-à-Binson) and passing through Oeuilly, Boursault, and Vauciennes before dropping down again to N3. The vineyards of the Côte des Blancs, where the aristocratic white chardonnay grapes grow, are traversed by D10 and D9 south of Epernay. The excursion—as far as Bergères-les-Vertus—is a peaceful and leisurely morning or afternoon drive begun by leaving Epernay on N51 and turning left onto D10 at Pierry. The boundary of the black grape area is at Cuis, where a 12th-century Romanesque church built on a terrace dominating the village affords a pretty view. The next town, Cramant, is one of the most renowned in the region for the quality of its white grapes. Cramant is a charming village, and if you detour up through its vineyards, you'll see the elegant and finely maintained *Château Saran* set imposingly on the hillside. South of Cramant, Avize, in the heart of the Côte des Blancs, has an interesting church, mostly 12th-century Romanesque but with a 15th-century Gothic transept and choir. Next comes Oger, also with an early church, and then Le Mesnil-sur-Oger, another village producing famous *blanc des blancs* with another interesting church, the *Eglise St-Nicolas*. Note particularly the 17th-century paneling inside and the Renaissance door. *Pierre Moncuit* (11 Rue Persault-Maheu; phone: 26-57-52-65; fax: 26-57-97-89), a local producer whose champagnes have won many awards, gives cellar tours by appointment year-round.

After D10 merges with D9, you'll reach Vertus, 13 miles (21 km) from Epernay.

BEST EN ROUTE

La Briqueterie A quiet place surrounded by gardens and vineyards, this hotel is in one of the area's nicest spots. Since it is only 4 miles (6 km) from Epernay (off N51 beyond Pierry), it makes a convenient base for touring. Its 40 rooms, two suites, and public areas have undergone extensive renovation, bringing the comfort level in line with the French government's four-star rating. On the premises are a pool, a sauna, a workout room, conference facilities, and an excellent one-Michelin-star restaurant with a superb wine list. The breakfast buffet is wonderful. During the summer have a drink outside on the lovely terrace. Closed one week in December. 4 Rte. de Sézanne, Vinay (phone: 26-59-99-99; fax: 26-59-92-10). Very expensive.

VERTUS This quiet little town with irregular streets and charming squares was once a fortified city. A medieval gate remains, as does the *Eglise St-Martin* (Pl. de l'Eglise), a remarkable example of the transition from Romanesque to Gothic style. Walk around the church to see the spot where springs form a mirror-like pond. Nearby are several small champagne operations that are worth a visit, such as *Champagne Guy Larmandier* (30 Rue Général-Koënig; phone: 26-52-12-41), a small place offering a friendly welcome in a flower-covered house, *Champagne Paul Goerg* (phone: 26-52-15-31), and *Champagne Michel Rogue* (phone: 26-52-15-68).

BEST EN ROUTE

Hostellerie de la Reine Blanche Looking something like an Alpine ski lodge, this 28-room hotel is well equipped and comfortable; there is a restaurant. Closed two weeks in February. 18 Av. Louis-Lenoir (phone: 26-52-20-76; fax: 26-52-16-59). Moderate.

En Route from Vertus Between Vertus and Bergères-les-Vertus, the Côte des Blancs ends and black grapes are seen again. Beyond Bergères, Mont-Aimé, the site of prehistoric, Roman, and feudal remains, offers a splendid view back over the Côte des Blancs vineyards and forward toward Châlons-sur-Marne, 18 miles (29 km) northeast on N33.

BEST EN ROUTE

Mont-Aimé All 29 rooms are simply yet tastefully furnished, and most overlook a charming garden with a swimming pool. The restaurant is highly touted by the locals, who come to feast on the excellent duck breast with Bouzy sauce.

4-6 Rue Vertus, Bergères-les-Vertus (phone: 26-52-21-31; fax: 26-52-21-39). Expensive.

CHÂLONS-SUR-MARNE Built on both sides of the Marne, this ancient crossroads town (pop. 54,300) is an administrative center of the Marne *département.* Attila the Hun was defeated on the Châlons plain in AD 451, and the town has played a significant role in military history ever since, especially under Napoleon III and during the two World Wars. It is still the home of an important military school. Châlons has a bourgeois look, with 17th- and 18th-century townhouses, tree-lined riverbanks, and 16th-century bridges (Pont de l'Arche-Mauvillan, Pont des Viviers, Pont des Mariniers) crossing canals formed by Marne tributaries. The tourist office is at 3 Quai des Arts (phone: 26-65-17-89).

Two of Châlons's many churches stand out. The *Cathédrale St-Etienne* (Rue de la Marne) is known for the pure Gothic style of its northern façade and for its beautiful stained glass windows, which span the 12th to the 16th century. Its 17th-century western portal is massive and impressive, and other sections—the chapels, the northern transept, and the treasury—also reveal superb artwork. The *Eglise Notre-Dame-en-Vaux* (Pl. Monseigneur-Tissier), a masterpiece of 12th-century Champenois architecture, shows characteristics of the Romanesque-Gothic transition period. Its interior is harmoniously proportioned and illuminated by beautiful 16th-century stained glass windows, and its carillon of 56 bells chimes out old melodies. Just north is the *Musée du Cloître* (Rue Nicolas-Durand; phone: 26-64-03-87), which contains some 50 carved columns, marvels of 12th-century art. It is open from 10 AM to noon and 2 to 5 PM (6 PM April through September); closed Tuesdays.

Many areas of the city are filled with ancient half-timbered houses; ask the tourist office (see above) for brochures on walking tours of the old districts. The 18th-century *Préfecture* (County Hall; Rue Carnot) is of architectural interest, and the *Musée Municipal* (Rue Carnot; phone: 26-64-38-42) has artifacts from the Stone Age to the Gallo-Roman era. There is no admission charge to the museum, which is open from 2 to 6 PM; closed Tuesdays and holidays. The *Bibliothèque Municipale* (Town Library; Passage Vendel; phone: 26-68-54-44), in an 18th-century residence, has a rich collection of antiquarian books and illuminated manuscripts. It is open from 9 AM to noon and 2 to 6 PM; closed Sundays, Mondays, and holidays.

BEST EN ROUTE

Hôtel Angleterre et Restaurant Jacky Michel In this charming hotel are 18 rooms and a garden where you may dine. The one-Michelin-star restaurant, named after its chef, offers attractive prix fixe menus, an extensive and excellent wine list, and good values, especially on champagne. Closed late December to early January and late July to early August; restaurant also closed Saturday lunch and Sundays. In the center of town, at 19 Pl. Monseigneur-Tissier (phone: 26-68-21-51; fax: 26-70-51-67). Expensive.

En Route from Châlons-sur-Marne Before driving the 48 miles (77 km) via N77 directly to Troyes, a short detour on N3 to L'Epine, 6 miles (10 km) east, is well worth the time.

L'EPINE As you drive toward L'Epine, its large *Basilique Notre-Dame-de-l'Epine* rises majestically in the midst of the Champagne flatlands, calling to mind the cathedral of Reims. Built in the 15th and early 16th centuries, the basilica is the site of a pilgrimage each May. The Flamboyant Gothic façade, graced with three sculptured doorways depicting Christ's birth, passion, and resurrection, is its glory, but note also the realistic, sometimes racy, gargoyles found all around the exterior (they symbolize the vices and evil spirits chased from the sanctuary by divine power). A laser-light-and-music show is offered here on Friday and Saturday nights at 10:30 PM from mid-June to mid-September. For information, contact *La Mairie* (City Hall; phone: 26-66-96-99).

BEST EN ROUTE

Aux Armes de Champagne The 35 rooms and two suites in this charming, recently renovated hotel are lovely, as is the garden, which has a new driving range. The neo-rustic dining room affords a view of the basilica; the cuisine, which has helped to win the place a star from Michelin, features nouvelle dishes and regional specialties, such as squab with Bouzy, *sandre* (pike) from the Marne, and snails with champagne. The *cave* is superlative (sample the native red wine), and the cheese tray is a must. The lunchtime prix fixe menu is a good deal. Closed January through mid-February; restaurant also closed Sunday dinner and Mondays from November through March. Pl. de la Basilique (phone: 26-66-96-79; fax: 26-66-92-31). Moderate.

TROYES The southern part of Champagne—including Troyes, the region's former capital—is all too often ignored by visitors. This was not so in the Middle Ages, when Troyes was a center of international commerce, one of the sites of the annual Champagne trade fairs (troy weight, one of the standards of measurement set by the fairs, persists today), and a famous center of the arts (a status it retained even after its commercial importance had waned). As the Renaissance superseded the Gothic age, the influence of a uniquely Troyen school of architecture spread over the entire region and into Burgundy. Troyen sculptors reached their finest hour, and Troyen stained glass craftsmen filled the city's churches with kaleidoscopic light. Today modern and prosperous—though there's a delightful old section of narrow streets and half-timbered houses—Troyes still is one of the great art towns of France. Many of the 64,800 inhabitants are employed in the manufacture of textiles, as residents have been since the 16th century. The *Office du Tourisme* is near the train station (16 Bd. Carnot; phone: 25-73-00-36).

The *Cathédrale St-Pierre-et-St-Paul* (Pl. de la Cathédrale) was a main beneficiary of the Troyen Renaissance. Built from the 13th to the 17th century, the church has a richly decorated 16th-century Flamboyant Gothic façade with a rose window above the central portal (carvings and statues missing from the tympana above the doors were destroyed during the French Revolution). Walk around to the doorway of the 13th-century north transept to see another rose window and four rosettes. Inside, the stained glass is stunning, from the 13th-century windows of the choir to the mainly 16th-century windows of the nave. The treasury of the church has a collection of beautiful 16th-century enamels, and the church tower affords a fine view of the town.

The *Basilique St-Urbain* (Pl. Vernier), built in the 13th century by Pope Urban IV on the spot where his father had a cobbler's shop, also is known for its splendid stained glass windows, which occupy so much wall space that it's hard to figure out how the edifice stays upright. It also is known for its many noteworthy statues, especially the *Vierge au Raisin* (Virgin of the Grape), a beautiful example of local 16th-century sculpture that once was brightly painted. A third church, the *Eglise Ste-Madeleine* (Rue de la Madeleine), dates from the 12th century. Though it is Troyes's oldest church, the marvelous stained glass in its choir is from the 16th century, as are its sculptured masterpieces: the intricately Flamboyant rood screen and the statue of St. Martha. If you wander around in the vicinity of the *Eglise St-Jean*, you'll see the picturesque old section of town, full of restored 16th-century houses. Walk along Rue Champeaux, and don't miss Rue des Chats, where the cantilevered gables of the houses almost touch each other across the narrow street.

To many the most interesting of Troyes's several museums is the *Musée d'Art Moderne* (Pl. St-Pierre; phone: 25-80-57-30). To the right of the cathedral in the former episcopal palace, the collection features some 1,500 works by Braque, Bonnard, Cézanne, Gauguin, Matisse, Picasso, and other artists; it's considered one of Europe's most important groups of 20th-century art. The museum is open from 11 AM to 6 PM; closed Tuesdays and holidays; there is an admission charge. The *Musée des Beaux-Arts et d'Histoire Naturelle* (in the 18th-century *Abbaye St-Loup;* 1 Rue Chrestien-de-Troyes; phone: 25-42-33-33) has a varied collection of art and artifacts, including some nice 15th- to 16th-century paintings. It is open from 10 AM to noon and 2 to 6 PM; closed Tuesdays and holidays; there is an admission charge. The *Musée de Historique de Troyes et de la Champagne* (in the *Hôtel de Vauluisant;* 4 Rue de Vauluisant; phone: 25-73-05-85) has good local sculptures, drawings, and paintings as well as exhibits tracing the history of the region's textile industry. Its hours are the same as those of the *Musée des Beaux-Arts,* with which there is a reciprocal entry arrangement. The *Maison de l'Outil et de la Pensée Ouvrière* (7 Rue de la Trinité; phone: 25-73-28-26) has tools and artisans' implements. It is open from 9 AM to noon and 2 to 6 PM; there is an admission charge. The *Musée de la Pharmacie* (in the *Hôtel Dieu le Comte;* Quai des Comtes de Champagne; phone: 25-80-98-97), in a beautiful old pharmacy that has been preserved to look as it did at the beginning of the 18th century, includes tools, faïence, and other objects used in the original pharmacy. There is an admission charge.

BEST EN ROUTE

Le Chanoine Gourmand A tiny dollhouse of an eatery whose bright young chef turns out such inventive, delicate dishes as langoustines with hot lime vinaigrette and *coq rouge* (a rare fish) in red wine sauce. In summer a pleasant garden behind the restaurant expands the seating capacity. Closed Sunday dinner, Mondays, and *Christmas* through early January. Reservations advised. Major credit cards accepted. Just behind the cathedral, at 32 Rue de la Cité (phone: 25-80-42-06). Expensive.

Relais St-Jean A quiet, cozy hotel, it offers 22 comfortable rooms but no restaurant. Closed December 20 to January 3. In the picturesque center of town, at 51 Rue Paillot-de-Montauber (phone: 25-73-89-90; fax: 25-73-88-60). Expensive.

Valentino The city's finest—and prettiest—restaurant emphasizes fish and the wines of Chablis. All the dishes are commendable; the sea bass preparations are remarkable. Closed Sunday dinner, Mondays, and mid-August through early September. Reservations necessary. Major credit cards accepted. In the old part of town, at 11 Cour de la Rencontre (phone: 25-73-14-14; fax: 25-73-74-04). Expensive.

Auberge de Sainte-Maure Overlooking a lake, this lovely country restaurant offers good nouvelle-influenced cooking, such as crayfish ravioli and smoked rabbit. Closed Sunday dinner and Mondays. Reservations advised. Major credit cards accepted. 99 Rte. de Méry, Sainte-Maure, 4 miles (6 km) north of Troyes via N19 and D91 (phone: 25-76-90-41). Moderate.

La Poste Its 26 smallish but well-equipped rooms are within striking distance of the old quarter of St-Jean, the *Basilique St-Urbain,* and other sights. It has two restaurants: one featuring seafood, the other a pizzeria. Restaurants closed Sunday dinner, Mondays, and late July through early August. 35 Rue Emile-Zola (phone: 25-73-05-05; fax: 25-73-80-76). Moderate.

En Route from Troyes The fourth vine-growing area of Champagne—the region of the Aube—is less esteemed in the making of champagne than the three areas described above. Our route traces a final loop eastward to encompass the Aube vineyards, picking up N71 farther along, at Bar-sur-Seine.

Leaving Troyes on N19, you'll come (in 13 miles/21 km) to the *Parc Régional de la Forêt d'Orient,* part of a large regional park and recreation area that includes reserves for birds and animals, and the Lac de la Forêt d'Orient (Orient Forest Lake), with water sports facilities popular with Troyens on weekend outings. Mesnil-St-Père, on the south side of the lake off N19, and Géraudot, on the north side on D1, are tiny villages with sand beaches. From Géraudot it is 17 miles (27 km) northeast via D1 and D11 to Brienne-le-Château, the birthplace of Jean de Brienne, who made a name for himself in the Crusades; Napoleon Bonaparte went to the military academy here from 1779 to 1784. A small museum, the *Musée Napoléon-I,* contains souvenirs of the young Napoleon and mementos of his nearby battles during the campaign of 1814. The museum is open from 9 AM to noon and 2 to 5:30 PM; closed Tuesdays, holidays, and December through February; there is an admission charge (phone: 25-92-82-41).

Another 15 miles (24 km), this time to the southeast (via D396 and N19), and you'll be in Bar-sur-Aube, in the center of one section of the Aube vineyards.

BAR-SUR-AUBE On the right bank of the river, this little town (pop. 7,000) already was famous in the Middle Ages, at the time of the great fairs of Champagne; today it is bordered by boulevards instead of ramparts. See the *Eglises St-Pierre* and *St-Maclou,* the former built in the 12th, 14th, and 16th centuries and surrounded by picturesque wooden galleries, the latter built in the 13th and 15th centuries.

A detour 9 miles (14 km) east via N19 will take you to the quiet village of Colombey-les-Deux-Eglises. Charles de Gaulle is buried here, and part of his private residence, *La Boisserie,* which he maintained from 1933 to his death in 1970, is open to visitors. From Bar you also can take a brief excursion south to Bayel, well known for its Cristalleries de Champagne glassworks (you'll see lots of crystal for sale) and of interest for several beautiful sculptures in the village church, including a 14th-century Virgin and Child and a 16th-century Pietà attributed to the same hand as the St. Martha in the *Eglise Ste-Madeleine* in Troyes.

BEST EN ROUTE

Relais des Gouverneurs Halfway between Bar's two historic churches is this establishment with 15 guestrooms and a good restaurant with a young and inventive chef. Try the broiled oysters, the calf sweetbreads, or the salad of sea scallops with truffle juice. Closed January; restaurant also closed Saturday lunch and Mondays in winter and Sunday dinner year-round. 38 Rue Nationale (phone: 25-27-08-76; fax: 25-27-20-80). Moderate.

En Route from Bar-sur-Aube Head southwest, winding 23 miles (37 km) on D4 across the region to pick up N71 at Bar-sur-Seine, the central town of the remaining section of the Aube vineyards. Besides some interesting 15th- and 16th-century houses, Bar-sur-Seine has the *Eglise St-Etienne,* whose stained glass windows and paintings representing the life of the Virgin are noteworthy. There also are a number of interesting, typical villages to the south of Bar-sur-Seine. Chaource, 13 miles (21 km) southwest on D443, besides being well known for its cheese, has some old houses on wooden stilts and, in its church, a 16th-century Entombment, possibly from the atelier of the St. Martha master. Les Riceys, a holiday resort off D452, turns out a tasty rosé wine and has several 16th-century churches. Essoyes, south of Bar-sur-Seine on N71 and east on D67, is associated with Renoir, who used to live here. In the village of Courteron, between Les Riceys and Essoyes on tiny D70, *Champagne Fleury* (43 Grande Rue; phone: 25-38-20-28) is a small, family-owned operation that has won many awards for its champagne produced without fertilizers or pesticides. At Courteron rejoin N71, a main route into the heart of Burgundy.

Corsica

Corsica, France's largest island and the third-largest in the Mediterranean (3,369 square miles), lies some 100 miles southeast of Nice, a six-hour boat trip or 35 minutes by air. But there the proximity ends; in just about every other way, Corsica and the Côte d'Azur are worlds apart. Although the chic, opulent Côte is where the beautiful people go to see and be seen, on Corsica wealth and good looks are not a prerequisite for fitting in. In fact, the only beauty that's seriously worshiped here is that of the landscape.

Corsica has been described as a mountain growing out of the sea. Except for the eastern coast, with its 190-mile stretch of white- and gold-sand beaches, the island is covered with mountains, from its coastal hills to the towering peaks of the central range (Monte Cinto is the highest, at 8,900 feet). Much of the mountainous center and northwest part of the island is deeply forested, though there are treeless, barren stretches as well, including the Agriates Desert in the north. Some of the most dramatic scenery anywhere can be found on the rocky western coast between Calvi and Ajaccio, with deep wooded gorges, sparkling gulf waters, and jagged precipices diving straight into the sea. Equally beautiful, though not quite as dramatic, are the mountains and seascapes of Cap Corse, a 30-mile peninsula projecting fingerlike from St-Florent and Bastia in the northwest.

The sun shines year-round in Corsica, and the summer can be unrelentingly hot. Spring is the gentler season, when the island becomes green and vivid with wild roses and *maquis,* a wild, white heather that blankets the landscape.

Although abundant in natural beauty, in many other ways Corsica is quite barren. There is very little culture or nightlife, and the island's 300 Romanesque churches dating from the 11th and 12th centuries constitute the only architecture of any significance. Even the population has dwindled over the years—it's just over 300,000 today—making this island the least densely populated in the Mediterranean. Part of the reason for this widespread emigration is the mechanization of farming on an island where tobacco growing accounts for roughly one-fourth of the economy. Another factor was the arrival of the French from Algeria after it gained its independence in 1962. Many Corsicans, claiming that outsiders obtained land unjustly, fled the island in anger.

Over the centuries Corsica has absorbed countless invasions; nearly every major town was once a fortress. Occupied by Greece in 560 BC, Corsica later became a colony of Rome, then Pisa. The Genoese came in the 13th century and held the island until 1768 (a year before Napoleon's birth here), when it was sold to France. Except for a brief British takeover—quashed by Napoleon and his troops in 1796—it has been under French rule ever since.

Centuries of political occupation, coupled with the hard and isolated life imposed by the landscape, have had a powerful influence on the character of Corsica's inhabitants. Generally speaking, they are an insular and fiercely independent people, despite numerous outside attempts to crush that independence. For years the French government tried to suppress the Corsican language (a form of Italian) by banning it in schools; it always was spoken at home, however, and though most residents do speak French, Corsican remains the preferred tongue.

During the past few decades the issue of separatism has reared its head, with Corsica demanding—sometimes violently—cultural recognition and greater autonomy. After a series of terrorist acts in 1992—the most infamous being the bombing of 30 tourist villas in southern Corsica—the island's interior minister instituted a crackdown on crime. Terrorist activity flared up again last year, but at press time the US State Department did not consider there to be any significant danger to US travelers abroad. Isolated attacks still occur, and most remain unsolved; a few may be attributed to the separatists, but most are believed to be linked to mobsters or generations-old vendettas and family rivalries.

With its wild, rugged terrain and vast, uninhabited stretches (and somewhat stabilized political situation), Corsica is truly a nature lover's paradise. If you want to get away from it all, this is the place to go.

TOURIST INFORMATION

Services on the island are most plentiful in the summer, so plan your trip accordingly. For information before visiting, contact the main tourist office on Boulevard Roi-Jérôme in Ajaccio (see below). Here is a list of major tourist offices in Corsica:

Ajaccio: 17 Bd. Roi-Jérôme (phone: 95-21-56-56; fax: 95-51-14-40) and *Hôtel de Ville,* 1 Pl. Maréchal-Foch, by the harbor (phone: 95-21-40-87 or 95-21-53-39).

Bastia: 3 Pl. St-Nicolas (phone: 95-31-00-89).

Bonifacio: Rue des 2 Moulins (phone: 95-73-11-88).

Calvi: Port de Plaisance (phone: 95-65-16-67 or 95-65-05-87).

Ile-Rousse: Pl. Paoli (phone: 95-60-04-35).

Porto: 9 Rte. de la Marine (phone: 95-26-10-55).

Porto-Vecchio: Pl. de l'Hotel de Ville (phone: 95-70-09-58).

Propriano: 17 Rue du Général-de-Gaulle (phone: 95-76-01-49).

Sartène: Rue Borgo (phone: 95-77-15-40).

LOCAL COVERAGE Among the excellent, free English-language publications available from local tourist offices is the *Guide to Corsica,* an illustrated index of hotels, restaurants, camping sites, and bungalows and apartments to rent. Supplement this with the *Guide to Hotels,* published by the *Corsican Tourist Office,* which lists hotels by region, including prices and amenities. The best map of Corsica is Michelin No. 90, available at any newsstand.

FOOD AND WINE Corsica's charcuterie includes *prisuttu* (dry-cured ham) and *figatellus* (smoked liver sausage). *Brocciu* is a soft cheese used in all sorts of dishes; often it's served with *fiandonu* (chestnut-flour pastries). Some main courses are *aziminu* (Corsica's version of bouillabaisse) and lamb kebabs in which the meat is skewered on myrtle twigs and barbecued over an aromatic wood fire. The island offers a wide variety of game in season and fresh fish year-round.

Corsican wines are greatly underestimated by the French. The best come from the vineyards of Patrimonio and Sartenais—robust reds and dry, aromatic whites and rosés.

TELEPHONE The area code for Corsica is 95, which is incorporated into all local eight-digit numbers. When calling a number in Corsica from the Paris region (including the Ile-de-France), dial 16, then the eight-digit number. When calling a number from outside Paris, dial only the eight-digit number.

GETTING AROUND

AIRPLANE *Air France* offers daily flights to Ajaccio and Bastia from Paris, Nice, and Marseilles, and there are weekly flights from Amsterdam and Brussels. *Air France*'s domestic carrier, *Air Inter,* flies from Paris, Nice, and Marseilles to Ajaccio, Bastia, and Calvi. From May through October *Air Alpes* flies from Nice and Hyères to Ajaccio, Bastia, Propriano, and Figari, near Bonifacio. *TAT* has regular flights to Figari, Ajaccio, Calvi, and Bastia.

BUS There is regular and inexpensive bus service to most villages; these generally run once a day.

CAR RENTAL A car is the most practical way to explore the island, but be extra careful: Though roads generally are well paved, they're also tortuous. Allow plenty of time to reach your destination—100 miles (160 km) through the mountains is a hard day's drive. Since some villages have neither a garage nor a gas station, carry a steel container (safer than plastic) of gas in the trunk. The following rental firms have offices on Corsica. In Ajaccio: *Avis* (4 Av. de Paris, phone: 95-21-01-86; and at the airport, phone: 95-23-25-14); *Europcar* (16 Cours Grandval, phone: 95-21-05-49; and at the airport, phone: 95-23-18-73); *Hertz* (8 Cours Grandval, phone: 95-21-70-94; and at the airport, phone: 95-23-24-17); and *Inter-Rent* (5 Montée St-Jean, phone: 95-22-61-79; and at the airport, phone: 95-23-19-42). In Bastia: *Avis* (9 Av. M.-Sébastiani, phone: 95-31-11-71; and at the airport, phone: 95-36-03-56); *Europcar* (1 Rue du Nouveau Port, phone: 95-31-59-29; and at the airport, phone: 95-36-03-55); *Hertz* (Pl. St-Victor, phone: 95-31-14-24; and at the airport, phone: 95-36-02-46); and *Inter-Rent* (2 Rue Notre-Dame-de-Lourdes; phone: 95-31-03-11). In Calvi: *Avis* (6 Av. de la République; phone: 95-65-06-74); *Europcar* (Av. de la République, phone: 95-65-10-35; and at the airport, phone: 95-65-10-19); *Hertz* (2 Rue Mal-Joffre, phone: 95-65-06-64;

and at the airport, phone: 95-65-02-96); and *Inter-Rent* (Pl. Christophe-Colombe; phone: 95-65-02-13).

FERRY The *Société Nationale Corse Maritime (SNCM)* serves the following ports: Ajaccio (Quai l'Herminier; phone: 95-29-66-99); Bastia (Nouveau Port, BP 40; phone: 95-54-66-99); Calvi (Quai Landry; phone: 95-65-01-38); Ile-Rousse (Av. J.-Calizi; phone: 95-60-09-56); and Propriano (Quai Commandant-l'Herminier; phone: 95-76-04-36). You can make a ferry connection to Corsica from Marseilles (61 Bd. des Dames; phone: 91-56-30-30); Nice (3 Av. Gustave-V, and Gare Maritime, Quai du Commerce; phone: 93-13-66-99); and Toulon (21 and 49 Av. de l'Infantène-de-Marine; phone: 94-16-66-66). The crossing takes from five to 12 hours, depending on the route you choose.

TOURS Numerous bus tours of the island, ranging from a half day to seven days, are organized by the *Service d'Autocars de la SNCF* (phone: 95-21-14-08). The following agencies also offer tours: *SAIB Bus Tours* (2 Rue Maréchal-Ornano, Ajaccio; phone: 95-21-53-74); *Autocars Bastiais* (40 Bd. Paoli, Bastia; phone: 95-31-01-79); *Autocars Balesi* (Rte. de Bastia, Porto-Vecchio; phone: 95-70-15-55); and *Corse Voyage Autocars Mariani* (Quai Landry, Calvi; phone: 95-46-00-35). Boat excursions ranging from one hour to all day depart daily from Ajaccio, Bonifacio, Calvi, Ile-Rousse, Porto, and Propriano. One of the most popular is the three-hour cruise from Ajaccio to the Iles-Sanguinaires (literally "Bloody Islands," so named because at sunset they're suffused with the red glow of the sun). It leaves from Ajaccio Harbor (Compagnie des Promenades en Mer; phone: 95-23-23-38).

TRAIN A scenic railway links Ajaccio, Corte, Bastia, Ile-Rousse, and Calvi, a distance of 145 miles (232 km). A tramway-train service runs 30 shuttles a day between the ports of Calvi and Ile-Rousse—a good way to visit the many beaches along this part of the coast. Train stations are located in Ajaccio (Pl. de la Gare; phone: 95-23-11-03); Bastia (Av. M.-Sébastiani; phone: 95-32-80-61); Calvi (Av. de la Gare; phone: 95-65-00-61); and Corte (Pl. de la Gare; phone: 95-46-00-97). For general information on train service on Corsica, call 95-23-11-03.

SPECIAL EVENTS

The biggest cultural event on the island is the *Milleli,* a festival of music, theater, and poetry held during July and August in Ajaccio. One of the best-known religious ceremonies is the *Catenacciu* procession, held on *Good Friday.* Penitents dressed in red hoods and shackled with heavy chains bear a large wooden cross through the cobbled streets of Sartène. The *Santa di u Niulu* is held on September 8 in Casamaccioli to celebrate the birth of the Virgin. After a procession, in which a painted, wooden statue of the Virgin is carried through the street, the celebrants—largely mountain folk and shepherds—recite poetry and improvise songs. For more details on special events on Corsica, contact the local tourist offices.

SPORTS AND FITNESS

BOATING Sailors insist that the best way to see Corsica is from the sea. Vessels ranging from sailboats to windsurfers can be rented at the following places: *Balagne Sport* (Ile-Rousse; phone: 95-60-05-17); *Cap Corse Voile* (Macinaggio, on the northeast of Cap Corse; phone: 95-35-41-47); *Europe Yachting* (Ajaccio, phone: 95-21-00-57; and Porto-Vecchio, phone: 95-70-18-69); and *Scim Corse* (Bonifacio; phone: 95-73-03-13).

For information on Corsica's many sailing schools and clubs, contact the *Ligue Corse de Voile* (Corsican Sailing League; Villa Suspirata, Bastelicaccia CP, Ajaccio 20000; phone: 95-21-90-33).

FISHING The waters of Corsica teem with some 200 species of fish. Trout can be caught in the fast-running mountain streams. Some rivers and parts of the coast are restricted, however. For more information, contact the *Fédération Départementale de Pêche et de Pisciculture* (7 Bd. Paoli, Bastia; phone: 95-31-47-31). If you speak some French, by inquiring in port town cafés, you will probably be able to find a fisherman willing to be a guide.

HIKING, CLIMBING, AND SKIING Corsica is a hiker's dream. The *Regional National Park* (phone: 95-21-56-54), a fine place to start, is accessible to pedestrians via GR20. In the park and its environs you can explore the Col de Vergio (Vergio Pass), Gorges de Resontica (Resontica Gorges), Forêt de Bavella (Bavella Forest), and Scala di Santa Regina (St. Regina's "Staircase"). On the west coast good hiking is possible around the gulfs of Girolata and Valinco and along the stunning Calanques of Piana, natural rock formations that resemble immense Henry Moore sculptures.

If you're serious about mountaineering or cross-country skiing, the island has 50 peaks that rise above 6,500 feet, snow-covered from November through May. For information, contact the *Comité Corse de Ski* (1 Bd. Auguste-Gandin, Bastia 20200; phone: 95-32-01-94). There are local climbing and cross-country skiing clubs in Ajaccio (phone: 95-22-09-86) and Bastia (phone: 95-31-17-32). The main resorts for downhill skiing are at Asco (phone: 95-31-02-04), Ghisoni (phone: 95-57-61-28, 95-56-02-72, or 95-56-12-12), and Col de Vergio (phone: 95-48-00-01). For cross-country skiing, the main resorts are at Val d'Ese (phone: 95-28-71-73) and the region of Coscione (Quenza, phone: 95-78-60-97 or 95-78-62-85; and Zicavo, phone: 95-24-40-05 or 95-24-42-13).

SCUBA DIVING The average sea temperature ranges from 55F in March to 74F in August, and the clear water abounds with grouper, multicolored rockfish, and red coral. Two diving schools on the island are the *Harpoon Club* at Ajaccio (phone: 95-22-23-78, 95-22-04-83, or 95-21-64-80) and the *Neptune Club* at Bastia (phone: 95-31-69-02). There also are a number of diving clubs in most of the main port cities. For more information, contact the *Centre d'Etudes Sous-Marines* (28 Rue du Four, Paris 75006; phone: 42-22-

52-66); *La Fédération Française d'Etude et des Sports Sous-Marins* (50 Av. Général-Graziani, Bastia; phone: 95-31-03-32); or the *Comité Corse de Plonger* (phone: 95-20-26-79).

SWIMMING The island has countless beaches. The east coast offers long stretches of golden sand. The west has a variety of large bays and small creeks; beaches that are half rock, half sand; and some spots where you can find solitude, even at the height of the season.

Ajaccio–Bonifacio–Corte–Calvi

The route outlined below begins on the western coast in Ajaccio, then dips south through coastal resorts and mountains to Bonifacio, at the island's southern tip. From there it runs along the eastern coast, with its miles and miles of beaches, then travels inland to the ancient capital, Corte. After a swing west to the port of Calvi, the route ends back in Ajaccio—a distance of some 340 miles (544 km). Allow yourself at least three or four days to make the trip.

Prices on Corsica generally are lower than those on the mainland of France. For a double room per night, expect to pay $100 or more in hotels listed as expensive; $70 to $100 in those listed as moderate; and under $70 in inexpensive places. Booking ahead isn't essential, even during the height of vacation season. Unless otherwise indicated, all hotels accept major credit cards and are open year-round. Almost all feature telephones, TV sets, and private baths in all of their rooms. However, some less expensive hotels may have private baths in only some rooms; it's a good idea to confirm when making a reservation whether your room has a private bath. Most hotels, except the more rustic variety, have air conditioned rooms. A meal for two will cost $100 or more in an expensive restaurant; $70 to $100 in a moderate one; and less than $75 at an inexpensive one. These prices include tax, service charge, and in some cases, wine. Fresh seafood is by far the best bargain. All restaurants are open for lunch and dinner unless otherwise noted. For each location hotels and restaurants are listed alphabetically by price category.

AJACCIO

Founded in the 15th century by the Genoese, Ajaccio is the capital of Corsica's Corse du Sud (Southern District); it and Bastia are the island's two largest cities. Ajaccio perhaps is best known as the birthplace of Napoleon Bonaparte. The three-story *Maison Bonaparte,* where Napoleon was born on August 15, 1769, can be seen on a guided tour that starts from the *Hôtel de Ville* (Town Hall; 1 Pl. Maréchal-Foch; phone: 95-21-90-15). The tour encompasses the 16th-century Baroque cathedral where Napoleon was baptized; its *Chapelle Impériale,* which served as a mausoleum for members of the Bonaparte family; and the *Musée Fesch* (50 Rue Fesch; phone: 95-21-48-17), with its fine collection of Italian paintings. The museum is closed during lunch hours and Sundays; there's an admission charge. For additional details, see *Memorable Museums and Monuments* in DIVERSIONS. The tour also takes you through the picturesque alleys of Ajaccio's old town, near the fishing port and its splendid bay. If you prefer to take it easy, there's a pleasant beach along Boulevard Lantivy.

BEST EN ROUTE

Cala di Sole On the beach with a superb view of the Gulf of Ajaccio, this small, 31-room, luxury hotel has a pool, water sports, tennis, and a dining room. Closed mid-October through March. Four miles (6 km) out of town on Rte. des Sanguinaires (phone: 95-52-01-36). Expensive.

Campo dell'Oro A comfortable, modern, 132-room hostelry in a garden setting, only minutes from the airport and the beach. The restaurant serves family-style fare (phone: 95-22-32-41; fax: 95-20-60-21). Expensive.

Eden Roc Sleek, modern elegance and comfort characterize this resort hotel with 48 balconied rooms and suites, all overlooking the sea. A state-of-the-art saltwater spa facility, an outdoor pool, a sheltered beach, tennis courts, and a restaurant *(La Toque Impériale)* and piano bar with a panoramic view make this garden paradise complete. Rte. des Sanguinaires (phone: 95-52-01-47; fax: 95-52-05-03). Expensive.

Le Maquis Hidden away on a sandy beach, this white stucco retreat is perhaps the most charming and romantic on the island. All 30 rooms, some with large terraces, have views of the sea. There are indoor and outdoor pools, a Jacuzzi, a solarium, and an excellent restaurant overlooking the gulf and Ajaccio. Restaurant closed February. In Porticcio, 11 miles (18 km) south of Ajaccio (phone: 95-25-05-55; fax: 95-25-11-70). Expensive.

Sofitel-Thalassa A modern, first class hotel, this place has 100 rooms, a heated pool, fine sandy beaches, and a very good restaurant serving French and Corsican fare. In Porticcio, 11 miles (18 km) south of Ajaccio, close to the Thalassa baths and spa (phone: 95-29-40-40; 800-763-4835; fax: 95-25-00-63). Expensive.

Albion Quiet and relaxed, it has 63 air conditioned rooms but no restaurant. Closed February. In the residential area, at 15 Av. Général-Leclerc (phone: 95-21-66-70). Moderate.

L'Amore Piattu A local favorite offering contemporary versions of Corsican specialties such as skate, grilled mussels with peppers, a *gâteau* (cake) of lamb and eggplant, and Middle Eastern–style chicken fricassee. Closed Sunday dinner and October. Reservations advised. Major credit cards accepted. 8 Pl. de Gaulle, Diamant II (phone: 95-51-00-53). Moderate.

Auberge du Prunelli A cozy fireplace and rustic antique furnishings make this a particularly appealing spot to try traditional Corsican dishes such as roast baby goat, hearty peasant soups, and *brocciu*. Closed Tuesdays, for lunch in summer, and October through November. Reservations advised. No credit cards accepted. Six miles (10 km) south of Ajaccio on the old Rte. de Sartène (phone: 95-20-02-75). Moderate.

Auberge Seta This ultramodern restaurant serving typical Corsican fare rises like a monolith in the heart of the tiny village of Bastelicaccia. The two-story glass-and-beam structure is actually an architect's clever expansion upward of the Seta family's old one-story *auberge*. Closed Sunday dinner and Mondays. Reservations advised. Major credit cards accepted. Seven miles (11 km) south of Ajaccio on the road to Porticcio, Bastelicaccia (phone: 95-20-00-16). Moderate.

En Route from Ajaccio Route N196 heads east before dipping south, through the ubiquitous mountains and charming villages like Petreto-Bicchisano and Olmeto. At nearly every turn along the winding road are views of deep, forested gorges. For a more panoramic view, stop at the Col de Celaccia, a mountain pass 38 miles (61 km) from Ajaccio. From there you can take D57 6 miles (10 km) to the archaeological site of Filitosa (phone: 95-74-00-91; open *Easter* to late October), where stone monoliths carved with human faces stare out to sea. Back on N196 it's a short (8-mile/13- km) drive to Propriano, a family resort with fine sand beaches.

From Propriano take N196 for 8 miles (13 km) inland to Sartène. The writer Prosper Mérimée, who was a government official in Corsica in the 1860s, called Sartène "the most Corsican of Corsican towns." He considered it severe and somber; perhaps he also was thinking of the town's 19th-century history of bloody vendettas among the feudal barons who controlled it. Today, however, Sartène is neither severe nor embattled; in fact, it would be difficult to find a more peaceful city. The oldest part of town is especially picturesque, with its narrow steps and alleyways, and the surrounding region is rich in prehistoric finds.

From Sartène continue on N196 for 34 miles (54 km) to Bonifacio. The sandy beaches off to the right are private enough for nude swimming and sunbathing.

BEST EN ROUTE

Miramar Perched on a hill overlooking the Gulf of Valinco, this cool stucco hotel is Propriano's most luxurious. All 28 rooms face the sea, and most have terraces. There is a pool and a restaurant. Closed October through April.

Rte. de la Corniche, Propriano (phone: 95-76-06-13; fax: 95-76-13-14). Expensive.

Auberge Santa Barbara Corsican specialties are served in the homey, beamed dining room or the flowered garden. There are also 40 guestrooms with panoramic valley views. Closed November to *Easter*. No reservations. Major credit cards accepted. Propriano (no phone). Moderate.

Le Beach In this hotel are 15 large rooms, each with a small terrace overlooking the bay. Just a few steps from the beach, on Av. Napoléon, Propriano (phone: 95-76-17-74; fax: 95-76-06-54). Moderate.

Le Lido This seaside sister establishment to *Le Beach* has 17 rooms and a restaurant that serves seafood specialties, including lobster. Av. Napoléon, Propriano (phone: 95-76-06-37). Moderate.

La Rascasse A simple spot featuring fresh fish and *aziminu,* the local version of bouillabaisse. Closed Sunday dinner and Mondays from October through April 15, and December 23 through January. Reservations unnecessary. Major credit cards accepted. About a block from the port, on Rue des Pêcheurs, Propriano (phone: 95-76-13-84). Moderate.

La Chaumière A charming and cozy place to sample regional fare. Closed January through mid-March. Reservations advised. Major credit cards accepted. 39 Rue Capitaine-Benedetti (phone: 95-77-07-13). Inexpensive.

BONIFACIO

Set on a peninsula of sheer limestone cliffs overlooking the port, this town at the southern tip of Corsica boasts one of the most dramatic sites in the Mediterranean. Founded as a fortress, Bonifacio is actually set on two levels. Atop the cliffs, rising more than 200 feet above the sea, are the houses and churches of the Haute Ville (Upper Town) in addition to the citadel, the ancient fortress now garrisoned by the French Foreign Legion. La Marine below can be reached from the Haute Ville by descending the *Escaliers du Roi d'Aragon* (King of Aragon Steps), a long stairway carved into the rocky cliffs. Most of Bonifacio's hotels, restaurants, and other tourist facilities are on this lower level.

The cliffs are full of caves and grottoes, and boat excursions can be arranged through a boat owners' association (phone: 95-73-05-43 or 95-73-03-76). The same group offers excursions to the nearby islands of Cavallo and Lavezzi, which have excellent beaches. *Tirrenia* (phone: 95-73-00-96) runs boats to the island of Sardinia, 8 miles (13 km) away, another good spot for a day trip.

If you turn right on D58 out of Bonifacio, you'll soon reach the *Sémaphore Phare de Pertusato,* a lighthouse that provides a sweeping coastal view.

La Caravelle A venerable old establishment overlooking the quaint port, with 30 comfortable rooms. The restaurant is known for its high-quality seafood. Closed December through *Easter*. 11 Quai Comparetti (phone: 95-73-00-03; fax: 95-73-11-10). Expensive.

Genovese This luxurious 14-room, salmon-colored stucco hotel, formerly a French Foreign Legion barracks, is set into the ramparts of the Haute Ville. It has a covered pool, a solarium, and conference rooms but no restaurant. There's a golf course nearby. Quartier de la Citadelle (phone: 95-73-12-34; fax: 95-73-09-03). Expensive.

Le Voilier This seafood restaurant at the port stands out among the Lower Town's most inviting dining spots. Closed January, February, Sunday dinner, and Mondays from October through December. Reservations advised. Major credit cards accepted. Quai Comparetti, La Marine (phone: 95-73-07-06). Expensive.

L'Albatros Excellent fish is served at this seaside eatery. Open daily. Reservations advised. Major credit cards accepted. Quai du Port (phone: 95-73-01-97). Moderate.

En Route from Bonifacio Take N198 north 17 miles (27 km) to Porto-Vecchio, a popular resort with great beaches along the gulf. In summer the water is crammed with sailboats and other pleasure craft.

Continue north on N198 for 36 miles (58 km) to the town of Ghisonaccia, then head inland 12 miles (19 km) on D344, approaching the gorges of Inzecca and Strette and their striking overhangs of rock. At nearby Ghisoni pick up D69, which winds through some glorious mountain scenery for some 12½ miles (20 km) to join N193, the main Ajaccio-Bastia road. Turn right to reach Corte, 14 miles (22 km) north.

BEST EN ROUTE

Le Bistrot du Port Offering slightly fancier seafood fare than the average bistro, this restaurant has a terrace overlooking the sea. Open daily year-round. Reservations advised. Major credit cards accepted. Quai Paoli, Porto-Vecchio (phone: 95-70-22-96). Expensive.

Grand Hôtel de Cala Rossa In a pine wood on a beach, this 50-room luxury establishment features a fine, one-Michelin-star restaurant. Closed November through mid-April. Carla Rossa, six miles (10 km) north of Porto-Vecchio by D468 via D568 and N198 (phone: 95-71-61-51; fax: 95-71-60-11). Expensive.

L'Orée du Maquis This intimate restaurant offers delicate cooking, evidenced in such dishes as langoustines in a sweet-and-sour sauce and scallops in port butter with asparagus. Open for dinner; closed Sundays except in July, August, and two weeks in March. Reservations advised. Major credit cards accepted. Rte. de la Lézardière, Trinité de Porto-Vecchio (phone: 95-70-22-21). Expensive.

Shegara Rugged stone and wrought-iron terraces overlooking the sea mark this old 30-room establishment. It offers simple comforts and easy access to the sea, as well as an open-air restaurant featuring lobster, fish, and grilled meat. Closed December through February. Porto-Vecchio (phone: 95-70-04-31; fax: 95-70-23-38). Moderate.

CORTE

The stillness of this hilltop town in the heart of the central mountains belies its somewhat rocky history. Occupied intermittently since ancient times, Corte became the capital of Corsica during the island's 18th-century War of Independence, which was fought against the ruling Genoese. No longer the capital, it's now slumberous, offering little to do except hiking in the gorges and forests of Tavignano and Restonica, just southwest of the city on D623.

BEST EN ROUTE

Auberge de la Restonica Staying in this rustic retreat is like being a guest in a Corsican country house. There's a cat in every armchair, a library full of books that guests are welcome to borrow, and a rambling dining room with a river view. Though the food can be disappointing, the warm welcome and secluded location are memorable. Thirty of the 36 rooms are in a new wing. Hotel open year-round; restaurant closed January 2 through February. Rte. de la Restonica (phone: 95-46-09-58; fax: 95-61-03-91). Moderate.

Pascal Paoli Named for the great 18th-century Corsican leader who established Corte as the island's capital, this is a relaxed, friendly place on the main square where you can sit at a sidewalk table and watch the world slowly pass by. The food is traditional Corsican, with an emphasis on grilled dishes. Closed mid-October through *Easter*. Reservations unnecessary. Major credit cards accepted. Pl. Paoli (phone: 95-46-13-48). Inexpensive.

U Palazzini Stop by this breezy café/restaurant for a simple meal of quiche, salad, or the daily special after a visit to the nearby citadel in the Haute Ville (Upper Town). Closed Sundays and two weeks in February. Reservations unnecessary. Major credit cards accepted. 3 Rue du Palais-National (phone: 95-46-03-87). Inexpensive.

En Route from Corte Follow N193 north for 15 miles (24 km) to Ponte Leccia, then pick up N197 headed northwest. As you get closer to the sea, the mountains become more rounded and wooded. At Lozari, 20 miles (32 km) away, head south on the coastal road, N197, for 16 miles (26 km)—through Ile-Rousse, a yachting port with good beaches—to Calvi.

Isola Rossa Just a few steps from the beach, this simple, white stucco, 23-room establishment is clean and homey. Ask for a room overlooking the bay, preferably one of those with a small balcony. No restaurant. Rte. Port, Ile-Rousse (phone: 95-60-01-32). Moderate.

Napoléon Bonaparte This renovated, elegant old seaside hotel is characterized by sweeping corridors, palatial pillars, and high ceilings. There are 106 rooms; request a refurbished one. No dining room. Ile-Rousse (phone: 95-60-06-09). Moderate.

CALVI

Corsica's chicest and most popular resort, Calvi is also a fortress town with a military history that dates back centuries. Occupied through the Roman era and the Middle Ages, it was resettled in the 15th century by the Genoese, who built the town's citadel on an immense rock towering above the sea. During the Napoleonic Wars, Calvi was taken by the British after two months of incessant combat during which Admiral Nelson lost an eye. Worth a visit is the *Oratoire St-Antoine* (no phone), within the walls of the fortified part of town. Built in the 15th century, it's now a museum of ancient and medieval religious art.

History aside, Calvi boasts some enticing long, white beaches. You also can take a boat trip on the *Colombo* line (phone: 95-65-03-40 or 95-65-32-10) to the Grotte des Veaux Marins (phone: 95-65-28-16 or 95-65-29-65), the well-known caves on the nearby Peninsula de la Revelata. Boats leave daily at 9:15 AM and 4:30 PM, April through September. For guided walks of the caves, call to make reservations (phone: 95-50-56-14). South of Calvi lies some of the island's most magnificent coastline—best appreciated when viewed from the sea.

Auberge de la Signoria A few miles from the beach, this pretty 17th-century estate with 11 comfortable rooms sits well back from the road amid eucalyptus trees and a garden-rimmed pool. There's a peacefulness here not found in the hotels closer to bustling Calvi. The restaurant serves such delicate dishes as warm turbot salad with truffle vinaigrette. Hotel closed mid-October through March; restaurant closed for lunch except weekends in July and August. Rte. de l'Aéroport (phone: 95-65-23-73; fax: 95-65-33-20). Expensive.

Comme Chez Soi On the lively waterfront strip, this place serves delicious fish. Open daily year-round. Reservations advised. Major credit cards accepted. Quai Landry (phone: 95-65-00-59). Expensive.

Ile de Beauté Also on the waterfront, this excellent spot specializes in lobster; the oysters with lime are popular too. Closed Wednesdays and October through April. Reservations advised. Major credit cards accepted. Quai Landry (phone: 95-65-00-46). Expensive.

Le Magnolia Formerly the home of a countess, this 19th-century mansion is graced by a lush garden where bougainvillea, hibiscus, and an immense magnolia tree bloom. Most of the 14 quaint, comfortable rooms overlook the garden, though one has a view of the bay. There's a dining room. Closed January and February. Pl. du Marché (phone: 95-65-19-16; fax: 95-65-34-52). Expensive.

Caravelle A pleasant beach hotel with 34 rooms; there's a restaurant. Closed October through April. On N197, just north of Calvi (phone: 95-65-01-21; fax: 95-65-00-03). Moderate.

Clos des Amandiers A charming place with 20 guest bungalows and four studios in a garden setting with a pool, tennis facilities, and a restaurant. Closed November through April. One mile (1.6 km) south of Calvi on N197 (phone: 95-65-08-32; fax: 95-65-37-76). Moderate.

En Route from Calvi Heading south on D81, the road ascends to 400 feet above the sea, providing a final panoramic view of the Peninsula de la Revelata, its caves, and its lighthouse. On the left is the belvedere of *Notre-Dame-de-la-Serra,* a tiny chapel that's the site of the *Santa di u Niulu,* an annual pilgrimage celebrating the birth of the Virgin (see *Special Events,* above).

The next 48-mile (77-km) stretch is, quite simply, breathtaking, even for an island so abundant in spectacular scenery. Driving along the rugged cliff road, mountains and rocky headlands rise on your left while the sea crashes on the right. From atop the Col de Bassa, 850 feet high and 17 miles (27 km) from Calvi, the long, isolated beach at Galeria is visible; or climb the nearby Col de Palmarella for a look at the Gulf of Girolata.

Porto, 32 miles (51 km) farther on, is a small beach resort where you can take a boat excursion to Girolata or, to the south, visit the famous Calanches de Piana. These are red-brown rock formations, the texture of giant coral, molded by nature into phantasmagorical shapes that plunge into bays of sparkling green and black water. From the road out of Porto, rising to 870 feet, the Calanches can be seen in all their glory. The village of Piana, 8 miles (13 km) from Porto, has a fine beach, Ficajola; it's a 2-mile (3-km) descent down D624—well paved but with a wicked hairpin turn.

From Piana D81 strikes inland for 12 miles (19 km) to rejoin the coast at Cargèse, a small Greek Orthodox community north of the Gulf of Sagone. The trip from Cargèse back to Ajaccio is 34 miles (54 km); for half that distance, it hugs the gulf coast before plunging into the mountains.

Capo Rosso A luxury, 57-room property overlooking the Calanches de Piana and the gulf. Sunning yourself by the pool, you feel as though you're part of this glorious landscape. The good restaurant serves fresh fish. Closed mid-October through March. Rte. des Calanches, Piana (phone: 95-27-82-40; fax: 95-27-80-00). Expensive.

Marina A modern, 60-room hotel with a pool, a sun deck, and a fine view of the sea and mountains but no restaurant. Closed October through April. Porto-Marine, Porto (phone: 95-26-10-34; fax: 95-26-12-97). Expensive.

Auberge de Ferayola Midway between Calvi and Porto is this quite comfortable hotel. The view from each of the 10 rooms is splendid, the restaurant is good, and there's a beach a mile (1.6 km) away at Argentella. Closed October · through May. D81, Ferayola (phone: 95-65-25-25). Moderate.

Dolce Vita This fine hilltop hostelry with 20 units is 2 miles (3 km) from a good sand beach. There is a restaurant. Closed November through March. Col de la Croix, Osani (phone: 95-27-31-86; fax: 95-27-31-57). Moderate.

U Campanile Crayfish and other gulf specialties are served on a terrace overlooking the village square. Closed October through March. Reservations unnecessary. Major credit cards accepted. Pl. de l'Eglise, Piana (phone: 95-27-81-71). Inexpensive.

Cap Corse

This much shorter route covers the Cap Corse, a narrow peninsula on the northeast that offers some of the island's most beautiful coastal and mountain scenery. It's an 80-mile (128-km) round trip from Bastia, on the eastern heel of the cape. For general information on hotels and restaurants, see the introduction to the route above.

BASTIA

A Genoese fortress from the 15th through the 18th century, Bastia today is the capital of Corsica's Haute Corse (Northern District) and the island's industrial center. In Terra-Vecchia, the 17th-century neighborhood north of the Vieux Port, is Bastia's landmark, the 17th-century *Eglise St-Jean-Baptiste,* with its simple, pretty façade. From here climb from the Quai du Sud up to the *Terra-Nova,* the Genoese citadel. Just inside the main gate is the *Musée d'Ethnographie Corse* (phone: 95-31-09-12), which, with artifacts spanning the island's history from prehistoric to medieval times, provides an excellent introduction to Corsica. Several exhibits illustrate Corsican customs, handicrafts, and folklore as well as 19th-century photographs and collections of Napoleon mementoes. More artifacts, including the emperor's death mask, are on the second floor. The museum is open weekdays from 9 AM to noon and 2 to 6 PM, Saturdays and Sundays from 10 AM to noon and 2 to 6 PM.

BEST EN ROUTE

Le Bistrot du Port Small and friendly, this restaurant prepares an excellent rendition of mussels with spinach, among other creative dishes. Closed Sundays and October. Reservations unnecessary. No credit cards accepted. Right off the Quai Martyrs-de-la-Libération on Rue Posta-Vecchia (phone: 95-32-19-83). Expensive.

Pietracap A modern, 40-room hotel set in a park of olive trees; its heated pool offers a view of the sea. No restaurant. Closed December through February. Rte. de San Martino, 2 miles (3 km) north of Bastia on the coast at Pietranera (phone: 95-31-64-63; fax: 95-31-39-00). Expensive.

Thalassa This small, quiet, 30-room hotel on the beach has an excellent restaurant serving regional specialties. Closed December through February. Rte. du Cap, Pietranera (phone: 95-31-56-63; fax: 95-32-32-79). Moderate.

En Route from Bastia Drive inland on D81, a mountain road that twists and curls its way across the base of the peninsula. At the midpoint, 6 miles (10 km) away, is the Col de Teghime, the site of a major battle during Corsica's liberation in World War II. Go another 9 miles (14 km) and you will reach the port of St-Florent, now a beach resort. Just to the east, and worth a look, is a 13th-century Pisan cathedral, practically all that remains of the medieval city of Nebbio. Some very good fish restaurants can be found in the port's Old Town, among them *Gaffe* (phone: 95-37-00-12). It's closed Mondays and from November to mid-December. In St-Florent you can take a motorboat across the gulf to explore the solitary beaches of the Agriates Desert and the salt lakes of Mortella.

Heading north, D81 swings inland to the vineyards of Patrimonio and then back to the coast. Twelve miles (19 km) from St-Florent is the village of Nonza, with a sand beach and a medieval fortress on a cliff. At the northwest corner of the cape, 35 miles (56 km) from Nonza, is tiny Centuri-Port, where you can get decent food and lodging. From Centuri go 7 miles (11 km) on D80 across the cape to the marina at Macinaggio. Driving the eastern length of the cape back to Bastia, the beaches aren't as attractive as those on the west, but the sight of the sea will sustain you.

BEST EN ROUTE

Le Vieux Moulin A dining spot featuring seafood, it also offers 14 guestrooms. Closed November through January. Reservations unnecessary. Major credit cards accepted. Centuri-Port (phone: 95-35-60-15). Moderate.

Glossary

Useful Words and Phrases

The French as a nation have a reputation for being snobbish and brusque to tourists, and, unfortunately, many Americans have allowed this stereotype to affect their appreciation of France. The more experienced traveler, however, knows that on an individual basis, the French people are usually cordial and helpful, especially if you speak a few words of their language. Don't be afraid of misplaced accents or misconjugated verbs—in most cases you will be understood.

The list below of commonly used words and phrases can help you get started.

Greetings and Everyday Expressions

Good morning/afternoon! (Hello!)	*Bonjour!*
Good evening!	*Bonsoir!*
How are you?	*Comment allez-vous?*
Pleased to meet you!	*Enchanté!*
Good-bye!	*Au revoir!*
See you soon!	*A bientôt!*
Good night!	*Bonne nuit!*
Yes!	*Oui!*
No!	*Non!*
Please!	*S'il vous plaît!*
Thank you!	*Merci!*
You're welcome!	*De rien!*
Excuse me!	*Excusez-moi* or *pardonnez-moi!*
It doesn't matter.	*Ça m'est égal.*
I don't speak French.	*Je ne parle pas français.*
Do you speak English?	*Parlez-vous anglais?*
Please repeat.	*Répétez, s'il vous plaît.*
I don't understand.	*Je ne comprends pas.*
Do you understand?	*Vous comprenez?*
My name is . . .	*Je m'appelle . . .*
What is your name?	*Comment vous appelez-vous?*
miss	*mademoiselle*
madame	*madame*
mister/sir	*monsieur*
open	*ouvert*
closed	*fermé*
entrance	*l'entrée*

exit	*la sortie*
push	*poussez*
pull	*tirez*
today	*aujourd'hui*
tomorrow	*demain*
yesterday	*hier*
Help!	*Au secours!*
ambulance	*l'ambulance*
Get a doctor!	*Appelez le médecin!*

Checking In

I have (don't have) a reservation.	*J'ai une (Je n'ai pas de) réservation.*
I would like . . .	*Je voudrais . . .*
a single room	*une chambre pour une personne*
a double room	*une chambre pour deux*
a quiet room	*une chambre tranquille*
with bath	*avec salle de bains*
with shower	*avec douche*
with a view of the Seine	*avec une vue sur la Seine*
with air conditioning	*avec une chambre climatisée*
with balcony	*avec balcon*
overnight only	*pour une nuit seulement*
a few days	*quelques jours*
a week (at least)	*une semaine (au moins)*
with full board	*avec pension complète*
with half board	*avec demi-pension*
Does that price include breakfast?	*Est-ce que le petit déjeuner est inclus?*
Are taxes included?	*Est-ce que les taxes sont comprises?*
Do you accept traveler's checks?	*Acceptez-vous les chèques de voyage?*
Do you accept credit cards?	*Acceptez-vous les cartes de crédit?*

Eating Out

ashtray	*un cendrier*
bottle	*une bouteille*
(extra) chair	*une chaise (en sus)*
cup	*une tasse*
fork	*une fourchette*
knife	*un couteau*
spoon	*une cuillère*
napkin	*une serviette*

plate	*une assiette*
table	*une table*
coffee	*café*
black coffee	*café noir*
coffee with milk	*café au lait*
cream	*crème*
fruit juice	*jus de fruit*
orange	*jus d'orange*
tomato	*jus de tomate*
juice	*jus*
lemonade	*citron pressé*
milk	*lait*
mineral water (non-carbonated)	*l'eau minérale non-gazeuse*
mineral water (carbonated)	*l'eau minérale gazeuse*
orangeade	*orange pressée*
tea	*thé*
water	*eau*
cold	*froid*
hot	*chaud*
bacon	*bacon*
bread	*pain*
butter	*beurre*
eggs	*oeufs*
soft boiled	*à la coque*
hard boiled	*durs*
fried	*sur le plats*
scrambled	*brouillés*
poached	*pochés*
ham	*jambon*
honey	*miel*
jam	*confiture*
omelette	*omelette*
pepper	*poivre*
salt	*sel*
sugar	*sucre*
beer	*bière*
port	*vin de Porto*
red wine	*vin rouge*
rosé	*rosé*
sherry	*vin de Xérès*
white wine	*vin blanc*
sweet	*doux*

(very) dry	(très) sec
Waiter!	Garçon!
Waitress!	Mademoiselle!
I would like	Je voudrais
a glass of	un verre de
a bottle of	une bouteille de
a half bottle of	une demi-bouteille
a liter of	un litre de
a carafe of	une carafe de

The check, please.	L'addition, s'il vous plaît.
Is the service charge included?	Le service, est-il compris?
I think there is a mistake in the bill.	Je crois qu'il y a une erreur avec l'addition.

Shopping

bakery	boulangerie
bookstore	librairie
butcher store	boucherie
camera shop	magasin de photographie
clothing store	magasin de vêtements
delicatessen	charcuterie
department store	grand magasin
drugstore (for medicine)	pharmacie
grocery	épicerie
jewelry store	bijouterie
newsstand	kiosque à journaux
notions (sewing supplies) shop	mercerie
pastry shop	pâtisserie
perfume (and cosmetics) store	parfumerie
pharmacy/drugstore	pharmacie
shoestore	magasin de chaussures
supermarket	supermarché
tobacconist	tabac

inexpensive	bon marché
expensive	cher

large	grand
larger	plus grand
too large	trop grand
small	petit
smaller	plus petit

too small	*trop petit*
long	*long*
short	*court*
old	*vieux*
new	*nouveau*
used	*d'occasion*
handmade	*fabriqué à la main* or *fait main*
Is it machine washable?	*Est-ce que c'est lavable à la machine?*
How much does this cost?	*Quel est le prix?/Combien?*
What is it made of?	*De quoi est-ce fait?*
camel's hair	*poil de chameau*
cotton	*coton*
corduroy	*velours côtelé*
filigree	*filigrane*
lace	*dentelle*
leather	*cuir*
linen	*lin*
silk	*soie*
suede	*suède*
synthetic	*synthétique*
wool	*laine*
brass	*cuivre jaune*
copper	*cuivre*
gold (plated)	*or (plaqué)*
silver (plated)	*argent (plaqué)*
wood	*bois*
May I have a sales tax rebate form?	*Puis-je avoir le formulaire pour la détaxe?*
May I pay with this credit card?	*Puis-je payer avec cette carte de crédit?*
May I pay with a traveler's check?	*Puis-je payer avec chèques de voyage?*

Colors

black	*noir*
blue	*bleu*
brown	*marron*
gray	*gris*

green	*vert*
orange	*orange*
pink	*rose*
purple	*violet*
red	*rouge*
yellow	*jaune*
white	*blanc*

Getting Around

north	*le nord*
south	*le sud*
east	*l'est*
west	*l'ouest*
right	*droite*
left	*gauche*
straight ahead	*tout droit*
far	*loin*
near	*proche*
airport	*l'aéroport*
bus stop	*l'arrêt de bus*
gas station	*station service*
train station	*la gare*
subway	*le métro*
map	*carte*
one-way ticket	*aller simple*
round-trip ticket	*un billet aller retour*
gate	*porte*
track	*voie*
in first class	*en première classe*
in second class	*en deuxième classe*
no smoking	*défense de fumer*
Does this subway/bus go to . . . ?	*Est-ce que ce métro/ bus va à . . . ?*
What time does it leave?	*A quelle heure part-il?*
gas	*essence*
regular (leaded)	*ordinaire*
super (leaded)	*super*
unleaded	*sans plomb*
diesel	*gas-oil*

Fill it up, please.	Le plein, s'il vous plaît.
the tires	pneus
the oil	huile
Danger	Danger
Caution	Attention
Detour	Déviation
Dead End	Cul-de-sac
Do Not Enter	Défense d'entrer
No Parking	Défense de stationner
No Passing	Défense de dépasser
No U-turn	Défense de faire demi-tour
One way	Sens unique
Pay toll	Péage
Pedestrian Zone	Zone piétonne
Reduce Speed	Ralentissez
Steep Incline	Côte à forte inclination
Stop	Stop; Arrêt
Use Headlights	Allumez les phares
Yield	Cédez le passage
Where is . . . ?	Où se trouve . . . ?
How many kilometers are we from . . . ?	A combien de kilomètres sommes-nous de . . . ?

Personal Items and Services

aspirin	aspirine
Band-Aids	pansement adhésif
barbershop	coiffeur pour hommes
bath	bain
bathroom	salle de bain
beauty shop	salon de coiffure
condom	préservatif
dentist	dentiste
disposable diapers	couches
dry cleaner	nettoyage à sec
hairdresser	coiffeur pour dames
laundromat	laundrette or blanchisserie automatique
post office	bureau de poste
postage stamps (airmail)	timbres (par avion)
razor	rasoir
sanitary napkins	serviettes hygiéniques
shampoo	shampooing
shaving cream	crème à raser

shower	*douche*
soap	*savon*
tampons	*tampons*
tissues	*mouchoirs en papier*
toilet	*toilettes* or *WC*
toilet paper	*papier hygiénique*
toothbrush	*brosse à dents*
toothpaste	*dentifrice*

Where is the men's/ladies' room?	*Où sont les toilettes?*

Days of the Week

Monday	*lundi*
Tuesday	*mardi*
Wednesday	*mercredi*
Thursday	*jeudi*
Friday	*vendredi*
Saturday	*samedi*
Sunday	*dimanche*

Months

January	*janvier*
February	*février*
March	*mars*
April	*avril*
May	*mai*
June	*juin*
July	*juillet*
August	*août*
September	*septembre*
October	*octobre*
November	*novembre*
December	*décembre*

Numbers

zero	*zéro*
one	*un*
two	*deux*
three	*trois*
four	*quatre*
five	*cinq*
six	*six*
seven	*sept*
eight	*huit*
nine	*neuf*
ten	*dix*

eleven	*onze*
twelve	*douze*
thirteen	*treize*
fourteen	*quatorze*
fifteen	*quinze*
sixteen	*seize*
seventeen	*dix-sept*
eighteen	*dix-huit*
nineteen	*dix-neuf*
twenty	*vingt*
twenty-one	*vingt-et-un*
thirty	*trente*
forty	*quarante*
fifty	*cinquante*
sixty	*soixante*
seventy	*soixante-dix*
eighty	*quatre-vingts*
ninety	*quatre-vingt-dix*
one hundred	*cent*
1995	**mille neuf cent quatre-vingt-cinq**

WRITING RESERVATIONS LETTERS

Restaurant/Hotel Name
Street Address
Postal Code, Paris
France

Dear Sir:

    I would like to reserve a table for (number of) persons for lunch/dinner on (day and month), 1995, at (hour) o'clock.

Monsieur:

    Je voudrais réserver une table pour (number) *personnes pour le déjeuner/dîner du* (day and month) *1995, à* (time using the 24-hour clock) *heures.*

or

    I would like to reserve a room for (number of) people for (number of) nights.

or

    Je voudrais réserver une chambre à (number) *personne(s) pour* (number) *nuits.*

and

    Would you be so kind as to confirm the reservation as soon as possible?

    I am looking forward to meeting you. (The French usually include a pleasantry such as this.)

and

    Auriez-vous la bonté de bien vouloir me confirmer cette réservation dès que possible?

    J'attends avec impatience le plaisir de faire votre connaissance.

    With my thanks,

    Avec tous mes remerciements,

    (Signature)

    (Signature)

(Print or type your name and address below your signature.)

Climate Chart

Average Temperatures (in °F)

	January	*April*	*July*	*October*
Aix-en-Provence	34–50	44–64	62–83	49–67
Avignon	34–49	45–67	61–87	49–68
Biarritz	39–52	46–61	61–73	52–66
Bordeaux	35–49	43–63	57–78	47–65
Cannes	37–54	46–63	63–81	52–68
Chartres	33–43	39–56	53–72	44–59
Dijon	28–39	41–61	57–77	43–59
Lyons	30–42	42–61	59–80	45–61
Marseilles	35–50	46–64	63–84	51–68
Monaco (and Monte Carlo)	46–54	54–61	72–79	61–68
Nice	40–55	48–63	65–80	54–69
Paris	34–43	43–60	58–76	46–60
Reims	30–41	39–59	55–75	43–59
Rouen	32–43	39–59	54–73	45–59
St-Tropez	33–41	41–59	62–82	43–61
Strasbourg	29–40	39–58	55–74	42–57

Weights and Measures

	Metric Unit	Abbreviation	US Equivalent
Length	1 millimeter	mm	.04 inch
	1 meter	m	39.37 inches
	1 kilometer	km	.62 mile
Capacity	1 liter	l	1.057 quarts
Weight	1 gram	g	.035 ounce
	1 kilogram	kg	2.2 pounds
	1 metric ton	MT	1.1 tons
Temperature	0° Celsius	C	32° Fahrenheit

CONVERSION TABLES

METRIC TO US MEASUREMENTS

	Multiply:	by:	to convert to:
Length	millimeters	.04	inches
	meters	3.3	feet
	meters	1.1	yards
	kilometers	.6	miles
Capacity (liquid)	liters	2.11	pints
	liters	1.06	quarts
	liters	.26	gallons
Weight	grams	.04	ounces
	kilograms	2.2	pounds

US TO METRIC MEASUREMENTS

	Multiply:	by:	to convert to:
Length	inches	25.0	millimeters
	feet	.3	meters
	yards	.9	meters
	miles	1.6	kilometers
Capacity	pints	.47	liters
	quarts	.95	liters
	gallons	3.8	liters
Weight	ounces	28.0	grams
	pounds	.45	kilograms

TEMPERATURE

Celsius to Fahrenheit	$(°C \times 9/5) + 32 = °F$
Fahrenheit to Celsius	$(°F - 32) \times 5/9 = °C$

Index